Why do smells trigger certain memories? **P. 141**

What else, besides antidepressant drugs, can boost moods? **P. 366**

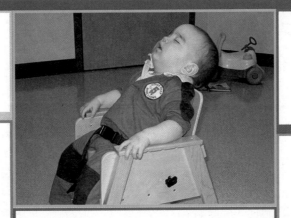

How can I be happier? **PP. 263–264**

Why do I need to sleep, and how much sleep do I need? **PP. 53–55**

How does stress affect my health and my ability to fight infections and disease, such as AIDS and cancer? **PP. 271–275**

Where do we draw the line between depression and understandable sadness? **PP. 314, 335**

Does modern life make us more vulnerable to psychological disorders, such as anxiety and depression? **PP. 322, 337**

How can I motivate myself and others to achieve more? **PP. 410–412**

What does my messy (or neat) room (or web site) say about my personality? **P. 304**

What should I do if I want to lose weight and keep it off? **PP. 245–246**

How can relaxation and meditation enhance my well-being? **PP. 281–283, 354–355**

Is intelligence all I need to be successful? **P. 220**

Are my personality traits evident in my musical taste? **P. 304**

How can I best remember what I'm learning in this course? **PP. xxix–xxxiii, 22, 200–201**

See inside back cover for complete list.

Psychology
in Everyday Life

David G. Myers

Hope College
Holland, Michigan

WORTH PUBLISHERS

Grateful acknowledgment is given for permission to reprint the following photos: p. 1: Lisa Pines / Photonica / Getty Images; p. 26: Photonica / Getty Images; p. 62: Taxi Japan / Getty Images; p. 102: moodboard/Corbis; p. 124: Tim Pannell/ Corbis; p. 156: AJA Productions / Getty Images; p. 180: Image Source Pink / Alamy; p. 204: John Lee / Masterfile; p. 234: Gulliver/ zefa/ Corbis; p. 268: Clifford White/ Corbis; p. 288: Patrick Ward/CORBIS; p. 312: Masterfile; p. 348: Jon Bradley / Stone / Getty Images; p. 374: Randy Faris/ Corbis.

Page 1 of front endpaper: Newscom (top right); Lisa B./Corbis (bottom right); Jens Koenig/Getty Images (top left); R. Ian Lloyd/Masterfile (bottom left). Page 2 of front endpaper: Christine Brune (top); Myrleen Ferguson Cate/Photo Edit (left); Howard Pyle/Veer (right); Gary Conner/Photo Edit (bottom).

Publisher: Catherine Woods
Senior Acquisitions Editor: Kevin Feyen
Executive Marketing Manager: Katherine Nurre
Development Editors: Christine Brune, Nancy Fleming
Media Editor: Peter Twickler
Photo Editor: Bianca Moscatelli
Photo Researcher: Patricia Cateura
Art Director, Cover Designer: Babs Reingold
Interior Designer: Charles Yuen
Photo Treatment: Lyndall Culbertson
Layout Designer: Lee Mahler-McKevitt
Associate Managing Editor: Tracey Kuehn
Project Editor: Dana Kasowitz
Illustration Coordinator: Bill Page
Illustrations: TSI Graphics, Keith Kasnot, Don Stewart
Production Manager: Sarah Segal
Composition: TSI Graphics
Printing and Binding: Quebecor
Cover Painting: Larry Williams/Larry Williams and Associates/Corbis

Library of Congress Control Number: 2008929130

paperback:
ISBN-13: 978-1-4292-0789-8
ISBN-10: 1-4292-0789-2

hardcover:
ISBN-13: 978-1-4292-2561-8
ISBN-10: 1-4292-2561-0

Printed in the United States of America

Second printing

All royalties from the sale of this book are assigned to the David and Carol Myers Foundation, which exists to receive and distribute funds to other charitable organizations.

Worth Publishers
41 Madison Avenue
New York, NY 10010
www.worthpublishers.com

In memory of Guy Edward Geraghty (1950–2008),
with gratitude and fond memories.

About the Author

DAVID MYERS RECEIVED his psychology Ph.D. from the University of Iowa. He has spent his career at Hope College, Michigan, where he has taught dozens of introductory psychology sections. Hope College students have invited him to be their commencement speaker and voted him "outstanding professor."

Myers' scientific articles have, with support from National Science Foundation grants, appeared in more than two dozen scientific periodicals, including *Science, American Scientist, Psychological Science,* and the *American Psychologist.* In addition to his scholarly writing and his textbooks for introductory and social psychology, he also digests psychological science for the general public. His writings have appeared in three dozen magazines, from *Today's Education* to *Scientific American.* He also has authored five general audience books, including *The Pursuit of Happiness* and *Intuition: Its Powers and Perils.*

David Myers has chaired his city's Human Relations Commission, helped found a thriving assistance center for families in poverty, and spoken to hundreds of college and community groups. Drawing on his experience, he also has written articles and a book (*A Quiet World*) about hearing loss, and he is advocating a transformation in American assistive listening technology (see hearingloop.org).

He bikes to work year-round and plays daily pick-up basketball. David and Carol Myers have raised two sons and a daughter.

Brief Contents

Contents

CHAPTER 9
Motivation and Emotion 234

CHAPTER 10
Stress, Health, and Human Flourishing 268

CHAPTER 11
Personality 288

Preface

PSYCHOLOGY IS FASCINATING, AND so relevant to our everyday lives. Psychology's insights can help us to be better students, more tuned-in friends, more effective co-workers, and wiser parents. With this new text, I hope to captivate students with what psychologists are learning about our human nature, to help them think more like psychological scientists, and, as the title implies, to help them relate psychology to their own lives—their thoughts, feelings, and behaviors.

For those of you familiar with my other introductory psychology texts, you may be surprised at how very different this new text is.

I have for years bounced around ideas with academic and publishing colleagues about new ways to reach students. How can we effectively share psychology's life-relevant, life-improving wisdom with today's academically and culturally diverse students? With input from 1000 instructors and 850 students (by way of surveys, focus groups, content and design reviews, and class testing), we have created what I think is a uniquely student-friendly book.

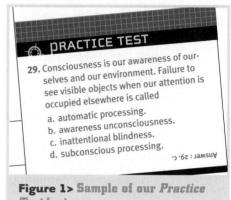

Figure 1> Sample of our *Practice Test* feature

Scattered throughout this book, students will find interesting and informative review notes and quotes from researchers and others that will encourage them to be active learners and to apply their new knowledge to everyday life.

Design

Our three-column format is rich with visual support. It responds to students' expectations, based on what they have told us about their reading, both online and in print. The magazinelike column width eliminates the strain of reading across a wide textbook page. Illustrations appear within the pertinent text column, which helps students see them in the appropriate context. Key terms are defined in page corners near where they are introduced.

Students in written reviews compared this new, three-column design with a traditional one-column design (without knowing which was ours). They unanimously preferred the three-column design. Students found the three-column design to be "less intimidating" and "less overwhelming" and said it "motivated" them to read on.

SQ3R Study Aids

Psychology in Everyday Life has been designed to help students pick out and remember key ideas and important terms with a **survey-question-read-rehearse-review (SQ3R)** format.

Chapter outlines allow students to *survey* what's to come. Main sections begin with a study *question* that encourages students to *read* actively. Periodic Practice Tests and chapter-ending Key Terms lists encourage students to *rehearse* their understanding. Chapter-ending visual concept maps *review* the material and help students make meaningful connections to reinforce what they have learned. (See **Figures 1** and **2** for practice test and concept map samples.)

Writing

Most important, I've written this book to be optimally accessible. The vocabulary is sensitive to students with widely varying reading levels and backgrounds. And this book is much briefer than many texts on the market, making it easier to fit into one-term courses. With only 14 chapters and 416 pages, this is not the book for those wanting encyclopedic coverage. Rather, my goal was to select the most humanly significant topics. I continually asked myself while working, "Would an educated person need to know this? Would this help students live better lives?"

key terms Look for complete definitions of each important term in a page corner near the term's introduction in the narrative.

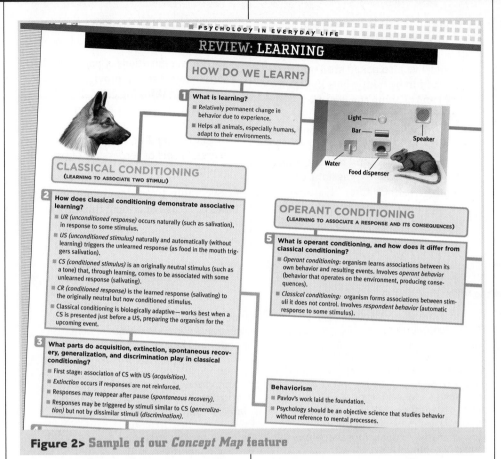

Figure 2> Sample of our *Concept Map* feature

Culture and Gender—No Assumptions

Even more than in my other texts, I have written *Psychology in Everyday Life* with the diversity of my student readers in mind.

- *Gender:* Extensive coverage of gender roles and the increasing diversity of choices men and women can make.

- *Cultural:* No assumptions about readers' cultural backgrounds or experiences.

- *Economic:* No references to back yards, summer camp, vacation cruises.

- *Educational:* No assumptions about past or current learning environments; writing is accessible for all.

- *Physical Abilities:* No assumptions about full vision, hearing, movement.

- *Life Experiences:* Examples are included from urban, suburban, and rural/outdoors settings.

- *Family Status:* Examples and ideas are made relevant for all students, whether they have children or are still living at home, are married or cohabiting or single; no assumptions about sexual orientation.

Four Big Ideas

I've often heard from instructors struggling to weave psychology's disparate parts into a cohesive whole for students, and from students struggling to make sense of all the pieces. In *Psychology in*

Everyday Life, I have introduced four of psychology's big ideas as one possible way to make connections among all the concepts. These ideas are presented in Chapter 1 and gently integrated throughout the text.

1. Critical Thinking Is Smart Thinking

I love to write in a way that gets students thinking and keeps them active as they read. I have tried to show students not just the outcome of research, but how the research process works. Students will see how the science of psychology can help them evaluate competing ideas and highly publicized claims—ranging from subliminal persuasion, ESP, and hypnosis, to astrology, alternative therapies, and repressed and recovered memories.

In *Psychology in Everyday Life,* students have many opportunities to learn or practice their critical thinking skills:

- *Chapter 1 takes a unique, critical thinking approach to introducing students to psychology's research methods.* Understanding the weak points of our everyday intuition and common sense helps students see the need for psychological science. *Critical thinking* is introduced as a key term in this chapter (page 5).

- *"Think Critically About . . ." boxes* are found throughout the book. This feature models for students a critical approach to some key issues in psychology. For example, see "Think Critically About: Lie Detectors" (Chapter 9) or "Think Critically About: How to Be a 'Successful' Astrologer" (Chapter 11). "Close-Up" boxes encourage application of the new concepts. For example, see "Close-Up: Some Weight-Loss Tips" in Chapter 9, or "Close-Up: The Relaxation Response" in Chapter 10.

- *Detective-style stories* throughout the text get students thinking critically about psychology's key research questions. In Chapter 2, for example, I present as a puzzle the history of discoveries about where and how language happens in the brain. I guide students through the puzzle, showing them how researchers put all the pieces together.

■ *"Try this"* and *"Think about it"* style discussions and side notes keep students active in their study of each chapter. I often encourage students to imagine themselves as participants in experiments. In Chapter 14, for example, students take the perspective of participants in a Solomon Asch conformity experiment, and later in one of Stanley Milgram's obedience experiments. I've also asked students to join the fun by taking part in activities they can try along the way. Here are a few examples: In Chapter 5, they try out a quick sensory adaptation activity. In Chapter 9, they try matching expressions to faces and test the effects of different facial expressions on themselves. In Chapter 11, students are asked to consider how they would construct a questionnaire for an Internet dating service.

■ *Critical examinations of pop psychology* spark interest and provide important lessons in thinking critically about everyday topics. For example, Chapter 5 includes a close examination of ESP, and Chapter 7 addresses the controversial topic of repression of painful memories.

See **Table 1** for a complete list of this text's coverage of critical thinking topics.

Table 1   Critical Thinking

Critical thinking coverage may be found on the following pages:

A scientific model for studying psychology, p. 163
Are intelligence tests biased?, pp. 230–231
Are people who use antidepressants more likely to commit suicide?, p. 366
Are personality tests able to predict behavior?, p. 304
Are there parts of the brain we don't use?, p. 42
Attachment style, development of, p. 78
Attention-deficit hyperactivity disorder (ADHD), p. 314
Causation and the violence-viewing effect, p. 176
Classifying psychological disorders, p. 317
Confirmation bias, pp. 206–207
Continuity vs. stage theories of development, pp. 89, 97–98
Correlation and causation, pp. 14–15, 80, 88
Critical thinking, defined, p. 5
Critiquing the evolutionary perspective on sexuality, pp. 119–120
Do animals think and have language?, pp. 215–218
Do lie detectors lie?, p. 253
Do video games teach, or release, violence?, p. 393
Does catharsis relieve, or worsen, anger?, p. 393
Does meditation enhance immunity?, pp. 282–283
Effectiveness of "alternative" therapies, pp. 361–362
Emotion and the brain, p. 37
Emotional intelligence, p. 222
Evolution and sexual orientation, p. 119
Evolutionary science and human origins, p. 120
Extrasensory perception, pp. 151–153

Fear of flying vs. probabilities, pp. 209–210
Freud's contributions, pp. 295–296
Genetic and environmental influences on schizophrenia, pp. 340–344
Group differences in intelligence, pp. 227–229
Heritability and weight, p. 245
Hindsight bias, pp. 9–10
Hindsight explanations, p. 119
How do nature and nurture shape prenatal development?, pp. 64–67
How do twin and adoption studies help us understand the effects of nature and nurture?, p. 69
How does the brain process language?, pp. 43–44
How much is gender socially constructed vs. biologically influenced?, pp. 105–108
How to be a "successful" astrologer, p. 302
How valid is the Rorschach inkblot test?, pp. 294–295
Human curiosity, p. 1
Humanistic perspective, pp. 298–299
Hypnosis: dissociation or social influence?, pp. 139–140
Illusory correlations, p. 16
Importance of checking fears against facts, pp. 209–210
Influence of cognitive processes on behavior, p. 169
Interaction of nature and nurture in overall development, pp. 83, 84
Is dissociative identity disorder a real disorder?, p. 323
Is psychotherapy effective?, pp. 359–362
Is repression a myth?, pp. 295–296
Limits of case studies, surveys, and naturalistic observation, pp. 12–14

Limits of intuition, p. 9
Nature and nurture's shared influence on gender and sexuality, p. 121
Nature, nurture, and perceptual ability, p. 148
Overconfidence, pp. 10, 208
Post-traumatic stress disorder (PTSD), pp. 320–321
Powers and perils of intuition, pp. 210–211
Problem-solving strategies, p. 206
Psychic phenomena, p. 11
Psychology: a discipline for critical thought, pp. 3, 9
Religious involvement and longevity, pp. 283–284
Scientific method, pp. 10, 11–12
Sex and human values, p. 113
Sexual desire and ovulation, p. 110
Similarities and differences between men and women, pp. 104–105
Stress and cancer, p. 274
Suggestive powers of subliminal messages, pp. 126–127
The discovery of the hypothalamus, p. 38
The divided brain, pp. 45–47
The powers and limits of parental involvement on development, p. 82
Using psychology to debunk popular beliefs, pp. 5, 8, 10
Values and psychology, p. 21
What does selective attention teach us about consciousness?, pp. 48–49
What factors influence sexual orientation?, pp. 114–117
What is the connection between the brain and the mind?, p. 35
Wording effects, pp. 13, 21

2. Behavior Is a Biopsychosocial Event

Students will learn that we can best understand human behavior if we view it from three levels—the biological, psycho-logical, and social-cultural. This concept is introduced in Chapter 1 and revisited throughout the text. Readers will see evidence of our human kinship—our shared biological heritage, our common mechanisms of seeing and learning, hungering and feeling, loving and hating. Yet they will also better understand the dimensions of our diversity—our *individual* diversity (in development and ability, temperament and personality, and disorders and health), our *gender* diversity (in emotions, abilities, and health), and our *cultural* diversity (in attitudes and expressive styles, childrearing and care for the elderly, and life priorities). **Table 2** provides a

Table 2	Culture and Multicultural Experience

Coverage of *culture and multicultural experience* may be found on the following pages:

"Abnormal" behavior, p. 315
Academic achievement, pp. 228–229, 279
Adolescence, onset of, p. 88
Aggression, p. 392
Anger, p. 259
Animal learning, p. 216
Animal research, views on, p. 20
Beauty ideals, p. 396
Biopsychosocial approach, pp. 5, 6–7, 83, 105–106, 110, 264, 315–316, 337, 369, 370, 394
Body image, p. 241
Cluster migration, p. 247
Cognitive development of children, p. 76
Collectivism, pp. 308, 376, 381
Contraceptive use among teens, p. 111
Crime and stress hormone levels, p. 324
Cultural values
  child-rearing and, pp. 80–81
  morality and, p. 86
  psychotherapy and, p. 363
Culture
  defined, pp. 6, 80, 106
  emotional expression and, pp. 256–257
  intelligence test bias and, p. 230
  the self and, pp. 308–309
Deindividuation, p. 385
Depression, risk of, p. 337
Developmental similarities across cultures, p. 83
Deviant behavior definitions, p. 314
Discrimination, pp. 388–389
Dissociative identity disorder, p. 323
Division of labor, p. 107
Divorce rate, p. 94
Dreams, p. 58
Enemy perceptions, pp. 400–401
Exercise, pp. 245, 280
Expressions of grief, p. 96
Family environment, p. 82
Family self, sense of, p. 81
Father care, p. 78
Father's presence
  pregnancy and, p. 112

violence and, p. 392
Flow, pp. 407–408
Foot-in-the-door phenomenon, pp. 377–378
Fundamental attribution error, pp. 376–377
Gender
  aggression and, p. 104
  phone communication and, p. 105
  sex drive and, p. 118
Gender roles, pp. 106–107, 121
General adaptation syndrome, p. 271
Global psychology, p. 4
Happiness, p. 264
HIV/AIDS, pp. 111, 274
Homosexuality, attitudes toward, p. 109
Hunger, p. 238
Identity formation, pp. 86–87
Individualism, pp. 308, 376, 381
  moral development and, p. 86
Ingroup bias, pp. 389–390
Intelligence, p. 218
  group differences in, pp. 227–229
Intelligence testing, p. 222
Job satisfaction, p. 410
Just-world phenomenon, pp. 388–389, 390
Language development, pp. 213–214
Leadership, p. 414
Learning, p. 169
Life satisfaction, p. 97
Mating preferences, pp. 118, 120
Meditation, p. 282
Mental disorders and stress, p. 315
Mere exposure effect, pp. 394–395
Motivation, pp. 236–237
Naturalistic observation, p. 14
Need to belong, p. 247
Obedience, pp. 381–383, 387
Optimism, p. 278
Ostracism, pp. 247–248
Parent-teen relations, p. 88
Partner selection, p. 398
Peer influence, p. 83
  on language development, p. 82
Personal control, p. 277
Personality traits, pp. 300, 301

Phobias, p. 322
Physical attractiveness, pp. 395–397
Poverty, explanations of, p. 377
Power differences between men and women, p. 104
Prejudice, pp. 388–390, 395
  automatic, p. 389
  cooperative contact and, p. 401
  group polarization and, p. 385
  racial, p. 378
  subtle versus overt, p. 388
Prosocial behavior, p. 174
Psychoactive drugs, p. 325
Psychological disorders, pp. 313, 316
Racial similarities, pp. 228–229
Religious involvement and longevity, p. 283
Risk assessment, p. 210
Scapegoat theory, p. 390
Self-esteem, p. 307
Self-serving bias, p. 307
Separation anxiety, p. 78
Serial position effect, p. 184
Shaping behavior of rats, p. 166
Situational influence, pp. 378, 380–386
Sleep patterns, p. 54
Social clock variation, p. 95
Social influence, p. 381
Social loafing, p. 384
Social trust, p. 81
Social-cultural psychology, pp. 4, 6, 333–334
Stereotype threat, p. 230
Stereotypes, pp. 388, 390
Stranger anxiety, p. 77
Substance abuse, p. 333
Survivor resiliency, p. 320
Susto, p. 315
Taijin-kyofusho, p. 315
Taste preference, pp. 240, 242
Terrorism, pp. 205, 209, 299, 377, 390, 392
Trauma, pp. 295–296, 360
Universal expressions, p. 7
Weight, p. 245

list of integrated coverage of the cross-cultural perspective on psychology. **Table 3** lists the coverage of the psychology of women and men. Significant gender and cross-cultural examples and research are presented within the narrative. In addition, an abundance of photos, especially in the *Diverse Yet Alike* photo feature, showcases the diversity of cultures within North America and across the globe. These photos and their informative captions bring the pages to life, broadening students' perspectives in applying psychological science to their own world and to the worlds across the globe.

3. We Operate With a Two-Track Mind (Dual Processing)

Today's psychological science explores our *dual-processing* capacity. Our perception, thinking, memory, and attitudes all operate on two levels: the level of fully aware, conscious processing, and the behind-the-scenes level of unconscious processing. Students may be surprised to learn how much information we process outside of our awareness! Discussions of sleep (Chapter 2), perception (Chapter 5), and attitudes and prejudice (Chapter 14) provide some particularly compelling examples of what goes on in our mind's downstairs.

4. Psychology Explores Human Strengths as Well as Challenges

Students will learn about the many troublesome behaviors and emotions psychologists study, as well as the ways in which psychologists work with those who need help. Yet students will also learn about the *beneficial* emotions and traits that psychologists study, and the ways psychologists (some as part of the new positive psychology movement) attempt to nurture those traits in others. After studying with this text, students may find themselves living improved

Table 3	Psychology of Women and Men

Coverage of the *psychology of women and men* may be found on the following pages:

Abusive relationships, p. 247
Age and decreased fertility, p. 91
Aggression, pp. 104, 391–394
  testosterone and, pp. 391–392
Alcohol dependence, pp. 326–327
Alcohol use and sexual assault, pp. 326, 328
Attraction, p. 394–398
Beauty ideals, p. 396
Bipolar disorder, p. 336
Body image, p. 241
Depression, pp. 335–338
  among girls, p. 87
  heart disease and, p. 275
Eating disorders, p. 241
Emotional expressiveness, p. 256
Emotion-detecting ability, p. 256
Empathy, p. 256
Father's presence, pregnancy rates and, p. 112
Freud's views on personality development, pp. 291–292, 296
Gender, pp. 6, 103
  anxiety and, p. 318
  biological Influences on, pp. 105–106
  changes in society's thinking about, pp. 103, 107, 108–109, 121, 388
  social-cultural influences on, pp. 6, 106–107
  weight discrimination and, p. 243
  widowhood and, p. 95
Gender differences, pp. 6–7, 104–106, 114
  emotional memory and, p. 338
  evolutionary perspectives on, pp. 117–119

intelligence and, pp. 229–230
  sexuality and, p. 118
Gender discrimination, p. 389
Gender identity, development of, pp. 107–108
Gender roles, pp. 106–107, 389, 393
Gender schema theory, pp. 107–108
Gender similarities, pp. 104–106
Gender typing, p. 107
HIV/AIDS, women's vulnerability to, p. 111
Homosexuality, attitudes towards, p. 109
Homosexuality's disorder classification, p. 314
Hormones and sexual behavior, pp. 109–110
Human sexuality, pp. 108–113
Leadership styles, pp. 104–105
Learned helplessness, p. 338
Life expectancy, p. 104
Marriage, pp. 94, 280, 284, 398
Mating preferences, pp. 118–119, 120
Maturation, pp. 84, 90
Menarche, pp. 84, 89
Menopause, p. 91
Obedience, p. 382
Obesity and heredity, p. 244
Partner selection, p. 398
Physical attractiveness, pp. 395–396
Post-traumatic stress disorder, p. 320
Puberty, p. 84
Puberty, early onset of, pp. 88–89
Relationship equity, p. 398
Religion and longevity, p. 283
Responses to stress, p. 272
Romantic love, pp. 397–398

Schizophrenia, p. 341
Seasonal affective disorder, p. 335
Sex, pp. 6, 109
Sex and gender, p. 106
Sex chromosomes, p. 106
Sex drive, p. 118
Sex hormones, p. 106
Sex-reassignment, p. 106
Sexual abuse, p. 79
Sexual activity and aging, p. 92
Sexual intercourse among teens, p. 108
Sexual orientation, pp. 113–117
Sexual response, alcohol-related expectation and, pp. 327–328
Sexual response cycle, p. 109
Sexual scripts, p. 393
Sexuality, natural selection and, pp. 117–120
Sexually explicit media, pp. 111–112, 393–394
Sexually transmitted infections, pp. 110–111
Similarities and differences between men and women, pp. 104–106
Social connectedness, p. 105
Social power, pp. 104–105
Stress and heart disease, p. 274
Substance abuse and addiction, p. 333
Teen pregnancy, pp. 111–112
Violent crime, p. 104
Vulnerability to psychological disorders, p. 104
Weight loss, p. 245
Women and work, p. 95
Women in psychology, p. 2

day-to-day lives. See, for example, tips for better sleep in Chapter 2, parenting suggestions throughout Chapter 3, information to help with romantic relationships in Chapter 4, and "Close-Up: Want to Be Happier?" in Chapter 9. Students may also find themselves doing better in their courses. See, for example, following this preface, "Time Management or, How to Be a Great Student and Still Have a Life!" and "Improving Memory" in Chapter 7.

Enhanced Clinical Coverage

Compared with my other texts, *Psychology in Everyday Life* has proportionately more coverage of clinical topics and a greater sensitivity to clinical issues throughout the text. For example, Chapter 12, Psychological Disorders, includes lengthy coverage of substance-related disorders complete with guidelines for determining substance abuse and substance dependence. The discussion of psychoactive drugs includes a special focus on alcohol and nicotine dependence. Chapter 12 also includes a more general table outlining the complete

process clinicians use to diagnose disorders with the DSM-IV-TR. See **Table 4** for a listing of coverage of clinical psychology concepts and issues throughout the text.

Currency and Everyday Life Applications

Few things dampen students' interest as quickly as the sense that they are reading stale news. While retaining psychology's classic studies and concepts, I also present the discipline's most important

Table 4	Clinical Psychology

Coverage of *clinical psychology* may be found on the following pages:

Abused children, risk of psychological disorder among, p. 162
Affluent children, risk of psychological disorder among, p. 261
Aggression, pp. 391–394
Alcohol use and aggression, p. 392
Alzheimer's disease, pp. 189, 242
Anxiety disorders, pp. 318–322
Autism, p. 219
Aversive conditioning, pp. 355–356
Behavior modification, p. 356
Behavior therapies, pp. 354–356
Bipolar disorder, pp. 335–336
Brain damage and memory loss, pp. 188–189
Brain scans, p. 35
Brain stimulation therapies, pp. 357–358
Childhood trauma, effect on mental health, p. 79
Client-centered therapy, pp. 352–353
Client-therapist relationship, pp. 299, 323, 350–353
Clinical psychologists, p. 3
Cognitive therapies, pp. 339, 356–358, 379
eating disorders and, p. 356
Culture and values in psychotherapy, p. 363
Depression
adolescence and, p. 87
heart disease and, p. 275
homosexuality and, p. 114
mood-memory connection and, p. 192
outlook and, pp. 338–339
self-esteem and, pp. 11–12, 16
social exclusion and, p. 88

unexpected loss and, p. 95
Dissociative and personality disorders, pp. 322–325
Dissociative identity disorder, pp. 322–323
Drug and alcohol treatment, pp. 162, 163
Drug therapies, pp. 17, 364–367
Eating disorders, p. 241
Emotional intelligence, p. 221
Exercise, therapeutic effects of, pp. 280–281, 366
Exposure therapy, pp. 354–355
Generalized anxiety disorder, p. 318
Grief therapy, p. 96
Group and family therapies, p. 358
Historical treatment of mental illness, pp. 315, 349–350
Humanistic therapies, pp. 352–353
Hypnosis and pain relief, pp. 138–140
Intelligence scales and stroke rehabilitation, p. 224
Loss of a child, psychiatric hospitalization and, p. 96
Major depressive disorder, p. 335
Medical model of mental disorders, p. 315
Mood disorders, pp. 334–339
Neurotransmitter imbalances and related disorders, p. 30
Nurturing strengths, p. 298
Obsessive-compulsive disorder, pp. 319–320
Operant conditioning in learned disordered behavior, pp. 356
Ostracism, pp. 247–248
Panic disorder, p. 319

Peer relationships and hotline counseling services, p. 88
Personality inventories, pp. 300–301
Personality testing, pp. 294–295
Phobias, p. 319
Physical and psychological treatment of pain, p. 138
Post-traumatic stress disorder, pp. 320–321
Psychiatric labels and bias, pp. 316–317
Psychoactive drugs, types of, pp. 326–332
Psychoanalysis, pp. 350–352
Psychodynamic theory, pp. 293–294
Psychological disorders, pp. 313–347
classification of, pp. 316–317, 390
Psychosurgery, pp. 368–369
Psychotherapy, pp. 350–358
effectiveness of, pp. 359–361
Rorshach inkblot test, pp. 294–295
Savant syndrome, pp. 218–219
Schizophrenia, pp. 340–344
parent-blaming and, p. 82
risk of, pp. 342–343
Self-actualization, p. 297
Sex reassignment therapy, p. 106
Sexual disorders, p. 110
Sexual orientation, p. 114
Sleep disorders, pp. 55–56
Spanked children, risk for aggression and depression among, p. 168
Substance-related disorders, pp. 325–334
Testosterone replacement therapy, p. 110
Tolerance, addiction, and dependence, pp. 325–326

recent developments. In this text, 362 references (16 percent) are dated 2004 or later. Some of the most exciting recent research has happened in the area of neuroscience, especially cognitive neuroscience and dual processing.

As the title of this text suggests, throughout—using stories, case histories, and hypothetical situations—I relate the findings of psychology's research to the real world. (See inside back cover for a listing of all of this text's applications to everyday life.) Where psychology can illuminate pressing human issues—bias and prejudice, health and happiness, violence and war—I have not hesitated to shine its light.

APA Learning Goals and Outcomes for Psychology Majors

In March 2002, an American Psychological Association (APA) Task Force created

Table 5 — *Psychology in Everyday Life* Corresponds to APA Goals

Relevant Feature from *Psychology in Everyday Life*	APA Goals				
	Knowledge Base of Psychology	Research Methods in Psychology	Critical Thinking Skills in Psychology	Application of Psychology	Values in Psychology
Text Content	✓	✓	✓	✓	✓
Four Big Ideas in Pyschology as Integrating Themes	✓	✓	✓	✓	✓
Think Critically boxes	✓	✓	✓	✓	✓
Close-Up boxes	✓			✓	✓
Study Questions previewing main sections	✓		✓	✓	
Practice Tests	✓		✓	✓	
Visual Concept Maps	✓				
"Try This" style activities integrated throughout	✓		✓	✓	
Diverse Yet Alike photo feature	✓		✓	✓	✓
Psychology at Work text appendix	✓		✓	✓	✓
PsychPortal	✓	✓	✓	✓	✓
ActivePsych	✓	✓	✓	✓	✓
Online Study Center	✓	✓	✓		✓
Companion Web site	✓	✓	✓	✓	✓
60-Second Psych (Scientific American podcast)	✓	✓	✓	✓	✓
Psych-2-Go (audio review and self-test files)	✓	✓	✓	✓	✓

a set of Learning Goals and Outcomes for students graduating with psychology majors from four-year schools (www.apa.org/ed/pcue/reports/html).

Psychology departments in many schools have since used these goals and outcomes to help them establish their own benchmarks.

Some instructors are eager to know whether a given text for the introductory course helps students get a good start at achieving these goals. **Table 5** outlines the way *Psychology in Everyday Life* and its supplements package could help you begin to address these goals in your department.

See www.worthpublishers.com/myers for a detailed guide to how *Psychology in Everyday Life* corresponds to the APA Outcomes.

| | APA Goals | | | |
Information and Technological Literacy	Communication Skills	Sociocultural and International Awareness	Personal Development	Career Planning and Development
✓	✓	✓	✓	✓
		✓	✓	
		✓	✓	
		✓	✓	
	✓			
✓	✓		✓	
✓	✓			
	✓	✓	✓	
	✓	✓	✓	
	✓	✓	✓	✓
✓	✓	✓	✓	✓
✓	✓	✓	✓	✓
✓	✓	✓	✓	✓
✓	✓	✓	✓	✓
✓	✓	✓	✓	✓
✓	✓	✓	✓	✓

Innovative Multimedia Supplements Package

Psychology in Everyday Life boasts impressive electronic and print supplements titles. For more information about any of these media and supplements titles, visit Worth Publishers' online catalog at worthpublishers.com.

PsychPortal

Integrating the best online material that Worth has to offer, PsychPortal is an innovative course space that combines a powerful quizzing engine with unparalleled media resources (see **Figure 3**). PsychPortal conveniently offers all the functionality you need to support your online or hybrid course. Yet it is flexible, customizable, and simple enough to enhance your traditional course. The following interactive learning materials contained within PsychPortal make it truly unique:

- **An interactive eBook** allows students to highlight, bookmark, and make their own notes just as they would with a printed textbook.

- Tom Ludwig's suite of interactive media—**PsychSim 5.0** and the new **Concepts in Action**—bring key topics to life.

- **Online Study Center 3.0** utilizes PsychPortal's powerful diagnostic quizzing engine. Students can generate their own personalized study plan, which will direct them to sections in the book and also to simulations, animations, and other resources to help them succeed in mastering the concepts. Instructors can access an overview of their students' understanding of the concepts (based on class quiz results) and browse suggestions for helpful presentation materials (from Worth's renowned videos and demonstrations) to address areas of weakness in lecture.

- **The Student Video Tool Kit for Introductory Psychology** allows instructors to assign videos for students to interact with outside of class, in an interactive assessible shell (**Figure 4**). Videos include classic experiments, current news footage, and cutting-edge research.

- *Scientific American's* news tidbits are updated regularly.

Additional Student Media

- Book Companion Site (includes "Careers in Psychology" supplement)

- 60-Second Psych (*Scientific American* podcasts)

- Psych2Go (audio review downloads)

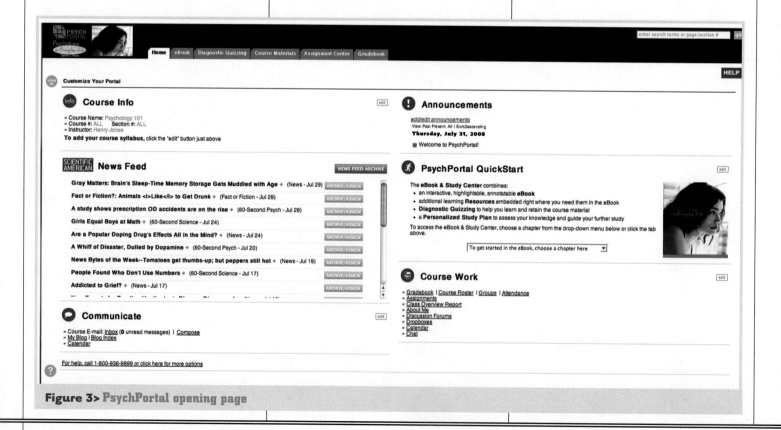

Figure 3> PsychPortal opening page

Rate this video!
Average rating: 4 stars | Views: 106 | Send us feedback

 ☆☆☆☆☆ Submit

Creating False Memories: A Laboratory Study expand ⌄

Is it possible we could remember a vivid childhood event that never occurred? Psychologists at Victoria University have demonstrated that such false memories can be

♡ Add Video to an Assignment

After you've read the description and watched the video, click the link below to answer questions about what you've learned.

View the Video Assessment Quiz!

HOT AIR

Marianne Gary:
No, we know that for a fact.

Creating False Memories A Laboratory Study

1. After a week of being asked about the false photo, what percent of students recalled having had a hot-air balloon ride?

- ○ a. 15
- ○ b. 35
- ○ c. 50
- ○ d. 75

Submit

Figure 4> Sample of our *Student Video Tool Kit*

- PsychSim 5.0 (on CD)
- Student Video Tool Kit for Introductory Psychology (on CD)

Course Management

- Enhanced Course Management Solutions

Assessment

- Printed Test Bank, Volumes 1 and 2
- Diploma Computerized Test Bank
- i>clicker Radio Frequency Classroom Response System

Presentation

- ActivePsych: Classroom Activities Projects and Video Teaching Modules (including Worth Digital Media and Scientific American Frontiers Teaching Modules, Third Edition)

- Instructor's Resource CD-ROM
- Worth Image and Lecture Gallery at worthpublishers.com/ilg
- Overhead Transparencies

Video and DVD

- Instructor Video Tool Kit
- Moving Images: Exploring Psychology Through Film
- Worth Digital Media Archive
- Psychology: The Human Experience Teaching Modules
- The Many Faces of Psychology Video
- *Scientific American* Frontiers Video Collection, Second Edition
- The Mind Video Teaching Modules, Second Edition
- The Brain Video Teaching Modules, Second Edition

Print Resources

- Instructor's Resources and Lecture Guides
- Instructor's Media Guide
- Study Guide
- Pursuing Human Strengths: A Positive Psychology Guide
- Critical Thinking Companion, Second Edition

Scientific American Resources

- Scientific American Mind
- Scientific American Reader to Accompany Myers
- Improving the Mind and Brain: A Scientific American Special Issue
- Scientific American Explores the Hidden Mind: A Collector's Edition

In Appreciation

Aided by input from 1000 instructors and 850 students, this has become a better, more effective, more accurate book than one author alone (this author, at least) could write.

I greatly appreciate the colleagues who contributed criticism, corrections, and creative ideas related to the content, pedagogy, and format of this new text. For their expertise and encouragement, and the gifts of their time to the teaching of psychology, I thank the reviewers listed below.

Tricia Alexander, *Long Beach City College*

Pamela Ansburg, *Metropolitan State College of Denver*

Randy Arnau, *University of Southern Mississippi*

Stacy Bacigalupi, *Mount San Antonio College*

Kimberly Bays-Brown, *Ball State University*

Diane Bogdan, *CUNY: Hunter College*

Robert Boroff, *Modesto Junior College*

Christia Brown, *University of Kentucky*

Alison Buchanan, *Henry Ford Community College*

Nicole Judice Campbell, *University of Oklahoma*

David Carlston, *Midwestern State University*

Kimberly Christopherson, *Morningside College*

Diana Ciesko, *Valencia Community College*

TaMetryce Collins, *Hillsborough Community College*

Patricia Crowe, *Hawkeye College*

George Diekhoff, *Midwestern State University*

Michael Drissman, *Macomb Community College*

Laura Duvall, *Heartland Community College*

Jennifer Dyck, *SUNY College at Fredonia*

Laura Engleman, *Pikes Peak Community College*

Warren Fass, *University of Pittsburgh*

Vivian Ferry, *Community College of Rhode Island*

Elizabeth Freeman-Young, *Bentley College*

Ann Fresoli, *Lehigh Carbon Community College*

Ruth Frickle, *Highline Community College*

Lenore Frigo, *Shasta College*

Gary Gargano, *Merced College*

Jo Anne Geron, *Antioch University*

Stephanie Grant, *Southern Nazarene University*

Raymond Green, *The Honors College of Texas*

Sandy Grossman, *Clackamas Community College*

Lisa Gunderson, *Sacramento City College*

Rob Guttentag, *University of North Carolina—Greensboro*

Gordon Hammerle, *Adrian College*

Mark Hartlaub, *Texas A&M University*

Sheyl Hartman, *Miami Dade College*

Brett Heintz, *Delgado Community College*

Alishia Huntoon, *Oregon Institute of Technology*

Cindy Hutman, *Elgin Community College*

Laurene Jones, *Mercer County Community College*

Charles "Ed" Joubert, *University of North Alabama*

Deana Julka, *University of Portland*

Richard Kandus, *Mount San Jacinto College, Menifree*

Elizabeth Kennedy, *University of Akron*

Norm Kinney, *Southeast Missouri University*

Gary Klatsky, *SUNY Oswego State University*

Dan Klaus, *Community College of Beaver County*

Gary Lewandowski, *Monmouth University*

Alicia Limke, *University of Central Oklahoma*

Leslie Linder, *Bridgewater State College*

Chris Long, *Ouachita Baptist University*

Martha Low, *Winston-Salem State University*

Mark Ludorf, *Stephen F. Austin State University*

Vince Markowski, *University of Southern Maine*

Dawn McBride, *Illinois State University*

Tammy Menzel, *Mott Community College*

Leslie Minor-Evans, *Central Oregon Community College*

Mar Navarro, *Valencia Community College*

David Neufeldt, *Hutchinson Community College*

Peggy Norwood, *Aurora Community College*

Fabian Novello, *Clark State Community College*

Ginger Osborne, *Santa Ana College*

Randall Osborne, *Texas State University—San Marcos*

Carola Pedreschi, *Miami-Dade College North Campus*

Jim Previte, *Victor Valley College*

Sean Reilley, *Morehead State University*

Vicki Ritts, *St. Louis Community College-Meramec*

R. Steven Schiavo, *Wellesley College*

Cynthia Selby, *California State University—Chico*

Jenifer Siciliani, *University of Missouri-St. Louis*

Barry Silber, *Hillsborough Community College*

Madhu Singh, *Tougaloo College*

Alice Skeens, *University of Toledo*

Jason Spiegalman, *Towson University*

Betsy Stern, *Milwaukee Area Technical College*

Eloise Thomas, *Ozarks Technical Community College*

Susan Troy, *Northeast Iowa Community College*

Jacqueline Remondet Wall, *University of Indianapolis*

Marc Wayner, *Hocking College*

Diane Webber, *Curry College*

Richard Wedemeyer, *Rose State College*

Peter Wooldridge, *Durham Technical Community College*

John Wright, *Washington State University*

Gabriel Ybarra, *University of North Florida*

I am also thankful to the 794 instructors who took the time to respond to our surveys. Their helpful and timely input was essential in the early formative stages of this text.

Sixty-two brave instructors agreed to class-test a chapter of this text in advance of its publication. For their interest and enthusiasm, and for their helpful feedback, I thank the following instructors and their students:

David Alfano, *Community College of Rhode Island*

Harold Arnold, *Judson College*

Stacy Bacigalupi, *Mt. San Antonio College*

Emily Balcetis, *Ohio University*

David Carlston, Midwestern State University

Richard Catrambone, Georgia Institute of Technology

Kathy Coiner, Scott Community College

TaMetryce Collins, Hillsborough Community College

Victoria Cooke, Erie Community College

Stephanie Deturk, University of Kansas

Mark Eastman, Diablo Valley College

Michael Feiler, Merritt College

Lenore Frigo, Shasta College

William Rick Fry, Youngstown State University

William Goggin, University of Southern Mississippi

Gary Grady, Connors State College

Jerry Green, Tarrant County College, Northwest Campus

Stephen Guerin, Motlow State Community College

Chuck Hallock, Pima County Community College

Lori Harris, Southeastern Iowa Community College

Catherine Hawkins, North Hennepin Community College

Ann Hennessey, Pierce College

Richard Kandus, Mt. San Jacinto College, Menifree Campus

Jason Kaufman, Inver Hills Community College

Kevin Keating, Broward Community College

Betsy Klopcic, Illinois Valley Community College

Ken Koenigshofer, Chaffey College

Larry Kollman, North Iowa Area Community College

Cindy Lahar, York County Community College

Mary Lofgren, Imperial Valley Community College

Brian MacKenna-Rice, Middlesex Community College

David Malcolm, Fordham University

John Mavromatis, St. John Fisher College

Christopher Mayhorn, North Carolina State University

Melissa McCeney, Montgomery College

Marcia McKinley-Baum, Mount St. Mary's University

Barbara McMillan, Alabama Southern University

Katy Neidhardt, California Polytechnic State University

Teri Nicoll-Johnson, Modesto Junior College

Patricia Nicosia, Kettering College of Medical Arts

Christopher Ostwinkle, Northeast Iowa Community College

William Pannell, El Paso Community College

Neophytos Papaneophytou, Borough of Manhattan Community College

David Payne, Wallace Community College

Julie Penley, El Paso Community College

John Pierce, Villanova University

Deborah Podwika, Kankakee Community College

Gregory Pool, St. Mary's University

Dennis Russell, Southeast Technical Institute

Brian Sexton, Georgia Court University

Donald Smith, Everett Community College

Jason Spiegalman, Towson University & Community College of Baltimore County

David Steitz, Nazareth College

Annette Kujawski Taylor, University of San Diego

Inger Thompson, Glendale Community College

Sarah Ting, Cerritos College

Susan Troy, Northeast Iowa Community College

Ada Wainwright, College of DuPage

Elizabeth Weiss, Ohio State University

Linda Weldon, Community College of Baltimore County—Essex

Jennifer Zwahr-Castro, St. Mary's University

My gratitude extends to more students who shared that most precious commodity—time—in order to help make this text a better learning tool for those who will follow. Students from the following schools gave up an afternoon to participate in one of our focus groups, or offered written feedback by way of their instructor.

Adrian College

Century College

Long Beach City College

Mount San Antonio College

Nassau Community College

Pikes Peak Community College

Shasta College

SUNY College at Fredonia

Southern Nazarene University

University of Akron

University of North Florida

University of Toledo

At Worth Publishers a host of people played key roles in creating this new text. The formal planning began as the author-publisher team gathered for a two-day retreat. This happy and creative gathering included John Brink, Martin Bolt, Thomas Ludwig, Richard Straub, and me from the author team, along with my assistants Kathryn Brownson and Sara Neevel. We were joined by Bedford-Freeman-Worth executives Tom Scotty, Elizabeth Widdicombe, and Catherine Woods; editors Christine Brune, Kevin Feyen, Nancy Fleming, Tracey Kuehn, Betty Probert, and Peter Twickler; artistic director Babs Reingold; and sales and marketing colleagues Kate Nurre, Tom Kling, Guy Geraghty, Sandy Manly, Amy Shefferd, Rich Rosenlof, and Brendan Baruth.

Senior Psychology Acquisitions Editor Kevin Feyen has become a valued team leader, thanks to his dedication, creativity, and sensitivity. Publisher Catherine Woods helped construct and execute the plan for this new text and its supplements. Catherine was also a trusted sounding board as we faced a seemingly unending series of discrete decisions along the way. Peter Twickler coordinated production of the huge supplements package for this edition. Betty Probert efficiently edited and produced the print supplements and, in the process, also helped fine-tune the whole book. Greg Bennetts and Lorraine Klimowich provided invaluable support in commissioning and organizing the multitude of reviews, mailing information to professors, and handling numerous other daily tasks related to the book's development and production. Lee Mahler-McKevitt did a splendid job of laying out each page. Bianca Moscatelli and Patty Cateura worked together to locate the myriad photographic illustrations.

Associate Managing Editor Tracey Kuehn and Project Editor Dana Kasowitz displayed tireless tenacity, commitment, and impressive organization in leading Worth's gifted artistic production team and coordinating editorial input throughout the production process. Production Manager Sarah Segal masterfully held the book to its tight schedule, and Babs Reingold skillfully envisioned and directed creation of the distinctive design and art program that lies at the heart of this project. Production Manager Stacey Alexander, along with supplements production editor Jenny Chiu, did their usual excellent work of producing the many supplements.

As you can see, although this book has one author it is a *team* effort. A special salute is due my two book development editors who have invested so much in creating *Psychology in Everyday Life*. My longtime editor Christine Brune saw the need for a very short, accessible, student-friendly introductory psychology text, and she energized and guided the rest of us in bringing her vision to reality.

Development editor Nancy Fleming is one of those rare editors who is gifted at "thinking big" about a chapter while also applying her sensitive, graceful, line-by-line touches. Her painstaking, deft editing was a key part of achieving the hoped-for brevity and accessibility.

To achieve our goal of supporting the teaching of psychology, this teaching package not only must be authored, reviewed, edited, and produced, but also made available to teachers of psychology. For their exceptional dedication to doing that, our author team is grateful to Worth Publishers' professional sales and marketing team. We are especially grateful to Executive Marketing Manager Kate Nurre, Associate Director of Marketing Development Carlise Stembridge, Marketing Manager Amy Shefferd, National Psychology and Economics Consultant Tom Kling, High School Executive Marketing Manager Cindi Weiss, and Marketing Assistant Kerri Knipper, both for their tireless attempts to inform our teaching colleagues of our efforts to assist their teaching, and for the joy of working with them.

At Hope College, the supporting team members for this edition included Kathryn Brownson, who researched countless bits of information and proofed hundreds of pages. Kathryn has become a knowledgeable and sensitive adviser on many matters, and Sara Neevel has become our high-tech manuscript developer, par excellence. Laura Myers created the cross-reference tables in this Preface, complete with page citations.

I gratefully acknowledge the influence and editing assistance of my writing coach, poet Jack Ridl, whose influence resides in the voice you will be hearing in the pages that follow. He, more than anyone, cultivated my delight in dancing with the language, and taught me to approach writing as a craft that shades into art.

After hearing countless dozens of people say that the Worth Publishers' supplements for my other texts have taken their teaching to a new level, I reflect on how fortunate I am to be a part of a team on which everyone produces on-time work marked by the highest professional standards (and how pleased I am that this new text will enjoy the same high-quality supplements). For their remarkable talents, their long-term dedication, and their friendship, I thank Martin Bolt, John Brink, Thomas Ludwig, and Richard Straub. I have worked with this wonderful team for 25 years now, and I continue to enjoy our collaborations.

Finally, I acknowledge my longtime friend and trusted adviser Guy Geraghty and dedicate this book to him. Guy joined the Worth Publishers sales team the same year I became a Worth author. He began introducing my work to colleagues across the country long before the first edition of my full-length text was published, and he continued doing so for 25 years, including during his later years as a technology expert. Guy attended all nine of our triennial book-planning retreats, and in our many conversations, meals, and meetings, he was a larger-than-life, exuberant, loving, encouraging friend. Although his life was claimed too soon, he remains indelibly alive in the minds of his many friends.

* * *

The day this book went to press was the day I started gathering information and ideas for the next edition. Your input will influence how this book continues to evolve. So, please, do share your thoughts.

David Myers

Hope College Holland, Michigan 49422-9000 USA davidmyers.org

Time Management
Or, How to Be a Great Student and Still Have a Life! —Richard O. Straub University of Michigan, Dearborn

1. **HOW ARE YOU USING YOUR TIME NOW?**

2. **DESIGN A NEW SCHEDULE**
   Plan the Term
   Develop a Weekly Schedule

   CLOSE-UP: More Tips for Effective Scheduling

3. **USE YOUR STUDY TIME EFFECTIVELY**
   Take Useful Class Notes
   Create a Study Space That Helps You Learn
   Set Up Daily Goals That Are Specific and Realistic
   Use SQ3R to Help You Master This Text
   Don't Forget About Rewards!

4. **DO YOU NEED TO REVISE YOUR NEW SCHEDULE?**

Dana John, on the campus of New Jersey City University

Alex Tehrani

So, you think you have a challenging schedule to juggle? In Chapter 10, you will learn about New Jersey City University basketball star Dana John, who balances time with his preschooler, a full-time job at the Post Office, college classes, *and* basketball! How does he do it? How do any of us balance our lives successfully? Time management. Manage the time you have so that you can find the time you need.

In this preface, I will outline a simple, four-step process for improving the way you make use of your time.

1. Focus on how you are spending your time now.

2. Set up a new, more efficient way to use your time.

3. Make the most of your study time so that your new schedule will work for you.

4. Consider ways that you can improve your schedule further based on what you've learned from this process.

How Are You Using Your Time Now?

Although everyone gets 24 hours in the day and seven days in the week, we fill those hours and days with different obligations and interests. If you are like most people, you probably use your time wisely in some ways, and not so wisely in others. To help you find the trouble spots—and hopefully more time for the things that matter most—start first by answering the questions in **TABLE 1**. This will give you a broad overview of the areas that may need more of your energy and attention over the next few weeks as you work to develop better time management and study skills.

Table 1	**Study Habits Survey**

Answer the following questions, writing *yes* or *no* on each line.

1. Do you usually set up a schedule to budget your time for studying, recreation, and other activities? _____

2. Do you often put off studying until time pressures force you to cram? _____

3. Do other students seem to study less than you do, but get better grades? _____

4. Do you usually spend hours at a time studying one subject, rather than dividing that time among several subjects? _____

5. Do you often have trouble remembering what you have just read in a textbook? _____

6. Before reading a chapter in a textbook, do you skim through it and read the section headings? _____

7. Do you try to predict test questions from your lecture notes and reading? _____

8. Do you usually try to summarize in your own words what you have just finished reading? _____

9. Do you find it difficult to concentrate for very long when you study? _____

10. Do you often feel that you studied the wrong material for a test? _____

Thousands of students have participated in similar surveys. Students who are fully realizing their academic potential usually respond as follows: (1) yes, (2) no, (3) no, (4) no, (5) no, (6) yes, (7) yes, (8) yes, (9) no, (10) no.
   Compare your responses to those of successful students. The greater the difference, the more you could benefit from a program to improve your time management and study habits. The questions are designed to identify areas of weakness. Knowing your trouble spots will help you set specific goals for improvement and a plan for reaching them.

Next you will need to record your activities in a time-use diary for one week. The important thing is to record how you *actually* spend your time—attending class, studying, working, commuting, meeting personal and family needs, fixing and eating meals, socializing, exercising, and anything else that occupies your time. Don't forget all of life's small practical tasks, which can take up plenty of your 24/7.

To help you get started, I've filled out a sample day for a student taking a full load of classes and working part time (TABLE 2). Using this simple format, prepare one diary page for each day of the week, including the weekend, and remember to carry the pages with you. You will need an accurate record of your activities in order to design your new schedule.

As you record your activities, jot down not only what you are doing at various times of the day, but also *how you are feeling* at those times. Careful recordkeeping will show you when your energy slumps and when you feel rested and energetic. Later, you'll want to schedule your activities to take full advantage of your most productive times. Many students don't get enough sleep to function effectively throughout their day. Your records may also reveal this need to "schedule" in more sleep time.

Are you finding times when you get distracted, as personal or job obligations invade the time you had set aside for school work? Be sure to record all these distractions. You will use this important information later, when you set up your new plan for managing your time more effectively.

Design a New Schedule

Take a close look at your time-use diary. Are there clear areas where time is wasted? Do you spend a lot of time commuting, for example? If it is not an option to live closer to school and/or work, or drive during a time with less traffic, you might consider getting audio review files so that you can make productive use of your travel time. (This text has audio review files available, for example, at worthpublishers.com/Psych2Go.)

Your diary should also give you a clear idea of how much time you need to allot for meals and other fixed activities.

Are you allowing enough time for sleep? Sleeping 7 to 8 hours per night at roughly the same time each night should provide you with the most energy.

Have you dedicated enough time for focused study? Although it may sound like more fun to study with friends, you may use less time on studying and have more time left over for socializing if you study alone.

| Table 2 | Sample Time-Use Diary |

Create a similar chart for each day of the week. Throughout the day, fill it in by writing down your activities, noting how much time was devoted to each and your energy level (where appropriate).

Monday

Activity	Time	Duration	Energy Level
Wake-up	6:30 a.m.		
Exercise	6:30–7:00 a.m.	30 minutes	
Shower, dress	7:00–7:30 a.m.	30 minutes	
Breakfast	7:30–8:15 a.m.	45 minutes	
Commute	8:15–8:40 a.m.	25 minutes	
Coffee	8:40–9:00 a.m.	20 minutes	
French	9:00–10:00 a.m.	1 hour	high
Check email, messages	10:00–10:40 a.m.	40 minutes	high
Study French	10:40–11:00 a.m.	20 minutes	high
Psychology	11:00 a.m.–12:00 noon	1 hour	medium
Lunch	12:00–12:25 p.m.	25 minutes	
Study chemistry	12:25–1:00 p.m.	35 minutes	low
Psychology lab	1:00–3:00 p.m.	2 hours	medium
Commute (with stop at the grocery store)	3:00–3:45 p.m.	45 minutes	
Social, dinner	3:45–5:15 p.m.	1.5 hours	
Commute	5:15–5:30 p.m.	15 minutes	
Work	5:30–9:00 p.m.	3.5 hours	medium
Commute	9:00–9:15 p.m.	15 minutes	
Social	9:15–9:45 p.m.	30 minutes	high
Online	9:45–10:15 p.m.	30 minutes	high
Study psychology	10:15–10:45 p.m.	30 minutes	high
Study French	10:45–11:00 p.m.	15 minutes	low
Sleep	11:00 p.m.	7.5 hours	

Table 3   Sample Weekly Schedule

This is a sample schedule for a student with a full load of classes and a part-time job. (If this were a real schedule, most of the "open" time slots would be filled in with real activities and personal commitments.) Using the guidelines outlined in this preface and this chart as an illustration, create your own weekly schedule.

Time	Monday	Tuesday	Wednesday	Thursday	Friday	Saturday	Sunday
7–8 a.m.	Shower, breakfast	Shower, breakfast	Shower, breakfast	Shower, breakfast	Shower, breakfast		
8–9 a.m.	Psychology class	Study Psychology	Psychology class	Study Psychology	Psychology lab	Shower, breakfast	Shower, breakfast
9–10 a.m.	English class	Study English	Study English	English class	Psychology lab	Study Biology	Work
10–11 a.m.	Study French	Open	Study French	Open	Study Statistics	Study Biology	Work
11–12 noon	French class	French lab	Open	French class	Study French	Study Statistics	Work
12–1 p.m.	Lunch	Lunch	Lunch	Lunch	Lunch	Lunch	Work
1–2 p.m.	Statistics class	Biology lab	Statistics class	Open	Study Statistics	Open	Work
2–3 p.m.	Biology class	Biology lab	Open	Biology class	Open	Open	Work
3–4 p.m.	Open	Open	Open	Open	Open	Open	Work
4–5 p.m.	Open	Open	Open	Open	Open	Open	Work
5–6 p.m.	Work	Work	Work	Work	Work	Open	Work
6–7 p.m.	Work	Work	Work	Work	Work	Open	Open
7–8 p.m.	Work	Work	Work	Work	Work	Open	Open
8–9 p.m.	Study English	Study Statistics	Study Psychology	Open	Open	Open	Open
9–10 p.m.	Open	Open	Open	Open	Open	Open	Open

Plan the Term

Having established and evaluated your current habits and time use, you are now ready to devise a more efficient schedule. Buy a portable calendar that covers the entire school term and has ample space for each day. Using the course outlines provided by your instructors, enter the dates of all tests, term-paper deadlines, and other important assignments. Also be sure to enter your own long-range personal plans (weekend trips, family events, etc.).

Develop a Weekly Schedule

Now that you have a general picture of the school term, develop a weekly schedule that includes all of your activities and re-sponsibilities. Aim for a schedule that you can live with for the entire school term. A sample weekly schedule, incorporating the following guidelines, is shown in **TABLE 3**.

1. Enter your class times, work hours, and any other fixed obligations first. *Be thorough.* Using information from your time-use diary, allow plenty of time for such things as commuting, meals, and laundry.

2. Set up a study schedule for each of your courses. The study habits survey (Table 1) and your time-use diary will help direct you. (See Close-Up: More Tips for Effective Scheduling for more guidance on the next page.)

3. After you have budgeted time for studying, fill in slots for other obligations, exercise, fun, and relaxation.

Carry your calendar daily, keep it up to date, and refer to it often. *Through this process, you are developing a regular schedule that will help you achieve success.*

Use Your Study Time Effectively

Finding a place for study time in your schedule is important, but knowing how to use that study time is even more important.

How do you study from a textbook? Studies show that many students simply read and reread in a *passive* manner. Unfortunately, this often leads to remembering the wrong things—only the catchy stories and not the main points that will

CLOSE-UP

MORE TIPS FOR EFFECTIVE SCHEDULING

There are a few other things you will want to keep in mind when you set up your schedule.

Spaced study is more effective than massed study. If you need 4 hours to study one subject, for example, it's best to divide that into shorter periods spaced over several days. If you cram your studying into one 4-hour block, what you attempt to learn in the third or fourth hour will interfere with what you studied in the first 2 hours. New knowledge is like wet cement. It needs some time to "set" to become memory.

Alternate subjects, but avoid interference. Alternating subjects will give you a chance to digest what you're learning, and will also help to prevent mental fatigue with any one topic. Studying similar topics back-to-back, however, such as two different foreign languages, could lead to interference in your learning.

Determine the amount of study time you need to do well in each course. The time you need depends upon the difficulty of your courses and the effectiveness of your study methods. You will probably want to spend at least 1 to 2 hours studying for each hour spent in class. If your time-use diary shows that you are studying less than that, do not plan to jump to a much higher level right away. Increase study time slowly by setting weekly goals that will gradually bring you up to the desired level.

Create a schedule that makes sense. Tailor your schedule to meet the demands of each course. For the course that emphasizes lecture notes, schedule time for a daily review soon after the class. This will give you a chance to revise your notes and clean up any hard-to-decipher scribbles while the material is still fresh in your mind. If you are evaluated for class participation (for example, in a language course), allow time for a review just before the class meets. Schedule study time for your most difficult (or least motivating) courses during hours when you are the most alert and distractions are fewest.

Schedule open study time. Life can be unpredictable. Emergencies and new obligations can throw off your schedule. Or you may simply need some extra time for a project or for review in one of your courses. Schedule several hours each week as "open" time to allow for some flexibility.

Following these guidelines will help you find a schedule that works for you!

---

show up in test questions. Here are some tips that will help you get the most from your class and your text.

Take Useful Class Notes

Are your class notes as useful as they might be? One way to determine their worth is to compare them with those taken by other good students. Are yours as thorough? Do they provide you with a sensible outline of each lecture? If not, you may need to change the way you take notes.

Keep Your Notes for Each Class in Separate Locations

If you have all your lecture notes for a subject in one main location, you'll be able to flip back and forth easily to find answers to questions you may have. One way to keep notes together is to have separate notebooks for each course. Another is to use a ring binder and set up notes in clearly marked sections. This method has the advantage of letting you reorganize material as needed, adding new information and weeding out past mistakes. In either case, pages with lots of space—8.5 inches by 11 inches—are a good choice because you can take ample notes and still leave a wide margin on the side of the page. You'll be able to add comments in that margin when you review and revise your notes after class.

Use an Outline Format

Use roman numerals for major points, letters for supporting arguments, and so on. (See **FIGURE 1** for a sample.) Taking notes will be easy in some courses. Instructors in those courses will deliver organized lectures. But other instructors may be a bit less organized, and you will have to work harder to form your outline.

Clean Up Your Notes After Class

Try to reorganize your notes soon after the lecture. Expand or clarify your scribbles while the material is fresh in your mind. Write important questions in the margin next to notes that answer them. This will help you when you review your notes before a test. These questions will be especially helpful if you state them so that they resemble the kinds of questions your instructor likes to ask on tests.

Create a Study Space That Helps You Learn

It's easier to study effectively if your work area is well designed.

Organize Your Space

Work at a desk or table, not in your bed or an extremely comfortable chair that might

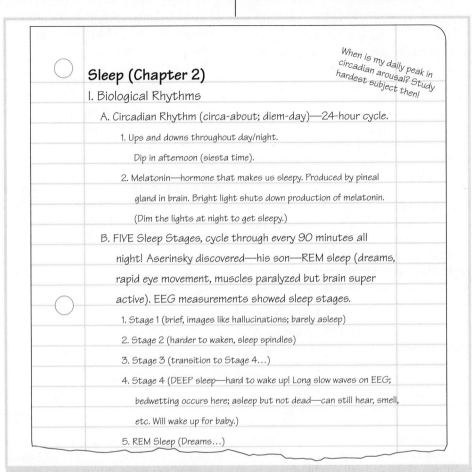

When is my daily peak in circadian arousal? Study hardest subject then!

Sleep (Chapter 2)

I. Biological Rhythms

  A. Circadian Rhythm (circa-about; diem-day)—24-hour cycle.

    1. Ups and downs throughout day/night.

      Dip in afternoon (siesta time).

    2. Melatonin—hormone that makes us sleepy. Produced by pineal

      gland in brain. Bright light shuts down production of melatonin.

      (Dim the lights at night to get sleepy.)

  B. FIVE Sleep Stages, cycle through every 90 minutes all

    night! Aserinsky discovered—his son—REM sleep (dreams,

    rapid eye movement, muscles paralyzed but brain super

    active). EEG measurements showed sleep stages.

    1. Stage 1 (brief, images like hallucinations; barely asleep)

    2. Stage 2 (harder to waken, sleep spindles)

    3. Stage 3 (transition to Stage 4…)

    4. Stage 4 (DEEP sleep—hard to wake up! Long slow waves on EEG;

      bedwetting occurs here; asleep but not dead—can still hear, smell,

      etc. Will wake up for baby.)

    5. REM Sleep (Dreams…)

Figure 1> **Sample lecture notes in outline form** Here is a sample from a student's notes taken in outline form from a lecture on sleep.

tempt you to nap. In an ideal world, you would do nothing but study in this space. If you can achieve that, the space will become so closely associated with studying that it will trigger your study habits, just as a mouth-watering aroma can trigger your appetite. If you need to work in a place away from your room or home, find a space that comes as close as possible to these conditions—for example, a quiet place you repeatedly use in the library.

Minimize Distractions

Keep your work area and the walls around it free from clutter. Do everything you can to eliminate distracting noises. Turn the TV off. If you must listen to music to mask outside noise, play soft instrumentals, not vocal selections that will draw your mind to the lyrics.

Study by yourself. Even when everyone in a group is studying, other students can distract you or break the pace at which *your* learning is most efficient. Worse, group studying can easily morph into a social event. You've reserved other times for socializing in your schedule. If you're going to do your best, you have to protect your study time.

Ask Others to Honor Your Quiet Time

If you have set up a schedule for studying, make roommates, family, and friends aware of this commitment. Ask them to honor your quiet study time. Close your door and post a "Do Not Disturb" sign.

Set Up Daily Goals That Are Specific and Realistic

Daily goals are necessary if you are going to accomplish all the course requirements for the term. But they have to be specific. The simple note "7–8 P.M.: Study psychology" is too broad to ensure that you will be using your time effectively. It's far better to break your studying into manageable tasks. For example, if you have course outlines with advance assignments, you could set systematic daily goals so that you would be able to cover 14 chapters before the final exam.

You won't achieve your daily goals if they are not realistic. Could you actually master a 30-page chapter in one session? Probably not. You'll have better results if you divide large tasks into smaller units. If you aren't used to studying for long periods, start with relatively short periods of concentrated study, with breaks in between. In this text, for example, you might decide to read one major section before each break. Limit your breaks to 5 or 10 minutes to stretch or move around a bit.

Your attention span is a good indicator of whether you are pacing yourself successfully. At this early stage, it's important to remember that you're in training. If your attention begins to wander, get up immediately and take a short break. It is better to study effectively for 15 minutes and then take a break than to fritter away 45 minutes out of your study hour. As your endurance develops, you can increase the length of study periods.

Use SQ3R to Help You Master This Text

David Myers organized this text by using a system called SQ3R (Survey, Question, Read, Rehearse, Review). Using SQ3R can

You will hear more about SQ3R in Chapter 1.

help you to understand what you read, and to retain that information longer. Applying SQ3R may feel at first as though it's taking more time and effort to "read" a chapter, but with practice, these steps will become automatic.

Survey

Before you read a chapter, survey its key parts. Note that main sections have numbered study questions to help you focus. Pay attention to the various headings, which indicate important subtopics, and to words that are set in bold type. Scan the last few pages of the chapter, where you will see a list of important terms and concepts. You will also find a concept map that provides a visual overview of main points in the chapter.

Surveying gives you the big picture of a chapter's content and organization. Getting a grasp on the chapter's logical sections will help you set your specific goals for daily study sessions, when you'll be reading the chapter more carefully.

Question

As you survey, you'll begin to notice some of the important questions covered in the chapter. These questions correspond to "mental files" into which you can sort knowledge for easy access. Don't limit yourself to the study questions that appear throughout the chapter. Jotting down additional questions of your own will cause you to look at the material in a new way. (You might, for example, scan this section's outline or headings, and ask "What does 'SQ3R' mean?") With your own questions in mind, you'll find that important points will be easier to remember, and to remember longer, because you've made them personally meaningful. You're now trying to answer your questions and fill your "mental files."

Read

When you have established "files" for each section of the chapter, begin reading. As you read a section, review your first question and continue reading until you discover its answer. If you come to

material that seems to answer an important question you don't have a file for, stop and write down that new question.

Be sure to read everything. Don't skip photo or art captions, graphs, or quotes or notes that appear periodically. In some cases, an idea that seems vague when you read about it becomes very clear when you see it in a simple graph. Keep in mind that instructors sometimes base their test questions on figures and tables.

Rehearse

When you have found the answer to one of your questions, close your eyes and mentally recite the question and its answer. Then *write* the answer next to the question. Use your own words, not the author's. Trying to explain something in your own words may show you that part of your understanding is vague or incomplete. Rehearsal has an added advantage. It tests the same skills you will need when you are taking exams, especially essay exams. If you study without ever putting your book and notes aside, you may develop false confidence about what you know. With the material available, you may be able to *recognize* the answer to your questions. But will you be able to *recall* it later, when you take an exam without having your mental props in sight?

Review

When you have answered the last question you formed on the material you are studying, go back and review. Read over your questions and your written answers. Study the concept map review at the end of the chapter. Take an extra few minutes to create a brief written summary covering all of your questions and answers. The few minutes you spend now will pay off in time saved when you do your final review of each chapter at the end of the term.

Don't Forget About Rewards!

If you have trouble studying regularly, giving yourself a reward may help. What kind of reward works best? That depends

on what you enjoy. You might start by making a list of 5 or 10 things that put a smile on your face. Taking a walk or going for a bike ride, relaxing with a magazine or novel, and catching a favorite television show or podcast are activities that can provide immediate rewards for achieving short-term study goals.

To motivate yourself when you're having trouble sticking to your schedule, allow yourself an immediate reward for completing a specific task. If running makes you smile, change your shoes, grab a friend, and head out the door! You deserve a reward for a job well done.

Do You Need to Revise Your New Schedule?

What if you've lived with your schedule for a few weeks, but you aren't making progress toward your academic and personal goals? What if your studying hasn't paid off in better grades? Don't let failure cause you to despair and abandon your program. But do take a little time to figure out what's gone wrong.

Are You Doing Well in Some Courses But Not in Others?

Perhaps you need to shift your priorities a bit. You may need to allow more time for Chemistry, for example, and less time for some other course.

Have You Received a Poor Grade on a Test?

Did your grade fail to reflect the effort you spent preparing for the test? This can happen to even the hardest-working student, often on a first test with a new instructor. This common experience can leave you feeling confused and abused. "What do I have to do to get an A?" "The test was unfair!" "I studied the wrong material!"

Before you decide you're wasting your time, try to figure out what went wrong.

Analyze the questions you missed, dividing them into two categories: lecture-based questions, and textbook-based questions. How many questions did you miss in each category? If you find far more errors in one category than in the other, you'll have some clues that will help you revise your schedule. Depending on the pattern you've found, you can add extra study time to lecture reviews or to textbook reviews.

Are You Trying to Study Regularly for the First Time and Feeling Overwhelmed?

Perhaps you've set your initial goals too high. Remember, the point of time management is to *identify a regular schedule that will help you achieve some success*. Like any skill, time management must be practiced to become effective. Accept your limitations and revise your schedule to work slowly up to where you know you

need to be—perhaps adding 15 minutes of study time per day.

I hope that these suggestions help make you more successful academically, and that they enhance the quality of your life in general. Having the necessary skills makes any job a lot easier and more pleasant. Let me repeat my warning not to attempt to make too drastic a change in your life-style immediately. Good habits require time and self-discipline to develop. Once established, they can last a lifetime.

REVIEW: TIME MANAGEMENT—OR HOW TO BE A GREAT STUDENT AND STILL HAVE A LIFE!

1 How Are You Using Your Time Now?
- Keep a Time-Use Diary for a week.
- Record the time you actually spend on activities.
- Record your energy levels to find your most productive times.

2 Design a Better Schedule
- Decide on your goals for the term and for each week.
- Enter class times, work times, social times (for family and friends), and time needed for other obligations and for practical activities.
- Tailor study times to avoid interference and to meet each course's needs.
- Set time aside for rest and recreation.

3 Use Your Study Time Effectively
- Take careful class notes that will help you recall and rehearse material covered in lectures.
- Try to eliminate distractions in your study area, and ask friends and family to help you focus on your work.
- Set specific daily goals to help you focus on each day's task.
- Use the SQ3R system (survey, question, read, rehearse, review) to master material covered in your text.
- When you achieve your daily goal, reward yourself with something that you value.

You will encounter these helpful concept maps at the end of each chapter. Use them as a visual aid to organize and review key topics.

4 Do You Need to Revise Your New Schedule?
- Poor test grades may indicate that you aren't using your study times effectively, or that your basic plan is too ambitious.
- Study your test results to help determine a more effective balance in your schedule.
- Make sure your schedule is not too ambitious. Work slowly to establish a schedule that will be effective for the long term.

1 Psychology's Roots, Big Ideas, and Critical Thinking Tools

HOPING TO FIGURE OUT THEMSELVES AND OTHERS, millions turn to psychology, as you now do. What do psychologists really know? "What's it like being married to a psychologist?" people have occasionally asked my wife. "Does he use his psychology on you?"

"So, does your Dad, like, analyze you?" my children have been asked many times by friends.

"What do you think of me?" asked one barber, hoping for an instant personality analysis after learning that I am a psychologist.

For these questioners, as for most people whose exposure to psychology comes from popular media, psychologists analyze personality, offer counseling, and dispense child-rearing advice.

Do they? Yes, and much more. Psychology's roots are broad, its ideas are big, and its investigations are scientific.

Psychology's Roots

Once upon a time, on a planet in your neighborhood of the universe, there came to be people. Soon thereafter, these creatures became intensely interested in themselves and in one another. They wondered, *"Who are we? Why do we think and feel and act as we do? And how are we to understand—and to manage—those around us?"*

To be human is to be curious about ourselves and the world around us. Before 300 B.C., the Greek naturalist and philosopher Aristotle wondered about learning and memory, motivation and emotion, perception and personality. Today we chuckle at some of his guesses, like his suggestion that a meal makes us sleepy by causing gas and heat to collect around the source of our personality, the heart. But credit Aristotle with asking the right questions.

Now, more than 2000 years later, psychology asks similar questions. But with its roots reaching back into philosophy and biology, and its branches spreading out across the world, psychology gathers its answers by scientifically studying how we act, think, and feel.

Psychological Science Is Born

1: How has psychology's focus changed over time?[1]

Psychology as we know it was born on a December day in 1879, in a small, third-floor room at a German university. There, Wilhelm Wundt and his assistants created a machine to measure how long it took people to press a telegraph key after hearing a ball hit a platform (Hunt, 1993).[2] (Most hit the key within about one-tenth of a second.) Wundt's attempt to measure "atoms of the mind"—the fastest and simplest mental processes—was psychology's first experiment. And that modest third-floor room took its place in history as the first psychological laboratory.

1. Throughout this book you will find numbered study questions that preview main sections. Keep the question in mind as you read the section to ensure that you are following the main point of the discussion. These questions are repeated and answered in the Review at the end of each chapter.
2. This book's information sources are cited in parentheses, with name and date. Every citation can be found in the end-of-book References, with complete documentation that follows American Psychological Association style.

Wilhelm Wundt :: Wundt (far left) established the first psychology laboratory at the University of Leipzig, Germany.

Psychology's earliest pioneers—"Magellans of the mind," Morton Hunt called them (1993)—came from many disciplines and countries. Wundt was both a philosopher and a physiologist. Charles Darwin, who proposed evolutionary psychology, was an English naturalist. Ivan Pavlov, who taught us much about learning, was a Russian physiologist. Sigmund Freud, a famous personality theorist, was an Austrian physician. Jean Piaget, who

Sigmund Freud :: The controversial ideas of this famous personality theorist and therapist influenced humanity's self-understanding.

showed us that children are not tiny adults, was a Swiss biologist. William James, who shared his love of psychology in an 1890 textbook, was an American philosopher.

Few of the early pioneers were women. In the late 1800s, psychology, like most fields, was a man's world. William James helped break that mold when he accepted Mary Calkins as his student. Although Calkins went on to outscore all the male students on the Ph.D. exams, Harvard denied her a degree. In its place, she was told, she could have a degree from Radcliffe, Harvard's sister school for women. Calkins turned down the offer but continued her work, which her colleagues honored by electing her the first

William James and Mary Whiton Calkins :: William James was a legendary teacher-writer of psychology. Among his students was Mary Whiton Calkins, who became famous for her memory research and for being the first woman president of the American Psychological Association.

female president of the American Psychological Association (APA). Animal behavior researcher Margaret Floy Washburn became the first woman to receive a psychology Ph.D. and the second to become an APA president.

The rest of the story of psychology— the story told by this book—develops at many levels, in the hands of many people, with interests ranging from therapy to the study of nerve cell activity. As you

Margaret Floy Washburn :: After Harvard refused to grant Calkins the degree she had earned, Washburn became the first woman to receive a psychology Ph.D. She focused on animal behavior research in *The Animal Mind.*

might expect, agreeing on a definition of *psychology* has not been easy.

For the early pioneers, psychology was "the science of mental life." And so it continued until the 1920s, when two larger-than-life American psychologists dismissed this idea. John B. Watson, and later B. F. Skinner, insisted that psychology

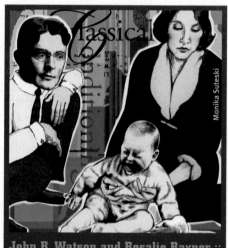

John B. Watson and Rosalie Rayner :: Working with Rayner, Watson championed psychology as the scientific study of behavior. He and Rayner showed fear could be learned, in experiments on a baby who became famous as "Little Albert."

B. F. Skinner :: This leading behaviorist rejected the idea of studying inner thoughts and feelings. He studied how consequences shape behavior.

must be "the scientific study of observable behavior." After all, science is rooted in observation. How can you observe a sensation, a feeling, or a thought? You *can*, however, observe and record people's *behavior* as they respond to different situations. Many agreed, and these **behaviorists**[3] were one of two major forces in psychology well into the 1960s.

The other major force was *Freudian psychology*. This reflected Sigmund Freud's teachings about unconscious sexual conflicts and the mind's defenses against its own wishes and impulses.

As the behaviorists had done in the early 1900s, two other groups rejected the definition of psychology that was current in the 1960s. The first, the **humanistic psychologists,** led by Carl Rogers and Abraham Maslow, found Freudian psychology and behaviorism too limiting. Rather than focusing on childhood memories or learned behaviors, Rogers and Maslow drew attention to ways that a positive environment can enhance our personal growth, and to our needs for love and acceptance.

3. Throughout the text, important concepts are **boldfaced.** As you study, you can find these terms defined nearby on the page and in the Glossary at the end of the book.

The rebellion of another group of psychologists during the 1960s is now known as the *cognitive revolution,* and it led the field back to its early interest in mental processes. But this new view differed in an important way. It intended to study internal thought processes *scientifically,* to find out how our minds perceive, process, and remember information. More recently *cognitive neuroscience* has enriched our understanding of brain activities underlying thought.

This long journey has led to our current definition: **Psychology** is *the scientific study of behavior and mental processes.* Let's unpack this definition.

Behavior is anything a human or nonhuman animal *does*—any action we can observe and record. Blinking, smiling, talking, and questionnaire marking are all observable behaviors. *Mental processes* are the internal states we infer from behavior—such as thoughts, beliefs, and feelings. For example, I may say that "I feel your pain," but in fact I infer it from the hints you give me—crying out, clutching your side, and gasping.

The key word in psychology's definition is *science.* Psychology, as I will stress again and again, is less a set of findings than a way of asking and answering questions. My aim, then, is not merely to report results but also to show you how psychologists play their game, evaluating opinions and ideas. And I hope you will learn how to play the game, too—to think smarter when explaining events and making choices in your own life.

Contemporary Psychology's Subfields

2: What are psychology's current subfields?

Psychologists' diverse interests make it hard to picture a psychologist at work. You might start by imagining a neuroscientist probing an animal's brain, an intelligence researcher studying how quickly infants become bored with a familiar scene, or a therapist listening closely to a

client's depressed thoughts. Psychology's many perspectives range from the biological to the social and cultural (see **TABLE 1.1** on the next page), and its settings range from the laboratory to the clinic. But they share a common goal: to describe and explain behavior, and the mind underlying it.

Psychology also relates to many fields. You'll find psychologists teaching in medical schools, law schools, and theological seminaries, and you'll see them working in hospitals, factories, and corporate offices.

In this course, you will hear about

- *biological psychologists* exploring the links between brain and mind.

- *developmental psychologists* studying our changing abilities from womb to tomb.

- *cognitive psychologists* experimenting with how we perceive, think, and solve problems.

- *personality psychologists* investigating our persistent traits.

- *industrial/organizational psychologists* studying and advising on behavior in the workplace.

- *counseling psychologists* helping people cope with personal and vocational challenges by recognizing their strengths and resources.

- *clinical psychologists* assessing and treating mental, emotional, and behavior disorders (as distinct from *psychiatrists,* medical doctors who also prescribe drugs when treating psychological disorders).

- *social psychologists* exploring how we view and affect one another.

behaviorism the view that psychology (1) should be an objective science that (2) studies behavior without reference to mental processes. Most research psychologists today agree with (1) but not with (2).

humanistic psychology emphasized the growth potential of healthy people and the individual's potential for personal growth.

psychology the scientific study of behavior and mental processes.

Table 1.1	Psychology's Current Academic Perspectives	
Perspective	**Focus**	**Sample Questions**
Neuroscience	How the body and brain enable emotions, memories, and sensory experiences	How are messages transmitted within the body? How is blood chemistry linked with moods and motives?
Evolutionary	How the natural selection of traits promotes the perpetuation of one's genes	How does evolution influence behavior tendencies?
Behavior genetics	How much our genes and our environment influence our individual differences	To what extent are psychological traits such as intelligence, personality, sexual orientation, and vulnerability to depression attributable to our genes? To our environment?
Psychodynamic	How behavior springs from unconscious drives and conflicts	How can someone's personality traits and disorders be explained in terms of sexual and aggressive drives or as the disguised effects of unfulfilled wishes and childhood traumas?
Behavioral	How we learn observable responses	How do we learn to fear particular objects or situations? What is the most effective way to alter our behavior, say, to lose weight or stop smoking?
Cognitive	How we encode, process, store, and retrieve information	How do we use information in remembering? Reasoning? Solving problems?
Social-cultural	How behavior and thinking vary across situations and cultures	How are we alike as members of one human family? How do we differ as products of different environmental contexts?

Psychology also influences modern culture. Knowledge transforms us. Learning about psychology's findings, people less often judge psychological disorders as moral failures. They less often regard women as men's inferiors. They less often view children as ignorant, willful beasts in need of taming. And as thinking changes, so do actions. "In each case," noted Hunt (1990, p. 206), "knowledge has modified attitudes, and, through them, behavior." Once aware of psychology's well-researched ideas—about how body and mind connect, how we construct our perceptions, how a child's mind grows, how people across the world differ (and are alike)—your own mind may never again be quite the same.

Global psychology :: Psychology is *growing* and it is *globalizing*. Today's psychologists are citizens of many lands—69 lands, according to the International Union of Psychological Science. From Albania to Zimbabwe, their number is mushrooming. In China, for example, five universities had psychology departments in 1985; by the last century's end, there were 40 (Zhang & Xu, 2006). And worldwide, ideas are working their way across borders now more than ever, as happened in 2007 at this international psychology conference in India. "We are moving rapidly towards a single world of psychological science," reports Robert Bjork (2000).

AP Photo/Ashwini Bhatia

⊕ PRACTICE TEST

Practice Tests appear at the end of main sections. Use them to check your understanding before moving on.

1. In 1879, in psychology's first laboratory experiment, _____ and his students measured the time lag between hearing a ball hit a platform and pressing a key.
   a. Charles Darwin
   b. William James
   c. Sigmund Freud
   d. Wilhelm Wundt

2. A prominent psychology text was published in 1890. Its author was
   a. Wilhelm Wundt.
   b. Mary Whiton Calkins.
   c. Charles Darwin.
   d. William James.

3. The definition of *psychology* has changed several times since the late 1800s. In the early twentieth century, _____ redefined *psychology* as "the scientific study of observable behavior."
   a. John B. Watson
   b. Margaret Floy Washburn
   c. William James
   d. Jean Piaget

4. The perspective in psychology that focuses on how behavior and thought differ from situation to situation and from culture to culture is the
   a. cognitive perspective.
   b. behavioral perspective.
   c. social-cultural perspective.
   d. neuroscience perspective.

5. The perspective in psychology that emphasizes how we learn observable responses is the
   a. cognitive perspective.
   b. behavioral perspective.
   c. social-cultural perspective.
   d. neuroscience perspective.

6. A psychologist who treats emotionally troubled adolescents at the local mental health agency is most likely to be a(an)
   a. biological psychologist.
   b. psychiatrist.
   c. industrial/organizational psychologist.
   d. clinical psychologist.

Answers: 1. d, 2. d, 3. a, 4. c, 5. b, 6. d.

Four Big Ideas in Psychology

3: What four big ideas run throughout this book?

I have used four of psychology's big ideas to organize material in this book.

1. *Critical Thinking* Science supports thinking that examines assumptions, uncovers hidden values, weighs evidence, and tests conclusions. Science-aided thinking is smart thinking.

2. *The Biopsychosocial Approach* We can best understand human behavior if we view it from three levels—the biological, psychological, and social-cultural. We share a biologically rooted human nature. Yet genes, culture, and other social influences fine-tune our assumptions, values, and behaviors.

3. *The Two-Track Mind* Today's psychological science explores our *dual-processing* capacity. Our perception, thinking, memory, and attitudes all operate on two levels: conscious (with awareness) and unconscious (without awareness). It has been a surprise to learn how much information processing happens without our awareness.

4. *Exploring Human Strengths* Psychology today focuses not only on understanding and offering relief from troublesome behaviors and emotions, but also on understanding and building beneficial emotions and traits.

Let's consider these four big ideas, one by one.

Big Idea 1: Critical Thinking Is Smart Thinking

Whether reading a news report or swapping ideas with others, **critical thinkers** ask questions. How do we know that? Who benefits from this? Is the conclusion based on guesswork and gut feelings, or on evidence? How do we know one event caused the other? How else could we explain things?

In psychology, critical thinking has led to some surprising findings. Believe it or not . . .

- massive losses of brain tissue early in life may have few long-term effects (see Chapter 2).

- within days, newborns can recognize their mother's odor and voice (see Chapter 3).

- some people with brain damage can learn new skills, yet at the mind's conscious level be unaware that they have these skills (see Chapter 7).

- diverse people—men and women, old and young, rich and working class, those with disabilities and without—report roughly the same levels of personal happiness (see Chapter 9).

- delivering an electric shock to the brain (electroconvulsive therapy) may snap people out of severe depression when all else has failed (see Chapter 13).

This same critical thinking has also debunked some popular beliefs. When we let the evidence speak for itself, we learn that . . .

- sleepwalkers are *not* acting out their dreams (see Chapter 2).

- our past is *not* precisely recorded in our brain. Neither brain stimulation nor hypnosis will let us "play the tape" and relive long-buried memories (see Chapter 7).

- most of us do *not* suffer from low self-esteem, and high self-esteem is not all good (see Chapter 11).

- opposites do *not* generally attract (see Chapter 14).

In later chapters, you'll see many more examples of research in which critical thinking has challenged our beliefs and triggered new ways of thinking.

critical thinking thinking that does not blindly accept arguments and conclusions. Rather, it examines assumptions, uncovers hidden values, weighs evidence, and assesses conclusions.

Big Idea 2: Behavior Is a Biopsychosocial Event

Each of us is part of a larger social system—a family, a group, a society. But each of us is also made up of smaller systems, such as our nervous system and body organs, which are composed of still smaller systems—cells, molecules, and atoms.

If we study this complexity with simple tools, we may end up with partial answers. Consider: Why do grizzly bears hibernate? Is it because hibernation helped their ancestors to survive and reproduce? Because their biology drives them to do so? Because cold climates hinder food gathering during winter?

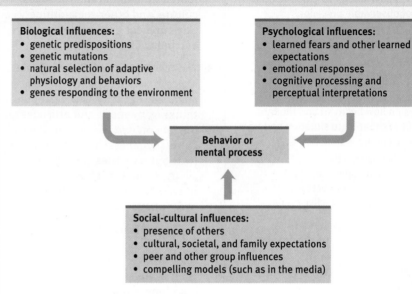

Figure 1.1> Biopsychosocial approach: Three paths to understanding Studying events from many viewpoints gives us a more complete picture than any one perspective could offer.

Biological influences:
• genetic predispositions
• genetic mutations
• natural selection of adaptive physiology and behaviors
• genes responding to the environment

Psychological influences:
• learned fears and other learned expectations
• emotional responses
• cognitive processing and perceptual interpretations

Behavior or mental process

Social-cultural influences:
• presence of others
• cultural, societal, and family expectations
• peer and other group influences
• compelling models (such as in the media)

Views of anger :: How would each of psychology's levels of analysis explain what's going on here?

Each of these is a partial truth, but no one is a full answer. For more complete answers, we need to use many *levels of analysis*. The **biopsychosocial approach** considers three sets of influences: biological, psychological, and social-cultural **(FIGURE 1.1)**. Each set gives us valuable insights into behavior, and together, they offer us the best possible view.

Let's assume we wanted to know more about gender differences. *Gender* is not the same as sex. *Gender* refers to the traits and behaviors we expect in a man or a woman. *Sex* refers to the biological characteristics we inherit, thanks to our genes. To study gender differences, we would want to know as much as possible about biological influences. But we would also want to understand how our **culture**—the ideas and behaviors shared by a group and passed on from one generation to the next—defines *male* and *female*. Even with this much information, our view would be incomplete without some understanding of the influence of the individual—differences due to personal abilities and learning.

Researchers studying all these influences have found gender differences—in what we dream, in how we express and detect emotion, and in our risk for alcoholism, depression, and eating disorders. Psychologically as well as biologically, women and men differ. But we are also alike. Whether female or male, we learn to walk at about the same age. We experience the same sensations of light and sound. We feel the same pangs of hunger, desire, and fear. We exhibit similar overall intelligence and well-being.

Psychology's biggest and most persistent issue is one part of the biopsychosocial approach: How do we judge the contributions of *nature* (biology) and *nurture* (experience)? Today's psychologists explore this age-old **nature-nurture issue** by asking, for example:

■ How are differences in intelligence, personality, and psychological disorders influenced by heredity and by environment?

■ Is sexual orientation biologically predisposed, or learned?

Diverse Yet Alike

A smile is a smile the world around :: Throughout this book, you will see examples not only of our cultural and gender diversity but also of our shared human nature. People in different cultures vary in when and how often they smile, but a naturally happy smile *means* the same thing anywhere in the world.

- Should we treat depression as a disorder of the brain or a disorder of thought—or both?

In most cases, *nurture works on what nature endows.* Our species has been graced with a great biological gift: an enormous ability to learn and adapt.

Moreover (and you will hear this over and over in the pages that follow), every psychological event—every thought, every emotion—is also a biological event. Thus, gender differences are products not only of our biology but also of our mind and our environment.

Big Idea 3: We Operate With a Two-Track Mind (Dual Processing)

From moment to moment we're consciously aware of little of what is happening around and within us. Our conscious mind *feels* like our body's chief executive. But mountains of new research reveal that our brain works on two tracks—the conscious track and a surprisingly large unconscious, automatic track (information that's processed without our awareness). Thinking, memory,

A nature-made nature-nurture experiment :: Identical twins (left) have the same genes. This makes them ideal participants in studies designed to shed light on hereditary and environmental influences on temperament, intelligence, and other traits. Fraternal twins (right) have different genes but often share the same environment. Twin studies provide a wealth of findings—described in later chapters—showing the importance of both nature and nurture.

biopsychosocial approach an integrated approach that incorporates different but complementary views from biological, psychological, and social-cultural perspectives.

culture the enduring behaviors, ideas, attitudes, and traditions shared by a group of people and transmitted from one generation to the next.

nature-nurture issue the longstanding controversy over the relative contributions that genes and experience make to the development of psychological traits and behaviors. Today's psychological science sees traits and behaviors arising from the interaction of nature and nurture.

perception, language, and attitudes all operate on these two tracks. Today's researchers call it **dual processing.** We know more than we know we know.

A fascinating scientific story illustrates the mind's two tracks. Sometimes science-aided critical thinking confirms widely held beliefs. But sometimes, as this story illustrates, the truth turns out to be stranger than fiction.

During my time spent at Scotland's University of St. Andrews, I came to know research psychologists Melvyn Goodale and David Milner (2004, 2006). A local woman, whom they call D. F., was overcome by carbon monoxide one day while showering. The resulting brain damage left her unable to recognize objects visually. Yet she was only partly blind, for she would act as if she could see. Asked to slip a postcard into a mail slot, she could do so without error. Although she could not report the width of a block in front of her, she could grasp it with just the right finger-thumb distance.

How could this be? Don't we have just one visual system? Goodale and Milner knew from animal research that the eye sends information to different brain areas, each of which has a different task. Sure enough, a scan of D. F.'s brain activity revealed normal activity in the area concerned with reaching for and grasping objects, but not in the area concerned with consciously recognizing objects. So, would the reverse damage lead to the opposite symptoms? Indeed, there are a few such patients—who can see and recognize objects but have difficulty pointing toward or grasping them.

We think of our vision as one system: We look, we see, we respond to what we see. Actually, vision is a great example of our dual processing. A *visual perception track* enables us to think about the world—to recognize things and to plan future actions. A *visual action track* guides our moment-to-moment actions.

This big idea that much of our everyday thinking, feeling, sensing, and acting operates outside our awareness may be a weird new idea for you. It was for me. I long believed that my own intentions and deliberate choices ruled my life. Of course, in many ways they do. But in the mind's downstairs, as you will see in later chapters, there is much, much more to being human.

Big Idea 4: Psychology Explores Human Strengths as Well as Challenges

Psychology's first hundred years focused on understanding and treating troubled states such as abuse and anxiety, depression and disease, prejudice and poverty. Much of today's psychology continues the exploration of such challenges. To balance psychology's focus on human problems, Martin Seligman and others (2002, 2005) have called for a more **positive psychology,** "the study of positive emotions, positive character traits, and enabling institutions." These psychologists believe that happiness is a by-product of a pleasant, engaged, and meaningful life. Thus, positive psychology focuses on building a "good life" that engages one's skills, and a "meaningful life" that points beyond oneself. We can view this movement as having three parts:

■ The first pillar, *positive emotions,* is built of satisfaction with the past, happiness with the present, and optimism about the future.

■ The bricks and mortar of the second pillar, *positive character*, are traits such as creativity, courage, compassion, integrity, self-control, leadership, wisdom, and spirituality. Current research examines the roots and fruits of such qualities, sometimes by studying the lives of individuals who offer striking examples.

■ The third pillar, *positive groups, communities, and cultures*, supports positive social forces, including healthy families, friendly neighborhoods, effective schools, socially responsible media, and civil discussions.

Martin E. P. Seligman :: "The main purpose of a positive psychology is to measure, understand, and then build the human strengths and the civic virtues."

Courtesy of Martin E.P. Seligman, Ph.D. Director, Positive Psychology Center/University of Pennsylvania

Will psychology have a more positive mission in this century? Can it help us all to flourish? Without slighting the need to repair damage and cure disease, an increasing number of scientists worldwide believe it can, and they are helping it happen right now.

◉ PRACTICE TEST

7. A newspaper article describes how a "cure for cancer has been found." A critical thinker probably will

  a. dismiss the article as untrue.

  b. accept the information as a wonderful breakthrough.

  c. question the article, evaluate the evidence, and assess the conclusions.

  d. question the article but quickly accept it as true if the author has an excellent reputation.

8. In the history of psychology, a major topic has been the relative influence of nature and nurture. Nature is to nurture as

  a. personality is to intelligence.

  b. biology is to experience.

  c. intelligence is to biology.

  d. psychological traits are to behaviors.

9. Which one of the following is NOT one of the four big ideas in psychology used to organize material in this book?

a. Exploring human strengths
b. The two-track mind
c. Industrial/organizational psychology
d. Biopsychosocial approach

Answers: 7. c, 8. b, 9. c.

Why Do Psychology?

Many people feel guided by their *intuition*—by what they feel in their gut. "Buried deep within each and every one of us, there is an instinctive, heartfelt awareness that provides—if we allow it to—the most reliable guide," offered Britain's Prince Charles (2000). Former U.S. President George W. Bush (2001), after meeting Russian President Vladimir Putin, had him sized up. "I looked the man in the eye. I was able to get a sense of his soul." And later, explaining his decision to launch the Iraq war, he noted, "I'm a gut player. I rely on my instincts" (Woodward, 2002).

The Limits of Intuition and Common Sense

4: Why are answers reached by thinking critically more reliable than ordinary common sense?

Prince Charles and President Bush have much company, judging from the long list of pop psychology books on "intuitive managing," "intuitive trading," and "intuitive healing." Intuition is indeed important. Research shows that, more than we realize, our thinking, memory, and attitudes operate on two tracks—conscious and unconscious. The larger part operates automatically, off-screen. Like jumbo jets, we fly mostly on autopilot.

But intuition can lead us astray. Our gut feelings may tell us that lie detectors work and that eyewitness recollections are accurate. But as you will see in chapters to come, hundreds of findings challenge these beliefs.

> "The first principle is that you must not fool yourself—and you are the easiest person to fool."
>
> Richard Feynman (1997)

Hunches are a good starting point, even for smart thinkers. But thinking critically means checking assumptions, weighing evidence, inviting criticism, and testing conclusions. Does the death penalty prevent murders? Whether your gut tells you "yes" or "no," you need more evidence. You might ask, do states with a death penalty have lower homicide rates? After states pass death-penalty laws, do their homicide rates drop? Do homicide rates rise in states that abandon the death penalty? Free to ignore the answers to such questions (which the evidence suggests are no, no, and no), our intuition can steer us down the wrong path.

With its standards for gathering and sifting evidence, psychological science helps us avoid errors and think smarter. Before moving on to our study of how psychologists use psychology's methods in their research, let's look more closely at two common flaws in intuitive thinking—*hindsight bias* and *overconfidence*.

Did We Know It All Along? Hindsight Bias

Some people think psychology merely proves what people already know and then dresses it in jargon: "So what else is new—you get paid for using fancy methods to tell me what my grandmother knew?" But consider how easy it is to draw the bull's eye *after* the arrow strikes. After the American occupation of Iraq led to a bloody civil war rather than a peaceful democracy, many saw the result as obvious. *Before* the invasion was launched, these results seemed anything but obvious. Few U.S. senators who voted for the Iraq invasion expected the chaos that broke out. But after learning the end of a story, an event, or a psychological finding, we tend to think the outcome was obvious—that we could have predicted it.

dual processing the principle that information is often simultaneously processed on separate conscious and unconscious tracks.

positive psychology the scientific study of human functioning, with the goals of discovering and promoting strengths and virtues that help individuals and communities to thrive.

Hindsight bias :: *After* the 2007 Virginia Tech massacre of 32 people, it seemed obvious that school officials should have locked down the school (despite its having the population of a small city) after the first two people were murdered. With 20/20 hindsight, everything seems obvious.

This tendency, known as **hindsight bias** (or the *I-knew-it-all-along phenomenon*), is easy to demonstrate: Give half the members of a group a true psychological finding, and give the other half an opposite result. Tell the first group, "Psychologists have found that separation weakens romantic attraction. As the saying goes, 'Out of sight, out of mind.'" Ask them to imagine why this might be true. Most people can, and nearly all will then view this true finding as unsurprising—just common sense.

Tell the second group just the opposite, "Psychologists have found that separation strengthens romantic attraction. As the saying goes, 'Absence makes the heart grow fonder.'" People given this false statement can also easily explain it, and most will also see it as unsurprising. When two opposite findings both seem like common sense, we have a problem!

This example illustrates why we need psychological research. People asked how and why they felt or acted as they did often give misleading answers. They don't mean to mislead us, but their common sense more easily describes what *has* happened than what *will* happen.

> "Prediction is very difficult, especially about the future."
>
> Physicist Neils Bohr, 1885–1962

Of course, many of psychology's findings have been foreseen. We're all behavior watchers, and sometimes we get it right. Many people believe that love breeds happiness, and it does. (We have what Chapter 9 calls a deep "need to belong.") But sometimes Grandmother's intuition, informed by countless casual observations, gets it wrong. Psychological research has overturned many popular ideas—that familiarity breeds contempt, that dreams predict the future, and that emotional reactions coincide with menstrual phase. It has also surprised us with discoveries we had not predicted—that the brain's chemical messengers control our moods and memories, that other animals can pass along their learned habits, that stress affects our capacity to fight disease.

Overconfidence

We humans also tend to be *overconfident*. Consider these three word puzzles (called anagrams), which people like you were asked to unscramble in one study (Goranson, 1978).

> WREAT → WATER
>
> ETRYN → ENTRY
>
> GRABE → BARGE

> Fun anagram solutions from Wordsmith.org:
>
> Elvis = lives
>
> Dormitory = dirty room
>
> Slot machines = cash lost in 'em

About how many seconds do you think it would have taken you to unscramble each of them? Once people know the target word, the answer seems obvious—so much so that they become overconfident. They think they would have seen the solution in only 10 seconds or so. In reality, the average problem solver spends 3 minutes, as you also might, given a similar anagram without the solution: OCHSA. (Turn the next page to check your answer.)

> "We don't like their sound. Groups of guitars are on their way out."
>
> Decca Records, in turning down a recording contract with the Beatles in 1962

Are we any better at predicting our social behavior? In one study (Vallone & others, 1990), students made predictions at the beginning of the school year. Would they drop a course, vote in an upcoming election, call their parents more than twice a month (and so forth)? On average, the students felt 84 percent sure of these self-predictions. But later quizzes about their actual behavior showed their predictions were correct only 71 percent of the time. Even when they were 100 percent sure of themselves, their self-predictions were wrong 15 percent of the time.

The point to remember: Hindsight bias and overconfidence often lead us to overestimate our intuition. But scientific inquiry can help us sift reality from illusion.

The Scientific Attitude

5: What are the three key attitudes of scientific inquiry?

What makes scientific inquiry so useful for detecting truth? The answer lies in three basic attitudes: *curiosity, skepticism,* and *humility.*

Underlying all science is, first, a hardheaded *curiosity*, a passion to explore and understand without misleading or being misled. Some questions (Is there life after death?) are beyond science. To answer them requires a leap of faith. With many other ideas (Can some people read minds?), the proof is in the pudding. No matter how crazy an idea sounds, the scientist asks, Does it work? When put to the test, can its predictions be confirmed?

Non Sequitur

THE IRRESISTIBLE FORCE MEETS THE IMMOVABLE OBJECT

THE FACTS AS THEY ARE

THE TRUTH AS I SEE IT

WILEY 5-16

Reprinted by permission of Universal Press Syndicate. © 1997 Wiley.

The amazing Randi :: Magician and skeptic James Randi has tested and debunked a variety of psychic phenomena.

Courtesy of the James Randi Education Foundation

Magician James Randi uses the scientific approach when testing those claiming to see auras around people's bodies:

Randi: Do you see an aura around my head?

Aura-seer: Yes, indeed.

Randi: Can you still see the aura if I put this magazine in front of my face?

Aura-seer: Of course.

Randi: Then if I were to step behind a wall barely taller than I am, you could determine my location from the aura visible above my head, right?

Randi has told me that no aura-seer has agreed to take this simple test.

When subjected to scientific tests, crazy-sounding ideas sometimes find support. More often, they become part of the mountain of forgotten claims of palm reading, miracle cancer cures, and out-of-body travels. For a lot of bad ideas, science is society's garbage disposal.

Sifting reality from fantasy, sense from nonsense, also requires us to be *skeptical*—not cynical, but also not gullible. "To believe with certainty," says a Polish proverb, "we must begin by doubting." As scientists, psychologists greet statements about behavior and mental processes by asking two questions: What do you mean? How do you know?

When ideas compete, skeptical testing can reveal which ones best match the facts. Do parental behaviors determine children's sexual orientation? Can astrologers predict your future based on the position of the planets at your birth? As you will see in later chapters, putting these two claims to the test has led most psychologists to doubt them.

A scientific attitude is more than curiosity and skepticism, however. It also requires *humility*—an awareness that we can make mistakes, and a willingness to be surprised and follow new roads. In the last analysis, what matters is not my opinion or yours, but the truths nature reveals in response to our questioning. If people or other animals don't behave as our ideas predict, then so much the worse for our ideas. This humble attitude was expressed in one of psychology's early mottos: "The rat is always right."

Historians of science tell us that these attitudes—curiosity, skepticism, and humility—helped make modern science possible.

PRACTICE TEST

10. *Hindsight bias* refers to our tendency to

a. perceive events as obvious after they happen.

b. assume that two events happened because we wished them to happen.

c. overestimate our abilities to predict the future.

d. make judgments that don't follow common sense.

11. As scientists, psychologists view theories with curiosity, skepticism, and humility. This means that they

a. have a negative, cynical approach to other people's research.

b. assume that an article published in a reputable journal must be true.

c. believe that every important human question can be tested scientifically.

d. are willing to ask questions and to reject testable claims that cannot be verified by research.

Answers: 10. a, 11. d.

How Do Psychologists Ask and Answer Questions?

Psychologists transform their scientific attitude into practice by using the *scientific method.* They observe events, form theories, and then refine their theories in the light of new observations.

The Scientific Method

6: How do psychologists construct theories?

Chatting with friends and family, we often use *theory* to mean "mere hunch." In science, a **theory** *explains* behaviors or events by offering ideas that *organize* what we have observed. By organizing isolated facts, a theory simplifies. There are too many facts about behavior to remember them all. By linking facts to underlying principles, a theory connects many small dots so that a larger picture can emerge.

Let's see how this might work with a theory of depression. Imagine that we observe over and over that people with depression describe their past, present, and future in gloomy terms. To organize these observations, we might state, *"Low self-esteem feeds depression."* So far so good: We've created a self-esteem principle that neatly summarizes a long list of facts about people with depression.

But wait—a theory must do more than organize observations. If a theory's principles reflect reality, they will also *predict* events. Thus, a good theory must produce

hindsight bias the tendency to believe, after learning an outcome, that one would have foreseen it. (Also known as the I-knew-it-all-along phenomenon.)

theory an explanation using an integrated set of principles that organizes observations and predicts behaviors or events.

hypotheses, predictions that let us test the theory. In this case, the hypothesis might be, *"People with low self-esteem will score higher on a depression test."*

Our next step is to ask people to take two different tests. One will assess self-esteem. On that test, people will indicate whether they agree with statements such as, "I have good ideas" and "I am fun to be with." On the second test, they will agree or disagree with statements that indicate depression.

If our hypothesis is correct, people who report poorer self-images will also score higher on the depression scale **(FIGURE 1.2)**. If not, we will need to reject or revise our theory.

Belief in a theory can bias observations. Believing that depression springs from low self-esteem, we may see what we expect. We may perceive depressed people's neutral comments as put-downs. As a check on their biases, psychologists use **operational definitions** when they report their studies. These exact descriptions will allow anyone to **replicate** (repeat) their research. Other people can

Solution to earlier OCHSA anagram Chaos.

then re-create the study with different participants and in different situations. If they get similar results, we can be confident that the findings are reliable.

Let's summarize. A good theory:

- effectively *organizes* a range of observations.

- leads to clear *predictions* that anyone can use to check the theory.

- often stimulates research that leads to a revised theory (such as the one in Chapter 13, which better organizes and predicts what we know about depression).

Let's look more closely now at methods for testing hypotheses and refining theories, using descriptions, correlations, and experiments. Recognizing these methods and knowing what conclusions they allow is an important part of thinking critically.

Description

7: What three techniques do psychologists use to observe and describe behavior?

In daily life, all of us observe and describe people, trying to understand why they behave as they do. Professional psychologists do much the same, though more objectively and systematically, using case studies, surveys, and naturalistic observation.

The Case Study

A **case study** examines one individual in great depth, in the hope of revealing things true of us all. Some examples: Medical case studies of people who lost specific abilities after damage to certain brain regions gave us much of our early knowledge about the brain. Piaget taught us about children's thinking after carefully watching and questioning just a few children. Studies of only a few chimpanzees jarred our beliefs about what other animals can understand and communicate. Intensive case studies are sometimes very revealing.

Case studies often suggest directions for further study, and they show us what *can* happen. But individual cases may also mislead us. The individual being studied may be *atypical* (not like those in the larger group). Viewing such cases as general truths can lead to false conclusions. Indeed, anytime a researcher mentions a finding ("Smokers die younger: 95 percent of men over 85 are nonsmokers"), someone is sure to offer an exception. These contradictory anecdotes—dramatic stories, personal experiences, even psychological case examples—often command attention. ("Well, I have an uncle who smoked two packs a day and lived to be 89.")

"Given a thimbleful of [dramatic] facts we rush to make generalizations as large as a tub."

Psychologist Gordon Allport, *The Nature of Prejudice,* 1954

The point to remember: Individual cases can suggest fruitful ideas. What is true of all of us (we all need to eat) can

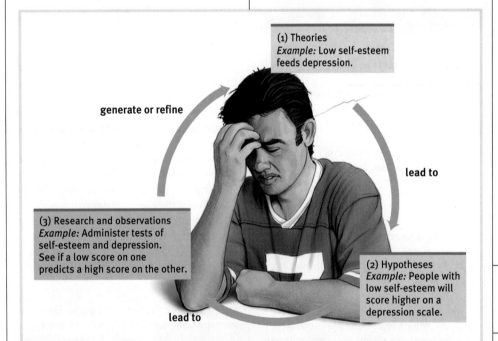

(1) Theories
Example: Low self-esteem feeds depression.

generate or refine

lead to

(3) Research and observations
Example: Administer tests of self-esteem and depression. See if a low score on one predicts a high score on the other.

(2) Hypotheses
Example: People with low self-esteem will score higher on a depression scale.

lead to

Figure 1.2> **The scientific method** A self-correcting process for asking questions and observing nature's answer.

The case of the conversational chimpanzee :: In case studies of chimpanzees, psychologists have asked whether language is uniquely human. Here Nim Chimpsky signs *hug* as his trainer, psychologist Herbert Terrace, shows him the puppet Ernie. But is Nim really using language? We'll explore that issue in Chapter 8.

"How would you like me to answer that question? As a member of my ethnic group, educational class, income group, or religious category?"

be seen in any one of us (I especially enjoy my afternoon snack with tea). But be careful about assuming the reverse of that statement. Just because something is true of one of us (the atypical uncle), that does not mean it will be true of all of us (most long-term smokers suffer ill health and early deaths). We look to methods beyond the case study to uncover general truths.

The Survey

A **survey** looks at many cases in less depth, asking people to report their behavior or opinions. Questions about everything from sexual practices to political opinions get put to the public. Harris and Gallup polls have revealed that 89 percent of Americans say they face high stress, 95 percent believe in God, and 96 percent would like to change something about their appearance. But asking questions is tricky, and your results often depend on the way you word your questions and on who answers them.

Wording Effects Even subtle changes in the order or wording of questions can have major effects. Should violence be allowed to appear in children's television

programs? People are much more likely to approve "not allowing" such things than "forbidding" or "censoring" them. In one national survey, only 27 percent of Americans approved of "government censorship" of media sex and violence, though 66 percent approved of "more restrictions on what is shown on television" (Lacayo, 1995). And people are much more approving of "aid to the needy" than of "welfare," and of "revenue enhancers" than of "taxes." Because wording is such a delicate matter, critical thinkers will reflect on whether the phrasing of a question might have affected the opinions people expressed.

Random Sampling For an accurate picture of a group's experiences and attitudes, there's only one game in town—*a representative sample*—a small group that accurately reflects a larger *population*.

So how do you obtain a representative sample to survey? How could you choose a group that would represent the whole group you want to study and describe—say, the total student population at your school? You would choose a **random sample,** in which every person in the

entire group has an equal chance of being picked. This means you would *not* send each student a questionnaire. (Those who believe it's their duty to return it would not be a random sample.)

hypothesis a testable prediction, often implied by a theory.

operational definition a statement of the procedures (operations) used to define research variables. For example, *human intelligence* may be operationally defined as what an intelligence test measures.

replication repeating the essence of a research study, usually with different participants in different situations, to see whether the basic finding extends to other participants and circumstances.

case study an observation technique in which one person is studied in depth in the hope of revealing universal principles.

survey a technique for ascertaining the self-reported attitudes or behaviors of people, usually by questioning a representative, random sample of them.

random sample a sample that fairly represents a population because each member has an equal chance of inclusion.

But you could use a table of random numbers to select your sample after assigning each student a number.

With very large samples, estimates become quite reliable. *E* is estimated to represent 12.7 percent of the letters in written English. *E,* in fact, is 12.3 percent of the 925,141 letters in Melville's *Moby-Dick,* 12.4 percent of the 586,747 letters in Dickens' *A Tale of Two Cities,* and 12.1 percent of the 3,901,021 letters in 12 of Mark Twain's works (*Chance News,* 1997).

Time and money will affect the size of your sample, but you would try to involve as many people as possible. Why? Because large representative samples are better than small ones. (But a small representative sample of 100 is better than an unrepresentative sample of 500.)

Political pollsters sample voters in national election surveys just this way. Using only 1500 randomly sampled people, drawn from all areas of a country, they can provide a remarkably accurate snapshot of the nation's opinions. Without random sampling, large samples—including call-in phone samples and TV Web site polls—often merely give misleading results.

The point to remember: Before believing survey findings, think critically: Consider the sample. The best basis for generalizing is from a representative sample of cases.

Naturalistic Observation

We can also describe behavior by watching, recording, and analyzing it in a natural environment. These **naturalistic observations** may describe parenting practices in different cultures, American students' self-seating patterns in lunchrooms, or chimpanzee family structures in their natural habitats.

In one study (Mehl & Pennebaker, 2003), researchers had 52 introductory psychology students don a belt-worn tape recorder. For up to four days, the machines captured 30-second snippets of the students' waking hours, turning on

Naturalistic observation of culture, climate, and pace of life :: Researchers operationally defined *pace of life* as walking speed, the speed with which postal clerks completed a simple request, and the accuracy of public clocks. After observing behavior in 31 countries, they concluded that life is fastest paced in Japan and Western Europe, and slower paced in economically less-developed countries (Levine & Norenzayan, 1999). People in colder climates, such as these people in Norway, also tend to live at a faster pace.

Sven Nackstrand/AFP/Getty Images

every 12.5 minutes. By the end of the study, researchers had eavesdropped on more than 10,000 half-minute life slices. On what percentage of the slices do you suppose they found the students talking

Courtesy of Gilda Morelli

Naturalistic observation :: For more than 20 years, psychologist Gilda Morelli has lived among the Efe people of Central Africa. Observing family members like the man and baby shown here, she has studied paternal and maternal care and children's development.

with someone? What percentage captured the students at a computer keyboard? The answers: 28 and 9 percent. (What percentage of *your* waking hours are spent in these activities?)

Like case studies and surveys, naturalistic observation does not *explain* behavior. It *describes* it. Nevertheless, descriptions can be revealing.

Correlation

8: Why do correlations permit prediction but not explanation, and what is an illusory correlation?

Describing behavior is a first step toward predicting it. Surveys and naturalistic observations often show us that one trait or behavior is related to another. In such cases, we say the two **correlate.** A statistical measure (the *correlation coefficient*) helps us figure how closely two things vary together, and thus how well either one *predicts* the other.

- A *positive correlation* (between 0 and +1.00) indicates a *direct* relationship, meaning that two things increase together or decrease together. In growing children, height correlates positively with weight.

- A *negative correlation* (between 0 and –1.00) indicates an *inverse* relationship: As one thing increases, the other decreases. Our earlier example, on the link between self-esteem and depression, might illustrate a negative correlation: If so, people who score low on self-esteem would tend to score high on depression. If the correlation is as low as –1.00, one set of scores goes down precisely as the other goes up, just like children on opposite ends of a teeter-totter.

- A coefficient near zero is a weak correlation, indicating little or no relationship.

To see how well you can spot positive and negative correlations, take the quiz in **TABLE 1.2**.

Psychology's correlations often catch our interest but fail to predict most human variations. In later chapters, you'll see, for example, that there is a positive correlation between parents' abusiveness and their children's later abusiveness when they become parents. Does this mean that most abused children become abusive? No! The correlation simply indicates a statistical association: Although most abused children *do not* grow into abusers, even fewer nonabused children become abusers. Correlations point us toward predictions, but usually imperfect ones.

The point to remember: A correlation coefficient helps us see the world more clearly by revealing the extent to which two things relate.

Correlation and Causation

Correlations help us predict. Self-esteem correlates negatively with (and therefore predicts) depression. But does that mean low self-esteem *causes* depression? If your answer is yes, you are not alone. A nearly irresistible error is thinking that such an association proves causation. But no matter how strong the relationship, it does not!

Correlation may not mean causation :: Length of marriage correlates with hair loss in men. Does this mean that marriage causes men to lose their hair (or that balding men make better husbands)? In this case, as in many others, a third factor obviously explains the correlation: Golden anniversaries and baldness both accompany aging.

R. Sidney/The Image Works

How else might we explain the negative correlation between self-esteem and depression? As **FIGURE 1.3** on the next page suggests, we'd get the same correlation between low self-esteem and depression if depression caused people to be down on themselves. And we'd also get that correlation if something else—a third factor such as heredity or brain chemistry—caused *both* low self-esteem and depression.

This point is so important—so basic to thinking smarter with psychology—that it merits one more example, this one from a survey of over 12,000 adolescents. The more teens feel loved by their parents, the less likely they are to behave in unhealthy ways—having early sex, smoking, abusing alcohol and drugs, behaving violently (Resnick & others, 1997). "Adults have a powerful effect on their children's behavior right through the high school years," gushed an Associated Press (AP) story on the study. But no correlation has a built-in cause-effect arrow. Thus, the AP could as well have said, "Well-behaved teens feel their parents' love and approval; out-of-bounds teens more often describe their parents as disapproving jerks."

The point to remember (turn up the volume here): Correlation indicates the *possibility* of a cause-effect relationship, but it *does not* prove causation. Knowing that two events are associated need not tell us anything about what causes what. Remember this principle and you will be wiser as you read and hear news of scientific studies.

Table 1.2	Name the Correlation

For each of the following news reports of correlational research, indicate in the blank whether the reported link is a positive (*P*) correlation or a negative (*N*) correlation.

1. The more TV is on in a young child's home, the less time the child spends reading (Kaiser, 2003). _____

2. The more sexual content teens see on TV, the more likely they are to have sex (Collins & others, 2004). _____

3. The longer children are breast-fed, the greater their later academic achievement (Horwood & Fergusson, 1998). _____

4. The more income rose among a sample of poor families, the fewer psychiatric symptoms their children experienced (Costello & others, 2003). _____

Answers: 1. negative, 2. positive, 3. positive, 4. negative.

naturalistic observation observing and recording behavior in naturally occurring situations without trying to manipulate and control the situation.

correlation a measure of the extent to which two factors vary together, and thus of how well either factor predicts the other. The *correlation coefficient* is the mathematical expression of the relationship, ranging from –1 to +1.

Figure 1.3> Three possible cause-effect relationships People low in self-esteem are more likely to report depression than are those high in self-esteem. One possible explanation of this negative correlation is that a bad self-image causes depressed feelings. But, as the diagram indicates, other cause-effect relationships are possible.

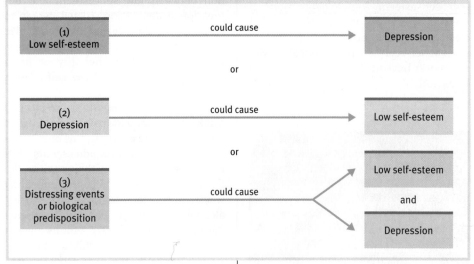

| (1) Low self-esteem | could cause → | Depression |

or

| (2) Depression | could cause → | Low self-esteem |

or

| (3) Distressing events or biological predisposition | could cause → | Low self-esteem **and** Depression |

Illusory Correlations

Correlation coefficients help us see relationships we might otherwise miss. They also help us to avoid "seeing" imaginary relationships. When we *believe* there is a link between two things, we are likely to *notice* and *recall* instances that confirm our belief (Trolier & Hamilton, 1986). These nonexistent relationships are **illusory correlations.**

Have you ever had a thought pop into your mind—say, that you were about to get an unlikely phone call—and then the unlikely event happened? We are especially likely to notice and remember such dramatic or unusual events occurring in sequence. When the call does not follow the thought, we are less likely to note and remember the nonevent.

Illusory correlations help explain many inaccurate beliefs, such as the idea that infertile couples who adopt become more likely to conceive (Gilovich, 1991). And they help explain why for so many years people believed (and many still do) that getting chilled and wet causes one to catch a cold, and that weather changes trigger arthritis pain. We are, in what poet Wallace Stevens called our "rage for

order," eager to perceive patterns, whether they're there or not.

The point to remember: When we notice random coincidences, we may forget that

Given enough random events, something weird will happen :: An event that happens to but one in 1 billion people every day occurs about six times a day, 2000 times a year. Angelo and Maria Gallina were the beneficiaries of one of those extraordinary chance events when they won two California lottery games on the same day.

they are random and instead see them as correlated. Thus, we can easily deceive ourselves by seeing what is not there.

Experimentation

9: How do experiments clarify or reveal cause-effect relationships?

Descriptions don't prove causation. Correlations don't prove causation. To isolate cause and effect, psychologists have to simplify the world. In our everyday lives, many things affect our actions and influence our thoughts. Psychologists sort out this complexity by using **experiments.** With experiments, researchers can focus on the possible effects of one or more items by (1) *manipulating the factors of interest* and (2) *holding constant ("controlling") other factors.* (You'll see the word *factor* often in descriptions of research. It refers to anything that contributes to a result.) Let's consider a few experiments to see how this works.

Random Assignment: Minimizing Differences

Researchers have compared breast-fed infants and infants bottle-fed with formula. One interesting set of findings shows children's intelligence scores are somewhat higher if they were breast-fed as infants (Angelsen & others, 2001; Mortensen & others, 2002; Quinn & others, 2001). So we can say that mother's milk correlates modestly but positively with later intelligence. But does this mean that smarter mothers (who more often breast-feed) have smarter children? Or that the nutrients in mother's milk contribute to brain development?

How might researchers isolate the effects of mother's milk from the effects of other factors, such as mother's age, education, and intelligence? The answer, as you've no doubt guessed, is to experiment. This is just what a British research team did, with parental permission. The researchers **randomly assigned** 424 hospital preterm infants either to formula feedings or to breast-milk feedings (Lucas & others, 1992). By doing this, the researchers created two groups: an **experimental group,** in which babies received the treatment (breast milk), and a **control group** without the treatment. Researchers were then fairly certain that the two groups were otherwise identical. Random assignment, like coin tossing, roughly equalizes the two groups in other characteristics (including mother's age, education, and so on). This eliminated alternative explanations and supported the conclusion that breast is indeed best for developing intelligence (at least for preterm infants). On intelligence tests taken at age 8, the children nourished with breast milk had significantly higher scores than their formula-fed counterparts.

Breast is also best nutritionally, notes the World Health Organization (2000). It is "an unequalled way of providing ideal food for the healthy growth and development of infants."

No single experiment is conclusive, of course. But *this study illustrates an important point:* If a behavior (such as test performance) changes when we vary an experimental factor (such as infant nutrition), then we know the factor is having an effect. Unlike correlational studies, which uncover naturally occurring relationships, an experiment manipulates (varies) a factor to determine its effect.

The Double-Blind Procedure: Eliminating Bias

Researchers in the breast-milk experiment were lucky—babies don't tend to have attitudes that affect the experiment's outcome. Adults do, and this can be a big problem, which may surface during tests of new drug treatments.

Consider: Three days into a cold, many of us start taking vitamin C tablets. If we find our cold symptoms lessening, we may credit the pills. But after a few days, a cold is naturally on its way out. Was the remedy truly effective? To find out, we could experiment.

And that is precisely how investigators evaluate new drug treatments and new methods of psychological therapy

(Chapter 13). Often, the participants in these studies are *blind* (uninformed) about what treatment, if any, they are receiving. The experimental group receives the treatment. The control group receives a **placebo** (an inactive substance—perhaps a pill with no drug in it).

Many studies use a **double-blind procedure**—neither the participant nor the research assistant collecting the data knows which group is receiving the treatment. In such studies, researchers can check a treatment's actual effects apart from the participants' belief in its healing powers and the staff's enthusiasm for its potential. Just *thinking* you are getting a treatment can boost your spirits, relax your body, and relieve your symptoms. This **placebo effect** is well documented in reducing pain, depression, and anxiety (Kirsch & Sapirstein, 1998). And that is why we can't know how effective a therapy really is unless we control for a possible placebo effect.

Independent and Dependent Variables

Here is an even more potent example: The drug Viagra was approved for use after 21 clinical trials. One trial was an experiment in which researchers randomly assigned 329 men with erectile dysfunction to either an experimental group (Viagra-takers) or a control group (placebo-takers). It was a double-blind procedure—neither the men nor the person who gave them the pills knew which drug they were receiving. The result: At peak doses, 69 percent of Viagra-assisted attempts at intercourse were successful, compared with 22 percent for men receiving the placebo (Goldstein & others, 1998). Viagra worked.

This simple experiment manipulated just one factor—the drug Viagra. This factor is called the **independent variable.** We can vary it independently—without concern for other factors, such as the men's age, weight, and personality, which, thanks to random assignment, should be equal in both groups. Experiments examine the effect of one or more independent variables on some measurable behavior.

This affected behavior is called the **dependent variable** because it can vary *depending* on what takes place during the experiment. Experimenters give both variables precise *operational definitions*, specifying exactly how they are manipulating the independent variable (the precise drug dosage and timing in this study) or measuring the dependent variable (the questions that assessed the men's responses). These definitions answer the "What do you mean?" question with a level of precision that enables others to repeat the study.

Note the distinction between random *sampling* in surveys and random *assignment* in experiments. Random sampling helps us generalize to a larger population. Random assignment controls extraneous influences, which helps us infer cause and effect.

illusory correlation the perception of a relationship where none exists.

experiment a method in which researchers vary one or more factors (independent variables) to observe the effect on some behavior or mental process (the dependent variable).

random assignment assigning participants to experimental and control groups by chance, thus minimizing any differences between them.

experimental group the group in an experiment that is exposed to the treatment, that is, to one version of the independent variable.

control group the group in an experiment that contrasts with the experimental condition and serves as a comparison for evaluating the effect of the treatment.

placebo [pluh-SEE-bo; Latin for "I shall please"] an inert substance or condition that is assumed to be an active agent.

double-blind procedure a procedure in which participants and research staff are ignorant (blind) about who has received the treatment or a placebo.

placebo effect results caused by expectations alone.

independent variable the experimental factor that is manipulated; the variable whose effect is being studied.

dependent variable the outcome factor; the variable that may change in response to manipulations of the independent variable.

Figure 1.4> Experimentation To study cause-effect, psychologists may randomly assign some participants to an experimental group, others to a control group. Measuring the dependent variable (intelligence score) will determine the effect of the independent variable (type of milk).

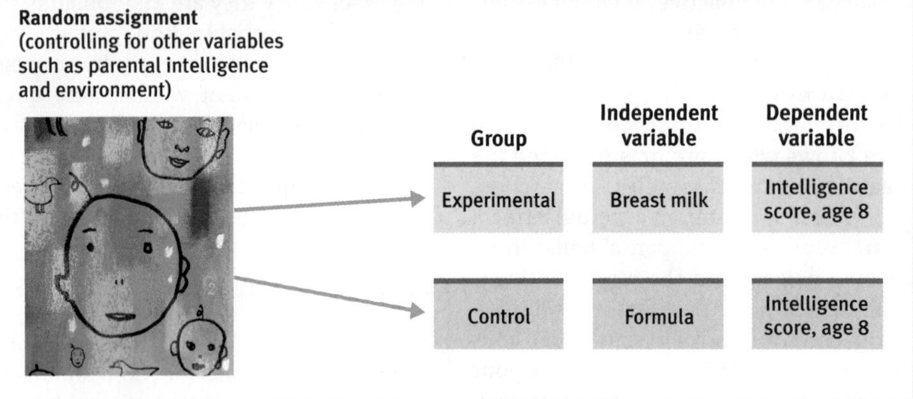

Random assignment (controlling for other variables such as parental intelligence and environment)

Group	Independent variable	Dependent variable
Experimental	Breast milk	Intelligence score, age 8
Control	Formula	Intelligence score, age 8

Let's see how this would work with the breast-milk experiment (**FIGURE 1.4**). A *variable* is anything that can vary (infant nutrition, intelligence, TV exposure). Experiments aim to *manipulate* an *independent* variable and *measure* the *dependent* variable. An experiment has at least two different groups: an *experimental group* and a *comparison* or *control group*. *Random assignment* works to control all other variables by equating the groups before any manipulation begins. In this way, an experiment tests the effect of at least one independent variable (what we manipulate) on at least one dependent variable (the outcome we measure).

Each of psychology's research methods has strengths and weaknesses (**TABLE 1.3**). Experiments show cause-effect relationships, but some experiments would not be ethical or practical. (To test the effects of parenting, we're just not going to take newborns and randomly assign them either to their biological parents or to orphanages.)

PRACTICE TEST

12. In psychology, a good theory leads to hypotheses, or predictions that can be tested. When hypotheses are tested, the result is typically

a. increased skepticism.
b. rejection of the theory.
c. confirmation or revision of the theory.
d. personal bias on the part of the investigator.

13. You wish to take an accurate poll in a certain country by questioning people who truly represent your country's adult population. Therefore, you need to make sure the people are

a. at least 50 percent males and 50 percent females.
b. a small but intelligent sample of the population.
c. a very large sample of the population.
d. a random sample of the population.

14. Suppose a psychologist finds that the more natural childbirth training classes a woman attends, the less pain medication she requires during childbirth. The relationship between the number of training sessions and the amount of pain medication required is a(an)

a. positive correlation.
b. negative correlation.
c. cause-effect relationship.
d. illusory correlation.

15. Knowing that two events are correlated does not tell us what is the cause and what is the effect. However, it does provide

a. a basis for prediction.
b. an explanation for why things happened the way they did.
c. proof that as one event increases, the other also increases.
d. an indication that some third factor is affecting both events.

Table 1.3 Comparing Research Methods

Research Method	Basic Purpose	How Conducted	What Is Manipulated	Weaknesses
Descriptive	To observe and record behavior	Do case studies, surveys, or naturalistic observations	Nothing	No control of variables; single cases may be misleading.
Correlational	To detect naturally occurring relationships; to assess how well one event predicts another	Compute statistical association, sometimes among survey responses	Nothing	Does not specify cause-effect.
Experimental	To explore cause-effect	Manipulate one or more factors; use random assignment	The independent variable(s)	Sometimes not possible for practical or ethical reasons. Results may not generalize to other contexts.

16. Some people wrongly perceive that their dreams predict future events. This is an example of a(an)
    a. negative correlation.
    b. positive correlation.
    c. illusory correlation.
    d. naturalistic observation.

17. Descriptive and correlational studies describe behavior, detect relationships, and predict behavior. But in order to begin to explain that behavior, psychologists use
    a. naturalistic observations.
    b. experiments.
    c. surveys.
    d. case studies.

18. A researcher wants to determine whether noise level affects the blood pressure of elderly people. In one group she varies the level of noise in the environment and records participants' blood pressure. In this experiment, the level of noise is the
    a. control condition.
    b. experimental condition.
    c. dependent variable (the factor being measured).
    d. independent variable (the factor being manipulated).

19. To test the effect of a new drug on depression, we randomly assign people to control and experimental groups. Those in the experimental group take a pink pill containing the new medication; those in the control group take a pink pill that contains no medication. Which statement is true?
    a. The medication is the dependent variable.
    b. Depression is the independent variable.
    c. Participants in the control group take a placebo.
    d. Participants in the experimental group take a placebo.

20. A double-blind procedure is often used to prevent a researcher's biases from influencing the outcome of an experiment. In this procedure
    a. only the participants will know whether they are in the control group or the experimental group.
    b. members of the experimental and control groups will be carefully matched to be sure they have the same age,

    sex, income, and level of education.
    c. neither the participants nor the researchers will know who is in the experimental and control groups.
    d. someone separate from the researcher will ask people to volunteer for either the experimental group or the control group.

Frequently Asked Questions About Psychology

We have reflected on how a scientific approach can restrain biases. We have seen how case studies, surveys, and naturalistic observations help us describe behavior. We have also noted that correlational studies assess the association between two factors, showing how well one predicts the other. We have examined the logic underlying experiments, which use controls and random assignment to isolate the effects of independent variables on dependent variables.

Hopefully, you are now prepared to understand what lies ahead and to think critically about psychological matters. Yet, even knowing this much, you may still have concerns. So before we plunge in, let's address some frequently asked questions about psychology.

10: How does research benefit from laboratory experiments?

Do you ever wonder whether people's behavior in the lab will predict their behavior in real life? For example, does detecting the blink of a faint red light in a dark room have anything useful to say about flying a plane at night? After viewing a violent, sexually explicit film, does an aroused man's increased willingness to push buttons that he thinks will electrically shock a woman really say anything about whether violent pornography makes a man more likely to abuse a woman?

Before you answer, consider: The experimenter *intends* to simplify reality—to create a mini-environment that imitates and controls important features of everyday life. Just as a wind tunnel lets airplane designers re-create airflow forces under controlled conditions, a laboratory experiment lets psychologists re-create psychological forces under controlled conditions.

In aggression studies, deciding whether to push a button that delivers a shock may not be the same as slapping someone in the face, but the *principle* is the same. The experiment's purpose is not to re-create the exact behaviors of everyday life but to test theoretical principles (Mook, 1983). *It is the resulting principles—not the specific findings—that help explain everyday behaviors.* And many investigations show that principles derived in the laboratory *do* typically generalize to the everyday world (Anderson & others, 1999).

The point to remember: Psychologists' concerns lie less with particular behaviors than with the general principles that help explain many behaviors.

11: What ethical guidelines safeguard human and animal research participants?

Many psychologists study animals because they find them fascinating. They want to understand how different species learn, think, and behave. Psychologists also study animals to learn about people, by doing experiments allowed only with animals. We humans are not *like* animals; we *are* animals, sharing a common biology. Animal experiments have therefore led to treatments for human diseases—insulin for diabetes, vaccines to prevent polio and rabies, transplants to replace defective organs.

"Rats are very similar to humans except that they are not stupid enough to purchase lottery tickets."

Dave Barry, July 2, 2002

Humans are complex. But, the same processes by which we learn are present in rats, monkeys, and even sea slugs. The simplicity of the sea slug's nervous system is precisely what makes it so revealing of the neural mechanisms of learning.

Sharing such similarities, should we not respect our animal relatives? "We cannot defend our scientific work with animals on the basis of the similarities between them and ourselves and then defend it morally on the basis of differences," noted Roger Ulrich (1991). The animal protection movement protests the use of animals in psychological, biological, and medical research. Researchers remind us that the world's 30 million mammals used each year in research are but a fraction of 1 percent of the billions of animals killed annually for food (which means the average person eats 20 animals a year). And for every dog or cat used in an experiment, 50 others are killed each year in animal shelters (Goodwin & Morrison, 1999).

Some animal protection organizations want to replace experiments on animals with naturalistic observations. Many animal researchers respond that this is not a question of good versus evil but of compassion for animals versus compassion for people.

Out of this heated debate, two issues emerge. The basic one is whether it is right to place the well-being of humans above that of animals. In experiments on stress and cancer, is it right that mice get tumors in the hope that people might not? Should some monkeys be exposed to an HIV-like virus in the search for an AIDS vaccine? Is our use of other animals as natural as the behavior of carnivorous hawks, cats, and whales? The answers to such questions vary by culture. In Gallup surveys in Canada and the United States, about 6 in 10 adults deem medical testing on animals "morally acceptable." In Britain, only 37 percent do (Mason, 2003).

If we give human life first priority, what safeguards should protect the well-being of animals in research? One survey of animal researchers gave an answer. Some 98 percent supported government regulations protecting primates, dogs, and cats, and 74 percent supported regulations providing for the humane care of rats and mice (Plous & Herzog, 2000). Many professional associations and funding agencies already have such guidelines. For example, British Psychological Society guidelines call for housing animals under reasonably natural living conditions, with companions for social animals (Lea, 2000). American Psychological Association (2002) guidelines state that researchers must ensure the "comfort, health, and humane treatment" of animals and minimize "infection, illness, and pain."

Animals have themselves benefited from animal research. One Ohio team of research psychologists measured stress hormone levels in samples of millions of dogs brought each year to animal shelters. They devised handling and stroking methods to reduce stress and ease the dogs' transition to adoptive homes (Tuber & others, 1999). Other studies have helped improve care and management in animals' natural habitats. By revealing our behavioral kinship with animals and the remarkable intelligence of chimpanzees, gorillas, and other animals, experiments have also led to increased empathy and protection for them. At its best, a psychology concerned for humans and sensitive to animals serves the welfare of both.

What about human participants? Does the image of white-coated scientists delivering electric shocks trouble you? If so, you'll be relieved to know that most psychological studies are free of such stress. With people, blinking lights, flashing words, and pleasant social interactions are more common.

Occasionally, though, researchers do temporarily stress or deceive people, but only when they believe it is essential to a justifiable end, such as understanding and controlling violent behavior or studying mood swings. Some experiments won't work if participants know everything beforehand. (Wanting to be helpful, the participants might try to confirm the researcher's predictions.)

The American Psychological Association (1992) and the British Psychological Society (1993) have developed ethical principles to guide investigators. They include (1) obtaining the participants' informed consent, (2) protecting them from harm and discomfort, (3) keeping information about individual participants confidential, and (4) fully explaining the

D. Shapiro, ©Wildlife Conservation Society

Animal research benefiting animals :: Thanks partly to research on the benefits of novelty, control, and stimulation, these gorillas are enjoying an improved quality of life in New York's Bronx Zoo. As they would in the wild, they now work for their supper (Stewart, 2002).

research afterward. Moreover, most universities now have an ethics committee that screens research proposals and safeguards participants' well-being.

12: How are researchers influenced by their own values, and what is psychology's ultimate purpose?

Psychology is definitely not value-free. Values affect what we study, how we study it, and how we interpret results. Consider: Researchers' values influence their choice of topics. Should we study worker productivity or worker morale? Sex discrimination or gender differences? Conformity or independence? Values can also color "the facts." As we noted earlier, what we want or expect to see can bias our observations and interpretations **(FIGURE 1.5)**.

Even the words we use to describe something can reflect our values. Are the sex acts we do not practice "perversions" or "sexual variations"? Labels describe and labels evaluate, whether in psychology or everyday speech. One person's

Figure 1.5> What do you see? Our expectations influence what we perceive. Did you see a duck or a rabbit? Before showing some friends this image, ask them if they can see the duck lying on its back (or the bunny in the grass). (From Shepard, 1990.)

"rigidity" is another's "consistency," one person's "faith" is another's "fanaticism." Our words—"firm" or "stubborn," "careful" or "picky," "discreet" or "secretive"—reveal as much about us as they do about those we label.

Applied psychology also contains hidden values. If you defer to "professional" guidance—on raising children, achieving self-fulfillment, coping with sexual feelings, getting ahead at work—you are accepting value-laden advice. A science of behavior and mental processes can certainly help us reach our goals, but it cannot decide what those goals should be.

Psychology is value-laden. Is it also dangerously powerful, as some worry? Is it an accident that astronomy is the oldest science and psychology the youngest? To some people, exploring the external universe seems far safer than exploring our own inner universe. Might psychology, they ask, be used to manipulate people?

Knowledge, like all power, can be used for good or evil. Nuclear power has been used to light up cities—and to demolish them. Persuasive power has been used to educate people—and to deceive and control them. Although psychology does indeed have the power to deceive, its purpose is to enlighten. Every day, psychologists are exploring ways to enhance learning, creativity, and compassion. Psychology speaks to many of our world's great problems—war, overpopulation, prejudice, family crises, crime—all of which involve attitudes and behaviors. Psychology also speaks to our deepest longings—for nourishment, for love, for happiness. And as you will see, one of the new developments in this field—positive psychology—has as its goal exploring and promoting human strengths. True, psychology cannot address all of life's great questions, but it speaks to some mighty important ones.

21. The laboratory environment is designed to
   a. exactly re-create the events of every-day life.
   b. re-create psychological forces under controlled conditions.
   c. create opportunities for naturalistic observation.
   d. minimize the use of animals and humans in psychological research.

22. Professional ethical standards provide guidelines about the treatment of people in research studies. Those guidelines include
   a. protecting the person from harm and discomfort.
   b. fully explaining the research after the experiment has been completed.
   c. keeping information about individual participants confidential.
   d. all of these answers.

23. In defending their experimental research with animals, psychologists have noted that
   a. animals' physiology and behavior can tell us much about our own.
   b. animal experimentation sometimes helps animals as well as humans.
   c. advancing the well-being of humans justifies animal experimentation.
   d. all of these answers.

Answers : 21. b, 22. d, 23. d

Close-Up: How to Be a Better Student, on the next page, provides study and learning tips for this and any other class you take.

CLOSE-UP: How to Be a Better Student

In this course, you will learn *how to ask and answer important questions*—how to think critically as you consider competing ideas and claims. Many of life's questions are beyond psychology, but even a first psychology course can shine a bright light on some very important ones.

Having your life enriched and your vision enlarged (and getting a decent grade) means you must actively process material. Your mind is not like your stomach, something to be filled passively. Your mind is more like a muscle that grows stronger with exercise. We learn and remember material best when we put it in our own words, rehearse it, and then review and rehearse it again.

The **SQ3R** study method—**S**urvey, **Q**uestion, **R**ead, **R**ehearse, **R**eview—uses these principles (Robinson, 1970).

- To study a chapter, first *survey*, taking a bird's-eye view as you scan the headings. Notice how the chapter is organized.

- As you prepare to read each section, form a *question* that you should answer. For this section, you might have asked, "How can I master the information in this book and become a better student while I'm at it?"

- Then *read*, actively searching for the answer to your question. At each sitting, read only as much of the chapter as you can absorb without tiring. Usually, a single main chapter section will do—the Frequently Asked Questions About Psychology section you just finished, for example. Relating what you are reading to your own life will help you understand and remember the material.

- When you finish reading a section, *rehearse* the section's main ideas putting them into your own words. Then test yourself by trying to answer your question. Glance back to see what you didn't recall.

- Finally, *review*: Read over any notes you have taken. As you do this, keep an eye on the chapter's organization. Then, quickly review the whole chapter.

Survey, question, read, rehearse, review. I have organized this book's chapters with the SQ3R study system in mind. Each chapter begins with a chapter outline that aids your *survey*. Headings and study *questions* suggest issues and concepts you should consider as you *read*. The material is organized into sections of readable length. Practice Tests at the end of the main sections will help you *rehearse* what you've learned before moving on. A visual concept map at the end of each chapter repeats and answers the study questions, and it can help you *review* the material. Finally, the list of key terms will help you check your mastery of important concepts.

You now have five SQ3R pointers to help you become a better student. Here are five more study tips drawn from psychology's research.

1. *Distribute your study time*. One of psychology's oldest findings is that *spaced practice* (perhaps an hour a day, six days a week) promotes better learning than trying to cram everything into one long study blitz. To space your study sessions, you'll need to learn to manage your time carefully. (Richard O. Straub explains time management in a helpful section at the front of this text. He has also written a very useful Study Guide to accompany this text.)

2. *Learn to think critically*. As you read and participate in class, think about people's *assumptions and values*. Do they have a strong perspective or even a bias in their arguments? *Evaluate evidence*. Is it just one person's story? Is it correlational? Is the evidence based on an experiment? *Assess conclusions*. Try to think of other explanations for what you are reading or hearing. Could you come up with another conclusion?

3. *In class, listen actively*. Listen for the main ideas of a lecture. Write them down. Ask questions during and after class. In class, as in your private study, process the information actively and you will understand and remember it better.

4. *Overlearn*. We tend to be overconfident about how much we know. You may understand a chapter as you read it. But you may not be able to hold on to that knowledge unless you devote extra study time to test yourself and review what you think you know.

5. *Be a smart test-taker*. If a test contains both multiple-choice questions and an essay question, turn first to the essay. Read the question carefully, noting exactly what the instructor is asking. On the back of a page, pencil in a list of points you'd like to make and then organize them. Before writing, put aside the essay and work through the multiple-choice questions. (As you do so, your mind may continue to mull over the essay question. Sometimes the other questions will bring important points to mind.) Then reread the essay question, rethink your answer, and start writing. When you finish, proofread your answer to fix spelling and other little mistakes that make you look less competent than you are. When reading multiple-choice questions, don't confuse yourself by trying to imagine how each choice might be the right one. Try instead to answer the question as if it were a fill-in-the-blank. First cover the answers, recall what you know, and complete the sentence in your mind. Then read the answers on the test and find the choice that best matches what you recall.

While connecting psychology to your everyday life, you will learn much more than effective study techniques. Psychology deepens our appreciation for how we perceive, think, feel, and act. By so doing it can indeed enrich our lives and enlarge our vision. Through this book I hope to help guide you toward that end. As educator Charles Eliot said a century ago: "Books are the quietest and most constant of friends, and the most patient of teachers."

SQ3R a study method incorporating five steps: **S**urvey, **Q**uestion, **R**ead, **R**ehearse, **R**eview.

terms and concepts to remember

behaviorism, p. 3

humanistic psychology, p. 3

psychology, p. 3

critical thinking, p. 5

biopsychosocial approach, p. 6

culture, p. 6

nature-nurture issue, p. 6

dual processing, p. 8

positive psychology, p. 8

hindsight bias, p. 10

theory, p. 11

hypothesis, p. 12

operational definition, p. 12

replication, p. 12

case study, p. 12

survey, p. 13

random sample, p. 13

naturalistic observation, p. 14

correlation, p. 14

illusory correlation, p. 16

experiment, p. 16

random assignment, p. 16

experimental group, p. 17

control group, p. 17

placebo [pluh-SEE-bo], p. 17

double-blind procedure, p. 17

placebo effect, p. 17

independent variable, p. 17

dependent variable, p. 17

SQ3R, p. 22

REVIEW: PSYCHOLOGY'S ROOTS, BIG IDEAS, AND CRITICAL THINKING TOOLS

PSYCHOLOGY'S ROOTS

1 **How has psychology's focus changed over time?**

- First psychological laboratory, 1879, studied the elements of mental experience.
- Early definition of *psychology:* the "science of mental life."
- Revised by *behaviorists* in 1920s to "scientific study of observable behavior."
- Current definition: "scientific study of behavior and mental processes."

2 **What are psychology's current subfields?**

- Biological
- Developmental
- Cognitive
- Personality
- Industrial/organizational
- Counseling
- Clinical
- Social

FOUR BIG IDEAS IN PSYCHOLOGY

3 **What four big ideas run throughout this book?**

- Critical thinking is smart thinking.
- Behavior is a biopsychosocial event. (Includes studying *nature-nurture* interaction and *cultural* influences.)
- We operate with a two-track mind (dual processing). (Our brains process a surprising amount without our awareness.)
- Psychology explores human strengths as well as challenges.

WHY DO PSYCHOLOGY?

4 **Why are answers reached by thinking critically more reliable than ordinary common sense?**

INTUITION AND COMMON SENSE ARE VULNERABLE TO

- *Hindsight bias* (the I-knew-it-all-along phenomenon)—believing, after learning the outcome, that we would have foreseen it.
- Overconfidence—bias for seeking evidence confirming our beliefs.

5 **What are the three key attitudes of scientific inquiry?**

- Curiosity
- Skepticism
- Humility

The scientific attitude carries into life as critical thinking.

HOW DO PSYCHOLOGISTS ASK AND ANSWER QUESTIONS?

6 **How do psychologists construct theories?**

- Use precise language in statements of procedures (*operational definitions*).
- Form *hypotheses* (predictions based on *theories*).
- Test hypotheses using descriptive, correlational, or experimental methods.
- Use research results to validate or refine the theory.
- Suggest practical applications when appropriate.
- *Replicate* (repeat) studies. (Similar results increase confidence in original conclusion.)

7 **What three techniques do psychologists use to observe and describe behavior?**

- Individual *case studies*.
- *Surveys* (among *random samples* of a population).
- *Naturalistic observation*.

8 **Why do correlations permit prediction but not explanation, and what is an illusory correlation?**

- *Correlations* tell us how well one event predicts another (using a measure called a correlation coefficient), but not whether one event *caused* the other, or whether some third factor influenced both events.
- We sometimes perceive relationships that are not there (*illusory correlations*).

9 **How do experiments clarify or reveal cause-effect relationships?**

EXPERIMENTS ENABLE

- Creation of a controlled, simplified version of reality.
- Manipulation of one factor (the *independent variable*) while controlling others.
- Measurement of changes in other factors (*dependent variables*).
- Minimizing differences between groups (through *random assignment*).
- Comparing *experimental group* results with *control group* results.

FREQUENTLY ASKED QUESTIONS ABOUT PSYCHOLOGY

10 **How does research benefit from laboratory experiments?**

- Studying specific examples in controlled environments can reveal important general principles.

11 **What ethical guidelines safeguard human and animal research participants?**

- Professional ethical standards, enforced by university ethics committees, protect participants' well-being.
- APA and other legal guidelines require animal researchers to minimize pain and distress.
- Researchers may only temporarily stress or deceive human participants to conceal a study's purpose and prevent biased responses.

12 **How are researchers influenced by their own values, and what is psychology's ultimate purpose?**

- Values influence choice of research topics, theories and observations, labels for behavior, and professional advice.
- Knowledge can be used for good or evil.
- Psychology's principles have been used mainly to enlighten and to achieve positive ends.

IMAGINE THAT JUST MOMENTS BEFORE YOUR death, someone removed your brain from your body and kept it alive by floating it in a tank of fluid while feeding it enriched blood. Would you still be in there? Further imagine that your still-living brain is transplanted into the body of a person whose own brain was severely damaged. To whose home should the recovered patient return?

"You're certainly a lot less fun since the operation."

If you answered that the patient should return to your home, you illustrated what most of us believe—that we reside in our head. An acquaintance of mine received a new heart from a woman who had needed a heart-lung transplant. When the two chanced to meet in their hospital ward, she introduced herself: "I think you have my heart." But only her heart; her self, she assumed, still resided inside her skull.

In this chapter, we explore the biology of the mind—the links between our brain and our behavior. No principle is more central to today's psychology, or to this book, than this: *Everything psychological—every idea, every mood, every urge—is simultaneously biological.* We may talk separately of biological and psychological influences, but to think, feel, or act without a body would be like running without legs.

Biological psychologists study the links between our biology and our behavior. These links are a key part of the biopsychosocial approach, which is one of the Four Big Ideas that you will hear about throughout this text. In later chapters, we'll look at some of the ways our thinking and emotions can influence our brain and our health. In this chapter, we start small and build from the bottom up—from nerve cells to the brain. Then we'll see how our brain states form the mind, as we take a closer look at waking and sleeping consciousness.

NEURAL COMMUNICATION

A Neuron's Structure

How Neurons Communicate

How Neurotransmitters Influence Us

THE NERVOUS SYSTEM

The Peripheral Nervous System

The Central Nervous System

THE ENDOCRINE SYSTEM

THE BRAIN

CLOSE-UP: The Tools of Discovery—Having Our Head Examined

Older Brain Structures

The Cerebral Cortex

Our Divided Brain

Right-Left Differences in the Intact Brain

BRAIN STATES AND CONSCIOUSNESS

Selective Attention

Sleep and Dreams

biological psychology a branch of psychology concerned with the links between biology and behavior.

Neural Communication

The human body is complexity built from simplicity. Part of this complexity is our amazing internal communication system, which makes the Internet look like a child's toy telephone. Across the world, researchers are unlocking the mysteries of how our brain uses electrical and chemical processes to take in, organize, interpret, store, and use information. The story begins with the system's basic building block, the **neuron,** or nerve cell. We'll look first at its structure, and then at how neurons work together.

A Neuron's Structure

1: What are neurons, and how do they transmit information?

Neurons differ, but all are variations on the same theme **(FIGURE 2.1).** Each consists of a cell body and branching fibers. The bushy **dendrite** fibers receive messages and conduct them toward the cell body. From there, the cell's **axon** sends out messages to other neurons or to muscles or glands. Dendrites listen. Axons speak.

The messages that neurons carry are nerve impulses called **action potentials.**

These electrical signals travel down axons inside your brain at different speeds. Researchers have tracked some trudging along at a sluggish 2 miles per hour, and others racing along at a breakneck 200 or more miles per hour. But even this top speed is 3 million times slower than electricity zipping through a wire. That helps explain why, unlike the nearly instant reactions of a high-speed computer, our "quick" reaction to a sudden event, such as a child darting in front of our car, may take a quarter-second or more. Our brain is vastly more complex than a computer, but not faster at executing simple responses.

Neurons interweave so tightly that even with a microscope you would have trouble seeing where one ends and another begins. But end they do, at meeting places called **synapses.** At these points, two neurons are separated by a tiny gap less than a millionth of an inch wide. "Like elegant ladies air-kissing so as not to muss their makeup, dendrites and axons don't quite touch," notes poet Diane Ackerman (2004). How then does a

> "All information processing in the brain involves neurons 'talking to' each other at synapses."
>
> Neuroscientist Solomon H. Snyder, 1984

neuron send information across the tiny synaptic gap? The answer is one of the important scientific discoveries of our age.

How Neurons Communicate

Each neuron is itself a miniature decision-making device as it receives signals from hundreds, even thousands, of other neurons. Most of these signals are *excitatory,* somewhat like pushing a neuron's gas pedal. Others are *inhibitory,* more like pushing its brake.

If excitatory signals minus inhibitory signals exceed a minimum intensity, or **threshold,** the combined signals trigger an action potential. (Think of it this way: If the excitatory party animals outvote the inhibitory party poopers, the party's on.) The action potential then travels down the axon of the sending neuron, carrying the information to the receiving cell.

> "What one neuron tells another neuron is simply how much it is excited."
>
> —Francis Crick, *The Astonishing Hypothesis,* 1994

A neuron's firing doesn't vary in intensity. The neuron's reaction is an **all-or-none response.** Like guns, neurons either fire or they don't. How then do we distinguish a big hug from a gentle touch? A

neuron a nerve cell; the basic building block of the nervous system.

dendrites neuron extensions that receive messages and conduct impulses toward the cell body.

axons neuron extensions that pass messages to other neurons or cells.

action potential a nerve impulse.

synapse [SIN-aps] the junction between the axon tip of the sending neuron and the dendrite or cell body of the receiving neuron.

threshold the level of stimulation required to trigger a neural impulse.

all-or-none response a neuron's reaction of either firing (with a full-strength response) or not firing.

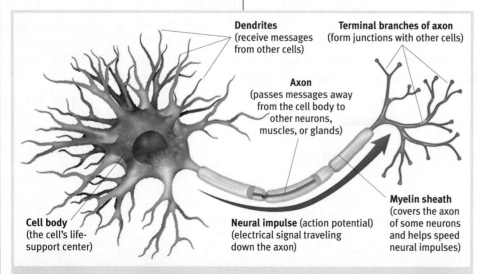

Dendrites (receive messages from other cells)

Terminal branches of axon (form junctions with other cells)

Axon (passes messages away from the cell body to other neurons, muscles, or glands)

Myelin sheath (covers the axon of some neurons and helps speed neural impulses)

Cell body (the cell's life-support center)

Neural impulse (action potential) (electrical signal traveling down the axon)

Figure 2.1> A typical neuron

Figure 2.2> How neurons communicate

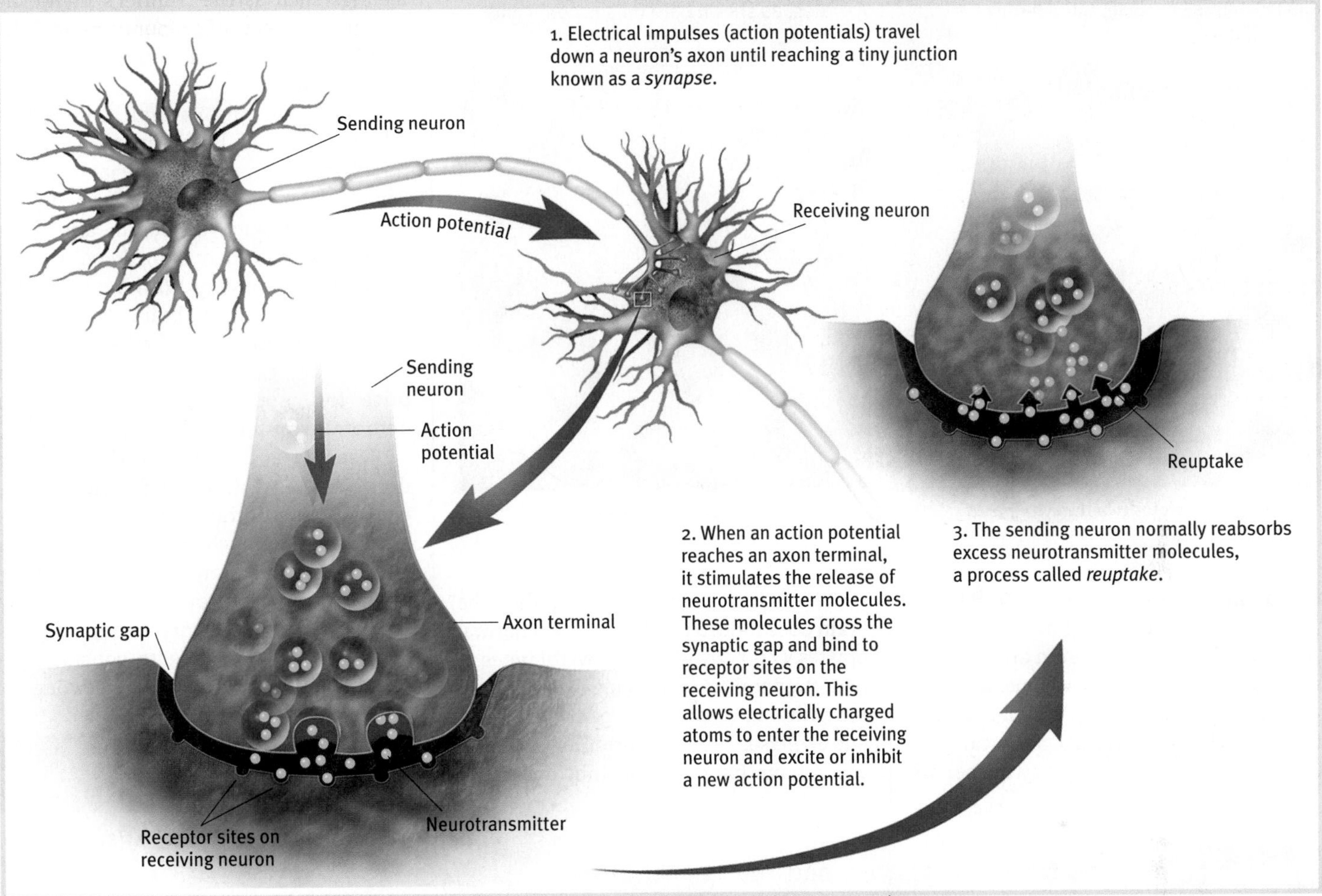

1. Electrical impulses (action potentials) travel down a neuron's axon until reaching a tiny junction known as a *synapse*.

Sending neuron

Action potential

Receiving neuron

Sending neuron

Action potential

Reuptake

Synaptic gap

Axon terminal

Receptor sites on receiving neuron

Neurotransmitter

2. When an action potential reaches an axon terminal, it stimulates the release of neurotransmitter molecules. These molecules cross the synaptic gap and bind to receptor sites on the receiving neuron. This allows electrically charged atoms to enter the receiving neuron and excite or inhibit a new action potential.

3. The sending neuron normally reabsorbs excess neurotransmitter molecules, a process called *reuptake*.

strong stimulus—a hug rather than a touch—can trigger *more* neurons to fire, and to fire more often. But it does not affect the action potential's strength or speed. Squeezing a trigger harder won't make a bullet bigger or faster.

When the action potential reaches the axon's end, your body performs an amazing trick. Your neural system converts an *electrical* impulse into a *chemical* message. At the synapse, the impulse triggers the release of **neurotransmitter** molecules (**FIGURE 2.2**). Within one 10,000th of a second, these chemical messengers cross the synaptic gap and bind to receptor sites on the receiving neuron. There, they act as excitatory or inhibitory signals, and the process begins again in this new

cell. Then, in another process called *reuptake*, the sending neuron absorbs any excess neurotransmitters left in the gap.

How Neurotransmitters Influence Us

2: How do neurotransmitters affect our mood and behavior?

Dozens of different neurotransmitters travel along their own pathways in the brain, carrying specific but different messages that affect our behavior and emotions (**FIGURE 2.3** on the next page). *Serotonin* levels, for example, can make us more or

less moody, hungry, sleepy, or aroused. *Dopamine* influences our movement, learning, attention, and emotions. **TABLE 2.1** on the next page shows the effects of some neurotransmitters.

In Chapter 1, I promised to show you how psychologists play their game. Let's do so now by taking a closer look at one exciting neurotransmitter discovery. Researchers attached a radioactive tracer to morphine, an **opiate** drug that elevates

neurotransmitters neuron-produced chemicals that cross synapses to carry messages to other neurons or cells.

opiates chemicals, such as opium, morphine, and heroin, that depress neural activity, temporarily lessening pain and anxiety.

Figure 2.3> Neurotransmitter pathways Each of the brain's differing chemical messengers has designated pathways where it operates, as shown here for serotonin and dopamine (Carter, 1998).

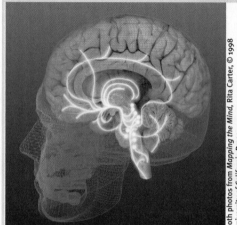

Serotonin pathways

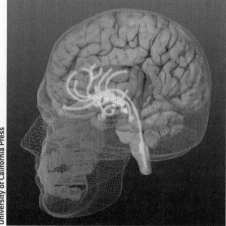

Both photos from *Mapping the Mind*, Rita Carter, © 1998 University of California Press

Dopamine pathways

mood and eases pain (Pert & Snyder, 1973). They noticed that the morphine "unlocked" receptors in brain areas linked with mood and pain sensations. But why would the brain have these "opiate receptors"? Why would it have a chemical lock, unless it also had a natural key to open it?

Researchers soon confirmed that the brain does indeed produce its own natural opiates. Our body releases several types of neurotransmitter molecules similar to morphine in response to pain and vigorous exercise. These **endorphins** (short for *endo*genous [produced within] m*orphine*),

as we now call them, help explain good feelings such as the "runner's high," the painkilling effects of acupuncture, and the indifference to pain in some severely injured people.

If indeed our natural endorphins lessen pain and boost mood, why not flood the brain with artificial opiates? One problem is that when flooded with opiate drugs such as heroin and morphine, the brain may shut down its own "feel-good" chemistry. Withdraw the artificial opiates and the brain will then be deprived of any form of relief. As you'll see in later chapters, nature charges a price for suppressing the body's own neurotransmitter production.

Research is, however, leading to new drugs for the treatment of disorders influenced by neurotransmitter imbalances. You will hear much more about this in later discussions of depression, addictions, and other disorders, as we follow the biology-of-mind story throughout this book. But now it's time to consider the body's larger communication network.

Table 2.1	Some Neurotransmitters and Their Functions	
Neurotransmitter	**Function**	**Examples of Imbalances**
Acetylcholine (ACh)	Enables muscle action, learning, and memory.	With Alzheimer's disease, ACh-producing neurons deteriorate.
Dopamine	Influences movement, learning, attention, and emotion.	Oversupply linked to schizophrenia. Undersupply linked to tremors and decreased mobility in Parkinson's disease.
Serotonin	Affects mood, hunger, sleep, and arousal.	Undersupply linked to depression. Some antidepressant drugs raise serotonin levels.
Norepinephrine	Helps control alertness and arousal.	Undersupply can depress mood.
GABA (gamma-aminobutyric acid)	A major inhibitory neurotransmitter.	Undersupply linked to seizures, tremors, and insomnia.
Glutamate	A major excitatory neurotransmitter; involved in memory.	Oversupply can overstimulate brain, producing migraines or seizures (which is why some people avoid MSG, monosodium glutamate, in food).

PRACTICE TEST

1. The neuron fiber that carries messages to other neurons is the
   a. dendrite.
   b. axon.
   c. cell body.
   d. synapse.

2. There is a tiny space between the axon of a sending neuron and the dendrite of a receiving neuron. This small space is called the
   a. axon.
   b. dendrite.
   c. synaptic gap.
   d. threshold.

3. The neuron's response to stimulation is an *all-or-none response*, meaning that the intensity of the stimulus determines
   a. whether or not an impulse is generated.
   b. how fast an impulse is transmitted.
   c. how intense an impulse will be.
   d. whether reuptake will occur.

4. When a neural impulse reaches the end of an axon, it triggers the release of chemical messengers called
   a. dendrites.
   b. synapses.
   c. action potentials.
   d. neurotransmitters.

5. Endorphins are released in the brain in response to
   a. morphine or heroin.
   b. pain or vigorous exercise.
   c. the all-or-none response.
   d. all of these answers.

Answers: 1. b, 2. c, 3. a, 4. d, 5. b.

The Nervous System

3: What are the major divisions of the nervous system, and what are their basic functions?

To live is to take in information from the world and the body's tissues, to make decisions, and to send back information and orders to the body's tissues. All this happens thanks to our body's nervous system (**FIGURE 2.4**). The brain and spinal cord form the **central nervous system (CNS),** the body's decision maker. The **peripheral nervous system (PNS)** is responsible for gathering information and for transmitting CNS decisions to other body parts. **Nerves,** electrical cables formed of bundles of axons, link the central nervous system with the body's sensory receptors, muscles, and glands. The optic nerve, for example, bundles a million axons into a single cable carrying the messages each eye sends to the brain (Mason & Kandel, 1991).

Neurons are the elementary units of the nervous system, and we have three types of them. **Sensory neurons** carry messages from the body's tissues and sensory receptors inward to the brain and spinal cord, for processing. The central nervous system then sends instructions out to the body's tissues via the **motor neurons.** In between the sensory input and motor output, **interneurons** process information within the CNS. Our complexity resides mostly in our interneuron systems. Our nervous system has a few million sensory neurons, a few million motor neurons, and billions and billions of interneurons.

The Peripheral Nervous System

Our peripheral nervous system has two parts: The **somatic nervous system** controls voluntary movements of our skeletal muscles. As you reach the end of this page, your somatic nervous system will trigger your hand to turn the page.

The **autonomic nervous system** controls your glands and the muscles of your internal organs, including those of your heart and digestive system. Like an automatic pilot, this system may be consciously overridden, but usually it operates on its own (autonomously). The autonomic nervous system has two divisions: the sympathetic and parasympathetic systems (**FIGURE 2.5** on the next page).

endorphins [en-DOR-fins] "morphine within"— natural, opiatelike neurotransmitters linked to pain control and to pleasure.

nervous system the body's speedy, electrochemical communication network, consisting of all the nerve cells of the peripheral and central nervous systems.

central nervous system (CNS) the brain and spinal cord.

peripheral nervous system (PNS) the sensory and motor neurons connecting the central nervous system (CNS) to the rest of the body.

nerves bundled axons that form neural "cables" connecting the central nervous system with muscles, glands, and sense organs.

sensory neurons neurons that carry incoming information from the sensory receptors to the central nervous system.

motor neurons neurons that carry outgoing information from the central nervous system to the muscles and glands.

interneurons neurons that communicate internally and intervene between the sensory inputs and motor outputs.

somatic nervous system the division of the peripheral nervous system that controls the body's skeletal muscles. Also called the *skeletal nervous system.*

autonomic [aw-tuh-NAHM-ik] **nervous system** the division of the peripheral nervous system that controls the glands and the muscles of the internal organs (such as the heart). Its sympathetic division arouses; its parasympathetic division calms.

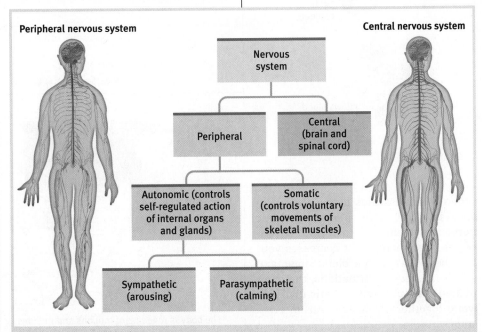

Figure 2.4> The functional divisions of the human nervous system

Figure 2.5> The autonomic nervous system arouses and calms Its sympathetic division arouses and expends energy. Its parasympathetic division calms and conserves energy, allowing routine maintenance activity. For example, sympathetic stimulation speeds up heartbeat, and parasympathetic stimulation slows it.

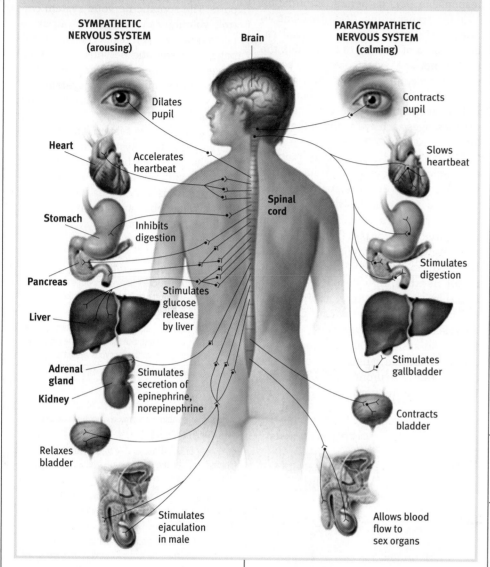

SYMPATHETIC NERVOUS SYSTEM (arousing)

Dilates pupil

Heart

Accelerates heartbeat

Stomach

Inhibits digestion

Pancreas

Liver

Stimulates glucose release by liver

Adrenal gland

Kidney

Stimulates secretion of epinephrine, norepinephrine

Relaxes bladder

Stimulates ejaculation in male

Brain

Spinal cord

PARASYMPATHETIC NERVOUS SYSTEM (calming)

Contracts pupil

Slows heartbeat

Stimulates digestion

Stimulates gallbladder

Contracts bladder

Allows blood flow to sex organs

The **sympathetic nervous system** arouses and expends energy. If something alarms or challenges you (such as a longed-for job interview), your sympathetic system will make you alert and prepare you for action. It will increase your heartbeat and your blood pressure, slow your digestion, raise your blood sugar, and cool you with perspiration.

When the stress dies down (the interview is over), your **parasympathetic nervous system** will calm you. It conserves your energy as it decreases your heartbeat, lowers your blood sugar, and so on. In everyday situations, the sympathetic and parasympathetic divisions work together to steady our internal state.

The Central Nervous System

From the simplicity of neurons "talking" to other neurons arises the complexity of the central nervous system's brain and spinal cord.

It is the brain that enables our humanity—our thinking, feeling, and acting. With some 40 billion neurons, each connecting with roughly 10,000 other neurons, we end up with perhaps 400 trillion synapses—places where neurons meet and greet their neighbors (de Courten-Myers, 2005). A grain-of-sand–sized speck of your brain contains 100,000 neurons and one billion "talking" synapses (Ramachandran & Blakeslee, 1998). Being human takes a lot of nerve.

All these neurons cluster into work groups called *neural networks*, much as people cluster into cities rather than spreading themselves evenly across the nation (Kosslyn & Koenig, 1992). Neurons network with close neighbors by means of short, fast connections. How these networks organize themselves into complex circuits capable of learning, feeling, and thinking remains one of the great remaining scientific mysteries: How does biology give birth to mind?

Stephen Colbert: "How does the brain work? Five words or less."
Steven Pinker: "Brain cells fire in patterns."
—The Colbert Report, February 8, 2007

"The body is made up of millions and millions of crumbs."

The spinal cord, which also is part of the central nervous system, is a two-way highway connecting the peripheral nervous system and the brain. Nerve fibers carry information from your senses to your brain, while others carry motor-control information to your body parts. When people suffer damage to the top of their spinal cord, their brain is literally out of touch with their body. They lose all sensation and voluntary movement in body regions that connect to the spinal cord below its injury. They feel no pain, no pleasure. Men paralyzed below the waist may be capable of an erection (a simple reflex) if their genitals are stimulated (Goldstein, 2000). Females similarly paralyzed may respond with vaginal lubrication. But, depending on where and how completely the spinal cord is severed, they may be genitally unresponsive to erotic images and have no genital feeling (Kennedy & Over, 1990; Sipski & Alexander, 1999). To produce physical pain or pleasure, the sensory information must reach the brain.

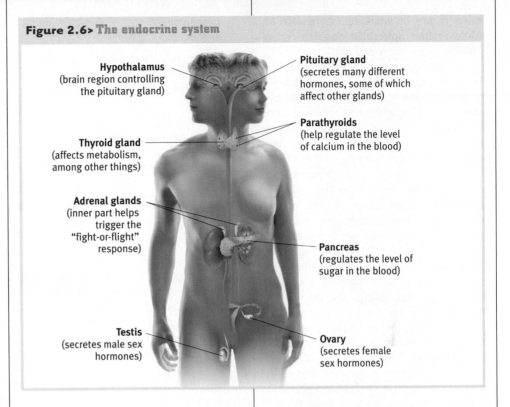

Figure 2.6> The endocrine system

Hypothalamus (brain region controlling the pituitary gland)

Pituitary gland (secretes many different hormones, some of which affect other glands)

Thyroid gland (affects metabolism, among other things)

Parathyroids (help regulate the level of calcium in the blood)

Adrenal glands (inner part helps trigger the "fight-or-flight" response)

Pancreas (regulates the level of sugar in the blood)

Testis (secretes male sex hormones)

Ovary (secretes female sex hormones)

PRACTICE TEST

6. The autonomic nervous system controls internal functions, such as your heart rate and glands. The word *autonomic* means
   a. peripheral.
   b. voluntary.
   c. operating on its own.
   d. arousing.

7. Usually, the sympathetic nervous system arouses us for action and the parasympathetic nervous system calms us down. Together, the two systems make up the
   a. autonomic nervous system.
   b. somatic nervous system.
   c. central nervous system.
   d. peripheral nervous system.

8. The spinal cord is part of the
   a. somatic nervous system.
   b. central nervous system.
   c. autonomic nervous system.
   d. peripheral nervous system.

Answers: 6. c, 7. a, 8. b.

The Endocrine System

4: How does the endocrine system—the body's slower information system—transmit its messages?

So far, we have focused on your body's electrochemical information system. But your body has a second communication system, the **endocrine system** (FIGURE 2.6). Glands in this system secrete **hormones,** another form of chemical messenger that influences our behaviors and emotions.

Some hormones are chemically identical to neurotransmitters. The endocrine system and nervous system are therefore close relatives. Both produce molecules that act on receptors elsewhere. Like many relatives, they also differ. The speedy nervous system zips messages from eyes to brain to hand in a fraction of a second. Endocrine messages trudge along in the bloodstream, taking several seconds or more to travel from the gland to the target tissue. If the nervous system's communication delivers messages rather like e-mail, the endocrine system is the body's snail mail.

But slow and steady sometimes wins the race. Endocrine messages tend to outlast the effects of neural messages. You've probably experienced this. Have you ever had angry feelings hang on, beyond your

sympathetic nervous system the division of the autonomic nervous system that arouses the body, mobilizing its energy in stressful situations.

parasympathetic nervous system the division of the autonomic nervous system that calms the body, conserving its energy.

endocrine [EN-duh-krin] **system** the body's "slow" chemical communication system; a set of glands that secrete hormones into the bloodstream.

hormones chemical messengers that are manufactured by the endocrine glands, travel through the bloodstream, and affect other tissues.

being aware of what set them off? As stress-related hormones linger, it takes time for us to "simmer down."

The endocrine system's hormones influence many aspects of our lives—growth, reproduction, metabolism, mood—working with our nervous system to keep everything in balance while we respond to stress, hard work, and our own thoughts. For example, if you almost collide with another car, your autonomic nervous system may order your **adrenal glands** to release *epinephrine* and *norepinephrine* (also called *adrenaline* and *noradrenaline*). In response, your heart rate, blood pressure, and blood sugar will rise, giving you a surge of energy. When the moment of danger passes, the hormones—and the feelings of excitement—will linger a while.

The endocrine gland control center is the **pituitary gland,** a pea-sized structure located in the core of the brain. Pituitary hormones influence growth, and they also send messages to other endocrine glands to release their hormones. For example, the pituitary directs your sex glands to release sex hormones, which in turn influence your brain and behavior.

But the pituitary has its own master—a nearby brain area, the *hypothalamus.* The pituitary doesn't send messages to the sex glands until it receives a signal from the hypothalamus. This feedback system (brain → pituitary → other glands → hormones → brain) reveals the interplay between the nervous and endocrine systems. The nervous system directs endocrine secretions, which then affect the nervous system. In charge of this whole electrochemical orchestra is that master conductor we call the brain.

⊙ PRACTICE TEST

9. The endocrine system produces chemical messengers that travel through the bloodstream and influence our behaviors and emotions. These chemical substances are

   a. hormones.
   b. neurotransmitters.
   c. endorphins.
   d. glands.

10. The pituitary gland releases hormones that influence growth and the activity of other glands. The pituitary gland is part of the

   a. endocrine system.
   b. peripheral nervous system.
   c. sympathetic nervous system.
   d. central nervous system.

Answers: 9. a, 10. a

The Brain

When you think about your brain, you're thinking *with* your brain—sending billions of neurotransmitter molecules across countless millions of synapses. Indeed, say neuroscientists, the *mind is what the brain does.*

> "I am a brain, Watson. The rest of me is a mere appendix."
>
> —Sherlock Holmes, in Arthur Conan Doyle's "The Adventure of the Mazarin Stone"

Even in a motionless body, the brain—and mind—may, in some cases, be active. One hospitalized 23-year-old woman showed no outward signs of conscious awareness after being in a traffic accident. Nevertheless, when researchers asked her to *imagine* playing tennis or moving around her home, brain scans revealed activity like that of healthy volunteers (Owen & others, 2006). As she imagined playing tennis, for example, an area of her brain controlling arm and leg movements became active.

Close-Up: The Tools of Discovery explains how scientists explore the brain-mind connection. For centuries, we had no tools high-powered yet sensitive enough to study the living brain. But we are living in the golden age of brain science, moving closer and closer to understanding where and how the mind's functions are tied to the brain. To be learning about the brain now is like studying geography while the early explorers were mapping the world. Let's begin our own exploration of the brain.

Older Brain Structures

Brain structures determine our abilities. In sharks and other primitive vertebrates (animals with backbones), a not-too-complex brain mainly handles basic survival functions: breathing, resting, and feeding. In lower mammals, such as rodents, a more complex brain enables emotion and greater memory. In advanced mammals, such as humans, a brain that processes more information enables foresight as well.

This increasing complexity arises from new brain systems built on top of the old, much as new layers cover old ones in the Earth's landscape. Digging down, one discovers the fossil remnants of the past—brainstem components performing for us much as they did for our distant ancestors. Let's start with the brain's basement and work up.

The Brainstem

5: What are the functions of the brainstem and its associated structures?

The brain's oldest and innermost region is the **brainstem.** It begins where the spinal cord swells slightly after entering the skull. This slight swelling is the **medulla,**

---

adrenal [ah-DREEN-el] **glands** a pair of endocrine glands that sit just above the kidneys and secrete hormones (epinephrine and norepinephrine) that help arouse the body in times of stress.

pituitary gland the endocrine system's most influential gland. Under the influence of the hypothalamus, the pituitary regulates growth and controls other endocrine glands.

brainstem the oldest part and central core of the brain, beginning where the spinal cord swells as it enters the skull; the brainstem is responsible for automatic survival functions.

medulla [muh-DUL-uh] the base of the brainstem; controls heartbeat and breathing.

CLOSE-UP

THE TOOLS OF DISCOVERY– HAVING OUR HEAD EXAMINED

In the past, brain injuries provided some clues to brain-mind connections. For example, damage to one side of the brain often caused paralysis on the body's opposite side. Noting this, physicians guessed that the body's right side is wired to the brain's left side, and vice versa. Others linked vision problems with damage to the back of the brain, and speech problems with damage to the left-front brain. Gradually, a map of the brain began to emerge.

Now a new generation of map makers is at work charting formerly unknown territory, stimulating various brain parts and watching the results. Some use microelectrodes to snoop on the messages of individual neurons. Some eavesdrop with an **EEG (electroencephalograph)** on the chatter of billions of neurons (see Figure 2.31 near the end of this chapter). Others use scans that peer into the thinking, feeling brain and give us a Supermanlike ability to see what's happening.

The **PET (positron emission tomography) scan** tracks the brain's favorite food, the sugar glucose. Active neurons are glucose hogs. Before a PET scan, a person is given a temporarily radioactive form of glucose. By locating and measuring the radioactivity, the PET scan can detect where this "food for thought" goes. "Hot spots" (which researchers may later render

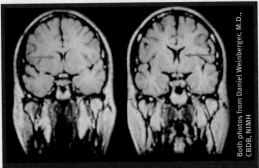

Figure 2.7> MRI scan of a healthy individual **(left)** and a person with schizophrenia **(right)** :: Note the enlarged fluid-filled brain region in the image on the right.

Both photos from Daniel Weinberger, M.D., CBDB, NIMH

in color for emphasis) show which brain areas are most active as the person performs math calculations, listens to music, or daydreams. (See Figure 2.22 later in this chapter for an example of PET scans.)

In **MRI (magnetic resonance imaging)** scans, the head is put in a strong magnetic field. Atoms of brain molecules are normally spinning. The MRI scan briefly disrupts this spinning with a brief pulse of radio waves. When the atoms begin spinning again, they release signals giving a detailed picture of soft tissues. These images of brain structures have revealed, for example, that some people with schizophrenia, a disabling psychological disorder, have enlarged fluid-filled brain area **(FIGURE 2.7)**.

A special application of MRI, **fMRI (functional MRI),** also reveals the brain's functions. Oxygen-laden blood flows to especially active brain areas. By comparing MRI scans taken less than a second apart, researchers can watch parts of the brain "light up" as a person thinks or acts in certain ways. As the person looks at a photo, for example, the fMRI shows blood rushing to the back of the brain, which processes visual information (see Figure 2.18 later in this chapter).

Using these tools, researchers are giving us new insights into how the brain divides its labor.

---

the control center for your heartbeat and breathing. Just above the medulla sits an area that helps coordinate movements. If a cat's brainstem is severed from the rest of the brain above it, the animal will still breathe. It will even run, climb, and groom (Klemm, 1990). But cut off from the brain's higher regions, it won't *purposefully* run or climb to get food.

The brainstem is a crossover point. Here, you'll find a peculiar sort of crosswiring, with most nerves to and from each side of the brain connecting to the body's opposite side. Thus, the right brain controls the left side of the body, and vice versa.

The Thalamus

Sitting at the top of the brainstem is the **thalamus (FIGURE 2.8** on the next page). This joined pair of egg-shaped structures acts as the brain's sensory switchboard. The thalamus receives information from all the senses except smell, and it forwards the messages to the brain regions that deal with seeing, hearing, tasting, and touching. You can think of the thalamus as something like an e-mail server. Messages flow through this hub on their way to their final destination. In addition to incoming messages from the senses, the thalamus receives replies from some

EEG (electroencephalograph) recording apparatus, using electrodes placed on the scalp, that records waves of electrical activity that sweep across the brain's surface. (The tracing of those brain waves is an *electroencephalogram*.)

PET (positron emission tomography) scan a view of brain activity showing where a radioactive form of glucose goes while the brain performs a given task.

MRI (magnetic resonance imaging) a technique that uses magnetic fields and radio waves to produce computer-generated images of soft tissue. MRI scans show brain anatomy.

fMRI (functional magnetic resonance imaging) a technique for revealing bloodflow and, therefore, brain activity by comparing successive MRI scans. fMRI scans show brain function.

thalamus [THAL-uh-muss] area at the top of the brainstem; directs sensory messages to the cortex and transmits replies to the cerebellum and medulla.

Figure 2.8> The brainstem and thalamus The brainstem, including the pons and medulla, is an extension of your spinal cord. The thalamus is attached to its top. The reticular formation passes through both structures.

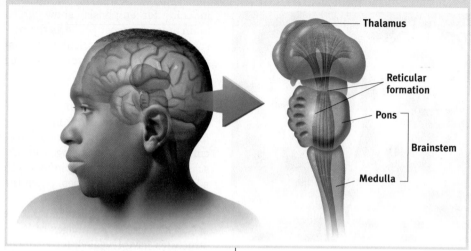

higher brain regions and forwards these replies to the medulla and to the cerebellum for processing.

The Reticular Formation

Inside the brainstem, between your ears, lies the **reticular** ("netlike") **formation.** This finger-shaped network of neurons extends upward from your spinal cord, through your brainstem, and into your thalamus (Figure 2.8). This long structure acts as a filter for some of the sensory messages traveling from the spinal cord to the thalamus, relaying important information to other areas of the brain.

In 1949, researchers discovered that electrically stimulating the reticular formation of a sleeping cat almost instantly produced an awake, alert animal (Moruzzi & Magoun, 1949). When a cat's reticular formation was severed from higher brain regions, without damaging the nearby sensory pathways, the effect was equally dramatic. The cat lapsed into a coma from which it never awakened. The conclusion? The reticular formation enables arousal.

The Cerebellum

At the rear of the brainstem is the **cerebellum,** meaning "little brain," which is what its two wrinkled halves resemble

(FIGURE 2.9). This baseball-sized structure plays an important role in a lot that happens just outside your awareness. Quickly, answer these questions. How much time has passed since you woke up this morning? Does this book's cover feel different from your shirt sleeve? How's

your mood? If you answered those questions easily, it's because your cerebellum helps you judge time, discriminate sounds and textures, and control your emotions (Bower & Parsons, 2003). It also coordinates voluntary movement. If you injured your cerebellum, your movements would be jerky, and you would have trouble walking, keeping your balance, or shaking hands. The cerebellum performs another task. It helps process and store memories for things we cannot consciously recall, such as why we link the sound of thunder to a flash of lightning. (Stay tuned for more about this in Chapter 7.)

> "Consciousness is a small part of what the brain does."
>
> —Neuroscientist Joseph LeDoux, in "Mastery of Emotions," 2006

Note: These older brain functions all occur without any conscious effort. Once again, we see one of our Big Ideas at work: *Our two-track brain processes most information outside of our awareness.* We are aware of the *results* of our brain's labor

Figure 2.9> The brain's organ of agility Hanging at the back of the brain, the cerebellum coordinates our voluntary movements, as when soccer star David Beckham leaps up to head the ball.

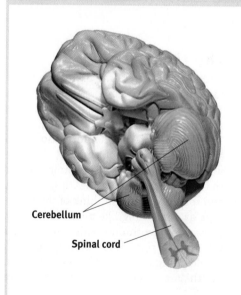

UPI Photo/Laura Cavanaugh

(say, our current visual experience) but not of *how* we construct the visual image. Likewise, whether we are asleep or awake, our brainstem manages its life-sustaining functions, freeing our newer brain regions to dream, think, talk, or savor a memory.

PRACTICE TEST

11. The part of the brainstem that controls heartbeat and breathing is the
    a. cerebellum.
    b. medulla.
    c. cortex.
    d. thalamus.

12. The thalamus receives information from the sensory neurons and routes it to the higher brain regions that control the senses. The thalamus functions as a
    a. memory bank.
    b. pleasure center.
    c. breathing regulator.
    d. switchboard.

13. The lower brain structure that governs arousal is the
    a. spinal cord.
    b. cerebellum.
    c. reticular formation.
    d. medulla.

14. The part of the brain that coordinates voluntary movement is the
    a. cerebellum.
    b. medulla.
    c. thalamus.
    d. reticular formation.

Answers: 11. b, 12. d, 13. c, 14. a.

The Limbic System

6: What are the functions of limbic system structures?

We've traveled through the brain's oldest parts, but we've not yet reached its highest regions, the *cerebral hemispheres* (the two halves of the brain.) In between these two brain areas lies the **limbic system** (*limbus* means "border"). This system contains the *amygdala*, the *hypothalamus*, and the *hippocampus* **(FIGURE 2.10)**. The

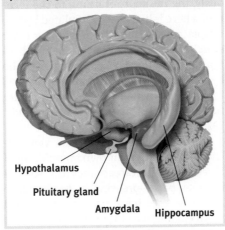

Figure 2.10> The limbic system
This neural system sits between your brain's older parts and its cerebral hemispheres. The limbic system, via the hypothalamus, controls the nearby pituitary gland.

Hypothalamus

Pituitary gland

Amygdala   Hippocampus

hippocampus processes conscious memories. Animals or humans who lose their hippocampus to surgery or injury also lose their ability to form new memories of facts and events. Chapter 7 explains how our two-track mind processes our memories. For now, let's look at the

Aggression as a brain state :: Back arched and fur fluffed, this cat is ready to attack. Electrical stimulation of a cat's amygdala provokes reactions such as the one shown here, suggesting its role in emotions such as rage.

Frank Siteman/Stock, Boston

limbic system's links to emotions such as fear and anger, and to basic motives such as those for food and sex.

The Amygdala The **amygdala** plays a role in emotion. Research has linked these two lima-bean–sized neural clusters in the limbic system to aggression and fear. In 1939, researchers surgically removed a rhesus monkey's amygdala, turning the normally ill-tempered animal into the most mellow of creatures (Klüver & Bucy, 1939). Gone were the ferocious responses. The animal remained placid.

What then might happen if we electrically stimulate the amygdala of a normally mellow domestic animal, such as a cat? Do so in one spot and the cat prepares to attack, hissing with its back arched, its pupils wide, its hair on end. Move the electrode only slightly within the amygdala, cage the cat with a small mouse, and now it cowers in terror.

These experiments confirm the amygdala's role in emotions such as rage and fear. Still, a critical thinker would be careful here. When we feel or act in aggressive and fearful ways, there is neural activity in all levels of our brain, not just in the amygdala. Stimulating limbic structures other than the amygdala can also trigger aggression or fear. If you charge your car's dead battery, you can activate the engine. Yet the battery is merely one link in an integrated system.

reticular formation a nerve network in the brainstem that plays an important role in controlling arousal.

cerebellum [sehr-uh-BELL-um] the "little brain" at the rear of the brainstem; functions include processing sensory input and coordinating movement output and balance.

limbic system neural system (including the *hippocampus, amygdala,* and *hypothalamus*) located below the cerebral hemispheres; associated with emotions and drives.

amygdala [uh-MIG-duh-la] two lima-bean–sized neural clusters in the limbic system; linked to emotion.

Figure 2.11> The hypothalamus This small but important structure, colored yellow-orange in this MRI scan photograph, helps keep your body's internal environment in a steady state by regulating thirst, hunger, and body temperature. Its activity also influences your experiences of pleasurable reward.

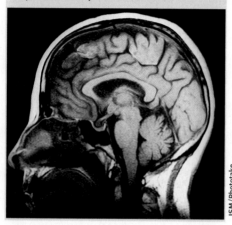

ISM/Phototake

The Hypothalamus Just below (*hypo*) the thalamus is the **hypothalamus (FIGURE 2.11)**, an important link in the chain of command governing bodily maintenance. Some neural clusters in the hypothalamus influence hunger. Others regulate thirst, body temperature, and sexual behavior. Together, they help you maintain a steady internal state.

As the hypothalamus monitors the state of your body, it tunes into your blood chemistry and any incoming orders from other brain parts. For example, picking up signals from your cerebral cortex that you are thinking about sex, your hypothalamus will secrete hormones. These hormones in turn trigger the nearby "master gland," the *pituitary* (see Figure 2.10), to influence your sex glands to release their hormones. These will intensify the thoughts of sex in your cerebral cortex. (Note the interplay between the nervous and endocrine systems: The brain influences the endocrine system, which in turn influences the brain.)

A true story: A remarkable discovery about the hypothalamus illustrates how progress in science often occurs—when curious, smart-thinking investigators

keep an open mind. Two young psychologists, James Olds and Peter Milner (1954), were trying to implant electrodes in rats' reticular formations when they made a magnificent mistake. In one rat, they placed the electrode incorrectly. Curiously, the rat kept returning to the location where it had been stimulated by this misplaced electrode, as if seeking more stimulation. On discovering they had actually placed the device in a region of the hypothalamus, Olds and Milner realized they had stumbled upon a brain center that provides pleasurable rewards (Olds, 1975).

In later studies, when rats were allowed to control their own stimulation in these and other areas, they did so at a feverish pace—pressing a pedal up to 7000 times an hour, until they dropped from exhaustion. Moreover, to get this stimulation, they would even cross an electrified floor that a starving rat would not cross to reach food **(FIGURE 2.12)**.

Similar reward centers in or near the hypothalamus were later discovered in many other species, including goldfish, dolphins, and monkeys. In fact, animal research has revealed both a general reward system that triggers the release of the neurotransmitter dopamine, and specific centers associated with the pleasures of eating, drinking, and sex. Animals, it seems, come equipped with

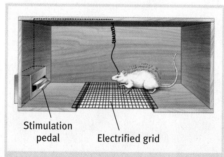

Stimulation pedal   Electrified grid

Figure 2.12> Pain for pleasure This rat has an electrode implanted in a reward center of its hypothalamus. It will cross an electric grid, accepting painful shocks, in order to press a lever that sends impulses to its reward center.

built-in systems that reward activities essential to survival.

Do we humans also have limbic centers for pleasure? Indeed we do. To calm violent patients, one neurosurgeon implanted electrodes in such areas. Stimulated patients reported mild pleasure. Unlike Olds' rats, however, they were not driven to a frenzy (Deutsch, 1972; Hooper & Teresi, 1986).

We've finished our tour of the older brain structures. **FIGURE 2.13** will help you place the key brain areas we've been discussing, as well as the cerebral cortex, our next topic.

PRACTICE TEST

15. The limbic system sits between the brain's older parts and the cerebral hemispheres. Two parts of the limbic system are the amygdala and the
    a. reticular formation.
    b. hippocampus.
    c. thalamus.
    d. medulla.

16. A cat's ferocious response to electrical brain stimulation would lead you to suppose that the electrode had been touching the
    a. medulla.
    b. pituitary.
    c. hypothalamus.
    d. amygdala.

17. The neural structure that most directly regulates eating, drinking, and body temperature is the
    a. cerebellum.
    b. hypothalamus.
    c. thalamus.
    d. amygdala.

18. The reward centers discovered by Olds and Milner were located in regions of the
    a. cerebral cortex.
    b. brainstem.
    c. hypothalamus.
    d. spinal cord.

Answers: 15, b, 16, d, 17, b, 18, c.

Figure 2.13> Review: Brain structures and their functions

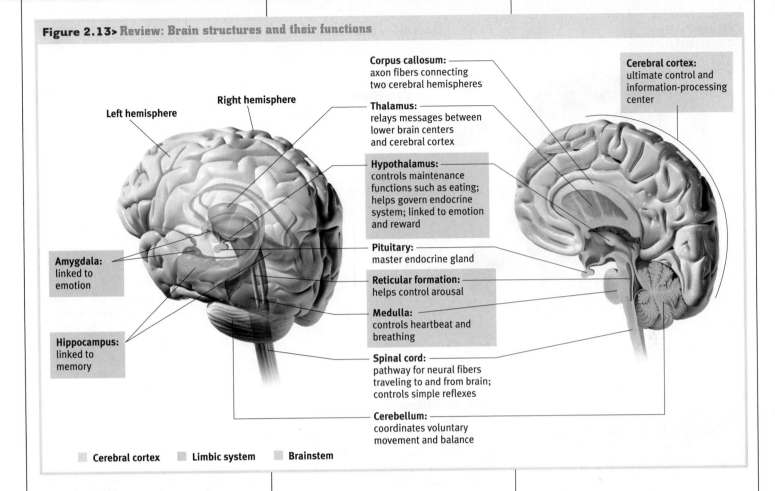

Corpus callosum: axon fibers connecting two cerebral hemispheres

Right hemisphere

Left hemisphere

Thalamus: relays messages between lower brain centers and cerebral cortex

Cerebral cortex: ultimate control and information-processing center

Hypothalamus: controls maintenance functions such as eating; helps govern endocrine system; linked to emotion and reward

Amygdala: linked to emotion

Pituitary: master endocrine gland

Reticular formation: helps control arousal

Medulla: controls heartbeat and breathing

Hippocampus: linked to memory

Spinal cord: pathway for neural fibers traveling to and from brain; controls simple reflexes

Cerebellum: coordinates voluntary movement and balance

■ Cerebral cortex   ■ Limbic system   ■ Brainstem

The Cerebral Cortex

7: What are the four lobes of the cerebral cortex, and where are they located?

Older brain networks sustain basic life functions and enable memory, emotions, and basic drives. High above these older structures is the *cerebrum*, consisting of two large hemispheres that contribute 85 percent of the brain's weight. Covering those hemispheres, like bark on a tree, is the **cerebral cortex,** a thin surface layer of interconnected neural cells. Its newer neural networks form specialized work teams that enable our perceiving, thinking, and speaking. The cerebral cortex is your brain's thinking crown, your body's ultimate control and information-processing center.

Structure of the Cortex

If you opened a human skull, exposing the brain, you would see a wrinkled organ, shaped somewhat like the meat of an oversized walnut. Without these wrinkles, a flattened cerebral cortex would require triple the area—roughly that of a very large pizza—to fit inside the skull. The brain's ballooning left and right hemispheres are filled mainly with axons connecting the cortex to the brain's other regions.

We can divide each hemisphere into four *lobes,* broad areas of cortex marked off by deep folds (**FIGURE 2.14** on the next page). You can roughly trace the four lobes, starting with both hands on your forehead. The **frontal lobes** lie directly behind your forehead. As you move your hands over the top of your head, toward the rear, you're sliding over your **parietal lobes.** Continuing to move down, toward

hypothalamus [hi-po-THAL-uh-muss] a neural structure lying below (*hypo*) the thalamus; directs several maintenance activities (eating, drinking, body temperature), helps govern the endocrine system via the pituitary gland, and is linked to emotion.

cerebral [seh-REE-bruhl] **cortex** thin layer of interconnected neurons covering the cerebral hemispheres; the body's ultimate control and information-processing center.

frontal lobes portion of the cerebral cortex lying just behind the forehead; involved in speaking and muscle movements and in making plans and judgments.

parietal [puh-RYE-uh-tuhl] **lobes** portion of the cerebral cortex lying at the top of the head and toward the rear; receives sensory input for touch and body position.

Figure 2.14> The cortex and its basic subdivisions Lobes define broad divisions of the cerebral cortex.

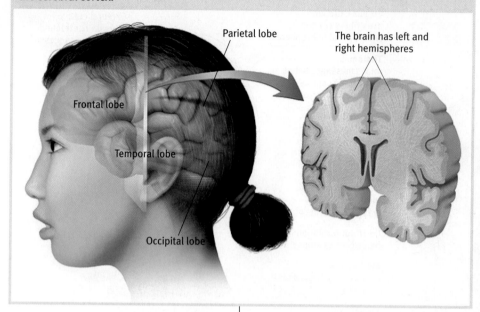

Frontal lobe

Temporal lobe

Parietal lobe

Occipital lobe

The brain has left and right hemispheres

Demonstration: Try moving your right hand in a circular motion, as if polishing a car. Now start your right foot doing the same motion synchronized with the hand. Now reverse the foot motion (but not the hand). Tough, huh? But easier if you try moving the *left* foot opposite to the right hand. The left and right limbs are controlled by opposite sides of the brain. So their opposed activities interfere less with one another.

the back of your head, you'll slide over your **occipital lobes.** Now move each hand forward, to the sides of your head, and just above each ear you'll find your **temporal lobes.** Each hemisphere has four lobes. Each lobe carries out many functions. And many functions require the cooperation of several lobes.

Functions of the Cortex

8: What are the functions of the cerebral cortex?

More than a century ago, surgeons found damaged cortical areas during autopsies of people who had been partially paralyzed or speechless. This rather crude evidence was interesting, but it did not prove that specific parts of the cortex control complex functions like movement or speech. After all, if the entire cortex controlled speech and movement, damage to almost any area might show up as a disability. A television with its power cord cut would go dead, but we would be fooling ourselves if we thought we had "localized" the picture in the cord.

Motor Functions Early scientists had better luck showing simpler brain-behavior links. In 1870, for example, German physicians Gustav Fritsch and Eduard Hitzig made an important discovery: By electrically stimulating parts of a dog's cortex, they could make parts of its body move. The movement happened only when they stimulated an arch-shaped region at the back of the frontal lobe, running roughly ear-to-ear across the top of the brain. Moreover, if they stimulated this region in the left hemisphere, the dog's right leg would move. And if they stimulated part of the right hemisphere, the opposite leg—on the left—reacted. Fritsch and Hitzig had discovered what is now called the **motor cortex.**

Lucky for brain surgeons and their patients, the brain has no sensory receptors. Knowing this, Otfrid Foerster and Wilder Penfield were able to map the motor cortex in hundreds of wide-awake patients, by stimulating different cortical areas and observing the body's responses. They discovered that body areas requiring precise control, such as

the fingers and mouth, occupied the greatest amount of cortical space.

Today's researchers are searching for the answer to a new puzzle. We know that electrically stimulating the motor cortex can cause body parts to move. Could such stimulation cause a robotic limb to move in, for example, soldiers who lost arms or legs during combat? Could such devices help a paralyzed person learn to command a cursor to write e-mail or surf the Internet? Some scientists believe all this will happen in the near future **(FIGURE 2.15).**

Rick Friedman

Figure 2.15> Mind over matter A research team led by John Donoghue (pictured here, holding a tiny brain implant) believes we can harness the power of computers to enable paralyzed people to control a computer, TV, and possibly even their own limbs. (*Discover,* 12/2006, p. 38.)

Figure 2.16> Left hemisphere tissue devoted to each body part in the motor cortex and the sensory cortex The amount of cortex devoted to a body part is not proportional to that part's size. Your brain devotes more tissue to sensitive areas and to areas requiring precise control. Thus, your fingers occupy more cortex space than does your upper arm.

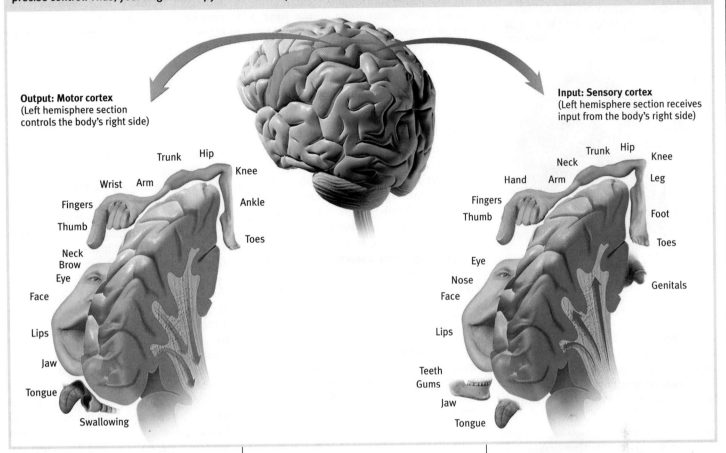

Output: Motor cortex
(Left hemisphere section controls the body's right side)

Trunk Hip
Wrist Arm Knee
Fingers Ankle
Thumb
Neck Toes
Brow
Eye
Face
Lips
Jaw
Tongue
Swallowing

Input: Sensory cortex
(Left hemisphere section receives input from the body's right side)

Trunk Hip
Neck Knee
Hand Arm Leg
Fingers Foot
Thumb Toes
Eye
Nose Genitals
Face
Lips
Teeth
Gums
Jaw
Tongue

Sensory Functions The motor cortex sends messages out to the body. What parts of the cortex receive incoming messages from our senses of touch and movement? Penfield supplied the answer. The **sensory cortex,** running parallel to the motor cortex and just behind it at the front of the parietal lobes, carries out this task. (**FIGURE 2.16** shows both motor and sensory cortex.) Stimulate a point on the top of this band of tissue, and a person reports being touched on the shoulder. Stimulate some point on the side, and the person feels something on the face.

The more sensitive a body region, the larger the area of sensory cortex devoted to it. Your supersensitive lips project to a larger brain area than do your arms (Figure 2.16). (That's one reason we kiss with our lips rather than rub elbows.) Similarly, rats have a large area of the brain devoted to their whisker sensations, and owls to their hearing sensations.

Your sensory cortex is a very powerful tool for processing information from your skin senses and from movements of your body parts. But it isn't the only area of the cortex that receives input from your senses. If you have normal vision, at this moment you are receiving visual information in the visual cortex in your occipital lobes, at the very back of your brain (**FIGURE 2.17** on the next page). A bad enough bash there would make you blind. Stimulated there, you might see flashes of light or dashes of color. (In a sense, we *do* have eyes in the back of our head!) From your occipital lobes, visual information goes to other

occipital [ahk-SIP-uh-tuhl] **lobes** portion of the cerebral cortex lying at the back of the head; includes areas that receive information from the visual fields.

temporal lobes portion of the cerebral cortex lying roughly above the ears; includes areas that receive information from the ears.

motor cortex area at the rear of the frontal lobe; controls voluntary movements.

sensory cortex area at the front of the parietal lobes that registers and processes body touch and movement sensations.

Figure 2.17> The visual cortex and auditory cortex The visual cortex of the occipital lobes at the rear of your brain receives input from your eyes. The auditory cortex, in your temporal lobes—above your ears—receives information from your ears.

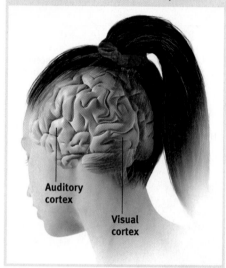

Auditory cortex

Visual cortex

areas that specialize in tasks such as identifying words, detecting emotions, and recognizing faces **(FIGURE 2.18)**.

Any sound you now hear is processed by your auditory cortex in your temporal

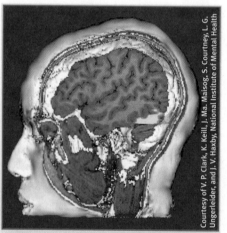

Courtesy of V. P. Clark, K. Keill, J. Ma. Maisog, S. Courtney, L. G. Ungerleider, and J. V. Haxby, National Institute of Mental Health

Figure 2.18> New technology shows the brain in action This fMRI (functional MRI) scan shows the visual cortex in the occipital lobes activated (color represents more bloodflow), as this person looks at a photo. When the person stops looking, the region instantly calms down.

lobes (see Figure 2.17). Most of this auditory information travels a roundabout route from one ear to the auditory receiving area above your opposite ear. If stimulated there, you alone might hear a sound. People with schizophrenia sometimes have auditory **hallucinations** (false sensory experiences). MRI scans taken during these hallucinations show active auditory areas in the temporal lobes (Lennox & others, 1999).

Association Areas So far, we have pointed out small areas of the cortex that receive messages from our senses, and other small areas that send messages to our muscles. Together, these areas occupy about one-fourth of the human brain's thin wrinkled cover. What then goes on in the vast remaining region of the cortex? Neurons in these **association areas** (the peach-colored areas in **FIGURE 2.19**) are busy with higher mental functions—many of the tasks that make us human.

Electrically probing an association area doesn't trigger any observable response. So, unlike the sensory and motor areas, association area functions can't be neatly mapped. Their silence has led to what Donald McBurney (1996, p. 44) calls "one of the hardiest weeds in the garden of psychology": that we ordinarily use only 10 percent of our brains. But—time for some critical thinking—the odds are

not 90 percent that a bullet to your brain would land in an area you don't use. Surgically lesioned animals and brain-damaged humans bear witness that association areas are not dormant. Rather, they interpret, integrate, and act on sensory information and link it with stored memories—a very important part of thinking.

Association areas are found in all four lobes. In the frontal lobes, they enable judgments, planning, and processing of new memories. People with damaged frontal lobes may have intact memories, high scores on intelligence tests, and great cake-baking skills. Yet they would not be able to plan ahead to *begin* baking a cake for a loved one's birthday.

Frontal lobe damage can have even more serious effects. It can alter personality and remove inhibitions. Consider the case of railroad worker Phineas Gage. One afternoon in 1848, Gage, then 25 years old, was packing gunpowder into a rock with an iron rod. A spark ignited the gunpowder, shooting the rod up through his left cheek and out the top of his skull **(FIGURE 2.20)**. To everyone's amazement, he was immediately able to sit up and speak, and after the wound healed he returned to work. But the friendly, soft-spoken Phineas Gage was now irritable, profane, and dishonest. Although his mental abilities and memories

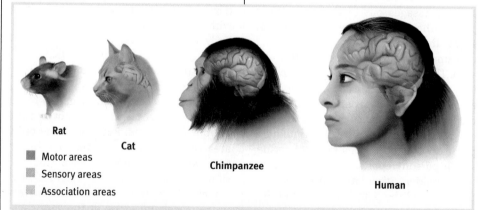

Rat

Cat

■ Motor areas
■ Sensory areas
■ Association areas

Chimpanzee

Human

Figure 2.19> Areas of the cortex in four mammals More intelligent animals have increased "uncommitted" or association areas of the cortex. These vast areas of the brain are responsible for integrating and acting on information received and processed by sensory areas.

Figure 2.20> *Phineas Gage reconsidered* Using measurements of his skull (which was kept as a medical record) and modern neuroimaging techniques, researchers (Damasio & others, 1994) have reconstructed the probable path of the rod through Gage's brain.

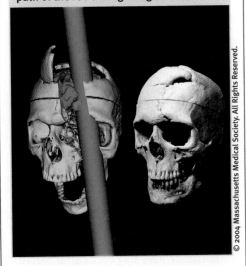

were intact, his personality was not. His frontal lobes had been massively damaged, and he was, said his friends, "no longer Gage." Gage eventually lost his job and ended up earning his living as a fairground exhibit. When his frontal lobes were ruptured, his moral compass was disconnected from his behavior.

Damage to association areas in other lobes would have different consequences. In the parietal lobes, you might lose mathematical and spatial reasoning. If a stroke or head injury destroyed an area on the underside of the right temporal lobe, which lets us recognize faces, you would still be able to describe facial features and to recognize someone's gender and approximate age. Yet you would be strangely unable to identify the person as, say, Queen Latifah or even your grandmother.

Language: Specialization and Integration So far, we have considered the effects of damage to some localized areas of the brain's cortex. But many of our complex abilities are spread across many areas of the brain.

Consider this curious finding: Damage to any one of several cortical areas can impair language. Even more curious, some people with brain damage can speak fluently but cannot read (despite good vision). Others can understand what they read but cannot speak. Still others can write but not read, read but not write, read numbers but not letters, or sing but not speak. This is puzzling, because we tend to think of speaking and reading, or writing and reading, or singing and speaking as merely different examples of one general ability. To sort out this puzzle required a lot of smart thinking by many different scientists, all working toward the same goal: How does the brain process language?

In 1865 French physician Paul Broca discovered that after damage to a specific area of the left frontal lobe (now called **Broca's area),** a person would struggle to form words, yet could often sing familiar songs with ease. A decade later, German investigator Karl Wernicke discovered that after damage to a specific area of the left temporal lobe **(Wernicke's area),** people could speak only meaningless words and were unable to understand others' words. Over the next century, other researchers—like archeologists unearthing dinosaur bones—revealed other fragments of the language-processing answer.

Norman Geschwind assembled all these clues into the explanation you can see in **FIGURE 2.21.** When you read aloud, the words (1) register in your visual cortex, (2) are relayed to another brain area, the *angular gyrus,* which transforms the words into an auditory code that (3) is received and understood in nearby Wernicke's area, and (4) is sent to Broca's area, which (5) controls the motor cortex as it directs

hallucinations false sensory experiences, such as hearing something in the absence of an external auditory stimulus.

association areas areas of the cerebral cortex that are primarily involved in higher mental functions such as learning, remembering, thinking, and speaking.

Broca's area an area of the frontal lobe, usually in the left hemisphere, that directs the muscle movements involved in speech; controls language expression.

Wernicke's area a brain area, usually in the left temporal lobe, involved in language comprehension and expression; controls language reception.

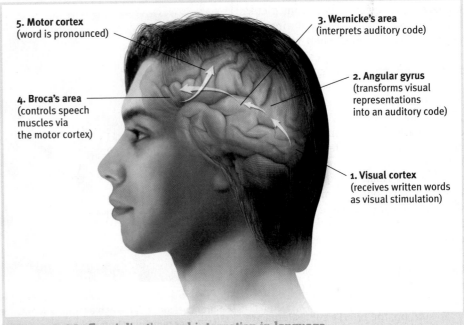

5. Motor cortex (word is pronounced)

3. Wernicke's area (interprets auditory code)

4. Broca's area (controls speech muscles via the motor cortex)

2. Angular gyrus (transforms visual representations into an auditory code)

1. Visual cortex (receives written words as visual stimulation)

Figure 2.21> *Specialization and integration in language*

Figure 2.22> Brain activity when hearing, seeing, and speaking words
PET scans such as these detect the activity of different areas of the brain.

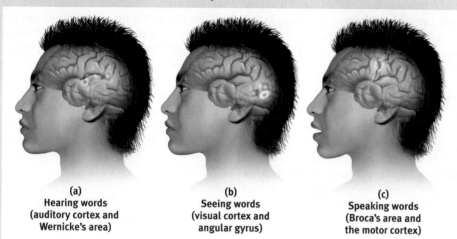

(a)	(b)	(c)
Hearing words (auditory cortex and Wernicke's area)	**Seeing words** (visual cortex and angular gyrus)	**Speaking words** (Broca's area and the motor cortex)

your muscles to pronounce the word. Any link in this chain can be damaged, and each would impair speech in a different way. With a damaged angular gyrus, you could speak and understand but you wouldn't be able to read. With a damaged Wernicke's area, you could speak and read, but you wouldn't understand the words. With a damaged Broca's area, you could read and understand, but you wouldn't be able to speak.

And the research continues, now at the level of the neuron. PET scans **(FIGURE 2.22)** can track brain activity during language processing. And when you read a word, your brain computes the word's form, sound, and meaning using different neural networks (Posner & Carr, 1992). Thus, fMRI scans show that jokes playing on meaning ("Why don't sharks bite lawyers? . . . Professional courtesy") are processed in a different brain area than jokes playing on words ("What kind of lights did Noah use on the ark? . . . Flood lights") (Goel & Dolan, 2001). Again, we encounter the theme of the two-track mind (dual processing): *What you experience as one continuous stream of perception is actually only the visible tip of a much larger iceberg. Most information processing takes place beneath the surface of conscious awareness.*

To sum up, the mind's subsystems are localized in particular brain regions, yet the brain acts as a unified whole. Moving your hand; recognizing a face; even perceiving color, motion, and depth—all depend on specific neural networks. Yet complex functions such as listening, learning, and loving involve the coordination of many brain areas. Together, these two principles—*specialization* and *integration*—describe the way our brain functions.

The Brain's Plasticity

Some of the effects of brain damage described earlier can be traced to two hard facts. (1) Severed neurons, unlike cut skin, usually do not repair themselves. (If your spinal cord were severed, you probably would be permanently paralyzed.) And (2) some brain functions seem forever linked to specific areas. One newborn who suffered damage to the facial recognition areas on both temporal lobes later remained unable to recognize faces (Farah & others, 2000).

But there is good news: The brain's impressive **plasticity** allows it to modify itself after some types of damage. Some brain tissue can *reorganize* in response to damage. Under the surface of our awareness, the brain is constantly changing, adjusting to little mishaps and new experiences. Our brains are most plastic when we are young children (Kolb, 1989; see **FIGURE 2.23**).

Plasticity may also occur after serious damage. Lose a finger and the sensory cortex that received its input will begin to pick up messages from the nearby fingers, which in turn become more sensitive (Fox, 1984). When one researcher

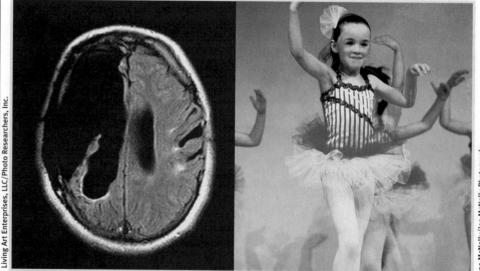

Living Art Enterprises, LLC/Photo Researchers, Inc.

Joe McNally/Joe McNally Photography

Figure 2.23> Brain plasticity This 6-year-old had surgery to end her life-threatening brain seizures. Although an entire hemisphere was removed (see MRI of hemispherectomy at left), her remaining hemisphere compensated by putting other areas to work.

stroked the arm of someone whose hand had been amputated, the person felt the sensations not only on the arm but also on the nonexistent ("phantom") hand. Sensory fibers sending messages from the arm had invaded the brain area vacated by the amputated hand. As Figure 2.16 showed us, the toes sit next to the genitals on the sensory cortex. So what do you suppose was the sexual intercourse experience of another patient whose lower leg had been amputated? "I actually experience my orgasm in my foot. And there it's much bigger than it used to be because it's no longer just confined to my genitals" (Ramachandran & Blakeslee, 1998, p. 36).

Our Divided Brain

9: What is a split brain, and what does it reveal about brain functioning?

We have seen that the left and right sides of our brain look very much alike. We have also seen that each of them has four lobes, and that the motor and sensory cortexes form arches that span both sides. Should we assume, then, that the two sides are identical? No—not if we trust the data collected over more than a century. An accident, stroke, or tumor in your left hemisphere could leave you unable to read, write, speak, do arithmetic, and understand others. Similar events in the right hemisphere seldom have such dramatic effects.

> "You wouldn't want to have a date with the right hemisphere."
>
> —Michael Gazzaniga, 2002

Does this mean that the right hemisphere is just along for the ride—a silent, "subordinate," or "minor" hemisphere? Many believed this was the case, until 1960, when researchers found that the "minor" right hemisphere was not so limited after all. The unfolding of this discovery is another one of psychology's fascinating stories.

Splitting the Brain

In 1961, two neurosurgeons speculated that the uncontrollable seizures of some patients with severe epilepsy were caused by abnormal brain activity bouncing back and forth between the two cerebral hemispheres. If so, could they put an end to this neurological tennis game by cutting through the **corpus callosum (FIGURE 2.24)**? This wide band of neural fibers connects the two hemispheres and carries messages between them. The neurosurgeons knew that psychologists Roger Sperry, Ronald Myers, and Michael Gazzaniga had divided the brains of cats and monkeys in this manner, with no serious ill effects.

So the surgeons operated. The result? The seizures all but disappeared. The patients with these **split brains** were surprisingly normal, their personality and intellect hardly affected. Waking from surgery, one even joked that he had a "splitting headache" (Gazzaniga, 1967). By sharing their experiences with us, these patients have greatly expanded our understanding of interactions between the intact brain's two hemispheres.

To appreciate these studies, we need to focus for a minute on the peculiar nature of our visual wiring. As **FIGURE 2.25** on the next page illustrates, information from the left half of your field of vision goes to your right hemisphere, and information from the right half of your visual field goes to your left hemisphere, which usually controls speech. Note, however, that each eye receives sensory information from both the right and left visual fields. Data received by either hemisphere are quickly transmitted to the other across the corpus callosum. In a person with a severed corpus callosum, this information sharing does not take place.

Knowing these facts, Sperry and Gazzaniga could send information to a patient's left hemisphere by having the person stare at a dot and then flashing a stimulus (a word or photo) to the right of

plasticity the brain's ability to change, especially during childhood, by reorganizing after damage or by building new pathways based on experience.

corpus callosum [KOR-pus kah-LOW-sum] large band of neural fibers connecting the two brain hemispheres and carrying messages between them.

split brain condition in which the brain's two hemispheres are isolated by cutting the fibers (mainly those of the corpus callosum) connecting them.

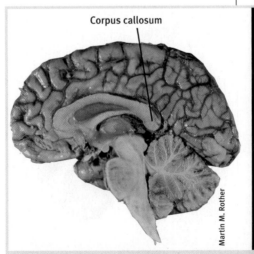
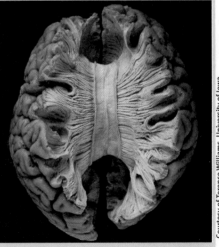

Martin M. Rother

Courtesy of Terence Williams, University of Iowa

Figure 2.24> The corpus callosum This large band of neural fibers connects the two brain hemispheres. To photograph the half brain shown at left, a surgeon separated the hemispheres by cutting through the corpus callosum and lower brain regions. In the view on the right, brain tissue has been cut back to expose the corpus callosum and bundles of fibers coming out from it.

Corpus callosum

Figure 2.25> The information pathway from eye to brain

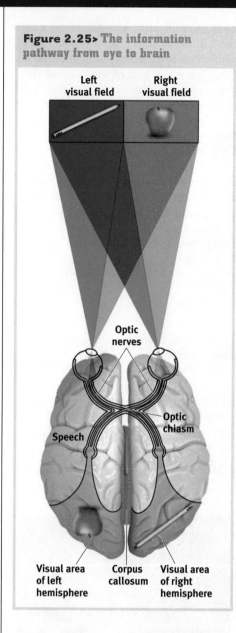

Left visual field
Right visual field

Optic nerves

Speech
Optic chiasm

Visual area of left hemisphere
Corpus callosum
Visual area of right hemisphere

the dot. To send a message to the right hemisphere, they would flash the item to the left of the dot.

They could do this with you, too, but in your intact brain the hemisphere receiving the information would instantly pass the news to the other hemisphere. But because the split-brain surgery had cut the communication lines between the hemispheres (the corpus callosum), the researchers could, with these patients, quiz each hemisphere separately. One way of doing this is to flash the word

HEART across the screen in such a way that *HE* appears to the left of the dot, and *ART* appears to the right **(FIGURE 2.26b)**. The patient then reports what they see. But there's a catch. Asked to *say* what they see, the person reports the letters transmitted to the left hemisphere—"ART". Asked to point with the left hand to what is seen, the person *points* to the letters transmitted to the right hemisphere—"HE" **(FIGURE 2.26c)**.

After split-brain surgery, a few people have been bothered for a time by the unruly independence of their left hand. It seemed the left hand truly didn't know what the right hand was doing. One hand might unbutton a shirt while the other

buttoned it, or put grocery store items back on the shelf after the other hand put them in the cart. It was as if each hemisphere was thinking "I've half a mind to wear my green (blue) shirt today." Indeed, said Sperry (1964), split-brain surgery leaves people "with two separate minds" **(FIGURE 2.27)**.

Who resolves disagreements when the "two minds" are at odds? If a split-brain patient follows an order sent to the right hemisphere ("Walk"), the left hemisphere won't know why it did so. But rather than say "I don't know," it instantly invents—and apparently believes—an explanation ("I'm going into the house to get a Coke"). Thus, Gazzaniga (1988), who

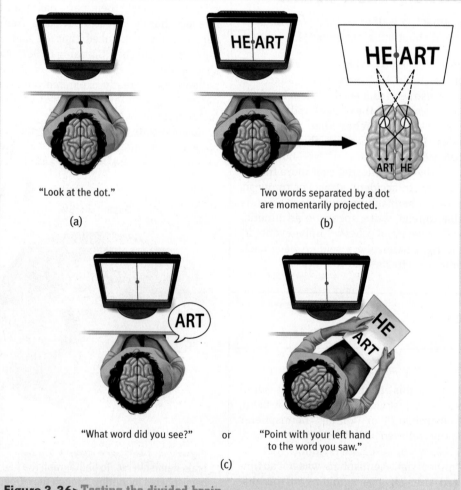

"Look at the dot."
(a)

Two words separated by a dot are momentarily projected.
(b)

"What word did you see?"   or

"Point with your left hand to the word you saw."
(c)

Figure 2.26> Testing the divided brain
(From Gazzaniga, 1983.)

Figure 2.27> Try this! Joe, a split-brain patient, can simultaneously draw two different shapes.

BBC

considers split-brain patients "the most fascinating people on earth," concludes that the conscious left hemisphere is an "interpreter" that instantly constructs theories to explain our behavior.

Question: If we flashed a red light to the right hemisphere of a split-brain patient and flashed a green light to the left hemisphere, would each observe its own color? Would the person be aware that the colors differ? What would the person verbally report seeing? (Answers on the next page.)

Right-Left Differences in the Intact Brain

So, what about the 99.99+ percent of us with undivided brains? Does each of *our* hemispheres also perform distinct functions? Several different types of studies indicate they do. When a person performs a *perceptual* task, for example, brain waves, bloodflow, and glucose

consumption reveal increased activity in the *right* hemisphere. When the person speaks or calculates, activity increases in the *left* hemisphere.

A dramatic demonstration of hemispheric specialization happens before some types of brain surgery. To check the location of language centers, the surgeon injects a sedative into the neck artery feeding blood to the left hemisphere. Before the injection, the patient is lying down, arms in the air, chatting with the doctor. Can you predict what happens when the drug puts the left hemisphere to sleep?

Within seconds, the person's right arm falls limp. If the person's left hemisphere controls language, the patient becomes speechless until the drug wears off.

To the brain, language is language, whether spoken or signed. Just as hearing people usually use the left hemisphere to process speech, deaf people usually use the left hemisphere to read sign language (Corina & others, 1992; Hickok & others, 2001). Thus, a stroke in the left hemisphere disrupts a deaf person's signing, much as it would disrupt a hearing person's speaking (Corina, 1998).

The left hemisphere is adept at making quick, literal interpretations of language. But the right hemisphere excels in high-level language processing (Beeman & Chiarello, 1998; Bowden & Beeman, 1998; Mason & Just, 2004). Given an insight problem—"What word goes with *high, district,* and *house?*"—the right hemisphere more quickly than the left recognizes the solution—*school.* As one patient explained after a right-hemisphere stroke, "I understand words, but I'm missing the subtleties." The right side of the brain surpasses the left at copying drawings, recognizing faces, perceiving differences, perceiving emotion, and expressing emotion through the more expressive left side of the face **(FIGURE 2.28).** Right-hemisphere damage can greatly disrupt these abilities.

Simply looking at the two hemispheres, so alike to the naked eye, who would suppose they contribute uniquely

Figure 2.28> Which one is happier? Look at the center of one face, then the other. Does one appear happier? Most people say the right face does. Some researchers think this is because the right hemisphere, which is skilled in emotion processing, receives information from the left half of each face (when looking at its center).

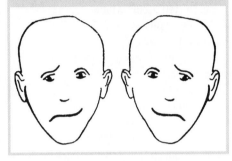

to the harmony of the whole? Yet a variety of observations—of people with split brains and people with normal brains—leaves little doubt that we have unified brains with specialized parts.

PRACTICE TEST

19. If a neurosurgeon stimulated your right motor cortex, you would most likely
   a. see light.
   b. hear a sound.
   c. feel a touch on the right arm.
   d. move your left leg.

20. The sensory cortex registers and processes body sensations, with the more sensitive body regions occupying the greatest amount of space. Which of the following occupies the greatest amount of space?
   a. Knee   c. Forehead
   b. Toes   d. Thumb

21. About three-fourths of the cerebral cortex is not committed to any specific sensory or muscular function. The "uncommitted" areas are called
   a. occipital lobes.
   b. temporal lobes.
   c. association areas.
   d. Wernicke's area.

22. Judging and planning are enabled by the
    a. occipital lobes.
    b. parietal lobes.
    c. frontal lobes.
    d. temporal lobes.

23. The area in the brain that, if damaged, might impair your ability to form words is
    a. Wernicke's area.
    b. Broca's area.
    c. the left occipital lobe.
    d. the angular gyrus.

24. Plasticity refers to the brain's ability to modify itself after damage. Especially plastic are the brains of
    a. split-brain patients.
    b. young adults.
    c. young children.
    d. right-handed people.

25. The brain structure that enables the right and left hemispheres to communicate is
    a. the medulla.
    b. Broca's area.
    c. Wernicke's area.
    d. the corpus callosum.

26. An experimenter flashes the word HERON across the visual field of a split-brain patient. HER is transmitted to his right hemisphere and ON to his left hemisphere. When asked to indicate what he saw, the patient
    a. says he saw HER but points to ON.
    b. says he saw ON but points to HER.
    c. says he saw HERON but points to HER.
    d. says he saw HERON but points to ON.

27. The study of split-brain patients has allowed us to observe the special functions of each hemisphere of the brain. The left hemisphere excels in
    a. processing language.
    b. visual perceptions.
    c. recognition of emotion.
    d. recognition of faces.

28. Damage to the brain's right hemisphere is most likely to reduce a person's ability to
    a. recite the alphabet rapidly.
    b. recognize the emotional content of facial expressions.
    c. understand verbal instructions.
    d. solve arithmetic problems.

Answers: 19. d, 20. d, 21. c, 22. c, 23. b, 24. c, 25. d, 26. b, 27. a, 28. b.

Brain States and Consciousness

In the lively field of neuroscience, researchers are addressing many exciting questions. Among the most interesting are those in the subfield of **cognitive neuroscience,** which includes the study of states of consciousness.

Consciousness is our awareness of ourselves and our environment. Consciousness lets us reflect on the past, plan for the future, and focus on the present. Psychologists study many aspects of consciousness. In this chapter we take a closer look at the role of attention, and at those altered states of consciousness we all experience—sleep and dreams.

Selective Attention

10: What is selective attention, and what does it teach us about consciousness?

Through **selective attention,** our awareness focuses, like a flashlight beam, on a *very* limited aspect of all that we experience. Until reading this sentence, you have been unaware that your shoes are pressing against your feet or that your nose is in your line of vision. Now, suddenly, the spotlight shifts. Your feet feel encased, your nose stubbornly intrudes on the page before you. While focusing on these words, you've also been blocking other parts of the room from your awareness, though your peripheral vision would let you see them easily. You can change that. As you stare at the X below, notice what surrounds the book (the edges of the page, your desktop, the floor).

X

Use your cellphone while driving and your attention will shift from road to phone and back again. We pay a toll for switching attentional gears, especially when we shift to complex tasks, like noticing and avoiding cars around us. The toll is a slight delay in coping (Rubenstein & others, 2001). In driving-simulation experiments, students talk-

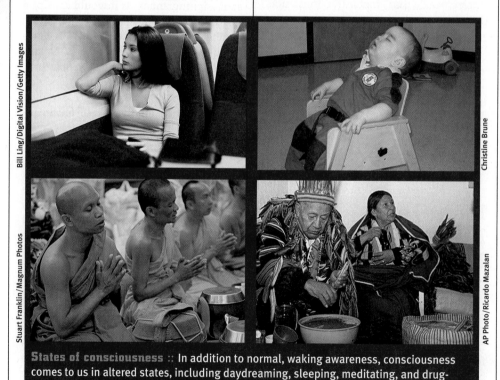

Bill Ling/Digital Vision/Getty Images

Stuart Franklin/Magnum Photos

Christine Brune

AP Photo/Ricardo Mazalan

States of consciousness :: In addition to normal, waking awareness, consciousness comes to us in altered states, including daydreaming, sleeping, meditating, and drug-induced hallucinating.

ing on cellphones—both hand-held and hands-free—have been slower to detect and respond to traffic signals, billboards, and other cars (Horrey & Wickens, 2006; Strayer & Johnston, 2001; Strayer & others, 2003). Multitasking comes at a cost.

We can process only a tiny sliver of the immense ocean of visual stimuli constantly before us. In one famous study, people watched a one-minute videotape in which images of three black-shirted men tossing a basketball were mixed with images of three white-shirted players; (Becklen & Cervone, 1983; Neisser, 1979). Researchers told the viewers to press a key each time they saw a black-shirted player pass the ball. Most were so intent on the game that they failed to notice a young woman carrying an umbrella stroll across the screen midway through the tape. During a replay they were amazed to see her! Their attention focused elsewhere, the viewers suffered from **inattentional blindness.** In a recent repeat of the experiment, smart-aleck researchers sent a gorilla-suited assistant through the swirl of players (Simons & Chabris, 1999) **(FIGURE 2.29).** During its 5- to 9-second cameo appearance, the gorilla paused to thump its chest. Still, half of the pass-counting participants failed to see it.

In other experiments, people have also exhibited *change blindness.* After a brief visual interruption, a big Coke bottle may disappear, a railing may rise, clothing color may change, but, more often than not, viewers won't notice (Resnick & others, 1997; Simons, 1996; Simons & Ambinder, 2005). **FIGURE 2.30**

Figure 2.29> Gorillas in our midst **When attending to one task (counting basketball passes by one of the three-person teams) about half the viewers display inattentional blindness by failing to notice a clearly visible gorilla passing through.**

Daniel Simons, University of Illinois

on the next page shows clips from one study in which two-thirds of the people giving directions to a construction worker failed to notice when he was replaced by another worker. Out of sight, out of mind.

Answers to earlier questions about flashing lights to a person with a split brain: Yes. No. Green.

PRACTICE TEST

29. Consciousness is our awareness of ourselves and our environment. Failure to see visible objects when our attention is occupied elsewhere is called
    a. automatic processing.
    b. awareness unconsciousness.
    c. inattentional blindness.
    d. subconscious processing.

Answer : 29. c.

cognitive neuroscience subfield of psychology that studies the connections between our brain activity and the processes of thinking, knowing, remembering, and communicating.

consciousness our awareness of ourselves and our environment.

selective attention focusing conscious awareness on a particular stimulus.

inattentional blindness failure to see visible objects when our attention is directed elsewhere.

SALLY FORTH

RESEARCH SHOWS EFFICIENCY IS CUT IN HALF WHEN YOU DO TWO THINGS AT ONCE.

I CAN DRIVE AND USE A CELL PHONE WITHOUT A PROBLEM.

BESIDES, I'M WIRED FOR MULTI-TASKING.

WELL, IT'S HARDER TO FOCUS ATTENTION THAN IT IS TO DIVIDE IT.

WHAT? SAY THAT AGAIN. NO, NOT YOU. I'M TALKING TO SALLY.

Figure 2.30> Change blindness While a man (white hair) provides directions to a construction worker, two experimenters rudely pass between them carrying a door. During this interruption, the original worker switches places with another person wearing different colored clothing. Most people, focused on their direction giving, do not notice the switch.

© 1998 Psychonomic Society, Inc. Images provided courtesy of Daniel J. Simons.

Sleep and Dreams

Now playing at an inner theater near you: the premiere showing of a sleeping person's vivid dream. This never-before-seen mental movie features captivating characters wrapped in a plot original and unlikely, yet intricate and seemingly real.

Waking from a troubling dream, we may wonder how our brain can so creatively, colorfully, and completely construct this inner-space world. Caught between our dreaming and waking consciousness, we may even for a moment be unsure which world is real.

> "I do not believe that I am now dreaming, but I cannot prove that I am not."
>
> Philosopher Bertrand Russell (1872–1970)

Sleep's mysteries have intrigued scientists for centuries. Now, in laboratories around the world, some of these mysteries are being solved as thousands sleep, attached to recording devices, while others observe. By recording brain waves and muscle movements, and by observing and waking sleepers from time to time, researchers are glimpsing things that a thousand years of common sense never told us.

> "I love to sleep. Do you? Isn't it great? It really is the best of both worlds. You get to be alive and unconscious."
>
> Comedian Rita Rudner, 1993

Biological Rhythms and Sleep

11: What are the stages of our nightly sleep cycle?

Like the ocean, life has its rhythmic tides. Let's look more closely at two of these biological rhythms—our 24-hour biological clock and our 90-minute sleep cycle.

At about age 20 (slightly earlier for women), we begin to shift from being evening-energized "owls" to being morning-loving "larks" (Roenneberg & others, 2004). Most university students are owls, with performance improving across the day (May & Hasher, 1998). Most older adults are larks, with performance declining as the day wears on. By mid-evening, when the night has hardly begun for many young adults, retirement homes are typically quiet.

Circadian Rhythm Try pulling an all-nighter, or working an occasional night shift. You will feel groggiest in the middle of the night but may get new energy around the time you would normally wake up. Your body is reacting in part to its own wake-up call. Our bodies are kept roughly in tune with the 24-hour cycle of day and night by an internal biological clock called the **circadian rhythm** (from the Latin *circa*, "about," and *diem*, "day"). As morning approaches, body temperature rises, then peaks during the day, dips for a time in early afternoon (when many people take siestas), and begins to drop again before we go to sleep. Thinking is sharpest and memory most accurate when we are at our daily peak in circadian arousal.

Bright light at night can disrupt this biological clock. Normally, the morning's bright light sounds an internal alarm by activating light-sensitive proteins in our eyes' retinas. These proteins trigger signals to neural clusters in the hypothalamus (Foster, 2004). As the brain's pineal gland picks up these signals, it decreases its production of the sleep-inducing hormone *melatonin*.

Sleep Stages Sooner or later, however, sleep overtakes us. As different parts of our brain's cortex stop communicating, consciousness fades (Massimini & others, 2005). But the sleeping brain does not emit a constant dial tone, for sleep has its own biological rhythm.

About every 90 minutes, we cycle through five distinct sleep stages. This elementary fact apparently was unknown until 8-year-old Armond Aserinsky went to bed one night in 1952. His father, Eugene, needed to test an electroencephalograph he had repaired that day (Aserinsky, 1988; Seligman & Yellen, 1987). Placing electrodes near Armond's eyes to record the rolling eye movements then believed to occur during sleep, Aserinsky watched the machine go wild, tracing deep zigzags on the graph paper. Could the machine still be broken? As the night proceeded and the activity recurred, Aserinsky realized that the periods of fast, jerky eye movements were accompanied by energetic brain activity. Awakened during one such episode, Armond reported having a dream. Aserinsky had discovered what we now know as **REM sleep** (rapid *eye movement* sleep).

Similar procedures used with thousands of volunteers showed the cycles

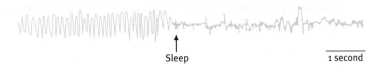

Figure 2.32> The moment of sleep We seem unaware of the moment we fall into sleep, but someone eavesdropping on our brain waves could tell. (From Dement, 1999.)

Sleep

1 second

were a normal part of sleep (Kleitman, 1960). To appreciate these studies, imagine yourself as a participant. As the hour grows late, you begin to fight sleepiness and yawn in response to reduced brain metabolism. (Yawning stretches your neck muscles and increases your heart rate, which increases your alertness [Moorcroft, 2003]). When you are ready for bed, the researcher tapes electrodes to your scalp (to detect your brain waves), on your chin (to detect muscle tension), and just outside the corners of your eyes (to detect eye movements) **(FIGURE 2.31).** Other devices allow the researcher to record your heart rate, respiration rate, and genital arousal.

When you are in bed with your eyes closed, the researcher in the next room sees on the EEG the relatively slow **alpha waves** of your awake but relaxed state **(FIGURE 2.32).** As you adapt to all this equipment, you grow tired and, in an unremembered moment, slip into **sleep.** The transition is marked by the slowed breathing and the irregular brain waves of *Stage 1 sleep* **(FIGURE 2.33** on the next page).

During this brief Stage 1 sleep you may experience fantastic images resembling *hallucinations*—sensory experiences that occur without a sensory stimulus. You may have a sensation of falling (at which moment your body may suddenly jerk) or of floating weightlessly. (These sensations may later be incorporated into memories. People who claim to have been abducted by aliens—often shortly after getting into bed—commonly recall being floated off their beds.)

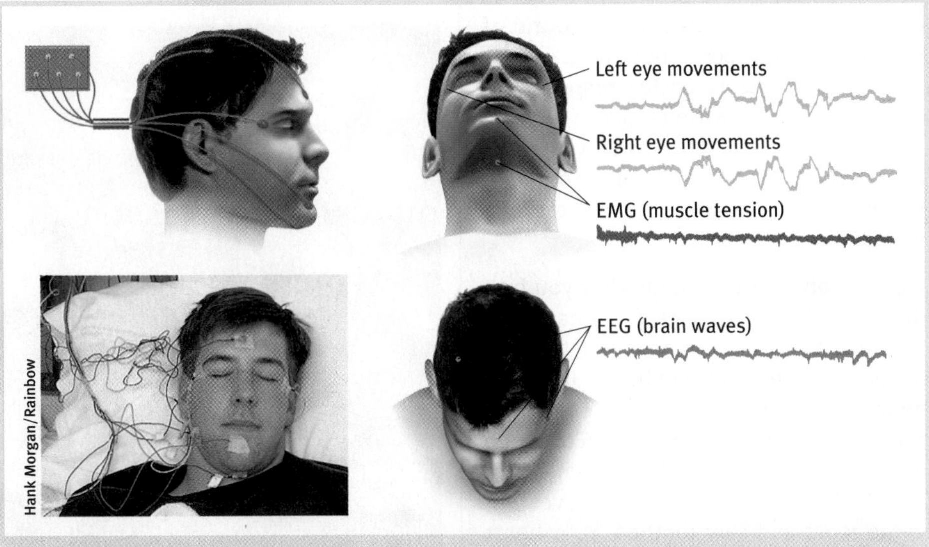

Left eye movements

Right eye movements

EMG (muscle tension)

EEG (brain waves)

Hank Morgan/Rainbow

Figure 2.31> Measuring sleep activity As this man sleeps, electrodes attached to an electroencephalograph are picking up weak electrical signals from his brain, eyes, and facial muscles. (From Dement, 1978.)

circadian [ser-KAY-dee-an] **rhythm** the biological clock; regular bodily rhythms (for example, of temperature and wakefulness) that occur on a 24-hour cycle.

REM (rapid eye movement) sleep recurring sleep stage during which vivid dreams commonly occur. Also known as *paradoxical sleep,* because the muscles are relaxed (except for minor twitches), but other body systems are active.

alpha waves relatively slow brain waves of a relaxed, awake state.

sleep periodic, natural, reversible loss of consciousness—as distinct from unconsciousness resulting from a coma, general anesthesia, or hibernation. (Adapted from Dement, 1999.)

Figure 2.33> Brain waves and sleep stages The regular alpha waves of an awake, relaxed state are quite different from the slower, larger delta waves of deep Stage 4 sleep. Although the rapid REM sleep waves resemble the near-waking Stage 1 sleep waves, the body is more aroused during REM sleep than during Stage 1 sleep. (From Dement, 1978.)

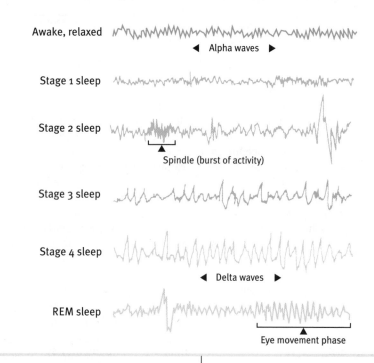

Awake, relaxed
◀ Alpha waves ▶

Stage 1 sleep

Stage 2 sleep
Spindle (burst of activity)

Stage 3 sleep

Stage 4 sleep
◀ Delta waves ▶

REM sleep
Eye movement phase

You then relax more deeply and begin about 20 minutes of *Stage 2 sleep,* with its periodic *sleep spindles*—bursts of rapid, rhythmic brain-wave activity (see Figure 2.33). Although you could still be awakened without too much difficulty, you are now clearly asleep.

Then, for the next few minutes, you go through the *transitional Stage 3* to the *deep sleep of Stage 4.* First in Stage 3, and even more so in Stage 4, your brain emits large, slow *delta* waves. These two slow-wave stages last about 30 minutes, during which you are hard to awaken. (It is at the end of the deep sleep of Stage 4 that children may wet the bed.)

Even when you are deeply asleep, your brain continues to monitor events. You move around on your bed, but you manage not to fall out. The roar of a passing motorcycle may leave deep sleep undisturbed, but a baby's cry can

quickly interrupt it, as can the sound of your name. EEG recordings confirm that the brain's auditory cortex responds to sound stimuli during sleep (Kutas, 1990). And one of this book's themes emerges again: *We process most information outside our conscious awareness (dual processing).*

REM Sleep About an hour after you first dive into sleep, a strange thing happens. You reverse course. From Stage 4, to Stage 3, and through Stage 2 (where you spend about half your night), you enter the most puzzling sleep phase—REM sleep **(FIGURE 2.34).** And the show begins. For about 10 minutes, your brain waves become rapid and saw-toothed. Your heart rate rises and your breathing becomes rapid and irregular. Every half-minute or so, your eyes dart around in a momentary burst of activity behind closed lids.

Except during very scary dreams, your genitals become aroused during REM sleep. You have an erection or increased vaginal lubrication and clitoral engorgement, regardless of whether the dream's content is sexual (Karacan & others, 1966). (Many men troubled by *erectile dysfunction* [impotence] still have sleep-related erections, suggesting the problem is not between their legs.)

Your brain's motor cortex is active during REM sleep, but your brainstem blocks its messages. This leaves your muscles relaxed, so much so that, except for an occasional finger, toe, or facial twitch, you are essentially paralyzed. Moreover, you cannot easily be awakened. Thus, REM sleep is sometimes called *paradoxical* sleep; the body is internally aroused and externally calm—except for those darting eyes. The rapid eye movements announce the beginning of a dream—often emotional, usually story-like, and richly hallucinatory.

Horses, which spend 92 percent of each day standing and can sleep standing, must lie down for muscle-paralyzing REM sleep (Morrison, 2003).

Luc Delahaye/Magnum Photos

Some sleep deeply, some not :: The fluctuating sleep cycle enables safe sleep for these soldiers on the battlefield. One benefit of communal sleeping is that someone will probably be awake or easily roused in the event of a threat during the night.

Figure 2.34> The stages in a typical night's sleep Most people pass through the five-stage sleep cycle (graph a) several times, with the periods of Stage 4 sleep and then Stage 3 sleep diminishing and REM sleep periods increasing. Graph b plots this increasing REM sleep and decreasing deep sleep based on data from 30 young adults. (From Cartwright, 1978; Webb, 1992.)

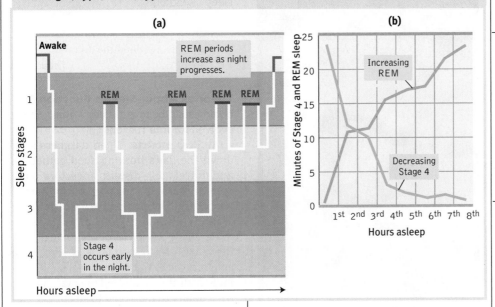

The sleep cycle repeats itself about every 90 minutes. As the night wears on, deep Stage 4 sleep grows shorter and disappears. REM sleep periods get longer (see Figure 2.34b). By morning, we have spent 20 to 25 percent of an average night's sleep—some 100 minutes—in REM sleep. Thirty-seven percent of people report rarely or never having dreams "that you can remember the next morning" (Moore, 2004). Yet even they, more than 80 percent of the time, will recall a dream if awakened during REM sleep.

People rarely snore during dreams. When REM starts, snoring stops.

Outside of conscious awareness, we spend about 600 hours a year experiencing some 1500 dreams, or more than 100,000 dreams over a typical lifetime—dreams mostly swallowed by the night but not acted out, thanks to REM's protective paralysis.

Why Do We Sleep?

12: How does sleep loss affect us? What are sleep's functions?

The idea that "everyone needs 8 hours of sleep" is untrue. Newborns sleep nearly two-thirds of their day, most adults no more than one-third. Still, there is more to our sleep differences than age. Allowed to sleep unhindered, most adults will regularly sleep at least 9 hours a night (Coren, 1996). Some, however, thrive with fewer than 6 hours a night.

2001 Gallup poll: "Usually, how many hours of sleep do you get at night?"	
5 or less	16%
6	27%
7	28%
8	28%
2001 average = 6.7 hours	
1942 average = 7.6 hours	

Genetics seems to play a role. When researchers checked sleep patterns among fraternal and identical twins, only the identical twins' were strikingly similar (Webb & Campbell, 1983).

But we must not stress biology too much. Remember another of this book's themes: *Individual and social-cultural forces also affect behavior.* Sleep patterns are culturally influenced. In industrialized nations, people now sleep less than they did a century ago. Thanks to modern light bulbs, shift work, and social diversions, those who would have gone to bed at 9:00 P.M. are now up until 11:00 P.M. or later. And sometimes we sleep *much* less.

Sleep and development :: During our first months, we spend less and less time asleep— from newborns' 16 hours a day down to 12 by age 2 (Snyder & Scott, 1972).

Dr. Carolyn Rovee-Collier, Rutgers University.

With a succession of 5-hour nights we accumulate a sleep debt that cannot be paid off by one long 10-hour sleep. "The brain keeps an accurate count of sleep debt for at least two weeks," says William Dement (1999, p. 64). With our body yearning for sleep, we will begin to feel terrible. Trying to stay awake, we will eventually lose. In the tiredness battle, sleep always wins.

The Effects of Sleep Loss Today more than ever, our sleep patterns leave us not only sleepy but also drained of energy and feelings of well-being. Teenagers now average less than 7 hours of sleep—nearly 2 hours less each night than their counterparts of 80 years ago enjoyed (Holden, 1993; Maas, 1999). And they regret it: Four in five American teens and three in five 18- to 29-year-olds wish they could get more sleep on weekdays (Mason, 2003, 2005). Small wonder so many fall asleep in class. When the going gets boring, the students start snoring. Even when awake, they often function below their peak.

Sleep deprivation is no joke. It can suppress immune cells that fight off viral infections and cancer (Beardsley, 1996; Irwin & others, 1994). Chronic sleep debt alters metabolism and hormonal functioning in ways that mimic aging. These effects can contribute to obesity, high blood pressure, and memory impairment (Spiegel & others, 1999; Taheri, 2004). Sleep deprivation also makes us irritable, slows performance, and impairs creativity, concentration, and communication (Harrison & Horne, 2000).

One study (Coren, 1996) demonstrated the high costs of sleep deprivation. Twice a year, most of us participate in a sleep-manipulation experiment—the "spring forward" to "daylight savings" time and "fall backward" to "standard" time. A search of millions of records showed that in both Canada and

"Tiger Woods said that one of the best things about his choice to leave Stanford for the professional golf circuit was that he could now get enough sleep."

Stanford sleep researcher William Dement, 1997

Sleepless :: After teaching a world record-breaking 72-hour English class in Shanghai, this teacher is clearly suffering. Sleep-deprived people experience a depressed immune system, impaired concentration, and greater vulnerability to accidents.

China Photos/Getty Images

the United States, accidents increase immediately after the time change that shortens sleep **(FIGURE 2.35)**.

So, nature charges us for our sleep debt. But why do we have this need for sleep? Read on.

"Sleep faster, we need the pillows."

Yiddish proverb

Theories About Sleep's Function Psychologists believe sleep may have evolved for four reasons.

1. *Sleep protects.* When darkness shut down the day's hunting, food gathering, and travel, our distant ancestors were better off asleep in a cave, out of harm's way. Those who didn't try to navigate around rocks and cliffs at night were more likely to leave descendants. This fits a broader principle: *A species' sleep patterns tend to suit its ecological niche.* Animals with the most need to graze and the least ability to hide tend to sleep less. Elephants and horses sleep 3 to 4 hours a day, gorillas 12 hours, and cats 14 hours.

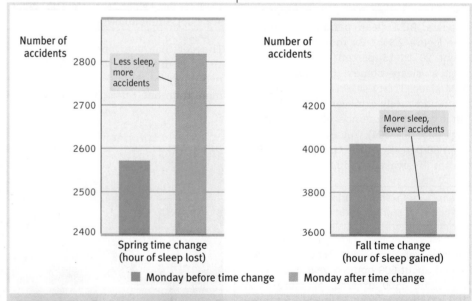

Figure 2.35> Canadian traffic accidents, 1991 and 1992 On the Monday after the spring time change, when people lose one hour of sleep, accidents increase as compared with the Monday before. In the fall, traffic accidents normally increase because of greater snow, ice, and darkness, but they diminish after the time change. (Adapted from Coren, 1996.)

For bats and eastern chipmunks, both of which sleep 20 hours, to live is hardly more than to eat and to sleep (Moorcroft, 2003).

> "Corduroy pillows make headlines."
>
> *Anonymous*

2. *Sleep helps us recover.* It helps restore and repair brain tissue. Bats and other animals with high waking metabolism burn a lot of calories, producing a lot of *free radicals,* molecules that are toxic to neurons. Sleeping a lot gives resting neurons time to repair themselves (Siegel, 2003). Think of it this way: When consciousness leaves the highway, brain road crews repair potholes while traffic is light.

3. *Sleep helps us remember.* During sleep, we restore and rebuild our memories of the day's experiences. People trained to perform tasks recall them better after a night's sleep than after several hours awake (Walker & Stickgold, 2006). Sleep also feeds creative thinking. After working on a task, then sleeping on it, people solve problems more insightfully than do those who stay awake (Wagner & others, 2004).

4. *Sleep may play a role in the growth process.* During deep sleep, the pituitary gland releases a growth hormone. As we age, we release less of this hormone and spend less time in deep sleep (Pekkanen, 1982).

Such discoveries are beginning to solve the ongoing riddle of sleep.

Sleep Disorders

13: What are some major sleep disorders?

No matter what their normal need for sleep, some 10 to 15 percent of adults complain of **insomnia.** These people have persistent problems in falling or staying asleep, not just an occasional loss of sleep when anxious or excited.

> "Sleep is like love or happiness. If you pursue it too ardently it will elude you."
>
> Wilse Webb, 1992 (p. 170)

The most popular quick fixes for true insomnia—sleeping pills and alcohol—can make things worse because they reduce REM sleep. Such aids also lead to *tolerance*—a state in which increasing doses are needed to produce an effect.

Scientists are searching for an ideal sleep aid—one that would mimic the natural chemicals that are abundant during sleep, without side effects. Until this magic pill is discovered, experts offer these tips for getting better quality sleep:

- Exercise regularly but not in the late evening. (Late afternoon is best.)

- Avoid caffeine, especially in the afternoon or later, and avoid food and drink near bedtime. The exception would be a glass of milk, which provides raw materials for the manufacture of serotonin, a neurotransmitter that promotes sleep.

- Relax before bedtime, using dimmer light.

- Sleep on a regular schedule (rise at the same time even after a restless night) and avoid naps.

- Reassure yourself that a temporary loss of sleep causes no great harm. Many people with insomnia overestimate—by about double—how long it takes them to fall asleep (Coren, 1996).

They also underestimate by nearly half how long they actually have slept. Even if we have been awake only an hour or two, we may *think* we have had very little sleep, because it's the waking part we remember.

- If all else fails, settle for less sleep, either going to bed later or getting up earlier.

Other sleep disorders include *narcolepsy, sleep apnea,* and *sleepwalking* and *sleeptalking.*

People with **narcolepsy** (from *narco,* "numbness," and *lepsy,* "seizure") have sudden attacks of overwhelming sleepiness. Narcolepsy attacks usually last less than 5 minutes but can occur at the worst times, perhaps just after taking a terrific swing at a softball or when laughing loudly, shouting angrily, or having sex (Dement, 1978, 1999). In severe cases, the person collapses directly into a brief period of REM sleep, with loss of muscle control. People with narcolepsy—1 in

insomnia recurring problems in falling or staying asleep.

narcolepsy sleep disorder in which a person has uncontrollable sleep attacks, sometimes lapsing directly into REM sleep.

Stress robs sleep :: Urban police officers, especially those under stress, report poorer sleep quality and less sleep than average (Neylan & others, 2002). The sleep of these Iraq war soldiers may also be disturbed.

Chris Hondros/Getty Images

2000 of us, estimates the Stanford University Center for Narcolepsy (2002)—must therefore live with extra caution. As a traffic menace, "snoozing is second only to boozing," says the American Sleep Disorders Association, and those with narcolepsy are especially at risk (Aldrich, 1989).

Sleep apnea also puts millions of people—1 in 20 of us—at increased risk of traffic accidents (Teran-Santos & others, 1999). *Apnea* means "with no breath," and people with this condition stop breathing during sleep. Then, after an airless minute or so, their blood oxygen drops enough to jolt them awake, and they snort in air for a few seconds. This process repeats hundreds of times each night, depriving them of slow-wave sleep. Apnea sufferers don't recall these episodes the next day, so many are unaware of their disorder.

Sleep apnea is linked with obesity, particularly among men. Other warning signs are loud snoring, sleepiness and irritability during the day, and (possibly) high blood pressure (Dement, 1999). If one doesn't mind looking a little goofy in the dark (imagine a snorkeler at a slumber party), the treatment—a masklike device with an air pump that keeps the sleeper's airway open—can be effective.

Sleepwalking and *sleeptalking* are usually childhood disorders, and they run in families. If a fraternal twin sleepwalks, the odds that the other twin will also sleepwalk are about one in three. But if the twins share identical genes, those odds increase to one in two. The same is true for sleeptalking (Hublin & others, 1997, 1998). Sleepwalking is usually harmless. After returning to bed on their own or with the help of a family member, few sleepwalkers recall their trip the next morning.

Several sleep disorders happen during Stage 4 sleep. Sleepwalking is one of them. Another is *night terrors*. Children have the deepest and longest Stage 4 sleep. So it's no surprise that children most often have these disorders. During an attack of night terrors, which are not nightmares, a child may sit up or walk around, talk nonsense, and appear terrified. The child's heart and

Did Brahms need his own lullabies? :: Cranky, overweight, and nap-prone, Johannes Brahms exhibited common symptoms of sleep apnea (Margolis, 2000).

Archivo Iconografico, S.A./Corbis

breathing rates may double. Luckily, children remember little or nothing of the fearful event the next day (Hartmann, 1981). As we grow older and spend less time in deep Stage 4 sleep, night terrors and sleepwalking are more and more rare.

PRACTICE TEST

30. Our body temperature tends to rise and fall in tune with a biological clock, which is referred to as

  a. the circadian rhythm.
  b. narcolepsy.
  c. REM sleep.
  d. an alpha wave.

31. Stage 1 sleep is a twilight zone of light sleep. During Stage 1 sleep, a person is most likely to experience

  a. sleep spindles.
  b. hallucinations.
  c. night terrors or nightmares.
  d. rapid eye movements.

32. In the deepest stage of sleep, the brain emits large, slow waves. This deep stage of sleep is called

  a. Stage 2.
  b. Stage 4.
  c. REM sleep.
  d. paradoxical sleep.

33. An electroencephalograph reading shows that during sleep we pass through a cycle of five stages, each with characteristic brain waves. As the night progresses, the REM stage

  a. gradually disappears.
  b. becomes briefer and briefer.
  c. remains about the same.
  d. becomes progressively longer.

34. Various theories have been proposed to explain why we need sleep. They include all but which of the following?

  a. Sleep has survival value.
  b. Sleep helps us restore and repair brain tissue.
  c. Sleep rests the eyes.
  d. Sleep plays a role in the growth process.

35. Narcolepsy is a sleep disorder in which a person _____; sleep apnea is a sleep disorder in which a person _____.

  a. has persistent problems falling asleep; experiences rising blood-oxygen levels
  b. experiences rising blood-oxygen levels; has persistent problems falling asleep
  c. repeatedly stops breathing; suffers attacks of overwhelming sleepiness
  d. suffers attacks of overwhelming sleepiness; repeatedly stops breathing

Answers : 30. a, 31. b, 32. b, 33. d, 34. c, 35. d.

Dreams

14: What are some explanations of why we dream?

Our two-track mind is clearly at work during sleep. Consider all the events happening outside our conscious awareness. We may stop breathing (sleep apnea), stroll around (sleepwalking), talk to imaginary people (sleeptalking), or *dream*.

Each of us spends about six years of our life in dreams—adventures that remain locked behind our moving eyelids and usually disappear from memory with the new day. The discovery of the link between REM sleep and dreaming gave us a key to that lock. Now instead of relying on a dreamer's hazy recall hours or days after waking, researchers can catch dreams as they happen. They can awaken people during or within 3 minutes after a REM sleep period and hear a vivid account.

What We Dream REM **dreams**—the sleeping mind's hallucinations—are vivid, emotional, and bizarre. Unlike daydreams, the dreams of REM sleep are so vivid we may confuse them with reality. Awakening from a nightmare, a 4-year-old may scream in fear of the bear in the house.

Few dreams are sweet. For both women and men, 8 in 10 dreams are bad dreams (Domhoff, 1999). Common themes are failing in an attempt to do something; being attacked, pursued, or rejected; or experiencing misfortune (Hall & others, 1982). Dreams with sexual imagery occur less often than you might think. In one study, only 1 in 10 dreams among young men and 1 in 30 among young women had sexual overtones (Domhoff, 1996). More commonly, the story line of our dreams—what Sigmund Freud called their **manifest content**—stars people and places from the day's experiences (De Koninck, 2000).

Our two-track mind is also monitoring our environment while we sleep. Sensory stimuli—a particular odor or the phone's ringing—may be instantly and ingeniously woven into a dream story. In a classic experiment, researchers lightly sprayed cold water on dreamers' faces (Dement & Wolpert, 1958). Compared with sleepers who did not get the cold-water treatment, these people were more likely to dream about a waterfall, a leaky roof, or even about being sprayed by someone.

> A popular sleep myth: If you dream you are falling and hit the ground (or if you dream of dying), you die. Unfortunately, those who could confirm these ideas are not around to do so. Some people, however, have had such dreams and are alive to report them.

Why We Dream Dream theorists have proposed several explanations of why we dream, including these:

MAXINE

www.maxine.net — © 2001 Marian Henley — mkhenley@prodigy.net

© 2001 Mariam Henley

Freud's wish-fulfillment theory. In 1900, offering what he thought was "the most valuable of all the discoveries it has been my good fortune to make," Freud proposed that dreams act as a safety valve, discharging feelings that cannot be expressed in public. He viewed a dream's remembered story line (its manifest content) as a censored, symbolic version of its **latent content,** the unconscious drives and wishes that would be threatening if expressed directly. Although most dreams have no overt sexual imagery, Freud nevertheless believed that most adult dreams can be "traced back by analysis to erotic wishes." Thus, a gun that appears in a dream could be a penis in disguise.

Freud's critics say it is time to wake up from Freud's dream theory, which is a scientific nightmare. Scientific studies offer "no reason to believe any of Freud's specific claims about dreams and their purposes," notes dream researcher William Domhoff (2000). Maybe a dream about a gun is really a dream about a gun. Legend has it that even Freud, who loved to smoke cigars, remarked that "sometimes, a cigar is just a cigar." Other critics note that dreams may be interpreted in many different ways.

Information-processing: The sleep-memory link. The *information-processing* perspective proposes that dreams may help sift, sort, and fix the day's events in our memory.

Studies support this view. When tested the next day after learning a task, those deprived of both slow-wave and REM sleep don't do as well as those who sleep undisturbed (Stickgold & others, 2000, 2001). Brain scans also confirm the link between REM sleep and memory. The brain regions that are active as rats learn to navigate a maze, or as people learn to perform a visual-discrimination task, are active again later during REM sleep (Louie & Wilson, 2001; Maquet, 2001). So precise are these activity patterns that scientists can tell where in the maze the rat would be if awake.

But why, ask some critics, do we sometimes dream about things we have not experienced?

Physiological function: Developing and preserving neural pathways. Perhaps dreams—or the brain activity linked to

sleep apnea a sleep disorder in which a sleeping person repeatedly stops breathing until blood oxygen is so low it awakens the person just long enough to draw a breath.

dream a sequence of images, emotions, and thoughts passing through a sleeping person's mind.

manifest content according to Freud, the remembered story line of a dream.

latent content according to Freud, the underlying meaning of a dream.

Diverse Yet Alike

People in hunter-gatherer tribes, such as these people in the Republic of Cameroon, often dream of animals; urban Japanese rarely do (Mestel, 1997). Yet they and we all dream repeatedly while asleep.

Patrick Bordes/Photo Researchers, Inc.

Urbanmyth/Alamy

REM sleep—give the sleeping brain a work-out that helps it develop. We know that stimulating experiences preserve and expand the brain's neural pathways. Infants, whose neural networks are fast developing, spend much of their abundant sleep time in REM sleep.

The activation-synthesis theory: Making sense of neural static. This theory proposes that dreams are born when random neural activity spreads upward from the brainstem (Antrobus, 1991; Hobson, 2003, 2004). Our ever-alert brain attempts to make sense of the activity, pasting the random bits of information into a meaningful image, much as children construct storybooks from snippets of magazine photos.

The cognitive-development perspective. Some dream researchers see dreams as a reflection of brain maturation and cognitive development (Domhoff, 2003; Foulkes, 1999). For example, before age 9, children's dreams seem more like a slide show and less like an active story in which the child is an actor. Dreams at all ages tend to feature the kind of thinking and talking we demonstrate when awake. They seem to draw on our current knowledge and concepts we understand.

There is one thing dream theorists agree on: We need REM sleep. Deprived of it in sleep labs or in real life, people return more and more quickly to the REM stage when finally allowed to sleep undisturbed. They literally sleep like babies—

with increased REM sleep, a phenomenon called **REM rebound.** Withdrawing REM-suppressing sleeping pills also increases REM sleep, often with nightmares.

There is no denying that a night of solid sleep (and dreaming) has an important place in our lives: To sleep, perchance to remember. Students, take note: Sleep researcher Robert Stickgold (2000) believes many of you suffer from a kind of sleep bulimia, binge-sleeping on the weekend. From his information-processing perspective he warns, "If you don't get good sleep and enough sleep after you learn new stuff, you won't integrate it effectively into your memories."

High-achieving secondary students with top grades average 25 minutes more sleep a night and go to bed 40 minutes earlier than their lower-achieving classmates (Wolfson & Carskadon, 1998).

◈ PRACTICE TEST

36. According to Sigmund Freud, dreams are the key to understanding our inner conflicts. In interpreting dreams, Freud was most interested in their
   a. information-processing function.
   b. physiological function.
   c. manifest content, or story line.
   d. latent content, or symbolic meaning.

37. Some theories of dreaming propose that dreams serve a physiological purpose. One such theory suggests that dreams
   a. are the brain's attempt to make sense of random neural activity.
   b. provide a rest period for overworked brains.
   c. serve as a safety valve for unfulfilled desires.
   d. prevent the brain from being disturbed by periodic stimulations.

38. The tendency for REM sleep to increase following REM sleep deprivation is referred to as
   a. paradoxical sleep.
   b. deep sleep.
   c. REM rebound.
   d. slow-wave sleep.

Answers : 36. d, 37. a, 38. c.

We have glimpsed the truth of this chapter's overriding principle: Everything psychological is simultaneously biological. You and I are privileged to live in a

REM rebound the tendency for REM sleep to increase following REM sleep deprivation (created by repeated awakenings during REM sleep).

time when the pace of discoveries about the interplay of our biology and our behavior and mental processes is truly breath-taking. Yet what is unknown still dwarfs what is known. We can describe the brain. We can learn the functions of its parts. We can study how the parts communicate. We can observe sleeping and waking brains. But how do we get mind out of meat? How does the electro-chemical whir in a hunk of tissue the size of a head of lettuce give rise to elation, a creative idea, or that crazy dream?

The mind seeking to understand the brain—that is indeed among the ultimate scientific challenges. And so it will always be. To paraphrase scientist John Barrow, a brain simple enough to be understood is too simple to produce a mind able to understand it.

Terms and concepts to Remember

biological psychology, p. 27

neuron, p. 28

dendrite, p. 28

axon, p. 28

action potential, p. 28

synapse [SIN-aps], p. 28

threshold, p. 28

all-or-none response, p. 28

neurotransmitters, p. 29

opiates, p. 29

endorphins [en-DOR-fins], p. 30

nervous system, p. 31

central nervous system (CNS), p. 31

peripheral nervous system (PNS), p. 31

nerves, p. 31

sensory neurons, p. 31

motor neurons, p. 31

interneurons, p. 31

somatic nervous system, p. 31

autonomic [aw-tuh-NAHM-ik] nervous system, p. 31

sympathetic nervous system, p. 32

parasympathetic nervous system, p. 32

endocrine [EN-duh-krin] system, p. 33

hormones, p. 33

adrenal [ah-DREEN-el] glands, p. 34

pituitary gland, p. 34

brainstem, p. 34

medulla [muh-DUL-uh], p. 34

thalamus [THAL-uh-muss], p. 35

EEG (electroencephalograph), p. 35

PET (positron emission tomography) scan, p. 35

MRI (magnetic resonance imaging), p. 35

fMRI (functional MRI), p. 35

reticular formation, p. 36

cerebellum [sehr-uh-BELL-um], p. 36

limbic system, p. 37

amygdala [uh-MIG-duh-la], p. 37

hypothalamus [hi-po-THAL-uh-muss], p. 38

cerebral [seh-REE-bruhl] cortex, p. 39

frontal lobes, p. 39

parietal [puh-RYE-uh-tuhl] lobes, p. 39

occipital [ahk-SIP-uh-tuhl] lobes, p. 40

temporal lobes, p. 40

motor cortex, p. 40

sensory cortex, p. 41

hallucinations, p. 42

association areas, p. 42

Broca's area, p. 43

Wernicke's area, p. 43

plasticity, p. 44

corpus callosum [KOR-pus kah-LOW-sum], p. 45

split brain, p. 45

cognitive neuroscience, p. 48

consciousness, p. 48

selective attention, p. 48

inattentional blindness, p. 49

circadian [ser-KAY-dee-an] rhythm, p. 50

REM (rapid eye movement) sleep, p. 51

alpha waves, p. 51

sleep, p. 51

insomnia, p. 55

narcolepsy, p. 55

sleep apnea, p. 56

dream, p. 57

manifest content, p. 57

latent content, p. 57

REM rebound, p. 58

:: Multiple-choice self-tests and more may be found at www.worthpublishers.com/myers

REVIEW: NEUROSCIENCE AND CONSCIOUSNESS

NEURAL COMMUNICATION

1 **What are neurons, and how do they transmit information?**

NEURONS:

- are basic units of the *nervous system.*
- transmit information to other cells in a chemistry-to-electricity process.
- send signals (action potentials) down their *axons.*
- receive incoming excitatory or inhibitory signals through their *dendrites* and cell body.
- fire in an *all-or-none response* when combined incoming signals are strong enough to pass a *threshold.* Response triggers release of chemical messengers (*neurotransmitters*) across the tiny gap (*synapse*) separating a sending neuron from a receiving cell.

2 **How do neurotransmitters affect our mood and behavior?**

SPECIFIC NEUROTRANSMITTERS, SUCH AS *SEROTONIN* AND *DOPAMINE,*

- travel designated pathways in the brain.
- affect particular behaviors and emotions, such as hunger, movement, and arousal.

THE NERVOUS SYSTEM

3 **What are the major divisions of the nervous system, and what are their basic functions?**

Central Nervous System (CNS)

CNS *interneurons* communicate with PNS *motor neurons* and *sensory neurons.*

Peripheral Nervous System (PNS)

Brain (enables thinking, feeling, and acting)

Spinal Cord (connects the PNS to the brain)

Somatic Nervous System controls voluntary movements of the skeletal muscles.

Autonomic Nervous System (ANS) controls the involuntary muscles and the glands.

Sympathetic division arouses.

Parasympathetic division calms.

Endorphins are natural *opiates* released in response to pain and exercise.

THE ENDOCRINE SYSTEM

4 **How does the endocrine system—the body's slower information system—transmit its messages?**

- *Endocrine system* glands secrete *hormones,* which affect the brain and other tissues.
- Stress or danger triggers the autonomic nervous system to activate the *adrenal glands.*
- The *pituitary* (the endocrine system's master gland) influences other glands, including sex glands, to release hormones.

THE BRAIN

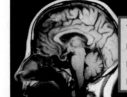

To study the brain, researchers

- study the effects of brain damage.
- use *MRI* scans to reveal brain structures.
- use *EEG, PET,* and *fMRI* (functional MRI) recordings to reveal brain activity.

5 **What are the functions of the brainstem and its associated structures?**

- The *brainstem* controls automatic survival functions.
- The *medulla* controls heartbeat and breathing.
- The *reticular formation* controls arousal and attention.
- The *thalamus* is the brain's sensory switchboard.
- The *cerebellum* processes sensory input and coordinates muscle movement.

6 **What are the functions of limbic system structures?**

THE *LIMBIC SYSTEM* IS LINKED TO EMOTIONS, DRIVES, AND MEMORY:

- The *amygdala* is involved in aggressive and fearful responses.
- The *hypothalamus* monitors various bodily maintenance activities, contains reward centers, and triggers the pituitary to influence other glands of the endocrine system.
- The hippocampus processes memories.

7 **What are the four lobes of the cerebral cortex, and where are they located?**

- *Frontal lobes:* enable speaking, muscle movement, planning, and judging
- *Parietal lobes:* receive sensory input
- *Occipital lobes:* receive input from visual fields
- *Temporal lobes:* receive input from the ears

8 **What are the functions of the cerebral cortex?**

- *Motor cortex* controls muscle movement, and *sensory cortex* receives sensory information.
- Cortex is mostly *association areas,* which integrate information related to learning, remembering, thinking, and other higher-level functions.
- Most higher-level functions require coordination of many brain areas.
- Language processing involves integration of specialized cortex areas, including *Broca's area, Wernicke's area,* and the angular gyrus.
- Brain damage may cause different types of language impairments, depending on which region is damaged.
- The brain's *plasticity* allows it to modify itself after some types of damage.

9 **What is a split brain, and what does it reveal about brain functioning?**

- The *corpus callosum* (large band of nerve fibers) normally connects the two brain hemispheres. If surgically severed (often to treat severe epilepsy), a *split brain* results.
- Through split-brain research we learned that most people have hemispheric specialization (though the hemispheres work together in a normal brain).
- Left hemisphere usually specializes in verbal processing.
- Right hemisphere usually specializes in visual perception and recognition of emotions.

BRAIN STATES AND CONSCIOUSNESS

10 **What is selective attention, and what does it teach us about consciousness?**

- *Consciousness* is our awareness of ourselves and our environment.
- *Selective attention* (for example *inattentional blindness*) happens as we focus attention on specific stimuli. We can focus our conscious awareness on only a small portion of the world around us.

11 **What are the stages of our nightly sleep cycle?**

- The *circadian rhythm's* 24-hour cycle regulates our daily schedule of alertness and sleepiness.
- Nightly sleep cycles through recurring stages, together lasting about 90 minutes.
- Stage 1: brief, near-waking; *hallucinations* (sensation of falling or floating, etc.) may occur.
- Stage 2: includes characteristic bursts of rapid, rhythmic brain-wave activity.
- Stages 3 and 4: deep sleep, with large, slow waves. Shortens as night goes on.
- *REM (rapid eye movement) sleep,* with internal arousal but outward paralysis. Begins after about one hour of sleep, replacing Stage 1 sleep. Includes most dreaming. Lengthens as night goes on.

12 **How does sleep loss affect us? What are sleep's functions?**

RISKS OF SLEEP DEPRIVATION:
- Fatigue, irritability
- Depressed immune system
- Impaired concentration, creativity, communication, and performance
- Obesity, high blood pressure, and memory impairment

POSSIBLE FUNCTIONS:
- Protection
- Maintenance
- Memory processing
- Growth and development

13 **What are some major sleep disorders?**

- *Insomnia* (recurring wakefulness)
- *Narcolepsy* (sudden uncontrollable sleepiness or lapsing into REM sleep)
- *Sleep apnea* (the stopping of breathing while asleep)
- Sleepwalking, sleeptalking, and night terrors

14 **What are some explanations of why we dream?**

REM REBOUND FOLLOWS REM DEPRIVATION, INDICATING THAT REM SLEEP AND DREAMING SERVE NEEDED FUNCTIONS. DREAM THEORIES INCLUDE:
- Freud's wish-fulfillment theory.
- information-processing: The sleep-memory link.
- physiological function: Developing and preserving neural pathways.
- the activation-synthesis theory: Making sense of neural static.
- the cognitive-development perspective.

3 | Developing Through the Life Span

MANY PSYCHOLOGISTS ONCE BELIEVED THAT CHILDHOOD sets our traits. Today's psychologists instead see development as lifelong. In some ways we become older versions of our former selves. An outgoing, playful 3-year-old, for example, may morph into a happy, wise-cracking 18-year-old, and finally into a jolly, playful grandparent. An abused and neglected child may later have difficulty forming close, trusting relationships.

But development also can bring surprises. My formerly shy little pre-schooler is now a young adult, living confidently in South Africa. There, Little-Miss-Hide-Behind-My-Legs does youth development work, often as a stand-up group leader who loves engaging adolescents from low-income townships.

The power of utterly unexpected life developments can be seen in the true story of Alexander (Bandura, 2008). Alexander was born in 1755, on a tiny Caribbean island. His parents were not married, and his father deserted the family. His mother was imprisoned and died. His guardian committed suicide. When his aunt, uncle, and grandfather also died, Alexander's few belongings were sold, leaving him penniless.

But his luck turned when a local minister raised funds to send Alexander to King's College (now Columbia University). From there, he went on to become one of the Founding Fathers of the United States and a leading author of the U.S. Constitution. As first Secretary of the Treasury, he helped create the country's banking and currency systems.

Alexander Hamilton :: A case example of change and consistency across the life span.

If you have ever had a ten-dollar bill, you have seen Alexander—Alexander Hamilton. His life—first as a penniless immigrant, and later as a respected statesman—shows how great achievements may arise from humble beginnings. In other ways, the apple did not fall far from the tree. His own stormy life, which ended after he was shot in a duel with Aaron Burr, was plagued by some of the instability and infidelity that also plagued his parents' lives.

1: **What are the three key issues studied by developmental psychologists?**

Developmental psychology is the study of how we change (physically, cognitively, and socially) as we, like Alexander Hamilton, journey from conception to death. We humans travel many of the same paths because we are alike in so many ways. We share most of our genes. As infants, we arrive able to sense and learn about our world. We begin walking around age 1 and talking by age 2. As children, we play together in preparation for life's work. As adults, we all smile and cry, love and loathe. And, eventually, we all die.

But we also differ. For better or worse, our experiences become part of who we are. In this chapter, we explore human development across the life span, from womb to tomb. Developmental psychologists' observations and experiments have shed light on three major issues.

1. *Nature and nurture:* How does our genetic inheritance (*our nature*) interact with our experiences (*the nurture we receive*) to influence our development?

> "Nature is all that a man brings with him into the world; nurture is every influence that affects him after his birth."
>
> Francis Galton, *English Men of Science*, 1874

2. *Continuity and stages:* What parts of development are gradual and continuous, like riding an escalator? What parts change abruptly in separate stages, like climbing rungs on a ladder?

3. *Stability and change:* Which of our traits persist through life? How do we change as we age?

You will read about these issues throughout this chapter. We also will focus on nature and nurture at the end of our Parents and Peers discussion; continuity and stages at the end of our adolescent development discussion; and stability and change at the end of our adult development discussion. Let's begin our journey.

Prenatal Development and the Newborn

Conception

2: **How does life develop before birth?**

Nothing is more natural than a species reproducing itself. Yet nothing is more wondrous. With humans, the process starts when a woman's ovary releases a mature egg—a cell roughly the size of the period at the end of this sentence. The 200 million or more sperm deposited during intercourse begin their race upstream, like space voyagers approaching a huge planet 85,000 times their own size. Only a small number will reach the egg. Those that do will release digestive enzymes that eat away its protective coating **(FIGURE 3.1a)**. As soon as one

sperm penetrates that coating **(FIGURE 3.1b)**, the egg's surface will block out the others. Before half a day passes, the egg nucleus and the sperm nucleus will fuse. The two have become one. Consider it your most fortunate of moments. Among 200 million sperm, the one needed to make you, in combination with that one particular egg, won the race.

The Heredity-Environment Dance Begins

Contained within the new single cell is a master code that will interact with your experience, creating you—a being in many ways like all other humans, but in other ways like no other human. Every cell in every part of your body will contain a copy of this genetic code.

Each of the trillions of cells you will eventually have will carry this message in its **chromosomes.** These threadlike structures contain the **DNA** we hear so much about. **Genes** are pieces of DNA, and they can be active (*expressed*) or inactive. Events in your environment can "turn them on," much as a cup of hot water "turns on" a teabag and lets it "express" itself as a refreshing cup of tea.

When turned on, your genes will guide your development. **FIGURE 3.2** summarizes these elements that make up your **heredity.**

Genetically speaking, every other human is close to being your identical twin. It is our shared genetic profile—our human **genome**—that makes us humans, rather than chimpanzees or tulips. Even

Diverse Yet Alike

The nurture of nature ::
Parents everywhere wonder: Will my baby grow up to be peaceful or aggressive? Homely or attractive? Successful or struggling at every step? What comes built in, and what is nurtured—and how? Research reveals that nature and nurture together shape our development— every step of the way.

Amy Etra/Photo Edit

Susan Van Etten/Photo Edit

Myrleen Ferguson Cate/Photo Edit

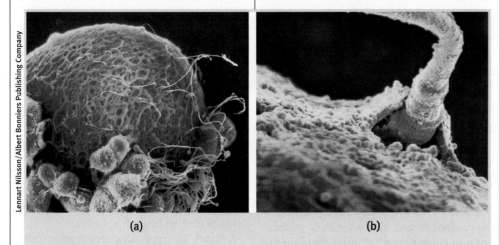

Figure 3.1> **Life is sexually transmitted** (a) Sperm cells surround an ovum. (b) As one sperm penetrates the egg's jellylike outer coating, a series of events begins that will cause sperm and egg to fuse into a single cell. If all goes well, that cell will subdivide again and again to emerge 9 months later as a 100-trillion-cell human being.

"Thanks for almost everything, Dad."

the person you like least is your near-clone, sharing about 99.9 percent of your DNA (Plomin & Crabbe, 2000). But that 0.1 percent difference, in interaction with differing environments, can give us a hero or a villain.

The slight person-to-person variations found at particular gene sites in the DNA give clues to our uniqueness—why one person has a disease that another does not, why one person is short and another tall, why one is happy and another depressed. Most human traits are influenced by many genes. How tall you are, for example, reflects the height of your face, the length of your leg bones, and so forth. Complex human traits such as intelligence, happiness, and aggressiveness are similarly influenced by groups of genes.

"We share half our genes with the banana."
Evolutionary biologist Robert May, president of Britain's Royal Society, 2001

Our human differences are also shaped by our **environment**—by every external influence, from maternal nutrition while in the womb, to social support

Nucleus
(the inner area of a cell that houses chromosomes and genes)

Chromosome
(threadlike structure made largely of DNA molecules)

Gene
(segment of DNA containing the code for a particular protein; determines our individual biological development)

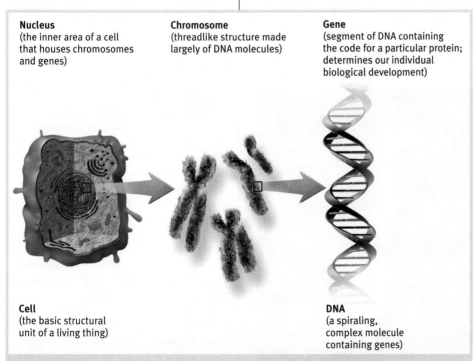

Cell
(the basic structural unit of a living thing)

DNA
(a spiraling, complex molecule containing genes)

Figure 3.2> **The genes: Their location and composition** Contained in the nucleus of each of the cells in your body are chromosomes. Each chromosome contains a coiled chain of the molecule DNA. Genes are DNA segments that, when expressed (turned on), direct the production of proteins and influence our individual biological development.

developmental psychology a branch of psychology that studies physical, cognitive, and social change throughout the life span.

chromosomes threadlike structures made of DNA molecules that contain the genes.

DNA (deoxyribonucleic acid) a molecule containing the genetic information that makes up the chromosomes.

genes the biochemical units of heredity that make up the chromosomes; a segment of DNA.

heredity the genetic transfer of characteristics from parents to offspring.

genome the complete instructions for making an organism, consisting of all the genetic material in that organism's chromosomes.

environment every external influence, from prenatal nutrition to social support in later life.

"I thought that sperm-bank donors remained anonymous."

while nearing the tomb. Your height, for example, may be influenced by your diet and even by accidental injuries during growth.

Heredity and environment are *both* important. More precisely, they **interact.** Let's imagine two babies with two very different sets of genes. Lorna is a beautiful baby and is also sociable and easygoing. Patty is plain, shy, and colicky. Lorna's pretty, smiling face elicits affectionate and stimulating care, which in turn helps her develop into an even warmer and more outgoing person. Patty's caretakers are often tired and stressed by her fussiness. As the two children grow older, Lorna, naturally outgoing, more often seeks activities and friends that increase her social confidence. Patty, shy and withdrawn, has few friends.

What has caused these differences? *Environments trigger gene activity. And our genetically influenced traits evoke significant responses in others.* Lorna and Patty were very different when they began life. Their appearances and characteristics caused other people to react differently to them. These responses, in turn, strengthened Lorna's and Patty's inborn tendencies. From conception onward, heredity and experience will dance together.

Prenatal Development

Fertilized eggs are called **zygotes.** Fewer than half of them survive beyond the first two weeks (Grobstein, 1979; Hall, 2004). But for you and me, good fortune prevailed. One cell became 2, then 4—each just like the first—until this cell division had produced some 100 identical cells within the first week. Then the cells began to specialize. How identical cells do this—as if one decides "I'll become a brain, you become intestines!"—is a puzzle that scientists are just beginning to solve.

About 10 days after conception, the zygote attaches to the wall of the mother's uterus. So begins about 37 weeks of the closest human relationship. The tiny clump of cells forms two parts now. The inner cells become the **embryo** (**FIGURE 3.3**). The outer cells become the *placenta,* the life-link between embryo and mother. Over the next 6 weeks, the embryo's organs begin to form and function. The heart begins to beat.

For about one in 270 sets of parents, though, there is a bonus. Two heartbeats will reveal that the zygote, during its early days of development, has split into two. If all goes well, two genetically identical babies will start life together some eight months later.

Identical twins develop from a single fertilized egg that splits in two (**FIGURE 3.4**). They are nature's own human clones. They share not only the same genes but also the same conception, uterus, birth date, and usually the same cultural history. **Fraternal twins** develop from separate fertilized eggs. They share the same fetal environment but not the same genes. Genetically, they are no more similar than ordinary brothers and sisters. (You will hear more about identical and fraternal twins later in this chapter.)

By 9 weeks after conception, an embryo looks unmistakably human. It is now a **fetus** (Latin for "offspring" or "young one"). By the sixth month, organs such as the stomach have developed enough to give the fetus a chance of survival if born prematurely.

Prenatal development	
zygote:	conception to 2 weeks
embryo:	2 weeks through 8 weeks
fetus:	9 weeks to birth

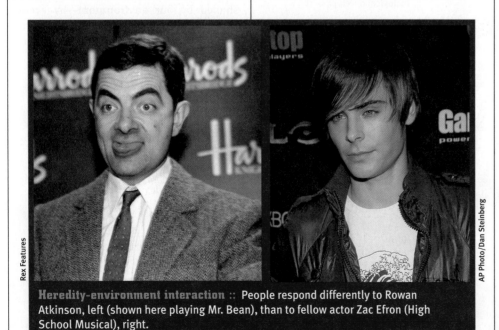

Heredity-environment interaction :: People respond differently to Rowan Atkinson, left (shown here playing Mr. Bean), than to fellow actor Zac Efron (High School Musical), right.

Rex Features

AP Photo/Dan Steinberg

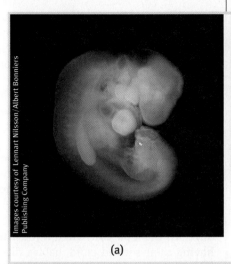  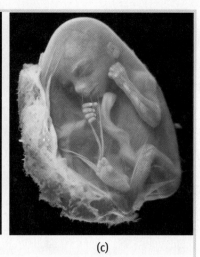

(a)   (b)   (c)

Figure 3.3> Prenatal development (a) The embryo grows and develops rapidly. At 40 days, the spine is visible and the arms and legs are beginning to grow. (b) By the end of the second month, when the fetal period begins, facial features, hands, and feet have formed. (c) As the fetus enters the fourth month, its 3 ounces could fit in the palm of your hand.

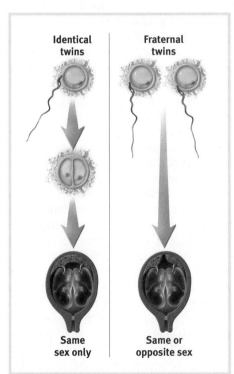

Identical twins / Fraternal twins

Same sex only / Same or opposite sex

Figure 3.4> Same fertilized egg, same genes; different eggs, different genes Identical twins develop from a single fertilized egg, fraternal twins from two different eggs.

Remember that heredity and environment *interact*. This is true even in the prenatal period. In addition to transferring nutrients and oxygen from mother to fetus, the placenta screens out many harmful substances. But some slip by. Among them are **teratogens,** agents such as viruses and drugs that can damage an embryo or fetus. This is one reason women who are pregnant are advised not to drink alcoholic beverages. A pregnant woman never drinks alone. As alcohol enters her bloodstream—and her fetus'— it depresses activity in both their central nervous systems. If she is a persistent heavy drinker, the fetus will be at risk for birth defects and mental retardation. For 1 in every 500 to 2000 infants (May & Gossage, 2001), the effects are visible as **fetal alcohol syndrome (FAS),** marked by a small, misproportioned head and lifelong brain abnormalities. Even light drinking can harm the fetal brain (Braun, 1996; Ikonomidou & others, 2000).

Some women's experience of nausea in the critical first three months of pregnancy may be an adaptation dating back to prehistoric times, say some evolutionary psychologists. Avoiding certain bitter, strongly flavored, and novel foods has survival value. They are the very foods most often toxic to embryonic development (Schmitt & Pilcher, 2004).

interaction in psychology, occurs when the effect of one factor (such as environment) depends on another factor (such as heredity).

zygote the fertilized egg; it enters a 2-week period of rapid cell division and develops into an embryo.

embryo the developing human organism from about 2 weeks after fertilization through the second month.

identical twins twins who develop from a single fertilized egg that splits in two, creating two genetically identical siblings.

fraternal twins twins who develop from separate fertilized eggs. They are genetically no closer than brothers and sisters, but they share a fetal environment.

fetus the developing human organism from 9 weeks after conception to birth.

teratogens agents, such as chemicals and viruses, that can reach the embryo or fetus during prenatal development and cause harm.

fetal alcohol syndrome (FAS) physical and cognitive abnormalities in children caused by a pregnant woman's heavy drinking. In severe cases, symptoms include noticeable facial misproportions.

Images courtesy of Lennart Nilsson/Albert Bonniers Publishing Company

Prepared to feed and eat :: Animals, including humans, offspring's are predisposed to respond to their offspring's cries for nourishment.

The Competent Newborn

3: What are some of the newborn's abilities and traits?

As newborns, we arrived with automatic **reflex** responses ideally suited for our survival. We withdrew our limbs to escape pain. If a cloth over our face interfered with our breathing, we turned our head from side to side and swiped at it. New parents are often in awe of the finely tuned set of reflexes by which their baby gets food. When something touches their cheek, babies turn toward that touch, open their mouth, and actively *root* for a nipple. Finding one, they quickly close on it and begin *sucking*. Sucking has its own set of reflexes—*tonguing, swallowing,* and *breathing*. Failing to find satisfaction, the hungry baby may *cry*—a behavior parents find highly unpleasant, and very rewarding to relieve.

Even as newborns, we seem to search out sights and sounds linked with other humans. We turn our heads in the direction of human voices. We gaze longer at a drawing of a facelike image **(FIGURE 3.5)**. We prefer to look at objects 8 to 12 inches away. And wonder of wonders, that just happens to be the approximate distance between a nursing infant's eyes and its mother's (Maurer & Maurer, 1988).

We seem especially attuned to that human who is our mother. Within days after birth, our brain has picked up and stored the smell of our mother's body. A week-old nursing baby, placed between a gauze pad from its mother's bra and one from another nursing mother, usually turns toward the pad that carries its mother's smell (MacFarlane, 1978). And what do you suppose happens if you give a 3-week-old a pacifier that sometimes

Figure 3.5> Newborns' preference for faces When shown these two forms with the same three elements, newborns spent nearly twice as long looking at the facelike image on the left (Johnson & Morton, 1991). Newborns—average age just 53 minutes in one study—seem to have an inborn preference for looking toward faces (Mondloch & others, 1999).

turns on recordings of its mother's voice and sometimes the voice of a stranger? The infant will suck more vigorously when it hears its now-familiar mother's voice (Mills & Melhuish, 1974).

Very young infants are competent, indeed. They see what they need to see. They smell and hear well. They are already using their sensory equipment to learn. Guided by biology and experience, those sensory and perceptual abilities will develop continuously over the next months.

Similar as newborns are, they also differ. As most parents will tell you after having their second child, babies differ even before gulping their first breath. This difference is **temperament,** or emotional excitability—whether reactive, intense, and fidgety, or easygoing, quiet, and placid. Anxious, inhibited infants have high and variable heart rates. Physically, they become very aroused when facing new or strange situations (Kagan & Snidman, 2004). From the first weeks of life, *difficult* babies are more irritable, intense, and unpredictable. *Easy* babies are cheerful, relaxed, and predictable in feeding and sleeping (Chess & Thomas, 1987).

Temperament, which seems to be rooted in our biology, is one aspect of our personality. Identical twins, who have identical genes, have more similar personalities, including temperament, than do fraternal twins. Such evidence supports the idea that our biologically rooted temperament helps form our enduring personality (McCrae & others, 2000; Rothbart & others, 2000). (To read more on how psychologists use twin studies to judge the influences of heredity and environment, see Close-Up: Twin and Adoption Studies.)

reflex an unlearned, automatic response to a sensory stimulus.

temperament a person's characteristic emotional reactivity and intensity.

CLOSE-UP

TWIN AND ADOPTION STUDIES

4: How do twin and adoption studies help us understand the effects of nature and nurture?

To tease apart the influences of nature and nurture, researchers would need to vary the home environment while controlling heredity, and to vary heredity while controlling the home environment. Happily for our purposes, nature has done this work for us.

Identical Versus Fraternal Twins

Identical twins have identical genes. Do these shared genes mean that identical twins also *behave* more similarly than fraternal twins (Bouchard, 2004)? Studies of thousands of twin pairs provide a consistent answer. Identical twins are more similar than fraternals in their abilities, personal traits, and interests (Loehlin & Nichols, 1976).

But could their shared experiences rather than their shared genes explain their similarities?

Separated Twins

On a chilly February morning in 1979, some time after divorcing his first wife, Linda, Jim Lewis awoke next to his second wife, Betty. Determined that this marriage would work, Jim left love notes to Betty around the house. As he lay there he thought about his son, James Alan, and his faithful dog, Toy.

Jim loved his basement woodworking shop where he had built furniture, including a white bench circling a tree. Jim also liked to drive his Chevy, watch stock-car racing, and drink Miller Lite beer.

Jim was healthy, except for an occasional migraine. His blood pressure was a little high, perhaps related to his chain-smoking. He had become overweight but had shed some of the pounds. After a vasectomy, he was done having children.

What was extraordinary about Jim Lewis, however, was that at that moment (I am not making this up) there was another man named Jim for whom all these things were also true.[1] This other Jim—Jim Springer—just happened, 38 years earlier, to have been Jim Lewis' womb-mate. Thirty-seven days after their birth, these genetically identical twins were separated and adopted by two blue-collar families. They grew up with no contact until the day Jim Lewis received a call from his genetic clone (who, having been told he had a twin, set out to find him).

One month later, the brothers became the first of many twin pairs tested by psychologist Thomas Bouchard and his colleagues. Given tests measuring their personality, intelligence,

Identical twins Jim Lewis and Jim Springer are people two.

©2006 Bob Sacha

heart rate, and brain waves, the Jim twins were virtually as alike as the same person tested twice. Their voice patterns were so similar that, hearing a playback of an earlier interview, Jim Springer guessed "That's me." Wrong—it was his brother.

This and other research on separated identical twins supports the idea that genes matter.

Twin similarities do not impress Bouchard's critics, however. If any two strangers were to spend hours comparing their behaviors and life histories, wouldn't they also discover many coincidental similarities? Moreover, because identical twins share an appearance and the responses it evokes, they have probably had similar experiences. Bouchard replies that the life choices made by separated fraternal twins are not as dramatically similar as those made by separated identical twins.

Biological Versus Adoptive Relatives

The separated twin studies control heredity while varying environment. Nature's second type of real-life experiment—adoption—controls environment while varying heredity. Adoption creates two groups of relatives: genetic (biological parents and siblings) and environmental (adoptive parents and siblings). For any given trait we study, we can therefore ask three questions:

- How much do adopted children resemble their biological parents, who contributed their genes?
- How much do they resemble their adoptive parents, who contribute a home environment?
- While sharing a home environment, do adopted siblings also come to share traits?

By providing children with loving, nurturing homes, adoption matters. Yet researchers asking these questions about *personality* agree on one stunning finding. Studies of hundreds of adoptive families show that non-twin siblings who grow up together, whether biologically related or not, do not much resemble one another in personality (McGue & Bouchard, 1998; Plomin & others, 1998; Rowe, 1990). In traits such as outgoingness and agreeableness, adoptees are more similar to their biological parents than to their caregiving adoptive parents. This heredity effect shows up in macaque monkeys' personalities as well (Maestripieri, 2003).

In the pages to come, twin and adoption study results will shed light on how nature and nurture influence intelligence, disordered behavior, and many other traits.

---

1. Actually, this description of the two Jims errs in one respect: Jim Lewis named his son James Alan. Jim Springer named his James Allan.

1. Developmental psychologists tend to focus on three major issues. Which of the following is NOT one of those issues?

   a. Nature and nurture
   b. Reflexes and unlearned behaviors
   c. Stability and change
   d. Continuity and stages

2. The first two weeks of prenatal development, the period of the _____, is a time of rapid cell division. The period of the _____ lasts from 9 weeks after conception until birth.

   a. zygote; embryo
   b. zygote; fetus
   c. embryo; fetus
   d. fetus; embryo

3. Teratogens are agents that pass through the placenta's screen and may harm an embryo or fetus. Which of the following is a known teratogen?

   a. Oxygen   c. Alcohol
   b. Sugar   d. Onions

4. From the very first weeks of life, some infants are intense and anxious, while others are easygoing and relaxed. These differences are usually explained as differences in

   a. automatic reflex responses.
   b. diet.
   c. temperament.
   d. parental responsiveness.

5. Adoption studies seek to understand genetic influences on personality. They do this mainly by

   a. comparing adopted children with non-adopted children.
   b. evaluating whether the personalities of adopted children more closely resemble the personalities of their adoptive parents or their biological parents.
   c. studying the effect of prior neglect on adopted children.
   d. studying the effect of one's age at adoption.

Answers: 1. b, 2. b, 3. c, 4. c, 5. b.

Infancy and Childhood

During infancy, a baby grows from newborn to toddler, and during childhood from toddler to teenager. We all traveled this path, with its physical, cognitive, and social milestones.

As a flower unfolds in accord with its genetic instructions, so did we, in the orderly biological growth process called **maturation.** Maturation dictates much of our shared path. We stand before we walk. We use nouns before adjectives. Some experiences, such as severe deprivation or abuse, can throw us off our path and slow development. Others, such as having caretakers who talk and read to us, can speed us on our way. Maturation (nature) sets the basic course of development; experience (nurture) adjusts it. Once again, we see genes and scene interacting.

Physical Development

5: How do the brain and motor skills develop during infancy and childhood?

Brain Development

In your mother's womb, your developing brain formed nerve cells at the explosive rate of nearly one-quarter million per *minute*. This brain-cell production line was so efficient that you arrived in the world with most of the brain cells you would ever have—or need. However, the wiring among these cells—your nervous system—was immature. After birth, these neural networks had a wild growth

> "It is a rare privilege to watch the birth, growth, and first feeble struggles of a living human mind."
>
> Annie Sullivan, in Helen Keller's *The Story of My Life*, 1903

"This is the path to adulthood. You're here."

spurt, branching and linking in patterns that would eventually enable you to walk, talk, and remember.

From ages 3 to 6, the most rapid brain growth was in your frontal lobes, the seat of rational planning. The frontal lobes continue developing into adolescence and beyond. The association areas—those linked with thinking, memory, and language—are the last to develop. As they do, mental abilities surge (Chugani & Phelps, 1986; Thatcher & others, 1987).

Neural pathways supporting language and agility continue their rapid growth into puberty. Then, a use-it-or-lose-it *pruning process* shuts down unused links and strengthens others (Paus & others, 1999; Thompson & others, 2000).

Our genes lay down the basic design of our brain, but experience directs the construction. Mark Rosenzweig and David Krech showed how early experiences leave their "marks" in the brain. They separated young rats into two groups. Rats in one group lived alone, with little to interest or distract them. The other rats shared a cage, complete with objects and activities that might exist in a natural "rat world" **(FIGURE 3.6).** The enriched environment made a difference. Those rats developed a heavier and thicker brain cortex (Rosenzweig, 1984; Renner & Rosenzweig, 1987).

This effect was so great that if you viewed brief video clips of rats, you could tell from their activity and curiosity

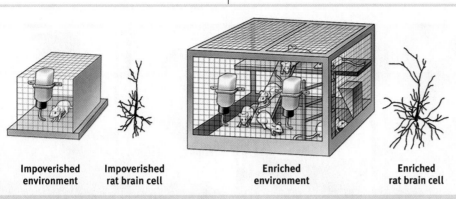

Figure 3.6> Experience affects brain development Mark Rosenzweig and his colleagues reared rats either alone in an environment without playthings, or with others in an environment enriched with playthings changed daily. In 14 of 16 repetitions of this experiment, rats in the enriched environment developed significantly more cerebral cortex (relative to the rest of the brain's tissue) than did those raised in an impoverished environment.

Impoverished environment   Impoverished rat brain cell   Enriched environment   Enriched rat brain cell

whether the rats had lived in solitary confinement or the enriched setting (Renner & Renner, 1993). After 60 days in an enriched environment, some rats' brain weight increased 7 to 10 percent. The number of synapses, forming the networks between the cells (see Figure 3.6), mushroomed by about 20 percent (Kolb & Whishaw, 1998).

Stringing the circuits young :: String musicians who started playing before age 12 have larger and more complex neural circuits controlling the note-making left-hand fingers than do string musicians whose training started later (Elbert & others, 1995).

Courtesy of C. Brune

Touching or massaging infant rats and premature babies has similar benefits (Field, 2001; Field & others, 2004). Neonatal intensive care units now know that massaging premature human infants helps them develop faster neurologically and gain weight more rapidly. And that means they can go home sooner.

Nature and nurture together sculpt our synapses. Brain maturation provides us with an abundance of neural connections. Experience—sights and smells, touches and tugs—activate and strengthen some neural pathways while others weaken from disuse. Similar to pathways through a forest, less-traveled paths gradually disappear and popular paths are broadened.

During early childhood—while excess connections are still on call—youngsters can most easily master such skills as the grammar and accent of another language. But we seem to have a **critical period** for some skills. Lacking any exposure to written or signed language before adolescence, a person will never master any language (see Chapter 8). Likewise, lacking visual experience during the early years, people whose vision is restored by cataract removal will never achieve

normal perceptions (see Chapter 5). In the pruning process, the brain cells normally assigned to vision have died or been diverted to other uses. For us to have optimum brain development, normal stimulation during the early years is critical. The maturing brain seems governed by a rule: Use it or lose it.

The brain's development does not, however, end with childhood. Throughout life, whether we are learning to type or skateboard, we perform with increasing skill as experience sculpts the neural tissue we were born with.

Motor Development

As their muscles and nervous system mature, infants begin to control their movements. With occasional exceptions, the sequence of physical (motor) development is universal. Babies sit unsupported before they crawl, and they walk before they run (**FIGURE 3.7** on the next page).

Heredity plays a major role in motor development. Identical twins typically begin sitting up and walking on nearly the same day (Wilson, 1979). The rapid development of the cerebellum (at the back of the brain; see Chapter 2) helps create our eagerness to walk at about age 1. Experience before that time has a limited effect. This is also true for other physical skills, including bowel and bladder control. If a child's muscles and brain have not yet matured, no amount of pleading or punishment will produce successful toilet training.

maturation biological growth processes leading to orderly changes in behavior, independent of experience.

critical period a period early in life when exposure to certain stimuli or experiences is needed for proper development.

Figure 3.7> Physical development :: Sit, crawl, walk, run—the sequence of these events is the same the world over. In the United States, 25 percent of all babies walk by age 11 months, 50 percent within a week after their first birthday, and 90 percent by age 15 months (Frankenburg & others, 1992). Depending on the culture, babies may reach these milestones sooner or later, but the *sequence* doesn't vary.

Cognitive Development

6: How did Piaget view the development of a child's mind, and how do current researchers' views differ?

"Who knows the thoughts of a child?" wondered poet Nora Perry. Developmental psychologists are more likely to ask, "How *can* we know the thoughts of a child?" To see how psychologists study learning in very young children, consider a surprise discovery made in 1965 by Carolyn Rovee-Collier, who was at that time finishing her doctoral work in psychology. She was also a new mom, whose colicky 2-month-old, Benjamin, could be calmed by moving a crib mobile. Weary of bonking the mobile, she strung a cloth ribbon connecting the mobile to Benjamin's foot. Soon, he was kicking his foot to move the mobile.

Thinking about her unintended home experiment, Rovee-Collier realized that, contrary to popular opinion in the 1960s, babies are capable of learning. To know for sure that little Benjamin wasn't just a whiz kid, Rovee-Collier had to repeat the experiment with other infants (Rovee-Collier, 1989, 1999). Sure enough, they, too, soon kicked more when linked to a mobile, both on the day of the experiment

and the day after. They had learned the link between moving legs and moving mobile. If, however, she hitched them to a different mobile the next day, the infants showed no learning. Their actions indicated that they remembered the original mobile and recognized the difference. Moreover, when tethered to a familiar mobile a month later, they remembered the association and again began kicking **(FIGURE 3.8).**

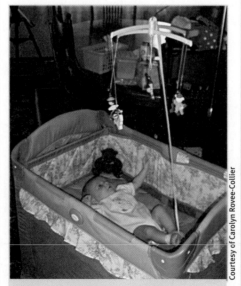

Figure 3.8> Developmental psychology in action (From Rovee-Collier, 1989, 1999.)

Jean Piaget (pronounced Pee-ah-ZHAY) spent a half-century doing as Rovee-Collier did—studying how a child's mind develops. Thanks partly to Piaget's work, we now understand that a child's mind is not a miniature model of an adult's. Children reason *differently*, in "wildly illogical ways about problems whose solutions are self-evident to adults" (Brainerd, 1996).

Piaget's interest began in 1920, when he was developing questions for children's

Jean Piaget (1896–1980) :: "If we examine the intellectual development of the individual or of the whole of humanity, we shall find that the human spirit goes through a certain number of stages, each different from the other" (1930).

Both photos: Courtesy Judy DeLoache

Figure 3.9> Scale errors Children age 18 to 30 months may fail to take the size of an object into account when trying to perform impossible actions with it. At left, a 21-month-old attempts to slide down a miniature slide. At right, a 24-month-old opens the door to a miniature car and tries to step inside (DeLoache, Uttal, & Rosengren, 2004).

intelligence tests in Paris. Looking over the test results, Piaget noticed something interesting. At certain ages, children made strikingly similar mistakes. Where others saw childish mistakes, Piaget saw intelligence at work.

Decades of observation convinced Piaget that a child's mind develops through a series of stages. This upward march begins with the newborn's simple reflexes, and ends with the adult's abstract reasoning power. Moving through these stages is like climbing a ladder. We can't easily move to a higher rung without first having a firm footing on the one below. Tools for thinking and reasoning differ in each stage. Thus, we can tell an 8-year-old that "getting an idea is like having a light turn on in your head," and the child

will understand. A 2-year-old won't get the analogy. Nor will she understand that a miniature slide is too small for sliding, or that a miniature car is much too small to get into **(FIGURE 3.9)**. But our adult minds likewise can reason in ways that 8-year-olds won't understand.

Piaget believed that the force driving us up this intellectual ladder is our struggle to make sense of our experiences. His core idea is that "children are active thinkers, constantly trying to construct more advanced understandings of the world" (Siegler & Ellis, 1996). Part of this active thinking is building **schemas,** concepts or mental molds into which we pour our experiences. By adulthood we have built countless schemas, ranging from what a dog is to what love is.

Let's stop now and look more closely at Piaget's stages. We'll examine them in the light of our current understandings about the development of **cognition**—all the mental activities associated with thinking, knowing, remembering, and communicating.

Piaget's Theory and Current Thinking

Piaget believed that children construct their understanding of the world from interactions with it. Their minds go through spurts of change, followed by times of stability as they move from one level to the next. The four stages Piaget proposed are summarized in **TABLE 3.1.**

schema a concept or framework that organizes and interprets information.

cognition all the mental activities associated with thinking, knowing, remembering, and communicating.

Milt and Patti Putnam/Corbis

Pretend play

Table 3.1	Piaget's Stages of Cognitive Development	
Typical Age Range	**Stage and Description**	**New Developments**
Birth to nearly 2 years	*Sensorimotor* Experiencing the world through senses and actions (looking, hearing, touching, mouthing, and grasping)	▪ Object permanence ▪ Stranger anxiety
2 to about 6 or 7 years	*Preoperational* Representing things with words and images; using intuitive rather than logical reasoning	▪ Pretend play ▪ Egocentrism
About 7 to 11 years	*Concrete operational* Thinking logically about concrete events; grasping concrete analogies and performing arithmetical operations	▪ Conservation ▪ Mathematical transformations
About 12 through adulthood	*Formal operational* Reasoning abstractly	▪ Abstract logic ▪ Potential for mature moral reasoning

Sensorimotor Stage The **sensorimotor stage** begins at birth and lasts to nearly age 2. In this stage, babies take in the world through their senses and actions—through looking, hearing, touching, mouthing, and grasping.

Very young babies seem to live in the present: Out of sight is out of mind. In one test, Piaget showed an infant an appealing toy and then flopped his hat over it. Before the age of 6 months, the infant acted as if the toy no longer existed. Such very young infants lack **object permanence**—the awareness that objects continue to exist when out of sight (FIGURE 3.10). By about 8 months, infants begin to show that they do remember things they can no longer see. If you hide a toy, an 8-month-old will momentarily look for it. Within another month or two, the infant will look for it even after several seconds have passed.

So does object permanence in fact blossom at 8 months, much as tulips blossom in spring? Today's researchers don't think it does. They believe object permanence unfolds gradually, and they view development as more continuous than Piaget did. They also think that young children are more competent than Piaget and his followers believed. For example, babies seem to have an inborn grasp of simple physics. Like adults staring in disbelief at a magic trick (the "Whoa!" look), infants look longer at an unexpected scene of a car seeming to pass through a solid object. They also stare longer at a ball stopping in midair, or at an object that seems to magically disappear (Baillargeon, 1995, 1998, 2004; Wellman & Gelman, 1992).

Preoperational Stage Piaget believed that until about age 6 or 7, children are in a **preoperational stage**—too young to perform mental operations (such as imagining an action and its reversible results). Consider a 5-year-old, who objects that there is too much milk in a tall, narrow glass. "Too much" may become an acceptable amount if you pour that milk into a short, wide glass. The child, focusing only on the height dimension, cannot perform the operation of mentally pouring the milk back. This happens because young children—younger than about age 6, said Piaget—lack the concept of **conservation**—the idea that quantity remains the same even if it changes shape (FIGURE 3.11).

A child who can perform mental operations can think in symbols and therefore begins to enjoy *pretend play*. Contemporary researchers have discovered that symbolic thinking appears at an earlier age than Piaget supposed. One researcher showed children a model of a room and hid a model toy in it (a miniature stuffed dog behind a miniature couch) (DeLoache & Brown, 1987). The 2½-year-olds easily remembered where to find the miniature toy in the model. But that knowledge didn't transfer to the real world. They could not use the model to locate an actual stuffed dog behind a couch in a real room. Three-year-olds—only 6 months older—usually went right to the actual stuffed animal in the real room, showing they *could* think of the model as a symbol for the room. Piaget did not view the change from one stage to another as an abrupt shift. But he probably would have been surprised to see symbolic thinking at such a young age.

Egocentrism. Piaget also believed that pre-school children are **egocentric:** They have difficulty imagining things from another's point of view. Asked to "show Mommy your picture," 2-year-old Gabriella holds the picture up facing her own eyes. Told to hide, 3-year-old Gray puts his hands over his eyes, assuming that if he can't see you, you can't see him.

Contemporary research supports preschoolers' egocentrism. This is helpful information when a TV-watching pre-schooler blocks your view of the screen. The child probably assumes that you see what she sees. At this age, children simply are not yet able to take another's viewpoint. Even we adults may overestimate the extent to which others share our views. Have you ever mistakenly assumed that something would be clear to a friend because it was clear to you? Or sent an e-mail mistakenly thinking that the receiver would "hear" your "just kidding" intent (Epley & others, 2004; Kruger & others, 2005)? Children are even more susceptible to this thinking error.

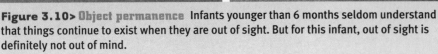

Figure 3.10> Object permanence Infants younger than 6 months seldom understand that things continue to exist when they are out of sight. But for this infant, out of sight is definitely not out of mind.

Doug Goodman

Figure 3.11> Piaget's test of conservation This preoperational child does not yet understand the principle of conservation of volume. When the milk is poured into a tall, narrow glass, it suddenly seems like "more" than when it was in the shorter, wider glass. In another year or so, she will understand that the volume stays the same even though it looks different.

Family Circus ® Bil Keane

©Bil Keane, Inc. Reprinted with special permission of King Features Syndicate.

*"Don't you remember, Grandma?
You were in it with me."*

Theory of Mind. When Little Red Riding Hood realizes her "grandmother" is really a wolf, she swiftly revises her ideas about the creature's intentions and races away. Preschoolers, although still egocentric, develop this ability to read others' mental states when they begin forming a **theory of mind.**

When children can imagine another person's viewpoint, all sorts of new skills emerge. They can tease, because they now understand what makes a playmate angry. They may be able to convince a sibling to share. Knowing what might make a parent buy a toy, they may try to persuade.

Between about 3½ and 4½, children worldwide use their new theory-of-mind

skills to realize that others may hold *false* beliefs (Callaghan & others, 2005; Sabbagh & others, 2006). Researchers illustrated this by asking preschoolers to tell them what was inside a Band Aids box (Jenkins & Astington, 1996). Expecting Band Aids, the children were surprised to see that the box actually contained pencils. Then came the theory-of-mind question. Asked what a child who had never seen the box would think was inside, 3-

year-olds typically answered "pencils." By age 4 to 5, children knew better. They anticipated their friends' false belief that the box would hold Band Aids.

Children with **autism** have an impaired theory of mind (Klein & Kihlstrom,

Autism :: For reasons still debated, autism diagnoses have been increasing in recent years. Both of Bobbie Gallagher's children were diagnosed with autism, which is marked by deficient social communication and difficulty in grasping others' states of mind.

sensorimotor stage in Piaget's theory, the stage (from birth to about 2 years of age) during which infants know the world mostly in terms of their sensory impressions and motor activities.

object permanence the awareness that things continue to exist even when not perceived.

preoperational stage in Piaget's theory, the stage (from about 2 to 6 or 7 years of age) during which a child learns to use language but does not yet comprehend the mental operations of concrete logic.

conservation the principle (which Piaget believed to be a part of concrete operational reasoning) that properties such as mass, volume, and number remain the same despite changes in the forms of objects.

egocentrism in Piaget's theory, the preoperational child's difficulty taking another's point of view.

theory of mind people's ideas about their own and others' mental states—about their feelings, perceptions, and thoughts, and the behaviors these might predict.

autism a disorder that appears in childhood and is marked by deficient communication, social interaction, and understanding of others' states of mind.

1998; Yirmiya & others, 1998). They have difficulty reading other people's thoughts and feelings. Most children learn that another child's pouting mouth signals sadness, and that twinkling eyes mean happiness or mischief. A child with autism fails to understand these signals (Frith & Frith, 2001). The underlying cause seems to be poor communication among brain regions that normally work together to let us take another's viewpoint. This effect appears to result from an unknown number of autism-related genes interacting with the environment (Blakeslee, 2005; Wickelgren, 2005).

Concrete Operational Stage By about 6 or 7 years of age, said Piaget, children enter the **concrete operational stage.** Given concrete materials, they begin to grasp conservation. Understanding that change in form does not mean change in quantity, they can mentally pour milk back and forth between glasses of different shapes. They also enjoy jokes that allow them to use this new understanding:

> Mr. Jones went into a restaurant and ordered a whole pizza for his dinner. When the waiter asked if he wanted it cut into 6 or 8 pieces, Mr. Jones said, "Oh, you'd better make it 6, I could never eat 8 pieces!" (McGhee, 1976)

Piaget believed that during the concrete operational stage, children fully gain the mental ability to understand simple math and conservation. When my daughter Laura was 6, I was astonished at her inability to reverse simple arithmetic. Asked, "What is 8 plus 4?" she required 5 seconds to compute "12," and another 5 seconds to then compute 12 minus 4. By age 8, she could answer a reversed question instantly.

As Piaget was forming his theory of stages of cognitive development, Russian psychologist Lev Vygotsky was also absorbed in how children think and learn. He noted that by age 7, children are more and more able to think in words and to use words to work out solutions to problems. They do this, he said, by no longer thinking aloud. Instead they internalize their culture's language and rely on inner speech. Parents who say "No, no!" when

Lev Vygotsky (1895–1934) :: Vygotsky, pictured here with his daughter, was a Russian developmental psychologist. He studied how children's minds feed on the language of social interaction.

James V. Wertsch/Washington University

pulling a child's hand away from a cake are giving the child a self-control tool. When the child later needs to resist temptation, he may likewise say "No!"

Talking to themselves, whether out loud or inside their heads, helps children control their behavior and emotions and master new skills. And when parents give children words, they provide, said Vygotsky, a *scaffold* upon which children can step to higher levels of thinking.

Formal Operational Stage By age 12, said Piaget, our reasoning expands to include abstract thinking. We are no longer limited to purely concrete reasoning, based on actual experience. As children approach adolescence, many become capable of *if . . . then* thinking. They can solve hypothetical propositions and deduce consequences. *If* this happens, *then* that will happen. Piaget called this new systematic reasoning ability **formal operational** thinking. (Stay tuned for more about adolescents' thinking abilities later in this chapter.)

Reflecting on Piaget's Theory What remains of Piaget's ideas about the child's mind? Plenty—enough to merit his being singled out by *Time* magazine as one of the last century's 20 most influential scientists and thinkers, and to be rated in a survey of British psychologists as the

greatest twentieth-century psychologist (*Psychologist,* 2003). Piaget identified significant cognitive milestones and stimulated worldwide interest in how the mind develops. His emphasis was less on the ages at which children typically reach specific milestones than on their sequence. Studies around the globe, from aboriginal Australia to Algeria to North America, have confirmed that human cognition unfolds basically in the sequence Piaget described (Lourenco & Machado, 1996; Segall & others, 1990).

Although today's researchers see development as more continuous than did Piaget, his insights can help teachers and parents understand young children. We will all be happier if we remember that young children cannot think with adult logic and cannot take another's viewpoint. What seems simple and obvious to us—getting off a teeter-totter will cause a friend on the other end to crash—may never occur to a 3-year-old. We should also remember that children are not empty containers waiting to be filled with knowledge. By building on what children already know, we can engage them in concrete demonstrations and stimulate them to think for themselves. And finally, psychologists remind us, we should realize that children's cognitive immaturity is adaptive (Bjorklund & Green, 1992). It is nature's strategy for keeping children close to protective adults and providing time for learning and socialization.

Social Development

7: How do the bonds of attachment form between parents and infants?

From birth, babies all over the world are social creatures, developing an intense bond with their caregivers. Infants come to prefer familiar faces and voices, then to coo and gurgle when given their mother's or father's attention. Soon after object permanence emerges and children become mobile, a curious thing happens. At about 8 months, they develop **stranger anxiety.** They may greet strangers by crying and reaching for familiar caregivers.

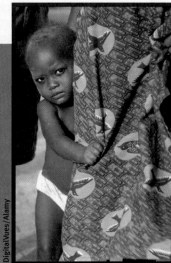

"No! Don't leave me!" their distress seems to say. At about this age, children have schemas for familiar faces—mental images of how caretakers should look. When the new face does not fit into one of these remembered images, they become distressed (Kagan, 1984). Once again, we see an important principle: *The brain, mind, and social-emotional behavior develop together.*

At 12 months, many infants cling tightly to a parent when they are frightened or expect separation. Reunited after being apart, they shower the parent with smiles and hugs. No social behavior is more striking than this intense and mutual infant-parent bond.

Origins of Attachment

The **attachment** bond is a powerful survival impulse that keeps infants close to their caregivers. Infants become attached to people—typically their parents—who are comfortable and familiar. For many years, psychologists reasoned that infants grew attached to those who satisfied their need for nourishment. It made sense. But an accidental finding—which forms another of psychology's fascinating stories—overturned this idea.

During the 1950s, University of Wisconsin psychologists Harry Harlow and Margaret Harlow bred monkeys for their learning studies. They separated the in-

fant monkeys from their mothers shortly after birth. To isolate them from diseases and ensure they were treated equally, each infant was put into a sanitary individual cage with a cheesecloth baby blanket (Harlow & others, 1971). Then came a surprise: When their blankets were taken to be laundered, the monkeys became distressed.

Imagine yourself as one of the Harlows, trying to figure out why the monkey infants were so intensely attached to their blankets. Remember, at the time, psychologists believed that infants became attached to those who nourish them. How could you test the idea that comfort might be the key? To pit the drawing power of a food source against the contact comfort of the blanket, the Harlows created two artificial mothers. One was a bare wire cylinder with a wooden head and an attached feeding bottle. The other was a cylinder wrapped with terry cloth.

For the monkeys, it was no contest. They overwhelmingly preferred the comfy cloth mother **(FIGURE 3.12)**. Like other infants clinging to their live mothers, the monkey babies would cling to their cloth mothers when anxious. When exploring their environment, they used her as a *secure base*, acting as though they were attached to her by an invisible elastic band that stretched only so far before

Figure 3.12> The Harlows' mothers The Harlows' infant monkeys much preferred contact with a comfortable cloth mother, even while feeding from a wire nourishing mother.

concrete operational stage in Piaget's theory, the stage of cognitive development (from about 6 or 7 to 11 years of age) during which children gain the mental operations that enable them to think logically about concrete events.

formal operational stage in Piaget's theory, the stage of cognitive development (normally beginning about age 12) during which people begin to think logically about abstract concepts.

stranger anxiety the fear of strangers that infants commonly display, beginning by about 8 months of age.

attachment an emotional tie with another person; shown in young children by their seeking closeness to the caregiver, and showing distress on separation.

pulling them back. Researchers soon learned that other qualities—rocking, warmth, and feeding—made the cloth mother even more appealing.

Human infants, too, become attached to parents who are soft and warm and who rock, feed, and pat. Much parent-infant emotional communication occurs via touch (Hertenstein, 2002), which can be either soothing (snuggles) or arousing (tickles). The human parent also provides a safe haven for a distressed child and a secure base from which to explore.

As we mature, our secure base and safe haven shift—from parents to peers and partners (Cassidy & Shaver, 1999). But at all ages we are social creatures. We gain strength when someone offers, by words and actions, a safe haven: "I will be here. I am interested in you. Come what may, I will actively support you" (Crowell & Waters, 1994).

Attachment Differences

What accounts for children's attachment differences? Trying to answer this question, Mary Ainsworth (1979) designed the *strange situation* experiment. She observed mother-infant pairs at home during their first six months. Later she observed the 1-year-old infants in a strange situation (usually a laboratory playroom) without their mothers. Such research shows that about 60 percent of infants display *secure attachment*. In their mother's presence, they play comfortably, happily exploring their new environment. When she leaves, they become upset. When she returns, they seek contact with her.

Other infants show *insecure attachment*, marked either by *anxiety* or *avoidance* of trusting relationships. They are less likely to explore their surroundings. They may even cling to their mother. When she leaves, some cry loudly and remain upset. Others seem not to notice or care about her departure and return (Ainsworth, 1973, 1989; Kagan, 1995; van IJzendoorn & Kroonenberg, 1988).

Ainsworth (1979) found that sensitive, responsive mothers—those who noticed what their babies were doing and responded appropriately—had infants who were securely attached. Insensitive, unresponsive mothers—mothers who attended to their babies when they felt like doing so but ignored them at other times—often had infants who were insecurely attached. The Harlows' monkey studies, with unresponsive artificial mothers, produced even more striking effects. When put in strange situations without their artificial mothers, the deprived infants were terrified **(FIGURE 3.13)**.

But is attachment style entirely the result of parenting? Or is attachment style also affected by our genetically influenced temperament? As we saw earlier in this chapter, some babies are, from the time of their birth, noticeably *difficult*—irritable, intense, and unpredictable. Others are *easy*—cheerful, relaxed, and feeding and sleeping on predictable schedules (Chess & Thomas, 1987). By neglecting such inborn differences, chides Judith Harris (1998), the parenting studies are like "comparing foxhounds reared in kennels with poodles reared in apartments." So, to separate nature and nurture, we would need to vary parenting while controlling temperament. (Pause and think: If you were a researcher, how might you do this?)

One researcher's solution was to randomly assign 100 temperamentally difficult infants to two groups. Half of the 6- to 9-month-olds were in the experimental group, in which mothers received personal training in sensitive responding. The other half were in a control group, in

Figure 3.13> Social deprivation and fear In the Harlows' experiments, monkeys raised with artificial mothers were terror-stricken when placed in strange situations without those mothers.

© Barry Hewlett

Father care :: Although "fathering a child" has meant impregnating and "mothering a child" has meant nurturing, fathers are not just mobile sperm banks. Across nearly 100 studies worldwide, father love has correlated with their offspring's health and well-being comparable to mother love (Rohner & Veneziano, 2001). Among the Aka people of Central Africa, fathers form an especially close bond with their infants and may be found holding or within reach of their babies 47 percent of the time (Hewlett, 1991).

which mothers did not receive this training (van den Boom, 1990). At 12 months of age, 68 percent of the infants in the first group were rated securely attached. Only 28 percent of the infants in the control group received this rating. Other studies support the idea that such programs can increase parental sensitivity and, to a lesser extent, infant attachment security (Bakermans-Kranenburg & others, 2003).

Whether children live with one parent or two, are cared for at home or in a day-care center, live in North America, Guatemala, or the Kalahari Desert, their anxiety over separation from parents peaks at around 13 months, then gradually declines **(FIGURE 3.14)**. As the power of early attachment relaxes, we begin to move out into a wider range of situations, communicate with strangers more freely, and stay attached emotionally to loved ones despite distance.

This made sense to developmental theorist Erik Erikson (1902–1994), who worked in collaboration with his wife, Joan Erikson. He believed that securely attached

Harlow Primate Laboratory, University of Wisconsin

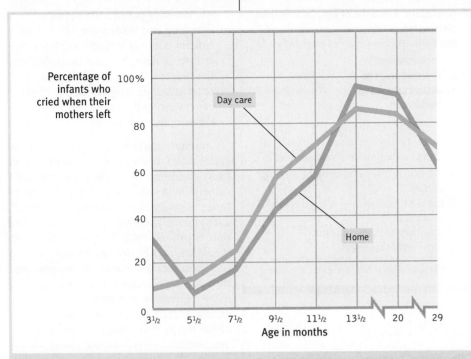

Percentage of infants who cried when their mothers left

Figure 3.14> Infants' distress over separation from parents In an experiment, two groups of infants were left by their mothers in an unfamiliar room. In both groups, the percentage who cried when the mother left peaked at about 13 months (from Kagan, 1976). Whether the infant had experienced day care made little difference.

children approach life with a sense of **basic trust**—a sense that the world is predictable and reliable. The Eriksons believed this lifelong attitude of trust rather than fear flows from children's interactions with sensitive, loving caregivers.

Our adult styles of romantic love likewise exhibit either secure, trusting attachment; insecure, anxious attachment; or the avoidance of attachment (Feeney & Noller, 1990; Mikulincer & Shaver, 2005; Rholes & Simpson, 2004). Although debate continues, many researchers now believe that our early attachments form the foundation for our adult relationships (Fraley, 2002).

Deprivation of Attachment

If secure attachment nurtures social competence, what happens when circumstances prevent a child from forming attachments? In all of psychology, there is no sadder research literature. Some of these babies were reared in institutions without the stimulation and attention of a regular caregiver. Others were locked away at home under conditions of abuse or extreme neglect. Most were withdrawn, frightened, even speechless. Those abandoned in Romanian orphanages during the 1980s looked "frighteningly like Harlow's monkeys" (Carlson, 1995). If institutionalized more than 8 months, they often bore lasting emotional scars (Chisholm, 1998; Malinosky-Rummell & Hansen, 1993; Rutter & others, 1998).

Harlow's monkeys bore similar scars if reared in total isolation, without even an artificial mother. As adults, when placed with other monkeys their age, they either cowered in fright or lashed out in aggression. When they reached sexual maturity, most were incapable of mating. Females who did have babies were often neglectful, abusive, even murderous toward them. In humans, too, the unloved sometimes become the

unloving. Some 30 percent of those who have been abused do later abuse their own children. This is four times the U.S. national rate of child abuse (Kaufman & Zigler, 1987; Widom, 1989a, b).

Extreme childhood trauma can leave footprints on the brain. Normally placid golden hamsters that are repeatedly threatened and attacked while young grow up to be cowards when caged with same-sized hamsters, or bullies when caged with weaker ones (Ferris, 1996). Young children who are terrorized through physical abuse or wartime atrocities (being beaten, witnessing torture, and living in constant fear) often suffer other lasting wounds—nightmares, depression, and an adolescence troubled by substance abuse, binge eating, or aggression (Kendall-Tackett & others, 1993; Polusny & Follette, 1995; Trickett & McBride-Chang, 1995). Child sexual abuse, especially if severe and prolonged, places children at increased risk for health problems, psychological disorders, substance abuse, and criminality (Freyd & others, 2005; Tyler, 2002).

It is true that most abusive parents—and many condemned murderers—were indeed abused. But it is also true that most children growing up in harsh conditions don't become violent criminals or abusive parents. They show great resilience and somehow go on to lead a better life.

6. The orderly biological growth process called maturation explains why
   a. children need training to learn bowel and bladder control.
   b. most children begin walking by about 12 to 15 months.
   c. enriching experiences may affect brain tissue.
   d. boys walk before they crawl.

basic trust according to Erik Erikson, a sense that the world is predictable and trustworthy; said to be formed during infancy by appropriate experiences with responsive caregivers.

7. Researchers raised some rats in an enriched environment and others in a deprived environment with no objects or activities to stimulate them. At the end of the experiment,

   a. the brains of the rats living in the enriched environment developed a heavier, denser cortex.

   b. the brains of the deprived rats developed a heavier, denser cortex.

   c. the brains of the two groups of rats showed no differences.

   d. the rats living in the deprived environment experienced a critical period.

8. As the infant's muscles and nervous system mature, more complicated skills emerge. Which of the following is true of motor-skill development?

   a. It is determined ONLY by genetic factors.

   b. The sequence is universal.

   c. The timing is universal.

   d. Environment determines maturation of muscles and nerves.

9. Piaget's preoperational stage extends from about age 2 to 6. During this period, the young child's thinking is

   a. abstract.

   b. negative.

   c. conservative.

   d. egocentric.

10. The principle of conservation explains why a pint of milk remains a pint, whether we pour it into a tall, thin pitcher or a low, wide one. Children gain the mental ability to understand conservation during the

   a. sensorimotor stage.

   b. preoperational stage.

   c. concrete operational stage.

   d. formal operational stage.

11. Piaget's theory of cognitive development has enriched our understanding of how children think. However, many researchers believe that

   a. development is more continuous than Piaget realized.

   b. children do not progress as rapidly as Piaget predicted.

   c. few children ever reach the concrete operational stage.

   d. there is no way of testing much of Piaget's theoretical work.

12. After about 8 months of age, infants show distress when faced with a new babysitter. Their response is an example of

   a. conservation.

   b. stranger anxiety.

   c. abstract thinking.

   d. maturation.

13. In a series of experiments, the Harlows found that monkeys raised with artificial mothers tended, when afraid, to cling to

   a. the wire mother who held the feeding bottle.

   b. the cloth mother who offered comfortable contact.

   c. only their real, live mother.

   d. other infant monkeys.

Answers: 6. b, 7. a, 8. b, 9. d, 10. c, 11. a, 12. b, 13. b.

Parents and Peers

8: To what extent are our lives shaped by parental and peer influences?

In procreation, a woman and a man shuffle their gene decks and deal a life-forming hand to their child-to-be, who is then subjected to countless influences beyond their control. One of these forces is the influence of the family and culture the child is born into. Another is the influence of peer interaction.

Parent Influence

Child-rearing practices vary. Some parents spank, some reason. Some are strict, some are lax. Some show little affection, some liberally hug and kiss. Do such differences affect children?

Parenting Styles

Investigators have identified three parenting styles:

1. *Authoritarian* parents impose rules and expect obedience: "Don't interrupt." "Keep your room clean." "Don't stay out late or you'll be grounded." "Why? Because I said so."

2. *Permissive* parents submit to their children's desires, make few demands, and use little punishment.

3. *Authoritative* parents are both demanding and responsive. They exert control not only by setting rules and enforcing them but also by explaining the reasons. And, especially with older children, they encourage open discussion and allow exceptions when making the rules.

Too hard, too soft, and just right, these styles have been called. Studies reveal that children with the highest self-esteem, self-reliance, and social competence usually have warm, concerned, *authoritative* parents (Baumrind, 1996; Buri & others, 1988; Coopersmith, 1967). Those with authoritarian parents tend to have less social skill and self-esteem, and those with permissive parents tend to be more aggressive and immature. But parenting doesn't happen in a vacuum. One of the forces that influences parents' values and behaviors is their culture.

A word of caution: *Correlation is not causation.* The association between certain parenting styles (being firm but open) and certain childhood outcomes (social competence) is correlational. Perhaps you can imagine other possible explanations for this parenting-competence link.

Culture and Child-Rearing

Culture is the set of behaviors, attitudes, values, and traditions shared by a group of people and transmitted from one generation to the next (Brislin, 1988). In Chapter 4, we'll explore the effects of culture on gender. In later chapters we'll consider the influence of culture on psychological disorders and social interactions. For now, let's look at the way that child-rearing practices reflect cultural values.

Cultural values vary from place to place and, even in the same place, from one time to another. Do you prefer children who are independent or children who comply with what others think? The Westernized culture of the United States today favors independence. "You are responsible for yourself," Western families and schools tell their children. "Follow

Cultures vary :: In Scotland's Orkney Islands' town of Stromness, social trust has enabled parents to park their toddlers outside shops.

Copyright Steve Reehl

brings honor to the family, brings honor to the self.

Children across place and time have thrived under various child-rearing systems. Upper-class British parents traditionally handed off routine caregiving to nannies, then sent their children off to boarding school at about age 10. These children generally grew up to be pillars of British society, just like their parents and their boarding-school peers. Sending children away would be shocking to an African Gusii family. Their babies nurse freely but spend most of the day on their mother's back, with lots of body contact but little face-to-face and language interaction. When the mother becomes pregnant, the toddler is weaned and handed over to someone else, often an older sibling. Westerners may wonder about the negative effects of the lack of verbal interaction, but then the African Gusii would in turn wonder about Western mothers pushing their babies around in strollers and leaving them in playpens and car seats (Small, 1997). Such diversity in child-rearing cautions us against presuming that our way is the only way to rear children successfully.

> **culture** the enduring behaviors, values, and traditions shared by a group of people and transmitted from one generation to the next.

your conscience. Be true to yourself. Discover your gifts. Think through your personal needs." But a half-century ago, Western cultural values placed greater priority on obedience, respect, and sensitivity to others (Alwin, 1990; Remley, 1988). "Be true to your traditions," parents then taught their children. "Be loyal to your heritage and country. Show respect toward your parents and other superiors." Cultures can change.

Many Asians and Africans live in cultures that value emotional closeness. Rather than being given their own bedrooms and entrusted to day care, infants and toddlers may sleep with their mothers and spend their days close to a family member (Morelli & others, 1992; Whiting & Edwards, 1988). These cultures encourage a strong sense of *family self*—a feeling that what shames the child shames the family, and what

Diverse Yet Alike

Parental involvement promotes development :: Parents in every culture facilitate their children's discovery of their world.

José Luis Pelaez, Inc./Corbis

Michael Newman/Photo Edit

How Much Credit (or Blame) Do Parents Deserve?

Parents usually feel enormous satisfaction in their children's successes, and guilt or shame over their failures. They beam over the child who wins an award. They wonder where they went wrong with the child repeatedly called into the principal's office. Freudian psychiatry and psychology have been among the sources of such ideas, by blaming problems from asthma to schizophrenia on "bad mothering." Society reinforces such parent-blaming. Believing that parents shape their offspring as a potter molds clay, people readily praise parents for their children's virtues and blame them for their children's vices.

But do parents really damage these future adults by being (take your pick from the toxic-parent lists) overbearing—or uninvolved? Pushy—or ineffectual? Overprotective—or distant? Are children really so easily wounded? If so, should we then blame our parents for our failings, and ourselves for our children's failings? Or does all the talk of wounding fragile children through normal parental mistakes trivialize the brutality of real abuse?

Parents do matter. The power of parenting is clearest at the extremes: the abused who become abusive, the neglected who become neglectful, the loved but firmly handled children who become self-confident and socially competent. The power of the family environment also

"So I blame you for everything—whose fault is that?"

appears in the remarkable academic and vocational successes of children of people who fled from Vietnam and Cambodia—successes attributed to close-knit, supportive, even demanding families (Caplan & others, 1992).

But how much does parenting matter? As twin and adoption studies show, shared environmental influences—including the home influences siblings share—typically account for less than 10 percent of children's personality differences. In the words of Robert Plomin and Denise Daniels (1987), "Two children in the same family [are on average] as different from one another as are pairs of children selected randomly from the population." To developmental psychologist Sandra Scarr (1993), this implies that "parents should be given less credit for kids who turn out great and blamed less for kids who don't." Knowing children are not easily sculpted by parental nurture, perhaps parents can relax a bit more and love their children for who they are.

Does this then mean that adoptive parenting is a fruitless venture? No. The genetic leash may limit the family environment's influence on personality, but parents do influence their children's attitudes, values, manners, faith, and politics (Brodzinsky & Schechter, 1990). A pair of adopted children or identical twins *will* have more similar religious beliefs, especially during adolescence, if reared together (Kelley & De Graaf, 1997; Koenig & others, 2005; Rohan & Zanna, 1996).

Child neglect, abuse, and parental divorce are rare in adoptive homes, in part because adoptive parents are carefully screened. Despite a somewhat greater risk of psychological disorder, most adopted children thrive, especially when adopted as infants (Benson & others, 1994; Wierzbicki, 1993). Seven in eight report feeling strongly attached to one or both adoptive parents. As children of self-giving parents, they themselves grow up to be more self-giving than average (Sharma & others, 1998). Many score higher than their biological parents on intelligence tests, and most grow into happier and more stable adults. Regardless of personality differences between parents and their adoptees, children benefit from adoption. Parenting matters!

Peer Influence

As children mature, what other experiences do the work of nurturing? At all ages, we are subject to group influences, as we seek to fit in with various groups (Harris, 1998):

- Preschoolers who reject a certain food despite parents' urgings often will eat the food if put at a table with a group of children who like it.

- A child who hears English spoken with one accent at home and another in the neighborhood and at school will invariably adopt the accent of the peers, not the parents.

- Teens who start smoking typically have friends who model smoking, suggest its pleasures, and offer cigarettes (Rose & others, 1999, 2003). Part of this peer similarity may result from a *selection effect,* as kids seek out peers with similar attitudes and interests. Those who smoke (or don't) may select as friends those who also smoke (or don't).

> "Men resemble the times more than they resemble their fathers."
>
> **Ancient Arab proverb**

Howard Gardner (1998) concludes that parents and peers are complementary:

> Parents are more important when it comes to education, discipline, responsibility, orderliness, charitableness, and ways of interacting with authority figures. Peers are more important for learning cooperation, for finding the road to popularity, for inventing styles of interaction among people of the same age. Youngsters may find their peers more interesting, but they will look to their parents when contemplating their own futures. Moreover, parents [often] choose the neighborhoods and schools that supply the peers.

Diverse Yet Alike

Peer power :: As we develop, we play, mate, and partner with peers. No wonder children and youths in varied cultures are sensitive and responsive to peer influences.

Ulana Swituucha/Alamy

Ole Graf/zefa/Corbis

The investment in raising a child buys many years not only of joy and love but of worry and irritation. Yet for most people who become parents, a child is one's biological and social legacy—one's personal investment in the human future. To paraphrase psychiatrist Carl Jung, we reach backward into our parents and forward into our children, and through their children into a future we will never see, but about which we must therefore care.

Thinking About Nature and Nurture

The unique gene combination created when our mother's egg engulfed our father's sperm helped form us, as individuals. Genes predispose both our shared humanity and our individual differences.

But it also is true that our experiences form us. In the womb, in our families, and in our peer social relationships, we learn ways of thinking and acting. Even differences initiated by our nature may be amplified by our nurture. We are not formed by nature or nurture, but by the interaction between them. Biological, psychological, and social-cultural forces interact during our development (FIGURE 3.15).

Mindful of how others differ from us, however, we often fail to notice the similarities stemming from our shared biology. Regardless of our culture, we humans share the same life cycle. We speak to our infants in similar ways and respond similarly to their coos and cries (Bornstein & others, 1992a,b). All over the world, the children of warm and supportive parents feel better about themselves and are less hostile than are the children of punishing and rejecting parents

(Rohner, 1986; Scott & others, 1991). Although Hispanic, Asian, Black, and White Americans differ in school achievement and delinquency, the differences are "no more than skin deep." To the extent that family structure, peer influences, and parental education predict behavior in one of these ethnic groups, they do so for the others as well. Compared with the person-to-person differences within groups, the differences between groups are small.

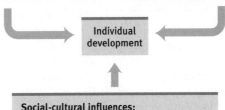

Biological influences:
• Shared human genome
• Individual genetic variations
• Prenatal environment

Psychological influences:
• Gene-environment interaction
• Neurological effect of early experiences
• Responses evoked by our own traits, etc.
• Beliefs, feelings, and expectations

Individual development

Social-cultural influences:
• Parental influences
• Peer influences
• Cultural emphasis on group or individual
• Chance events

Figure 3.15> The biopsychosocial approach to development

Adolescence

During **adolescence,** we morph from child to adult. Adolescence starts with a physical event—bodily changes that mark the beginning of sexual maturity. It ends with a social event—independent adult status.

Physical Development

9: What major physical changes occur during adolescence?

Adolescence begins with **puberty,** the time when we are maturing sexually. Puberty follows a surge of hormones, which may intensify moods. This outpouring of hormones triggers two years of rapid physical development, usually beginning at about age 11 in girls and at about age 13 in boys.

A girl's puberty starts with breast development, often beginning by age 10 (Brody, 1999). The first menstrual period, called **menarche** (meh-NAR-key), usually occurs within a year of age 12. Girls who have been prepared for menarche usually experience it as a positive event. As adults, most remember having had mixed feelings—pride, excitement, embarrassment, and a tinge of fear—in response to this important life transition (Greif & Ulman, 1982; Woods & others, 1983).

Most men similarly recall their first ejaculation (*spermarche*). This landmark event usually occurs as a nocturnal emission at about age 14 (Fuller & Downs, 1990).

Just as in the earlier life stages, we all go through the same *sequence* of changes in puberty. All girls, for example, develop breast buds and visible pubic hair before they have their first period. The timing of such changes is less predictable. Some girls start their growth spurt at 9, others as late as age 16. Maturing earlier or later than your peers has little effect on adult physical features, such as your final height. But it can have important psychological consequences. It is not only when we mature that counts, but how people react to our genetically influenced physical development. Remember: *Heredity and environment interact.* For boys, early maturation pays dividends: Being stronger and more athletic during their early teen years, they tend to be more popular, self-assured, and independent, though also more at risk for alcohol use and premature sexual activity (Steinberg & Morris, 2001). But for girls, early maturation can be stressful (Mendle & others, 2007). If a young girl's body is out of sync with her own emotional maturity and her friends' physical development and experiences, she may begin associating with older adolescents or may suffer teasing or sexual harassment.

Adolescents' brains are a work in progress. Frontal lobe maturation brings improved judgment, impulse control, and the ability to plan for the long term. But this maturation lags behind the emotional limbic system's development. When puberty's hormonal surge combines with limbic system development and unfinished frontal lobes, it's no wonder teens feel stressed. Impulsiveness, risky behaviors, and emotional storms— slamming doors and turning up the music—happen. Not yet fully equipped for making long-term plans and curbing impulses, young teens sometimes give in to the lure of smoking, which adult smokers could tell them they will later regret.

> "If a gun is put in the control of the prefrontal cortex of a hurt and vengeful 15-year-old, and it is pointed at a human target, it will very likely go off."
>
> National Institutes of Health brain scientist Daniel R. Weinberger, "A Brain Too Young for Good Judgment," 2001

So, when Junior drives recklessly and academically self-destructs, should his parents reassure themselves that "he can't help it; his frontal cortex isn't yet fully grown"? They can at least take hope: The brain with which Junior begins his teens differs from the brain with which he will end his teens. In fact, his frontal lobes will continue maturing until about age 25 (Beckman, 2004). In 2004, the American Psychological Association joined seven other medical and mental health associations in filing briefs with the U.S. Supreme Court. These petitions argued against the death penalty for 16- and 17-year-olds. They presented evidence for the teen brain's immaturity "in areas that bear upon adolescent decision-making." Teens are "less guilty by reason of adolescence," suggested psychologist Laurence Steinberg and law professor Elizabeth Scott (2003). In 2005, by a 5-to-4 margin, the Court agreed, declaring juvenile death penalties unconstitutional.

"Young man, go to your room and stay there until your cerebral cortex matures."

Cognitive Development

10: How did Piaget and Kohlberg describe cognitive and moral development during adolescence?

During the early teen years, reasoning is often self-focused. Adolescents may think their private experiences are unique, something parents just couldn't understand: "But, Mom, *you* don't really know how it feels to be in love" (Elkind, 1978). Capable of thinking about their own thinking and about other people's thinking, they also begin imagining what other people are thinking about *them.* (They might worry less if they knew how similarly self-absorbed their peers are.) Gradually, though, most begin to reason more abstractly.

Developing Reasoning Power

When adolescents achieve the intellectual summit Jean Piaget called *formal operations,* they apply their new abstract-thinking tools to the world around them. They may debate human nature, good and evil, truth and justice. Having left behind the concrete images of early childhood, they may search for a deeper meaning of God and existence (Elkind, 1970; Worthington, 1989). They can now reason hypothetically and deduce consequences. And they can spot hypocrisy and detect inconsistencies in others' reasoning (Peterson & others, 1986). (Can you remember having a heated debate

Demonstrating their reasoning ability :: Although on opposite sides of the Iraq war debate, these teens are all demonstrating their ability to think logically about abstract topics. According to Piaget, they are in the final cognitive stage, formal operations.

with your parents? Did you perhaps even vow silently never to lose sight of your own ideals and "be like them"?)

Developing Morality

A crucial task of childhood and adolescence is developing the psychological muscles for controlling impulses. Much of our morality is rooted in unconscious, gut-level reactions, such as disgust or liking. Our conscious mind then tries to make sense of these reactions (Haidt, 2006). Yet to be a moral person is to *think* morally (sorting right from wrong) and to *act* accordingly.

Moral Thinking Piaget (1932) believed that children's moral judgments build on their cognitive development. Agreeing with Piaget, Lawrence Kohlberg (1981, 1984) sought to describe the development

of *moral reasoning,* the thinking that occurs as we consider right and wrong. Kohlberg posed moral dilemmas—for example, should a man steal medicine to save his wife's life? He then asked children, adolescents, and adults whether the action was right or wrong. He believed their answers would give evidence of stages of moral thinking. His findings led him to propose three basic levels of moral thinking.

- *Preconventional morality* Before age 9, most children's morality focuses on self-interest. They obey rules either to avoid punishment ("If you let your wife die, you will get in trouble") or to gain concrete rewards ("If you save your wife, you will be a hero").

- *Conventional morality* By early adolescence, morality focuses on caring for others and on upholding laws and social rules simply because they are the laws and rules. At this stage, people

"Ben is in his first year of high school, and he's questioning all the right things."

"This might not be ethical. Is that a problem for anybody?"

adolescence the transition period from childhood to adulthood, extending from puberty to independence.

puberty the period of sexual maturation, during which a person becomes capable of reproducing.

menarche [meh-NAR-key] the first menstrual period.

may favor actions that gain social approval or help maintain the social order. ("If you steal the drug, everyone will think you are a criminal.")

■ *Postconventional morality* With the abstract reasoning of formal operational thought, people may reach a third moral level. Actions are judged "right" because they flow from people's rights ("People have a right to live") or from self-defined, basic ethical principles ("If you steal the drug, you won't have lived up to your own ideals").

Kohlberg claimed these levels form a moral ladder. As with all stage theories, the sequence never changes. We begin on the bottom rung and rise to varying heights.

What does cross-cultural research tell us about Kohlberg's theory? In various cultures, children do move from Kohlberg's preconventional level into his conventional level (Edwards, 1981, 1982; Snarey, 1985, 1987). Evidence of the postconventional level is less convincing. This stage appears mostly among people who prize *individualism*—giving priority to one's own goals rather than to group goals (Eckensberger, 1994; Miller & Bersoff, 1995). These people are found mostly in the European and North American educated middle class. This doesn't mean that Europeans and North Americans are moral and others are immoral. Instead, say the critics, it means that Kohlberg's theory is biased against *collectivist* (group-centered) societies, such as China and India. With different cultural values, these societies may have different definitions of what is morally right or wrong.

Moral Action Today's character-education programs focus both on moral reasoning and on *doing* the right thing. They teach children *empathy* for others' feelings. They also teach the self-discipline needed to restrain one's own impulses—to delay small pleasures now to earn bigger rewards later. Those who do learn to *delay gratification* become more socially responsible, academically successful, and productive (Funder & Block, 1989; Mischel

Moral reasoning :: New Orleans' Hurricane Katrina victims were faced with a moral dilemma: Should they steal household necessities? Their reasoning likely reflected different levels of moral thinking, even if they behaved similarly.

AP Photo/Eric Gray

& others, 1988, 1989). In service-learning programs, teens tutor, clean up their neighborhoods, and assist the elderly. Everyone seems to benefit. The teens' sense of competence and their desire to serve increase, while their school absenteeism and drop-out rates decrease (Andersen, 1998; Piliavin, 2003). Moral action feeds moral attitudes.

Social Development

11: What social tasks and challenges do adolescents face on the path to mature adulthood?

Erik Erikson (1963) believed that we must resolve a specific crisis at each stage of life. Thus, each stage has its own *psychosocial* task **(TABLE 3.2).** Young children wrestle with issues of *trust,* then *autonomy* (independence), then *initiative.* School-age children strive for *competence*—feeling able and productive. The adolescent's task is to blend past, present, and future possibilities into a clearer sense of self. Adolescents wonder, "Who am I as an individual? What do I want to do with my life? What values should I live by? What do I believe in?" Such questions, said Erikson, are part of the adolescent's *search for identity.*

Forming an Identity

To refine their sense of identity, adolescents in Western cultures usually try out different "selves" in different situations. They may act out one self at home, another with friends, and still another at school or on the Internet. But sometimes these separate worlds overlap. If friends and family bump into each other at a school play, for example, the confused teen may worry, "Which self should I be? Which is the real me?" In time, however, most of us make peace with our various selves, blending them into a stable and comfortable sense of who we are—an **identity.**

But not always. Erikson noticed that some adolescents bypass this period. Some forge their identity early, simply by taking on their parents' values and expectations. Others may adopt the identity of a particular peer group—jocks, preppies, geeks, goths.

Cultural values may influence teens' search for an identity. Traditional, less individualistic cultures tend to inform adolescents about who they are, rather than

identity our sense of self; according to Erikson, the adolescent's task is to solidify a sense of self by testing and integrating various roles.

Table 3.2 — Erikson's Stages of Psychosocial Development

Stage (approximate age)	Issues	Description of Task
Infancy (to 1 year)	If needs are dependably met, infants develop a sense of basic trust.	Trust vs. mistrust
Toddlerhood (1 to 2 years)	Toddlers learn to exercise their will and do things for themselves, or they doubt their abilities.	Autonomy vs. shame and doubt
Preschooler (3 to 5 years)	Preschoolers learn to initiate tasks and carry out plans, or they feel guilty about efforts to be independent.	Initiative vs. guilt
Elementary school (6 years to puberty)	Children learn the pleasure of applying themselves to tasks, or they feel inferior.	Competence vs. inferiority
Adolescence (teen years into 20s)	Teenagers work at refining a sense of self by testing roles and then blending them into a single identity, or they become confused about who they are.	Identity vs. role confusion
Young adulthood (20s to early 40s)	Young adults struggle to form close relationships and to gain the capacity for intimate love, or they feel socially isolated.	Intimacy vs. isolation
Middle adulthood (40s to 60s)	In middle age, people discover a sense of contributing to the world, usually through family and work, or they may feel a lack of purpose.	Generativity vs. stagnation
Late adulthood (late 60s and up)	When reflecting on his or her life, the older adult may feel a sense of satisfaction or failure.	Integrity vs. despair

John Eastcott/Yves Momatiuk/The Image Works

Competence vs. inferiority

Jeff Greenberg/Photo Edit

Intimacy vs. isolation

encouraging them to decide on their own. In individualistic Western cultures, young people may continue to try out possible roles well into their late teen years, when many people begin attending college or working full time. During the early to mid-teen years, self-esteem falls and, for girls, depression scores often increase. Then, during the late teens and twenties, self-image bounces back (Robins & others, 2002; Twenge & Campbell, 2001; Twenge & Nolen-Hoeksema, 2002).

Diverse Yet Alike

Who shall I be today? :: By varying the way they look, adolescents try out different "selves." Although we eventually form a consistent and stable sense of identity, the self we present may change with the situation.

Michael Wong/Getty Images

Jeff Greenberg/Photo Edit

"How was my day? How was my day? Must you micromanage my life?"

Erikson believed that the adolescent identity stage is followed in young adulthood by a developing capacity for **intimacy,** the ability to form emotionally close relationships. With a clear and comfortable sense of who you are, said Erikson, you are ready for close relationships. Such relationships are, for most of us, a source of great pleasure.

Parent and Peer Influence

When researchers used a beeper to sample the daily experiences of American teens, they found them unhappiest when alone and happiest when with friends (Csikszentmihalyi & Hunter, 2003). As ancient Greek philosopher Aristotle long ago recognized, we humans are "the social animal." For Western adolescents forming their own identities, this means pulling away from their parents (Shanahan & others, 2007). The preschooler who can't be close enough to her mother, who loves to touch and cling to her, gradually becomes the 14-year-old who wouldn't be caught dead holding hands with Mom. By adolescence, arguments occur more often, usually over ordinary things—household chores, bedtime, homework (Tesser & others, 1989).

For a minority of parents and their adolescents, differences lead to real splits and great stress (Steinberg & Morris, 2001). But most disagreements are at the level of harmless bickering. And most adolescents—6000 of them in 10 countries, from Australia to Bangladesh to Turkey—say they like their parents (Offer & others, 1988). "We usually get along but . . . ," adolescents often report (Galambos, 1992; Steinberg, 1987)

"I love u guys."

Colorado school hostage Emily Keyes' final text message to her parents before being murdered, 2006.

Positive parent-teen relations and positive peer relations often go hand-in-hand. High school girls who have the most affectionate relationships with their mothers tend also to enjoy the most intimate friendships with girlfriends (Gold & Yanof, 1985). And teens who feel close to their parents tend to be healthy and happy and to do well in school (Resnick & others, 1997). But pause now to think critically. Look what happens if you state this association another way: Teens in trouble are more likely to have tense relationships with parents and other adults. Remember: *Correlations don't prove cause and effect.*

As we saw earlier in this chapter, our peers are part of our environment, and they help form us. Teens are herd animals. They talk, dress, and act more like their peers than their parents. What their friends are—what "Everybody's Doing"—they often become. In teen calls to hotline counseling services, peer relationships are the most discussed topic (Boehm & others, 1999).

Nine times out of ten, it's all about peer pressure.

For those who feel excluded, the pain is acute. "The social atmosphere in most high schools is poisonously clique-driven and exclusionary," observes social psychologist Elliot Aronson (2001). Most excluded teens "suffer in silence. . . . A small number act out in violent ways against their classmates." Those who withdraw are vulnerable to loneliness, low self-esteem, and depression (Steinberg & Morris, 2001). Peer approval matters.

Teens see their parents as having more influence in other areas—for example, in shaping their religious faith and practices and in thinking about college and career choices (*Emerging Trends,* 1997). A Gallup Youth Survey reveals that most share their parent's political views, too (Lyons, 2005).

Emerging Adulthood

In the Western world, adolescence now roughly equals the teen years. At earlier times, and in other parts of the world today, this has not always been the case (Baumeister & Tice, 1986). Shortly after sexual maturity, such young people would assume adult responsibilities and status. The event might be celebrated with an elaborate initiation—a public *rite of passage.* The new adult would then work, marry, and have children.

In the Western world, when schooling became compulsory, independence was put on hold until after graduation. Educational goals rose, and so did the age of independence. Now, from Europe to Australia, adolescents are taking more time to finish college, leave the nest, and establish careers. In the United States, the average age at first marriage has increased more than 4 years since 1960 (to 27 for men, 25 for women).

Delayed independence has overlapped with an earlier onset of puberty. Earlier puberty seems to be related both to girls' increased body fat (which can support pregnancy and nursing) and to weakened parent-child bonds, including absent fathers (Ellis, 2004).

Together, later independence and earlier sexual maturity have stretched the once-brief interlude between child

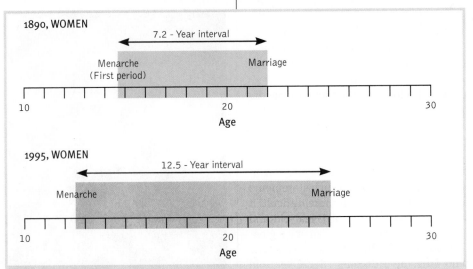

1890, WOMEN

7.2 - Year interval

Menarche
(First period)　　　　　　　　　Marriage

10　　　　　　　20　　　　　　　30
Age

1995, WOMEN

12.5 - Year interval

Menarche　　　　　　　　　　　Marriage

10　　　　　　　20　　　　　　　30
Age

Figure 3.16> Transition to adulthood is being stretched from both ends In the 1890s, the average time between a woman's first menstrual period and marriage, which typically marked a transition to adulthood, was about 7 years. Today, in industrialized countries it is about 12 years (Guttmacher, 1994, 2000). Although many adults are unmarried, later marriage combines with prolonged education and earlier menarche to help stretch out the transition to adulthood.

and adult (**FIGURE 3.16**). In prosperous communities, the time from 18 to the mid-twenties is an increasingly not-yet-settled phase of life, which some now call **emerging adulthood** (Arnett, 2000). No longer adolescents, these young people ease their way into their independent adult status. After high school, those who enter the job market or go to college may be managing their own time and priorities more than ever before. Yet they may be doing so from their parents' home—unable to afford their own place and perhaps still emotionally dependent as well. Adulthood emerges, gradually.

Thinking About Continuity and Stages

Let's stop now and consider the second developmental issue introduced at the beginning of this chapter—*continuity and stages*. Adults differ from infants as a giant redwood differs from its seedling. Is this difference mostly created by constant, gradual growth? Or do we change in some ways like the caterpillar that becomes a butterfly—in distinct stages?

Generally speaking, researchers who emphasize experience and learning view development as a slow, ongoing process. Those who emphasize the influence of our biology tend to see development as a process of maturation, as we pass through a series of stages or steps, guided by instructions programmed into our genes. Progress through the various stages may be quick or slow, but we all pass through the stages in the same order, crawling before standing, and walking before running.

Are there clear-cut stages of psychological development, as there are physical stages such as walking before running? We have considered the stage theories of Jean Piaget on cognitive development, Lawrence Kohlberg on moral development, and Erik Erikson on psychosocial development. And we have seen their stage theories criticized: Young children have some abilities Piaget attributed to later stages. Kohlberg's work reflected a worldview found primarily in individualistic cultures, and he emphasized thinking over acting. And as you will see in the next section, adult life does not progress through the fixed, predictable series of steps Erikson outlined. Chance events can influence us in ways we would never have predicted.

Although research casts doubt on the idea that life proceeds through neatly defined, age-linked stages, the concept of *stage* remains useful. The human brain does experience growth spurts during childhood and puberty that correspond roughly to Piaget's stages (Thatcher & others, 1987). And stage theories help us focus our attention on the forces and interests that affect us at different points in the life span. This close attention can help us understand how people of one age think and act differently when they arrive at a later age.

intimacy in Erikson's theory, the ability to form close, loving relationships; a primary developmental task in early adulthood.

emerging adulthood a period from about age 18 to the mid-twenties, when many in Western cultures are no longer adolescents but have not yet achieved full independence as adults.

DOONESBURY　　　　　　　　　　　**Garry Trudeau**

⊙ PRACTICE TEST

16. Adolescence is marked by the onset of

    a. an identity crisis.
    b. puberty.
    c. separation anxiety.
    d. parent-child conflict.

17. Puberty is the time of maturing sexually. Girls begin puberty at about the age of _____, boys at about the age of _____.

    a. 13; 11   c. 11; 13
    b. 13; 12   d. 12; 13

18. According to Piaget, the ability to think abstractly indicates

    a. concrete operational thought.
    b. egocentrism.
    c. formal operational thought.
    d. conservation.

19. According to Kohlberg, preconventional morality focuses on _____; conventional morality is more concerned with _____.

    a. upholding laws and social rules; self-interest
    b. self-interest; basic ethical principles
    c. upholding laws and social rules; basic ethical principles
    d. self-interest; upholding laws and social rules

20. Erikson contended that each stage of life has its own special psychosocial task or challenge. The primary task during adolescence is to

    a. attain formal operations.
    b. search for an identity.
    c. develop a sense of intimacy with another person.
    d. live independent of parents.

21. Earlier sexual maturity and delayed social independence have stretched the time between childhood and adulthood in many Western countries. As a result, some developmental psychologists now refer to this period as

    a. emerging adulthood.
    b. adolescence.
    c. formal operations.
    d. young adulthood.

Answers: 16. b, 17. c, 18. c, 19. d, 20. b, 21. a.

Adulthood

At one time, psychologists viewed the center-of-life years between adolescence and old age as one long plateau. No longer. Those who follow the unfolding of people's adult lives now believe our development continues across the life span.

Earlier in this chapter, we considered many qualities and events we all share in life's early years. Making such statements about adult life is much more difficult. If we know that James is a 1-year-old and Jamal is a 10-year-old, we can say a great deal about each child. Not so with adults who differ by a decade. The 20-year-old may be a parent who supports a child or a child who gets an allowance. The new mother may be 25 or 45. The boss may be 30 or 60.

Nevertheless, our life courses are in some ways similar. Physically, cognitively, and especially socially, we are at age 60 different from our 25-year-old selves. In the discussion that follows, we recognize these differences and use three terms: *early adulthood* (roughly twenties and thirties), *middle adulthood* (to age 65), and *late adulthood* (the years after 65). Remember, though, that within each of these stages, people vary widely in physical, psychological, and social development.

TOO MUCH COFFEE MAN BY SHANNON WHEELER

Stages of the life cycle

Rick Doyle/Corbis

Adult abilities vary widely :: Eighty-seven-year-olds: Don't try this. In 2002, George Blair became the world's oldest barefoot water skier, 18 days after his eighty-seventh birthday.

"I am still learning."

Michelangelo, 1560, at age 85

Physical Development

12: How do our bodies change from early to late adulthood?

Young Adulthood

Our physical abilities—muscular strength, reaction time, sensory keenness, and cardiac output—all crest by our mid-twenties. Like the declining daylight at the end of summer, the pace of our physical decline is a slow creep. Athletes are often the first to notice. World-class sprinters and swimmers peak by their early twenties. Women, who mature earlier than men, also peak earlier. But few of us notice. Unless our daily lives require us to be in top physical condition, we hardly perceive the early signs of decline.

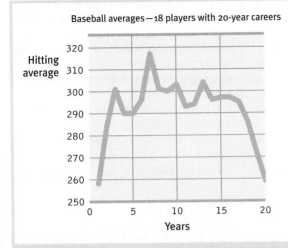

Baseball averages—18 players with 20-year careers

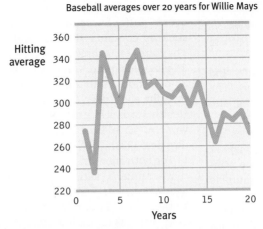

Baseball averages over 20 years for Willie Mays

Figure 3.17> Gradually accelerating decline An analysis of aging and batting averages of all twentieth-century major league baseball players revealed a gradual but accelerating decline in players' later years (Schall & Smith, 2000). The career performance record of the great Willie Mays followed this curve.

Middle Adulthood

During early and middle adulthood, physical vigor has less to do with age than with a person's health and exercise habits. Many of today's sedentary 25-year-olds find themselves huffing and puffing up two flights of stairs. When they make it to the top and glance out the window, they may see their physically fit 50-year-old neighbor jog by on a daily 4-mile run.

Physical decline is gradual, but as most athletes know, the pace of that decline gradually picks up **(FIGURE 3.17)**. As a 65-year-old whose daily exercise is usually playing basketball, I now catch myself wondering whether my team really needs me down court. The good news is that even diminished vigor is enough for normal activities.

Aging also brings a gradual decline in fertility. For a 35- to 39-year-old woman, the chances of getting pregnant after a single act of intercourse are only half those of a woman 19 to 26 (Dunson & others, 2002). A woman's foremost biological sign of aging is the onset of **menopause,** the end of the menstrual cycle, usually within a few years of age 50. Does she see this as a sign that she is

"Happy fortieth. I'll take the muscle tone in your upper arms, the girlish timbre of your voice, your amazing tolerance for caffeine, and your ability to digest french fries. The rest of you can stay."

losing her femininity and growing old? Or does she view it as liberation from menstrual periods and fears of pregnancy? The answer depends on her expectations and attitudes.

There is no male menopause—no end of fertility or sharp drop in sex hormones. Men do experience a more gradual decline in sperm count, testosterone level, and speed of erection and ejaculation.

Late Adulthood

Is old age "more to be feared than death" (Juvenal, *Satires*)? Or is life "most delightful when it is on the downward slope" (Seneca, *Epistulae ad Lucilium*)? What is it like to grow old?

Although physical decline begins in early adulthood, we are not usually acutely aware of it until later life. Vision changes. We have trouble seeing fine details, and our eyes take longer to adapt to changes in light levels. As the eye's pupil shrinks and its lens grows cloudy, less light reaches the *retina*—the light-sensitive inner portion of the eye. In fact, a 65-year-old retina receives only about one-third as much light as its 20-year-old counterpart (Kline & Schieber, 1985). Thus, to see as well as a 20-year-old when reading or driving, a 65-year-old needs three times as much light—a reason for buying cars with untinted windshields. This also explains why older people sometimes ask younger people, "Don't you need better light for reading?"

menopause the end of menstruation. In everyday use, it can also mean the biological transition a woman experiences from before to after the end of menstruation.

> "For some reason, possibly to save ink, the restaurants had started printing their menus in letters the height of bacteria."
>
> Dave Barry, *Dave Barry Turns Fifty,* 1998

Muscle strength, reaction time, and stamina also diminish noticeably. The fine-tuned senses of smell, hearing, and distance perception that we took for granted in our twenties and thirties are now distant memories (FIGURE 3.18). In later life, the stairs get steeper, the print gets smaller, and people seem to mumble more.

Clever manufacturers have found a new market in this age-related difference in hearing. One convenience store has reduced teen loitering by installing a device that emits a shrill, high-pitched sound that almost no one over 30 can hear (Lyall, 2005). Other teens have learned they can use that pitch to their advantage by downloading cellphone ring tones that their middle-aged instructors cannot hear (Vitello, 2006).

In late adulthood, there is both bad and good news about health. The bad news: The body's disease-fighting immune system weakens, putting older adults at higher risk for life-threatening ailments, such as cancer and pneumo-nia. The good news: Thanks partly to a lifetime's collection of antibodies, those over 65 suffer fewer short-term ailments, such as common flu and cold viruses. They are, for example, half as likely as 20-year-olds and one-fifth as likely as preschoolers to suffer upper respiratory flu each year (National Center for Health Statistics, 1990). No wonder older workers have lower absenteeism rates (Rhodes, 1983).

For both men and women, sexual activity remains satisfying after middle age. When people over 60 were surveyed by the National Council on Aging, 39 percent expressed satisfaction with the amount of sex they were having and 39 percent said they wished for sex more frequently (Leary, 1998).

> "The things that stop you having sex with age are exactly the same as those that stop you riding a bicycle (bad health, thinking it looks silly, no bicycle)."
>
> Alex Comfort, *The Joy of Sex,* 2002

Aging does, however, levy a tax on the brain. A small, gradual net loss of brain cells begins in young adulthood. By age 80, the brain has lost about 5 percent of its former weight. This loss is a bit slower in women, who worldwide live an average four years longer than men (CIA, 2008). But in both women and men, some of the brain regions that shrink during aging are the areas important to memory (Schacter, 1996).

Let's turn now to one of the most controversial questions in the study of the human life span: Do adult cognitive abilities, such as memory, intelligence, and creativity, decline as body and brain age?

Cognitive Development

Aging and Memory

13: In what ways do memory and intelligence change as we age?

As we age, we remember some things well. Looking back in later life, people asked to recall the one or two most important events over the last half-century tend to name events from their teens or twenties (Conway & others, 2005; Rubin & others, 1998). Whatever one experienced around this time of life—World War II, the civil rights movement, the Vietnam war, or the Iraq war—becomes pivotal

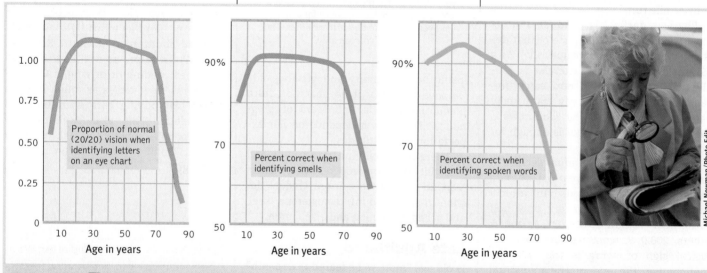

Figure 3.18> The aging senses Sight, smell, and hearing all are less acute among those over age 70. (From Doty & others, 1984.)

(Pillemer, 1998; Schuman & Scott, 1989). Our teens and twenties are also the time when we experience many memorable "firsts"—first date, first job, first day at college, first meeting your parents-in-law. This period is indeed a peak time for some types of learning and remembering.

If you are within five years of 20, what experiences from your last year will you likely never forget? (When you are 70, this is the time of your life you may best remember.)

Up through the teen years, we process information with greater and greater speed (Fry & Hale, 1996; Kail, 1991). This neural processing slows in late adulthood. Compared with teens and young adults, older people take a bit more time to react, to solve perceptual puzzles, even to remember names (Bashore & others, 1997; Verhaeghen & Salthouse, 1997). The lag is greatest on complex tasks (Cerella, 1985; Poon, 1987). At video games, most 70-year-olds are no match for a 20-year-old.

Consider one experiment in which 1205 people were invited to learn some names (Crook & West, 1990). These people watched videotapes in which 14 individuals said their names, using a common format: "Hi, I'm Larry." Then the same individuals reappeared and gave additional details. For example, saying "I'm from Philadelphia" gave viewers visual and voice cues for remembering the person's name. After a second and third replay of the introductions, all viewers remembered more names, but younger adults were consistently better than older adults on this memory task.

Perhaps it is not surprising, then, that nearly two-thirds of people over age 40 say their memory is worse than it was 10 years ago (KRC, 2001). But how well older people remember depends on whether they are being asked to *recognize* what they have tried to memorize (minimal decline) or to *recall* it without clues (greater decline) **(FIGURE 3.19).**

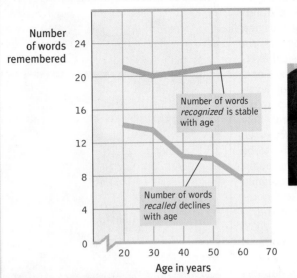

Figure 3.19> Recall and recognition in adulthood In this experiment, the ability to *recall* new information declined during early and middle adulthood, but the ability to *recognize* new information did not. (From Schonfield & Robertson, 1966.)

Aging and Intelligence

What happens to our broader intellectual powers as we age? The answer depends on what we assess and how we assess it (Cattell, 1963; Horn, 1982).

- **Crystallized intelligence**—one's accumulated knowledge, as reflected in vocabulary and analogies tests—*increases* up to middle age.

- **Fluid intelligence**—one's ability to reason speedily and abstractly, as when solving novel logic problems—*decreases* slowly up to age 75 or so, then more rapidly, especially after age 85.

We can see this pattern in the intelligence scores of a national sample of adults. After adjustments for education, word power scores (reflecting crystallized intelligence) increase until later life (Salthouse, 2004). Nonverbal, puzzle-solving intelligence declines (Park & others, 2002). With age we lose and we win. We lose recall memory and processing speed, but we gain vocabulary and knowledge.

These cognitive differences help explain some age-related findings about creativity. Mathematicians and scientists produce much of their most creative work during their late twenties or early thirties. In literature, history, and philosophy, people tend to produce their best work in their forties, fifties, and beyond, after accumulating more knowledge (Simonton, 1988, 1990). For example, poets (who depend on fluid intelligence) reach their peak output earlier than prose authors (who need a deeper knowledge reservoir). This finding holds in every major literary tradition, for both living and dead languages.

"In youth we learn, in age we understand."
Marie Von Ebner-Eschenbach, *Aphorisms*, 1883

crystallized intelligence our accumulated knowledge and verbal skills; tends to increase with age.

fluid intelligence our ability to reason speedily and abstractly; tends to decrease during late adulthood.

Despite age-related cognitive changes, health and exercise can make a difference. In addition to enhancing muscles, bones, and energy and helping prevent obesity and heart disease, physical exercise feeds the brain (Coleman & Flood, 1986). Exercise stimulates brain cell development and connections, thanks perhaps to increased oxygen and nutrient flow (Kempermann & others, 1998). Across 20 studies, active older adults tended to be mentally quick older adults. When sedentary older adults were randomly assigned to aerobic exercise programs, their memory improved and their judgment sharpened (Colcombe & Kramer, 2003; Colcombe & others, 2004; Weuve & others, 2004). "Use it or lose it" is sound advice.

Studies in several countries support the idea that age is only a modest predictor of abilities such as memory and intelligence. Tell me whether someone is 60, 70, or 80, and you haven't told me much about their mental sharpness. Mental ability more strongly correlates with proximity to death. Thus, tell me whether someone is 8 months or 8 years from death and, regardless of age, you've given me a better clue to that person's mental ability. Researchers call this near-death drop the *terminal-decline phenomenon* (Backman & MacDonald, 2006).

Social Development

14: What are adulthood's two primary commitments, and how do the social clock and chance events influence us in these areas?

Adulthood's Commitments

Two basic aspects of our lives dominate adulthood. Erik Erikson called them *intimacy* (forming close relationships) and *generativity* (being productive and supporting future generations). Sigmund Freud (1935) put it most simply: The healthy adult, he said, is one who can *love* and *work*.

Love We flirt, fall in love, and commit— one person at a time. "Pair-bonding is a trademark of the human animal," observed anthropologist Helen Fisher (1993).

Love :: Intimacy, attachment, commitment—love by whatever name—is central to healthy and happy adulthood.

Lisa B./Corbis

From an evolutionary perspective, this pairing makes sense. Parents who cooperated to nurture their children to maturity were more likely to have their gene-carrying children survive and reproduce.

Bonds of love are most satisfying and enduring when two adults share similar interests and values and offer mutual emotional and material support. One of the ties that binds couples is *self-disclosure*—revealing intimate aspects of oneself to others (see Chapter 14).

The chances that a marriage will last also increase when couples marry after age 20 and are well educated. Shouldn't this mean that fewer marriages would end in divorce today? Compared with their counterparts of 40 years ago, people in Western countries *are* better educated and marrying later. But no—ironically, we are twice as likely to divorce today. Both Canada and the United States now have about one divorce for every two marriages. In Europe, divorce is only slightly less common. The divorce rate partly reflects women's increased ability to support themselves. But men and women also now expect more than an enduring bond when they marry. Most hope for a mate who is a wage earner, caregiver, intimate friend, and warm and responsive lover.

Might test-driving a relationship with a live-in "trial marriage" minimize divorce risk? In a 2001 Gallup survey of American twenty-somethings, 62 percent thought it would (Whitehead & Popenoe, 2001). In reality, in Europe, Canada, and the United States, those who lived together before marriage had *higher* rates of divorce and marital troubles than those who had not cohabited (Dush & others, 2003; Popenoe & Whitehead, 2002). The risk appears greatest for those who live together before becoming engaged (Kline & others, 2004). These couples tend to be initially less committed to the ideal of enduring marriage, and they become even less marriage-supporting while living together.

Nonetheless, the institution of marriage endures. Worldwide, reports the United Nations, 9 in 10 heterosexual adults marry. And marriage is a predictor of happiness, health, sexual satisfaction, and income. Neighborhoods with high marriage rates typically have low rates of crime, delinquency, and emotional disorders among children (Myers & Scanzoni, 2005). Surveys of more than 40,000 Americans since 1972 reveal that 40 percent of married adults, though only 23 percent of unmarried adults, report being "very happy." Part of this happiness seems to come from having a partner who is a close, supportive companion—someone who sees you as special. Lesbian couples, too, report greater well-being than those who are alone (Wayment & Peplau, 1995).

Often, love bears children. For most people, this most enduring of life changes is a happy event. "I feel an overwhelming love for my children unlike anything I feel for anyone else," said 93 percent of American mothers in a national survey (Erickson & Aird, 2005). Many fathers feel the same. A few weeks after the birth of my first child I was suddenly struck by a realization: "So *this* is how my parents felt about me!"

But children eventually leave home. This departure is a significant and sometimes difficult event. For most people in middle adulthood, though, an empty nest is a happy place (Adelmann & others,

1989; Glenn, 1975). Compared with middle-aged women with children still at home, those living in an empty nest report greater happiness and greater enjoyment of their marriage. Many parents experience a "postlaunch honeymoon," especially if they maintain close relationships with their children (White & Edwards, 1990). As Daniel Gilbert (2006) concludes, "The only known symptom of 'empty nest syndrome' is increased smiling."

Work Having work that fits your interests provides a sense of competence and accomplishment. For many adults, the answer to "Who are you?" depends a great deal on the answer to "What do you do?" But choosing a career path is difficult, especially in today's changing work environment. (See Appendix: Psychology at Work for more on building work satisfaction.)

For women the once-rigid sequence—of student to worker to wife to at-home mom to worker again—has loosened. Contemporary women occupy these roles in any order or all at once. Nevertheless, for both men and women, there exists a **social clock**—the definition of "the right time" to leave home, get a job, marry, have children, and retire. It's the expectation people have in mind when saying "I married early" or "I started college late." Today the clock still ticks, but people feel freer about being out of sync with it. The social clock also varies from culture to culture. In Western Europe, fewer than 10 percent of men over 65 remain in the work force. That figure rises to 16 percent in the United States, 36 percent in Japan, and 69 percent in Mexico (Davies & others, 1991).

Chance Events

A new job means new relationships, new expectations, and new demands. Marriage brings the joy of intimacy and the stress of merging your life with another's. The birth of a child introduces responsibilities and alters your life focus. These significant events are not triggered by our genes. Simple chance, not maturation, often sends us down one road rather than another (Bandura, 1982). Romantic attraction, for example, is often influenced by chance encounters. Psychologist Albert Bandura (2005) recalls the ironic true story of a book editor who came to one of Bandura's lectures on the "Psychology of Chance Encounters and Life Paths"—and ended up marrying the woman who happened to sit next to him.

Consider one study of identical twins and their spouses. Twins, especially identical twins, make similar choices of friends, clothes, vacations, jobs, and so on. So, if your identical twin became engaged to someone, wouldn't you (being in so many ways the same as your twin) expect to also feel attracted to this person? Surprisingly, only half the identical twins recalled really liking their co-twin's selection, and only 5 percent said, "I could have fallen for my twin's partner." Researchers David Lykken and Auke Tellegen (1993) offer this explanation of romantic love: Given repeated exposure to someone after childhood, you may become attached to almost any available person who has a roughly similar background and level of attractiveness and who returns your affections.

Death and Dying

Perhaps the saddest event most of us will have to cope with is the death of a close relative or friend. Usually, the most difficult separation is from one's spouse or partner—a loss suffered by five times more women than men. When, as usually happens, death comes at an expected late-life time—the "right time" on the social clock—the grieving will pass (**FIGURE 3.20** on the next page).

> "Love—why, I'll tell you what love is: It's you at 75 and her at 71, each of you listening for the other's step in the next room, each afraid that a sudden silence, a sudden cry, could mean a lifetime's talk is over."
>
> Brian Moore, *The Luck of Ginger Coffey*, 1960

When the death of a loved one comes suddenly and before its expected time, grief is especially severe. The sudden illness that claims a 45-year-old life partner, or the accidental death of a child, may trigger a year or more of mourning flooded with memories. Eventually, this may give way to a mild depression, sometimes

Job satisfaction and life satisfaction :: Work can provide us with a sense of identity and competence and opportunities for accomplishment. Perhaps this is why challenging and interesting occupations enhance people's happiness.

social clock the culturally preferred timing of social events such as marriage, parenthood, and retirement.

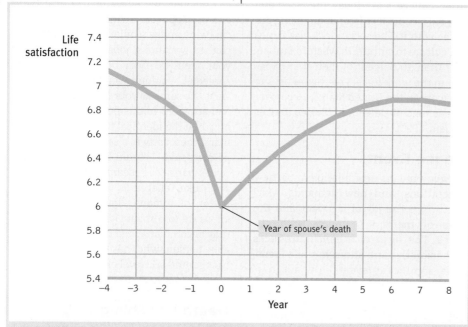

Figure 3.20> Life satisfaction before, during the year of, and after a spouse's death In periodic lifetime surveys of more than 30,000 Germans, researchers identified 513 married people who had not remarried after the death of a spouse. They found that life satisfaction began to dip during the prewidowhood year, dropped significantly during the year of the spouse's death, and then eventually rebounded to nearly the earlier level (Lucas & others, 2003).

lasting for several years (Lehman & others, 1987). But for some, the loss is unbearable. One study tracked more than 17,000 people who had suffered the death of a child under 18. In the five years following that death, 3 percent of them were hospitalized in a psychiatric unit. This rate is 67 percent higher than the rate found in a control group of parents who had not lost a child (Li & others, 2005).

Grief reactions cover a wide range. Some cultures encourage public weeping and wailing. Others expect mourners to hide their emotions. In all cultures, some individuals grieve more intensely and openly. Contrary to popular beliefs, however,

- those who immediately express the strongest grief do not purge their grief faster (Bonanno & Kaltman, 1999; Wortman & Silver, 1989).

- for most people, grief therapy and self-help groups are little better than the healing power of time and supportive friends (Bonanno, 2001, 2004; Genevro, 2003; Stroebe & others, 2001, 2002, 2005).

- terminally ill and grief-stricken people do not go through predictable stages, such as denial, anger, and so forth (Nolen-Hoeksema & Larson, 1999). Given similar losses, some people grieve hard and long, others more lightly and briefly.

Well-Being Across the Life Span

15: What factors affect our well-being in later life?

To live is to grow older. This moment marks the oldest you have ever been and the youngest you will henceforth be. That

Diverse Yet Alike

Grief reactions vary across cultures. A hired brass band may lead the funeral procession in Chinatown (San Francisco), or mourners may gather at a graveside service in Washington D.C. Yet people everywhere grieve loss, especially when death strikes ahead of the social clock.

Dwayne Newton/Photo Edit

Cleve Bryant/Photo Edit

means we all can look back with satisfaction or regret, and forward with hope or dread. When asked what they would have done differently if they could relive their lives, people most often answer, "Taken my education more seriously and worked harder at it" (Kinnier & Metha, 1989; Roese & Summerville, 2005). Other regrets—"I should have told my father I loved him," "I regret that I never went to Europe"—also focus less on mistakes made than on the things one *failed* to do (Gilovich & Medvec, 1995).

> How will you look back on your life 10 years from now? Are you making choices that someday you will recollect with satisfaction?

From early adulthood to midlife, people typically experience a strengthening sense of identity, confidence, and self-esteem (Miner-Rubino & others, 2004; Robins & Trzesniewski, 2005). In later life, challenges arise. Income shrinks as work is often taken away. The body deteriorates, recall fades, and energy wanes. Family members and friends die or move away. The great enemy, death, looms ever closer. Small wonder that many presume the over-65 years must be the worst of times. But they are not, as data collected from nearly 170,000 people in 16 nations show (Inglehart, 1990). Older people report as much happiness and satisfaction with life as younger people do **(FIGURE 3.21)**.

> "At 20 we worry about what others think of us. At 40 we don't care what others think of us. At 60 we discover they haven't been thinking about us at all."
>
> Anonymous

If anything, positive feelings grow after midlife and negative feelings give way (Charles & others, 2001; Mroczek, 2001). Older adults increasingly express positive emotions (Pennebaker & Stone, 2003). Compared with younger adults, they pay less attention to negative information and are slower to perceive

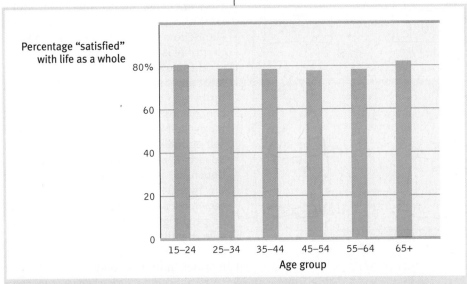

Figure 3.21> Age and life satisfaction With the tasks of early adulthood behind them, many older adults have more time to pursue personal interests. No wonder their satisfaction with life remains high, and may even rise if they are healthy and active. As this graph based on multinational surveys shows, age differences in life satisfaction are trivial. (Data from Inglehart, 1990.)

negative faces (Mather & Carstensen, 2003). Brain areas that process emotions show less activity in response to negative events, but they continue to respond at the same levels to positive events (Mather & others, 2004).

Throughout the life span, the bad feelings tied to negative events fade faster than the good feelings linked with positive events (Walker & others, 2003). This contributes to most older people's sense that life, on balance, has been mostly good. The positivity of later life is comforting. As the years go by, feelings mellow (Costa & others, 1987; Diener & others, 1986). Highs become less high, lows less low.

> "The best thing about being 100 is *no peer pressure.*"
>
> Lewis W. Kuester, 2005, on turning 100

For all of us, life eventually ends. Although death may be unwelcome, facing death with dignity and openness helps people complete the life cycle with a sense of life's meaningfulness and unity. Many treasure the feeling that their existence has been good and that life and death are parts of an ongoing cycle. Erik Erikson called this feeling a sense of *integrity*—an ability to look back with satisfaction, knowing one's life has been meaningful and worthwhile.

Thinking About Stability and Change

It's time to address the third developmental issue introduced at the beginning of this chapter. As we follow lives through time, do we find more evidence for stability or change? If reunited with a long-lost grade-school friend, do we instantly realize that "it's the same old Andy"? Or do people we befriend during one period of life seem like total strangers at a later period? (At least one man would choose the second option. He failed to recognize a former classmate at his 40-year college reunion. That angry classmate eventually pointed out that she was his long-ago first wife!)

BEFORE   AFTER

As adults grow older, there is continuity of self.

Developmental psychologists' research reveals that we experience both stability and change. Some of our characteristics, such as temperament, are very stable. As we noted earlier in this chapter, temperament seems to be something we're born with. When a research team studied 1000 people from age 3 to 26, they were struck by the consistency of temperament and emotionality across time (Caspi & others, 2003). "As at seven, so at seventy," says a Jewish proverb.

We cannot, however, predict all of our eventual traits based on our first three years of life (Kagan & others, 1978, 1998). Some traits, such as social attitudes, are much less stable than temperament (Moss & Susman, 1980). And older children and adolescents can learn new ways of coping. It is true that delinquent children have high rates of work problems, substance abuse, and crime. But many confused and troubled children have blossomed into mature, successful adults (Moffitt & others, 2002; Roberts & others, 2001; Thomas & Chess, 1986). Happily for them, life is a process of becoming.

In some ways, we *all* change with age. Most shy, fearful toddlers begin opening up by age 4. In the years after adolescence, most people become calmer and more self-disciplined, agreeable, and self-confident (McCrae & Costa, 1994; Roberts & others, 2003, 2006). Conscientiousness increases especially during the twenties, and agreeableness during the thirties (Srivastava & others, 2003). As people grow older, personality gradually stabilizes (Terracciano & others, 2006). Many a 20-year-old goof-off has matured into a 40-year-old business or cultural leader. *Such changes can occur without changing a person's position relative to others of the same age.* The hard-driving young adult may mellow by later life, yet still be a relatively hard-driving senior citizen.

Life requires *both* stability and change. Stability gives us our identity. It lets us depend on others and be concerned about the healthy development of the children in our lives. Our trust in our ability to change gives us hope for a brighter future and lets us adapt and grow with experience.

PRACTICE TEST

22. Our physical abilities tend to peak by our
- a. late teens.
- b. mid-twenties.
- c. mid-thirties.
- d. late forties.

23. By age 65, a person would be most likely to experience a decline in the ability to
- a. recall and list all the items on a grocery list.
- b. remember important events from their teens or twenties.
- c. decide whether a statement is true or false.
- d. do well on a vocabulary test.

24. Freud defined the healthy adult as one who is able to love and work. Erikson agreed, observing that the adult struggles to attain intimacy and
- a. affiliation.
- b. identity.
- c. competence.
- d. generativity.

25. Most older adults report
- a. more depression than younger people.
- b. less confidence than younger people.
- c. satisfaction levels comparable to those of younger people.
- d. more negative thinking than younger people experience.

26. Which statement is true about stability and change throughout the life span?
- a. Once we reach adolescence, our attitudes are set for life and do not change.
- b. Our temperament takes a while to develop as we learn through experience.
- c. Our temperament tends to be very stable throughout our lives.
- d. A shy child usually becomes an outgoing adult.

Answers: 22. b, 23. a, 24. d, 25. c, 26. c.

Terms and Concepts to Remember

developmental psychology, p. 64
chromosomes, p. 64
DNA (deoxyribonucleic acid), p. 64
genes, p. 64
heredity, p. 64
genome, p. 65
environment, p. 65
interaction, p. 66
zygote, p. 66
embryo, p. 66
identical twins, p. 66
fraternal twins, p. 66
fetus, p. 66
teratogens, p. 67
fetal alcohol syndrome (FAS), p. 67
reflex, p. 68
temperament, p. 68
maturation, p. 70
critical period, p. 71
schema, p. 73
cognition, p. 73
sensorimotor stage, p. 74
object permanence, p. 74
preoperational stage, p. 74
conservation, p. 74
egocentrism, p. 74
theory of mind, p. 75
autism, p. 75
concrete operational stage, p. 76
formal operational stage, p. 76
stranger anxiety, p. 76
attachment, p. 77
basic trust, p. 79
culture, p. 80
adolescence, p. 84
puberty, p. 84
menarche [meh-NAR-key], p. 84
identity, p. 86
intimacy, p. 88
emerging adulthood, p. 89
menopause, p. 91
crystallized intelligence, p. 93
fluid intelligence, p. 93
social clock, p. 95

:: Multiple-choice **self-tests** and more may be found at www.worthpublishers.com/myers

REVIEW: DEVELOPING THROUGH THE LIFE SPAN

Developmental psychologists study physical, cognitive, and social changes throughout the life span.

1 **What are the three key issues studied by developmental psychologists?**

- Nature and nurture
- Continuity and stages
- Stability and change

PRENATAL DEVELOPMENT AND THE NEWBORN

2 **How does life develop before birth?**

- At conception, one sperm cell fuses with one egg cell to form a *zygote*.
- By 6 weeks, the *embryo's* body organs begin to form and function.
- By 9 weeks, the *fetus* is recognizably human.
- *Identical twins* develop from a single fertilized egg that splits into two; *fraternal twins* develop from separate fertilized eggs.
- *Teratogens* are potentially harmful agents that can pass through the placental screen.
- *Genes* (*DNA* segments that form the *chromosomes*) are the basic units of *heredity*. When expressed in particular *environments*, genes guide development.
- Heredity and environment *interact* to influence development.

3 **What are some of the newborn's abilities and traits?**

- Newborns' sensory systems and *reflexes* aid their survival and social interactions with adults.
- Inborn *temperament*—emotional excitability—heavily influences developing personality.

4 **How do twin and adoption studies help us understand the effects of nature and nurture?**

- Studies of separated identical twins allow researchers to maintain the same genes while testing the effects of different home environments. Studies of adoptive families let them maintain the same home environment while studying the effects of genetic differences.
- Twin and adoption studies offer an ethical way to study the c ontributions of heredity (nature) and environment (nurture) on development.

INFANCY AND CHILDHOOD

5 **How do the brain and motor skills develop during infancy and childhood?**

- Brain cells form before birth. With *maturation* and experience, their interconnections multiply rapidly after birth.
- Complex motor skills—sitting, standing, walking—develop in a predictable sequence. Timing may vary with individual maturation and with culture.

6 **How did Piaget view the development of a child's mind, and how do current researchers' views differ?**

- Piaget believed that children actively construct and modify their understanding of the world as they interact with it. He proposed that children's reasoning develops in four stages.
- *Sensorimotor stage:* first two years; develop *object permanence*.
- *Preoperational stage:* age 2 to about 6 or 7; preschoolers are *egocentric* but begin to develop a *theory of mind* (except for those with *autism*, whose theory of mind is impaired).
- *Concrete operational stage:* about 7 to 11 years; master conservation and simple math.
- *Formal operational stage:* age 12 and up; reasoning expands to abstract thinking.

CURRENT RESEARCH

- supports the sequence Piaget proposed.
- shows that young children are more capable, and their development more continuous, than Piaget believed.

7 **How do the bonds of attachment form between parents and infants?**

- Infants demonstrate *stranger anxiety* after developing object permanence.
- Infants form *attachments* with caregivers who are comfortable, familiar, and responsive.
- Attachment styles differ (secure or insecure) due to the child's individual temperament and the responsiveness of the child's caregivers.
- Neglect or abuse can disrupt the attachment process and put children at risk for physical, psychological, and social problems.

PARENTS AND PEERS

8 To what extent are our lives shaped by parental and peer influences?

- Parenting styles—permissive, authoritative, and authoritarian—often reflect cultural influences. Children with the highest self-esteem, self-reliance, and social competence tend to have authoritative parents.
- Parents heavily influence their children's political and religious beliefs.
- Peers are especially influential in learning to cooperate with one another, achieve popularity, and interact with people of a similar age.
- *Nature and nurture:* Both nature and nurture—genes and experiences—guide our development.

ADOLESCENCE

9 What major physical changes occur during adolescence?

- *Puberty* is a time of sexual maturation.
- Boys seem to benefit psychologically from "early" maturation, girls from "late" maturation.
- The brain's frontal lobes mature during adolescence and the early twenties, enabling improved judgment, impulse control, and long-term planning.

10 How did Piaget and Kohlberg describe cognitive and moral development during adolescence?

- In Piaget's view, formal operations (abstract reasoning) develop in adolescence. Research indicates that these abilities begin to emerge earlier than Piaget believed.
- Kohlberg proposed a stage theory of moral thinking, from a preconventional morality of self-interest, to a conventional morality concerned with gaining others' approval or doing one's duty, to (in some people) a post-conventional morality of agreed-upon rights or universal ethical principles.
- Kohlberg's critics point out that true morality is both moral actions and moral thinking. They also note that the postconventional level represents morality from the perspective of an individualist, middle-class group.

11 What social tasks and challenges do adolescents face on the path to mature adulthood?

- Erikson's stages of psychosocial development suggest that developing an *identity* is a major task of adolescence.
- During adolescence, parental influence diminishes and peer influence increases.
- *Emerging adulthood* is the period from age 18 to the mid-twenties, when many young people in Western cultures are not yet fully independent.
- *Continuity and stages:* Development is more continuous than stage theorists believed. Still, it is important to consider the effects of growth spurts and the changing forces and interests that affect us at different points in our lives.

ADULTHOOD

12 How do our bodies change from early to late adulthood?

- Muscular strength, reaction time, sensory abilities, and cardiac output begin to decline in the late twenties.
- Around age 50, *menopause* ends women's period of fertility. Men do not undergo a similar sharp drop in hormone levels or fertility.

13 In what ways do memory and intelligence change as we age?

- Recall begins to decline, especially for meaningless information. Recognition memory remains strong.
- *Fluid intelligence* (speedy, abstract reasoning) declines in later life. *Crystallized intelligence* (accumulated knowledge) does not.

14 What are adulthood's two primary commitments, and how do the social clock and chance events influence us in these areas?

- Adulthood's two major commitments are love (Erikson's intimacy—forming close relationships, especially with family) and work (productive activity, or what Erikson called generativity).
- Marriage seems more likely to last when people marry after age 20 and are well educated.
- Chance encounters affect many of our important decisions, such as our choice of romantic partners.
- Death of a loved one is much harder to accept when it comes before its expected time.

15 What factors affect our well-being in later life?

- Most older people retain a sense of well-being, partly due to the tendency to focus more on positive emotions and memories later in life.
- Many find what Erikson called integrity—a feeling that one's life has been meaningful.
- *Stability and change:* Development is lifelong. People's traits continue to change in later life. There is also an underlying consistency to most people's temperament and personality traits.

4 Gender and Sexuality

IN 1972, AS THE YOUNG CHAIR of our psychology department, I was proud to make the announcement: We had concluded our search for a new colleague, and we had found just who we were looking for—a bright, warm, enthusiastic woman about to receive her Ph.D. in developmental psychology. The vote was unanimous. Thus, we were stunned when our elderly chancellor rejected our recommendation. He explained, "As a mother of a preschooler, she should be home with her child, *not* working full time." No amount of pleading or arguing (for example, that it might be possible to parent a child while employed) could change his mind. So, with a heavy heart, I drove to her city to explain, face to face, my embarrassment in being able to offer her only a temporary position.

In this case, all's well that ends well—she accepted and quickly became a beloved, tenured colleague who went on to found our college's women's studies program. But today, she and I marvel at the swift transformation in our culture's thinking about gender. In a thin slice of history, little more than 35 years, our ideas about the "proper" behavior for women and men have undergone an extreme makeover. Both women and men are now recognized as "fully capable of effectively carrying out organizational roles at all levels," note Wendy Wood and Alice Eagly (2002). Women's employment in formerly male occupations and men's employment in formerly female occupations have increased. And as this was happening, our views of what is "masculine" and what is "feminine" have also changed, as have our ideas about what we seek in a mate (Twenge, 1997).

In this chapter, we'll look at some of the ways nature and nurture form us as males and females. We'll see what researchers tell us about how much males and females are alike, and how and why they differ. Along the way, we'll take a close look at human sexuality. As part of that close look, we'll see how *evolutionary psychologists* explain some aspects of our sexuality. Our gender similarities, gender differences, and sexual motivation fascinate these psychologists, who use principles of *natural selection* to understand behaviors and mental processes.

Let's start by considering what gender is and how it develops.

Gender Development

Humans everywhere share an irresistible urge to organize the world into simple categories. Among the ways we classify people—as tall or short, slim or fat, smart or dull—one stands out. At your birth, everyone wanted to know, "Boy or girl?" From that time on, your biological sex helped define your **gender,** the characteristics our society defines as *male* or *female.*

How much does biology contribute to these characteristics? And what portion of our differences is socially constructed, influenced by our culture and by how we are socialized as children? Before we try to answer those questions, we need to consider some gender similarities and differences.

gender in psychology, the biologically and socially influenced characteristics by which people define *male* and *female.*

GENDER DEVELOPMENT

How Are We Alike? How Do We Differ?

The Nature of Gender: Our Biology

The Nurture of Gender: Our Culture

HUMAN SEXUALITY

The Physiology of Sex

The Psychology of Sex

THINK CRITICALLY ABOUT: Sex and Human Values

SEXUAL ORIENTATION

Environment and Sexual Orientation

Biology and Sexual Orientation

AN EVOLUTIONARY EXPLANATION OF HUMAN SEXUALITY

Gender Differences in Sexuality

Natural Selection and Mating Preferences

Critiquing the Evolutionary Perspective

CLOSE-UP: For Those Troubled by the Scientific Understanding of Human Origins

THINKING ABOUT GENDER, SEXUALITY, AND NATURE–NURTURE INTERACTION

How Are We Alike? How Do We Differ?

1: What are some of the similarities and differences between men and women?

In most ways, we are alike. Men and women are not from different planets—Mars and Venus—but from the same planet Earth. Tell me whether you are male or female and you tell me almost nothing. You give me no clue to your intelligence. You tell me little about the mechanisms by which you see, hear, learn, and remember. Why? Because your "opposite" sex is, in reality, your very similar sex. At conception, you received 23 chromosomes from your mother and 23 from your father. Of those 46 chromosomes, 45 are *unisex*— the same for males and females. (More about that other chromosome later in this chapter.)

But males and females also differ, and differences command attention. Some differences are obvious. Compared with the average man, the average woman enters puberty two years sooner, and her life span is five years longer. She carries 70 percent more fat, has 40 percent less muscle, and is 5 inches shorter. Women differ in other ways, too. They are more likely to dream equally of men and women. They can become sexually re-aroused immediately after orgasm. They smell fainter odors, express emotions more freely, and are offered help more often. Women are also doubly vulnerable to depression and anxiety, and their risk of developing an eating disorder is 10 times greater. But, then, men are some 4 times more likely to commit suicide or suffer alcoholism and are far more often diagnosed with autism, color-blindness, ADHD (as children), and antisocial personality disorder (as adults). Choose your gender and pick your vulnerability.

Psychologists have been especially interested in three areas of male-female differences: aggression, social power, and social connectedness.

Gender and Aggression

In surveys, men admit to more **aggression** than do women. And in experiments, men tend to behave more aggressively, such as by administering what they believe are more painful electric shocks (Bettencourt & Kernahan, 1997). The aggression gender gap pertains to harmful *physical* aggression rather than verbal, *relational* aggression (such as excluding someone). The gap appears in everyday life in various cultures and at various ages (Archer, 2004). Violent crime rates illustrate the difference. The male-to-female arrest ratio for murder, for example, is 9 to 1 in the United States and 7 to 1 in Canada (FBI, 2004; Statistics Canada, 2003).

Throughout the world, hunting, fighting, and warring are primarily men's activities (Wood & Eagly, 2002). Men also express more support for war. In a 2007 Gallup survey, 46 percent of American men but only 37 percent of American women said that sending troops to Iraq was *not* a mistake (Newport, 2007).

Gender and Social Power

Around the world, from Nigeria to New Zealand, people perceive power differences between men and women (Williams & Best, 1990). Who is viewed as more dominant, forceful, and independent? Men. Who is viewed as more likely to be submissive, nurturing, and socially connected? Women. Indeed, in most societies men *are* socially dominant. When political leaders are elected, they usually are men, who held 84 percent of the seats in the world's governing parliaments in 2005 (IPU, 2005). When groups form, whether as juries or companies, leadership tends to go to males (Colarelli & others, 2006). And when salaries are paid, those in traditionally male occupations receive more.

As leaders, men tend to be more directive, even authoritarian, issuing orders for others to follow. Women tend to be more democratic and more welcoming of subordinates' participation in decision making (Eagly & Johnson, 1990; van Engen & Willemsen, 2004). When people

Gender difference in aggression :: Around the world, fighting, violent crime, and blowing things up are mostly men's activities. The terrorists who bombed the U.S. Embassy in Nairobi (left), killing 200 people and wounding over 4000 were males, as were the robbers (right) who killed two people and critically injured one in a hold-up of a convenience store in Nashville.

AP Photo/Sayyid Azim

AP Photo/Nashville Police Department

Gender and power :: At the 2007 European Union leaders summit, there was a sea of suits, but one (Germany's Angela Merkel) was not like the others.

AP Photo/Jan Bauer

interact, men are more likely to utter opinions, women to express support (Aries, 1987; Wood, 1987). Men tend to act as powerful people often do. They smile less often than women do, and they are more likely to talk assertively, interrupt, initiate touches, and stare (Hall, 1987; Major & others, 1990). Such behaviors help sustain social power inequities.

Gender differences in power do grow smaller as we age. With maturity, middle-aged women become more assertive, and men become more empathic (Maccoby, 1998).

Gender and Social Connectedness

Men and women differ not only in aggression and in power, but also in reaching out to others. Many psychologists view adolescence as a time when we struggle to create a separate *identity*—a unique, independent self. To Carol Gilligan and her colleagues (1982, 1990), this "normal" struggle describes males more than females. Gilligan believes females differ from males in two important ways. Females are less concerned with viewing themselves as separate individuals. And

they are more concerned with relationships, with *making connections*.

These male-female differences surface early, in children's play. Boys typically play in large groups. Their games tend to be active and competitive, with little intimate discussion. Girls usually play in smaller groups, often with one friend. Their play is less competitive, and they tend to act out social relationships. Both in play and in other settings, females are more open to feedback than are males, and more likely to react to it (Maccoby, 1990; Roberts, 1991).

These differences continue with age. In their teen years, girls spend more time with friends and in clubs and less time alone watching TV or playing video games (Pryor & others, 2006; Wong & Csikszent-mihalyi, 1991). As adults, men enjoy doing activities *side-by-side,* and they tend to talk with others to communicate solutions. Women take more pleasure in talking *face-to-face* (Wright, 1989), and they tend to talk with others to explore relationships (Tannen, 1990). As friends, women also talk more often and more openly (Berndt, 1992; Dindia & Allen, 1992). This may help explain a finding about gender differences

in phone communication in France, where women make 63 percent of telephone calls. When talking to a woman, female callers stay connected longer (7.2 minutes) than men do when talking to another man (4.6 minutes) (Smoreda & Licoppe, 2000).

Perhaps we should not be surprised, then, that relationship-oriented women provide most of the care to the very young and the very old. In their interests and vocations, women emphasize caring and relate more to people and less to things (Lippa, 2005, 2006). They also purchase 85 percent of greeting cards (*Time,* 1997). Although many people (69 percent) say they have a close relationship with their father, most (90 percent) feel close to their mother (Hugick, 1989). When wanting someone who will understand them and share their worries and hurts, both men and women usually turn to women. Both also report their friendships with women to be more intimate, enjoyable, and nurturing (Rubin, 1985; Sapadin, 1988).

What explains our male-female differences? Are we shaped by our biology? By our experiences? A biopsychosocial view suggests both are at work. Gender diversity, like so many other aspects of our development, is a byproduct of the interplay of our biology, our personal history, and our current situation (Wood & Eagly, 2002).

The Nature of Gender: Our Biology

2: How do nature and nurture interact to define us as male or female?

In areas where we face similar challenges—regulating heat with sweat, developing food tastes that nourish, growing calluses where the skin meets friction—men and women are similar. Even when describing the ideal mate, both put traits such as "kind," "honest," and "intelligent" at the top of their lists.

aggression physical or verbal behavior intended to hurt someone.

But in mating-related areas, evolutionary psychologists contend, guys act like guys whether they are elephants or elephant seals, rural peasants or corporate presidents. Our biology may influence our gender differences in two ways: genetically, through our differing *sex chromosomes,* and physiologically, from our differing concentrations of *sex hormones.*

As we noted earlier, males and females are variations on a single form—of 46 chromosomes, 45 are unisex. So great is this similarity that until seven weeks after conception, you were anatomically the same as someone of the other sex. Then that forty-sixth chromosome kicked in. Male or female, your sex was determined by your father's contribution to your twenty-third pair of chromosomes, the two sex chromosomes. Like all of us, you received an **X chromosome** from your mother. From your father, you received the one chromosome that is not unisex—either an X chromosome, making you a girl, or a **Y chromosome,** making you a boy.

The Y chromosome includes a single gene that, about the seventh week after conception, throws a master switch triggering the testes to develop and to produce the principal male hormone, **testosterone.** This hormone starts the development of external male sex organs. Females also have testosterone, but not enough to throw this developmental switch.

Another key period for the development of male-female differences falls

Courtesy of Nick Downes.

during the fourth and fifth prenatal months. During this period, sex hormones bathe the fetal brain and influence its wiring. Different patterns for males and females develop under the influence of the male's greater testosterone and the female's ovarian hormones (Hines, 2004; Udry, 2000). In adulthood, male and female brains differ in some areas. For example, parts of the frontal lobes (an area involved in verbal fluency) are reportedly thicker in women. Part of the parietal cortex, a key area for space perception, is thicker in men.

Sometimes, despite normal male hormones and testes, male infants are born without a penis or with a very small one. In such cases, biology's power to influence gender development is clear. Until recently, pediatricians and other medical experts sometimes recommended surgery to create a female identity for these children. One study reviewed 14 cases of boys who had undergone early sex-reassignment surgery and had been raised as girls. Six later declared themselves to be males, 5 were living as females, and 3 had unclear sexual identity (Reiner & Gearhart, 2004).

The dramatic difference between *gender* (the characteristics that people associate with male and female) and *sex* (the biology of male and female) was equally and tragically clear in another case, in which a little boy had lost his penis during a botched circumcision. His parents followed a psychiatrist's advice to raise him as a girl rather than as a damaged boy. Alas, "Brenda" Reimer was not like other girls. "She" didn't like dolls. She tore her dresses with rough-and-tumble play. At puberty she wanted no part of kissing boys. Finally, Brenda's parents explained what had happened, whereupon this young person immediately rejected the assigned female identity. He cut his hair and took a male name, David. He eventually married a woman and became a stepfather. And, sadly, he later committed suicide (Colapinto, 2000).

Sex-reassignment surgery is no longer recommended for genetic males in cases like these. Indeed, "Sex matters," concludes the National Academy of Sciences

David Reimer :: Sex-reassignment tragedy

Fred Greenslade/Reuters

(2001). In combination with the environment, sex-related genes and physiology "result in behavioral and cognitive differences between males and females."

The Nurture of Gender: Our Culture

If nurture cannot undo biology in cases like David Reimer's, does this mean that biology is destiny? No. For most of us, nurture finishes the job that biology begins.

Gender Roles

Sex indeed matters. But from a bio-psychosocial perspective, culture and the immediate situation matter, too. *Culture* is everything shared by a group and transmitted across generations. We can see culture's shaping power in the social expectations that guide men's and women's behavior.

In psychology, as in the theater, a **role** refers to a cluster of actions, the behaviors we expect of those who occupy a particular social position. **Gender roles** are the behaviors a culture expects of its men and women. Traditionally, American men were expected to initiate dates, drive the car, and pick up the check, and women were expected to decorate the

"Sex brought us together, but gender drove us apart."

home, buy and care for the children's clothes, and select the wedding gifts. About 90 percent of the time in two-parent families, Mom has stayed home with a sick child, arranged for the baby-sitter, and called the doctor (Maccoby, 1995). Even today, compared with employed women, employed men in the United States spend about one hour more on the job and about one hour less on household activities and caregiving each day (Bureau of Labor Statistics, 2004).

The gendered tsunami :: In Sri Lanka, Indonesia, and India, the gendered division of labor helps explain the excess of female deaths from the 2004 tsunami. In some villages, 80 percent of those killed were women, who were mostly at home while the men were more likely to be out at sea fishing or doing out-of-the-home chores (Oxfam, 2005).

Gender roles can smooth social relations, saving irritating discussions about whose job it is to get the car fixed, and who should make the kids breakfast before they leave for school. But these quick and easy assumptions come at a cost. If we don't fit into these roles, we may feel anxious.

Gender roles vary from culture to culture. Nomadic societies of food-gathering people have only a minimal division of labor by sex. Boys and girls receive much the same upbringing. In agricultural societies, where women work in the fields close to home, and men roam more freely herding livestock, children are typically guided into more distinct gender roles (Segall & others, 1990; Van Leeuwen, 1978).

Among industrialized countries, gender roles and attitudes nevertheless vary widely. Would you say life is more satisfying when both spouses work for pay and share child care? If so, you would agree with most people in 41 of 44 countries, according to a Pew Global Attitudes survey (2003). Even so, the culture-to-culture differences were huge, ranging from Egypt, where people disagreed 2 to 1, to Vietnam, where people agreed 11 to 1.

Gender ideas also vary across generations. When families emigrate from Asia to Canada and the United States, their children often grow up with peers whose ideas about what it means to be a man or a woman differ from those of the immigrant parents. Daughters, especially, may feel torn between the "old ways" and "new ways" (Dion & Dion, 2001).

Even within the same culture, attitudes about gender roles vary over time. In 1960, of every 30 U.S. students entering law school, one was a woman. By 2005, half were (Cynkar, 2007; Glater, 2001). Today, virtually no college administrator would make the statement that women should not be full-time faculty members. Ideas about men's and women's roles have changed.

How Do We Learn to Be Male or Female?

In time, most boys display masculine traits and interests, and most girls display feminine ones. How does this happen? How do we acquire our **gender identity?**

Social learning theory assumes that children learn gender-linked behaviors by observing and imitating others, and by being rewarded or punished for certain behaviors. "Nicole, you're such a good mommy to your dolls"; "Big boys don't cry, Alex." But modeling and rewarding by parents can't be the whole story, say some critics. Differences in the way parents rear boys and girls aren't enough to explain **gender typing**—the way some children seem more attuned than others to traditional male or female roles (Lytton & Romney, 1991). In fact, even when their families discourage traditional gender-typing, children organize themselves into "boy worlds" and "girl worlds," each guided by rules for what boys and girls do.

Gender schema theory combines social learning theory with cognition. In your own childhood, as you struggled to understand the world, you—like other children—formed *schemas,* or concepts that helped you make sense of your

X chromosome the sex chromosome found in both men and women. Females have two X chromosomes; males have one X chromosome and one Y chromosome.

Y chromosome the sex chromosome found only in males. When paired with an X chromosome from the mother, it produces a male child.

testosterone the most important male sex hormone. Stimulates the growth of the male sex organs in the fetus and the development of the male sex characteristics during puberty. Females have testosterone, but less of it.

role a set of expectations about a social position, defining how those in the position ought to behave.

gender role a set of expected behaviors for males or for females.

gender identity one's sense of being male or female.

social learning theory the theory that we learn social behavior by observing and imitating and by being rewarded or punished.

gender typing taking on a traditional masculine or feminine role.

gender schema theory the theory that children learn from their cultures a concept of what it means to be male and female, and that they adjust their behavior accordingly.

Figure 4.1> Two theories of gender typing

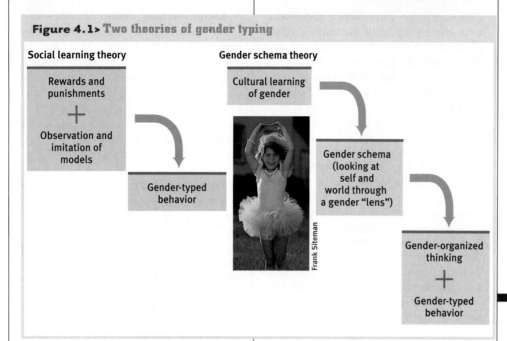

3. Gender roles vary across cultures and over time. *Gender role* refers to our
   a. sense of being male or female.
   b. expectations about the way males and females behave.
   c. biological sex.
   d. beliefs about how men and women should earn a living.

4. When children have developed a *gender identity,* they
   a. exhibit traditional masculine or feminine behaviors.
   b. have a masculine or feminine appearance.
   c. have a sense of being male or female.
   d. have an unclear biological sex.

Answers: 1. c, 2. d, 3. b, 4. c.

world. One of these was a schema for your own gender (Bem, 1987, 1993). This gender schema then became a lens through which you viewed your experiences **(FIGURE 4.1).**

Gender schemas begin to form early in life, and social learning helps to form them. Before age 1, you began to discriminate male and female voices and faces (Martin & others, 2002). After age 2, language forced you to begin organizing your world on the basis of gender. English, for example, uses the pronouns *he* and *she;* other languages classify objects as masculine ("*le train*") or feminine ("*la table*").

Young children are "gender detectives," explain Carol Lynn Martin and Diane Ruble (2004). Once they grasp that two sorts of people exist—and that they are of one sort—they search for clues about gender, and they find them in language, dress, toys, and songs. Girls, they may decide, are the ones with long hair. Having divided the human world in half, 3-year-olds will then like their own kind better and seek them out for play. And having compared themselves with their concept of gender, they will adjust their behavior accordingly. ("I am male—thus,

masculine, strong, aggressive," or "I am female—therefore, feminine, sweet, and helpful.") These rigid boy-girl comparisons peak at about age 5 or 6. If the new neighbor is a boy, a 6-year-old girl may assume he just cannot share her interests. For young children, gender schemas loom large.

PRACTICE TEST

1. Females and males are very similar to each other. But one way they differ is that
   a. women are more physically aggressive than men.
   b. men are more democratic than women in their leadership roles.
   c. girls tend to play in small groups, while boys tend to play in large groups.
   d. men can detect faint odors better than women.

2. The fertilized egg will develop into a boy if it receives
   a. an X chromosome from its mother.
   b. an X chromosome from its father.
   c. a Y chromosome from its mother.
   d. a Y chromosome from its father.

Human Sexuality

One aspect of our gender is our sexuality. As we have seen, gender roles vary from place to place and from time to time within the same place. It's not surprising, then, that sexual expression also varies dramatically with time and culture. Among American women born before 1900, a mere 3 percent had experienced premarital sex by age 18 (Smith, 1998). A century later, about half of U.S. ninth- to twelfth-graders reported having had sexual intercourse, as did 42 percent of Canadian 16-year-olds (Boroditsky & others, 1995; CDC, 2004). Teen intercourse rates have been higher in Western Europe but much lower in Arab and Asian countries and among North Americans of Asian descent (McLaughlin & others, 1997; Wellings & others, 2006). One survey of nearly 5000 unmarried Chinese students reported rates even lower (2.5 percent) than those of early twentieth-century Americans (Meston & others, 1996).

In recent U.S. history, the pendulum of sexual values has swung back and forth. The European eroticism of the early 1800s gave way to the conservative Victorian era of the late 1800s. The libertine flapper era of the 1920s was replaced by the family-values period of the 1950s. The pendulum may have begun a new swing toward commitment in the twenty-first century, with declining teen birth rates since 1991, and virgins (54 percent in 2002) now outnumbering nonvirgins among U.S. 15- to 19-year-olds (CDC, 2004; Mohn & others, 2003).

Attitudes toward homosexuality also vary with time and culture. In U.S. Gallup surveys, support for gay marriage increased from 27 percent in 1996 to 46 percent in 2007. Homosexuality "should be accepted in society," agree only 1 in 10 people in some predominantly Muslim countries and more than 3 in 4 people in several west European countries (Speulda & McIntosh, 2004).

Later in this chapter, we'll return to these topics. But first, let's look at some of the biological and psychological aspects of our sexuality.

The Physiology of Sex

The first extensive descriptions of sexual behavior in the United States appeared in mid-twentieth-century surveys (Kinsey & others, 1948, 1953). In the 1960s, the studies of gynecologist-obstetrician William Masters and his collaborator Virginia Johnson (1966) made headlines.

The Sexual Response Cycle

3: What are the stages of the human sexual response cycle?

Masters and Johnson recorded the physiological responses of 382 female and 312 male volunteers who masturbated or had intercourse. With the help of this somewhat atypical sample (people able and willing to display arousal and orgasm while being observed in a laboratory), Masters and Johnson identified a four-stage **sexual response cycle,** similar in men and women. Here are the stages:

1. *Excitement:* The genital areas become engorged with blood. A woman's vagina expands and secretes lubricant, and her breasts and nipples may enlarge.

2. *Plateau:* Excitement peaks as breathing, pulse, and blood pressure rates continue to increase. A man's penis becomes fully engorged. A woman's vaginal secretion continues to increase and her clitoris retracts. Orgasm feels imminent.

3. *Orgasm:* Muscle contractions appear all over the body and are accompanied by further increases in breathing, pulse, and blood pressure rates. (Later studies showed that a woman's arousal and orgasm aid conception by helping propel semen from the penis, positioning the uterus to receive sperm, and drawing the sperm further inward [Furlow & Thornhill, 1996].) In the excitement of the moment, men and women are hardly aware of all this as their rhythmic genital contractions create a pleasurable feeling of sexual release. The feeling apparently is much the same for both sexes. One panel of experts could not reliably distinguish between descriptions of orgasm written by men and those written by women (Vance & Wagner, 1976). In another study, PET scans showed that the same brain regions were active when men and women were having orgasms (Holstege & others, 2003a,b).

4. *Resolution:* The body gradually returns to its unaroused state as the engorged genital blood vessels release their accumulated blood. This happens relatively quickly if orgasm has occurred, relatively slowly otherwise. (It's like the nasal tickle that goes away rapidly if you have sneezed, slowly otherwise.) Men then enter a **refractory period,** lasting from a few minutes to a day or more, during which they are incapable of another orgasm. A woman's much shorter refractory period may enable her to have another orgasm if restimulated during or soon after resolution.

Hormones and Sexual Behavior

4: How do sex hormones influence human sexual development and arousal?

Among the forces driving the sexual response cycle are the *sex hormones.* The main male sex hormone, as we saw earlier, is *testosterone.* The main female sex hormones are the **estrogens,** such as estradiol. Sex hormones influence us at many points in the life span.

- During the prenatal period, they direct our development as males or females.

- During puberty, a surge in sex hormones ushers us into adolescence.

- After puberty and well into the late adult years, sex hormones help activate sexual behavior.

In most mammals, fertility and sex overlap. Females become sexually receptive ("in heat") when their estrogen peaks at ovulation. In experiments, researchers cause female animals to become receptive by injecting them with estrogen. Researchers cannot so easily manipulate the sexual behavior of male animals (Feder, 1984). Nevertheless, male rats that have had their testes (which manufacture testosterone) surgically removed will gradually lose much of their interest in receptive females. They gradually regain it if injected with testosterone.

sexual response cycle the four stages of sexual responding described by Masters and Johnson—excitement, plateau, orgasm, and resolution.

refractory period a resting period after orgasm, during which a man cannot achieve another orgasm.

estrogens sex hormones, such as estradiol, secreted in greater amounts by females than by males. In nonhuman female mammals, estrogen levels peak during ovulation, promoting sexual receptivity.

"I love the idea of there being two sexes, don't you?"

Hormones do influence human sexual behavior, but in a looser way. Sexual desire does rise slightly at ovulation among women with mates (Pillsworth & others, 2004). "How do we know this?" a critical thinker might ask. We know because of studies like the one that invited women who had partners to keep a diary of their sexual activity. On the days around ovulation, intercourse was 24 percent more frequent (Wilcox & others, 2004). But women's sexuality differs from that of other mammalian females. Women are more responsive to testosterone level than to estrogen level (Meston & Frohlich, 2000; Reichman, 1998). You may recall that women have testosterone, at lower levels than are found in men. If a woman's natural testosterone level drops, as happens with removal of the ovaries or adrenal glands, her sexual interest may wane. But testosterone-replacement therapy can often restore sexual activity, arousal, and pleasure (Davis & others, 2003; Kroll & others, 2004).

In men, testosterone levels fluctuate normally, from man to man and hour to hour, with little effect on sexual drive (Byrne, 1982). Indeed, male hormones sometimes vary in response to sexual stimulation. Researchers had heterosexual male volunteers talk separately with a male student and with a female student. In both cases, the volunteers' testosterone levels rose with the social arousal, but especially after talking with the female (Dabbs & others, 1987, 2000). Thus, sexual arousal can be a *cause* as well as a result of increased testosterone levels.

Although normal short-term hormonal changes have little effect on men's

"Fill'er up with testosterone."

and women's desire, large hormonal shifts have a greater effect. These tend to occur at two predictable points in the life span, and sometimes at an unpredictable third point.

1. *During puberty, a surge in sex hormones triggers the development of sex characteristics.* Interest in dating and sexual stimulation usually increases at this time. If the hormonal surge is prevented—as it was during the 1600s and 1700s for boys who were castrated to preserve their soprano voices for Italian opera—sex characteristics and sexual desire do not develop normally (Peschel & Peschel, 1987).

2. *In later life, estrogen levels fall, and women experience menopause* (see Chapter 3). As sex hormone levels decline, the frequency of sexual fantasies and intercourse declines as well (Leitenberg & Henning, 1995).

3. *For some, surgery or drugs may cause hormonal shifts.* When adult men are castrated, sex drive typically falls as testosterone levels decline (Hucker & Bain, 1990). If male sex offenders take a drug that reduces testosterone level to that of a boy's before puberty, they also lose much of their sexual urge (Money & others, 1983).

Sexual Disorders

5: What are sexual disorders?

Like so much else, sexual behavior is a biopsychosocial phenomenon. An inability to complete the sexual response cycle may stem from biological or psychological factors or both. **Sexual disorders** are problems that consistently impair sexual functioning. Some involve sexual motivation, especially lack of sexual energy and arousability. For men, common problems are *premature ejaculation* and *erectile dysfunction* (inability to have or maintain an erection). For women, the problem may be *orgasmic dysfunction* (infrequently or never experiencing orgasm). Most women who experience sexual distress relate it to their emotional relationship

with their partner during sex, not to physical aspects of the activity (Bancroft & others, 2003).

People with sexual disorders can often be helped by receiving therapy. A therapist may, for example, help men learn ways to control their urge to ejaculate, or help women learn to bring themselves to orgasm. In some areas, drug therapy is the answer. For men with abnormally low testosterone levels, testosterone-replacement therapy often increases sexual desire and also energy and vitality (Yates, 2000). Starting with the introduction of Viagra in 1998, erectile dysfunction has been treated effectively by taking a pill.

Two other kinds of sexual problems can radically change people's lives. These are not sexual disorders. Rather, they are problems arising from unprotected sex—sexually transmitted infections and unwanted teen pregnancies.

Sexually Transmitted Infections

6: What are STIs and how can they be prevented?

Rates of *sexually transmitted infections* (STIs, also called STDs for *sexually transmitted diseases*) are rising. Two-thirds of new infections occur in people under 25 (ASHA, 2003). Teenage girls, because of their less mature biological development and lower levels of protective antibodies, seem especially vulnerable (Guttmacher, 1994; Morell, 1995). About 40 percent of sexually experienced 14- to 19-year-old U.S. females have an STI (CDC, 2008).

To comprehend the mathematics of sexually transmitted infection, imagine this scenario. Over the course of a year, Pat has sex with 9 people. Over the same period, each of Pat's partners has sex with 9 other people, who in turn have sex with 9 others. How many "phantom" sex partners (past partners of partners) will Pat have? The actual number—511—is more than five times the estimate given by the average student (Brannon & Brock, 1994).

Condoms offer no protection against certain skin-to-skin STIs and only partial

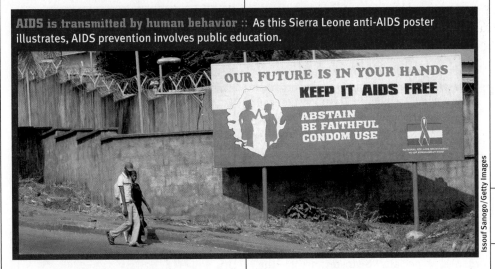

AIDS is transmitted by human behavior :: As this Sierra Leone anti-AIDS poster illustrates, AIDS prevention involves public education.

protection against the human papillomaviruses (HPV), most of which can now be prevented by vaccination (Medical Institute, 1994; NIH, 2001). Condoms do, however, reduce other risks. The risk of getting HIV (*human immunodeficiency virus*—the virus that causes **AIDS**) from an infected partner is 10 times higher for those who do not use condoms (Pinkerton & Abramson, 1997). Although AIDS is also transmitted by other means, such as needle sharing during drug use, its sexual transmission is most common.

Women's AIDS rates are increasing fastest, partly because the virus is passed from male to female much more often than from female to male. A man's semen can carry more of the virus than can a woman's vaginal and cervical secretions. The HIV-infected semen can also linger for days in the woman's vagina and cervix, increasing the time of exposure (Allen & Setlow, 1991; WHO, 2004).

In 2005, most U.S. AIDS cases were people in midlife and younger—ages 25 to 44 (U.S. Centers for Disease Control and Prevention, 2007). Given AIDS' long incubation period, many would have been infected as teens. In 2007, the death of 2 million AIDS victims worldwide left behind countless grief-stricken partners and millions of orphaned children (UNAIDS, 2008). Sub-Saharan Africa is home to 6 in

10 of those carrying the HIV virus, and medical treatment and care for the dying are sapping the region's social resources.

Teen Pregnancy

7: What factors influence teenagers' sexual behaviors and use of contraceptives?

Compared with European teens, American teens have lower rates of intercourse, but higher rates of teen pregnancy and abortion (Call & others, 2002). Why? One reason is that they have lower rates of contraceptive use. Only one-third of sexually active male teens use condoms consistently (Sonenstein, 1992). Some findings:

Ignorance Half of sexually active Canadian teen girls have had mistaken ideas about which birth control methods will protect them from pregnancy and STIs (Immen, 1995). Most teens also overestimate their peers' sexual activity. The idea that "everybody is doing it" may influence their own behavior (Child Trends, 2001).

Guilt related to sexual activity One survey found that 72 percent of sexually active 12- to 17-year-old American girls said they regretted having had sex (Reuters, 2000). Such feelings can reduce sexual activity. But if passion overwhelms intentions, they can also reduce attempts at birth control (Gerrard & Luus, 1995).

Minimal communication about birth control Many teens have been uncomfortable talking about contraception with their parents, partners, and peers (Kotva & Schneider, 1990; Milan & Kilmann, 1987). Those who talk freely with friends or parents, and are in an exclusive relationship with a partner with whom they communicate openly, are more likely to use contraceptives.

"Condoms should be used on every conceivable occasion."

Anonymous

Alcohol use Sexually active teens are typically alcohol-using teens (Albert & others, 2003; National Research Council, 1987). For teens, a few pre-sex drinks often translate into not using condoms (Kotchick & others, 2001). Alcohol depresses the brain centers that control judgment, inhibition, and self-awareness. As a result, it tends to break down normal restraints, a fact well known to sexually coercive males.

TV and movies model unsafe sex An hour of prime-time TV on the three major U.S. networks contains on average 15 sexual acts, words, and innuendos. The partners are usually unmarried, with no prior romantic relationship. Few communicate any concern for birth control or STIs (Brown & others, 2002; Kunkel, 2001).

"All of us who make motion pictures are teachers, teachers with very loud voices."

Film producer George Lucas,
Academy Award ceremonies, 1992

---

sexual disorder a problem that consistently impairs sexual arousal or functioning.

AIDS (acquired immune deficiency syndrome) a life-threatening, sexually transmitted infection caused by the *human immunodeficiency virus* (HIV). AIDS depletes the immune system, leaving the person vulnerable to infections.

Planned Parenthood contends that such portrayals of unsafe sex without consequence amounts to a campaign of sex disinformation. Carefully controlled studies have compared adolescents who view extensive sexual content with similar teens who don't. Those viewing the sexual material are more likely to perceive their peers as sexually active, to develop permissive attitudes, and to have early intercourse (Escobar-Chaves & others, 2005; Martino & others, 2005).

One response to these facts of life has been a greater emphasis on teen abstinence within some comprehensive sex education programs. A National Longitudinal Study of Adolescent Health among 12,000 teens found several predictors of sexual restraint. These include high intelligence, religiosity, the presence of the teen's father in the home, and participation in service learning programs.

Teens with high (rather than average) intelligence test scores are more likely to delay sex. They evidently appreciate the risk of pregnancy and other negative outcomes. They also tend to be more focused on future achievement than on here-and-now pleasures (Halpern & others, 2000). Actively religious teens and young adults have lower pregnancy rates because they more often reserve sex for marital commitment (Rostosky & others, 2004; Smith, 1998).

The link between a father's presence and low pregnancy rates comes from studies like one that followed hundreds of New Zealand and U.S. girls from age 5 to 18. A father's absence was linked to sexual activity before age 16 and teen pregnancy (Ellis & others, 2003). These associations held even after adjusting for other adverse influences, such as poverty.

Several experiments have compared pregnancy rates among teens volunteering as tutors or teachers' aides or participating in community projects with comparable teens randomly assigned to control conditions (Kirby, 2002; O'Donnell & others, 2002). Pregnancy rates were lower among the teen volunteers. Does service learning promote a sense of personal competence, control, and responsibility? Does it encourage more future-oriented thinking?

Or does it simply reduce opportunities for unprotected sex? Researchers are currently searching for these answers.

We have seen that exposure to mass media portrayals of sexual behavior correlates with teen pregnancy. On a broader level, sexually explicit material influences our expectations about our own sexuality.

The Psychology of Sex

8: How do external and imagined stimuli contribute to sexual arousal?

We might compare human sex hormones, especially testosterone, to the fuel in a car. Without fuel, a car will not run. Our hormonal fuel is equally essential. But our sexual motivation is fueled by more than hormones. It also requires the psychological stimuli—external and imagined—that turn on the engine, keep it running, and shift it into high gear.

External Stimuli

Many studies confirm that men become aroused when they see, hear, or read erotic material. It should not be surprising, then, to hear that most sexually explicit materials are sold to men. What may be surprising, though, is that most women—at least the less-inhibited women who volunteer to participate in such studies—report or exhibit nearly as much arousal to the same stimuli (Heiman, 1975; Stockton & Murnen, 1992).

With repeated exposure, the emotional response to any erotic stimulus often grows weaker. During the 1920s, when Western women's hemlines first rose to the knee, an exposed leg was a mildly erotic stimulus. So were modest (by today's standards) two-piece swimsuits and movie scenes of a mere kiss. Today, few Westerners would be aroused by such images.

Repeatedly viewing images of women being sexually coerced—and seeming to enjoy it—appears to follow a similar path. Viewers become more accepting of the false idea that women enjoy rape. They also tend to be more willing to

hurt women (Malamuth & Check, 1981; Zillmann, 1989).

Sexually explicit material is not the only form of external sexual stimuli. Simply looking at images of sexually attractive women and men can affect people's attitudes toward their own partners and relationships. After male collegians view sexually attractive women on TV or in magazines, they often find an average woman, or their own girlfriend or wife, less attractive (Kenrick & Gutierres, 1980; Kenrick & others, 1989; Weaver & others, 1984). Viewing X-rated sex films similarly tends to diminish people's satisfaction with their own sexual partners (Zillmann, 1989). Some sex researchers suspect that reading or watching erotica may create expectations that few men and women can fulfill.

Imagined Stimuli

The brain, it has been said, is our most important sex organ. The stimuli inside our heads—our imagination—can influence sexual arousal and desire. People who, because of a spinal cord injury, have no genital sensation, can still feel sexual desire (Willmuth, 1987).

Wide-awake people become sexually aroused not only by memories of prior sexual activities but also by fantasies. In one survey of masturbation-related fantasies (Hunt, 1974), 19 percent of women

THINK CRITICALLY ABOUT:

SEX AND HUMAN VALUES

Recognizing that values are both personal and cultural, most sex researchers and educators try to keep their writings on sexual behavior value-free. But the very words we use to describe behavior can reflect our personal values. Whether we label certain sexual behaviors as "perversions" or as part of an "alternative sexual life-style" depends on our attitude toward the behaviors. Labels describe, but they also evaluate.

Yet sex education separated from the context of human values may give some students the idea that sexual intercourse is simply a recreational activity. Diana Baumrind (1982), a University of California child-rearing expert, has observed that an implication that adults are neutral about adolescent sexual activity is unfortunate, because "promiscuous recreational sex poses certain psychological, social, health, and moral problems that must be faced realistically."

Perhaps we can agree that the knowledge provided by sex research is preferable to ignorance, and yet also agree that researchers' values should be stated openly, enabling us to debate them and to reflect on our own values.

and 10 percent of men reported imagining being "taken" by someone overwhelmed with desire for them. Fantasy is not reality, however. There's a big difference between fantasizing that Orlando Bloom just won't take no for an answer and having a hostile stranger actually force himself on you (Brownmiller, 1975).

About 95 percent of both men and women say they have had sexual fantasies. But men (whether gay or straight) fantasize about sex more often, more physically, and less romantically. They also prefer less personal and faster-paced sexual content in books and videos (Leitenberg & Henning, 1995).

* * *

We have considered some of the research on the biological and psychological aspects of human sexuality. It's important to remember, though, that scientific research on human sexuality does not aim to define the personal meaning of sex in our own lives. (See Think Critically About: Sex and Human Values.) You could know every available fact about sex—that the initial spasms of male and female orgasm come at 0.8-second intervals, that the female nipples expand 10 millimeters at the peak of sexual arousal, that systolic blood

pressure rises some 60 points, and respiration rate to 40 breaths per minute—but fail to understand the human significance of sexual intimacy.

Surely one significance of sexual intimacy is its expression of our profoundly social nature. Sex is a socially significant act. Men and women can achieve orgasm alone, yet most people find greater satisfaction while embracing their loved one. Our sexuality fuels a yearning for closeness. At its human best, sex is life-uniting and love-renewing.

In the remaining pages of this chapter, we'll consider two special topics: *sexual orientation* (the direction of our sexual interests), and evolutionary psychology's explanation of our sexual motivation.

PRACTICE TEST

5. In describing the sexual response cycle, Masters and Johnson noted that
   a. a plateau phase follows orgasm.
   b. men experience a refractory period during which they cannot experience orgasm.
   c. the feeling that accompanies orgasm is stronger in men than in women.

   d. testosterone is released equally in women and men.

6. A striking effect of hormonal changes on human sexual behavior is the
   a. end of sexual desire in men over 60.
   b. sharp rise in sexual interest at puberty.
   c. decrease in women's sexual desire at the time of ovulation.
   d. increase in testosterone levels in castrated males.

7. The use of condoms during sex
   a. protects against all STIs.
   b. reduces the risk of getting HIV.
   c. protects against skin-to-skin STIs.
   d. increases the risk of getting a human papillomavirus.

8. Factors contributing to unplanned teen pregnancies include ignorance, guilt, lack of communication about options, mass media modeling of promiscuity, and
   a. the "just say no" attitude.
   b. higher intelligence level.
   c. the decreased rates of sexually transmitted diseases.
   d. alcohol use.

9. An example of an external stimulus that might influence sexual behavior is
   a. blood level of testosterone.
   b. the onset of puberty.
   c. a sexually explicit film.
   d. an erotic fantasy or dream.

Answers: 5. b, 6. b, 7. b, 8. d, 9. c.

Sexual Orientation

9: What does current research tell us about why some people are attracted to members of their own sex and others are attracted to members of the other sex?

We express the *direction* of our sexual interest in our **sexual orientation**—our enduring sexual attraction toward members of our own sex (*homosexual orientation*)

sexual orientation an enduring sexual attraction toward members of either our own sex (homosexual orientation) or the other sex (heterosexual orientation).

or the other sex (*heterosexual orientation*). As far as we know, all cultures in all times have been predominantly heterosexual (Bullough, 1990). Some cultures have condemned homosexuality. Other have accepted it. But in both cases, heterosexuality prevails and homosexuality survives.

In one British survey of 18,876 people, 1 percent reported being *asexual,* having "never felt sexually attracted to anyone at all" (Bogaert, 2006).

Estimates based on data from the 2000 U.S. Census suggest that 2.5 percent of the population is gay or lesbian (Tarmann, 2002). About 3 or 4 percent of men and 1 or 2 percent of women are exclusively homosexual (Smith, 1998). A much smaller number (fewer than 1 percent) report being actively bisexual, and many of them say they had an isolated homosexual experience (Mosher & others, 2005). Most people surveyed say they have had an occasional homosexual fantasy.

Studies indicate that men who describe themselves as bisexual tend to respond like homosexual men; they typically have genital arousal mostly to same-sex erotic stimuli (Rieger & others, 2005).

The overwhelming majority of the U.S. population—some 97+ percent—is heterosexual, or *straight*. What does it feel like to be the "odd man (or woman) out" in a straight culture? If you are heterosexual, one way to understand is to imagine how you would feel if you were socially isolated or fired for openly admitting or displaying your feelings toward someone of the other sex. How would you react if you overheard people making crude jokes about heterosexual people? How would you feel if most movies, TV shows, and advertisements showed homosexuals going about their normal daily life? And how would you answer if your family members were pleading with you to change your heterosexual life-style and to enter into a homosexual marriage?

Facing such reactions, homosexual people often struggle with their sexual orientation. They may at first try to ignore or deny their desires, hoping they will go away. But they don't. Some may try to change, through psychotherapy, willpower, or prayer. But the feelings typically persist, as do those of heterosexual people—who are similarly incapable of becoming homosexual (Haldeman, 1994, 2002; Myers & Scanzoni, 2005).

Most of today's psychologists therefore view sexual orientation as neither willfully chosen nor willfully changed. In 1973, the American Psychiatric Association dropped homosexuality from its list of "mental illnesses." In 1993, the World Health Organization did the same, as did Japan's and China's psychiatric associations in 1995 and 2001. Some have noted that rates of depression and attempted suicide are higher among gays and lesbians. Many psychologists believe, however, that these symptoms may result from experiences with bullying, harassment, and discrimination (Sandfort & others, 2001; Warner & others, 2004).

Thus, sexual orientation in some ways is like handedness: Most people are one way, some the other. A very few are ambidextrous. Regardless, the way one is endures.

There are, however, some gender differences in sexual orientation. Women's orientation tends to be less strongly felt and may be more variable than men's (Diamond, 2000, 2003; Peplau & Garnets, 2000). Men's lesser *erotic plasticity* (sexual variability) is apparent across time, across cultures, across situations, and across differing levels of education, religiosity, and peer influence (Baumeister, 2000). Adult women's sexual drive and interests are more flexible and changing than are adult men's. Women, more than men, for example, prefer to alternate periods of high sexual activity with periods of almost none. They are also somewhat more likely than men to feel bisexual attractions.

AP Photo/Stephen J. Carerra

Personal values affect sexual orientation less than they affect other forms of sexual behavior. :: Compared with people who rarely attend religious services, for example, those who attend regularly are one-third as likely to have lived together before marriage, and they report having had many fewer sex partners. But (if male) they are just as likely to be homosexual (Smith, 1998).

Environment and Sexual Orientation

If our sexual orientation is indeed something we do not choose and seemingly cannot change, then where do these enduring preferences—heterosexual or homosexual—come from? Let's look first at possible environmental influences on sexual orientation. To see if you can predict the findings that have emerged from hundreds of studies, try answering (yes or no) the following questions:

1. Is homosexuality linked with problems in a child's relationships with parents, such as with a domineering mother and an ineffectual father, or a possessive mother and a hostile father?

2. Does homosexuality involve a fear or hatred of people of the other gender, leading individuals to direct their sexual desires toward members of their own sex?

3. Is sexual orientation linked with levels of sex hormones currently in the blood?

4. As children, were many homosexuals molested, seduced, or otherwise sexually victimized by an adult homosexual?

The answer to all these questions appears to be *no* (Storms, 1983). In a search for possible environmental influences on sexual orientation, Kinsey Institute investigators interviewed nearly 1000 homosexuals and 500 heterosexuals. They assessed nearly every imaginable psychological cause of homosexuality—parental relationships, childhood sexual experiences, peer relationships, dating experiences (Bell & others, 1981; Hammersmith, 1982). Their findings: Homosexuals were no more likely than heterosexuals to have been sexually abused, smothered by maternal love, or neglected by their father. Consider this: If "distant fathers" were more likely to produce homosexual sons, then shouldn't boys growing up in father-absent homes more often be gay? (They are not.) And shouldn't the rising number of such homes have led to a noticeable increase in the gay population? (It has not.)

The bottom line from a half-century's theory and research: If there are environmental factors that influence sexual orientation, we do not yet know what they are.

Biology and Sexual Orientation

The lack of evidence for environmental causes of homosexuality has led researchers to explore possible biological influences. Some areas under study include homosexuality in other species, gay-straight brain differences, and the influence of genetics and prenatal hormones.

Same-Sex Attraction in Other Species

New York City's Central Park Zoo penguins Silo and Roy spent several years as devoted same-sex partners. In Boston's Public Gardens, caretakers recently solved the mystery of why a much-loved swan couple's eggs never hatched. Both swans are female. At least occasional

Juliet and Juliet, Boston

©The Boston Globe/John Tlumacki

same-sex relations have been observed in several hundred species (Bagemihl, 1999). Grizzlies, gorillas, monkeys, flamingos, and owls are all on the long list. Among rams, for example, some 6 to 10 percent (to sheep-breeding ranchers, the "duds") display same-sex attraction by shunning ewes and seeking to mount other males (Perkins & Fitzgerald, 1997). Some degree of homosexuality seems to be a natural part of the animal world.

Gay-Straight Brain Differences

Researcher Simon LeVay (1991) studied sections of the hypothalamus taken from deceased heterosexual and homosexual people. (The hypothalamus is a brain structure linked to emotion.) As a gay man, LeVay wanted to do "something connected with my gay identity." As a scientist, he knew he had to avoid biasing the results. He therefore conducted a *blind* study, without knowing which donors were gay. After nine months of peering through his microscope at a cell cluster that seemed to come in different sizes, he consulted the records to see which samples came from which donors. One cell cluster was reliably larger in heterosexual men than in women and homosexual men. "I was almost in a state of shock," LeVay said (1994). "I took a walk

by myself on the cliffs over the ocean. I sat for half an hour just thinking what this might mean."

It should not surprise us that brains differ with sexual orientation. Remember our maxim: *Everything psychological is simultaneously biological.* But when did the brain difference begin? At conception? During childhood or adolescence? Did experience produce the difference? Or was it genes or prenatal hormones (or genes via prenatal hormones)?

LeVay does not view this cell cluster as an "on-off button" for sexual orientation. Rather, he believes it is an important part of a brain pathway active during sexual behavior. He agrees that sexual behavior patterns could influence the brain's anatomy. (Neural pathways in our brain do tend to strengthen with use.) In fish, birds, rats, and humans, brain structures vary with experience—including sexual experience (Breedlove, 1997). But LeVay believes it more likely that brain anatomy influences sexual orientation. His hunch seems confirmed by the discovery of a similar difference found between the 6 to 10 percent of male sheep that display same-sex attraction and the 90+ percent attracted to females (Larkin & others, 2002; Roselli & others, 2002, 2004). Moreover, such differences seem to develop soon after birth, perhaps even before birth (Rahman & Wilson, 2003).

> "Gay men simply don't have the brain cells to be attracted to women."
>
> Simon LeVay, *The Sexual Brain*, 1993

Since LeVay's discovery, other researchers have reported additional gay-straight brain differences. One is an area of the hypothalamus that governs sexual arousal (Savic & others, 2005). When straight women are given a whiff of a scent derived from men's sweat, which contains traces of male hormones, this area becomes active. Gay men's brains respond similarly to the men's scent. Straight men's brains do not; they show the arousal response only to a female hormone sample. In a similar study, lesbians' responses differed from those of straight women (Martins & others, 2005).

A third brain difference appears in the fibers connecting the right and left hemispheres. A section of the anterior commissure (similar to the corpus callosum) is one-third larger in homosexual men than in heterosexual men (Allen & Gorski, 1992). These and other studies support the idea that, in some areas, homosexual men's brains are similar to women's brains in ways not found in heterosexual men (Gladue, 1994).

Genetic Influences

Three lines of evidence suggest a genetic influence on sexual orientation.

- "Homosexuality does appear to run in families," note Brian Mustanski and Michael Bailey (2003). Homosexual men have more homosexual relatives on their mother's side than on their father's. And these maternal relatives produce more offspring than do the maternal relatives of heterosexual men. Perhaps genes that convey a reproductive advantage in mothers and aunts somehow influence the sexual orientation of their sons and nephews (Camperio-Ciani & others, 2004).

- Twin studies support the idea that genes influence sexual orientation. Identical twins (who have identical genes) are somewhat more likely than fraternal twins (who have different genes) to share a homosexual orientation. However, sexual orientations differ in many identical twin pairs (especially female twins). This means that other factors besides genes play a role.

- Laboratory experiments on fruit flies have altered a single gene and changed the flies' sexual orientation and behavior (Dickson, 2005). During courtship, females acted like males (pursuing other females) and males acted like females (Demir & Dickson, 2005).

Brain anatomy and genetics are two of the biological influences on sexual orientation. The third appears to be prenatal exposure to hormones or other biochemical substances in the womb.

Prenatal Influences

Twins share not only genes, but also a prenatal environment. Two sets of findings indicate that the prenatal environment matters.

> "Modern scientific research indicates that sexual orientation is . . . partly determined by genetics, but more specifically by hormonal activity in the womb."
>
> Glenn Wilson and Qazi Rahman, *Born Gay: The Psychobiology of Sex Orientation*, 2005

First, exposure to the hormone levels typically experienced by female fetuses during a critical period of brain development may predispose a person (female or male) to be attracted to males in later life. When pregnant sheep are injected with testosterone during a critical period of fetal development, their female offspring later show homosexual behavior (Money, 1987). In humans, this critical period seems to fall between the middle of the second and fifth months after conception (Ellis & Ames, 1987; Gladue, 1990; Meyer-Bahlburg, 1995).

Second, the mother's immune system may play a role in the development of sexual orientation. Men who have older brothers are somewhat more likely to be gay (Blanchard, 1997, 2001; Bogaert, 2003). Assuming the odds of homosexuality are roughly 3 percent among first sons, they rise to about 4 percent among second sons, 5 percent or a little more for third sons, and so on for each additional older brother. The reason for this curious effect—called the *older-brother* or *fraternal birth-order effect*—is unclear. But the explanation does seem biological because the older-brother effect does not occur among adopted brothers (Bogaert, 2006). Researchers suspect the mother's immune system may have a defensive response to substances produced by male fetuses. After each pregnancy with a male fetus, the maternal antibodies may become stronger and may prevent the fetus' brain from developing in a typical male pattern.

Women with older sisters, and women who were womb-mates of twin brothers, exhibit no such sibling effect (Rose & others, 2002).

Gay-Straight Trait Differences

On several traits, homosexual individuals of both sexes appear to fall midway between heterosexual females and males. Consider, for example, the spatial abilities of gay and straight people (Cohen, 2002; Gladue, 1994; McCormick & Witelson, 1991; Sanders & Wright, 1997). On mental rotation tasks such as the one illustrated in **FIGURE 4.2,** the scores of homosexual

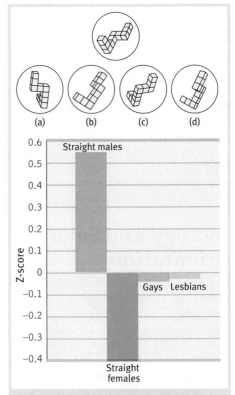

Figure 4.2> Spatial abilities and sexual orientation Which two of the four figures can be rotated to match the target figure at the top? Straight males tend to find this an easier task than do straight females, with gays and lesbians scoring somewhere in between. (From Rahman, Wilson, & Abrahams, 2003, with 60 people tested in each group.)

Answer: (a) and (d).

Table 4.1   Biological Factors in Sexual Orientation

Gay-straight trait differences

Studies—some in need of replication—indicate that homosexuals and heterosexuals differ in the following biological and behavioral traits.

- spatial abilities
- fingerprint ridge counts
- auditory system development
- handedness
- occupational preferences
- relative finger lengths
- gender nonconformity
- age of onset of puberty in males
- male body size
- sleep length
- physical aggression
- walking style

On average (the evidence is strongest for males), results for gays and lesbians fall between those of straight men and straight women. Three biological influences—brain, genetic, and prenatal—may contribute to these differences.

Brain differences

- One hypothalamic cell cluster is smaller in women and gay men than in straight men.
- Anterior commissure is larger in gay men than in women or straight men.
- Gay men's hypothalamus reacts as do straight women's to the smell of sex-related hormones.

Genetic influences

- Shared sexual orientation is higher among identical twins than among fraternal twins.
- Sexual attraction in fruit flies can be genetically manipulated.
- Male homosexuality often appears transmitted from the mother's side of the family.

Prenatal influences

- Altered prenatal hormone exposure may lead to homosexuality in humans and other animals.
- Men with several older biological brothers are more likely to be gay, possibly due to a maternal immune-system reaction.

males and females fall in between those of heterosexual males and heterosexual females. **TABLE 4.1** lists some biological and behavioral traits that show similar gay-straight differences.

* * *

The consistency of the genetic, prenatal, and brain findings has swung the pendulum toward a biological explanation of sexual orientation (Rahman & Wilson, 2003). This helps explain why sexual orientation is so difficult to change. Our sexual orientation is, it now appears, a natural and enduring disposition.

An Evolutionary Explanation of Human Sexuality

10: How do evolutionary psychologists use natural selection to explain human sexuality?

Hunger and sex are different sorts of motivations. Hunger responds to a need. If we do not eat, we die. Sex is not in this sense a need. If we do not have sex, we may feel like dying, but we do not. Why, then, is our sexuality so important to us? **Evolutionary psychologists** have proposed an answer. They ask us to remember that life is sexually transmitted. As the pleasure we take in eating is nature's inventive method of getting our body nourishment, so the pleasure of sex is our genes' way of preserving and spreading themselves. When two people are attracted, they hardly stop to think of themselves as guided by their genes. But sexual motivation is nature's clever way of making people procreate, thus enabling our species' survival.

At the dawn of human history, some of those ancestors faced certain questions: Who is my ally, who my foe? What food should I eat? With whom should I mate? Some individuals answered those questions more successfully than others.

In generations past, men who were attracted to young, healthy women would have produced more offspring than those who were as attracted to older or less healthy women. That helps explain why today's men, across 37 cultures studied (**FIGURE 4.3** on the next page), would have eyes for women whose age and features imply fertility (Buss, 1994). That, say evolutionary psychologists, is because of **natural selection**—nature selects traits and appetites that contribute to survival and reproduction.

Douglas Kenrick and his colleagues (in press) suggest that what men across the world are really attracted to is "female features that were associated with fertility in the ancestral past." As carriers of our prehistoric ancestors' genes, we are biologically prepared to act in ways that promoted their survival and reproduction.

Having faced many similar challenges throughout history, evolutionary psychologists reason, men and women have

evolutionary psychology the study of how our behavior and mind have changed in adaptive ways over time using principles of natural selection.

natural selection the adaptive process; among the range of inherited trait variations, those that lead to increased reproduction and survival will most likely be passed on to succeeding generations.

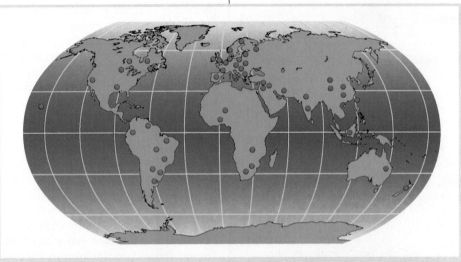

Figure 4.3> *Worldwide mating preferences* In 37 cultures studied (indicated by the red dots), men more than women preferred physical features suggesting youth and health—and reproductive potential—and women more than men preferred mates with resources and social status. Researchers credit (or blame) natural selection (Buss, 1994).

Gender Differences in Sexuality

And differ we do. Consider women's and men's sex drive. Who desires more frequent sex? Thinks more about sex? Masturbates more often? Sacrifices more to gain sex? Initiates more sex? The answers: Men, men, men, men, and men (Baumeister & others, 2001). Crosscultural psychologist Marshall Segall and his colleagues (1990, p. 244) agree: "With few exceptions anywhere in the world, males are more likely than females to initiate sexual activity." This is one of the largest gender differences in sexuality, but there are others. To see if you can predict some of these differences, take the quiz in **TABLE 4.2.**

Evolutionary psychologists summarize findings like those in Table 4.2 by saying

adapted in similar ways. Whether male or female, we eat the same foods, avoid the same predators, and perceive, learn, and remember in much the same ways. Only in areas where men and women faced differing adaptive challenges—most obviously in behaviors related to reproduction—do we differ.

that men have a more *recreational* approach to sex, while women have a more *relational* approach (Schmitt, 2005). This difference also appears in surveys that compare homosexual men and women.

Gay men (like straight men) report more interest in uncommitted sex, more responsiveness to visual sexual stimuli, and more concern with their partner's physical attractiveness (Bailey & others, 1994; Doyle, 2005).

> "It's not that gay men are oversexed; they are simply men whose male desires bounce off other male desires rather than off female desires."
>
> Steven Pinker, *How the Mind Works*, 1997

Natural Selection and Mating Preferences

Evolutionary psychologists use natural selection to explain why men and women differ more in the bedroom than in the boardroom. Our natural yearnings are our genes' way of reproducing themselves. "Humans are living fossils—collections of mechanisms produced by prior selection pressures," says evolutionary psychologist David Buss (1995).

Table 4.2	Predict the Responses		

Researchers asked samples of U.S. men and women whether they agreed or disagreed with the following statements. For each item below, give your best guess about the percentage of men and women who agreed with the statement.

Percentage of men who agreed	Percentage of women who agreed	Statement
_____	_____	1. If two people really like each other, it's all right for them to have sex even if they've known each other for a very short time.
_____	_____	2. I can imagine myself being comfortable and enjoying "casual" sex with different partners.
_____	_____	3. Affection was the reason I first had intercourse.
_____	_____	4. I think about sex every day, or several times a day.

Answers: (1) men, 58 percent; women, 34 percent; (2) men, 48 percent; women, 12 percent; (3) men, 25 percent; women, 48 percent; (4) men, 54 percent; women, 19 percent.

Sources: (1) Pryor & others, 2005; (2) Bailey & others, 2000; (3 and 4) Adapted from Laumann & others, 1994.

The explanation goes like this. Most women incubate and nurse one infant at a time. Men, however, can spread their genes by mating with many females. In our ancestral history, men most often sent their genes into the future by pairing widely, women by pairing wisely. Thus, women often feel attracted to men who seem mature, dominant, bold, and affluent—traits that reflect a capacity to support and protect (Buss, 1996, 2000; Geary, 1998; Singh, 1995). Women also prefer stick-around dads over walk-away cads. Long-term mates contribute protection and support, which give their offspring greater survival prospects (Gangestad & Simpson, 2000). Women's more relational approach to sex has adaptive benefits. A woman's best chances for sending her genes into the future lie in finding a long-term mate who will protect her offspring.

For a man, there is a genetic tradeoff between seeking to distribute his genes widely and being willing to co-parent to ensure his offspring's success. Even so, say evolutionary psychologists, the same principle is at work: Nature selects behaviors that increase the likelihood of sending one's genes into the future. As

The mating game :: Evolutionary psychologists are not surprised that older men, and not just Michael Douglas (pictured here with his wife, Catherine Zeta-Jones), often prefer younger women whose features suggest fertility.

mobile gene machines, we are designed to prefer whatever worked for our ancestors in their environments. They were predisposed to act in ways that would leave grandchildren. Had they not been, we wouldn't be here. And as carriers of their genetic legacy, we are similarly predisposed.

How, then, do evolutionary psychologists explain why "gay genes" might exist? Given that same-sex couples cannot naturally reproduce, how could such genes have survived in the human gene pool? One possible answer is that many of our genes also reside in our biological relatives. Perhaps, then, gay people's genes live on through their supporting the survival and reproductive success of their nieces, nephews, and other relatives, who also carry many of the same genes. Or perhaps different genes produce different adaptive traits that, when combined by chance, result in same-sex attraction.

Critiquing the Evolutionary Perspective

Most critics of evolutionary psychology's explanation of human sexuality accept Charles Darwin's theory of evolution, which has been an organizing principle for biology for a long time. As Jared Diamond (2001) notes, "Virtually no contemporary scientists believe that Darwin was basically wrong." Evolutionary psychologists have adapted Darwin's theory and applied evolutionary principles to psychology. Darwin would have been pleased. In concluding *On the Origin of Species*, he predicted "open fields for far more important researches. Psychology will be based on a new foundation" (1859, p. 346).

But critics say there is a weakness in the reasoning used by evolutionary psychologists. Evolutionary psychology often starts with an effect (such as the gender sexuality difference) and works backward to propose an explanation. To see the problems, let's imagine a different

"I had a nice time, Steve. Would you like to come in, settle down, and raise a family?"

observation and reason backward. If men were uniformly loyal to their mates, might we not reason that the children of these committed, supportive fathers would more often survive to pass on their fathers' genes? Might not this bond with one woman also increase the otherwise slim odds of conceiving a child, while preventing her from mating with competing men? Might not a ritualized bond—a marriage—also spare women from male advances and chronic harassment? Such suggestions are, in fact, evolutionary explanations for why humans tend to pair off monogamously. One can hardly lose at hindsight explanation, which is, said Stephen Jay Gould (1997), mere "speculation [and] guesswork."

Some also worry about the social consequences of evolutionary psychology's approach. Does it suggest that genes *are* destiny? Does it mean that any effort to remake society is useless (Rose, 1999)? Does it mean that men don't need to take responsibility for their sexual behavior? Could it be used to justify "high-status men marrying a series of young, fertile women" (Looy, 2001)?

Other critics remind us that cultural expectations can bend the genders. If men are socialized to value lifelong commitment, they may sexually bond with one partner. If women are socialized to accept casual sex, they may willingly have sex with many partners.

Cultural expectations can also shape our mate preferences. Show Alice Eagly and Wendy Wood (1999; Wood & Eagly, 2002) a culture with gender inequality—where men are providers and women are homemakers—and they will show you a culture where men strongly desire youth and domestic skill in their potential mates, and where women seek status and earning potential in their mates. Show Eagly and Wood a culture with gender equality, and they will show you a culture with smaller gender differences in mate preferences.

Evolutionary psychologists agree that much of who we are is not hard-wired.

What's considered attractive varies somewhat with time and place. And they reassure us that the sexes, having faced similar adaptive problems, are far more alike than different. They stress that the tight genetic leash that predisposes a dog's retrieving, a cat's pouncing, or an ant's building is looser on humans. The genes selected during our ancestral history give us a great capacity to learn and to adapt and survive, whether living in igloos or tree houses.

But they ask us to remember the power of evolutionary principles to explain by offering testable predictions. We can, for example, scientifically test whether we will favor others to the extent that they share our genes or can later return our favors. And they remind us that

our great capacity to learn gives us hope. The study of how we came to be need not dictate how we *ought* to be. Understanding what we are capable of doing can help us become better people. Genes and experience together wire the brain.

10. Current research suggests several possible influences on male sexual orientation. Which of the following is NOT one of those influences?
    a. Certain cell clusters in the hypothalamus
    b. A domineering mother and ineffectual father

CLOSE-UP

■ FOR THOSE TROUBLED BY THE SCIENTIFIC UNDERSTANDING OF HUMAN ORIGINS

I know from my mail that some readers feel troubled by the naturalism and evolutionism of contemporary science. They worry that a science of behavior (and evolutionary science in particular) will destroy our sense of the beauty, mystery, and spiritual significance of the human creature. For those concerned, I offer some reassuring thoughts.

When Isaac Newton explained the rainbow in terms of light of differing wavelengths, the poet Keats feared that Newton had destroyed the rainbow's mysterious beauty. Yet, nothing about the science of optics need diminish our appreciation for the drama of a rainbow arching across a rain-darkened sky.

When Galileo assembled evidence that the Earth revolved around the Sun, not vice versa, he did not offer absolute proof for his theory. Rather he offered an explanation that pulled together a variety of observations, such as the changing shadows cast by the Moon's mountains. His explanation eventually won the day because it described and explained things in a way that made sense, that hung together. Darwin's theory of evolution likewise offers an organizing principle that makes sense of many observations.

Some people of faith may find the scientific idea of human origins troubling. Many others find it fits with their own spirituality. Pope John Paul II in 1996 welcomed a science-religion dialogue, finding it noteworthy that evolutionary theory "has been progressively accepted by researchers, following a series of discoveries in various fields of knowledge."

Meanwhile, many people of science are awestruck at the emerging understanding of the universe and the human creature. It boggles the mind—the entire universe popping out of a point some 14 billion years ago, and instantly inflating to cosmological size. Had the energy of this Big Bang been the tiniest

bit less, the universe would have collapsed back on itself. Had it been the tiniest bit more, the result would have been a soup too thin to support life. Had gravity been a teeny bit stronger or weaker, or had the weight of a carbon proton been a wee bit different, our universe just wouldn't have worked.

What caused this almost-too-good-to-be-true, finely tuned universe? Why is there something rather than nothing? How did it come to be, in the words of Harvard-Smithsonian astrophysicist Owen Gingerich (1999), "so extraordinarily right, that it seemed the universe had been expressly designed to produce intelligent, sentient beings"? Is there a benevolent superintelligence behind it all? On such matters, a humble, awed, scientific silence is appropriate, suggested philosopher Ludwig Wittgenstein: "Whereof one cannot speak, thereof one must be silent."

Rather than fearing science, we can welcome its enlarging our understanding and awakening our sense of awe. In a short 4 billion years, life on Earth has come from nothing to structures as complex as a 6-billion-unit strand of DNA and the incomprehensible intricacy of the human brain. Nature seems cunningly and ingeniously devised to produce extraordinary, self-replicating, information-processing systems—us (Davies, 1992, 1999, 2004). Although we appear to have been created from dust, over eons of time, the end result is a priceless creature, one rich with potentials beyond our imagining.

> "The causes of life's history [cannot] resolve the riddle of life's meaning."
>
> Stephen Jay Gould,
> *Rocks of Ages: Science and Religion in the Fullness of Life,* 1999

c. A section of fibers connecting the right and left hemispheres of the brain

d. Exposure to hormone levels typically experienced by female fetuses

11. Evolutionary psychologists are most likely to focus on
    a. how we differ from one another.
    b. the social consequences of sexual behaviors.
    c. natural selection of the fittest adaptations.
    d. cultural expectations about the "right" ways for men and women to behave.

Answer: 10. b, 11. c.

Thinking About Gender, Sexuality, and Nature-Nurture Interaction

Our ancestral history helped form us as a species. Where there is variation, natural selection, and heredity, there will be evolution. Our genes form us. This is a great truth about human nature.

But our culture and experiences also form us. If their genes and hormones predispose males to be more physically aggressive than females, culture may magnify this gender difference by encouraging males to be macho and females to be the kinder, gentler sex. If men are encouraged toward roles that demand physical power, and women toward more nurturing roles, each may act accordingly. By exhibiting the actions expected of those who fill such roles, they will shape their own behaviors. Presidents in time become more presidential, servants more servile. Gender roles similarly shape us.

> "Genes, by themselves, are like seeds dropped onto pavement: powerless to produce anything."
> Primatologist Frans B. M. de Waal, 1999

Today, in our culture, gender roles are converging. Brute strength has become increasingly irrelevant to power and status (think Bill Gates and Oprah Winfrey). From 1960 to the century's end, women soared from 6 percent to 50 percent of U.S. medical students (AMA, 2004). In the mid-1960s, U.S. married women devoted *seven times* as many hours to housework as did their husbands; by 2003 this gap had shrunk to two times as much (Bianchi & others, 2000, 2006). Such swift change signals that biology does not fix gender roles.

If nature and nurture jointly form us, are we "nothing but" the product of nature and nurture? Are we rigidly determined?

We *are* the product of nature and nurture, but we are also an open system. Genes are all-pervasive but not all-powerful; people may defy their genetic bent to reproduce, by electing celibacy. Culture, too, is all-pervasive but not all-powerful; people may defy peer pressures and do the opposite of the expected. To excuse our failings by blaming our nature is handing over responsibility for our fate to bad genes or bad influences.

In reality, we are both the creatures and the creators of our worlds. So many things about us—including our gender identity and mating behaviors—are the product of our genes and environments. Nevertheless, the stream of causation that shapes the future runs through our present choices. Our decisions today design our environments tomorrow. Mind matters. The human environment is not like the weather—something that just happens. We are its architects. Our hopes, goals, and expectations influence our future. And that is what enables cultures to vary and to change so quickly.

TERMS AND CONCEPTS TO REMEMBER

gender, p. 103

aggression, p. 104

X chromosome, p. 106

Y chromosome, p. 106

testosterone, p. 106

role, p. 106

gender role, p. 106

gender identity, p. 107

social learning theory, p. 107

gender typing, p. 107

gender schema theory, p. 107

sexual response cycle, p. 109

refractory period, p. 109

estrogens, p. 109

sexual disorder, p. 110

AIDS, p. 111

sexual orientation, p. 113

evolutionary psychology, p. 117

natural selection, p. 117

:: Multiple-choice **self-tests** and more may be found at www.worthpublishers.com/myers.

REVIEW: GENDER AND SEXUALITY

GENDER DEVELOPMENT

1 What are some of the similarities and differences between men and women?

- *Sex* is a biological definition based on physical characteristics. *Gender* is a social definition of what it means to be male or female in a particular culture.
- Males and females are similar in their overall genetic makeup.
- Male-female differences include size, age of onset of puberty, and life expectancy.
- Psychological differences include the greater tendencies for men to express physical *aggression* and to hold social power, and for women to form social connections.

2 How do nature and nurture interact to define us as male or female?

- Different sex chromosomes lead to differing concentrations of sex hormones.
- *Gender roles* vary depending on cultural expectations.
- *Social learning theory:* Children learn male and female behaviors through imitation and reinforcement.
- *Gender schema theory:* Children's concepts of male and female influence their perceptions and behavior.

HUMAN SEXUALITY

3 What are the stages of the human sexual response cycle?

- Excitement
- Plateau
- Orgasm
- Resolution: Males enter a *refractory period* in which renewed arousal and orgasm are impossible.

5 What are sexual disorders?

- Impaired sexual arousal or functioning.
- Treatments include drugs and behavior therapy.

7 What factors influence teenagers' sexual behaviors and use of contraceptives?

- Ignorance of facts
- Guilt about sexual behavior
- Poor communication about options
- Alcohol use
- Media modeling of casual unsafe sex

6 What are STIs and how can they be prevented?

- Using condoms helps protect against most STIs (especially *AIDS*), but not those that are transmitted skin-to-skin.
- HPV may be prevented by vaccination.

"Fill'er up with testosterone."

4 How do sex hormones influence human sexual development and arousal?

- The main sex hormones are *testosterone* (greater in males) and the *estrogens* (greater in females).
- These hormones direct sexual development in the prenatal period; trigger development of sexual characteristics in adolescence; and help activate sexual behavior from puberty to late adulthood.

8 How do external and imagined stimuli contribute to sexual arousal?

- Erotic material and other external stimuli can trigger sexual arousal in both men and women.
- Viewing sexually coercive material can lead to increased acceptance of violence toward women.
- Viewing sexually explicit materials can cause men to devalue their own partners.
- Imagined stimuli (fantasies) help trigger sexual arousal.

SEXUAL ORIENTATION

9 **What does current research tell us about why some people are attracted to members of their own sex and others are attracted to members of the other sex?**

■ About 3 or 4 percent of men and 1 or 2 percent of women are homosexual, and *sexual orientation* seems to be enduring.

■ There is no evidence that environmental factors influence sexual orientation.

■ Evidence for biological influences on homosexuality comes from same-sex attraction in other species; gay-straight differences in brain characteristics and other traits; higher rates of homosexuality in certain families and among twins; and higher rates among individuals exposed to abnormal levels of hormones during critical periods of prenatal development.

THINKING ABOUT GENDER, SEXUALITY, AND NATURE-NURTURE INTERACTION

Nature and nurture interact in the development of our gender-related traits and our mating behaviors.

AN EVOLUTIONARY EXPLANATION OF HUMAN SEXUALITY

10 **How do evolutionary psychologists use natural selection to explain human sexuality?**

■ *Evolutionary psychologists* attempt to understand how *natural selection* has shaped behaviors found in all people.

■ They reason that men's more recreational attitude toward sex results from their ability to spread their genes widely by mating with many females, and women's more relational approach to sex results from their need to incubate and nurse one infant at a time.

■ Critics point out the problem in starting with an effect (male/female differences in sexuality) and working back to an explanation and suggest that cultural and social factors are being underestimated.

5 | Sensation and Perception

HEATHER SELLERS, AN ACCLAIMED WRITER and teacher, cannot recognize faces. Her vision is perfect, but her perception is not. In her book, *Face First* (2008), Sellers tells of awkward moments resulting from her lifelong *prosopagnosia*—face blindness.

> In college . . . I returned from the bathroom and plunked myself down in the wrong booth, facing the wrong man. I remained unaware he was not my date even as my date (a stranger to me) accosted Wrong Booth Guy, and then stormed out. . . . I do not recognize myself in photos or videos. I can't recognize my step-sons in the soccer pick-up line; I failed to determine which husband was mine at a party, in the mall, at the market.

People sometimes see Sellers as snobby. "Why did you walk past me?" a neighbor might later say. Hoping to avoid offending others, Sellers sometimes fakes recognition. She smiles at people she passes, in case she knows them, and may pretend to know the person with whom she is talking. But there is an upside to these perception failures. When encountering someone who previously irritated her, she typically won't feel ill will. She doesn't recognize the person.

This curious mix of "perfect vision" and face blindness illustrates the distinction between *sensation* and *perception*. When Sellers looks at a friend, her **sensation** is normal. Her senses detect the same information yours would, and they transmit that information to her brain. And her **perception**—the processes by which her brain organizes and interprets the sensory input—is *almost* normal. Thus, she may recognize people from their hair, walk, voice, or peculiar build—just not from their face. Her experience is much like yours or mine if we were struggling to recognize a specific penguin in a group of waddling penguins.

Most of us have an area on the underside of our brain's right hemisphere that helps us recognize a familiar human face as soon as we detect it—in only one-seventh of a second (Jacques & Rossion, 2006). This ability is an example of a broader principle. Nature's sensory gifts are tailored to each animal's survival needs. Some examples:

- Frogs, which feed on flying insects, have cells in their eyes that fire only in response to small, dark, moving objects. A frog could starve to death knee-deep in motionless flies. But let one zoom by and the frog's "bug detector" cells snap awake.
- Male silkworm moths' odor receptors can detect one-billionth of an ounce of sex attractant per second released by a female one mile away. That is why there continue to be silkworms.
- Human ears are most sensitive to sound frequencies that include human voices, especially a baby's cry.

We begin our exploration of such sensory gifts by considering questions that cut across all our sensory systems.

SENSING THE WORLD
From Energy to Neural Impulse
Thresholds
Sensory Adaptation

VISION
Stimulus Input: Light Energy
The Eye
Visual Information Processing

OTHER SENSES
Hearing
Touch
Pain
Taste
Smell
Body Position and Movement

PERCEPTUAL ORGANIZATION
Form Perception
Depth Perception
Perceptual Constancy

PERCEPTUAL INTERPRETATION
Sensory Deprivation and Restored Vision
Perceptual Adaptation
Perceptual Set

ESP
Claims of ESP
Facts or Fantasies?
Testing ESP

sensation the process by which our sensory receptors and nervous system take in stimulus energies from our environment.

perception the process by which our brain organizes and interprets sensory information, transforming it into meaningful objects and events.

Sensing the World: Some Basic Principles

Twenty-four hours a day, all kinds of stimuli from the outside world bombard your body. Meanwhile, in a silent, cushioned, inner world, your brain floats in utter darkness. By itself, it sees nothing. It hears nothing. It feels nothing. *So, how does the world out there get in?* How do we normally construct our representations of the external world?

From Energy to Neural Impulse

1: What three steps are basic to all our sensory systems?

Every second of every day, your sensory systems perform an amazing feat: They convert one sort of energy into another. Vision processes light energy. Hearing processes sound waves. All your senses:

- *receive* sensory stimulation, often using specialized receptor cells.

- *transform* that stimulation into neural impulses.

- *deliver* the neural information to your brain.

The process of converting one form of energy into another form that your brain can use is called **transduction.** Later in this chapter, we'll be asking more detailed questions. How do the senses work? How do we see? Hear? Smell? Taste? Feel pain? Keep our balance? In each case, we'll consider these three steps—receiving, transforming, and delivering the information that your brain uses to form your perceptions.

First, though, let's explore some of the characteristics of the stimuli we can detect in the vast sea of energy around us.

Thresholds

2: What are absolute thresholds and difference thresholds?

At this moment, you and I are being struck by x-rays and radio waves, ultraviolet and infrared light, and sound waves of very high and very low frequencies. To all of these we are blind and deaf. Other animals with differing needs detect a world that lies beyond our experience (Hughes, 1999). Birds stay on course using a magnetic compass. Bats and dolphins locate prey with the help of sonar, bouncing sounds off objects. On cloudy days, bees navigate by detecting aspects of sunlight we cannot see. The shades on our senses are open just a crack, giving us only a tiny glimpse of the energy around us. But for our needs, this is enough.

Absolute Thresholds

To some kinds of stimuli we are amazingly sensitive. From a mountain peak on an utterly dark, clear night, most of us could see a candle flame atop another mountain 30 miles away. We could feel the wing of a bee falling on our cheek. We could even smell a single drop of perfume in a three-room apartment (Galanter, 1962).

Our awareness of these faint stimuli illustrates our **absolute thresholds**—the minimum stimulation needed to detect a particular light, sound, pressure, taste, or odor 50 percent of the time. To test your absolute threshold for sounds, for example, a hearing specialist would send tones, at varying levels, into each of your ears. The tester would then record whether or not you could hear each tone. The test results would show the point where half the time you could detect the sound and half the time you could not. That 50-50 point would define your absolute threshold for that sound.

Subliminal Stimulation

Hoping to penetrate our unconscious, marketers offer audio and video programs to help us lose weight, stop smoking, or improve our memories. Soothing ocean sounds may mask messages we cannot consciously hear, such as "I am thin," "Cigarettes taste bad," or "I do well on tests. I have total recall of information." These **subliminal** messages, below our absolute threshold of awareness, can, we are told, change our lives. Such claims make two assumptions: (1) We can unconsciously sense subliminal stimuli **(FIGURE 5.1).** (2) Without our awareness, these stimuli have extraordinary suggestive powers. Can we? Do they?

Can we be affected by stimuli so weak that we don't notice them? Under certain conditions, yes. An unnoticed image or word can briefly **prime** your response to a later question. Let's see how this might work in a laboratory experiment. You've been asked to view a series of slides of people and to give them either positive or negative ratings. But the trickster researchers also flash another image an instant before showing you each slide. Some of the flashed images will be emotionally positive (kittens, a romantic couple) and some will be negative (a werewolf, a dead body). You will consciously perceive these images only as flashes of light. Will they affect your ratings?

In this real experiment (Krosnick & others, 1992), participants gave more positive ratings to people paired with positive images. People somehow looked nicer if their photo immediately followed unperceived kittens rather than an unperceived werewolf. This *priming effect* happened even though the viewer's brain did not have enough time to fully process the images and consciously perceive them. Once again, we see the two-track mind at work: *Much of our information processing occurs automatically, out of sight, off the radar screen of our conscious mind.*

So subliminal *sensation* is a fact. But does this mean that claims of subliminal *persuasion* are also facts? Can subliminal recordings really help us make lasting behavioral changes, such as eating less or quitting smoking? Research results from 16 experiments on the influence of subliminal self-help recordings reached the same conclusion. Not one of the recordings helped more than a placebo

Figure 5.1> Do I taste it or not? Stimuli that we detect less than 50 percent of the time are "subliminal."

Kurt Scholz/Superstock

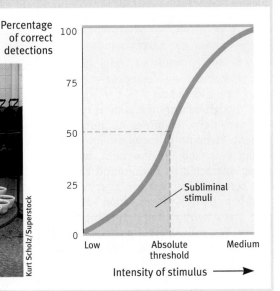

Percentage of correct detections

Intensity of stimulus →

just noticeable difference [jnd].) We define this as the minimum difference a person can detect between any two stimuli half the time. That detectable difference increases with the size of the stimulus. Thus, if you add 1 ounce to a 10-ounce weight, you will detect the difference. If you add 1 ounce to a 100-ounce weight, you will not. More than a century ago, Ernst Weber noted something so simple but so true that we refer to it as **Weber's law** and still apply it. This law states that for an average person to perceive a difference, two stimuli must differ by a constant minimum *proportion*—not a constant amount. The exact proportion varies, depending on the stimulus. Two lights, for example, must differ in intensity by 8 percent. Two objects must differ in weight by 2 percent. And two tones must differ in frequency by only 0.3 percent (Teghtsoonian, 1971).

(Greenwald & others, 1991, 1992). And placebos, you may remember, work only because we *believe* they will work.

Difference Thresholds

To function effectively, we need absolute thresholds low enough to allow us to detect important sights, sounds, textures, tastes, and smells. We also need to detect small differences among stimuli. A musician must detect tiny differences when tuning an instrument. Parents must detect the sound of their own child's voice amid other children's voices.

Psychologists call the minimum difference the **difference threshold** (or the

Sensory Adaptation

3: What function does sensory adaptation serve?

Entering your neighbors' living room, you smell a musty odor. You wonder how they can stand it, but within minutes you

The LORD is my shepherd;
I shall not want.
He maketh me to lie down
in green pastures:
he leadeth me
beside the still waters.
He restoreth my soul:
he leadeth me
in the paths of righteousness
for his name's sake.
Yea, though I walk through the valley
of the shadow of death,
I will fear no evil:
for thou art with me;
thy rod and thy staff
they comfort me.
Thou preparest a table before me
in the presence of mine enemies:
thou anointest my head with oil,
my cup runneth over.
Surely goodness and mercy
shall follow me
all the days of my life:
and I will dwell
in the house of the LORD
for ever.

The difference threshold :: In this computer-generated copy of the Twenty-third Psalm, each line of the typeface changes imperceptibly. How many lines did you read before detecting a just noticeable difference?

transduction changing one form of energy into another. In sensation, the transforming of stimulus energies, such as sights, sounds, and smells, into neural impulses our brains can interpret.

absolute threshold the minimum stimulation needed to detect a particular stimulus 50 percent of the time.

subliminal below our absolute threshold for conscious awareness.

priming activating, often unconsciously, associations in our mind, thus setting us up to perceive or remember objects or events in certain ways.

difference threshold the minimum difference between two stimuli required for detection 50 percent of the time. We experience the difference threshold as a *just noticeable difference* (or jnd).

Weber's law the principle that, to be perceived as different, two stimuli must differ by a constant minimum proportion (rather than a constant amount).

no longer notice it. **Sensory adaptation** has come to your rescue. When we are constantly exposed to a stimulus that does not change, we become less aware of it because our nerve cells fire less frequently. (To experience sensory adaptation, move your watch up your wrist an inch. You will feel it—but only for a few moments.)

Why, then, if we stare at an object without flinching, does it *not* vanish from sight? Because, unnoticed by us, our eyes are always moving. This continual quivering ensures that stimulation on the eyes' receptors is always changing.

What if we actually could stop our eyes from moving? Would sights seem to vanish, as odors do? To find out, psychologists have devised clever instruments that maintain a constant image on the eye's inner surface. Imagine that we have fitted a volunteer, Mary, with one of these instruments—a miniature projector mounted on a contact lens **(FIGURE 5.2a)**. When Mary's eye moves, the image from the projector moves as well. So everywhere that Mary looks, the scene is sure to go.

If we project images through this instrument, what will Mary see? At first, she will see the complete image. But within a few seconds, as her sensory system begins to tire, things get weird. Bit by

> "My suspicion is that the universe is not only queerer than we suppose, but queerer than we can suppose."
>
> J.B.S. Haldane, *Possible Worlds*, 1927

bit, the image vanishes, only later to reappear and then disappear—often in fragments **(FIGURE 5.2b)**.

Although sensory adaptation reduces our sensitivity, it offers an important benefit: Freedom to focus on *informative* changes in our environment without being distracted by background chatter. Our sensory receptors are alert to novelty; bore them with repetition and they free our attention for more important things. We will see this principle again and again: *We perceive the world not exactly as it is, but as it is useful for us to perceive it.*

Our sensitivity to changing stimulation helps explain television's attention-getting power. Cuts, edits, zooms, pans, and sudden noises demand attention. Even TV researchers marvel at its attention-grabbing power. One noted that even during interesting conversations, "I cannot for the life of me stop from periodically glancing over to the screen" (Tannenbaum, 2002).

Transduction, sensory thresholds, and sensory adaptation are features shared by our senses. Let's turn now to the ways

our sensory systems are unique. We'll start with vision, the sense that people prize the most.

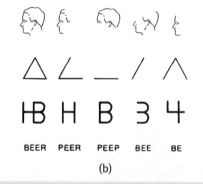

(a)   (b)

BEER   PEER   PEEP   BEE   BE

Figure 5.2> **Sensory adaptation: Now you see it, now you don't!** (a) A projector mounted on a contact lens makes the projected image move with the eye. At first, the person sees the whole image, but soon it begins to break into fragments that fade and reappear, like those in frame (b). (From "Stabilized images on the retina" by R. M. Pritchard. Copyright © 1961 Scientific American, Inc. All Rights Reserved.)

Vision

Your eyes receive light energy and transform it into neural messages that your brain then processes into what you consciously see. How does such a taken-for-granted yet remarkable thing happen?

The Stimulus Input: Light Energy

4: What are the characteristics of the energy we see as light?

When you see a red-breasted robin, what strikes your eyes are not bits of the colors gray or red but pulses of energy that your visual system perceives as these colors. What we see as visible light is but a thin slice of the wide spectrum of electromagnetic energy shown in **FIGURE 5.3**. On one end of this spectrum are the short gamma waves, no longer than the diameter of an atom. On the other end of the spectrum are the mile-long waves of radio transmission. In between is the narrow band we can see as visible light. Other portions are visible to other animals. Bees, for instance, cannot see red but can see ultraviolet light.

The light we see travels in waves, and the shape of those waves influences what we see. Light's **wavelength**—the distance from one wave peak to the next **(FIGURE 5.4a** on the next page)—determines its **hue** (the color we experience, such as the robin's red breast). A light wave's *amplitude,* or height, determines its **intensity**—the amount of energy it contains. Intensity influences brightness **(FIGURE 5.4b).**

Understanding the characteristics of the physical energy we see as light is one part of understanding vision. But to appreciate how we transform that energy into color and meaning, we need to know more about vision's window, the eye.

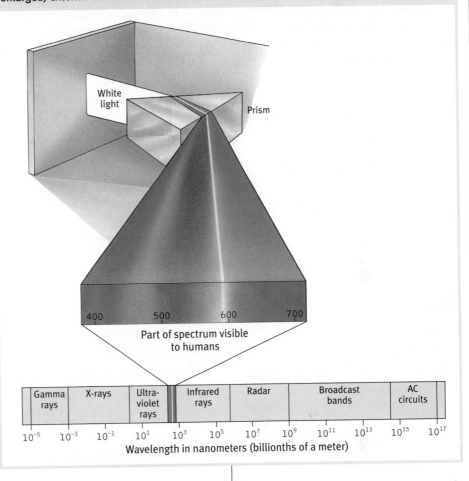

Figure 5.3> The wavelengths we see What we see as light is only a tiny slice of a wide spectrum of electromagnetic energy. The wavelengths visible to the human eye (shown enlarged) extend from the shorter waves of blue-violet light to the longer waves of red light.

White light

Prism

400   500   600   700

Part of spectrum visible to humans

Gamma rays	X-rays	Ultra-violet rays		Infrared rays	Radar	Broadcast bands	AC circuits
10^{-5}	10^{-3}	10^{-1}	10^{1}	10^{3} 10^{5}	10^{7} 10^{9}	10^{11} 10^{13}	10^{15} 10^{17}

Wavelength in nanometers (billionths of a meter)

Adaptive eyes :: You don't normally need to see well at night, unless you are a soldier. Night vision goggles (left) allow soldiers to see infrared rays (heat) in order to maneuver in the dark. When it comes to flowers, we see the ones in the middle. Bees, however, can detect ultraviolet light (right), which allows them to detect a "landing field" of pollen.

Chris Hondros/Getty Images

Edward Kinsman/Photo Researchers, Inc.

Edward Kinsman/Photo Researchers, Inc.

sensory adaptation reduced sensitivity in response to constant stimulation.

wavelength the distance from the peak of one light or sound wave to the peak of the next.

hue the dimension of color that is determined by the wavelength of light; what we know as the color names *blue, green,* and so forth.

intensity the amount of energy in a light or sound wave, which we perceive as brightness or loudness, as determined by the wave's amplitude.

Figure 5.4> The physical properties of waves (a) Waves vary in *wavelength*, the distance between successive peaks. *Frequency*, the number of complete wavelengths that can pass a point in a given time, depends on the length of the wave. The shorter the wavelength, the higher the frequency. (b) Waves also vary in *amplitude*, the height from peak to trough. Wave amplitude determines the *intensity* of colors and sounds.

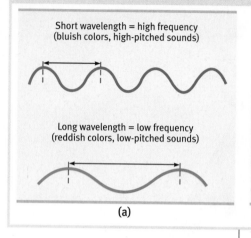

(a)

(b)

The Eye

5: How does the eye transform light energy into neural messages?

What color are your eyes? Asked this question, most people describe the color of their *irises*. This doughnut-shaped ring of muscle adjusts the size of your *pupil*, which controls the amount of light entering your eye. After passing through your cornea (the eyeball's protective covering) and pupil, light hits the *lens* in your eye. The lens then focuses the light into an image on your eyeball's inner surface, the **retina.**

For centuries, scientists knew that when an image of an object passes through a small opening, it casts an inverted mirror image on a dark wall behind. If the retina receives this sort of upside-down image, as in **FIGURE 5.5,** how

can we see the world right side up? Eventually, the answer became clear: The retina doesn't "see" a whole image. Rather, its millions of receptor cells behave like the prankster engineering students who make news by taking a car apart and rebuilding it in a friend's third-floor bedroom. The retina's cells convert the stream of light energy into neural impulses and forward those to the brain, where they are reassembled into what we perceive as an upright object.

The Retina

Let's follow a single light-energy particle into your eye. First, it makes its way through the retina's outer layer of cells to its buried receptor cells, the **rods** and **cones** (**FIGURE 5.6**). Striking the rods and cones, the light energy triggers chemical changes. These chemical reactions nudge nearby *bipolar cells*, causing them to send out neural signals. These signals in turn activate neighboring *ganglion cells*, whose axons twine together like strands of a rope to form the **optic nerve.** That nerve will carry the information to your brain, where your *thalamus* stands ready to distribute the information. The optic nerve can send nearly 1 million messages at once through its nearly 1 million ganglion fibers. We pay a small price for this high-speed eye-to-brain highway. Where the optic nerve leaves the eye, there are no receptor cells—creating a **blind spot** (**FIGURE 5.7**).

Rods and cones differ in where they're found and in what they do (**FIGURE 5.8**). *Cones* cluster around the retina's area of central focus. Many have their own hotline to the brain—each one connects to a single bipolar cell that helps relay the cone's individual message to the visual cortex. These direct connections preserve the cones' precise information, making them better able to detect fine detail.

Rods have no such hotline; they share bipolar cells with other rods, sending combined messages. Stop for a minute and experience this rod-cone difference in sensitivity to details. Pick a word in this sentence and stare directly at it, focusing its image on the cones in the center of your eye. Notice that words a few

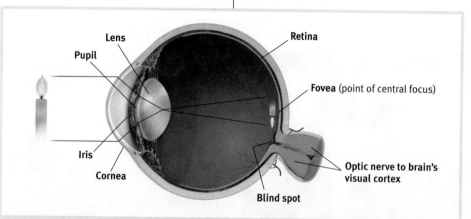

Figure 5.5> The eye Light rays reflected from a candle pass through the cornea, pupil, and lens. The curve and thickness of the lens change to bring nearby or distant objects into focus on the retina. Rays from the top of the candle strike the bottom of the retina and those from the left side of the candle strike the right side of the retina. The candle's image appears on the retina upside-down and reversed.

Figure 5.6> The retina's reaction to light

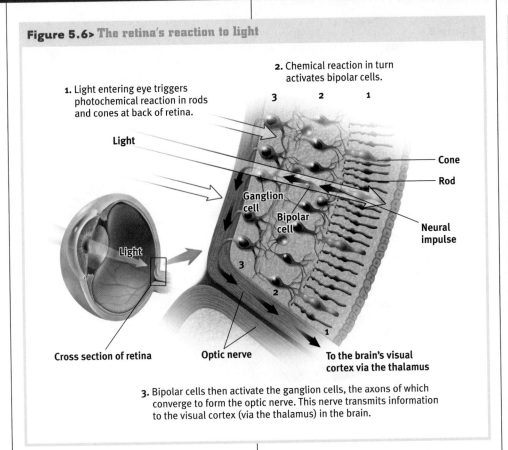

1. Light entering eye triggers photochemical reaction in rods and cones at back of retina.

2. Chemical reaction in turn activates bipolar cells.

Light

Ganglion cell

Bipolar cell

Light

Cone

Rod

Neural impulse

Cross section of retina

Optic nerve

To the brain's visual cortex via the thalamus

3. Bipolar cells then activate the ganglion cells, the axons of which converge to form the optic nerve. This nerve transmits information to the visual cortex (via the thalamus) in the brain.

Figure 5.8> Rod-shaped rods and cone-shaped cones As the scanning electron microscope shows, rods and cones are well named. The rods are more sensitive to light than are the color-sensitive cones, which is why the world looks colorless at night. Some night-loving animals, such as toads, mice, rats, and bats, have retinas made up almost entirely of rods, allowing them to function well in dim light. These creatures probably have very poor color vision.

Omikron/Photo Researchers, Inc.

inches off to the side appear blurred? Their image is striking the outer regions of your retina, where most rods are found.

Cones also enable you to see color. But in dim light, they don't function well, which is why you can't see colors in dark places. This is when rods, which enable black-and-white vision, take the lead. Rods remain sensitive in dim light. Several rods will funnel their faint energy output onto a single bipolar cell. Thus,

Figure 5.7> The blind spot There are no receptor cells where the optic nerve leaves the eye (Figure 5.6). This creates a blind spot in our vision. To demonstrate, close your left eye, look at the spot, and move the page to a distance from your face (about a foot) at which the car disappears. The blind spot does not normally impair your vision, because your eyes are moving and because one eye catches what the other misses.

retina the light-sensitive inner surface of the eye; contains the receptor rods and cones plus layers of neurons that begin the processing of visual information.

rods retinal receptors that detect black, white, and gray; necessary for peripheral and twilight vision, when cones don't respond.

cones retinal receptor cells that are concentrated near the center of the retina; in daylight or well-lit conditions, cones detect fine detail and give rise to color sensations.

optic nerve the nerve that carries neural impulses from the eye to the brain.

blind spot the point at which the optic nerve leaves the eye; this part of the retina is "blind" because it has no receptor cells.

Table 5.1	Receptors in the Human Eye	
	Cones	Rods
Number	6 million	120 million
Location in retina	Center	Periphery
Sensitivity in dim light	Low	High
Color sensitive?	Yes	No
Detail sensitive?	Yes	No

cones and rods each provide a special sensitivity—cones to detail and color, and rods to faint light (**TABLE 5.1**).

Visual Information Processing

6: How is visual information processed in the brain?

After processing by the retina's receptor cells, information travels up the optic nerve to the brain. Any given retinal area relays its information to a corresponding location in the visual cortex in the back of your brain (**FIGURE 5.9**).

Feature Detection

David Hubel and Torsten Wiesel (1979) received a Nobel prize for their work on **feature detectors.** These specialized nerve cells in the brain's visual cortex receive information from individual ganglion cells in the retina. Feature detector cells get their name from their ability to respond to a scene's specific features—to particular edges, lines, and angles. These cells pass this information to other cortical areas, where teams of cells respond to more complex patterns, such as recognizing faces. The brain activity that results is so specific that, with the help of brain scans, "we can tell if a person is looking at a shoe, a chair, or a face," noted one researcher (Haxby, 2001).

Figure 5.9> Pathway from the eyes to the visual cortex The retina's ganglion axons form the optic nerve, which runs to the thalamus to connect with neurons that run to the visual cortex.

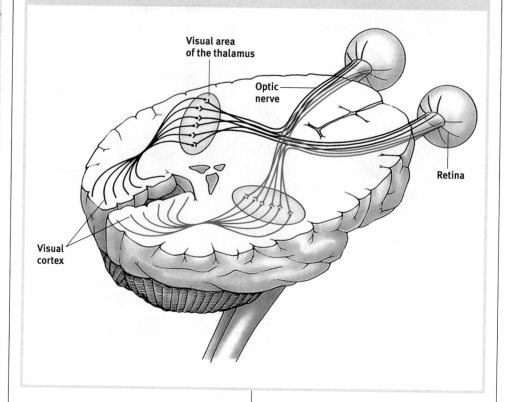

Parallel Processing

One of the most amazing aspects of visual information processing is the brain's ability to divide a scene into its parts. Using **parallel processing,** the brain assigns different teams of nerve cells to process simultaneously a scene's color, movement, form, and depth (**FIGURE 5.10**). We then construct our perceptions by integrating the work of these different visual teams (Livingstone & Hubel, 1988).

Figure 5.10> Parallel processing Studies of patients with brain damage suggest that the brain delegates the work of processing a robin's color, motion, form, and depth to different areas. After taking a scene apart, the brain integrates these parts into a whole perceived image.

Destroy or disable the neural workstation for a visual subtask, and something peculiar results, as happened to "Mrs. M." (from Hoffman, 1998). Since a stroke damaged areas near the rear of both sides of her brain, she can no longer perceive movement. People in a room seem "suddenly here or there but I have not seen them moving." Pouring tea into a cup is a challenge because the fluid appears frozen—she cannot perceive it rising in the cup.

* * *

Think about the wonders of visual processing. As you look at that robin, information enters your eyes, where it is taken apart and turned into millions of neural impulses that are sent to your brain. As your brain buzzes with activity, various areas focus on different aspects of the image of the robin. Finally, in some as yet mysterious way, these separate teams pool their work to produce a meaningful image. You compare this

> "I am fearfully and wonderfully made."
>
> King David, Psalms 139:14

with previously stored images and recognize it—a beautiful robin. The whole process **(FIGURE 5.11)** is much more complex than the prank of "transporting" and rebuilding a car. That all of this happens instantly, effortlessly, and continuously is indeed awesome.

PRACTICE TEST

6. The characteristic of light that determines the color we experience, such as blue or green, is
   a. intensity.
   b. wavelength.
   c. amplitude.
   d. rods.

7. The blind spot in your retina is located where

   a. there are rods but no cones.
   b. there are cones but no rods.
   c. the optic nerve leaves the eye.
   d. the bipolar cells meet the ganglion cells.

8. Rods and cones are the eye's receptor cells. Cones are especially sensitive to _____ light and are responsible for our _____ vision.
   a. bright; black-and-white
   b. dim; color
   c. bright; color
   d. dim; black-and-white

9. The cells in the visual cortex that respond to certain lines, edges, and angles are called
   a. rods and cones.
   b. feature detectors.
   c. bug detectors.
   d. ganglion cells.

10. The brain is capable of processing many aspects of an object or problem at the same time. We call this ability
    a. parallel processing.
    b. movement processing.
    c. sensory adaptation.
    d. priming.

Answers: 6. b, 7. c, 8. c, 9. b, 10. a.

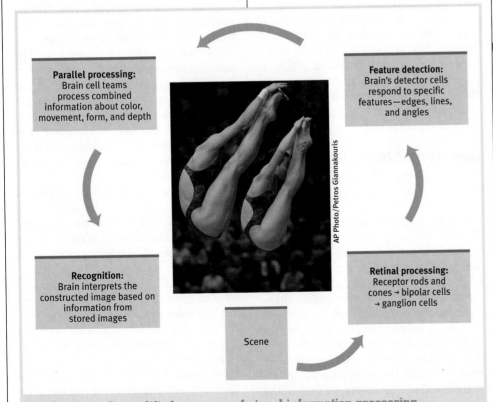

Parallel processing: Brain cell teams process combined information about color, movement, form, and depth

Feature detection: Brain's detector cells respond to specific features—edges, lines, and angles

Recognition: Brain interprets the constructed image based on information from stored images

Retinal processing: Receptor rods and cones → bipolar cells → ganglion cells

Scene

AP Photo/Petros Giannakouris

Figure 5.11> A simplified summary of visual information processing

The Other Senses

For humans, vision is the major sense. More of our brain cortex is devoted to vision than to any other sense. Yet without our senses of hearing, touch, taste, smell, and body motion and position, our experience of the world would be vastly diminished.

feature detectors nerve cells in the brain that respond to specific features of a stimulus, such as edges, lines, and angles.

parallel processing the processing of many aspects of a problem or scene at the same time; the brain's natural mode of information processing for many functions, including vision.

Hearing

Like our other senses, our hearing, or **audition,** helps us adapt and survive. We hear a wide range of sounds, but the ones we hear best are those in a range similar to that of the human voice. We also are remarkably sensitive to faint sounds, such as a child's whimper. Our ancestors' survival may also have depended on this keen hearing when hunting or being hunted. (If our ears were much more sensitive, we would hear a constant hiss from the movement of air molecules.) We are also acutely sensitive to differences in sounds. Among thousands of possible voices, we easily detect a friend's on the phone, from the moment she says "Hi." A fraction of a second after such events stimulate receptors in the ear, millions of neurons have worked together to extract the essential features, compare them with past experience, and identify the sound (Freeman, 1991). For hearing as for seeing, we will consider the fundamental question: How do we do it?

The Stimulus Input: Sound Waves

7: What are the characteristics of the air pressure waves that we hear as meaningful sounds?

Hit a piano key and you will unleash the energy of sound waves—jostling molecules of air, each bumping into the next, creating waves of compressed and expanded air. These waves are like the ripples on a pond circling out from where a stone has been tossed. As we swim in our pond of moving air molecules, our ears detect these brief air pressure changes.

Like light waves, sound waves vary in shape. The *amplitude* of sound waves determines their *loudness.* Their length, or **frequency,** determines the **pitch** we experience. Long waves have low frequency—and low pitch. Short waves have high frequency—and high pitch. Sound waves produced by a piccolo are much shorter and faster than those produced by a bass guitar.

The sounds of music :: A violin's short, fast waves create a high pitch. A cello's longer, slower waves create a lower pitch. Differences in the waves' height, or amplitude, also create differing degrees of loudness.

We measure sounds in *decibels,* with zero decibels representing the absolute threshold for hearing. Normal conversation registers at about 60 decibels. A whisper falls at about 20 decibels, and a passing subway train at about 100 decibels. Prolonged exposure to any sounds above 85 decibels—whether from a frenzied sports event or a bagpipe band—can produce hearing loss.

Decoding Sound Waves

8: How does the ear transform sound energy into neural messages?

Our hearing system transforms vibrating air into nerve impulses, which our brain decodes as sounds. This happens by means of an intricate mechanical chain reaction. The process begins when sound waves enter the outer ear, which channels them into the auditory canal to the *eardrum,* a tight membrane that vibrates with the waves **(FIGURE 5.12a).** In the middle ear, a piston made of three tiny bones then transmits the eardrum's vibrations to the **cochlea,** a snail-shaped tube in the inner ear. The incoming vibrations cause the cochlea's membrane (the *oval window*) to vibrate **(FIGURE 5.12b).** The resulting ripples in the cochlea's fluid bends the *hair cells* lining its surface, not unlike wind bending a wheat field. The hair cell movements trigger impulses in nerve cells. Axons from those nerve cells combine to form the *auditory nerve,* which carries the neural messages to the *auditory cortex* in the brain's temporal lobe. From vibrating air to moving piston to fluid waves to electrical impulses to the brain: We hear!

My vote for the most magical part of the hearing process is the hair cells— "quivering bundles that let us hear" thanks to their "extreme sensitivity and extreme speed" (Goldberg, 2007). A cochlea has 16,000 of them, which sounds like a lot until we compare that with an eye's 130 million or so receptors. But consider their responsiveness. Deflect the tiny bundles of *cilia* on the tip of a hair cell by the width of an atom—the equivalent of displacing the top of the Eiffel Tower by half an inch—and the alert hair cell triggers a neural response (Corey & others, 2004).

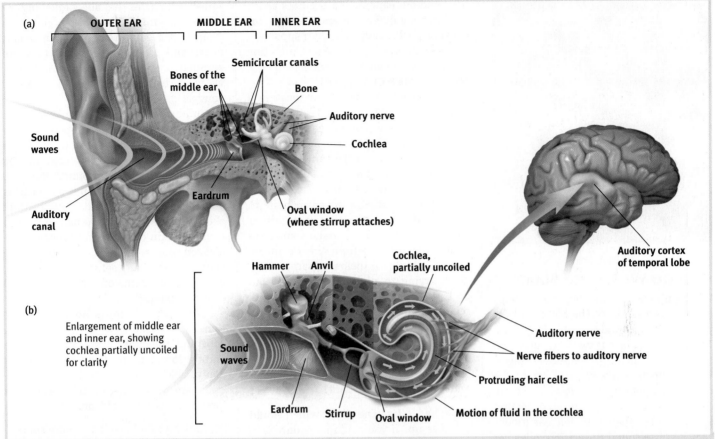

(a)

OUTER EAR   MIDDLE EAR   INNER EAR

Semicircular canals

Bones of the middle ear

Bone

Auditory nerve

Sound waves

Cochlea

Auditory canal

Eardrum

Oval window (where stirrup attaches)

Auditory cortex of temporal lobe

(b)

Enlargement of middle ear and inner ear, showing cochlea partially uncoiled for clarity

Hammer   Anvil   Cochlea, partially uncoiled

Sound waves

Auditory nerve

Nerve fibers to auditory nerve

Protruding hair cells

Eardrum   Stirrup   Oval window   Motion of fluid in the cochlea

Figure 5.12> Hear here: How we transform sound waves into nerve impulses that our brain interprets (a) The outer ear funnels sound waves to the eardrum. The bones of the middle ear (hammer, anvil, and stirrup) amplify and relay the eardrum's vibrations through the oval window into the fluid-filled cochlea. (b) As shown in this detail of the middle and inner ear, the resulting pressure changes in the cochlear fluid cause the hair cells to bend. Hair cell movements trigger impulses at the base of the nerve cells, whose fibers join together to form the auditory nerve. That nerve sends neural messages to the thalamus and on to the auditory cortex.

At the highest perceived frequency, hair cells can turn neural current on and off a thousand times per second! As you might expect of something so sensitive, they are, however, delicate. Blast them with hunting rifle shots or blaring iPods and the hair cells' cilia will begin to wither or fuse.

Damage to hair cells accounts for most hearing loss. They have been likened to shag carpet fibers. Walk around on them and they will spring back with a quick vacuuming. But leave a heavy piece of furniture on them for a long time and they may never rebound. As a general rule, any noise we cannot talk over may be harmful, especially if we are exposed to it often or for a long time (Roesser, 1998). And if our ears ring after exposure to loud machinery or music, we have been bad to our unhappy hair cells. As pain alerts us to possible bodily harm, ringing of the ears alerts us to possible hearing damage. It is hearing's version of bleeding. People who spend many hours behind a power mower, above a jackhammer, or in a loud nightclub should wear earplugs. "Condoms or, safer yet, abstinence," say sex educators. "Earplugs or walk away," say hearing educators.

audition the sense or act of hearing.

frequency the number of complete wavelengths that pass a point in a given time (for example, per second).

pitch a tone's experienced highness or lowness; depends on frequency.

cochlea [KOHK-lee-uh] a coiled, bony, fluid-filled tube in the inner ear; sound waves traveling through the cochlear fluid trigger nerve impulses.

Protect your inner ear's hair cells :: When vibrating in response to sound, the hair cells (shown here) lining the cochlea produce an electrical signal.

Dr. Fred Hossler/Visuals Unlimited

How Do We Locate Sounds?

Why don't we have one big ear—perhaps above our one nose? "The better to hear you," as the wolf said to Red Riding Hood. The placement of our two ears allows us to hear two slightly different messages. We benefit in two ways. If a car to the right honks, your right ear receives a more *intense* sound, and it receives sound slightly *sooner* than your left ear **(FIGURE 5.13).** Because sound travels 750 miles per

Sound shadow

Air

Figure 5.13> Why two ears are better than one Sound waves strike one ear sooner and more intensely than the other. From this information, our nimble brain can compute the sound's location. As you might therefore expect, people who lose all hearing in one ear often have difficulty locating sounds.

hour and our ears are but 6 inches apart, the intensity difference and the time lag are very small. Lucky for us, our supersensitive sound system can detect such tiny differences (Brown & Deffenbacher, 1979; Middlebrooks & Green, 1991).

So how well do we do at locating a sound that comes from directly ahead, behind, overhead, or beneath us? Not very well. Why? Because such sounds strike the two ears at the same time. You can try this yourself by sitting with closed eyes while a friend snaps fingers around your head. You will easily point to the sound when it comes from either side, but you will likely make some mistakes when it comes from directly ahead, behind, above, or below. That is why, when trying to pinpoint a sound, you cock your head, so that your two ears will receive slightly different messages.

Touch

9: How do we sense touch and feel pain, and how can we treat pain?

If you had to lose one sense, which would you give up? If you could have only one, which would you keep?

Although not the first sense to come to mind, touch might be a good choice for keeping. Right from the start, touch is essential to our development. Infant monkeys allowed to see, hear, and smell—but not touch—their mothers become desperately unhappy. Those separated by a

screen with holes that allow touching are much less miserable. As we noted in Chapter 3, premature babies gain weight faster and go home sooner if they are stimulated by hand massage. As lovers, we yearn to touch—to kiss, to stroke, to snuggle.

Humorist Dave Barry may be right to jest that your skin "keeps people from seeing the inside of your body, which is repulsive, and it prevents your organs from falling onto the ground." But skin does much more. Our "sense of touch" is actually a mix of at least four distinct skin senses—*pressure, warmth, cold,* and *pain.* Our skin has different types of specialized nerve endings, so that some spots are especially sensitive to pressure, others to warmth, others to cold, still others to pain.

Surprisingly, there is no simple relationship between what we feel at a given spot and the type of specialized nerve ending found there. Only pressure has identifiable receptors. Other skin sensations are variations of the basic four (pressure, warmth, cold, and pain):

- Stroking side-by-side pressure spots creates a tickle.

- Repeated gentle stroking of a pain spot creates an itching sensation.

- Touching side-by-side cold and pressure spots triggers a sense of wetness, which you can experience by touching dry, cold metal.

Bruce Ayres/Stone/Getty Images

Robert Brenner/Photo Edit

The precious sense of touch :: As William James wrote in his *Principles of Psychology* (1890), "Touch is both the alpha and omega of affection."

Touch sensations involve more than the feelings on our skin, however. A self-produced tickle activates a smaller area of the brain's cortex than the same tickle would from something or someone else (Blakemore & others, 1998). (The brain is wise enough to be most sensitive to unexpected stimulation.)

Pain

Be thankful for occasional pain. Pain is your body's way of telling you something has gone wrong. When drawing your attention to a burn, a break, or a rupture, pain tells you to change your behavior immediately. The rare people born without the ability to feel pain may experience severe injury or even die before early adulthood. Without the discomfort that makes us shift positions, their joints can fail from excess strain. Without the warnings of pain, infections can run wild, and injuries can accumulate (Neese, 1991).

Many more people live with chronic pain, which is rather like an alarm that won't shut off. The suffering of those who cannot escape the pain of backaches, arthritis, headaches, and cancer-related problems prompts two questions: What is pain? And how might we control it?

Figure 5.14> The rubber hand illusion When Dublin researcher Deirdre Desmond simultaneously touches a volunteer's real and fake hands, the volunteer feels as though the seen fake hand is her own.

Understanding Pain

Pain experiences vary widely from person to person. The pain we feel is in part a property of our senses, of the region where we feel it. But pain is also a product of our culture, our attention, and our expectations. The brain-pain connection was clear in a clever "rubber hand" study. The participants' own hands were hidden beneath a shell that contained a clearly visible fake hand **(FIGURE 5.14)**. The researcher then bent a finger slightly backward on a volunteer's real but unseen hand while at the same time "hurting" (severely bending) a finger on the fake hand (Armel & Ramachandran, 2003). The volunteers felt as if their real finger was being severely bent, and they responded with increased skin perspiration.

With pain, as with sights and sounds, the brain sometimes gets its signals crossed. Consider people's experiences of *phantom limb sensations*. After having a limb amputated, some 7 in 10 people feel pain or movement in limbs that no longer exist (Melzack, 1992, 1993). Some try to step off a bed onto a phantom leg or to lift a cup with a phantom hand. Even those born without a limb sometimes feel sensations in the missing part. The brain, notes Ronald Melzack, comes prepared to anticipate "that it will be getting information from a body that has limbs" (1998).

AP Photo/Stephen Morton

A pain-free, problematic life :: Ashlyn Blocker (right), shown here with her mother and sister, has a rare genetic disorder. She feels neither pain nor extreme hot and cold. She must frequently be checked for accidentally self-inflicted injuries that she herself cannot feel. "Some people would say [that feeling no pain is] a good thing," says her mother. "But no, it's not. Pain's there for a reason. It lets your body know something's wrong and it needs to be fixed. I'd give anything for her to feel pain" (quoted by Bynum, 2004).

Phantoms may haunt our other senses, too. People with hearing loss often experience the sound of silence: *tinnitus*, a phantom sound of ringing in the ears. Those who lose vision to glaucoma, cataracts, diabetes, or macular degeneration may experience phantom sights—nonthreatening hallucinations (Ramachandran & Blakeslee, 1998). And damage to nerves in the systems for tasting and smelling can give rise to phantom tastes or smells, such as ice water that seems sickeningly sweet or fresh air that reeks of rotten food (Goode, 1999). The point to remember: *We see, hear, taste, smell, and feel pain with our brain.*

In other ways, however, our pain system differs from some of our other senses. We don't have a simple neural cord running from a sensing device on our skin to a specific area in our brain. No one type of stimulus triggers pain (as light triggers vision). And we have no special receptors (like the retina's rods and cones) for pain. In fact, at low intensities, the stimuli that produce pain also cause other sensations, including warmth or coolness, smoothness or roughness.

Controlling Pain

If pain is where body meets mind—if it is indeed a physical and a psychological event—then it should be treatable both physically and psychologically. We have some built-in pain controls. Our brain releases a natural painkiller—*endorphins*—in response to severe pain or even vigorous exercise. Soothed by the release of endorphins, our experience of pain may be greatly diminished. People who carry a gene that boosts the normal supply of endorphins are less bothered by pain, and their brains are less responsive to it (Zubieta & others, 2003).

When endorphins combine with distraction, amazing things can happen. Sports injuries may go unnoticed until the after-game shower (thus demonstrating that the pain in sprain is mainly in the brain). During a 1989 basketball game, Ohio State University player Jay Burson broke his neck—and kept playing.

Playing with pain :: In a 2008 NBA championship series game, Boston Celtics star Paul Pierce screamed in pain after an opposing player stepped on his right foot, causing his knee to twist and pop. After being carried off the court, he came back and played through the pain, which reclaimed his attention after the game's end.

Tim Heitman/NBAE via Getty Images

> "Pain is increased by attending to it."
> Charles Darwin, *Expression of Emotions in Man and Animals*, 1872

Health-care professionals understand the value of distractions and may divert attention with a pleasant image ("Think of a warm, comfortable environment") or a request to perform some task ("Count backward by 3s") (Fernandez & Turk, 1989; McCaul & Malott, 1984). A well-trained nurse may distract needle-shy patients by chatting with them and asking them to look away when the needle is inserted. For burn victims receiving excruciating wound care, an even more effective distraction comes from immersion in a computer-generated 3-D world **(FIGURE 5.15)**. Functional MRI (fMRI) scans reveal that playing in the virtual reality reduces the brain's pain-related activity (Hoffman, 2004).

The brain-pain connection is also clear in our *memories* of pain. The pain we experience may not be the pain we remember. In experiments, and after medical procedures, people tend to overlook a pain's duration. Their memory snapshots may instead record its *peak* moment and also how much pain they felt at the *end*. Researchers discovered this when they asked people to put one hand in painfully cold water for 60 seconds, and then the other hand in the same painfully cold water for 60 seconds, followed by a slightly less painful 30 seconds more (Kahneman & others, 1993). Curiously, when asked which trial they would prefer to repeat, most preferred the longer trial, with more net pain—but less pain at the end. A physician used this principle with patients undergoing colon exams—lengthening the discomfort by a minute, but lessening its intensity at the end (Kahneman, 1999). Patients experiencing this taper-down treatment later recalled the exam as less painful than those whose pain ended abruptly.

Because pain is in the brain, hypnosis may also bring relief.

Hypnosis and Pain Relief

Imagine you are about to be hypnotized. The hypnotist invites you to sit back, fix your gaze on a spot high on the wall, and

Figure 5.15> Virtual-reality pain control For burn victims undergoing painful skin repair, escaping into virtual reality (like the icy playground shown here) can be a powerful distraction. With attention focused elsewhere, pain and the brain's response to painful stimulation decrease, as shown in the fMRI scans on the right. The calmer brain on the lower right belongs to a person playing in a virtual reality environment.

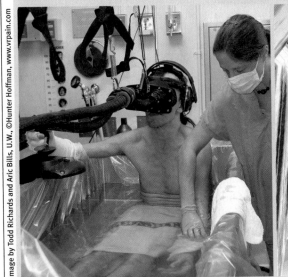  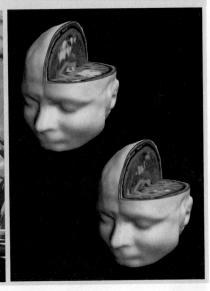

Image by Todd Richards and Aric Bills, U.W., ©Hunter Hoffman, www.vrpain.com

relax. In a quiet, low voice the hypnotist suggests, "Your eyes are growing tired. . . . Your eyelids are becoming heavy . . . now heavier and heavier. . . . They are beginning to close. . . . You are becoming more deeply relaxed. . . . Your breathing is now deep and regular. . . . Your muscles are becoming more and more relaxed. Your whole body is beginning to feel like lead."

After a few minutes of this *hypnotic induction,* you may experience **hypnosis.** Hypnotists have no magical mind-control power; they merely focus people on certain images or behaviors. To some extent, we are all open to suggestion. But highly hypnotizable people—such as the 20 percent who can carry out a suggestion not to smell or react to an open bottle of ammonia—are especially suggestible and imaginative (Barnier & McConkey, 2004; Silva & Kirsch, 1992).

Hypnosis has proved useful in relieving pain (Druckman & Bjork, 1994; Patterson, 2004). When unhypnotized people put their arms in an ice bath, they feel intense pain within 25 seconds. When hypnotized people do the same after being given suggestions to feel no pain, they indeed report feeling little pain. As some dentists know, even light hypnosis can reduce fear, and thus hypersensitivity to pain.

Nearly 10 percent of us can become so deeply hypnotized that even major surgery can be performed without anesthesia. Half of us can gain at least some pain relief from hypnosis. Hypnosis inhibits pain-related brain activity. In surgical experiments, hypnotized patients have required less medication, recovered sooner, and left the hospital earlier than unhypnotized controls (Lang & others, 2000; Patterson & Jensen, 2003).

How can this be? Psychologists have proposed two explanations for how hypnosis works. One theory proposes that hypnosis produces a *dissociation*—a split—between normal sensations and conscious awareness. Dissociation theory seeks to explain why hypnotized people may carry out posthypnotic suggestions when no one is watching. It also offers an explanation for why people hypnotized for pain relief may show brain activity in areas that receive sensory information, but not in areas that normally process pain-related information.

Those who reject the hypnosis-as-dissociation view believe that hypnosis is a form of normal *social influence* (Lynn & others, 1990; Spanos & Coe, 1992). In this view, hypnosis is a by-product of normal social and mental processes. Like actors caught up in their roles, people begin to feel and behave in ways appropriate for "good hypnotic subjects." They may allow the hypnotist to direct their attention and fantasies away from pain.

hypnosis a social interaction in which one person (the hypnotist) suggests to another (the subject) that certain perceptions, feelings, thoughts, or behaviors will spontaneously occur.

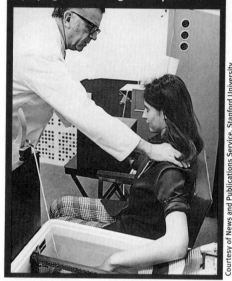

Dissociation or social influence? ::
This hypnotized woman tested by famous researcher Ernest Hilgard showed no pain when her arm was placed in an ice bath. But asked to press a key if some part of her felt the pain, she did so. To Hilgard (1986, 1992), this was evidence of dissociation, or divided consciousness. The social influence perspective, however, maintains that people responding this way are caught up in playing the role of "good subject."

Taste

10: How are our senses of taste and smell similar, and what is sensory interaction?

Our sense of taste involves several basic sensations, which until recently were thought to be *sweet, sour, salty,* and *bitter* (McBurney & Gent, 1979). In recent decades, many researchers have searched for specialized fibers that might act as nerve pathways for the four taste sensations. During this search, they discovered a receptor for a fifth basic taste sensation—the meaty taste of *umami.* You may have experienced umami as the flavor enhancer monosodium glutamate, often used in Chinese or Thai food (Chaudhari & others, 2000; Nelson & others, 2001; Smith & Margolskee, 2001).

Good food tastes great, but our sense of taste exists for more than our pleasure. Nice tastes attracted our ancestors to energy-rich foods that enabled their survival. Unpleasant tastes warned them away from new foods that might contain toxins and lead to food poisoning, especially deadly for children. We see the inheritance of this biological wisdom in today's 2- to 6-year-olds. At this age, children are typically fussy eaters and often turn away from new meat dishes or bitter-tasting vegetables, such as spinach and Brussels sprouts (Cooke & others, 2003). But another tool in our early ancestors' survival kit was learning. Across the globe, frustrated parents are happy to see that, given repeated small tastes of disliked new foods, children typically learn to accept these foods (Wardle & others, 2003).

Taste is a chemical sense. You've surely noticed the little bumps on the top and sides of your tongue. Inside each bump are 200 or more taste buds. Each bud contains a pore. Projecting into each of these taste bud pores are antennalike hairs from 50 to 100 taste receptor cells. These hairs carry information about molecules of food chemicals back to your taste receptor cells. Some receptors respond mostly to sweet-tasting molecules, others to salty- , sour-, umami-, or bitter-tasting ones. It doesn't take much to trigger a response that alerts your brain's temporal lobe. If a stream of water is pumped across your tongue, the addition of a concentrated salty or sweet taste for but one-tenth of a second will get your attention (Kelling & Halpern, 1983). When a friend asks for "just a taste" of your soft drink, you can squeeze off the straw after an eyeblink.

Taste receptors reproduce themselves every week or two, so if you burn your tongue with hot food it hardly matters. However, as you grow older, it may matter more, because the number of taste buds in your mouth will decrease, as will your taste sensitivity (Cowart, 1981). (No wonder adults enjoy strong-tasting foods that children resist.) Smoking and alcohol can speed up the loss of taste buds.

Essential as taste buds are, there's more to taste than meets the tongue. Hold your nose, close your eyes, and have someone feed you various foods. You may not be able to tell a slice of apple from a slice of raw potato. To savor a taste, we normally breathe its aroma through our nose—which is why eating is not much fun when you have a bad cold. Smell can also change our perception of taste. Add a strawberry odor and a drink will seem sweeter. This is **sensory interaction** at work—the principle that one sense may influence another. Smell plus texture plus taste equals flavor.

Sensory interaction also influences what we hear (FIGURE 5.16). If I (as a person with hearing loss) watch a video with subtitles, I have no trouble hearing the words I am seeing. If I then mistakenly think I don't need these captions and turn them off, I suddenly realize I really do need them. But what do you suppose happens if we *see* a speaker saying one syllable while *hearing* another? Surprise: We may perceive a third syllable that blends both inputs. Seeing the mouth movements for *ga* while hearing *ba,* we may perceive *da.* This peculiar interaction is known as the *McGurk effect,* after its discoverers, psychologist Harry McGurk and his assistant John MacDonald (1976).

Tasting, smelling, hearing, seeing, touching—our senses are not totally separate information channels. In interpreting the world, our brain blends their inputs.

Figure 5.16> Sensory interaction
When a hard-of-hearing listener *sees* an animated face forming words being spoken at the other end of a phone line, the words become easier to understand (Knight, 2004).

Smell

Inhale, exhale. Inhale, exhale. Breaths come in pairs—except at two moments: birth and death. Between those two moments, you will daily inhale and exhale nearly 20,000 breaths of life-sustaining air, bathing your nostrils in a stream of scent-laden molecules. This experience of smell (*olfaction*) is strikingly intimate. We inhale something of whatever or whoever it is we smell.

Smell, like taste, is a chemical sense. We smell something when molecules of a substance carried in the air reach a tiny cluster of 5 million or more receptor cells at the top of each nasal cavity. These olfactory receptor cells, waving like sea anemones on a reef, respond selectively—to the aroma of a cake baking, to a wisp of smoke, to a friend's fragrance. Instantly they alert the brain.

Aided by smell, a mother fur seal returning to a beach crowded with pups will find her own. Human mothers and nursing infants also quickly learn to recognize each other's scents (McCarthy, 1986). Our sense of smell is, however, less impressive than our senses of seeing and hearing. Looking out across a garden, we see its forms and colors in wonderful detail and hear a variety of birds singing.

The nose knows :: Humans have 10 to 20 million olfactory receptors. A bloodhound has some 200 million (Herz, 2001).

Figure 5.17> Taste, smell, and memory Information from the taste buds (green arrow) travels to an area of the temporal lobe. It registers in an area not far from where the brain receives information from our sense of smell, which interacts with taste. The brain's circuitry for smell (red arrow) also connects with areas involved in memory storage, which helps explain why a smell can trigger a memory.

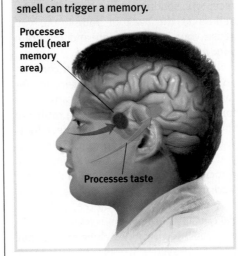

Processes smell (near memory area)

Processes taste

Yet we smell few of the garden's scents without sticking our nose into the blossoms.

Odor molecules come in many shapes and sizes—so many, in fact, that it takes hundreds of different receptors, designed by a large family of genes, to recognize these molecules (Miller, 2004). We do not have one distinct receptor for each detectable odor. Instead, different combinations of receptors send messages to the brain's olfactory cortex. As the English alphabet's 26 letters can combine to form many words, so olfactory receptors can produce different patterns to identify the 10,000 odors we can detect (Malnic & others, 1999). It is these combinations that allow us to smell the difference between a cup of fresh-brewed coffee and one that is hours old.

Odors can evoke emotions **(FIGURE 5.17)**. Though it's difficult to recall odors by name, we have a remarkable capacity to recognize long-forgotten odors and their associated personal tales (Engen, 1987; Schab, 1991). Pleasant odors can call up pleasant memories (Ehrlichman

& Halpern, 1988). The smell of the sea, the scent of a perfume, or an aroma of a favorite relative's kitchen can bring to mind a happy time. It's a link one British travel agent chain understands well. To evoke memories of lounging on sunny, warm beaches, the company has piped the aroma of coconut sunscreen into its shops (Fracassini, 2000).

Body Position and Movement

11: How do our senses monitor our body's position and movement?

With only the five familiar senses we have so far considered, we could not put food in our mouth, stand up, or reach out and touch someone. To know just how to move your arms to grasp someone's hand, you need a sixth sense. You need to know the current position of your arms and hands and then to be aware of their changing positions as you move them. For you to take just one step requires feedback from, and instructions to, some 200 muscles. The brain power engaged in all this dwarfs even that involved in reasoning. Let's take a closer look.

You came equipped with millions of position and motion sensors. They are all over your body—in your muscles, tendons, and joints—and they are continually feeding information to your brain. Twist your wrist one degree, and these sensors provide an immediate update. This sense of your body parts' position and movement is **kinesthesis.**

One can momentarily imagine being blind or deaf. Close your eyes, plug your ears, and experience the dark stillness. But what would it be like to live without being able to sense the positions of your limbs when you wake during the night?

sensory interaction the principle that one sense may influence another, as when the smell of food influences its taste.

kinesthesis [kin-ehs-THEE-sehs] the system for sensing the position and movement of individual body parts.

AP Photo/The Charlotte Observer, Layne Bailey

Ian Waterman of Hampshire, England, knows. In 1972, at age 19, Waterman contracted a rare viral infection that destroyed the nerves that enabled his sense of light touch and of body position and movement. People with this condition report feeling disconnected from their body, as though it is dead, not real, not theirs (Sacks, 1985). With prolonged practice, Waterman has learned to walk and eat—by visually focusing on his limbs and directing them accordingly. But if the lights go out, he crumples to the floor (Azar, 1998).

For all of us, vision interacts with kinesthesis. Stand with your right heel in front of your left toes. Easy. Now close your eyes and you will probably wobble.

Working hand-in-hand with kinesthesis is our **vestibular sense.** This companion sense monitors your head's (and thus your body's) position and movement.

The intricate vestibular sense ::
These Cirque du Soleil performers can thank their inner ears for the information that enables their brains to monitor their bodies' position so expertly.

Michal Cizek/AFP/Getty Images

Controlling this sense of equilibrium are two structures in your inner ear. The first is your *semicircular canals,* which look like a three-dimensional pretzel (Figure 5.12a). The second is your *vestibular sacs,* which connect the canals with the cochlea. These sacs contain fluid that moves when your head rotates or tilts. When this movement stimulates hairlike receptors, sending messages to the cerebellum at the back of your brain, you sense your body position and maintain your balance.

If you twirl around and then come to an abrupt halt, it takes a few seconds for the fluid in your semicircular canals and for your kinesthetic receptors to return to their neutral state. The aftereffect fools your dizzy brain with the sensation that you're still spinning. This illustrates a principle underlying perceptual illusions: *Mechanisms that normally give us an accurate experience of the world can, under special conditions, fool us.* Understanding how we get fooled provides clues to how our perceptual system works.

◈ PRACTICE TEST

11. The amplitude of a light wave determines our perception of brightness. The amplitude of a sound wave determines our perception of
    a. loudness.
    b. pitch.
    c. audition.
    d. frequency.

12. The frequency of sound waves determines their pitch. The _____ the waves are, the lower their frequency is and the _____ their pitch.
    a. shorter; higher
    b. longer; lower
    c. lower; longer
    d. higher; shorter

13. The snail-shaped tube in the inner ear, where sound waves are converted into neural activity, is called the
    a. piston.
    b. cilia.
    c. cochlea.
    d. auditory nerve.

14. Of the four skin senses that make up our sense of touch, only ———— has its own identifiable receptor cells.
    a. pressure
    b. warmth
    c. cold
    d. pain

15. Which of the following options has NOT been proven to reduce pain?
    a. Distraction
    b. Hypnosis
    c. Phantom limb sensations
    d. Endorphins

16. The taste of the food we eat is greatly enhanced by its smell or aroma. This influence of one sense on another is an example of
    a. sensory adaptation.
    b. chemical sensation.
    c. kinesthesis.
    d. sensory interaction.

17. The receptors for the vestibular sense are located in the
    a. skin.
    b. brain.
    c. inner ear.
    d. skeletal muscles.

Answers: 11. a, 12. b, 13. c, 14. a, 15. c, 16. d, 17. c.

Perceptual Organization

12: **What was the main message of Gestalt psychology, and how do the principles of figure-ground and grouping contribute to our perception of form?**

We have examined the processes by which we sense sights and sounds, tastes and smells, touch and movement. Now our central question is how do we see not just shapes and colors, but a rose in bloom, a familiar face, a sunset? How do we hear not just a mix of pitches and rhythms, but a child's cry of pain? In short, how do we organize and interpret our sensations so that they become meaningful perceptions?

Early in the twentieth century, a group of German psychologists noticed that when given a cluster of sensations, people tend to organize them into a **gestalt**, a German word meaning a "form" or a "whole." For example, look at **FIGURE 5.18**. Note that the individual elements of the figure are really nothing but eight blue circles, with three white lines meeting near the center. When we view these elements all together, however, we see a *whole*, a form, a *Necker cube*.

Over the years, the Gestalt psychologists demonstrated some principles we use to organize our sensations into perceptions. As you read on, keep in mind the basic truth they illustrate: *Our brain does more than merely register information about the world. Perception is not just opening a shutter and letting a picture print itself on the brain. We constantly filter incoming information and construct perceptions. Mind matters.*

Figure 5.18> A Necker cube What do you see: circles with white lines, or a cube? If you stare at the cube, you may notice that it reverses location, moving the tiny X in the center from the front edge to the back. At times the cube may seem to float in front of the page, with circles behind it. At other times, the circles may become holes in the page through which the cube appears, as though it were floating behind the page. There is far more to perception than meets the eye. (From Bradley & others, 1976.)

Form Perception

Imagine designing a video-computer system that, like your eye-brain system, can recognize faces at a glance. What abilities would it need?

Figure and Ground

To start with, the video-computer system would need to separate faces from their backgrounds. Likewise, in our eye-brain system, our first perceptual task is to perceive any object (the *figure*) as distinct from its surroundings (the *ground*). Among the voices you hear at a party, the one you attend to becomes the figure; all others are part of the ground. As you read, the words are the figure; the white paper is the ground. In **FIGURE 5.19**, the **figure-ground** relationship continually reverses—but always we organize the forms into a figure seen against a ground. Such reversible figure-and-ground illustrations demonstrate that the same stimulus can trigger more than one perception.

Grouping

Able to tell figure from ground, we (and our video-computer system) now have to organize the figure into a *meaningful* form. Some basic features of a scene—such as

Figure 5.19>
Reversible figure and ground

Time Saving Suggestion, © 2003 Roger Shepherd.

color, movement, and light-dark contrast—we process instantly and automatically (Treisman, 1987). Our mind brings order and form to stimuli by following certain rules for **grouping.** These rules, identified by the Gestalt psychologists, illustrate the idea that the perceived whole differs from the sum of its parts (Quinn & others, 2002; Rock & Palmer, 1990). Three examples:

Proximity We group nearby figures together. We see not six separate lines, but three sets of two lines.

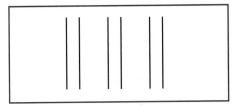

Proximity

Continuity We perceive smooth, continuous patterns rather than discontinuous ones. This pattern could be a series of alternating semicircles, but we perceive it as two continuous lines—one wavy, one straight.

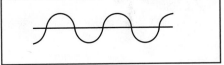

Continuity

vestibular sense the sense of body movement and position, including the sense of balance.

gestalt an organized whole. Gestalt psychologists emphasized our tendency to integrate pieces of information into meaningful wholes.

figure-ground the organization of the visual field into objects (the *figures*) that stand out from their surroundings (the *ground*).

grouping the perceptual tendency to organize stimuli into meaningful groups.

Closure We fill in gaps to create a complete, whole object. Thus, we assume that the circles on the left are complete but partially blocked by the (illusory) triangle. Add nothing more than little lines to close off the circles, and your brain stops constructing a triangle.

Closure

Usually, these and other grouping principles help us construct reality. Sometimes, however, they lead us astray, as when we look at the doghouse in **FIGURE 5.20**.

Figure 5.20> Grouping principles
What's the secret to this impossible doghouse? You probably perceive this doghouse as a gestalt—a whole (though impossible) structure. Actually, your brain imposes this sense of wholeness on the picture. As you will see in Figure 5.27, Gestalt grouping principles such as closure and continuity are at work here.

Depth Perception

13: **How do we see the world in three dimensions?**

Our eyes receive two-dimensional images (height and width). But somehow our brain organizes these images into three-dimensional perceptions (height, width, and depth). **Depth perception** lets us estimate an object's distance from us. At a glance, we can, for example, estimate the distance of an oncoming car. This ability is partly present at birth. Eleanor Gibson and Richard Walk (1960) discovered this using a model of a cliff with a drop-off area (which was covered by sturdy glass). These experiments were a product of Gibson's scientific curiosity, which kicked in while she was picnicking on the rim of the Grand Canyon. She wondered: Would a toddler peering over the rim perceive the dangerous drop-off and draw back?

Back in their laboratory, Gibson and Walk placed 6- to 14-month-old infants on the edge of a safe canyon—a **visual cliff** (**FIGURE 5.21**). Their mothers then coaxed them to crawl out onto the glass. Most infants refused to do so, indicating that they could perceive depth. Had they *learned* to perceive depth? Learning seemed to be part of the answer, because crawling, no matter when it begins, seems to increase an infant's fear of heights. Yet newborn animals with no visual experience—including young kittens, a day-old goat, and newly hatched chicks—respond similarly, the researchers observed. Thus, the full answer seems to be that biological maturation prepares us to be wary of heights, and experience amplifies that fear.

How do we do it? *How* do we perceive depth—transforming two differing two-dimensional retinal images into a single three-dimensional perception? Our brain constructs these perceptions using information supplied by one or both eyes.

Binocular Cues

Binocular cues depend on information provided by both eyes. Here's an example. With both eyes open, hold two pens or pencils in front of you and touch their tips together. Now do so with one eye closed. With one eye, the task becomes more difficult.

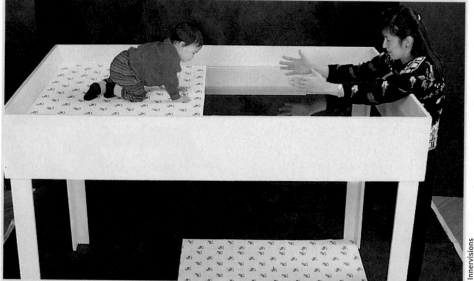

Figure 5.21> Visual cliff Eleanor Gibson and Richard Walk devised this miniature cliff with a glass-covered drop-off to determine whether crawling infants and newborn animals can perceive depth. Even when coaxed, infants are reluctant to climb onto the glass over the cliff.

Figure 5.22> The floating finger sausage Hold your two index fingers about 5 inches in front of your eyes, with their tips half an inch apart. Now look beyond them and note the weird result. Move your fingers out farther and the retinal disparity—and the finger sausage—will shrink.

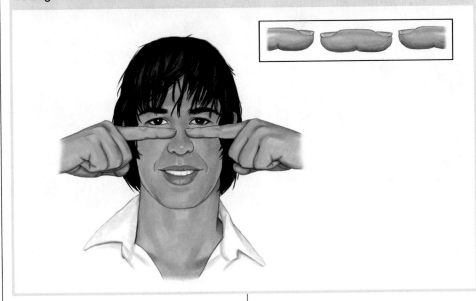

We use binocular cues to judge the distance of nearby objects. One such cue is **retinal disparity.** Because your eyes are about 2½ inches apart, your retinas receive slightly different images of the world. By comparing these two images, your brain can judge how close an object is to you. The greater the difference between the two retinal images, the closer the object. Try it yourself. Hold your fingers directly in front of your nose, and your retinas will receive quite different views. You can see the difference if you close one eye and then the other. (You will also create a finger sausage, as in **FIGURE 5.22.**) At a greater distance—say, when you hold your fingers at arm's length—the disparity, or difference, is smaller.

We could easily build this feature into our seeing computer. Movie makers can exaggerate retinal disparity by filming a scene with two cameras placed a few inches apart. Viewers then wear glasses that allow the left eye to see only the image from the left camera, and the right eye to see only the image from the right camera. The resulting 3-D effect mimics normal retinal disparity.

Monocular Cues

How do we judge whether a person is 10 or 100 yards away? Retinal disparity won't help us here, because there won't be much difference between the images cast on our right and left retinas. At such distances, we depend on **monocular cues** (depth cues available to each eye separately), such as those in **FIGURE 5.23** on the next page.

Perceptual Constancy

14: How do perceptual constancies help us construct meaningful perceptions?

So far, we have noted that our video-computer system must perceive objects as we do—as having a distinct form, location, and perhaps motion. Its next task is to recognize objects without being deceived by changes in their color, shape, brightness, and size—an ability we call **perceptual constancy.**

Color Constancy

Color does not reside in an object. Our experience of color depends on an object's context. If you viewed an isolated tomato through a paper tube, its color would seem to change as the light—and thus the wavelengths reflected from its surface—changed. But if you viewed that tomato without the tube, as one item in a bowl of fresh vegetables, its color would remain roughly constant as the lighting shifts. This perception of consistent color is known as **color constancy.**

"From there to here, from here to there, funny things are everywhere."

Dr. Seuss, *One Fish, Two Fish, Red Fish, Blue Fish,* 1960

Though we take color constancy for granted, this ability is truly remarkable. A chip colored blue under indoor lighting will, in sunlight, reflect wavelengths that match those reflected by a sunlit gold chip (Jameson, 1985). Yet bring a goldfinch indoors and it won't look like a bluebird.

depth perception the ability to see objects in three dimensions, although the images that strike the retina are two-dimensional; allows us to judge distance.

visual cliff a laboratory device for testing depth perception in infants and young animals.

binocular cues depth cues, such as retinal disparity, that depend on the use of two eyes.

retinal disparity a binocular cue for perceiving depth: By comparing images from the two eyeballs, the brain computes distance—the greater the disparity (difference) between the two images, the closer the object.

monocular cues depth cues, such as interposition and linear perspective, available to either eye alone.

perceptual constancy perceiving objects as unchanging (having consistent color, brightness, shape, and size) even as illumination and retinal images change.

color constancy perceiving familiar objects as having consistent color, even if changing illumination alters the wavelengths reflected by the object.

Relative height

We perceive objects higher in our field of vision as farther away. Because we assume the lower part of a figure-ground illustration is closer, we perceive it as figure (Vecera & others, 2002). Invert the illustration above and the black will become ground, like a night sky.

Relative size

If we assume two objects are similar in size, *most* people perceive the one that casts the smaller retinal image as farther away.

Interposition

If one object partially blocks our view of another, we perceive it as closer. The depth cues provided by interposition make this an impossible scene.

Relative motion

As we move, objects that are actually stable may appear to move. If while riding on a bus you fix your gaze on some object—say, a house—the objects beyond the fixation point appear to move with you; objects in front of the fixation point appear to move backward. The farther those objects are from the fixation point, the faster they seem to move.

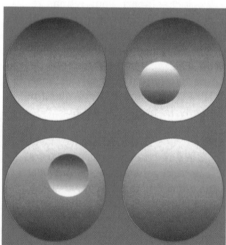

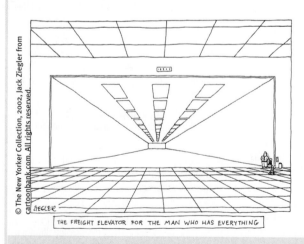

Linear perspective

Parallel lines appear to meet in the distance. The more they converge, the greater their perceived distance.

Light and shadow

Shading produces a sense of depth consistent with our assumption that light comes from above. Invert the illustration above and the hollow will become a hill.

Figure 5.23> Monocular depth cues

Figure 5.24> Color depends on context Believe it or not, these three blue disks are identical in color.

R. Beau Lotto at University College, London

The color is not in the bird's feathers. You and I see color thanks to our brain's ability to decode the meaning of the light reflected by an object *relative to the objects surrounding it.* **FIGURE 5.24** dramatically illustrates the ability of a blue object to appear very different in three different contexts. Yet we have no trouble seeing these disks as blue. Paint manufacturers have learned this lesson. Knowing that your perception of a paint color will be determined by other colors in your home, many now offer trial samples you can test in that context. The take-home lesson: *Comparisons govern our perceptions.*

Shape and Size Constancies

Thanks to *shape constancy,* we usually perceive the form of familiar objects, like the door in **FIGURE 5.25,** as constant even while our retinas receive changing images of them.

Thanks to *size constancy,* we perceive objects as having a constant size, even while our distance from them varies. We assume a car is large enough to carry people, even when we see its tiny image from two blocks away. This assumption also shows the close connection between perceived *distance* and perceived *size.* Per-

Figure 5.25> Shape constancy A door casts an increasingly trapezoidal image on our retinas as it opens. Yet we still perceive it as rectangular.

ceiving an object's distance gives us cues to its size. Likewise, knowing its general size—that the object is, say, a car—provides us with cues to its distance.

Even in size-distance judgments, however, we consider an object's context. The monsters in **FIGURE 5.26** cast identical images on our retinas, but each monster appears in a different context. Using linear perspective as a cue, our brain assumes that the pursuing monster is farther away. We therefore perceive it as larger. It isn't.

From Shepard (1990)

Figure 5.26> Fooling our size-distance perceptions Which monster is bigger? Measure them to see.

The interplay between perceived size and perceived distance helps explain several well-known illusions. For example, the Moon looks up to 50 percent larger near the horizon than when high in the sky. Can you imagine why? One reason is that cues to objects' distances make the horizon Moon—like the distant monster in Figure 5.26—appear farther away. If it's farther away, our brain assumes, it must be larger than the Moon high in the night sky (Kaufman & Kaufman, 2000). Take away the distance cues—by looking at the horizon Moon (or each monster) through a paper tube—and the object will immediately shrink.

Mistaken judgments like these reveal the workings of our normally effective perceptual processes. The perceived relationship between distance and size is generally valid, but under special circumstances it can lead us astray—as when helping to create the Moon illusion.

Form perception, depth perception, and perceptual constancy illuminate how

Photo by Walter Wick. Reprinted from GAMES Magazine. © 1983

Figure 5.27> The solution Another view of the impossible doghouse in Figure 5.20 reveals the secrets of this illusion. From the photo angle in Figure 5.20, the grouping principle of closure leads us to perceive the boards as continuous.

we organize our visual experiences. Perceptual organization applies to other senses, too. It explains why we perceive a clock's steady tick not as a tick-tick-tick-tick but as grouped sounds, say, TICK-tick, TICK-tick. Perception though, is more than organizing stimuli. Perception also requires what would be a challenge to our video-computer system: interpretation—finding meaning in what we perceive.

18. Gestalt psychologists identified the principles by which we organize our perceptions. Our minds bring order and form to stimuli by following certain rules for
    a. color constancy.
    b. depth perception.
    c. shape constancy.
    d. grouping.

19. In listening to a concert, you attend to the solo instrument and perceive the orchestra as accompaniment. This illustrates the organizing principle of
    a. figure-ground.
    b. shape constancy.
    c. grouping.
    d. depth perception.

20. The visual cliff experiments suggest that
    a. infants have not yet developed depth perception.
    b. crawling human infants and very young animals perceive depth.
    c. we have no way of knowing whether infants can perceive depth.
    d. humans differ significantly from animals in being able to perceive depth in infancy.

21. Depth perception is our ability to
    a. group similar items in a gestalt.
    b. perceive objects as having a constant shape or form.
    c. judge distances.
    d. fill in the gaps in a figure.

22. Two examples of monocular cues are interposition and
    a. closure.
    b. retinal disparity.
    c. linear perspective.
    d. continuity.

23. Perceiving a radish as consistently red, despite lighting shifts, is an example of
    a. shape constancy.
    b. color constancy.
    c. a binocular cue.
    d. feature detection.

Answers: 18. d, 19. a, 20. b, 21. c, 22. c, 23. b.

Perceptual Interpretation

The debate over whether our perceptual abilities spring from our nature or our nurture has a long history. To what extent do we *learn* to perceive? German philosopher Immanuel Kant (1724–1804) maintained that knowledge comes from our *inborn* ways of organizing sensory experiences. Psychology's findings support this idea. We do come equipped to process sensory information. But British philosopher John Locke (1632–1704) argued that through our experiences we also *learn* to perceive the world. Psychology also supports *this* idea. We do learn to link an object's distance with its size. So, just how important is experience? How much does it shape our perceptual interpretations?

Sensory Deprivation and Restored Vision

15: What does research on sensory deprivation and restored vision reveal about the effects of experience on perception?

Writing to John Locke, a friend asked a question that would test the idea that experience shapes perceptions. If "a man *born* blind, and now adult, [was] taught by his *touch* to distinguish between a cube and a sphere" could he, if made to see, visually distinguish the two? Locke's answer was no, because the man would never have *learned* to see the difference.

This clever question has since been put to the test with a few dozen adults who, though blind from birth, have

Learning to see :: At age 3, Mike May lost his vision in an explosion. Decades later, after a new cornea restored vision to his right eye, he got his first look at his wife and children. Alas, although signals were now reaching his visual cortex, it lacked the experience to interpret them. May could not recognize expressions, or faces, apart from features such as hair. Yet he can see an object in motion and is gradually learning to navigate his world and to marvel at such things as dust floating in sunlight (Abrams, 2002).

Mike May, Allison Aliano Photography

gained sight (Gregory, 1978; von Senden, 1932). Most were born with *cataracts*—clouded lenses that allowed them to see only light and shadows, rather as someone might see a foggy image through a Ping-Pong ball sliced in half. After surgery, the patients could tell the difference between figure and ground and could sense colors. This suggests that we are born with these aspects of perception. But much as Locke supposed, they often could not by sight recognize objects that were familiar by touch.

In experiments with infant kittens and monkeys, researchers have outfitted the young animals with goggles through which they could see only diffuse, unpatterned light (Wiesel, 1982). After infancy, when the goggles were removed, these animals' reactions were much like those of humans born with cataracts. Their eyes were healthy. Their retinas still sent signals to their visual cortex. But the brain's cortical cells had not developed normal connections. Thus, the animals remained functionally blind to shape. Experience guides and sustains the brain's development as it forms pathways that affect our perceptions.

In both humans and animals, similar sensory restrictions later in life do no permanent damage. When researchers cover an adult animal's eye for several months, its vision will be unaffected after the eye patch is removed. When surgeons remove cataracts that develop during late adulthood, most people are thrilled at the return to normal vision. The effect of sensory restriction on infant cats, monkeys, and humans suggests there is a *critical period* (Chapter 3) for normal sensory and perceptual development. Nurture sculpts what nature has endowed.

Perceptual Adaptation

16: What is perceptual adaptation?

Given a new pair of glasses, we may feel a little strange, even dizzy. Within a day or two, we adjust. Our **perceptual adaptation** to changed visual input makes the world seem normal again. But imagine a far more dramatic new pair of glasses—one that shifts the apparent location of objects 40 degrees to the left. When you first put them on and toss a ball to a friend, it sails off to the left. Walking forward to shake hands with the person, you veer to the left.

Could you adapt to this distorted world? Chicks cannot. When fitted with such lenses, they continue to peck where food grains *seem* to be (Hess, 1956; Rossi, 1968). But we humans adapt to distorting lenses quickly. Within a few minutes, your throws would again be accurate, your stride on target. Remove the lenses and you would experience an aftereffect. At first your throws would err in the *opposite* direction, sailing off to the right. But again, within minutes you would adjust.

Indeed, given an even more radical pair of glasses—one that literally turns the world upside down—you could still

Perceptual adaptation :: "Oops, missed," thinks researcher Hubert Dolezal as he views the world through inverting goggles. Yet, believe it or not, kittens, monkeys, and humans can adapt to an upside-down world.

Courtesy of Hubert Dolezal

adapt. Psychologist George Stratton (1896) experienced this when he invented, and for eight days wore, a device that flipped left to right *and* up to down, making him the first person to experience a right-side-up retinal image while standing upright. The ground was up, the sky was down.

At first, when Stratton wanted to walk, he found himself searching for his feet, which were now "up." Eating was nearly impossible. He became nauseated and depressed. But Stratton persisted, and by the eighth day he could comfortably reach for an object in the right direction and walk without bumping into things. When Stratton finally removed the headgear, he readapted quickly.

In later experiments, people wearing the optical gear have even been able to ride a motorcycle, ski the Alps, and fly an airplane (Dolezal, 1982; Kohler, 1962). The world around them still seemed above their heads or on the wrong side. But by actively moving about in these topsy-turvy worlds, they adapted to the context and learned to coordinate their movements.

Perceptual Set

17: How do our assumptions, expectations, and contexts affect our perceptions?

As everyone knows, to see is to believe. As we also know, but less fully appreciate, to believe is to see. Through experience, we come to expect certain results. Those expectations may give us a **perceptual set,** or mental tendencies and assumptions that greatly influence what we perceive. Consider: Is the image in the center frame of **FIGURE 5.28** on the next page a man playing a saxophone or a woman's face? What we see in such a drawing can be influenced by first looking at either the left or right drawing, where the meaning is clear (Boring, 1930).

When shown the phrase:

*Mary had a
a little lamb*

many people perceive what they expect, and miss the repeated word. Did you?

IT'S AMAZING HOW PEOPLE SLOW DOWN WHEN YOU POINT A HAIR DRYER AT THEM.

perceptual adaptation in vision, the ability to adjust to an artificially displaced or even inverted visual field.

perceptual set a mental predisposition to perceive one thing and not another.

Figure 5.28> Perceptual set Show a friend either the left or right image. Then show the center image and ask, "What do you see?" Whether your friend reports seeing a saxophonist or a woman's face will likely depend on which of the other two drawings was viewed first. In each of those images, the meaning is clear, and it will establish perceptual expectations.

Perceptual set can influence what we hear, taste, feel, and see. In 1972, a British newspaper published photos of a "monster" in Scotland's Loch Ness—"the most amazing pictures ever taken," stated the paper. If this information creates in you the same expectations it did in most of the paper's readers, you, too, will see the monster in the photo in **FIGURE 5.29.** But when a skeptical researcher approached the photos with different expectations, he saw a curved tree trunk—as had others the day the photo was shot (Campbell,

1986). With this different perceptual set, you may now notice that the object is floating motionless, with no ripples in the water around it—hardly what we would expect of a lively monster.

Consider also the kindly airline pilot who, on a takeoff run, looked over at his unhappy co-pilot and said, "Cheer up." Expecting to hear the usual "Gear up," the co-pilot promptly raised the wheels—before they left the ground (Reason & Mycielska, 1982). Perceptual set also influenced some bar patrons invited to sample free beer (Lee

& others, 2006). When researchers added a few drops of vinegar to a brand-name beer, the tasters preferred it—unless they had been told they were drinking vinegar-laced beer and thus expected, and usually experienced, a worse taste. Clearly, much of what we perceive comes not just from the world "out there" but also from what's behind our eyes and between our ears.

Context Effects

Our perceptions are influenced partly by our perceptual set, but the immediate context (including the cultural context, as in **FIGURE 5.30**) also plays a role. Two examples:

■ Imagine hearing a noise, perhaps a cough, immediately followed by the words "eel is on the wagon." Likely, you would actually perceive the first word as *wheel*. Given "eel is on the orange," you would hear *peel*. This curious finding suggests that the brain can allow a later stimulus to determine how we perceive an earlier one (Grossberg, 1995; Warren, 1984). The context creates an expectation, a sort of detour that sends our incoming signals down one path or another.

■ Did the pursuing monster in Figure 5.26 look aggressive? Did the pursued one seem frightened? If so, you experienced a context effect, because the images are identical.

Even hearing sad rather than happy music can tilt our minds toward hearing a sad meaning in spoken words—*mourning* rather than *morning*, *die* rather than *dye*, *pain* rather than *pane* (Halberstadt & others, 1995).

Similarly, our emotions can shove our social perceptions in one direction or another. Spouses who feel loved and appreciated perceive less threat in stressful marital events—"He's just having a bad day" (Murray & others, 2003). Professional referees, if told a soccer team has a history of aggressive behavior, will assign more penalty cards when watching recorded play (Jones & others, 2002). Lee Ross invites us to recall our own perceptions in

Figure 5.29> Believing is seeing What do you perceive in these photos? Is this Nessie, the Loch Ness monster, or a log?

Figure 5.30> *Culture and context effects* What is above the woman's head? When East Africans were asked this question, most said the woman was balancing a metal box or can on her head and that the family was sitting under a tree. Most Westerners, for whom corners and boxlike architecture are more common, said the woman was sitting under a window, indoors with her family. (Adapted from Gregory & Gombrich, 1973.)

different contexts: "Ever notice that when you're driving you hate pedestrians, the way they saunter through the crosswalk, almost daring you to hit them, but when you're walking you hate drivers?" (Jaffe, 2004).

The effects of perceptual set and context show how experience helps us construct perception. In everyday life, for example, we may filter our thoughts about a new baby through our gender stereotypes. Without the obvious cues of pink or blue, people will struggle over whether to call the new baby "he" or "she." But told an infant is "David," people (especially children) may perceive "him" as bigger and stronger than if told the same infant is called "Diana" (Stern & Karraker, 1989). Some differences, it seems, exist merely in the eyes of their beholders.

* * *

We have learned that perception is both inborn and learned. The river of perception is fed by two streams: our sensations and our thought processes. "Simple" perceptions are the brain's creative products. If we accept the statement that perception is the product of sensation and cognition, what can we say about extrasensory perception (ESP), which claims that perception can occur apart from sensory input?

PRACTICE TEST

24. In some cases, surgeons have restored vision to patients who have been blind from birth. The newly sighted individuals were able to sense colors but had difficulty
    a. recognizing objects by touch.
    b. recognizing objects by sight.
    c. distinguishing figure from ground.
    d. distinguishing between bright and dim light.

25. Experiments in which volunteers wear glasses that turn their visual fields upside down show that, after a period of disorientation, people learn to function quite well. This ability is called

a. context effect.
b. perceptual set.
c. sensory interaction.
d. perceptual adaptation.

26. Our perceptual set influences what we perceive. This mental tendency reflects our
    a. experiences, assumptions, and expectations.
    b. perceptual adaptation.
    c. skill at extrasensory perception.
    d. perceptual constancy.

Answers: 24. b, 25. d, 26. a.

ESP: Perception Without Sensation?

18: How do ESP claims hold up when put to the test by scientists?

Without sensory input, are we capable of **extrasensory perception (ESP)?** Are there indeed people—*any* people—who can read minds, see through walls, or foretell the future? Before we evaluate claims of ESP, let's review them.

Claims of ESP

The most testable and, for this chapter, most relevant ESP claims focus on:

Telepathy: mind-to-mind communication.

Clairvoyance: perceiving remote events, such as a house on fire in another state.

Precognition: perceiving future events, such as an unexpected death in the next month.

Closely linked with these are claims of *psychokinesis,* or "mind over matter," such as levitating a table or influencing the roll of a die. (The claim is illustrated by the wry request, "Will all those who believe in psychokinesis please raise my hand?")

extrasensory perception (ESP) the controversial claim that perception can occur apart from sensory input, such as through *telepathy, clairvoyance,* and *precognition.*

Facts or Fantasies?

Most research psychologists and scientists—including 96 percent of the scientists in one U.S. National Academy of Sciences survey—are skeptical of ESP claims (McConnell, 1991). No greedy—or charitable—psychic has been able to predict the outcome of a lottery jackpot, or to make billions on the stock market. The new-century psychics failed to anticipate the big-news events such as the horror of 9/11. In 26 years, unusual predictions have almost never come true, and psychics have virtually never anticipated any of the year's headline events (Emery, 2004).

Moreover, the hundreds of visions offered by psychics working with the police are no more accurate than guesses made by others (Reiser, 1982). Their sheer volume does increase the odds of an occasional correct guess, however, which psychics can then report to the media.

> "A person who talks a lot is sometimes right."
>
> Spanish proverb

Police departments are wise to all this. When researchers asked the police departments of America's 50 largest cities whether they ever had used psychics, 65 percent said no (Sweat & Durm, 1993). Of those that had, not one had found them helpful.

Are the spontaneous "visions" of everyday people any more accurate? Do our dreams foretell the future, or do they only seem to do so when we recall or reconstruct dreams in light of what has happened? Two Harvard psychologists (Murray & Wheeler, 1937) tested the prophetic power of dreams after aviator Charles Lindbergh's baby son was kidnapped and murdered in 1932, but before the body was discovered. When invited to report their dreams about the child, 1300 visionaries replied. How many accurately saw the child dead? Five percent. And how many also correctly anticipated the body's location—buried among trees? Only 4 of the 1300. Although this number was surely no better than chance, to those 4 dreamers the accuracy of their *apparent* prior knowledge must have seemed uncanny.

Given the billions of events in the world each day, and given enough days, some stunning coincidences are sure to occur. By one careful estimate, chance alone would predict that more than a thousand times a day someone on Earth will think of another person and then within the next five minutes will learn of that person's death (Charpak & Broch, 2004). With enough time and people, the improbable becomes inevitable.

That became the experience of comics writer John Byrne (2003). Six months after his Spider-Man story about a New York blackout appeared, New York suffered its massive 1977 blackout. A later Spider-Man storyline involved a major earthquake in Japan "and again," he recalls, "the real thing happened in the month the issue hit the stands." When working on a Superman comic book, Byrne "had the Man of Steel fly to the rescue when disaster beset the NASA space shuttle. The 1986 *Challenger* tragedy happened almost immediately thereafter" (with time for the issue to be redrawn). "Most recent, and chilling, came when I was writing and drawing Wonder Woman and did a story in which the title character was killed as a prelude to her becoming a goddess." The issue cover "was done as a newspaper front page, with the headline 'Princess Diana Dies.' (Diana is Wonder Woman's real name.) That issue went on sale on a Thursday. The following Saturday . . . I don't have to tell you, do I?"

Testing ESP

When faced with claims of mind reading or out-of-body travel or communication with the dead, how can we separate bizarre ideas from those that sound bizarre but are true? At the heart of science is a simple answer: *Test them to see if they work.* If they do, so much the better for the ideas. If they don't, so much the better for our skepticism.

How might we test ESP claims in a controlled experiment? An experiment differs from a staged demonstration. In the laboratory, the experimenter controls

Testing psychic powers in the British population :: Psychologist Richard Wiseman created a "mind machine" to see if people can influence or predict a coin toss. Using a touch-sensitive screen, visitors to British festivals were given four attempts to call heads or tails playing against a computer that kept score. By the time the experiment ended, nearly 28,000 people had predicted 110,972 tosses—with 49.8 percent correct (not beating chance, which would be 50 percent).

what the "psychic" sees and hears. On stage, the "psychic" controls what the audience sees and hears.

The search for a valid and reliable test of ESP has resulted in thousands of experiments. One controlled procedure invited "senders" to telepathically transmit one of four visual images to "receivers" deprived of sensation in a nearby chamber (Bem & Honorton, 1994). The result? A 32 percent accurate response rate, surpassing the chance rate of 25 percent. But follow-up studies have (depending on who was summarizing the results) either failed to replicate the phenomenon or produced mixed results (Bem & others, 2001; Milton & Wiseman, 2002; Storm, 2000, 2003).

One skeptic, magician James Randi, has a longstanding offer that expires in 2010—$1 million—"to anyone who proves

> "A psychic is an actor playing the role of a psychic."
>
> Psychologist magician Daryl Bem, 1984

a genuine psychic power under proper observing conditions" (Randi, 1999). French, Australian, and Indian groups have similar offers of up to 200,000 euros (CFI, 2003). And $50 million was made available for information leading to Osama bin Laden's capture. Large as these sums are, the scientific seal of approval would be worth far more. To silence those who say there is no ESP, one need only produce a single person who can demonstrate a single, reproducible ESP event. (To silence those who say pigs can't talk would take but one talking pig.) So far, no such person has emerged.

PRACTICE TEST

27. There is some evidence to suggest that the following ESP phenomenon may have a scientific base of support.
    a. Telepathy
    b. Clairvoyance
    c. Precognition
    d. None of these answers

Answer: 27. d.

* * *

Within our ordinary perceptual experiences lies much that is truly extraordinary. A century of research has revealed many of the secrets of sensation and perception, yet for future generations of researchers there remain profound and genuine mysteries to solve.

Terms and Concepts to Remember

sensation, p. 125

perception, p. 125

transduction, p. 126

absolute threshold, p. 126

subliminal, p. 126

priming, p. 126

difference threshold, p. 127

Weber's law, p. 127

sensory adaptation, p. 128

wavelength, p. 129

hue, p. 129

intensity, p. 129

retina, p. 130

rods, p. 130

cones, p. 130

optic nerve, p. 130

blind spot, p. 130

feature detectors, p. 132

parallel processing, p. 132

audition, p. 134

frequency, p. 134

pitch, p. 134

cochlea [KOHK-lee-uh], p. 134

hypnosis, p. 139

sensory interaction, p. 140

kinesthesis [kin-ehs-THEE-sehs], p. 141

vestibular sense, p. 142

gestalt, p. 143

figure-ground, p. 143

grouping, p. 143

depth perception, p. 144

visual cliff, p. 144

binocular cues, p. 144

retinal disparity, p. 145

monocular cues, p. 145

perceptual constancy, p. 145

color constancy, p. 145

perceptual adaptation, p. 149

perceptual set, p. 149

extrasensory perception (ESP), p. 151

:: Multiple-choice self-tests and more may be found at www.worthpublishers.com/myers

REVIEW: SENSATION AND PERCEPTION

Through *sensation*, we receive, transform, and deliver input from our environment to our brain. Through *perception*, we organize and interpret sensory information.

SENSING THE WORLD: SOME BASIC PRINCIPLES

1 What three steps are basic to all our sensory systems?

- Receiving sensory input.
- Transforming that input into neural impulses (*transduction*).
- Delivering neural information to our brain.

2 What are absolute thresholds and difference thresholds, and how do they help us function effectively?

- An *absolute threshold* is the minimum stimulation needed to be consciously aware of a stimulus 50 percent of the time.
- A *difference threshold* is the minimum change needed to detect the difference between two stimuli.
- We can process some information from *subliminal* stimuli, which are too weak to be recognized reliably.
- Our difference threshold increases in proportion to the stimulus (*Weber's law*).

3 What function does sensory adaptation serve?

- We grow less sensitive to constant sensory input.
- *Sensory adaptation* makes us aware of changes in our environment.

VISION

4 What are the characteristics of the energy we see as light?

- The visible light we experience is a thin slice of the broad spectrum of electromagnetic energy.
- The *hue* (blue, green, etc.) and brightness we perceive depend on the light's *wavelength* and *intensity*.

5 How does the eye transform light energy into neural messages?

- Light entering the eye is focused on our *retina*—the inner surface of the eye.
- The retina's light-sensitive *rods* and color-sensitive *cones* convert the light energy into neural impulses.
- Those impulses travel along the *optic nerve* to the brain.

6 How is visual information processed in the brain?

- In the visual cortex, *feature detectors* respond to specific features of the visual information (lines, edges, etc.).
- Through *parallel processing*, the brain processes different aspects of visual information (color, movement, depth, and form) separately but at the same time.

THE OTHER SENSES

7 What are the characteristics of the air pressure waves that we hear as meaningful sounds?

- Sound waves vary in *amplitude* (perceived as loudness) and in *frequency* (perceived as *pitch*—a tone's highness or lowness).
- Sound energy is measured in decibels.

8 How does the ear transform sound energy into neural messages?

- Sound waves travel through the auditory canal, causing tiny vibrations in the eardrum.
- The bones of the middle ear transmit the vibrations to the *cochlea,* causing waves of movement in hair cells.
- This movement triggers nerve cells to send signals along the auditory nerve to the brain's auditory cortex.
- Small differences in the loudness and timing of the sounds received by each ear allow us to locate sounds.

9 How do we sense touch and feel pain, and how can we treat pain?

- Our sense of touch involves pressure, warmth, cold, and pain. Only pressure has identifiable receptors.
- Pain is a combination of biological, psychological, and social-cultural influences. Treatments may manage pain from any or all of these perspectives.
- *Hypnosis*, which increases our response to suggestions, can help relieve pain.

10 How are our senses of taste and smell similar, and what is sensory interaction?

- Both taste and smell are chemical senses.
- Taste involves five basic sensations—sweet, sour, salty, bitter, and umami.
- Taste receptors in the taste buds carry messages to the brain's temporal lobe.
- Receptors for smell, located at the top of each nasal cavity, send messages to the brain. These cells work together, combining their messages into patterns that vary, depending on the different odors they detect.
- *Sensory interaction* is the influence of one sense on another.

11 How do our senses monitor our body's position and movement?

- Our *kinesthetic sense* monitors the position and movement of individual body parts. Sensors all over the body send messages to the brain.
- Our *vestibular sense* monitors the position and movement of our head (and therefore our whole body). Its receptors in the inner ear send messages to the cerebellum.

PERCEPTUAL ORGANIZATION

12 **What was the main message of Gestalt psychology, and how do the principles of figure-ground and grouping contribute to our perception of form?**

- Gestalt psychologists showed that the brain organizes bits of sensory information into meaningful forms.

- To recognize an object, we must first perceive it as distinct (see it as a *figure*) from its surroundings (the *ground*).

- We bring order and form to sensory input by organizing it into meaningful *groups*, following such rules as proximity, continuity, and closure.

PERCEPTUAL INTERPRETATION

13 **How do we see the world in three dimensions?**

- Humans and many other species perceive the world in three dimensions at, or very soon after, birth. Learning intensifies our fear of heights.

- We transform two-dimensional retinal images into three-dimensional depth perceptions by use of *binocular cues* (such as *retinal disparity*) and *monocular cues* (such as relative height, relative size, interposition, relative motion, linear perspective, and light and shadow).

14 **How do perceptual constancies help us construct meaningful perceptions?**

- *Perceptual constancy* is the ability to recognize an object regardless of its changing angle, distance, or illumination. This ability lets us perceive objects as unchanging despite the changing images they cast on our retina.

- *Color constancy* is our ability to perceive consistent color under changing light. It shows that our brains construct our experience of color through comparisons with surrounding objects.

- *Shape and size constancies* help explain visual illusions, such as the Moon illusion.

15 **What does research on sensory deprivation and restored vision reveal about the effects of experience on perception?**

- Some perceptual abilities (such as color and figure-ground perception) are inborn.

- A critical period exists for other abilities (such as perceiving shapes visually). Without early experience, these abilities (and brain areas associated with them) do not develop normally.

16 **What is perceptual adaptation?**

- Given eyeglasses that shift the world slightly to the left or right, turn it upside down, or reverse it, people can learn to *adapt* their movements and move about with ease.

17 **How do our assumptions, expectations, and contexts affect our perceptions?**

- Perception is influenced by our *perceptual set*—our mental tendencies and assumptions.

- Physical, emotional, and cultural context can create expectations about what we will perceive, thus affecting those perceptions.

ESP: PERCEPTION WITHOUT SENSATION?

18 **How do ESP claims hold up when put to the test by scientists?**

- Researchers have not been able to replicate (reproduce) *extrasensory perception* (ESP) effects under controlled conditions.

IN THE EARLY 1940S, UNIVERSITY OF Minnesota graduate students Marian Breland and Keller Breland witnessed the power of a new learning technology. Their mentor, B. F. Skinner, would become famous for *shaping* rat and pigeon behaviors, delivering well-timed rewards as the animals inched closer and closer to a desired behavior. Impressed with Skinner's results, the Brelands began shaping the behavior of cats, chickens, parakeets, turkeys, pigs, ducks, and hamsters (Bailey & Gillaspy, 2005). The rest is history. The company they formed spent the next half-century training more than 15,000 animals from 140 species for movies, traveling shows, amusement parks, corporations, and the government. And along the way, the Brelands themselves mentored others, including Sea World's first director of training.

While writing a book about such animal trainers, Amy Sutherland wondered if shaping had uses closer to home (2006a,b). If baboons could be trained to skateboard and elephants to paint, might "the same techniques . . . work on that stubborn but lovable species, the American husband"? Step by step, she "began thanking Scott if he threw one dirty shirt into the hamper. If he threw in two, I'd kiss him [and] as he basked in my appreciation, the piles became smaller." After two years of "thinking of my husband as an exotic animal species," she reports, "my marriage is far smoother, my husband much easier to love."

Like husbands and other animals, much of what we do we learn from experience. Indeed, nature's most important gift may be our *adaptability*—our capacity to learn new behaviors that help us cope with our changing world. We can learn how to build grass huts or snow shelters, submarines or space stations, and thereby adapt to almost any environment.

Learning breeds hope. What is learnable we may be able to teach—a fact that encourages animal trainers, and also parents, educators, and coaches. What has been learned we may be able to change by new learning—an assumption underlying stress management and counseling programs. No matter how unhappy or unloving we are, that need not be the end of our story.

No topic is closer to the heart of psychology than **learning,** a relatively permanent change in behavior due to experience. In earlier chapters we considered the learning of sleep patterns, of visual perceptions, of gender roles. In later chapters we will see how learning shapes our thoughts, our emotions, our personalities, and our attitudes. This chapter examines some core processes of three types of learning: *classical conditioning, operant conditioning,* and *observational learning.*

HOW DO WE LEARN?

CLASSICAL CONDITIONING

Pavlov's Experiments

Extending Pavlov's Understanding

Pavlov's Legacy

OPERANT CONDITIONING

Skinner's Experiments

Extending Skinner's Understanding

Skinner's Legacy

Contrasting Classical and Operant Conditioning

LEARNING BY OBSERVATION

Bandura's Experiments

Applications of Observational Learning

learning a relatively permanent change in behavior due to experience.

How Do We Learn?

1: What is learning?

Our minds naturally connect events that occur in sequence. We learn by *association.* Suppose you see and smell freshly baked bread, eat some, and find it satisfying. The next time you see and smell fresh bread, that experience will lead you to expect that eating it will again be satisfying. So, too, with sounds. If you associate a sound with a frightening consequence, hearing the sound alone may trigger your fear. As one 4-year-old said after watching a TV character get mugged, "If I had heard that music, I wouldn't have gone around the corner!" (Wells, 1981).

Other animals also learn by association. To protect itself, the sea slug *Aplysia* withdraws its gill when squirted with water. If the squirts continue, as happens naturally in choppy water, the withdrawal response weakens. But if the sea slug repeatedly receives an electric shock just after being squirted, its response to the squirt instead grows stronger. The animal has learned that the squirt signals an upcoming shock.

Complex animals can learn to link outcomes with their own responses. An aquarium seal will repeat behaviors, such as slapping and barking, that prompt people to toss it a herring.

By linking two events that occur close together, both animals are exhibiting **associative learning.** The sea slug associates the squirt with an upcoming shock; the seal associates slapping and barking with a herring treat. Each animal has learned something important to its survival: predicting the immediate future.

This process of learning associations is *conditioning,* and it takes two main forms:

■ In *classical conditioning,* we learn to associate two stimuli and thus to anticipate events. (A **stimulus** is any event or situation that evokes a response.) We learn that a flash of lightning will be followed by a crack of thunder, so when lightning flashes nearby, we start to brace ourselves (FIGURE 6.1).

■ In *operant conditioning,* we learn to associate a response (our behavior) and its consequence, and thus to repeat acts followed by good results (FIGURE 6.2) and avoid acts followed by bad results.

Figure 6.1> Classical conditioning

Two related events:

Stimulus 1:
Lightning

Stimulus 2:
Thunder

Result after repetition:

Stimulus:
We see
lightning

Response:
We wince,
anticipating
thunder

(a) Response: balancing a ball

(b) Consequence: receiving food

(c) Behavior strengthened

Figure 6.2> Operant conditioning

Conditioning is not the only form of learning. Through *observational learning*, we learn from others' experiences. Chimpanzees, for example, sometimes learn behaviors merely by watching others perform them. If one animal sees another solve a puzzle and gain a food reward, the observer may perform the trick more quickly.

By conditioning and by observation we humans learn and adapt to our environments. We learn to expect and prepare for significant events such as food or pain (*classical conditioning*). We learn to repeat acts that bring good results and to avoid acts that bring bad results (*operant conditioning*). By watching others, we learn new behaviors (*observational learning*). And through language we also learn things we have neither experienced nor observed.

Classical Conditioning

For many people, the name Ivan Pavlov (1849–1936) rings a bell. His early twentieth-century experiments—now psychology's most famous research—are classics. The process he explored we justly call **classical conditioning.**

Pavlov's Experiments

2: How does classical conditioning demonstrate associative learning?

For his studies of digestion, Pavlov (who held a medical degree) earned Russia's first Nobel prize in 1904. But his novel experiments on learning, which consumed the last three decades of his life, earned this feisty scientist his place in history.

Pavlov's new direction came when his creative mind seized on an incidental observation. Without fail, putting food in a dog's mouth caused the animal to salivate. Moreover, the dog began salivating not only to the taste of the food but also to the mere sight of the food or the food

Ivan Pavlov :: "Experimental investigation . . . should lay a solid foundation for a future true science of psychology" (1927).

Sovfoto

dish or the person delivering the food, or even the sound of that person's approaching footsteps. At first, Pavlov considered these "psychic secretions" an annoyance—until he realized they pointed to a simple but important form of learning.

Pavlov and his assistants tried to imagine what the dog was thinking and feeling as it drooled in anticipation of the food. This only led them into fruitless debates. So to make their studies more objective, they experimented. To rule out other possible influences, they isolated the dog in a small room, placed it in a harness, and attached a device to measure its saliva. From the next room, they presented food—first by sliding in a food bowl, later by blowing meat powder into the dog's mouth at a precise moment. They then paired various *neutral events*—unrelated stimuli that the dog could see

or hear—with food in the dog's mouth. If a sight or sound regularly signaled the arrival of food, would the dog learn the link? If so, would it begin salivating in anticipation of the food?

The answers proved to be yes and yes. Just before placing food in the dog's mouth to produce salivation, Pavlov sounded a tone. After several pairings of tone and food, the dog got the message. Anticipating the meat powder, it began salivating to the tone alone. In later experiments, a buzzer, a light, a touch on the leg, even the sight of a circle set off the drooling.

A dog doesn't *learn* to salivate in response to food in its mouth. Food in the mouth automatically, *unconditionally*, triggers this response. Thus, Pavlov called the drooling an **unconditioned response (UR).** And he called the food an **unconditioned stimulus (US).**

---

associative learning learning that certain events occur together. The events may be two stimuli (as in classical conditioning) or a response and its consequences (as in operant conditioning).

stimulus any event or situation that evokes a response.

classical conditioning a type of learning in which we learn to link two or more stimuli and anticipate events.

unconditioned response (UR) in classical conditioning, the unlearned, naturally occurring response to the unconditioned stimulus (US), such as salivation when food is in the mouth.

unconditioned stimulus (US) in classical conditioning, a stimulus that unconditionally—naturally and automatically—triggers a response (UR).

PEANUTS

PEANUTS reprinted by permission of United Feature Syndicate, Inc.

Figure 6.3> Pavlov's classic experiment Pavlov presented a neutral stimulus (a tone) just before an unconditioned stimulus (food in mouth). The neutral stimulus then became a conditioned stimulus, producing a conditioned response.

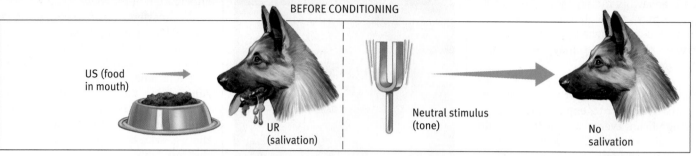

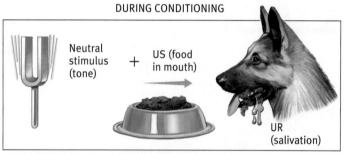

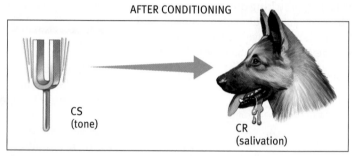

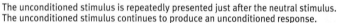

Salivating in response to a tone, however, is learned. Because it is *conditional* upon the dog's linking the tone with the food (FIGURE 6.3), we call this response the **conditioned response (CR).** The stimulus that used to be neutral (in this case, a tone that had no meaning before conditioning, but that now triggers drooling) is the **conditioned stimulus (CS).** Remembering the difference between these two kinds of stimuli and responses is easy: Conditioned = learned; *unconditioned* = *unlearned*.

A second example, drawn from more recent experiments, may help. An experimenter sounds a tone just before delivering an air puff to your eye. After several repetitions, you blink to the tone alone. What is the US? The UR? The CS? The CR?[1]

Remember:

US = Unconditioned Stimulus
UR = Unconditioned Response
CS = Conditioned Stimulus
CR = Conditioned Response

If Pavlov's demonstration of associative learning was so simple, what did he do for the next three decades? What discoveries did his research factory publish in his 532 papers on salivary conditioning (Windholz, 1997)? He and his associates identified five major conditioning processes: *acquisition, extinction, spontaneous recovery, generalization,* and *discrimination*.

Acquisition

3: What parts do acquisition, extinction, spontaneous recovery, generalization, and discrimination play in classical conditioning?

Acquisition is the first stage in classical conditioning. This is the point when Pavlov's dogs learned the link between the neutral stimulus (the tone, the light, the touch) and the US (the food). To understand this stage, Pavlov and his associates had to confront the question of timing: How much time should pass between presenting the neutral stimulus and the food? In most cases, not much—half a second usually works well.

What do you suppose would happen if the food (US) appeared *before* the tone (CS) rather than after? Would conditioning occur? Not likely. With but a few exceptions, conditioning doesn't happen when the CS follows the US. Remember, classical conditioning is biologically adaptive because it helps humans and other animals *prepare* for good or bad events. To Pavlov's dogs, the tone (CS) signaled an important biological event— the arrival of food (US). To deer in the forest, the snapping of a twig (CS) may signal a predator's approach (US). If the good or bad event has already occurred, the tone or the sound won't help the animal prepare.

1. US = air puff; UR = blink to air puff; CS = tone; CR = blink to tone

Check yourself: If the aroma of cake baking sets your mouth to watering, what is the US? The CS? The CR? (See the next page for the answer.)

More recent research on male Japanese quail shows how a CS can signal another important biological event, sexual arousal (Domjan, 1992, 1994, 2005). Just before presenting an approachable female, the researchers turned on a red light. Over time, as the red light continued to announce the female's arrival, the light caused the male quail to become excited. They developed a preference for their cage's red-light district. When a female appeared, they mated with her more quickly and released more semen and sperm (Domjan & others, 1998). All in all, the quail's capacity for classical conditioning gives it a reproductive edge.

In humans, too, objects, sights, and smells (even the unlikely smell of onion breath) associated with sexual pleasure can become conditioned stimuli for sexual arousal (Byrne, 1982) (FIGURE 6.4). The larger lesson: *Conditioning helps an animal survive and reproduce—by responding to cues that help it gain food, avoid dangers, locate mates, and produce offspring* (Hollis, 1997).

Figure 6.5> Acquisition, extinction, and spontaneous recovery The rising curve (simplified here) shows that the CR rapidly grows stronger as the CS and US are repeatedly paired (*acquisition*). The CS weakens when it is presented alone (*extinction*). After a pause, the CR reappears (*spontaneous recovery*).

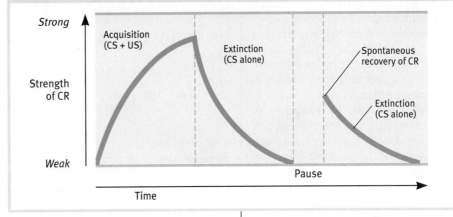

Extinction and Spontaneous Recovery

What would happen, Pavlov wondered, if after conditioning, the CS occurred repeatedly without the US? If the tone sounds again and again, but no food appears, would the tone still trigger drooling? The answer was mixed. The dogs salivated less and less, a reaction known as **extinction,** a drop-off in responses when a CS (tone) no longer signals an upcoming US (food). But when Pavlov allowed several hours to pass before sounding the tone, the dogs would again begin drooling to the tone (FIGURE 6.5). This **spontaneous recovery**—the reappearance of a (weakened) CR after a pause—suggested to Pavlov that extinction was suppressing the CR rather than eliminating it.

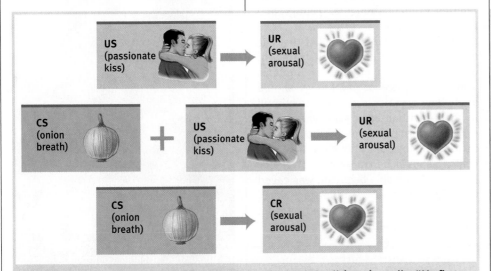

Figure 6.4> An unexpected CS Psychologist Michael Tirrell (1990) recalls: "My first girlfriend loved onions, so I came to associate onion breath with kissing. Before long, onion breath sent tingles up and down my spine. Oh what a feeling!"

conditioned response (CR) in classical conditioning, the learned response to a previously neutral (but now conditioned) stimulus (CS).

conditioned stimulus (CS) in classical conditioning, an originally irrelevant stimulus that, after association with an unconditioned stimulus (US), comes to trigger a conditioned response (CR).

acquisition in classical conditioning, the initial stage, when we link a neutral stimulus and an unconditioned stimulus so that the neutral stimulus begins triggering the conditioned response. (In operant conditioning, the strengthening of a reinforced response.)

extinction in classical conditioning, the weakening of a conditioned response when an unconditioned stimulus does not follow a conditioned stimulus. (In operant conditioning, the weakening of a response when it is no longer reinforced.)

spontaneous recovery the reappearance, after a pause, of an extinguished conditioned response.

Generalization

Pavlov and his students noticed that a dog conditioned to the sound of one tone also responded somewhat to the sound of a new and different tone. Likewise, a dog conditioned to salivate when rubbed would also drool a bit when scratched (Windholz, 1989) or when touched on a different body part. This tendency to respond to stimuli similar to the CS is called **generalization.**

Generalization can be adaptive, as when toddlers taught to fear moving cars also become afraid of moving trucks and motorcycles. And generalized fears can linger. One Argentine writer who had been tortured still flinches when he sees black shoes—his first glimpse of his torturers when they approached his cell. This generalized fear response was found in laboratory studies comparing abused with nonabused children. When an angry face appears on a computer screen, abused children's brain-wave responses are dramatically stronger and longer lasting (FIGURE 6.6) (Pollak & others, 1998).

Discrimination

Pavlov's dogs also learned to respond to the sound of a particular tone and *not* to other tones. **Discrimination** is the learned

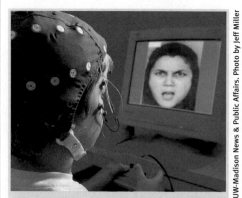

Figure 6.6> Why child abuse puts children at risk Seth Pollak (University of Wisconsin-Madison) reports that abused children's sensitized brains react more strongly to angry faces. This generalized anxiety response may help explain their greater risk of psychological disorder.

Stimulus generalization

"I don't care if she's a tape dispenser. I love her."

ability to *distinguish* between a conditioned stimulus (which predicts the US) and other irrelevant stimuli. Being able to recognize differences is adaptive. Slightly different stimuli can be followed by vastly different results. Confronted by a pit bull, your heart may race; confronted by a golden retriever, it probably will not.

Extending Pavlov's Understanding

4: What areas did Pavlov tend to overlook, and why is his work still important?

John B. Watson was one of many psychologists who built on Pavlov's work. Watson and Pavlov rejected "mentalistic" concepts (such as consciousness) that referred to inner thoughts, feelings, and motives (Watson, 1913). The two researchers also shared a belief that the basic laws of learning were the same for all animals—whether dogs or humans. Thus, the science of psychology should study how organisms respond to stimuli in their environments, said Watson. "Its theoretical goal is the prediction and control of behavior." This view, that psychology should be an objective science based on observable behavior, was called **behaviorism,** and it influenced North American psychology during the first half of the twentieth century.

Answer to questions on the previous page: The cake (and its taste) are the US. The associated aroma is the CS. Salivation to the aroma is the CR.

Later research has shown that Pavlov's and Watson's views of learning underestimated two important sets of influences. The first is *cognitive processes,* our thoughts, perceptions, and expectations. For example, people being treated for alcohol dependence may be given alcohol spiked with a nauseating drug. However, their *awareness* that the drug, not the alcohol, causes the nausea tends to weaken the association between drinking alcohol and feeling sick. Even in classical conditioning, it is (especially with humans) not simply the CS–US pairing, but also the thought that counts.

There also are *biological constraints* on learning. Each species comes prepared to learn those things crucial to its survival. The idea that environments are the whole story—that almost any stimulus (whether a taste, sight, or sound) can serve equally well as a CS—ended in the 1960s, with a discovery by John Garcia and Robert Koelling (1966). They noticed that rats would avoid a taste—but not sights or sounds—associated with becoming sick, even hours later. This

John Garcia :: As the laboring son of California farmworkers, Garcia attended school only in the off-season during his early childhood years. After entering junior college in his late twenties, and earning his Ph.D. in his late forties, he received the American Psychological Association's Distinguished Scientific Contribution Award "for his highly original, pioneering research in conditioning and learning." He was also elected to the National Academy of Sciences.

makes adaptive sense, because for rats the easiest way to identify tainted food is to taste it. If sickened after sampling a new food, rats thereafter avoid it. This response, which psychologists call *taste aversion,* makes it tough to wipe out an invasion of "bait-shy" rats by poisoning.

Humans, too, seem biologically prepared to learn some things rather than others. If you become violently ill four hours after eating a tainted hamburger, you will probably develop an aversion to the taste of hamburger but not to the sight of the associated restaurant, its plates, the people you were with, or the music you heard there.

Garcia and Koelling's taste-aversion research is but one instance in which experiments that began with the discomfort of some laboratory animals enhanced the welfare of many others. In another study, coyotes and wolves that were tempted into eating sheep carcasses laced with a sickening poison thereafter

Taste aversion :: If you became violently ill after eating mussels, you probably would have a hard time eating them again. Their smell and taste would have become a CS for nausea. This learning occurs readily because our biology prepares us to learn taste aversions to toxic foods.

avoided sheep meat (Gustavson & others, 1974, 1976). Two wolves penned with a live sheep seemed actually to fear it. The study not only saved the sheep from their predators, but also saved the sheep-shunning coyotes and wolves from angry ranchers and farmers who had wanted to destroy them. In later experiments, conditioned taste aversion has successfully prevented baboons from raiding African gardens, raccoons from attacking chickens, and ravens and crows from feeding on crane eggs. In all cases, research helped preserve both the prey and their predators, who occupy an important ecological niche (Garcia & Gustavson, 1997).

Such research supports Charles Darwin's principle that natural selection favors traits that aid survival. Our ancestors who readily learned taste aversions were unlikely to eat the same toxic food again and were more likely to survive and leave descendants. Nausea, like anxiety, pain, and other bad feelings, serves a good purpose. Like a low-oil warning on a car dashboard, each alerts the body to a threat (Neese, 1991).

Pavlov's Legacy

What, then, remains of Pavlov's ideas? A great deal. Most psychologists now agree that classical conditioning is a basic form of learning. Judged by today's knowledge of the interplay of our biology, psychology, and social-cultural environment, Pavlov's ideas were incomplete. But if we see further than Pavlov did, it is because we stand on his shoulders.

Why does Pavlov's work remain so important? If he had taught us only that old dogs can learn new tricks, his experiments would long ago have been forgotten. Why should we care that dogs can be conditioned to drool at the sound of a tone? The importance lies first in this finding: *Many other responses to many other stimuli can be classically conditioned in many other creatures*—in fact, in every species tested, from earthworms to fish to dogs to monkeys to people (Schwartz, 1984). Thus, classical conditioning is one way

that virtually all animals learn to adapt to their environment.

Second, *Pavlov showed us how a process such as learning can be studied objectively.* He was proud that his methods were not based on guesswork about what was going on in a dog's mind. The salivary response is a behavior we can measure in cubic centimeters of saliva. Pavlov's success therefore suggested a scientific model for how the young field of psychology might proceed—by isolating the basic building blocks of complex behaviors and studying them with objective laboratory procedures.

Applications of Classical Conditioning

Other chapters in this text—on motivation and emotion, stress and health, psychological disorders, and therapy—show how Pavlov's principles can influence human health and well-being. Two examples:

- Drugs used to treat cancer can trigger nausea and vomiting more than an hour following treatment. Patients may then develop classically conditioned nausea (and sometimes anxiety) to the sights, sounds, and smells associated with the clinic (Hall, 1997). Merely entering the clinic's waiting room or seeing the nurses can provoke these feelings (Burish & Carey, 1986).

- Former crack cocaine users often feel a craving when they are again with people or in places they associate with previous highs. Thus, drug counselors advise addicts to steer clear of people and settings that may trigger these cravings.

generalization in classical conditioning, the tendency, after conditioning, to respond similarly to stimuli that resemble the conditioned stimulus.

discrimination in classical conditioning, the learned ability to distinguish between a conditioned stimulus and other irrelevant stimuli.

behaviorism the view that psychology (1) should be an objective science that (2) studies behavior without reference to mental processes. Most research psychologists today agree with (1) but not with (2).

Could Pavlov's work help us understand our own emotions? Watson thought so. He believed that human emotions and behavior, though biologically influenced, are mainly a bundle of conditioned responses (1913). Working with an 11-month-old, Watson and Rosalie Rayner (1920; Harris, 1979) showed how specific fears might be conditioned. Like most infants, "Little Albert" feared loud noises but not white rats. Watson and Rayner presented a white rat and, as Little Albert reached to touch it, struck a hammer against a steel bar just behind his head. After seven repeats of seeing the rat and hearing the frightening noise, Albert burst into tears at the mere sight of the rat. Five days later, he had generalized this startled-fear reaction to the sight of a rabbit, a dog, and a sealskin coat, but not to dissimilar objects, such as toys.

The treatment of Little Albert would be unacceptable by today's ethical standards. Also, some psychologists, noting that the infant's fear wasn't learned

John B. Watson :: Watson (1924) admitted to "going beyond my facts" when offering his famous boast: "Give me a dozen healthy infants, well-formed, and my own specified world to bring them up in and I'll guarantee to take any one at random and train him to become any type of specialist I might select—doctor, lawyer, artist, merchant-chief, and, yes, even beggar-man and thief, regardless of his talents, penchants, tendencies, abilities, vocations, and race of his ancestors."

Brown Brothers

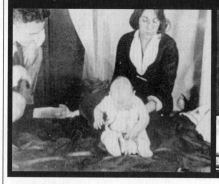
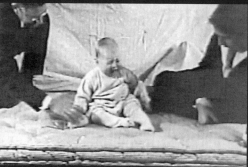

Little Albert's classically conditioned fear :: In Watson and Rayner's experiments, "Little Albert" learned to fear a white rat after repeatedly experiencing a loud noise as the rat was presented.

Archives of the History of American Psychology, The University of Akron

In Watson and Rayner's experiment, what was the US? The UR? The CS? The CR? (See 3 pages ahead.)

quickly, had difficulty repeating Watson and Rayner's findings with other children. Nevertheless, Little Albert's learned fears led many psychologists to wonder whether each of us might be a walking storehouse of conditioned emotions. If so, might extinction procedures or even new conditioning help us change our unwanted responses to emotion-arousing stimuli? One patient, who for 30 years had feared going into an elevator alone, did just that. Following his therapist's advice, he forced himself to enter 20 elevators a day. Within 10 days, his fear had nearly vanished (Ellis & Becker, 1982). In Chapter 13 we will see more examples of how psychologists use behavioral techniques to treat emotional disorders and promote personal growth.

⊙ PRACTICE TEST

1. *Learning* is defined as "a relatively permanent change in behavior due to
   a. instinct."
   b. mental processes."
   c. experience."
   d. formal education."

2. Two forms of associative learning are classical conditioning, in which we associate _____, and operant conditioning, in which we associate _____.
   a. two responses; a response and a consequence
   b. two stimuli; two responses
   c. two stimuli; a response and a consequence
   d. two responses; two stimuli

3. In Pavlov's experiments, dogs learned to drool in response to a tone. The tone is therefore a(n)
   a. conditioned stimulus.
   b. unconditioned stimulus.
   c. conditioned response.
   d. unconditioned response.

4. Dogs can learn to respond (by salivating) to one kind of stimulus (a circle, for example) and not to another (a square). This process is an example of
   a. generalization.
   b. discrimination.
   c. acquisition.
   d. spontaneous recovery.

5. Taste-aversion research showed that when rats get sick after sampling a new food, they learn to avoid certain tastes but not the sights or sounds connected to the place they became sick. This finding supports the idea that
   a. animals learn to react to similar stimuli in similar ways.
   b. conditioning has survival value by helping animals adapt to their environment.
   c. psychologists should only study observable behavior.
   d. organisms can be conditioned to any stimulus.

6. After Watson and Rayner classically conditioned a small child named Albert to fear a white rat, the child later showed some fear in response to a rabbit, a dog, and a sealskin coat. Little Albert's fear of objects resembling the rat illustrates

   a. extinction.
   b. generalization.
   c. spontaneous recovery.
   d. discrimination between two stimuli.

Answers: 1. c, 2. c, 3. a, 4. b, 5. b, 6. b.

Operant Conditioning

5: What is operant conditioning, and how does it differ from classical conditioning?

It's one thing to classically condition a dog to drool at the sound of a tone, or a child to fear moving cars. To teach an elephant to walk on its hind legs or a child to say *please*, we must turn to another type of learning—*operant conditioning*.

Classical conditioning and operant conditioning are both forms of associative learning, yet their difference is straightforward:

- In classical conditioning, an animal (dog, child, sea slug) forms associations between two events it does not control. This type of learning involves **respondent behavior**—actions that are automatic responses to a stimulus (such as salivating in response to meat powder and later in response to a tone).

- In **operant conditioning,** animals associate their own actions with consequences. Actions followed by a rewarding event increase; those followed by a punishing event decrease. Behavior that *operates* on the environment to *produce* rewarding or punishing events is called **operant behavior.**

We can therefore distinguish classical from operant conditioning by asking: *Is the animal learning associations between events it does not control (classical conditioning)? Or is it learning associations between its behavior and resulting events (operant conditioning)?*

Skinner's Experiments

In college, B. F. Skinner (1904–1990) was an English major and aspiring writer. Seeking a new direction, he entered graduate school in psychology. This decision led to pioneering studies in control, in which he taught pigeons such unpigeonlike behaviors as walking in a figure eight, playing Ping-Pong, and keeping a missile on course by pecking at a target on a screen.

For his studies, Skinner designed an **operant chamber,** popularly known as a Skinner box (FIGURE 6.7). The box has a bar or button that an animal presses or pecks to release a reward of food or water. An attached recording device tracks these responses. This design creates a stage on which rats and other animals act out Skinner's concept of **reinforcement:** any event that strengthens (increases the frequency of) a preceding response. What is reinforcing depends on the animal and the conditions. For people, it may be praise, attention, or a paycheck. For hungry and thirsty rats, food and water work well. Skinner's operant conditioning experiments have done far more than teach us how to pull habits out of a rat. They have explored the precise conditions that foster efficient and enduring learning.

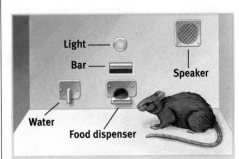

Figure 6.7> A Skinner box Inside the box, the rat presses a bar or button for a food reward. Outside, a measuring device (not shown here) records the animal's accumulated responses.

Reinforcers vary with circumstances :: What is reinforcing (a heat lamp) to one animal (a cold meerkat) may not be to another (an overheated child). What is reinforcing in one situation (a cold snap at the Taronga Zoo in Sydney) may not be in another (a sweltering summer day).

Reuters/Corbis

Shaping Behavior

Imagine that you wanted to condition a hungry rat to press a bar. Like Skinner, you could tease out this action with **shaping,** gradually guiding the rat's actions toward the desired behavior. First, you would watch how the animal naturally behaves, so that you could build on its existing

---

respondent behavior behavior that occurs as an automatic response to some stimulus.

operant conditioning a type of learning in which behavior is strengthened if followed by a reinforcer or diminished if followed by a punisher.

operant behavior behavior that operates on the environment, producing consequences.

operant chamber a box (also known as a *Skinner box*) with an attached recording device to track the rate at which an animal presses the box's bar to obtain a reinforcer. Used in operant conditioning research.

reinforcement in operant conditioning, any event that *strengthens* the behavior it follows.

shaping an operant conditioning procedure in which reinforcers guide actions closer and closer toward a desired behavior.

Shaping rats to save lives :: This Gambian giant pouched rat has been shaped to sniff out and approach the smell of land mines. After successfully locating a mine during training in Mozambique it receives a bite of banana.

behaviors. You might give the rat a bit of food each time it approaches the bar. Once the rat is approaching regularly, you would give the treat only when it moves close to the bar, then closer still. Finally, you would require it to touch the bar to get food. With this method of *successive approximations,* you reward responses that are ever-closer to the final desired behavior. By giving rewards only for desired behaviors and ignoring all other responses, researchers and animal trainers gradually shape complex behaviors.

Shaping can also help us understand what nonverbal organisms perceive. Can a dog see red and green? Can a baby hear the difference between soft and loud tones? If we can shape them to respond to one stimulus and not to another, then we know they can perceive the difference. Such experiments have even shown some animals can, remarkably, form concepts. If an experimenter reinforces a pigeon for pecking after seeing a human face, but not after seeing other images,

HI AND LOIS

the pigeon learns to recognize human faces (Herrnstein & Loveland, 1964). After being trained to discriminate among classes of events or objects—flowers, people, cars, chairs—pigeons can usually identify the category in which a new pictured object belongs (Bhatt & others, 1988; Wasserman, 1993).

In everyday life, we continually reward and shape others' behavior, said Skinner, though we may not mean to do so. Billy's whining, for example, annoys his parents, but look how they typically deal with Billy:

Billy: Could you tie my shoes?

Father: (Continues reading paper.)

Billy: Dad, I need my shoes tied.

Father: Uh, yeah, just a minute.

Billy: DAAAAD! TIE MY SHOES!

Father: How many times have I told you not to whine? Now, which shoe shall we do first?

Billy's whining is reinforced, because he gets something desirable—his dad's attention. Dad's response is reinforced

because it ends something unpleasant—Billy's whining.

Or consider a teacher who pastes gold stars on a wall chart after the names of children scoring 100 percent on spelling tests. As everyone can then see, some children always score 100 percent. The others, who take the same test and may have worked harder than the academic all-stars, get no stars. The teacher would be better advised to apply operant conditioning principles of shaping—to reinforce all spellers for gradual improvements.

Types of Reinforcers

6: What are the basic types of reinforcers?

Up to now, we've mainly been discussing **positive reinforcement,** which strengthens a response by *presenting* a typically pleasurable stimulus after a response. But, as we saw in the whining Billy story, there are *two* basic kinds of reinforcement (TABLE 6.1). **Negative reinforcement** strengthens a response by *reducing or removing* something undesirable or

Table 6.1	Ways to Increase Behavior	
Operant Conditioning Term	Description	Examples
Positive reinforcement	Give something that's desired.	Praise a dog that comes when you call it. Pay a person who paints your house.
Negative reinforcement	End something that's undesired.	End pain by taking painkillers. Fasten seatbelt to end beeping noise.

unpleasant. Billy's whining was *positively* reinforced, because Billy got something desirable—his father's attention. His dad's response to the whining (doing what Billy wanted) was *negatively* reinforced, because it got rid of Billy's annoying whining. Similarly, taking aspirin may relieve your headache and pushing the snooze button will silence your annoying alarm. These welcome results provide negative reinforcement and increase the odds that you will repeat these behaviors. For drug addicts, the negative reinforcement of escaping withdrawal pangs can be a compelling reason to resume using (Baker & others, 2004). Note that negative reinforcement is *not* punishment; rather, it *removes* a punishing event. Whether it works by getting rid of something we don't enjoy, or by giving us something we do enjoy, *reinforcement is any consequence that strengthens behavior.*

Primary and Conditioned Reinforcers

Getting food when hungry or having a painful headache go away is innately satisfying. These **primary reinforcers** are unlearned. **Conditioned reinforcers,** also called *secondary reinforcers,* get their power through learned associations with primary reinforcers. If a rat in a Skinner box learns that a light reliably signals a food delivery, the rat will work to turn on the light. The light has become a secondary reinforcer linked with food. Our lives are filled with conditioned reinforcers— money, good grades, a pleasant tone of voice—each of which has been linked with a more basic reward. Conditioned reinforcers greatly enhance our ability to influence one another.

Immediate and Delayed Reinforcers

Unlike rats, which are shaped by immediate reinforcers, humans respond to delayed reinforcers: the paycheck at the end of the week, the good grade at the end of the semester, the trophy at the end of the season. Indeed, to function effectively we must learn to delay our rewards, as some 4-year-olds did in laboratory testing. In choosing a candy, they preferred having a big reward tomorrow to munching on a small one right now. Learning to control one's impulses in order to achieve more valued rewards is a big step toward maturity (Logue, 1998a,b). No wonder children who make such choices tend to become socially competent and high-achieving adults (Mischel & others, 1989).

Sometimes, however, small but immediate pleasures (the enjoyment of watching late-night TV, for example) blind us to big but delayed consequences (tomorrow's sluggishness). For many teens, the immediate gratification of risky, unprotected sex in passionate moments prevails over the delayed gratification of safe sex or saved sex (Loewenstein & Furstenberg, 1991). And for too many of us, the immediate rewards of today's gas-guzzling vehicles prevail over the bigger consequences of tomorrow's global warming, rising seas, and extreme weather.

Reinforcement Schedules

7: How do continuous and partial reinforcement schedules affect behavior?

In most of our examples, the desired response has been reinforced every time it occurs. But **reinforcement schedules** vary, and they influence our learning. With **continuous reinforcement,** learning occurs rapidly, which makes this the best choice for mastering a new behavior. But there's a catch: Extinction also occurs rapidly. When reinforcement stops—when we stop delivering food after the rat presses the bar—the behavior soon stops. If a normally dependable candy machine fails to deliver a chocolate bar twice in a row, we stop putting money into it (although a week later we may exhibit spontaneous recovery by trying again).

Real life rarely provides continuous reinforcement. Salespeople don't make a sale with every pitch. But they persist because their efforts are occasionally rewarded. And that's the good news about **partial (intermittent) reinforcement** schedules, in which responses are

"Oh, not bad. The light comes on, I press the bar, they write me a check. How about you?"

sometimes reinforced, sometimes not (Nevin, 1988). Learning is slower to appear, but *resistance to extinction* is greater than with continuous reinforcement. Imagine a pigeon that has learned to peck a key to obtain food. If you gradually phase out the delivery of food until it occurs only rarely, in no predictable pattern, the pigeon may peck 150,000 times without a reward (Skinner, 1953). Slot machines reward gamblers in much the same way—occasionally and unpredictably. And like pigeons, slot payers keep trying, time and time again. With intermittent reinforcement, hope springs eternal.

positive reinforcement increases behaviors by presenting positive stimuli, such as food. A positive reinforcer is anything that, when *presented* after a response, strengthens the response.

negative reinforcement increases behaviors by stopping or reducing negative stimuli, such as shock. A negative reinforcer is anything that, when *removed* after a response, strengthens the response. (Note: negative reinforcement is *not* punishment.)

primary reinforcer an event that is innately reinforcing, often by satisfying a biological need.

conditioned reinforcer (also known as *secondary reinforcer*) an event that gains its reinforcing power through its link with a primary reinforcer.

reinforcement schedule a pattern that defines how often a desired response will be reinforced.

continuous reinforcement reinforcing a desired response every time it occurs.

partial (intermittent) reinforcement reinforcing a response only part of the time; results in slower acquisition but much greater resistance to extinction than does continuous reinforcement.

Lesson for parents: Partial reinforcement also works with children: *Occasionally giving in to children's tantrums for the sake of peace and quiet intermittently reinforces the tantrums.* This is the very best procedure for making a behavior persist.

Animal behaviors differ, yet Skinner (1956) contended that operant conditioning principles are universal. It matters little, he said, what response, what reinforcer, or what species you use. The effect of a given reinforcement schedule is pretty much the same: "Pigeon, rat, monkey, which is which? It doesn't matter. . . . Behavior shows astonishingly similar properties."

Punishment

8: How does punishment affect behavior?

Reinforcement increases a behavior; **punishment** does the opposite. A punisher is any consequence that *decreases* the frequency of the behavior it follows. Swift and sure punishers can powerfully restrain behaviors. The rat that is shocked after touching a forbidden object and the child who is burned by touching a hot stove will learn not to repeat those behaviors.

Should we physically punish children to change their behavior? Many psychologists and supporters of nonviolent parenting say no, pointing out four major drawbacks of physical punishment (Gershoff, 2002; Marshall, 2002).

1. *Punished behavior is suppressed, not forgotten, but this temporary state may (negatively) reinforce parents' punishing behavior.* The child swears, the parent swats, the parent hears no more swearing and feels the punishment successfully stopped the behavior. No wonder spanking is a hit with so many U.S. parents of 3- and 4-year-olds—more than 9 in 10 of whom acknowledge spanking their children (Kazdin & Benjet, 2003).

2. *Punishment teaches discrimination.* Was the punishment effective in putting an end to the swearing? Or did the child simply learn that it's not okay to swear around the house, but it is okay to swear elsewhere?

3. *Punishment can teach fear.* The child may associate the fear not only with the undesirable behavior but also with the person who delivered the punishment or the place it occurred. Thus, children may learn to fear a punishing teacher and try to avoid school. For such reasons, most European countries now ban hitting children in schools and child-care institutions (Leach, 1993, 1994). Eleven countries, including those in Scandinavia, further outlaw hitting by parents, giving children the same legal protection given to spouses (EPOCH, 2000).

4. *Physical punishment may increase aggressiveness by modeling aggression as a way to cope with problems.* We know that many aggressive delinquents and abusive parents come from abusive families (Straus & Gelles, 1980; Straus & others, 1997). But some researchers note a problem with studies that find that spanked children are at increased risk for aggression (and depression and low self-esteem). Well, yes, they say, just as people who have undergone psychotherapy are more likely to suffer depression—because they had preexisting problems that triggered the treatments (Larzelere, 1996, 2000, 2004). Which is the chicken and which is the egg? The correlations don't hand us an answer.

If one adjusts for preexisting antisocial behavior, then an occasional single swat or two to misbehaving 2- to 6-year-olds looks more effective (Baumrind & others, 2002; Larzelere, 2004). That is especially so if the swat is used only as a backup when milder disciplinary tactics (such as a *time-out,* removing them from reinforcing surroundings) fail, and when the swat is combined with a generous dose of reasoning and reinforcing. Remember: *Punishment tells you what not to do; reinforcement tells you what to do.* This dual approach can be effective. Children

Children see, children do? :: Children who often experience physical punishment tend to display more aggression.

David Strickler/The Image Works

with self-destructive behaviors may be mildly punished (say, with a squirt of water in the face) when they bite themselves, or bang their heads, but also rewarded (with positive attention and food) when they behave well. In high school classrooms, teachers can give feedback on papers by saying "No, but try this . . ." and "Yes, that's it!" Such responses reduce unwanted behavior while reinforcing more desirable alternatives.

Parents of delinquent youths may not know how to reinforce desirable behavior without screaming or hitting (Patterson & others, 1982). Training programs can help them translate dire threats into positive incentives—turning "You clean up your room this minute or no dinner!" to "You're welcome at the dinner table after you get your room cleaned up." Stop and think about it. Aren't many threats of punishment just as forceful, and perhaps more effective, when rephrased positively? Thus, "If you don't get your homework done, there'll be no car!" would better be phrased as . . .

What punishment often teaches, said Skinner, is how to avoid it. Most psychologists now favor an emphasis on reinforcement: *Notice people doing something right and affirm them for it.*

Extending Skinner's Understanding

9: What areas did Skinner overlook, and why is his work still important?

Skinner granted the existence of private thought processes and the biological underpinnings of behavior. Nevertheless, many psychologists criticized him for discounting the importance of these influences.

Cognition and Operant Conditioning

A mere eight days before dying of leukemia in 1990, Skinner stood before the American Psychological Association convention. In this final address, he again rejected the growing belief that cognitive processes (thoughts, perceptions, expectations) have a necessary place in the science of psychology and even in our understanding of conditioning. (Skinner regarded thoughts and emotions as behaviors that follow the same laws as other behaviors.)

Nevertheless, the mounting evidence of cognitive processes cannot be ignored. For example, rats exploring a maze, given no obvious rewards, seem to develop a **cognitive map,** a mental representation of the maze. When an experimenter then places food in the maze's goal box, the rats run the maze as quickly and efficiently as other rats that were previously reinforced with food for this result. Like people sightseeing in a new town, the exploring rat seemingly experienced **latent learning** during earlier tours. That learning became apparent only when there was some reason to demonstrate it.

The cognitive perspective has also shown us the limits of rewards: Promising people a reward for a task they already enjoy can backfire. Excessive rewards can destroy **intrinsic motivation**—the desire to do something well, for its own sake. In experiments, children promised a payoff for playing with an interesting puzzle or toy later play with the toy *less* than other children do (Deci & others, 1999; Tang & Hall, 1995). It is as if they think, "If I have to be bribed into doing this, it must not be worth doing for its own sake."

To sense the difference between intrinsic motivation and **extrinsic motivation** (behaving to gain external rewards or avoid threatened punishment), think about your experience in this course. Are you feeling pressured to finish this reading before a deadline? Worried about your grade? Eager for the credits that will count toward graduation? If yes, then you are extrinsically motivated (as, to some extent, almost all students must be). Are you also finding the material interesting? Does learning it make you feel more competent? If there were no grade at stake, might you

Tiger Woods' intrinsic motivation :: "I remember a daily ritual that we had: I would call Pop at work to ask if I could practice with him. He would always pause a second or two, keeping me in suspense, but he'd always say yes. . . . In his own way, he was teaching me initiative. You see, he never pushed me to play" (quoted in *USA Weekend*, 1997).

punishment an event that *decreases* the behavior it follows.

cognitive map a mental image of the layout of one's environment.

latent learning learning that is not apparent until there is an incentive to demonstrate it.

intrinsic motivation a desire to perform a behavior for its own sake.

extrinsic motivation a desire to perform a behavior to gain a reward or avoid a punishment.

Diverse Yet Alike

We learn from our experience—whether in a Chinese shopping mall or the Amazon jungle—and form cognitive maps of our environments.

AP Photo/Rob Carr

Greg Elms/Lonely Planet/Getty Images

Victor Englebert/Photo Researchers, Inc

be curious enough to want to learn the material for its own sake? If yes, intrinsic motivation also fuels your efforts.

Nevertheless, rewards can be effective if used neither to bribe nor to control but to signal a job well done (Boggiano & others, 1985). "Most improved player" awards, for example, can boost feelings of competence and increase enjoyment of a sport. Rightly administered, rewards can raise performance and spark creativity (Eisenberger & Rhoades, 2001; Henderlong & Lepper, 2002).

Biological Predispositions

As with classical conditioning, nature sets limits on each species' capacity for operant conditioning. We most easily learn and retain behaviors that reflect our biological predispositions. Thus, using food as a reinforcer, you can easily condition a hamster to dig or to rear up, because these are among the animal's natural food-searching behaviors. But you won't be so successful if you use food to try to shape other hamster behaviors, such as face washing, that normally have no link to food or hunger (Shettleworth, 1973). Similarly, you could easily teach pigeons to flap their wings to avoid being shocked, and to peck to obtain food, because fleeing with their wings and eating with their beaks are natural pigeon

Natural athletes :: Animals can most easily learn and retain behaviors that draw on their biological predispositions, such as dolphins' inborn ability to leap out of the water.

behaviors. However, pigeons have a hard time learning to peck to avoid a shock, or to flap their wings to obtain food (Foree & LoLordo, 1973). The principle: *Our biology predisposes us to learn associations that are naturally adaptive.*

> "Never try to teach a pig to sing. It wastes your time and annoys the pig."
>
> Mark Twain (1835–1910)

Skinner's Legacy

B. F. Skinner stirred a hornet's nest with his outspoken beliefs. He repeatedly insisted that external influences (not internal thoughts and feelings) shape behavior. And he urged people to use operant principles to influence others' behavior at school, work, and home. Knowing that behavior is shaped by its results, he said we should use rewards to evoke more desirable behavior.

Skinner's critics objected, saying that he dehumanized people by neglecting their personal freedom and trying to control their actions. Skinner's reply: External consequences already haphazardly control people's behavior. Why not steer those consequences toward human betterment? Wouldn't reinforcers be more humane than the punishments used in homes, schools, and prisons? And if it is humbling to think that our history has shaped us, doesn't this very idea also give us hope that we can shape our future?

Applications of Operant Conditioning

In later chapters we will see how psychologists apply operant conditioning principles to help people moderate high blood pressure or gain social skills. Reinforcement technologies are also at work in schools, workplaces, and homes (Flora, 2004).

At School A generation ago, Skinner and others worked toward a day when machines and textbooks would shape learning in small steps, immediately reinforcing correct responses. Such machines and texts, they said, would

B. F. Skinner :: "I am sometimes asked, 'Do you think of yourself as you think of the organisms you study?' The answer is yes. So far as I know, my behavior at any given moment has been nothing more than the product of my genetic endowment, my personal history, and the current setting" (1983).

revolutionize education and free teachers to focus on each student's special needs.

Stand in Skinner's shoes for a moment and imagine two math teachers, each with a class of students ranging from whiz kids to slow learners. Teacher A gives the whole class the same lesson, knowing that the bright kids will breeze through the math concepts and slower ones will be frustrated and fail. With so many different children, how could one teacher guide them individually?

Teacher B, faced with a similar class, paces the material according to each student's rate of learning and provides prompt feedback, with positive reinforcement, to both the slow and the fast learners. Thinking as Skinner did, how might you achieve the individualized instruction of Teacher B?

Computers were Skinner's final hope. "Good instruction demands two things," he said. "Students must be told immediately whether what they do is right or wrong and, when right, they must be directed to the step to be taken next." Thus, the computer could be Teacher B—

Computer-assisted learning :: Computers have helped realize Skinner's goal of individually paced instruction with immediate feedback.

pacing math drills to the student's rate of learning, quizzing the student to find gaps in understanding, giving immediate feedback, and keeping flawless records.

To the end of his life, Skinner (1986, 1988, 1989) believed his ideal was achievable. Although the predicted education revolution has not occurred, today's interactive student software, Web-based learning, and online testing bring us closer than ever before to achieving this ideal.

At Work Skinner's ideas are also showing up in the workplace. Knowing that reinforcers influence productivity, many organizations have invited employees to share the risks and rewards of company ownership. Others focus on reinforcing a job well done. Rewards are most likely to increase productivity if the desired performance has been well-defined and is achievable. The message for managers? *Reward specific, achievable behaviors, not vaguely defined "merit."*

OH! THAT WAS A WONDERFUL REPORT, BOB. A WONDERFUL, WONDERFUL REPORT.

THE VICE-PRESIDENT IN CHARGE OF SINCERITY

Operant conditioning also reminds us that reinforcement should be *immediate*. IBM legend Thomas Watson understood. When he observed an achievement, he wrote the employee a check on the spot (Peters & Waterman, 1982). But rewards need not be material, or lavish. An effective manager may simply walk the floor and sincerely affirm people for good work, or write notes of appreciation for a completed project. As Skinner said, "How much richer would the whole world be if the reinforcers in daily life were more effectively contingent on productive work?"

At Home As we have seen, parents can learn from operant conditioning practices. Parent-training researchers (Wierson & Forehand, 1994) remind us that by saying "Get ready for bed" but caving in to protests or defiance, parents reinforce such whining and arguing. Exasperated, they may then yell or gesture menacingly. When the child, now frightened, obeys, that in turn reinforces the parents' angry behavior. Over time, a destructive parent-child relationship develops.

To disrupt this cycle, parents should remember the basic rule of shaping: *Notice people doing something right and affirm them for it.* Give children attention and other reinforcers when they are behaving *well* (Wierson & Forehand, 1994). Target a specific behavior, reward it, and watch it increase. When children misbehave or are defiant, do not yell at or hit them. Simply explain the misbehavior and give them a time-out.

Finally, we can use operant conditioning to build our own strengths. To reinforce your own desired behaviors and extinguish the undesired ones, psychologists suggest taking these steps:

1. *State your goal*—to stop smoking, eat less, or study or exercise more—in measurable terms, and announce it. You might, for example, aim to boost your study time by an hour a day and share that goal with some close friends.

2. *Monitor* how often you engage in your desired behavior. You might log your current study time, noting under what conditions you do and don't

"I wrote another five hundred words. Can I have another cookie?"

study. (When I began writing textbooks, I logged how I spent my time each day and was amazed to discover how much time I was wasting.)

3. *Reinforce* the desired behavior. To increase your study time, give yourself a reward (a snack or some activity you enjoy) only after you finish your extra hour of study. Agree with your friends that you will join them for weekend activities only if you have met your realistic weekly studying goal.

4. *Reduce the rewards* gradually. As your new behaviors become habits, give yourself a mental pat on the back instead of a cookie.

Contrasting Classical and Operant Conditioning

Both classical and operant conditioning are forms of *associative learning* (TABLE 6.2 on the next page). In both, we *acquire* behaviors that may later become *extinct* and then *spontaneously reappear*. We often *generalize* our responses but learn to *discriminate* among different stimuli. But these two forms of learning differ in important ways: Through classical conditioning, we associate different events that we don't control, and we respond automatically (*respondent behaviors*). Through operant conditioning, we link our own behaviors that act on our environment to produce rewarding or punishing events (*operant behaviors*) with their consequences. Our *thought processes* and our *biology* influence both classical and operant conditioning.

Table 6.2 **Comparison of Classical and Operant Conditioning**

	Classical Conditioning	Operant Conditioning
Basic idea	Learning associations between events we don't control.	Learning associations between our own behavior and its consequences.
Response	Involuntary, automatic.	Voluntary, operates on environment.
Acquisition	Associating events; CS announces US.	Associating response with a consequence (reinforcer or punisher).
Extinction	CR decreases when CS is repeatedly presented alone.	Responding decreases when reinforcement stops.
Spontaneous recovery	The reappearance, after a rest period, of an extinguished CR.	The reappearance, after a rest period, of an extinguished response.
Generalization	Responding to stimuli similar to the CS.	Responses to similar stimuli are also reinforced.
Discrimination	Learning to distinguish between a CS and other stimuli that do not signal a US.	Learning that some responses, but not others, will be reinforced.
Cognitive processes	Expecting the CS to signal the arrival of the US.	Expecting a response will be reinforced or punished; also, latent learning, without reinforcement.
Biological predispositions	Biological tendencies to associate some stimuli more easily than others.	Biological tendency to learn behaviors similar to the species' natural behaviors.

PRACTICE TEST

7. Salivating in response to a tone paired with food is a (an) _____; pressing a bar to obtain food is a (an) _____.
   a. primary reinforcer; conditioned reinforcer
   b. conditioned reinforcer; primary reinforcer
   c. operant behavior; respondent behavior
   d. respondent behavior; operant behavior

8. The pioneer researcher in operant conditioning was
   a. Ivan Pavlov.
   b. John Garcia.
   c. B. F. Skinner.
   d. John B. Watson.

9. One way to change behavior is to reward natural behaviors in small steps, as they get closer and closer to the desired behavior. This process is called
   a. shaping.
   b. punishment.
   c. taste aversion.
   d. classical conditioning.

10. Your dog is barking so loudly that it's making your ears ring. You clap your hands, the dog stops barking, your ears stop ringing, and you think to yourself, "I'll have to do that when he barks again!" The end of the dog's barking was for you a
    a positive reinforcer.
    b. negative reinforcer.
    c. secondary reinforcer.
    d. primary reinforcer.

11. Continuous reinforcement is reinforcing the desired response every time it occurs. _____ reinforcement is reinforcing a desired response only some of the times it occurs.
    a. Negative
    b. Partial
    c. Delayed
    d. Aversive

12. An old saying states that "a burnt child dreads the fire." In operant conditioning, the burning would be an example of a
    a. conditioned reinforcer.
    b. negative reinforcer.
    c. punisher.
    d. positive reinforcer.

13. We now know that cognitive processes (thoughts, perceptions, and expectations) play an important role in learning. Evidence for the effect of these processes comes from studies in which rats
    a. spontaneously recover previously learned behavior.
    b. develop cognitive maps.
    c. exhibit respondent behavior.
    d. generalize responses.

14. Rats were carried through a maze without any opportunity to walk around or explore, and they were given no reward when they left the maze. In later trials in which food was given at the end of the maze, these rats immediately did as well as others that had received rewards for running the maze. The rats that had learned without reinforcement demonstrate
    a. modeling.
    b. biological predisposition.
    c. shaping.
    d. latent learning.

Answers: 7. d, 8. c, 9. a, 10. b, 11. b, 12. c, 13. b, 14. d.

Learning by Observation

10: What is observational learning, and how does it differ from associative learning?

From drooling dogs, running rats, and pecking pigeons we have learned much about the basic processes of learning. But conditioning principles don't tell us the whole story. Higher animals, especially humans, can learn without direct experience, through **observational learning,** by watching and imitating others. A child who sees his sister burn her fingers on a hot stove learns not to touch it. We learn all kinds of specific behaviors by observing and imitating models, a process called **modeling.**

The brain's **mirror neurons** may be the key to observational learning. When a monkey performs a task such as grasping, holding, or tearing, these neurons fire (become active) (Rizzolatti & others, 2002). But they also fire *when the monkey observes another monkey performing the same task.* When one monkey sees, these neurons mirror what another monkey does.

It's not just monkey business. In humans, mirror neurons help give rise to children's empathy and to their ability to pick up clues to another's mental state. As adults, we often feel what another feels, and we find it harder to frown when viewing a smile than when viewing a frown (Dimberg & others, 2000, 2002). Seeing a loved one's pain, it's not just our faces that mirror their emotion, but also our brains. As FIGURE 6.8 shows, the pain imagined by a caring partner triggers some of the same brain activity experienced by the one actually having the pain (Singer & others, 2004).

The imitation of models shapes even very young children's behavior. Shortly after birth, a baby may imitate an adult who sticks out his tongue. By 9 months, infants imitate novel play behaviors. And by age 14 months, children imitate acts modeled on television (Meltzoff, 1988; Meltzoff & Moore, 1989, 1997). Children see, children do.

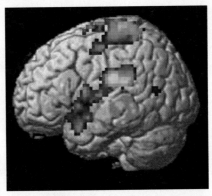

Pain

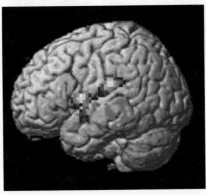

Empathy

Figure 6.8> **Experienced and imagined pain in the brain** Brain activity related to actual pain (top) is mirrored in the brain of an observing loved one (bottom). Empathy in the brain shows up in areas that process emotions, but not in the areas that register physical pain.

Bandura's Experiments

Picture this scene from an experiment by Albert Bandura, the pioneering researcher of observational learning (Bandura & others, 1961). A preschool child works on a drawing. An adult in another part of the room is building with Tinkertoys. As the child watches, the adult gets up and for nearly 10 minutes pounds, kicks, and throws around the room a large, inflated Bobo doll, yelling, "Sock him in the nose. . . . Hit him down. . . . Kick him."

Courtesy of Albert Bandura, Stanford University

Albert Bandura :: "The Bobo doll follows me wherever I go. The photographs are published in every introductory psychology text and virtually every undergraduate takes introductory psychology. I recently checked into a Washington hotel. The clerk at the desk asked, 'Aren't you the psychologist who did the Bobo doll experiment?' I answered, 'I am afraid that will be my legacy.' He replied, 'That deserves an upgrade. I will put you in a suite in the quiet part of the hotel'" (2005).

"Children need models more than they need critics."

Joseph Joubert, *Pensées,* 1842

The child is then taken to another room filled with appealing toys. Soon the experimenter returns and tells the child she has decided to save these good toys "for the other children." She takes the now-frustrated child to a third room containing a few toys, including a Bobo doll. Left alone, what does the child do?

Compared with other children in the study, those who viewed the model's actions were much more likely to lash

observational learning learning by observing others.

modeling the process of observing and imitating a specific behavior.

mirror neurons neurons that fire when we perform certain actions or observe others doing so.

Figure 6.9> The famous Bobo doll experiment Notice how the children's actions directly imitate the adult's.

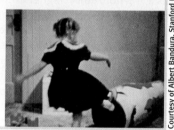

Courtesy of Albert Bandura, Stanford University

out at the doll. Apparently, observing the aggressive outburst lowered their inhibitions. But something more was also at work, for the children imitated the very acts they had observed and used the very words they had heard (**FIGURE 6.9**).

Applications of Observational Learning

The big news from Bandura's studies is that we look and we learn. Models—in our family or neighborhood, or on TV— may have effects—good or bad.

Prosocial Effects

The good news is that **prosocial behavior** (positive, helpful) models can have prosocial effects. To encourage children to read, read to them and surround them with books and people who read. To increase the odds that your children will practice your religion, worship and attend religious activities with them. People who model nonviolent, helpful behavior can prompt similar behavior in others. India's Mahatma Gandhi and America's Martin Luther King Jr., both drew on the power of modeling, making nonviolent action a powerful force for social change in both countries. Parents are also powerful models. European Christians who risked their lives to rescue Jews from the Nazis usually had a close relationship with at least one parent who modeled a strong moral or humanitarian concern. This was also true for U.S. civil rights activists in the 1960s (London, 1970; Oliner & Oliner, 1988).

Antisocial Effects

The bad news is that observational learning may have *antisocial effects*. This helps us understand how abusive parents might have aggressive children, and why many men who beat their wives had wife-battering fathers (Stith & others, 2000). Critics note that being aggressive could be passed along by parents' genes.

Models of giving :: Children, such as this boy helping out in a soup kitchen, learn positive behaviors and attitudes from the prosocial models in their lives.

Michael Newman/Photo Edit Inc.

But in monkeys, we know it can also be environmental. In study after study, young monkeys reared apart from their mothers and subjected to high levels of aggression grew up to be aggressive themselves (Chamove, 1980). The lessons we learn as children are not easily unlearned as adults, and they are sometimes visited on future generations.

TV programs teach powerful lessons to young observers. While watching, children may "learn" that bullying is an effective way to control others, that free and easy sex brings pleasure without later misery or disease, or that men should be tough and women gentle. And they have ample time to learn such lessons. During their first 18 years, most children in developed countries spend more time watching TV than they spend in school. In the United States, where 9 in 10 teens watch TV daily, someone who lives to 75 will have spent 9 years staring at the tube (Gallup, 2002; Kubey & Csikszentmihalyi, 2002).

TV viewers are learning about life from a rather peculiar storyteller, one reflecting the culture's mythology but not its reality. Before finishing elementary school, they will have observed some 8,000 TV murders and 100,000 other acts of violence (Huston & others, 1992). During one closely studied year, nearly 6 in 10 U.S. network and cable programs featured violence, 74 percent of those acts went unpunished, and the victims usually showed no pain. Nearly half the violence was portrayed as "justified," and nearly half the attackers were attractive (Donnerstein, 1998). To see how these conditions fit the recipe for the *violence-viewing effect*, read on.

Was the judge who in 1993 tried two British 10-year-olds for their murder of a 2-year-old right to suspect that the pair had been influenced by "violent video films"? Were the American media right to think that the teen assassins who killed 13 of their Columbine High School classmates had been influenced by repeated exposure to *Natural Born Killers* and splatter games such as *Doom*? To understand whether violence viewing leads to violent behavior, researchers have done both correlational and experimental studies (Anderson & others, 2003).

Correlational studies do support this link.

- In the United States and Canada, homicide rates doubled between 1957 and 1974, just when TV was introduced and spreading. Moreover, census regions with later dates for TV service also had homicide rates that jumped later.

- Elementary-school children with heavy exposure to media violence (via TV, videos, and video games) also tend to get into more fights (FIGURE 6.10).

> TV's greatest effect may stem from what it displaces. Children and adults who spend four hours a day watching TV spend four fewer hours in active pursuits—talking, studying, playing, reading, or socializing with friends. What would you have done with your extra time if you had never watched TV, and how might you therefore be different?

prosocial behavior positive, constructive, helpful behavior. The opposite of antisocial behavior.

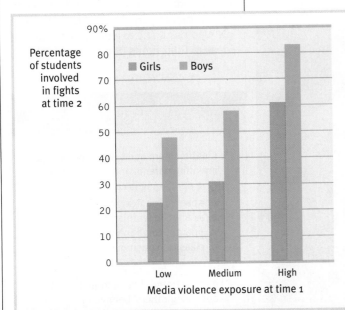

Figure 6.10> Media violence experience predicts future aggressive behavior
After controlling for existing differences in hostility and aggression, researchers studying more than 400 third- to fifth-graders reported increased aggression in those heavily exposed to violent TV, videos, and video games (Gentile & others, 2004).

But as we know from Chapter 1, correlation does not prove causation. So these studies do not *prove* that viewing violence *causes* aggression (Freedman, 1988; McGuire, 1986). Maybe aggressive children prefer violent programs. Maybe abused or neglected children are both more aggressive and more often left in front of the TV.

Critical thinking leads to smart thinking. To pin down causation, psychologists use experiments. In this case, researchers randomly assigned some viewers to observe violence and others to watch entertaining nonviolence. Does viewing cruelty prepare people, when irritated, to react more cruelly? To some extent, it does. "Most of the research community [agrees] that violence on television does lead to aggressive behavior by children and teenagers who watch the programs," reported the National Institute of Mental Health (1982). This is especially so when an attractive person commits seemingly justified, realistic violence that goes unpunished and causes no visible pain or harm (Donnerstein, 1998).

This *violence-viewing effect* seems to stem from at least two factors. One is *imitation*

(Geen & Thomas, 1986). Violent play increased sevenfold immediately after children viewed the "Power Rangers" (Boyatzis & others, 1995). As happened in the Bobo experiment, children often precisely imitated the model's violent acts, in this case, flying karate kicks.

Prolonged exposure to violence also *desensitizes* viewers. They become more indifferent to it when later viewing a brawl, whether on TV or in real life (Rule & Ferguson, 1986). Adult males who spent three evenings watching sexually violent movies became progressively less bothered by the rapes and slashings. Compared with those in a control group, the film watchers later expressed less sympathy for domestic violence victims, and they rated the victims' injuries as less severe (Mullin & Linz, 1995).

Indeed, an evil psychologist could hardly imagine a better way to make people indifferent to brutality than to expose them to a graded series of scenes, from fights to killings to the mutilations in slasher movies (Donnerstein & others, 1987). Watching cruelty fosters indifference.

"Don't you understand? This is life, this is what is happening. We can't switch to another channel."

* * *

Our knowledge of learning principles comes from the work of thousands of investigators. This chapter has focused on the ideas of a few pioneers—Ivan Pavlov, John Watson, B. F. Skinner, and Albert Bandura—who defined the issues and impressed on us the importance of learning. They illustrate the impact that can result from single-minded devotion to a few well-defined problems and concepts. Intellectual history is often made by people who risk going to extremes in pushing ideas to their limits (Simonton, 2000).

Violence viewing leads to violent play :: Research has shown that viewing media violence does lead to increased expression of aggression in the viewers, as with these boys imitating pro wrestlers.

Bob Daemmrich/The Image Works

Glassman/The Image Works

PRACTICE TEST

15. Children learn many social behaviors by imitating parents and other models. This type of learning is called

- a. observational learning.
- b. reinforced learning.
- c. operant conditioning.
- d. classical conditioning.

16. _____ famous Bobo doll experiments demonstrated that children learn by observing others' behaviors.

- a. Skinner's
- b. Watson's
- c. Bandura's
- d. Pavlov's

17. Correlational studies show a link between viewing violence on TV and behaving aggressively, but they don't *prove* that violence *causes* aggression. However, most experts agree that repeated viewing of TV violence

a. makes all viewers significantly more aggressive.
b. has little effect on viewers.
c. dulls the viewers' sensitivity to violence.
d. makes viewers angry and frustrated.

Answers: 15. a, 16. c, 17. c.

TERMS AND CONCEPTS TO REMEMBER

learning, p. 157
associative learning, p. 158
stimulus, p. 158
classical conditioning, p. 159
unconditioned response (UR), p. 159
unconditioned stimulus (US), p. 159
conditioned response (CR), p. 160
conditioned stimulus (CS), p. 160
acquisition, p. 160
extinction, p. 161
spontaneous recovery, p. 161
generalization, p. 162
discrimination, p. 162

behaviorism, p. 162
respondent behavior, p. 165
operant conditioning, p. 165
operant behavior, p. 165
operant chamber, p. 165
reinforcement, p. 165
shaping, p. 165
positive reinforcement, p. 166
negative reinforcement, p. 166
primary reinforcer, p. 167
conditioned reinforcer, p. 167
reinforcement schedule, p. 167
continuous reinforcement, p. 167

partial (intermittent) reinforcement, p. 167
punishment, p. 168
cognitive map, p. 169
latent learning, p. 169
intrinsic motivation, p. 169
extrinsic motivation, p. 169
observational learning, p. 173
modeling, p. 173
mirror neurons, p. 173
prosocial behavior, p. 174

REVIEW: LEARNING

HOW DO WE LEARN?

1 **What is learning?**

- Relatively permanent change in behavior due to experience.
- Helps all animals, especially humans, adapt to their environments.

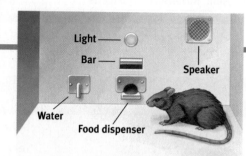

Light ——— ○
Bar ———
Speaker
Water
Food dispenser

CLASSICAL CONDITIONING
(LEARNING TO ASSOCIATE TWO STIMULI)

2 **How does classical conditioning demonstrate associative learning?**

- *UR (unconditioned response)* occurs naturally (such as salivation), in response to some stimulus.
- *US (unconditioned stimulus)* naturally and automatically (without learning) triggers the unlearned response (as food in the mouth triggers salivation).
- *CS (conditioned stimulus)* is an originally neutral stimulus (such as a tone) that, through learning, comes to be associated with some unlearned response (salivating).
- *CR (conditioned response)* is the learned response (salivating) to the originally neutral but now conditioned stimulus.
- Classical conditioning is biologically adaptive—works best when a CS is presented just before a US, preparing the organism for the upcoming event.

3 **What parts do acquisition, extinction, spontaneous recovery, generalization, and discrimination play in classical conditioning?**

- First stage: association of CS with US (*acquisition*).
- *Extinction* occurs if responses are not reinforced.
- Responses may reappear after pause (*spontaneous recovery*).
- Responses may be triggered by stimuli similar to CS (*generalization*) but not by dissimilar stimuli (*discrimination*).

4 **What areas did Pavlov tend to overlook, and why is his work still important?**

- Pavlov underestimated the power of expectations and biological predispositions.
- Yet all animals learn to adapt to their environment via classical conditioning.
- Pavlov also taught us how to study a process objectively.

OPERANT CONDITIONING
(LEARNING TO ASSOCIATE A RESPONSE AND ITS CONSEQUENCES)

5 **What is operant conditioning, and how does it differ from classical conditioning?**

- *Operant conditioning*: organism learns associations between its own behavior and resulting events. Involves *operant behavior* (behavior that operates on the environment, producing consequences).
- *Classical conditioning*: organism forms associations between stimuli it does not control. Involves *respondent behavior* (automatic response to some stimulus).

Behaviorism

- Pavlov's work laid the foundation.
- Psychology should be an objective science that studies behavior without reference to mental processes.

B. F. Skinner and others

■ *Shaped* the behavior of rats and pigeons placed in *operant chambers* (Skinner boxes) by rewarding closer and closer approximations of desired behavior.

LEARNING BY OBSERVATION
(LEARNING BY WATCHING OTHERS' EXPERIENCES AND EXAMPLES)

10 **What is observational learning, and how does it differ from associative learning?**

■ Watching and imitating others' behavior, which does not require the direct experience of associative learning.

■ *Mirror neurons* in the frontal lobes may be involved.

WE ARE MORE LIKELY TO IMITATE

■ actions that go unpunished.

■ attractive models.

CHILDREN IMITATE

■ what a model both does *and* says, whether that behavior is *prosocial* or antisocial.

Albert Bandura's pioneering research

■ In *observational learning* showed that preschoolers learn (by watching) to imitate adults' interactions with a Bobo doll.

6 **What are the basic types of reinforcers?**

ALL REINFORCERS STRENGTHEN THE BEHAVIOR THEY FOLLOW:

■ *Positive reinforcers*: presented after a desired response.

■ *Negative reinforcers*: cause an aversive stimulus to be withdrawn.

■ *Primary reinforcers*: unlearned.

■ *Conditioned reinforcers*: learned through association with primary reinforcers.

■ Reinforcers may be immediate or delayed.

7 **How do continuous and partial reinforcement schedules affect behavior?**

PARTIAL REINFORCEMENT:

■ Slower acquisition

■ Greater resistance to extinction

CONTINUOUS REINFORCEMENT:

■ Faster acquisition

■ Less resistance to extinction

9 **What areas did Skinner overlook, and why is his work still important?**

SKINNER UNDERESTIMATED THE EFFECTS OF COGNITIVE PROCESSES AND BIOLOGICAL CONSTRAINTS.

■ *Cognitive mapping* and *latent learning* point to learning that occurs despite lack of immediate consequences.

■ Despite training, animals will revert to biologically predisposed patterns.

■ Excess rewards can undermine *intrinsic motivation* for an activity.

EDUCATORS, BUSINESS MANAGERS, AND OTHER INDIVIDUALS STILL APPLY OPERANT CONDITIONING.

■ Teachers can shape students' behaviors.

■ Interactive media can provide immediate feedback.

■ Managers can boost productivity and morale by rewarding well-defined and achievable behaviors.

■ Parents can reward desirable behaviors.

■ We can use these principles to reinforce our own desired behaviors and extinguish undesirable ones.

8 **How does punishment affect behavior?**

PUNISHMENT:

■ Administering undesirable consequence (spanking) or withdrawing something desirable (favorite toy)

■ Aims to decrease frequency of a behavior (child's disobedience)

UNDESIRABLE SIDE EFFECTS:

■ Suppressing rather than changing behavior

■ Teaching aggression

■ Creating fear

■ Encouraging discrimination (undesirable behavior appears when the punisher is not present)

■ Fostering depression and feelings of hopelessness

IMAGINE LIFE WITHOUT BEING ABLE TO form new conscious memories. In the 50+ years since he had brain surgery to stop severe seizures, this has been life for H. M., as psychologists know him. H. M. is intelligent and still does daily crossword puzzles. Yet, reports neuroscientist Suzanne Corkin (2005), "I've known H. M. since 1962, and he still doesn't know who I am."

My own father suffered a similar problem after a small stroke at age 92. His upbeat personality was intact. He enjoyed poring over family photo albums and telling stories about his pre-stroke life. But he could not tell me what day of the week it was, or what he'd had for dinner. Told repeatedly of his brother-in-law's death, he was surprised and saddened each time he heard the news.

At the other extreme are people who would be gold medal winners in a memory Olympics. Russian journalist Shereshevskii, or S, had merely to listen while other reporters scribbled notes (Luria, 1968). You and I could parrot back a string of 7 or so numbers. S could repeat up to 70, if they were read about 3 seconds apart in an otherwise silent room. Moreover, he could recall these numbers (and words, too) backward as easily as forward. His accuracy was perfect, even when recalling a list 15 years later. "Yes, yes," he might recall. "This was a series you gave me once when we were in your apartment. . . . You were sitting at the table and I in the rocking chair. . . . You were wearing a gray suit. . . ."

Amazing? Yes, but consider your own impressive memory. You remember countless voices, sounds, and songs; tastes, smells, and textures; faces, places, and happenings. Imagine viewing 2500 slides of faces and places for 10 seconds each. Later, you see 280 of these slides, paired with others you've never seen before. Actual participants in this experiment recognized 90 percent of the slides they had viewed in the first round (Haber, 1970).

WELL, FOR CRYING OUT LOUD! AL TOWBRIDGE! WHAT IS IT, NINE YEARS, SEVEN MONTHS, AND TWELVE DAYS SINCE I LAST RAN INTO YOU? TEN-THIRTY-TWO A.M., A SATURDAY, FELCHER'S HARDWARE STORE. YOU WERE BUYING SEALER FOR YOUR BLACKTOP DRIVEWAY. TELL ME, AL, HOW DID THAT SEALER WORK? DID IT HOLD UP?

MR. TOTAL RECALL

Memory is learning we retain over time. How does our brain pluck information out of the world around us and tuck that information away for later use? How can we remember things we have not thought about for years, yet forget the name of someone we just met? How can two people's memories of an event be so different? Why will you be likely later in this chapter to misrecall this sentence: *"The angry rioter threw the rock at the window"*? In this chapter, we'll consider these fascinating questions and more—including how we can improve our own memories.

memory the persistence of learning over time through the storage and retrieval of information.

Studying Memory: An Information-Processing Model

1: How do psychologists describe our memory system?

Architects build miniature models of houses to help clients imagine living in their future homes. Similarly, psychologists build models of memory to help us think about how our brain forms and retrieves memories. One such memory model is based on information processing.

Building a memory is somewhat like the way I processed information in creating this book. First, I viewed countless items of information, including some 100,000 journal article titles. Most of it I ignored, but I *selected* some things for *temporary storage* in my briefcase, to process later. Most of those items I eventually threw out. The rest—about 3,000 articles and news items—I organized and filed for long-term storage. Later, I *retrieved* that information and drew from it as I spun this story of today's psychology. We build memories in a similar way. To remember any event, we must

- *get information into our brain,* a process called **encoding.**
- *retain* that information, a process called **storage.**
- later *get the information back out,* a process called **retrieval.**

Richard Atkinson and Richard Shiffrin (1968) proposed a three-stage memory model to show how information might move from encoding to storage to retrieval. Other psychologists have updated this model to include more recent findings **(FIGURE 7.1).**

1. We first record to-be-remembered information as a fleeting **sensory memory.**

2. From there, we process information into **short-term memory,** where we encode it through *rehearsal.* But short-term memory does more than temporarily store information. It is a **working memory** that uses and actively maintains information.

3. Finally, information moves into **long-term memory** for later retrieval.

But note that some information takes a short-cut on its way to long-term storage. These memories are formed through *unconscious processing,* without our awareness. As we have seen so many times in this text, our mind operates on two tracks, processing some information out in the open, with our full attention. But another show is quietly going on behind the scenes.

PRACTICE TEST

1. The psychological terms for taking in information, retaining it, and later getting it back out are
   a. retrieval, encoding, and storage.
   b. encoding, storage, and retrieval.

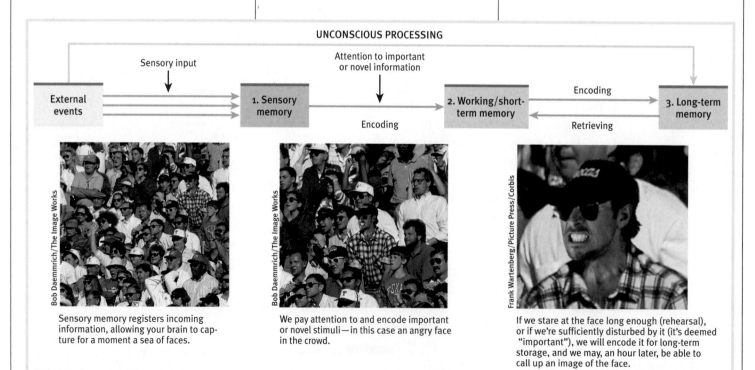

UNCONSCIOUS PROCESSING

Sensory input

Attention to important or novel information

External events → 1. Sensory memory

Encoding

2. Working/short-term memory

Encoding → 3. Long-term memory

Retrieving

Bob Daemmrich/The Image Works — Sensory memory registers incoming information, allowing your brain to capture for a moment a sea of faces.

Bob Daemmrich/The Image Works — We pay attention to and encode important or novel stimuli—in this case an angry face in the crowd.

Frank Wartenberg/Picture Press/Corbis — If we stare at the face long enough (rehearsal), or if we're sufficiently disturbed by it (it's deemed "important"), we will encode it for long-term storage, and we may, an hour later, be able to call up an image of the face.

Figure 7.1> A modified three-stage processing model of memory

c. storage, encoding, and retrieval.
d. retrieval, storage, and encoding.

2. In what order do our brains process an external event into a memory that can last a lifetime?
   a. Long-term memory, sensory memory, short-term memory
   b. Short-term memory, sensory memory, long-term memory
   c. Short-term memory, long-term memory, sensory memory
   d. Sensory memory, short-term memory, long-term memory

Answers: 1. b, 2. d.

Encoding: Getting Information In

How We Encode: The Two-Track Mind

2: How do automatic and effortful processing help us encode sights, sounds, and other sensations?

As you walked to class today, your mind processed your journey without your awareness. But your mind would have switched into another gear if a friend had called to give you her new cellphone number or a last-minute change in a meeting place. With the help of our two-track minds, we **automatically process** vast amounts of everyday information. And we remember new and important information through **effortful processing** (FIGURE 7.2).

What Do We Process Automatically?

With little or no conscious effort, you automatically process information about

- *space.* While studying, you often encode the place on a page where certain material appears. Later, when you try to recall the difference between automatic and effortful processing, you may picture the text on this page.

- *time.* While going about your day, your mind is working behind the scenes, jotting down the sequence of the day's events. Later, when you realize you've left your coat somewhere, you can call up that sequence and retrace your steps.

- *frequency.* Your behind-the-scenes mind also takes notes about how many times things have happened, thus enabling you to realize, "This is the third time I've run into her today!"

Automatic processing happens so effortlessly that it is difficult to shut off. When you see words in your native language, perhaps on the side of a delivery truck, you can't help but register their meaning. Learning to read wasn't automatic. You may recall working hard to pick out letters and connect them to certain sounds. But with experience and practice, your reading became automatic. Imagine now learning to read reversed sentences like this:

.citamotua emoceb nac gnissecorp luftroffE

Figure 7.2> Automatic versus effortful processing

Encoding

Automatic

(Where you ate dinner yesterday)

Effortful

(This chapter's concepts)

© Bananastock/Alamy

Spencer Grant/Photo Edit

At first, reading reversed sentences also requires attention and effort. After enough practice, you can perform this task, and many others, from driving to rollerblading, much more automatically.

What Requires Effortful Processing?

The close attention and effort we put into the effortful processing of people's names (or this chapter's information) often produces durable and accessible memories. We can boost our memory of new information through **rehearsal** (conscious repetition). A pioneering researcher, Hermann Ebbinghaus (1850–1909), showed this long ago by studying his own learning and forgetting of new verbal material.

encoding the processing of information into the memory system—for example, by extracting meaning.

storage the retention of encoded information over time.

retrieval the process of getting information out of memory storage.

sensory memory the immediate, very brief recording of sensory information in the memory system.

short-term memory activated memory that holds a few items briefly, such as the seven digits of a phone number while dialing, before the information is stored or forgotten.

working memory a newer understanding of short-term memory that involves conscious, active processing of incoming information, and of information retrieved from long-term memory.

long-term memory the relatively permanent and limitless storehouse of the memory system. Includes knowledge, skills, and experiences.

automatic processing unconscious encoding of everyday information, such as space, time, frequency, and well-learned word meanings.

effortful processing encoding that requires attention and conscious effort.

rehearsal the conscious repetition of information, either to maintain it in consciousness or to encode it for storage.

Put yourself in Ebbinghaus' shoes. How could you produce new items to learn without becoming familiar with them before your experiment? Ebbinghaus' answer was to form a list of all possible nonsense syllables by sandwiching a vowel between two consonants. Then, for a particular experiment, he would randomly select a sample of the syllables, practice them, and test himself. To get a feel for his experiments, rapidly read aloud the following list, repeating it eight times (from Baddeley, 1982). Then, without looking, try to recall the items:

JIH, BAZ, FUB, YOX, SUJ, XIR, DAX, LEQ, VUM, PID, KEL, WAV, TUV, ZOF, GEK, HIW.

> "He should test his memory by reciting the verses."
>
> Abdur-Rahman Abdul Khaliq, "Memorizing the Quran"

The day after learning such a list, Ebbinghaus recalled only a few of the syllables. But were they entirely forgotten? No. The more often he practiced the list aloud on day 1, the fewer times he would have to practice it to learn it on day 2 **(FIGURE 7.3)**. Here, then, was a simple beginning principle: *The amount we remember depends on the time we spend learning.* Even after we think we know material, additional rehearsal (*overlearning*) increases learning. For novel verbal information, practice—effortful processing—does indeed make perfect.

We retain information (such as our new classmates' names) even better if we spread rehearsal over time. This **spacing effect** (Bjork, 1999; Dempster, 1988) is the reason teachers have urged you to study regularly throughout the term rather than only cramming the night before an exam. In life, as in your studies, spreading out learning helps you retain information far into the future.

Even with rehearsal, however, we won't remember all items in a list equally well. As we struggle to recall the list, we will probably remember the last and first items better than those in the middle **(FIGURE 7.4)**. This is the **serial position effect** (Reed,

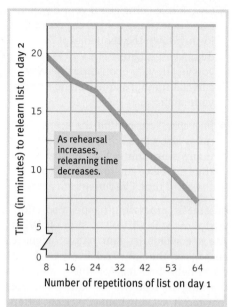

Figure 7.3> Ebbinghaus' retention curve **The more times he practiced a list of nonsense syllables on day 1, the less time he would need to relearn it on day 2. (From Baddeley, 1982.)**

2000). Perhaps we remember the last items better because they are still in working memory, and we briefly have access to them. After a delay—after we shift our attention away from those last items—our recall is best for the first items.

Time spent rehearsing is one factor in how well we remember. But it doesn't explain why we encode some things easily and others only with difficulty—or not at all.

Encoding Effectively

Processing our experiences is like sorting through e-mail. Some items we instantly trash. Others we open, read, and retain, encoding their meaning or image and mentally organizing the information.

Encoding Meaning

While processing verbal information, our active mind makes connections between new information and what we already know or imagine. These connections guide us as we interpret and encode sounds. For example, whether we hear *eye-screem* as "ice cream" or "I scream" depends on both the context (snack shop or horror film) and our experience. This all happens in our working memory, a temporary work site where we organize information and solve problems.

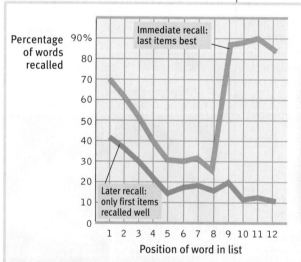

Figure 7.4> The serial position effect **Which names will Hu Jintao (General Secretary of the Central Committee of the Communist Party of China) remember best when he finishes making his way through this long line of dignitaries from Taiwan? (Turn the next page to check your answer.)**

> Here is another sentence I will ask you about later: *The fish attacked the swimmer.*

Can you repeat the sentence about the rioter (from this chapter's opening page)? Was the sentence "The angry rioter threw the rock *through* the window" or "The angry rioter threw the rock *at the window*"? If the first looks more correct, you—like the participants in the original study—may have recalled the meaning you encoded, not the words that were written (Brewer, 1977). In making such mistakes, our minds are like theater directors who, given a raw script, imagine a finished stage production (Bower & Morrow, 1990). Asked later what we heard or read, we recall not the text itself but *the meaning we encoded* while listening or reading. Thus, studying for an exam, you may remember your lecture notes with your encoded meaning rather than the lecture itself.

Given too raw a script, we may have trouble finding any meaning, as students did when asked to remember the following recorded passage (Bransford & Johnson, 1972):

> The procedure is actually quite simple. First you arrange things into different groups. Of course, one pile may be sufficient depending on how much there is to do. . . . After the procedure is completed one arranges the materials into different groups again. Then they can be put into their appropriate places. Eventually they will be used once more and the whole cycle will then have to be repeated. However, that is part of life.

Hearing the paragraph you just read, without a meaningful context, students remembered little of it. But when they were told the paragraph described doing laundry (something meaningful to them), they remembered much more of it—as you probably could now if you read it again.

Such research illustrates a second principle: *You will more easily remember what you read and hear if you translate it into personally meaningful information.* From his experiments on himself, Ebbinghaus estimated that learning meaningful material required one-tenth the effort needed to learn nonsense material. As memory researcher Wayne Wickelgren (1977, p. 346) noted, "The time you spend thinking about material you are reading and relating it to previously stored material is about the most useful thing you can do in learning any new subject matter."

Visual Encoding

If you still recall the rock-throwing rioter sentence, it is probably not only because of the meaning you encoded but also because that sentence lent itself to a visual image. We more easily remember things we can process *visually* as well as meaningfully (Marschark & others, 1987; Paivio, 1986). Our earliest memories—probably of something that happened at age 3 or 4—involve visual **imagery.** As adults, we may struggle to remember formulas, definitions, and dates, yet we can easily remember mental pictures—where we were yesterday, who was with us, where we sat, and what we wore. High-imagery words—those that lend themselves to visual encoding—are more easily remembered than low-imagery words. (When I quiz you later, which three of these words—*typewriter, void, cigarette, known, fire, process*—will you most likely recall?)

PRACTICE TEST

3. Rehearsal—the conscious repetition of information you want to remember—is part of
   a. automatic processing.
   b. effortful processing.
   c. forgetting.
   d. retrieval.

4. When we are tested immediately after viewing a list of words, we tend to recall the first and last items more readily than those in the middle. This tendency is called the _____ effect.

   a. serial position
   b. spacing
   c. rehearsal
   d. effortful processing

5. The process of forming mental images as we encode information in memory is called
   a. picturing.
   b. visual encoding.
   c. rehearsing.
   d. imagining.

Answers: 3. b, 4. a, 5. b.

Storage: Retaining Information

3: What are the limits of our memory, and how are memories stored in the brain?

At the heart of memory is storage. If you later recall something you experienced, you must, somehow, have stored and retrieved it. How much can we store in our memory, and how does our brain change as we store our memories?

Storage Capacities

Working/Short-Term Memory

Sensory memory is truly fleeting—like lightning flashes in the brain. One clever experiment showed people three rows of three letters each for only 1/20th of a second (**FIGURE 7.5** on the next page). After the nine letters disappeared from the screen, people could recall only about half of them.

spacing effect the tendency for distributed study or practice to yield better long-term retention than is achieved through massed study or practice.

serial position effect the tendency to recall best the last and first items in a list.

imagery mental pictures; a powerful aid to effortful processing, especially when combined with encoding meaning.

Answer to question in Figure 7.4: Immediately, Hu Jintao would probably remember best the first and last people he greeted. Later, he probably would remember best the first people in line.

Was it because they had insufficient time to see them? No—George Sperling demonstrated that people actually *can* see and recall all the letters, but only for a moment. Rather than ask them to recall all nine letters at once, he sounded a high, medium, or low tone immediately *after* flashing the nine letters. This cue directed participants to report only the letters of the top, middle, or bottom row, respectively. Now they rarely missed a letter, showing that all nine letters were briefly available for recall.

Unless our working memory rehearses or meaningfully encodes sensory information, it quickly disappears. During your finger's trip from phone book to phone, your memory of a telephone number may evaporate. To find out how quickly a short-term memory will disappear, researchers asked people to remember three-consonant groups, such as *CHJ* (Peterson & Peterson, 1959). To prevent rehearsal, the participants were distracted, for example, by counting backward from

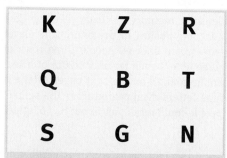

Figure 7.5> Momentary photographic memory When George Sperling (1960) flashed a group of letters similar to this for 1/20th of a second, people could recall only about half of the letters. But when signaled to recall a particular row *immediately* after the letters had disappeared, they could do so with near-perfect accuracy.

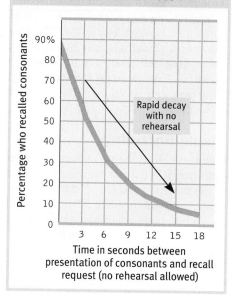

Figure 7.6> Short-term memory decay Unless rehearsed, verbal information may be quickly forgotten. (From Peterson & Peterson, 1959.)

Percentage who recalled consonants (y-axis: 0, 10, 20, 30, 40, 50, 60, 70, 80, 90%)

Rapid decay with no rehearsal

Time in seconds between presentation of consonants and recall request (no rehearsal allowed) (x-axis: 3, 6, 9, 12, 15, 18)

100 by threes. Without active processing, memories of the consonants disappeared. After 3 seconds, people recalled the letters only about half the time; after 12 seconds, they seldom recalled them at all **(FIGURE 7.6)**. Our short-term memories have a very limited life.

Short-term memory capacity is also limited. Typically, we can store about seven bits of information (give or take two) in short-term memory. George Miller (1956) enshrined this recall capacity as the *Magical Number Seven, plus or minus two*. Not surprisingly, when some phone companies began requiring callers to dial a three-digit area code in addition to a seven-digit number, people had trouble retaining the just-looked-up number.

The Magical Number Seven has become psychology's contribution to an intriguing list of magic sevens—the seven wonders of the world, the seven seas, the seven deadly sins, the seven primary colors, the seven musical scale notes, the seven days of the week—seven magical sevens.

Earlier in this chapter, in the discussion of encoding imagery, I gave you six words and told you I would quiz you about them later. How many of these words can you now recall? Of these, how many are high-imagery words? How many are low-imagery?

Long-Term Memory

In Arthur Conan Doyle's *A Study in Scarlet*, Sherlock Holmes offers a popular theory of memory capacity:

> I consider that a man's brain originally is like a little empty attic, and you have to stock it with such furniture as you choose. . . . It is a mistake to think that that little room has elastic walls and can distend to any extent. Depend upon it, there comes a time when for every addition of knowledge you forget something that you knew before.

Contrary to Holmes' belief, our capacity for storing long-term memories has no real limit. The point is vividly shown by those who have performed amazing memory feats.

Clark's Nutcracker :: Among animals, one contender for the gold medal for memory would be a mere birdbrain—the Clark's Nutcracker. During winter and early spring, this bird can locate up to 6000 caches of pine seeds it had buried earlier. (Shettleworth, 1993.)

R. J. Erwin/Photo Researchers

Memories Changing the Brain

I marveled at my aging mother-in-law, a retired pianist and organist. At age 88 her blind eyes could no longer read music. But let her sit at a keyboard and she would flawlessly play any of hundreds of songs, including some she had not thought of for 20 years. Where did her brain store those thousands of note patterns?

Synaptic Changes

Memories begin as impulses whizzing through neural circuits, somehow leaving permanent tracks in our brain. Where do these changes occur? The available clues point to the *synapses*—the sites where nerve cells communicate with one another by means of chemical messengers. We know that experience modifies the brain's neural networks. With increased activity in a particular pathway, connections between neurons form or strengthen (see Chapter 3).

Eric Kandel and James Schwartz (1982) were able to catch a memory leaving tracks in neurons of the California sea slug. This simple animal's nerve cells are unusually large and accessible, and researchers have been able to observe how they change during learning. Using electric shocks, they have classically conditioned sea slugs to withdraw their gills when squirted with water, much as we might jump when lightning strikes nearby. By observing the slugs' neural connections before and after conditioning, Kandel and Schwartz pinpointed changes. As a slug learns, its neurons release more of the neurotransmitter *serotonin* at certain synapses. These synapses then become more sensitive and transmit signals more efficiently.

As synapses become more efficient, so do neural circuits. Sending neurons now

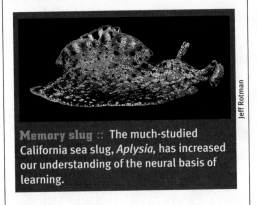

Memory slug :: The much-studied California sea slug, *Aplysia,* has increased our understanding of the neural basis of learning.

Jeff Rotman

release their neurotransmitters more easily. Receiving neurons may grow additional receptor sites **(FIGURE 7.7)**. This process is called **long-term potentiation (LTP),** and it is important because it helps us understand *how* our brain learns and remembers (Lynch, 2002). Blocking LTP interferes with learning (Lynch & Staubli,

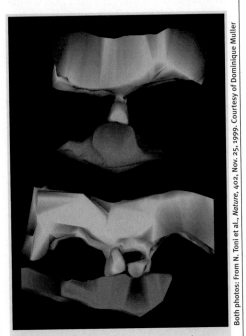

Figure 7.7> Doubled receptor sites Before LTP (top), electron microscope images show just one receptor site (gray) reaching toward a sending neuron. After LTP, the receptor site has doubled, increasing the neuron's sensitivity for detecting the neurotransmitter. (From Toni & others, 1999.)

Both photos: From N. Toni et al., *Nature,* 402, Nov. 25, 1999. Courtesy of Dominique Muller

1991). Mutant mice that lack an enzyme needed for LTP can't learn their way out of a maze (Silva & others, 1992). And rats given a drug that enhances LTP can learn a maze with half the usual number of mistakes (Service, 1994).

After LTP has occurred, an electric current passing through the brain won't disrupt old memories. Before LTP, very recent memories can be wiped out. This often happens when depressed people are given electroconvulsive therapy (Chapter 13). A blow to the head can do the same. Football players and boxers knocked unconscious typically have no memory of events just before the knockout (Yarnell & Lynch, 1970). Their working memory had no time to process the information into long-term memory before the shut-down.

Stress-Related Memories

Arousal can sear certain events into the brain (Birnbaum & others, 2004; Strange & Dolan, 2004). Excitement or stress triggers our glands to produce stress hormones. These hormones make more glucose energy available to fuel brain activity, signaling the brain that something important has happened. At the same time, emotion-processing clusters in the brain boost activity in memory-forming areas (Dolcos & others, 2004; Hamann & others, 2002). The result is "stronger, more reliable memories" (McGaugh, 1994, 2003). After horrific experiences—a wartime ambush, a house fire, a rape—vivid memories of the event may intrude again and again.

Weaker emotion means weaker memories. Given a drug that blocks stress-hormone effects, people later have trouble remembering the details of an upsetting story (Cahill, 1994). Research is under way on a drug that could blunt intrusive memories if taken soon after a traumatic experience.

long-term potentiation (LTP) an increase in a synapse's firing potential. Believed to be a neural basis for learning and memory.

Severe stress sears in memories :: Significantly stressful events, such as the disastrous 2007 California wildfires, may become a permanent part of survivors' memories.

Spencer Platt/Getty Images

Which is more important—your experiences or your memories of them?

Emotion-triggered hormonal changes help explain why we long remember exciting or shocking events. Ask any adult American where he or she first heard the news on 9/11—that fateful day that the

THE FAR SIDE® BY GARY LARSON

© 1993 FarWorks, Inc. All Rights Reserved./Dist. by Creators Syndicate

The Far Side® by Gary Larson © 1993 FarWorks, Inc. All Rights Reserved. The Far Side® and the Larson® signature are registered trademarks of FarWorks, Inc. Used with permission.

More facts of nature: All forest animals, to this very day, remember exactly where they were and what they were doing when they heard that Bambi's mother had been shot.

New York Times called "one of those moments in which history splits and we define the world as 'before and after.'" Five years later, 95 percent of Americans surveyed said they remembered where they were (Pew, 2006). The exceptionally clear memories we have of surprising, significant events lead some psychologists to call them **flashbulb memories.** It's as if the brain commands, "Capture this!"

Our memories of dramatic experiences remain bright and clear for another reason. We tend to rehearse them, thinking about them and describing them to others. But as we will see later in this chapter, rehearsal can feed the construction of false memories. Thus, sometimes, even our flashbulb memories err (Talarico & Rubin, 2003).

Two-Track Storage: Facts and Skills

A memory-to-be enters by way of the senses, then makes its way into the brain's depths. Precisely where it goes depends on the type of information. This is dramatically illustrated by those who, as in the case of my father mentioned earlier, suffer brain damage that leaves them unable to form new memories.

Neurologist Oliver Sacks (1985, pp. 26–27) describes one such patient, Jimmie, who was stuck in the year of his injury, 1945. Jimmie had formed no new memories after that year. Asked in 1975 to name the U.S. President, he replied, "FDR's dead. Truman's at the helm." When Jimmie gave his age as 19, Sacks set a mirror before him: "Look in the mirror and tell me what you see. Is that a 19-year-old looking out from the mirror?"

Jimmie turned pale, gripped the chair, cursed, then became frantic: "What's going on? What's happened to me? Is this a nightmare? Am I crazy? Is this a joke?" When his attention was directed to some children playing baseball, his panic ended, the dreadful mirror forgotten.

Sacks showed Jimmie a photo from *National Geographic.* "What is this?" he asked.

"It's the Moon," Jimmie replied.

"No, it's not," Sacks answered. "It's a picture of the Earth taken from the Moon."

"Doc, you're kidding? Someone would've had to get a camera up there!"

"Naturally."

"Hell! You're joking—how the hell would you do that?" Jimmie's wonder was that of a bright young man from the 1940s amazed by his travel back to the future.

Careful testing of people with injuries like Jimmie's reveals something even stranger. Although they are unable to recall new facts or anything they have done recently, they can learn new skills and can be classically conditioned. Shown hard-to-find figures in pictures (in the *Where's Waldo?* series), they can quickly spot them again later. They can master mirror-image writing, jigsaw puzzles, and even complicated job skills (Schacter, 1992, 1996; Xu & Corkin, 2001). However, *they do all these things with no awareness of having learned them.*

Memory is clearly not a single, unified, conscious system. Our two-track memory system is evident in people with Jimmie's type of brain injury **(FIGURE 7.8).** Whatever has destroyed their conscious recall has left their unconscious capacity

Figure 7.8> Two-track memory We process and store our memories for facts and skills separately. Thus, we may lose conscious (explicit) memory, yet retain memory for material we cannot consciously recall (implicit memory).

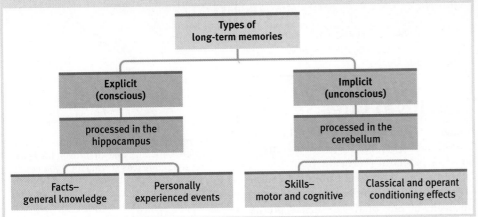

for learning intact. They can learn *how* to do something—to play golf, for example. And they can form an **implicit** (unconscious) **memory** of their new skill. But they may not *be aware* that they can play golf. They won't form **explicit** (conscious) **memories** of learning the sport or playing on a particular golf course. If they continue to practice, their game will improve steadily. Yet this will all happen out of their awareness. They will have new skills, but no conscious memories of the facts associated with their new achievements. Even Alzheimer's patients, whose explicit memories for people and events are lost, have shown an ability to form new implicit memories (Lustig & Buckner, 2004).

Our explicit and implicit memory systems involve separate brain regions. We know this from scans of the brain in action, and from autopsies of people who had suffered from different types of memory loss. New explicit memories of names, images, and events are laid down via the *hippocampus,* a neural center in the limbic system. When brain scans capture the brain forming an explicit memory, they reveal hippocampus activity. The hippocampus seems to act as a loading dock where the brain registers and temporarily stores the elements of a remembered episode. But then, like

older files shifted to a basement store-room, memories migrate for storage elsewhere.

Although your hippocampus is a temporary processing site for your explicit memories, you could lose it and still lay down memories for skills, such as golfing, and conditioned associations. Joseph LeDoux (1996) recounts the story of a brain-damaged patient whose memory loss left her unable to recognize her physician as, each day, he shook her hand and introduced himself. One day, after reaching for his hand, she yanked hers back, for the physician had pricked her with a tack in his palm. The next time he returned to introduce himself she refused to shake his hand but couldn't explain why. Having been classically conditioned, she just wouldn't do it.

The *cerebellum,* the brain region extending out from the rear of the brainstem, plays a key role in forming and storing the implicit memories created by classical conditioning. Humans with a damaged cerebellum are unable to develop certain conditioned reflexes, such as associating a tone with an oncoming puff of air—and thus blinking in anticipation of the puff (Daum & Schugens, 1996; Green & Woodruff-Pak, 2000). Implicit memory formation needs the cerebellum.

Retrieval: Getting Information Out

4: What is involved in retrieving information from our memory?

Remembering an event requires more than getting information into our brain and storing it there. To most people,

flashbulb memory a clear memory of an emotionally significant moment or event.

implicit memory retaining learned skills or conditioning, often without conscious awareness of this learning.

explicit memory memories of facts and personal events that you can consciously retrieve.

memory is **recall,** the ability to draw information out of storage and into conscious awareness. To a psychologist, memory is more than that. **Recognizing** or more quickly **relearning** information also shows that something was learned and retained.

Long after you cannot recall most of your high school classmates, you could probably recognize their yearbook pictures from a photo lineup and pick them out from a list of names. One research team found that people who had graduated 25 years earlier could not *recall* many of their old classmates, but they could *recognize* 90 percent of their pictures and names (Bahrick & others, 1975).

Our recognition memory is quick and vast. "Is your friend wearing a new or old outfit?" "Old." "Is this five-second movie clip from a film you've ever seen?" "Yes." "Have you ever before seen this person—this minor variation on the same old human features (two eyes, one nose, and so on)?" "No." Before our mouth can form an answer to any of millions of such questions, our mind knows, and knows that it knows.

Speed of relearning also reveals memory. If you once learned something and then forgot it, you probably will relearn it more quickly. When you re-study material for a final exam or resurrect a language you used in early childhood, mastering the material is easier the second time around. Tests of recognition and of time spent relearning show that we remember more than we can recall.

Remembering things past :: Even if Oprah Winfrey and Brad Pitt had not become famous, their high school classmates would most likely still recognize their yearbook photos.

Questions:
Multiple-choice questions test our
  a. recall.
  b. recognition.
  c. relearning.
Fill-in-the-blank questions test our
_____. (Turn the next page to check your answers.)

Retrieval Cues

Imagine a spider suspended in the middle of her web, held up by the many strands extending outward from her in all directions to different points. To trace a pathway to the spider, you would need to begin at one of these anchor points and follow the attached strand down into the web.

Retrieving a memory is similar. Memories are held in storage by a web of associations, each piece of information connected to many others. Here's a simplified example of how a memory web is constructed. Suppose you encode into your memory the name of the person sitting next to you in class. With that name, you will also encode other bits of information, such as your surroundings, mood, seating position, and so on. These other bits act as **retrieval cues,** anchor points for pathways you can follow to access your classmate's name when you need to recall it later. The more retrieval cues you've encoded, the better your chances of finding a path to the memory suspended in this web of information.

The best retrieval cues come from associations formed at the time we encode a memory. Tastes, smells, and sights often open pathways to our memories. To recall something, we may mentally place ourselves in the original context. Doing so gives us visual cues that can lead us to the searched-for memory. After losing his sight, British theologian John Hull (1990, p. 174) described his difficulty recalling such details: "I knew I had been somewhere, and had done particular things with certain people, but where? I could not put the conversations . . . into a context. There was no background, no features against which to identify the place.

"Let me refresh your memory. It was the night before Christmas and all through the house not a creature was stirring until you landed a sled, drawn by reindeer, on the plaintiff's home, causing extensive damage to the roof and chimney."

Normally, the memories of people you have spoken to during the day are stored in frames which include the background."

Here's a question to test your memory. Do you recall the second sentence I asked you to remember (earlier in this chapter)? If not, does the word *shark* open a pathway? Experiments show that *shark* (likely the image you visualized and stored) is a better retrieval cue than the sentence's actual word, *fish* (Anderson & others, 1976). *(The fish attacked the swimmer.)*

Context Effects

Returning to the context where you experienced something can *prime* (activate) your memory of it. Researchers discovered this when they had scuba divers listen to a list of words in two different settings, either 10 feet underwater or sitting on the beach (Godden & Baddeley, 1975). The divers recalled more words when they were retested in the same place (FIGURE 7.9).

You may have experienced similar context effects. Imagine this: While taking notes from this book, you realize you need to sharpen your pencil. You get up and walk to another room. When you get there, however, you cannot recall why you made the trip. You give up and return to your desk. As you sit down to work again, it hits you: "I wanted to sharpen this pencil!" What happens to create this

Figure 7.9> The effect of context on memory
Words heard underwater were best recalled underwater; words heard on land were best recalled on land. (Adapted from Godden & Baddeley, 1975.)

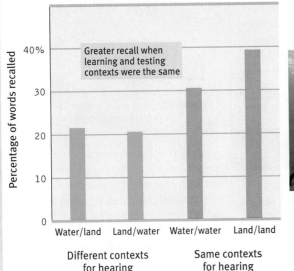

Greater recall when learning and testing contexts were the same

Percentage of words recalled

40%

30

20

10

0

Water/land   Land/water   Water/water   Land/land

Different contexts for hearing and recall

Same contexts for hearing and recall

Alexis Rosenfeld/Photo Researchers, Inc.

frustrating experience? In one context (desk, reading psychology), you realize your pencil needs sharpening. In another room, in a different context, you have few cues to lead you back to that thought. When you are once again seated at your desk, you are back in the context in which you encoded the thought ("This pencil is dull").

Sometimes, being in a context similar to one we've been in before may trigger feelings of **déjà vu** (French for "already seen"). Two-thirds of us have had this fleeting, eerie sense that "I've been in this exact situation before." Well-educated, imaginative young adults are most likely to experience déjà vu, especially when tired or stressed (Brown, 2003, 2004; McAneny, 1996). Some wonder, "How could I recognize a situation I'm now in for the first time?" Others may suspect extraordinary causes: "Could I have experienced this in a previous life?" or "Did I dream of this place?"

Posing the question differently—"Why do I feel as though I recognize this situation?"—we can see how our memory system might produce déjà vu (Alcock,

"Do you ever get that strange feeling of vujà dé? Not déjà vu; vujà dé. It's the distinct sense that, somehow, something just happened that has never happened before. Nothing seems familiar. And then suddenly the feeling is gone. Vujà dé."

George Carlin, *Funny Times*, December 2001

1981). Our current situation may be loaded with retrieval cues that take us down paths leading to earlier, similar experiences. Thus, if you are in a restaurant where you often meet a friend for lunch, and you see a stranger who walks and talks like that friend, the similarity may trigger an eerie feeling of recognition. Having awakened a shadow of that earlier experience, you may think, "I've seen that person in this situation before."

Or perhaps a situation seems familiar because it resembles several other similar experiences (Lampinen, 2002). Imagine you briefly encountered my dad, my brothers, my sister, and my children. Then, a few weeks later, you meet me. You might think, "I've been with this guy before." Although no one in my family looks or acts just like me (lucky them),

their looks and gestures are somewhat like mine, and I might form a "global match" to what you had experienced.

Moods and Memories

Words, images, and contexts are not our only retrieval cues. An event in the past may have aroused a specific *emotion*, such as fear, anger, or joy. Later, when we again feel that emotion, we may recall the event associated with it (Fiedler & others, 2001).

We have all experienced mood effects. If you have a terrible evening—your date canceled, you lost your iPod, and now you've absent-mindedly washed your colored clothes with bleach instead of detergent—your sour mood will surely bring to mind memories of other unhappy times. If a friend or family member walks in at this point, your mind may fill with bad memories of that person. Being angry or depressed sours memories. This tendency to recall events that are consistent with our mood is called **mood-congruent memory.** If put in a great mood—whether under hypnosis or just by the day's events (a World Cup soccer victory for the German participants in one study)—people recall the world through rose-colored glasses (DeSteno & others, 2000; Forgas & others, 1984; Schwarz & others, 1987). They judge themselves competent and effective, other people as kind and giving, and happy events as more common than unhappy ones.

recall memory demonstrated by retrieving information learned earlier, as on a fill-in-the-blank test.

recognition memory demonstrated by identifying items previously learned, as on a multiple-choice test.

relearning memory demonstrated by time saved when learning material a second time.

retrieval cue any stimulus (event, feeling, place, and so on) linked to a specific memory.

déjà vu that eerie sense that "I've experienced this before." Cues from the current situation may unconsciously trigger retrieval of an earlier experience.

mood-congruent memory the tendency to recall experiences that are consistent with your current good or bad mood.

Answers to questions two pages back: Multiple-choice questions test recognition. Fill-in-the-blank questions test recall.

Knowing this mood-memory connection, we should not be surprised that in some studies *currently* depressed people recall their parents as rejecting, punitive, and guilt-promoting. *Formerly* depressed people describe their parents in more positive ways—much as do those who have never suffered depression (Lewinsohn & Rosenbaum, 1987; Lewis, 1992). Similarly, adolescents' ratings of parental warmth in one week give little clue to how they will rate their parents six weeks later (Bornstein & others, 1991). When teens are down, their parents seem inhuman. As the teens' moods brighten, those devil parents sprout wings and become angels.

Our mood's effect on retrieval helps explain why our moods persist. When happy, we recall happy events and therefore see the world as a happy place, which helps prolong our good mood. When depressed, we recall sad events, which darkens our interpretations of current events. For those with a predisposition to depression, this process can help maintain a vicious, dark cycle.

CALLAHAN

"I wonder if you'd mind giving me directions. I've never been sober in this part of town before."

Distributed by Levin Represents.

Mood-congruent memory is part of a larger concept called *state-dependent memory*. What we learn in one state may be more easily recalled when we are again in that state. What people learn when drunk, for example, they don't recall well in *any* state (alcohol disrupts storage). But they recall it slightly better when again drunk. Someone who hides money when drunk may forget the location until drunk again.

⬡ PRACTICE TEST

10. To access a memory, we think of things associated with that memory, such as odors, images, or emotions, which are all examples of
    a. relearning.
    b. storage.
    c. imagery.
    d. retrieval cues.

11. The feeling that "I've been here before" is known as
    a. déjà vu.
    b. retrieval.
    c. relearning.
    d. an explicit memory.

12. The tendency to recall experiences consistent with our current emotions is called
    a. emotional memory.
    b. déjà vu.
    c. automatic processing.
    d. mood-congruent memory.

Answers: 10. d, 11. a, 12. d.

Forgetting

5: Why do we forget? At what points in the memory system can our memory fail us?

If a memory-enhancing pill becomes available, it had better not be too effective. To discard the clutter of useless or out-of-date information—where we

"Waiter, I'd like to order, unless I've eaten, in which case bring me the check."

parked the car yesterday, a friend's old phone number, restaurant orders already cooked and served—is surely a blessing. Remember the Russian memory whiz S whom we met earlier in this chapter? His junk heap of memories dominated his consciousness. He had difficulty thinking abstractly—generalizing, organizing, evaluating. So did a woman named A. J., who reports that her extraordinary memory interferes with her life, with one memory cuing another (Parker & others, 2006). "It's like a running movie that never stops."

More often, however, our quirky memories fail us when we least expect it. My own memory can easily call up such episodes as that wonderful first kiss with the woman I love, or trivial facts like the air mileage from London to Detroit. Then it abandons me when I'm trying to recall that new colleague's name or where I left my hat, and I discover I have failed to encode, store, or retrieve the information. Memory researcher Daniel Schacter (1999) lists seven ways our memories fail us—the seven sins of memory, he calls them.

Three sins of forgetting (encoding failure):

1. *Absent-mindedness*—inattention to details leads to encoding failure (our mind is elsewhere as we lay down the car keys).

2. *Transience*—memory loss (we forget former classmates, as that unused information fades).

Figure 7.10> Forgetting as encoding failure We cannot remember what we have not encoded.

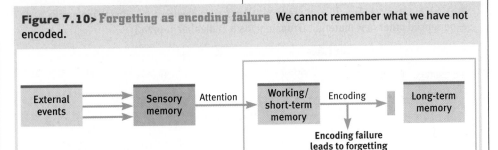

3. *Blocking*—stored information can't be accessed (seeing an actor in an old movie, we feel the name on the tip of our tongue but cannot get it out).

Three sins of distortion (storage decay):

4. *Misattribution*—confusing the source of information (forgetting who said what or remembering a dream as an actual event).

5. *Suggestibility*—the lingering effects of misinformation (a leading question— "Did Mr. Jones touch your private parts?"—later becomes a young child's false memory).

6. *Bias*—belief-colored recollections (current bad feelings toward a friend may change our memory of initial good feelings).

One sin of intrusion (retrieval failure):

7. *Persistence*—unwanted memories (being haunted by images of a sexual assault).

Let's first consider encoding failures, then storage decay and retrieval failures.

Encoding Failure

Much of what we sense we never notice, and what we fail to encode, we will never remember **(FIGURE 7.10)**. Age can affect encoding efficiency. The brain areas that jump into action when young adults encode new information are less responsive in older adults. This slower encoding helps explain age-related memory decline (Grady & others, 1995).

But no matter how young we are, we pay conscious attention to only a limited portion of the vast number of sights and sounds bombarding us. Consider something you have looked at countless times: What letters accompany the number 5 on your phone? For most of us, the question is surprisingly tough. This detail is not personally meaningful, and few of us have made the effort to encode it. We encode some information—where we had dinner yesterday—automatically. Other types of information—like the concepts in this chapter—require effort and attention. Without this effortful processing, many memories never form.

Storage Decay

Even after encoding something well, we sometimes later forget it. That master of nonsense-syllable learning Hermann Ebbinghaus (1885) also studied the durability of stored memories. After learning lists of nonsense syllables, he measured how much he had retained from 20 minutes to 30 days later. The result was his famous *forgetting curve*: The course of forgetting is rapid at first, then levels off with time (Wixted & Ebbesen, 1991). People studying Spanish as a foreign language showed this forgetting curve for Spanish vocabulary (Bahrick, 1984). Compared with others who had just completed a high school or college Spanish course, people 3 years out of school had forgotten much of what they had learned **(FIGURE 7.11)**. However, what people remembered then, they still remembered 25 and more years later. Their forgetting had leveled off.

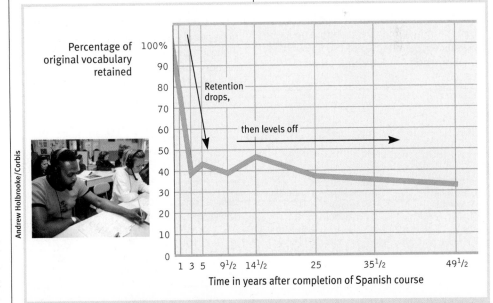

Andrew Holbrooke/Corbis

Figure 7.11> The forgetting curve for Spanish learned in school Compared with others just completing a Spanish language-learning course, people 3 years out of the course remembered much less. Compared with the 3-year group, however, those who studied Spanish even longer ago did not forget much more. (Adapted from Bahrick, 1984.)

One explanation for these forgetting curves is a gradual fading of the physical **memory trace.** Researchers are getting closer to solving the mystery of the physical storage of memory and are increasing our understanding of how memory storage could decay. But memories fade for many reasons, including other learning that disrupts our retrieval.

Retrieval Failure

We can compare forgotten events to books you can't find in your local library. Some aren't available for use because they were never acquired (not encoded). Others have been discarded (stored memories decay).

But there is a third possibility. The book may be stored and available but out of reach because we don't have enough information to look it up and retrieve it. How frustrating when you know information is "in there," even on the tip of your tongue, but you cannot get it out **(FIGURE 7.12).** Given retrieval cues ("It begins with an M"), you may easily retrieve the memory. Forgetting is often not memories discarded but memories unretrieved.

Deaf people fluent in sign language experience a parallel "tip of the fingers" phenomenon (Thompson & others, 2005).

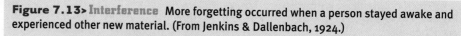

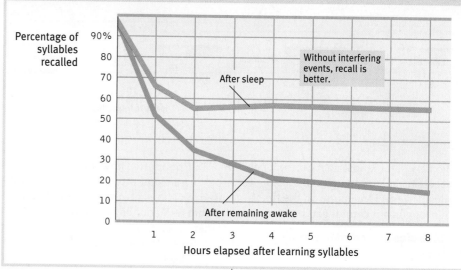

Figure 7.13> Interference More forgetting occurred when a person stayed awake and experienced other new material. (From Jenkins & Dallenbach, 1924.)

Interference

Old and new items, especially similar items, sometimes compete for your attention when you try to retrieve a memory. This process is called **interference,** and it is an important cause of forgetting. For example, if you're at a party and someone gives you a phone number, you may be able to recall it the next day. But if two more people give you their numbers, each of those numbers will interfere with your memory of the ones that went before. Likewise, if you get a new combination

lock, your memory of the old one may block out the new set of numbers. As you collect more and more information, your mental attic never fills, but it certainly gets cluttered.

What we learn in the hour before falling asleep is protected from interference. During that hour, fewer distractions interfere with our learning. Researchers discovered this in a now-classic experiment (Jenkins & Dallenbach, 1924). Day after day, two people each learned some nonsense syllables. When they tried to recall them after up to eight hours of being asleep at night, they could retrieve more than half of the items **(FIGURE 7.13).** But when they learned the material and then stayed awake and involved with other activities, they forgot more items, and they forgot them sooner. Later experiments have confirmed that the hour before a night's sleep is a good time to commit information to memory (Benson & Feinberg, 1977; Fowler & others, 1973; Nesca & Koulack, 1994). But not the *seconds* just before sleep. Information presented then doesn't have a chance to get encoded, so we seldom remember it later (Wyatt & Bootzin, 1994). Nor do we remember recorded information played during sleep, although our ears register it

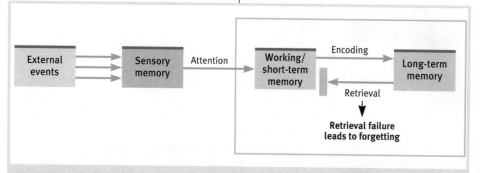

Figure 7.12> Retrieval failure We store in long-term memory what's important to us or what we've rehearsed. But sometimes even stored information cannot be accessed, which leads to forgetting.

(Wood & others, 1992). Without opportunity for rehearsal, most learning doesn't occur.

But we should not overstate the point. Sometimes old information can help us learn new information. Knowing Latin may actually help us to learn French. It is when old and new information compete with each other, as in learning Spanish soon after learning French, that interference occurs.

Motivated Forgetting

To remember our past is often to revise it. Years ago, the huge cookie jar in our kitchen was jammed with freshly baked chocolate chip cookies. Still more were cooling across racks on the counter. Twenty-four hours later, not a crumb was left. Who had taken them? During that time, my wife, three children, and I were the only people in the house. So while memories were still fresh, I conducted a little memory test. Andy admitted wolfing down as many as 20. Peter thought he had eaten 15. Laura guessed she had stuffed her then-6-year-old body with 15 cookies. My wife, Carol, recalled eating 6, and I remembered consuming 15 and taking 18 more to the office. We sheepishly accepted responsibility for 89 cookies. Still, we had not come close; there had been 160.

Why were we so far off in our estimates of the number of cookies we had eaten? As **FIGURE 7.14** reminds us, we automatically encode sensory information in amazing detail. So was it an encoding problem? Did we just not notice what we had eaten? Or was it a storage problem? Might our memories of cookies, like Ebbinghaus' memory of nonsense syllables, have melted away almost as fast as the cookies themselves? Or was the information still intact but not retrievable because it would be embarrassing to remember?[1]

Sigmund Freud might have argued that our memory systems self-censored this information. He proposed that we **repress**

1. One of my cookie-scarfing sons, on reading this in his father's textbook years later, confessed he had fibbed "a little."

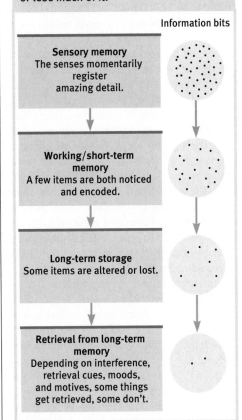

Figure 7.14> When do we forget?
Forgetting can occur at any memory stage. As we process information, we filter, alter, or lose much of it.

Information bits

Sensory memory
The senses momentarily register amazing detail.

Working/short-term memory
A few items are both noticed and encoded.

Long-term storage
Some items are altered or lost.

Retrieval from long-term memory
Depending on interference, retrieval cues, moods, and motives, some things get retrieved, some don't.

painful memories to protect our self-concept and to minimize anxiety. But the repressed memory lingers, he believed, and can be retrieved by some later cue or during therapy. Repression was central to Freud's theory (see Chapter 11) and, especially in the mid-twentieth century, it was a popular idea in psychology. In one fairly recent study, 9 in 10 university students agreed that "memories for painful experiences are sometimes pushed into unconsciousness" (Brown & others, 1996). Therapists often assume it. Yet increasing numbers of memory researchers think repression rarely, if ever, occurs. More typically, we have trouble truly forgetting traumatic experiences. Before turning to that topic, however, let's look at some of the ways our memories become distorted.

memory trace enduring physical changes in the brain as a memory forms.

interference the blocking of recall as old or new learning disrupts the recall of other memories.

repression in psychoanalytic theory, the basic defense mechanism that banishes from consciousness anxiety-arousing thoughts, feelings, and memories.

Memory Construction

6: **What factors affect the accuracy of our memories?**

Picture yourself having this experience:

> You go to a fancy restaurant for dinner. You are seated at a table with a white tablecloth. You study the menu. You tell the server you want broiled salmon, a baked potato with sour cream, and a salad with blue cheese dressing. You also order some white wine from the wine list. A few minutes later the server returns with your salad. Later the rest of the meal arrives. You enjoy it all, except the salmon is a bit overdone.

Were I immediately to quiz you on this paragraph (adapted from Hyde, 1983), you could surely retrieve plenty of details. For example, without looking back, answer the following questions:

1. What kind of salad dressing did you order?

2. Was the tablecloth red-checked?

3. What did you order to drink?

4. Did the server give you a menu?

You were probably able to recall exactly what you ordered, and maybe even the color of the tablecloth. We do have a large capacity for storing and reproducing the little details of our daily experience. But did the server give you a menu? Not in the paragraph given. Nevertheless, many answer yes. We often *construct* our memories as we encode them. We may also *alter* our memories as we withdraw them from our memory bank. Like scientists who infer a dinosaur's appearance from its remains, we infer our past from stored tidbits of information plus what we now assume. By filtering information and filling in missing pieces, your concept of restaurants directed your memory construction.

Misinformation and Imagination Effects

In more than 200 experiments, involving more than 20,000 people, Elizabeth Loftus has shown how eyewitnesses reconstruct their memories when questioned after a crime or an accident. For example, two groups of people watched a film of a traffic accident and then answered questions about what they had seen (Loftus and Palmer, 1974). Those asked, "How fast were the cars going when they *smashed* into each other?" gave higher speed estimates than those asked, "How fast were the cars going when they *hit* each other?" A week later, when asked whether they recalled seeing any broken glass, people who had heard *smashed* were more than twice as likely to report seeing glass fragments **(FIGURE 7.15)**. In fact, the film showed no broken glass.

In many follow-up experiments, others have witnessed an event, received or not received misleading information about it, and then taken a memory test. The repeated result is a **misinformation effect.** Exposed to misleading information, we tend to misremember. As our memories fade over time, we are even more easily misled (Loftus, 1992). (This tendency makes older adults vulnerable to scams, as when a repairperson overcharges by falsely claiming "I told you it would cost X and you agreed to pay" [Jacoby & others, 2005].)

Because the misinformation effect happens outside our awareness, it's nearly impossible to sift the suggested ideas out of the larger pool of real memories (Schooler & others, 1986). Perhaps you can recall describing a childhood experience to a friend, and filling in memory gaps with reasonable guesses and assumptions. We all do it, but after more retellings, those guessed details—now absorbed into our memories—may feel as real as if we had actually observed them (Roediger & others, 1993).

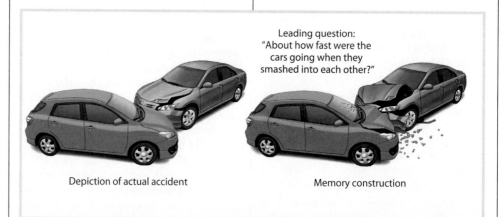

Depiction of actual accident

Leading question: "About how fast were the cars going when they smashed into each other?"

Memory construction

Figure 7.15> Memory construction When people who had seen the film of a car accident were later asked a leading question, they recalled a more serious accident than they had witnessed. (From Loftus, 1979.)

DOONESBURY

Just hearing a vivid retelling of an event may implant false memories. Should we be surprised that digitally altered photos produced the same result? In one experiment, researchers altered photos from a family album to show some family members taking a hot-air balloon ride. After viewing these childhood photos three times over two weeks, half the participants "remembered" the faked experience, often in rich detail (Wade & others, 2002).

"Memory is insubstantial. Things keep replacing it. Your batch of snapshots will both fix and ruin your memory. . . . You can't remember anything from your trip except the wretched collection of snapshots."

Annie Dillard, "To Fashion a Text," 1988

Such experiments can help us understand why "hypnotically refreshed" memories of crimes often contain errors. If the hypnotist asks leading questions ("Did you hear loud noises?"), witnesses may weave that false information into their memory of the event.

Even repeatedly *imagining* nonexistent actions and events can create false memories. One in four American and British university students asked to imagine certain childhood events, such as breaking a window with their hand or having a skin sample removed from a finger, later recalled the imagined event as something that had really happened (Garry & others, 1996; Mazzoni & Memon, 2003).

"It isn't so astonishing, the number of things I can remember, as the number of things I can remember that aren't so."

Mark Twain (1835–1910)

This effect occurs partly because visualizing something and actually perceiving it activate similar brain areas (Gonsalves & others, 2004). Imagined events also later seem more familiar, and familiar things seem more real. The more vividly we can imagine things, the more likely they are to become memories (Loftus, 2001; Porter & others, 2000).

Source Amnesia

Among the frailest parts of a memory is its source. Thus, we may recognize someone but have no idea where we have seen the person. Or we may dream an event and later be unsure whether it really happened. Or we may hear something and later recall seeing it (Henkel & others, 2000). In each case, we are experiencing **source amnesia**—we retain the memory of the event but not of the context in which we acquired it. Source amnesia, along with the misinformation effect, is at the heart of many false memories.

Authors and songwriters sometimes suffer source amnesia. They think an idea came from their own creative imagination, when in fact they are unintentionally plagiarizing something they earlier read or heard.

misinformation effect a memory that has been corrupted by misleading information.

source amnesia linking the wrong source with an event you have experienced, heard about, read about, or imagined.

Psychologist Donald Thompson became part of his own research on memory distortion when police brought him in for questioning about a rape. Although he was a near-perfect match to the victim's memory of the rapist, Thompson had an airtight alibi. Just before the rape occurred, he was being interviewed on live TV and could not possibly have made it to the crime scene. Then it came to light that the victim had been watching the interview—ironically about face recognition—and had experienced source amnesia. She had confused her memories of Thompson with those of the rapist (Schacter, 1996).

Children's Eyewitness Recall

Constructed memories *feel* like real memories. If memories can be sincere, yet sincerely wrong, how can jurors decide cases in which children's memories of sexual abuse are the only evidence?

Stephen Ceci (1993) thinks "it would be truly awful to ever lose sight of the enormity of child abuse." Yet, as we have seen, asking leading questions can plant false memories. Ceci and Maggie Bruck's (1993, 1995) studies have made them aware of how easily children's memories can be molded. For example, they asked 3-year-olds to show on anatomically correct dolls where a pediatrician had touched them. Of the children who had not received genital examinations, 55 percent pointed to either genital or anal areas.

In other studies, the researchers used suggestive interviewing techniques. Influenced by the questions, most preschoolers and many older children reported false events, such as seeing a thief steal food in their day-care center (Bruck & Ceci, 1999, 2004). In one study, children chose a card from a deck of possible happenings, and an adult then read the card to them. For example, "Think real hard, and tell me if this ever happened to you. Can you remember going to the hospital with a mousetrap on your finger?" In weekly interviews, the same adult repeatedly asked children to think about several

real and fictitious events. After 10 weeks of this, a new adult asked the same questions. The stunning result: 58 percent of preschoolers produced false (often vivid) stories about one or more events they had never experienced (Ceci & others, 1994). Here's one of those stories.

> My brother Colin was trying to get Blowtorch [an action figure] from me, and I wouldn't let him take it from me, so he pushed me into the wood pile where the mousetrap was. And then my finger got caught in it. And then we went to the hospital, and my mommy, daddy, and Colin drove me there, to the hospital in our van, because it was far away. And the doctor put a bandage on this finger.

Given such detailed stories, professional psychologists who specialize in interviewing children could not reliably separate the real memories from the false ones. Nor could the children themselves. The above child, reminded that his parents had told him several times that the mousetrap event never happened—that he had imagined it—protested, "But it really did happen. I remember it!"

Does this then mean that children can never be accurate eyewitnesses? No. If a neutral person asks nonleading questions in words the children can understand, children often accurately recall what happened and who did it (Goodman & others, 1990; Howe, 1997; Pipe, 1996). Children are especially accurate if they have not talked with involved adults before the interview. When interviewers use less suggestive, more effective techniques, even 4- to 5-year-olds produce more accurate recall (Holliday & Albon, 2004; Pipe & others, 2004).

Repressed or Constructed Memories of Abuse?

Many therapists have guided people in "recovering" memories of childhood abuse. In one survey, 7 in 10 therapists said they had used techniques such as

hypnosis or drugs for this purpose (Poole & others, 1995). These clinicians believe they are addressing a widespread problem. In another survey, therapists estimated that 11 percent of the population—some 34 million people—have repressed memories of childhood sexual abuse (Kamena, 1998). Are these well-intentioned therapists triggering false memories that damage innocent adults, or are they uncovering the truth?

The research on source amnesia and the misinformation effect raises concerns. Some therapists have reasoned with patients that "people who've been abused often have your symptoms, so you probably were abused. Let's see if, aided by hypnosis or drugs, or helped to dig back and visualize your trauma, you can recover it." Patients exposed to such techniques may then form an image of a threatening person. With rehearsal and visualization, the image grows more vivid, as it did for the little boy who came to believe he had caught his finger in a mousetrap. The patient ends up stunned, angry, and ready to confront or sue the equally stunned parent, relative, or clergy member, who then vigorously denies the accusation.

Scientific critics are not questioning the professionalism of most therapists. Their charge is specifically directed against clinicians who use "memory work" techniques, such as "guided imagery," hypnosis, and dream analysis to recover memories. These therapists, say Elizabeth Loftus and her colleagues (1995), "are nothing more than merchants of mental chaos, and, in fact, constitute a blight on the entire field of psychotherapy." Irate clinicians counter that those who argue that recovered memories of abuse never happen are adding to abused people's trauma and playing into the hands of child molesters. Loftus' scientist colleagues disagree. They elected her president of the science-oriented Association for Psychological Science, awarded her psychology's biggest prize ($200,000), and elected her to the U.S. National Academy of Sciences and the Royal Society of Edinburgh.

Elizabeth Loftus :: "The research findings for which I am being honored now generated a level of hostility and opposition I could never have foreseen. People wrote threatening letters, warning me that my reputation and even my safety were in jeopardy if I continued along these lines. At some universities, armed guards were provided to accompany me during speeches." (Elizabeth Loftus, on receiving the Association for Psychological Science's William James Fellow Award, 2001.)

Don Shrubshell

In an effort to find a sensible common ground that might resolve psychology's "memory war," professional organizations (the American Medical, American Psychological, and American Psychiatric Associations, among others) have set up study panels and issued public statements. Those committed to protecting abused children and those committed to protecting wrongly accused adults agree on the following.

- *Injustice happens.* Some innocent people have been falsely convicted. Some guilty people have avoided punishment by casting doubt on their truth-telling accusers.

- *Incest and other sexual abuse happen.* And they happen more often than we once supposed. Sexual abuse can leave its victims at risk for problems ranging from sexual dysfunction to depression. Yet there is no characteristic "survivor syndrome"—no group of symptoms that lets us spot victims of sexual abuse (Kendall-Tackett & others, 1993).

- *Forgetting happens.* Forgetting isolated past events, both negative and positive, is an ordinary part of everyday life. Those who have forgotten being abused were either very young when it happened or may not have understood the meaning of their experience—circumstances under which forgetting is "utterly common."

- *Recovered memories are commonplace.* Cued by a remark or an experience, all of us sometimes recover memories of long-forgotten events, both pleasant and unpleasant. What many psychologists question is whether the unconscious mind *forcibly represses* painful experiences, and whether these can be retrieved by certain therapist-aided techniques.

"When memories are 'recovered' after long periods of amnesia, particularly when extraordinary means were used to secure the recovery of memory, there is a high probability that the memories are false."

Royal College of Psychiatrists Working Group on Reported Recovered Memories of Child Sexual Abuse (Brandon & others, 1998)

- *Memories of things happening before age 3 are unreliable.* We cannot reliably recall happenings of any sort from our first three years. This *infantile amnesia* happens because our brain pathways are not yet developed enough to form the kinds of memories we will form later in life. Psychologists are therefore skeptical of "recovered" memories of abuse during infancy (Gore-Felton & others, 2000; Knapp & Vande Creek, 2000). The older a child is when suffering sexual abuse, and the more severe it was, the more likely it is to be remembered (Goodman & others, 2003).

- *Memories "recovered" under hypnosis are especially unreliable.* Under hypnosis, people will incorporate all kinds of suggestions into their memories.

- *Memories, whether real or false, can be emotionally upsetting.* Both the accuser and the accused may suffer when what was born of mere suggestion becomes, like an actual trauma, a stinging memory that drives bodily stress (McNally, 2003). This has happened to people knocked unconscious in unremembered accidents. They have developed stress disorders after being haunted by memories they constructed from photos, news reports, and friends' accounts (Bryant, 2001).

So, does repression of threatening memories ever occur? Or is this concept—the cornerstone of Freud's theory and of so much popular psychology—misleading? In Chapter 11, we will return to this hotly debated issue. For now, this

TODAY'S SPECIAL GUEST

BRUNDAGE MORNALD, OF BATTLE CREEK, MONTANA UNDER HYPNOSIS, MR. MORNALD RECOVERED LONG-BURIED MEMORIES OF A PERFECTLY NORMAL, HAPPY CHILDHOOD.

much appears certain: The most common response to a traumatic experience (witnessing a loved one's murder, being terrorized by a hijacker or a rapist, losing everything and everyone in a natural disaster) is not banishing the experience into the unconscious. Rather, such experiences are typically etched on the mind as vivid, persistent, haunting memories. As Robert Kraft (2002) said of the experience of those trapped in the Nazi death camps, "Horror sears memory, leaving . . . the consuming memories of atrocity."

PRACTICE TEST

17. The tendency to alter information as we encode it, and to fill in gaps when we try to recall something, is known as
    a. interference.
    b. memory construction.
    c. the déjà vu effect.
    d. the eyewitness recall effect.

18. You recognize a face in a crowd, but you can't recall how you know this person. This is an example of
    a. the misinformation effect.
    b. interference.
    c. source amnesia.
    d. repression.

19. Children may be accurate eyewitnesses if
    a. interviewers use suggestive interviewing techniques.
    b. a neutral person asks nonleading questions in words the children can understand.
    c. the children have talked with involved adults before the interview.
    d. interviewers use words that are slightly beyond the children's vocabulary.

20. Psychologists involved in the study of memories of abuse tend to disagree about which of the following statements?
    a. Memories for things that happened before age 3 are not reliable.
    b. We tend to repress extremely upsetting memories.
    c. Memories can be emotionally upsetting.
    d. Incest and sexual abuse happen.

Answers: 17, b, 18, c, 19, b, 20, b.

Improving Memory

7: How can you improve your memory so that you do better in this and other courses?

Much as biology benefits medicine, and botany benefits agriculture, the psychology of memory can benefit your education and class performance. Sprinkled throughout this chapter and summarized here for easy reference are concrete suggestions that could help you remember information when you need it.

Study repeatedly to boost long-term recall. Overlearn. To learn a name, say it to yourself after being introduced. Wait a few seconds and say it again. Wait a bit longer and say it a third time. To learn a concept, give yourself many separate study sessions. Take advantage of life's little intervals—riding on the bus, walking across campus, waiting for class to start.

"I have discovered that it is of some use when you lie in bed at night and gaze into the darkness to repeat in your mind the things you have been studying. Not only does it help the understanding, but also the memory."

Leonardo da Vinci (1452–1519)

Space out study. Cramming just before a test produces overconfidence. Spreading out your studying over many days and weeks produces better results.

Spend more time rehearsing or actively thinking about the material. New memories are weak; exercise them and they will strengthen. Skimming complex material won't give you enough time to rehearse what you're learning or to think critically about how it applies to you. Instead, study actively. To memorize specific facts or figures, Thomas Landauer (2001) suggests: "rehearse the name or number you are trying to memorize, wait a few seconds, rehearse again, wait a little

Thinking and memory :: Actively thinking as we read, by rehearsing and relating ideas, and by making the material meaningful, yields the best retention.

© LWA-Dann Tardiff/Corbis

longer, rehearse again, then wait longer still and rehearse yet again. The waits should be as long as possible without losing the information."

"Knit each new thing on to some acquisition already there."

William James, *Principles of Psychology*, 1890

Make the material personally meaningful. You can build a network of retrieval cues by taking thorough text and class notes in your own words. You can increase retrieval cues by forming as many associations as possible. Apply the concepts to your own life. Form images. Understand and organize information. Relate the material to what you already know or have experienced. Restate it in your own words. Mindlessly repeating someone else's words won't provide such cues. On an exam, you may find yourself stuck when a question uses phrasing different from the words you memorized.

Refresh your memory by activating retrieval cues. Mentally re-create the situation and the mood in which your original learning occurred. Return to the same location. Jog your memory by allowing one thought to cue the next.

Minimize interference. Study before sleeping. Do not schedule back-to-back study times for topics that are likely to interfere with each other, such as Spanish and French.

Test your own knowledge, both to rehearse it and to find out what you don't yet know. Test your learning using the Practice Tests at the end of text sections and in this book's study guide or on its Web site (www.worthpublishers.com/myers). But don't let your ability to recognize information fool you. Outline sections on a blank page. Try defining the terms and concepts listed at each chapter's end before turning back to their definitions.

PRACTICE TEST

21. Which of the following is NOT a good suggestion for improving your memory?
    a. Cram just before a test rather than spacing out your studying.
    b. Make the material you are reading as personally meaningful as possible.
    c. Overlearn by studying repeatedly.
    d. Study in a way that reduces the interference of other topics and distractions.

Answer: 21. a.

Terms and concepts to Remember

memory, p. 181
encoding, p. 182
storage, p. 182
retrieval, p. 182
sensory memory, p. 182
short-term memory, p. 182
working memory, p. 182
long-term memory, p. 182
automatic processing, p. 183
effortful processing, p. 183

rehearsal, p. 183
spacing effect, p. 184
serial position effect, p. 184
imagery, p. 185
long-term potentiation (LTP), p. 187
flashbulb memory, p. 188
implicit memory, p. 189
explicit memory, p. 189
recall, p. 190
recognition, p. 190

relearning, p. 190
retrieval cue, p. 190
déjà vu, p. 191
mood-congruent memory, p. 191
memory trace, p. 194
interference, p. 194
repression, p. 195
misinformation effect, p. 196
source amnesia, p. 197

REVIEW: MEMORY

STUDYING MEMORY: AN INFORMATION-PROCESSING MODEL

1 **How do psychologists describe our memory system?**

■ *Memory* is the persistence of learning over time through the *encoding, storage,* and *retrieval* of information.

■ Atkinson-Shiffrin's classic three-stage model of memory: (1) We register fleeting *sensory memories*; (2) some are processed into *short-term memories*; (3) even fewer are encoded for *long-term memory* and later retrieval.

■ Today's researchers note that we register much information unconsciously, bypassing the first two stages (sensory and short-term).

■ The term *working memory* is better than short-term memory for describing the more active role in this second stage, where we work to connect new input with older stored memories.

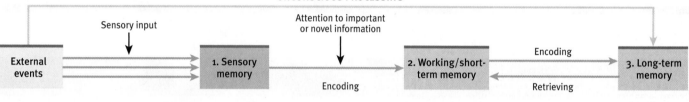

UNCONSCIOUS PROCESSING

Sensory input

Attention to important or novel information

External events → 1. Sensory memory → Encoding → 2. Working/short-term memory → Encoding → 3. Long-term memory

Retrieving

ENCODING: GETTING INFORMATION IN

2 **How do automatic and effortful processing help us encode sights, sounds, and other sensations?**

■ We unconsciously and *automatically process* some types of information, such as space, time, and frequency.

■ *Effortful processing*, including *rehearsal* that is *spaced* out over time, requires conscious attention and deliberate effort.

■ When learning a list, our later recall is often best for items learned first, which we may have rehearsed more (the *serial position effect*).

■ Effortful encoding of meaning and *imagery* improves long-term retention.

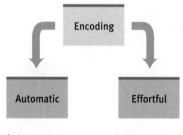

Encoding

Automatic — (Where you ate dinner yesterday)

Effortful — (This chapter's concepts)

STORAGE: RETAINING INFORMATION

3 **What are the limits of our memory, and how are memories stored in the brain?**

■ We lose sensory memories almost immediately, unless those memories are further processed.

■ In our working memory, we can focus on and process only about seven items of information. Without rehearsal, information disappears from working memory within seconds.

■ We have an unlimited capacity for storing information permanently in long-term memory.

■ *Long-term potentiation* (*LTP*) is a neural basis of our memory storage.

■ Stress triggers hormonal changes that arouse brain areas and can produce strong memories.

■ Vivid events form *flashbulb memories.*

■ *Explicit* (conscious) *memories* of general knowledge, facts, and experiences are processed by the hippocampus.

■ *Implicit* (unconscious) *memories* of skills and conditioned responses are processed by other parts of the brain, including the cerebellum.

RETRIEVAL: GETTING INFORMATION OUT

4 **What is involved in retrieving information from our memory?**

- *Recall:* retrieving information we learned earlier (fill-in-the-blank test).
- *Recognition:* identifying items previously learned (multiple-choice test).
- *Relearning:* more quickly mastering material that has been previously learned.
- *Retrieval cues,* such as context and *mood,* are information bits linked with the original encoded memory.

FORGETTING

5 **Why do we forget? At what points in the memory system can our memory fail us?**

- Encoding failure (information is never entered into memory system) from absent-mindedness, transience, or blocking.
- Storage decay (encoded information is later forgotten) through misattribution, suggestibility, or bias; measured by a gradual fading of the *memory trace* in the brain.
- Retrieval failure (lacking the right cues to access stored memories) through persistence; includes *interference.* Freud believed, but modern research does not support, the idea that we *repress* painful memories.

MEMORY CONSTRUCTION

6 **What factors affect the accuracy of our memories?**

- We construct our memories, using both stored and new information.
- *Misinformation* (exposure to misleading information) and *source amnesia* (attributing an event to the wrong source) both lead to false memories.
- Incest and abuse happen more than was once supposed. But unless the victim was a child too young to remember, such traumas are usually remembered vividly, not repressed.

IMPROVING MEMORY

7 **How can you improve your memory so that you do better in this and other courses?**

- Study repeatedly.
- Schedule spaced (not crammed) study times.
- Actively rehearse information to be learned.
- Make well-organized, vivid, and personally meaningful associations.
- Return to contexts and moods that are rich with association.
- Minimize interference.
- Self-test to rehearse information and find gaps in your memory.

TERROR ALERTS. IMAGES OF FATED PLANES. Security lines. Confinement in stuffed planes lifting off from planet Earth. It's enough to drive many passengers to take anti-anxiety drugs before flying.

When Gallup pollsters asked Americans to give their views of flying, only 40 percent chose the "not afraid at all" answer (Saad, 2006). Terrorism is near or at the top of Americans' list of concerns, far ahead of problems such as global climate change (Pew, 2007). Would it surprise you to find out that this epidemic of fear has little basis in fact? During the three years following 9/11 (2001 to 2003), Americans were, mile-per-mile, 37 times safer on commercial flights than in passenger vehicles (National Safety Council, 2008). Even earthbound trains put us at greater risk than do airlines.

Meanwhile, some 4 in 10 Americans worried that they or their family would be victims of a terrorist attack (Nacos & Shapiro, 2007). The odds that more terrorist attacks will occur are great. The odds that they will occur in the precise place we live or work or fly are tiny.

What drives us to fret about remote risks and to ignore bigger threats? Why do governments spend so much money to protect us against slim possibilities while ignoring higher probabilities? In this chapter, we consider these questions and more. In earlier chapters, we have studied the human brain—3 pounds of wet tissue the size of a small cabbage, yet containing circuitry more complex than the planet's telephone networks. From this complex circuitry emerge two images—the rational, thoughtful, and competent human, and the irrational, not-so-wise human prone to foolish judgments. We saw the thoughtful and competent human take form in the amazing abilities of newborns. We relished the power of the human sensory system, translating light and shapes into clear and colorful perceived images. We assessed our memory's almost unlimited capacity and the ease with which we process information, with and without awareness. Little wonder that our species has had the collective genius to invent the camera, the car, and the computer; to unlock the atom and crack the genetic code; to travel out to space and into the oceans' depths.

Yet we have also seen that our species is kin to the other animals, influenced by the same principles that produce learning in rats and pigeons. We have noted that we not-so-wise humans are easily fooled by perceptual illusions, fake psychic claims, and false memories.

In this chapter, we find more examples of these two images—the rational and the irrational human. We will consider how our active brain uses and misuses the information it receives, perceives, stores, and retrieves. We will look at our flair for language, and we will reflect on how deserving we are of the meaning of our species' name, *Homo sapiens*—wise human.

> "Fearful people are more dependent, more easily manipulated and controlled, more susceptible to deceptively simple, strong, tough measures and hard-line postures."
>
> Communications researcher George Gerbner, Congressional testimony, 1981

Thinking

Psychologists who study **cognition** focus on the mental activities associated with processing, understanding, remembering, and communicating information. Among these activities are the ways we solve problems, make decisions, form judgments, and assess risk.

Solving Problems

1: What strategies do we use to solve problems?

One tribute to our rationality is our impressive skill in solving problems and coping with new situations. What's the best route around this traffic jam? How should we respond to a friend's criticism? How can we get into the house when we've lost our keys?

Some problems we solve through trial and error. Thomas Edison tried thousands of light bulb filaments before stumbling upon one that worked. For other problems, we use **algorithms,** step-by-step procedures that guarantee a solution. But following the steps in an algorithm takes time and effort—sometimes a lot of time and effort. To find a word using the 10 letters in *SPLOYOCHYG*, for example, you could construct a list, with each letter in each of the 10 positions. But your list of 907,200 different combinations would be very long! In such cases, we often resort to **heuristics,** simpler thinking strategies. Thus, you might reduce the number of options in the *SPLOYOCHYG* example by grouping letters that often appear together (CH and GY) and avoiding rare combinations (such as YY). By using heuristics and then applying trial and error, you may hit on the answer. Have you guessed it? Turn the next page to check your answer.

Sometimes, our problem-solving strategy seems to be no strategy at all. We puzzle over a problem, and the pieces suddenly fall together as the solution hits us in a flash of **insight.** Ten-year-old Johnny Appleton's insight solved a problem that had stumped many adults: how

Heuristic searching To search for a certain kind of energy drink, you could search every supermarket aisle (an algorithm). Or you could check the bottled beverage and natural foods sections (heuristics). The heuristic approach is often speedier, but an algorithmic search guarantees you will find it eventually.

B₂M Productions/Digital Vision/Getty Images

to rescue a young robin that had fallen into a narrow, 30-inch-deep hole in a cement-block wall. Johnny's solution: slowly pour in sand, giving the bird enough time to keep its feet on top of the constantly rising mound (Ruchlis, 1990).

Insight gives us a sense of satisfaction, a feeling of happiness. The joy of a joke is similarly a sudden "I get it!" reaction to a surprise ending or a double meaning. See for yourself, with these two jokes rated funniest (among 2 million ratings of 40,000 submitted jokes) in an Internet humor study (Wiseman, 2002). First, the runner-up:

> Sherlock Holmes and Dr. Watson are going camping. They pitch their tent under the stars and go to sleep. Sometime in the middle of the night Holmes awakens Watson.
>
> *Holmes:* "Watson, look up at the stars, and tell me what you deduce."
>
> *Watson:* "I see millions of stars and even if a few of those have planets, it's quite likely there are some planets like Earth, and if there are a few planets like Earth out there, there might also be life. What does it tell you, Holmes?"
>
> *Holmes:* "Watson, you idiot, somebody has stolen our tent!"

And drum roll, please, for the winner:

> A couple of New Jersey hunters are out in the woods when one of them falls to the ground. He doesn't seem to be breathing, his eyes are rolled back in his head. The other guy whips out his cellphone and calls the emergency services. He gasps to the operator: "My friend is dead! What can I do?" The operator, in a calm, soothing voice says: "Just take it easy. I can help. First, let's make sure he's dead." There is a silence, then a shot is heard. The guy's voice comes back on the line: "OK, now what?"

Making Good (and Bad) Decisions and Judgments

2: What obstacles hinder smart thinking?

Each day holds hundreds of judgments and decisions. Is it worth the bother to take an umbrella? Can I trust this person? Should I shoot the basketball or pass to the player who's hot? As we judge the odds and make our decisions, we seldom take the time and effort to reason systematically. We just follow our *intuition,* our gut feeling. After interviewing leaders in government, business, and education, social psychologist Irving Janis (1986) concluded that these leaders "often do not use a reflective problem-solving approach. How do they usually arrive at their decisions? If you ask, they are likely to tell you . . . they do it mostly by *the seat of their pants.*"

Confirmation Bias

Have you ever had an argument with someone and searched for evidence to support your views? We all seek evidence for our ideas more eagerly than we seek evidence *against* them (Klayman & Ha, 1987; Skov & Sherman, 1986). This tendency is **confirmation bias,** and Peter Wason (1960) demonstrated it in a now-classic study. He gave students a three-number sequence (2-4-6) and told them the sequence was based on a rule. Their task was to guess the rule. (It was simple: Each of the three numbers must be larger than the one it follows.) Before giving their answers, students formed their own three-number sets, and Wason told them whether their sets worked with his rule. Once they felt certain they had the rule, they were to announce it. The result? They were seldom right but never in doubt. Most students formed a wrong idea ("Maybe it's counting by twos") and then searched only for evidence confirming the wrong rule (by testing 6-8-10, 100-102-104, and so forth).

In real-life disagreements, said Wason (1981), "ordinary people evade facts, become inconsistent, or systematically defend themselves against the threat of new information." The process can have grave results. The U.S. war against Iraq was launched on the belief that the late Saddam Hussein was hiding weapons of mass destruction (WMDs). That belief turned out to be false. When a U.S. Senate committee (with members from both political parties) investigated, they found flaws in the judgment process, including confirmation bias (U.S. Senate Select Committee on Intelligence, 2004). Administration analysts "had a tendency to accept information which supported [their beliefs] . . . more readily than information which contradicted" them. Sources denying such weapons were viewed to be "either lying or not knowledgeable about Iraq's problems, while those sources who reported ongoing WMD activities were seen as having provided valuable information."

Quick-Thinking Heuristics

When we need to act quickly, those mental shortcuts we call *heuristics* often do help us overcome analysis paralysis.

"In creating these problems, we didn't set out to fool people. All our problems fooled us, too." (Amos Tversky, 1985)

Courtesy of Greymayer Award, University of Louisville and the Tversky family

Without awareness, we make automatic intuitive judgments. But cognitive psychologists Amos Tversky and Daniel Kahneman (1974) showed how these shortcuts can lead even the smartest people into quick but dumb judgments, as when fearing the wrong things.

"Intuitive thinking [is] fine most of the time. . . . But sometimes that habit of mind gets us in trouble." (Nobel laureate Daniel Kahneman, 2005)

Courtesy of Greymayer Award, University of Louisville and Daniel Kahneman

"The problem is I can't tell the difference between a deeply wise, intuitive nudge from the Universe and one of my own bone-headed ideas!"

The **availability heuristic** operates when we base our judgments on how quickly and easily an event comes to mind. The faster we can remember an instance of some event (a broken promise, for example), the more we expect it to happen again (MacLeod & Campbell, 1992). Mentally available events *are* more likely to repeat—but not always. To see this, try answering this question: Does the letter *k* appear more often as the first or third letter in English words?

cognition the mental activities associated with thinking, knowing, remembering, and communicating.

algorithm a methodical, logical rule or procedure that guarantees you will solve a particular problem. Contrasts with the usually speedier—but also more error-prone—use of *heuristics*.

heuristic a simple thinking strategy that often allows us to make judgments and solve problems efficiently; usually speedier but also more error-prone than *algorithms*.

insight a sudden realization of the solution to a problem; it contrasts with strategy-based solutions.

confirmation bias a tendency to search for information that confirms our preconceptions.

availability heuristic estimating the likelihood of an event based on its availability in memory; if instances come readily to mind (perhaps because of their vividness), we assume such events are common.

Answer to SPLOYOCHYG problem presented earlier: PSYCHOLOGY.

Did you guess that *k* occurs more frequently as the first letter? Most people do, because words beginning with *k* come to mind more easily than words having *k* as their third letter. Actually, *k* appears more often as the third letter. So far in this chapter, words such as *know, kingdom,* and *kin* are outnumbered 22 to 5 by words such as *make, likely, asked,* and *acknowledged.*

The availability heuristic can lead us astray in our judgments of other people, too. Anything that makes information "pop" into mind—how recently we heard about an event, how vivid and concrete it was, or how distinctive—can make it more available to our memory. If someone from a particular ethnic group commits a terrorist act, our readily available memory of the dramatic event may shape our impression of the whole group. When statistical reality is pitted against a single vivid case, the vivid case often wins.

Sometimes heuristics can lead to **fixation**—an inability to see a problem from a fresh perspective. Once we get hung up on an incorrect view of a problem, it's hard to approach it from a different angle. If you can't solve the matchstick problem in **FIGURE 8.1,** you may be experiencing fixation. (Turn the next page to see the solution in **FIGURE 8.3.**)

Figure 8.1> The matchstick problem
How would you arrange six matches to form four equilateral triangles?

Overconfidence: Was There Ever Any Doubt?

Using heuristics and relying on our intuition often feels so right that we become **overconfident.** We overestimate the accuracy of our beliefs and decisions. Too often, however, we're more confident than correct. When answering such questions as, "Is absinthe a liqueur or a precious stone?" only 60 percent of people in one study answered correctly. (It's a licorice-flavored liqueur.) But correct or not, those answering felt 75 percent confident. Even those who felt 100 percent certain of their answer were wrong about 15 percent of the time (Fischhoff & others, 1977).

> "Don't believe everything you think."
> **Bumper sticker**

History is full of leaders who were more confident than correct. It was an overconfident Lyndon Johnson who waged war with North Vietnam and an overconfident George W. Bush who marched into Iraq to save us from supposed weapons of mass destruction. And classrooms are full of overconfident students who expect to finish assignments and write papers ahead of schedule (Buehler & others, 1994). In fact, the projects generally take about twice the number of days predicted.

We tend to overestimate our future free time (Zauberman & Lynch, 2005). Thinking we will have more free time next month than we do today, we happily accept invitations, only to discover we're just as busy when the day rolls around.

Despite our painfully wrong estimates, we remain overly confident of our next prediction. And overconfidence does have adaptive value. Self-confident people, believing that their decisions are right and they have time to spare, live more happily, make tough decisions more easily, and seem more believable than others (Baumeister, 1989; Taylor, 1989). Moreover, given prompt and clear feedback—as weather forecasters receive after each day's predictions—people can learn to be more realistic about the accuracy of their

Predict your own behavior :: When will you finish reading this chapter?

judgments (Fischhoff, 1982). The wisdom to know when we know a thing and when we do not is born of experience.

> "When you know a thing, to hold that you know it; and when you do not know a thing, to allow that you do not know it; this is knowledge."
> **Confucius (551–479 B.C.),** *Analects*

Framing: Let Me Put It This Way . . .

Framing is the way we present an issue, and its effects can be striking. Imagine two surgeons discussing the risk of surgery, presenting the issue in two different but equally logical ways. One tells patients that 10 percent of people will die while undergoing this surgery. The other tells patients that 90 percent will survive. In surveys, both patients and physicians said the risk seems greater when they hear that 10 percent will die (Marteau, 1989; McNeil & others, 1988; Rothman & Salovey, 1997). Similarly, 9 in 10 college students rate a condom as effective if told it has a "95 percent success rate" in stopping the HIV virus. Only 4 in 10 judge it effective when told it has a "5 percent failure rate" (Linville & others, 1992).

Those who understand the power of framing can use it to influence our decisions. For example, politicians may frame survey questions to gather support for a particular viewpoint or to spread fear. People told that a chemical exposure will kill 10 of every 10 million people (imagine 10 dead people!) feel more frightened than if told the fatality risk is an infinitesimal .000001 (Kraus & others, 1992). Retailers who understand the power of framing may mark up their "regular prices" to appear to offer huge savings on "sale prices." A $100 coat marked down from $150 by Store X can seem like a better deal than the same coat priced regularly at $100 by Store Y (Urbany & others, 1988). Try it yourself. Would you rather have a hamburger that is "75 percent lean" or one that is "25 percent fat" (Levin & Gaeth, 1988; Sanford & others, 2002)? The information is the same. The effect is not.

Our Beliefs Live On— Despite the Evidence

That our judgments can flip-flop dramatically is startling. Equally startling is our unwillingness to give up our beliefs even when the evidence proves us wrong. **Belief perseverance** often fuels social conflict, as it did in one study of people with opposing views of the death penalty (Lord & others, 1979). Both sides were asked to read the same material—two reports on new research. One report showed that the death penalty lowers the crime rate. The other report showed that the death penalty has no effect on the crime rate. Were people's views changed by reading these studies? Not a bit. Each side was very impressed by the study supporting its own beliefs, and each was quick to criticize the other study. Thus, showing the two groups the same mixed evidence actually *increased* their disagreement about the value of capital punishment.

So how can we avoid belief perseverance? A simple remedy is to *consider the opposite*. In a repeat of the capital-punishment study, researchers (Lord & others, 1984) asked some participants to be "as *objective* and *unbiased* as possible." This plea did nothing to reduce people's biases in judging the evidence. They also asked another group to consider "whether you would have made the same

high or low evaluations had exactly the same study produced results on the *other* side of the issue." These people did imagine and ponder *opposite* findings, and their evaluations of the evidence were much less biased.

The more we come to appreciate why our beliefs might be true, the more tightly we cling to them. Once we have explained to ourselves why we believe a child is "gifted" or "learning disabled" or why candidate X or Y will be more likely to help working folks, we tend to ignore evidence that challenges our belief. Prejudice persists. Once beliefs form and get justified, it takes more compelling evidence to change them than it did to create them.

Assessing Risk

3: How can we improve our risk assessment?

Why do we fear the wrong things? Why do we judge terrorism to be a greater risk than accidents? In the United States alone, accidents kill nearly as many people in

one week as terrorists killed worldwide in all of the 1990s (2527 people) (Johnson, 2001). Even with the horror of 9/11, more Americans in 2001 died of food poisoning (which scares few) than of terrorism (which scares many).

Nevertheless, after 9/11, many people feared safe flying more than riskier driving. Indeed, in the last three months of 2001, there were significantly more U.S. traffic fatalities than in the same three months in the previous five years (Gigerenzer, 2004; see **FIGURE 8.2**). Long after 9/11, the dead terrorists were still

fixation the inability to see a problem from a new perspective; an impediment to problem solving.

overconfidence the tendency to be more confident than correct—to overestimate the accuracy of your beliefs and judgments.

framing the way an issue is posed; framing can significantly affect decisions and judgments.

belief perseverance clinging to beliefs and ignoring evidence that proves they are wrong.

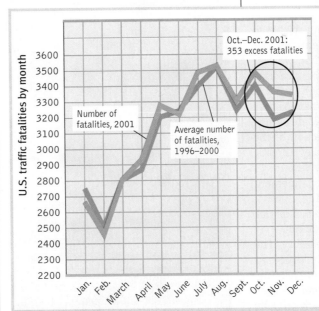

Figure 8.2> Scaring us onto deadly highways Images of 9/11 etched a sharper image in our minds than did the millions of fatality-free flights on U.S. airlines during 2002 and after. Such dramatic events, being readily available to memory, shape our perceptions of risk. In the three months after 9/11, those faulty perceptions led more people to travel, and some to die, by car. (Adapted from Gigerenzer, 2004.)

Figure 8.3> Solution to the match-stick problem Were you, by chance, fixated on two-dimensional solutions? Solving problems often requires taking a new angle on the situation.

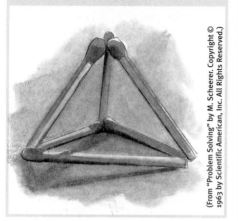

killing Americans by sending them back to their cars. During 2002, 2003, and 2004, air travel gradually recovered. Nearly 2 billion passengers flew on U.S. commercial flights. How many of them died? Only 34—none on a major airline's big jet (Miller, 2005). Meanwhile, traffic accidents claimed 128,000 American lives.

How can our intuition about risk be so wrong? Psychologists have identified four forces that feed our fears. First, we fear *what our ancestral history has prepared us to fear.* Human emotions were road-tested in the Stone Age. Yesterday's risks prepare us to fear snakes, lizards, and spiders (which combined now kill a tiny fraction of the number killed by modern-day threats, such as cars and cigarettes). Yesterday's risks also prepare us to fear confinement and heights, and therefore flying.

Second, we fear *what we cannot control.* Driving we control, flying we do not.

Third, we fear *what is immediate.* The dangers of flying are mostly squeezed into the moments of takeoff and landing. The dangers of driving are spread across many moments to come, each trivially dangerous.

Fourth, we fear *what is most readily available in memory.* Powerful, available memories—like the image of United Flight 175 slicing into the World Trade Center—

serve as our measuring tapes as we intuitively judge risks. Thousands of car trips lull us into a comfortable safe feeling.

Numbers can be numbing. Vivid images we remember, and they distort our comprehension of risks and probable outcomes. We comprehend disasters that kill people dramatically, in bunches, as hurricanes and earthquakes kill. But we fear too little those threats that claim lives undramatically, one by one, and in the distant future. As Bill Gates has noted, each year a half-million children worldwide die quietly, one by one, from rotavirus. This is the equivalent of four 747s full of children *every day,* and we hear nothing of it (Glass, 2004). Dramatic outcomes capture our attention; probabilities don't.

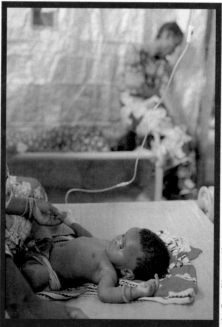

Less dramatic deaths :: The memorable South Asian tsunami in 2004 that killed some 300,000 people stirred an outpouring of concern and new tsunami-warning technology. Meanwhile, a "silent tsunami" of poverty-related malaria was killing about that many of the world's children every couple of months, noted Jeffrey Sachs, the head of a United Nations project aiming to cut extreme poverty in half by 2015 (Dugger, 2005).

The point to remember: It is perfectly normal to fear violence from those who hate us. When terrorists strike again, we will all fall back in horror. But try to remember this: *Check your fears against the facts, and resist people who serve their own purposes by feeding a culture of fear.* By thinking smart, we can take away the terrorists' most powerful weapon: exaggerated fear.

The Perils and Powers of Intuition

4: When is intuition useful?

We have seen how our irrational thinking can plague our efforts to solve problems, make wise decisions, form valid judgments, and assess risks. Moreover, these perils of *intuition* appear even when people are offered extra pay for thinking smart, even when they are asked to justify their answers, and even when they are expert physicians or clinicians (Shafir & LeBoeuf, 2002). From this we might conclude that we fail to live up to our species' name, *Homo sapiens* (wise human).

But we must not abandon hope for human rationality. Throughout this book, you have also seen intuition's powers. For the most part, our instant, intuitive reactions enable us to react quickly and *usually* adaptively.

In showing how everyday heuristics usually make us smart (and only sometimes make us dumb), researchers asked both American and German university students, "Which city has more inhabitants: San Diego or San Antonio?" (Gigerenzer, 2004). After thinking a moment, 62 percent of the Americans guessed right: San Diego. Many German students had not heard of San Antonio (apologies to our Texas friends). Instead, they used a fast and intuitive heuristic: Pick the name you recognize. With less knowledge but an adaptive heuristic, 100 percent of the German students answered correctly.

In summary: *Intuition is huge.* More than we realize, thinking occurs off-screen, with the results occasionally

"I'm happy to say that my final judgment of a case is almost always consistent with my prejudgment of the case."

displayed on-screen. *Intuition is adaptive.* It feeds our expertise, our creativity, our love, and our spirituality. *Intuition is born of experience.* Playing "blitz chess," where every move is made after barely more than a glance, chess masters can look at a board and intuitively know the right move (Burns, 2004). Sorting chicks, experienced chicken sexers can tell you a bird's sex at a glance, yet cannot tell you how they do it. In each case, what feels like instant intuition is a speedy use of expert skill and knowledge. Experienced nurses, firefighters, art critics, car mechanics, hockey players, and you, for anything in which you develop a deep and special knowledge, learn to size up

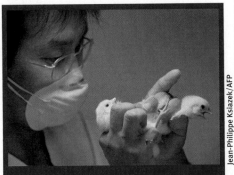

Chick sexing :: When acquired expertise becomes an automatic habit, as it is for experienced chick sexers, it feels like intuition. At a glance, they just know.

many a situation in an eyeblink. And *intuition is recognition*. As Nobel laureate psychologist-economist Herbert Simon (2001) observed, it is analysis "frozen into habit."

Mindful of intuition's perils and powers, we can think smarter. Our gut intuitions are terrific at some things, such as instantly reading emotions in others' faces, but not so good at others, such as assessing risks. Wisdom comes with knowing the difference.

PRACTICE TEST

1. The most systematic procedure for solving a problem is
   a. a heuristic.
   b. an algorithm.
   c. insight.
   d. intuition.

2. A major obstacle to problem solving is *fixation,* which is
   a. a tendency to base our judgments on vivid memories.
   b. the art of framing the same question in two different ways.
   c. an inability to view a problem from a new perspective.
   d. the tendency to overestimate the accuracy of our own beliefs and judgments.

3. After the 9/11 attacks by foreign-born terrorists, some people initially assumed that the 2003 East Coast blackout was probably also the work of foreign-born terrorists. This assumption illustrates
   a. belief perseverance.
   b. the availability heuristic.
   c. fixation.
   d. confirmation bias.

4. The way an issue is presented can affect our decisions and judgments. This is called
   a. belief perseverance.
   b. fixation.
   c. confirmation bias.
   d. framing.

Answers: 1. b, 2. c, 3. b, 4. d.

Language

The most obvious indication of our thinking power is **language**—our spoken, written, or signed words and the ways we combine them as we think and communicate. Humans have long and proudly proclaimed that language sets us above all other animals. "When we study human language," asserted linguist Noam Chomsky (1972), "we are approaching what some might call the 'human essence,' the qualities of mind that are, so far as we know, unique [to humans]."

Imagine an alien species that could pass thoughts from one head to another merely by setting air molecules in motion between them. Perhaps these weird creatures could star in a future Spielberg movie? Actually, we are those creatures! When we speak, we send air pressure waves banging against other people's eardrums—as we transfer thoughts from our brain into theirs. As Steven Pinker (1998) notes, we sometimes sit for hours "listening to other people make noise as they exhale, because those hisses and squeaks contain *information*." And thanks to all those funny sounds created from the air pressure waves we send out, we get people's attention, we get them to do things, and we maintain relationships (Guerin, 2003).

When our capacity for language evolved, it catapulted our species forward (Diamond, 1989). Whether spoken, written, or signed, language enables us not only to communicate but to transmit civilization's knowledge from one generation

"The average newspaper boy in Pittsburgh knows more about the universe than did Galileo, Aristotle, Leonardo, or any of those other guys who were so smart they only needed one name."

Daniel Gilbert, *Stumbling on Happiness*, 2006

language our spoken, written, or signed words and the ways we combine them to communicate meaning.

to the next. Monkeys mostly know what they see. Thanks to language, we know much that we've never seen.

Language Development

5: When do children acquire language, and how do they master this complex task?

Make a quick guess: How many words did you learn during the years between your first birthday and your high school graduation? Ready? The answer is about 60,000 (Bloom, 2000). That averages nearly 3500 words each year, or 10 each day! How you did it—how the 3500 words could so far outnumber the roughly 200 words your schoolteachers consciously taught you each year—is one of the great human wonders.

> Although you probably know between 60,000 and 80,000 words in your native language, you use only 150 words for about half of what you say.

Could you even now state all your language's rules of *syntax* (the correct way to string words together to form sentences)? Most of us cannot. Yet, before you were able to add 2 + 2, you were creating your own original sentences and applying these rules. As a preschooler, your ability to understand and speak your language was so great it would put to shame high schoolers struggling to learn a foreign language.

We humans have a knack for language. Without blinking, we sample tens of thousands of words in our memory, effortlessly combine them with near-perfect syntax, and spew them out three words a second (Vigliocco & Hartsuiker, 2002). We also fine-tune our language to our social and cultural setting, following rules for speaking (How far apart should we stand?) and listening (Is it OK to interrupt?). Given how many ways there are to mess up, it is amazing that we effortlessly master this social dance. So, when and how does it happen?

When Do We Learn Language?

Children's language development moves from simplicity to complexity. Infants start without language (*in fantis* means "not speaking"). Yet by 4 months of age, babies are reading lips and sorting out speech sounds. They prefer to look at a face that matches a sound, so we know they can recognize that *ah* comes from wide open lips and *ee* from a mouth with corners pulled back (Kuhl & Meltzoff, 1982). This marks the beginning of the development of babies' *receptive language,* their ability to understand what is said to and about them. Babies' receptive language abilities begin to mature before their *productive language,* their ability to produce words.

Around 4 months of age, babies enter a **babbling stage** in which they seem to sample all the sounds they can make, such as *ah-goo.* Babbling is not an imitation of adult speech. We know this because babbling includes sounds from various languages, including those not spoken in the household. From this early babbling, a listener could not identify an infant as being, say, French, Korean, or Ethiopian.

By the time infants are about 10 months old, their babbling has changed so that a trained ear can identify the language of the household (de Boysson-Bardies & others, 1989). Deaf infants who observe their deaf parents signing begin to babble more with their hands (Petitto & Marentette, 1991). Without exposure to other languages, babies lose their ability to hear and produce sounds and tones found outside their native language (Pallier & others, 2001). Thus, by adulthood those who speak only English cannot discriminate certain sounds in Japanese speech. Nor can Japanese adults with no training in English hear the difference between the English *r* and *l*. Thus, *la-la-ra-ra* may sound like the same repeated syllable to a Japanese-speaking adult. This makes life challenging for a Japanese speaker who is told the train station is "just after the next light." The next what? After the street veering right, or farther down, after the traffic light?

"Got idea. Talk better. Combine words. Make sentences."

© 1994 by Sidney Harris.

Around their first birthday, most children enter the **one-word stage.** They already know that sounds carry meanings. They now begin to use sounds—usually only one barely recognizable syllable, such as *ma* or *da*—to communicate meaning. But family members quickly learn to understand, and gradually the infant's language sounds more like the family's language. At this one-word stage, a single word ("Doggy!") may equal a sentence ("Look at the dog out there!").

At about 18 months, children's word learning explodes from about a word per week to a word per day. By their second birthday, most have entered the **two-word stage.** They start uttering two-word sentences **(TABLE 8.1)** in **telegraphic speech.** Like today's text messages or yesterday's telegrams that charged by the word (TERMS ACCEPTED. SEND MONEY.), a 2-year-old's speech contains mostly nouns and verbs (*Want juice*). Also like telegrams, it follows rules of syntax; the words are in a sensible order. English-speaking children typically place adjectives before nouns—*white house* rather than *house white*. Spanish adjectives usually come after nouns, so a Spanish speaker says *casa blanca.*

Moving out of the two-word stage, children quickly begin speaking in longer phrases (Fromkin & Rodman, 1983). By early elementary school, they understand

Table 8.1	Summary of Language Development
Month (approximate)	Stage
4	Babbles many speech sounds ("ah-goo").
10	Babbling resembles household language ("ma-ma").
12	One-word stage ("Kitty!").
24	Two-word, telegraphic speech ("Get ball.").
24+	Language develops rapidly into complete sentences.

complex sentences and can enjoy a joke with a double meaning: "You never starve in the desert because of all the sand-which-is there."

How Do We Learn Grammar?

Chomsky argues that all languages share a *universal grammar,* and that we humans are born with a built-in readiness to learn grammar rules. Thus, all human languages have the same grammatical building blocks, such as nouns and verbs, subjects and objects, negations and questions. This readiness to learn grammar rules helps explain why preschoolers pick up language so readily and use grammar so well. It happens so naturally—as naturally as birds learn to fly—that training hardly helps. Once again, we see biology and experience working together.

We are not, however, born with a built-in *specific* language. Babies born in Mexico learn to speak Spanish, not Chinese. We learn readily the specific grammar of the language we experience, whether it is spoken or signed (Bavelier & others, 2003). No matter what that language is, we start speaking mostly in nouns (*kitty, da-da*) rather than verbs and adjectives (Bornstein & others, 2004).

Childhood seems to represent a *critical period* for mastering certain aspects of language. Deaf children who gain hearing with *cochlear implants* by age 2 develop better oral speech than do those who receive implants after age 4 (Greers, 2004). For deaf or hearing children, later-than-usual exposure to language—at age 2 or 3—unleashes their brain's idle language capacity, producing a rush of language. But there is no similar rush of learning for children who are not exposed to either a spoken or a signed language until age 7. Such deprived children lose their ability to master *any* language.

Creating a language :: Young deaf children in Nicaragua were brought together as if on a desert island (actually a school). They drew upon sign gestures from their own home to create their own Nicaraguan Sign Language, complete with words and intricate grammar. Our biological predisposition for language does not create language in a vacuum. But activated by a social context, nature and nurture work creatively together (Osborne, 1999; Sandler & others, 2005; Senghas & Coppola, 2001).

Susan Meiselas/Magnum Photos

After the window for learning language closes, even learning a second language becomes more difficult. If you learn a second language as an adult, you will almost certainly speak it with the accent of your first. Learning the grammar of the second language will also take effort. In one study (Johnson & Newport, 1991), Korean and Chinese immigrants read 276 English sentences, such as "Yesterday the hunter shoots a deer." They scored each sentence as either grammatically correct or incorrect. Some test-takers had arrived in the United States in early childhood, others as adults, but all had been in the country for approximately 10 years. Nevertheless, as **FIGURE 8.4** on the next page reveals, those who learned their second language early learned it best. The older we are when moving to a new country, the harder it will be to learn the new language (Hakuta & others, 2003).

> "Childhood is the time for language, no doubt about it. Young children, the younger the better, are good at it; it is child's play. It is a onetime gift to the species."
>
> Lewis Thomas, *The Fragile Species,* 1992

The impact of early experiences is also evident in language learning in the 90+ percent of deaf children born to hearing-nonsigning parents. These children typically do not experience language during their early years. Compared

babbling stage beginning at about 4 months, the stage of speech development in which the infant spontaneously utters various sounds at first unrelated to the household language.

one-word stage the stage in speech development, from about age 1 to 2, during which a child speaks mostly in single words.

two-word stage beginning about age 2, the stage in speech development during which a child speaks mostly two-word statements.

telegraphic speech early speech stage in which a child speaks like a telegram—"go car"—using mostly nouns and verbs.

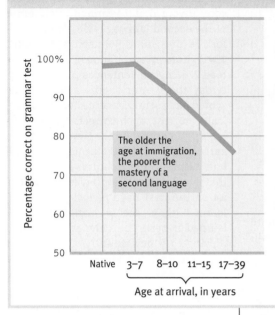

Figure 8.4> New language learning gets harder with age Young children have a readiness to learn language. Ten years after coming to the United States, Asian immigrants took a grammar test. Those who arrived before age 8 understood American English grammar as well as native speakers did. Those who arrived later did not. (From Johnson & Newport, 1991.)

The older the age at immigration, the poorer the mastery of a second language

with children exposed to sign language from birth, those who learn to sign as teens or adults are like immigrants who learn a new language after childhood. They can master the basic words and learn to order them, but they never become as fluent as native signers in producing and comprehending subtle grammatical differences (Newport, 1990).

Moreover, natively deaf children who do not learn sign language until after age 9 learn it better if they have been previously exposed to a language such as English. And natively deaf children who learn to sign in infancy have an easier time learning English (Mayberry & others, 2002). The striking conclusion: When a young brain does not learn *any* language, its language-learning capacity never fully develops. Brain scans show the difference. The late-learners show less brain activity in right-hemisphere regions that are active as native signers read sign language (Newman & others, 2002). As a flower's growth will be stunted without nourishment, so, too, will children become linguistically stunted if isolated from language during the critical period for its acquisition.

How deserving are we of our name *Homo sapiens?* Let's pause to issue an interim report card. On decision making and judgment, our error-prone species might rate a C+. On problem solving, where humans are inventive yet subject to confirmation bias and fixation, we would probably receive better marks, perhaps a B. On cognitive efficiency, our fallible but quick heuristics earn us an A. And when it comes to learning and using language, the awestruck experts would surely award the human species an A+.

Thinking Without Language

6: How can thinking in images be useful?

To turn on the cold water in your bathroom, in which direction do you turn the handle? To answer this question, you probably thought not in words but in images—perhaps a mental picture of your hand turning the faucet.

Indeed, we often think in images. Pianist Liu Chi Kung showed the value of this process. One year after placing second in a worldwide piano competition, Liu was imprisoned during China's cultural revolution. Soon after his release, after seven years without touching a piano, he was back on tour. The critics judged his playing to be better than ever, and his fans wondered how he had continued to develop without practice. "I did practice," said Liu, "every day. I rehearsed every piece I had ever played, note by note, in my mind" (Garfield, 1986).

Mental practice is now an accepted part of training for many athletes, including Olympic athletes (Suinn, 1997). One experiment observed the University of Tennessee women's basketball team (Savoy & Beitel, 1996). Over 35 games, researchers tracked the team's skill at shooting free throws following standard physical practice or mental practice. After physical practice, the team scored about 52 percent of their shots. After mental practice, that score rose to 65 percent. During mental practice, players had repeatedly imagined making foul shots under various conditions, including being "trash-talked" by their opposition. In a dramatic conclusion, Tennessee won that season's national championship game in overtime, thanks in part to their foul shooting.

So how does mental practice work its magic? Once you have learned a skill, even *watching* that event will flip a switch in the brain, triggering activity in the same areas that are active when you are actually using that skill. One research team showed this in functional MRI scans (fMRIs) as ballet dancers watched ballet videos (Calvo-Merino & others, 2004).

Even imagining an event can trigger brain activity. **FIGURE 8.5** shows an fMRI of a person imagining the experience of pain, activating neural networks that are active during actual pain (Grèzes & Decety, 2001).

Knowing all this, you can use mental rehearsal to help achieve your academic goals. One study (Taylor & others, 1998) demonstrated this with two groups of introductory psychology students facing a midterm exam one week later. (A third control group did not engage in any mental simulation.) The first group spent five minutes each day imagining themselves scanning the posted grade list, seeing their A, beaming with joy, and feeling proud. This daily *outcome simulation* had little effect, adding only 2 points to their average exam score. A second group spent five minutes each day imagining themselves effectively studying—reading the chapters, going over notes, eliminating distractions, declining an offer to go out. This daily *process simulation* paid off—this second group began studying sooner, spent more time at it, and beat the other students' average by 8 points. *The point to remember:* Mental practice is more effective if you spend your fantasy time planning how to get somewhere, rather than focusing on the imagined destination.

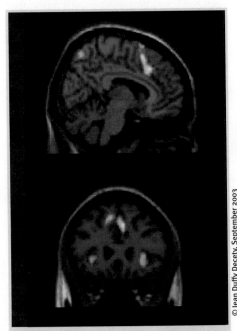

© Jean Duffy Decety, September 2003

Figure 8.5> The power of imagination These fMRIs show a person imagining the experience of pain, which activates some of the same areas in the brain as the actual experience of pain.

A thoughtful art :: Playing the piano engages thinking without language. In the absence of a piano, mental practice can sustain one's skill.

Courtesy Christine Brune

Experiments on thinking without language bring us back to a principle we've seen in earlier chapters: Much of our information processing occurs outside of consciousness and beyond language. Inside our ever-active brain, many streams of activity flow at once, function automatically, are remembered without our awareness, and only occasionally surface as conscious words.

PRACTICE TEST

5. The one-word stage of speech development is usually reached at about
   a. 4 months.
   b. 6 months.
   c. 1 year.
   d. 2 years.

6. According to Chomsky, we _____ to learn the grammar rules of language.
   a. must receive instruction
   b. are born with a built-in readiness
   c. need rewards for babbling and other early verbal behaviors
   d. must imitate and drill

Answers: 5. c, 6. b.

Animal Thinking and Language

7: Do animals—in some sense we can identify with—think? Do they even exhibit language?

If in our use of language we humans are, as the psalm says, "little lower than God," where do other animals fit in the scheme of things? Are they "little lower than human"? Let's see what the research on animal thinking and language can tell us.

Do Animals Think?

Animals display remarkable capacities for thinking. This is especially true of the *great apes*—a category that includes chimpanzees and gorillas. They can, for example, *form concepts,* such as "cat" and "dog." After monkeys learn these concepts, certain frontal lobe neurons in their brains fire in response to new "catlike" images, others to new "doglike" images (Freedman & others, 2001). Even pigeons—mere birdbrains—can sort objects (pictures of cars, cats, chairs, flowers) into groups of similar items. Shown a picture of a never-before-seen chair, the pigeon will reliably peck a key that represents the category "chairs" (Wasserman, 1995).

We also are not the only creatures to display *insight,* as psychologist Wolfgang Köhler (1925) demonstrated in an experiment with Sultan, a chimpanzee. Köhler placed a piece of fruit and a long stick well beyond Sultan's reach, and a short stick inside his cage. Spying the short stick, Sultan grabbed it and tried to reach the fruit. After several failed attempts, Sultan dropped the stick and seemed to survey the situation. Then suddenly, as if thinking "Aha!" he jumped up, seized the short stick again, and used it to pull in the longer stick—which he then used to reach the fruit. This was clear evidence of animal thinking, said Köhler, showing that there is more to their learning than conditioning.

Conditioning does play a role in animal behavior, of course. Operant conditioning principles say that we will repeat

Figure 8.6> Cultural transmission (a) On the western bank of one Ivory Coast river, a youngster watches as its mother uses a stone hammer to open a nut. On the river's other side, a few miles away, chimpanzees do not follow this custom. (b) This bottlenose dolphin in Shark Bay, Western Australia, is a member of a small group that uses marine sponges as a protective nose guard when probing the sea floor for fish.

Copyright Amanda K. Coakes

(a)

Michael Nichols/National Geographic Image Collection

(b)

behaviors that have good results. Searching for a solution to a problem, chimpanzees, like humans, are *shaped by reinforcement.* For example, forest-dwelling chimpanzees have become natural tool users (Boesch-Achermann & Boesch, 1993). They select different tools for different purposes—a heavy stick for making holes, a light, flexible stick for fishing for termites (Sanz & others, 2004). They break off the reed or stick, strip off any leaves, and carry it to a termite mound. Then they twist it just so and carefully remove it. Termites for lunch! (This is very reinforcing for a chimpanzee.) One anthropologist, trying to mimic the animal's deft fishing moves, failed miserably.

Researchers have found at least 39 local customs related to chimpanzee tool use, grooming, and courtship (Whiten & Boesch, 2001). One group may slurp termites directly from a stick, another group may pluck them off individually. One group may break nuts with a stone hammer, another with a wooden hammer. Such group differences, along with differing styles of communication and hunting, seem not to be genetic. Rather, they are the chimpanzee version of cultural diversity. Like humans, chimpanzees invent behaviors and *transmit cultural patterns to* their peers and offspring **(FIGURE 8.6a).** So do orangutans (van Schaik & others, 2003). And so do some Australian dolphins **(FIGURE 8.6b),** which have learned to break off and wear sponges to protect their snouts when probing the sea floor for fish (Krützen & others, 2005).

Several experiments (Horner & others, 2006) have brought chimpanzee cultural transmission into the laboratory. If Chimpanzee A obtains food either by sliding or by lifting a door, Chimpanzee B will then typically do the same to get food. And so will Chimpanzee C after observing Chimpanzee B. Across a chain of six animals, chimpanzees see, and chimpanzees do.

Do Animals Have Language?

Without doubt, animals communicate. Consider vervet monkeys. They sound different alarm cries for different predators: a barking call for a leopard, a cough for an eagle, and a chuttering for a snake. Hearing the leopard alarm, other vervets climb the nearest tree. Hearing the eagle alarm, they rush into the bushes. Hearing the snake chutter, they stand up and scan the ground (Byrne, 1991). And it won't surprise dog owners to hear that dogs can connect human words with certain objects. Rico, a border collie, knows and can fetch 200 items by name. Moreover, if asked to retrieve a novel toy with a name he has never heard, Rico will pick out the novel item from among a group of familiar items (Kaminski & others, 2004). Hearing that novel word for the second time four weeks later, Rico as often as not retrieves the object.

Such feats show animals' impressive comprehension and communication. But is this language? Or are we humans the only language-using species? This question has launched thousands of studies.

The Case of the Apes In the late 1960s, psychologists Allen Gardner and Beatrix Gardner (1969) challenged humans' claim to language—and aroused enormous scientific and public interest—when they taught sign language to Washoe, a chimpanzee. After four years, Washoe could use 132 signs; by age 32, Washoe was using 181 signs (Sanz & others, 1998). One *New York Times* reporter, having learned sign language from his deaf parents, visited Washoe and exclaimed, "Suddenly I realized I was conversing with a member of another species in my native tongue."

Further evidence of gestured "ape language" surfaced during the 1970s. Usually, apes sign just single words such as *that* or *gimme* (Bowman, 2003). But sometimes they string signs together to form sentences. Washoe signed, "You me go out,

Copyright Baus/Krzeslowski

Comprehending canine :: Rico, a border collie with a 200-word vocabulary, can infer that an unfamiliar sound refers to a novel object.

"Although humans make sounds with their mouths and occasionally look at each other, there is no solid evidence that they actually communicate with each other."

please." Some word combinations used by the great apes seemed very creative—saying *water bird* for "swan" or *elephant baby* for a long-nosed Pinocchio doll, or *apple which-is orange* for "orange" (Patterson, 1978; Rumbaugh, 1977). These vocabularies and sentences are simple, rather like those of a 2-year-old child. Yet as more and more reports of ape language came in, it seemed they might indeed be "little lower than human."

But Can Apes Really Talk? By the late 1970s, some psychologists were skeptical of the "talking apes." Were the chimps language champs or were the researchers chumps? Critics raised the following arguments:

- Unlike speaking or signing children, who easily soak up dozens of new words a week, apes gain their limited vocabularies only with great difficulty (Wynne, 2004). Saying that apes can learn language because they can sign words is like saying humans can fly because they can jump.

- Chimpanzees can make signs or push buttons in sequence to get a reward, but pigeons, too, can peck a sequence of keys to get grain (Straub & others, 1979). The apes' signing might be nothing more than aping their trainers' signs and learning that certain arm movements produce rewards (Terrace, 1979).

- Studies of perceptual set show that when information is unclear, we tend to see what we want or expect to see.

Interpreting chimpanzee signs as language may be little more than the trainers' wishful thinking (Terrace, 1979). When Washoe signed *water bird*, she may have been separately naming *water* and *bird*.

- "Give orange me give eat orange me eat orange . . ." is a far cry from the exquisite syntax of a 3-year-old (Anderson, 2004; Pinker, 1995). To the child, "You tickle" and "Tickle you" communicate different ideas. A chimpanzee, lacking human syntax, might use the same sequence of signs for both phrases.

Controversy can stimulate progress, and in this case, it triggered more evidence of chimpanzees' abilities to think and communicate. One surprising finding was that Washoe trained her adopted son Loulis to use the signs she had learned. It started like this. After her second infant died, Washoe became withdrawn when told, "Baby dead, baby gone, baby finished." Two weeks later, caretaker-researcher Roger Fouts (1992, 1997) signed better news: "I have baby for you." Washoe reacted with instant excitement, hair on end, swaggering and panting while signing over and again, "Baby, my baby." It took several hours for Washoe and the foster infant, Loulis, to

But is this language? :: Chimpanzees' ability to express themselves in American Sign Language raises questions about the very nature of language. Here, the trainer is asking, "What is this?" The sign in response is "Baby." Does the response constitute language?

warm to each other. But then she broke the ice by signing, "Come baby" and cuddling Loulis.

In the months that followed, Loulis picked up 68 signs simply by observing Washoe and three other language-trained chimps. Signing together, without human assistance, the chimps asked one another to *chase, tickle, hug, come,* or *groom*. People who sign were in near-perfect agreement about what the chimps were saying, 90 percent of which related to social interaction, reassurance, or play (Fouts & Bodamer, 1987). The chimps could even translate some spoken English words into signs (Shaw, 1989–1990).

Even more stunning was a report that Kanzi, a bonobo, could understand *syntax* in English spoken to him (Savage-Rumbaugh & others, 1993). Kanzi appears to have the grammatical abilities of a human 2-year-old. He happened onto language while observing his adoptive mother during her language training. To those who don't understand syntax "Can you show me the light?" and "Can you bring me the [flash]light?" and "Can you turn the light on?" would all seem the same. Kanzi knows the difference. He also knows the spoken words *snake, bite,* and *dog*. Given stuffed animals and asked—for the first time—to "make the dog bite the snake," he put the snake to the dog's mouth. Furthermore, for chimpanzees as for humans, early life is a critical time for learning language. Without early exposure to speech or word symbols, adult chimpanzees will not gain language competence (Rumbaugh & Savage-Rumbaugh, 1994).

Most psychologists now agree that humans alone possess language, if by the term we mean verbal or signed expression of complex grammar. If we mean, more simply, an ability to communicate through a meaningful sequence of symbols, then apes are indeed capable of language. But all of these studies on animal thinking and language have moved psychologists toward a greater appreciation of the remarkable abilities of other species and of our own (Friend, 2004;

Rumbaugh & Washburn, 2003). In the past we doubted that animals could plan, form concepts, count, use tools, show compassion, or use language (Thorpe, 1974). Today, we know better. Animal researchers have shown us that primates exhibit insight, show family loyalty, communicate with one another, care for one another, transmit cultural patterns across generations, and sometimes even understand the syntax of human speech. Accepting and working out what this means in terms of the moral rights of other animals is an unfinished task for our own thinking species.

Intelligence

So far, we have considered how humans as a group think and communicate. But we humans also differ from one another in these abilities. One of the most heated questions in psychology is whether each of us has some general mental capacity that can be measured and assigned a number. School boards, courts, and scientists debate the usefulness of intelligence and aptitude tests. Is it fair to use such tests to rank individuals and decide who can enter a particular training program, college, or job? How shall we interpret group differences? Do they reflect nature (heredity) or nurture (environment)? What about our other not-so-easily-measured abilities? Let's consider some findings from a century of research.

What Is Intelligence?

8: Is intelligence a single general ability or several distinct abilities?

In many research studies, *intelligence* has been defined as whatever intelligence tests measure, which has tended to be school smarts. But we have developed a broader understanding of this concept. Intelligence is not a quality like height or weight, which has the same meaning in all generations, all around the globe. People assign the term *intelligence* to the qualities that enable success in their own time and in their own culture (Sternberg & Kaufman, 1998). In the Amazon rain forest, *intelligence* may be understanding the medicinal qualities of local plants. In a Minnesota high school, it may be mastering difficult concepts in tough courses. In both locations, **intelligence** is the ability to learn from experience, solve problems, and use knowledge to adapt to new situations.

You probably know some people with talents in science or history, and others gifted in athletics, art, music, or dance. You may also know a talented artist who is stumped by the simplest math problem, or a brilliant math student with little talent for literary discussion. Are all of these people intelligent? Could you rate their intelligence on a single scale? Or would you need several different scales? Simply put: Is intelligence a single overall ability or several specific abilities?

Hands-on healing :: The meaning of *intelligence* varies from culture to culture. This folk healer in Peru displays intelligence in his knowledge about medicinal plants and the needs of the people he is helping.

© Maya Goded/Magnum Photos

One General Intelligence or Multiple Intelligences?

Charles Spearman (1863–1945) believed we have one **general intelligence** (often shortened to **g**) that is at the heart of all of our intelligent behavior, from navigating the sea to excelling in school. He granted that people often have special, outstanding abilities. But he noted that those who score high in one area, such as verbal intelligence, typically score higher than average in other areas, such as spatial or reasoning ability. Spearman's belief stemmed in part from his work with *factor analysis,* a statistical tool that searches for clusters of related items.

Other psychologists have rejected this idea of a *g factor,* or common skill set. Howard Gardner (1983, 1999), for example, views intelligence as multiple abilities that come in several packages. He asks us to consider studies of people with brain damage, who may lose one ability while

Islands of genius: Savant syndrome :: Savant syndrome is the presence of an exceptional skill despite otherwise limited abilities. Most people (4 in 5) with this syndrome are males. (left) Matt Savage, a 16-year-old award-winning jazz pianist, has his own band—the Matt Savage Trio. (middle) Kim Peek, the inspiration for the character Raymond Babbit in the movie *Rain Man,* knows more than 7600 books by heart, as well as all U.S. area codes, Zip codes, and TV stations. (right) Alonzo Clemons can create perfect replicas of any animal he briefly sees. His bronze figures have earned him a national reputation.

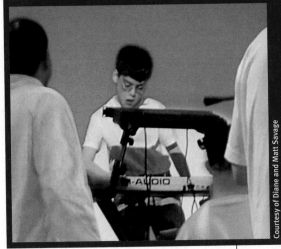

Courtesy of Diane and Matt Savage

© Darold A. Treffert, M.D. www.savantsyndrome.com

© Darold A. Treffert, M.D. www.savantsyndrome.com

others remain intact. And he sees evidence of multiple intelligences in people with **savant syndrome,** which sometimes accompanies *autism,* a developmental disorder (see Chapter 3). People with savant syndrome often score low on intelligence tests—and may have limited or no language ability—but have an island of brilliance (Treffert & Wallace, 2002). Some can compute numbers as quickly and accurately as an electronic calculator, or identify almost instantly the day of the week that matches any given date in history. Others can render incredible works of art or musical performances (Miller, 1999).

Gardner identifies a total of eight *relatively independent intelligences,* including the verbal and mathematical aptitudes assessed by standard tests **(TABLE 8.2).** Thus, the computer programmer, the poet, the street-smart adolescent who becomes a crafty executive, and the point guard on the basketball team exhibit different kinds of intelligence (Gardner, 1998). To Gardner, a general intelligence score is like the overall rating of a city—which doesn't give you much specific information about its schools, streets, or nightlife.

"You have to be careful, if you're good at something, to make sure you don't think you're good at other things that you aren't necessarily so good at. . . . Because I've been very successful at [software development] people come in and expect that I have wisdom about topics that I don't."

Bill Gates, 1998

Wouldn't it be wonderful if the world were so just that a weakness in one area would be compensated by genius in

intelligence mental quality consisting of the ability to learn from experience, solve problems, and use knowledge to adapt to new situations.

general intelligence (*g*) a general intelligence factor that, according to Spearman and others, underlies specific mental abilities and is therefore measured by every task on an intelligence test.

savant syndrome a condition in which a person otherwise limited in mental ability has an exceptional specific skill, such as in computation or drawing.

Table 8.2	Gardner's Eight Intelligences
Aptitude	**Example**
1. Linguistic	T. S. Eliot, poet
2. Logical-mathematical	Albert Einstein, scientist
3. Musical	Igor Stravinsky, composer
4. Spatial	Pablo Picasso, artist
5. Bodily-kinesthetic	Martha Graham, dancer
6. Intrapersonal (self)	Sigmund Freud, psychiatrist
7. Interpersonal (other people)	Mahatma Gandhi, leader
8. Naturalist	Charles Darwin, naturalist

Spatial intelligence genius :: In 1998, World Checkers Champion Ron "Suki" King of Barbados set a new record by simultaneously playing 385 players in 3 hours and 44 minutes. Thus, while his opponents often had hours to plot their game moves, King could only devote about 35 seconds to each game. Yet he still managed to win all 385 games!

Courtesy of Cameras on Wheels

some other area? Alas, says intelligence researcher Sandra Scarr (1989), the world is not just. People with mental disadvantages, for example, often have lesser physical abilities as well. Special Olympics gives them and others a chance to enjoy fair competition. *G* matters. General intelligence scores predict performance on various complex tasks and in various jobs (Gottfredson, 2002a,b, 2003a,b; Reeve & Hakel, 2002). In one overview of 127 studies, an academic intelligence score that predicted graduate school success also predicted later job success (Kuncel & others, 2004).

But the recipe for success has more than one ingredient. High intelligence may get you into a profession (via the schools and training programs that take you there). Grit makes you successful once you're there. Highly successful people also tend to be conscientious, well-connected, and doggedly energetic. Researchers found one common ingredient in expert performances in chess, dancing, sports, computer programming, music, and medicine: a decade of intense, daily practice (Ericsson, 2002; Ericsson & Lehmann, 1996).

After picking up a Nobel prize in Stockholm, physicist Richard Feynman stopped in Queens, New York, to look at his high school record. "My grades were not as good as I remembered," he reported, "and my IQ was [a good, though unexceptional] 124" (Faber, 1987).

Is Intelligence the Same as Creativity?

9: What is creativity, and what fosters this ability?

There was no question about the intelligence of seventeenth-century genius Pierre de Fermat. He dared scholars of his day to solve various mathematical problems. Three centuries later, one of those problems continued to baffle the greatest mathematical minds, even after a $2 million prize had been offered if someone could crack the puzzle.

Like countless others, math professor Andrew Wiles had searched for the answer. After more than 30 years, he was on the brink of a solution. Then, one morning,

out of the blue, an "incredible revelation" struck him. "It was so indescribably beautiful; it was so simple and so elegant. I couldn't understand how I'd missed it and I just stared at it in disbelief for 20 minutes. Then during the day I walked around the department, and I'd keep coming back to my desk looking to see if it was still there. It was still there. I couldn't contain myself, I was so excited. It was the most important moment of my working life" (Singh, 1997, p. 25).

Wiles' incredible revelation illustrates **creativity**—the ability to produce ideas that are both novel and valuable. Studies suggest that creativity requires a certain level of aptitude, a score of about 120 on a standard intelligence test. But the link stops there. Intelligence test scores of exceptionally creative architects, mathematicians, scientists, and engineers are usually no higher than those of their less creative peers (MacKinnon & Hall, 1972; Simonton, 2000). Moreover, when researchers use scanning tools to pinpoint brain activity, they find different areas become active during creative thinking than during academic problem solving.

Robert Sternberg views creative intelligence as a separate form of intelligence, with five necessary parts, in addition to sufficient aptitude (Sternberg, 1988; Sternberg & Lubart, 1991, 1992).

1. *Expertise* is a well-developed base of knowledge, which furnishes the ideas, images, and phrases we use as mental building blocks. The more blocks we have, the more chances we have to combine them in novel ways. Wiles' well-developed base of mathematical knowledge gave him access to many different combinations of ideas and methods.

2. *Imaginative thinking skills* let us see things in novel ways, recognize patterns, and make connections. Having mastered a problem's basic elements, we can redefine or explore the problem in a new way. Wiles' imaginative solution combined two important but incomplete solutions.

Imaginative thinking :: Cartoonists often display creativity as they see things in new ways or make unusual connections.

FURIOUS GEORGE

Everyone held up their crackers as David threw the cheese log into the ceiling fan.

3. **A *venturesome personality*** seeks new experiences rather than following the pack, tolerates gray areas, takes risks, and continues despite obstacles. Wiles said he worked in near-isolation from the mathematics community, partly to stay focused and avoid distraction.

> "If you would allow me any talent, it's simply this: I can, for whatever reason, reach down into my own brain, feel around in all the mush, find and extract something from my persona, and then graft it onto an idea."
>
> Cartoonist Gary Larson, *The Complete Far Side*, 2003

4. ***Intrinsic motivation*** is linked to our most creative moments. When we are intrinsically motivated, we are driven by our internal feelings rather than by outside rewards (Amabile & Hennessey, 1992). Creative people focus on the pleasure and challenge of the work itself, not on meeting deadlines, impressing people, or making money. As Wiles said: "I was so obsessed by this problem that for eight years I was thinking about it all the time—when I woke up in the morning to when I went to sleep at night" (Singh & Riber, 1997).

5. **A *creative environment*** sparks, supports, and refines creative ideas. One study of 2026 prominent scientists and inventors found that the most well-known of them had been mentored, challenged, and supported by their relationships with colleagues (Simonton, 1992). Even Wiles stood on the shoulders of others and wrestled with his problem with the collaboration of a former student.

Emotional Intelligence: Feeling Smarts

10: Is our ability to manage our own emotions and to empathize with others a form of intelligence?

Is being in tune with yourself and others also a form of intelligence? Some psychologists think it is. *Social intelligence* is the know-how involved in comprehending social situations and managing ourselves successfully (Cantor & Kihlstrom, 1987). More recently, researchers (Mayer & others, 2002; Salovey & Grewal, 2005) have focused on a critical part of social intelligence, **emotional intelligence,** with its four components. These are the abilities to

- *perceive* emotions (to recognize them in faces, music, and stories).

- *understand* emotions (to predict them and how they change and blend).

- *manage* emotions (to know how to express them in varied situations).

- *use* emotions to enable adaptive or creative thinking.

Emotionally intelligent people are self-aware. Those who score high on emotional intelligence tests enjoy higher-quality interactions with friends of both sexes (Lopes & others, 2004). They avoid being hijacked by overwhelming depression, anxiety, or anger. They can read others' emotions and know what to say to soothe a grieving friend, encourage a workmate, and manage a conflict. These high-scorers also exhibit modestly better job performance (Van Rooy & Viswesvaran, 2004). They can delay gratification in pursuit of long-range rewards, rather than being overtaken by immediate impulses. Simply said, they are emotionally smart, and thus they often succeed in career, marriage, and parenting situations where academically smarter (but emotionally less intelligent) people fail.

creativity the ability to produce new and valuable ideas.

emotional intelligence the ability to perceive, understand, manage, and use emotions.

"You're wise, but you lack tree smarts."

But is this intelligence? Gardner (1999) suggests that we respect emotional sensitivity, creativity, and motivation as important but different. Stretch a word—*intelligence* or any other word—to include everything we prize, and that word will lose its meaning.

To summarize, we might compare mental abilities to physical abilities. Athleticism is not one thing but many. The ability to run fast is distinct from the strength needed for power lifting, which is distinct from the eye-hand coordination required to throw a ball on target. A champion weightlifter rarely has the potential to be a skilled ice skater. Yet there remains some tendency for good things to come packaged together—for running speed and throwing accuracy to correlate—thanks to general athletic ability. Similarly, intelligence involves several distinct abilities, which correlate enough to define a small general intelligence factor. Let's turn next to how psychologists have designed tests to assess these mental abilities.

Assessing Intelligence

How do we assess intelligence? As noted earlier, *intelligence* can be considered to be whatever **intelligence tests** measure. So, what are these tests, and what makes them trustworthy? Answering those questions begins with a look at why psychologists created tests of mental abilities and how they have used those tests.

What Do Intelligence Tests Test?

11: When and why were intelligence tests created?

"No two persons are born exactly alike; but each differs from the other in natural endowments, one being suited for one occupation and the other for another." Although Plato recorded these thoughts in *The Republic* more than 2000 years ago, it was barely more than a century ago that psychologists undertook to assess people's **aptitude** (ability to learn) as well as their **achievement** (what they have already learned).

Alfred Binet: Predicting School Achievement Modern intelligence testing traces its birth to early twentieth-century France, where a new law required all children to attend school. French officials knew that some children, including many newcomers to Paris, would need special classes. But how could the schools make fair judgments about children's learning potential? Teachers might assess children who had little prior education as slow learners. Or they might assign children to

classes on the basis of their social backgrounds. To minimize bias, France's minister of public education in 1904 gave Alfred Binet and others, including Théodore Simon, the task of studying this problem.

Binet and Simon began by assuming that all children follow the same course of intellectual development but that some develop more rapidly. A "dull" child's test results should therefore be the same as a typical younger child's, and a "bright" child's results the same as a typical older child's. Binet and Simon now had a clear goal: measuring each child's **mental age,** the level of performance typically associated with a certain chronological age. The average 9-year-old, for example, has a mental age of 9. A 9-year-old with a below-average mental age (perhaps performing at the level of a typical 7-year-old) would struggle with schoolwork considered normal for 9-year-olds.

> "The IQ test was invented to predict academic performance, nothing else. If we wanted something that would predict life success, we'd have to invent another test completely."
>
> Social psychologist Robert Zajonc, 1984b

Binet and Simon tested a variety of reasoning and problem-solving questions on Binet's two daughters, and then on "bright" and "backward" Parisian schoolchildren. The items they developed eventually predicted how well French children would handle their schoolwork.

Lewis Terman: Measuring Innate IQ Soon after Binet's death in 1911, others adapted his tests for wider use. Lewis Terman (1877–1956), a Stanford University professor, tried to use Binet's test as a numerical measure of inherited intelligence with poor results. The Paris-developed age groupings worked poorly for California schoolchildren. Terman then adapted some of Binet's original items, added others, and established new standards for various ages. Terman extended the upper end of the test's range from teenagers to "superior adults." He gave his revision the name it retains today—the **Stanford-Binet.**

Alfred Binet (1857–1911) :: "Some recent philosophers have given their moral approval to the deplorable verdict that an individual's intelligence is a fixed quantity, one which cannot be augmented. We must protest and act against this brutal pessimism" (Binet, 1909, p. 141).

William Stern's contribution to intelligence testing was the famous term **intelligence quotient,** or **IQ.** The IQ was simply a person's mental age divided by chronological age and multiplied by 100 to get rid of the decimal point:

$$IQ = \frac{\text{mental age}}{\text{chronological age}} \times 100$$

Thus, an average child, whose mental and chronological ages are the same, has an IQ of 100. But an 8-year-old who answers questions as would a typical 10-year-old has an IQ of 125.

The original IQ formula worked fairly well for children but not for adults. (Should a 40-year-old who does as well on the test as an average 20-year-old be assigned an IQ of only 50?) Most current intelligence tests, including the Stanford-Binet, no longer compute an IQ (though the term "IQ" still lingers in everyday vocabulary as short for "intelligence test score"). Instead, they represent the test-taker's performance *relative to the average performance of others the same age.* This average performance is arbitrarily assigned a score of 100, and about two-thirds of all test-takers fall between 85 and 115.

David Wechsler: Separate Scores for Separate Skills Psychologist David Wechsler created what is now the most widely used intelligence test, the **Wechsler Adult Intelligence Scale (WAIS),** with a version for school-age children (the *Wechsler Intelligence Scale for Children,* "WISC"), and another for preschool children. The WAIS consists of 11 subtests broken into verbal and performance areas **(FIGURE 8.7)**. It yields not only an overall intelligence score, as does the Stanford-Binet, but also separate scores for verbal comprehension, perceptual organization, working memory, and processing speed. Striking differences among these scores can provide clues to strengths or weaknesses. For example, a

Matching patterns :: Block design puzzles test the ability to analyze patterns. Wechsler's individually administered intelligence test comes in forms suited for adults (WAIS) and children (WISC).

Lew Merrim/Photo Researchers, Inc.

VERBAL (samples from the six subtests)

Similarities
  In what way are wool and cotton alike?

Arithmetic Reasoning
  If eggs cost 60 cents a dozen, what does 1 egg cost?

Comprehension
  Why do people buy fire insurance?

PERFORMANCE (samples from the five subtests)

Picture Arrangement
  The pictures below tell a story. Put them in the right
  order to tell the story.

Block Design
  Using the four blocks, make one just like this.

Figure 8.7> Sample items from the Wechsler Adult Intelligence Scale (WAIS) subtests (Adapted from Thorndike & Hagen, 1977.)

intelligence test a method for assessing an individual's mental aptitudes and comparing them with those of others, using numerical scores.

aptitude test a test designed to predict a person's future performance; *aptitude* is the capacity to learn.

achievement test a test designed to assess what a person has learned.

mental age a measure of intelligence test performance devised by Binet; the chronological age that most typically corresponds to a given level of performance. Thus, a child who does as well as the average 8-year-old is said to have a mental age of 8.

Stanford-Binet the widely used American revision (by Terman at Stanford University) of Binet's original intelligence test.

intelligence quotient (IQ) defined originally as the ratio of mental age *(ma)* to chronological age *(ca)* multiplied by 100 (thus, IQ = *ma/ca* × 100). On contemporary intelligence tests, the average performance for a given age is assigned a score of 100.

Wechsler Adult Intelligence Scale (WAIS) the WAIS is the most widely used intelligence test; contains verbal and performance (nonverbal) subtests.

low verbal comprehension score combined with high scores on other subtests could indicate a reading or language disability. Other comparisons can help a psychologist or psychiatrist establish a rehabilitation plan for a stroke patient. In such ways, tests help realize Binet's aim: to identify opportunities for improvement and strengths that teachers or employers can build upon.

Three Tests of a "Good" Test

12: By what criteria can we judge intelligence tests?

To be widely accepted, a psychological test must be *standardized, reliable,* and *valid.* The Stanford-Binet and Wechsler tests meet these requirements.

Was the Test Standardized? The number of correct answers you score on an intelligence test would tell you almost nothing. To know how well you performed, you need some basis for comparison. This is the reason test-makers give new tests to a representative sample of people. The scores from this pretested group become the basis for future comparisons. If you later take the test following the same procedures, your score will be meaningful when compared with others. This process is called **standardization.**

If we make a graph of test-takers' scores, they typically form a bell-shaped pattern called the **normal curve.** No matter what we measure—heights, weights, or mental aptitudes—people's scores tend to form this shape. The highest point is the midpoint, or the average score. On an intelligence test, we give this average score a value of 100 **(FIGURE 8.8).** Moving out from the average, toward either extreme, we find fewer and fewer people. For the Stanford-Binet and the Wechsler tests, a person's score indicates whether that person's performance fell above or below the average. A performance higher than all but 2 percent of all scores earns an intelligence score of 130. A performance lower than 98 percent of all scores earns an intelligence score of 70.

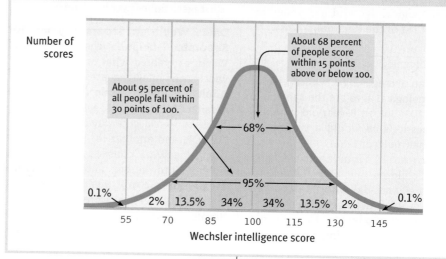

Figure 8.8> The normal curve Scores on aptitude tests tend to form a normal, or bell-shaped, curve around an average score. For the Wechsler scale, for example, the average score is 100.

Number of scores

About 95 percent of all people fall within 30 points of 100.

About 68 percent of people score within 15 points above or below 100.

0.1% 2% 13.5% 34% 34% 13.5% 2% 0.1%

55 70 85 100 115 130 145

Wechsler intelligence score

Is the Test Reliable? Knowing where you stand in comparison to the standardizing group still won't tell you much unless the test has **reliability.** A reliable test gives consistent scores, no matter who takes the test or when they take it. To check a test's reliability, researchers test many people many times. They may retest people using the same test or they may split the test in half and see whether odd-question scores and even-question scores agree. If the two sets of scores generally agree, the test is reliable. The tests we have considered so far—the Stanford-Binet, the WAIS, and the WISC—all score very high for reliability. When retested, people's scores generally match their first score closely.

Is the Test Valid? High reliability does not ensure a test's **validity**—the extent to which the test actually measures or predicts what it promises. Imagine cutting six inches off the end of a tape measure and then using it to measure people's heights. Your results would be very reliable. No matter how many times you measured, people's heights would be the same. But your results would not be valid—you wouldn't be giving the information you promised—real heights.

We expect intelligence tests to have *predictive validity.* They should predict future performance. To some extent, intelligence tests do have predictive ability. As critics are fond of noting, their predictive power is fairly strong in the early school years, but later it weakens. Past grades, which reflect both aptitude and motivation, are better predictors of future achievements.

PRACTICE TEST

9. The existence of savant syndrome seems to support
   a. Stern's concept of IQ.
   b. Spearman's notion of general intelligence, or *g* factor.
   c. Gardner's theory of multiple intelligences.
   d. Binet's concept of mental age.

10. Which of the following is NOT a characteristic of a creative person?
    a. Expertise
    b. Extrinsic motivation
    c. A venturesome personality
    d. Imaginative thinking skills

11. Emotionally intelligent people are characterized by

a. the tendency to seek immediate gratification.
b. the ability to understand their own emotions but not those of others.
c. high academic intelligence.
d. self-awareness.

12. The intelligence quotient, or IQ, of a 6-year-old with a mental age of 9 would be
   a. 67.   c. 86.
   b. 133.   d. 150.

13. The Wechsler Adult Intelligence Scale (WAIS) is best able to tell us
   a. what part of an individual's intelligence is determined by genetic inheritance.
   b. whether the test-taker will succeed in a job.
   c. how the test-taker compares with other adults in vocabulary and arithmetic reasoning.
   d. whether the test-taker has specific skills for music and the performing arts.

14. The Stanford-Binet, the Wechsler Adult Intelligence Scale, and the Wechsler Intelligence Scale for Children are known to have very high reliability. This means that
   a. a pretest has been given to a representative sample.
   b. the test yields consistent results, for example on retesting.

c. the test measures what it is supposed to measure.
d. the results of the test will predict future behavior, such as college grades or success in business.

Answers: 9. c, 10. b, 11. d, 12. d, 13. c, 14. b.

The Nature and Nurture of Intelligence

13: Is intelligence influenced more by heredity or by environment?

Intelligence runs in families. But why? Are our intellectual abilities mostly inherited? Or are they molded by our environment? Few issues in psychology arouse so much passion. Let's look at some of the evidence.

What Do Twin and Adoption Studies Tell Us?

Does sharing the same genes also mean sharing the same mental abilities? As you can see from **FIGURE 8.9,** which summarizes

many studies, the answer is clearly yes. Identical twins who grow up together have intelligence test scores fully as similar as those of the same person taking the same test twice (Lykken, 1999; Plomin, 2001). (Fraternal twins, who typically share only half their genes, have much less similar scores.) Even when identical twins are adopted by two different families, their scores are very similar. Genes matter.

But shared environment matters, too. Fraternal twins, who are genetically no

standardization defining meaningful scores by comparison with the performance of a pretested standardization group.

normal curve the symmetrical bell-shaped curve that describes the distribution of many physical and psychological attributes. Most scores fall near the average, and fewer and fewer scores lie near the extremes.

reliability the extent to which a test yields consistent results, as assessed by the consistency of scores on two halves of the test, on alternate forms of the test, or on retesting.

validity the extent to which a test measures or predicts what it is supposed to.

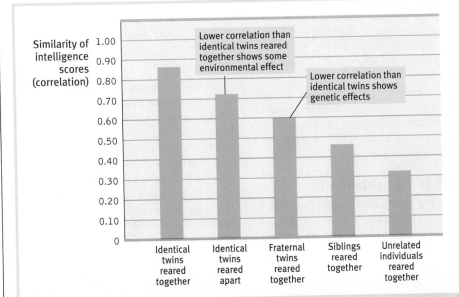

Corbis Images/Picture Quest

Similarity of intelligence scores (correlation)

Lower correlation than identical twins reared together shows some environmental effect

Lower correlation than identical twins shows genetic effects

Categories (x-axis): Identical twins reared together / Identical twins reared apart / Fraternal twins reared together / Siblings reared together / Unrelated individuals reared together

Figure 8.9> Intelligence: Nature and nurture The most genetically similar people have the most similar intelligence scores. Remember: 1.0 indicates a perfect correlation; zero indicates no correlation at all. (Data from McGue & others, 1993.)

more alike than any other siblings—but who are treated more alike because they are the same age—tend to score more alike than other siblings. And studies show that adoption of mistreated or neglected children enhances their intelligence scores (van IJzendoorn & Juffer, 2005, 2006). So, should we expect unrelated children in adoptive families to share similar aptitudes?

Seeking to disentangle genes and environment, researchers have compared the intelligence test scores of adopted children with those of their family members. These include their *biological parents* (the providers of their genes), their *adoptive parents* (the providers of their home environment), and their *adoptive siblings* (who share that environment). During childhood, the test scores of adoptive siblings correlate modestly. What do you think happens as the years go by and adopted children settle in with their adoptive families? Would you expect the effect of family environment to grow stronger and the genetic effect to shrink?

If you said yes, you have a surprise in store. Mental similarities between adopted children and their adoptive families *lessen* with age, dropping to roughly zero by adulthood (McGue & others, 1993). Similarities with *biological* parents become more

"I told my parents that if grades were so important they should have paid for a smarter egg donor."

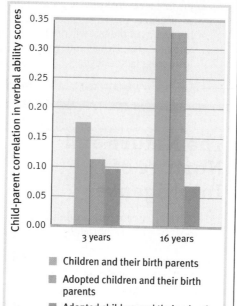

Figure 8.10> Adopted children resemble birth parents **As the years went by in their adoptive families, children's verbal ability scores became modestly more like their *biological* parents' scores. (Adapted from Plomin & DeFries, 1998.)**

apparent as adopted children gain life experience (Bouchard, 1995, 1996b). Adopted children's verbal ability scores, for example, become more like those of their biological parents over time **(FIGURE 8.10)**. Further evidence of the power of genetic influences comes from studies of identical twins, whose similarities continue or increase into their eighties (McClearn & others, 1997; Plomin & others, 1997).

What Is Heritability?

Heritability of intelligence is the portion of test-score variation that can be assigned to genetic factors. This genetically influenced portion is often estimated to be about 50 percent. Does this mean your genes are responsible for 50 percent of your intelligence and your environment for the rest? No. It means we credit heredity with 50 percent of the *variation* in intelligence among people being studied.

This point is so often misunderstood that I repeat: Heritability never applies to an *individual,* only to *why people differ from one another.*

The influence of heredity on the range of test scores varies from study to study. Where environments vary widely, as they do among children of less-educated parents, environmental differences are more predictive of intelligence scores (Rowe & others, 1999). To see why, consider humorist Mark Twain's proposal to raise boys in barrels until age 12, feeding them through a hole. Let's take his joke a step further and say we'll give all those boys an intelligence test at age 12. Since their environments were all equal, any differences in their test scores could only be due to their heredity. In this "study," heritability would be nearly 100 percent. But if we clone an equal number of boys and raise them in drastically different environments (some in barrels and others in mansions), the environmental effect will be 100 percent, and heritability will be zero.

A check on your understanding of heritability: If environments become more equal, the heritability of intelligence would

a. increase.
b. decrease.
c. be unchanged.
(Turn the next page to check your answer.)

In the real world, your genes and your environment work together. Suppose that (thanks to your genes) you are just slightly taller and quicker than others (Flynn, 2003). If you try out for a basketball team, you will more likely be picked. Once on the team, you will probably play more often than others (getting more practice and experience) and you will receive more coaching. The same would be true for your separated identical twin—who might, *not just for genetic reasons,* also come to excel at basketball. Our genes shape the experiences that shape us. If you have a natural aptitude for academics, you will more likely stay in school, read books, and ask questions—all of which will increase your brain power. In these gene-environment interactions, small genetic advantages can trigger social experiences that multiply our original skills.

How Does Environment Influence Intelligence?

We have seen that biology and experience intertwine. Nowhere is this more apparent than in the most hopeless human environments. Severe life experiences can leave footprints on the brain, as J. McVicker Hunt (1982) observed in one Iranian orphanage. The typical child Hunt observed there could not sit up unassisted at age 2 or walk at age 4. The little care the infants received was not in response to their crying, cooing, or other behaviors, so the children developed little sense of personal control over their environment. They were instead becoming passive "glum lumps." Extreme deprivation was crushing native intelligence.

Hunt was aware of both the dramatic effects of early experiences and the impact of early intervention. He began a training program for caregivers, teaching them to play language-fostering games with 11 infants. They learned to imitate the babies' babbling. They engaged them in vocal follow-the-leader. And, finally, they taught the infants sounds from the Persian language. The results were dramatic. By 22 months of age, the infants could name more than 50 objects and

Devastating neglect :: Romanian orphans who had minimal interaction with caregivers, such as this child in the Lagunul Pentro Copii orphanage in 1990, suffered delayed development.

Josef Polleross / The Image Works

body parts. They so charmed visitors that most were adopted—an impressive new success rate for the orphanage.

Do studies of such early interventions indicate that an "enriched" environment can "give your child a superior intellect," as some popular books claim? Most experts are doubtful (Bruer, 1999). Malnutrition, sensory deprivation, and social isolation can retard normal brain development, but there is no environmental recipe for fast-forwarding a normal infant into a genius. All babies should have normal exposure to sights, sounds, and speech. Beyond that, Sandra Scarr's (1984) verdict still is widely shared: "Parents who are very concerned about providing special educational lessons for their babies are wasting their time."

Group Differences in Intelligence Test Scores

14: How, and why, do ethnic and gender groups differ in their intelligence test scores?

If there were no group differences in aptitude scores, psychologists could politely debate hereditary and environmental influences in their ivory towers. But there are group differences. What are they? And what do they mean?

Ethnic Differences

Fueling this discussion of group differences are two disturbing but agreed-upon facts:

- Racial groups differ in their average scores on intelligence tests.

- High-scoring people (and groups) are more likely to have high levels of education and income.

A 1994 statement by 52 intelligence researchers explained: "The bell curve for Whites is centered roughly around IQ 100; the bell curve for American Blacks roughly around 85; and those for different subgroups of Hispanics roughly midway

between those for Whites and Blacks" (Avery & others, 1994). In recent years, the Black-White difference has shrunk to about 10 points (Dickens & Flynn, 2006). Yet a test-score gap stubbornly persists.

There are differences among other groups as well (Steele, 1990; Zeidner, 1990). In New Zealand, people of European descent outscore people of native Maori descent. In Israel, Jews outscore Arabs. In Japan, most Japanese outscore the Burakumin, a stigmatized minority group.

One more agreed-upon fact is that *group* differences provide little basis for judging individuals. Women outlive men by six years, but knowing this book's editor is a woman doesn't tell me how long she will live. Even Charles Murray and Richard Herrnstein (1994), whose writings drew attention to Black-White intelligence-score differences, reminded us that "millions of Blacks have higher IQs than the average White."

So what shall we make of these group differences in intelligence scores? As we have seen, heredity contributes to *individual* differences in intelligence. Does that mean it also contributes to *group* differences? Some psychologists believe it does, perhaps because of the world's differing climates and survival challenges (Herrnstein & Murray, 1994; Lynn, 1991, 2001; Rushton, 1998, 2003).

In prosperous country X everyone eats all they want. In country Y the rich are well fed, but the semistarved poor are often thin. In which country will the heritability of body weight be greater? (Turn the page to check your answer.)

But we have also seen that group differences in a heritable trait may be entirely environmental, as in our earlier boys-in-barrels versus boys-in-mansions example. Consider one of nature's experiments: Allow some children to grow up

heritability the portion of variation among individuals that we can attribute to genes. The heritability of a trait may vary, depending on the range of populations and environments studied.

hearing their culture's dominant language, while others, born deaf, do not. Then give both groups an intelligence test rooted in the dominant language, and (no surprise) those with expertise in that language will score highest. In group comparisons on such tests, people who can hear outscore those who were born deaf (Braden, 1994). Within each group, the differences between individuals are mainly a reflection of genetic differences. Between the two groups, the difference is mainly environmental **(FIGURE 8.11)**.

Might the racial gap be similarly environmental? Consider:

Genetics research reveals that under the skin, the races are remarkably alike (Cavalli-Sforza & others, 1994; Lewontin, 1982). The average genetic difference between two Icelandic villagers or between two Kenyans greatly exceeds the group difference between Icelanders and Kenyans. Moreover, looks can deceive. Genetic studies show that light-skinned Europeans and dark-skinned Africans are more closely related than are dark-skinned Africans and dark-skinned Aboriginal Australians.

Race is not a neatly defined biological category. Some scholars argue that there is a reality to race, noting that there are genetic markers for race and that medical risks (such as skin cancer or high blood pressure) vary by race (Rowe, 2005). Other social scientists think race is no longer a meaningful term. They view race as primarily a social category, without well-defined biological boundaries (Helms & others, 2005; Smedley & Smedley, 2005; Sternberg

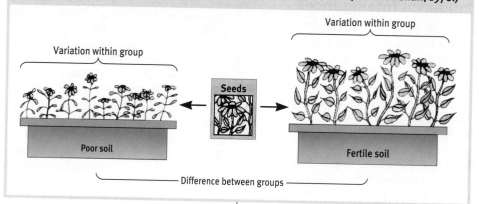

Figure 8.11> Group differences and environmental impact Even if the variation between members within a group reflects genetic differences, the average difference between groups may be wholly due to the environment. Imagine that seeds from the same mixture are sown in different soils. Although height differences *within* each window box will be genetic, the height difference *between* the two groups will be environmental. (From Lewontin, 1976.)

& others, 2005). People from many different ancestries may label themselves as members of the same race. Moreover, with increasingly mixed ancestries, fewer and

Nature's own morphing :: Nature draws no sharp boundaries between races, which blend gradually one into the next around the Earth. But the human urge to classify causes people to socially define themselves in racial categories, which become catch-all labels for physical features, social identity, and nationality.

© Paul Almasy/Corbis; © Rob Howard/ Corbis; © Barbara Bannister; Gallo Images/ Corbis; © David Turnley/Corbis; © Dave Bartruff/Corbis; © Haruyoshi Yamaguchi/Corbis; © Richard T. Nowitz/Corbis; © Owen Franken/Corbis; © Paul Almasy/Corbis; © John-Francis Bourke/zefa/Corbis

fewer people fit neatly into any one category. (What race is Tiger Woods?)

Within the same population, there are generation-to-generation differences in intelligence test scores. Test scores of today's better-fed, better-educated, and more test-prepared population exceed the scores of the 1930s population. The two generations differ by the same margin that the intelligence test score of the average White today exceeds that of the average Black. No one attributes the generational group difference to genetics.

White and Black infants tend to score equally well on an infant intelligence measure (preference for looking at novel stimuli— a crude predictor of future intelligence scores [Fagan, 1992]).

Asian students outperform North American students on math achievement and aptitude tests. This difference may reflect culture more than inborn abilities. Compared with Americans, Asian students attend school 30 percent more days per year and spend much more time in school and at home studying math (Geary & others, 1996; Larson & Verma, 1999; Stevenson, 1992).

In different eras, different ethnic groups have experienced golden ages—periods of remarkable achievement. Twenty-five-hundred years ago, it was the Greeks and the Egyptians, then the Romans. In the eighth and ninth centuries, genius seemed to

The culture of scholarship :: Researchers who studied the children of Indochinese refugee families found that they typically excel in school (Caplan, Choy & Whitmore, 1992). On weekday nights after dinner, the family clears the table and begins homework. Family cooperation is valued, and older siblings help younger ones.

reside in the Arab world. Five hundred years ago, the Aztec Indians and the peoples of Northern Europe took the lead. Today, we marvel at Asians' technological genius. Cultures rise and fall over centuries; genes do not. That fact makes it difficult to believe in the natural genetic superiority of any race.

"Do not obtain your slaves from Britain, because they are so stupid and so utterly incapable of being taught."

Cicero, 106–43 B.C.

Gender Differences

In science, as in everyday life, differences, not similarities, excite interest. Compared with the many ways men and women are physically alike, our physical sex differences are relatively minor. Similarly, in the ways we think and feel and act, gender similarities vastly outnumber gender differences. In a 1932 testing of all Scottish 11-year-olds, for example, girls' average intelligence score was 100.6 and boys' was 100.5 (Deary & others, 2003). So far as *g* is concerned, boys and girls, men and women, are the same species. Yet most people find differences, such as those that follow, more newsworthy.

Spelling Females are better spellers: By the end of high school, only 30 percent of males spell better than the average female (Lubinski & Benbow, 1992).

Verbal ability Females excel at verbal fluency and remembering words. And, year after year, among nearly 200,000 students taking Germany's Test for Medical Studies, young women surpass men in remembering facts from short medical case descriptions (Stumpf & Jackson, 1994). (My wife, who remembers many of my experiences for me, tells me that if she died I'd be a man without a past.)

Nonverbal memory Females have an edge in locating objects (Halpern, 2000). In studies of more than 100,000 adolescents, females also modestly surpassed males in memory for picture associations (Hedges & Nowell, 1995).

Sensation Females are more sensitive to touch, taste, and odor.

Emotion-detecting ability Females are better emotion detectors. This fact emerged from studies in which hundreds of men and women viewed brief film clips of portions of a person's emotionally expressive face or body, sometimes with a garbled voice added (McClure, 2000; Rosenthal & others, 1979). For example, they watched a 2-second scene revealing only the face of an upset woman, and then they guessed whether the woman was criticizing someone for being late or was talking about her divorce. Women guessed right more often than men did.

Underachievement Males outnumber females at the low extremes of school achievement, and therefore also outnumber females in special education classes (Kleinfeld, 1998). They also tend to talk later and to stutter more often.

Math and spatial aptitudes On math tests, males and females have nearly identical average scores. This was the finding in 100 independent studies, with more than 3 million representatively sampled people (Hyde & others, 1990). But again—despite greater diversity within the genders than between them—group differences make the news. Females tend to display an edge in math computation, but males score higher in math problem solving (Bronner, 1998; Hedges & Nowell, 1995). In Western countries, almost all participants in the International Mathematics Olympiad have been males. (More females have, however, reached the top levels in non-Western countries, such as China [Halpern, 1991]). The score differences are sharpest at the extremes. Among 12- to 14-year-olds scoring extremely high on the math part of the SAT college entrance exam, boys outnumber girls 13 to 1. Within that group, the boys more often go on to earn a degree in the inorganic sciences and engineering (Benbow & others, 2000).

The most reliable male edge appears in spatial ability tests like the one shown in **FIGURE 8.12** on the next page, which involves speedily rotating three-dimensional objects in one's mind (Collins & Kimura, 1997; Halpern, 2000). Such skills help when fitting suitcases into a car trunk, playing chess, or doing certain types of geometry problems. From an evolutionary perspective, those same skills would have helped our ancestral fathers track prey and make their way home (Geary, 1995, 1996; Silverman & others, 1992, 1998). The survival of

World Math Olympics champs :: After outscoring 350,000 of their U.S. peers, these boys all had perfect scores in competition with math whizzes from 68 other countries.

Which two circles contain a configuration of blocks identical to the one in the circle on the left?

Standard

Responses

Figure 8.12> The mental rotation test This is a test of spatial abilities. Which two responses show a rotated view of the standard? (From Vandenberg & Kuse, 1978.)

Answers: first and fourth alternatives

our ancestral mothers may have benefited more from a keen memory for the location of edible plants—a legacy that lives today in women's superior memory for objects and their location.

AP Photo/Paul Sakuma

Nature or nurture? :: At this 2005 Google Inc.-sponsored computer coding competition, programmers competed for cash prizes and possible jobs. What do you think accounted for the fact that only one of the 100 finalists was female?

Are Test Questions Biased?

15: Are intelligence tests biased and discriminatory?

Knowing there are group differences in intelligence test scores leads us to wonder whether intelligence tests are biased. The answer depends on how we define bias.

One way a test can be biased is if scores are influenced by a person's cultural experience. This in fact happened to Eastern European immigrants in the early 1900s. Lacking the experience to answer questions about their new culture, many were classified as feeble-minded.

The *scientific* meaning of *bias* hinges on the test's validity. For an intelligence test, this means it should predict future behavior for all groups of test-takers, not just for some. For example, if the SAT accurately predicted the college achievement of women but not that of men, then the test would be biased. Almost all psychologists agree that the major U.S. aptitude tests are *not* biased in this scientific meaning of the term (Neisser & others, 1996; Wigdor & Garner, 1982). Their predictive validity is roughly the same for women and men, for Blacks and Whites, and for rich and poor. If an intelligence test score of 95 predicts slightly below-average grades, that rough prediction usually applies equally to both genders and all ethnic and economic groups.

Test-Takers' Expectations Our expectations and attitudes can influence our performance on tests, just as they influence our perceptions and behaviors in other areas. Sometimes we are driven by **stereotype threat**—the fear that we will be judged not by our own actions but by the negative feelings that others have about our group or category. In one study, for example, Black students performed at a lower level on verbal aptitude tests under conditions designed to make them feel threatened (Steele & others, 2002). And when equally capable men and women took a difficult math test, the women did not perform as well as the men—except when they had been led to expect that women usually do as well as men on the test (Spencer & others, 1999). Without this helpful hint, the women seem to have been concerned about their

ability to do well, and this feeling influenced them to live down to their own expectations. Stereotype threat helps explain why women have scored higher on math tests when no male test-takers were in the group, and why Blacks have scored higher when tested by Blacks than when tested by Whites (Danso & Esses, 2001; Inzlicht & Ben-Zeev, 2000).

All of these findings show that intelligence test scores reflect many things—the test-takers' innate abilities, their attitudes and expectations, and their cultural experience. In this sense, the tests are biased. But they are not biased in the scientific sense of making valid predictions for all groups.

What time is it now? Earlier in this chapter, did you underestimate or overestimate how quickly you would finish the chapter?

So, are the tests also discriminatory? Again, the answer can be yes or no. In one sense, yes, their purpose is to discriminate—to distinguish among individuals according to their abilities. But in another sense, intelligence tests are designed to reduce discrimination. Recall that intelligence testing began with Alfred Binet. The French government hired him to avoid relying on teachers' personal judgments about how well children would do in school programs. Aptitude tests are meant to give people a fair chance at school and job placement, replacing judgments about who you know, how you dress, or whether you are the "right kind of person." Civil service aptitude tests, for example, were devised to select people for government jobs more fairly and objectively, by reducing the political, racial, and ethnic discrimination that preceded their use. Without access to aptitude test scores, those who award jobs and admissions would rely more on other considerations, such as their personal opinions or intuitions.

stereotype threat a self-confirming concern that we will be evaluated based on a negative stereotype.

Perhaps, then, our goals for tests of mental abilities should be threefold. First, we should realize the benefits Binet foresaw—to enable schools to recognize who might profit most from early intervention. Second, we must remain alert to misinterpreting intelligence test scores as measures of a person's worth and fixed potential. And finally, we must remember that the competence sampled by general intelligence tests is important; it helps people succeed in some life paths. But it reflects only one aspect of personal competence. Our emotional intelligence matters, too, as do other forms of creativity, talent, and character. The carpenter's spatial ability differs from the programmer's logical ability, which differs from the poet's verbal ability. Because there are many ways of being successful, our differences are variations of human adaptability.

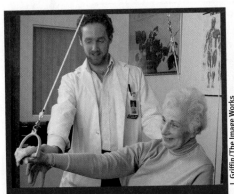

J. Griffin/The Image Works

Untestable compassion :: Intelligence test scores are only one part of the picture of a whole person. They don't measure the abilities, talent, and commitment of, for example, people who devote their lives to helping others.

PRACTICE TEST

15. The strongest support for heredity's influence on intelligence is the finding that
   a. identical twins, but not other siblings, have nearly identical intelligence test scores.
   b. the correlation between intelligence test scores of fraternal twins is higher than that for other siblings.
   c. separated fraternal twins living in different environments tend to have similar intelligence test scores.
   d. rich children have higher intelligence test scores than impoverished children.

16. To say that the heritability of intelligence is about 50 percent means that 50 percent of
   a. an individual's intelligence is due to genetic factors.
   b. the similarities between men and women are attributable to genes.
   c. the variation in intelligence within a group of people is attributable to genetic factors.
   d. intelligence is due to the mother's genes and the rest is due to the father's genes.

17. The experience that has the clearest, most profound effect on intellectual development is
   a. being enrolled in school by age 4.
   b. growing up in an economically disadvantaged home or neighborhood.
   c. being raised in a very neglectful home or institution.
   d. being exposed to very stimulating toys and lessons in infancy.

Answers: 15. a, 16. c, 17. c.

TERMS AND CONCEPTS TO REMEMBER

cognition, p. 206

algorithm, p. 206

heuristic, p. 206

insight, p. 206

confirmation bias, p. 207

availability heuristic, p. 207

fixation, p. 208

overconfidence, p. 208

framing, p. 208

belief perseverance, p. 209

language, p. 211

babbling stage, p. 212

one-word stage, p. 212

two-word stage, p. 212

telegraphic speech, p. 212

intelligence, p. 218

general intelligence (*g*), p. 218

savant syndrome, p. 219

creativity, p. 220

emotional intelligence, p. 221

intelligence test, p. 222

aptitude test, p. 222

achievement test, p. 222

mental age, p. 222

Stanford-Binet, p. 222

intelligence quotient (IQ), p. 223

Wechsler Adult Intelligence Scale (WAIS), p. 223

standardization, p. 224

normal curve, p. 224

reliability, p. 224

validity, p. 224

heritability, p. 226

stereotype threat, p. 230

:: Multiple-choice **self-tests** and more may be found at www.worthpublishers.com/myers

REVIEW: THINKING, LANGUAGE, AND INTELLIGENCE

THINKING

COGNITION: ALL THE MENTAL ACTIVITIES ASSOCIATED WITH THINKING, KNOWING, REMEMBERING, AND COMMUNICATING.

1 What strategies do we use to solve problems?

- *Algorithms:* Time-consuming but thorough strategies (such as a step-by-step description for evacuating a building during a fire) that guarantee a solution to a problem.
- *Heuristics:* Strategies that are simpler and quicker (such as running for an exit if you smell smoke), but can lead to incorrect solutions.
- *Insight:* An Aha! reaction, a sudden flash of inspiration that is not based on any strategy.

3 How can we improve our risk assessment?

- Realize that we are predisposed to fear what our ancestors feared, what we feel we cannot control, what is immediate, and what is most available to our memories.
- Measure the actual danger by today's reality.

2 What obstacles hinder smart thinking?

- *Confirmation bias:* Searching for evidence that confirms rather than challenges our ideas.
- *The availability heuristic:* Judging the likelihood of events based on how readily they come to mind (not on how likely they are to actually occur).
- *Fixation:* Inability to take fresh perspectives on a problem.
- *Overconfidence:* Believing we know more than we do.
- *Framing:* The wording of questions, which affects how we respond to them.
- *Belief perseverance:* Our tendency to cling to our ideas, ignoring evidence that disproves them.

4 When is intuition useful?

- Despite our capacity for error and bias, human intuition can be efficient and adaptive, as when we gain expertise in a field and grow adept at making quick, shrewd judgments.

LANGUAGE

LANGUAGE: WORDS AND THE WAYS WE COMBINE THEM TO COMMUNICATE MEANING.

5 When do children acquire language, and how do they master this complex task?

- By about 4 months of age, infants *babble,* making a wide range of sounds found in languages all over the world.
- By about 10 months, babbling contains only the sounds of the household language.
- By about 12 months, babies speak in *one-word* sentences.
- *Two-word (telegraphic)* phrases happen around 24 months, followed by full sentences soon after.
- We are predisposed to learn language, but the particular language we learn is the result of our experience.
- Childhood is a critical period for learning language.

6 How can thinking in images be useful?

- Thinking in images can provide useful mental practice if we focus on the steps needed to reach our goal rather than fantasizing about having achieved the goal.

7 Do animals—in some sense we can identify with—think? Do they even exhibit language?

- Primates form concepts, display insight, use and create tools, and transmit cultural innovations.
- Animals do communicate, but research reveals important differences between primates' and humans' abilities to use language, especially in ordering words grammatically.

INTELLIGENCE

INTELLIGENCE: THE ABILITY TO LEARN FROM EXPERIENCE, SOLVE PROBLEMS, AND ADAPT TO NEW SITUATIONS.

8 **Is intelligence a single general ability or several distinct abilities?**

- A *general intelligence* (*g*) factor seems to run through many aptitudes.
- *Savant syndrome* and abilities lost after brain injuries suggest that we have multiple types of mental aptitudes.
- Gardner proposed eight intelligences (linguistic, logical-mathematical, musical, spatial, bodily-kinesthetic, intrapersonal, interpersonal, and naturalist).

10 **Is our ability to manage our own emotions and to empathize with others a form of intelligence?**

- *Emotional intelligence* is the ability to perceive, understand, manage, and use emotions.
- Critics suggest this concept stretches the idea of intelligence too far.

11 **When and why were intelligence tests created?**

- *Intelligence tests* measure *aptitude* (ability to learn), and *achievement tests* measure what we have already learned.
- In the early 1900s, Alfred Binet and Théodore Simon developed tests to measure children's *mental age* and predict their progress in the Paris school system.
- Lewis Terman's *Stanford-Binet* test was an adaptation of Binet's work for use in the United States. William Stern devised a formula (the *intelligence quotient*) to state test scores as a single number.
- David Wechsler designed the most widely used individual intelligence tests, the *Wechsler Adult Intelligence Scale (WAIS)* and the Wechsler Intelligence Scale for Children (WISC).

9 **What is creativity, and what fosters this ability?**

- *Creative* people produce novel and valuable ideas.
- Creativity correlates with developed expertise, imaginative thinking skills, a venturesome personality, intrinsic motivation, and a creative environment.
- Beyond an intelligence score of about 120, test scores don't predict creativity.

12 **By what criteria can we judge intelligence tests?**

- All good tests must be *standardized* by comparisons with a pre-tested group. Test-takers' scores usually form a bell-shaped *normal curve*.
- Tests must also be *reliable* (yielding dependably consistent scores) and *valid* (measuring or predicting what they are supposed to).

13 **Is intelligence influenced more by heredity or by environment?**

- *Heritability* is the amount of variation among individuals that can be attributed to genes.
- Twin and adoption studies reveal an important genetic contribution to intelligence.
- Studies of children raised in impoverished, enriched, or culturally different environments show that life experiences also affect intelligence test performance.

14 **How, and why, do ethnic and gender groups differ in their intelligence test scores?**

- Environmental differences predict racial gaps in test scores.
- Girls score higher on spelling tests; verbal ability; nonverbal memory; sensitivity to touch, taste, and odor; and on reading others' emotions. Boys score higher on some math tests and on spatial relations tests, and they outnumber girls at the low extreme of school achievement.
- Evolutionary and cultural factors influence gender differences in specific abilities.

15 **Are intelligence tests biased and discriminatory?**

- Aptitude tests need to be sensitive to performance differences caused by cultural experience.
- Expectations influence our performance on tests, as when we feel a *stereotype threat* (fearing others' negative judgment of our group).
- Experts consider the major aptitude tests to be unbiased, in the sense that they predict as well for one group as for another.

9 Motivation and Emotion

HAVING BAGGED NEARLY ALL OF COLORADO'S tallest peaks, many of them solo and in winter, experienced climber Aron Ralston went canyon hiking alone one Saturday spring morning in 2003. The outing seemed so risk-free he did not bother to tell anyone where he was going. In Utah's narrow Bluejohn Canyon, just 150 yards above his final drop, he was climbing over an 800-pound rock when disaster struck. The rock shifted and pinned his right wrist and arm. He was, as the title of his book says, caught *Between a Rock and a Hard Place.*

Realizing that no one would be rescuing him, Ralston tried with all his might to dislodge the rock. Then, with his dull pocket knife, he tried chipping away at the rock. When that failed, he rigged up ropes to lift the rock. Alas, nothing worked. Hour after hour, then cold night after cold night, he was stuck. By Tuesday, he had run out of food and water. On Wednesday, as thirst and hunger gnawed, he began saving and sipping his own urine. Using his video recorder, he said his good-byes to family and friends, for whom he now felt intense love. "So again love to everyone. Bring love and peace and happiness and beautiful lives into the world in my honor. Thank you. Love you."

On Thursday, surprised to find himself still alive, Ralston had a seemingly divine insight into his reproductive future. In his vision, he saw a preschool boy being scooped up by a one-armed man. With this inspiration, he summoned his remaining strength and his enormous will to live. Over the next hour, he willfully broke his bones and then proceeded to use that dull knife to cut off his arm. The

AP Photo/E Pablo Kosmicki

Aron Ralston

next moment was spent putting on a tourniquet, chopping the last piece of skin, and breaking free. Then, holding his bleeding half-arm close, he climbed down the 65-foot cliff and hiked 5 miles before finding someone. He describes the moment when he broke free. "[I was] just reeling with this euphoria . . . having been dead and standing in my grave, leaving my last will and testament, etching 'Rest in peace' on the wall, all of that, gone and then replaced with having my life again. It was undoubtedly the sweetest moment that I will ever experience" (Ralston, 2004).

Aron Ralston's thirst and hunger, his sense of belonging to others, and his underlying will to live and become a father highlight the force of **motivation:** a need or desire that *energizes* behavior and *directs* it toward a goal. His intense emotional experiences of love and joy demonstrate the close ties between our feelings, or *emotions,* and our motivated behaviors. In this chapter, we explore both of these human forces—our motivations and our emotions.

motivation a need or desire that energizes and directs behavior.

Motivational Concepts

1: What are three key perspectives on motivation, and how do they help us understand motivated behaviors?

Our motivations arise from the interplay between nature (the bodily "push") and nurture (the "pulls" from our thought processes and culture). Let's consider three perspectives psychologists have used in their attempt to understand motivated behaviors. *Drive-reduction theory* focuses on how our inner pushes and external pulls interact. *Arousal theory* focuses on our search for the "right" level of stimulation. And Abraham Maslow's *hierarchy of needs* describes how some of our needs can be more compelling than others.

Drive-Reduction Theory

Drive-reduction theory assumes that our unmet **physiological needs** (such as hunger or thirst) create an aroused state. This physical arousal translates into a psychological **drive**—a motivated state that *pushes* us to reduce the need by, say, eating or drinking.

We also are *pulled* by **incentives**—environmental stimuli that attract or repel us, depending on our individual learning histories. Thus, the aroma of good food will motivate a hungry person. Whether

"What do you think . . . should we get started on that motivation research or not?"

that aroma comes from fresh-baked bread or toasted ants will depend on your culture and experience.

When there is both a need and an incentive, we feel strongly driven. If I skip lunch and then smell baking bread, I will feel a strong hunger drive. In the presence of that drive, the baking bread becomes a powerful incentive. *For each motive, we can therefore ask, "How is it pushed by our inborn bodily needs and pulled by incentives in the environment?"*

Arousal Theory

When we are motivated to satisfy our basic needs, we are *aroused* (physically energized or tense). Behaviors that meet these needs, such as eating when we're hungry, reduce our feelings of arousal. (Imagine sitting lazily around the table after Thanksgiving dinner.) But other motivated behaviors actually increase arousal **(FIGURE 9.1)**. Well-fed animals with

no clear, need-based drive will leave safe shelter to explore. From taking such risks, animals gain information and resources (Renner, 1992).

Curiosity drives monkeys to monkey around trying to figure out how to unlock a latch that opens nothing or how to open a window that allows them to see outside their room (Butler, 1954). It drives the 9-month-old infant who checks out every corner of the house. It drives the scientists whose work this text discusses. And it drives adventurers such as Aron Ralston. Asked why he wanted to climb Mount Everest, George Mallory answered, "Because it is there." Those who, like Mallory and Ralston, enjoy high arousal are most likely to enjoy intense music, novel foods, and risky behaviors (Zuckerman, 1979).

So, when we humans find that all our biological needs are met, we may feel bored and seek stimulation to increase our arousal. But not *too* much stimulation, for that brings stress, and we then look for a way to decrease arousal. This search for just the right level of arousal thus energizes and directs our behavior.

A Hierarchy of Needs

Some needs are more important than others. At this moment, with your needs for air and water satisfied, other motives are directing your behavior. If you were deprived of water, your thirst would take over your thoughts. Just ask Aron Ralston. But if your air supply was cut off, your thirst would disappear.

Figure 9.1> These Israeli college students exploring at an archeological site (left) and this Berber shepherd boy meeting a digital camera for the first time (right) are all driven by their curiosity, and they are maintaining a desired level of arousal.

Bill Aron/Photo Edit

David Samuel Robbins/Corbis

"Hunger is the most urgent form of poverty."

Alliance to End Hunger, 2002

Abraham Maslow (1970) viewed these and other motives as a pyramid he called a **hierarchy of needs (FIGURE 9.2)**. At the pyramid's base are our physiological needs, such as those for food and water. Only after these needs are met, said Maslow (1971), do we try to meet our need for safety, and then to satisfy the uniquely human needs to give and receive love and to enjoy self-esteem. At the very peak of the pyramid are the highest human needs. At the *self-actualization* level, people seek to realize their own potential. At the *self-transcendence* level, which Maslow proposed near the end of his life, some people strive for *transpersonal* meaning, purpose, and identity that is beyond (*trans*) the self (Koltko-Rivera, 2006).

There are exceptions to Maslow's hierarchy. For example, people have starved themselves to make a political statement. Nevertheless, the simple idea that some needs are more basic than others gives us a framework for thinking about motivation. Surveys in 39 nations support this basic idea (Oishi & others, 1999). In poorer nations, money, and the food and shelter it buys, more strongly commands attention and predicts feelings of well-being. In wealthy nations, where most are able to meet basic needs, home-life satisfaction is a better predictor of well-being.

Let's take a closer look now at two specific motives, beginning at the physiological level with *hunger* and working up to the higher-level *need to belong*. At each level, we will see how incentives (the psychological "pull") interact with bodily needs (the biological "push").

1. An example of a physiological need is _____. An example of a psychological drive is _____.
   a. hunger; a "push" to find food
   b. a "push" to find food; hunger
   c. curiosity; a "push" to reduce arousal
   d. a "push" to reduce arousal; curiosity

2. Motivated behaviors satisfy a variety of needs. When feeling bored, we may look for ways to
   a. reduce physiological needs.
   b. search out respect from others.
   c. increase arousal.
   d. ensure stability.

3. Jan walks into a friend's kitchen, smells bread baking, and begins to feel very hungry. The smell of baking bread is a(n)
   a. psychological drive.
   b. physiological need.
   c. incentive.
   d. aroused state.

4. According to Abraham Maslow, our most basic needs are physiological needs, including the need for food, water, and oxygen; just above these are
   a. safety needs.
   b. self-esteem needs.
   c. belongingness needs.
   d. psychological needs.

Answers: 1. a, 2. c, 3. c, 4. a.

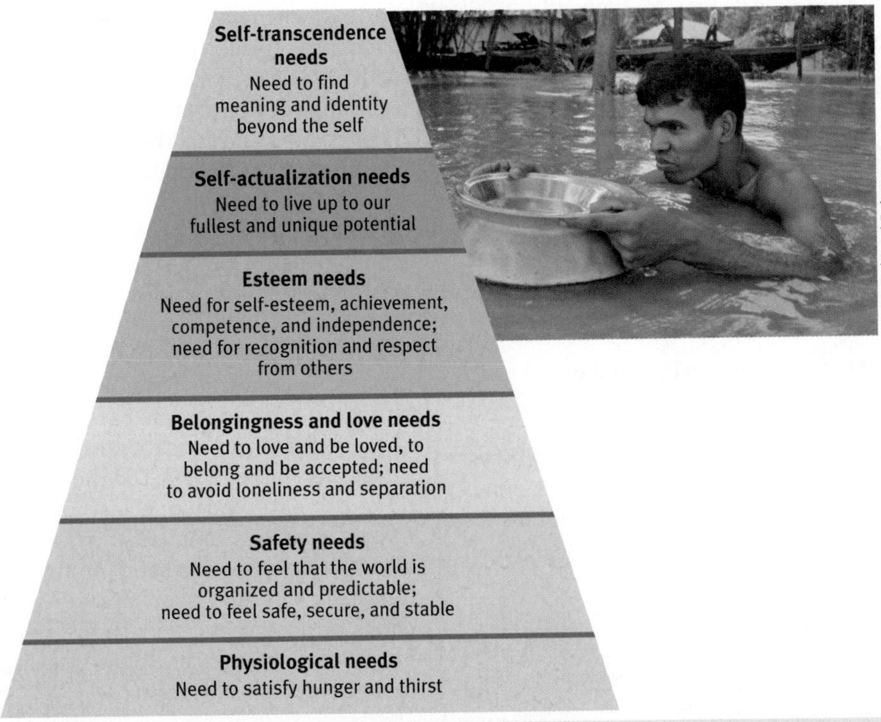

Self-transcendence needs
Need to find meaning and identity beyond the self

Self-actualization needs
Need to live up to our fullest and unique potential

Esteem needs
Need for self-esteem, achievement, competence, and independence; need for recognition and respect from others

Belongingness and love needs
Need to love and be loved, to belong and be accepted; need to avoid loneliness and separation

Safety needs
Need to feel that the world is organized and predictable; need to feel safe, secure, and stable

Physiological needs
Need to satisfy hunger and thirst

AP Photo/Pavel Rahman

Figure 9.2> Maslow's hierarchy of needs Once our lower-level needs are met, we are prompted to satisfy our higher-level needs (from Maslow, 1970). For survivors of the disastrous 2007 Bangladeshi flood, such as this man carefully carrying his precious load of clean water, satisfying very basic needs for water, food, and safety became top priority. Higher-level needs, such as respect, self-actualization, and meaning often take a back seat during such times.

drive-reduction theory the idea that a physiological need creates an aroused tension state (a drive) that motivates an organism to satisfy the need.

physiological needs basic bodily requirements.

drive aroused, motivated state often created by deprivation of a needed substance.

incentive a positive or negative environmental stimulus that motivates behavior.

hierarchy of needs Maslow's pyramid of human needs; at the base are physiological needs that must be satisfied before higher-level safety needs, and then psychological needs, become active.

Hunger

The power of physiological needs was vividly demonstrated in World War II prison camps. David Mandel (1983), a Nazi concentration camp survivor, recalled how a starving "father and son would fight over a piece of bread. Like dogs." One father, whose 20-year-old son stole his bread from under his pillow while he slept, went into a deep depression, asking over and over how his son could do such a thing. The next day the father died. "Hunger does something to you that's hard to describe," Mandel explained.

> "The full person does not understand the needs of the hungry."
>
> Irish proverb

To learn more about the results of semistarvation, scientist Ancel Keys and his colleagues (1950) fed 36 male volunteers just enough to maintain their initial weight. Then, for six months, they cut this food level in half. The effects soon became visible. Without thinking about it, the men began conserving energy. They appeared sluggish and dull. They lost weight rapidly, until they had shed about 25 percent of their starting weights. As Maslow would have guessed, the men became obsessed with food. They talked food. They daydreamed food. They collected recipes, read cookbooks, and feasted their eyes on tasty but forbidden food. Preoccupied with their unmet basic need, they lost interest in sex and social activities. As one man reported, "If we see a show, the most interesting part of it is contained in scenes where people are eating. I couldn't laugh at the funniest picture in the world, and love scenes are completely dull."

> "Nobody wants to kiss when they are hungry."
>
> Dorothea Dix (1801–1887)

The Physiology of Hunger

2: What physiological factors cause us to feel hungry?

Deprived of a normal food supply, Keys' volunteers were clearly hungry. What precisely triggers feelings of hunger? Are the pangs of an empty stomach the source of hunger? So it seemed to A. L. Washburn. Working with Walter Cannon (Cannon & Washburn, 1912), Washburn agreed to swallow a balloon that was attached to a recording device **(FIGURE 9.3)**. When inflated in his stomach, the balloon tracked his stomach contractions. Washburn supplied information about his *feelings* of hunger by pressing a key each time he felt a hunger pang. The discovery: Washburn was indeed having stomach contractions whenever he felt hungry.

Can hunger exist without stomach pangs? To answer that question, researchers removed some rats' stomachs and created a direct path to their small intestines (Tsang, 1938). Did the rats continue to eat? Indeed they did. Some hunger persists similarly in humans whose stomachs have been removed as a treatment for ulcers or cancer. So, the pangs of an empty stomach are not the only source of hunger. What else might fuel our feelings of hunger?

Body Chemistry and the Brain

Somehow, somewhere, your body is keeping tabs on the energy it takes in and the energy it uses. If this weren't true,

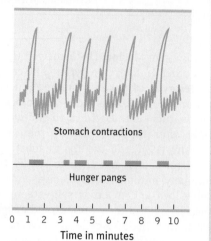
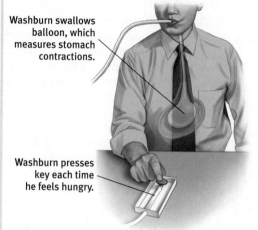

Figure 9.3> Monitoring stomach contractions

Washburn swallows balloon, which measures stomach contractions.

Washburn presses key each time he feels hungry.

Stomach contractions

Hunger pangs

Time in minutes

GARFIELD

THE TV ADVERTISERS DIDN'T WASTE ANY TIME

I'VE BEEN ON A DIET ONE DAY AND THEY'RE ALREADY RUNNING MORE FOOD COMMERCIALS

JPM DAVIS
© 1986 PAWS, INC./Distributed by Universal Press Syndicate

3-19

you would be unable to maintain a stable body weight. A major source of energy in your body is the blood sugar **glucose.** If your blood glucose level drops, your stomach, intestines, and liver will send messages to your brain. Your brain, which is automatically monitoring your blood chemistry and your body's internal state, will then trigger feelings of hunger.

How does the brain integrate these messages and sound the alarm? Researchers began unraveling this puzzle when they located hunger controls within the hypothalamus, buried deep in the brain **(FIGURE 9.4)**. This tiny, complex neural traffic intersection contains two distinct centers that help control eating. Activity along the sides of the hypothalamus (the *lateral hypothalamus*) brings on hunger. If electrically stimulated there, well-fed animals begin to eat. If the area is destroyed, even starving animals have no interest in food.

Activity in the second center—the lower mid-hypothalamus (the *ventromedial hypothalamus*)—depresses hunger. Stimulate this area and an animal will stop eating. Destroy the area and the animal's stomach and intestines will process food more rapidly, causing it to become extremely fat (Duggan & Booth, 1986; Hoebel & Teitelbaum, 1966) **(FIGURE 9.5)**.

Blood vessels connect the hypothalamus to the rest of the body, so it can respond to our current blood chemistry

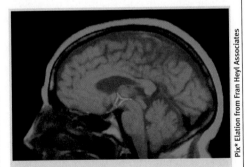

Figure 9.4> The hypothalamus The hypothalamus (colored red) performs various body maintenance functions. One of these functions is control of hunger.

Pix Elation from Fran Heyl Associates*

Figure 9.5> Evidence for the brain's control of eating Destroying the ventromedial hypothalamus caused this rat's weight to triple.

Richard Howard

Over the next 40 years you will eat about 20 tons of food. If during those years you increase your daily intake by just .01 ounce more than required for your energy needs, you will gain 24 pounds (Martin & others, 1991).

---

and other incoming information. One of its tasks is monitoring levels of appetite hormones, such as *ghrelin,* a hunger-arousing hormone secreted by an empty stomach. During bypass surgery for severe obesity, surgeons seal off part of the stomach. The remaining stomach then produces much less ghrelin, and the person's appetite lessens (Lemonick, 2002). Other appetite hormones include insulin, leptin, orexin, and PYY **(FIGURE 9.6** on the next page).

The interaction of appetite hormones and brain activity suggests that we have a sort of "weight thermostat." When semistarved rats fall below their normal weight, this system signals the body to restore the lost weight. The rats' hunger increases and their energy output decreases. If body weight rises—as happens when rats are force-fed—hunger

decreases and energy output increases. In this way, rats (and humans) tend to hover around a stable weight, or **set point,** influenced in part by heredity (Keesey & Corbett, 1983).

We humans vary in our **basal metabolic rate,** a measure of how much energy we use to maintain basic body functions when our body is at rest. But we share a common response to a decrease in food intake: Our basal metabolic rate decreases. By the end of their 24 weeks of semistarvation, the participants in Keys' experiment had stabilized at three-quarters of their normal weight, while taking in only half their previous calories. They managed this by reducing the amount of energy they used, partly through inactivity but partly because of a 29 percent drop in their basal metabolic rate.

Some researchers have suggested that the idea of a biologically *fixed* set point is too rigid. They note that slow, steady changes in body weight can alter one's set point (Assanand & others, 1998). Given unlimited access to various tasty foods, people and other animals tend to overeat and gain weight (Raynor & Epstein, 2001). Psychological factors also influence hunger. For all these reasons, some researchers prefer the looser term *settling point* to indicate the level at which a person's weight settles in response to caloric intake and energy use. As we will see next, these factors are influenced by environment as well as biology.

---

glucose the form of sugar that circulates in the blood and provides the major source of energy for body tissues. When its level is low, we feel hunger.

set point the point at which an individual's "weight thermostat" is supposedly set. When the body falls below this weight, an increase in hunger and a lowered metabolic rate may act to restore the lost weight.

basal metabolic rate the body's resting rate of energy expenditure.

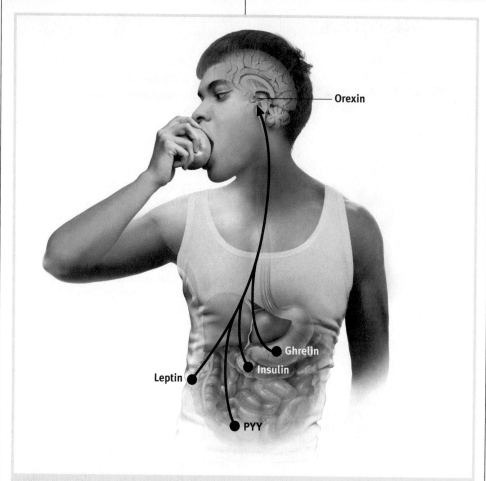

Figure 9.6> The appetite hormones
Insulin: Hormone secreted by pancreas; controls blood glucose.
Leptin: Protein secreted by fat cells; when abundant, causes brain to increase metabolism and decrease hunger.
Orexin: Hunger-triggering hormone secreted by hypothalamus.
Ghrelin: Hormone secreted by empty stomach; sends "I'm hungry" signals to the brain.
PYY: Digestive tract hormone; sends "I'm *not* hungry" signals to the brain.

"*Never get a tattoo when you're drunk and hungry.*"

The Psychology of Hunger

3: What psychological factors affect our eating behavior and feelings of hunger?

We have seen that our eagerness to eat is pushed by our body chemistry and brain activity. Yet there is more to hunger than meets the stomach. This was strikingly apparent when trickster researchers tested two patients who had no memory for events occurring more than a minute ago (Rozin & others, 1998). If offered a second lunch 20 minutes after eating a normal lunch, both patients readily consumed it . . . and usually a third meal offered 20 minutes after the second was finished. This suggests that one part of our decision to eat is our memory of the time of our last meal. As time passes, we think about eating again, and that thought triggers feelings of hunger.

Psychological influences on eating behavior are most striking when an abnormal desire to be thin overrides normal reactions to hunger (see Close-Up: Eating Disorders).

Taste Preference: Biology or Culture?

Both body chemistry and environment play a role in our feelings of hunger and in what we hunger for—our taste preferences. When feeling tense or depressed, do you crave starchy, carbohydrate-laden foods (chips, sweets, fast food)? Carbohydrates help boost levels of the neurotransmitter serotonin, which has calming effects. When stressed, even rats find it extra rewarding to scarf Oreos (Artiga & others, 2007; Boggiano & others, 2005).

Our preferences for sweet and salty tastes are genetic and universal. Other taste preferences are learned. People given highly salted foods, for example, develop a liking for excess salt (Beauchamp, 1987). A very effective learning experience is violent illness after eating a particular food, which we will avoid after that. (The frequency of children's illnesses provides many chances for them to learn to avoid certain foods.)

Culture affects taste preferences, too. Bedouins enjoy eating the eye of a camel, which most North Americans would find repulsive. Most North Americans and Europeans shun horse, dog, and rat meat, all of which are prized elsewhere.

Rats themselves tend to avoid unfamiliar foods (Sclafani, 1995). So do we, especially those that are animal-based.

CLOSE-UP

EATING DISORDERS

The power of psychological influences to overwhelm biological wisdom is painfully clear in eating disorders.

Our bodies are naturally disposed to maintain a normal weight, storing some energy reserves in case food becomes unavailable for a time. Yet people with **anorexia nervosa**—usually adolescents and 9 out of 10 times females—starve themselves. Anorexia begins as a weight-loss diet, but even when the person drops far below normal weight (typically, by 15 percent or more), the feeling of being fat and needing to lose weight remains.

Bulimia nervosa may also be triggered by a weight-loss diet, broken by gorging on forbidden foods. In the binge-purge cycle that follows, overeating alternates with vomiting, laxative use, fasting, and excessive exercise. Unlike anorexia, however, bulimia is marked by weight shifts within or above normal ranges, making this disorder easier to hide. Binge-purge eaters—mostly women in their late teens or early twenties—are preoccupied with food (craving sweet and high-fat foods) and obsessed with their weight and appearance. They experience bouts of depression and anxiety, most severe during and following binges (Hinz & Williamson, 1987; Johnson & others, 2002).

About half of those with anorexia also display the binge-purge-depression symptoms of bulimia. People with anorexia often come from competitive, high-achieving families. They tend to have low self-esteem, set impossible standards, and fret about falling short of expectations (Polivy & Herman, 2002; Striegel-Moore & others, 1993).

"*Skeletons on parade*" :: A recent newspaper article used this headline in criticizing superthin models. Do such models make self-starvation fashionable?

©Newscom

Heredity may bend some people in the direction of eating disorders. Identical twins share the disorder somewhat more often than fraternal twins do (Fairburn & others, 1999; Kaplan, 2004).

But environment plays a bigger role. Body ideals vary across culture and time. In India, women students rate their ideal body size as close to their actual shape. In much of Africa—where plump means prosperous and thinness can signal poverty and AIDS—bigger is better (Knickmeyer, 2001).

Bigger is not better in Western cultures, where the rise in eating disorders over the last 50 years has coincided with a dramatic increase in women having a poor body image (Feingold & Mazzella, 1998). Part of the pressure on women surely stems from the doctored images of unnaturally thin models and celebrities (Tovee & others, 1997). Viewing such images, women often feel ashamed, depressed, and dissatisfied with their own bodies (Stice & Shaw, 1994; Posavac & others, 1998).

> "Diana remained . . . almost childlike in her desire to do good for others, so she could release herself from deep feelings of unworthiness, of which her eating disorders were merely a symptom."
>
> **Charles, Ninth Earl of Spencer, eulogizing his sister Princess Diana, 1997**

Testing this link, researchers gave some adolescent girls (but not others) a 15-month subscription to a teen fashion magazine (Stice & others, 2001). Vulnerable girls (those who were already dissatisfied, idealized thinness, and lacked social support) who received the magazine showed increased body dissatisfaction and eating disorder tendencies.

The eating disorders of today's Western world seem to be reflecting a weight-obsessed culture.

"Gee, I had no idea you were married to a supermodel."

The New Yorker Collection, 1999, Michael Maslin from cartoonbank.com. All Rights Reserved.

anorexia nervosa an eating disorder in which a person (usually an adolescent female) maintains a starvation diet despite being significantly (15 percent or more) underweight.

bulimia nervosa an eating disorder in which a person alternates binge-eating (usually of high-calorie foods) with purging (by vomiting or laxative use), fasting, or excessive exercise.

Diverse Yet Alike

People everywhere learn to enjoy the fatty, bitter, or spicy foods common in their culture. For Alaska Natives (left), but not for most other North Americans, whale blubber is a tasty treat. For these Campa Indians in Peru (right), roasted ants are similarly delicious.

This surely was adaptive for our ancestors by protecting them from potentially toxic substances.

We also may learn to prefer some tastes because they are adaptive. The spices most commonly used in the recipes of hot climates (where food spoils more quickly) inhibit the growth of bacteria **(FIGURE 9.7)**. India averages nearly 10 spices per meat recipe, Finland 2 spices. Pregnancy-related nausea is another example of adaptive taste preferences. Food aversions stemming from this nausea peak about the tenth week, when the developing embryo is most vulnerable to toxins.

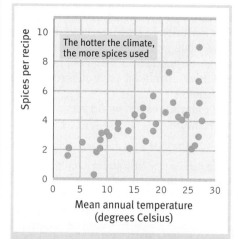

Spices per recipe

The hotter the climate, the more spices used

Mean annual temperature (degrees Celsius)

Figure 9.7> Hot cultures like hot spices (Sherman & Flaxman, 2001).

Obesity and Weight Control

4: What factors predispose some people to become and remain obese?

Why are so many of us (65 percent of Americans, according to the Centers for Disease Control) overweight, while others who eat the same amount don't add a pound? And why do so few overweight people win the battle of the bulge?

Part of the answer lies in our history. Fat is an ideal form of stored energy, a fuel reserve that can carry us through times when food is scarce. This was a common state in the feast-or-famine world of our prehistoric ancestors. (Think of that spare tire around the middle as an energy storehouse—biology's counterpart to a hiker's waist-borne snack pack.) In Europe in earlier centuries, obesity signaled wealth and social status, as it does in other parts of the world today (Furnham & Baguma, 1994). But the rule that once served our hungry distant ancestors (When you find energy-rich fat or sugar, eat it!) now works against us. In many parts of the world today, food and sweets are abundant, and 60 percent of the world's people are overweight (Booth & Neufer, 2005).

Being slightly overweight poses only modest health risks (Gibbs, 2005). Fitness matters more than carrying a little extra weight. But significant obesity **(FIGURE 9.8)** can shorten your life and reduce your quality of life. It increases the risk of diabetes, high blood pressure, heart disease, gallstones, joint pain, arthritis, and certain types of cancer (Olshansky & others, 2005). The risks are greater for apple-shaped people who carry their weight in pot bellies than for pear-shaped people with ample hips and thighs (Greenwood, 1989). New research also has linked women's obesity to the risk of late-life Alzheimer's disease and brain tissue loss (Gustafson & others, 2003, 2004).

The Social Effects of Obesity

Obesity can also be socially toxic, by affecting both how others treat you and how you feel about yourself. Obese people know the unfair stereotype: slow, lazy, and sloppy (Crandall, 1994, 1995; Ryckman & others, 1989). Widen people's images on a video monitor, making them look fatter, and observers suddenly rate them as less sincere, less friendly, meaner, and more obnoxious (Gardner & Tockerman, 1994). The social effects of obesity were clear in a study that followed 370 obese 16- to 24-year-old women (Gortmaker & others, 1993). When restudied seven years later, two-thirds of the women were still obese. And they were making less money—$7000 a year less—than an equally intelligent

Figure 9.8> Obesity measured as body mass index (BMI) U.S. government guidelines encourage a body mass index (BMI) under 25. The World Health Organization and many countries define obesity as a BMI of 30 or more. The zones in this graph are based on BMI measurements for these heights and weights. BMI is calculated by using the following formula:

$$\frac{\text{Weight in kg (pounds} \times .45)}{\text{Squared height in meters (inches} \div 39.4)^2} = \text{BMI}$$

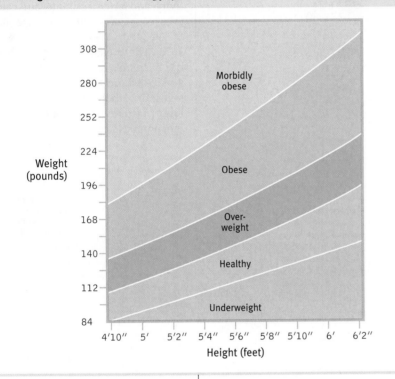

comparison group of some 5000 women who were not obese. They also were less likely to be married. In personal ads, men often state their preference for slimness, and women often advertise it (Miller & others, 2000; Smith & others, 1990).

In one clever experiment, viewers rated applicants in videotaped mock job interviews. In fact, the "applicants" were professional actors, who appeared as either normal-weight or overweight, thanks to makeup and body padding that made them look 30 pounds heavier (Pingitore & others, 1994). When appearing to be overweight, the same person—using the same sentences, voice, and gestures—was rated less worthy of hiring. The weight bias was especially strong against women applicants (FIGURE 9.9). Weight discrimination, though hardly

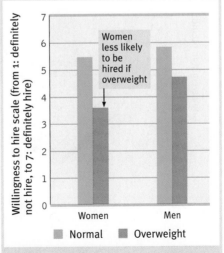

Figure 9.9> Gender and weight discrimination by employers

discussed, occurs at every stage of the employment cycle—hiring, placement, promotion, compensation, discipline, and discharge (Roehling, 1999). Anti-fat prejudice even extends to job seekers who are *seen* with an obese person (Hebl & Mannix, 2003).

So, why don't obese people just drop that excess baggage? Because their bodies fight back. Let's consider some of the evidence.

The Losing Battle

Research on obesity challenges the stereotype of severely overweight people being weak-willed gluttons. First, consider the arithmetic of weight gain: People get fat by taking in more calories than they use. The energy equivalent of a pound of fat is 3500 calories. Many dieters therefore believe they will lose a pound for every 3500 calories they cut from their diet. Surprise: This conclusion is false. Our bodies are designed to survive periods of famine.

An Explosion of Fat Cells Our body fat depends on the size and number of our fat cells. A typical adult has 30 to 40 billion of these mini fuel tanks, half of which lie near the skin's surface. The total number of fat cells depends on our heredity and personal history. Each fat cell can vary from nearly empty, like a dead balloon, to stuffed full. In an obese person, fat cells may swell to two or three times their normal size. Then—surprise—they divide, or they trigger nearby immature fat cells to divide, resulting in up to 75 billion total fat cells (Hirsch, 2003). That new total never decreases (FIGURE 9.10 on the next page). A dieter's fat cells may shrink, but they won't disappear (Sjöstrum, 1980).

A Sluggish Metabolism The body adapts to starvation by burning off fewer calories. Compared with other tissue, fat takes less food energy to maintain. An obese person's body has been maintaining body weight at a higher-than-average settling point. When a diet forces weight to drop below this range, the dieter's hunger increases and metabolism decreases.

Figure 9.10> Fat cells Our bodies store energy in fat cells, which become larger and more numerous if we are obese. If we then lose weight, the fat cells become smaller, but their number doesn't decrease. (Adapted from Jules Hirsch, 2003.)

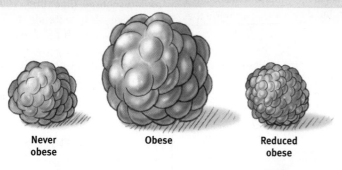

Never
obese

Obese

Reduced
obese

This effect was dramatically demonstrated in a month-long experiment in which obese patients' daily food intake was reduced from 3500 to 450 calories (Bray, 1969). Despite this drastic cut, participants lost only 6 percent of their weight. Their bodies reacted as though they were being starved, and their metabolic rates dropped about 15 percent **(FIGURE 9.11)**. That is why reducing food intake by 3500 calories may not reduce our weight by 1 pound. That is also why further weight loss comes slowly following the early rapid losses of a rigorous diet. And that is why we can regain weight by eating amounts of food that only maintained weight before we dieted. After a diet ends, our body is still in famine mode, trying to conserve energy.

A Genetic Handicap Studies reveal that the genes we inherit have a lot to do with the size of our jeans. Consider:

- Adopted children share meals with their adoptive siblings and parents. Yet their body weights most closely resemble those of their biological family (Grilo & Pogue-Geile, 1991).

- Identical twins have closely similar weights, even when reared apart (Plomin & others, 1997; Stunkard & others, 1990). The much less similar weights of fraternal twins suggest that genes explain two-thirds of our person-to-person differences in body mass (Maes & others, 1997).

- Given an obese parent, a boy is three times, and a girl six times more likely to be obese than their counterparts with normal-weight parents (Carrière, 2003).

Too Little Activity, Too Much Food
Most of us overestimate our physical activity and underestimate our caloric intake, especially if we are obese (Brownell & Wadden, 1992; Lichtman & others, 1992). That's easy to do in a culture that has become a lot like an animal feedlot—a place where farmers fatten animals by restricting their movement and offering lots of fattening food. One way to restrict movement is to sit still and watch TV. A

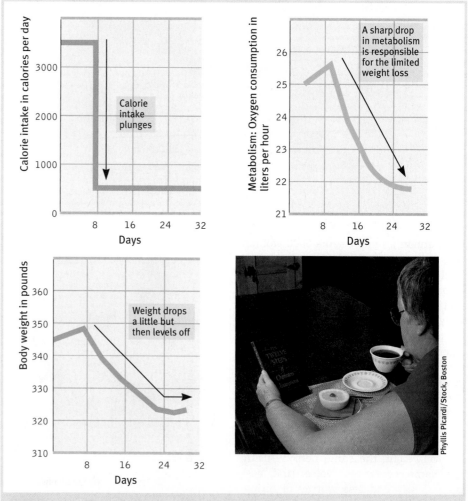

Figure 9.11> The effects of a severe diet on obese patients' body weight and metabolism (From Bray, 1969.)

Phyllis Picardi/Stock, Boston

long-term study of 50,000 nurses found that TV watching correlates with obesity. This link held even after the researchers controlled for exercise, smoking, age, and diet. For every two-hour increase in daily TV watching, there was a corresponding 23 percent increase in obesity and a 7 percent increase in diabetes (Hu & others, 2003). The TV watching–obesity link is found in children, too **(FIGURE 9.12)**.

Traveling by car also helps us hoard fat. People who live in many urban centers and other walking-dependent communities tend to weigh less than more sedentary folks in car-dependent suburbs (Ewing & others, 2003). Among Ontario's Old Order Amish, where farming and gardening are labor intensive, men walk an average nine miles a day, and women walk seven miles. The obesity rate in this community is one-seventh the U.S. rate (Bassett & others, 2004).

Lack of exercise means we expend fewer calories. At the same time, compared with people in the early 1900s, we are eating a higher-fat, higher-sugar diet and suffering higher rates of diabetes at younger ages (Brody, 2003; Thompson, 1998). The ready availability of all-you-can-eat food buffets, make-your-own waffles, and free-refill soft drinks offers a fast path to weight gain. The average adult American has grown one inch since 1960 and gained 23 pounds (Ogden & others, 2004). Taken together, Big Macs, Double Whoppers, sugar-laden 16-ounce drinks, and inactivity form a weapon of mass inflation.

New stadiums, theaters, and subway cars are offering wider seats for our growing population (Hampson, 2000). Washington State Ferries abandoned a 50-year-old standard of 18 inches per person. "Eighteen-inch butts are a thing of the past," explained a spokesperson (Shepherd, 1999). New York City has mostly replaced its 17.5-inch bucket-style subway seats with bucketless seats for Big Apple bottoms (Hampson, 2000). The "bottom" line: Today's people need more room.

Note how these findings reinforce a familiar lesson from Chapter 8's study of intelligence: There can be high levels of *heritability* (genetic influence on individual differences) without heredity being the only explanation of group differences. Genes mostly determine why you are heavier or leaner than your friends. Environment mostly determines why you and your friends are heavier than your parents and grandparents were at your age. Our eating behavior also demonstrates the now-familiar interaction among biological, psychological, and social-cultural factors.

Setting Realistic Goals

Fighting obesity is an enormous business. Americans spend $40 billion a year on diet foods and drinks (Kolata, 2004). Two-thirds of women and half of men say they want to lose weight; about half of those women and men say they are "seriously trying" (Moore, 2003). So what are their chances?

We have seen that many forces conspire against those seeking to shed excess pounds. Indeed, an obese person's body, held under its normal settling point, "thinks" it is starving. Having lost weight, that body may look normal, but its fat cells will be abnormally small and its metabolism will be slowed. Short of drastic surgery to tie off part of the stomach and small intestine, most who succeed on a weight-loss program eventually regain most of the weight (Garner & Wooley, 1991; Jeffery & others, 2000).

So what advice can psychology offer? Permanent weight loss is not easy. Those who manage to lose weight and keep it off set realistic and moderate goals. They modify their life-style and ongoing eating behavior. They realize that being moderately heavy is less risky than being extremely thin (Ernsberger & Koletsky, 1999). They lose weight gradually, and they exercise regularly. Lack of exercise helps explain why many fail to lose weight permanently. In a Centers for Disease Control study of 107,000 adults, only 1 in 5 of those trying to lose weight was following the government recommendation for both calories and exercise (Serdula & others, 1999). For other helpful hints, see Close-Up: Waist Management on the next page.

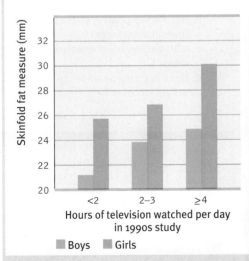

Figure 9.12> American idle: Couch potatoes beware—TV watching correlates with obesity (Robinson, 1999).

"It works as well as most other diet plans. . . . I've lost over $200 in less than three weeks."

CLOSE-UP

■ WAIST MANAGEMENT

People struggling with extreme obesity should seek medical help. For others seeking to lose less weight, researchers offer these tips.

Begin only if you feel motivated and self-disciplined. For most people, permanent weight loss requires a lifelong change in eating habits. Gradually increased exercise will also be needed.

Minimize exposure to tempting food cues. Keep tempting foods out of the house. Food shop only on a full stomach, and avoid the sweets and chips aisles. Limit meals to a few simple foods. Given more variety, we eat more.

Take steps to boost your metabolism. Inactive people are often overweight. Exercise, such as brisk walking, running, and swimming, empties fat cells, builds muscle, and makes you feel better. It also temporarily speeds up metabolism and can help lower your settling point (Bennett, 1995; Kolata, 1987; Thompson & others, 1982). Even brief bouts of exercise—four 10-minute walks a day—provide benefits (Jakicic & others, 1999).

Eat healthy foods. Whole grains, fruits, vegetables, and healthy fats, such as those found in olive oil and fish, help regulate appetite and artery-clogging cholesterol (Taubes, 2001, 2002). Better crispy greens than Krispy Kremes.

Don't starve all day and eat a lot at night. This eating pattern, common among overweight people, slows metabolism. By late morning, most of us are more alert and less fatigued if we have eaten a balanced breakfast (Spring & others, 1992).

Beware of the binge. Drinking alcohol or feeling anxious or depressed can unleash your urge to eat (Herman & Polivy, 1980). So can being distracted from monitoring your eating (Ward & Mann, 2000). (Ever notice that you eat more when out with friends?) Once you break your diet, you may think "What the heck," and then binge (Polivy & Herman, 1985, 1987). But a lapse doesn't have to become a full collapse. You can stray from a healthy diet without abandoning it.

Joe R. Liuzzo

Long-term success :: Tammy and Jeffrey Munson are in the National Weight Control Registry, which tracks people who have lost at least 30 pounds and kept the weight off for at least a year. She lost 147 pounds, and he lost 100 pounds. "We broke the bed when we were first married," said Jeffrey. They had, at the time the second photo was taken, been slim for 8 years, thanks to healthier eating and exercise. "You eat a lot of good stuff and a little bad stuff, and you'll be fine, but you've got to have the little bad stuff, too," noted Tammy (*New York Times*, May 25, 1999).

⊙ PRACTICE TEST

5. Hunger occurs in response to
 a. high blood glucose and low levels of ghrelin.
 b. low blood glucose and high levels of ghrelin.
 c. a low basal metabolic rate.
 d. a high basal metabolic rate.

6. Which of the following is a genetically disposed response to food?
 a. An aversion to eating cats and dogs
 b. An interest in novel foods
 c. A preference for sweet and salty foods
 d. An aversion to carbohydrates

7. Which of the following is true of the eating disorder bulimia nervosa?
 a. People with bulimia continue to want to lose weight even when they are underweight.
 b. Bulimia is marked by weight fluctuations within or above normal ranges.
 c. Bulimia patients often come from competitive and high-achieving families.
 d. If one twin is diagnosed with bulimia, the chances of the other twin's sharing the disorder are greater if they are fraternal rather than identical twins.

8. Obese people find it very difficult to lose weight permanently for several reasons, including the fact that
 a. with dieting, fat cells shrink and then disappear.
 b. the settling point of obese people is lower than average.
 c. with dieting, basal metabolic rate increases.
 d. there is a genetic influence on body weight.

Answers: 5. b, 6. c, 7. b, 8. d.

The Need to Belong

5: Why do we have a need to belong—to affiliate with others?

The social stigma attached to obesity may bother us as much or more than the health concerns. Why? We are what

Greek philosopher Aristotle called the *social animal*. Cut off from friends or family—alone in prison or at a new school or in a foreign land—most people feel keenly their lost connections with important others. This deep *need to belong* seems a basic human motivation (Baumeister & Leary, 1995). We are by nature social creatures.

The Benefits of Belonging

Social bonds boosted our ancestors' chances of survival. These bonds helped keep children close to their caregivers, protecting them from many threats. As adults, those who formed attachments were more likely to come together to reproduce and to stay together to nurture their offspring to maturity. To be "wretched" literally means, in its Middle English origin (*wrecche*), to be without kin nearby.

Cooperation in groups also enhanced survival. In solo combat, our ancestors were not the toughest predators. But as hunters, they learned that six hands were better than two. As food gatherers, they gained protection from their enemies by traveling in groups. Those who felt a need to belong survived and reproduced most successfully, and their genes now rule.

The need to connect :: Six days a week, women from the Philippines work as "domestic helpers" in 154,000 Hong Kong households. On Sundays, they throng to the central business district to picnic, dance, sing, talk, and laugh. "Humanity could stage no greater display of happiness," reported one observer (*Economist*, 2001).

People in every society on Earth belong to groups (and, as Chapter 14 explains, prefer and favor "us" over "them"). With the need to belong satisfied by close, supportive relationships, we feel included, accepted, and loved, and our self-esteem rides high. Indeed, *self-esteem* is a measure of how valued and accepted we feel (Leary & others, 1998).

Is it surprising, then, that so much of our social behavior aims to increase our feelings of belonging? To win friendship and avoid rejection, we generally conform to group standards. We monitor our behavior, hoping to make a good impression. We spend billions on clothes, cosmetics, and diet and fitness aids—all motivated by our quest for love and acceptance.

By drawing a sharp circle around "us," the need to belong feeds both deep attachments and menacing threats. Out of our need to define a "we" come loving families, faithful friendships, and team spirit, but also teen gangs, ethnic rivalries, and fanatic nationalism.

For good or for bad, we work hard to form and maintain our relationships. Familiarity breeds liking, not contempt. Thrown together in groups at school, at work, in a tornado shelter, we behave like magnets, moving closer, forming bonds. Parting, we feel distress. We promise to call, to write, to come back for reunions.

Even when bad relationships break, people suffer. In one 16-nation survey, separated and divorced people were only half as likely as married people to say they were "very happy" (Inglehart, 1990). After such separations, feelings of loneliness and anger—and sometimes even a strange desire to be near the former partner—linger. For those in abusive relationships, the fear of being alone sometimes seems worse than the certainty of emotional or physical pain. Children who move through a series of foster homes also know the fear of being alone. After repeated disruptions of budding attachments, they may have difficulty forming deep attachments. The evidence is clearest in the most extreme cases, when children grow up in institutions without a sense of belonging to anyone, or are locked away at home and severely neglected. They become pathetic creatures, withdrawn, frightened, speechless.

When something threatens or dissolves our social ties, negative emotions—anxiety, loneliness, jealousy, guilt—overwhelm us. Life may feel empty, pointless. For those moving alone to new places, the stress and loneliness can be depressing. But if feelings of acceptance and connection build, so do self-esteem, positive feelings, and desires to help rather than hurt others (Buckley & Leary, 2001).

Such findings have influenced U.S. policies. After years of placing individual refugee and immigrant families in isolated communities, U.S. agencies today encourage *cluster migration* (Pipher, 2002). The second refugee Sudanese family settling in a town generally has an easier adjustment than the first.

The Pain of Being Shut Out

Sometimes the need to belong is denied. Perhaps you can recall such a time, when you felt excluded or ignored or shunned. Perhaps you received the silent treatment. Perhaps others avoided you, looked away, mocked you, or shut you out in some other way.

This is *ostracism*—social exclusion (Williams, 2002, 2007). Worldwide, humans use many forms of ostracism—exile, imprisonment, solitary confinement—to punish, and therefore control, social behavior. For children, even a brief time-out in isolation can be punishing. To be shunned is to have one's need to belong threatened (Williams & Zadro, 2001). Lea, a lifelong victim of the silent treatment by her mother and grandmother, described the effect. "It's the meanest thing you can do to someone, especially if you know they can't fight back. I never should have been born." Like Lea, people often respond to ostracism with depressed moods, initial

AFP/Getty Images

efforts to restore their acceptance, and then withdrawal. After two years of silent treatment by his employer, Richard reported, "I came home every night and cried. I lost 25 pounds, had no self-esteem, and felt that I wasn't worthy."

Rejected and powerless, people may turn nasty, as did college students made to feel rejected in one series of experiments (Baumeister & others, 2002; Twenge & others, 2001, 2002). Some students were told that a personality test they had taken showed that they were "the type likely to end up alone later in life." Others heard that people they had met didn't want them in a group that was forming. Still others heard good news: They would have "rewarding relationships throughout life," or "everyone chose you as someone they'd like to work with." Students who were told they weren't wanted or would end up alone were much more likely to engage in self-defeating behaviors and to underperform on aptitude tests. They also were more likely to act in mean or aggressive ways (blasting people with noise, for example) when given the chance to interact with

those who had excluded them. "If intelligent, well-adjusted, successful . . . students can turn aggressive in response to a small laboratory experience of social exclusion," noted the research team, "it is disturbing to imagine the aggressive tendencies that might arise from . . . chronic exclusion from desired groups in actual social life." (At the end of such experiments, the study is fully explained and the participants leave feeling reassured.)

◎ PRACTICE TEST

9. Decades of evidence indicate that we normally have a strong need to belong. Which of the following is NOT part of this evidence?
   a. Students made to feel rejected and unwanted developed aggressive tendencies.
   b. Social exclusion—such as exile or solitary confinement—is considered a severe form of punishment.
   c. Gang members are not subject to the need to belong.
   d. Children who are extremely neglected become withdrawn, frightened, and speechless.

Answer: 9. c.

Theories of Emotion

6: What are the components of an emotion, and what three theories help us to understand more about those components?

Motivated behavior is often connected to powerful emotions. I will never forget the day I went to a huge store to drop off film and brought along Peter, my toddler first-born child. As I set Peter down on his feet and prepared to complete the paperwork, a passerby warned, "You'd better be careful or you'll lose that boy!" Not more than a few breaths later, after dropping the film in the slot, I turned and found no Peter beside me.

With mild anxiety, I peered around one end of the counter. No Peter in sight. With slightly more anxiety, I peered around the other end. No Peter there, either. Now, with my heart pounding, I circled the neighboring counters. Still no Peter anywhere. As anxiety turned to panic, I began racing up and down the store aisles. He was nowhere to be found. Hearing my alarm, the store manager used the public-address system to ask customers to assist in looking for a missing child. Soon after, I passed the customer who had warned me. "I told you that you were going to lose him!" he scorned. With visions of kidnapping (strangers routinely adored that beautiful child), I braced for the possibility that my neglect had caused me to lose what I loved above all else, and—dread of all dreads—that I might have to return home and face my wife without our only child.

But then, as I passed the customer service counter yet again, there he was, having been found and returned by some obliging customer! In an instant, the arousal of dread spilled into ecstasy. Clutching my son, with tears suddenly flowing, I found myself unable to speak my thanks and stumbled out of the store awash in grateful joy.

Where do such emotions come from? Why do we have them? What are they made of? Emotions don't exist just to give us interesting experiences. They are our body's adaptive response, increasing our chances of survival. When we face challenges, emotions focus our attention and energize our action. Our heart races. Our pace quickens. All our senses go on high alert. Receiving unexpected good news, we may find our eyes tearing up. We raise our hands in triumph. We feel joy and a newfound confidence.

As my panicked search for Peter illustrates, **emotions** are a mix of (1) *bodily arousal* (heart pounding), (2) *expressive behaviors* (quickened pace), and (3) *conscious experience,* including thoughts (Is this a kidnapping?) and feelings (panic, fear, and later joy). The puzzle for psychologists has been figuring out how these three pieces fit together.

There are two major questions about the interplay of our arousal, behaviors, and conscious experience in emotions. The first is a chicken-and-egg debate: Does your bodily arousal come *before* or *after* your emotional feelings? (Did I first notice my heart racing and my faster step, and then feel anxious dread about losing Peter? Or did my sense of fear come first, stirring my heart and legs to respond?) The second question focuses on the interaction between *thinking* and *feeling*: Does thinking—cognition—always come before emotion? (Did I consciously perceive a kidnapping threat before I reacted emotionally?)

Common sense tells most of us that we cry because we are sad, lash out because we are angry, tremble because we are afraid. First comes conscious awareness, then the feeling. But to pioneering psychologist William James, this commonsense view of emotion was wrong. According to James, "We feel sorry because we cry, angry because we strike, afraid because we tremble" (1890, p. 1066). James' idea was also proposed by Danish physiologist Carl Lange, and thus is called the **James-Lange theory.** Perhaps you can recall a time when your car skidded on slick pavement. As it veered crazily you counter-steered and regained

The joys of friendship :: According to the James-Lange theory, we don't just smile because we share a friend's joy. We also share the joy because we are smiling with them.

control. Just after the skid ended, you noticed your racing heart and *then,* shaking with fright, you felt the whoosh of emotion. Your feeling of fear *followed* your body's response.

Physiologist Walter Cannon (1871–1943) disagreed with James and Lange. Does a racing heart signal fear, anger, or love? The body's responses are not distinct enough, said Cannon, to cause the different emotions. Also, heart rate, perspiration, and body temperature change too slowly to trigger sudden feelings of emotion. Cannon, and later another physiologist, Philip Bard, concluded that bodily arousal and our emotional experience occur together. In their view, the emotion-triggering stimulus travels to our brain's cortex, causing our awareness of emotion, at the same time that it travels to the sympathetic nervous system, causing our body's arousal. So, according to the **Cannon-Bard theory,** your heart begins pounding *as you* experience fear. The pounding heart does not cause the feeling of fear, nor does the feeling of fear cause the pounding heart.

Let's check your understanding of the James-Lange and Cannon-Bard theories. Imagine that your brain could not sense your heart pounding or your stomach churning. According to each theory, how would this affect your experienced emotions?

Cannon and Bard would have expected you to experience emotions normally. They believed emotions occur separately from (though simultaneously with) the body's arousal. James and Lange would have expected greatly diminished emotions. They believed that to experience emotion you must first perceive your body's arousal.

The James-Lange theory finds support in studies of people with severed spinal cords, including a survey of 25 soldiers who suffered such injuries in World War II (Hohmann, 1966). Those with lower-spine injuries, who had lost sensation only in their legs, reported little change in the intensity of their emotions before and after their spinal injuries. Those with high spinal-cord injury, who could feel nothing below the neck, reported a difference, however. After their injury, the intensity of

some of their reactions had decreased considerably, as James and Lange would have expected. Anger, one man confessed, "just doesn't have the heat to it that it used to. It's a mental kind of anger." But other emotions, those that are expressed mostly in body areas above the neck, were felt more intensely by the men with high spinal-cord injury. Virtually all the men reported increases in weeping, lumps in the throat, and getting choked up when saying good-bye, worshipping, or watching a touching movie. Such evidence has led some researchers to view feelings as "mostly shadows" of our bodily responses and behaviors (Damasio, 2003).

But most researchers now agree with Cannon and Bard on another point. Our experienced emotions involve cognition (Averill, 1993). Whether we fear the man behind us on the dark street depends entirely on whether we interpret his actions as threatening or friendly.

So, with James and Lange we can say that our body's reactions are an important ingredient of emotion. And with Cannon and Bard we can say that there is more to the experience of emotion than reading our body's responses.

Stanley Schachter and Jerome Singer (1962) proposed a third theory: that our physical reactions and our thoughts—perceptions, memories, and interpretations—together create emotion. In their **two-factor theory,** emotions therefore have two ingredients: physical arousal and cognitive appraisal. Like James and

emotion a response of the whole organism, involving (1) physiological arousal, (2) expressive behaviors, and (3) conscious experience.

James-Lange theory the theory that our experience of emotion is our awareness of our physiological responses to emotion-arousing stimuli.

Cannon-Bard theory the theory that an emotion-arousing stimulus simultaneously triggers (1) physiological responses and (2) the subjective experience of emotion.

two-factor theory Schachter-Singer's theory that to experience emotion we must (1) be physically aroused and (2) cognitively label the arousal.

Tom McCarthy/Photo Edit

Figure 9.13> Theories of emotion

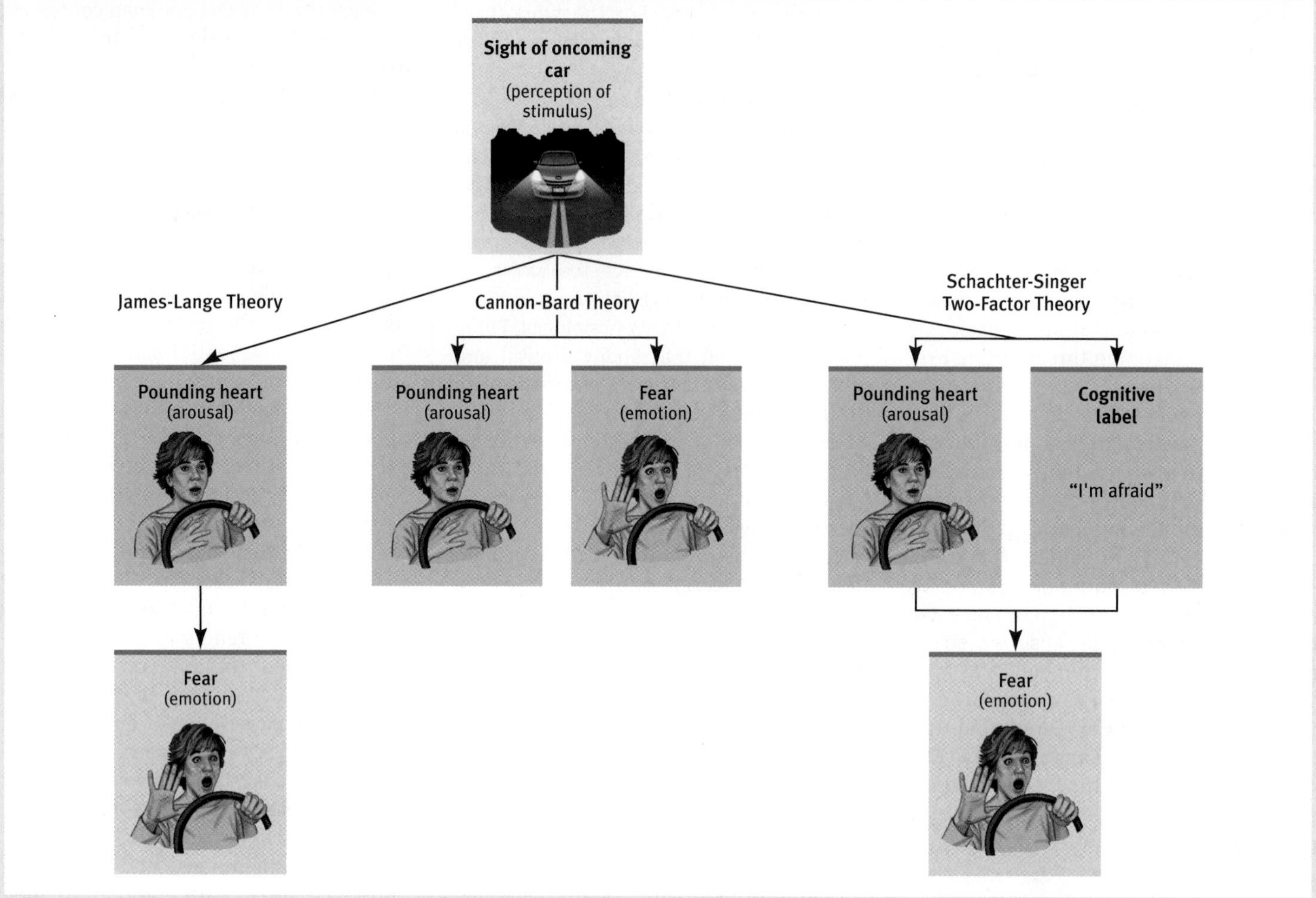

Lange, Schachter and Singer believed that our experience of emotion grows from our awareness of our body's arousal. Yet like Cannon and Bard, Schachter and Singer also believed that our physical reactions to emotions are similar **(FIGURE 9.13)**. Thus, in their view, an emotional experience requires a conscious interpretation of the arousal.

To assess the James-Lange, Cannon-Bard, and two-factor theories, let's consider the answers researchers have gleaned to two questions:

- Are different emotions marked by distinct bodily responses?
- What is the connection between what we *think* and how we *feel*?

PRACTICE TEST

10. The James-Lange theory states that our experience of an emotion is a result of our physiological response to a stimulus; we are afraid because our heart pounds. The Cannon-Bard theory proposes that the physiological response (like heart pounding) and the subjective experience of, say, fear

a. are unrelated.
b. occur simultaneously.
c. occur in the opposite order (with feelings of fear first).
d. are cognitive functions.

11. When you pick up your mail, you see a long-awaited letter from your school's financial aid office. Your breathing and heart rate increase as you open the letter with anticipation. Yes! Your scholarship request has been approved! The two-factor theory of emotion would explain that your feelings of joy are

a. a result of your increased breathing and heart rate.
b. a result of the increased breathing and heart rate *and* your labeling of that arousal.
c. causing the increased breathing and heart rate.
d. unrelated to your increased breathing and heart rate.

Answers: 10, b, 11, b.

Embodied Emotion

7: What bodily changes accompany emotions, and how do they differ?

Whether you are falling in love or grieving a loved one's death, you need little convincing that emotions involve the body. Feeling without a body is like breathing without lungs. Some physical responses are easy to notice, others happen without your awareness. Indeed, many take place at the level of neurons in your brain.

Emotions and the Autonomic Nervous System

As you learned in Chapter 2, in a crisis your *autonomic nervous system (ANS)* mobilizes your body for action **(FIGURE 9.14)**. Alarmed by the sound of a motorcycle slowing down behind you on a dark street, your muscles tense, your stomach develops butterflies, your mouth becomes dry. To provide energy, your liver pours extra sugar into your bloodstream. To help burn the sugar, your breathing increases to supply needed oxygen. Your digestion slows, allowing blood to move away from your internal organs and toward your muscles. With blood sugar driven into the large muscles, running becomes easier. Your pupils open wider, letting in more light. To cool your stirred-up body, you perspire. If wounded, your blood would clot more quickly. After your next crisis, think of this: Without any conscious effort, your body's response to danger was wonderfully coordinated and adaptive—preparing you to fight or flee. When the crisis passes, the ANS gradually calms the body, as stress hormones slowly leave your bloodstream.

The Physiology of Emotions

Imagine another scene. You are conducting an experiment, measuring the body's responses to different emotions. In each of four rooms, you have someone watching a movie. In the first, the person is viewing a horror show. In the second, the viewer watches an anger-provoking film. In the third, someone is watching a sexually arousing film. In the fourth, the person is viewing an utterly boring movie. From the control center you track each person's physical responses, measuring perspiration, breathing, and heart rates. Do you think you could tell who is frightened? Who is angry? Who is sexually aroused? Who is bored?

With training, you could probably pick out the bored viewer. But the bodily differences among fear, anger, and sexual arousal would be much more difficult to spot by measuring perspiration, breathing, and heart rates (Barrett, 2006; Cacioppo & others, 1997).

> "No one ever told me that grief felt so much like fear. I am not afraid, but the sensation is like being afraid. The same fluttering in the stomach, the same restlessness, the yawning. I keep on swallowing."
>
> C. S. Lewis, *A Grief Observed*, 1961

Autonomic Nervous System Controls Physiological Arousal

Sympathetic division (arousing)		Parasympathetic division (calming)
Pupils dilate	EYES	Pupils contract
Decreases	SALIVATION	Increases
Perspires	SKIN	Dries
Increases	RESPIRATION	Decreases
Accelerates	HEART	Slows
Inhibits	DIGESTION	Activates
Secrete stress hormones	ADRENAL GLANDS	Decrease secretion of stress hormones
Reduced	IMMUNE SYSTEM FUNCTIONING	Enhanced

Figure 9.14> Emotional arousal Emotional arousal involves autonomic nervous system activation.

Emotional arousal :: Elated excitement and panicky fear involve similar bodily arousal. That allows us to flip rapidly between the two emotions.

AP Photo/HO

Despite similar bodily responses, sexual arousal, fear, and anger *feel* different. If sexually stimulated, you will experience a genital response. If afraid, you may feel a clutching, sinking sensation in your chest and a knot in your stomach. If angry, you may feel "hot under the collar" and be aware of a pressing inner tension. Fear and anger also *look* different. People may appear "paralyzed with fear" or "ready to explode."

So, does research pinpoint any distinct body- or brain-pattern indicators of each emotion? Yes. With the help of some sophisticated laboratory tools, you could find some indicators. For example, the finger temperatures and hormone secretions that accompany fear and rage do sometimes differ (Ax, 1953; Levenson, 1992). Fear and joy, although they prompt similar increased heart rate, stimulate different facial muscles. During fear, your brow muscles tense. During joy, muscles in your cheeks and under your eyes pull into a smile (Witvliet & Vrana, 1995).

Brain scans show that emotions differ in the brain circuits they use (Kalin, 1993; Panksepp, 1982). When you experience negative emotions such as disgust, your right frontal cortex is more active than your left frontal cortex. This general area is also more active in depression-prone people and in those with generally nega-tive personalities (Harmon-Jones & others, 2002). One man, having lost part of his right frontal lobe in brain surgery, became (his not-unhappy wife reported) less irritable and more affectionate (Goleman, 1995). My father, after a right-hemisphere stroke at age 92, lived the last two years of his life with happy gratitude and nary a complaint or negative emotion.

Your left frontal lobe will be more active when you experience positive moods. When people are enthusiastic, energized, and happy, brain scans and EEG recordings reveal more left frontal lobe activity. Again, this pattern is found in people with positive personalities—jolly infants and alert, energetic, and persistently goal-directed adults (Davidson, 2000, 2003; Urry & others, 2004). Indeed, the more a person's baseline frontal lobe activity tilts left, the more upbeat the person typically is. (When you're happy and you know it, your brain will surely show it.)

To sum up, we can't easily see differences in emotions from tracking heart rate, breathing, and perspiration. But facial expressions and brain activity do vary with the emotion. (Given the physical indicators of emotion, might we, like Pinocchio, give off telltale signs when we lie? See Think Critically About: Do Lie Detectors Lie?)

Cognition and Emotion

8: How do our thinking and feelings interact?

How does what we *think* affect how we *feel?* Can we experience emotion apart from thinking? Or do we become what we think?

Cognition Can Define Emotion

Sometimes our general feeling of arousal spills over from one event to the next, influencing our response. Imagine arriving home after a fast run and finding a message that you got a longed-for job. With arousal lingering from the run, would you feel more excited than if you received this news after awakening from a nap?

To find out whether this *spillover effect* exists, researchers injected college men with the hormone epinephrine, which triggers feelings of arousal (Schachter & Singer, 1962). Picture yourself as a participant: After receiving the injection, you go to a waiting room. You find yourself with another person (actually an accomplice of the experimenters) who is acting either joyful or irritated. As you observe this person, you begin to feel your heart race, your body flush, and your breathing become more rapid. If you had been told to expect these effects from the injection, what would you feel? The actual volunteers felt little emotion—because they attributed their arousal to the drug. But if you had been told the injection would produce no effects, what would you feel? Perhaps you would react as another group of participants did. They "caught" the apparent emotion of the person they were with, becoming happy when the accomplice was acting joyful, and testy when the accomplice was acting irritated.

This discovery—that we can experience a stirred-up state as one emotion or another very different one, depending on how we interpret and label it—has been repeated in dozens of experiments. Insult people who have just been aroused by

THINK CRITICALLY ABOUT:

DO LIE DETECTORS LIE?

Do we in any way give ourselves away when we lie? The creators and users of the lie *detector,* or **polygraph,** believe we do. Polygraphs are sensitive machines that measure breathing, heart rate, and perspiration. Changes indicate an emotional response. Attached to the machine, you would try to relax, while an examiner monitors your responses to questions. Some items, called *control questions,* aim to make everyone a little nervous. If asked, "In the last 20 years, have you ever taken something that didn't belong to you?" many people lie and say, "No!" But their nervousness will register as arousal, which the polygraph will detect. This baseline will be useful when you respond to *critical questions* ("Did you ever steal anything from your previous employer?"). If your responses to critical questions are weaker than to control questions, the examiner infers you are telling the truth. The underlying idea is that only a thief becomes nervous when denying a theft.

Critics of this idea point out two problems. First, our physiological arousal is much the same from one emotion to another. Our bodies react to anxiety, irritation, and guilt in very similar ways. Second, many innocent people *do* get nervous when accused of a crime or bad act. Many rape victims, for example, "fail" these tests because they have strong emotional reactions while telling the truth about their assailant (Lykken, 1991). About one-third of the time, polygraph test results are wrong **(FIGURE 9.15).**

A 2002 U.S. National Academy of Sciences report noted that "no spy has ever been caught [by] using the polygraph." It is not for lack of trying. The CIA is one of several U.S. agencies that together have spent millions of dollars testing tens of thousands of employees. Did the test catch Aldrich Ames, a Russian spy within

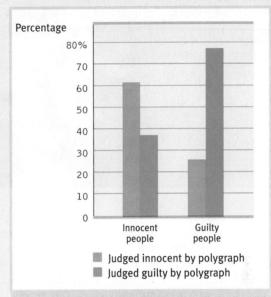

Percentage

Figure 9.15> How often do lie detectors lie? In one study, polygraph experts interpreted the test results of 100 people who had been suspects in theft crimes (Kleinmuntz & Szucko, 1984). Half of the suspects were guilty and had confessed. The other half had been proven innocent. Had the polygraph experts been the judges, more than one-third of the innocent would have been declared guilty, and almost one-fourth of the guilty would have been declared innocent.

the CIA who enjoyed an unexplained lavish life-style? Ames "took scores of polygraph tests and passed them all," notes Robert Park (1999). "Nobody thought to investigate the source of his sudden wealth—after all, he was passing the lie detector tests."

A more effective approach to lie detection uses the *guilty knowledge test,* which also assesses a suspect's physiological responses. But in this test, the questions focus on specific crime-scene details known only to the police and the guilty person (Ben-Shakhar & Elaad, 2003). If a camera and computer had been stolen, for example, only the person guilty of the crime should react strongly to the brand names of the stolen items. Given enough such specific probes, an innocent person will seldom be wrongly accused.

Stock Connections/Newscom

Can polygraph tests like this identify liars? :: Not reliably. Guilty knowledge tests are more accurate.

polygraph a machine, commonly used in attempts to detect lies, that measures several of the physiological responses accompanying emotion (such as changes in perspiration, heart rate, and breathing).

pedaling an exercise bike or watching rock videos, and they interpret and label their arousal as a response to the insult. Their feelings of anger will be greater than those of people who were similarly provoked but not previously aroused. Likewise, sexually aroused people have angrier reactions in anger-provoking situations. So what do you think might happen if a person who has just experienced an angry or fearful event becomes sexually involved? The lingering arousal may intensify sexual passion (Palace, 1995). Just as the Schachter-Singer two-factor theory predicts, arousal + label = emotion. Arousal—from emotions as diverse as anger, fear, and sexual excitement—can indeed spill from one emotion to another (Reisenzein, 1983; Sinclair & others, 1994; Zillmann, 1986).

Cognition Does Not Always Precede Emotion

So if arousal fuels emotion and cognition channels it, does this mean that we need to interpret our arousal before we can experience an emotion? No, says Robert Zajonc (pronounced ZI-yence; 1980, 1984a). He contends that we actually have many emotional reactions apart from, or even before, our interpretation of a situation. Perhaps you can recall liking something or someone immediately, without knowing why. Research on neurological processes shows how we can

experience emotion unconsciously, before cognition. The answer lies in the dual processing that takes place in our two-track mind.

Our emotional responses are the final step in a process that can follow two different kinds of pathways in our brain. Some emotions (especially our more complex feelings, like hatred and love) travel the "high road." A stimulus following the

high road would travel (by way of the thalamus) to the brain's cortex (FIGURE 9.16b). There, it would be analyzed and labeled before our body sends out an order, via the amygdala, to respond.

But sometimes our emotions (especially simple likes, dislikes, and fears) take what Joseph LeDoux (2002) calls the "low road," a neural shortcut that bypasses the cortex (FIGURE 9.16a). Following

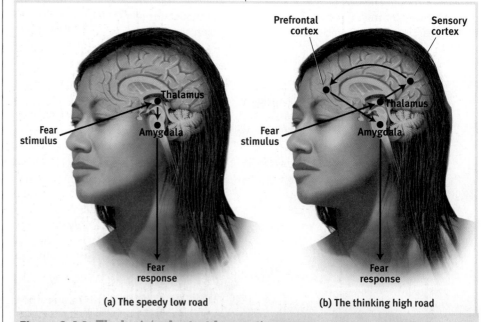

(a) The speedy low road

(b) The thinking high road

Figure 9.16> The brain's shortcut for emotions Sensory input may be routed (a) directly to the amygdala (via the thalamus) for an instant emotional reaction or (b) indirectly to the amygdala by way of the thalamus and cortex (for analysis).

the low-road pathway, a fear-provoking stimulus would travel (again by way of the thalamus) *directly* to the amygdala, an emotion-control center. This shortcut, bypassing the conscious cortex, enables our greased-lightning emotional response ("Life in danger!") before our brain interprets the exact source of danger. So speedy is the amygdala response that we may not be aware of what's happened (Dimberg & others, 2000). In one fascinating experiment, researchers used fMRI (functional MRI) scans to observe the amygdala's response to subliminally presented fearful eyes (FIGURE 9.17) (Whalen & others, 2004). Although the fearful eyes were flashed too quickly for people to perceive them, they did trigger increased amygdala activity. A control condition that presented the whites of happy eyes did not trigger this activity.

The amygdala's structure makes it easier for our feelings to hijack our thinking than for our thinking to rule our feelings (LeDoux & Armony, 1999). It sends

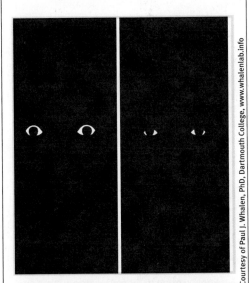

Figure 9.17> The brain's sensitivity to threats Researchers flashed fearful eyes (left) too briefly for viewers to consciously perceive them. But fMRI scans revealed that they did get the message: Their alert amygdala became more active—a response not triggered when happy eyes (right) were presented (Whalen & others, 2004).

Courtesy of Paul J. Whalen, PhD, Dartmouth College, www.whalenlab.info

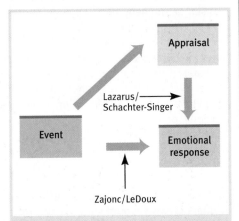

Figure 9.18> Two routes to emotion Zajonc and LeDoux emphasized that some emotional responses are immediate, before any conscious appraisal. Lazarus, Schachter, and Singer emphasized that our appraisal and labeling of events also determine our emotional responses.

more neural projections up to the cortex than it receives back. Thus, in the forest, we can jump when we hear rustling in the bushes nearby, and leave it to our cortex (via the high road) to decide later whether the sound was made by a snake or by the wind. Such an experience supports Zajonc's belief that *some* of our emotional reactions involve no deliberate thinking, and that cognition is not always necessary for emotion. The heart is not always subject to the mind.

Emotion researcher Richard Lazarus (1991, 1998) agreed that our brains process vast amounts of information outside of our conscious awareness and that some emotional responses do not require *conscious* thinking. But, he asked, how would we *know* what we are reacting to if we did not in some way appraise the situation? The appraisal may be effortless and we may not be conscious of it, but it is still a mental function. Emotions arise when we *appraise* an event as harmless or dangerous, he said, whether we truly *know* it is or not. We appraise the sound of the rustling bushes as the presence of a threat. Later, we learn that it was "just the wind."

Let's sum up. As Zajonc and LeDoux have demonstrated, some emotional responses—especially simple likes, dislikes, and fears—involve no conscious thinking (FIGURE 9.18). We may fear a big spider, even if we "know" it is harmless. Such responses are difficult to alter by changing our thinking.

Other emotions—including moods such as depression and complex feelings such as hatred and love—are, as Lazarus, Schachter, and Singer predicted, greatly affected by our interpretations, memories, and expectations. For these emotions, as you will see in Chapter 12, learning to *think* more positively about ourselves and the world around us helps us *feel* better.

PRACTICE TEST

12. Research on arousal indicates that if we are physically aroused by swimming, then heckled by an onlooker, we may interpret our arousal as anger and
   a. become less physically aroused.
   b. feel angrier than usual.
   c. feel less angry than usual.
   d. act joyful.

13. Zajonc and LeDoux maintain that some of our emotional reactions occur before we have had the chance to label or interpret them. Lazarus disagreed. These psychologists differ about whether emotional responses occur in the absence of
   a. physical arousal.
   b. the hormone epinephrine.
   c. cognitive processing.
   d. learning.

Answers: 12. b, 13. c.

Expressed Emotion

There is a simple method of detecting people's emotions: Read their body language, listen to their voice tones, and study their faces. People's expressive behavior reveals their emotion. Does this nonverbal language vary with culture, or is it the same everywhere? And do our expressions influence what we feel?

Detecting Emotion in Others

9: How do we communicate nonverbally?

All of us communicate without words. Westerners "read" a firm handshake as evidence of an outgoing, expressive personality (Chaplin & others, 2000). A glance or a stare can communicate intimacy, submission, or dominance (Kleinke, 1986). When two people are passionately in love, gazing into each other's eyes is typically prolonged and mutual (Rubin, 1970). Would these intimate gazes stir such feelings between strangers? To find out, researchers (Kellerman & others, 1989) asked unacquainted male-female pairs to gaze intently for two minutes either at each other's hands or into each other's eyes. After separating, the eye-gazers reported feeling a tingle of attraction and affection.

Most of us read nonverbal cues well enough to detect the emotions in an old silent film. We are especially good at detecting nonverbal threats. A single angry face will "pop out" of a crowd faster than a single happy one (Fox & others, 2000;

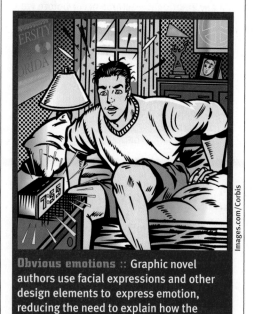

Obvious emotions :: Graphic novel authors use facial expressions and other design elements to express emotion, reducing the need to explain how the characters are feeling.

Hansen & Hansen, 1988; Öhman & others, 2001). Even when hearing another language, most people can easily detect anger (Scherer & others, 2001).

Some of us are especially sensitive to expressive cues. In one study, hundreds of people watched brief film clips showing portions of a person's emotionally expressive face or body (sometimes accompanied by a garbled voice) and named the emotion (Rosenthal & others, 1979). For example, after viewing a 2-second scene revealing only the face of an upset woman, viewers would state whether the woman was criticizing someone for being late or was talking about her divorce. Given such "thin slices," women generally surpass men at reading people's emotional cues (Hall, 1984, 1987). This nonverbal sensitivity gives women an edge in spotting lies (DePaulo, 1994). Women also surpass men in other assessments of emotional cues, such as deciding whether a male-female couple is a genuine romantic couple or a posed phony couple, or selecting the supervisor in a photo of two people who work together (Barnes & Sternberg, 1989).

Women's skill at decoding emotions may contribute to their greater emotional responsiveness in both positive and negative situations (Grossman & Wood, 1993; Sprecher & Sedikides, 1993; Stoppard & Gruchy, 1993). Some studies have focused on gender differences in *empathy.* If you have empathy, you identify with others and imagine what it must be like to walk in their shoes. You rejoice with those who rejoice and weep with those who weep. In surveys, women are far more likely than men to describe themselves as empathic. Actually, measures of body responses, such as one's heart rate while seeing another's distress, reveal a much smaller gender gap (Eisenberg & Lennon, 1983).

Nevertheless, females are more likely to *express* empathy—to cry and to report distress when observing someone in distress. As **FIGURE 9.19** shows, this gender difference was clear in videotapes of men and women watching film clips that were sad (children with a dying parent), happy (slapstick comedy), or frightening (a man nearly falling off the ledge of a tall building) (Kring

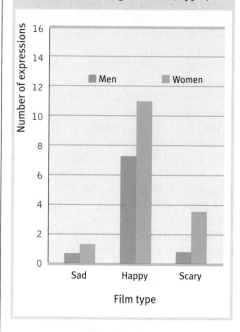

Figure 9.19> Gender and expressiveness Male and female film viewers did not differ dramatically in self-reported emotions or physiological responses. But the women's faces *showed* much more emotion. (From Kring & Gordon, 1998.)

& Gordon, 1998). Women also tend to experience emotional events (such as viewing pictures of mutilation) more deeply—with more brain activation in areas sensitive to emotion—and then to remember the scenes better three weeks later (Canli & others, 2002).

Culture and Emotional Expression

10: Are nonverbal expressions of emotion universally understood, and do they influence our feelings?

The meaning of *gestures* varies with culture. Former U.S. President Richard Nixon learned this while traveling in Brazil. He made the North American "A-OK" sign, but in Brazil that meant, "Let's have sex." The importance of cultural definitions of gestures was again demonstrated in 1968, when North Korea publicized photos of supposedly happy officers from a captured U.S. Navy spy ship. In the photo, three men had raised their middle fingers, telling their captors it was a "Hawaiian good luck sign" (Fleming & Scott, 1991).

Do *facial expressions* also have different meanings in different cultures? To find out, researchers showed photographs of different facial expressions to people in different parts of the world and asked them to guess the emotion (Ekman & others, 1975, 1987, 1994; Izard, 1977, 1994). You can try this matching task yourself by pairing the six emotions with the six faces of **FIGURE 9.20**.

Regardless of your cultural background, you probably did pretty well. A smile's a smile the world around. Ditto for anger, and to a lesser extent the other basic expressions (Elfenbein & Ambady, 1999). (There is no culture where people frown when they are happy.) We do slightly better when judging emotional displays from our own culture (Elfenbein & Ambady, 2002, 2003a,b). Nevertheless, cultures and languages tend to categorize emotions—as anger, fear, and so on—in similar ways.

Do these shared categories reflect shared cultural experiences, such as American and European movies and TV programs? Apparently not. Paul Ekman and his team asked isolated people in New Guinea to display various emotions in response to such statements as, "Pretend your child has died." When North American collegians viewed the videotapes, the students read the New Guineans' facial reactions easily.

"For news of the heart, ask the face."
Guinean proverb

So we can say that facial muscles speak a fairly universal language. This discovery would not have surprised Charles Darwin, the pioneering emotion researcher who wrote *The Expression of the Emotions in Man and Animals* in 1872. Darwin believed that in prehistoric times, before our ancestors communicated in words, they communicated threats, greetings, and submission with facial expressions. That ability helped them survive and became part of our shared heritage, explaining why all humans express basic emotions with similar facial expressions. A sneer, for example, retains elements of an animal's baring its teeth in a snarl. Emotional expressions may enhance our survival in other ways, too. Surprise raises the eyebrows and widens the eyes, helping us take in more information. Disgust wrinkles the nose, closing it from foul odors.

Smiles are social as well as emotional events. Bowlers seldom smile when they score a strike; they smile when they turn to face their companions (Jones & others, 1991; Kraut & Johnston, 1979). Even Olympic gold-medal winners typically don't smile when they are awaiting their ceremony. But they wear broad grins when interacting with officials and facing the crowd and cameras (Fernández-Dols & Ruiz-Belda, 1995).

The Effects of Facial Expressions

As famed psychologist William James struggled with feelings of depression and grief, he came to believe that we can control our emotions by going "through the outward movements" of any emotion we want to experience. "To feel cheerful," he advised, "sit up cheerfully, look around cheerfully, and act as if cheerfulness were already there."

Was James right? Let's test his hypothesis: Fake a big grin. Now scowl. Can you feel the "smile therapy" difference? Participants in dozens of experiments have felt a difference. For example, researchers (Laird & others, 1974, 1984, 1989) tricked students into making a frowning expression by asking them to "contract these muscles" and "pull your brows together"

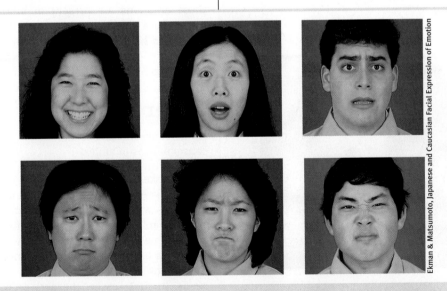

Figure 9.20> Culture-specific or culturally universal expressions? As people of differing cultures, do our faces speak differing languages? Which face expresses disgust? Anger? Fear? Happiness? Sadness? Surprise? Turn the page to check your answers. (From Matsumoto and Ekman, 1989.)

Ekman & Matsumoto, Japanese and Caucasian Facial Expression of Emotion

"Refuse to express a passion and it dies. . . . If we wish to conquer undesirable emotional tendencies in ourselves, we must . . . go through the outward movements of those contrary dispositions which we prefer to cultivate."

William James, *Principles of Psychology*, 1890

Answers to the questions in Figure 9.20: From left to right, top to bottom: happiness, surprise, fear, sadness, anger, disgust.

(supposedly to help the researchers attach facial electrodes). The result? The students reported feeling a little angry. Students similarly tricked into smiling felt happier, found cartoons funnier, and recalled happier memories than did the frowners. So, too, with other basic emotions **(FIGURE 9.21)**. For example, people reported feeling more fear than anger, disgust, or sadness when made to construct a fearful expression: "Raise your eyebrows. And open your eyes wide. Move your whole head back, so that your chin is tucked in a little bit, and let your mouth relax and hang open a little" (Duclos & others, 1989).

In the absence of competing emotions, this **facial feedback effect** is subtle yet detectable. Just activating one of the smiling muscles by holding a pen in the teeth (rather than with the lips, which activates a frowning muscle) is enough to make cartoons seem more amusing (Strack & others, 1988). A heartier smile—made not just with the mouth but with raised cheeks that crinkle the eyes—enhances positive feelings even more when you are reacting to something pleasant or funny (Soussignan, 2001). The face is more than a billboard that displays our feelings; it also feeds our feelings. No wonder depressed patients reportedly feel better after between-the-eyebrows Botox injections that immobilize their frown muscles (Finzi & Wasserman, 2006).

Other studies note a similar *behavior feedback effect* (Snodgrass & others, 1986). You can duplicate the participants' experience. Walk for a few minutes with short, shuffling steps, keeping your eyes downcast. Now walk around taking long strides, with your arms swinging and your eyes looking straight ahead. Can you feel your mood shift? Going through the motions awakens the emotions.

One small way to become more empathic—to feel what others feel—is to let your own face mimic another person's expression (Vaughn & Lanzetta, 1981). Acting as another acts helps us feel what another feels. Indeed, natural mimicry of others' emotions helps explain why emotions are contagious (Dimberg & others, 2000; Neumann & Strack, 2000).

Experienced Emotion

How many distinct emotions are there? Carroll Izard (1977) isolated 10 basic emotions (joy, interest-excitement, surprise, sadness, anger, disgust, contempt, fear, shame, and guilt). Most of these emotions are present in infancy. Let's take a closer look at two of them: anger and happiness. What functions do they serve? What influences our experience of each?

Anger

11: What are the causes and consequences of anger?

What makes us angry? People asked to recall or keep careful records of their experiences with anger reported becoming at least mildly angry several times a week, some several times a day (Averill, 1983). The anger was often a response to friends' or loved ones' perceived misdeeds. In most cases, the acts seemed willful, unjustified, and avoidable.

What do we do with our anger? And what *should* we do with our anger? In a Gallup survey of teens, boys more than

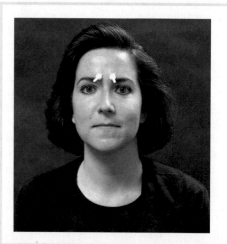 

Courtesy of Louis Schakel/Michael Kausman/The New York Times Pictures

Figure 9.21> How to make people frown without telling them to frown Here's one solution: Attach two golf tees above the participants' eyebrows and ask them to make the tee tips touch. Participants felt sad while viewing scenes of war, sickness, and starvation, and even sadder with their "sad face" muscles activated (Larsen, Kasimatis, & Frey, 1992).

"I thought it would be nice if we had a forum where we could get together and have screaming tantrums."

© The New Yorker Collection,1999, Bruce Eric Kaplan from cartoonbank.com. All Rights Reserved.

girls reported walking away from the situation or working it off with exercise. Girls more often reported talking with a friend, listening to music, or writing (Ray, 2005).

Like a boomerang, our anger can come back to strike us if it fuels physically or verbally aggressive acts we later regret. Anger can also prime prejudice. After 9/11, Americans who responded with more anger than fear also displayed more intolerance for immigrants and Muslims (DeSteno & others, 2004; Skitka & others, 2004).

Anger can harm us in another way. Chronic anger is linked to heart disease (Chapter 10). Does this mean that we should, as some popular books and articles advise, release our angry feelings by lashing out at those who offend us? Should children be told to "vent" angry feelings? Are "recovery" therapists right to encourage us to rage at our dead parents, imaginatively curse the boss, or confront our childhood abuser?

The vent-your-anger advice assumes that we can achieve emotional release, or **catharsis,** through aggressive action or fantasy. Experimenters report that *sometimes* when people lash out at a provoker, they may indeed calm down. But this tends to be true only *if* they direct their strike at the provoker, *if* their behavior seems justified, and *if* their target is not threatening (Geen & Quanty, 1977; Hokanson & Edelman, 1966). In short, expressing anger can be *temporarily* calming *if* it does not leave us feeling guilty or anxious.

More often, expressing anger breeds more anger. For one thing, it may trigger another round of angry interactions, turning a minor conflict into a major confrontation. For another, expressing anger can magnify anger. (Recall the behavior feedback research: *Acting* angry can make us *feel* angrier.) The backfire potential of catharsis appeared in one study of 100 frustrated engineers and technicians just laid off by an aerospace company (Ebbesen & others, 1975). Researchers asked some workers questions that released angry feelings, such as, "What instances can you think of where the company has not been fair with you?" After expressing their anger, the workers later filled out a questionnaire that assessed their attitudes toward the company. Had the opportunity to "drain off" their feelings reduced their anger? Quite the contrary. These people in fact showed more anger than those who had discussed neutral topics.

"Anger will never disappear so long as thoughts of resentment are cherished in the mind."

The Buddha, 500 B.C.

Other studies support this finding. For example, researchers asked people who had been provoked to wallop a punching bag while thinking about the person who had angered them. Later, when given a chance for revenge, these people became even more aggressive. "Venting to reduce anger is like using gasoline to put out a fire," concluded the researcher, Brad Bushman (2002).

Retaliation sometimes reduces tension temporarily and gives a squirt of pleasure (Ramirez & others, 2005). But in the long run, any such pleasure reinforces the outbursts, reduces inhibitions, and may be habit forming. If stressed teachers find they can drain off some of their tension by berating a student, then the next time they feel irritated and tense they may be more likely to explode again. Think about it: The next time you

facial feedback effect the tendency of facial muscle states to trigger corresponding feelings such as fear, anger, or happiness.

catharsis emotional release. The catharsis hypothesis maintains that "releasing" aggressive energy (through action or fantasy) relieves aggressive urges.

A cool culture :: Domestic violence is rare in Micronesia. This photo of community life on Pulap Island suggests one possible reason: Family life takes place in the open on this island. Relatives and neighbors who witness angry outbursts can step in before the emotion escalates into child, spouse, or elder abuse.

Wolfgang Kaehler

are angry you are likely to do whatever has relieved your anger in the past.

Anger is not always wrong. Used wisely, it can communicate strength and competence (Tiedens, 2001). It can benefit a relationship when it expresses a complaint in ways that help solve the conflict rather than give it a fresh start. This means not only keeping silent about trivial irritations but also communicating important ones clearly and firmly. A nonaccusing statement of feeling—perhaps letting your housemates know that "I get irritated when I have to wash everyone's dirty dishes"—can help end the conflicts that cause anger.

What if someone else's behavior really hurts you, and you cannot resolve the conflict? The age-old response of forgiveness may be your best answer. Without letting the offender off the hook or inviting further harm, forgiveness releases anger and can calm the body. To explore the bodily effects of forgiveness, researchers invited college students to recall an incident where someone had hurt them (Witvliet & others, 2001). As the students mentally rehearsed forgiveness, their negative feelings—and their perspiration, blood pressure, heart rate, and facial tension—all were lower than when they rehearsed their grudges.

Happiness

12: What are the causes and consequences of happiness?

Our state of happiness or unhappiness colors our thoughts and our actions. Happy people perceive the world as a safer place. They make decisions and cooperate more easily. They live healthier and more energized and satisfied lives (Lyubomirsky & others, 2005; Myers, 1993). When your mood is gloomy, life as a whole seems depressing. Let your mood brighten and your thinking broadens and becomes more playful and creative (Fredrickson, 2002, 2003). Your relationships, your self-image, and your hopes for the future seem more promising.

Moreover—and this is one of psychology's most consistent findings—when we

feel happy we are more willing to help others. In study after study, a mood-boosting experience (finding money, succeeding on a challenging task, recalling a happy event) has made people more likely to give money, pick up someone's dropped papers, volunteer time, and do other good deeds. Psychologists call it the **feel-good, do-good phenomenon** (Salovey, 1990). Happiness doesn't just feel good, it does good.

Doing good also promotes good feeling. Some happiness coaches and instructors harness this force by asking their clients to perform a daily "random act of kindness" and to record how it made them feel.

William James was writing about the importance of happiness ("the secret motive for all [we] do") as early as 1902. With the rise of positive psychology in the twenty-first century, the study of happiness has become a significant area of research and is a key part of one of our big ideas in this text—psychology explores human strengths as well as challenges. Part of happiness research is the study of **subjective well-being**—our feelings of happiness (sometimes defined as a high ratio of positive to negative feelings) or sense of satisfaction with life. This information, combined with measures of *objective well-being,* such as a person's physical and economic condition, is helping us understand how people judge their quality of life.

The Short Life of Emotional Ups and Downs

When you are down, can you usually depend on rebounding within a day or two? How about when you're feeling up? Is that mood also hard to sustain? Over the long run, our emotional ups and downs tend to balance out. This is true even over the course of the day. Positive emotion rises over the early to middle part of most days and then

> "Weeping may tarry for the night, but joy comes with the morning."
>
> Psalm 30:5

Take heart! Tomorrow will be a new day :: Car trouble can happen at the worst possible times. But this woman's bad mood will almost certainly clear by tomorrow, when she may even experience a better-than-normal good mood.

Myrleen Ferguson Cate/Photo Edit

drops off (Kahneman & others, 2004; Watson, 2000). So, too, with day-to-day moods. A stressful event—an argument, a sick child, a car problem—triggers a bad mood. No surprise there. But by the next day, the gloom nearly always lifts (Affleck & others, 1994; Bolger & others, 1989; Stone & Neale, 1984). If anything, people tend to rebound from bad days to a *better*-than-usual good mood the following day.

Even when negative events drag us down for longer periods, the pattern continues. Romantic breakups feel devastating, but eventually the wound heals. Faculty members denied tenure expect their lives to be deflated. Actually, 5 to 10 years later, their happiness level is about the same as for those who were awarded tenure (Gilbert & others, 1998).

Grief over the loss of a loved one or anxiety after a severe trauma can linger. But usually, even tragedy is not permanently depressing. Those who learn that they are HIV-positive are devastated. But after five weeks of adapting to the grim

Human resilience :: Seven weeks after her 1994 wedding, Anna Putt of South Midlands, England, shown here with her husband, Des, suffered a brainstem stroke that left her "locked-in." For months afterward, she recalls, "I was paralyzed from the neck down and was unable to communicate. These were VERY frightening times. But with encouragement from family, friends, faith, and medical staff, I tried to keep positive." In the ensuing three years, she became able to "talk" (by nodding at letters), to steer an electric wheelchair with her head, and to use a computer (by nodding while wearing spectacles that guide a cursor). Despite her paralysis, she reports that "I enjoy going out in the fresh air. My motto is 'Don't look back, move forward.' God would not want me to stop trying and I have no intention of doing so. Life is what you make of it!"

Courtesy of Anna Putt

news, they are in less emotional pain than they had expected (Sieff & others, 1999). Similarly, people who become blind or paralyzed or are placed on kidney dialysis usually recover near-normal levels of day-to-day happiness (Gerhart & others, 1994; Myers, 1993; Riis & others, 2005). "If you are a paraplegic," explains Daniel Kahneman (2005), "you will gradually start thinking of other things, and the more time you spend thinking of other things the less miserable you are going to be." A major disability does often leave people somewhat less happy than the average person, yet considerably hap-

pier than able-bodied people with depression (Kübler & others, 2005; Lucas, 2005; Schwartz & Estrin, 2004). And, contrary to what many people believe, most patients "locked-in" a motionless body do not say they want to die (Smith & Delargy, 2005). The surprising reality: *We overestimate the duration of our emotions and underestimate our resilience.*

Wealth and Well-Being

The emotional impact of dramatically positive events also fades sooner than we might expect. Once the rush wears off, lottery winners typically find their overall happiness little changed (Brickman & others, 1978; Lau & Kramer, 2005). For them, as for others, there is much more to well-being than being well-off. Nevertheless, many people, including most new American collegians **(FIGURE 9.22)**, believe they would be happier if they had more money (Carroll, 2006; Csikszentmihalyi, 1999).

They probably would be—temporarily. Yet in the long run, wealth is like health. Its utter absence can breed misery, yet having it is no guarantee of happiness. Researchers find that people in some Indian and Pakistani slums "are more satisfied than one might expect" (Biswas-Diener & Diener, 2001; Suhail & Chaudry, 2004).

"But on the positive side, money can't buy happiness—so who cares?"

© H. L. Schwadron

Growing up poor puts one at risk for certain problems, but so does growing up rich. Children of affluence are at greater-than-normal risk for substance abuse, anxiety, and depression (Luthar & Latendresse, 2005).

During the last four decades, the average U.S. citizen's buying power tripled. Did this greater wealth—enabling twice as many cars per person, not to mention

feel-good, do-good phenomenon our tendency to be helpful when already in a good mood.

subjective well-being self-perceived happiness or satisfaction with life. Used along with measures of objective well-being (for example, physical and economic indicators) to evaluate our quality of life.

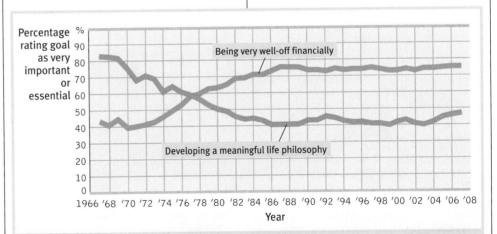

Figure 9.22> The changing materialism of entering college students Yearly surveys of more than 200,000 entering U.S. college students have, since 1970, revealed an increasing desire for wealth. (From *The American Freshman* surveys, UCLA, 1966 to 2007.)

iPods, laptops, Wii's, and Blackberries—also buy more happiness? As **FIGURE 9.23** shows, the average American, though richer, is not a bit happier.

Indeed, given mushrooming depression and the doubled rates of divorce and teen suicide, contemporary Americans—and Europeans and Australians and Japanese—seem to be more often miserable. These people, who enjoy better nutrition, health care, education, and science, are somewhat happier than people in very poor countries (Diener & Biswas-Diener, 2002; Eckersley, 2000). Yet their happiness has not kept pace with their wealth. Such findings lob a bombshell at modern materialism: *Economic growth in wealthy countries has provided no apparent boost to morale or social well-being.*

Why Can't Money Buy Happiness?

Why is it that, beyond poverty, more and more money does not buy more and more happiness? More generally, why do our emotions seem to be attached to elastic bands that pull us back from highs or lows? Psychology has proposed two answers. Each of them suggests that happiness is relative.

My Happiness Is Relative to My Own Experience The **adaptation-level phenomenon** describes our tendency to judge events in comparison to our past experiences. We draw on our past experience to establish *neutral* levels, points at which sounds seem neither loud nor soft, temperatures neither hot nor cold,

"*Money won't make you happy, Waldron. So instead of a raise, I'm giving a Prozac.*"

"No happiness lasts for long."

Seneca, *Agamemnon*, A.D. 60

events neither pleasant nor unpleasant. We then notice and react to variations up or down from these levels.

So, could we ever create a permanent social paradise? Probably not (Campbell, 1975). If you woke up tomorrow with all your wishes granted—perhaps a world with no bills, no ills, perfect grades, someone who loves you unreservedly—you would feel great joy and satisfaction, for a time. But then you would gradually adapt, and you would adjust your neutral level to include these new experiences. Before long, you would again sometimes feel joy and satisfaction (when events exceed your expectations), sometimes feel let down (when they fall below), and sometimes feel neutral. *The point to remember:* The feelings of satisfaction and dissatisfaction, success and failure are judgments we make about ourselves, based on our prior experience. As we add new experiences to the mix, those self-judgments may change.

My Happiness Is Relative to Your Success We are always comparing ourselves with others. And whether we feel good or bad depends on our perception of just how successful those others are (Lyubomirsky, 2001). We are slow-witted or clumsy only when others are smart or agile. This sense that we are worse off than others with

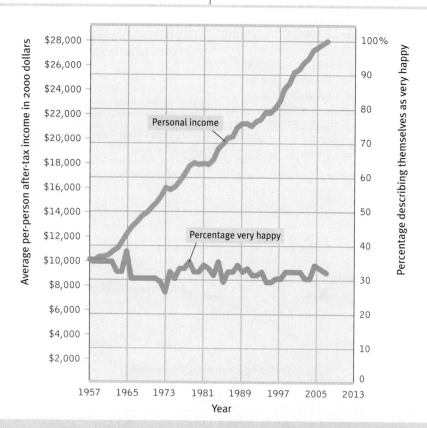

Figure 9.23> Does money buy happiness? Money surely helps us to avoid certain types of pain. Yet, though buying power has almost tripled since the 1950s, the average American's reported happiness has remained almost unchanged. (Happiness data from National Opinion Research Center surveys; income data from *Historical Statistics of the United States* and *Economic Indicators*.)

HI & LOIS

whom we compare ourselves is the concept of **relative deprivation.**

Some examples: During World War II, U.S. Air Corps soldiers experienced a relatively rapid promotion rate. Nevertheless, individual soldiers were frustrated about their own comparatively slow promotion rates (Merton & Kitt, 1950). Seeing so many others being promoted apparently inflated the soldiers' expectations. And when expectations soar above achievements, the result is disappointment. Relative deprivation showed up again when Alex Rodriguez achieved a 10-year, $252 million baseball contract. His deal surely made him temporarily happy, but it also lowered other star players' satisfaction with their mere multimillion-dollar contracts. And here's a third, larger example. The economic surge that has made some urban Chinese newly wealthy appears to have fueled among others a sense of relative deprivation (Burkholder, 2005a,b). In each of these three examples, people climbing the ladder of success were

"Researchers say I'm not happier for being richer, but do you know how much researchers make?"

doing what we all do: comparing themselves mostly with peers at or above their current level (Gruder, 1977; Suls & Tesch, 1978). "Beggars do not envy millionaires, though of course they will envy other beggars who are more successful," noted Bertrand Russell (1930, p. 90).

> "I have also learned why people work so hard to succeed: It is because they envy the things their neighbors have. But it is useless. It is like chasing the wind. . . . It is better to have only a little, with peace of mind, than be busy all the time with both hands, trying to catch the wind."
>
> Ecclesiastes 4:4

Just as comparing ourselves with those who are better off creates envy, so counting our blessings as we compare ourselves with those less well off boosts our contentment. In one study, University of Wisconsin–Milwaukee women considered others' deprivation and suffering (Dermer & others, 1979). They viewed vivid depictions of how grim life was in Milwaukee in 1900. They imagined and then wrote about various personal tragedies, such as being burned and disfigured. Later, the women expressed greater satisfaction with their own lives. Similarly, when mildly depressed people read about someone who is even more depressed, they feel somewhat better (Gibbons, 1986). "I cried because I had no shoes," states a Persian saying, "until I met a man who had no feet."

Predictors of Happiness

Happy people share many characteristics **(TABLE 9.1).** But what makes one person, day after day, so filled with joy and others so gloomy? Here, as in so many other areas, the answer is found in the interplay between nature and nurture.

adaptation-level phenomenon our tendency to form judgments (of sounds, of lights, of income) relative to a neutral level defined by our prior experience.

relative deprivation the perception that we are worse off relative to those with whom we compare ourselves.

Table 9.1	Happiness Is . . .	
Researchers Have Found That Happy People Tend To	**However, Happiness Seems Not Much Related to Other Factors, Such As**	
Have high self-esteem (in individualistic countries).	Age.	
Be optimistic, outgoing, and agreeable.	Gender (women are more often depressed, but also more often joyful).	
Have close friendships or a satisfying marriage.	Education level.	
Have work and leisure that engage their skills.	Parenthood (having children or not).	
Have a meaningful religious faith.	Physical attractiveness.	
Sleep well and exercise.		

Source: Summarized from DeNeve & Cooper (1998), Diener & others (2003), Lucas & others (2004), Myers (1993, 2000), and Myers & Diener (1995, 1996).

"I could cry when I think of the years I wasted accumulating money, only to learn that my cheerful disposition is genetic."

Genes matter. Studies of 254 identical and fraternal twins indicate that heredity accounts for 50 percent of the difference among people's happiness ratings (Lykken & Tellegen, 1996). Identical twins raised apart are often similarly happy.

But our personal history and our culture matter, too. On the personal level, as we saw earlier, our emotions tend to balance around our adaptation level, as defined by our experiences. On the cultural level, groups vary in the traits they value. Self-esteem matters more to Westerners, who value individualism. Social acceptance matters more to those in other cultures that stress family and community (Diener & others, 2003).

Depending on our genes, our outlook, and our recent experiences, our happiness seems to fluctuate around our "happiness set point," which disposes some people to be ever upbeat and others more negative. Even so, our satisfaction with life is not fixed (Fujita & Diener, 2005; Mroczek & Spiro, 2005). As researchers studying human strengths will tell you, happiness rises and falls, and it can be influenced by factors that are under our control. (See Close-Up: Want to Be Happier?)

Anger, happiness, and other emotions have this in common: They are biopsychosocial phenomena. Our genetic predispositions, brain activity, outlooks, experiences, relationships, and cultures jointly form us.

CLOSE-UP

■ WANT TO BE HAPPIER?

Happiness, like cholesterol level, is genetically influenced. Yet as cholesterol is also influenced by diet and exercise, so our happiness is to some extent under our personal control. Here are some research-based suggestions for building your personal strengths to increase your satisfaction with life.

Realize that enduring happiness doesn't come from financial success. We adapt to change by adjusting our expectations. Neither wealth, nor any other circumstance we long for, will guarantee happiness.

Take control of your time. Happy people feel in control of their lives. To master your use of time, set goals and break them into daily aims. This may be frustrating at first because we all tend to overestimate how much we will accomplish in any given day. The good news is that we generally underestimate how much we can accomplish in a year, given just a little progress every day.

Act happy. We can sometimes act ourselves into a happier frame of mind. Manipulated into a smiling expression, people feel better; when they scowl, the whole world seems to scowl back. So put on a happy face. Talk as if you feel positive self-esteem, are optimistic, and are outgoing.

Seek work and leisure that engage your skills. Happy people often are in a zone called *flow*—absorbed in tasks that challenge but don't overwhelm them. The most expensive forms of leisure (sitting on a yacht) often provide less flow experience than simpler forms, such as gardening, socializing, or craft work.

Join the "movement" movement. Aerobic exercise can relieve mild depression and anxiety as it promotes health and energy. Sound minds reside in sound bodies. Off your duffs, couch potatoes!

Give your body the sleep it wants. Happy people live active lives yet save time for renewing sleep. Many people—high school and college students, especially—suffer from sleep debt, with resulting fatigue, diminished alertness, and gloomy moods.

"Flowing" with the music, and enjoying time with friends

Solus Photography/Veer

Give priority to close relationships. Intimate friendships with those who care deeply about you can help you weather difficult times. Resolve to nurture your closest relationships by not taking your loved ones for granted, by displaying to them the sort of kindness you display to others, by affirming them, by playing together and sharing together.

Focus beyond self. Reach out to those in need. Happiness increases helpfulness (those who feel good do good). But doing good also makes us feel good.

Be grateful. Keeping a gratitude journal can heighten well-being. Try pausing each day to reflect on some positive aspect of your life (health, friends, family, freedom, education, senses, natural surroundings, and so on).

Nurture your spiritual self. For many people, faith provides a support community, a reason to focus beyond self, and a sense of purpose and hope. That helps explain why people active in faith communities report greater-than-average happiness and often cope well with crisis.

Digested from David G. Myers, *The Pursuit of Happiness* (Harper).

PRACTICE TEST

16. When you move into a new apartment, you find the street noise irritatingly loud, but after a while, it no longer bothers you. This illustrates the
a. relative deprivation principle.
b. adaptation-level principle.
c. feel-good, do-good phenomenon.
d. catharsis principle.

17. Those who support catharsis believe that we can get rid of anger by venting—by expressing our feelings in actions or words directed at the person who offended us. Such expressions of anger can
a. be temporarily calming if they do not produce feelings of guilt or anxiety.
b. strengthen the original feelings of anger and cause disagreements to escalate.
c. teach people that anger is a rewarding response that can be repeated on other occasions.
d. All of these answers are correct.

18. There will always be someone more successful, more accomplished, or richer with whom to compare yourself. In psychology, this observation is embodied in the
a. relative deprivation principle.
b. adaptation-level principle.
c. need to belong.
d. feel-good, do-good phenomenon.

19. One of the most consistent findings of psychological research is that happy people are also
a. more likely to express anger.
b. generally luckier than others.
c. concentrated in the wealthier nations.
d. more likely to help others.

Answers: 16. b, 17. d, 18. a, 19. d.

TERMS AND CONCEPTS TO REMEMBER

motivation, p. 235

drive-reduction theory, p. 236

physiological needs, p. 236

drive, p. 236

incentive, p. 236

hierarchy of needs, p. 237

glucose, p. 239

set point, p. 239

basal metabolic rate, p. 239

anorexia nervosa, p. 241

bulimia nervosa, p. 241

emotion, p. 248

James-Lange theory, p. 249

Cannon-Bard theory, p. 249

two-factor theory, p. 249

polygraph, p. 253

facial feedback effect, p. 258

catharsis, p. 259

feel-good, do-good phenomenon, p. 260

subjective well-being, p. 260

adaptation-level phenomenon, p. 262

relative deprivation, p. 263

:: Multiple-choice **self-tests** and more may be found at www.worthpublishers.com/myers

REVIEW: MOTIVATION AND EMOTION

MOTIVATIONAL CONCEPTS

MOTIVATION: THE ENERGIZING AND DIRECTING OF OUR BEHAVIOR.

HUNGER

1 What are three key perspectives on motivation, and how do they help us understand motivated behaviors?

- *Drive-reduction theory*: We feel motivated when pushed by a *physiological need* to reduce a *drive* (such as thirst), or when pulled by an *incentive* in our environment (ice cold drink).

- Arousal theory: We also feel motivated to behave in ways that maintain arousal (for example, curiosity-driven behaviors).

- Maslow's *hierarchy of needs*: Our levels of motivation form a pyramid shape. Lower-level needs (hunger, thirst, safety) must be met before we attend to higher-level needs (love, respect, self-actualization, meaning).

2 What physiological factors cause us to feel hungry?

- Empty-stomach pangs and low levels of blood *glucose* motivate hunger.

- The brain's hypothalamus is involved in hunger control.

- Appetite hormones heighten or reduce hunger.

- To maintain a stable weight (*set point*), the body adjusts its *basal metabolic rate* of energy use according to how much food we eat.

3 What psychological factors affect our eating behavior and feelings of hunger?

- Our memory of when we last ate affects our expectation of when we should eat again.

- We universally prefer certain tastes (such as sweet and salty).

- We learn taste preferences from family and culture.

- Some taste aversions (such as to foods that have made us ill) have survival value.

- Cultural pressures, low self-esteem, negative emotions, and perhaps a genetic factor seem to interact with stressful life experiences to produce *anorexia* and *bulimia*.

4 What factors predispose some people to become and remain obese?

- Fat cells store a concentrated fuel reserve for our bodies—perfect for feast/famine times, but no longer adaptive.

- Genes influence the number and size of our fat cells and our body weight.

- Weight loss challenges: The size but not the number of fat cells is reduced by a diet, fat cells require less energy than muscle cells to maintain, and metabolism decreases (and hunger increases) when body weight drops.

- Ways to increase odds of success: Reduce exposure to food cues, boost energy use through exercise, set realistic goals, and make a lifelong change in eating patterns.

THEORIES OF EMOTION

EMBODIED EMOTION

6 What are the components of an emotion, and what three theories help us to understand more about those components?

- *Emotion*: whole body response involving physiological arousal, expressive behaviors, and conscious experience.

- *James-Lange theory*: Emotional feelings follow our body's response to the emotion-arousing stimuli. (Our heart pounds, then we feel fear.)

- *Cannon-Bard theory*: Our body responds to emotion at the same time that we experience that emotion. (Neither one causes the other.)

- *Two-factor theory*: Emotions involve physical arousal (pounding heart), which is given a cognitive label ("I'm afraid").

7 What bodily changes accompany emotions, and how do they differ?

- Our autonomic nervous system controls the body changes that accompany emotions.

- The large-scale body changes that accompany sexual arousal, fear, and anger are very similar (increased perspiration, breathing, and heart rate), though they feel different.

- The small-scale body changes are different. For example, fear stimulates different facial muscles than joy does.

- Emotions use different circuits in the brain. For example, greater activity in the left frontal lobe signals positive rather than negative moods.

- *Polygraphs* (lie detectors) attempt to measure physical evidence of emotions, but they are not accurate enough to justify widespread use.

8 How do our thinking and feelings interact?

- Zajonc and LeDoux showed that simple emotions (such as likes, dislikes, and fears) may occur instantly, without conscious appraisal. Such responses are difficult to change by thinking.

- Lazarus, Schachter, and Singer found that conscious appraisal and labeling are key parts of more complex emotions (such as moods, hatred, and love). These emotions are therefore more open to change by thinking.

THE NEED TO BELONG

5 **Why do we have a need to belong—to affiliate with others?**

- Social bonds boosted our ancestors' chances for survival.
- When shunned by others, people suffer from stress and depression and may engage in self-defeating or antisocial behavior.
- Those who are socially secure in their relationships tend to be healthier and happier.

EXPRESSED EMOTION

9 **How do we communicate nonverbally?**

- We are good at detecting emotions from body language (expressions, gestures), especially if the message is a threat.
- Women tend to be better than men at reading people's emotional cues.

10 **Are nonverbal expressions of emotion universally understood, and do they influence our feelings?**

- Facial expressions, such as those of happiness and fear, are roughly similar all over the world.
- The meaning of gestures varies by culture.
- Expressions communicate emotion to others but also amplify the feelings we experience (*facial feedback effect*).

EXPERIENCED EMOTION

11 **What are the causes and consequences of anger?**

- Anger is caused by frustrating or insulting events that we interpret as willful, unjustified, and avoidable.
- Venting our anger (*catharsis*) may be temporarily calming, but expressing anger can actually make us angrier.

12 **What are the causes and consequences of happiness?**

- Good moods boost our perception of the world, ability to think creatively, health, energy levels, and willingness to help others (the *feel-good, do-good phenomenon*).
- Even significantly good or bad events don't usually change happiness levels for long.
- Our happiness level depends on our comparisons with our own experiences, including recent ones (the *adaptation-level phenomenon*), and on our comparisons with others (*relative deprivation*).
- Tips for increasing happiness levels: Act happy, seek meaningful work and leisure, exercise, sleep enough, nurture friendships, and focus beyond the self.

10 Stress, Health, and Human Flourishing

CONSIDER: HOW OFTEN DO YOU EXPERIENCE stress in your daily life? Never? Rarely? Sometimes? Or frequently?

When Gallup pollsters put that question to a national sample in late 2007, fewer than one in four Americans said "rarely" or "never." More than three in four said "sometimes" or "frequently" (Carroll, 2008). And you?

For many students, the transition to college (or back to college), with its new relationships and more demanding challenges, proves stressful. Debt piles up. Deadlines loom. Family demands continue. A big exam or a class presentation makes you tense. Then, stuck in traffic and late to class or work, your mood turns sour. It's enough to give you a headache or to disrupt your sleep.

Stress tends to be most intense when responsibilities overlap, such as while trying to be a good student, earn some money, and fulfill family responsibilities. An extreme case is Dana John, a student who began college in his mid-twenties. In high school, John didn't play sports "because everyone in our family worked . . . to take a little burden off my mother and my father" (Novin, 2006). But sports would become an important part of his life when he reached New Jersey City University, where he be-

Alex Tehrani

Dana John with his son, Dana Jr.

came a star basketball player. In 2007, ESPN featured John as "The Most Exhausted Man in Sports." A typical weekday: After spending the day on campus, he heads for a late afternoon practice. Two hours later, he heads home to eat and spend time with his four-year-old son. Sometime after 8 P.M., he's into his short night's sleep, which, five days a week, ends around 11 P.M., when he's off to his midnight to 8 A.M. post office job. Leaving work, he heads back to campus for the next day's classes and study, sometimes managing a training table nap just before practice. Whew!

In this chapter we explore stress—what it is and how it affects us. We also take a close look at some ways we can reduce the stress in our lives, so that we can flourish in both body and mind.

Stress: Some Basic Concepts

1: What is *stress,* and what are some of the ways we respond to stress?

Stress is a slippery concept, and we use this word in many different ways. To a psychologist, **stress** is a process of appraising and responding to a threatening or challenging event. That event is a *stressor.* Our physical and emotional responses are *stress reactions.* To see these differences, imagine that you're about to take a math test that will count for 25 percent of your final grade.

Stress arises less from the event itself than from how we appraise it (Lazarus, 1998). If you have prepared for the test, you may see it as a welcome challenge, an opportunity to nail down one-quarter of your grade for the course. You will be aroused and focused, and you will probably do well **(FIGURE 10.1).** When perceived as challenges, stressors can have positive effects, motivating us to conquer problems. Championship athletes, successful entertainers, and great teachers and leaders all thrive and excel when aroused by a challenge (Blascovich & others, 2004). Bouncing back from a serious illness or a lost job, we may feel a stronger sense of self-esteem and a deeper sense of purpose.

Tough challenges, especially early in life, can foster personal growth and emotional resilience (Landauer & Whiting, 1979).

Stressors that we appraise as threats, not challenges, can instead lead to strong *negative* reactions. Suppose a personal crisis prevents you from preparing for your math test. You will appraise this event as a threat that could destroy your hope for a good grade, and your response will be distress.

Severe or prolonged stress can harm us. Children who suffer severe or repeated abuse are later at risk of chronic disease (Repetti & others, 2002). Troops who had stress reactions after heavy combat in the Vietnam War later suffered high rates of circulatory, digestive, respiratory, and infectious diseases (Boscarino, 1997). There is an interplay between our heads and our health. Before we explore that interplay, however, let's take a closer look at stressors and stress reactions.

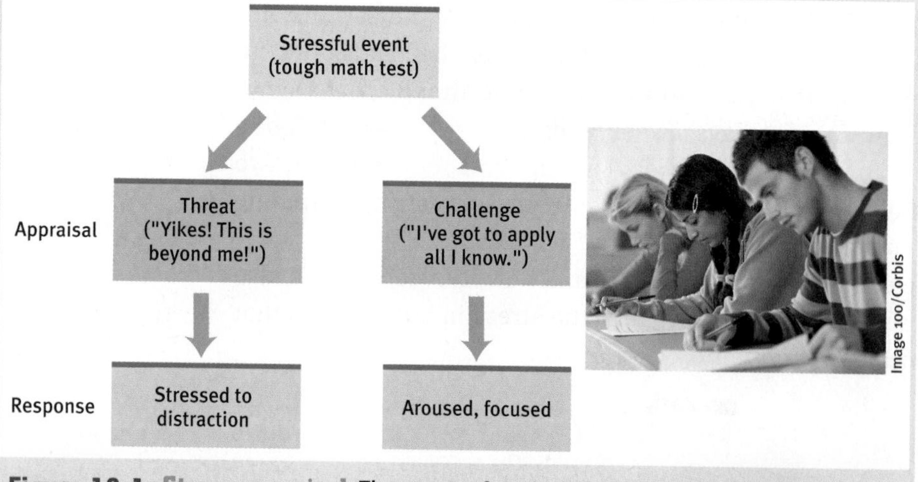

Stressors—Things That Push Our Buttons

2: What are three main types of stressors?

Stressors fall into three main types: catastrophes, significant life changes, and daily hassles. All can be toxic.

Toxic stress :: On the day of its 1994 earthquake, Los Angeles experienced a fivefold increase in sudden-death heart attacks. Most occurred in the first two hours after the quake and near its center. Physical exertion (running, lifting debris) contributed to only 13 percent of the deaths. The likely trigger for the others was stress (Muller & Verrier, 1996).

Les Stone/Corbis

Catastrophes are unpredictable large-scale events, such as wars, earthquakes, and famines. Nearly everyone appraises catastrophes as threatening. We often give aid and comfort to one another after such events, but the damage to emotional and physical health can be significant. In surveys taken in the three weeks after the 9/11 terrorist attacks, for example, two-thirds of Americans said they were having some trouble concentrating and sleeping (Wahlberg, 2001). New Yorkers were especially likely to report such symptoms (NSF, 2001).

Misery often has company during catastrophes, but *significant life changes* may leave us experiencing stress alone. Even happy life events, such as getting married, can be stressful. Such changes—leaving home, losing a job, getting married, being divorced, having a loved one die—often happen during young adulthood. The stress of those years was clear in a survey that asked whether "you are trying to take on too many things at once." The youngest adults reported the highest stress levels. In other studies, half of all adults under age 50 report "frequent" stress, compared with fewer than 30 percent of those over 50 (Saad, 2001).

Stressful event
(tough math test)

Appraisal

Threat
("Yikes! This is beyond me!")

Challenge
("I've got to apply all I know.")

Response

Stressed to distraction

Aroused, focused

Image 100/Corbis

Figure 10.1> Stress appraisal The events of our lives flow through a psychological filter. How we appraise an event influences how much stress we experience and how effectively we respond.

What are the health effects of life-change–related stress? Long-term studies indicate that people recently widowed, fired, or divorced are more vulnerable to disease (Dohrenwend & others, 1982). In one study of 96,000 widowed people, their risk of death doubled in the week following their partner's death (Kaprio & others, 1987). Experiencing a cluster of crises (perhaps losing a job while falling behind in school work *and* losing a relationship) puts one even more at risk.

Events don't have to remake our lives to cause stress. *Daily hassles*—rush-hour traffic, irritating housemates, long lines at the store, too many things to do, e-mail spam, loud cellphone talkers—may be significant sources of stress (Kohn & Macdonald, 1992; Lazarus, 1990; Ruffin, 1993). Some people can simply shrug off such hassles. For others, however, they are like having your skin sand-papered,

> "It's not the large things that send a man to the madhouse . . . no, it's the continuing series of small tragedies . . . not the death of his love but the shoelace that snaps with no time left."
>
> Charles Bukowski, cited by Lazarus in Wallis, 1983

and these little stressors add up and take a toll on health and well-being.

Many Americans experience more significant daily hassles: low wages; stretching to make ends meet; poor health; no or poor health insurance; solo parenting; day care, school, and neighborhood problems; and overcrowding in substandard housing. Any of these stressors can lead to high blood pressure and other health problems.

Stress Reactions— From Alarm to Exhaustion

3: How does the body respond to stress?

The stress response is part of a unified mind-body system. Walter Cannon (1929) first realized this in the 1920s, when he found that extreme cold, lack of oxygen, and emotion-arousing incidents all trigger an outpouring of stress hormones from the adrenal glands. You may recall (Chapters 2 and 9) that when your brain sounds an alarm, your *sympathetic nervous system* responds. It increases your heart rate and respiration, diverts blood from your digestive organs to your skeletal muscles, dulls your feeling of pain, and releases sugar and fat from your body's stores. Combined with the outpouring of stress hormones, this prepares your body for the wonderfully adaptive **fight-or-flight** response (see Figure 9.14 in Chapter 9).

Hans Selye's (1936, 1976) studies of animals' reactions to various stressors, such as electric shock and surgery, extended Cannon's findings and helped make stress a major concept in both psychology and medicine. Selye discovered that the body's adaptive response to stress was so general that it was like a single burglar alarm that sounds, no matter what intrudes. He named this response the **general adaptation syndrome (GAS),** and he saw it as a three-stage process **(FIGURE 10.2).** Let's say

stress the process by which we perceive and respond to certain events, called *stressors,* that we appraise as threatening or challenging.

fight-or-flight an emergency response, including activity of the sympathetic nervous system, that mobilizes energy and activity for attacking or escaping a threat.

general adaptation syndrome (GAS) Selye's concept of the body's adaptive response to stress in three stages—alarm, resistance, exhaustion.

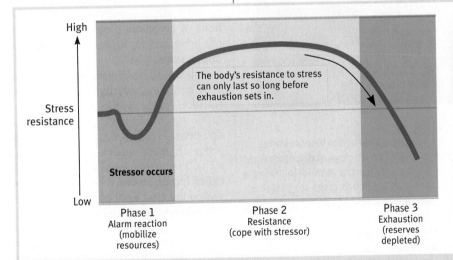

The body's resistance to stress can only last so long before exhaustion sets in.

High

Stress resistance

Stressor occurs

Low

Phase 1
Alarm reaction
(mobilize
resources)

Phase 2
Resistance
(cope with stressor)

Phase 3
Exhaustion
(reserves
depleted)

EPA/Yuri Kochetkov/Landov

Figure 10.2> Selye's general adaptation syndrome These girls are being carried to freedom and medical attention. They were held captive in a three-day attack on a school in Chechnya in 2004. After such a trauma, the body enters an alarm phase of temporary shock. From this it rebounds, as stress resistance rises. If the stress is prolonged, as it was for the 400 school hostages and their waiting loved ones, wear and tear may lead to exhaustion.

you suffer a physical or emotional trauma. In Phase 1, you have an *alarm reaction,* as your sympathetic nervous system is suddenly activated. Your heart rate zooms. Blood flows to your skeletal muscles. You feel the faintness of shock.

With your resources mobilized, you are ready to fight back. During Phase 2, *resistance,* your temperature, blood pressure, and respiration remain high, and stress hormones pour out from your adrenal glands into your bloodstream. You are fully engaged, summoning all your resources to meet the challenge.

As time passes, with no relief from stress, your body's reserves begin to run out. You have reached Phase 3, *exhaustion.* With exhaustion, you become more vulnerable to illness or even, in extreme cases, collapse and death. Although our body copes well with temporary stress, prolonged stress can damage us. So, too, with rats. The most fearful and easily stressed rats die sooner (after about 600 days) than their more confident siblings, which average 700-day life spans (Cavigelli & McClintock, 2003).

Fortunately, there are other options for dealing with stress. One is a common response to a loved one's death: Withdraw. Pull back. Conserve energy. Another, found especially among women, is to seek and give support (Taylor & others, 2000, 2006). This **tend-and-befriend** response is demonstrated in the outpouring of help after natural disasters.

It often pays to spend our resources in fighting or fleeing an external threat. But we do so at a cost. When our stress is momentary, the cost is small. When stress persists, we may pay a much higher price, with lowered resistance to infections and other threats to mental and physical health.

PRACTICE TEST

1. _____ are events that we appraise as challenging or threatening.
   a. Adrenals
   b. Stress reactions
   c. Stressors
   d. Fight-or-flight responses

Cleo Photography/Photo Edit

Michael Newman/Photo Edit

Every man for himself, or tend and befriend? Gender differences in the way we interact with others begin to appear at a very young age.

2. The number of short-term illnesses and stress-related psychological disorders was higher than usual in the months following an earthquake. Such findings suggest that
   a. daily hassles can ruin our health.
   b. experiencing a very stressful event makes us more vulnerable to illness and death.
   c. the amount of stress we feel is not related to the number of bad events we experience.
   d. small, bad events don't stress us, but large ones can be toxic.

3. In Selye's general adaptation syndrome (GAS), the first stage, an alarm reaction, is followed by
   a. fight or flight.
   b. resistance then exhaustion.
   c. challenge then recovery.
   d. stressful life events.

Answers: 1, c, 2, b, 3, b.

Stress Effects and Health

4: How does stress make us more vulnerable to disease?

Throughout this text, we have considered the many ways that our mind and our body interact. We have seen that everything psychological is at the same time biological. To experience this, think for a moment about biting into a section of a perfectly ripe orange. Imagine the sweet, tangy juice flooding across your tongue. Did you begin to salivate a bit? Our psychological states have real effects on other parts of our body, too. Stress correlates with specific illnesses, including high blood pressure and some headaches. Stress also leaves us less able to fight off disease. The relatively new field of **psychoneuroimmunology (PNI)** has emerged to study these mind-body interactions.

You can think of your immune system as a complex security system. When it functions properly, it keeps you healthy by capturing and destroying bacteria, viruses, and other invaders. Four types of cells are active in these search-and-destroy missions. Two are types of white blood cells, called **lymphocytes.** *B lymphocytes* release antibodies that fight bacterial infections. *T lymphocytes* attack cancer cells, viruses, and foreign substances—even "good" ones, such as transplanted organs. The third agent is the *macrophage* ("big eater"), which identifies, pursues, and ingests harmful invaders and worn-out cells **(FIGURE 10.3)**. And, finally, the *natural killer cells* (NK cells) pursue diseased

Figure 10.3> The immune system in action A large macrophage (at top) is about to trap and destroy a tiny bacterium (lower right). Macrophages constantly patrol our bodies in search of invaders—such as this *Escherichia coli* bacterium—and debris, such as worn-out red blood cells.

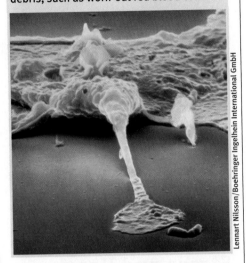

Lennart Nilsson/Boehringer Ingelheim International GmbH

cells (such as those infected by viruses or cancer). Age, nutrition, genetics, body temperature, and stress all influence the immune system's activity.

When your immune system doesn't function properly, it can err in two directions. Responding too strongly, it may attack the body's own tissues, causing arthritis or an allergic reaction. Underreacting, it may allow a dormant herpes virus to erupt or cancer cells to multiply. Women have stronger immune systems, making them less likely than men to get infections. But this very strength also makes women more susceptible to self-attacking diseases, such as lupus and multiple sclerosis (Morell, 1995; Pido-Lopez & others, 2001).

Your immune system becomes less active when your body is flooded with stress hormones. This effect appears when animals are stressed by physical restraints, unavoidable electric shocks, noise, crowding, cold water, social defeat, or separation from their mothers (Maier & others, 1994). In one such study (Cohen & others, 1992), monkeys were stressed by being housed with new roommates—three or four new monkeys—each month for six months. If you know the stress of adjusting to a new roommate, you can imagine how stressful it would be to repeat this experience monthly. By the end of the experiment, the socially stressed monkeys' immune systems were weaker than those of other monkeys left in stable groups. Human immune systems react similarly. Two examples:

- Surgical wounds heal more slowly in stressed people. In one experiment, two groups of dental students received punch wounds (small holes punched in the skin). The group wounded three days before a major exam healed 40 percent slower than the group wounded during summer vacation (Kiecolt-Glaser & others, 1998).

- Colds are more likely to develop in stressed people. Researchers dropped a cold virus in the noses of stressed and relatively unstressed people **(FIGURE 10.4)**. How many developed colds? Among those living stress-filled lives, 47 percent did. Among those living relatively free of stress, only 27 percent got colds (Cohen & others, 1999, 2003, 2006a,b).

The stress effect on immunity makes sense (Maier & others, 1994). It takes energy to track down invaders, produce swelling, and maintain fevers, and stress hormones drain this energy away from the disease-fighting white blood cells. When we are ill, our bodies demand inactivity and increased sleep, in part to cut back on the energy our muscles usually use. Stress does the opposite. It creates a competing energy need. During an aroused fight-or-flight reaction, stress responses draw energy away from the disease-fighting immune system and send it to the muscles and brain (see Figure 9.14 in Chapter 9). This leaves us more vulnerable to illness. *The bottom line: Stress does not make us sick, but it does reduce our immune system's ability to function, which leaves us open to foreign invaders.*

Let's look now at some ways that stress can affect three specific illnesses—AIDS, cancer, and heart disease.

tend and befriend under stress, people (especially women) often provide support to others *(tend)* and bond with and seek support from others *(befriend).*

psychoneuroimmunology (PNI) the study of how psychological, neural, and endocrine processes combine to affect our immune system and health.

lymphocytes the two types of white blood cells that are part of the body's immune system: *B lymphocytes* release antibodies that fight bacterial infections; *T lymphocytes* attack cancer cells, viruses, and foreign substances.

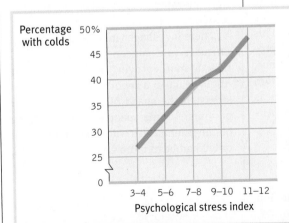

Laurent Bsip/Yakou/Photo Library

Figure 10.4> Stress and colds People with the highest life-stress scores were also most vulnerable when exposed to an experimentally delivered cold virus (Cohen & others, 1999).

Stress and AIDS

We know that stress suppresses immune functioning. What does this mean for people suffering from AIDS (acquired immune deficiency syndrome)? People with AIDS already have a damaged immune system. The name of the virus that triggers AIDS tells us that. "HIV" stands for *human immunodeficiency virus*. Stress can't give people AIDS. But could stress and negative emotions speed the transition from HIV infection to AIDS in someone already infected? Might stress predict a faster decline in those with AIDS? The answer to both questions seems to be "yes" (Bower & others, 1998; Kiecolt-Glaser & Glaser, 1995; Leserman & others, 1999). HIV-infected men who experience stressful events, such as the loss of a partner, show somewhat greater immune suppression and travel a faster course in this disease.

Could reducing stress help control AIDS? The answer again appears to be yes. Educational programs, grief support groups, talk therapy, and exercise programs that reduce distress have all had good results for HIV-positive people (Baum & Posluszny, 1999; Schneiderman, 1999). But we must be realistic about these results. The benefits of stress-reduction programs are small, compared with available drug treatments. Although AIDS is now more treatable than ever before, preventing HIV infection is a far better option. This is the focus of many educational programs, such as the ABC (abstinence, being faithful, condom use) program that has been used with notable success in the African country of Uganda (Altman, 2004; USAID, 2004).

Stress and Cancer

Stress does not create cancer cells. But in a healthy, functioning immune system, lymphocytes, macrophages, and NK cells search out and destroy cancer cells and cancer-damaged cells. If stress weakens the immune system, might this weaken a person's ability to fight off cancer or to recover from that disease? Experiments on humans would be impossible, of course, but researchers have explored such questions in rodents, by implanting tumor cells or giving them *carcinogens* (cancer-producing substances). They then exposed some of the rodents to uncontrollable stress, such as inescapable shocks, which weakened their immune systems. These rodents were indeed more prone to developing cancer (Sklar & Anisman, 1981). Their tumors developed sooner and grew larger than in nonstressed rodents.

Does this stress-cancer link also hold with humans? The results are mixed. Some studies find that people are at increased risk for cancer within a year after experiencing depression, helplessness, or grief. In one large study, the risk of colon cancer was 5.5 times greater among people with a history of workplace stress than among those who reported no such problems. This difference was not due to group differences in age, smoking, drinking, or physical characteristics (Courtney & others, 1993). Other studies, however, find no link between stress and human cancer (Edelman & Kidman, 1997; Fox, 1998; Petticrew & others, 1999, 2002). Concentration camp survivors and former prisoners of war, for example, do not have elevated cancer rates. So this research story is still being written.

There is a danger in hyping reports on attitudes and cancer. Can you imagine how a mother dying of breast cancer might react to a report on the effects of stress on the speed of decline in cancer patients? Some people may wrongly blame themselves for their illness: "If only I had been more expressive, relaxed,

> "I didn't give myself cancer."
>
> Mayor Barbara Boggs Sigmund (1939–1990), Princeton, New Jersey

and hopeful." Another danger is a "wellness macho" among the healthy, who may take credit for their "healthy character" and lay a guilt trip on the ill: "She has cancer? That's what you get for holding your feelings in and being so nice." Dying thus becomes the ultimate failure. It's important enough to repeat: *Stress does not create cancer cells*. At worst, it may affect their growth by weakening the body's natural defenses against multiplying cancer cells. Although a relaxed, hopeful state may enhance these defenses, we should be aware of the thin line that divides science from wishful thinking. The powerful biological processes at work in advanced cancer or AIDS are not likely to be completely derailed by avoiding stress or maintaining a relaxed but determined spirit (Anderson, 2002; Kessler & others, 1991).

Stress and Heart Disease

Stress is much more closely linked to **coronary heart disease,** the leading cause of death in North America today. In this disease, the blood vessels that nourish the heart muscle close. High blood pressure and a family history of the disease increase the risk of heart disease. So do smoking, obesity, a high-fat diet, physical inactivity, and a high cholesterol level. Stress and personality also play a big role, as Meyer Friedman, Ray Rosenman, and their colleagues discovered in 1956 (Friedman & Ulmer, 1984).

While studying the eating behavior of White San Francisco women and their husbands, Friedman and Rosenman stumbled upon an interesting fact. The women consumed as much cholesterol and fat as their husbands did, yet they were far less likely to get heart disease. Was it because of their female sex hormones? No, because African-American women, with those same female hormones, were as prone to heart disease as their husbands.

In search of an answer to the differences in heart attack rates, Friedman and Rosenman began a series of tests. They measured the blood cholesterol level and clotting speed of 40 U.S. male tax accountants at different times of year. From January through March, the test results were completely normal. Then, as the accountants began scrambling to finish their clients' tax returns before the April 15 filing deadline, their cholesterol and clotting measures rose to dangerous levels. In May and June, with the deadline past, the measures returned to normal. Stress predicted heart attack risk for the accountants, with rates going up during their most stressful times. The researchers' hunch had paid off, launching a classic nine-year study of more than 3000 healthy men, aged 35 to 59.

At the start of the study, Friedman and Rosenman interviewed each man for 15 minutes, noting his work and eating habits, manner of talking, and other behavioral patterns. Some men, they discovered, reacted very strongly and were competitive, hard-driving, impatient, time-conscious, supermotivated, verbally aggressive, and easily angered. They labeled these men **Type A.** The roughly equal number who were more easygoing they called **Type B.** Which group do you suppose turned out to be the most coronary-prone?

Nine years later, 257 men in the study had suffered heart attacks, and 69 percent of them were Type A. Moreover, not one of the "pure" Type Bs—the most mellow and laid-back of their group—had suffered a heart attack.

As often happens in science, this exciting discovery provoked enormous public interest. But after that initial honeymoon period, researchers wanted to know more. Was the finding reliable? If so, what exactly is so toxic about the Type A profile: Time-consciousness? Competitiveness? Anger? Further research revealed the answer. Type A's toxic core is negative emotions—especially anger (Smith & Ruiz, 2002; Williams, 1993). Type A individuals are more often "combat ready." When these people are harassed or challenged by a stressor, they react aggressively. As their often-active sympathetic nervous system redistributes bloodflow to the muscles, it pulls blood away from internal organs. One of these internal organs, the liver, which normally removes cholesterol and fat from the blood, can't do its job. Excess cholesterol and fat continue to circulate in the blood and later get deposited around the heart. Further stress—sometimes conflicts brought on by their own abrasiveness—may trigger altered heart rhythms. In people with weakened hearts, this altered pattern can cause sudden death (Kamarck & Jennings, 1991). We see again that our hearts and minds interact in important ways.

TYPE **A** PERSONALITY   TYPE **B** PERSONALITY

Because it's there!

Because it's there!

Bannerman © 7/94

> "The fire you kindle for your enemy often burns you more than him."
>
> Chinese proverb

Other studies of young and middle-aged men and women confirm the finding that people who react with anger over little things are the most coronary-prone. One study followed 13,000 middle-aged people for five years. Among those with normal blood pressure, people who had scored high on anger were three times more likely to have had heart attacks, even after researchers controlled for smoking and weight (Williams & others, 2000). Another study followed 1055 male medical students over an average of 36 years. Those who had reported being hot-tempered were five times more likely to have had a heart attack by age 55 (Chang & others, 2002). As Charles Spielberger and Perry London (1982) put it, rage "seems to lash back and strike us in the heart muscle."

Depression, too, can be lethal, as the accumulated evidence from 57 studies indicates (Wulsin & others, 1999). One study focused on women age 67 or older. Among those with no symptoms of depression, 7 percent died within six years. When six or more symptoms were present, 24 percent died within six years (Whooley & Browner, 1998). The trend continues in the years following a heart attack. People with high scores for depression are four times more likely than their low-scoring counterparts to develop further heart problems (Frasure-Smith & Lesperance, 2005). Although explanations of the depression–heart disease association range from unhealthy life-style habits to a biological clogging of the arteries, this much seems clear: Depression is disheartening. A healthy balance is key—prolonged stress can take a serious toll.

* * *

We can view the stress effect on our disease resistance as a price we pay for the benefits of stress (**FIGURE 10.5** on the next page). Yet stress invigorates our

coronary heart disease the clogging of the vessels that nourish the heart muscle; the leading cause of death in many developed countries, such as those in North America.

Type A Friedman and Rosenman's term for competitive, hard-driving, impatient, verbally aggressive, and anger-prone people.

Type B Friedman and Rosenman's term for easygoing, relaxed people.

Figure 10.5> Stress can have a variety of health-related consequences This is especially so when experienced by angry, depressed, or anxious people.

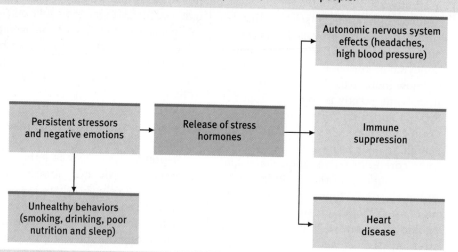

Persistent stressors and negative emotions → Release of stress hormones

Release of stress hormones → Autonomic nervous system effects (headaches, high blood pressure)

Release of stress hormones → Immune suppression

Release of stress hormones → Heart disease

Persistent stressors and negative emotions → Unhealthy behaviors (smoking, drinking, poor nutrition and sleep)

Michael NewmN/PPhoto Edit

---

lives. It arouses and motivates us. An un-stressed life would not be challenging or productive.

a. living a fast-paced life-style.
b. working in a competitive job.
c. meeting deadlines and challenges.
d. often feeling angry and negative.

Answers: 4. d, 5. c, 6. d.

PRACTICE TEST

4. Stress hormones suppress immune system cells that ordinarily attack bacteria, viruses, cancer cells, and other foreign substances. Which of the following is NOT one of those cell types?

a. Lymphocytes   c. NK cells
b. Macrophages   d. Neurons

5. People are at increased risk for cancer a year or so after experiencing depression, helplessness, or grief. In describing this link between negative emotions and cancer, researchers are quick to point out that

a. accumulated stress causes cancer.
b. anger is the negative emotion most closely linked to cancer.
c. stress does not create cancer cells, but it weakens the body's natural defenses against them.
d. feeling optimistic about the chances of survival ensures that a cancer patient will get well.

6. Heart attacks occur more often in Type A people, who are hard-driving, verbally aggressive, and anger-prone. The "toxic ingredient" most closely linked to coronary heart disease is

Human Flourishing

Stressors are unavoidable. That's a fact we have to live with. One way we can develop our strengths is to learn better ways to cope with our stress and to manage it as we try to avoid health problems. Again, though the finding is correlational, one study indicates that managing stress may be life-sustaining. The one personality trait shared by 169 people over the age of 100 was their ability to manage stress well (Perls & others, 1999).

Coping with Stress

5: What are some of the things that influence our ability to cope with stress?

To prevent illness and promote our well-being, we need to find new ways to feel, think, and act when we are dealing with stressors. We address some stressors directly, with **problem-focused coping.** For example, if our impatience leads to a

family fight, we may go directly to that family member to work things out. We tend to use problem-focused strategies when we feel a sense of control over a situation and think we can change the circumstances, or at least change ourselves to more capably deal with the circumstances. We turn to **emotion-focused coping** when we cannot—or *believe* we cannot—change a situation. If, despite our best efforts, we cannot get along with that family member, we may search for relief from stress by confiding in friends and reaching out for social support and comfort.

Emotion-focused strategies can be adaptive when they move us toward better long-term health, as when we attempt to gain emotional distance from a damaging relationship or keep busy with hobbies to avoid thinking about an old addiction. Emotion-focused strategies can be nonadaptive, however, as when students worried about not keeping up with the reading in class go out to party to get it off their minds. Sometimes a problem-focused strategy (catching up with the reading) more effectively reduces stress and promotes long-term health and satisfaction.

Our success in coping depends on several factors. Let's look at four of them: personal control, outlook, social support, and the search for meaning.

Personal Control

Personal control is our sense of seeing ourselves in control of our environment. Psychologists study the effect of personal control (or any personality factor) in two ways:

1. *Correlate* people's feelings of control with their behaviors and achievements.

2. *Experiment,* by raising or lowering people's sense of control and noting the effects.

Both methods have helped us understand that personal control matters.

Control, Morale, and Health Facing an ongoing series of bad events beyond our control can lead us to feel helpless, hopeless, and depressed. Psychologists call this passive resignation **learned helplessness.** Researcher Martin Seligman (1975, 1991) and others studied learned helplessness in animals and people **(FIGURE 10.6).** For example, dogs were strapped in a harness and given repeated shocks, with no opportunity to avoid them. When later placed in another situation where they *could* escape the punishment by simply leaping a hurdle, the dogs cowered as if without hope. Other dogs that were able to escape the shocks in Seligman's first situation did not react this way. They learned they were in control, and they easily escaped the shocks in the new situation.

Animal studies show—and human studies confirm—that feelings of losing control trigger physical symptoms. Stress hormone levels rise, blood pressure increases, and immune responses drop (Rodin, 1986; Sapolsky, 2005). Feelings of loss of control happen when rats cannot avoid shocks. They happen when people in high-density neighborhoods, prisons, and even college dorms are crowded together (Fleming & others, 1987; Ostfeld & others, 1987).

Perceived loss of control can be a predictor of health problems. Captive animals experience more stress and are more vulnerable to disease than are wild animals (Roberts, 1988).

People given little control over their world in prisons, factories, colleges, and nursing homes also experience lower morale and increased stress. Knowing this, psychologists have proposed measures that increase control and noticeably improve health and morale (Miller & Monge, 1986; Ruback & others, 1986; Wener & others, 1987). These include allowing prisoners to move chairs and control room lights and the TV; having workers participate in decision making; and offering nursing home patients choices about their environment. In one famous study, 93 percent of nursing home patients who were encouraged to exert more control became more alert, active, and happy (Rodin, 1986). "Perceived control is basic to human functioning," observed researcher Ellen Langer (1983, p. 291). "For the young and old alike," environments should enhance people's sense of control over their world. No wonder iPods and TiVos, which enhance our control of the content and timing of our entertainment, are so popular.

The verdict of these studies is reassuring on a larger scale. Under conditions of personal freedom and empowerment, people thrive. Indeed, the citizens of stable democracies report higher levels of happiness (Inglehart, 1990). Shortly before the democratic revolution in the former East Germany, researchers compared the telltale body language of working-class men in East and West Berlin bars

Happy to have control :: These joyous East Berliners were crossing over to freedom in West Berlin after the wall came down in 1989.

Peter Turnley/Corbis

(Oettingen & Seligman, 1990). Compared with their counterparts on the other side of the Wall, the empowered West Berliners much more often laughed, sat upright rather than slumped, and had up-turned rather than down-turned mouths.

So, some freedom and control is better than none, but does ever-increasing choice breed ever-happier lives? Barry Schwartz (2000, 2004) suggests that the "excess of freedom" in today's Western cultures contributes to decreasing life satisfaction, increased depression, and, sometimes, paralysis. Consumers may be staggered by the choices. After choosing among 30 brands of jam or chocolate, people express less satisfaction than do

problem-focused coping attempting to alleviate stress directly—by changing the stressor or the way we interact with that stressor.

emotion-focused coping attempting to alleviate stress by avoiding or ignoring a stressor and attending to emotional needs related to our stress reaction.

personal control our sense of controlling our environment rather than feeling helpless.

learned helplessness the hopelessness and passive resignation an animal or human learns when unable to avoid repeated aversive events.

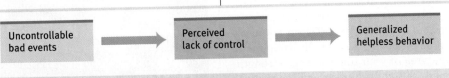

| Uncontrollable bad events | → | Perceived lack of control | → | Generalized helpless behavior |

Figure 10.6> Learned helplessness When animals and people experience no control over repeated bad events, they often learn helplessness.

those who made their choices from only 6 options (Iyengar & Lepper, 2000). This *tyranny of choice* brings information overload and a greater likelihood that we will feel regret over some of the things we left behind.

Who's at the Controls? Do you believe that your life is out of control? That the world is run by a few powerful people? That getting a good job depends mainly on being in the right place at the right time? Or do you more strongly believe that you control your own fate? That each of us can influence our government's decisions? That being a success is a matter of hard work, not luck?

Hundreds of studies have compared people who differ in their perceptions of control. On the one side are those who have what psychologist Julian Rotter called an **external locus of control**—the view that chance or outside forces control their fate. On the other are those who perceive an **internal locus of control** and believe that to a great extent they control their own destiny. Do these feelings make a difference outside the laboratory? Apparently they do. In study after study, "internals" achieve more in school and work, act more independently, enjoy better health, and feel less depressed than

do "externals" (Lachman & Weaver, 1998; Lefcourt, 1982; Ng & others, 2006). Moreover, they are better able to delay gratification and cope with various stressors, including marital problems (Miller & others, 1986).

If *feeling* an internal locus of control lowers stress, does *actively* controlling or self-managing our behavior likewise reduce stress? *Self-control*—the ability to control impulses and delay gratification—in turn predicts good adjustment, better grades, and social success (Tangney & others, 2004). Students who plan their day's activities and then live out their day as they had planned are also at low risk for depression (Nezlek, 2001).

Self-control is not a constant state, like having brown eyes. Rather, self-control, like a muscle, temporarily weakens after being used, regains energy with rest, and grows stronger with exercise (Baumeister & Exline, 2000). Hungry people who had exercised self-control and resisted the temptation to eat chocolate chip cookies gave up sooner when later performing a tedious task. This decrease in mental energy also appeared in other experiments. For example, people have spent willpower on laboratory tasks that demanded their full attention and energy, as when they have seen the word green printed in red ink and must quickly state the color of the printed word ("red," not "green"). After focusing on such tasks, these people are temporarily less restrained in their aggressive responses when provoked and in their sexual thoughts and behaviors (De Wall & others, 2007; Gaillot & Baumeister, 2007). These are short-term effects. In the long run, disciplined exercise and study strengthen self-control, as work-out programs strengthen muscles. This result appears both in people's performance on laboratory tasks and in their improved self-management of eating, drinking, smoking, and household chores (Oaten & Cheng, 2006a,b). Develop your self-discipline in one area of your life and your strengthened self-control may spill over into other areas as well, making for a less stressed life.

Is the Glass Half Full or Half Empty?

Another part of coping with stress is our outlook—what we expect from the world. **Optimists** agree with statements such as, "In uncertain times, I usually expect the best" (Scheier & Carver, 1992). People with an optimistic outlook expect to have more control and to cope better with stressful events. **Pessimists** expect things to go badly. If they perform poorly, they see it as evidence of their lack of ability or of a situation that is beyond their control (Noel & others, 1987; Peterson & Barrett, 1987). They often make statements like, "I can't do this!" or "There is nothing I can do about it."

Optimists tend to enjoy better health than pessimists do. During the last month of a semester, students previously identified as optimistic reported less fatigue and fewer coughs, aches, and pains. And during the stressful first few weeks of law school, those who are optimistic ("It's unlikely that I will fail") enjoy better moods and stronger

Robert Biswas-Diener/The Strengths Project

Optimism against all odds :: *The Strengths Project* profiled "Gita" in India, who remains upbeat and is flourishing despite having lost her daughter to suicide. She is shown here with her beloved granddaughter, whose blood disorder requires frequent, expensive treatments that have left them impoverished. Yet she still finds joy in life's small pleasures. "We are a community," she says proudly. "We respect one another and help each other during hard times."

Rubes®   By Leigh Rubin

"YOU SEEM TO HAVE TROUBLE ACCEPTING RESPONSIBILITY."

"IT'S MY PARENTS' FAULT."

7-6

Creators Syndicate, Inc.
© 1993 Leigh Rubin!

Creators Syndicate, Inc. © Leigh Rubin

immune systems (Segerstrom & others, 1998). Optimists also respond to stress with smaller increases in blood pressure, and they recover more quickly from heart bypass surgery.

Does optimists' better health translate into a longer life span? Possibly. One study asked 795 Americans aged 64 to 79 years if they were "hopeful about the future." Five years later, 29 percent of those answering "no" had died—more than double the 11 percent of deaths among those who said "yes" (Stern & others, 2001). The optimism–long-life correlation also appeared in a study of 180 Catholic nuns. At about 22 years of age, each of these women had written a brief autobiography. In the decades that followed, they lived similar life-styles. Those who had expressed happiness, love, and other positive feelings in their autobiographies lived an average seven years longer than did the more negative nuns (Danner & others, 2001). By age 80, only 24 percent of the most positive-spirited had died, compared with 54 percent of those expressing few positive emotions.

Positive thinking pays dividends, but so does a dash of realism (Schneider, 2001). Can you remember a time when you were *realistically anxious* about failing in some future event? Perhaps you were short of money and worried about being able to

Positive expectations often motivate eventual success.

"We just haven't been flapping them hard enough."

Laughter among friends is good medicine :: Laughter arouses us, massages muscles, and then leaves us feeling relaxed (Robinson, 1983). Humor (though not hostile sarcasm) may defuse stress and strengthen immune activity (Berk & others, 2001; Kimata, 2001). People who laugh a lot also tend to have lower rates of heart disease (Clark & others, 2001).

pay a bill on time, or you had fallen behind on your reading and feared you would do badly on an exam. Did your anxiety cause you to try extra hard to avoid failure? Realistic anxiety over possible *future* failures often has this effect (Goodhart, 1986; Norem, 2001; Showers, 1992). Students concerned about failing an upcoming exam may study more, and therefore outperform equally able but more confident peers. This may help explain the impressive academic achievements of some Asian-American students. Compared with European-Americans, these students express somewhat greater pessimism (Chang, 2001). Success requires enough optimism to provide hope and enough pessimism to keep us on our toes.

> "God grant us the serenity to accept the things we cannot change, courage to change the things we can, and wisdom to know the difference."
>
> Alcoholics Anonymous Serenity Prayer
> (attributed to Reinhold Niebuhr)

Excessive optimism can also blind us to real risks (Weinstein, 1980, 1982, 1996). Most college students display an *unrealistic optimism*. They view themselves as less

likely than their average classmate to develop drinking problems, drop out of school, or have a heart attack by age 40. Most older adolescents see themselves as much less vulnerable than their peers to the AIDS virus (Abrams, 1991). Blinded by optimism, people young and old deny the effects of smoking, venture into ill-fated relationships, and engage in unprotected sex. As famed basketball player Magic Johnson said (1993) after contracting the HIV virus, "I didn't think it could happen to me."

Social Support

Social support—feeling liked and encouraged by intimate friends and family—is another coping strategy that promotes both happiness and health. Consider Linda and Emily, who participated in a study by psychologist Shelley Taylor (1989). The women had similar histories. Both lived in Los Angeles, had married, and had raised three children. Both had been diagnosed with comparable breast tumors and had recovered from surgery and six months of chemotherapy. But there was a difference. Linda, a widow in her early fifties, was living alone, her children scattered in Atlanta, Boston, and Europe. "She had become odd in ways that people sometimes do when they are isolated," reported Taylor. "Having no one with whom to share her thoughts on a daily basis, she unloaded them somewhat inappropriately with strangers, including our interviewer."

Interviewing Emily was difficult in a different way. Phone calls interrupted the

---

external locus of control the perception that chance or outside forces beyond our personal control determine our fate.

internal locus of control the perception that we control our own fate.

optimism the anticipation of positive outcomes. Optimists are people who expect the best and expect their efforts to lead to good things.

pessimism the anticipation of negative outcomes. Pessimists are people who expect the worst and doubt that their goals will be achieved.

interview. Her children, all living nearby, were in and out of the house, dropping things off with a quick kiss. Her husband called from his office for a brief chat. Two dogs roamed the house, greeting visitors enthusiastically. All in all, Emily "seemed a serene and contented person, basking in the warmth of her family."

Three years later, the researchers tried to interview the women again. Linda, they learned, had died two years before. Emily was still lovingly supported by her family and friends and was as happy as ever. No two cancers are identical, so we can't be certain that different social situations led to Linda's and Emily's fates. But their cases illustrate a striking fact that emerged in seven massive investigations. For several years, each study followed thousands of people—some with and others without close social ties. The studies reached similar conclusions. People are less likely to die early if supported by close relationships with friends, family, fellow workers, members of a faith community, or other support groups (Cohen, 1988; House & others, 1988; Nelson, 1988).

Social support helps us fight illnesses in at least two ways. First, it calms our *cardiovascular system,* lowering blood pressure and stress hormones (Uchino & others, 1996, 1999). Second, social support fosters stronger *immune functioning.* Cancer patients' spouses who received ample social support showed this stronger immune functioning (Baron & others, 1990). So did volunteers in studies of resistance to cold viruses (Cohen & others, 1997, 2004). In those studies, two groups of healthy volunteers inhaled nose drops loaded with a cold virus and were quarantined and observed for five days. (The volunteers received $800 each to endure this experience.) The researchers then took a cold, hard look at the results, after controlling for age, race, sex, smoking, and other health habits. People with close social ties in their everyday lives were least likely to catch a cold. If they did catch one, they produced less mucus. The effect of social ties is nothing to sneeze at.

Many people find their support system in a happy marriage. People in low-conflict marriages live longer, healthier lives than the unmarried (Kaplan & Kronick, 2006; Wilson & Oswald, 2002). This correlation holds regardless of age, sex, race, and income (National Center for Health Statistics, 2004). One seven-decades–long study found that at age 50, healthy aging is better predicted by a good marriage than by a low cholesterol level (Vaillant, 2002).

Finding Meaning

For many people, an important part of coping with stress is making sense of bad events and finding some redeeming purpose in their suffering (Taylor, 1983). Those with a strong sense of meaning have a purpose for which to live, strong values, and a sense of personal competence and self-worth. Close relationships offer an opportunity for "open heart therapy," a chance to *confide* painful feelings (Frattaroli, 2006). Confiding is good for both soul and body. Talking or writing about our experiences helps us make sense of our stress and find meaning in it (Esterling & others, 1999). This effect is clear in studies of Holocaust survivors, victims of childhood sexual trauma, and other trauma survivors (Pennebaker & others, 1984, 1989, 1990). In one study, researchers contacted the surviving spouses of people who had committed suicide or died in car accidents. Those who bore their grief alone had more health problems than those who could express it openly. In other studies, people who managed to find meaning in a family member's death and to draw something positive out of it were less distressed a year and more later (Nolen-Hoeksema & Davis, 2002).

So we see that a strong sense of meaning can have health consequences (Baumeister & Vohs, 2002). One study looked at this effect in 40 HIV-positive men who had recently lost a partner to AIDS. Those who said they had found meaning in the loss showed stronger immune system functioning, and they were also less likely to die during a follow-up period (Bower & others, 1998). Likewise, psychiatrist Viktor Frankl (1962), who had been imprisoned in a Nazi concentration camp, observed that his fellow inmates who retained a sense of meaning were more likely to survive.

Managing Stress Effects

6: What tactics can we use to manage stress?

Having a sense of control, nurturing an optimistic outlook, building our base of social support, and finding meaning in hard times can help us *experience* less stress and thus improve our health. But when we cannot avoid stress, we need to *manage* it in a healthful way. Aerobic exercise, biofeedback, relaxation, meditation, and spirituality may help us gather inner strength and lessen the effects of stress.

Aerobic Exercise

Aerobic exercise is sustained activity—such as jogging, swimming, or biking—that increases heart and lung fitness. It's hard to find bad things to say about exercise. By one estimate, moderate exercise adds not only to your quantity of life—two additional years, on average—but also to your quality of life—as more energy and better mood (Seligman, 1994).

Exercise helps fight heart disease. It strengthens your heart, increases blood flow, keeps blood vessels open, and lowers both blood pressure and the blood pressure reaction to stress (Ford, 2002; Manson, 2002). Compared with inactive adults, people who exercise suffer half as many heart attacks (Powell & others, 1987). Exercise makes the muscles hungry for the "bad fats" that, if not used by the muscles, contribute to clogged arteries (Barinaga, 1997).

Can aerobic exercise also reduce stress, depression, and anxiety? Many studies suggest it can. For example, 3 in 10 Americans and Canadians, and 2 in 10 Britons do aerobic exercises three times a week or more. In studies, these active people also manage stressful events better, are more self-confident and energetic, and feel less depressed and fatigued than their inactive peers (McMurray, 2004;

The mood boost :: When energy or spirits are sagging, few things reboot the day better than exercising (as I can vouch from my daily noontime basketball).

Kathryn Brownson

Puetz & others, 2006). But we could state this observation another way: Stressed and depressed people exercise less. It's that old correlation problem again—cause and effect are not clear.

To sort out cause and effect, researchers experiment. They randomly assign stressed, depressed, or anxious people either to an aerobic exercise group or to a control group. One such experiment sorted a group of mildly depressed female college students this way. One-third were randomly assigned to a program of aerobic exercise. Another third were assigned to a program of relaxation exercises, and the remaining third (the control group) were assigned to a no-treatment group (McCann & Holmes, 1984). As **FIGURE 10.7** shows, 10 weeks later the women in the aerobic exercise program reported the greatest decrease in depression. Many of them had, quite literally, run away from their troubles.

More than 150 other studies have confirmed that exercise reduces depression and anxiety. Some findings indicate that aerobic exercise counteracts depression in two ways. First, it increases arousal. Second, it does naturally what some prescription drugs do chemically: It increases serotonin activity in the brain. Aerobic exercise has therefore taken a place, along with antidepressant drugs and psychotherapy, on the list of effective treatments for depression and anxiety (Arent & others, 2000; Berger & Motl, 2000; Dunn & others, 2005).

Biofeedback, Relaxation, and Meditation

Aerobic exercise reduces depression and anxiety. But did you notice in Figure 10.7 that women in the relaxation-treatment group also had a drop in their depression scores? Indeed, more than 60 studies have found that relaxation procedures can provide relief from headaches, high blood pressure, anxiety, and insomnia (Stetter & Kupper, 2002).

Training people to counteract stress by bringing their heart rate and blood pressure under conscious control was once considered a foolish idea. After all, these functions are controlled by the autonomic ("involuntary") nervous system. That tide turned in the late 1960s, when respected psychologists began experimenting with **biofeedback,** a system of recording, amplifying, and feeding back information about subtle bodily responses (Miller & Brucker, 1979). This feedback allows people to see whether their efforts to control a particular bodily response are working.

Though they did not use biofeedback techniques, Meyer Friedman and his colleagues later used relaxation in a program designed to help Type A heart attack survivors reduce their risk of future attacks. They randomly assigned hundreds of these middle-aged men to one of two

aerobic exercise sustained activity that increases heart and lung fitness; may also reduce depression and anxiety.

biofeedback a system for electronically recording, amplifying, and feeding back information about a subtle physiological state, such as blood pressure or muscle tension.

Figure 10.7> Aerobic exercise reduced depression (From McCann & Holmes, 1984.)

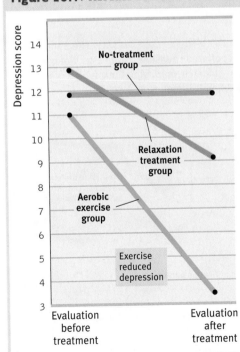

Newscom

groups. The first group received standard advice from cardiologists about medications, diet, and exercise habits. The second group received similar advice, but they also were taught ways of modifying their life-style. They learned to slow down and relax by walking, talking, and eating more slowly. They learned to smile at others and laugh at themselves. They learned to admit their mistakes, to take time to enjoy life, and to renew their religious faith. The training paid off **(FIGURE 10.8)**. During the next three years, the group that learned to modify their life-style had half as many repeat heart attacks as did the first group. This, wrote Friedman, was a truly spectacular reduction.

Cardiologist Herbert Benson (1996) became intrigued with reports that experienced meditators could lower their blood pressure, heart rate, and oxygen consumption and raise their fingertip temperature. Benson calls this the *relaxation response.* (If you'd like to try to relax and shed your feelings of stress, see Close-Up: The Relaxation Response.) Tibetan Buddhists deep in meditation and Franciscan nuns deep in centering prayer report a diminished sense of self, space, and time. Brain scans reveal the footprints these

CLOSE-UP

■ THE RELAXATION RESPONSE

The relaxation response is a state of calm marked by relaxed muscles, slowed breathing and heart rate, and decreased blood pressure. Advocates such as cardiologist Herbert Benson claim lasting stress-reducing benefits when relaxation is practiced once or twice daily.

To experience the relaxation response, the Benson-Henry Institute for Mind Body Medicine recommends these steps: Sit quietly in a comfortable position. Close your eyes. Relax your muscles, starting with your feet, then your calves, and upward through your thighs, shoulders, neck, and head. Breathe slowly. As you exhale each breath, repeat a focus word, phrase, or prayer—something drawn from your own belief system. When other thoughts intrude, don't worry. Just return to your repetition and continue for 10 to 20 minutes. When finished, sit quietly for another minute or two, then open your eyes and sit for a few more moments.

mystical experiences leave in the brain. A part of the brain that tracks our location in space is less active than usual, and an area involved in focused attention is more active (Newberg & D'Aquili, 2001). Another difference appears in the brain's left frontal lobe. In Buddhist monks who are experienced in meditation, this brain area shows a high level of activity that is usually associated with positive emotions.

Was this high rate of activity a result of meditation, or simply a correlation that had nothing to do with cause and effect? To find out, researchers experimented, comparing "before" and "after" brain scans of volunteers who were *not* experienced meditators. First, they took baseline scans of the volunteers' normal levels of brain activity. Then they randomly assigned people either to a control group or

Figure 10.8> **Recurrent heart attacks and life-style modification** The San Francisco Recurrent Coronary Prevention Project offered counseling from a cardiologist to survivors of heart attacks. Those who were also guided in modifying their Type A life-style suffered fewer repeat heart attacks. (From Friedman & Ulmer, 1984.)

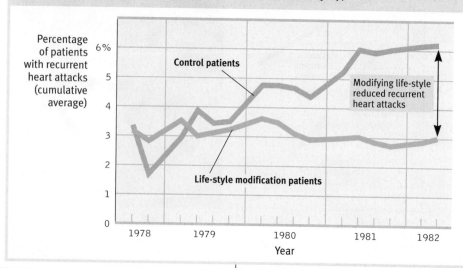

Ghislain and Marie David De Lossy/ Getty Images

to an eight-week course in "mindfulness meditation" (Davidson & others, 2003). Finally, they compared the meditation participants with both the control group and with their own pre-course baseline. The meditation group showed noticeably more left-hemisphere brain activity, and they also had improved immune functioning after the training.

Spirituality and Health

A wealth of studies has revealed another curious correlation, called the *faith factor*. Religiously active people tend to live longer than those who are not religiously active. For example, one 16-year study tracked 3900 Israelis living in one of two groups of communities. The first group contained 11 religiously orthodox collective settlements. The second contained 11 matched, nonreligious collective settlements (Kark & others, 1996). Researchers found that "belonging to a religious collective was associated with a strong protective effect" not explained by age or economic differences. In every age group, religious community members were about half as likely to have died as were their nonreligious counterparts.

How should we interpret such findings? Skeptical researchers remind us, of course, that correlations can leave many factors uncontrolled (Sloan & others, 1999, 2000, 2002, 2005). Here's one obvious possibility: Women are more religiously active than men, and women outlive men. Could religious involvement reflect this gender-longevity link? No. Although the religiosity-longevity correlation is stronger among women, it is also found among men (McCullough & others, 2000, 2005). In study after study—some lasting 28 years, and some studying more than 20,000 people—the faith factor holds (Hummer & others, 1999). And it holds after researchers control for age, sex, race, ethnicity, education, and region. In one study, this effect translated into a life expectancy at age 20 of 83 years for frequent attenders at religious services (more than weekly) and 75 years for infrequent attenders **(FIGURE 10.9)**.

These correlational findings do not mean that nonattenders who start attending services and change nothing else will live 8 years longer. But they do indicate that as a *predictor* of health and longevity, religious involvement rivals nonsmoking and exercise. Such findings demand explanation. Can you imagine what might account for the correlation?

First, religiously active people have healthier life-styles; for example, they smoke and drink less (Lyons, 2002; Strawbridge & others, 2001). Health-oriented, vegetarian Seventh Day Adventists have a longer-than-usual life expectancy (Berkel & de Waard, 1983). Religiously orthodox Israelis eat less fat than do their nonreligious compatriots.

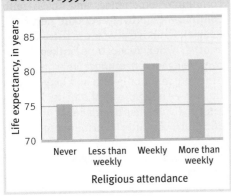

Figure 10.9> Religious attendance and life expectancy (Data from Hummer & others, 1999.)

Such differences may help explain why the religiously active have healthier immune functioning and fewer hospital admissions, or, if they are AIDS patients, why they have lower stress hormone levels and longer survival times (Ironson & others, 2002; Koenig & Larson, 1998; Lutgendorf & others, 2004). But life-style differences are not great enough to explain the dramatically reduced mortality in the religious settlements, say the Israeli researchers. In the American studies, too, about 75 percent of the longevity difference remains after controlling for unhealthy behaviors such as inactivity and smoking (Musick & others, 1999).

Diverse Yet Alike

The faith factor :: Across diverse cultures, people experience and express their spirituality in faith communities.

Could social support explain the faith factor (George & others, 2002)? In Judaic, Christian, and Islamic religions, faith is a communal experience, and these faith communities provide support networks. Religiously active people are there for one another when misfortune strikes. Moreover, religion encourages marriage, another predictor of health and longevity. In the Israeli religious settlements, for example, divorce has been almost nonexistent. But even after controlling for social support, gender, unhealthy behaviors, and preexisting health problems, much of the original correlation remains (George & others, 2000; Powell & others, 2003).

Researchers therefore speculate about a third set of influences. Stress protection and enhanced well-being may come from a stable worldview, a sense of hope for the long-term future, feelings of ultimate acceptance, and the relaxed meditation of prayer or Sabbath observance (**FIGURE 10.10**).

Although the religion-health correlation has yet to be fully explained, Harold Pincus (1997), deputy medical director of the American Psychiatric Association, believes these findings "have made clear that anyone involved in providing health care services . . . cannot ignore . . . the important connections between spirituality, religion, and health."

* * * * *

Let's summarize: Sustained emotional reactions to stressful events can be damaging. However, a sense of control, an optimistic outlook, healthy habits, social support, relaxation, a sense of meaning, and spirituality can all help us flourish by making us emotionally and physically stronger (**FIGURE 10.11**).

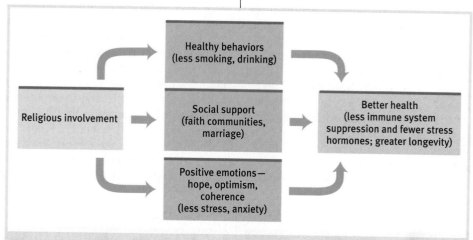

Figure 10.10> Possible explanations for the correlation between religious involvement and health/longevity

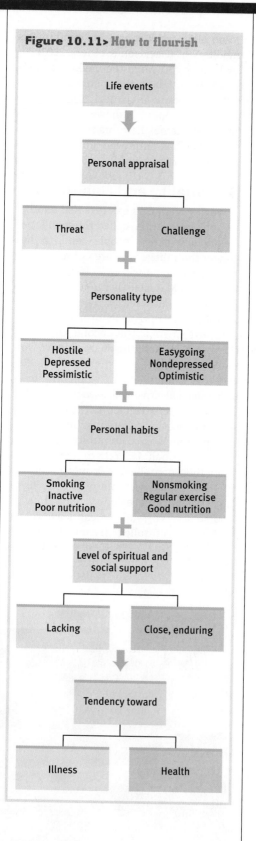

Figure 10.11> How to flourish

PRACTICE TEST

7. To cope with stress, we tend to use _____ strategies when we feel in control of our world, and to use _____ strategies when we believe we cannot change a situation.

   a. emotion-focused; problem-focused
   b. problem-focused; emotion-focused
   c. internal locus; external locus
   d. external locus; internal locus

8. People who have a strong social support system tend to live longer than those who do not, supporting the idea that

   a. social ties can be a source of stress.
   b. gender influences longevity.
   c. Type A behavior is responsible for many premature deaths.
   d. social support has a beneficial effect on health.

9. A dog will respond with learned helplessness if it has received repeated shocks and has had

   a. the opportunity to escape.
   b. no control over the shocks.
   c. ample social support.
   d. biofeedback training.

10. The *faith factor* is a research finding that

   a. optimists tend to be healthier than pessimists.
   b. our expectations influence our feelings of stress.
   c. religiously active people tend to live longer than those who are not religiously active.
   d. our mind and our body interact to influence our health and well-being.

Answers: 7. b, 8. d, 9. b, 10. c.

TERMS AND CONCEPTS TO REMEMBER

stress, p. 270

fight-or-flight, p. 271

general adaptation syndrome (GAS), p. 271

tend and befriend, p. 272

psychoneuroimmunology (PNI), p. 272

lymphocytes, p. 272

coronary heart disease, p. 274

Type A, p. 275

Type B, p. 275

problem-focused coping, p. 276

emotion-focused coping, p. 276

personal control, p. 277

learned helplessness, p. 277

external locus of control, p. 278

internal locus of control, p. 278

optimism, p. 278

pessimism, p. 278

aerobic exercise, p. 280

biofeedback, p. 281

REVIEW: STRESS, HEALTH, AND HUMAN FLOURISHING

STRESS: SOME BASIC CONCEPTS

1 What is *stress,* and what are some of the ways we respond to stress?

- *Stress* is the process by which we appraise and respond to stressors—events that challenge or threaten us.
- If we appraise an event as challenging, we will be aroused and focused in preparation for success.
- If we appraise an event as a threat, we will experience a stress reaction, and our health may suffer.

2 What are three main types of stressors?

- *Catastrophes* are unpredictable, large-scale events.
- *Significant life changes* include leaving home or losing a job.
- *Daily hassles* are small problems, with negative effects adding up over time.

3 How does the body respond to prolonged stress?

- Cannon viewed our body's response to stress as *fight-or-flight.*
- Selye saw our response as a three-stage (alarm-resistance-exhaustion) *general adaptation syndrome (GAS).*
- People (especially women) may also show a *tend-and-befriend* response to stress, such as when helping others after natural disasters.

STRESS EFFECTS AND HEALTH

4 **How does stress make us more vulnerable to disease?**

■ Stress takes energy away from the immune system, inhibiting the activities of its B and T *lymphocytes*, macrophages, and NK cells. This leaves us more vulnerable to illness and disease.

■ *Psychoneuroimmunology* is the study of these mind-body interactions.

■ Although stress does not cause diseases such as AIDS and cancer, it may affect their progression.

■ Stress is more directly connected to *coronary heart disease*, North America's number one cause of death.

■ Heart disease has been linked with the competitive, hard-driving, impatient, and (especially) anger-prone *Type A* personality. *Type B* personalities are more relaxed and easygoing and less likely to experience heart disease.

HUMAN FLOURISHING

5 **What are some of the things that influence our ability to cope with stress?**

■ Direct, *problem-focused coping* strategies are usually best, but *emotion-focused coping* can also be helpful.

■ Having a sense of *personal control*, developing a more optimistic outlook (and avoiding *learned helplessness*), building our base of social support, and finding meaning in difficult times can help us reduce stress.

6 **What tactics can we use to manage stress?**

■ *Aerobic exercise, biofeedback,* and relaxation can help us manage stress in a healthful way.

■ Counseling Type A heart attack survivors to slow down and relax has helped lower rates of recurring attacks.

■ Social support and religious involvement also help people manage their stress.

11 Personality

LORD OF THE RINGS HOBBIT-HERO Frodo Baggins knew that throughout his difficult journey there was one who would never fail him—his loyal and ever-cheerful companion, Sam Gamgee. Even before they left their beloved hometown, Frodo warned Sam that the journey would not be easy.

> "It is going to be very dangerous, Sam. It is already dangerous. Most likely neither of us will come back."
>
> "If you don't come back, sir, then I shan't, that's certain," said Sam. "[The Elves told me] 'Don't you leave him!' Leave him! I said. I never mean to. I am going with him, if he climbs to the Moon; and if any of those Black Riders try to stop him, they'll have Sam Gamgee to reckon with." (J. R. R. Tolkien, *The Fellowship of the Ring*, p. 96)

And so they did! Later in the story, when it becomes clear that Frodo's path will lead him into the dreaded land of Mordor, Sam insists he will be at Frodo's side, come what may. It is Sam who lifts Frodo's spirits with songs and stories from their boyhood. And it is Sam whom Frodo leans upon when he can barely take another step. When Frodo is overcome by the evil of the ring he carries, it is Sam who saves him. In the end, it is Sam who helps Frodo successfully complete his journey. Sam Gamgee—cheerful, optimistic, emotionally stable—never falters in his faithfulness or his belief that they will overcome the darkness.

As he appears throughout the series, Tolkien's Sam Gamgee exhibits the distinctive and enduring behaviors that define **personality**—our characteristic ways of thinking, feeling, and acting. Earlier chapters have focused on our shared paths—our similar ways of developing, perceiving, learning, remembering, thinking, and feeling. This chapter focuses on what makes us unique.

Much of this book deals with personality. In earlier chapters, we considered biological influences on personality, personality development across the life span, and personality-related aspects of learning, motivation, emotion, and health. In later chapters we will study disorders of personality and social influences on personality. In this chapter, we focus on the topic of personality itself—what it is and how researchers study it. We begin with two grand theories of personality that have become part of our culture. The first, Sigmund Freud's *psychoanalytic* theory, proposed that childhood sexuality and unconscious motivations influence personality. The second, the *humanistic* perspective, focused on our inner capacities for growth and self-fulfillment.

The chapter then explores today's more scientific approach to the study of personality. We'll look at the traits that define our differences. We'll see how biology, psychology, and environment together influence personality. Finally, we'll note how our concept of *self* helps organize our thoughts, feelings, and actions.

personality an individual's characteristic pattern of thinking, feeling, and acting.

The Psychoanalytic Perspective

1: What was Sigmund Freud's view of human personality and its development and dynamics?

In the popular mind, Sigmund Freud is to psychology's history what Elvis Presley is to rock music's history. Ask 100 people on the street to name a notable deceased psychologist, suggests Keith Stanovich (1996, p. 1), and "Freud would be the winner hands down." His influence lingers in books and movies and in the treatment of psychological disorders. So, who was this early personality theorist, and what did he teach?

After graduating from the University of Vienna medical school, Freud set up a private practice. His specialty was nervous disorders. Before long, he began hearing complaints that made no medical sense. One patient had lost all feeling in one hand. Yet there is no nerve pathway that, if damaged, would numb the entire hand and nothing else. What, wondered Freud, could cause such disorders? His search for the answer led in a direction that would challenge our self-understanding.

Sigmund Freud (1856–1939) :: "I was the only worker in a new field."

Exploring the Unconscious

Could these strange disorders have mental rather than physical causes? Freud decided they could. Many meetings with patients led to Freud's "discovery" of the **unconscious.** In Freud's view, this deep well keeps unacceptable thoughts, wishes, feelings, and memories hidden away, beyond our awareness. But despite our attempts, bits and pieces of these ideas seep out. Thus, patients might have an odd loss of feeling in their hand because they have an unconscious fear of touching their genitals. Or their unexplained blindness might be caused by unconsciously not wanting to see something that makes them anxious.

Basic to Freud's theory was his belief that the mind is mostly hidden. Below the surface is this large unconscious region in which unacceptable passions and thoughts lurk. Freud believed we *repress,* or forcibly block, these unconscious feelings and ideas from awareness because admitting them would be too unsettling. Nevertheless, these repressed feelings and ideas powerfully influence us.

For Freud, nothing was ever accidental. He saw the unconscious seeping not only into people's troubling symptoms, but also in disguised forms into the work they chose, the beliefs they held, and their daily habits. He also glimpsed the unconscious in slips of the tongue and pen, as when a financially stressed patient, not wanting any large pills, said, "Please do not give me any bills, because I cannot swallow them." Jokes, too, were expressions of repressed sexual and aggressive tendencies traveling in disguise. Dreams, he said, were the "royal road to the unconscious." He thought the part we remember is really a censored version of our unconscious wishes.

"I know how hard it is for you to put food on your family."

George W. Bush, 2000

"*Good morning, beheaded—uh, I mean beloved.*"

Hoping to unlock the door to the unconscious, Freud first tried hypnosis, with poor results. He then turned to **free association,** telling patients to relax and say whatever comes to mind, no matter how unimportant or silly it might seem. Freud believed that free association would trace a path from the troubled present into a patient's distant past. The chain of thought would lead back into the patient's unconscious, the hiding place of painful past memories, often from childhood. His goal was to find these forbidden thoughts and release them. In his analysis of dreams, Freud searched for the nature of his patients' inner conflicts and tried to find ways to relieve the tension caused by the conflicts.

Personality Structure

Freud called his treatment and the underlying theory of personality **psychoanalysis.** He believed that we are born with aggressive, pleasure-seeking biological impulses. As we are socialized, we internalize social restraints against these basic urges. Personality is the result of our efforts to resolve this basic conflict—to express these impulses in ways that bring satisfaction without guilt or punishment.

To understand the mind's conflicts, Freud proposed three interacting systems: the *id, ego,* and *superego.* Psychologists have found it useful to view the mind's structure as an iceberg **(FIGURE 11.1).**

The **id** stores unconscious energy. It tries to satisfy our basic drives to survive,

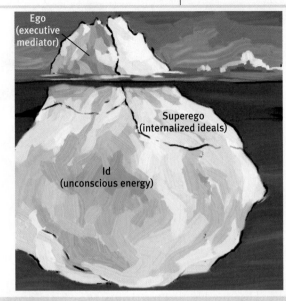

Figure 11.1> Freud's idea of the mind's structure Psychologists have used an iceberg image to illustrate Freud's idea that the mind is mostly hidden beneath the conscious surface. Note that the id is totally unconscious, but the ego and superego operate both consciously and unconsciously. Unlike the parts of a frozen iceberg, however, the id, ego, and superego interact.

reproduce, and be aggressive. The id operates on the *pleasure principle:* It seeks immediate gratification. To see the power of the id, think of newborn infants, crying out the moment they feel a need, wanting satisfaction without care for the adult world's conditions and demands. Or think of people who abuse drugs, partying now rather than sacrificing today's pleasure for future success and happiness (Keough & others, 1999).

A second part of the mind, the **ego,** operates on the *reality principle.* The ego is the conscious part of personality. It tries to satisfy the id's impulses in realistic ways that will bring long-term pleasure rather than pain or destruction.

As the ego develops, the young child learns to cope with the real world. Beginning around age 4 or 5, Freud theorized, a child's ego begins to recognize the demands of the **superego,** the voice of our moral compass or *conscience.* The superego forces the ego to consider not only the real but the ideal. It focuses on how one *ought* to behave in a perfect world. It judges actions and produces positive feelings of pride or negative feelings of guilt.

"Fifty is plenty."   "Hundred and fifty."

The ego struggles to reconcile the demands of superego and id, said Freud.

The superego's demands often oppose the id's. It is the ego's job to reconcile the two. As the personality "executive," the ego juggles the impulsive demands of the id, the restraining demands of the superego, and the real-life demands of the external world. If a man feels sexually attracted to someone, he may satisfy both id and superego by joining a volunteer organization to which the person belongs.

Personality Development

Freud was convinced that personality forms during life's first few years. Again and again his patients' symptoms seemed rooted in unresolved early childhood conflicts. He concluded that children pass through a series of **psychosexual stages,** from oral to genital (**TABLE 11.1** on the next page). In each

unconscious according to Freud, a reservoir of mostly unacceptable thoughts, wishes, feelings, and memories. According to contemporary psychologists, information processing of which we are unaware.

free association in psychoanalysis, a method of exploring the unconscious in which the person relaxes and says whatever comes to mind, no matter how trivial or embarrassing.

psychoanalysis Freud's theory of personality that attributes thoughts and actions to unconscious motives and conflicts; the techniques used in treating psychological disorders by seeking to expose and interpret unconscious tensions.

id a reservoir of unconscious psychic energy that, according to Freud, strives to satisfy basic sexual and aggressive drives. The id operates on the *pleasure principle,* demanding immediate gratification.

ego the largely conscious, "executive" part of personality that, according to Freud, balances the demands of the id, superego, and reality. The ego operates on the *reality principle,* satisfying the id's desires in ways that will realistically bring pleasure rather than pain.

superego the part of personality that, according to Freud, represents internalized ideals and provides standards for judgment (the conscience).

psychosexual stages the childhood stages of development (oral, anal, phallic, latency, genital) during which, according to Freud, the id's pleasure-seeking energies focus on distinct erogenous zones.

Table 11.1	Freud's Psychosexual Stages
Stage	**Focus**
Oral (0–18 months)	Pleasure centers on the mouth—sucking, biting, chewing
Anal (18–36 months)	Pleasure focuses on bowel and bladder elimination; coping with demands for control
Phallic (3–6 years)	Pleasure zone is the genitals; coping with incestuous sexual feelings
Latency (6 to puberty)	Dormant sexual feelings
Genital (puberty on)	Maturation of sexual interests

"Oh, for goodness' sake! Smoke!"

stage, the id's pleasure-seeking energies focus on an *erogenous zone,* a distinct pleasure-sensitive area of the body.

Freud believed that during the third stage, the *phallic stage,* boys seek genital stimulation, and they develop unconscious sexual desires for their mother. They feel jealousy and hatred for their father, who is a rival for their mother's attention. These feelings lead to guilt and a lurking fear that their father will punish them, perhaps by castration. Freud called this collection of feelings the **Oedipus complex,** after the Greek legend of Oedipus, who unknowingly killed his father and married his mother.

Children learn to cope with these feelings by repressing them, said Freud. They identify with the "rival" parent and try to become like him or her. It's as though something inside the child decides, "If you can't beat 'em [the same sex parent], join 'em." Through this **identification** process, children's superegos gain strength as they take on many of their parent's values. Freud believed that identification with the same-sex parent provides what psychologists now call our *gender identity*—our sense of being male or female.

The identification process described here illustrates how a conflict might be resolved at the phallic stage. Other conflicts could arise at other stages. But whatever the stage, a conflict that isn't resolved in childhood may cause trouble in adulthood. The result, Freud believed, would be **fixation,** locking the person's pleasure-seeking energies at the unresolved stage. A child who is either orally overindulged or orally deprived (perhaps by abrupt, early weaning) might become stalled at the oral stage, for example. As an adult, this orally fixated person might continue to seek oral gratification by smoking and excessive eating. In such ways, Freud suggested, the twig of personality is bent at an early age.

Identification :: I want to be like Dad.

From the K. Vandervelde private collection

Defense Mechanisms

2: What are defense mechanisms?

Anxiety, said Freud, is the price we pay for civilization. As members of social groups, we must control our sexual and aggressive impulses, not act them out. But sometimes the ego fears losing control of this inner war between the demands of the id and the superego. The result is a dark cloud of generalized anxiety. We feel unsettled but are unsure why.

Freud proposed that the ego distorts reality in an effort to protect itself from anxiety. **Defense mechanisms** achieve this goal by disguising threatening impulses and preventing them from reaching consciousness. Here are six examples.

- **Repression** banishes anxiety-arousing wishes and feelings from consciousness. According to Freud, *repression underlies all the other defense mechanisms.* However, because repression is often incomplete, repressed urges may appear as symbols in dreams or as slips of the tongue in casual conversation.

"For seven and a half years I've worked alongside President Reagan. We've had triumphs. Made some mistakes. We've had some sex . . . uh . . . setbacks."

George H. W. Bush, 1988

- **Regression** allows us to retreat to an earlier stage of development. Facing the anxious first days of school, a child may regress to the oral comfort of thumb-sucking. Young monkeys, when anxious, retreat to infantile clinging to their mothers or to one another (Suomi, 1987).

- In **reaction formation,** the ego transforms unacceptable impulses into their opposites. Without our awareness, the unacceptable thought "I hate him" becomes "I love him." Timidity becomes daring.

- **Projection** disguises threatening impulses by assigning them to others. Thus, the person saying "He doesn't trust me" may unconsciously be feeling "I don't trust him" or "I don't trust myself." An El Salvadoran saying captures the idea: "The thief thinks everyone else is a thief."

- **Rationalization** is explaining our actions in ways that make us look good. Thus, heavy drinkers may describe the addiction they unconsciously fear by saying that they drink with friends "just to be sociable." Students who fail to study may rationalize, "All work and no play makes Jack [or Jill] a dull person."

- **Displacement** turns sexual or aggressive impulses toward a target that is easier or more acceptable than the one that aroused the feelings. Children who fear expressing anger against their parents may displace it by kicking the family pet. Road rage may release pent-up frustrations from a family fight.

Note that *all these defense mechanisms function indirectly and unconsciously.* They lower anxiety by disguising our threatening impulses. Just as the body unconsciously defends itself against disease, so also, believed Freud, does the ego unconsciously defend itself against anxiety.

Neo-Freudians and Psychodynamic Theory

3: Who were the neo-Freudians, and what is psychodynamic theory?

Freud's writings caused a lot of debate, but he soon attracted followers. Several young, ambitious physicians formed an inner circle around the strong-minded Freud. These *neo-Freudians,* such as Alfred Adler, Karen Horney [HORN-eye], and Carl Jung [Yoong], accepted Freud's basic ideas:

Personality is made up of id, ego, and superego. The unconscious is key. Personality is shaped in childhood. We use defense mechanisms to ward off anxiety.

But the neo-Freudians veered away from Freud in two important ways. First, they placed more emphasis on the role of the *conscious* mind. And second, they doubted that sex and aggression were all-consuming motivations. Instead, they tended to emphasize loftier motives and social interactions.

Since Freud's death, some of his ideas have been incorporated into **psychodynamic theory.** Theorists and clinicians

Oedipus [ED-uh-puss] **complex** according to Freud, a boy's sexual desires toward his mother and feelings of jealousy and hatred for the rival father.

identification the process by which, according to Freud, children incorporate their parents' values into their developing superegos.

fixation according to Freud, a lingering focus of pleasure-seeking energies at an earlier psychosexual stage, in which conflicts were unresolved.

defense mechanisms in psychoanalytic theory, the ego's protective methods of reducing anxiety by unconsciously distorting reality.

repression in psychoanalytic theory, the basic defense mechanism that banishes anxiety-arousing thoughts, feelings, and memories from consciousness.

regression psychoanalytic defense mechanism in which an individual faced with anxiety retreats to an earlier stage of development.

reaction formation psychoanalytic defense mechanism by which the ego unconsciously switches unacceptable impulses into their opposites. Thus, we may express feelings that are the opposite of our anxiety-arousing unconscious feelings.

projection psychoanalytic defense mechanism by which we disguise our own threatening impulses by attributing them to others.

rationalization psychoanalytic defense mechanism that offers self-justifying explanations in place of the real, but more threatening, unconscious reasons for our actions.

displacement psychoanalytic defense mechanism that shifts sexual or aggressive impulses toward a more acceptable or less threatening object or person, as when redirecting anger toward a safer outlet.

psychodynamic theory a Freud-influenced perspective that sees behavior, thinking, and emotions as reflecting unconscious motives.

Regression :: Faced with a mild stressor, children and young orangutans will regress, retreating to the comfort of earlier behaviors.

VStock/Alamy

Barbara Von Hoffmann/Animals Animals

Alfred Adler (1870–1937)
Adler believed that childhood feelings of insecurity can drive behavior, triggering strivings for power and superiority. Adler coined the term *inferiority complex*.

National Library of Medicine

Karen Horney (1885–1952)
Horney proposed that children's feelings of dependency give rise to feelings of helplessness and anxiety. These feelings trigger adult desires for love and security. Horney believed Freud's views of personality showed a masculine bias.

The Bettmann Archive/Corbis

Carl Jung (1875–1961)
Jung shared Freud's view of the power of the unconscious. He also proposed a human *collective unconscious*, derived from our species' experiences in the distant past. Today's psychology does not believe that experiences can be inherited.

Archive of the History of American Psychology/University of Akron

who study personality from a psychodynamic perspective assume, with Freud, that much of our mental life is unconscious. They believe we often struggle with inner conflicts among our wishes, fears, and values. And they agree that childhood shapes our personality and ways of becoming attached to others. But in other ways, they differ from Freud. "Most contemporary dynamic theorists and therapists are not wedded to the idea that sex is the basis of personality," notes psychologist Drew Westen (1996). They "do not talk about ids and egos, and do not go around classifying their patients as oral, anal, or phallic characters."

Assessing Unconscious Processes

4: What are projective tests, and what do clinicians in the Freudian tradition hope to learn from them?

Personality tests reflect the basic ideas of particular personality theories. So, what might be the tool of choice for someone working in the Freudian tradition?

To find a way into the unconscious mind, you would need a sort of psychological x-ray. The test would have to see through the top layer of social politeness, revealing hidden conflicts and impulses. **Projective tests** aim to provide this view by asking test-takers to describe an unclear image or tell a story about it. The image itself has no real meaning. Anything test-takers read into it can be considered a projection of their unconscious feelings and conflicts. (Recall that *projection* disguises threatening impulses by assigning them elsewhere.)

"We don't see things as they are; we see things as we are."

The Talmud

The most widely used projective test, the **Rorschach inkblot test,** was introduced in 1921. Swiss psychiatrist Hermann Rorschach [ROAR-shock] based it on a game he and his friends played as children. They would drip ink on paper, fold it, and then say what they saw in the resulting blot (Sdorow, 2005). The assumption is that what you see in a series of 10 inkblots reflects your inner feelings

and conflicts **(FIGURE 11.2).** Do you see an attacking animal? Perhaps you feel like attacking someone.

Is this a reasonable assumption? Let's see how well the Rorschach test measures up to the two primary criteria of a good test (see Chapter 8):

- *Reliability* (consistency of results): Raters trained in different Rorschach scoring systems show little agreement (Sechrest & others, 1998).

"*The forward thrust of the antlers shows a determined personality, yet the small sun indicates a lack of self-confidence. . . .*"

© 1983 by Sidney Harris; American Scientist Magazine.

Figure 11.2> The Rorschach test In this projective test, people tell what they see in a series of symmetrical inkblots.

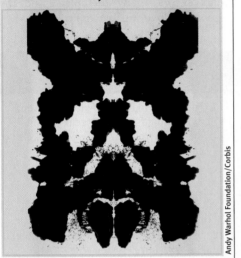

Andy Warhol Foundation/Corbis

- *Validity* (predicting what it's supposed to): The Rorschach test is not very successful at predicting behavior or at discriminating between groups (for example, identifying who is suicidal and who is not). Inkblot results diagnose many normal adults as disordered (Wood & others, 2003, 2006).

Thus, the test has neither much reliability nor great validity. A research-based, computer-aided coding and interpretation tool aims to improve agreement among raters and enhance the test's validity (Erdberg, 1990; Exner, 2003). But Freud himself might have been uncomfortable with a tool that tried to diagnose patients based on tests. He probably would have been more interested in the therapist-patient interactions that take place during the test.

Evaluating the Psychoanalytic Perspective

5: How does the psychoanalytic perspective hold up to contemporary psychology's findings?

"Many aspects of Freudian theory are indeed out of date, and they should be: Freud died in 1939, and he has been slow to undertake further revisions," observed Westen (1998). In Freud's time, there were no neurotransmitter or DNA studies. Seven decades of research—all the scientific breakthroughs in human development, thinking, and emotion announced during your parents' and your grandparents' time—were yet to come. Criticizing Freud's theory by comparing it with current concepts is therefore, some say, like comparing Henry Ford's Model T with today's hybrid cars.

Nevertheless, as smart thinkers, we must ask the same question about Freud's theory that we ask about other theories. You may recall from Chapter 1 that a good theory organizes observations and predicts behaviors or events. How does Freudian theory stand up to the test?

Freud's theory rests on few objective observations, and it has produced few hypotheses to verify or reject. (For Freud, his own memories and interpretations of patients' free associations, dreams, and slips were evidence enough.) Moreover, say the critics, Freud's theory offers after-the-fact explanations of behaviors and traits, but it fails to predict them. If you feel angry at your mother's death, you illustrate his theory because "your unresolved childhood dependency needs are threatened." If you do not feel angry, you again illustrate his theory because "you are repressing your anger." That, said Calvin Hall and Gardner Lindzey (1978, p. 68), "is like betting on a horse after the race has been run."

Freud's supporters object. To criticize Freudian theory for not making testable predictions is, they say, like criticizing baseball for not being an aerobic exercise, something it was never intended to be. Freud never claimed that psychoanalysis was predictive science. He merely claimed that, looking back, psychoanalysts could find meaning in our state of mind (Rieff, 1979).

In response, the critics ask that we look at current research on the idea that was Freud's foundation. Psychoanalytic theory rests on the assumption that the human mind often *represses* threatening wishes (as Freud believed) or painful experiences (as his later followers believed). Repression supposedly banishes emotions into the unconscious until they resurface, like long-lost books in a dusty attic. Today's memory researchers disagree. "Repression folklore is . . . partly refuted, partly untested, and partly untestable," says Elizabeth Loftus (1995).

Repression, when it occurs, is a rare mental response to terrible trauma. One death camp survivor reportedly forgot for more than 30 years the snatching and shooting of her infant son (Kraft, 1996). Some researchers believe that extreme, prolonged stress, such as the stress some severely abused children experience, might disrupt memory by causing brain damage (Schacter, 1996). But the far more common reality is that high stress (and associated stress hormones) enhances memory (see Chapter 7). Those who have witnessed a parent's murder or survived Nazi death camps retain their unrepressed

projective test a personality test, such as the Rorschach test, that provides an unclear image designed to trigger projection of the test-taker's unconscious thoughts or feelings.

Rorschach inkblot test the most widely used projective test, a set of 10 inkblots, designed by Hermann Rorschach; seeks to identify people's inner feelings by analyzing their interpretations of the blots.

PEANUTS reprinted by permission of UFS, Inc.

memories of the horror (Helmreich, 1992, 1994; Malmquist, 1986; Pennebaker, 1990). Traumatic events, such as rape and torture, haunt survivors as unwanted flashbacks. They are seared into the soul. "You see the babies," said Holocaust survivor Sally H. (1979). "You see the screaming mothers. You see hanging people. . . . It's something you don't forget."

On other specific questions, Freud's admirers and his critics agree.

■ More recent research provides evidence that our development is lifelong, not fixed in childhood as Freud suggested.

■ Infants' neural networks are not mature enough to process emotional trauma in the ways Freud assumed.

■ Conscience and gender identity are not offshoots of the Oedipus complex at age 5 or 6. We gain our gender identity earlier and become masculine or feminine even without a same-sex parent present.

■ Freud's ideas about childhood sexuality have a shaky basis, in part because Freud didn't believe his female patients' stories of childhood sexual abuse. Some scholars believe he therefore thought the stories reflected childhood sexual wishes and conflicts (Esterson, 2001; Powell & Boer, 1994).

■ New ideas about why we dream (see Chapter 2) dispute Freud's belief that dreams disguise unfulfilled wishes.

■ Slips of the tongue can be explained as competition between similar verbal choices in our memory network. Someone who says "I don't want to do that—it's a lot of brothel" may simply be blending *bother* and *trouble* (Foss & Hakes, 1978).

■ History fails to support the idea that suppressed sexuality causes psychological disorders. From Freud's time to ours, sexual inhibition has decreased; psychological disorders have not.

Freud's supporters, however, note that some of his ideas *are* enduring. It was Freud who drew our attention to the unconscious and the irrational. We indeed have limited access to all that goes on in our minds (Erdelyi, 1985, 1988; Kihlstrom, 1990). The unconscious processes studied by today's researchers differ greatly from Freud's idea of the unconscious. Today's scientists do not think of the unconscious as a place to store anxiety-causing thoughts that we are "censoring." Instead, we view the unconscious today as a place for routine information processing. Yet we agree with Freud that the unconscious mind is huge.

> "Two passengers leaned against the ship's rail and stared at the sea. 'There sure is a lot of water in the ocean,' said one. 'Yes,' answered his friend, 'we've only seen the top of it.'"
>
> Psychologist George A. Miller, 1962

Recent research has also provided some support for Freud's idea of defense mechanisms. For example, people tend to see their actions and attitudes in others (Baumeister & others, 1998). Freud called this *projection*. Today's researchers call it the *false consensus effect*—the tendency to overestimate how much others share our beliefs and behaviors. People who cheat on their taxes or break speed limits tend to think many others do the same. Defense mechanisms don't work exactly as Freud supposed. They seem motivated less by the seething impulses he imagined than by our need to protect our self-image.

Freud also drew our attention to the importance of human sexuality, and to the tension between our biological impulses and our social well-being. He challenged our self-righteousness and reminded us of our potential for evil.

No wonder, then, that in popular culture, Freud's legacy lives on. Can you see his influence in the idea that childhood experiences mold personality? That dreams have meaning? That many behaviors have disguised motives? His early twentieth-century concepts have crept into our twenty-first-century language. Without realizing their source, we may speak of *ego, repression, projection, sibling rivalry, Freudian slips,* and *fixation.*

Freud's ideas may not stand up as current psychological science, but as Martin Seligman noted (1994), "Hollywood, the talk shows, many therapists, and the general public still love them."

PRACTICE TEST

1. Freud believed that we block unacceptable thoughts, wishes, feelings, and memories from our consciousness. He called this process of blocking
   a. free association.
   b. repression.
   c. anxiety.
   d. reaction formation.

2. In Freud's view of personality structure, the "executive" system, the _____, seeks to gratify the impulses of the _____ in more acceptable ways.
   a. id; ego
   b. ego; superego
   c. ego; id
   d. id; superego

3. Freud called the *conscience,* or the part of the personality that internalizes ideals,
   a. the ego.
   b. the superego.
   c. the reality principle.
   d. repression.

4. According to the psychoanalytic view, conflicts unresolved at any of the psychosexual stages may lead to
   a. dormant sexual feelings.
   b. fixation in that stage.
   c. conscious blocking of impulses.
   d. a distorted identity.

5. All defense mechanisms distort or disguise reality, and all are
   a. conscious.
   b. unconscious.
   c. fixated.
   d. rationalizations.

6. The projective test that asks people to describe the meaning of inkblots was created by
   a. Alfred Adler.
   b. Karen Horney.
   c. Sigmund Freud.
   d. Hermann Rorschach.

7. In general, neo-Freudians such as Adler and Horney accepted many of Freud's views but placed more emphasis on
   a. motives beyond sex and aggression.
   b. social interactions.
   c. the role of the conscious mind.
   d. all of these answers.

8. Psychodynamic theorists and therapists tend to reject Freud's view that sex is the basis of personality, but they tend to agree with Freud about
   a. the existence of unconscious mental processes.
   b. the Oedipus complex.
   c. the predictive value of Freudian theory.
   d. the superego's role as the executive part of personality.

9. Contemporary psychologists dispute the Freudian idea that
   a. we have limited access to all that goes on in our minds.
   b. we use some defenses to protect our self-image.
   c. life involves tension between biological impulses and social restraint.
   d. we often repress the memory of traumatic events.

Answers: 1.b, 2.c, 3.b, 4.b, 5.b, 6.d, 7.d, 8.a, 9.d.

The Humanistic Perspective

6: What were Abraham Maslow's and Carl Rogers' contributions to humanistic psychology?

In the 1960s, some psychologists decided that psychology needed some fresh ideas and a new direction. They thought Freud's views of human development were too negative. They were equally uncomfortable with the strict behaviorism of John Watson and B. F. Skinner (see Chapter 6), judging it to be too mechanical. This movement helped produce *humanistic psychologists* such as Abraham Maslow (1908–1970) and Carl Rogers (1902–1987). In contrast to Freud's emphasis on disorders born out of dark conflicts, the humanistic psychologists focused on the ways "healthy" people strive for self-determination and self-realization. In contrast to behaviorism's objective laboratory experiments, they asked people to report their own experiences and feelings.

Abraham Maslow's Self-Actualizing Person

Abraham Maslow proposed that human motivations form a pyramid-shaped **hierarchy of needs** (see Chapter 9). At the base are bodily needs. If those are met, we become concerned with the next-higher level of needs, personal safety. If we feel secure, we then seek to love, to be loved, and to love ourselves. With our love needs satisfied, we seek self-esteem. Having achieved self-esteem, we seek the top-level needs for **self-actualization** and **self-transcendence.** These motives sit at the pyramid's peak and involve reaching our full potential.

Maslow (1970) formed his ideas by studying healthy, creative people rather than troubled clinical cases. His description of self-actualization grew out of his study of people who had lived rich and

Abraham Maslow :: "Any theory of motivation that is worthy of attention must deal with the highest capacities of the healthy and strong person as well as with the defensive maneuvers of crippled spirits" (*Motivation and Personality,* 1970).

Ted Polumbaum/Time Pix/Getty Images

productive lives. Among them were Abraham Lincoln, Thomas Jefferson, and Eleanor Roosevelt, who all shared certain traits. They were self-aware and self-accepting. They were open and spontaneous. They were loving and caring. They didn't worry too much about other people's opinions. But these people were not self-centered. Curious about the world, they focused their energies on a particular task, often regarding that task as their life mission. Most enjoyed a few deep relationships rather than many shallow ones. Many had been moved by spiritual or personal *peak experiences* that were beyond normal consciousness.

These, said Maslow, are mature adult qualities. These healthy people had learned about life. They knew the value of being compassionate. They had outgrown their mixed feelings toward their parents. They had found their calling. They had "acquired enough courage to be unpopular, to be unashamed about being openly virtuous." Who is likely to become a self-actualizing adult? Maslow's work with college students led him to believe that the best candidates were likable, caring young people who are "privately affectionate to those of their elders who deserve it," and "secretly uneasy about the cruelty, meanness, and mob spirit so often found in young people."

Carl Rogers' Person-Centered Perspective

Carl Rogers agreed that people have self-actualizing tendencies. Rogers believed that people are basically good. Like

hierarchy of needs Maslow's pyramid of human needs; at the base are physiological needs that must be satisfied before higher-level safety needs, and then psychological needs, become active.

self-actualization according to Maslow, the psychological need that arises after basic physical and psychological needs are met and self-esteem is achieved; the motivation to fulfill our potential.

self-transcendence according to Maslow, the striving for identity, meaning, and purpose beyond the self.

acorns, we are primed to reach our potential if we are given a growth-promoting environment. People nurture our growth, and we nurture theirs, in three ways (Rogers, 1980).

- If we are *genuine* to another person, we are open with our own feelings. We drop our false fronts and are transparent and self-disclosing.

- If we are *accepting,* we offer the other person what Rogers called **unconditional positive regard.** This is an attitude of total acceptance. We value the person even knowing the person's failings. We all find it a huge relief to drop our pretenses, confess our worst feelings, and discover that we are still accepted. In a good marriage, a close family, or an intimate friendship, we are free to be ourselves without fearing what others will think.

- If we are *empathic,* we share another's feelings and reflect that person's meanings back to them. "Rarely do we listen with real understanding, true empathy," said Rogers. "Yet listening, of this very special kind, is one of the most potent forces for change that I know."

The picture of empathy :: Being open and sharing confidences is easier when the listener shows real understanding. Within such relationships people can relax and fully express their true selves.

"Just remember, son, it doesn't matter whether you win or lose—unless you want Daddy's love."

A father *not* offering unconditional positive regard.

Genuineness, acceptance, and empathy are the water, sun, and nutrients that enable people to grow like vigorous oak trees, according to Rogers. For "as persons are accepted and prized, they tend to develop a more caring attitude toward themselves" (Rogers, 1980, p. 116). As persons are empathically heard, "it becomes possible for them to listen more accurately to the flow of inner experiencing."

Rogers called for genuineness, acceptance, and empathy in the relationship between therapist and client. But he also believed that these three qualities nurture growth between any two human beings—between leader and group, teacher and student, manager and staff member, parent and child, friend and friend.

Writer Calvin Trillin (2006) recalls an example of parental genuineness and acceptance at a camp for children with severe disorders, where his wife, Alice, worked. L., a "magical child," had genetic diseases that meant she had to be tube-fed and could walk only with difficulty. Alice recalled,

> . . . One day, when we were playing duck-duck-goose, I was sitting behind her and she asked me to hold her mail for her while she took her turn to be chased around the circle. It took her a while to make the circuit, and I had time to see that on top of the pile [of mail] was a note from her mom. Then I did something truly awful. . . . I simply had to

know what this child's parents could have done to make her so spectacular, to make her the most optimistic, most enthusiastic, most hopeful human being I had ever encountered. I snuck a quick look at the note, and my eyes fell on this sentence: "If God had given us all of the children in the world to choose from, L., we would only have chosen you." Before L. got back to her place in the circle, I showed the note to Bud, who was sitting next to me. "Quick. Read this," I whispered. "It's the secret of life." . . .

From "Alice, Off the Page" by Calvin Trillin. Originally appeared in *The New Yorker.* Copyright ©2006 by Calvin Trillin. Reprinted by permission of Lescher & Lescher, Ltd. All rights reserved.

Maslow and Rogers would have smiled knowingly. For these two humanistic psychologists, a central feature of personality is one's **self-concept**—all the thoughts and feelings we have in response to the question, "Who am I?" If our self-concept is positive, we tend to act and perceive the world positively. If it is negative—if in our own eyes we fall far short of our *ideal self*—we feel dissatisfied and unhappy. A worthwhile goal for all of us—therapists, parents, teachers, and friends—is therefore to help others know, accept, and be true to themselves, said Rogers.

Evaluating the Humanistic Perspective

7: What have critics said about humanistic psychology?

Humanistic psychology's message has been heard, and its impact has been far-reaching. Maslow's and Rogers' ideas have influenced counseling, education, child rearing, and management.

These theorists have also influenced—sometimes in ways they did not intend—much of today's popular psychology. Is a positive self-concept the key to happiness and success? Do acceptance and empathy nurture positive feelings about ourselves? Are people basically good and capable of improving? Many would answer yes, yes, and yes. Nine in ten people responding to

"We do pretty well when you stop to think that people are basically good."

a 1992 *Newsweek* Gallup poll rated self-esteem as very important for "motivating a person to work hard and succeed."

Many psychologists have been critics of the humanistic perspective, despite its popularity. First, said the critics, its concepts are vague and based on the theorists' personal opinions, rather than on scientific methods. Consider Maslow's description of self-actualizing people as open, spontaneous, loving, self-accepting, and productive. Is this a scientific description? Or is it merely a description of Maslow's own values and ideals, as viewed in his own personal heroes (Smith, 1978)? Imagine another theorist who had a different set of heroes, such as Napoleon and former Vice President Dick Cheney. This theorist may describe self-actualizing people as "not held back by the needs of others," "desiring power," and "self-assured."

Other critics objected to the attitudes encouraged by humanistic psychology. Rogers, for example, said, "The only question which matters is, 'Am I living in a way which is deeply satisfying to me, and which truly expresses me?'" (quoted by Wallach & Wallach, 1985). Could such attitudes—trusting and acting on our feelings, being true to ourselves, fulfilling ourselves—lead to

self-indulgence, selfishness, and a lack of moral restraints (Campbell & Specht, 1985; Wallach & Wallach, 1983)?

Humanistic psychologists have countered that a secure, nondefensive self-acceptance is actually the first step toward loving others. Indeed, people who feel liked and accepted—for who they are, not just for their achievements—show less-defensive attitudes (Schimel & others, 2001).

A final criticism is that humanistic psychology fails to appreciate the reality of our human capacity for evil. Faced with global climate change, overpopulation, terrorism, and the spread of nuclear weapons, we may be paralyzed by either of two ways of thinking. One is a naive optimism that denies the threat ("People are basically good; everything will work out"). The other is a dark despair ("It's hopeless; why try?"). Action requires enough realism to fuel concern and enough optimism to provide hope. Humanistic psychology, said the critics, encourages the needed hope but not the equally necessary realism about evil.

PRACTICE TEST

10. Maslow based his description of self-actualizing people on

a. Freudian theory.

b. case histories of people with disorders.

c. controlled laboratory experiments.

d. his study of healthy, creative people.

11. Rogers believed that we can help people reach their full potential by providing an environment of total acceptance, which he called

a. self-esteem.

b. unconditional positive regard.

c. self-actualization.

d. the "ideal self."

12. In the humanistic perspective, a central feature of personality is the

a. human capacity for evil.

b. reality principle.

c. unconscious.

d. self-concept.

Answers: 10. d, 11. b, 12. d.

The Trait Perspective

8: How do psychologists use traits to describe personality? Which traits seem to provide the most useful information about personality variation?

Both the Freudian perspective and the humanistic psychology perspective viewed personality as the product of forces acting upon us, forming us much as a diamond is formed when carbon is subjected to great pressure. Both perspectives attempt to *explain* how personality develops. **Trait** researchers are less concerned with *explaining* individual traits than with *describing* them. To them, personality is a *stable and enduring pattern of behavior,* such as Sam Gamgee's consistent loyalty and optimism.

Searching for Basic Personality Traits

Imagine that you've been hired by an Internet dating service. Your job is to construct a questionnaire that will help people describe themselves to those seeking dates and mates. What personality traits might give an accurate sense of the person filling out the questionnaire? You might begin by thinking of how we describe an apple. We place it along several trait dimensions. It's relatively large or small; it's red or yellow; it's sweet or sour. By likewise placing people on trait dimensions, we can begin to describe them.

An even better way to identify a person's personality is to identify **factors**—

unconditional positive regard according to Rogers, an attitude of total acceptance toward another person.

self-concept all our thoughts and feelings about ourselves, in answer to the question, "Who am I?"

trait a characteristic pattern of behavior or a tendency to feel and act in a certain way, as assessed by self-reports on a personality test.

factor a cluster of behavior tendencies that occur together.

Figure 11.3> Two personality factors Mapmakers can tell us a lot by using two axes (north–south and east–west). Two primary personality factors—extraversion–introversion and stability–instability—are similarly useful as axes for describing personality variation. Varying combinations define other, more specific traits. (From Eysenck & Eysenck, 1963.)

Michael Newman/Photo Edit

UNSTABLE

INTROVERTED	EXTRAVERTED
Moody	Touchy
Anxious	Restless
Rigid	Aggressive
Sober	Excitable
Pessimistic	Changeable
Reserved	Impulsive
Unsociable	Optimistic
Quiet	Active
Passive	Sociable
Careful	Outgoing
Thoughtful	Talkative
Peaceful	Responsive
Controlled	Easygoing
Reliable	Lively
Even-tempered	Carefree
Calm	Leadership

STABLE

Howard Pyle/Veer

clusters of behavior tendencies that occur together. People who describe themselves as outgoing, for example, may also say that they like excitement and practical jokes and dislike quiet reading. This cluster of behaviors

Tyra Banks: the extravert :: Trait labels such as *extraversion* can describe our temperament and typical behaviors.

AP Photo/Seth Wenig

reflects a basic factor, or trait—in this case, *extraversion*.

So how many traits will be just the right number for your Internet-dating questionnaire? If psychologists Hans Eysenck and Sybil Eysenck [EYE-zink] had been hired to do your job, they would have said two. They believed that we can reduce many normal human variations to the two shown in **FIGURE 11.3**: *extraversion–introversion* and *emotional stability–instability*. People in 35 countries around the world, from China to Uganda to Russia, have taken the *Eysenck Personality Questionnaire*. In their answers, the extraversion and emotionality factors emerged as basic personality dimensions (Eysenck, 1990, 1992).

The Eysencks believed that extraversion and emotionality are genetically influenced. Recent research supports this belief. Brain-activity scans show that extraverts seek stimulation because their normal brain arousal is relatively low. For example, a frontal lobe area involved in restraining behavior is less active in extraverts than in introverts (Johnson & others, 1999).

As you may recall from the discussion of twin and adoption studies in Chapter 3, our genes have much to say about the temperament and behavioral style that help define our personality. Developmental psychologist Jerome Kagan, for example, attributes differences in children's shyness to differences in their autonomic nervous systems. An infant with a reactive autonomic nervous system responds quickly and dramatically to stress, with greater anxiety. A less fearful and more curious child often has a less reactive autonomic nervous system.

The Big Five Factors

Knowing that a potential date is an introvert or an extravert, or even that the person is emotionally stable or unstable, may be somewhat helpful. But as the designer of the dating questionnaire, you'd probably prefer a little more information about the test-taker's personality. The *Minnesota Multiphasic Personality Inventory (MMPI)* might help. *Personality inventories,* including the famous MMPI, are long sets of questions covering a wide range of

Table 11.2   The "Big Five" Personality Factors

(*Memory tip:* Picturing a **CANOE** will help you recall these.)

Trait Dimension	Endpoints of the Dimension		
Conscientiousness	Organized	⟷	Disorganized
	Careful	⟷	Careless
	Disciplined	⟷	Impulsive
Agreeableness	Soft-hearted	⟷	Ruthless
	Trusting	⟷	Suspicious
	Helpful	⟷	Uncooperative
Neuroticism (emotional stability vs. instability)	Calm	⟷	Anxious
	Secure	⟷	Insecure
	Self-satisfied	⟷	Self-pitying
Openness	Imaginative	⟷	Practical
	Prefers variety	⟷	Prefers routine
	Independent	⟷	Conforming
Extraversion	Sociable	⟷	Retiring
	Fun-loving	⟷	Sober
	Affectionate	⟷	Reserved

Source: Adapted from McCrae & Costa (1986, p. 1002).

feelings and behaviors. Although the MMPI was originally developed to identify emotional disorders, it also assesses people's personality traits. But for a dating questionnaire, this might be too much information, so let's see what else personality researchers have to offer.

Today's trait researchers often use an expansion of the Eysencks' introverted–extraverted and stable–unstable factors. It's called the *Big Five* (John & Srivastava, 1999; McCrae & Costa, 1999). Where people fall on each of its five dimensions—*conscientiousness, agreeableness, neuroticism, openness,* and *extraversion* (**TABLE 11.2**)—says much of what there is to say about their personality.

The recent wave of Big Five research explores various questions:

- *How stable are these traits?* In adulthood, the Big Five traits are quite stable. Some tendencies (emotional instability, extraversion, and openness) fade a bit during early and middle adulthood. Others (conscientiousness and agreeableness) increase (McCrae & others, 1999; Vaidya & others, 2002). Conscientiousness typically rises most during our twenties, as we mature and learn to manage our jobs and relationships. Agreeableness increases the most during people's thirties and continues to increase through their sixties (Srivastava & others, 2003).

- *Do we inherit these traits?* Roughly 50 percent of our individual differences on the Big Five can be credited to our genes (Loehlin & others, 1998).

- *How well do these traits apply to various cultures?* The Big Five dimensions describe personality in various cultures reasonably well (McCrae, 2001; Yamagata & others, 2006). "Features of personality traits are common to all human groups," infer Robert McCrae and 79 co-researchers (2005) from their recent 50-culture study. Around the world, people describe others in terms roughly consistent with this list.

Can astrology give us clues to people's traits? See Think Critically About: How to Be a "Successful" Astrologer on the next page.

Diverse Yet Alike

Whether we are at Doshisha University in Kyoto, Japan, or at the University of California, in Los Angeles, our personality traits can be described using the Big Five dimensions.

THINK CRITICALLY ABOUT:

HOW TO BE A "SUCCESSFUL" ASTROLOGER

Can we figure out people's traits from the alignment of the stars and planets at the time of their birth? From their handwriting?

Astronomers scoff at astrology. The stars and planets have shifted in the thousands of years since astrologers first made their predictions (Kelly, 1997, 1998). Humorists mock it. "No offense," writes Dave Barry, "but if you take the horoscope seriously your frontal lobes are the size of Raisinets." Psychologists instead ask questions. Can astrologers beat chance when given someone's birth date and asked to identify the person from a short list of personality descriptions? Can people pick out their own horoscope from such a list?

The consistent answers have been: No and no (British Psychological Society, 1993; Carlson, 1985; Kelly, 1997). Can handwriting experts do better than chance at telling people's jobs after examining several pages of their handwriting? Again, the answer is no (Beyerstein & Beyerstein, 1992; Dean & others, 1992). Still, experts—and introductory psychology students—often *perceive* correlations between personality and handwriting even where there are none (King & Koehler, 2000).

How do astrologers persuade thousands of newspapers and millions of people worldwide to buy their advice? Ray Hyman (1981), palm reader turned research psychologist, revealed some tricks of the trade.

The first technique is the "stock spiel." Each of us is in some ways like no one else and in other ways just like everyone. That some things are true of us all allows the "seer" to offer statements that seem impressively accurate. "I sense that you worry about things more than you let on, even to your best friends."

A second technique is to "read" our clothing, physical features, gestures, and reactions. An expensive wedding ring and black dress might, for example, suggest a wealthy woman who was recently widowed.

I SEE BY YOUR HANDWRITING YOU LIKE BANANAS.

© 2000 by Rob Pudim

You, too, could read such clues, says Hyman. If people seek you out for a reading, start with some safe sympathy: "I sense you're having some problems lately. You seem unsure what to do. I get the feeling another person is involved." Then give them what they want to hear and tell people it is their duty to cooperate by relating your message to their specific experiences. Later they will recall that you predicted those specific details. Phrase statements as questions, and when you detect a positive response assert the statement strongly. Finally, be a good listener, and later, in different words, reveal to people what they earlier revealed to you.

Better yet, beware of those who, by exploiting people with these techniques, are fortune takers rather than fortune tellers.

If you work the Big Five traits into your dating questionnaire, your mission should be accomplished—assuming people act the same way at all times and in all situations. Next, we ask, do they?

13. Trait theory often describes personality in terms of clusters of characteristic behaviors, or traits that tend to occur together. These clusters are called

  a. lobe areas.
  b. axes.
  c. factors.
  d. dimensions.

14. A personality inventory is a(an)

  a. set of questions covering a wide range of feelings and behaviors.

  b. image designed to trigger the test-taker's repressed thoughts and feelings.

  c. pyramid illustrating the range of human needs, from the most basic to the most complex.

  d. humanistic test of the range of a person's capacity for unconditional positive regard.

15. Most trait researchers today believe that the Big Five factors offer the best descriptions of personality. Which of the following is NOT one of the Big Five?

  a. Conscientiousness
  b. Empathy
  c. Extraversion
  d. Agreeableness

Answers: 13. c, 14. a, 15. b.

The Social-Cognitive Perspective

9: How does the social-cognitive perspective view personality?

In some ways, our personality seems to stay reliably the same. Cheerful, friendly children tend to become cheerful, friendly adults. But it's also true that a fun-loving jokester can suddenly be serious and respectful at a job interview. Do the personality traits we express change from one situation to another? The short answer is yes.

> "There is as much difference between us and ourselves, as between us and others."
>
> Michel de Montaigne, *Essays*, 1588

The **social-cognitive perspective** on personality is especially interested in the many ways our individual traits and thoughts interact with our social world as we move from one situation to another. Let's take a closer look at this idea.

We bring a lot of baggage to any social situation we enter. We bring our past learning, picked up either through conditioning or by observing others and modeling our behavior after theirs. We also bring our ways of thinking about specific situations. But situations themselves place different demands on us. Most of us know the general social rules for acceptable behavior at a grandparent's funeral, for example. We also know that a different set of rules outlines what's acceptable at a friend's New Year's Eve party. In the end, our behavior in any situation is in part the result of our own characteristics and in part the result of the demands of the situation. For psychologists studying personality from a social-cognitive perspective, this interaction is a fascinating area of research. Roughly speaking, the short-term, outside influences on behavior are the focus of social psychology (see Chapter 14), and

the lasting, inner influences are the focus of personality psychology. In actuality, behavior always depends on the interaction of persons with situations. So let's consider how the person, the situation, and their interaction create behavior.

The Person

Are some people dependably conscientious and others unreliable, some cheerful and others grumpy, some friendly and outgoing and others shy? To be useful indicators of personality, traits would have to persist over time. Friendly people, for example, would have to act friendly at different times and places. In such cases, we could say that personality is stable.

Some researchers who have followed lives through time (especially those who have studied infancy) are impressed with personality change. Others are struck by personality stability during adulthood. Data from 152 long-term studies reflect both of these trends. The studies compared early trait scores with scores for the same traits seven years later. The scores were positively correlated **(FIGURE 11.4).** But the correlations were strongest for comparisons done in adulthood. For young children, the correlation was +0.3. For 70-year-olds, the correlation was +0.73. (Remember that 0 indicates no relationship, and +1.0 would mean that one score perfectly predicts the other.)

"Mr. Coughlin over there was the founder of one of the first motorcycle gangs."

As people grow older, their personality stabilizes. Interests may change—the devoted collector of tropical fish may become the devoted gardener. Careers may change—the determined salesperson may become a determined social worker. Relationships may change—the hostile spouse may start over with a new partner. But most of us know that some things change, and some stay the same.

The consistency of specific *behaviors* from one situation to the next is another matter. As Walter Mischel (1968, 1984, 2004) points out, people are not always

social-cognitive perspective views behavior as influenced by the interaction between persons (and their thinking) and their social context.

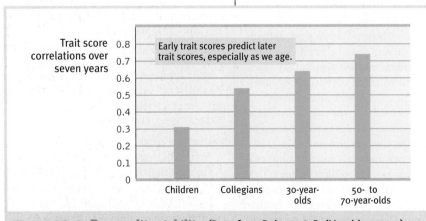

Figure 11.4> Personality stability (Data from Roberts & DelVecchio, 2000.)

Trait score correlations over seven years

Early trait scores predict later trait scores, especially as we age.

0.8
0.7
0.6
0.5
0.4
0.3
0.2
0.1
0

Children | Collegians | 30-year-olds | 50- to 70-year-olds

Our spaces express our personalities :: Even at "zero acquaintance," people can catch a glimpse of others' personality from looking at their Web site, dorm room, or office. So, what's your read on University of Texas researcher Samuel Gosling?

John Langford Photography

predictable. What relationship would you expect to find between a student's being conscientious on one occasion (say, showing up for class on time) and being conscientious on another occasion (say, turning in assignments on time)? If you've noticed how outgoing you are in some situations and how reserved you are in others, perhaps you said, "very little." That's what Mischel found—only a small correlation. This inconsistency in behaviors makes personality test scores weak predictors of behaviors. If you are extraverted, you are friendly and outgoing. A person's score on an extraversion test predicts that person's behavior across *many different situations*. It does not neatly predict how sociable that individual will be on *any given occasion*.

If we remember such results, says Mischel, we will be more careful about labeling other people. We will be slower to respond when asked whether someone is likely to violate parole, commit suicide, or be an effective employee. Years in advance, science can tell us the phase of the Moon for any given date. A day in advance, meteorologists can often predict the weather. But we are much further from being able to predict how *you* will feel and act tomorrow.

Does this mean that psychological science has nothing meaningful to say about personality traits? No! People's *average* outgoingness, happiness, or carelessness over *many* situations is predictable (Epstein, 1983a, b). Extraverts really do talk more. We know this because researchers collected snippets of people's daily experience via wearable recording devices (Mehl & others, 2006). People who know us well can agree on our distinctive shyness or agreeableness (Kenrick & Funder, 1988).

Even when we try to restrain them, our traits may assert themselves. During my noontime pickup basketball games with friends, I keep vowing to cut back on my jabbering and joking. But without fail, the irrepressible chatterbox reoccupies my body moments later.

Our personality traits influence our health, our thinking, and our job performance (Deary & Matthews, 1993; Hogan, 1998). Our traits even lurk in our

■ *music preferences.* Classical, jazz, blues, and folk music lovers tend to be open to experience and verbally intelligent. Country, pop, and religious music lovers tend to be cheerful, outgoing, and conscientious (Rentfrow & Gosling, 2003).

■ *dorm rooms and offices.* In our personal spaces, our scattered laundry or neat desktop displays our personality. After just a few minutes' inspection of someone's living and working spaces, you could give a fairly accurate summary of their conscientiousness, openness to new experience, and even emotional stability (Gosling & others, 2002).

■ *personal Web sites.* We all know that some people use the Internet to present themselves in false or misleading ways. But we might be surprised to find out how quickly visitors to personal Web sites gain important clues to the owner's extraversion, conscientiousness, and openness to experience. Personal Web sites are a canvas for self-expression (Vazire & Gosling, 2004; see also Marcus & others, 2006).

To sum up, averaging our behavior across many occasions reveals distinct personality traits. Personality traits exist, and they leave tracks in our lives. We differ. And our differences matter.

The Situation

Situations also differ. And as powerful as our personality traits are, they don't give us control over every situation. At any moment, the immediate situation powerfully influences our behavior, especially when the situation makes clear demands. We can better predict drivers' behavior at traffic lights from knowing the color of the lights than from knowing the drivers' personalities.

Sometimes, in unfamiliar, formal situations—perhaps as a guest in the home of a person from another culture—our traits remain hidden as we carefully attend to social cues. In familiar, informal situations—just hanging out with friends—we feel more relaxed, and our traits emerge (Buss, 1989). In these informal situations, our expressive styles—our animation, manner of speaking, and gestures—are impressively consistent. Viewing even very "thin slices" of someone's behavior—such as three 2-second clips of a teacher—can tell us a lot about the person's basic traits (Ambady & Rosenthal, 1992, 1993).

The Interaction

So our personal traits interact with our environment to influence our behavior. Albert Bandura called this process **reciprocal determinism.** "Behavior, internal personal factors, and environmental influences," he said, "all operate as interlocking determinants of each other" **(FIGURE 11.5).** We can see this in children's TV-viewing habits. Their history of watching TV (past behavior) influences their viewing preferences (internal factor), which influence how TV (environmental factor) affects their current behavior. Where a behaviorist might assume that environment *determines* behavior, a social-cognitive theorist explores the *interaction* among the three sets of influences.

1. *Different people choose different environments.* Choices are part of life. What school do you attend? What do you read? What shows do you watch? What music do you download? With whom do you enjoy spending time? All these choices are part of an environment you are choosing, based partly on your personality (Ickes & others, 1997). You choose your environment, and then it shapes you.

2. *Our personalities shape how we interpret and react to events.* For example, anxious people pay more attention to potentially threatening events (Eysenck & others, 1987). If you perceive the world as threatening, you will watch for threats and be prepared to defend yourself.

3. *Our personalities help create situations to which we react.* How we view and treat people influences how they then treat us. If you expect a family member to be angry, you may give that person a cold shoulder, touching off the very anger you expect. If you have an easygoing, upbeat personality, you will probably enjoy close, supportive friendships (Donnellan & others, 2005; Kendler, 1997).

In such ways, we are both the products and the architects of our environments. Boiling water turns an egg hard and a potato soft. A threatening environment turns one person into a hero, another into a scoundrel. *At every moment,* we are influenced by past behavior, our social context, and our personality.

Exploring the Self

10: What is self-esteem, and how does it influence us?

We can think of our *self-image* as our internal view of our personality. Underlying this idea is the notion that the **self** is the center of personality—the organizer of our thoughts, feelings, and actions.

Consider the concept of *possible selves* (Cross & Markus, 1991; Markus & Nurius, 1986). Your possible selves include your

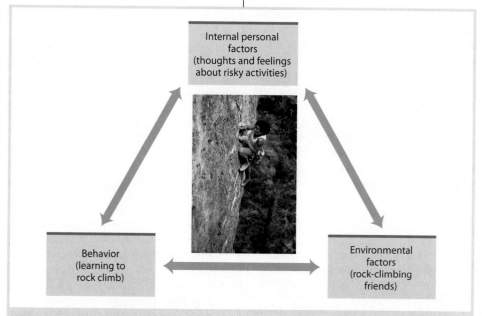

Figure 11.5> Reciprocal determinism

Internal personal factors
(thoughts and feelings about risky activities)

Behavior
(learning to rock climb)

Environmental factors
(rock-climbing friends)

reciprocal determinism the interacting influences of behavior, internal personal factors, and environment.

self your image and understanding of who you are; in modern psychology, the idea that this is the center of personality, organizing your thoughts, feelings, and actions.

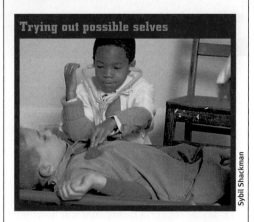

Trying out possible selves

visions of the self you dream of becoming—the rich self, the successful self, the loved and admired self. Your possible selves also include the self you fear becoming—the unemployed self, the lonely self, the academically failed self. Possible selves motivate us by laying out specific goals and calling forth the energy to work toward them. University of Michigan students in a combined undergraduate and medical school program earn higher grades if they have a clear vision of themselves as successful doctors.

> "The first step to better times is to imagine them."
>
> Chinese fortune cookie

Carried too far, a self-focused perspective can lead us to fret that others are always noticing and evaluating us. Researchers demonstrated this **spotlight effect** by having some students wear Barry Manilow T-shirts and enter a room filled with other students (Gilovich, 1996). Feeling self-conscious, the T-shirt wearers guessed that nearly half of the other students would notice the shirt as they walked in. How many did notice? Fewer than one in four. We stand out less than we imagine, even with dorky clothes or bad hair, and even after a blunder like setting off a library alarm. This is true no matter how nervous, irritated, or attractive we are (Gilovich & Savitsky, 1999; Savitsky & others, 2001).

Knowing about the spotlight effect can be empowering. When public speakers understand that their natural nervousness is not obvious to the audience, their speaking performance improves (Savitsky & Gilovich, 2003).

Self-Esteem: The Good News and the Bad

If we like our self-image, we'll probably have high **self-esteem.** This feeling of high self-worth will translate into fewer sleepless nights and less pressure to conform. We'll be more persistent at difficult tasks. We'll be less shy and lonely and just plain happier (Murray & others, 2002; Swann & others, 2007; Watson & others, 2002).

Can we inspire high self-esteem in others who have feelings of low self-worth? Could we accomplish this by, for example, repeatedly reminding them of their good points? Much research challenges the idea that high self-esteem is really "the armor that protects kids" from life's problems (Baumeister & others, 2003, 2005; Damon, 1995; Dawes, 1994; Leary, 1999; Seligman, 1994, 2002). Problems and failures lower self-esteem. So, maybe self-esteem simply reflects reality. Maybe it's a side effect of meeting challenges and getting through difficulties. Maybe self-esteem is a gauge that reports the state of our relationships with others. If so, isn't pushing the gauge artificially higher much like forcing a car's low-fuel gauge to display "full"? If feeling good *follows* doing well, the best boost will come from children's own effective coping and hard-won achievements, not from repeatedly telling them how wonderful they are.

> "There's a lot of talk about self-esteem these days. It seems pretty basic to me. If you want to feel proud of yourself, you've got to do things you can be proud of."
>
> Oseola McCarty, Mississippi laundry worker, after donating $150,000 to the University of Southern Mississippi

Dear diary, Sorry to bother you again.

LOW SELF-ESTEEM

There is, however, an important *effect* of low self-esteem. People who feel negative about themselves also tend to be negative toward others (Amabile, 1983; Baumgardner & others, 1989; Pelham, 1993). Researchers have temporarily deflated people's self-image—for example, by telling them they did poorly on a test or by insulting them. These participants were then more likely to insult others or to express racial prejudice (Ybarra, 1999).

> "If you compare yourself with others, you may become vain and bitter; for always there will be greater and lesser persons than yourself."
>
> Max Ehrmann, "Desiderata," 1927

Inflated self-esteem also causes problems, as Roy Baumeister discovered when studying insult-triggered aggression. He found that "conceited, self-important individuals turn nasty toward those who puncture their bubbles of self-love."

Some researchers have separated self-esteem into two categories—*defensive* and *secure* (Jordan & others, 2003; Kernis, 2003; Lambird & Mann, 2006; Ryan & Deci, 2004).

- *Defensive self-esteem* is fragile. Its goal is to sustain itself, which makes failures and criticism feel threatening. Defensive self-esteem feeds anger and disorder (Crocker & Park, 2004). Like low self-esteem, it correlates with aggressive and antisocial behavior (Donnellan & others, 2005).

■ *Secure self-esteem* is less fragile. It relies less on other people's evaluations. If we feel accepted for who we are, and not for our looks, wealth, or fame, we are free of pressures to succeed. We can focus beyond ourselves, losing ourselves in relationships and purposes larger than self. Secure self-esteem thus leads to greater quality of life. Such findings are in line with Maslow's and Rogers' ideas about the benefits of a healthy self-image.

If deflating people's self-image can lower self-esteem, will groups that have faced discrimination—members of minority groups, for example—have low self-esteem? The evidence says no. Comparisons of more than a half-million people reveal slightly *higher* self-esteem scores for Black than for White children, adolescents, and young adults (Gray-Little & Hafdahl, 2000; Twenge & Crocker, 2002).

Members of stigmatized groups (people of color, those with disabilities, and, in some cases, women) appear to maintain their self-esteem in three ways (Crocker & Major, 1989):

■ They value the things at which they excel.

■ They attribute problems to prejudice.

■ They do as everyone does—they compare themselves to people in their own group.

Despite the realities of prejudice, people in minority groups report levels of happiness roughly comparable to those of members of majority groups.

Self-Serving Bias

11: What is the self-serving bias?

Carl Rogers (1958) once objected to the idea that humanity's problems arise from too much self-love, or pride. He noted that most people he had known "despise themselves, regard themselves as worthless and unlovable."

One of psychology's most surprising but firmly established recent conclusions disagrees. Most of us have a good reputation with ourselves. We have a potent **self-serving bias**—a readiness to perceive ourselves favorably (Mezulis & others, 2004; Myers, 2005). Consider these findings:

People accept more responsibility for good deeds than for bad, and for successes than for failures. Athletes often privately credit their victories to their own talent. Their losses are surely the result of bad breaks, lousy officials, or the other team's amazing performance. In a half-dozen studies, most students who received poor grades on an exam criticized the exam, not themselves. On insurance forms, drivers have explained accidents in such words as: "An invisible car came out of nowhere, struck my car, and vanished." "As I reached an intersection, a hedge sprang up, obscuring my vision, and I did not see the other car." "A pedestrian hit me and went under my car." The question "What have I done to deserve this?" is one we usually ask of our troubles, not our successes.

Most people see themselves as better than average. This is true for nearly any testable and socially desirable personality trait. In national surveys, most business executives say they are more ethical than the average executive. Most business managers and college professors (90 percent or more of each) rated their performance as superior to that of their average peer. This tendency is less striking in Asia, where people value modesty (Heine & Hamamura, 2007). Yet self-serving biases have been observed worldwide: among Dutch, Australian, and Chinese students; Japanese drivers; Indian Hindus; and French people of most walks of life.

We even see ourselves as more immune than others to self-serving bias (Pronin & others, 2002). We also are quicker to believe flattering descriptions of ourselves than unflattering ones, and we are impressed with psychological tests that make us look good. Whether justifying our past actions, touting our beliefs and judgments, or predicting our own actions in situations where most people behave badly, we think we're way above average (Myers, 2005). So are our pets. Three in four pet owners are sure their pet is smarter than average (Nier, 2004; also El-Alayli & others, 2006).

Self-serving bias often underlies conflicts. Some blame their spouse for marriage problems. All of us tend to see our own group (whether it's a school, an age group, an ethnic group, or a country) as superior. "Aryan pride" fueled Nazi horrors. No wonder religion and literature so often warn against the perils of self-love and pride.

If self-serving bias is so common, why do so many people put themselves down? For three reasons: First, self-directed putdowns are sometimes meant to prompt positive feedback. Saying "No one likes me" may at least get you "But not everyone has met you!" Second, these putdowns help prepare us for possible failure—before a game or an exam, for example. The coach who talks about the superior strength of the upcoming opponent makes a loss understandable, a victory noteworthy. Finally, we may put ourselves down when we mean to be critical of our distant past selves, not our current selves—even when we have not changed (Wilson & Ross, 2001). Chumps yesterday, but champs today: "At 18, I was a jerk; today I'm more sensitive."

Even so, it's true: All of us some of the time, and some of us much of the time, do feel inferior. As we saw in Chapter 9, this

---

"If you are like most people, then like most people, you don't know you're like most people. Science has given us a lot of facts about the average person, and one of the most reliable of these facts is the average person doesn't see herself as average."

Daniel Gilbert, *Stumbling on Happiness*, 2006

---

spotlight effect overestimating others' noticing and evaluating our appearance, performance, and blunders (as if we presume a spotlight shines on us).

self-esteem your feelings of high or low self-worth.

self-serving bias our readiness to perceive ourselves favorably.

often happens when we compare ourselves with those who are a step or two higher on the ladder of status, looks, income, or ability. The deeper and more frequently we have such feelings, the more unhappy, even depressed, we are. But for most people, thinking has a naturally positive bias.

Culture and the Self

12: How does the view of self differ in individualist and collectivist cultures?

The meaning of *self* varies from culture to culture. Imagine that someone were to rip away your social connections, leaving you alone in a foreign land. How much of your identity would remain intact? Your answer may depend on your culture, and whether it gives greater priority to the *independent self* or to the *interdependent self*.

If you are an **individualist,** alone in a foreign land, you would retain a lot of your identity. The very core of your being, the sense of "me," the awareness of your personal convictions and values would be intact. Individualists give higher priority to personal goals. They define their identity mostly in terms of personal traits. They strive for personal control and individual achievement.

The United States, with its relatively big "I" and small "we," is mostly an individualist culture. Some 85 percent of

Americans say it is possible "to pretty much be who you want to be" (Sampson, 2000). Being more self-contained, individualists also move in and out of social groups more easily. They feel relatively free to switch places of worship, leave one job for another, or even leave their extended families and migrate to a new place. Marriage is often for as long as they both shall love.

If set adrift in a foreign land as a **collectivist,** you might experience a much greater loss of identity. Cut off from family, groups, and loyal friends, you would lose the connections that have defined who you are. *Group identifications* provide a sense of belonging and a set of values in collectivist cultures. In Korea, for example, people place less value on expressing a consistent, unique self-concept, and more on tradition and shared practices (Choi & Choi, 2002).

Collectivists are like athletes who take more pleasure in their team's victory than in their own performance. They find satisfaction in advancing their groups' interests, even at the expense of personal needs. Preserving group spirit and avoiding social embarrassment are important goals. Collectivists therefore avoid direct confrontation, blunt honesty, and uncomfortable topics. They often defer to others' wishes and display polite humility (Markus & Kitayama, 1991). In new groups, they may be shy and more easily

embarrassed than individualists are (Singelis & others, 1995, 1999). Compared with Westerners, people in Japanese and Chinese cultures, for example, show greater shyness toward strangers and greater concern for social harmony and loyalty (Bond, 1988; Cheek & Melchior, 1990; Triandis, 1994). Elders and superiors receive respect, and duty to one's family may trump personal career preference.

People in competitive, individualist cultures have more personal freedom **(TABLE 11.3)**. They take more pride in personal achievements, are less geographically bound to their families, and enjoy more privacy. But these benefits come at the cost of more loneliness, divorce, homicide, and stress-related disease (Popenoe, 1993; Triandis & others, 1988). People in individualist cultures also demand more romance and personal fulfillment in marriage, which puts relationships under more pressure (Dion & Dion, 1993). In one survey, "keeping romance alive" was rated as important to a good marriage by 78 percent of U.S. women but only 29 percent of Japanese women (*American Enterprise,* 1992).

individualism giving priority to our own goals over group goals and defining our identity in terms of personal traits rather than group membership.

collectivism giving priority to goals of our group (often our extended family or work group) and defining our identity accordingly.

Table 11.3	Value Contrasts Between Individualism and Collectivism	
Concept	Individualism	Collectivism
Self	Independent (identity from individual traits)	Interdependent (identity from belonging)
Life task	Discover and express our uniqueness	Maintain connections, fit in, perform role
What matters	Me—personal achievement and fulfillment; rights and liberties; self-esteem	Us—group goals and solidarity; social responsibilities and relationships; family duty
Coping method	Change reality	Adjust to reality
Morality	Defined by individuals (self-based)	Defined by social networks (duty-based)
Relationships	Many, often temporary or casual; confrontation acceptable	Few, close and enduring; harmony valued
Attributing behavior	Behavior reflects our personality and attitudes	Behavior reflects social norms and roles

Sources: Adapted from Thomas Schoeneman (1994) and Harry Triandis (1994).

Collectivism :: The collectivist support system in Pakistan may have helped these people survive the chaos that followed the 2005 Kashmir earthquake, which leveled the house behind them.

Kyodo News

Individualist proverb: "The squeaky wheel gets the grease."

Collectivist proverb: "The quacking duck gets shot."

* * *

From Freud's psychoanalysis and Maslow and Rogers' humanistic perspective, to the trait and social-cognitive theories, to today's study of the self, our understanding of personality has come a long way! This is a good base from which to explore Chapter 12's questions: How and why do some people suffer from disordered thinking and emotions?

PRACTICE TEST

19. The *spotlight effect* is our tendency to
a. perceive ourselves favorably and perceive others unfavorably.
b. try out many possible selves.
c. become excessively critical when made to feel insecure.
d. overestimate others' attention to and evaluation of our appearance, performance, and blunders.

20. People tend to accept responsibility for their successes and to blame circumstances or bad luck for their failures. This is an example of
a. defensive self-esteem.
b. secure self-esteem.
c. self-serving bias.
d. possible selves.

21. Researchers have found a correlation between low self-esteem and life problems. This finding proves
a. that life problems cause low self-esteem.
b. that low self-esteem leads to life problems.
c. that some third factor causes both low self-esteem and life problems.
d. nothing—correlations allow predictions, but they don't prove cause and effect.

Answers: 19. d, 20. c, 21. d.

TERMS AND CONCEPTS TO REMEMBER

personality, p. 289
unconscious, p. 290
free association, p. 290
psychoanalysis, p. 290
id, p. 290
ego, p. 291
superego, p. 291
psychosexual stages, p. 291
Oedipus [ED-uh-puss] complex, p. 292
identification, p. 292
fixation, p. 292
defense mechanisms, p. 292

repression, p. 292
regression, p. 293
reaction formation, p. 293
projection, p. 293
rationalization, p. 293
displacement, p. 293
psychodynamic theory, p. 293
projective test, p. 294
Rorschach inkblot test, p. 294
hierarchy of needs, p. 297
self-actualization, p. 297
self-transcendence, p. 297

unconditional positive regard, p. 298
self-concept, p. 298
trait, p. 299
factors, p. 299
social-cognitive perspective, p. 303
reciprocal determinism, p. 305
self, p. 305
spotlight effect, p. 306
self-esteem, p. 306
self-serving bias, p. 307
individualism, p. 308
collectivism, p. 308

:: Multiple-choice **self-tests** and more may be found at www.worthpublishers.com/myers

REVIEW: PERSONALITY

Personality—an individual's characteristic pattern of thinking, feeling, and acting.

PSYCHOANALYTIC PERSPECTIVE

1 **What was Sigmund Freud's view of human personality and its development and dynamics?**

■ Freud's *psychoanalysis:* Disorders spring from *unconscious* dynamics; Freud analyzed by using *free associations* and dreams.

■ Personality includes *id* (pleasure-seeking impulses), *ego* (reality-oriented executive), and *superego* (internalized set of ideals).

■ Children develop through *psychosexual stages*—oral, anal, phallic, latency, and genital stages. Freud believed that our personalities are influenced by how we have resolved conflicts at each stage, and whether we have remained *fixated* at any stage.

2 **What are defense mechanisms?**

■ Tensions between the demands of id and superego cause anxiety.

■ The ego copes by using *defense mechanisms,* such as *repression, regression, reaction formation, projection, rationalization,* and *displacement.*

3 **Who were the neo-Freudians, and what is psychodynamic theory?**

■ Neo-Freudians Adler, Horney, and Jung accepted many of Freud's ideas, but they argued that we have motives other than sex and aggression, and that the ego's conscious control is greater than Freud thought.

■ *Psychodynamic theory* is a modern perspective that retains Freud's focus on unconscious motives.

4 **What are projective tests, and what do clinicians in the Freudian tradition hope to learn from them?**

■ *Projective tests,* such as the *Rorschach inkblots,* attempt to assess personality by showing people vague stimuli with many possible interpretations; answers reveal unconscious motives.

■ Most projective tests have low reliability and validity.

5 **How does the psychoanalytic perspective hold up to contemporary psychology's findings?**

■ Freud rightly drew our attention to the vast unconscious, to the struggle to cope with anxiety and sexuality, and to the conflict between biological impulses and social restraints.

■ There is support for some of Freud's defense mechanisms.

■ Freud's view of the unconscious as a collection of repressed and unacceptable thoughts, wishes, feelings, and memories has not survived scientific scrutiny.

■ Freud offered after-the-fact explanations, which are hard to test scientifically.

■ Researchers question whether repression ever occurs.

■ Research does not support many of Freud's specific ideas, such as development being fixed in childhood. (We now know it is lifelong.)

HUMANISTIC PERSPECTIVE
SOUGHT TO TURN PSYCHOLOGY'S ATTENTION TOWARD HUMAN GROWTH POTENTIAL.

6 **What were Abraham Maslow's and Carl Rogers' contributions to humanistic psychology?**

■ Maslow: If basic human needs are fulfilled, people will strive toward *self-actualization* and *self-transcendence.*

■ Rogers: Being genuine, accepting, and empathic helps others develop a more realistic and positive *self-concept.*

7 **What have critics said about humanistic psychology?**

■ Humanistic psychology did help renew interest in the concept of self.

■ Humanistic psychology's concepts were vague and subjective, values Western and self-centered, and assumptions naively optimistic.

TRAIT PERSPECTIVE

8 How do psychologists use traits to describe personality? Which traits seem to provide the most useful information about personality variation?

■ *Trait* theorists see personality as a stable and enduring pattern of behavior. They describe our differences rather than trying to *explain* them.

■ The Big Five personality dimensions—conscientiousness, agreeableness, neuroticism, openness, and extraversion (CANOE)—offer a broad picture of personality.

SOCIAL-COGNITIVE PERSPECTIVE

9 How does the social-cognitive perspective view personality?

■ The *social-cognitive perspective* applies principles of learning, cognition, and social behavior to personality.

■ *Reciprocal determinism*: Personal-cognitive factors interact with the environment to influence people's behavior.

■ Social-cognitive researchers study how our behaviors and beliefs both affect and are affected by situations.

EXPLORING THE SELF

SELF—THE CENTER OF PERSONALITY, ORGANIZING OUR THOUGHTS, FEELINGS, AND ACTIONS.

10 What is self-esteem, and how does it influence us?

■ *Self-esteem:* Our feeling of self-worth.

■ High self-esteem is beneficial, but unrealistically high self-esteem is dangerous (linked to aggressive behavior) and fragile.

11 What is the self-serving bias?

■ *Self-serving bias:* Perceiving ourselves favorably, as when viewing ourselves as better than others, or when accepting credit for our successes but not blame for our failures.

12 How does the view of self differ in individualist and collectivist cultures?

■ *Individualism:* Self-reliant; defines the self in terms of personal goals and attributes.

■ *Collectivism:* Socially connected; gives priority to group goals, social identity, and commitments.

I felt the need to clean my room at home in Indianapolis every Sunday and would spend four to five hours at it. I would take every book out of the bookcase, dust and put it back. At the time I loved doing it. Then I didn't want to do it anymore, but I couldn't stop. The clothes in my closet hung exactly two fingers apart. . . . I made a ritual of touching the wall in my bedroom before I went out because something bad would happen if I didn't do it the right way. I had a constant anxiety about it as a kid, and it made me think for the first time that I might be nuts.

Marc, diagnosed with obsessive-compulsive disorder
(from Summers, 1996)

Whenever I get depressed it's because I've lost a sense of self. I can't find reasons to like myself. I think I'm ugly. I think no one likes me. . . . I become grumpy and short-tempered. Nobody wants to be around me. I'm left alone. Being alone confirms that I am ugly and not worth being with. I think I'm responsible for everything that goes wrong.

Greta, diagnosed with depression
(from Thorne, 1993, p. 21)

Voices, like the roar of a crowd came. I felt like Jesus; I was being crucified. It was dark. I just continued to huddle under the blanket, feeling weak, laid bare and defenseless in a cruel world I could no longer understand.

Stuart, diagnosed with schizophrenia
(from Emmons & others, 1997)

NOW AND THEN, ALL OF US feel, think, or act the way disturbed people do much of the time. We, too, get anxious, depressed, withdrawn, or suspicious, just less intensely and more briefly. It's no wonder, then, that we sometimes see ourselves in the psychological disorders we study. "To study the abnormal is the best way of understanding the normal," proposed William James (1842–1910).

Either personally or through friends or family, many of us will know the confusion and pain of unexplained physical symptoms, irrational fears, or a feeling that life is not worth living. Worldwide, some 450 million people suffer psychological disorders (WHO, 2008). The National Institute of Mental Health (2008) estimates that 26 percent of adult Americans "suffer from a diagnosable mental disorder in a given year" (TABLE 12.1 on the next page). Rates and symptoms vary by culture, but no known society is free of two terrible disorders: depression and schizophrenia (Castillo, 1997; Draguns, 1990a,b, 1997). This chapter examines these and other disorders, and the next chapter considers their *treatment*. But first, let's address some basic questions.

Table 12.1	Percentage of Americans Reporting Certain Psychological Disorders in the Past Year

Disorder	Percentage
Generalized anxiety	3.1
Social phobia	6.8
Phobia of specific object or situation	8.7
Mood disorder	9.5
Obsessive-compulsive disorder (OCD)	1.0
Schizophrenia	1.1
Post-traumatic stress disorder (PTSD)	3.5
Attention-deficit hyperactivity disorder (ADHD)	4.1
Any mental disorder	26.2

Source: National Institute of Mental Health, 2008.

What Is a Psychological Disorder?

Most of us would agree that a family member who is depressed and refuses to get out of bed for three months has a psychological disorder. But what should we say about a grieving mother who can't resume her usual social activities three months after her child has died of cancer? Where do we draw the line between depression and understandable sadness? Between bizarre irrationality and zany creativity? Between abnormality and normality? Let's consider how psychologists define, understand, and classify disorders.

"They're trying to figure out whether it's a chemical thing or I'm just a crybaby."

©The New Yorker Collection 2002 Bruce Eric Kaplan from cartoonbank.com. All Rights Reserved.

Defining Psychological Disorders

1: How do psychologists draw the line between normal behavior and disordered behavior, and what is a psychological disorder?

To a psychologist, a **psychological disorder** is an ongoing pattern of thoughts, feelings, and actions that is *deviant, distressful,* and *dysfunctional* (Comer, 2004).

Deviant Behavior Being *deviant* means being different from most other people in your culture. What people consider deviant varies with the situation, even within a culture. Depending on the situation—a battlefield or a children's playground—mass killing may be viewed as heroic or horrific. In our Western culture, hearing voices is deviant. But in cultures that practice ancestor worship, people claiming to talk with the dead may be seen as gifted, not disordered (Friedrich, 1987).

What people consider deviant also varies with time. In 1952, the American Psychiatric Association listed homosexuality as a psychological disorder. In 1973, it dropped homosexuality as a disorder because fewer and fewer mental health workers viewed homosexuality as a psychological problem. Also in the 1950s, many viewed high-energy children as normal children running wild. Today, many of these children are diagnosed with *attention-deficit hyperactivity disorder (ADHD)*. Times change, and views of what's deviant change with them.

Distressful Behavior But there is more to a disorder than being deviant. Olympic gold medalists differ from most of us in their physical abilities, and society honors them. For deviant behavior to be considered disordered, it must also cause *distress* to the person or to others. Marc, Greta, and Stuart were all clearly distressed by their behaviors. If the distress becomes extreme, the disordered behavior may also be judged dangerous. If Greta's depression deepens, for example, she may develop suicidal thoughts and be considered a danger to herself.

Dysfunctional Behavior *Dysfunctional* behaviors interfere with normal day-to-day life. Dysfunction is key to defining a disorder. An intense fear of spiders may be deviant, but if it doesn't interfere with your life, it isn't a disorder. Marc's obsessive cleaning and other rituals interfered with his work and leisure. Even typical behaviors can become dysfunctional. Many students have occasional sad moods. If these feelings persist and become disabling, they may signal a disorder.

Understanding Psychological Disorders

2: How can our perspectives on psychological disorders affect our understanding of these conditions?

The way we view a problem influences how we try to solve it. In earlier times, people often thought that strange behaviors were evidence that strange forces were at work. "The devil made him do it," you might have said had you lived during the Middle Ages. To drive out demons,

Diverse Yet Alike

Young men of the West African Wodaabe tribe put on elaborate makeup and costumes to attract women. Young American men may buy flashy cars with loud stereos to do the same. Each culture would view the other's behavior as abnormal.

Carol Beckwith

Jens Koenig/Getty Images

mad people were sometimes caged or given "therapies" such as beatings, genital mutilations, removal of teeth or lengths of intestine, or transfusions of animal blood (Farina, 1982).

Reformers such as Philippe Pinel (1745–1826) in France opposed such brutal treatments. Madness is not demon possession, he insisted, but a sickness of the mind caused by severe stress and inhumane conditions. Curing the sickness requires "moral treatment," including boosting patients' morale by unchaining them and talking with them. He and others worked to replace brutality with gentleness, isolation with activity, and filth with clean air and sunshine.

George Wesley Bellows, *Dance in a Madhouse*, 1907.
© 1997 The Art Institute of Chicago

"Moral treatment" :: Under Philippe Pinel's influence, hospitals sometimes sponsored patient dances, such as the "Lunatic Ball" depicted in this painting by George Bellows *(Dance in a Madhouse)*.

The Medical Model

By the 1800s, a medical breakthrough prompted further reform. Researchers discovered that syphilis, a sexually transmitted disease, infects the brain and distorts the mind. This discovery triggered an excited search for physical causes of other mental disorders, and for treatments that would cure them. Hospitals replaced madhouses, and the **medical model** of mental disorders was born. This model is reflected in words we still use today. We speak of the mental *health* movement. A mental *illness* needs to be *diagnosed* on the basis of its *symptoms*. It needs to be *cured* through *therapy*, which may include *treatment* in a psychiatric *hospital*. Recent discoveries that abnormal brain structures and biochemistry contribute to a number of disorders have brought new life to the medical perspective.

The Biopsychosocial Approach

To call psychological disorders "sicknesses" tilts research heavily toward the influence of biology and away from the influence of our personal histories and social and cultural surroundings. But as we have seen throughout this text, our

"It's no measure of health to be well adjusted to a profoundly sick society."
Krishnamurti (1895–1986)

behaviors, our thoughts, and our feelings are formed by the interaction of our biology, our psychology, and our social-cultural environment.

Evidence of the effects of a person's environment, thinking, habits, or social skills comes from links between specific disorders and cultures (Beardsley, 1994; Castillo, 1997). People differ in the amount of stress they experience and in their ways of coping with stress. Cultures also differ in their sources of stress, and they produce different ways of coping.

Disorders may share an underlying dynamic, such as anxiety, while exhibiting differing symptoms in given cultures. The eating disorders *anorexia nervosa* and *bulimia nervosa*, for example, occur mostly in North American and other Western cultures. In Latin American cultures, people may suffer from *susto*, a condition marked by severe anxiety, restlessness, and a fear of black magic. In Japanese culture, people may experience *taijin-kyofusho*, social anxiety about their appearance, combined with a readiness to blush and a fear of eye contact.

psychological disorder deviant (atypical), distressful, and dysfunctional thoughts, feelings, or behaviors.

medical model the concept that diseases, in this case psychological disorders, have physical causes that can be *diagnosed, treated*, and, in most cases, *cured*, often through *treatment* in a *hospital*.

Depression and schizophrenia, however, occur worldwide. From Asia to Africa and across the Americas, people with schizophrenia often act irrationally and speak in disorganized ways (Brislin, 1993; Draguns, 1990b). But disorders that appear only in one culture remind us to consider all of the possible influences. For disorders, this means we should try to understand not only genes and physiology, but also inner psychological dynamics and social and cultural circumstances. The biopsychosocial approach recognizes that mind and body are inseparable. We are mind embodied.

Classifying Disorders—and Labeling People

3: How and why do clinicians classify psychological disorders, and why do some psychologists criticize the use of diagnostic labels?

In biology and the other sciences, classification creates order and helps us communicate. To say that an animal is a "mammal" tells us a great deal—that it is warm-blooded, has hair or fur, and produces milk to feed its young. In psychiatry and psychology, classification serves the same ends. To classify a person's disorder as "schizophrenia" also tells us a great deal. It says that the person speaks in a disorganized way, has bizarre beliefs, shows either little emotion or inappropriate emotion, or is socially withdrawn. "Schizophrenia" is a quick way of describing a complex set of behaviors.

But diagnostic classification does more than give us a thumbnail sketch of a person's disordered behavior. In psychiatry and psychology, classification also attempts to predict the disorder's future course and suggest treatment. It prompts research into causes. Indeed, to study a disorder we must first name and describe it.

Our current best scheme for describing disorders and estimating how often they occur is the American Psychiatric Association's *Diagnostic and Statistical Manual of Mental Disorders,* now in its updated, text-

"I'm always like this, and my family was wondering if you could prescribe a mild depressant."

revised fourth edition (**DSM-IV-TR**). Many of the examples used in this chapter are drawn from case illustrations accompanying the DSM-IV-TR.

The DSM-IV-TR categories and diagnostic guidelines are fairly reliable (**TABLE 12.2**). If one psychiatrist or psychologist diagnoses someone as having, say, "catatonic schizophrenia," the chances are good that another mental health worker will independently give the same diagnosis. To reach a diagnosis, clinicians answer a series of objective questions about observable behaviors, such as, "Is the person afraid to leave home?"

In one study, 16 psychologists used DSM guidelines in interviews with 75 patients with disorders. The psychologists' task was to diagnose each patient as having (1) depression, (2) generalized anxiety, or (3) some other disorder (Riskind & others, 1987). Another psychologist then viewed a videotape of each interview and offered a second, independent opinion.

Table 12.2	How Are Psychological Disorders Diagnosed?

Based on assessments, interviews, and observations, many clinicians diagnose by answering the following questions from the five levels, or *axes,* of the DSM-IV-TR. (Chapters in parentheses locate the topics discussed elsewhere in this text.)

Axis I Is a *Clinical Syndrome* present?
Using specifically defined criteria, clinicians may select none, one, or more syndromes from the following list:

- Disorders usually first diagnosed in infancy, childhood, and adolescence
- Delirium, dementia, amnesia, and other cognitive disorders (Chapter 7)
- Mental disorders due to a general medical condition
- Substance-related disorders
- Schizophrenia and other psychotic disorders
- Mood disorders
- Anxiety disorders
- Somatoform disorders
- Factitious disorders (intentionally faked)
- Dissociative disorders
- Eating disorders (Chapter 9)
- Sexual disorders and gender identity disorder (Chapter 4)
- Sleep disorders (Chapter 2)
- Impulse-control disorders not classified elsewhere
- Adjustment disorders
- Other conditions that may be a focus of clinical attention

Axis II Is a *Personality Disorder* or *Mental Retardation* present?
Clinicians may or may not also select one of these two conditions.

Axis III Is a *General Medical Condition,* such as diabetes, hypertension, or arthritis, also present?

Axis IV Are *Psychosocial* or *Environmental Problems,* such as school or housing issues, also present?

Axis V What is the *Global Assessment* of this person's functioning?
Clinicians assign a code from 0–100.

For 83 percent of the patients, the two opinions agreed.

Nevertheless, the DSM has its critics. Some believe it casts too wide a net and brings "almost any kind of behavior within the compass of psychiatry" (Eysenck & others, 1983). Others note that as the number of disorder categories has swelled (from 60 in the 1950s DSM to 400 today), so has the number of adults who meet the criteria for at least one of them. In one year, that number reached nearly 30 percent of the U.S. population, according to one survey (Regier & others, 1998).

Other critics register a more basic complaint—that these labels are just society's value judgments. Once we label a person, we view that person differently (Farina, 1982). We then are on the alert for evidence that confirms our view. When this happens, labels can change reality. When teachers are told certain students are "gifted," when students expect someone to be "hostile," or when interviewers check to see whether someone is "extraverted," they may act in ways that bring out the very behavior expected (Snyder, 1984). If you hear that your new co-worker is a difficult person, you may treat him suspiciously. He may in turn respond to you as a difficult person would. Labels can be self-fulfilling.

> "One of the unpardonable sins, in the eyes of most people, is for a man to go about unlabeled. The world regards such a person as the police do an unmuzzled dog, not under proper control."
>
> T. H. Huxley, *Evolution and Ethics*, 1893

In a now-classic study, David Rosenhan (1973) and seven others demonstrated the biasing power of labels. They went to hospital admissions offices, complaining of "hearing voices" saying *empty, hollow,* and *thud.* Apart from this complaint and giving false names and occupations, they answered questions truthfully. All eight normal people were misdiagnosed with disorders.

Should we be surprised? As one psychiatrist noted, if someone swallowed blood, went to an emergency room, and spat it up, would we blame a doctor for diagnosing a bleeding ulcer? Perhaps not. But what followed the diagnosis was startling. Until being released (an average of 19 days later), the "patients" showed no other symptoms. Yet after analyzing the (quite normal) life histories of these eight people, clinicians were able to "discover" the causes of their disorders, such as having mixed emotions about a parent. Even the patients' routine note-taking behavior was misinterpreted as a symptom.

In another study, people watched videotaped interviews. Some were told the people being interviewed were job applicants, and the viewers perceived them as normal (Langer & others, 1974, 1980). Others were told they were watching psychiatric or cancer patients. Are you surprised to hear that these viewers perceived these same people as "different from most people"? Labels matter. Therapists who thought the person being interviewed was a psychiatric patient described him as "frightened of his own aggressive impulses," a "passive, dependent type," and so forth. As Rosenhan discovered, a label can have "a life and an influence of its own."

The power of labels is just as real outside the laboratory. Getting a job or finding a place to rent can be a challenge for people who have just been released from a mental hospital. The shame seems to be lifting as people better understand that many psychological disorders are diseases of the brain, not failures of character (Solomon, 1996). Public figures have helped foster this understanding by speaking openly about their own struggles with disorders such as depression. The more contact we have with people with disorders, the more accepting our attitudes are (Kolodziej & Johnson, 1996).

Despite their risks, we can't forget the *benefits* of diagnostic labels. Mental health professionals have good reasons for using labels. These shortcuts help them communicate about their cases, pinpoint underlying causes, and share information about effective treatments.

Accurate portrayal :: Popular movies, such as "Silence of the Lambs" and "Psycho," have often portrayed those with psychological disorders as aggressive and dangerous. The TV show "ER" has portrayed more typical suffering and personal disruption. Here Abby (Maura Tierney) confronts her mother (Sally Fields), who is suffering from bipolar disorder.

PRACTICE TEST

1. Although some psychological disorders appear in only one culture, others are universal. For example, in every known culture some people have
   a. bulimia nervosa.
   b. anorexia nervosa.
   c. schizophrenia.
   d. susto.

2. If a lawyer washes his hands 100 times a day for no apparent reason and has no time left to meet with his clients, the hand washing will probably be labeled disordered because it is, among other things,
   a. distressing and dysfunctional.
   b. not explained by the medical model.
   c. harmful to others.
   d. untreatable.

DSM-IV-TR the American Psychiatric Association's *Diagnostic and Statistical Manual of Mental Disorders,* a widely used system for classifying psychological disorders. Presently available in an updated, text-revised fourth edition.

3. A psychologist focusing mostly on disorders as sicknesses and suggesting they should be treated in hospitals is using a
   a. social-cultural perspective.
   b. biopsychosocial approach.
   c. medical model.
   d. diagnostic model.

4. A psychologist working with a distressed person is trying to get more information on the person's medical history, personal background, and social environment. This psychologist is using a _____ approach.
   a. medical
   b. deviant-dysfunctional
   c. biopsychosocial
   d. diagnostic labels

5. Most psychologists and psychiatrists currently use _____ to classify psychological disorders.
   a. the DSM-IV-TR
   b. in-depth histories of patients
   c. input from patients' family and friends
   d. the theories of Pinel, Rosenhan, and others

Answers: 1. c, 2. a, 3. c, 4. c, 5. a.

Anxiety Disorders

4: What are anxiety disorders, and how do they differ from the ordinary worries and fears we all experience?

Anxiety is part of life. Speaking in front of a class, peering down from a high ledge, or waiting to play in a big game, any one of us might feel anxious. At times we may feel enough anxiety to avoid making eye contact or talking with someone—"shyness," we call it. Fortunately for most of us, our uneasiness is not intense and persistent. If it becomes so, we may have one of the **anxiety disorders,** marked by distressing, persistent anxiety or maladaptive behaviors that reduce anxiety. For example, a man with a fear of social settings may avoid going out. This behavior is maladaptive because it reduces his

Coping with disorder :: "The only way I knew how to deal with it was to write a song about it," musician Billie Joe Armstrong of Green Day explained, referring to his song "Basket Case," which relates a personal struggle with anxiety disorders.

AP Photo/Robert E. Klein

anxiety but does not help him cope with his world.

In this section we focus on five anxiety disorders:

■ *Generalized anxiety disorder,* in which a person is constantly tense and uneasy for no apparent reason.

■ *Panic disorder,* in which a person experiences sudden episodes of intense dread.

■ *Phobias,* in which a person feels irrationally and intensely afraid of a specific object or situation.

■ *Obsessive-compulsive disorder,* in which a person is troubled by repetitive thoughts or actions.

■ *Post-traumatic stress disorder,* in which a person has lingering memories, nightmares, and possibly other symptoms for weeks after a severely threatening, uncontrollable event.

Generalized Anxiety Disorder

Tom is a 27-year-old electrician. For the past two years, he has had periods of dizziness, sweating palms, irregular heartbeats, and ringing in his ears. He feels edgy and sometimes finds himself shaking. With reasonable success he hides his symptoms from his family and co-workers. But he allows himself few other social contacts, and sometimes he has to leave work. Neither his family doctor nor a neurologist has been able to find any physical problem.

Tom's unfocused, out-of-control, negative feelings suggest **generalized anxiety disorder.** The symptoms of this disorder are commonplace; their persistence is not. People with this condition (two-thirds are women) worry continually, and they are often jittery, on edge, and sleep-deprived. Concentration is difficult, as attention switches from worry to worry. Their tension may leak out through furrowed brows, twitching eyelids, trembling, sweating, or fidgeting. One of the worst features of this disorder is that the person cannot identify, and therefore cannot deal with or avoid, the cause of this tension. To use Sigmund Freud's term, the anxiety is *free-floating.* Generalized anxiety disorder and depression often go hand-in-hand, but even without depression this disorder tends to be disabling (Hunt & others, 2004). Moreover, it may lead to physical problems, such as ulcers and high blood pressure.

Gender and anxiety: Eight months after 9/11, more U.S. women (34 percent) than men (19 percent) told Gallup (2002) they were still less willing than before 9/11 to go into skyscrapers or fly on planes. In early 2003, more women (57 percent) than men (36 percent) were "somewhat worried" about becoming a terrorist victim (Jones, 2003).

Panic Disorder

Panic disorder is to anxiety what a tornado is to a windy day. It strikes suddenly, does its damage, and disappears. Anxiety suddenly escalates into a terrifying *panic attack*—a minutes-long feeling of intense fear that something horrible is about to happen. Irregular heartbeat, chest pains, shortness of breath, choking, trembling, or dizziness may accompany the panic. The symptoms are often misinterpreted as a heart attack or other serious physical ailment. Smokers have at least a doubled risk of a first-time panic attack (Zvolensky & others, 2005). Because nicotine is a stimulant, lighting up doesn't lighten up.

One woman recalled suddenly feeling "hot and as though I couldn't breathe. My heart was racing and I started to sweat and tremble and I was sure I was going to faint. Then my fingers started to feel numb and tingly and things seemed unreal. It was so bad I wondered if I was dying and asked my husband to take me to the emergency room. By the time we got there (about 10 minutes) the worst of the attack was over and I just felt washed out" (Greist & others, 1986).

Phobias

Phobias are anxiety disorders in which a persistent, irrational fear causes the person to avoid some object, activity, or situation. We all live with some fears, but people with phobias are consumed by their efforts to avoid the feared object or situation. Marilyn, an otherwise healthy and happy 28-year-old, so fears thunderstorms that she feels anxious as soon as a weather forecaster mentions possible storms later in the week. If her husband is away and a storm is forecast, she may stay with a close relative. During a storm, she hides from windows and buries her head to avoid seeing the lightning. *Specific phobias* such as Marilyn's typically focus on particular animals, insects, heights, blood, or closed spaces **(FIGURE 12.1)**.

Not all phobias are so specific. *Social phobia* is shyness taken to an extreme. Those with a social phobia have an intense fear of being judged by others. They avoid threatening social situations, such as speaking up in a group, eating out, or going to parties. Finding themselves in such a situation, they will sweat, tremble, or have diarrhea.

People who have experienced several panic attacks may come to fear the fear itself. If the fear is intense enough, it may become *agoraphobia*, fear or avoidance of situations in which panic may strike and escape might be difficult or help unavailable. People with agoraphobia may avoid being outside the home, in a crowd, on a bus, or on an elevator.

Obsessive-Compulsive Disorder (OCD)

As with generalized anxiety and phobias, we can see aspects of our own behavior in **obsessive-compulsive disorder (OCD)**. *Obsessive thoughts* (recall Marc's focus on cleaning his room) are unwanted and so repetitive it may seem they will never go away. *Compulsive behaviors* are responses to those thoughts (cleaning and cleaning and cleaning).

All of us are at times obsessed with senseless or offensive thoughts that will

anxiety disorders psychological disorders characterized by distressing, persistent anxiety or maladaptive behaviors that reduce anxiety.

generalized anxiety disorder an anxiety disorder in which a person is continually tense, fearful, and in a state of autonomic nervous system arousal.

panic disorder an anxiety disorder marked by unpredictable minutes-long episodes of intense dread in which a person experiences terror and accompanying chest pain, choking, or other frightening sensations.

phobia an anxiety disorder marked by a persistent, irrational fear and avoidance of a specific object or situation.

obsessive-compulsive disorder (OCD) an anxiety disorder characterized by unwanted repetitive thoughts (obsessions) and/or actions (compulsions).

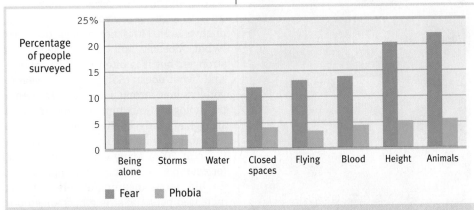

Dr. Morley Read/Science Photo Library

Figure 12.1> Some common and uncommon specific fears Researchers surveyed people to identify the most common events or objects they feared. A strong fear becomes a phobia if it provokes a compelling but irrational desire to avoid the dreaded object or situation. (From Curtis & others, 1998.)

Snapshots

Obsessing about obsessive-compulsive disorder.

not go away. All of us sometimes engage in compulsive behaviors, rigidly checking, ordering, and cleaning before guests arrive, or lining up books and pencils "just so" before studying. But obsessive thoughts and compulsive behaviors cross the fine line between normality and disorder when they interfere with everyday living and cause us distress. Checking to see if you locked the door is normal; checking 10 times is not. Washing your hands is normal; washing so often that your skin becomes raw is not. Normal rehearsals and fussy behaviors become a disorder when the obsessive thoughts become so haunting, the compulsive rituals so senselessly time-consuming, that effective functioning becomes impossible.

Post-Traumatic Stress Disorder (PTSD)

As an Army infantry scout during the Iraq war, Jesse "saw the murder of children and women. It was just horrible for anyone to experience." After calling in a helicopter strike on one house where he had seen ammunition crates carried in, he heard the screams of children from within. "I didn't know there were kids there," he recalls. Back home in Texas, he suffered "real bad flashbacks" (Welch, 2005).

Jesse is not alone. Many other battle-scarred veterans have complained of recurring haunting memories and nightmares, a numb feeling of social withdrawal, jumpy anxiety, and trouble sleeping. So have survivors of accidents, disasters, and violent and sexual assaults (including an estimated two-thirds of prostitutes) (Brewin & others, 1999; Farley & others, 1998; Taylor & others, 1998). These symptoms are typical of **post-traumatic stress disorder (PTSD)** (Hoge & others, 2004; Kessler, 2000).

The Iraq war has taken its toll on U.S. combat infantry. About 17 percent of them have reported symptoms of PTSD, depression, or severe anxiety in the months after returning home (Hoge & others, 2004). Similar rates were found in other groups. A month after the 9/11 terrorist attacks, 20 percent of the people who lived near the World Trade Center reported nightmares, severe anxiety, and fear of public places (Susser & others, 2002). Nineteen percent of Vietnam veterans reported PTSD symptoms. Among those who had never seen combat, the rate was 10 percent, compared with 32 percent among veterans who had experienced heavy combat (Dohrenwend & others, 2006; U.S. Centers for Disease Control Vietnam Experience Study, 1988).

Toxic trauma :: U.S. Army Reserve Sgt. Jared Myers is shown here with his mother, Judy Smith, at a Veterans Administration Medical Center, where he spent three weeks being diagnosed and treated for post-traumatic stress disorder in 2005.

The greater one's emotional distress during a trauma, the higher the risk for post-traumatic symptoms (Ozer & others, 2003). Sensitivity of the emotion-processing limbic system also seems to make some people more vulnerable by flooding the body with stress hormones (Ozer & Weiss, 2004). The more frequent and severe the trauma, the worse the long-term outcomes tend to be (Golding, 1999).

About half of us will experience at least one traumatic event in our lifetime, but we won't all develop PTSD. For women, the odds of getting this disorder after a traumatic event are about 1 in 10. For men, the odds drop to 1 in 20 (Ozer & Weiss, 2004). After severe stress, most people display an impressive *survivor resiliency*, or ability to recover (Bonanno, 2004, 2005, 2006). For example, more than 9 in 10 New Yorkers, although stunned and grief-stricken by 9/11, did not have a dysfunctional stress reaction. By the following January, the stress symptoms of those who did were mostly gone (Person & others, 2006). Even in groups of combat-stressed veterans and political rebels who have survived dozens of episodes of torture, most do not later exhibit PTSD (Mineka & Zinbarg, 1996).

Psychologist Peter Suedfeld (1998, 2000) has documented this resilience among Holocaust survivors. As a boy, Suedfeld survived the Holocaust, though his mother did not. His research shows that most Holocaust survivors have lived productive lives. "It is not always true that 'What doesn't kill you makes you stronger,' but it is often true," he reports. And "what doesn't kill you may reveal to you just how strong you really are." Other psychologists join him in believing that struggling with challenging crises can lead to *post-traumatic growth* (Tedeschi & Calhoun, 2004). Many who survive cancer, for example, report a greater appreciation for life, more meaningful relationships, increased personal strength, changed priorities, and a richer spiritual life. Suffering can lead to new sensitivity and strength.

Other psychologists believe that PTSD has been overdiagnosed, due partly to a broader definition of *trauma* (McNally, 2003).

If PTSD is actually infrequent, say these critics, common treatments—though well-intentioned—may only make people feel worse (Wakefield & Spitzer, 2002). For example, survivors may be "debriefed" right after a trauma and asked to revisit the experience and vent their emotions. This tactic has been generally ineffective and sometimes harmful (Devilly & others, 2006; McNally & others, 2003; Rose & others, 2003).

Understanding Anxiety Disorders

5: What are the sources of the anxious feelings and thoughts that characterize anxiety disorders?

Anxiety is both a feeling and a thought—a doubt-laden appraisal of one's safety or social skill. How do these anxious feelings and thoughts arise? Sigmund Freud's psychoanalytic theory (Chapter 11) proposed that, beginning in childhood, people repress certain impulses, ideas, and feelings. He thought this submerged mental energy sometimes leaks out, appearing as odd symptoms, such as anxious hand washing. Few of today's psychologists interpret anxiety disorders this way. Most believe that two modern perspectives—learning and biological—offer a more complete understanding.

The Learning Perspective

Fear Conditioning When bad events happen unpredictably and uncontrollably, anxiety often develops (Chorpita & Barlow, 1998). In experiments, researchers have shown how classical conditioning can produce feelings of fear and anxiety. You may recall from Chapter 6 that infants have learned to fear furry objects that were paired with loud noises. And by giving rats unpredictable electric shocks, researchers have created anxious, ulcer-prone animals (Schwartz, 1984). The rats—like assault victims who report feeling anxious when returning to the scene of the crime—then become uneasy in their lab environment. That environment has become a cue for fear.

Such research helps explain how panic-prone people come to associate anxiety with certain cues and why anxious people are so attentive to possible threats (Field, 2006; Mineka & Zinbarg, 2006). In one survey, 58 percent of those with social phobia said their disorder began after a traumatic event (Ost & Hugdahl, 1981).

How might conditioning magnify a single painful and frightening event into a full-blown phobia? The answer lies in two specific learning processes: stimulus generalization and reinforcement.

Stimulus generalization occurs when a person experiences a fearful event and later develops a fear of similar events. For example, my car was once struck by another whose driver missed a stop sign. For months afterward, I felt a twinge of unease when any car approached from a side street. My fear eventually disappeared, but for others, fear may linger and grow. Marilyn's phobia may have similarly generalized after a terrifying or painful experience during a thunderstorm.

Once phobias and compulsions arise, *reinforcement* helps maintain them. Anything that helps a person avoid or escape from a feared situation reduces anxiety. This feeling of relief can reinforce phobic behaviors. Fearing a panic attack, a person may decide not to leave the house. Reinforced by feeling calmer, the person is likely to repeat that maladaptive behavior in the future (Antony & others, 1992). So, too, with compulsive behaviors. If washing your hands relieves your feelings of anxiety, you may wash your hands again when those feelings return.

Observational Learning We may also learn fear by observing others' fears. The watchful offspring of wild monkeys pick up their parents' fear of snakes (Mineka, 1985). Human parents also transmit fears to their children. Moreover, just observing someone receiving a mild electric shock after a conditioned stimulus produces fear learning. What the observer learns by watching is very similar to what the shocked person learns from direct experience (Olsson & Phelps, 2004).

Fearless :: The biological perspective helps us understand why most people would be terrified in this situation. Snowboarder Shaun White (the "Flying Tomato") is less vulnerable to a fear of heights than most of us!

Doug Pensinger/Getty Images

The Biological Perspective

There is, however, more to anxiety than simple conditioning or observational learning. Few of us develop lasting phobias after suffering traumas or seeing them. The biological perspective can help us understand why some of us are more vulnerable to learned fears, and why all of us learn some fears more easily than others.

post-traumatic stress disorder (PTSD) an anxiety disorder characterized by haunting memories, nightmares, social withdrawal, jumpy anxiety, and/or insomnia that lingers for four weeks or more after a traumatic experience.

Genes Genes matter. Among monkeys, fearfulness runs in families. A monkey reacts more strongly to stress if its close biological relatives have sensitive, high-strung temperaments (Suomi, 1986). So, too, with people. Some of us more than others seem predisposed to anxiety. If one identical twin has an anxiety disorder, the other is also likely to develop this disorder (Barlow, 1988; Hettema & others, 2001; Kendler & others, 1992, 1999, 2002a,b). Even when raised separately, identical twins also may develop similar phobias (Carey, 1990; Eckert & others, 1981). One pair of separated identical twins independently became so afraid of water that, even at age 35, they would wade into the ocean backward and only up to the knees.

The Brain Pair a genetic predisposition with a traumatic event, and the result may be an anxiety disorder. Brain research demonstrates that our experiences alter our brain, paving new pathways. Fear-learning experiences can leave tracks in the brain. These fear pathways create easy inroads for more fear experiences (Armony & others, 1998).

Generalized anxiety, panic attacks, and even obsessions and compulsions are biologically measurable. Brain scans of people with OCD, for example, reveal higher-than-normal activity in brain areas involved in impulse control and habitual behaviors. Specific brain areas become very active during behaviors such as compulsive hand washing, checking, ordering, or hoarding (Mataix-Cols & others, 2004, 2005). When the disordered brain detects that something is amiss, it seems to generate a mental hiccup of repeating thoughts or actions (Gehring & others, 2000).

Natural Selection No matter how fearful or fearless we are, we humans seem biologically prepared to fear the threats faced by our ancestors: spiders and snakes, closed spaces and heights, storms and darkness. (In the distant past, those who did not fear these threats were less likely to survive and leave descendants.) It is easy to condition and hard to extinguish those fears (Davey, 1995;

Öhman, 1986). Many of our modern fears may also have an evolutionary explanation. For example, a modern fear of flying may have grown from a fear of confinement and heights, which can be traced to our biological past.

Moreover, consider what people tend *not* to learn to fear. World War II air raids produced remarkably few lasting phobias. As the air strikes continued, the British, Japanese, and German populations did not become more and more panicked. Rather they grew more indifferent to planes outside their immediate neighborhood (Mineka & Zinbarg, 1996). Evolution has not prepared us to fear bombs dropping from the sky.

Just as our phobias focus on dangers faced by our ancestors, our compulsive acts typically exaggerate behaviors that had survival value. Grooming had value; it helped our ancestors detect insects and infections. Gone wild, it becomes compulsive hair pulling. Cleaning up helped people stay healthy; out of control, it becomes ritual hand washing. Checking territorial boundaries helped ward off enemies; in OCD, it becomes checking and rechecking an already locked door (Rapoport, 1989).

The biological perspective explains a great deal, but it cannot explain all aspects of anxiety disorders. It cannot, for example, explain the sharp increase in the anxiety levels of U.S. children and college students over the last half-century. That increase appears related to modern-day concerns—unrealistic expectations, a greater focus on the self rather than the community, and a loss of social support (Twenge, 2000). Nevertheless, it is clear that biology underlies anxiety.

PRACTICE TEST

6. The anxiety disorder that takes the form of an irrational fear of a specific object or situation is called
   a. a phobia.
   b. a panic attack.
   c. generalized anxiety.
   d. an obsessive-compulsive disorder.

7. An episode of intense dread, accompanied by feelings of terror and trembling, dizziness, chest pains, or choking sensations, is called
   a. a specific phobia.
   b. a compulsion.
   c. a panic attack.
   d. an obsessive fear.

8. Marina has become consumed with the need to clean the entire house each day. This behavior may indicate
   a. obsessive-compulsive disorder.
   b. generalized anxiety disorder.
   c. a phobia.
   d. a panic attack.

9. The ability to recover after experiencing severe stress is called
   a. post-traumatic stress disorder.
   b. an anxiety disorder.
   c. fear conditioning.
   d. survivor resiliency.

10. Psychologists who study phobias from a learning perspective explain phobias as
   a. the result of individual genetic makeup.
   b. a way of repressing unacceptable impulses.
   c. conditioned fears.
   d. evidence of the natural selection process.

Answers: 6. a, 7. c, 8. a, 9. d, 10. c.

Dissociative and Personality Disorders

Dissociative Disorders

6: What are dissociative disorders, and why are they controversial?

Among the most bewildering disorders are the rare **dissociative disorders.** The person's conscious awareness is said to become separated—*to dissociate*—from painful memories, thoughts, and feelings. In this state, people may suddenly lose their memory or change their identity, often in response to an overwhelmingly stressful situation.

Dissociation itself is not so rare. Now and then, any one of us may have a fleeting sense of being unreal, of being separated from our body, of watching ourselves as if in a movie. Only when such experiences are severe and prolonged do they suggest a dissociative disorder.

A massive dissociation of self from ordinary consciousness occurs in **dissociative identity disorder (DID)**. At different times, two or more distinct identities seem to control the person's behavior, each with its own voice and mannerisms. Thus, the person may be prim and proper one moment, loud and flirtatious the next. Typically, the original personality denies any awareness of the other(s).

Skeptics have raised some serious questions about DID. First, they find it suspicious that this disorder has such a short history. Between 1930 and 1960, the number of DID diagnoses in North America was 2 per decade. By the 1980s, when the DSM contained the first formal code for this disorder, the number of reported cases had exploded to more than 20,000 (McHugh, 1995a). The average number of displayed personalities also mushroomed—from 3 to 12 per patient (Goff & Simms, 1993).

"Would it be possible to speak with the personality that pays the bills?"

Second, note the skeptics, DID is much less common outside North America, although in other cultures some people are said to be "possessed" by an alien spirit (Aldridge-Morris, 1989; Kluft, 1991). In Britain, DID—which some consider "a wacky American fad" (Cohen, 1995)—is rare. In India and Japan, it is essentially nonexistent. Such findings, say skeptics, point to a cultural explanation. They propose that this disorder is created by therapists in a particular social context (Merskey, 1992).

Third, instead of being a real disorder, some ask, could DID be an extension of the way we vary the "selves" we present, as when we display a goofy, loud self while hanging out with friends, and a subdued, respectful self around grandparents? If so, say the critics, clinicians who discover multiple personalities may merely have triggered role-playing by fantasy-prone people. After all, patients do not enter therapy saying, "Allow me to introduce myselves." Rather, note these skeptics, some therapists go fishing for multiple personalities: "Have you ever felt like another part of you does things you can't control? Does this part of you have a name? Can I talk to the angry part of you?" Once patients permit a therapist to talk, by name, "to the part of you that says those angry things," they begin acting out the fantasy. Like actors who lose themselves in their roles, vulnerable patients may "become" the parts they are acting out. The result may be the experience of another self.

Not everyone agrees with the skeptics. Some researchers and clinicians believe DID is a real disorder. They find support for this view in the distinct brain and body states associated with differing personalities (Putnam, 1991).

If DID is a real disorder, how can we best understand it? Both the psychoanalytic and the learning perspectives interpret DID symptoms as ways of dealing with anxiety. Psychoanalysts see them as defenses against the anxiety caused by unacceptable impulses. For example, an immoral second personality would allow the discharge of forbidden impulses. Learning theorists see dissociative disorders as behaviors reinforced by anxiety reduction.

Other psychologists include dissociative disorders under the umbrella of post-traumatic disorders. In this view, DID would be a natural, protective response to traumatic experiences during childhood (Putnam, 1995). Many DID patients have suffered physical, sexual, or emotional abuse as children (Gleaves, 1996; Kihlstrom, 2005; Lilienfeld & others, 1999). In one study of 12 murderers diagnosed with DID, 11 had suffered severe child abuse, even torture (Lewis & others, 1997). One had been set afire by his parents. Another had been used in child pornography and was scarred from being made to sit on a stove burner.

So the debate continues. On one side are those who believe multiple personalities are the desperate efforts of people trying to detach from a horrific existence. On the other are the skeptics who think DID is a condition constructed out of the therapist–patient interaction and acted out by fantasy-prone, emotionally vulnerable people.

dissociative disorders disorders in which conscious awareness becomes separated (dissociated) from previous memories, thoughts, and feelings.

dissociative identity disorder (DID) a rare dissociative disorder in which a person exhibits two or more distinct and alternating personalities. Also called *multiple personality disorder.*

Multiple personalities :: Chris Sizemore's story told in the book and movie, *The Three Faces of Eve*, gave early visibility to what is now called *dissociative identity disorder.*

Lois Bernstein/Gamma Liaison

Personality Disorders

7: What characteristics are typical of personality disorders?

There is little debate about the reality of **personality disorders.** These disruptive, inflexible, and enduring behavior patterns interfere with a person's social functioning. Some people with these disorders withdraw and avoid social contact. Others interact but do so without responding emotionally.

The most troubling and heavily researched personality disorder is **antisocial personality disorder.** (You may have heard the older terms *sociopath* or *psychopath*.) A person with this disorder is typically a male who shows no conscience in his actions, even toward friends and family. When an antisocial personality combines a keen intelligence with no conscience, the result may be a charming and clever con artist—or worse.

Antisocial personality? :: Dennis Rader, known as the "BTK killer" in Kansas, was convicted in 2005 of killing 10 people over a 30-year span. Rader exhibited the extreme lack of conscience that marks antisocial personality disorder.

Lack of conscience usually becomes plain before age 15, as the person begins to lie, steal, fight, or display unrestrained sexual behavior (Cale & Lilienfeld, 2002). Not all such children become antisocial adults. Those who do (about half of them) will generally be unable to keep a job, irresponsible as a spouse and parent, and violent or otherwise criminal (Farrington, 1991).

Criminal behavior alone does not define antisocial personality disorder. Most criminals show concern for their friends and family members. Antisocial personalities feel and fear little, and the results can be horrifying, as they were in the case of Henry Lee Lucas. He killed his first victim when he was 13. He felt little regret then or later. He confessed that, during his 32 years of crime, he had brutally beaten, suffocated, stabbed, shot, or mutilated some 360 women, men, and children. For the last 6 years of his reign of terror, Lucas teamed with Elwood Toole, who reportedly slaughtered about 50 people he "didn't think was worth living anyhow" (Darrach & Norris, 1984).

Antisocial personality disorder is woven of both biological and psychological strands. No single gene codes for a complex behavior such as crime. There does, however, seem to be a genetic tendency toward an uninhibited approach to life.

Twin and adoption studies reveal that biological relatives of people with antisocial and unemotional tendencies are at increased risk for antisocial behavior (Rhee & Waldman, 2002; Viding & others, 2005). Their genetic vulnerability appears as low levels of arousal. Awaiting events that most people would find unnerving, such as electric shocks or loud noises, they show little bodily arousal (Hare, 1975). Even as youngsters, before committing any crime, they produce lower levels of stress hormones than do others their age **(FIGURE 12.2)**.

Genetic influences help wire the brain. One researcher compared PET scans of 41 murderers' brains with those from people of similar age and sex (Raine, 1999). He found reduced activity in the murderers' frontal lobes, an area of the brain that helps control impulses **(FIGURE 12.3)**.

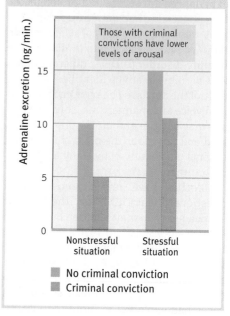

Figure 12.2> Cold-blooded arousability and risk of crime Levels of the stress hormone adrenaline were measured in two groups of 13-year-old Swedish boys. In both stressful and nonstressful situations, those later convicted of a crime (as 18- to 26-year-olds) showed relatively low arousal. (From Magnusson, 1990.)

This reduction was especially apparent in those who murdered impulsively. In a follow-up study, researchers found that violent repeat offenders had 11 percent less frontal lobe tissue than normal

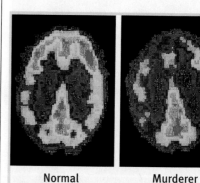

Figure 12.3> Murderous minds PET scans illustrate reduced activation (less red and yellow) in a murderer's frontal lobes—a brain area that helps brake impulsive, aggressive behavior. (From Raine, 1999.)

(Raine & others, 2000). This helps explain another finding. People with antisocial personality disorder fall far below normal in aspects of thinking such as planning, organization, and inhibition, which are all frontal lobe activities (Morgan & Lilienfeld, 2000).

PRACTICE TEST

11. Psychologists debate whether dissociative identity disorder is a real disorder because
    a. people in other cultures are possessed by alien spirits.
    b. it was reported frequently in the 1920s but rarely today.
    c. it is almost never reported outside North America.
    d. its symptoms are nearly identical to those of obsessive-compulsive disorder.

12. A personality disorder, such as antisocial personality, is characterized by
    a. the presence of multiple personalities.
    b. disorganized thinking.
    c. enduring and maladaptive personality traits.
    d. an elevated level of autonomic nervous system arousal.

Answers: 11. c, 12. c.

Substance-Related Disorders

8: What is a substance-related disorder, and what are tolerance, addiction, and dependence?

As we will see in the next chapter, psychiatrists sometimes prescribe drugs to help alleviate the disorders we've been discussing. But there is another category of disorder that actually involves drug use itself.

Most of us manage to use some nonprescription drugs—caffeine, alcohol, and painkillers, for example—in moderation

Table 12.3 — Drug Use or Abuse?

The following DSM guidelines are used to determine when a person crosses the line from drug use to substance abuse.

Maladaptive use of a substance is shown by one of the following:
- Failure to meet obligations.
- Repeated use in situations where it is physically dangerous.
- Continued use despite problems caused by the substance.
- Repeated substance-related legal problems.

and without disrupting our lives. But some of us develop self-harming **substance-related disorders.** People with these disorders may have trouble completing school work, maintaining healthy relationships, or holding a job. Frequent conflicts over getting, using, or not using the drug may interfere with daily life. They may be unable to care for their children. They may drive dangerously or lose control of machinery while under the influence of the substance.

Psychoactive drugs are chemicals that change perceptions and mood. A drug's overall effect depends not only on its *biological* effects but also on the *psychology* of the user's expectations, which vary with *cultures* (Ward, 1994). If one culture assumes that a particular drug produces good feelings or aggression or sexual arousal, and another does not, each culture may find its expectations fulfilled. In the pages that follow, we'll take a closer look at these interacting forces in the use and potential abuse of particular psychoactive drugs. (See **TABLE 12.3** for the DSM guidelines for substance abuse.) But first, let's see how our bodies react to the ongoing use of psychoactive drugs, which helps explain why these substances can lead to deviant, distressful, and dysfunctional behaviors.

Tolerance, Addiction, and Dependence

Why might a person who rarely drinks alcohol get tipsy on one can of beer, while a long-term drinker shows few effects until the second six-pack? The answer is **tolerance.** With continued use of alcohol and some other drugs, the user's brain chemistry adapts to offset the drug's effect. So, to experience the same result, the user needs to take larger and larger doses of the substance. These ever-increasing doses can become a serious threat to health. In some cases, they lead to **addiction:** The user craves the substance despite possible unpleasant consequences.

Regular users often try to fight their addiction. But abruptly stopping the use of a drug can lead to undesirable side effects known as **withdrawal.** Heavy coffee

personality disorders psychological disorders characterized by inflexible and enduring behavior patterns that impair social functioning.

antisocial personality disorder a personality disorder in which the person (usually a man) exhibits a lack of conscience for wrongdoing, even toward friends and family members. May be aggressive and ruthless or a clever con artist.

substance-related disorders a maladaptive pattern of substance use leading to clinically significant impairment or distress.

psychoactive drug a chemical substance that alters perceptions and mood.

tolerance the diminishing effect with regular use of the same dose of a drug, requiring the user to take larger and larger doses before experiencing the drug's effect.

addiction compulsive drug craving and use.

withdrawal the discomfort and distress that follow discontinuing the use of an addictive drug.

| Table 12.4 | What Is Substance Dependence? |

According to the DSM, presence of three or more of the following indicates *dependence* on a substance.

- Tolerance (a lessening effect requires larger doses).
- Withdrawal (aversive symptoms when discontinued).
- Taking the substance for a longer time, or in a greater amount, than intended.
- Little desire or effort to regulate use.
- Much time spent in activities related to obtaining the substance.
- Normal activities given up or reduced.
- Use continues despite knowing that it worsens problems.

drinkers who skip their usual caffeine fix know the feeling when a headache or grogginess strikes. With more serious drugs like heroin, the physical pain and intense cravings of withdrawal are evidence of **physical dependence.**

People can also develop **psychological dependence,** particularly for stress-relieving drugs, such as alcohol. Although not always physically addictive, such drugs may nevertheless become an important part of the user's life, often as a way of relieving negative emotions. For someone who is either physically or psychologically dependent, obtaining and using the drug can become the main focus of the day, interfering with other activities **(TABLE 12.4).**

Types of Psychoactive Drugs

9: What are the three main types of psychoactive drugs, and what are their effects?

Psychoactive drugs include *depressants, stimulants,* and *hallucinogens.* Drugs in all three categories do their work at the brain's synapses. They achieve their effect by increasing, decreasing, or mimicking the activity of neurotransmitters, the brain's chemical messengers. But our expectations also play a role in the ways these drugs affect us.

Depressants

Depressants are drugs such as alcohol and opiates that calm neural activity and slow body functions. Let's take a closer look at alcohol.

Alcohol True or false? In large amounts, alcohol is a depressant; in small amounts, it is a stimulant.

False. Low doses of alcohol may, indeed, enliven a drinker, but they do so by acting as a *disinhibitor*—they slow brain activity that controls judgment and inhibitions. (This activity is part of what happens when you think about doing something, decide it's a *really* bad idea, and then don't do it.) Alcohol is an equal-opportunity drug. It increases harmful tendencies—as when sexually aggressive college men lower their dates' inhibitions by getting them to drink (Abbey, 1991;

"That is not one of the seven habits of highly effective people."

Mosher & Anderson, 1986). And it increases helpful tendencies, as when tipsy restaurant patrons leave big tips (M. Lynn, 1988). *The urges you would feel if sober are the ones you will more likely act upon after drinking.*

A University of Illinois campus survey showed that before sexual assaults, 80 percent of the male attackers and 70 percent of the female victims had been drinking (Camper, 1990). Another survey of 89,874 American collegians found alcohol or drugs involved in 79 percent of unwanted sexual intercourse experiences (Presley & others, 1997).

Low doses of alcohol relax the drinker by slowing sympathetic nervous system activity. With larger doses, reactions slow, speech slurs, and skilled performance declines. Paired with lack of sleep, alcohol is a potent sedative. Add these physical effects to lowered inhibitions, and the result can be deadly. Worldwide, several hundred thousand lives are lost each year in alcohol-related accidents and violent crime. When sober, most drinkers believe that driving under the influence of alcohol is wrong, and they insist they would not do so. That belief disappears as blood-alcohol level rises and moral judgments become fuzzy. Most will drive home from a bar, even if given a breathalyzer test and told they are intoxicated (Denton & Krebs, 1990; MacDonald & others, 1995).

Some people drink to forget their troubles. And forget they do—alcohol disrupts the processing of recent experiences into long-term memories. Thus, heavy drinkers may not recall people they met the night before or what they said or did while drunk. These blackouts result partly from the way alcohol suppresses REM sleep, which normally would help fix the day's experiences into permanent memories.

Alcohol can affect thinking in a more permanent way, especially in those with **alcohol dependence.** Such prolonged and excessive drinking can shrink the brain,

Facts: College and university students drink more alcohol than their nonstudent peers, and they spend more on alcohol than on books and other beverages combined. Fraternity and sorority members drink three times as much as other students (Atwell, 1986; Malloy, 1994; Slutske, 2005). Although few university students believe they have an alcohol problem, many meet the criteria for alcohol abuse (Marlatt, 1991). As students mature with age, they drink less.

Drinking disaster demo :: Firefighters re-enacted the trauma of an alcohol-related car accident, providing a memorable demonstration for these high school students. Alcohol consumption leads to feelings of invincibility, which become especially dangerous behind the wheel of a car.

Lon C. Diehl/Photo Edit

most intensely in women **(FIGURE 12.4),** who have less of a stomach enzyme that digests alcohol (Wuethrich, 2001). Girls and young women can also become addicted to alcohol more quickly than boys and young men do. They also suffer lung, brain, and liver damage at lower consumption levels (CASA, 2003).

A strong correlation between early drinking and later dependence shows in a national survey of 43,000 adults. Of those who began drinking alcohol before age 14, about half (47 percent) later became alcohol dependent (Hingson & others, 2006). Of those who began drinking at age 21 or after, only 9 percent showed this dependency. These correlations held after controlling for smoking, family alcohol history, and antisocial behaviors.

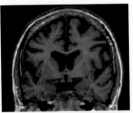

Scan of woman
with alcoholism

Daniel Hommer, NIAAA, NIH, HHS

Scan of woman
without alcoholism

Figure 12.4> Alcoholism shrinks the brain MRI scans show brain shrinkage in women with alcoholism (top) compared with women in a control group (bottom).

Warning signs of alcohol dependence

- Drinking binges
- Regretting things done or said when drunk
- Feeling low or guilty after drinking
- Failing to honor a resolve to drink less
- Drinking to alleviate depression or anxiety
- Avoiding family or friends when drinking

As with other psychoactive drugs, users' behavior depends in part on their expectations. When people *believe* that alcohol affects social behavior in certain ways, and *believe*, rightly or wrongly, that they have been drinking alcohol, they will behave accordingly (Leigh, 1989). Consider one such experiment. Researchers gave college men who volunteered for a study on "alcohol and sexual stimulation"

Fact: In a Harvard School of Public Health survey of 18,000 students at 140 colleges and universities, almost 9 in 10 students reported abuse by intoxicated peers, including sleep and study interruption, insults, sexual advances, and property damage (Wechsler & others, 1994). In a follow-up survey, 44 percent of students admitted binge drinking within the previous two weeks (Wechsler & others, 2002).

either an alcoholic or a nonalcoholic drink (Abrams & Wilson, 1983). (Both had strong tastes that masked any alcohol.) In each group, half the participants thought

physical dependence a physiological need for a drug, marked by unpleasant withdrawal symptoms when the drug is discontinued.

psychological dependence a psychological need to use a drug, such as to relieve negative emotions.

depressants drugs (such as alcohol, barbiturates, and opiates) that reduce neural activity and slow body functions.

alcohol dependence (popularly known as alcoholism). Alcohol use marked by tolerance, withdrawal if suspended, and a drive to continue use.

Fact: Drinking contributes to 1400 annual U.S. college student deaths, 70,000 sexual assaults, and 500,000 injuries (Hingson & others, 2002).

they were drinking alcohol and half thought they were not. After watching an erotic movie clip, the men who *thought* they had consumed alcohol were more likely to report having strong sexual fantasies and feeling guilt-free. Being able to *attribute* their sexual responses to alcohol released their inhibitions—whether or not they had actually been drinking. If, as commonly believed, liquor is the quicker pick-her-upper, the effect lies partly in that powerful sex organ, the mind.

Barbiturates Like alcohol, the **barbiturate** drugs, or *tranquilizers,* depress nervous system activity. Barbiturates such as Nembutal, Seconal, and Amytal are sometimes prescribed to induce sleep or reduce anxiety. In larger doses, they can impair memory and judgment. If combined with alcohol, the total depressive effect on body functions can lead to death. This sometimes happens when people take a sleeping pill after an evening of heavy drinking.

Opiates The **opiates**—opium and its offshoots, morphine and heroin—also depress nervous system activity. Pupils constrict, breathing slows, and a feeling of extreme relaxation sets in, as blissful pleasure replaces pain and anxiety. But for this short-term pleasure, opiate users may pay a long-term price: a gnawing craving for another fix, a need for progressively larger doses (as tolerance develops), and the extreme discomfort of withdrawal. When repeatedly flooded with an artificial opiate, the brain eventually stops producing *endorphins,* its own feel-good opiates. If the artificial opiate is then withdrawn, the brain lacks the normal level of these natural painkillers. Those who cannot or choose not to endure this state may pay an ultimate price—death by overdose. Methadone, a synthetic opiate drug prescribed as a substitute for heroin or for relief of chronic pain, can also produce tolerance and dependence.

Stimulants

A **stimulant's** effect is opposite to that of a depressant. A stimulant excites neural activity and speeds up body functions. Pupils dilate. Heart and breathing rates increase. Blood-sugar levels rise, causing a drop in appetite. Energy and self-confidence also rise.

This category of drugs includes caffeine, nicotine, the **amphetamines,** cocaine, methamphetamine, and Ecstasy (NIDA, 2002, 2005). People use stimulants to feel alert, lose weight, or boost mood or athletic performance. Unfortunately, stimulants can be addictive. You may know this if you are one of the many people who use caffeine daily in your coffee, tea, soda, chocolate, or energy drinks. Cut off from their usual dose, caffeine drinkers may crash into fatigue, headaches, irritability, and depression (Silverman & others, 1992).

"There is an overwhelming medical and scientific consensus that cigarette smoking causes lung cancer, heart disease, emphysema, and other serious diseases in smokers. Smokers are far more likely to develop serious diseases, like lung cancer, than nonsmokers."

Philip Morris Companies Inc., 1999

Nicotine One of the most addictive stimulants is **nicotine,** found in cigarettes and other tobacco products. If you are a smoker who has tried to kick your habit, you won't be surprised to hear that tobacco products are as addictive as heroin and cocaine. Addicted customers are loyal customers. As with other addictions, smokers become *dependent,* and they develop *tolerance.* But nicotine is not only mood-altering, it is also reinforcing.

Asked "If you had to do it all over again, would you start smoking?" more than 85 percent of adult smokers answer No (Slovic & others, 2002).

A burning cigarette is a portable nicotine dispenser. Within 7 seconds, a rush of nicotine signals the central nervous system

Nic-a-teen :: Virtually nobody starts smoking past the vulnerable teen years. Eager to hook customers whose addiction will give them business for years to come, cigarette companies target teens. Portrayals of tough, appealing, socially adept smokers in popular movies (such as Sarah Michelle Gellar, pictured here in *I Know What You Did Last Summer*) entice teens to imitate.

Columbia Pictures/courtesy Everett Collection

to release a flood of neurotransmitters **(FIGURE 12.5).** Epinephrine and norepinephrine diminish appetite and boost alertness and mental efficiency. Dopamine and opioids calm anxiety and reduce sensitivity to pain (Nowak, 1994; Scott & others, 2004).

"A cigarette in the hands of a Hollywood star on screen is a gun aimed at a 12- or 14-year-old."

Screenwriter Joe Eszterhas, 2002

These rewards keep people smoking even when they wish they could stop. Each year, fewer than 1 in 7 smokers who want to quit will be able to resist nicotine withdrawal symptoms, which include craving, insomnia, anxiety, and irritability. Even those who know they are committing slow-motion suicide may be unable to stop (Saad, 2002).

Nevertheless, repeated attempts seem to pay off. Half of all Americans who have

"To cease smoking is the easiest thing I ever did; I ought to know because I've done it a thousand times."

Mark Twain (1835–1910)

Figure 12.5> Where there's smoke . . . : The physiological effects of nicotine

Nicotine reaches the brain within 7 seconds, twice as fast as intravenous heroin. Within minutes, the amount in the blood soars.

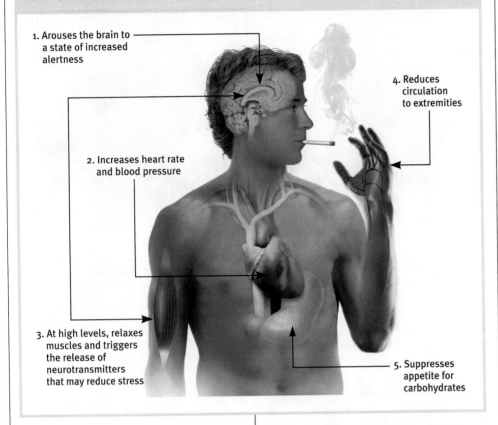

1. Arouses the brain to a state of increased alertness

2. Increases heart rate and blood pressure

3. At high levels, relaxes muscles and triggers the release of neurotransmitters that may reduce stress

4. Reduces circulation to extremities

5. Suppresses appetite for carbohydrates

ever smoked have quit, and more than 90 percent did so on their own. The acute craving and withdrawal symptoms do go away gradually over six months (Ward & others, 1997).

Cocaine Cocaine users travel a fast track from flying high to crashing to earth. Cocaine is snorted, injected, or smoked. It enters the bloodstream quickly, producing a rush that continues until the brain's supply of the neurotransmitters dopamine, serotonin, and norepinephrine drops off (**FIGURE 12.6** on the next page).

The recipe for Coca-Cola originally included an extract of the coca plant, creating a cocaine tonic for tired elderly people. Between 1896 and 1905, Coke was indeed "the real thing."

Then, within a mere 15 to 30 minutes, a crash of agitated depression follows. Many regular cocaine users chasing this high become addicted. In the lab, cocaine-addicted monkeys have pressed levers more than 12,000 times to gain one cocaine injection (Siegel, 1990).

"Cocaine makes you a new man. And the first thing that new man wants is more cocaine."

Comedian George Carlin (1937–2008)

In national surveys, 5 percent of U.S. high school seniors and 5 percent of British 18- to 24-year olds reported having tried cocaine during the past year (Home Office, 2003; Johnston & others, 2005). Nearly half of the drug-using

seniors had smoked *crack*. These faster-working, potent cocaine crystals produce a briefer but more intense high followed by a more intense crash. The craving for more wanes after several hours, only to return several days later (Gawin, 1991).

Cocaine's psychological effects depend in part on the dosage and form consumed. But as with all psychoactive drugs, the situation and the user's expectations and personality play a role. Given a placebo, cocaine users who *think* they are taking cocaine often have a cocaine-like experience (Van Dyke & Byck, 1982).

Methamphetamine This drug is more addictive than most stimulants. **Methamphetamine** triggers the release of the neurotransmitter dopamine, which stimulates brain cells that enhance energy and mood. The drug's powerful effects include eight or so hours of heightened energy and mood. Its aftereffects may include irritability, insomnia, high blood pressure, seizures, periods of disorientation, and occasional violent behavior. Over time, methamphetamine use appears to permanently reduce the brain's normal output of dopamine.

barbiturates drugs that depress the activity of the central nervous system, reducing anxiety but impairing memory and judgment.

opiates opium and its derivatives, such as morphine and heroin; they depress neural activity, temporarily lessening pain and anxiety.

stimulants drugs (such as caffeine, nicotine, and the more powerful amphetamines, cocaine, and Ecstasy) that excite neural activity and speed up body functions.

amphetamines drugs that stimulate neural activity, causing speeded-up body functions and associated energy and mood changes.

nicotine a stimulating and highly addictive psychoactive drug in tobacco.

methamphetamine a powerfully addictive drug that stimulates the central nervous system with speeded-up body functions and associated energy and mood changes; over time, appears to reduce baseline dopamine levels.

Figure 12.6> Cocaine euphoria and crash

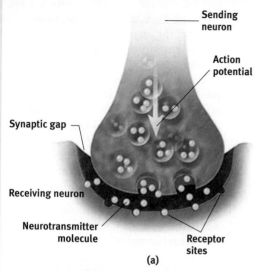

Sending neuron

Action potential

Synaptic gap

Receiving neuron

Neurotransmitter molecule

Receptor sites

(a)

Neurotransmitters carry a message from a sending neuron across a synapse to receptor sites on a receiving neuron.

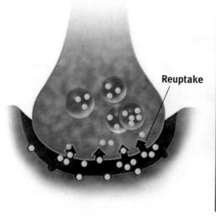

Reuptake

(b)

The sending neuron normally reabsorbs excess neurotransmitter molecules, a process called reuptake.

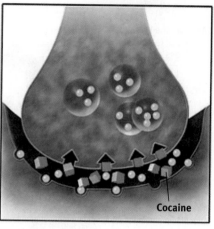

Cocaine

(c)

By binding to the sites that normally reabsorb neurotransmitter molecules, cocaine blocks reuptake of dopamine, norepinephrine, and serotonin (Ray & Ksir, 1990). The extra neurotransmitter molecules therefore remain in the synapse, intensifying their normal mood-altering effects and producing a euphoric rush. When the cocaine level drops, the absence of these neurotransmitters produces a crash.

Ecstasy **Ecstasy** is the street name for **MDMA** (methylenedioxymethamphetamine). This powerful drug is both a stimulant and a mild hallucinogen. (*Hallucinogens*, as we will see in the next section, distort perceptions and lead to false sensory images.) Ecstasy is an amphetamine derivative. Like many other drugs, it affects neurotransmitters. It triggers the release of dopamine. But its major effect is achieved by influencing the serotonin system. It releases stored serotonin and blocks its reuptake, thus prolonging serotonin's feel-good flood (Braun, 2001). Users feel the effect about a half-hour after taking an Ecstasy pill. For three or four hours, they experience feelings of euphoria. They feel intimately connected to the people around them. ("I love everyone.")

During the late 1990s, Ecstasy's popularity soared as a "club drug" taken at night clubs and all-night raves (Landry, 2002). There are, however, reasons not to be ecstatic about Ecstasy. One is its ability

The hug drug :: MDMA, known as Ecstasy, produces a euphoric high and feelings of intimacy. But repeated use destroys serotonin-producing neurons and may permanently deflate mood and impair memory.

AP Photo/Dale Sparks

to cause dehydration. With prolonged dancing, Ecstasy's side effects can lead to severe overheating, increased blood pressure, and death. Long-term, repeated use can also damage serotonin-producing neurons. This decreased output can be permanent and can lead to a permanently depressed mood (Croft & others, 2001; McCann & others, 2001; Roiser & others, 2005). Serotonin does more than just make us feel good. It helps regulate our body rhythms (including sleep), our disease-fighting immune system, and our memory and other cognitive functions (Biello & Dafters, 2001; Pacifici & others, 2001; Reneman & others, 2001). Ecstasy interferes with all of these functions. It delights for the night but darkens our tomorrows.

Hallucinogens

Among the least addictive drugs are the **hallucinogens.** These substances distort perceptions and call up sensory images

THE FAR SIDE® BY GARY LARSON

Before

After

And then suddenly, I saw this bright light at the end of a tunnel!

(such as sounds or sights) without any input from the senses. This helps explain why these drugs are also called *psychedelics*, meaning "mind-manifesting." Some are synthetic. The best known synthetic hallucinogens are MDMA (Ecstasy), discussed earlier, and LSD. Others, such as the mild hallucinogen marijuana, are natural substances.

LSD In 1943, Albert Hofmann reported perceiving "an uninterrupted stream of fantastic pictures, extraordinary shapes with an intense, kaleidoscopic play of colors" (Siegel, 1984). Hofmann, a chemist, had created and accidentally ingested **LSD** (lysergic acid diethylamide). LSD, like Ecstasy, interferes with the serotonin neurotransmitter system. LSD and other powerful hallucinogens are chemically similar to one type of serotonin and can therefore block its actions (Jacobs, 1987). An LSD "trip" can take users to unexpected places. Emotions may vary from euphoria to detachment to panic, depending in part on the person's current mood and expectations.

Even so, the perceptual distortions and hallucinations have some things in common. Psychologist Ronald Siegel (1982) reports that whether you provoke your brain to hallucinate by drugs, loss of

oxygen, or extreme sensory deprivation, "it will hallucinate in basically the same way." The experience typically begins with simple geometric forms, such as a criss-cross, a cobweb, or a spiral. The next phase consists of more meaningful images. Some may be seen in front of a tunnel, others may be replays of past emotional experiences. As the hallucination peaks, users frequently feel separated from their bodies. Dreamlike scenes feel so real that people may become panic-stricken or harm themselves.

These sensations are strikingly similar to the **near-death experience.** This altered state of consciousness is reported by about one-third of those who survive a brush with death, as when revived from cardiac arrest (Moody, 1976; Ring, 1980; Schnaper, 1980). Many experience visions of tunnels **(FIGURE 12.7),** bright lights or beings of light, a replay of old memories, and out-of-body sensations (Siegel, 1980). Oxygen deprivation and other insults to the brain can produce hallucinations. Following temporal lobe seizures, for example, patients have reported similarly

Figure 12.7> Near-death vision or hallucination? Psychologist Ronald Siegel (1977) reported that people under the influence of hallucinogenic drugs often see "a bright light in the center of the field of vision. . . . The location of this point of light create[s] a tunnel-like perspective." This is very similar to others' reported near-death experiences.

profound mystical experiences. So have solitary sailors and polar explorers while enduring monotony, isolation, and cold (Suedfeld & Mocellin, 1987). Under stress, the brain can manufacture seeming near-death experiences.

Marijuana For 5000 years, hemp has been cultivated for its fiber. The leaves and flowers of this plant, which are sold as *marijuana,* contain **THC** (delta-9-tetrahydrocannabinol). Whether smoked (getting to the brain in a mere 7 seconds) or eaten (producing slower, less intense effects), THC produces a mix of effects that makes marijuana a difficult drug to classify. Like alcohol, marijuana relaxes, disinhibits, and may produce a euphoric high. But marijuana is also a mild hallucinogen, increasing sensitivity to colors, sounds, tastes, and smells.

The odds of getting hooked after trying various drugs:

Marijuana:	9 percent
Alcohol:	15 percent
Cocaine:	17 percent
Heroin:	23 percent
Tobacco:	32 percent

Source: National Academy of Science, Institute of Medicine (Brody, 2003).

Ecstasy (MDMA) a synthetic stimulant and mild hallucinogen. Produces euphoria and social intimacy, but with short-term health risks and longer-term harm to serotonin-producing neurons and to mood and cognition.

hallucinogens psychedelic ("mind-manifesting") drugs, such as LSD, that distort perceptions and evoke sensory images in the absence of sensory input.

LSD a powerful hallucinogenic drug; also known as *acid (lysergic acid diethylamide).*

near-death experience an altered state of consciousness reported after a close brush with death (such as through cardiac arrest); often similar to drug-induced hallucinations.

THC the major active ingredient in marijuana; triggers a variety of effects, including mild hallucinations.

Marijuana is like alcohol in other ways. Both impair the motor coordination, perceptual skills, and reaction time necessary for safely operating an automobile or other machine. "THC causes animals to misjudge events," reports Ronald Siegel (1990, p. 163). "Pigeons wait too long to respond to buzzers or lights that tell them food is available for brief periods; and rats turn the wrong way in mazes."

But unlike alcohol, which the body eliminates within hours, THC and its byproducts linger in the body for a month or more. Thus, regular users may achieve a high with smaller amounts of the drug than would be needed by an occasional user. This is contrary to the usual path of tolerance, in which repeat users need to take larger doses to feel the same effect. Marijuana also disrupts memory formation and interferes with immediate recall of information learned only a few minutes before. Such effects on thinking outlast the period of smoking (Pope & Yurgelun-Todd, 1996; Smith, 1995).

A user's experience can vary with the situation. If the user feels anxious or depressed, marijuana may intensify these feelings. The more often the person uses it, the greater the risk of anxiety, depres-

sion, or, possibly, schizophrenia. These correlations held even after controlling for other drug use and personal traits (Arseneault & others, 2002; Patton & others, 2002; Zammit & others, 2002).

How does marijuana alter thought processes, movements, and moods? Scientists shed light on this question when they made an exciting discovery. Dense groups of THC-sensitive receptors exist in our brain's frontal lobes, limbic system, and motor cortex (Iversen, 2000). Why would our brain be equipped with THC-sensitive receptors? The answer had to be that something very much like THC regularly passes through the brain and binds with these receptors. These THC-like molecules may naturally control pain. If so, this would help explain why marijuana can relieve the pain, nausea, and severe weight loss associated with diseases such as AIDS (Watson & others, 2000). Some states have passed laws allowing marijuana to be used for medical purposes. In such cases, the Institute of Medicine recommends medical inhalers to deliver the THC, thereby avoiding the toxic marijuana smoke, which, like cigarette smoke, can cause cancer and other conditions.

* * *

TABLE 12.5 summarizes many of the psychoactive drugs discussed in this section. All of them share some common features. They trigger negative aftereffects that counter the drug's immediate positive effects. These negative aftereffects grow stronger with repetition. Except with marijuana, as the opposing, negative aftereffects grow stronger, it takes larger and larger doses to produce the desired positive effect. (This process is *tolerance*.) These increasingly larger doses produce even worse aftereffects in the drug's absence. (This process is *withdrawal*.) The worsening aftereffects in turn create a need to switch off the withdrawal symptoms by taking yet more of the drug. (This process is *addiction*.)

Understanding Substance Abuse

10: Why do some people abuse mind-altering drugs?

Substance abuse by North American youth increased during the 1970s. Then, with increased drug education and a shift toward more realism in media portrayals

Table 12.5	A Guide to Selected Psychoactive Drugs		
Drug	**Type**	**Pleasurable Effects**	**Negative Aftereffects**
Alcohol	Depressant	Initial high followed by relaxation and disinhibition	Impaired reactions, depression, memory loss, organ damage
Heroin	Depressant	Rush of euphoria, relief from pain	Depressed physiology, agonizing withdrawal
Caffeine	Stimulant	Increased alertness and wakefulness	In high doses, anxiety, restlessness, and insomnia; uncomfortable withdrawal
Nicotine	Stimulant	Arousal and relaxation, sense of well-being	Heart disease, cancer
Cocaine	Stimulant	Rush of euphoria, confidence, energy	Cardiovascular stress, suspiciousness, depressive crash
Methamphetamine	Stimulant	Euphoria, alertness, energy	Irritability, insomnia, high blood pressure, seizures
Ecstasy (MDMA)	Stimulant; mild hallucinogen	Euphoria, disinhibition	Dehydration, overheating, depressed mood, impaired cognitive and immune functioning
LSD	Hallucinogen	Visual "trip"	Risk of panic
Marijuana	Mild hallucinogen	Enhanced sensation, relief of pain, distortion of time, relaxation	Impaired learning and memory, increased risk of psychological disorders, lung damage from smoke

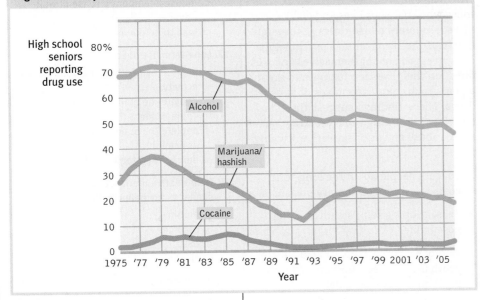

Figure 12.8> Trends in drug use The percentage of U.S. high school seniors who report having used alcohol, marijuana, or cocaine during the past 30 days peaked in the late 1970s. After declining for more than a decade, drug use partially rebounded in 1992, and remained higher for a few years before another slight decline. (From Johnston & others, 2008.)

of the effects of drugs, substance abuse declined sharply. After the early 1990s, the cultural antidrug voice softened, and drugs for a time were again glamorized in some music and films **(FIGURE 12.8)**.

For some adolescents, occasional drug use represents thrill seeking. Why, though, do other adolescents become regular drug abusers? In search of answers, researchers have tried to sort out biological, psychological, and social-cultural influences.

Biological Influences

Are some of us biologically vulnerable to particular drugs? Some evidence indicates we are (Crabbe, 2002).

- Adopted individuals are more likely to develop alcohol dependence if one or both biological parents have a history of it.

- Having an identical twin with alcohol dependence puts one at increased risk for alcohol problems (Kendler & others, 2002). This increased risk is not found among fraternal twins. In marijuana use also, identical twins more closely resemble each other than do fraternal twins.

- Boys who at age 6 are excitable, impulsive, and fearless (genetically influenced traits) are more likely as teens to smoke, drink, and abuse other drugs (Masse & Tremblay, 1997).

- Researchers have bred rats and mice that prefer alcoholic drinks to water. One such strain has low levels of a brain chemical called *NPY*. Mice bred to *overproduce* NPY are very sensitive to alcohol's sedating effect and drink little (Thiele & others, 1998).

- Some genes are more common among people and animals predisposed to alcohol dependence. These genes may, for example, produce deficiencies in the brain's natural dopamine reward system.

Psychological and Social-Cultural Influences

Throughout this text, you have seen a recurring theme. Biological, psychological, and social-cultural influences interact to produce behavior. So, too, with substance abuse. Feeling that one's life

is meaningless and directionless is a psychological influence that puts youth and young adults at risk (Newcomb & Harlow, 1986). This feeling is common among school dropouts who try to make their way in life without job skills, without privilege, and with little hope. The ups and downs of marijuana usage among young people seem predicted by another psychological factor—their perception of the risk involved in using marijuana. When perceived risk rises, usage falls (Johnston & others, 2007).

Sometimes, the psychological influence is more obvious. Many heavy users of alcohol, marijuana, and cocaine have experienced significant stress or failure and are depressed. Monkeys develop a taste for alcohol when stressed by permanent separation from their mothers at birth (Small, 2002). Girls with a history of depression, eating disorders, or sexual or physical abuse are at risk for substance addiction. So are youth undergoing school or neighborhood transitions (CASA, 2003; Logan & others, 2002). By temporarily dulling the pain of self-awareness, alcohol and other drugs may offer a way to avoid coping with depression, anger, anxiety, or insomnia. As Chapter 6 explains, behavior is often controlled more by its immediate consequences than by its later ones.

Especially for teenagers, substance abuse can also have social roots. Rates of substance abuse vary across cultural and ethnic groups. Among the Amish, Mennonites, Mormons, and Orthodox Jews, alcohol and other substance addiction rates are extremely low (Trimble, 1994). Among African-American teens, rates of drinking, smoking, and cocaine use are sharply lower than among other U.S. teens (Bass & Kane-Williams, 1993; ISR, 2003; Kann & others, 1993).

For those whose genetic predispositions nudge them toward substance abuse, location makes a difference. Cities offer more opportunities and less supervision (Legrand & others, 2005). Relatively drug-free small towns and rural areas tend to exert an influence in the opposite direction.

SNAPSHOTS

Once upon a time, peer pressure caused Bob to start smoking.

RESTAURANT

Twenty years later, it forces him to quit.

(C) Love A|4

© Jason Love

In the real world, alcohol accounts for one-sixth or less of beverage use. In TV land, drinking alcohol occurs more often than the combined drinking of coffee, tea, soft drinks, and water (Gerbner, 1990).

Regardless of location, peers influence attitudes about drugs. They throw the parties and provide (or don't provide) the drugs. If an adolescent's friends abuse drugs, the odds are that he or she will, too. If the friends do not, the opportunity may not even arise. But peer influence is more than what friends do and say. Adolescents' expectations—what they *believe* their friends are doing and favoring—influence their behavior. In one study covering 22 U.S. states, 14 percent of the sixth-graders surveyed believed their friends had smoked marijuana. How many of those friends said they had smoked it? Only 4 percent (Wren, 1999). When the substance is alcohol, young adolescents consume more after overestimating their friends' use (Aas & Klepp, 1992; Graham & others, 1991). College students are not immune to such misperceptions. Drinking dominates social occasions partly because students overestimate their fellow students' enthusiasm

for alcohol (Prentice & Miller, 1993; Self, 1994). As always with correlations, the traffic between friends' drug use and our own may be two-way: Our friends influence us, but we also select as friends those who share our likes and dislikes.

People rarely abuse drugs if they understand the physical and psychological costs, feel good about themselves and the direction their lives are taking, and are in a peer group that disapproves of abusing drugs. These findings suggest three tactics for preventing and treating substance abuse and addiction among young people.

■ Educate people about the long-term costs of a drug's temporary pleasures.

■ Boost people's self-esteem and purpose in life.

■ Modify peer associations or "inoculate" youth against peer pressures by training them in refusal skills.

In Chapter 13, we'll consider treatments for substance abuse in more detail.

PRACTICE TEST

13. Continued use of a psychoactive drug produces tolerance. This usually means that the user will

a. feel physical pain and intense craving.
b. be irreversibly addicted to the substance.
c. need to take larger doses to get the desired effect.
d. be able to take smaller doses to get the desired effect.

14. The depressants include alcohol, barbiturates,

a. and opiates.
b. cocaine, and morphine.
c. caffeine, nicotine, and marijuana.
d. and amphetamines.

15. Because alcohol _____, it may make a person more helpful or more aggressive.

a. causes alcoholic blackouts
b. destroys REM sleep
c. produces hallucinations
d. lowers inhibitions

16. Nicotine and cocaine stimulate neural activity, speed up body functions, and

a. induce sensory hallucinations.
b. interfere with memory.
c. induce a temporary sense of well-being.
d. lead to heroin use.

17. Long-term use of Ecstasy can

a. depress sympathetic nervous system activity.
b. deplete the brain's supply of epinephrine.
c. deplete the brain's supply of dopamine.
d. damage serotonin-producing neurons.

18. Near-death experiences are strikingly similar to the hallucinations evoked by

a. heroin.
b. cocaine.
c. LSD.
d. alcohol.

19. Use of marijuana

a. impairs motor coordination, perception, reaction time, and memory.
b. inhibits people's emotions.
c. leads to dehydration and overheating.
d. stimulates brain cell development.

20. Social explanations for drug use often focus on the effect of peer influence. An important *psychological* contributor to drug use is

a. inflated self-esteem.
b. the feeling that life is meaningless and directionless.
c. genetic predispositions.
d. overprotective parents.

Answers: 13. c, 14. a, 15. d, 16. c, 17. d, 18. c, 19. a, 20. b.

Mood Disorders

11: What are mood disorders, and what forms do they take?

Just as most of us have indirectly or directly had some experience with substance-related disorders, many of us have also had close encounters with **mood disorders.** These disorders are characterized by emotional extremes. They appear in two principal forms.

Major depressive disorder is a prolonged state of hopeless depression. *Bipolar disorder* is a chronic alternation between depression and overexcited hyperactivity.

Anxiety is a response to the threat of future loss. Depressed mood is often a response to past and current loss. To feel bad in reaction to very sad events (such as the death of a loved one) is to be in touch with reality. In such times, depression is like a car's oil light—a signal that warns us to stop and take protective measures.

Perhaps you, like many students, have experienced some of the symptoms of depression. Perhaps you wanted to go to college right out of high school, but you couldn't afford it, and now you are struggling to find time for school amid family and work responsibilities. Perhaps social stresses, such as a relationship gone sour, or a feeling of being excluded from a group, have made you feel isolated or plunged you into despair. And perhaps you find yourself dwelling on these thoughts. You may feel deeply discouraged about your life or your future. You may lack the energy to get things done or even to force yourself out of bed. You may be unable to concentrate, eat, or sleep normally; or even occasionally wonder if you would be better off dead. These feelings are more likely to strike during the dark months of winter than the bright days of summer.

For some people, recurring depression during winter's dark months constitutes a "seasonal affective disorder." For others, winter darkness means more blue moods. When asked "Have you cried today?" Americans answered "yes" more often in the winter:

	Percentage answering yes	
	Men	Women
August	4%	7%
December	8%	21%

Source: Time/CNN survey, 1994.

From an evolutionary perspective, depression makes sense. Biologically speaking, life's purpose is survival and reproduction, not happiness. Coughing, vomiting, and various forms of pain protect our body from dangerous toxins. Similarly, depression protects our mind. It slows us down, defuses aggression, and cuts back on risk taking (Allen & Badcock, 2003). Grinding temporarily to a halt and thinking hard, as we do when depressed, give us time to consider our options when we feel threatened. After reassessing our life, we may redirect energy in more promising ways. But sometimes, depression becomes seriously maladaptive. How do we recognize the fine line between normal and abnormal behavior?

> "If someone offered you a pill that would make you permanently happy, you would be well advised to run fast and run far. Emotion is a compass that tells us what to do, and a compass that is perpetually stuck on NORTH is worthless."
>
> Daniel Gilbert, *The Science of Happiness*, 2006

Major Depressive Disorder

Joy, contentment, sadness, and despair are different points on a continuum, points at which any of us may be found at any given moment. The difference between a blue mood after bad news and **major depressive disorder** is like the difference between gasping for breath for a few minutes after a hard run and being always short of breath. Major depressive disorder occurs when signs of depression last two or more weeks and are not caused by drugs or a medical condition. These signs include lethargy (extreme lack of energy), feelings of worthlessness, or loss of interest in family, friends, and activities. To sense what major depression feels like, suggest some clinicians, imagine combining the anguish of grief with the exhaustion you feel after pulling an all-nighter.

Although phobias are more common, depression is the number one reason people seek mental health services. Worldwide, it is the leading cause of disability. In any given year, 5.8 percent of men and 9.5 percent of women will have a depressive episode (World Health Organization, 2001). With or without therapy, most of these people will temporarily or permanently return to their previous behavior patterns.

Bipolar Disorder

In **bipolar disorder,** when the depressive episode ends, people fly to the opposite emotional extreme. This intensely happy, hyperactive, wildly optimistic state is called **mania.** If depression is living in slow motion, mania is fast forward. But before long, the elated mood either returns to normal or plunges into a depression.

During the manic phase of bipolar disorder, people are typically overtalkative, overactive, and elated (though easily irritated if crossed). They feel little need for sleep. They show fewer sexual inhibitions. One of mania's maladaptive symptoms is extreme optimism and self-esteem. Thus, at the same time that people need protection from their own poor judgment (which may lead to reckless spending or unsafe sex) they find advice irritating.

> "All the people in history, literature, art, whom I most admire: Mozart, Shakespeare, Homer, El Greco, St. John, Chekhov, Gregory of Nyssa, Dostoevsky, Emily Brontë: not one of them would qualify for a mental-health certificate."
>
> Madeleine L'Engle, *A Circle of Quiet*, 1972

mood disorders psychological disorders characterized by emotional extremes. See *major depressive disorder, mania,* and *bipolar disorder.*

major depressive disorder a mood disorder in which a person experiences, in the absence of drugs or a medical condition, two or more weeks of significantly depressed moods, feelings of worthlessness, and diminished interest or pleasure in most activities.

bipolar disorder a mood disorder in which the person alternates between the hopelessness and lethargy of depression and the overexcited state of mania. (Formerly called manic-depressive disorder.)

mania a mood disorder marked by a hyperactive, wildly optimistic state.

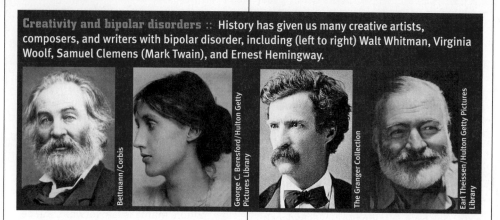

Creativity and bipolar disorders :: History has given us many creative artists, composers, and writers with bipolar disorder, including (left to right) Walt Whitman, Virginia Woolf, Samuel Clemens (Mark Twain), and Ernest Hemingway.

In milder forms, mania's energy and free-flowing thinking can fuel creativity. George Frideric Handel (1685–1759), who many believe suffered a mild form of bipolar disorder, composed his nearly four-hour-long *Messiah* during three weeks of intense, creative energy (Keynes, 1980). Bipolar disorder strikes more often among people who rely on emotional expression and vivid imagery, such as poets and artists, and less often among those who rely on precision and logic, such as architects, designers, and journalists (Jamison, 1993, 1995; Kaufman & Baer, 2002; Ludwig, 1995).

Bipolar disorder is as maladaptive as major depressive disorder, but it is much less common. It afflicts as many men as women.

Understanding Mood Disorders

12: What causes mood disorders?

From thousands of studies of the causes, treatment, and prevention of mood disorders, researchers have pulled out some common threads. Any theory of depression must explain at least the following (Lewinsohn & others, 1985, 1998).

Many changes in behavior and cognition accompany depression. People trapped in a depressed mood are inactive and feel unmotivated. They are sensitive to negative happenings. They recall negative information. And they expect negative outcomes (my team will lose, my grades will fall, my love will fail). When the mood lifts, these behaviors and thoughts disappear. Nearly half the time, people with depression also have symptoms of another disorder, such as anxiety or substance abuse.

Depression is widespread. Depression is one of two disorders found worldwide. (The other is schizophrenia.) This suggests that depression's causes, too, must be common.

Compared with men, women are nearly twice as vulnerable to major depression (FIGURE 12.9). In general, women are most vulnerable to disorders involving internal states, such as depression, anxiety, and inhibited sexual desire. Men's disorders tend to be more external—alcohol abuse, antisocial conduct, lack of impulse control. When women get sad, they often get sadder than men do. When men get mad, they often get madder than women do.

Most major depressive episodes end, with or without therapy. Therapy tends to speed recovery, but with or without it, most people eventually return to normal after a major depressive episode. The plague of depression comes and, a few weeks or months later, it usually goes. Sometimes it recurs later. About 50 percent will suffer another episode within two years. Recovery is more likely to be permanent the later the first episode strikes, the longer the person stays well, the fewer the previous episodes, the less stress experienced, and the more social support received (Belsher & Costello, 1988; Fergusson & Woodward, 2002; Kendler & others, 2001).

Stressful events related to work, marriage, and close relationships often precede depression. A family member's death, a job loss, a marital crisis, or a physical assault increase one's risk of depression. One long-term study tracked rates of depression in 2000 people (Kendler, 1998). Among those who had experienced no stressful life event in the preceding month, the risk of depression was less than 1 percent. Among those who had experienced three such events in that month, the risk was 24 percent.

The emotional lives of men and women?

Figure 12.9> Gender and major depression Interviews with 38,000 adults in 10 countries confirm what many smaller studies have found: Women's risk of major depression is nearly double that of men's. Lifetime risk of depression also varies by culture—from 1.5 percent in Taiwan to 19 percent in Beirut. (Data from Weissman & others, 1996.)

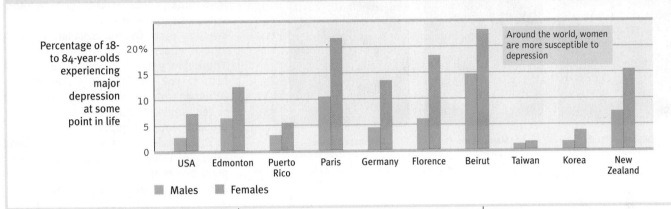

Percentage of 18- to 84-year-olds experiencing major depression at some point in life

Around the world, women are more susceptible to depression

■ Males ■ Females

With each new generation, depression is striking earlier (now often in the late teens) and affecting more people. This has been true in Canada, the United States, Germany, Italy, France, Lebanon, New Zealand, Taiwan, and Puerto Rico (Cross-National Collaborative Group, 1992). In North America, today's young adults are three times more likely than their grandparents to report having recently—or ever—suffered depression.

> "I see depression as the plague of the modern era."
>
> Lewis Judd, former chief, National Institute of Mental Health, 2000

This is true even though their grandparents have been at risk for many more years. The increased risk among young adults appears partly real, but it may also reflect cultural differences between generations. Today's young people are more willing to disclose depression. Psychological processes may also be at work. We tend to forget many negative experiences over time, so older generations may overlook depressed feelings they had in earlier years. Both of these tendencies are examples of reasons why the biopsychosocial perspective is so useful in studying psychological disorders.

Biological Influences

Depression is a whole-body disorder. It involves genetic predispositions and biochemical imbalances as well as negative thoughts and a gloomy mood.

Genes and Depression We have long known that mood disorders run in families. The risk of major depression and bipolar disorder increases if you have a parent or sibling with the disorder (Sullivan & others, 2000). If one identical twin is diagnosed with major depressive disorder, the chances are about 1 in 2 that at some time the other twin will be, too. If one identical twin has bipolar disorder, the chances are 7 in 10 that the other twin will at some point be diagnosed similarly. Among fraternal twins, the corresponding odds are just under 2 in 10 (Tsuang & Faraone, 1990). The greater similarity among identical twins holds even among twins reared apart (DiLalla & others, 1996). Moreover, adopted people who suffer a mood disorder often have close biological relatives who suffer mood disorders, become dependent on alcohol, or commit suicide (Wender & others, 1986). "Emotions are postcards from our genes," observed Henry Plotkin (1994).

The Depressed Brain Scanning devices open a window on the brain, giving researchers a view of activity during depressed and manic states. During periods of depression, brain activity slows. During mania, it increases (**FIGURE 12.10** on the next page). The left frontal lobe, which is active during positive emotions, is less active during depressed times (Davidson & others, 2002).

At least two neurotransmitter systems are at work during these periods of activity and inactivity. The first, *norepinephrine,* increases arousal and boosts mood. It is scarce during depression and overabundant during mania.

The second neurotransmitter, *serotonin,* is also scarce during depression. Recent research has revealed how genes and stress can interact to produce depression. Some genes provide codes for a protein that controls serotonin activity (Plomin & McGuffin, 2003). Researchers tracked one such gene in a large study of young adults who had experienced several major stresses (such as a relationship breakup or a family death). Those who carried a variation of the serotonin-controlling gene were much more likely to suffer depression (Caspi & others, 2003). When significant stress and the gene combined, the result was depression. As we have seen so often throughout this book, genes interacting with environments—the dance of nature and nurture—forms us.

Figure 12.10> The ups and downs of bipolar disorder PET scans show that brain energy consumption rises and falls with the patient's emotional switches. Red areas are where the brain is using energy most rapidly.

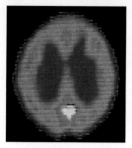

Depressed state
(May 17)

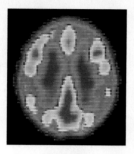

Manic state
(May 18)

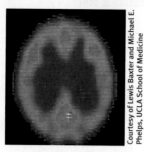

Depressed state
(May 27)

Courtesy of Lewis Baxter and Michael E. Phelps, UCLA School of Medicine

In Chapter 13, we will see how drugs that relieve depression tend to make more norepinephrine or serotonin available to the depressed brain. Repetitive physical exercise, such as jogging, which increases serotonin, can have a similar effect (Jacobs, 1994).

Psychological and Social Influences

Biological influences contribute to depression, but in the nature-nurture dance, thinking and acting also play a part. The *social-cognitive perspective* reminds us that people's assumptions and expectations influence what they perceive.

Depressed people see life through dark glasses. They have intensely negative views of themselves, their situation, and their future. Expecting the worst, they magnify bad experiences and minimize good ones. Listen to Norman, a college professor, recalling his depression (Endler, 1982, pp. 45–49).

I [despaired] of ever being human again. I honestly felt subhuman, lower than the lowest vermin. Furthermore, I . . . could not understand why anyone would want to associate with me, let alone love me. . . . I was positive that I was a fraud and a phony and that I didn't deserve my Ph.D. . . . I didn't deserve the research grants I had been

awarded; I couldn't understand how I had written books and journal articles. . . . I must have conned a lot of people.

Negative Thoughts and Negative Moods Interact Self-defeating beliefs may arise from *learned helplessness.* As we saw in Chapter 10, both dogs and humans act depressed, passive, and withdrawn after experiencing uncontrollable painful events. Learned helplessness is more common in women, who may respond more strongly to stress (Hankin & Abramson, 2001; Mazure & others, 2002; Nolen-Hoeksema, 2001, 2003). This gender difference appeared in a survey of women and men entering American colleges. Asked to agree or disagree with the statement that "I feel frequently overwhelmed by all I have to do," 38 percent of the women agreed. Only 17 percent of the men agreed (Pryor & others, 2006).

Such findings may help explain why, beginning in their early teens, women are nearly twice as vulnerable to depression (Kessler, 2001). This higher risk of depression may relate to women's tendency to *overthink,* to ruminate (Nolan-Hoeksema, 2003). Women often vividly recall both wonderful and horrid experiences. Men recall their experiences more vaguely (Seidlitz & Diener, 1998). This gender difference in emotional memory may feed women's greater tendency to linger men-

tally on the meaning of negative events. It may also help explain why fewer men than women report being frequently overwhelmed on entering college.

But why do life's unavoidable failures lead some people—women or men—and not others to become depressed? The answer lies partly in their *explanatory style—* who or what they blame for their failures. Think how you might feel if you failed a test. If you can blame someone else (What an unfair test!), you are more likely to feel angry. If you blame yourself, you probably will feel stupid and depressed.

Depressed people tend to blame themselves. As **FIGURE 12.11** illustrates, they explain bad events in terms that are *stable* ("I'll never get over this"), *global* ("I can't do anything right"), and *internal* ("It's all my fault"). Their explanations are pessimistic, overgeneralized, self-focused, and self-blaming. The result may be a depressing sense of hopelessness (Abramson & others, 1989). As Martin Seligman notes, "A recipe for severe depression is preexisting pessimism encountering failure" (1991, p. 78).

Critics point out a chicken-and-egg problem nesting in the social-cognitive explanation of depression. Which comes first? The bad feelings, or the depressed mood? Certainly, the negative explanations *coincide* with a depressed mood, and they are *indicators* of depression (Barnett & Gotlib, 1988). But do they *cause* depression, any more than a speedometer's reading 70 mph *causes* a car's speed? Before or after being depressed, people's thoughts are less negative. Perhaps a depressed mood *triggers* negative thoughts. If you temporarily put people in a bad or sad mood, their memories, judgments, and expectations do become more pessimistic.

Depression's Vicious Cycle No matter which comes first, rejection and depression feed each other. Depression, as we have seen, is often brought on by anything that disrupts our sense of who we are and why we are worthy. The stressful experience may be losing a job, getting divorced or rejected, suffering physical trauma—almost any bad event. This disruption in turn leads to brooding, which

Figure 12.11> Outlook and depression

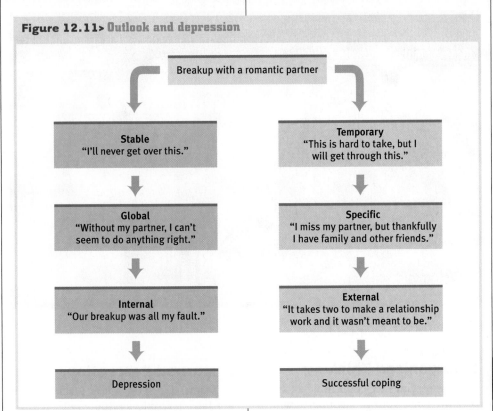

Breakup with a romantic partner

Stable
"I'll never get over this."

Global
"Without my partner, I can't seem to do anything right."

Internal
"Our breakup was all my fault."

Depression

Temporary
"This is hard to take, but I will get through this."

Specific
"I miss my partner, but thankfully I have family and other friends."

External
"It takes two to make a relationship work and it wasn't meant to be."

Successful coping

is rich soil for growing negative feelings. And that negativity—being withdrawn, self-focused, and complaining—can cause others to reject us (Furr & Funder, 1998; Gotlib & Hammen, 1992). Indeed, people with depression are at high risk for divorce, job loss, and other stressful life events. Weary of the person's fatigue, hopeless attitude, and lethargy, a spouse may threaten to leave, or a boss may begin to question the person's competence. New losses and stress then plunge the already depressed person into even deeper misery. Misery may love another's company, but company does not love another's misery.

We can now assemble pieces of the depression puzzle **(FIGURE 12.12):** (1) Negative, stressful events interpreted through (2) a brooding, pessimistic explanatory style create (3) a hopeless, depressed state that (4) hampers the way the person thinks and acts. These thoughts and actions in turn fuel (1) negative experiences such as rejection. Depression is a snake that bites its own tail.

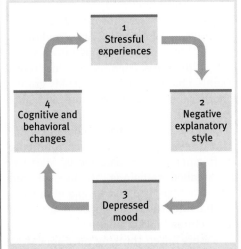

1 Stressful experiences

2 Negative explanatory style

3 Depressed mood

4 Cognitive and behavioral changes

Figure 12.12> The vicious cycle of depressed thinking Cognitive therapists attempt to break this cycle, as we will see in Chapter 13, by changing the way depressed people process events. Psychiatrists prescribe medication to try to alter the biological roots of persistently depressed moods.

It is a cycle we can all recognize. When we *feel* down, we *think* negatively and remember bad experiences. On the brighter side, if we recognize the cycle, we can break out of it. Each of the four points offers an exit. We could move to a different environment. We could reverse our self-blame and negative attributions. We could turn our attention outward. We could engage in more pleasant activities and more competent behavior.

Britain's Prime Minister Winston Churchill called depression a "black dog" that periodically hounded him. President Abraham Lincoln was so withdrawn and brooding as a young man that his friends feared he might take his own life (Kline, 1974). As their lives remind us, people can and do struggle through depression. Most regain their capacity to love, to work, to hope, and even to succeed at the highest levels.

PRACTICE TEST

21. The most common reason for seeking mental health services is
    a. substance abuse.
    b. depression.
    c. bipolar disorder.
    d. obsessive-compulsive disorder.

22. Bipolar disorder is as maladaptive as depression, but it is much less common. It affects
    a. more women than men.
    b. more men than women.
    c. women and men equally.
    d. primarily scientists and doctors.

23. Rates of depression
    a. are higher among women than among men.
    b. vary by culture.
    c. are rising with each new generation.
    d. All of these answers are correct.

24. Psychologists who emphasize the importance of negative perceptions, beliefs, and thoughts in depression are working within the _____ perspective.
    a. psychoanalytic   c. behavioral
    b. biological   d. social-cognitive

Answers: 21. b, 22. c, 23. d, 24. d.

Schizophrenia

During their most severe periods, people with **schizophrenia** live in a private inner world, preoccupied with the strange ideas and images that haunt them. Literally translated, *schizophrenia* means "split mind." The mind is not split into multiple personalities. Rather, the mind has suffered a split from reality that shows itself in disorganized thinking, disturbed perceptions, and inappropriate emotions and actions.

As you can imagine, these traits profoundly disrupt social relationships and make it difficult to hold a job. Given a supportive environment, some eventually recover to enjoy a normal life or to experience only occasional bouts of schizophrenia. Others remain socially withdrawn and isolated throughout much of their life.

Symptoms of Schizophrenia

13: What patterns of thinking, perceiving, feeling, and behaving characterize schizophrenia, and what are the two basic types of schizophrenia?

The term *schizophrenia* covers a cluster of disorders that share some features and differ in others. One difference is between those who have *positive symptoms* and those who have *negative symptoms*. Symptoms are "positive" in the sense that inappropriate behaviors are present. People may have hallucinations or talk in disorganized and deluded ways. They may laugh or cry or lash out in rage at inappropriate times.

Symptoms are "negative" in the sense that actions or feelings are absent when you might expect them to be present. People may have toneless voices, expressionless faces, or mute and rigid bodies. Because schizophrenia is a cluster of disorders, these varied symptoms may have more than one cause.

Art by people diagnosed with schizophrenia :: Commenting on the kind of art work shown here, poet and art critic John Ashbery wrote: "The lure of the work is strong, but so is the terror of the unanswerable riddles it proposes."

August Natterer, Witch's Head. The Prinzhorn Collection, University of Heidelberg

Photos of paintings by Krannert Museum, University of Illinois at Urbana-Champaign

Disorganized Thinking

Imagine trying to communicate with Maxine, a young woman whose thoughts spill out in no logical order. Her biographer, Susan Sheehan (1982, p. 25), observed her saying aloud to no one in particular, "This morning, when I was at Hillside [Hospital], I was making a movie. I was surrounded by movie stars. . . . I'm Mary Poppins. Is this room painted blue to get me upset? My grandmother died four weeks after my eighteenth birthday."

As this strange speech illustrates, the thinking of a person with schizophrenia is fragmented and distorted by false beliefs called **delusions.** Maxine believed she was Mary Poppins. People with *paranoid* tendencies often believe they are being threatened or pursued.

Disorganized thinking may appear as *word salad*, jumbled ideas that make no sense even within sentences. One young man begged for "a little more allegro in the treatment," and suggested that "liberationary movement with a view to the widening of the horizon" will "ergo extort some wit in lectures."

Disturbed Perceptions

Delusions are false *beliefs. Hallucinations* are false *perceptions.* People with schizophrenia sometimes see, feel, taste, or smell things that are not there. Most often, however, the hallucinations are sounds, often voices making insulting remarks or giving orders. The voices may tell the patient that she is bad or that she must burn herself with a cigarette lighter. Imagine your own reaction if a dream broke into your waking consciousness. When the unreal seems real, the resulting perceptions are at best bizarre, at worst terrifying.

"When someone asks me to explain schizophrenia I tell them, you know how sometimes in your dreams you are in them yourself and some of them feel like real nightmares? My schizophrenia was like I was walking through a dream. But everything around me was real. At times, today's world seems so boring and I wonder if I would like to step back into the schizophrenic dream, but then I remember all the scary and horrifying experiences."

Stuart Emmons, with Craig Geisler, Kalman J. Kaplan, and Martin Harrow, *Living With Schizophrenia*, 1997

Inappropriate Emotions and Actions

The emotions of schizophrenia are often utterly inappropriate, split off from reality. Maxine laughed after recalling her grandmother's death. On other occasions, she cried when others laughed, or became angry for no apparent reason. Other people with schizophrenia lapse into an emotionless *flat affect,* a zombielike state of no apparent feeling.

Inappropriate motor behavior takes many forms. Some patients perform senseless, compulsive acts, such as continually rocking or rubbing an arm. Others may remain motionless for hours (a condition called *catatonia*) and then become agitated.

Onset and Development of Schizophrenia

Nearly 1 in 100 people will develop schizophrenia this year, joining the estimated 24 million worldwide who suffer this dreaded disorder (WHO, 2008). It typically strikes as young people are maturing into adulthood. It knows no national boundaries, and it affects both men and women. Men tend to be struck earlier, more severely, and slightly more often (Aleman & others, 2003).

For some, schizophrenia will appear suddenly, seemingly as a reaction to stress. For others, as was the case with Maxine, schizophrenia develops gradually, emerging from a long history of social inadequacy. This may help explain why people predisposed to schizophrenia often end up in the lower socioeconomic levels, or even homeless.

One rule holds true around the world (World Health Organization, 1979): When schizophrenia is a slow-developing process (called *chronic,* or *process, schizophrenia*), recovery is doubtful. Social withdrawal, a negative symptom, is common among those with chronic schizophrenia. Men, whose schizophrenia develops on average four years earlier than women's, more often exhibit negative symptoms and chronic schizophrenia (Räsänen & others, 2000).

Recovery is much more likely when a well-adjusted person develops schizophrenia rapidly (called *acute,* or *reactive, schizophrenia*) following some sort of stress. People with reactive schizophrenia more often have the positive symptoms that respond to drug therapy (Fenton & McGlashan, 1991, 1994; Fowles, 1992).

Understanding Schizophrenia

14: What do we know about the causes of schizophrenia?

Schizophrenia is the most dreaded psychological disorder. It is also one of the most heavily researched. Most of the new research studies link it with abnormal brain tissue and activity, and with genetic predispositions. Schizophrenia is a disease of the brain exhibited in symptoms of the mind.

Brain Abnormalities

Could chemical imbalances in the brain explain the symptoms of schizophrenia? Scientists have long known that strange behavior can have strange chemical causes. Have you ever heard the phrase "mad as a hatter"? The saying dates back to the behavior of British hatmakers whose brains were slowly poisoned as they moistened the brims of mercury-laden felt hats with their lips (Smith, 1983). Could schizophrenia symptoms have some similar biochemical key? Scientists are tracking the mechanisms by which chemicals produce hallucinations and other symptoms.

Dopamine Overactivity One possible answer emerged when researchers examined schizophrenia patients' brains after death. They found an excess number of *dopamine* receptors (Seeman & others, 1993; Wong & others, 1986). What could this mean? Perhaps a high level of dopamine could intensify brain signals, creating positive symptoms such as hallucinations and paranoia. Sure enough, other evidence confirmed this idea. Drugs that block dopamine receptors often lessen the positive symptoms of schizophrenia. Drugs that increase dopamine levels, such as amphetamines and cocaine, sometimes intensify them (Swerdlow & Koob, 1987). Dopamine overactivity may help explain patients' strong reactions to some external and internal stimuli.

About 60 percent of schizophrenia patients smoke, often heavily. Nicotine apparently stimulates certain brain receptors, which helps focus attention (Javitt & Coyle, 2004).

Abnormal Brain Activity and Anatomy Brain scans show that people with schizophrenia have abnormal brain activity and brain structures. Some have abnormally low activity in the brain's frontal lobes, which are critical for reasoning, planning, and problem solving (Morey & others, 2005; Pettegrew & others, 1993; Resnick, 1992). For some, brain-wave patterns indicate the frontal-lobe neurons are not firing normally (Spencer & others, 2004; Symond & others, 2005). Out-of-sync neuron firing may contribute to schizophrenia symptoms.

One study took PET scans of brain activity while people were hallucinating (Silbersweig & others, 1995). When patients heard a voice or saw something,

schizophrenia a group of severe disorders characterized by disorganized and delusional thinking, disturbed perceptions, and inappropriate emotions and actions.

delusions false beliefs, often of persecution or grandeur, that may accompany schizophrenia and other disorders.

Studying schizophrenia :: Psychiatrist E. Fuller Torrey is collecting the brains of hundreds of those who died as young adults and suffered disorders such as schizophrenia and bipolar disorder. Torrey is making tissue samples available to researchers worldwide.

Chris Usher

their brain became vigorously active in several core regions. One active area was the thalamus, the structure deep in the brain that filters incoming sensory signals and transmits them to the cortex. Another PET scan study of people with paranoia found increased activity in the fear-processing center, the amygdala (Epstein & others, 1998).

Many studies have found enlarged, fluid-filled areas and a corresponding shrinkage of cerebral tissue in people with schizophrenia (Wright & others, 2000). The greater the shrinkage, the more severe the thought disorder (Collinson & others, 2003; Nelson & others, 1998; Shenton, 1992). Most remarkably, one study found abnormal structures in the brains of people who would *later* develop this disorder (Pantelis & others, 2002). The bottom line of various studies is clear. Schizophrenia involves not one isolated brain abnormality but problems with several brain regions and their interconnections (Andreasen, 1997, 2001).

Prenatal Environment and Risk

What causes the brain abnormalities that appear in schizophrenia? Some researchers blame low birth weight or lack of oxygen during delivery (Buka & others, 1999; Zornberg & others, 2000). Famine may also increase risks. For people conceived during the peak of the Dutch famine of World War II, their risk of developing schizophrenia was twice the normal rate. Those conceived during the famine of 1959 to 1961 in eastern China also displayed this doubled rate (St. Clair & others, 2005; Susser & others, 1996).

Let's consider another possible culprit. Might a midpregnancy viral infection impair fetal brain development? Can you imagine some ways to test this fetal-virus idea? Scientists have asked these questions.

■ *Are people at increased risk of schizophrenia if, during the middle of their fetal development, their country experienced a flu epidemic?* The repeated answer is yes (Mednick & others, 1994; Murray & others, 1992; Wright & others, 1995).

■ *Are people who are born in densely populated areas, where viral diseases spread more readily, at greater risk for schizophrenia?* The answer, confirmed in a study of 1.75 million Danes, is yes (Jablensky, 1999; Mortensen, 1999).

■ *Are people born during the winter and spring months—after the fall-winter flu season—also at increased risk?* The answer is again yes, at 5 to 8 percent increased risk (Torrey & others, 1997, 2002).

■ *In the Southern Hemisphere, where the seasons are the reverse of the Northern Hemisphere, are the months of above-average schizophrenia births similarly reversed?* Again, the answer is yes. In Australia, people born between August and October are at greater risk—unless they migrated from the Northern Hemisphere. For those immigrants, the risk is greater if they

were born between January and March (McGrath & others, 1995, 1999).

■ *Are mothers who report being sick with influenza during pregnancy more likely to bear children who develop schizophrenia?* In one study of nearly 8000 women, the answer was yes. The schizophrenia risk increased from the customary 1 percent to about 2 percent. But that increase applied only to mothers who were infected during their second trimester (Brown & others, 2000).

■ *Does blood drawn from pregnant women whose offspring develop schizophrenia suggest a viral infection?* The answer was yes in a huge California study, which collected blood samples from some 20,000 pregnant women during the 1950s and 1960s. Some children born of those pregnancies were later diagnosed with schizophrenia. When antibodies in the mother's blood indicated she had been exposed to influenza during the first half of the pregnancy, the child's risk of developing schizophrenia tripled. Flu during the second half of the pregnancy produced no such increase (Brown & others, 2004).

These converging lines of evidence suggest a key to the schizophrenia puzzle: Prenatal viral infections can contribute to the development of schizophrenia. This finding also strengthens the U.S. government recommendation that "women who will be more than three months pregnant during the flu season" have a flu shot (CDC, 2003).

Genetics and Risk

Although prenatal viruses increase the odds that a child will develop schizophrenia, they don't answer all the questions. Many women get the flu during their second trimester of pregnancy. The children of 98 percent of these women do *not* develop schizophrenia. Why does exposure to the virus put some children at risk but not others? Could the answer be that some people are more vulnerable

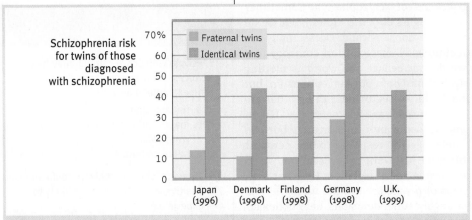

Figure 12.13> Risk of developing schizophrenia The lifetime risk of developing schizophrenia varies with one's genetic relatedness to someone having this disorder. Across countries, barely more than 1 in 10 fraternal twins, but some 5 in 10 identical twins, share a schizophrenia diagnosis. (Adapted from Gottesman, 2001.)

The Genain quadruplets :: The odds of any four people picked at random all being diagnosed with schizophrenia are 1 in 100 million. But genetically identical sisters Nora, Iris, Myra, and Hester Genain all have the disease. Two of the sisters have more severe forms of the disorder than the others, suggesting the influence of environmental as well as biological factors.

Courtesy of Genain family

because they have inherited a predisposition to this disorder? The evidence strongly suggests that the answer is yes. For most people, the odds of being diagnosed with schizophrenia are nearly 1 in 100. For those who have a sibling or parent with schizophrenia, the odds increase to 1 in 10. And if the affected sibling is an identical twin, the odds are close to 1 in 2 **(FIGURE 12.13)**. That 1-in-2 chance is unchanged even when the twins are reared apart (Plomin & others, 1997). (Only a dozen or so of these cases are on record.)

But wait! Identical twins also share a prenatal environment. So it is possible that shared germs as well as shared genes produce identical twin similarities. And there is some evidence to support this idea.

About two-thirds of identical twins also share a placenta and the blood it supplies. The other sets of identical twins have two separate placentas. If an identical twin has schizophrenia, the co-twin's chances of having the disorder are 6 in 10 if they shared a placenta. If they had separate placentas, the chances are only 1 in 10 (Davis & others, 1995a,b; Phelps & others, 1997). A likely explanation: Identical twins who share a placenta are more likely to share the same prenatal viruses.

How, then, could we untangle the genetic influences from the environmental influences on this disorder? Adoption studies offer some clues. Children adopted by someone who develops schizophrenia seldom "catch" the disorder. Rather, adopted children have a higher risk of developing schizophrenia if one of their *biological* parents has this disorder. Adoption studies confirm that the genetic link is real (Gottesman, 1991).

The search is on for specific genes that might lead to schizophrenia-related brain abnormalities (Callicott & others, 2005;

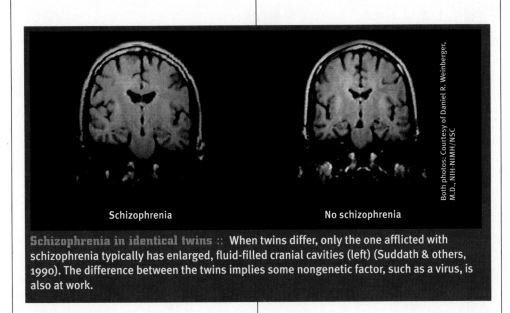

Schizophrenia in identical twins :: When twins differ, only the one afflicted with schizophrenia typically has enlarged, fluid-filled cranial cavities (left) (Suddath & others, 1990). The difference between the twins implies some nongenetic factor, such as a virus, is also at work.

Both photos: Courtesy of Daniel R. Weinberger, M.D., NIH-NIMH/NSC

Egan & others, 2004). Some of these genes influence the activity of dopamine and other neurotransmitters in the brain. Multiple genes, each exerting small effects, seem to interact to produce schizophrenia. And environmental factors—such as prenatal viral infections, nutritional deprivation, and oxygen deprivation at birth—may somehow help to "turn on" the genes that make some of us more vulnerable to this disease. As we have seen in so many different contexts, our genes sculpt our brain, and our brain interacts with our environment to direct our behavior. Neither hand claps alone.

* * *

Most of us can relate more easily to the ups and downs of mood disorders than to the strange thoughts, perceptions, and behaviors of schizophrenia. Sometimes our thoughts do jump around, but we do not talk nonsensically. Occasionally we feel unjustly suspicious of someone, but we do not believe the world is plotting against us. Often our perceptions err, but rarely do we see or hear things that are not there. We have felt regret after laughing at someone's misfortune, but we rarely giggle in response to bad news. At times we just want to be alone, but we do not live in social isolation. However, millions of people around the world do talk strangely, suffer delusions, hear nonexistent voices, see things that are not there, laugh or cry at inappropriate times, or withdraw into private imaginary worlds. The quest to solve the cruel puzzle of schizophrenia therefore continues, more vigorously than ever.

PRACTICE TEST

25. People with schizophrenia may hear voices when no one is speaking. This is an example of a(n)
   a. flat emotion.
   b. inappropriate emotion.
   c. word salad.
   d. hallucination.

26. A person who has schizophrenia and has positive symptoms is most likely to experience
   a. catatonia.
   b. delusions.
   c. withdrawal.
   d. flat emotion.

27. Chances for recovery from schizophrenia are best when
   a. onset is sudden, in response to stress.
   b. deterioration occurs gradually.
   c. no environmental causes can be identified.
   d. there is a detectable brain abnormality.

Answers: 25. d, 26. b, 27. a.

terms and concepts to remember

psychological disorder, p. 314

medical model, p. 315

DSM-IV-TR, p. 316

anxiety disorders, p. 318

generalized anxiety disorder, p. 318

panic disorder, p. 319

phobia, p. 319

obsessive-compulsive disorder (OCD), p. 319

post-traumatic stress disorder (PTSD), p. 320

dissociative disorders, p. 322

dissociative identity disorder (DID), p. 323

personality disorders, p. 324

antisocial personality disorder, p. 324

substance-related disorders, p. 325

psychoactive drug, p. 325

tolerance, p. 325

addiction, p. 325

withdrawal, p. 325

physical dependence, p. 326

psychological dependence, p. 326

depressants, p. 326

alcohol dependence, p. 326

barbiturates, p. 328

opiates, p. 328

stimulants, p. 328

amphetamines, p. 328

nicotine, p. 328

methamphetamine, p. 329

Ecstasy (MDMA), p. 330

hallucinogens, p. 330

LSD, p. 331

near-death experience, p. 331

THC, p. 331

mood disorders, p. 334

major depressive disorder, p. 335

bipolar disorder, p. 335

mania, p. 335

schizophrenia, p. 340

delusions, p. 340

REVIEW: PSYCHOLOGICAL DISORDERS

1 How do psychologists draw the line between normal behavior and disordered behavior, and what is a psychological disorder?

- What is considered "abnormal" varies with context, culture, and time in history.
- Psychologists define *psychological disorder* as an ongoing pattern of thoughts, feelings, or behaviors that are deviant (different from your cultural norm), distressful, and dysfunctional (interfering with everyday life).

2 How can our perspectives on psychological disorders affect our understanding of these conditions?

- The *medical model*: Psychological disorders are considered mental illnesses, diagnosed based on symptoms, and cured through therapy, sometimes in a hospital.
- The biopsychosocial approach: Disordered behavior comes from the interaction of genes and physiology, psychological dynamics, and social-cultural circumstances.

3 How and why do clinicians classify psychological disorders, and why do some psychologists criticize the use of diagnostic labels?

- The APA's most recent *Diagnostic and Statistical Manual of Mental Disorders (DSM-IV-TR)* lists and describes psychological disorders.
- Diagnostic labels provide a common language and shared concepts for communications and research.
- Labels can create preconceptions that cause us to view a person differently, and then look for evidence to confirm that view.

ANXIETY DISORDERS

4 What are anxiety disorders, and how do they differ from the ordinary worries we all experience?

- *Anxiety disorders*: distressing, persistent anxiety or maladaptive behaviors that reduce anxiety.
- *Generalized anxiety disorder*: continuing state of tension and apprehension for no apparent reason.
- *Panic disorder:* anxiety escalating into episodes of intense dread.
- *Phobia:* irrational fear of a specific object or situation.
- *Obsessive-compulsive disorder:* Persistent and repetitive thoughts (obsessions) and actions (compulsions).
- *Post-traumatic stress disorder:* four or more weeks of haunting memories, nightmares, social withdrawal, jumpy anxiety, and sleep problems following a traumatic event.

5 What are the sources of the anxious feelings and thoughts that characterize anxiety disorders?

- Freud's now-dated view: Anxiety disorders discharge repressed impulses.
- The learning perspective: Anxiety disorders come from fear conditioning, stimulus generalization, and reinforcement of fearful behaviors.
- The biological perspective: Anxiety disorders result from inherited temperament differences; learned fears that have altered brain pathways; and outdated, inherited responses that had survival value for our ancestors.

DISSOCIATIVE AND PERSONALITY DISORDERS

6 What are dissociative disorders, and why are they controversial?

- *Dissociative disorders:* conscious awareness becomes separated from previous memories, thoughts, and feelings.
- Skeptics say: *Dissociative identity disorder (DID;* multiple personality disorder) increased dramatically in the late twentieth century. DID is rarely found outside North America. DID may reflect role-playing by people who are vulnerable to therapists' suggestions.

7 What characteristics are typical of personality disorders?

- *Personality disorders:* enduring, maladaptive patterns of behavior that impair social functioning.
- *Antisocial personality disorder:* lack of conscience and, sometimes, aggressive and fearless behavior.

SUBSTANCE-RELATED DISORDERS

8 What is a substance-related disorder, and what are tolerance, addiction, and dependence?

Substance-related disorder: Maladaptive substance use that leads to clinical self-harm or distress.

- *Tolerance:* requiring larger doses of a drug to achieve the same effect; produced by continued use of the drug.
- *Addiction:* compulsive drug craving and use.
- In *physical dependence,* the need for the drug is physiological, and ending the drug use may produce *withdrawal* symptoms.
- In *psychological dependence,* the person relies on the drug to relieve stress or negative emotions.

9 What are the three main types of psychoactive drugs, and what are their effects?

- *Depressants* (alcohol, *barbiturates, opiates*) dampen neural activity and slow body functions.
- Alcohol disinhibits, increasing the likelihood that we will act on our impulses, whether helpful or harmful.
- *Stimulants* (caffeine, *nicotine,* amphetamines, *methamphetamine,* cocaine, *Ecstasy*) excite neural activity and speed up body functions. All are highly addictive.
- Methamphetamine may permanently reduce dopamine levels, and Ecstasy (MDMA) may damage serotonin-producing neurons.
- *Hallucinogens* (*LSD,* marijuana) distort perceptions and evoke hallucinations (sensory images in the absence of sensory input), some of which resemble the altered consciousness of *near-death experiences.*

10 Why do some people abuse mind-altering drugs?

- Some people are biologically more vulnerable to drugs.
- Psychological factors (stress, depression, hopelessness) and social-cultural influences (peer pressure, cultural values) also affect drug use.

MOOD DISORDERS

11 What are mood disorders, and what forms do they take?

- *Mood disorders:* characterized by emotional extremes.
- *Major depressive disorder:* two or more weeks of seriously depressed moods and feelings of worthlessness, with little interest in most activities. Not caused by drugs or a medical condition.
- *Bipolar disorder:* mood swings between depression and *mania* (hyperactive and wildly optimistic, impulsive behavior).

12 What causes mood disorders?

- Biological influences: Genetic predispositions and abnormalities in brain structures and functions.
- Psychological and social influences: Cycles of self-defeating beliefs, learned helplessness, a negative outlook, and stressful experiences.

SCHIZOPHRENIA

13 What patterns of thinking, perceiving, feeling, and behaving characterize schizophrenia, and what are the two basic types of schizophrenia?

- *Schizophrenia:* a group of disorders that typically strike during late adolescence.
- Symptoms include disorganized and *delusional* thinking (with false beliefs), disturbed perceptions, and inappropriate emotions and actions.
- Positive symptoms are defined as the presence of inappropriate behaviors; negative symptoms, as the absence of appropriate behaviors.
- Chronic, or process, schizophrenia is slow-developing and difficult to treat. Acute, or reactive, schizophrenia comes on rapidly following stress and is more likely to respond to treatment.

14 What do we know about the causes of schizophrenia?

- People with schizophrenia have more receptors for dopamine, which may intensify the positive symptoms of schizophrenia.
- Brain scans reveal abnormal activity in the frontal lobes, thalamus, and amygdala.
- Brain abnormalities associated with schizophrenia include enlarged, fluid-filled cerebral cavities and corresponding decreases in the cortex.
- A mid-pregnancy virus may contribute to fetal brain impairment.
- A genetic predisposition seems to interact with environmental factors to produce schizophrenia.

Kay Redfield Jamison, an award-winning clinical psychologist and world expert on bipolar disorder, knows her subject firsthand. "For as long as I can remember," she recalls in *An Unquiet Mind,* "I was frighteningly, although wonderfully, beholden to moods. Intensely emotional as a child, mercurial as a young girl, first severely depressed as an adolescent, and then unrelentingly caught up in the cycles of manic-depressive illness by the time I began my professional life, I became, both by necessity and intellectual inclination, a student of moods" (1995, pp. 4–5). Her life was blessed with times of intense sensitivity and passionate energy. But like her father's, it was also at times plagued by reckless spending, racing conversation, and sleeplessness, alternating with swings into "the blackest caves of the mind."

Then, "in the midst of utter confusion," she made a sane and profoundly helpful decision. Risking embarrassment, she made an appointment with a therapist, a psychiatrist she would visit weekly for years to come.

> He kept me alive a thousand times over. He saw me through madness, despair, wonderful and terrible love affairs, disillusionments and triumphs, recurrences of illness, an almost fatal suicide attempt, the death of a man I greatly loved, and the enormous pleasures and aggravations of my professional life. . . . He was very tough, as well as very kind, and even though he understood more than anyone how much I felt I was losing—in energy, vivacity, and originality—by taking medication, he never was seduced into losing sight of the overall perspective of how costly, damaging, and life threatening my illness was. . . . Although I went to him to be treated for an illness, he taught me . . . the total beholdenness of brain to mind and mind to brain (pp. 87–89).

Jamison reports, "psychotherapy heals. It makes some sense of the confusion, reins in the terrifying thoughts and feelings, returns some control and hope and possibility from it all."

Treating Psychological Disorders

1: What are the two main types of treatments for psychological disorders?

The long history of efforts to treat psychological disorders has included a bewildering mix of harsh and gentle methods. Well-meaning individuals have cut holes in people's heads and restrained, bled, or "beat the devil" out of people. They have administered drugs and electric shocks. But they also have given warm baths and massages and placed people in sunny, serene environments. And they have talked with their patients about childhood experiences, current feelings, and maladaptive thoughts and behaviors.

Reformers Philippe Pinel, Dorothea Dix, and others pushed for gentler, more humane treatments and for constructing

Culver Pictures

Dorothea Dix (1802–1887) :: "I . . . call your attention to the state of the Insane Persons confined within this Commonwealth, in cages."

mental hospitals to house people in distress. Since the 1950s, the introduction of effective drug therapies and community-based treatment programs have emptied most of those hospitals.

Today's therapies can be classified into two main categories. Both the disorder and the therapist's viewpoint influence the choice of treatment. **Psychotherapy,** for example, is often the treatment for learning-related disorders, such as phobias. A therapist trained in the use of psychological techniques will try to help the person overcome difficulties or achieve personal growth. Biologically rooted disorders, such as schizophrenia, will probably be treated with **biomedical therapy.** In these cases, the treatment will be prescribed medication or a medical procedure that acts directly on the patient's brain.

Some therapists combine techniques. Jamison received psychotherapy in her meetings with her psychiatrist, and she took medications to control her wild mood swings. Indeed, half of all psychotherapists describe themselves as taking an **eclectic approach,** using a blend of therapies (Beitman & others, 1989; Castonguay & Goldfried, 1994). Closely related to eclecticism is *psychotherapy integration.* Rather than picking and choosing methods, integration advocates aim to combine them into a single, coherent system.

Let's take a closer look now at some of the options available to therapists and the people who seek their help. Although dozens of types of therapy are available, we'll look at only the most influential.

The Psychological Therapies

Each form of psychotherapy is built on one or more of psychology's major theories: psychoanalytic, humanistic, behavioral, and cognitive. Most of these techniques can be used one-on-one or in groups.

Psychoanalysis

2: What are the aims and methods of psychoanalysis, and how have they been adapted in psychodynamic therapy?

Sigmund Freud's **psychoanalysis** was the first of the psychological therapies, and its terminology has crept into our modern vocabulary. Few clinicians today practice therapy exactly as Freud did. Some of his techniques and assumptions survive, however, especially in the *psychodynamic therapies.*

Aims

What do you think ever happened to all those forbidden impulses and conflicts you felt as a child? Did maturity cause them to disappear? Or did punishment and disapproval force them underground? Freud believed these impulses and urges live submerged in our unconscious, where they act as fuel for the psychological problems of our adult years. He and his followers therefore tried to bring these repressed feelings into patients' conscious awareness. By digging back into their childhood, patients might gain insight into a disorder's origins. They would then be able to work through the buried feelings and take responsibility for their own growth. Healthier, less anxious living would become possible if people could release the energy they had previously devoted to dealing with inner conflicts.

Methods

Psychoanalysis is historical reconstruction. It aims to unearth the past in hope of unmasking the present. But how?

The Granger Collection

The history of treatment :: Visitors to mental hospitals in the eighteenth century paid to gawk at patients, as though they were viewing zoo animals. William Hogarth's (1697–1764) engraving (left) captured one of these visits to London's St. Mary of Bethlehem hospital (commonly called Bedlam). Benjamin Rush (1746–1813), a founder of the movement for more humane treatment of the mentally ill, designed the chair on the right "for the benefit of maniacal patients." He believed the restraints would help them regain their sanity.

Freud's consulting room :: Freud's office was rich with antiquities from around the world, including artwork related to his ideas about unconscious motives. His famous couch was piled high with pillows. It placed patients in a comfortable reclining position facing away from him to help them focus inward.

Might hypnosis do the trick? Freud tried it and discarded it as unreliable.

Freud found his preferred method in *free association.* Imagine yourself as a patient using free association. First you relax, perhaps by lying on a couch. To help you focus on your own thoughts and feelings, the psychoanalyst may sit out of your line of vision. You say aloud whatever comes to your mind, at one moment a childhood memory, at another a dream or recent experience. It sounds easy, but soon you notice how often you edit your thoughts as you speak. You omit what seems trivial, off the point, or shameful. Even in the safe presence of the analyst, you may pause before uttering an embarrassing thought. You may joke or change the subject to something less threatening. Sometimes your mind goes blank, or you find yourself unable to remember important details.

To the psychoanalyst, the pauses, the jokes, the change of subject indicate **resistance.** They hint that you are defending yourself against the anxiety that you would feel if you allowed this sensitive material to enter your conscious mind. After pointing out your resistances, the analyst will **interpret** their meaning, providing *insight* into your underlying wishes, feelings, and conflicts. If offered at the right moment, this deep, new understanding—of, say, your not wanting to

talk about your mother—may illuminate what you are avoiding and may even show how other pieces of your psychological puzzle fit together.

Freud also believed that unconscious conflicts leak out in dreams. After inviting you to report a dream, the analyst may offer a dream analysis, drawing your attention to the dream's *latent content*— its underlying but censored meaning.

During many such sessions, you will probably disclose to your analyst more of yourself than you have ever revealed to anyone else. Much of it will focus on your earliest memories. As you share your inner thoughts and feelings, you may find yourself experiencing strong positive or negative feelings for your analyst. Your analyst may suggest that you experienced these same emotions in earlier

relationships with family members or other important people. By exposing feelings you have previously defended against, such as dependency or mingled love and anger, this **transference** will give you a belated chance to work through them, with your analyst's help. Examining your feelings may also give you insight into your current relationships, not just those of your childhood.

Psychoanalysts' interpretations are hard to refute because they cannot be proven or disproven. Psychoanalysts acknowledge this criticism, but they insist that interpretations often are a great help to patients. Psychoanalysis, they say, is therapy, not science.

"In the mental-health profession, we try to avoid negative labels, like 'a hundred and fifty bucks an hour—that's crazy!' or 'three fifty-minute sessions a week—that's insane!'"

psychotherapy treatment involving psychological techniques; consists of interactions between a trained therapist and someone seeking to overcome psychological difficulties or achieve personal growth.

biomedical therapy prescribed medications or medical procedures.

eclectic approach an approach to psychotherapy that, depending on the client's problems, uses techniques from various forms of therapy.

psychoanalysis Sigmund Freud's therapeutic technique. Freud believed the patient's free associations, resistances, dreams, and transferences—and the therapist's interpretations of them—released previously repressed feelings, allowing the patient to gain self-insight.

resistance in psychoanalysis, the blocking from consciousness of anxiety-laden material.

interpretation in psychoanalysis, the analyst's noting supposed dream meanings, resistances, and other significant behaviors and events in order to promote insight.

transference in psychoanalysis, the patient's transfer to the analyst of emotions linked with other relationships (such as love or hatred for a parent).

"You say, 'Off with her head' but what I'm hearing is, 'I feel neglected.'"

Psychoanalysis takes time, up to several years of several sessions a week, and it is expensive. (Three times a week for just two years at more than $100 per hour comes to at least $30,000.) Outside of France, Germany, Quebec, and New York City, relatively few therapists offer traditional psychoanalysis (Goode, 2003). Most managed U.S. health-care plans won't cover such high bills for such long periods.

> "I haven't seen my analyst in 200 years. He was a strict Freudian. If I'd been going all this time, I'd probably almost be cured by now."
>
> Woody Allen, after awakening from suspended animation in the movie *Sleeper*

Psychodynamic Therapy

Some of Freud's ideas have been melded into today's **psychodynamic** approach. These therapists try to understand a patient's current symptoms by focusing on themes across important relationships, including childhood experiences and the therapist relationship. They also draw attention to thoughts and feelings the person seems to be avoiding, and they help the person explore and gain perspective in these areas. But these therapists may talk to the patient face to face (rather than out of the line of vision). They often meet once a week (rather than several times weekly) for only a few weeks or months (rather than several years).

No brief excerpt can offer a full view of the way psychodynamic therapy interprets a patient's conflict. But the following interaction between therapist David Malan and a depressed patient gives us a quick glimpse at how a psychodynamic therapist might help a person gain insight by looking for common, recurring themes, especially in relationships. Note how Malan interprets the woman's earlier remarks (when she did most of the talking) and suggests that her relationship with him reveals a characteristic pattern of behavior (1978, pp. 133–134).

Malan: I get the feeling that you're the sort of person who needs to keep active. If you don't keep active, then something goes wrong. Is that true?

Patient: Yes.

Malan: I get a second feeling about you and that is that you must, underneath all this, have an awful lot of very strong and upsetting feelings. Somehow they're there but you aren't really quite in touch with them. Isn't this right? I feel you've been like that as long as you can remember.

Patient: For quite a few years, whenever I really sat down and thought about it I got depressed, so I tried not to think about it.

Malan: You see, you've established a pattern, haven't you? You're even like that here with me, because in spite of the fact that you're in some trouble and you feel that the bottom is falling out of your world, the way you're telling me this is just as if there wasn't anything wrong.

Interpersonal psychotherapy, a brief (12- to 16-session) variation of psychodynamic therapy, has been effective in treating depression (Weissman, 1999). Interpersonal psychotherapy also tries to help people gain insight into the roots of their difficulties. Rather than focusing mostly on undoing past hurts and offering interpretations, the therapist focuses primarily on understanding current relationships and improving relationship skills. The goal is symptom relief in the here and now.

Humanistic Therapies

3: What are the basic themes of humanistic therapy, such as Rogers' client-centered approach?

The humanistic perspective (Chapter 11) has emphasized people's inherent potential for self-fulfillment. Not surprisingly, humanistic therapists aim to boost self-fulfillment by helping people grow in self-awareness and self-acceptance. Like psychoanalytic therapies, humanistic therapies attempt to reduce the conflicts that interfere with natural development and growth. But humanistic therapists differ from psychoanalytic therapists in other ways. For them,

- the *present and future* are more important than the past. The goal is to explore feelings as they occur, rather than achieving insights into the childhood origins of the feelings.

- *conscious thoughts* are more important than the unconscious.

- the path to growth is taking immediate responsibility for our feelings and actions, rather than uncovering possible hidden causes.

- *promoting growth,* not curing illness, is the focus. Thus, those in therapy are called "clients" or just "persons" rather than "patients" (a change many other therapists have adopted).

Carl Rogers (1961, 1980) developed the widely used humanistic technique he called **client-centered therapy** (now often called *person-centered therapy*), which focuses on the person's conscious self-perceptions. This therapy is *nondirective*—the therapist listens, without judging or interpreting, and refrains from directing the client toward certain insights.

Rogers believed that most people already possess the resources for growth. He encouraged therapists to exhibit *genuineness, acceptance,* and *empathy.* By being genuine, therapists will express their true feelings. By providing a nonjudgmental, grace-filled environment and showing

Active listening :: Carl Rogers (right) empathized with a client during this group therapy session.

Michael Rougier/*Life* Magazine © Time Warner, Inc.

people *unconditional positive regard*, a therapist may help clients accept even their worst traits and feel valued and whole. By showing empathy, by sensing and reflecting their clients' feelings, therapists can help clients experience a deeper self-understanding and self-acceptance (Hill & Nakayama, 2000). As Rogers (1980, p. 10) explained,

> Hearing has consequences. When I truly hear a person and the meanings that are important to him at that moment, hearing not simply his words, but him, and when I let him know that I have heard his own private personal meanings, many things happen. There is first of all a grateful look. He feels released. He wants to tell me more about his world. He surges forth in a new sense of freedom. He becomes more open to the process of change.

> I have often noticed that the more deeply I hear the meanings of the person, the more there is that happens. Almost always, when a person realizes he has been deeply heard, his eyes moisten. I think in some real sense he is weeping for joy. It is as though he were saying, "Thank God, somebody heard me. Someone knows what it's like to be me."

To Rogers, "hearing" was **active listening.** In this technique, the therapist echoes, restates, and seeks clarification

"We have two ears and one mouth that we may listen the more and talk the less."

Zeno (335–263 B.C.), *Diogenes Laertius*

of what the person expresses (verbally or nonverbally). The therapist also acknowledges those expressed feelings. Active listening is now an accepted part of counseling practices in many schools, colleges, and clinics. Counselors listen attentively. They interrupt only to restate and confirm feelings, to accept what is being expressed, or to seek clarification. The following brief excerpt between Rogers and a male client illustrates how he sought to provide a psychological mirror that would help clients see themselves more clearly.

Rogers: Feeling that now, hm? That you're just no good to yourself, no good to anybody. Never will be any good to anybody. Just that you're completely worthless, huh?—Those really are lousy feelings. Just feel that you're no good at all, hm?

Client: Yeah. (*Muttering in low, discouraged voice*) That's what this guy I went to town with just the other day told me.

Rogers: This guy that you went to town with really told you that you were no good? Is that what you're saying? Did I get that right?

Client: M-hm.

Rogers: I guess the meaning of that if I get it right is that here's somebody that—meant something to you and what does he think of you? Why, he's told you that he thinks you're no good at all. And that just really knocks the props out from under you. (*Client weeps quietly.*) It just brings the tears. (*Silence of 20 seconds*)

Client: (*Rather defiantly*) I don't care though.

Rogers: You tell yourself you don't care at all, but somehow I guess some part of you cares because some part of you weeps over it. (Meador & Rogers, 1984, p. 167)

Can a therapist be a perfect mirror, critics have asked, without selecting and interpreting what is reflected? Rogers agreed that no one can be *totally* nondirective. Nevertheless, he said, the therapist's most important contribution is to accept and understand the client.

To develop your own communication strengths, you may want to listen more actively in your own relationships. Three hints may help:

1. *Summarize.* Check your understanding by repeating the speaker's statements in your own words.

2. *Invite clarification.* "What might be an example of that?" may encourage the speaker to say more.

3. *Reflect feelings.* "It sounds frustrating" might mirror what you're sensing from the speaker's body language and intensity.

psychodynamic therapy a Freud-influenced perspective that sees behavior, thinking, and emotions in terms of unconscious motives.

client-centered therapy a humanistic therapy, developed by Carl Rogers, in which the therapist uses techniques such as active listening within a genuine, accepting, empathic environment to promote clients' growth. (Also called *person-centered therapy.*)

active listening empathic listening in which the listener echoes, restates, and clarifies. A feature of Rogers' client-centered therapy.

Behavior Therapies

4: What are the assumptions and techniques of the behavior therapies?

The therapies we have considered so far assume that self-awareness and psychological well-being go hand in hand. Traditional psychoanalysts expect people's problems to begin to go away as they gain insight into their unresolved and unconscious tensions. Humanistic therapists expect people's problems to lessen as they get in touch with their feelings. **Behavior therapists,** however, doubt the healing power of self-awareness. (You can become aware of why you are highly anxious during exams and still be anxious.) They assume that problem behaviors *are* the problems, and that learning principles are useful tools for eliminating problems. Rather than searching beneath the surface for inner causes, behavior therapists take maladaptive symptoms at face value. In this view, phobias or sexual disorders, for example, are learned behaviors that can be replaced by new and more useful behaviors learned through classical or operant conditioning.

Classical Conditioning Techniques

One cluster of behavior therapies derives from principles developed in Ivan Pavlov's early-twentieth-century conditioning experiments (Chapter 6). As Pavlov and others showed, we learn various behaviors and emotions through classical conditioning. If we're attacked by a dog, we may thereafter have a conditioned fear response when other dogs approach. (Our fear generalizes, and all dogs become conditioned stimuli.)

Could maladaptive symptoms also be examples of conditioned responses? If so, might reconditioning be a solution? Learning theorist O. H. Mowrer thought so. He developed a successful conditioning therapy for chronic bed-wetters, using a liquid-sensitive pad connected to an alarm. If the sleeping child wets the pad (which is in the bed), moisture triggers the alarm, waking the child. With

sufficient repetition, this association of urinary relaxation with waking stops the bed-wetting. In three out of four cases, the treatment is effective, and the success provides a boost to the child's self-image (Christophersen & Edwards, 1992; Houts & others, 1994).

Another example: Assume that a claustrophobic fear of elevators is a learned fear response to the stimulus of being in a confined space. Would it be possible for the person to unlearn the fear response through new conditioning? **Counterconditioning** pairs the trigger stimulus (in this case, the enclosed space of the elevator) with a new response (relaxation) that cannot coexist with fear. And indeed, behavior therapists have successfully counterconditioned people with a fear of confined spaces.

Two counterconditioning techniques that are often used are *exposure therapies* and *aversive conditioning*. The goal of both is replacing unwanted responses with new responses.

Exposure Therapies Picture this scene. Behaviorist psychologist Mary Cover Jones is working with 3-year-old Peter, who is petrified of rabbits and other furry objects. To rid Peter of his fear of rabbits, Jones plans to associate the fear-evoking rabbit with the pleasurable, relaxed response associated with eating. As Peter begins his midafternoon snack, she introduces a caged rabbit on the other side of the huge room. Peter, eagerly munching away on his crackers and drinking his milk, hardly notices. On succeeding days, she gradually moves the rabbit closer and closer. Within two months, Peter is holding the rabbit in his lap, even stroking it while he eats. Moreover, his fear of other furry objects has also gone away, having been *countered,* or replaced, by a relaxed state that cannot coexist with fear (Fisher, 1984; Jones, 1924).

Unfortunately for many who might have been helped by Jones' procedures, her story of Peter and the rabbit did not enter psychology's lore when it was reported in 1924. It was more than 30 years before psychiatrist Joseph Wolpe (1958; Wolpe & Plaud, 1997) refined Jones'

Professor Gallagher and his controversial technique of simultaneously confronting the fear of heights, snakes, and the dark.

counterconditioning technique into the **exposure therapies** used today. These therapies, in a variety of ways, try to change people's reactions by repeatedly exposing them to stimuli that trigger unwanted reactions. We all experience this process in everyday life. A person may move to a new apartment and at first be very annoyed by the sound of a train passing by. But with repeated exposure, the person gets used to the sound. So, too, with people who have fear reactions to specific events. Exposed repeatedly to the situation that once terrified them, they can learn to react less anxiously (Deacon & Abramowitz, 2004).

One widely used exposure therapy is **systematic desensitization.** You cannot be anxious and relaxed at the same time. Therefore, if you can repeatedly relax when facing anxiety-provoking stimuli, you can gradually eliminate your anxiety. The trick is to proceed in slow stages. Imagine yourself afraid of public speaking. A behavior therapist might first ask for your help in making a list of anxiety-triggering speaking situations. Your list would range from situations that cause you to feel mildly anxious (perhaps speaking up in a small group of friends) to those that provoke feelings of panic (having to address a large audience).

Using *progressive relaxation*, the therapist would then train you to relax one muscle group after another, until you achieve a drowsy state of complete relaxation and comfort. Then the therapist asks you to imagine, with your eyes closed, a mildly anxiety-arousing situation: You are having coffee with a group of friends and are trying to decide whether to speak up. If imagining the scene causes you to feel any anxiety, you signal your tension by raising your finger. Seeing the signal, the therapist instructs you to switch off the mental image and go back to deep relaxation. This imagined scene is repeatedly paired with relaxation until you feel no trace of anxiety.

The therapist then moves to the next item on your list and again uses relaxation techniques to desensitize you to each imagined situation. After several sessions, you move to actual situations and practice what you had only imagined before. You begin with relatively easy tasks and gradually move to more anxiety-filled ones. Conquering your anxiety in an actual situation, not just in your imagination, raises your self-confidence (Foa & Kozak, 1986; Williams, 1987). Eventually, you may even become a confident public speaker.

A newer option is **virtual reality exposure therapy.** Wearing a head-mounted display unit that projects a three-dimensional virtual world, you would view a lifelike series of scenes. As your head turns, motion sensors adjust the scene. Experiments led by several research teams have treated people for a number of fears, including fear of flying, heights, particular animals, and public speaking (Gershon & others, 2002; Rothbaum & others, 2002). If you fear flying, for example, you could peer out a virtual window of a simulated plane, feel the vibrations, and hear the engine roar as the plane taxis down the runway and takes off. In studies comparing control groups with people participating in virtual reality exposure

Virtual reality exposure therapy :: Within the confines of a room, virtual reality technology exposes people to vivid simulations of feared stimuli, such as a plane's takeoff.

Bob Mahoney The Image Works

therapy, the therapy has provided greater relief from real-life fear (Hoffman, 2004; Krijn & others, 2004).

Aversive Conditioning Systematic desensitization substitutes a positive response for a negative response to a *harmless* stimulus. (You learn to relax in front of an audience, or on an airplane.) **Aversive conditioning** substitutes a negative response for a positive response to a *harmful* stimulus. (You learn to avoid driving while under the influence of alcohol.) Systematic desensitization helps you learn what you *should* do. Aversive conditioning helps you to learn what you *should not* do.

The procedure is simple: It associates the unwanted behavior with unpleasant feelings. To treat nail biting, one can paint the fingernails with a yucky-tasting nail polish (Baskind, 1997). To treat alcohol dependence (popularly known as alcoholism), the therapist offers the client appealing drinks laced with a drug that produces severe nausea. By linking alcohol with violent nausea (recall the taste-aversion experiments with rats and coyotes in Chapter 6), the therapist seeks to transform the person's reaction to alcohol from positive to negative (**FIGURE 13.1** on the next page).

Does aversive conditioning work? In the short run it may. In one classic study, 685 patients with alcoholism completed an aversion therapy program at a hospital (Wiens & Menustik, 1983). One year later, after returning for several booster treatments of alcohol-sickness pairings, 63 percent were still successfully abstaining. But after three years, only 33 percent had remained abstinent.

The problem, as we saw in Chapter 6, is that our thoughts can interfere with

behavior therapy therapy that applies learning principles to the elimination of unwanted behaviors.

counterconditioning a behavior therapy procedure that uses classical conditioning to evoke new responses to stimuli that are triggering unwanted behaviors; includes *exposure therapies* and *aversive conditioning*.

exposure therapies behavioral techniques, such as systematic desensitization, that treat anxieties by exposing people (in imagination or actual situations) to the things they fear and avoid.

systematic desensitization a type of exposure therapy that associates a pleasant relaxed state with gradually increasing, anxiety-triggering stimuli. Commonly used to treat phobias.

virtual reality exposure therapy an anxiety treatment that progressively exposes people to electronic simulations of their greatest fears, such as airplane flying, spiders, or public speaking.

aversive conditioning a type of counterconditioning that associates an unpleasant state (such as nausea) with an unwanted behavior (such as drinking alcohol).

Figure 13.1> Aversion therapy for alcohol dependence After repeatedly imbibing an alcoholic drink mixed with a drug that produces severe nausea, some people with a history of alcohol abuse develop at least a temporary conditioned aversion to alcohol.

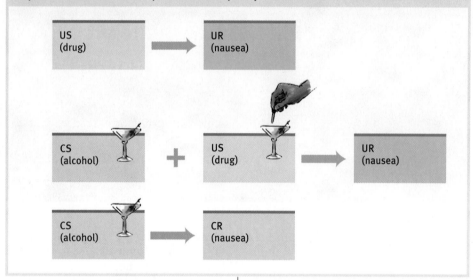

conditioning processes. People know that outside the therapist's office they can drink without fear of nausea. Their ability to isolate the aversive conditioning situation from all other situations can limit the treatment's effectiveness. Thus, aversive conditioning is often used in combination with other treatments.

Operant Conditioning

A basic concept in operant conditioning (Chapter 6) is that our behaviors are strongly influenced by their consequences. Knowing this, behavior therapists can practice *behavior modification*. They reinforce behaviors they consider desirable. And they fail to reinforce—or sometimes punish—behaviors they consider undesirable.

Using operant conditioning to solve specific behavior problems has raised hopes for some cases thought to be hopeless. Children with mental retardation have been taught to care for themselves. Socially withdrawn children with autism have learned to interact. People with schizophrenia have been helped to behave more rationally in their hospital ward. In such cases, therapists use positive reinforcers to shape behavior in a step-by-step manner, rewarding closer and closer approximations of the desired behavior.

In extreme cases, treatment must be intensive, as it was in a study of 19 withdrawn, uncommunicative 3-year-olds with autism. For two years, 40 hours each week, the parents of these children attempted to shape their behavior (Lovaas, 1987). They positively reinforced desired behaviors and ignored or punished aggressive and self-abusive behaviors. The combination worked wonders for some children. By first grade, 9 of the 19 were functioning successfully in school and exhibiting normal intelligence. Only one child in a group of 40 comparable children who did not undergo this treatment showed similar improvement.

The rewards used to modify behavior vary, because the things each of us considers rewarding vary. For some people, the reinforcing power of attention or praise is enough. Others require concrete rewards, such as food. In institutional settings, therapists may create a **token economy.** When people display appropriate behavior, such as getting out of bed, washing, dressing, eating, talking meaningfully, cleaning their rooms, or playing cooperatively, they receive a token or plastic coin. Later, they can exchange a number of these tokens for rewards, such as candy, TV time, day trips, or better living quarters. Token economies have been used successfully in various settings (homes, classrooms, hospitals, institutions for the delinquent) and among members of various populations (including disturbed children and people with schizophrenia and other mental disabilities).

Cognitive Therapies

5: What are the goals and techniques of the cognitive therapies?

People with specific fears and problem behaviors respond to behavior therapy. But how would you modify the wide assortment of behaviors that accompany major depression? Or those associated with generalized anxiety, where unfocused anxiety doesn't lend itself to a neat list of anxiety-triggering situations? The same *cognitive revolution* that has profoundly changed other areas of psychology during the last five decades has influenced the practice of therapy in these areas.

Cognitive therapy for eating disorders aided by journaling :: Cognitive therapists guide people toward new ways of explaining their good and bad experiences. By recording each day's positive events and how they enabled them, for example, people may become more mindful of their self-control.

Figure 13.2> A cognitive perspective on psychological disorders The person's emotional reactions are produced not directly by the event but by the person's thoughts in response to the event.

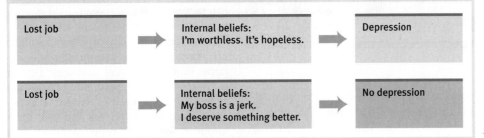

The **cognitive therapies** assume that our thinking colors our feelings (**FIGURE 13.2**), that between the event and our response lies the mind. Self-blaming and overgeneralized explanations of bad events are often an important part of the vicious cycle of depression (see Chapter 12). The depressed person interprets a suggestion as criticism, disagreement as dislike, praise as flattery, friendliness as pity. Dwelling on such thoughts sustains the bad mood. Cognitive therapists aim to help people change their minds with new ways of thinking.

> "Life does not consist mainly, or even largely, of facts and happenings. It consists mainly of the storm of thoughts that are forever blowing through one's mind."
>
> Mark Twain (1835–1910)

Beck's Therapy for Depression

Cognitive therapist Aaron Beck's original training was in Freudian techniques, including dream analysis. Depressed people, he found, often reported dreams with negative themes of loss, rejection, and abandonment. These thoughts extended into their waking thoughts, even into therapy, as clients recalled and rehearsed their failings and worst impulses (Kelly, 2000). How, Beck and his colleagues (1979) wondered, could they reverse their clients' negativity about themselves, their situations, and their futures? Their answer was the approach we call cognitive therapy. With gentle questioning intended to reveal irrational thinking, they persuaded depressed people to take off the dark glasses through which they view life (Beck & others, 1979, pp. 145–146):

Client: I agree with the descriptions of me but I guess I don't agree that the way I think makes me depressed.

Beck: How do you understand it?

Client: I get depressed when things go wrong. Like when I fail a test.

Beck: How can failing a test make you depressed?

Client: Well, if I fail I'll never get into law school.

Beck: So failing the test means a lot to you. But if failing a test could drive people into clinical depression, wouldn't you expect everyone who failed the test to have a depression? . . . Did everyone who failed get depressed enough to require treatment?

Client: No, but it depends on how important the test was to the person.

Beck: Right, and who decides the importance?

Client: I do.

Beck: And so, what we have to examine is your way of viewing the test (or the way that you think about the test) and how it affects your chances of getting into law school. Do you agree?

Client: Right.

Beck: Do you agree that the way you interpret the results of the test will affect you? You might feel depressed, you might have trouble sleeping, not feel like eating, and you might even wonder if you should drop out of the course.

Client: I have been thinking that I wasn't going to make it. Yes, I agree.

Beck: Now what did failing mean?

Client: (tearful) That I couldn't get into law school.

Beck: And what does that mean to you?

Client: That I'm just not smart enough.

Beck: Anything else?

Client: That I can never be happy.

Beck: And how do these thoughts make you feel?

Client: Very unhappy.

Beck: So it is the meaning of failing a test that makes you very unhappy. In fact, believing that you can never be happy is a powerful factor in producing unhappiness. So, you get yourself into a trap—by definition, failure to get into law school equals "I can never be happy."

We often think in words. Therefore, getting people to change what they say to themselves is an effective way to change their thinking. Perhaps you can identify with students who become anxious before taking an exam. It's easy to make matters worse with self-defeating thoughts. "This exam's probably going to be impossible. All these other students seem so relaxed and confident. I wish I were better prepared. Anyhow, I'm so nervous I'll forget everything." To change

token economy an operant conditioning procedure in which people earn a token for exhibiting a desired behavior and can later exchange the tokens for privileges or treats.

cognitive therapy therapy that teaches people new, more adaptive ways of thinking and acting; based on the assumption that thoughts intervene between events and our emotional reactions.

PEANUTS

Drawing by Charles Schulz; © 1956 Reprinted by permission of United Feature Syndicate, Inc.

such negative self-talk, therapists teach people to alter their thinking in stressful situations (Meichenbaum, 1977, 1985). Sometimes it may be enough simply to say more positive things to yourself. "Relax. The exam may be hard, but it will be hard for everyone else, too. I studied harder than most people. Besides, I don't need a perfect score to get a good grade." Experiments show that such training can be effective. Depression-prone children and college students who were trained to dispute their negative thoughts showed a greatly reduced (by half) rate of future depression (Seligman, 2002). To a great extent, it is the thought that counts.

Cognitive-Behavior Therapy

Cognitive-behavior therapy takes a double-barreled approach to depression and other disorders. This integrated approach aims not only to alter the way people think but also to alter the way they act. Like other cognitive therapies, it seeks to make people aware of their irrational negative thinking and to replace it with new ways of thinking. Like other behavior therapies, it trains people to practice the more positive approach in everyday settings.

In one study, people with obsessive-compulsive behaviors learned to relabel their compulsive thoughts (Schwartz & others, 1996). Feeling the urge to wash their hands again, they would tell themselves, "I'm having a compulsive urge." They would explain to themselves that it was a result of their brain's abnormal activity, which they had previously viewed in PET scans. Then, instead of giving in to the urge, they would spend 15 minutes in an enjoyable, alternative behavior, such as practicing an instrument, taking a walk, or gardening. This helped "unstick" the brain by shifting attention and engaging other

parts of the brain. For two or three months, the weekly therapy sessions continued, with relabeling and refocusing practice at home. By the study's end, most participants' symptoms had diminished, and their PET scans revealed normalized brain activity.

Group and Family Therapies

6: What are the benefits of group therapy?

Except for traditional psychoanalysis, most therapies may also occur in small groups. Group therapy does not provide the same degree of therapist involvement with each client. However, it saves therapists' time and clients' money, and it often is no less effective than individual therapy (Fuhriman & Burlingame, 1994). Therapists frequently suggest group therapy for people who are having family conflicts or for those whose behavior is distressing to others. Up to 90 minutes a week, the therapist guides the interactions of 6 to 10 people as they confront issues and react to one another.

The social context of group sessions offers some unique benefits. People discover that others have problems similar to their own. It can be a relief to find that others, despite their apparent composure, share your problems and your troublesome feelings. Group members can also receive feedback as they try out new ways of behaving. Hearing that you look poised, even though you feel anxious and self-conscious, can be very reassuring.

One special type of group interaction, **family therapy,** assumes that no person is an island, that we live and grow in relation to others, especially our families. We work to find an identity outside of our family, yet we also need to connect with family members emotionally. These two opposing tendencies can create stress for the individual and the family. This helps explain why therapists tend to view families as systems, in which each person's actions trigger reactions from others. To change these negative interactions, the therapist often attempts to guide family members toward positive relationships and improved communication.

Family therapy :: The therapist helps family members understand how their ways of relating to one another create problems. The treatment's emphasis is not on changing the individuals, but on changing their relationships and interactions.

Michael Newman/Photo Edit

PRACTICE TEST

1. A psychotherapist who encourages people to relate their dreams, and who searches for the unconscious roots of their problems is drawing from
   a. psychoanalysis.
   b. humanistic therapies.
   c. client-centered therapy.
   d. nondirective therapy.

2. According to psychoanalytic theory, developing strong feelings for the analyst is an important part of the psychoanalytic process and is called
   a. transference.
   b. resistance.
   c. interpretation.
   d. empathy.

3. Compared with psychoanalysts, humanistic therapists are more likely to emphasize
   a. hidden or repressed feelings.
   b. childhood experiences.
   c. psychological disorders.
   d. self-fulfillment and growth.

4. Especially important to Rogers' client-centered therapy is the technique of active listening, in which the therapist
   a. engages in free association.
   b. exposes the patient's resistances.
   c. restates and clarifies the client's statements.
   d. directly challenges the client's self-perceptions.

5. Behavior therapists apply learning principles to the treatment of problems such as phobias and alcohol dependence. In such treatment, the goal is to
   a. identify and treat the underlying causes of the problem.
   b. improve learning and insight.
   c. eliminate the unwanted behavior.
   d. improve communication and social sensitivity.

6. To produce new responses to old stimuli, behavior therapists often use counterconditioning techniques, such as systematic desensitization and
   a. resistance.
   b. aversive conditioning.
   c. transference.
   d. active listening.

7. Systematic desensitization is commonly used in the treatment of
   a. phobias.
   b. depression.
   c. alcoholism.
   d. bed-wetting.

8. Token economies are an application of
   a. classical conditioning.
   b. counterconditioning.
   c. cognitive therapy.
   d. operant conditioning.

9. Cognitive therapy has been effective in treating
   a. mental retardation.
   b. phobias.
   c. alcoholism.
   d. depression.

10. In family therapy, the therapist assumes that
    a. only one family member needs to change.
    b. each person's actions trigger reactions from other family members.
    c. dysfunctional families must improve their interactions or give up their children.
    d. all of these answers are true.

Answers: 1. a, 2. a, 3. d, 4. c, 5. c, 6. b, 7. a, 8. d, 9. d, 10. b.

Evaluating Psychotherapies

Many Americans have great confidence in psychotherapy's effectiveness. "Seek counseling" or "ask your mate to find a therapist," advice columnists often advise. Before 1950, psychiatrists were the primary providers of mental health care. Today, surging demands for psychotherapy still occupy the time and attention of psychiatrists, but also of many others. Psychotherapy is now offered by many clinical and counseling psychologists; clinical social workers; pastoral, marital, abuse, and school counselors; and psychiatric nurses. In 2004, 7.4 percent of Americans reported "undergoing counseling for mental or emotional problems," a 25 percent increase since 1991 (Smith, 2005).

Is the faith that millions of people worldwide place in these therapists justified? The question, though simply put, is not simply answered.

Is Psychotherapy Effective?

7: Does psychotherapy work? How do we know? Are some therapies more effective than others?

Measuring therapy's effectiveness is not like taking your body's temperature to see if your fever has gone away. If you and I were to undergo psychotherapy, how would we gauge its effectiveness? By how we feel about our progress? By how our therapist feels about it? By how our friends and family feel about it? By how our behavior has changed?

Clients' Perceptions

If clients' testimonials were the only measuring stick, we could strongly assert that psychotherapy is effective. Consider 2900 *Consumer Reports* readers who reported on their experiences with mental health professionals (1995; Kotkin & others, 1996; Seligman, 1995). How many were at least "fairly well satisfied"? Almost 90 percent (as was Kay Redfield Jamison, as you saw at this chapter's beginning). Among those who recalled feeling *fair* or *very poor* when beginning therapy, 9 in 10 now were feeling *very good, good,* or at least *so-so.* We have their word for it—and who should know better?

But client testimonials don't persuade everyone. Critics point out some reasons for skepticism.

---

cognitive-behavior therapy a popular integrated therapy that combines cognitive therapy (changing self-defeating thinking) with behavior therapy (changing behavior).

family therapy therapy that treats the family as a system. Views an individual's unwanted behaviors as influenced by or directed at other family members.

- *People often enter therapy in crisis.* When, with the normal ebb and flow of events, the crisis passes, people may assume their improvement was a result of the therapy.

- *Clients may need to justify their investment of effort and money.* People will be powerfully motivated to be able to say their therapy was worth the time and money.

- *Clients generally speak kindly of their therapists.* Even if their problems remain, clients "work hard to find something positive to say. The therapist had been very understanding, the client had gained a new perspective, he learned to communicate better, his mind was eased, anything at all so as not to have to say treatment was a failure" (Zilbergeld, 1983, p. 117).

Clinicians' Perceptions

If clinicians' perceptions were proof of therapy's effectiveness, we would have even more reason to celebrate. Case studies of successful treatment abound. Furthermore, therapists are like the rest of us. They treasure compliments from people they've tried to help—in this case, clients saying good-bye or later expressing their gratitude. The problem is that clients justify entering psychotherapy by emphasizing their unhappiness. They justify leaving by emphasizing their well-being. And they stay in touch only if they are satisfied. This means that therapists are most aware of the failures of *other* therapists—those whose clients, having experienced only temporary relief, are now seeking a new therapist for their recurring problems. Thus, the same person, suffering from the same old anxiety, depression, or marital difficulty, may be a "success" story in several therapists' files.

Outcome Research

How, then, can we objectively assess psychotherapy's effectiveness? What types of people and problems are best helped, and by what type of psychotherapy? These questions are important both academically and personally. If you feel anxious or depressed, or someone close to you shows these or other symptoms, you'll want to know the best way to get help.

In search of answers, psychologists have turned to controlled research studies. This is a well-traveled path. In the 1800s, skeptical medical doctors asking similar questions transformed their field into a science. These skeptics began to realize that many patients got better on their own, that most of the fashionable treatments (bleeding, purging) were doing no good. Sorting fact from superstition required following illnesses closely, and keeping records of what happened with and without a particular treatment. Typhoid fever patients, for example, often improved after being bled, convincing most doctors that the treatment worked. Not until a control group was given mere bed rest—and 70 percent were observed to improve after five weeks of fever—did doctors learn, to their shock, that the bleeding treatment was worthless (Thomas, 1992).

In psychology, Hans Eysenck (1952) was first to challenge the effectiveness of psychotherapy. He summarized studies showing that two-thirds of those receiving psychotherapy for disorders not involving hallucinations or delusions improved markedly. To this day, no one disputes that optimistic estimate.

Why, then, are we still debating psychotherapy's effectiveness? Because Eysenck also reported similar improvement among *untreated* persons, such as those who were on waiting lists for treatment. With or without psychotherapy, he said, roughly two-thirds improved noticeably. Time was a great healer.

An avalanche of criticism greeted Eysenck's conclusions. Some critics pointed out errors in his analysis. Others noted that he based his ideas on only 24 studies. Now, more than a half-century later, those who want proof of psychotherapy's effectiveness have hundreds of outcome studies to analyze. The best of these are *randomized clinical trials.* Researchers randomly assign people on a waiting list to therapy, and then at some later point, they compare the outcomes to those of people not receiving therapy.

Trauma :: These women are mourning the tragic loss of family members in Tanzanian mines that were flooded by heavy rains in 2008. Those who suffer through such trauma may benefit from counseling, though many people recover on their own, or with the help of supportive relationships with family and friends.

Simon Maina/AFP/Getty Images

When researchers used statistical methods to combine the results of 475 investigations (Smith & others, 1980), psychotherapists welcomed the result **(FIGURE 13.3)**. The average therapy client ends up better off than 80 percent of the untreated individuals on waiting lists. This claim is more modest than it first appears. By definition, about 50 percent of people who receive no treatment are also better off than the average untreated person.

Newer research summaries confirm that psychotherapy works (Kopta & others, 1999; Shadish & others, 2000). Consider one ambitious study done by the National Institute of Mental Health. Experienced therapists at three research sites were trained in one of three depression treatment methods: cognitive therapy, interpersonal therapy, and a standard drug therapy. Then, 239 participants suffering from depression were randomly assigned to one of these therapists or to a control group. People in the control group received a placebo (a sugar pill) and supportive attention, encouragement, and advice. Participants in all three treatment groups improved more than did those in the control group. At the end of the full 16-week program, the depression lifted for slightly more than half the people in each of the three treatment groups. Only

Figure 13.3> Treatment versus no treatment In 475 studies, the outcome for the average therapy client was better than that for 80 percent of the untreated people. (Adapted from Smith & others, 1980.)

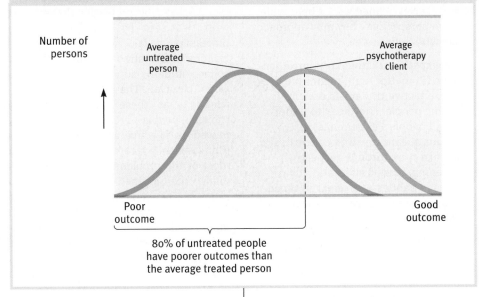

29 percent of those in the control group showed similar improvement (Elkin & others, 1989). The results echo the earlier outcome studies: *Those not undergoing therapy often improve, but those undergoing therapy are more likely to improve.*

It's good to know that psychotherapy, in general at least, is somewhat effective. But what distressed people—and those paying for their therapy—really want to know is not the *average* effectiveness of *all* therapy but the *particular* effectiveness of a treatment for *specific* problems. So what can we tell these people?

Which Therapies Work Best?

The early statistical summaries and surveys did not find that any one type of therapy is generally better than others (Smith & others, 1977, 1980). Newer studies have had similarly generalized results. There is little if any connection between clinicians' experience, training, supervision, and licensing and their clients' outcomes (Bickman, 1999; Luborsky & others, 2002). Clients sharing their views with

Consumer Reports agree. Were they treated by a psychiatrist, psychologist, or social worker? Were they seen in a group or individual context? Did the therapist have extensive or relatively limited training and experience? It didn't matter. They seemed equally satisfied (Seligman, 1995).

So was the dodo bird in *Alice in Wonderland* right: "Everyone has won and all must have prizes"? Not quite. Some forms of therapy get prizes for *particular* problems. Behavioral conditioning therapies, for example, have had especially good results with specific behavior problems, such as bed-wetting, phobias, compulsions, marital problems, and sexual disorders (Bowers & Clum, 1988; Hunsley & DiGiulio, 2002; Shadish & Baldwin, 2005). And newer studies confirm cognitive therapy's effectiveness in coping with depression and reducing suicide risk (Brown & others, 2005; DeRubeis & others, 2005; Hollon & others, 2005).

"Different sores have different salves."

English proverb

But no prizes—and little or no scientific support—go to other therapies (Arkowitz & Lilienfeld, 2006). We would all therefore be wise to avoid the following unsupported approaches.

- *Energy therapies* propose to manipulate people's invisible energy fields.

- *Recovered memory therapies* aim to unearth "repressed memories" of early child abuse. (See Chapter 7.)

- *Rebirthing therapies* engage people in reenacting the supposed trauma of their birth.

- *Facilitated communication* has an assistant touch the typing hand of a child with autism.

- *Crisis debriefing* forces people to rehearse and "process" their recent traumatic experiences.

But this raises another question. Who should decide which therapies get prizes and which do not? This question lies at the heart of a controversy—some call it psychology's civil war—over the role science should play in clinical practice and the extent to which science should guide health-care providers and insurers in setting payment policies for psychotherapy. On one side are research psychologists using scientific methods to extend the list of well-defined and validated therapies for various disorders. On the other side are the nonscientist therapists who view their practices as more art than science, not something that can be described in a manual or tested in an

"I utilize the best from Freud, the best from Jung, and the best from my Uncle Marty, a very smart fellow."

experiment. People are too complex and therapy too intuitive for a cookie-cutter approach, many therapists say. Between them stand the science-oriented clinicians. If we base practice on evidence and make mental health professionals accountable for effectiveness, everyone gains, say these clinicians. The public will be protected from false therapies, and therapists will be protected from accusations of sounding like snake-oil salesmen—"Trust me, I know it works, I've seen it work."

How Do Psychotherapies Help People?

8: What three elements are shared by all forms of effective psychotherapy? How do differences in culture and values influence the relationship between a therapist and a client?

How can it be that therapists' training and experience do not seem to influence clients' outcomes? The answer seems to be that all therapies offer three basic benefits (Frank, 1982; Goldfried & Padawer, 1982; Strupp, 1986; Wampold, 2001).

■ *Hope for demoralized people.* People seeking therapy typically feel anxious, depressed, self-disapproving, and not capable of turning things around. What any therapy offers is the expectation that, with commitment from the therapy seeker, things can and will get better. This belief, apart from any therapy technique, may help improve morale, create feelings of inner strength, and reduce symptoms (Prioleau & others, 1983). Each therapy, in its own way, may therefore harness the person's own healing powers. And that helps us understand why all sorts of treatments—including some folk-healing rites with no scientific support for their effectiveness—may in their own time and place produce cures (Frank, 1982).

■ *A new perspective.* Every therapy offers people an explanation of their symptoms. Therapy can also offer new experiences. These new windows on the world can help people change their behaviors and their views of themselves. Armed with a believable fresh perspective, they may approach life with new energy.

■ *An empathic, trusting, caring relationship.* No matter what technique they use, effective therapists are empathic people. They seek to understand people's experience, to communicate care and concern, and to earn trust through respectful listening, reassurance, and advice. These qualities were clear in taped therapy sessions from 36 recognized master therapists (Goldfried & others, 1998). Some were cognitive-behavior therapists. Others were psychodynamic-interpersonal therapists. Regardless, they were *strikingly similar* during the most significant parts of their sessions. At key moments, the empathic therapists of both types would help clients evaluate themselves, link one aspect of their life with another, and gain insight into their interactions with others. Warmth and empathy are hallmarks of effective healers everywhere, whether psychiatrists, witch doctors, or shamans (Torrey, 1986).

A caring relationship :: Effective therapists form a bond of trust with their patients.

Mary Kate Denny/Photo Edit

An analysis of 39 studies supports this idea that effective therapies offer *hope* through a *fresh perspective* offered by a *caring person.* Each study compared treatment offered by professional therapists with treatment by laypeople: friendly professors, others with a few hours' training in empathic listening skills, and college students supervised by a professional clinician. The result? The *paraprofessionals,* as these and other briefly trained people are called, typically proved as effective as the professionals (Christensen & Jacobson, 1994). Although most of the problems they treated were mild, the trained paraprofessionals were—believe it or not—as effective as professionals even when dealing with more disturbed adults, such as those diagnosed with serious depression.

Let's recap. People who seek help usually improve. So do many of those who do not undergo psychotherapy, and that is a tribute to our human resilience and our capacity to care for one another. Nevertheless, though the therapist's orientation and experience appear not to matter much, people who receive some psychotherapy usually improve more than those who do not. People with clear-cut, specific problems tend to improve the most.

These three common ingredients of effective therapy—hope, a fresh way of looking at life, and an empathic, caring relationship—may explain why a paraprofessional's empathy and friendly counsel can be as helpful as professional psychotherapy. They may also explain another finding. People who feel supported by close relationships, who enjoy the fellowship and friendship of caring people, are less likely to need or seek therapy (Frank, 1982; O'Connor & Brown, 1984).

"Fortunately, [psycho]analysis is not the only way to resolve inner conflicts. Life itself still remains a very effective therapist."

Karen Horney, *Our Inner Conflicts,* 1945

Culture and Values in Psychotherapy

All therapies offer hope. Nearly all therapists attempt to enhance their clients' sensitivity, openness, personal responsibility, and sense of purpose (Jensen & Bergin, 1988). But in matters of cultural and moral diversity, therapists differ from one another and may differ from their clients (Kelly, 1990).

These differences can create a mismatch when a therapist from one culture interacts with a client from another. In North America, Europe, and Australia, for example, many therapists reflect the majority culture's *individualism*, which often gives priority to personal desires and identity. Clients with a *collectivist* perspective, as may be the case in those with Asian ancestry, for example, may assume people will be more mindful of others' expectations. These clients may have trouble relating to therapies that require them to think only of their own well-being. Such differences help explain why some minority populations are less likely to use mental health services (Sue, 2006). In one experiment, Asian-American clients matched with counselors who shared their cultural values (rather than mismatched with those who did not) perceived more counselor empathy and felt more alliance with the counselor (Kim & others, 2005).

Another area of potential value conflict is religion. Highly religious people may prefer religiously similar therapists, and they may have trouble establishing an emotional bond with a therapist who does not share their values (Wade & others, 2007; Worthington & others, 1996).

Albert Ellis, a well-known therapist, and Allen Bergin, co-editor of the *Handbook of Psychotherapy and Behavior Change*, illustrated how sharply therapists can differ, and how those differences can affect their view of a healthy person. Ellis (1980) assumed that "no one and nothing is supreme," that "self-gratification" should be encouraged, and that "unequivocal love, commitment, service, and . . . fidelity to any interpersonal commitment, especially marriage, leads to harmful consequences." Bergin (1980) assumed the opposite—that "because God is supreme, humility and the acceptance of divine authority are virtues," that "self-control and committed love and self-sacrifice are to be encouraged," and that "infidelity to any interpersonal commitment, especially marriage, leads to harmful consequences."

Bergin's and Ellis' values differ more radically than those of most therapists. However, their example helps illustrate an important point. *Psychotherapists' personal beliefs and values influence their practice.* Because clients tend to adopt their therapists' values (Worthington & others, 1996), some psychologists believe therapists should express those values more openly. (For therapy options see Close-Up: A Consumer's Guide to Psychotherapists.)

CLOSE-UP

A CONSUMER'S GUIDE TO PSYCHOTHERAPISTS

Life for everyone is marked by a mix of serenity and stress, blessing and bereavement, good moods and bad. So, when should a person seek the help of a mental health professional? When troubling thoughts, emotions, or behaviors interfere with your normal living, you might consider talking to a professional. The American Psychological Association offers these common trouble signals:

- Feelings of hopelessness
- Deep and lasting depression
- Self-destructive behavior, such as alcohol and drug abuse
- Disruptive fears
- Sudden mood shifts
- Thoughts of suicide
- Compulsive rituals, such as hand washing
- Sexual difficulties

In looking for a therapist, you may want to have a preliminary consultation with two or three. You can describe your problem and learn each therapist's treatment approach. You can ask questions about the therapist's values, credentials (TABLE 13.1), and fees. And you can assess your own feelings about each of them. The emotional bond between therapist and client is perhaps the most important factor in effective therapy.

Table 13.1	Therapists and Their Training
Type	**Description**
Counselors	Marriage and family counselors specialize in family relations problems. Pastoral counselors provide counseling to countless people.
Clinical or psychiatric social workers	A social work graduate program plus post-graduate supervision prepares professionals to offer psychotherapy, mostly to people with everyday personal and family problems. About half have earned the National Association of Social Workers' designation of clinical social worker.
Clinical psychologists	Most are psychologists with a Ph.D. or Psy.D., supplemented by a supervised internship. About half work in agencies and institutions, half in private practice.
Psychiatrists	Psychiatrists are medical doctors who specialize in the treatment of psychological disorders and who, as M.D.s, can prescribe medications.

The Biomedical Therapies

Psychotherapy is one way to treat psychological disorders. The other, often used with the most serious disorders, is *biomedical therapy*. This form of treatment changes the brain's functioning by altering its chemistry with drugs, or affecting its circuitry with electrical stimulation, magnetic impulses, or psychosurgery. Although psychologists can provide psychological therapies, only psychiatrists (as medical doctors) offer most biomedical therapies.

Drug Therapies

9: What are the most common forms of biomedical therapies? What criticisms have been leveled against drug therapies?

By far the most widely used biomedical treatments today are the drug therapies. Since the 1950s, drug researchers have written a new chapter in the treatment of people with severe disorders. Thanks to drug therapies and support from community mental health programs, hundreds of thousands of people have been freed from hospital confinement. The resident population of U.S. state and county mental hospitals is now a fraction of what it was a half-century ago **(FIGURE 13.4)**.

Almost any new treatment, including drug therapy, is greeted by an initial wave of enthusiasm as many people apparently improve. But that enthusiasm often diminishes on closer examination. To judge the effectiveness of a new treatment, we also need to know the rates of

■ normal recovery among untreated people.

■ recovery due to the *placebo effect,* which arises from the positive expectations of patients and mental health workers alike.

To control for these influences when testing a new drug, researchers give half the patients the drug, and the other half a similar-appearing placebo. Because neither the staff nor the patients know who gets which, this is called a *double-blind technique.* The good news: In double-blind studies, several types of drugs have proven useful in treating psychological disorders.

Antipsychotic Drugs

Accidents sometimes launch revolutions. When physicians accidentally discovered that certain drugs, used for other medical

"If this doesn't help you don't worry, it's a placebo."

purposes, calmed *psychotic* patients, they launched a revolution in treatment for these patients. People with psychoses show a split from reality, with symptoms such as hallucinations and delusions. **Antipsychotic drugs,** such as chlorpromazine (sold as Thorazine), reduce patients' overreaction to irrelevant stimuli. Thus, they provide the most help to schizophrenia patients experiencing positive symptoms, such as auditory hallucinations and paranoia (Lehman & others, 1998; Lenzenweger & others, 1989). People with negative symptoms, such as apathy and withdrawal, often do not respond well to antipsychotic drugs. Another drug, clozapine (marketed since 1989 as Clozaril), does sometimes enable "awakenings" in these individuals. It may also help those who have positive symptoms but have not responded to other drugs.

Antipsychotic drugs mimic certain neurotransmitters. Molecules of antipsychotic drugs can occupy dopamine receptor sites and block its activity (Pickar & others, 1984; Taubes, 1994). This finding reinforced the idea that an overactive dopamine system contributes to schizophrenia.

Perhaps you can guess an occasional side effect of L-dopa, a drug that raises dopamine levels for Parkinson's patients: hallucinations.

Antipsychotics are powerful drugs with powerful side effects. Some produce sluggishness, tremors, and twitches similar to those of Parkinson's disease (a disease in which a person produces too little dopamine) (Kaplan & Saddock, 1989). Long-term use of antipsychotics can also produce *tardive dyskinesia*, with involuntary movements of the facial muscles (such as grimacing), tongue, and limbs. Newer antipsychotics have fewer of these side effects, but they may increase the risk of obesity and diabetes (Lieberman & others, 2005). Despite their drawbacks, antipsychotics, combined with life-skills programs and family support, have given new hope to many people with schizophrenia. Hundreds of

Figure 13.4> The emptying of U.S. mental hospitals After the widespread introduction of antipsychotic drugs, starting in about 1955, the number of residents in state and county mental hospitals declined sharply. But in the rush to deinstitutionalize the mentally ill, many people who were ill-equipped to care for themselves were left homeless on city streets. (Data from the U.S. National Institute of Mental Health and Bureau of the Census, 2004.)

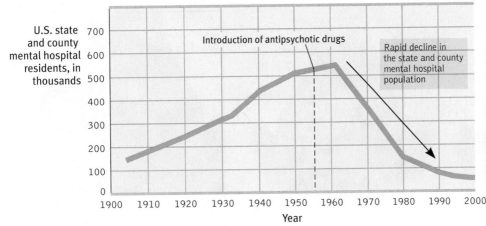

Les Snider/The Image Works

thousands of patients have left the wards of mental hospitals and returned to work and to near-normal lives (Leucht & others, 2003).

Antianxiety Drugs

Like alcohol, **antianxiety drugs,** such as Xanax or Ativan, depress central nervous system activity (and so should not be used in combination with alcohol). These drugs are often used in combination with psychological therapy, calming anxiety as the person learns to cope with frightening situations and fear-triggering stimuli.

One criticism made of antianxiety drugs is that they may reduce symptoms without resolving underlying problems, especially if these substances are used as an ongoing treatment. "Popping a Xanax" at the first sign of tension can produce psychological dependence; the immediate

On U.S. college campuses, the 9 percent of counseling center visitors taking psychiatric medication in 1994 nearly tripled, to 24.5 percent in 2004 (Duenwald, 2004).

relief reinforces a person's tendency to take drugs when anxious. Heavy use can also lead to physical dependence. People who then stop taking antianxiety drugs may experience increased anxiety, insomnia, and other withdrawal symptoms.

Antidepressant Drugs

The **antidepressant drugs** were named for their ability to lift people up from a state of depression, and this was their main use until recently. But now that name doesn't tell it all. These drugs are also used to treat anxiety disorders such as obsessive-compulsive disorder. They work by increasing the availability of norepinephrine or serotonin. These neurotransmitters elevate arousal and mood and appear scarce during depression. Fluoxetine, which tens of millions of users worldwide have known as Prozac, partially blocks the normal reuptake of excess serotonin from synapses (**FIGURE 13.5** on the next page).

Prozac, and its cousins Zoloft and Paxil, are called *selective-serotonin-reuptake-inhibitors (SSRIs)* because they slow (inhibit) the synaptic vacuuming up

(reuptake) of serotonin. Other antidepressants similarly work by blocking the reuptake or breakdown of serotonin and another neurotransmitter—norepinephrine. These *dual-action drugs* are effective, but they have more potential side effects, such as dry mouth, weight gain, high blood pressure, or dizzy spells (Anderson, 2000; Mulrow, 1999). To reduce these effects, the dual-action drugs are sometimes given in a patch (much like the nicotine patches used by people trying to stop smoking), which keeps them out of the digestive system (Bodkin & Amsterdam, 2002).

One side effect of SSRI drugs can be decreased sexual appetite, which has led to their occasional prescription to control sexual behavior (Slater, 2000).

antipsychotic drugs drugs used to treat schizophrenia and other forms of severe thought disorders.

antianxiety drugs drugs used to control anxiety and agitation.

antidepressant drugs drugs used to treat depression and some anxiety disorders. Different types work by altering the availability of various neurotransmitters.

Figure 13.5> Biology of antidepressants   Shown here is the action of Prozac, which partially blocks the reuptake of serotonin.

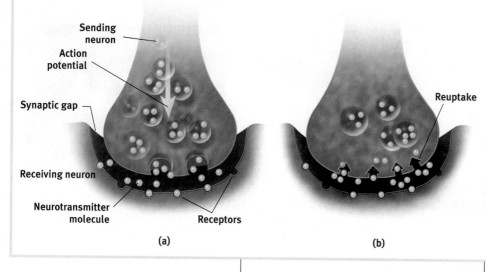

Message is sent across synaptic gap.

Message is received; excess neurotransmitter molecules are reabsorbed by sending neuron.

Prozac partially blocks normal reuptake of the neurotransmitter serotonin; excess serotonin in synapse enhances its mood-lifting effect.

Sending neuron
Action potential
Synaptic gap
Receiving neuron
Neurotransmitter molecule
Receptors

(a)

Reuptake

(b)

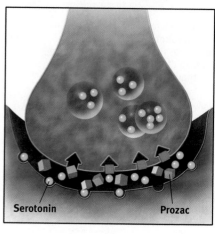

Serotonin   Prozac

(c)

In 1987, the year before SSRI drugs were introduced, 7 in 10 patients being treated for depression received medication. In 2001, nearly 9 in 10 were being treated with drug therapy (Olfson & others, 2003; Stafford & others, 2001). Although SSRIs begin to influence neurotransmission within hours, their full psychological effect may take four weeks.

Antidepressant drugs are not the only way to give our mood a lift. Aerobic exercise helps calm people who feel anxious and energize those who feel depressed. For people with mild to moderate depression, aerobic exercise seems to do about as much good as drugs, and it has additional positive side effects (see Chapter 10). Cognitive therapy, which helps people reverse their habits of thinking negatively, can boost the drug-aided relief from depression and reduce post-treatment relapses (Hollon & others, 2002; Keller & others, 2000). The best approach seems to be attacking depression from both above and below (Goldapple & others, 2004; TADS, 2004). Antidepressant drugs work, bottom-up, on the emotion-forming limbic system.

Cognitive behavior therapy works, top-down, by changing thought processes.

Everyone agrees that people with depression often improve after a month on antidepressants. But after allowing for natural recovery (the return to normal called *spontaneous recovery*) and the placebo effect, how big is the drug effect? Not big, report some researchers (Kirsch & others, 1998, 2002). In double-blind clinical

"I think the dosage needs adjusting. I'm not nearly as happy as the people in the ads."

trials, placebos produced improvement comparable to about 75 percent of the active drug's effect. Analysis of data from 45 studies showed similar results. When people with depression were given antidepressants, about 4 in 10 of them improved. When given placebos, about 3 in 10 improved (Khan & others, 2000).

The effects of drug therapy may be less exciting than many TV ads suggest, but they also are less frightening than other stories have warned. Some people taking Prozac, for example, have committed suicide, but their numbers seem fewer than we would expect from the millions of depressed people who take the medication. Prozac users who commit suicide are like cellphone users who get brain cancer. Given the millions of people taking Prozac or using cellphones, alarming anecdotes tell us nothing. The question critical thinkers want answered is this: Do people in these groups have a *higher rate* of suicide or brain cancer? In each case, the answer appears to be no (Grunebaum & others, 2004; Paulos, 1995; Søndergård & others, 2006a,b).

Mood-Stabilizing Medications

In addition to antipsychotic, antianxiety, and antidepressant drugs, psychiatrists have *mood-stabilizing* drugs in their arsenal. The simple salt *lithium* can effectively level the emotional highs and lows of bipolar disorder. Australian physician John Cade discovered this in the 1940s when he administered lithium to a patient with severe mania. Cade's reasoning was misguided. He thought lithium had calmed excitable guinea pigs, when actually it had made them sick. But less than a week after taking the lithium, Cade's patient became perfectly well (Snyder, 1986).

> Depakote, a drug originally used to treat epilepsy, has also been found effective in the control of manic episodes associated with bipolar disorder.

Although we do not understand why, lithium works. About 7 in 10 people with bipolar disorder benefit from a long-term daily dose of this cheap salt (Solomon & others, 1995). Their risk of suicide is but one-sixth that of bipolar patients not taking lithium (Tondo & others, 1997). Kay Redfield Jamison (1995, pp. 88–89) describes the effect. "Lithium prevents my seductive but disastrous highs, diminishes my depressions, clears out the wool and webbing from my disordered thinking, slows me down, gentles me out, keeps me from ruining my career and relationships, keeps me out of a hospital, alive, and makes psychotherapy possible."

"First of all I think you should know that last quarter's sales figures are interfering with my mood-stabilizing drugs."

Brain Stimulation

10: How is brain stimulation used as a treatment for depression? Under what conditions might psychosurgery be considered for changing behavior or mood?

Electroconvulsive Therapy

A more controversial form of biomedical treatment, **electroconvulsive therapy (ECT),** manipulates the brain by shocking it. When ECT was first introduced in 1938, the wide-awake patient was strapped to a table and jolted with roughly 100 volts of electricity to the brain, producing racking convulsions and brief unconsciousness. ECT therefore gained a barbaric image, one that lingers still. Today, however, the patient receives a general anesthetic and a muscle relaxant to prevent convulsions. A psychiatrist then delivers a series of brief electrical pulses to the patient's brain. Within 30 minutes, the patient wakens and remembers nothing of the treatment or of the hours preceding it (**FIGURE 13.6** on the next page).

Does this treatment work? Yes. Shocking as it may seem, study after study confirms that ECT is an effective treatment for severe depression in patients who have not responded to drug therapy (Consensus Conference, 1985; UK ECT Review Group, 2003). After three such sessions each week for two to four weeks, 80 percent or more of those who receive ECT improve markedly. They show some memory loss for the treatment period but no apparent brain damage (Bergsholm & others, 1989; Coffey, 1993). A *Journal of the American Medical Association* editorial concluded that "the results of ECT in treating severe depression are among the most positive treatment effects in all of medicine" (Glass, 2001). ECT reduces suicidal thoughts and is credited with saving many from suicide (Kellner & others, 2005).

How does ECT relieve severe depression? After more than 50 years, no one knows for sure. One patient compared

"I used to . . . be unable to shake the dread even when I was feeling good, because I knew the bad feelings would return. ECT has wiped away that foreboding. It has given me a sense of control, of hope."
Kitty Dukakis, *Shock: The Healing Power of Electroconvulsive Therapy,* 2006

ECT to the smallpox vaccine, which was saving lives before we knew how it worked. Perhaps the shock-induced seizures cause the brain to react by calming neural centers where overactivity produces depression.

Given this ignorance about how ECT works, the idea of electrically shocking people still strikes many as barbaric. Although it is now administered with briefer pulses, often only to the right side, and although it disrupts memory less (Fink, 1998; Kho & others, 2003), its Frankensteinlike image continues. Moreover, ECT-treated patients, like other patients with a history of depression, may have relapses. Nevertheless, ECT is, in the minds of many psychiatrists and patients, a lesser evil than severe depression's misery, anguish, and risk of suicide.

> **electroconvulsive therapy (ECT)** a biomedical therapy for severely depressed patients in which a brief electric current is sent through the brain of an anesthetized patient.

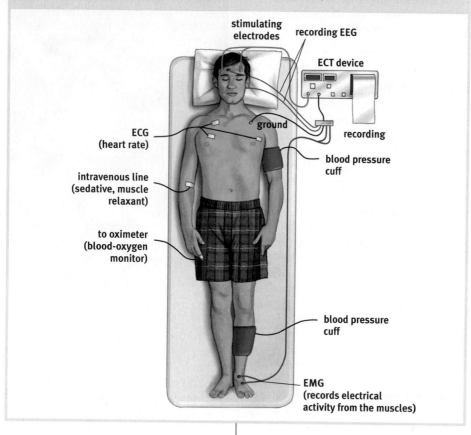

Figure 13.6> Electroconvulsive therapy Although controversial, ECT is often an effective treatment for depression that does not respond to drug therapy. "Electroconvulsive" is no longer accurate because patients are now given a drug that prevents convulsions.

stimulating electrodes

recording EEG

ECT device

ground

recording

ECG (heart rate)

blood pressure cuff

intravenous line (sedative, muscle relaxant)

to oximeter (blood-oxygen monitor)

blood pressure cuff

EMG (records electrical activity from the muscles)

Alternatives to ECT

Hopes are now rising for gentler alternatives for jump-starting the depressed brain. One treatment that has brought relief to some is an electrical device that is implanted in the chest of a person with chronic depression. The device periodically stimulates the vagus nerve, which sends signals to the brain's mood-related limbic system (Marangell & others, 2002; Rush & others, 2005).

Another new experimental procedure, *deep stimulation,* is administered by a pacemaker that controls implanted electrodes (Mayberg & others, 2005). The stimulation inhibits activity in a brain area that feeds negative emotions and thinking. Patients whose depression has not responded to drugs or ECT have

found their depression lifting in response to this stimulation.

Depressed moods also seem to improve when repeated pulses of magnetic energy are applied to a person's brain. In a painless procedure called **repetitive transcranial magnetic stimulation (rTMS),** a coiled wire held close to the skull sends a magnetic field through the skull to the brain **(FIGURE 13.7).** Unlike deep brain stimulation, the magnetic energy penetrates only to the brain's surface. And unlike ECT, the rTMS procedure produces no seizures, memory loss, or other side effects. Wide-awake patients receive this treatment daily for two to four weeks.

After studies confirmed the benefit of this therapy, two large, multilocation rTMS clinical experiments began in 2005

(Cohen & others, 2005; Janicak, 2005; Martin & others, 2005). How rTMS works is not yet clear. One possible explanation is that the stimulation energizes the brain's left frontal lobe, which is relatively inactive during depression (Helmuth, 2001). Repeated stimulation may cause nerve cells to form new functioning circuits through the process of long-term potentiation. (See Chapter 7 for more details on LTP.) Will rTMS fulfill its promise as a valuable new treatment for depression? Data from the two big clinical trials should soon help answer that question.

Psychosurgery

Because its effects are irreversible, **psychosurgery**—surgery that removes or destroys brain tissue—is the most drastic and the least-used biomedical intervention for changing thoughts and behaviors. In the 1930s, Portuguese physician Egas Moniz developed what became the best-known psychosurgical operation: the **lobotomy.** Moniz found that cutting the nerves connecting the frontal lobes with the emotion-controlling centers of the inner brain calmed uncontrollably emotional and violent patients. His crude but easy and inexpensive procedure took only about 10 minutes. After shocking the patient into a coma, a neurosurgeon would hammer an instrument shaped like an icepick through each eye socket into the brain, and wiggle it to sever connections running up to the frontal lobes. Tens of thousands of severely disturbed people were "lobotomized" during the 1940s and 1950s, and Moniz was honored with a Nobel prize (Valenstein, 1986).

Although the intention was simply to disconnect emotion from thought, the effect was often more drastic. A lobotomy usually produced a permanently listless, immature, impulsive personality. During the 1950s, after some 35,000 people had been lobotomized in the United States alone, calming drugs became available and psychosurgery was largely abandoned. Today, lobotomies are history, and other psychosurgery is used only in extreme

Figure 13.7> Magnets for the mind In rTMS, a painless magnetic field is sent through the skull to the surface of the brain. Pulses can stimulate or dampen activity in various areas. (From George, 2003.)

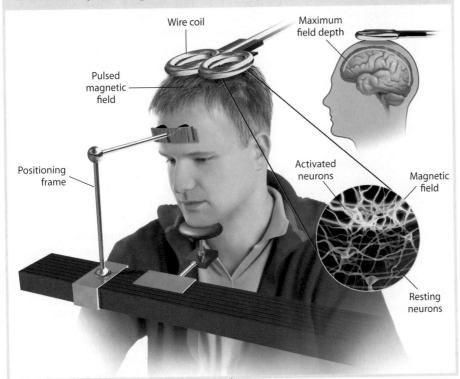

Wire coil

Maximum field depth

Pulsed magnetic field

Positioning frame

Activated neurons

Magnetic field

Resting neurons

Failed lobotomy :: This 1940 photo shows Rosemary Kennedy (center) at age 22 with brother (and future U.S. president) John and sister Jean. A year later her father, on medical advice, approved a lobotomy that was promised to control her reportedly violent mood swings. The procedure left her institutionalized with an infantile mentality until her death in 2005 at age 86.

New York Times Co./Getty Images

cases. For example, if a patient suffers uncontrollable seizures, surgeons can destroy the specific nerve clusters that cause or transmit the convulsions. MRI-guided precision surgery is also occasionally done to cut the circuits involved in severe obsessive-compulsive disorder (Sachdev & Sachdev, 1997). Because these procedures are irreversible, however, neurosurgeons perform them only as a last resort.

* * *

The effectiveness of the biomedical therapies reminds us of one of our big ideas. Behavior is a biopsychosocial event. We find it convenient to talk of separate psychological and biological influences, but everything psychological is also biological **(FIGURE 13.8)**. Every thought and feeling depends on the functioning brain. Every creative idea, every moment of joy or anger, every period of depression emerges from the electrochemical activity of the

living brain. The influence is two-way: When psychotherapy relieves obsessive-compulsive behavior, PET scans reveal a calmer brain (Schwartz & others, 1996).

TABLE 13.2 on the next page summarizes the problems, goals, and techniques of the types of therapies discussed in this chapter.

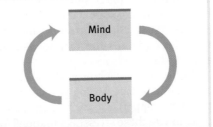

Mind

Body

Figure 13.8> Mind-body interaction The biomedical therapies assume that mind and body are a unit: Affect one and you will affect the other.

repetitive transcranial magnetic stimulation (rTMS) the application of repeated pulses of magnetic energy to the brain; used to stimulate or suppress brain activity.

psychosurgery surgery that removes or destroys brain tissue in an effort to change behavior.

lobotomy a psychosurgical procedure once used to calm uncontrollably emotional or violent patients. The procedure cut the nerves connecting the frontal lobes to the emotion-controlling centers of the inner brain.

Table 13.2	Comparing Therapies		
Therapy	**Presumed Problem**	**Therapy Aim**	**Therapy Technique**
Psychodynamic	Unconscious conflicts and urges	Promote insight into repressed material.	Psychoanalysis; therapist's interpretations of patient's memories and feelings.
Client-centered	Blocking of self-acceptance	Enable growth via unconditional positive regard, genuineness, and empathy.	Active reflective listening.
Behavior	Dysfunctional behaviors	Relearn adaptive behaviors; extinguish problem ones.	Classical conditioning via exposure or aversion therapy; operant conditioning, as in token economies.
Cognitive	Self-harmful thoughts	Promote positive thinking.	Training people to dispute negative thoughts and attributions.
Biomedical	Brain or neurotransmitter malfunctions	Restore healthy biological state.	Drugs; brain stimulation; exercise.

Preventing Psychological Disorders

11: What is the purpose of preventive mental health programs?

Psychotherapies and biomedical therapies tend to locate the cause of psychological disorders within the person. We assume that people who act cruelly must be cruel, and that people who act "crazy" must be "sick." We attach labels to such people, thereby distinguishing them from "normal" folks. It follows, then, that we try to treat "abnormal" people. We try to give them insight into their problems, to change their thinking, to help them gain control with drugs or brain stimulation.

There is an alternative viewpoint: We could interpret many psychological disorders as understandable responses to a disturbing and stressful society. In this view, it is not just the person who needs treatment, but also the person's social context. Better to prevent a problem by reforming a sick situation and by developing people's coping skills than to wait for a problem to arise.

A story about the rescue of a drowning person from a rushing river illustrates this viewpoint. Having successfully given first aid to the first victim, the rescuer spots another struggling person and pulls her out, too. After a half-dozen repetitions, the rescuer suddenly turns and starts running away while the river sweeps yet another floundering person into view. "Aren't you going to rescue that fellow?" asks a bystander. "Heck no," the rescuer replies. "I'm going upstream to find out what's pushing all these people in."

Preventive mental health is upstream work. It seeks to prevent psychological casualties by identifying and wiping out the conditions that cause them. Poverty, meaningless work, constant criticism, unemployment, racism, and sexism can undermine people's sense of competence, personal control, and self-esteem (Albee, 1986). Such stresses increase their risk of depression, alcohol dependence, and suicide.

To prevent psychological casualties, George Albee says, caring people should therefore support programs that control or eliminate these stressful situations. We eliminated smallpox not by treating the afflicted but by vaccinating the healthy. We conquered yellow fever by controlling mosquitoes. Prevention of psychological problems means empowering those who have learned an attitude of helplessness and changing environments that breed loneliness. It means renewing the disintegrating family and bolstering parents' and teachers' skills at nurturing children's achievements and resulting self-esteem. Indeed, "Everything aimed at improving the human condition, at making life more fulfilling and meaningful, may be considered part of primary prevention of mental or emotional disturbance" (Kessler & Albee, 1975, p. 557).

There is, however, more to the story of psychological disorders than toxic environments and pessimism. Anxiety disorders, major depression, bipolar disorder, and schizophrenia are in part biological events. Again, we see one of this book's big ideas. *A human being is an integrated biopsychosocial system.* We now know that stress affects body chemistry and health. And chemical imbalances, whatever their cause, can produce schizophrenia and depression. As an ancient Latin saying advised long ago, our goal must be "a healthy mind in a healthy body."

"It is better to prevent than to cure."
Peruvian folk wisdom

"Mental disorders arise from physical ones, and likewise physical disorders arise from mental ones."

The Mahabharata, c. A.D. 200

PRACTICE TEST

14. The expectation that a treatment will be effective can by itself cause some improvement. Psychologists call this the _____ effect.
    a. placebo
    b. biomedical
    c. spontaneous recovery
    d. psychotic

15. Despite their benefits in treating symptoms of schizophrenia, some antipsychotic drugs have unpleasant side effects, including
    a. hyperactivity.
    b. convulsions and momentary memory loss.
    c. sluggishness, tremors, and twitches.
    d. paranoia.

16. The _____ drugs can cause death if they are taken in combination with alcohol because both alcohol and these drugs depress central nervous system activity.
    a. antipsychotic
    b. antianxiety
    c. antidepressant
    d. SSRI

17. One substance that often brings relief to patients suffering the highs and lows of bipolar disorder is
    a. rTMS.
    b. Xanax.
    c. lithium.
    d. clozapine.

18. Electroconvulsive therapy (ECT) can be an effective treatment for
    a. severe obsessive-compulsive disorder.
    b. severe depression.
    c. schizophrenia.
    d. generalized anxiety disorder.

19. _____ seeks to identify and alleviate conditions that put people at risk for psychological disorders.
    a. Biomedical therapy
    b. The cognitive approach
    c. Empathic active listening
    d. Preventive mental health

Answers: 14. a, 15. c, 16. b, 17. c, 18. b, 19. d.

TERMS AND CONCEPTS TO REMEMBER

psychotherapy, p. 350

biomedical therapy, p. 350

eclectic approach, p. 350

psychoanalysis, p. 350

resistance, p. 351

interpretation, p. 351

transference, p. 351

psychodynamic therapy, p. 352

client-centered therapy, p. 352

active listening, p. 353

behavior therapy, p. 354

counterconditioning, p. 354

exposure therapies, p. 354

systematic desensitization, p. 354

virtual reality exposure therapy, p. 355

aversive conditioning, p. 355

token economy, p. 356

cognitive therapy, p. 357

cognitive-behavior therapy, p. 358

family therapy, p. 358

antipsychotic drugs, p. 364

antianxiety drugs, p. 364

antidepressant drugs, p. 365

electroconvulsive therapy (ECT), p. 367

repetitive transcranial magnetic stimulation (rTMS), p. 368

psychosurgery, p. 368

lobotomy, p. 368

REVIEW: THERAPY

TREATING PSYCHOLOGICAL DISORDERS

1 What are the two main types of treatments for psychological disorders?

- *Psychotherapy* involves psychological techniques.
- *Biomedical therapy* involves treatment with drugs or medical procedures.
- Therapists who take an *eclectic approach* combine several different techniques.

THE PSYCHOLOGICAL THERAPIES

EVALUATING PSYCHOTHERAPIES

2 What are the aims and methods of psychoanalysis, and how have they been adapted in psychodynamic therapy?

- Freud's *psychoanalysis* aimed to help people (1) gain insight into the unconscious origins of their disorders, and (2) work through the accompanying feelings.
- Methods included free association, dream analysis, *interpretation* of *resistance*, and *transference* to the therapist of long-repressed feelings.
- Today's *psychodynamic therapy* is briefer and less expensive. It focuses on themes in important relationships, including childhood experiences and interactions with the therapist. Interpersonal therapy is even briefer and deals mostly with current symptoms rather than the origins of unconscious conflicts.

3 What are the basic themes of humanistic therapy, such as Rogers' client-centered approach?

- The present and future are more important than the past.
- Conscious thoughts are more important than the unconscious.
- Take responsibility for personal growth.
- Focus on promoting growth rather than curing illness.
- *Client-centered therapy:* therapists use *active listening* to provide a growth-fostering environment of unconditional positive regard (genuineness, acceptance, and empathy).

4 What are the assumptions and techniques of the behavior therapies?

- *Behavior therapists* attempt to modify the problem behaviors themselves.
- *Counterconditioning* helps people learn new responses to troublesome stimuli, such as learning not to feel afraid in an elevator.
- *Exposure therapies*, *aversive conditioning*, or *token economies* may also be used.

5 What are the goals and techniques of the cognitive therapies?

- *Cognitive therapies*, such as Beck's therapy for depression, aim to train people to think in healthier ways.
- *Cognitive-behavior therapy* helps clients to develop new, healthier ways of acting as well as thinking.

6 What are the benefits of group therapy?

- *Group therapy* can help more people for less money.
- Clients may benefit from knowing others have similar problems and from getting feedback and reassurance.
- *Family therapy* attempts to guide family members toward positive relationships and better communication.

7 Does psychotherapy work? How do we know? Are some therapies more effective than others?

- Clients and therapists both tend to claim success from psychotherapy, but they may be biased.
- Outcome research has found that people who remain untreated often improve, but those who receive psychotherapy (any kind, for any length of time) are more likely to improve.
- No one psychotherapy is superior to all others, but some therapies seem best-suited to specific disorders. (Cognitive therapy, for example, is effective in reducing depression and suicide risk.)

8 What three elements are shared by all forms of effective psychotherapy? How do differences in culture and values influence the relationship between a therapist and a client?

- All effective psychotherapies offer (1) new hope; (2) a fresh perspective; and (3) an empathic, trusting, caring relationship.
- A person seeking therapy should ask about a potential therapist's treatment approach and values in order to avoid clashing cultural or religious perspectives.

THE BIOMEDICAL THERAPIES

9 **What are the most common forms of biomedical therapies? What criticisms have been leveled against drug therapies?**

- Drug therapy is the most widely used biomedical therapy.

- *Antipsychotic drugs*, used in treating schizophrenia, block dopamine activity. Side effects can include tardive dyskinesia or increased risk of obesity and diabetes.

- *Antianxiety drugs*, which depress central nervous system activity, are used to treat anxiety disorders. These drugs can be physically and psychologically addictive.

- *Antidepressant drugs*, which increase the availability of serotonin and norepinephrine, are used for depression and anxiety disorders.

- Mood-stabilizing drugs, such as lithium, are often prescribed for those with bipolar disorder.

"If this doesn't help you don't worry, it's a placebo."

PREVENTING PSYCHOLOGICAL DISORDERS

11 **What is the purpose of preventive mental health programs?**

- These programs aim to prevent psychological disorders by turning destructive environments into more nurturing places that foster individual growth.

- The biopsychosocial approach considers social-cultural influences as well as biological and individual factors in psychological disorders.

10 **How is brain stimulation used as a treatment for depression? Under what conditions might psychosurgery be considered for changing behavior or mood?**

- In *electroconvulsive therapy (ECT)*, a brief electric current is sent through the brain.

- ECT remains an effective treatment for severely depressed people who have not responded to other therapy.

- Newer alternative treatments for depression include *repetitive transcranial magnetic stimulation (rTMS)* and implants that directly stimulate some nerves.

- The irreversible *psychosurgical* procedures are used only in the rare, extreme cases when no other treatment is effective. *Lobotomies* are no longer performed.

On September 11, 2001, shortly after terrorists flew hijacked planes into the World Trade Center, I spoke by phone with my daughter, Laura. She was on the street in her Manhattan neighborhood, describing the scene, when suddenly she yelled, "Oh my gosh! Oh my gosh!" as the second massive tower collapsed before her eyes. By almost anyone's definition, this catastrophic violence—accomplished by a mere 19 men with box cutters—was an evil act. And the communal response it evoked from millions of stunned Americans was fear mixed with outrage and a lust for revenge.

But this horrific event also triggered an outpouring of love and compassion. From around the country and the world, money and countless truckloads of food, clothing, and teddy bears—more than New Yorkers could possibly use—poured in. People in Toledo, Fargo, and Stockholm wept for those who wept. There on 6th Avenue and 24th Street, strangers hugged and talked, trying to make sense of the senseless destruction. Although few transfusions would be needed, willing donors formed long lines at blood banks. "Everywhere I go I see concern," Laura wrote that evening.

> I see compassion. I see people with many differences united. I don't see violence. I don't see impatience. I don't see cruelty. Except when I look at that cloud of smoke, a constant backdrop all day. People are helping each other. People are desperate to do whatever they can.
>
> In the midst of this nightmare, I am utterly filled with love for the people of this city. It is incredible to witness their response. I am covered in goose bumps. My faith in humanity rises over that cloud and I see goodness and respect.

We watch and we wonder. What drives people to feel such hatred and to destroy so many innocent lives? And what motivates the unselfish concern for strangers—the heroism of those who died trying to save others and the many acts of kindness toward those coping with loss?

As the events of 9/11 so compellingly demonstrate, we are social animals. We may assume the best or the worst in others. We may approach them with closed fists or open arms. But as the novelist Herman Melville remarked, "We cannot live for ourselves alone. Our lives are connected by a thousand invisible threads." **Social psychologists** explore these connections by scientifically studying how we *think about, influence,* and *relate to* one another.

social psychology the scientific study of how we think about, influence, and relate to one another.

Social Thinking

Was the horror of 9/11 the work of crazed people, or of ordinary people corrupted by life events? When the unexpected occurs, we want to understand, to explain why people act as they do. Our search for answers—whether in a crisis or in everyday life—often leaves us with two choices. We can attribute (give credit or blame for) the behavior to the person's stable, enduring traits. Or we can attribute it to the situation (Heider, 1958).

Recall from Chapter 11 that personality psychologists study the enduring, inner determinants of behavior that help to explain why *different people* act differently *in a given situation.* Social psychologists study the social influences that help explain why *the same person* will act differently in *different situations.*

The Fundamental Attribution Error

1: How do we tend to explain others' behavior? How do we explain our own behavior?

In class, we notice that Juliette seldom talks. Over coffee, Jack talks nonstop. That must be the sort of people they are, we decide. Juliette must be shy and Jack outgoing. Are they? Perhaps. People do have enduring personality traits. But all too often, our explanations are wrong. We fall prey to the **fundamental attribution error,** overestimating the influence of personality, and underestimating the influence of situations. In class, Jack may be as quiet as Juliette. Catch Juliette at a party and you may hardly recognize your quiet classmate.

Researchers demonstrated this tendency in an experiment with college students (Napolitan & Goethals, 1979). They had students talk, one at a time, with a young woman who acted either cold and critical or warm and friendly.

The fundamental attribution error :: If a new friend acts grouchy, we may decide that she's a grouchy person. She may be more likely to explain her behavior as a result of losing sleep over a family worry, getting a flat tire on the way to work, or having a fight with her boyfriend.

Alloy Photography/Veer

Before the talks, the researchers told half the students that the woman's behavior would be normal and natural. They told the other half the truth—that they had instructed her to *act* friendly (or unfriendly).

Did hearing the truth affect students' impressions of the woman? Not at all! If the woman acted friendly, both groups decided she really was a warm person. If she acted unfriendly, both decided she really was a cold person. In other words, they attributed her behavior to her personal traits, *even when they were told that her behavior was part of the experimental situation.*

The fundamental attribution error appears more often in some cultures than in others. Individualistic Westerners more often attribute behavior to people's dispositions. People in East Asian cultures are more sensitive to the power of situations (Masuda & Kitayama, 2004). This difference appears in experiments in which people were asked to view scenes, such as a big fish swimming. Americans focus more on the individual fish, but Japanese people are more attentive to the whole situation (Chua & others, 2005; Nisbett, 2003).

To see how easy it is to make the fundamental attribution error, answer this question. Consider: Is your psychology instructor shy or outgoing? If you're tempted to answer "outgoing," remember that you know your instructor in only one situation—the classroom, which demands outgoing behavior. Catch your instructor in a different situation and you might be surprised.

When explaining *our own* behavior, we are sensitive to how behavior changes with the situation (Idson & Mischel, 2001). Your instructor (who observes his or her own behavior not only in the classroom, but also with family, friends, and colleagues) might say, "Me, outgoing? It all depends on the situation. In class or with good friends, yes, I'm outgoing. But at professional meetings I'm really rather shy." We also are sensitive to the power of the situation when we explain the behavior of people we know well and have seen in many different contexts.

We are most likely to commit the fundamental attribution error when a stranger acts badly. Having never seen this person in other situations, we leap to conclusions about his or her personality. Outside their assigned roles, terrorists seem less terrifying, professors less professorial, students less studious.

The way we explain others' actions, attributing them to the person or the situation, can have important real-life effects (Fincham & Bradbury, 1993; Fletcher & others, 1990). A jury must decide whether a shooting was malicious or in self-defense. A voter must judge whether

"Otis, shout at that man to pull himself together."

a candidate's promises will be kept or forgotten. A partner must decide whether a loved one's tart-tongued remark reflects a bad day or a mean disposition.

In the workplace, attributions can lead to the end of a job or the end of poor working conditions. Managers are likely to attribute an employee's poor performance to the person's low ability, lack of motivation, or some other personal trait. But workers doing poorly on a job tend to see situational influences, such as bad working conditions, difficult co-workers, or impossible demands (Rice, 1985).

Finally, consider the political effects of attribution. How can we explain poverty or unemployment? In Britain, India, Australia, and the United States (Furnham, 1982; Pandey & others, 1982; Wagstaff, 1982; Zucker & Weiner, 1993), political conservatives tend to place the blame on the personal traits of the poor and unemployed. "People generally get what they deserve. Those who don't work are often freeloaders. Anybody who takes the initiative can still get ahead." Political liberals (and social scientists) are more likely to blame past and present situations. "If you or I had to live with the same poor education, lack of opportunity, and discrimination, would we be any better off?" To understand and prevent terrorism, they say, consider the situations that

breed terrorists. Better to drain the swamps than swat the mosquitoes.

The point to remember: Our attributions—to the person's disposition or to the situation—have real consequences.

Attitudes and Actions

2: Does what we think predict what we will do? Or does what we do shape what we will think?

Attitudes are feelings, based on our beliefs, that set us up to react in certain ways to objects, people, and events. If we *believe* someone is mean, we may *feel* dislike for the person and *act* unfriendly.

Attitudes Can Affect Actions

Attitudes affect our behavior, but they don't reliably predict it. Other factors, including the situation, also influence behavior. Strong social pressures can weaken the attitude-behavior connection (Wallace & others, 2005). For example, the American public overwhelmingly supported President George W. Bush's preparation to invade Iraq. Feeling this pressure, Democratic leaders voted to support Bush's war plan, despite their private reservations (Nagourney, 2002).

Attitudes are most likely to affect behavior when

- other influences are minimal.
- the attitude is specific to the behavior.
- we are keenly aware of our attitudes.

Actions Can Affect Attitudes

People also come to believe in what they have stood up for. Many streams of evidence confirm that *attitudes follow behavior* (FIGURE 14.1).

The Foot-in-the-Door Phenomenon How would you react if someone forced you to act against your beliefs? In many cases, people change their attitudes. During the Korean War, many U.S. prisoners

Figure 14.1> **Attitudes follow behavior** Cooperative actions, such as those performed by people on sports teams, feed mutual liking. Such attitudes, in turn, promote positive behavior.

Actions

Attitudes

AP Photo/Wichita Falls Times Record News, Jason Palmer

of war were held in camps run by Chinese communists. Without using brutality, the captors convinced hundreds of these prisoners to cooperate in various activities. Some merely ran errands or accepted favors. Others made radio appeals and false confessions. Still others informed on other prisoners and revealed military information. When the war ended, 21 prisoners chose to stay with the communists. More returned home "brainwashed"—convinced that communism was a good thing for Asia.

How did the Chinese captors achieve these amazing results? A key ingredient

An attribution question :: Some people blamed the New Orleans residents for not getting out before the predicted Hurricane Katrina. Others attributed people's inaction to the situation—to their not having access to transportation.

AP Photo/LM Otero

fundamental attribution error the tendency, when analyzing another's behavior, to overestimate the influence of personal traits and underestimate the effects of the situation.

attitude feelings, often based on our beliefs, that predispose us to respond in a particular way to objects, people, and events.

was their effective use of the **foot-in-the-door phenomenon.** They knew that people who agree to a small request will find it easier to agree later to a larger one. The Chinese began with harmless requests, such as copying a trivial statement, but gradually made bigger demands on the prisoners (Schein, 1956). The next statement to be copied might contain a list of flaws of capitalism. Then, to gain privileges, the prisoners took part in group discussions, wrote self-criticisms, or made public confessions. After taking this series of small steps, the Americans often changed their beliefs to be more in line with their public acts. The point is simple. To get people to agree to something big, start small and build (Cialdini, 1993). A trivial act makes the next act easier. Give in to a temptation and you will find the next temptation harder to resist.

In dozens of experiments, researchers have coaxed people into acting against their attitudes or violating their moral standards, with the same result. Doing becomes believing. After giving in to a request to harm an innocent victim—by making nasty comments or delivering electric shocks—people begin to look down on their victim. After speaking or writing in support of a position they have doubts about, they begin to believe their own words.

Fortunately, the attitudes-follow-behavior principle works as well for good deeds as for bad. After U.S. schools were desegregated and the Civil Rights Act was passed in 1964, American Whites expressed lower levels of racial prejudice. And as Americans in different regions came to act more alike—thanks to more uniform national standards against discrimination—they began to think more alike. Experiments confirm the observation: Moral action strengthens moral convictions.

Role-Playing Affects Attitudes How many new **roles** have you adopted recently? Becoming a college student is a new role. Perhaps you've started a new relationship or even become engaged or married. If so, you may have realized that people expected you to behave a little differently. At first, your behaviors may have felt phony, because you were *acting* a role. Soldiers may feel that they are playing war games. Newlyweds may feel they are "playing house." Before long, however, what began as play-acting in the theater of life becomes *you*.

> "Fake it until you make it."
>
> Alcoholics Anonymous saying

This happened in one famous study, where male college students volunteered to spend time in a mock prison (Zimbardo, 1972). Psychologist Philip Zimbardo randomly assigned some volunteers to be guards. He gave them uniforms, clubs, and whistles and instructed them to enforce certain rules. Others became prisoners, locked in barren cells and forced to wear humiliating outfits. For a day or two, the volunteers self-consciously played their roles. Then it became clear that the "play" had become real—too real. Most guards developed bad attitudes. Some set up cruel and degrading routines. One by one, the prisoners broke down, rebelled, or became passively resigned. After only six days, Zimbardo called off the study.

Role-playing can train people to become torturers in the real world, too (Staub, 1989). One instance occurred in Greece in the early 1970s. There, the military government eased men into their roles. First, a trainee stood guard outside an interrogation cell. After this "foot-in-the-door" step, he stood guard inside. Only then was he ready to become actively involved in the questioning and torture. What we do, we gradually become.

Cognitive Dissonance: Relief From Tension We have seen that actions can affect attitudes, sometimes turning prisoners into collaborators, doubters into believers, and guards into abusers. But why? One explanation is that when we become aware of a mismatch between our attitudes and actions, we experience mental discomfort, or *cognitive dissonance*. To relieve this tension, according to Leon Festinger's **cognitive dissonance theory,**

Diverse Yet Alike

The power of the situation :: In his 1972 Stanford Prison simulation, Philip Zimbardo created a toxic situation. Those assigned to the guard role soon degraded the prisoners. In real life in 2004, some U.S. military guards abused Iraqi prisoners at the U.S.-run Abu Ghraib prison. To Zimbardo (2004, 2007), it was a bad barrel rather than a few bad apples that led to the atrocities. "When ordinary people are put in a novel, evil place, such as most prisons, Situations Win, People Lose."

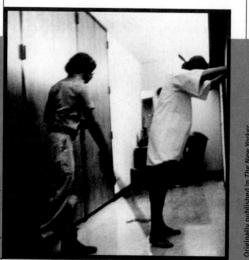

Philip G. Zimbardo, Inc.

Originally published in *The New Yorker*

we often bring our attitudes into line with our actions. It is as if we tell ourselves, "If I chose to do it (or say it), I must believe in it." The greater the clash between attitudes and actions, the more motivated we are to find consistency. Thus, we may change our attitudes to help justify the act.

Some believe that the pressure to reduce dissonance helps explain the evolution of American attitudes toward the U.S. invasion of Iraq. When the war began, the stated reason for the invasion was the presumed threat of Saddam Hussein's weapons of mass destruction (WMD). Would the war be justified if Iraq did not have WMD? Only 38 percent of Americans said it would be (Gallup, 2003). Nearly 80 percent believed such weapons would be found (Duffy, 2003; Newport & others, 2003). When no WMD were found, many Americans felt dissonance. These feelings deepened as information about the war's human and financial costs poured in. Scenes of chaos in Iraq, and inflamed anti-American and pro-terrorist sentiments in some parts of the world, increased the tension.

To reduce dissonance, some Americans revised their memories of the main reason for going to war. The invasion now became a movement to liberate an oppressed people and promote democracy in the Middle East. Before long, the once-minority opinion became the majority view: 58 percent of Americans said they supported the war even if no WMD were found (Gallup, 2003). Support for the war continued above 50 percent until late 2004, then fell when hopes for a flourishing peace faded.

Dozens of experiments have explored cognitive dissonance by making people feel responsible for behavior that clashes with their attitudes. As a participant in one of these experiments, you might agree for a mere $2 to help a researcher by writing an essay that supports something you don't believe in (perhaps a tuition increase). Feeling responsible for the statements (which are not consistent with your attitudes), you would probably feel dissonance, especially if you thought an administrator would be reading your essay. How could

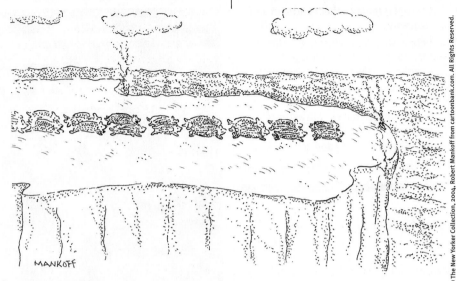

"Look, I have my misgivings, too, but what choice do we have except stay the course?"

you reduce the uncomfortable tension? One way would be to start believing your phony words. Your pretense could become your reality.

The attitudes-follow-behavior principle has a heartening implication. We cannot directly control all our feelings, but we can influence them by altering our behavior. (Recall from Chapter 9 the emotional effects of facial expressions and of body postures.) If we are down in the dumps, we can do as cognitive therapists advise and talk in more positive, self-accepting ways with fewer self–put-downs. If we are unloving, we can become more loving by behaving as if we were loving—by doing thoughtful things, expressing affection, giving support. *The point to remember:* Cruel acts shape the self. But so do acts of good will. Act as though you like someone, and you soon will. Changing our behavior can change how we think about others and how we feel about ourselves.

PRACTICE TEST

1. You see a community theater's presentation of "Alice in Wonderland," in which the wicked Queen of Hearts is played by a neighbor you don't know very well. If you make the fundamental attribution error, you will assume that

a. she must be a mean person to be able to play that role so well.
b. she may be a nice person outside her role.
c. she could just as easily have played the part of sweet Alice.
d. she was highly influenced by the costume, set, and fellow actors' expectations.

2. During the Korean War, the Chinese "brainwashed" captured American soldiers to think that communism was a good thing for Asia. A key ingredient in this process was their use of

a. the fundamental attribution error.
b. the foot-in-the-door phenomenon.
c. the behavior-follows-attitudes principle.
d. role-playing.

foot-in-the-door phenomenon the tendency for people who have first agreed to a small request to comply later with a larger request.

role a set of expectations about a social position, defining how those in the position ought to behave.

cognitive dissonance theory the theory that we act to reduce the discomfort (dissonance) we feel when two of our thoughts (cognitions) clash. For example, when we become aware that our attitudes and our actions don't match, we may change our attitudes so that we feel more comfortable.

3. Cognitive dissonance theory attempts to explain why

a. people who act against their attitudes tend to change their attitudes.

b. people who act against their attitudes tend to change their behavior.

c. agreeing to a small request increases the likelihood that we will agree to a larger request.

d. people talk one way and act another.

Answers: 1. a, 2. b, 3. a.

Social Influence

Social psychology's great lesson is the enormous power of social influence. We conform to the desires of those around us. We follow orders. We behave as others in our group behave. On campus, jeans are the dress code; on New York's Wall Street, dress suits are the norm. Let's examine the pull of these social strings. How strong are they? How do they operate? When do we break them?

Conformity and Obedience

3: What do experiments on conformity and compliance reveal about the power of social influence?

Fish swim in schools. Birds fly in flocks. And humans, too, tend to go with their group, to think what it thinks and do what it does. Behavior is contagious. If one of us laughs, coughs, yawns, or stares at the sky, others in our group will soon do the same. We are natural mimics, unconsciously imitating others' expressions, postures, and voice tones.

Researchers call this the *chameleon effect,* and they demonstrated it in a clever experiment (Chartrand & Bargh, 1999). They had students work in a room beside another person. Although the students didn't know it, the person was actually the experimenter's assistant. Sometimes the assistants rubbed their own face. At other times, they shook their foot. Sure enough, the students tended to rub their face

Conforming to nonconformity :: Are these students asserting their individuality, or identifying themselves with others of the same microculture?

R. Ian Lloyd/Masterfile

when they were with the face-rubbing person and shake their foot when they were with the foot-shaking person.

Automatic mimicry helps us to *empathize,* to feel what others feel. This helps explain why we feel happier around happy people than around depressed ones. Like the chameleon lizards that take on the color of their surroundings, we humans take on the emotional tones of those around us (Totterdell & others, 1998). And the more we mimic, the greater our empathy, and the more people tend to like us.

Group Pressure and Conformity

Why do we clap when others clap, eat as others eat, believe what others believe, even see what others see? **Conformity**— adjusting our behavior or thinking toward some group standard—is often an attempt to avoid rejection or gain social approval.

To study conformity, Solomon Asch (1955) devised a simple test. As a participant in what you believe is a study of

visual perception, you arrive in time to take a seat at a table with five other people. The experimenter asks the group to state, one by one, which of three comparison lines is identical to a standard line. You see clearly that the answer is Line 2, and you await your turn to say so. Your boredom begins to show when the next set of lines proves equally easy.

Now comes the third trial, and the correct answer seems just as clear-cut **(FIGURE 14.2).** But the first person gives what strikes you as a wrong answer: "Line 3." When the second person and then the third and fourth give the same wrong answer, you sit up straight and squint. When the fifth person agrees with the first four, you feel your heart begin to pound. The experimenter then looks to you for your answer. Torn between the agreement voiced by the five other respondents and the evidence of your own eyes, you feel tense and suddenly unsure of yourself. You hesitate before answering, wondering whether you should suffer the pain of being the oddball. What answer do you give?

In the experiments Asch and others conducted, thousands of college students experienced this conflict. Answering questions alone, the students were wrong less than 1 percent of the time. Answering after several others had answered incorrectly, they were wrong more than one-third of the time. Asch reports that these "intelligent and well-meaning" college students were then "willing to call white black" by going along with the group. Though the exact percentages varied in later investigations, the act of conforming did not.

Experiments reveal that we are more likely to conform when we

■ are made to feel incompetent or insecure.

■ are in a group with at least three people.

■ are in a group in which everyone else agrees. (If just one other person disagrees, the odds that we also will disagree greatly increase.)

Figure 14.2> Asch's conformity experiments Which of the three comparison lines on the right is equal to the standard line? The photo on the left (from one of the experiments) was taken after five people, who were actually working for Asch, had answered, "Line 3." The student in the center shows the severe discomfort that comes from disagreeing with the responses of other group members.

William Vendivert/*Scientific American*

Standard line   Comparison lines
                                   1   2   3

- admire the group's status and attractiveness.
- have not already committed ourselves to any response.
- know that others in the group will observe our behavior.
- are from a culture that strongly encourages respect for social standards.

When we conform, we are giving in to social influence. Is conformity good or bad? The answer depends on our values. When people conform to influences that support what we approve, we applaud them for being "open-minded" and "sensitive" enough to be "responsive." When they conform to influences that support what we disapprove, we scorn their "blind, thoughtless willingness" to give in to others' wishes. Our values, as we saw in Chapter 11, are influenced by our culture. Western Europeans and people in most English-speaking countries tend to

Ilan Rosen/Alamy

Tattoos: Yesterday's nonconformity, today's conformity? :: As tattoos become perceived as fashion conformity, their popularity may wane.

prize individualism. People in many Asian, African, and Latin American countries place a higher value on honoring group standards. It's perhaps not surprising, then, that in social influence experiments across 17 countries, conformity rates are lower in individualist cultures (Bond & Smith, 1996).

Obedience

Social psychologist Stanley Milgram (1963, 1974), a student of Solomon Asch, knew that people often give in to social pressure. But how would they respond to outright commands? To find out, he undertook experiments that have become social psychology's most famous and most hotly debated.

Imagine yourself as one of the nearly 1000 people who took part in Milgram's 20 experiments. You have responded to an ad for participants in a Yale University psychology study of the effect of punishment on learning. Professor Milgram's assistant asks you and another person to draw slips from a hat to see who will be the "teacher" and who will be the "learner." You draw the "teacher" slip and are asked to sit down in front of a machine, which has a series of labeled switches. The "learner" is led to a nearby room and strapped into a chair. From the chair, wires run through the wall to "your" machine. You are given your task: Teach and then test the learner on a list

conformity adjusting our behavior or thinking to coincide with a group standard.

Stanley Milgram (1933–1984) :: This social psychologist's obedience experiments "belong to the self-understanding of literate people in our age" (Sabini, 1986).

of word pairs. If the learner gives a wrong answer, you are to flip a switch to deliver a brief electric shock. For the first wrong answer, you are told to flip the switch labeled "15 Volts—Slight Shock." With each succeeding error, you are to move to the next higher voltage. The researcher demonstrates by flipping the first switch. Lights flash, relay switches click on, and an electric buzzing fills the air.

The experiment begins, and you deliver the shocks after the first and second wrong answers. If you continue, you hear the learner grunt when you flick the third, fourth, and fifth switches. After you flip the eighth switch ("120 Volts—Moderate Shock"), the learner cries out that the shocks are painful. After the tenth switch ("150 Volts—Strong Shock"), he begins shouting. "Get me out of here! I won't be in the experiment anymore! I refuse to go on!" You draw back, but the experimenter prods you. "Please continue—the experiment requires that you continue." You resist, but the experimenter insists, "It is absolutely essential that you continue," or "You have no other choice, you *must* go on."

If you obey, you hear the learner shriek in agony as you continue to raise the shock level after each new error. After the 330-volt level, the learner refuses to

answer and falls silent. Still, the experimenter pushes you toward the final, 450-volt switch. Ask the question, he says, and if no correct answer is given, administer the next shock level.

How far do you think you would follow the experimenter's commands? Milgram asked that question in a survey before he started his experiments. Most people were sure they would stop playing such a sadistic-seeming role soon after the learner first indicated pain, certainly before he shrieked in agony. Forty psychiatrists agreed with that prediction when Milgram asked them to guess the outcome. Were the predictions accurate? Not even close. When Milgram actually conducted the experiment with men aged 20 to 50, he was astonished. More than 60 percent complied fully—right up to the last switch. Even when Milgram ran a new study, with 40 new teachers, and the learner complained of a "slight heart condition," the results were the same. A full 65 percent of the new teachers obeyed every one of the experimenter's commands **(FIGURE 14.3).**

How can we explain these findings? Could they reflect some aspect of gender behavior found only in males? No. In 10 later studies, women obeyed at rates similar to men (Blass, 1999).

Did the teachers figure out the hoax—that no real shock was being delivered and the learner was in fact an assistant who was pretending to feel pain? Did they realize the experiment was really testing their willingness to obey commands to inflict punishment? No, the

"Drive off the cliff, James, I want to commit suicide."

teachers typically displayed genuine distress. They perspired, trembled, laughed nervously, and bit their lips.

In later experiments, Milgram discovered some things that did influence people's behavior. When he varied some details of the situation, the percentage of participants who fully obeyed ranged from 0 to 93 percent. Obedience was highest when

- the person giving the orders was close at hand and was perceived to be a legitimate authority figure.

- the authority figure was supported by a respected, well-known institution (Yale University).

- the victim was depersonalized or at a distance, even in another room. (Similarly, many soldiers in combat either do not fire their rifles at an enemy they can see or do not aim them properly. Such refusals to kill are rare among soldiers who operate long-distance artillery or aircraft weapons [Padgett, 1989].)

- there were no role models for defiance. (Teachers did not see any other participant disobey the experimenter.)

The power of legitimate, close-at-hand authorities is dramatically apparent in stories of those who followed orders to carry out the Holocaust atrocities. Obedience alone does not explain the Holocaust. Anti-Semitic ideology produced eager killers as well (Mastroianni, 2002). But obedience was a factor. In the summer of 1942, nearly 500 middle-aged German reserve police officers were dispatched to German-occupied Jozefow, Poland. On July 13, the group's visibly upset commander informed his recruits, mostly family men, of their orders. They were to round up the village's Jews, who were said to be aiding the enemy. Able-bodied men would be sent to work camps, and all the rest were to be shot on the spot.

The commander gave the recruits a chance to refuse to participate in the executions. Only about a dozen immediately did so. Within 17 hours, the remaining 485 officers killed 1500 helpless women,

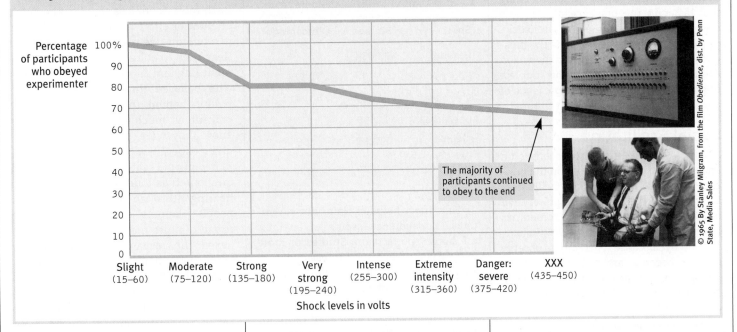

Figure 14.3> Milgram's follow-up obedience experiment In a repeat of the earlier experiment, 65 percent of the adult male "teachers" fully obeyed the experimenter's commands to continue. They did so despite the "learner's" earlier mention of a heart condition and despite hearing cries of protest after they administered what they thought were 150 volts and agonized protests after 330 volts. (Data from Milgram, 1974.)

Percentage of participants who obeyed experimenter

The majority of participants continued to obey to the end

Shock levels in volts

Slight (15–60), Moderate (75–120), Strong (135–180), Very strong (195–240), Intense (255–300), Extreme intensity (315–360), Danger: severe (375–420), XXX (435–450)

© 1965 By Stanley Milgram, from the film *Obedience*, dist. by Penn State, Media Sales

children, and elderly, shooting them in the back of the head as they lay face down. Hearing the pleadings of the victims, and seeing the gruesome results, some 20 percent of the officers did eventually disobey. They did so either by missing their victims or by wandering away and hiding until the slaughter was over (Browning, 1992). But in real life, as in Milgram's experiments, those who resisted did so early, and they were the minority.

Another story was being played out in the French village of Le Chambon. There, French Jews were being sheltered by villagers who openly defied orders to cooperate with the "New Order." The villagers' ancestors had themselves been persecuted. Their pastors had been teaching them to "resist whenever our adversaries will demand of us obedience contrary to the orders of the Gospel" (Rochat, 1993). Ordered by police to give a list of sheltered Jews, the head pastor modeled defiance. "I don't know of Jews, I only know of human beings." These resistors had no

Standing up for democracy :: Some individuals—roughly one in three in Milgram's experiments—resist social coercion. This unarmed man in Beijing single-handedly challenged an advancing line of tanks the day after the 1989 Tiananmen Square student uprising was suppressed.

AP/Wide World Photos

idea how long and terrible the war would be, or how much punishment and poverty they would suffer. But early on, they made a commitment to resist. After that, they drew support from their beliefs, their role models, their interactions with one another, and their own early actions. They remained defiant to the war's end.

Group Influence

4: How does the presence of others influence our actions? How does our behavior change when we act as part of a group?

Imagine yourself standing in a room, holding a fishing pole. You are once again participating in a psychology experiment, and this time your task is to wind the reel as fast as you can. You're winding very quickly, and perhaps you're wondering how long you'll have to do this. Suddenly, the door opens and the experimenter introduces you to another participant, who stands nearby and also begins turning his reel. Will this affect your own behavior?

In one of social psychology's first experiments, Norman Triplett (1898) found that adolescents *would* wind a fishing reel faster in the presence of someone doing the same thing. He and later social psychologists have studied how the presence of others affects our behavior. Group influences operate in the simplest of groups—one person in the presence of another—and in more complex groups.

Social Facilitation

Triplett's finding—that our responses on an individual task are stronger in the presence of others—is called **social facilitation.** Later studies revealed that the presence of others sometimes helps and sometimes hurts performance (Guerin, 1986; Zajonc, 1965). Why? Because when others observe us, we become aroused. This arousal strengthens our most *likely* response—the correct one on an easy task, an incorrect one on a difficult task. Thus, when others observe us, we perform well-learned tasks *more* quickly and accurately. But on new and difficult tasks, we perform *less* quickly and accurately.

Social facilitation :: Skilled athletes often find they are "on" before an audience. What they do well, they do even better when people are watching.

Table 14.1	Home Advantage in Major Team Sports	
Sport	Games Studied	Home Team Winning Percentage
Baseball	23,034	53.5%
Football	2,592	57.3
Ice hockey	4,322	61.1
Basketball	13,596	64.4
Soccer	37,202	69.0

From Courneya & Carron (1992).

This effect helps explain why an enthusiastic audience seems to energize the home sports team. Studies of more than 80,000 college and professional athletic events in Canada, the United States, and England point to a home team advantage **(TABLE 14.1)**. Home teams win about 6 in 10 games (somewhat fewer for baseball and football, somewhat more for basketball and soccer).

The point to remember: What you do well, you are likely to do even better in front of an audience, especially a friendly audience. What you normally find difficult may seem all but impossible when you are being watched.

Social facilitation also helps explain a funny effect of crowding. Comedians and actors know that a "good house" is a full one. What they may not know is that crowding triggers arousal, which in turn amplifies other reactions. Comedy records that are mildly amusing to people in an uncrowded room seem funnier in a densely packed room (Aiello & others, 1983; Freedman & Perlick, 1979). And in other experiments, participants seated close to one another liked a friendly person even more, an unfriendly person even less (Schiffenbauer & Schiavo, 1976; Storms & Thomas, 1977). *The practical lesson:* At social gatherings, you can increase the chances of lively interaction by choosing a room or setting up seating that will just barely hold everyone.

Social Loafing

Does the presence of others have the same effect when people perform a task as a group? In a team tug-of-war, for example, do you suppose a person will put forth more than, less than, or the same amount of effort he or she would exert in a one-on-one tug-of-war? If you said, "less than," you're right. In one experiment (Ingham & others, 1974), students who believed three others were also pulling behind them exerted only 82 percent as much effort as when they knew they were pulling alone. In another experiment (Latané, 1981), blindfolded people seated in a group clapped or shouted as loud as they could while hearing (through headphones) other people clapping or shouting. In one round of noise making, participants believed the researchers could identify their individual sounds. In another round, they believed their clapping and shouting was blended with other people's. Believing they were part of a group effort, the participants produced about one-third less noise than when clapping "alone."

This diminished effort is called **social loafing** (Jackson & Williams, 1988; Latané, 1981). Experiments in the United States, India, Thailand, Japan, China, and Taiwan have recorded social loafing on various tasks. It was especially common among men in individualistic cultures (Karau & Williams, 1993).

What causes social loafing? First, people acting as part of a group feel less accountable, so they worry less about what others think of them. Second, they may not believe their contribution makes a difference (Harkins & Szymanski, 1989; Kerr & Bruun, 1983). If you've worked on group assignments, you are probably already aware of the third cause of social loafing, and that's the loafing itself! When group members share equally in the benefits regardless of how much they contribute, some may slack off. People who are not highly motivated, who don't identify strongly with the group, may free-ride on others' efforts.

Working hard, or hardly working? :: In group projects, such as car washes, social loafing often occurs, as individuals free-ride on the efforts of others.

Tony Freeman/Photo Edit

Deindividuation

We've seen that the presence of others can arouse people or it can make them feel less responsible. But sometimes the presence of others does both. The uninhibited behavior that results can range from a food fight in the dining hall to vandalism or rioting in the streets. This process of losing self-awareness and self-restraint is called **deindividuation,** and it often occurs when group participation makes people feel aroused and anonymous. In one experiment, some female students dressed in depersonalizing Ku Klux Klan-style hoods. Others in a control group did not wear the hoods. Those whose identities were hidden delivered twice as much electric shock to a victim (Zimbardo, 1970). (As in all such experiments, the "victim" did not actually receive the shocks.) Similarly, tribal warriors who depersonalize themselves with face paints or masks are more likely than those with exposed faces to kill, torture, or mutilate captured enemies (Watson, 1973). Whether in a mob, at a rock concert, at a ballgame, or at worship, to shed self-awareness and self-restraint is to become more responsive to the group experience. *Interacting* with others can similarly have both bad and good effects.

Group Polarization

Over time, differences between groups of college students tend to grow. If the first-year students at College X tend to be more artistic and those at College Y tend to be business-savvy, those differences will probably be even greater by the time they graduate.

In each case, the beliefs and attitudes students brought to the group grew stronger when they discussed their views with people who shared them. This process, called **group polarization,** can have positive results, as when low-prejudice students become even more accepting while discussing racial issues. But sometimes the results are far from positive. As **FIGURE 14.4** shows, when high-prejudice students discuss racial issues, they become *more* prejudiced (Myers & Bishop, 1970).

social facilitation stronger responses on simple or well-learned tasks in the presence of others.

social loafing the tendency for people in a group to exert less effort when pooling their efforts toward attaining a common goal than when individually accountable.

deindividuation the loss of self-awareness and self-restraint occurring in group situations that foster arousal and anonymity.

group polarization the enhancement of a group's prevailing inclinations through discussion within the group.

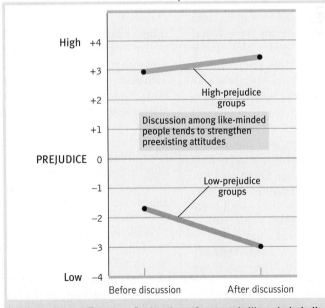

Figure 14.4> Group polarization If a group is like-minded, discussion strengthens its prevailing opinions. Talking about racial issues increased prejudice in a high-prejudice group of high school students and decreased it in a low-prejudice group (Myers & Bishop, 1970).

Researchers captured group polarization in a 2005 "Deliberation Day" experiment (Schkade & others, 2006). They chose a random sample of people from the voter rolls of liberal Boulder, Colorado. They then divided the sample into five-person groups to discuss global climate change, affirmative action, and same-sex civil unions. In Colorado Springs, the researchers followed the same procedure with its more conservative voters. After the discussions, those in Boulder had moved further left, and those in Colorado Springs further right.

The polarizing effect of interaction among the like-minded applies also to suicide terrorists. The terrorist mentality does not erupt suddenly on a whim (McCauley, 2002; McCauley & Segal, 1987; Merari, 2002). It usually begins slowly, among people who get together because of a grievance. As group members interact in isolation (sometimes with other "brothers" and "sisters" in camps), their views grow more and more extreme. Increasingly, they divide the world into "us" against "them" (Moghaddam, 2005; Qirko, 2004).

The Internet provides a medium for group polarization. In thousands of virtual groups, people who share interests in government conspiracies, visitors from space, or White supremacy have found support from kindred spirits (McKenna & Bargh, 1998). But so have grief-stricken parents, peacemakers, and teachers working to make the world a better place.

Groupthink

Does group interaction ever distort important decisions? Consider what is now known as the Bay of Pigs fiasco. In 1961, President John F. Kennedy and his advisers decided to invade Cuba with 1400 CIA-trained Cuban exiles. The invaders were easily captured and soon linked to the U.S. government. President Kennedy wondered in hindsight, "How could we have been so stupid?"

"One's impulse to blow the whistle on this nonsense was simply undone by the circumstances of the discussion."

Arthur M. Schlesinger, Jr., *A Thousand Days*, 1965

Reading a historian's account of the ill-fated blunder, social psychologist Irving Janis (1982) thought the decision-making procedures leading to the invasion might give some clues. Here's what he discovered. The morale of the popular and recently elected president and his advisers was soaring. Their confidence was almost unlimited. To preserve the good feeling, group members with differing views kept quiet, especially after President Kennedy voiced his enthusiasm for the scheme. Since no one spoke strongly against the idea, everyone assumed the support was unanimous. **Groupthink** was at work. The desire for harmony had replaced realistic judgment.

Since then, other instances of groupthink have been described, including the escalation of the Vietnam War, the Chernobyl nuclear reactor accident (Reason, 1987), and the U.S. space shuttle *Challenger* explosion (Esser & Lindoerfer, 1989). Most recently, groupthink surfaced in discussions of the Iraq war. The bipartisan U.S. Senate Intelligence Committee (2004) reported that "personnel involved in the Iraq WMD [weapons of mass destruction] issue demonstrated several aspects of groupthink: examining few alternatives, selective gathering of information, pressure to conform within the group or withhold criticism, and collective rationalization." This mode of thinking led analysts to "interpret ambiguous evidence as conclusively indicative of a WMD program as well as ignore or minimize evidence that Iraq did not have [WMD] programs." In this case, as in others, groupthink was fed by overconfidence, conformity, self-justification, and group polarization.

How can we prevent groupthink? Knowing that two heads are better than one in solving many problems, leaders can make better decisions. They can welcome open debate, invite experts' critiques of developing plans, and assign people to identify possible problems. *The point to remember:* None of us is as smart as all of us, especially when we engage in open debate.

"Truth springs from argument among friends."

Philosopher David Hume (1711–1776)

Lessons From the Social Influence Studies

5: What do the social influence studies teach us about ourselves? How much power do we have as individuals?

How do the laboratory experiments on social influence relate to everyday social behavior? Recall from Chapter 1 that psychological experiments aim not to re-create the exact behaviors of everyday life but to capture and explore the underlying processes that shape those behaviors. Solomon Asch and Stanley Milgram devised experiments that explored a dilemma we all face frequently. Participants had to choose between honoring their own standards and being responsive to others.

In Milgram's experiments, participants were also torn between what they should respond to—the pleas of the victim or the orders of the experimenter. Their moral sense warned them not to harm another. But that same sense also prompted them to obey the experimenter and to be a good research participant. With kindness and obedience on a collision course, obedience usually won.

"I was only following orders."

Adolf Eichmann, Director of Nazi deportation of Jews to concentration camps

Such experiments demonstrate that strong social influences can make people conform to falsehoods or give in to cruelty. Milgram saw this as the most basic lesson of his work. "Ordinary people, simply doing their jobs, and without any particular hostility on their part, can become agents in a terrible destructive process" (1974, p. 6). Using the foot-in-the-door effect, Milgram began with a little tickle of electricity and escalated step by step. In the minds of those throwing the switches, the small action became justified, making the next act tolerable.

In any society, great evils sometimes grow out of people's acceptance of lesser evils. The Nazi leaders suspected that most German civil servants would resist shooting or gassing Jews directly. But they found them surprisingly willing to handle the paperwork of the Holocaust (Silver & Geller, 1978). Milgram found a similar reaction in his experiments. When he asked 40 men to administer the learning test while someone else did the shocking, 93 percent complied. Cruelty does not require devilish villains. All it takes is ordinary people corrupted by an evil situation. Ordinary soldiers may follow orders to torture prisoners. Ordinary students may follow orders to haze initiates into their group. Ordinary employees may follow orders to produce and market harmful products.

In Jozefow and Le Chambon, as in Milgram's experiments, those who resisted usually did so early. After the first acts of obedience or resistance, attitudes began to follow and justify behavior.

What have social psychologists learned about the power of the individual? *Social control* (the power of the situation) and *personal control* (the power of the individual) interact. Much as water dissolves salt but not sand, so rotten situations turn some people into bad apples while others resist (Johnson, 2007).

People may resist coercion. When feeling pressured, perhaps in a situation where groupthink threatens decision making, we may react by doing the opposite of what is expected (Brehm & Brehm, 1981). Without Rosa Parks' assertion of freedom—her refusal to sit at the back of the bus—the U.S. civil rights movement would not have been ignited at that time.

The power of one or two individuals to sway majorities is *minority influence* (Moscovici, 1985). In studies of groups in which one or two individuals consistently express a controversial attitude or an unusual perceptual judgment, one finding repeatedly stands out. When you are the

Gandhi :: As the life of Mahatma Gandhi powerfully testifies, a consistent and persistent minority voice can sometimes sway the majority. The nonviolent appeals and fasts of the Hindu nationalist and spiritual leader were instrumental in winning India's independence from Britain in 1947.

Margaret Bourke-White/Life Magazine. © 1946 Time Warner, Inc.

minority, you are far more likely to sway the majority if you hold firmly to your position and don't waffle. This tactic won't make you popular, but it may make you influential, especially if your self-confidence stimulates others to consider *why* you react as you do. Even when a minority's influence is not yet visible, people may privately develop sympathy for the minority position and rethink their views (Wood & others, 1994). The powers of social influence are enormous, but so are the powers of the committed individual.

PRACTICE TEST

4. We are *most likely* to conform to a group if
   a. the group members have many different opinions.
   b. we are feeling competent and secure.

   c. the group consists of at least three people.
   d. other group members cannot observe our behavior.

5. In Milgram's experiments, the "teachers" were most likely to obey the commands to deliver high-voltage shocks to "learners" when
   a. the learner was at a distance from the teacher.
   b. the learner was close at hand.
   c. other teachers refused to go along with the experimenter.
   d. the person giving the order was another teacher.

6. *Social facilitation*—improved performance in the presence of others—occurs with
   a. any physical task.
   b. any mental task.
   c. a well-learned task.
   d. new learning.

7. When people are part of a group working toward a common goal, their individual efforts decrease. This process is called
   a. minority influence.
   b. social facilitation.
   c. social loafing.
   d. group polarization.

8. Deindividuation—losing self-awareness and self-control in a group situation that fosters arousal and anonymity—is best illustrated by
   a. performing better in front of an audience.
   b. rioting at a mass rally.
   c. avoiding responsibility in a group clean-up effort.
   d. denying your own opinions in the face of a unanimous group opinion.

9. In like-minded groups, discussion strengthens the prevailing opinion. This effect is called
   a. groupthink.
   b. minority influence.
   c. group polarization.
   d. social facilitation.

groupthink the mode of thinking that occurs when the desire for harmony in a decision-making group overrides a realistic appraisal of alternatives.

10. When a group's desire for harmony over-
    rides its realistic analysis of other op-
    tions, _____ has occurred.
    a. group polarization
    b. groupthink
    c. social facilitation
    d. deindividuation

Answers: 4. c, 5. a, 6. c, 7. c, 8. b, 9. c, 10. b.

Social Relations

We have sampled how we *think about* and *influence* one another. Now we come to social psychology's third focus— how we *relate* to one another. What causes us to harm or to help or to fall in love? How can we transform the closed fists of aggression into the open arms of compassion? We will ponder the bad and the good: from prejudice and aggression to attraction, altruism, and peacemaking.

Prejudice

6: What are the social, emotional, and cognitive roots of prejudice?

Prejudice means "prejudgment." It is an un-justifiable and usually negative attitude toward a group—often a different cultural, ethnic, or gender group. **Prejudice** is a three-part mixture of

■ *beliefs* (called **stereotypes**).

■ *emotions* (for example, hostility, envy, or fear).

■ predispositions to *action* (to discriminate).

To *believe* that obese people are glut-tonous, to *feel* dislike for an obese person, and to be hesitant to hire or date an obese person is to be prejudiced. Preju-dice is a negative *attitude*. **Discrimination** is a negative *behavior*.

The ideas we bring to the table influ-ence what we notice and how we inter-pret events. In one 1970s study, most White participants who saw a White man shoving a Black man said they were "horsing around." When they saw a Black man shoving a White man, they inter-preted the same act as "violent" (Duncan, 1976). Our preconceived ideas color our perceptions.

How Prejudiced Are People?

To learn about levels of prejudice, we can assess what people say and what they do. Americans say that gender and racial at-titudes have changed dramatically in the last half-century. Nearly everyone agrees that women and men should receive the same pay for doing the same job and that children of all races should attend the same schools.

The one-third of Americans who in 1937 told Gallup they would vote for a qualified woman whom their party nom-inated for president soared to 89 percent in 2007 (Gallup Brain, 2008; Jones & Moore, 2003). Support for all forms of racial contact, including voting "for a Black candidate" for president and inter-racial marriage **(FIGURE 14.5)**, has also dra-matically increased.

Yet as *overt* prejudice wanes, *subtle* prej-udice lingers. Despite increased verbal support for interracial marriage, many people admit that in socially intimate set-tings (dating, dancing, marrying) they would feel uncomfortable with someone of another race. Recent experiments illustrate

that prejudice can be not only subtle but also automatic and unconscious (see Close-Up: Automatic Prejudice).

Social Roots of Prejudice

Why does prejudice arise? Social in-equalities and social divisions are partly responsible.

Social Inequalities Some people have money, power, and prestige. Others do not. In this situation, the "haves" usually develop attitudes that justify things as they are. The **just-world phenomenon** assumes that good is rewarded and evil is punished. From this it is but a short leap to assume that those who succeed must be good and those who suffer must be

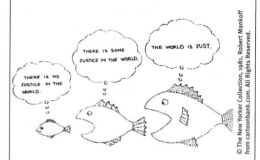

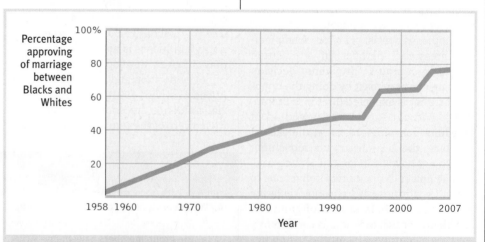

Figure 14.5> Prejudice over time Americans' approval of interracial marriage has soared over the past half-century. (Gallup surveys reported by Carroll, 2007.)

CLOSE-UP

AUTOMATIC PREJUDICE

Again and again throughout this book, we have seen that the human mind processes thoughts, memories, and attitudes on two different tracks. Sometimes that processing is *explicit*—on the radar screen of our awareness. More often, it is *implicit*—below the radar, out of sight. Modern studies indicate that prejudice is often implicit, an automatic attitude that is more of an unthinking knee-jerk response than a decision. Consider these findings on U.S. racial prejudice.

Implicit racial associations Even people who deny harboring racial prejudice may carry negative associations (Greenwald & others, 1998). For example, 9 in 10 White respondents took longer to identify pleasant words (such as *peace* and *paradise*) as "good" when presented with Black-sounding names (such as *Latisha* and *Darnell*) rather than White-sounding names (such as *Katie* and *Ian*).

Race-influenced perceptions Our expectations influence our perceptions. An unarmed man was shot in the doorway of his Bronx apartment building when officers mistook his wallet for a gun. Curious about this shooting, two research teams reenacted the situation (Correll & others, 2002; Greenwald & others, 2003). They asked people to press buttons quickly to "shoot" or not shoot men who suddenly appeared on screen. Some of the on-screen men held a gun. Others held a harmless object, such as a flashlight or bottle. People (both Blacks and Whites, in one of the studies) more often mistakenly shot Black men.

Reflexive bodily responses Even people who *consciously* express little prejudice may give off telltale signals as their body responds selectively to another person's race. Neuroscientists can detect these signals when people look at images of White and Black faces. The viewers' implicit prejudice shows up in different responses in their facial muscles and in their amygdala, an emotion-processing center (Cunningham & others, 2004; Eberhardt, 2005; Vanman & others, 2004).

If your own gut check sometimes reveals feelings you would rather not have about other people, remember this: It is what we do with our feelings that matters. We can monitor our feelings and actions and replace old habits with new ones based on new friendships.

---

bad. Such reasoning enables the rich to see both their own wealth and the poor's misfortune as justly deserved.

In an extreme case, slave "owners" developed attitudes that "justified" slavery. They perceived the people they enslaved as innately lazy, ignorant, and irresponsible. More commonly, women are perceived as unassertive but sensitive. These traits just happen to "justify" holding women responsible for the caretaking tasks they have traditionally performed (Hoffman & Hurst, 1990). Prejudice rationalizes inequalities.

Being a victim of discrimination can produce either self-blame or anger (Allport, 1954). Either reaction can increase prejudice through the classic *blame-the-victim* dynamic. Do the circumstances of poverty breed a higher crime rate? If so, that higher crime rate can be used to justify discrimination against those who live in poverty.

Us and Them: Ingroup and Outgroup
We have inherited our ancestors' need to belong, to live and love in groups. We cheer for our groups, kill for them, die for them. Indeed, we define who we are partly in terms of our groups. Through our *social identities* we associate ourselves with certain groups and contrast ourselves with others (Hogg, 1996; Turner, 1987). When Marc identifies himself as a man, an American, a political Independent, a Hudson Community College student, a Catholic, and a part-time letter carrier, he knows who he is, and so do we.

Mentally drawing a circle defines "us," the **ingroup.** But the social definition of who you are also states who you are not. People outside that circle are "them," the **outgroup.** An **ingroup bias**—a favoring of our own group—soon follows. Even creating us-them groups with the toss of a coin creates this bias. In experiments, people show favoritism to their own new group when dividing any rewards (Tajfel, 1982; Wilder, 1981).

Sorting enemies from friends and wanting our own group to be dominant sets us up to be prejudiced against strangers (Whitley, 1999). Many high

"All good people agree,
And all good people say
All nice people, like Us, are We
And everyone else is They."

Rudyard Kipling, "We and They," 1926

---

prejudice an unjustifiable and usually negative attitude toward a group and its members. Prejudice generally involves stereotyped beliefs, negative feelings, and a predisposition to discriminatory action.

stereotype a generalized (sometimes accurate but often overgeneralized) belief about a group of people.

discrimination unjustifiable negative behavior toward a group and its members.

just-world phenomenon the tendency of people to believe the world is just and that people therefore get what they deserve and deserve what they get.

ingroup "us"—people with whom we share a common identity.

outgroup "them"—those perceived as different or apart from our group.

ingroup bias the tendency to favor our own group.

The ingroup :: Scotland's famed "Tartan Army" soccer fans, shown here during a match against archrival England, share a social identity that defines "us" (the Scottish ingroup) and "them" (the English outgroup).

Mike Hewitt/Getty Images

school students form cliques—jocks, goths, skaters, gangsters, freaks, geeks— and look down on those outside their group. Even chimpanzees touched by a chimp from another group have been seen wiping the spot clean (Goodall, 1986).

Emotional Roots of Prejudice

Prejudice springs not only from the divisions of society but also from the passions of the heart. Facing the terror of death heightens patriotism and produces anger and aggression toward "them"— those who threaten our world (Pyszczynski & others, 2002). **Scapegoat theory** proposes that when things go wrong, finding someone to blame can provide an outlet for anger. Following 9/11, negative stereotypes blossomed. Some outraged people lashed out at innocent Arab-Americans. Others called for eliminating Saddam Hussein, the Iraqi leader whom Americans had been grudgingly tolerating. "Fear and anger create aggression, and aggression against citizens of different ethnicity or race creates racism and, in turn, new forms of terrorism," noted Philip Zimbardo (2001).

Evidence for the scapegoat theory of prejudice comes from two sources: high prejudice levels among economically frustrated people, and experiments in which a temporary frustration increases prejudice. In experiments, students made to feel insecure often restore their self-esteem by speaking badly of a rival school or another person (Cialdini & Richardson, 1980; Crocker & others, 1987). By contrast, those made to feel loved and supported become more open to and accepting of others who differ (Mikulincer & Shaver, 2001).

Cognitive Roots of Prejudice

We have seen that prejudice springs from the divisions of society and the passions of the heart. The by-products of the mind's natural workings form a third force that feeds prejudice.

Forming categories. One way we simplify our world is to sort things into categories. A chemist sorts molecules into categories of "organic" and "inorganic." Therapists discuss symptoms of psychological disorders and treatments by referring to diagnostic categories. But when we categorize people into social or ethnic

groups, we often overestimate their similarities. "They"—the members of that other group—seem to be alike in appearance, personality, and attitudes, while "we" differ from one another (Bothwell & others, 1989).

Remembering vivid cases. Cognitive psychologists tell us that we often judge the frequency of events by instances that readily come to mind. In a classic experiment, researchers showed two groups of student volunteers lists containing information about 50 men (Rothbart & others, 1978). The first group's list included 10 men arrested for *nonviolent* crimes, such as forgery. The second group's list included 10 men arrested for *violent* crimes, such as assault. Later, both groups were asked how many men on their list had committed *any* sort of crime. The second group overestimated the number. Vivid (violent) cases are readily available to our memory and feed our stereotypes **(FIGURE 14.6)**.

Believing the world is just. A final thought process that helps build stereotypes is the just-world phenomenon. If the world is just, "people must get what they deserve." As one German civilian is said to have remarked when visiting the Bergen-Belsen concentration camp shortly after World War II, "What terrible criminals these prisoners must have been to receive such treatment."

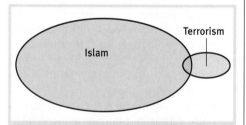

Figure 14.6> Vivid cases feed stereotypes The 9/11 Muslim terrorists created, in many minds, an exaggerated stereotype of Muslims as terror-prone. Actually, reported a National Research Council panel on terrorism, when offering this inexact illustration, most terrorists are not Muslim. "The vast majority of Islamic people have no connection with and do not sympathize with terrorism" (Smelser & Mitchell, 2002).

Aggression

7: What biological factors predispose us to be aggressive, and what psychological factors can trigger aggressive behavior?

The most destructive force in our social relations is aggression. In psychology, **aggression** is any verbal or physical behavior intended to hurt or destroy, be it passing along a vicious rumor or engaging in a physical assault.

Aggressive behavior emerges when biology interacts with experience. For a gun to fire, the trigger must be pulled. With some people, as with hair-trigger guns, it doesn't take much to trip an explosion. Let's look first at some biological factors that influence our thresholds for aggressive behavior. Then we'll turn to the psychological factors that pull the trigger.

In the last 25 years, guns caused some 800,000 suicidal, homicidal, and accidental deaths in the United States. Compared with people of the same sex, race, age, and neighborhood, those who keep a gun in the home (ironically, often for protection) are nearly three times more likely to be murdered in the home—nearly always by a family member or close acquaintance. For every self-defense use of a gun in the home, there are 4 unintentional shootings, 7 criminal assaults or homicides, and 11 attempted or completed suicides (Kellermann & others, 1993, 1997, 1998).

The Biology of Aggression

Is aggression an unlearned instinct? The wide variation from culture to culture, era to era, and person to person argues against that idea. But biology does *influence* aggression at three levels—genetic, neural, and biochemical.

Genetic Influences Genes influence aggression. We know this because animals have been bred for aggressiveness—sometimes for sport, sometimes for research. The effect of genes also appears in human twin studies. If one identical twin admits to "having a violent temper," the other twin will often independently admit the same (Miles & Carey, 1997; Rowe & others, 1999). Fraternal twins are much less likely to respond similarly.

Neural Influences There is no one spot in the brain that controls aggression. Aggression is a complex behavior, and it occurs in particular contexts. But animal and human brains do have neural systems that, when stimulated, either inhibit or produce aggressive behavior (Moyer, 1983). Consider:

- Researchers implanted a radio-controlled electrode in the brain of the domineering leader of a caged monkey colony. The electrode was in a brain area that, when stimulated, inhibits aggression. When researchers placed the control button for the electrode in the colony's cage, one small monkey learned to push it every time the boss became threatening.

- Neurosurgeons implanted an electrode in the brain of a mild-mannered woman to diagnose a disorder. The electrode was in her amygdala, in her limbic system. Because the brain has no sensory receptors, she did not feel the stimulation. But at the flick of a switch she snarled, "Take my blood pressure. Take it now," then stood up and began to strike the doctor.

- Studies of violent criminals have revealed diminished activity in the frontal lobes, which play an important role in controlling impulses. If this system is damaged, inactive, disconnected, or not yet fully mature, aggression may be more likely (Amen & others, 1996; Davidson & others, 2000; Raine, 1999).

Biochemical Influences Our genes engineer our individual nervous systems, which operate electrochemically. The hormone testosterone, for example, circulates in the bloodstream and influences the neural systems that control aggression. A raging bull will become a gentle Ferdinand when castration reduces its testosterone level. The same is true of castrated mice. When injected with testosterone, the castrated mice once again become aggressive.

Humans are less sensitive than mice to hormonal changes. But as men age, their testosterone levels—and their aggressiveness—drop off. Also, violent criminals tend to be muscular young males with lower-than-average intelligence scores, low levels of the neurotransmitter serotonin, and higher-than-average testosterone levels (Dabbs & others, 2001a; Pendick, 1994). Drugs that sharply reduce their testosterone also subdue their aggressive tendencies.

"We could avoid two-thirds of all crime simply by putting all able-bodied young men in cryogenic sleep from the age of 12 through 28."

David T. Lykken, *The Antisocial Personalities,* 1995

"It's a guy thing."

scapegoat theory the theory that prejudice offers an outlet for anger by providing someone to blame.

aggression any physical or verbal behavior intended to hurt or destroy.

A lean, mean fighting machine—the testosterone-laden female hyena :: Unusual prenatal development pumps testosterone into female hyena fetuses. The result is revved-up young females that seem born to fight.

Misuaki Iwago/Minden Pictures

Another substance that circulates in the bloodstream—alcohol—*unleashes* aggressive responses to frustration. Its effects are both biological and psychological (Bushman, 1993; Ito & others, 1996; Taylor & Chermack, 1993). (Just *thinking* you've imbibed alcohol has some effect; but so, too, does drinking alcohol unknowingly in a drink.) In police data and prison surveys, as in experiments, aggression-prone people are more likely to drink, and to become violent when they are intoxicated (White & others, 1993). People who have been drinking commit 4 in 10 violent crimes and 3 in 4 acts of spousal abuse (Greenfeld, 1998).

The Psychology of Aggression

Biological factors create the hair trigger for aggression. But what psychological factors pull that trigger?

Aversive Events Suffering sometimes builds character. Too often, however, when we are made miserable, we make others miserable (Berkowitz, 1983, 1989). This reaction is called the **frustration-aggression principle.** Frustration creates anger, which can spark aggression. (You

may recall from Chapter 10 that organisms often respond to stress with a *fight-or-flight reaction*.) After the frustration and stress of 9/11, Americans responded with a readiness to fight. Terrorism similarly may spring from a desire for revenge, following the death or injury of a friend or family member.

Another aversive event, rejection, can also trigger aggression (Catanese & Tice, 2005; Gaertner & Iuzzini, 2005). In a series of studies (Twenge & others, 2001, 2002, 2003), researchers told participants that some people they had met didn't want them in their group, or that a personality test indicated they "were likely to end up alone later in life." People led to feel socially excluded were later more likely to put down those who had insulted them, or even deliver a blast of noise to them. Rejection-induced aggression was a theme in various North American and European school shootings, committed by youths who had been shunned and mocked by peers.

Learning That Aggression Is Rewarding Experience can teach us that aggression pays. Animals that have successfully fought to get food or mates become increasingly ferocious. Children whose aggression successfully intimidates other children may become more aggressive. Terrorism, which aims to terrorize, is rewarded by massive publicity and frightened and inconvenienced people. "Kill one, frighten ten thousand," asserts an ancient Chinese proverb. Once established, aggressive behavior patterns are difficult to change.

> "Why do we kill people who kill people to show that killing people is wrong?"
> **National Coalition to Abolish the Death Penalty, 1992**

Observing Models of Aggression As Chapter 6 points out, we observe and we learn. We often imitate what a model, even an aggressive model, says and does. To foster a kinder, gentler world we had best model and reward sensitivity and cooperation from an early age.

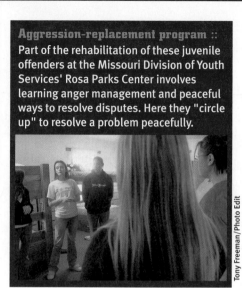

Aggression-replacement program :: Part of the rehabilitation of these juvenile offenders at the Missouri Division of Youth Services' Rosa Parks Center involves learning anger management and peaceful ways to resolve disputes. Here they "circle up" to resolve a problem peacefully.

Tony Freeman/Photo Edit

Parent-training programs often advise parents to avoid modeling violence by screaming and hitting. Instead, parents should reinforce desirable behaviors and frame statements positively. ("When you finish loading the dishwasher you can go play," rather than "If you don't load the dishwasher, there'll be no playing.") Parents of delinquent youngsters typically discipline with beatings and give in to (reward) their children's tears and temper tantrums (Patterson & others, 1982, 1992).

One *aggression-replacement program* worked with juvenile offenders and gang members and their parents. It taught both generations new ways to control anger, and more thoughtful approaches to moral reasoning (Goldstein & others, 1998). The result? The youths' rearrest rates dropped.

Different cultures model, reinforce, and evoke different tendencies toward violence. For example, crime rates are higher (and average happiness is lower) in countries marked by a wide gulf between rich and poor (Triandis, 1994). In the United States, cultures and families that experience minimal father care also have high violence rates (Myers, 2000; Triandis, 1994). But parents are not the only aggression models. In the United States and elsewhere, TV, films, and video games offer supersized portions of violence. (See Think Critically About: Do Video Games Teach, or Release, Violence?)

THINK CRITICALLY ABOUT:

DO VIDEO GAMES TEACH, OR RELEASE, VIOLENCE?

Violent video games became an issue for public debate after teen assassins in Paducah, Kentucky; Littleton, Colorado; and more than a dozen other places seemed to mimic the carnage in the splatter games they had so often played (Anderson, 2004a). In 2002, two Grand Rapids, Michigan, teens and a man in his early twenties spent part of a night drinking beer and playing Grand Theft Auto III. They used cars to run down pedestrians in cyberspace, then beat them with fists, leaving a bloody body behind (Kolker, 2002). These same teens and man then went out for a real drive. Spotting a 38-year-old man on a bicycle, they ran him down with their car, got out, stomped and punched him, and returned home to play the game some more. (The victim, a father of three, died six days later.)

Most youths who spend hundreds of hours with mass-murder simulators won't become teen assassins. Still, we wonder: What will be the effect of actively role-playing aggression? Although very few will commit slaughter, how many will become less sensitive to violence and more open to violent acts?

Thirty-eight recent studies of more than 7000 people hint at the answer. Video games can prime aggressive thoughts and increase aggression (Anderson & others, 2004). University men who have spent the most hours playing violent video games also tend to be the most physically aggressive (Anderson & Dill, 2000). (For example, they more often acknowledge having hit or attacked someone else.) And people randomly assigned to play a game involving bloody murders with groaning victims (rather than to play nonviolent Myst) became more hostile. On a follow-up task, they also were more likely to blast intense noise at a fellow student.

Studies of young adolescents reveal that those who play a lot of violent video games see the world as more hostile (Gentile & others, 2004). Compared with nongaming kids, they get into more arguments and fights and get worse grades.

Desensitizing people to violence

AP Photo/Damian Dovarganes

Ah, but is this merely because naturally hostile kids are drawn to such games? Apparently not. Comparisons of gamers and nongamers who scored low in hostility revealed a real difference in the number of fights they reported. Almost 4 in 10 violent-game players had been in fights. Only 4 in 100 of the nongaming kids reported fights (Anderson, 2004a). In part, due to the more repetitive and active participation of game play, violent video games seem to have even greater effects than exposure to violent television and movies.

Much remains to be learned, but one thing seems clear. We don't feel better if we "blow off steam" by venting our emotions (Chapter 9). Instead, playing violent video games increases aggressive thoughts, emotions, and behaviors. As the Greek philosopher Aristotle observed, "We are what we repeatedly do."

Repeatedly viewing violence on screen tends to make us less sensitive to cruelty. It also primes us to respond aggressively when provoked. And it teaches us **social scripts**—culturally provided mental files for how to act. When we find ourselves in new situations, uncertain how to behave, we rely on social scripts. After so many games and action films, youngsters may acquire a script that plays in their head when they face real-life conflicts. Challenged, they may "act like a man" by intimidating or eliminating the threat.

Likewise, after exposure to the sexual commentary and behavior in the short-term relationships featured in many prime-time TV shows, youths may acquire *sexual scripts* they later enact in real-life relationships (Kunkel & others, 2001; Sapolsky & Tabarlet, 1991).

Sexual scripts depicted in X-rated films are often toxic. People heavily exposed to televised crime perceive the world as more dangerous. People heavily exposed to pornography see the world as more sexual. Repeatedly watching X-

rated films, even nonviolent films, has many effects. One's own partner seems less attractive (Chapter 4). Extramarital sex seems less troubling (Zillmann, 1989).

frustration-aggression principle the principle that frustration—the blocking of an attempt to achieve some goal—creates anger, which can generate aggression.

social script culturally modeled guide for how to act in various situations.

Women's friendliness seems more sexual. Sexual aggression seems less serious (Harris, 1994).

In one experiment (Zillmann & Bryant, 1984), some undergraduates viewed six brief, sexually explicit films each week for six weeks. A control group viewed films with no sexual content during the same six-week period. Three weeks later, both groups read a newspaper report about a man convicted but not yet sentenced for raping a hitchhiker. They were then asked to suggest an appropriate prison term. Did viewing the sexually explicit films affect that group's suggestions? Yes. Sentences recommended by those viewers were only half as long as the sentences recommended by the control group.

Research on the effects of violent versus nonviolent erotic films points to one conclusion. It's not the sexual content of films that most directly affects men's acceptance and performance of aggression against women. It's the behavior modeled in the depictions of sexual *violence,* whether in R-rated slasher films or X-rated films. A statement by 21 social scientists (Surgeon General, 1986) noted, "Pornography that portrays sexual aggression as pleasurable for the victim increases the acceptance of the use of coercion in sexual relations." Contrary to much popular opinion, viewing such depictions does not provide an outlet for bottled-up impulses. Rather, "in laboratory studies measuring short-term effects, exposure to violent pornography increases punitive behavior toward women."

* * *

To sum up, research reveals biological, psychological, and social-cultural influences on aggressive behavior. Complex behaviors, including violence, have many causes, making any single explanation an oversimplification. Asking what causes violence is therefore like asking what causes cancer. Those who study the effects of asbestos exposure on cancer rates may remind us that asbestos is indeed a cancer cause, but it is only one among many. Like so much else, aggression is a biopsychosocial phenomenon.

Attraction

8: Why do we befriend or fall in love with some people but not with others? Does our love for a partner remain the same as time passes?

Pause a moment and think about your relationships with two people—a close friend, and someone who stirs in you feelings of romantic love. These special sorts of attachments help us cope with all other relationships. What is the psychological chemistry that binds us together? Social psychology suggests some answers.

The Psychology of Attraction

We endlessly wonder how we can win others' affection and what makes our own affections flourish or fade. Does familiarity breed contempt, or affection? Do birds of a feather flock together, or do opposites attract? Is beauty only skin deep, or does attractiveness matter greatly? Let's address these questions by considering three ingredients of our liking for one another: proximity, physical attractiveness, and similarity.

Proximity Before friendships become close, they must begin. *Proximity*—geographic nearness—is friendship's most powerful predictor. Being near another person gives us opportunities for aggression, but much more often it breeds liking. Study after study reveals that people are most inclined to like, and even to marry, those who are nearby. We are drawn to those who live in the same neighborhood, sit nearby in class, work in the same office, share the same parking lot, eat in the same dining hall. Look around.

Psychologists call this the **mere exposure effect.** Repeated exposure to novel stimuli increases our liking for them. This applies to nonsense syllables, musical selections, geometric figures, Chinese characters, human faces, and the letters of our own name (Moreland & Zajonc, 1982; Nuttin, 1987; Zajonc, 2001). People are even somewhat more likely to marry someone whose first or last name resembles their own (Jones & others, 2004).

Familiarity breeds acceptance :: When this rare white penguin was born in the Sydney, Australia, zoo, his tuxedoed peers shunned him. Zookeepers thought they would need to dye him black to gain acceptance. But after three weeks of contact, the other penguins came to accept him.

Rex USA

So, within certain limits, familiarity breeds fondness (Bornstein, 1989, 1999). Researchers demonstrated this by having four equally attractive women silently attend a 200-student class for zero, 5, 10, or 15 class sessions (Moreland & Beach, 1992). At the end of the course, students were shown slides of each woman and

The mere exposure effect :: The mere exposure effect applies even to ourselves. Because the human face is not perfectly symmetrical, the face we see in the mirror is not the same as the one our friends see. Most of us prefer the familiar mirror image, while our friends like the reverse (Mita & others, 1977). The Hillary Clinton known to us all is at left. The person she sees in the mirror each morning is shown at right, and that's the photo she would probably prefer.

Stan Honda/Getty Images

asked to rate her attractiveness. The most attractive? The ones they'd seen most often. These ratings would come as no surprise to the young Taiwanese man who wrote more than 700 letters to his girlfriend, urging her to marry him. She did marry—the mail carrier (Steinberg, 1993).

No face is more familiar than your own. And that helps explain a curious finding about voter preferences in a study using images of the two leading candidates in the 2004 presidential campaign. Researchers showed people images of the candidates, John Kerry and George W. Bush. What the researchers did not tell these voters was that the images had been altered. They were actually blends of the voter's own features and a candidate's features **(FIGURE 14.7)**. Which candidate did these voters prefer? The one whose face incorporated some of their own features (Bailenson & others, 2008). In me I trust.

The mere exposure effect had survival value for our ancestors. What was familiar was generally safe and approachable. What was unfamiliar was more often dangerous and threatening. Evolution may have hard-wired into us the tendencies to bond with those who are familiar and to be wary of those who are unfamiliar (Zajonc, 1998). If so, gut-level prejudice against those who are culturally different could be a primitive, automatic emotional response (Devine, 1995). It's what we do

"I'm going to have to recuse myself."

with our knee-jerk prejudice that matters, suggest researchers. Do we let those feelings control our behavior? Or do we monitor our feelings and act in ways that reflect our conscious valuing of human equality?

Physical Attractiveness Once proximity offers contact, what most affects your first impressions? The person's sincerity? Intelligence? Personality? The answer—physical appearance—is unnerving for those of us who were taught that "beauty is only skin deep" and that "appearances can be deceiving." In one early study, researchers randomly matched new students for a Welcome Week dance (Walster & others, 1966). Before the dance, the researchers gave each student a battery of personality and aptitude tests, and they rated each student's level of physical attractiveness. On the night of the blind

date, the couples danced and talked for more than two hours and then took a brief intermission to rate their dates. What determined whether they liked each other? Only one thing seemed to matter: Appearance. Both the men and the women liked good-looking dates best. Although women are more likely than men to say that another's looks don't affect them, research shows that a man's looks do affect women's behavior (Feingold, 1990; Sprecher, 1989; Woll, 1986).

Physical attractiveness has wide-ranging effects. It predicts how often people date and how popular they feel. It affects initial impressions of people's personalities. We may not assume that attractive people are more honest or compassionate, but we do perceive them as healthier, happier, more sensitive, more successful, and more socially skilled (Eagly & others, 1991; Feingold, 1992; Hatfield & Sprecher, 1986). Attractive, well-dressed people make a more favorable impression on potential employers, and they tend to be more successful in their jobs (Cash & Janda, 1984; Langlois & others, 2000; Solomon, 1987). There is a premium for beauty in the workplace, and a penalty for plainness or obesity (Engemann & Owyang, 2005).

Percentage of Men and Women Who "Constantly Think About Their Looks"		
	Men	Women
Canada	18%	20%
United States	17	27
Mexico	40	45
Venezuela	47	65

From Roper Starch survey, reported by McCool (1999).

Judging from their gazing times, even babies seem to prefer attractive over unattractive faces (Langlois & others, 1987).

  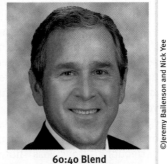

| Voter | "George Bush" | 60:40 Blend |

Figure 14.7> I like the candidate who looks a bit like dear old me Voters viewed images of presidential candidates. Researchers had secretly incorporated some of the voters' features into the blended photos (Bailenson & others, 2008). Without conscious awareness of their own features, the participants became more likely to favor the candidate who shared those features.

mere exposure effect the phenomenon that repeated exposure to novel stimuli increases liking of them.

So do some blind people. University of Birmingham professor John Hull (1990, p. 23) discovered this after going blind himself. A colleague's remarks about a woman's beauty can strangely affect his feelings. He finds this "deplorable . . . but I still feel it. . . . What can it matter to me what sighted men think of women . . . yet I do care what sighted men think, and I do not seem able to throw off this prejudice."

For those of us who find the importance of looks unfair and unenlightened, two other findings about attractiveness may be reassuring. First, people's attractiveness is surprisingly unrelated to their self-esteem and happiness (Diener & others, 1995; Major & others, 1984). Except after comparing ourselves with superattractive people, few of us (thanks, perhaps, to the mere exposure effect) view ourselves as unattractive (Thornton & Moore, 1993). Second, strikingly attractive people are sometimes suspicious that praise for their work may simply be a reaction to their looks. Less attractive people are more likely to accept praise as sincere (Berscheid, 1981).

In the end, however, beauty is in the eye of the culture. Hoping to look attractive, people across the globe have pierced their nose, lengthened their neck, bound their feet, and dyed or painted their skin and hair. Cultural ideals also change over time.

...So I told my plastic surgeon, "Do whatever it takes — just make me look YOUNG again.

Dan Piraro, Bizarro.com

Extreme makeover :: In affluent, beauty-conscious cultures, increasing numbers of people, such as this woman from the American TV show *Extreme Makeover*, have turned to cosmetic surgery to improve their looks. If money were no concern, might you ever do the same?

© ABC TV. Courtesy: Everett Collection

In the United States, the soft, voluptuous Marilyn Monroe ideal of the 1950s has been replaced by today's lean yet busty ideal.

If we're not born attractive, we may try to buy beauty. Americans now spend more on beauty supplies than on education and social services combined. Still not satisfied, millions undergo plastic surgery, Botox skin smoothing, teeth-capping or whitening, and laser hair removal (Wall, 2002).

Do any aspects of attractiveness cross place and time? Yes. As we noted in Chapter 4, men in 37 cultures, from Australia to Zambia, find women more attractive if they have a youthful appearance. Women are attracted to healthy looking men, but especially to those who seem mature, dominant, and affluent (Cunningham & others, 2005; Langlois & others, 2000).

Our feelings also influence our judgment of whether a person is attractive. In a Rodgers and Hammerstein musical, Prince Charming asks Cinderella, "Do I love you because you're beautiful, or are you beautiful because I love you?" Chances are it's both. As we see our loved ones again and again, their physical imperfections grow less noticeable and their attractiveness grows more apparent (Beaman & Klentz, 1983; Gross & Crofton, 1977). Shakespeare said it in *A Midsummer Night's Dream*: "Love looks not with the eyes, but with the mind." Come to love someone and watch beauty grow.

Similarity So you've met someone, and your appearance has made a decent first impression. What now influences whether you will become friends? As you get to know each other, will the chemistry be better if you are opposites or if you are alike? In real life, birds that flock together usually are of a feather. Compared with randomly paired people, friends and couples are far more likely to share attitudes, beliefs, and interests (and, for that matter, age, religion, race, education, intelligence, smoking behavior, and economic status). Journalist Walter Lippmann was right to suppose that love lasts "when the lovers love many things together, and not merely each other."

Proximity, attractiveness, and similarity are not the only forces that influence attraction. We also like those who like us, especially when our self-image is low. When we believe someone likes us, we respond to them more warmly. Our warm response in turn leads them to like us even more (Curtis & Miller, 1986). To be liked is powerfully rewarding.

Indeed, all the findings we have considered so far can be explained by a simple *reward theory of attraction*. We will like those whose behavior is rewarding to us, and we will continue relationships that offer more rewards than costs. When people live or work in close proximity with us, it costs less time and effort to

Diverse Yet Alike

In the eye of the beholder :: Conceptions of attractiveness vary by culture and over time. Yet some adult physical features, such as a youthful form and face, seem attractive everywhere.

arabianEye/Getty Images

Bill Bachmann/Alamy

Jamie Grill/Getty Images

develop the friendship and enjoy its benefits. When people are attractive, they are aesthetically pleasing, and associating with them can be socially rewarding. When people share our views, they reward us by confirming our own.

Romantic Love

Sometimes people move from initial impressions, to friendship, to the more intense, complex, and mysterious state of romantic love. If love endures, temporary passionate love will mellow into a lingering companionate love (Hatfield, 1988).

© The New Yorker Collection, 2005, Paul Noth from cartoonbank.com. All Rights Reserved.

"I can't wait to see what you're like online."

Passionate Love A key ingredient of **passionate love** is arousal. The two-factor theory of emotion (Chapter 9) can help us understand this intense positive absorption in another (Hatfield, 1988). That theory makes two assumptions:

■ Emotions have two ingredients—physical arousal plus thoughtful appraisal.

■ Arousal from any source can enhance an emotion, depending on how we interpret and label the arousal.

In tests of this theory, college men have been aroused by fright, by running in place, by viewing erotic materials, or by listening to humorous or repulsive monologues. They were then introduced to an attractive woman and asked to rate her (or their girlfriend). Unlike unaroused men, these men interpreted their stirred-up state as a response to the woman or girlfriend, and they felt more attracted to her (Carducci & others, 1978; Dermer & Pyszczynski, 1978; White & Kight, 1984).

A sample experiment: Researchers (Dutton & Aron, 1974, 1989) studied people crossing two bridges above British Columbia's rocky Capilano River. One, a swaying footbridge, was 230 feet above the rocks. The other bridge was low and solid. They had an attractive young woman stop men coming off each bridge

and ask their help in filling out a short questionnaire. She then offered her phone number in case they wanted to hear more about her project. Which men accepted the number and later called the woman? Far more of those who had just crossed the high bridge—which left their hearts pounding. To be revved up and to associate some of that arousal with a desirable person is to feel the pull of passion. Adrenaline makes the heart grow fonder.

Companionate Love Passionate romantic love seldom endures. The intense absorption in the other, the thrill of the romance, the giddy "floating on a cloud" feeling typically fades. Does this mean the French are correct in saying that "love

"When two people are under the influence of the most violent, most insane, most delusive, and most transient of passions, they are required to swear that they will remain in that excited, abnormal, and exhausting condition continuously until death do them part."

George Bernard Shaw, "Getting Married," 1908

passionate love an aroused state of intense positive absorption in another, usually present at the beginning of a love relationship.

MATRIMONY

Courtship and Matrimony (From the collection of Werner Nekes)

COURTSHIP
Sometimes passionate love becomes enduring companionate love, sometimes not (turn the picture upside-down) :: What, in addition to similar attitudes and interests, predicts long-term loving attachment?

makes the time pass and time makes love pass"? Not really. The evidence indicates that, as love matures, it becomes a steadier **companionate love**—a deep, affectionate attachment (Hatfield, 1988).

There may be adaptive wisdom to this change from passion to affection. Passionate love often produces children, whose survival is aided by the parents' waning obsession with one another. Failure to appreciate passionate love's limited half-life can doom a relationship (Berscheid & others, 1984). Indeed, recognizing the short duration of passionate love, some societies judge such feelings to be a poor reason for marrying. Better, these cultures say, to choose (or have someone choose for you) a partner who shares your background and interests. Non-Western cultures, where people rate love less important for marriage, do have lower divorce rates (Levine & others, 1995).

One key to a gratifying and enduring relationship is **equity.** When equity exists, when both partners receive in proportion to what they give—the chances for sustained and satisfying companionate love are good (Gray-Little & Burks, 1983; Van Yperen & Buunk, 1990). Mutually sharing self and possessions, making

decisions together, giving and getting emotional support, promoting and caring about one another's welfare—all of these acts are at the core of every type of loving relationship (Sternberg & Grajek, 1984). It's true for lovers, for parent and child, and for intimate friends.

Another vital ingredient of loving relationships is **self-disclosure,** revealing intimate details about ourselves—our likes and dislikes, our dreams and worries, our proud and shameful moments. As one person reveals a little, the other returns the gift. The first then reveals more, and on and on, as friends or lovers move to deeper and deeper intimacy (Baumeister & Bratslavsky, 1999).

One study marched pairs of students through 45 minutes of increasingly self-disclosing conversation—from "When did you last sing to yourself" to "When did you last cry in front of another person? By yourself?" Others spent the time with small-talk questions, such as "What was your high school like?" (Aron & others, 1997). By the experiment's end, those

AP Photo/Archaeological Society SAP, ho

Love is an ancient thing :: In 2007, skeletons of a 5000- to 6000-year-old "Romeo and Juliet" young couple were unearthed, locked in an embrace, near Rome.

experiencing the escalating intimacy felt remarkably close to their conversation partner, much closer than did the small-talkers.

In the mathematics of love, self-disclosing intimacy + mutually supportive equality = enduring companionate love.

Altruism

9: Why do we help others? When are we most—and least—likely to help?

Altruism is an unselfish concern for the welfare of others. A heroic example of altruism occurred in an underground New York City subway station. Construction worker Wesley Autrey and his 6- and 4-year old daughters were waiting for their train when they saw a nearby man collapse in a convulsion. The man then got up, stumbled to the platform's edge, and fell onto the tracks. With train headlights approaching, Autrey later recalled, "I had to make a split decision" (Buckley, 2007). His decision, as his girls looked on in horror, was to leap onto the track, push the man off the rails and into a foot-deep space between them, and lie on top of him. As the train screeched to a halt, five cars traveled just above his head, leaving grease on his knit cap. When Autrey cried out, "I've got two daughters up there. Let them know their father is okay," the onlookers erupted into applause.

Such selfless goodness made New Yorkers proud to call that city home. Another New York story, four decades earlier, had a different ending. In 1964, a stalker repeatedly stabbed Kitty Genovese, then raped her as she lay dying outside her Queens, New York, apartment at 3:30 A.M. "Oh, my God, he stabbed me!" Genovese screamed into the early morning stillness. "Please help me!" Windows opened and lights went on as her neighbors (38, said an initial *New York Times* report, though that number was later disputed) heard her screams. Her attacker fled. Then he returned to stab her eight more times and rape her again. Not until he had fled for good did anyone so much as call the police, at 3:50 A.M.

Subway hero Wesley Autrey :: "I don't feel like I did something spectacular; I just saw someone who needed help."

AP Photo/Newsday, Nick Brooks

Bystander Intervention

In an emergency, why do some people intervene, as Wesley Autrey did, but others, like the Genovese bystanders, fail to offer help? Social psychologists John Darley and Bibb Latané (1968b) have offered an answer. They believe bystanders will help only under three conditions.

- The situation enables them first to notice the incident.

- They interpret the event as an emergency.

- They assume responsibility for helping **(FIGURE 14.8).**

At each step, the presence of others can turn people away from the path that leads to helping. Darley and Latané (1968a) reached these conclusions after interpreting the results of a series of experiments. For example, they staged a fake emergency in their laboratory as students participated in a discussion over an intercom. Each student was in a separate cubicle, and only the person whose microphone was switched on could be heard. When his turn came, one of the students (an accomplice of the experimenters) made sounds as though he were having an epileptic seizure, and he called for help.

How did the other students react? As **FIGURE 14.9** on the next page shows, those who believed only they could hear the victim—and therefore thought they alone had responsibility for helping him—usually went to his aid. Students who thought others also could hear the victim's cries were more likely to react as Kitty Genovese's neighbors had. When more people shared responsibility for helping—when no one person was clearly responsible—each listener was less likely to help.

Hundreds of additional experiments have confirmed this **bystander effect.** For example, researchers and their assistants took 1497 elevator rides in three cities and "accidentally" dropped coins or pencils in front of 4813 fellow passengers (Latané & Dabbs, 1975). When alone with the person in need, 40 percent helped; in the presence of five other bystanders, only 20 percent helped.

Observations of behavior in tens of thousands of situations—relaying an emergency phone call, aiding a stranded motorist, donating blood, picking up dropped books, contributing money, giving time, and more—show that the *best* odds of our helping someone occur when

- the person appears to need and deserve help.

- the person is in some way similar to us.

- the person is a woman.

- we have just observed someone else being helpful.

- we are not in a hurry.

- we are in a small town or rural area.

- we are feeling guilty.

- we are focused on others and not preoccupied.

- we are in a good mood.

companionate love the deep affectionate attachment we feel for those with whom our lives are intertwined.

equity a condition in which people receive from a relationship in proportion to what they give to it.

self-disclosure revealing intimate aspects of yourself to others.

altruism unselfish concern for the welfare of others.

bystander effect the tendency for any given bystander to be less likely to give aid if other bystanders are present.

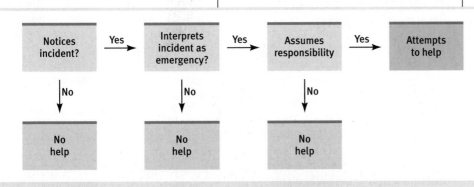

Viviane Moos/Corbis

Figure 14.8> The decision-making process for bystander intervention Before helping, one must first notice an emergency, then correctly interpret it, and then feel responsible. For Wesley Autrey, the quick answer to each question was *yes.* (From Darley & Latané, 1968b.)

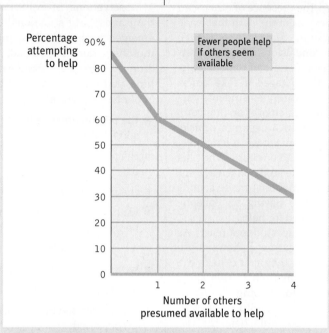

Percentage attempting to help

Fewer people help if others seem available

Number of others presumed available to help

Figure 14.9> Responses to a simulated physical emergency **When people thought they alone heard the calls for help from a person they believed to be having an epileptic seizure, they usually helped. But when they thought four others were also hearing the calls, fewer than a third responded. (From Darley & Latané, 1968a.)**

This last result, that happy people are helpful people, is one of the most consistent findings in all of psychology. As poet Robert Browning (1868) observed, "Oh, make us happy and you make us good!" It doesn't matter how we are cheered.

Whether by being made to feel successful and intelligent, by thinking happy thoughts, by finding money, or even by receiving a posthypnotic suggestion, we become more generous and more eager to help (Carlson & others, 1988).

Conflict and Peacemaking

10: What social processes fuel conflict? How can we transform feelings of prejudice, aggression, and conflict into attributes that promote peace?

We live in surprising times. With astonishing speed, late-twentieth-century democratic movements swept away totalitarian rule in Eastern European countries. Hopes for a new world order displaced the Cold War chill. Yet the twenty-first century began with terrorist acts and war. *Every* day the world continues to spend

$2 billion for arms and armies—money that could be used for housing, nutrition, education, and health care. Knowing that wars begin in human minds, psychologists have wondered: What in the human mind causes destructive conflict? How might the perceived threats of our differences be replaced by a spirit of cooperation?

To a social psychologist, a **conflict** is the perception that actions, goals, or ideas are incompatible. The elements of conflict are much the same, whether we are speaking of nations at war, cultural groups feuding within a society, or partners sparring in a relationship. In each situation, people become tangled in a destructive process that can produce results no one wants.

Enemy Perceptions

Psychologists have noticed a curious tendency: People in conflict form diabolical images of one another. These distorted images are so similar that we call them **mirror-image perceptions.** As we see "them"—untrustworthy, with evil intentions—so "they" see us. Each sees a demon in the other.

Mirror-image perceptions can feed a vicious cycle of hostility. In 2001, newly elected President George W. Bush spoke of Saddam Hussein. "Some of today's tyrants are gripped by an implacable hatred of the United States of America. They hate our friends, they hate our values, they hate democracy and freedom and individual liberty. Many care little for the lives of their own people." Hussein mirrored the perception in 2002. The United States, he said, is "an evil tyrant," with Satan as its protector. It lusts for oil and aggressively attacks those who "defend what is right."

The point is not that truth must lie midway between two such views (one may be more accurate). The point is that enemy perceptions often form mirror images. Moreover, as enemies change, so do perceptions. During World War II, Americans viewed the Japanese as "bloodthirsty, cruel, treacherous." Three decades later, American minds and media lauded

PLEASE GIVE TO ALTRUISM RESEARCH

©Nick Downes

those same people as our "intelligent, hardworking, self-disciplined, resourceful allies" (Gallup, 1972).

How can we change perceptions and make peace? Can cooperation transform the anger and fear fed by prejudice and conflicts into attitudes that promote peace? Research indicates that, in some cases, they can.

Cooperation

Does it help to put two conflicting parties into close contact? It depends. When that contact is free of competition and between parties with equal status, such as fellow store clerks, it may help. Initially prejudiced co-workers of different races have, in such circumstances, usually come to accept one another. Among North Americans and Europeans, friendly contact with ethnic minorities has similarly led to less prejudice (Pettigrew, 1969, 2004). This has also been true when heterosexual people knowingly have gay friends.

However, mere contact is not always enough. In most desegregated schools, ethnic groups resegregate themselves in the lunchrooms and on the school grounds (Clack & others, 2005; Schofield, 1986). People in each group often think they would welcome more contact with the other group, but they assume the other group is not interested in more contact with them (Shelton & Richeson, 2005). When these mirror-image untruths are corrected, friendships can form and prejudices melt.

> "You cannot shake hands with a clenched fist."
>
> Indira Gandhi, 1971

To see if enemies could overcome their differences, researcher Muzafer Sherif (1966) set a conflict in motion. He separated 22 boys into two separate camp areas. Then he had the two groups compete for prizes in a series of activities. Before long, each group became intensely proud of itself and hostile to the other group's "sneaky," "smart-alecky stinkers." Food wars broke out. Cabins were ransacked. Fistfights had to be broken up by camp counselors. Brought together, the two groups avoided each other, except to taunt and threaten. Little did they know that within a few days, they would be friends.

Sherif accomplished this by giving them **superordinate goals**—shared goals that could be achieved only through cooperation. When he arranged for the camp water supply to "fail," all 22 boys had to work together to restore water. To rent a movie in those pre-DVD days, they all had to pool their resources. To move a stalled truck, all the boys had to combine their strength, pulling and pushing together. Sherif used shared predicaments and goals to turn enemies into friends. What reduced conflict was not mere contact, but *cooperative* contact.

A shared predicament likewise had a powerfully unifying effect in the weeks after 9/11. Sharing a fearsome external threat and an overriding desire to overcome it, Americans pulled together. "We" were under attack. Gallup-surveyed approval of "our President" shot up from 51 percent the week before the attack to a highest-ever level of 90 percent just 10 days after (Newport, 2002). In chat groups and everyday speech, even the word *we* (relative to *I*) surged in the immediate aftermath (Pennebaker, 2002).

At such times, cooperation can lead people to define a new, inclusive group that dissolves their former subgroups (Dovidio & Gaertner, 1999). If this were a social psychology experiment, you might seat members of two groups not on opposite sides, but alternately around a table. Give them a new, shared name. Have them work together. Then watch "us" and "them" become "we." After 9/11, one 18-year-old New Jersey man described this shift in his own social identity. "I just thought of myself as Black. But now I feel like I'm an American, more than ever" (Sengupta, 2001).

If cooperative contacts between members of rival groups encourage positive attitudes, might this principle bring people together in multicultural schools? Could interracial friendships replace competitive classroom situations with cooperative ones? Could cooperative learning maintain or even enhance student achievement? Many educational researchers have asked these questions, and many experiments have confirmed that, in each case, the answer is yes (Johnson & Johnson, 1989, 1994; Slavin & others, 2003). In the classroom as in the sports arena, members of interracial groups who form teams and work together typically come to feel friendly toward one another. Knowing this, thousands of teachers have made interracial cooperative learning part of their classroom experience.

> "Most of us have overlapping identities which unite us with very different groups. We *can* love what we are, without hating what—and who—we are *not*. We can thrive in our own tradition, even as we learn from others."
>
> U.N. Secretary General Kofi Annan, Nobel Prize Lecture, 2001

The power of cooperative activity to make friends of former enemies has led psychologists to urge increased international exchange and cooperation (Klineberg, 1984). Let us engage in mutually beneficial trade, working together to protect our common destiny on this fragile planet and becoming more aware that our hopes and fears are shared. By taking such steps, we can change misperceptions that drive us

conflict a perceived incompatibility of actions, goals, or ideas.

mirror-image perceptions mutual views of each other often held by people in conflict.

superordinate goals shared goals that override differences among people and require their cooperation.

apart and instead join together in a common cause based on common interests. As working toward shared goals reminds us, we are more alike than different.

PRACTICE TEST

11. When things go wrong, _____ gives us someone to blame.
   a. ingroup bias
   b. creating a scapegoat
   c. an aversive event
   d. the just-world phenomenon

12. If several well-publicized murders are committed by members of a particular group, we tend to react with fear and suspicion toward all members of that group. In other words, we
   a. blame the victim.
   b. overgeneralize from vivid, memorable cases.
   c. create a scapegoat.
   d. rationalize inequality.

13. Evidence of a biological influence on aggression is the finding that
   a. aggressive behavior varies widely from culture to culture.
   b. animals can be bred for aggressiveness.
   c. the brain has a violence center in the frontal lobes.
   d. men who commit violent crimes have low levels of testosterone.

14. A conference of social scientists studying the effects of pornography unanimously agreed that violent pornography
   a. has little effect on most viewers.
   b. is the primary cause of reported and unreported rapes.
   c. leads viewers to be more accepting of coercion in sexual relations.
   d. has no effect, other than short-term arousal and entertainment.

15. The mere exposure effect helps explain why people tend to marry someone
   a. about as attractive as themselves.
   b. who lives or works nearby.
   c. of similar religious or ethnic background.
   d. who has similar attitudes and habits.

16. According to the two-factor theory of emotion, emotions such as passionate love consist of physical arousal plus
   a. a reward.
   b. proximity.
   c. companionate love.
   d. our interpretation of that arousal.

17. Companionate love is described as a deep, affectionate attachment. _____ is/are vital to the maintenance of such loving relationships.
   a. Equity and self-disclosure
   b. Physical attraction
   c. Intense positive absorption
   d. Passionate love

18. The bystander effect states that a particular bystander is less likely to give aid if
   a. the victim is similar to the bystander in appearance.
   b. no one else is present.
   c. other people are present.
   d. the incident occurs in a deserted or rural area.

19. One way of fostering cooperation is by providing groups with superordinate goals, which are
   a. the goals of friendly competition.
   b. shared goals that override differences.
   c. goals for winning at negotiations.
   d. goals for reducing conflict through increased contact.

Answers: 11. b, 12. b, 13. b, 14. c, 15. b, 16. d, 17. a, 18. c, 19. b.

Terms and Concepts to Remember

REVIEW: SOCIAL PSYCHOLOGY

Social psychologists study how people think about, influence, and relate to one another.

SOCIAL THINKING

1 **How do we tend to explain others' behavior? How do we explain our own behavior?**

■ We often commit the *fundamental attribution error* when explaining others' behavior—underestimating the influence of the situation and over-estimating the effects of personality.

■ When we explain our own behavior, however, we more often recognize the influence of the situation.

2 **Does what we think predict what we will do? Or does what we do shape what we will think?**

■ *Attitudes* predict behavior best when (1) other influences are minimized, (2) the attitude is specific to the behavior, and (3) we are aware of our attitudes.

■ Actions also modify our attitudes, especially when we feel responsible for those actions. This can be seen in the *foot-in-the-door phenomenon* and *role-playing*.

■ When our attitudes don't fit with our actions, *cognitive dissonance theory* suggests that we will reduce tension by changing our attitudes to match our actions.

SOCIAL INFLUENCE

3 **What do experiments on conformity and compliance reveal about the power of social influence?**

■ Asch and others have found that we are most likely to *conform* to a group standard when (1) we feel incompetent or insecure, (2) our group has at least three people, (3) everyone else agrees, (4) we admire the group's status, (5) we have not committed to another response, (6) we are being ob-served, and (7) our culture respects social standards.

■ In Milgram's famous experiments, people usually obeyed the experi-menter's orders even when they thought they were harming another per-son. Obedience was highest when (1) the experimenter was nearby and was a legitimate authority figure supported by an important institution, (2) the victim was not nearby, and (3) there were no role models for defiance.

4 **How does the presence of others influence our actions? How does our behavior change when we act as part of a group?**

■ *Social facilitation:* The presence of others arouses us, improving performance on easy tasks but hindering it on difficult ones.

■ *Social loafing:* In a group project, we may free-ride on others' efforts.

■ *Deindividuation:* In a big, energetic group, we may feel anonymous and become less self-aware and less self-restrained.

■ *Group polarization:* In a group, discussions with like-minded others cause us to feel more strongly about our shared beliefs and attitudes.

■ *Groupthink:* A desire for harmony within a group can cause its members to overlook important alternatives.

5 **What do the social influence studies teach us about ourselves? How much power do we have as individuals?**

■ The power of the group is great, but so is the power of the individual.

■ Even a small minority sometimes sways a group, especially when the minority expresses its views consistently.

SOCIAL RELATIONS

6 **What are the social, emotional, and cognitive roots of prejudice?**

- *Prejudice* is an unjustifiable, usually negative attitude toward a group, consisting of beliefs (often *stereotypes*), emotions, and predispositions to action (*discrimination*).

- Social roots: Social inequalities and social divisions feed prejudice. Favored social groups often rationalize their higher status with the *just-world phenomenon*. We tend to experience *ingroup bias* as we divide ourselves into us versus them.

- Emotional roots: We may use prejudice to protect our self-esteem, such as when focusing anger on a *scapegoat*.

- Cognitive roots: Our natural way of processing information tends to feed prejudice. We form categories, remember vivid cases, and believe the world is just.

7 **What biological factors predispose us to be aggressive, and what psychological factors can trigger aggressive behavior?**

- Biological factors: *Aggression* is influenced by genes and biochemical events in the brain.

- Psychological factors: Frustration *(frustration-aggression principle)*, rejection, getting rewarded for aggression, and seeing an aggressive role model can all contribute to aggression. Viewing sexual violence contributes to greater aggression toward women.

8 **Why do we befriend or fall in love with some people but not with others? Does our love for a partner remain the same as time passes?**

- Three factors affect attraction: (1) Proximity (geographical nearness) increases liking; even repeated *mere exposure* to novel stimuli increases liking of those stimuli. (2) Physical attractiveness increases social opportunities and improves the way we are perceived. (3) Similarity of attitudes and interests greatly increases liking, especially as relationships develop.

- Intimate love relationships start with *passionate love*—an intensely aroused state. Over time, the strong affection of *companionate love* often develops, enhanced by an *equitable* relationship and by intimate *self-disclosure*.

9 **Why do we help others? When are we most—and least—likely to help?**

- *Altruism* is unselfish regard for the well-being of others.

- According to the *bystander effect,* we are most likely to help if (1) we notice the incident, (2) we interpret the event as an emergency, and (3) we assume responsibility for helping.

- Other factors, including our mood and our similarity to the victim, also affect our willingness to help.

10 **What social processes fuel conflict? How can we transform feelings of prejudice, aggression, and conflict into attributes that promote peace?**

- *Conflicts* between individuals and cultures are often fed by distorted *mirror-image perceptions*—each party views itself as moral and the other as untrustworthy and evil-intentioned.

- Peace can result when individuals or groups cooperate to achieve *superordinate* (shared) *goals*.

THERE IS SOME JUSTICE IN THE WORLD.

THE WORLD IS JUST.

THERE IS NO JUSTICE IN THE WORLD.

Psychology at Work

FOR MOST OF US, TO LIVE is to work. Work is life's biggest single waking activity, helping to satisfy several levels of our needs. Work supports us, giving us food, water, and shelter. Work connects us, meeting our social needs. Work defines us, satisfying our self-esteem needs. Work helps us understand someone we've met for the first time. Wondering, "Who are you?" we may instead ask, "So, what do you do?"

The answer, however, may give us only a fleeting snapshot of that person at a particular time and place. On the day we retire from the work force, few of us will look back and say we have followed a predictable career path. We will have changed jobs, some of us often. The trigger for those changes may have been a desire for better pay, happier on-the-job relationships, or more fulfilling work.

Work and Life Satisfaction

1: What is *flow*?

Across various occupations, attitudes toward work tend to fall into one of three categories (Wrzensniewski & others, 1997, 2001). Some people view their work as a *job*. They work to make money, but the work itself is not a positive and fulfilling activity. Others view their work as a *career*. Their present position may not be ideal, but it is at least a rung on a ladder leading to increasingly better positions. The third group views their work as a *calling*. For them, work is a fulfilling and socially useful activity. Of all these groups, those who see their work as a calling report the highest satisfaction with their work and their lives.

This finding would not surprise Mihaly Csikszentmihalyi (1990, 1999), who has observed that people's quality of life increases when they are purposefully engaged. Between the anxiety of being overwhelmed and stressed, and the lethargy of being underwhelmed and bored, lies **flow.** In this intense, focused state, our skills are totally engaged, and we lose our awareness of self and time. Csikszentmihalyi (Chick-SENT-me-hi) came up with the flow concept after studying artists who spent hour after hour wrapped up in a project. After hours of painting or sculpting as if nothing else mattered, they promptly forgot about the project once they finished. The artists seemed driven less by the external rewards of producing their art—money, praise, promotion—than by the internal rewards of creating the work.

Fascinated, Csikszentmihalyi broadened his observations. He studied dancers, chess players, surgeons, writers, parents, mountain climbers, sailors, and farmers. His research included Australians, North Americans, Koreans, Japanese, and Italians. Participants ranged from

Sometimes, notes Gene Weingarten (2002), a humor writer knows "when to just get out of the way." Here are some sample job titles from the U.S. Department of Labor *Dictionary of Occupational Titles:* Animal impersonator, human projectile, banana ripening-room supervisor, impregnator, impregnator helper, dope sprayer, finger waver, rug scratcher, egg smeller, bottom buffer, cookie breaker, brain picker, hand pouncer, bosom presser, mother repairer.

flow a completely involved, focused state, with lowered awareness of self and time; results from full engagement of our skills.

Have you ever noticed that when you are immersed in an activity, time flies? And that when you are watching the clock, time seems to move more slowly? Researchers have confirmed that the more we attend to an event's duration, the longer it seems to last (Couli & others, 2004).

the teenage years to the golden years. A clear principle emerged. An activity that fully engages our skills leads to a state of flow, which boosts our sense of self-esteem, competence, and well-being. How did the researchers discover this? They beeped people at random intervals and asked them to report what they were doing and how much they were enjoying themselves. People reported more positive feelings when beeped while doing something active—work or play that engaged their skills. Those interrupted while passive usually reported little sense of flow and low satisfaction.

Other research supports these findings. In almost every developed nation, unemployed people have reported much lower well-being (Inglehart, 1990) **(FIGURE 1)**. Idleness may sound like bliss, but purposeful work enriches our lives. (For some tips on enriching your own work life, see Close-Up: Finding Your Own Flow.)

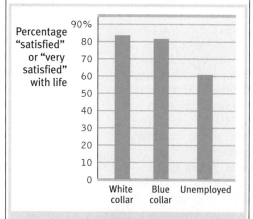

Figure 1> Unemployment and life satisfaction To want work but not have it is to feel less satisfied with life. (Data from 169,776 adults in 16 nations—Inglehart, 1990.)

Industrial-Organizational Psychology

2: What are the three subfields of industrial-organizational psychology?

In developed nations, work has been changing, from farming to manufacturing to "knowledge work." More and more work is *outsourced* to temporary employees. Consultants in remote locations now communicate electronically with the main office and with one another. (This book project is developed and produced by a team of people in a dozen cities, from Alaska to Florida.)

As work changes, will our attitudes toward our work also change? Will our satisfaction with work increase or decrease? What will happen to the *psychological contract*—that feeling of duty between workers and employers? Will our relationship with work become more or less trusting and secure? These are just a few of the many questions that fascinate those interested in **industrial-organizational (I/O) psychology,** a fast-growing profession that applies psychology's principles to the workplace.

I/O psychology has three subfields (see Close-Up: I/O Psychologists on the Job). **Human factors psychology** explores how machines and environments can best be designed to fit human abilities **(FIGURE 2)**. **Personnel psychology** applies psychology's methods and principles to selecting, placing, training, and evaluating workers. **Organizational psychology** is the primary focus of this appendix. This subfield considers an organization's goals, work environments, and management styles, and their influence on worker motivation, satisfaction, and productivity.

Figure 2> How not to go mad while going to Mars Future astronauts headed to Mars will be confined in conditions of monotony, stress, and weightlessness for months on end. To help design a workable human environment, such as for this Transit Habitation (Transhab) Module, NASA engages human factors psychologists (Weed, 2001; Wichman, 1992).

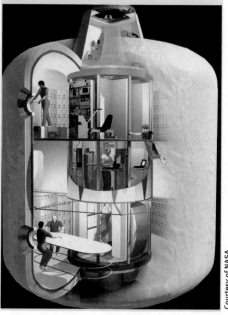

Courtesy of NASA

industrial-organizational (I/O) psychology the application of psychological concepts and methods to human behavior in workplaces.

human factors psychology a subfield of I/O psychology that explores how people and machines interact and how machines and physical environments can be made safe and easy to use.

personnel psychology a subfield of I/O psychology that focuses on employee selection, placement, training, and appraisal.

organizational psychology a subfield of I/O psychology that examines organizational influences on worker satisfaction and productivity and facilitates organizational change.

CLOSE-UP

FINDING YOUR OWN FLOW

Want to identify your own path to flow? You can start by pinpointing your strengths and the types of work that may prove satisfying and successful. Marcus Buckingham and Donald Clifton (2001) suggest asking yourself four questions.

1. What activities give me pleasure? (Bringing order out of chaos? Playing host? Helping others? Challenging sloppy thinking?)
2. What activities leave me wondering, "When can I do this again?" (Rather than "When will this be over?")
3. What sorts of challenges do I relish? (And which do I dread?)
4. What sorts of tasks do I learn easily? (And which do I struggle with?)

There are no "right" answers to these questions, but considering possible answers may lead you to your own zone of flow. You may find your skills engaged and time flying when teaching or selling or writing or cleaning or consoling or creating or repairing. If an activity feels good, if it comes easily, if you look forward to it, then look deeper. You'll see your strengths at work.

Top performers are "rarely well rounded," Buckingham and Clifton found. Satisfied and successful people devote far less time to correcting their weaknesses than to sharpening their existing skills. Given how stable our traits and temperaments are, this is probably wise. There may be limits to the benefits of assertiveness training if you are shy, or of public speaking courses if you tend to be nervous and soft-spoken. Drawing classes may not help much if you express your artistic side in stick figures.

But identifying your talents can help you recognize the activities you learn quickly and find absorbing. Knowing your strengths, you can develop them further.

As Robert Louis Stevenson said in *Familiar Studies of Men and Books* (1882), "To be what we are, and to become what we are capable of becoming, is the only end of life."

CLOSE-UP

I/O PSYCHOLOGISTS ON THE JOB

As scientists, consultants, and management professionals, I/O psychologists are found working in varied areas.

Human Factors (Engineering) Psychology

- Designing optimum work environments
- Optimizing person-machine interactions
- Developing systems technologies

Personnel Psychology

Selecting and placing employees

- Developing and validating assessment tools for selecting and placing workers
- Analyzing job content
- Optimizing worker placement

Training and developing employees

- Identifying needs
- Designing training programs
- Evaluating training programs

Appraising performance

- Developing criteria
- Measuring individual performance
- Measuring organizational performance

Organizational Psychology

Developing organizations

- Analyzing organizational structures
- Maximizing worker satisfaction and productivity
- Facilitating organizational change

Enhancing quality of work life

- Expanding individual productivity
- Identifying elements of satisfaction
- Redesigning jobs

Adapted from the Society of Industrial and Organizational Psychology (siop.org).

Motivating Achievement

3: Why is it important to motivate achievement?

Organizational psychologists help motivate employees and keep them engaged. But what motivates any of us to pursue high standards or difficult goals?

Grit

Think of someone you know who seems driven to be the best—to excel at any task where performance can be judged. Now think of someone who is less driven. For psychologist Henry Murray (1938), the difference between these two people is a reflection of their **achievement motivation.** If you score high in achievement motivation, you have a desire for significant accomplishment, for mastering skills or ideas, for control, and for meeting a high standard.

Achievement motivation matters. Just how much it matters was demonstrated in a study that followed the lives of 1528 California children. The children all scored in the top 1 percent on an intelligence test. Forty years later, researchers compared those who were most and least successful professionally. The most successful were ambitious, energetic, and persistent. As children, these highly motivated individuals had enjoyed more active hobbies. As adults, they participated in more groups and preferred *playing* sports over watching sports (Goleman, 1980).

Other studies of both high school and college students have also found motivation-based differences. Self-discipline, not intelligence score, has been the best predictor of school performance, attendance, and graduation honors. "Discipline outdoes talent," concluded researchers Angela Duckworth and Martin Seligman (2005). For example, by their early twenties, top violinists have fiddled away 10,000 hours of their life practicing. This is double the practice time of other violin

Grit feeds achievement :: B. F. Skinner knew he was far behind other students when beginning his graduate education in psychology. So, he devised a daily discipline of rising at 6:00 A.M., studying until breakfast, then going to classes, labs, and the library. After dinner he studied some more, leaving no more than 15 unscheduled minutes each day. Continuing this disciplined daily routine, he became one of the twentieth century's most influential psychologists.

Ken Heyman/Woodfin Camp & Associates

students aiming to be teachers (Ericsson & others, 1993, 2001).

Similarly, a study of outstanding scholars, athletes, and artists found that all were highly motivated and self-disciplined. They dedicated hours every day to the pursuit of their goals (Bloom, 1985). These achievers became superstars through daily discipline, not just natural talent. Great achievement, it seems, mixes a teaspoon of inspiration with a gallon of perspiration.

Duckworth and Seligman have a name for this passionate dedication to an ambitious, long-term goal: *grit*. Intelligence scores and many other physical and psychological traits can be displayed as a *bell-shaped curve*. Most scores cluster around an average, and fewer scores fall at the two far ends of the bell shape. Achievement scores don't follow this pattern. And that is why organizational psychologists seek ways to engage and motivate ordinary people to be superstars in their own jobs.

Satisfaction and Engagement

I/O psychologists know that everyone wins when workers are satisfied with their jobs. For employees, satisfaction with work feeds satisfaction with life. Moreover, lower job stress feeds improved health (Chapter 10).

Employers also benefit from worker satisfaction. Positive moods can translate into greater creativity, persistence, and helpfulness (Brief & Weiss, 2002). The positive correlation between individual job satisfaction and performance is modest but real (Judge & others, 2001; Parker & others, 2003). One recent analysis tracked 4500 employees at 42 British manufacturing companies. The most productive workers tended to be those in satisfying work environments (Patterson & others, 2004). In the United States, the *Fortune* "100 Best Companies to Work For" have also produced much higher-than-average returns for their investors (Dickler, 2007).

The biggest-ever study of worker satisfaction and job performance was an analysis of Gallup data **(TABLE 1)** from more than 198,000 employees (Harter & others, 2002). These people were employed in nearly 8000 business units of 36 large companies, including some 1100 bank branches, 1200 stores, and 4200 teams or departments. The study focused on links between various measures of organizational success and *employee engagement*—the extent of workers' involvement, satisfaction, and enthusiasm **(TABLE 2)**. The researchers found that engaged workers

- know what's expected of them.
- have what they need to do their work.
- feel fulfilled in their work.
- have regular opportunities to do what they do best.
- perceive that they are part of something significant.
- have opportunities to learn and develop.

achievement motivation a desire for significant accomplishment; for mastery of things, people, or ideas; and for attaining a high standard.

Engaged employees and organizational success :: Best Buy's 400 electronic goods stores have nearly identical product layout and operations manuals. Yet some stores have much more engaged employees—and more profitable performance. The store with the highest worker-engagement scores has been in the top tenth of stores in having profits beyond budget. And the store with the least-engaged employees has been in the bottom tenth (Buckingham, 2001).

Capital-Journal/David Eulitt/AP/WideWorld Photos

Table 2	Three Types of Employees

Engaged: working with passion and feeling a profound connection to their company or organization.

Not-engaged: putting in the time but investing little passion or energy into their work.

Actively disengaged: unhappy workers undermining what their colleagues accomplish.

(*Source:* Adapted from Crabtree, 2005.)

Researchers have also found that business units with engaged employees have more loyal customers. Their turnover is lower. Their productivity is higher, and so are their profits. A separate analysis for a company with 275 retail stores found a dramatic difference in employee turnover (Harter, 2000). In stores where employee engagement was in the top quarter, annual turnover was 55 percent. In stores where employee engagement was in the bottom quarter, annual turnover was 75 percent. Worker satisfaction matters.

Table 1	The Gallup Workplace Audit

Overall satisfaction—On a 5-point scale, where 5 is extremely satisfied and 1 is extremely dissatisfied, how satisfied are you with (name of company) as a place to work? _____

On a scale of 1 to 5, where 1 is strongly disagree and 5 is strongly agree, please indicate your agreement with the following items.

1. I know what is expected from me at work.
2. I have the materials and equipment I need to do my work right.
3. At work, I have the opportunity to do what I do best every day.
4. In the last seven days, I have received recognition or praise for doing good work.
5. My supervisor, or someone at work, seems to care about me as a person.
6. There is someone at work who encourages my development.
7. At work, my opinions seem to count.
8. The mission/purpose of my company makes me feel my job is important.
9. My associates (fellow employees) are committed to doing quality work.
10. I have a best friend at work.
11. In the last six months, someone at work has talked to me about my progress.
12. This last year, I have had opportunities at work to learn and grow.

Note: These statements are proprietary and copyrighted by The Gallup Organization. They may not be printed or reproduced in any manner without the written consent of The Gallup Organization. Reprinted here by permission.

Leadership

4: How can leaders be most effective?

The best leaders want their organization to be successful. They also want the people who work for them and with them to be satisfied, engaged, and productive. To achieve these ends, effective leaders harness people's strengths, set goals, and choose an appropriate leadership style.

Harness Strengths

Engaged employees don't just happen. Effective leaders engage their employees' interests and loyalty. They figure out people's natural talents, adjust roles to suit their talents, and develop those talents into great strengths (**FIGURE 3** on the next page). Consider, for example, instructors at a given school. Should they all be expected to teach the same load? To advise the same number of students? To serve on the same number of committees? To take on the same number of additional responsibilities in the department? Or should their job descriptions be tailored to their specific strengths? Would most schools and their students be better served if instructors' tasks were matched to their strengths?

Trying to create talents that are not there can be a waste of time. Leaders who excel spend more time developing and drawing out talents that already exist. Great managers share certain traits (Tucker, 2002). They

- start by helping people identify and measure their talents.

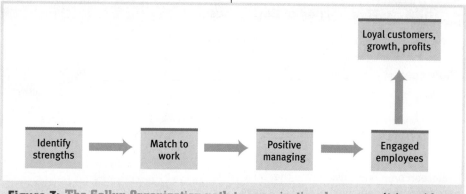

Figure 3> The Gallup Organization path to organizational success **(Adapted from Fleming, 2001.)**

- match tasks to talents and then give people freedom to do what they do best.

- care how people feel about their work.

- reinforce positive behaviors through recognition and reward.

Imagine that you're a manager with a limited budget for training your employees. You have two choices. You can focus on people's weaknesses and send them

Positive coaching :: NBA coach Larry Brown has been an adviser to "The Positive Coaching Alliance." He has been observed during practices to offer his players 4 to 5 positive comments for every negative comment (Insana, 2005). In 2004, his underdog Detroit Pistons won the National Basketball Association championship.

to training seminars to fix those problems. Or you can focus training time on educating people about their strengths and building upon them. Good managers choose the second option. They also try not to promote people into roles ill-suited to their strengths.

Does all this sound familiar? Bringing out the best in people within an organization builds upon a basic principle of operant conditioning (Chapter 6). To teach a behavior, catch a person doing something right and reinforce it. It sounds simple, but too many managers are like the bad parents who focus on the one low score when a child returns home with an almost perfect report card. As a report by the Gallup Organization (2004) observed, "65 percent of Americans received *no* praise or recognition in their workplace last year."

Set Specific, Challenging Goals

Good managers also know how to motivate people. In study after study, people merely asked to do their best do not do so. A better way to motivate higher achievement is to set specific, challenging goals. For example, you might state your own goal in this course as "Finish studying the Appendix by Friday." Specific goals focus our attention and stimulate us to work hard, persist, and try creative strategies. Such goals are especially effective

when people share in setting them. Achieving goals that are challenging yet within our reach boosts our self-evaluation (White & others, 1995).

Stated goals are most effective when combined with progress reports (Locke & Latham, 2002). Action plans that specify when, where, and how to achieve a goal will increase the chances of completing a project on time (Burgess & others, 2004; Koestner & others, 2002; Koole & Spijker, 2000). (Before writing this book, my editors, my associates, and I agreed on target dates for completing each draft of each chapter.) Creating your own action plans can help you become a more effective manager and leader. To motivate high productivity, you can work with people to define goals, make a plan for achieving those goals, and provide feedback on progress.

Choose an Appropriate Leadership Style

What qualities produce a great leader? Psychologists and others once believed that all great leaders share certain traits. That *great person theory of leadership* now seems overstated. But a leader's personality does matter. Effective leaders of laboratory groups, work teams, and large corporations tend to be self-confident. They also have *charisma,* which seems to have three main ingredients (House & Singh, 1987; Shamir & others, 1993). They have a *vision* of some goal. They are able to *communicate* that vision clearly and simply. They have enough optimism and faith to *inspire* their group to follow them.

One study rated company morale at 50 Dutch firms. Those with the highest ratings had chief executives who inspired their colleagues "to transcend their own self-interests for the sake of the collective" (de Hoogh & others, 2004). This ability to motivate others to commit themselves to a group's mission is *transformational leadership.* Transformational leaders are often natural extraverts. They set their standards high, and they inspire others to share their vision. They pay attention to

CLOSE-UP

DOING WELL WHILE DOING GOOD—"THE GREAT EXPERIMENT"

At the end of the 1700s, there were more than 1000 workers in the cotton mill at New Lanark, Scotland. Many of them were children drawn from Glasgow's poorhouses. They worked 13-hour days and lived in grim conditions. Education and sanitation were neglected. Theft and drunkenness were common. Most families occupied just one room.

On a visit to Glasgow, Welsh-born Robert Owen—an idealistic young cotton-mill manager—chanced to meet and fall in love with the mill owner's daughter. After their marriage, Owen, with several partners, purchased the mill. On the first day of the 1800s he took control as its manager. Before long, he began what he said was "the most important experiment for the happiness of the human race that had yet been instituted at any time in any part of the world" (Owen, 1814). The abuse of child and adult labor was, he observed, producing unhappy and inefficient workers. Owen believed that better working and living conditions could pay economic dividends.

Owen showed transformational leadership skills when he bravely began many new practices. He started a nursery for preschool children, and education (with encouragement rather than corporal punishment) for older children. Workers had Sundays off. They received health care, paid sick days, and unemployment pay for days when the mill could not operate. He set up a company store, selling goods at reduced prices. When his partners resisted his changes, he bought their shares in the mill.

Owen also designed a goals and worker-assessment program, with detailed records of daily productivity and costs. By each employee's workstation, one of four colored boards indicated that person's performance for the previous day. Owen could walk through the mill and at a glance see how individuals were performing. There was, he said, "no beating, no abusive language. . . . I merely looked at the person and then at the color. . . . I could at once see by the expression [which color] was shown."

The financial success of Owen's mill supported a reform movement for better working and living conditions. Owen believed he had demonstrated "that society may be formed so as to exist without crime, without poverty, with health greatly improved, with little if any misery, and with intelligence and happiness increased a hundredfold." Although that vision has not been fulfilled, Owen's great experiment did lay the groundwork for employment practices that are accepted in much of the world today.

Courtesy of New Lanark World Heritage Site

The great experiment :: New Lanark Mills showed that industries could do well while doing good. In its time, Owen's mill was visited by many European royals and reformers who came to observe its vibrant work force and prosperous business. New Lanark has been preserved as a World Heritage Site (www.newlanark.org).

other people (Bono & Judge, 2004). The frequent result is a work force that is more engaged, trusting, and effective (Turner & others, 2002). (For an impressive example of transformational leadership skills, see Close-up: Doing Well While Doing Good.)

Leadership styles vary, depending both on the demands of the situation and on the qualities of the leader. In some situations (think of a commander leading troops into battle), a *directive* style may be needed (Fiedler, 1981). In other situations, the strategies that work on the battlefield may smother creativity. In the creation of a new comedy show, for example, a better approach would be the *democratic* style, which shares power with team members and welcomes their participation.

Leaders also differ in the personal qualities they bring to the job. Some excel at **task leadership**—setting standards, organizing work, and focusing attention on goals. To keep the group centered on its mission, task leaders typically use a directive style. This style can work well if the leader is smart enough to give good orders (Fiedler, 1987).

task leadership goal-oriented leadership that sets standards, organizes work, and focuses attention on goals.

Other managers excel at **social leadership.** They can help group members solve their conflicts and build teams that work well together (Evans & Dion, 1991). Social leaders often have a democratic style. They share authority and welcome the opinions of team members. Social leadership is good for morale. We usually feel more satisfied and motivated when we can participate in decision making (Burger, 1987; Spector, 1986).

> "Good leaders don't ask more than their constituents can give, but they often ask—and get—more than their constituents intended to give or thought it was possible to give."
>
> John W. Gardner, *Excellence,* 1984

Effective managers often exhibit a high degree of *both* task and social leadership. This finding applies in many locations, including coal mines, banks, and government offices in India, Taiwan, and Iran (Smith & Tayeb, 1989). As achievement-minded people, effective managers certainly care about how well people do their work. Yet they are sensitive to their workers' needs. That sensitivity is often repaid by worker loyalty. In one national survey of American workers, those in family-friendly organizations offering flexible hours reported feeling greater loyalty to their employers (Roehling & others, 2001).

Employee participation in decision making is common in Sweden, Japan, the United States, and elsewhere (Cawley & others, 1998; Sundstrom & others, 1990). Giving workers a chance to voice their opinion before a decision is made engages them in the process. They then tend to respond more positively to the final decision (van den Bos & Spruijt, 2002). And, as we noted earlier, positive, engaged employees are a mark of thriving organizations.

Sharing vision and decisions :: As CEO, Jeffrey Bleustein helped Harley-Davidson thrive, in part by involving workers in planning and decision making.

Harley-Davidson management and employees worked together to drive their company from rags to riches (Teerlink & Ozley, 2000). In 1987, the struggling company began transforming its management process. The aim: "To push decision-making, planning, and strategizing from a handful of people at the top, down throughout the organization. We wanted all the employees to think every day about how to improve the company," reported CEO Jeffrey Bleustein (2002). In the mid-1990s, Harley-Davidson signed a cooperative agreement with its unions that included them "in decision-making in virtually every aspect of the business." Shared decision making can take longer, Bleustein noted. But "when the decision is made, it gets implemented quickly and the commitment is by the group." Satisfied stockholders agreed. Every $1 of Harley-Davidson stock purchased at the beginning of 1988 was worth more than $100 by 2008. For Harley-Davidson, an engaged work force was a win-win solution.

PRACTICE TEST

1. People who report great satisfaction with their work often experience _____, a focused state in which they lose awareness of themselves and of time.
   a. stress
   b. apathy
   c. flow
   d. facilitation

2. The three main divisions within I/O psychology are _____, _____, and _____ psychology.
   a. motivational; management; small group
   b. human factors; personnel; organizational
   c. motivational; personnel; human factors
   d. personnel; management; small group

social leadership group-oriented leadership that builds teamwork, resolves conflict, and offers support.

3. When people at similar intelligence levels are compared, those with higher achievement motivation tend to
   a. be more successful.
   b. be less successful.
   c. be less satisfied.
   d. have less grit.

4. Which of the following is NOT a quality of an effective leader?
   a. Helping people identify and measure their talents.
   b. Setting specific, challenging goals.
   c. Focusing on people's weaknesses with training to fix the problems.
   d. Reinforcing positive behaviors.

5. Task leadership is goal-oriented, whereas social leadership is group-oriented. Research indicates that effective managers exhibit
   a. mainly task leadership.
   b. mainly social leadership.
   c. both task and social leadership, depending on the situation and the person.
   d. task leadership for building teams and social leadership for setting standards.

Answers: 1. c, 2. b, 3. a, 4. c, 5. c.

Terms and Concepts to Remember

flow, p. 407

industrial-organizational (I/O) psychology, p. 408

human factors psychology, p. 408

personnel psychology, p. 408

organizational psychology, p. 408

achievement motivation, p. 410

task leadership, p. 413

social leadership, p. 414

REVIEW: PSYCHOLOGY AT WORK

INDUSTRIAL-ORGANIZATIONAL PSYCHOLOGY

WORK AND LIFE SATISFACTION

1 What is *flow*?

■ Having our skills fully engaged; losing awareness of self and time.

■ Work may be just a job, a somewhat fulfilling career, or a calling, which produces the highest levels of satisfaction.

2 What are the three subfields of industrial-organizational psychology?

■ *Human factors psychologists* explore how people and machines interact for optimal safety and effectiveness.

■ *Personnel psychologists* use psychology's principles to select, place, train, and evaluate workers.

■ *Organizational psychologists* consider an organization's goals, environments, and management styles in an effort to improve worker motivation, satisfaction, and productivity.

MOTIVATING ACHIEVEMENT

3 Why is it important to motivate achievement?

■ Those with grit have high *achievement motivation*, which leads to greater success.

■ The most satisfied and engaged employees tend to be the most productive and successful.

■ Managers motivate most effectively when they make clear what is expected, provide needed materials, allow employees to do what they do best, recognize employees, and ensure opportunities to learn and develop.

LEADERSHIP

4 How can leaders be most effective?

■ Harness strengths, by matching tasks to talents and reinforcing positive behaviors.

■ Set specific, challenging goals that stretch employees, but not beyond what they can do.

■ Choose an appropriate leadership style for the situation, such as *task leadership* when a more directive style is needed, or *social leadership* when a more democratic style fits best.

Glossary

absolute threshold the minimum stimulation needed to detect a particular stimulus 50 percent of the time. (p. 126)

achievement motivation a desire for significant accomplishment; for mastery of things, people, or ideas; and for attaining a high standard. (p. 408)

achievement test a test designed to assess what a person has learned. (p. 222)

acquisition in classical conditioning, the initial stage, when we link a neutral stimulus and an unconditioned stimulus so that the neutral stimulus begins triggering the conditioned response. (In operant conditioning, the strengthening of a reinforced response.) (p. 160)

action potential a nerve impulse. (p. 28)

active listening empathic listening in which the listener echoes, restates, and clarifies. A feature of Rogers' client-centered therapy. (p. 353)

adaptation-level phenomenon our tendency to form judgments (of sounds, of lights, of income) relative to a neutral level defined by our prior experience. (p. 262)

addiction compulsive drug craving and use. (p. 325)

adolescence the transition period from childhood to adulthood, extending from puberty to independence. (p. 84)

adrenal [ah-DREEN-el] **glands** a pair of endocrine glands that sit just above the kidneys and secrete hormones (epinephrine and norepinephrine) that help arouse the body in times of stress. (p. 34)

aerobic exercise sustained activity that increases heart and lung fitness; may also reduce depression and anxiety. (p. 280)

aggression physical or verbal behavior intended to hurt someone. (pp. 104, 391)

AIDS (acquired immune deficiency syndrome) a life-threatening, sexually transmitted infection caused by the *human immunodeficiency virus* (HIV). AIDS depletes the immune system, leaving the person vulnerable to infections. (p. 111)

alcohol dependence (popularly known as alcoholism). Alcohol use marked by tolerance, withdrawal if suspended, and a drive to continue use. (p. 326)

algorithm a methodical, logical rule or procedure that guarantees you will solve a particular problem. Contrasts with the usually speedier—but also more error-prone—use of *heuristics*. (p. 206)

all-or-none response a neuron's reaction of either firing (with a full-strength response) or not firing. (p. 28)

alpha waves relatively slow brain waves of a relaxed, awake state. (p. 51)

altruism unselfish concern for the welfare of others. (p. 398)

amphetamines drugs that stimulate neural activity, causing speeded-up body functions and associated energy and mood changes. (p. 328)

amygdala [uh-MIG-duh-la] two lima-bean–sized neural clusters in the limbic system; linked to emotion. (p. 37)

anorexia nervosa an eating disorder in which a person (usually an adolescent female) maintains a starvation diet despite being significantly (15 percent or more) underweight. (p. 241)

antianxiety drugs drugs used to control anxiety and agitation. (p. 364)

antidepressant drugs drugs used to treat depression and some anxiety disorders. Different types work by altering the availability of various neurotransmitters. (p. 365)

antipsychotic drugs drugs used to treat schizophrenia and other forms of severe thought disorder. (p. 364)

antisocial personality disorder a personality disorder in which the person (usually a man) exhibits a lack of conscience for wrongdoing, even toward friends and family members. May be aggressive and ruthless or a clever con artist. (p. 324)

anxiety disorders psychological disorders characterized by distressing, persistent anxiety or maladaptive behaviors that reduce anxiety. (p. 318)

aptitude test a test designed to predict a person's future performance; *aptitude* is the capacity to learn. (p. 222)

association areas areas of the cerebral cortex that are primarily involved in higher mental functions such as learning, remembering, thinking, and speaking. (p. 42)

associative learning learning that certain events occur together. The events may be two stimuli (as in classical conditioning) or a response and its consequences (as in operant conditioning). (p. 158)

attachment an emotional tie with another person; shown in young children by their seeking closeness to the caregiver and showing distress on separation. (p. 77)

attitude feelings, often based on our beliefs, that predispose us to respond in a particular way to objects, people, and events. (p. 377)

audition the sense or act of hearing. (p. 134)

autism a disorder that appears in childhood and is marked by deficient communication, social interaction, and understanding of others' states of mind. (p. 75)

automatic processing unconscious encoding of everyday information, such as space, time, frequency, and well-learned word meanings. (p. 138)

autonomic [aw-tuh-NAHM-ik] **nervous system** the division of the peripheral nervous system that controls the glands and the muscles of the internal organs (such as the heart). Its sympathetic division arouses; its parasympathetic division calms. (p. 31)

availability heuristic estimating the likelihood of an event based on its availability in memory; if instances come readily to mind (perhaps because of their vividness), we assume such events are common. (p. 207)

aversive conditioning a type of counterconditioning that associates an unpleasant state (such as nausea) with an unwanted behavior (such as drinking alcohol). (p. 355)

axons neuron extensions that pass messages to other neurons or cells. (p. 28)

B

babbling stage beginning at about 4 months, the stage of speech development in which the infant spontaneously utters various sounds at first unrelated to the household language. (p. 212)

barbiturates drugs that depress the activity of the central nervous system, reducing anxiety but impairing memory and judgment. (p. 328)

basal metabolic rate the body's resting rate of energy expenditure. (p. 239)

basic trust according to Erik Erikson, a sense that the world is predictable and trustworthy; said to be formed during infancy by appropriate experiences with responsive caregivers. (p. 79)

behavior therapy therapy that applies learning principles to the elimination of unwanted behaviors. (p. 354)

behaviorism the view that psychology (1) should be an objective science that (2) studies behavior without reference to mental processes. Most research psychologists today agree with (1) but not with (2). (pp. 3, 162)

belief perseverance clinging to beliefs and ignoring evidence that proves they are wrong. (p. 209)

binocular cues depth cues, such as retinal disparity, that depend on the use of two eyes. (p. 144)

biofeedback a system for electronically recording, amplifying, and feeding back information about a subtle physiological state, such as blood pressure or muscle tension. (p. 281)

biological psychology a branch of psychology concerned with the links between biology and behavior. (p. 27)

biomedical therapy prescribed medications or medical procedures. (p. 350)

biopsychosocial approach an integrated approach that incorporates different but complementary views from biological, psychological, and social-cultural perspectives. (p. 6)

bipolar disorder a mood disorder in which the person alternates between the hopelessness and lethargy of depression and the overexcited state of mania. (Formerly called manic-depressive disorder.) (p. 335)

blind spot the point at which the optic nerve leaves the eye; this part of the retina is "blind" because it has no receptor cells. (p. 130)

brainstem the oldest part and central core of the brain, beginning where the spinal cord swells as it enters the skull; the brainstem is responsible for automatic survival functions. (p. 34)

Broca's area an area of the frontal lobe, usually in the left hemisphere, that directs the muscle movements involved in speech; controls language expression. (p. 43)

bulimia nervosa an eating disorder in which a person alternates binge-eating (usually of high-calorie foods) with purging (by vomiting or laxative use), fasting, or excessive exercise. (p. 241)

bystander effect the tendency for any given bystander to be less likely to give aid if other bystanders are present. (p. 399)

C

Cannon-Bard theory the theory that an emotion-arousing stimulus simultaneously triggers (1) physiological responses and (2) the subjective experience of emotion. (p. 249)

case study an observation technique in which one person is studied in depth in the hope of revealing universal principles. (p. 12)

catharsis emotional release. The catharsis hypothesis maintains that "releasing" aggressive energy (through action or fantasy) relieves aggressive urges. (p. 259)

central nervous system (CNS) the brain and spinal cord. (p. 31)

cerebellum [sehr-uh-BELL-um] the "little brain" at the rear of the brainstem; functions include processing sensory input and coordinating movement output and balance. (p. 36)

cerebral [seh-REE-bruhl] **cortex** thin layer of interconnected neurons covering the cerebral hemispheres; the body's ultimate control and information-processing center. (p. 39)

chromosomes threadlike structures made of DNA molecules that contain the genes. (p. 64)

circadian [ser-KAY-dee-an] **rhythm** the biological clock; regular bodily rhythms (for example, of temperature and wakefulness) that occur on a 24-hour cycle. (p. 50)

classical conditioning a type of learning in which we learn to link two or more stimuli and anticipate events. (p. 159)

client-centered therapy a humanistic therapy, developed by Carl Rogers, in which the therapist uses techniques such as active listening within a genuine, accepting, empathic environment to promote clients' growth. (Also called *person-centered therapy*.) (p. 352)

cochlea [KOHK-lee-uh] a coiled, bony, fluid-filled tube in the inner ear; sound waves traveling through the cochlear fluid trigger nerve impulses. (p. 134)

cognition all the mental activities associated with thinking, knowing, remembering, and communicating. (pp. 73, 206)

cognitive dissonance theory the theory that we act to reduce the discomfort (dissonance) we feel when two of our thoughts (cognitions) clash. For example, when we become aware that our attitudes and our actions don't match, we may change our attitudes so that we feel more comfortable. (p. 378)

cognitive map a mental image of the layout of one's environment. (p. 169)

cognitive neuroscience subfield of psychology that studies the connection between our brain activity and the processes of thinking, knowing, remembering, and communicating. (p. 48)

cognitive therapy therapy that teaches people new, more adaptive ways of thinking and acting; based on the assumption that thoughts intervene between events and our emotional reactions. (p. 357)

cognitive-behavior therapy a popular integrated therapy that combines cognitive therapy (changing self-defeating thinking) with behavior therapy (changing behavior). (p. 358)

collectivism giving priority to goals of our group (often our extended family or work group) and defining our identity accordingly. (p. 308)

color constancy perceiving familiar objects as having consistent color, even if changing illumination alters the wavelengths reflected by the object. (p. 145)

companionate love the deep affectionate attachment we feel for those with whom our lives are intertwined. (p. 398)

concrete operational stage in Piaget's theory, the stage of cognitive development (from about 6 or 7 to 11 years of age) during which children gain the mental operations that enable them to think logically about concrete events. (p. 76)

conditioned reinforcer (also known as *secondary reinforcer*) an event that gains its reinforcing power through its link with a primary reinforcer. (p. 167)

conditioned response (CR) in classical conditioning, the learned response to a previously neutral (but now conditioned) stimulus (CS). (p. 160)

conditioned stimulus (CS) in classical conditioning, an originally irrelevant stimulus that, after association with an unconditioned stimulus (US), comes to trigger a conditioned response. (p. 160)

cones retinal receptor cells that are concentrated near the center of the retina; in daylight or well-lit conditions, cones detect fine detail and give rise to color sensations. (p. 130)

confirmation bias a tendency to search for information that confirms our preconceptions. (p. 207)

conflict a perceived incompatibility of actions, goals, or ideas. (p. 400)

conformity adjusting our behavior or thinking to coincide with a group standard. (p. 380)

consciousness our awareness of ourselves and our environment. (p. 48)

conservation the principle (which Piaget believed to be a part of concrete operational reasoning) that properties such as mass, volume, and number remain the same despite changes in the forms of objects. (p. 74)

continuous reinforcement reinforcing a desired response every time it occurs. (p. 167)

control group the group in an experiment that contrasts with the experimental condition and serves as a comparison for evaluating the effect of the treatment. (p. 17)

coronary heart disease the clogging of the vessels that nourish the heart muscle; the leading cause of death in many developed countries, such as those in North America. (p. 274)

corpus callosum [KOR-pus kah-LOW-sum] large band of neural fibers connecting the two brain hemispheres and carrying messages between them. (p. 45)

correlation a measure of the extent to which two factors vary together, and thus of how well either factor predicts the other. The *correlation coefficient* is the mathematical expression of the relationship, ranging from –1 to +1. (p. 14)

counterconditioning a behavior therapy procedure that uses classical conditioning to evoke new responses to stimuli that are triggering unwanted behaviors; includes *exposure therapies* and *aversive conditioning*. (p. 354)

creativity the ability to produce new and valuable ideas. (p. 220)

critical period a period early in life when exposure to certain stimuli or experiences is needed for proper development. (p. 71)

critical thinking thinking that does not blindly accept arguments and conclusions. Rather, it examines assumptions, uncovers hidden values, weighs evidence, and assesses conclusions. (p. 5)

crystallized intelligence our accumulated knowledge and verbal skills; tends to increase with age. (p. 93)

culture the enduring behaviors, ideas, attitudes, and traditions shared by a group of people and transmitted from one generation to the next. (pp. 6, 80)

D

defense mechanisms in psychoanalytic theory, the ego's protective methods of reducing anxiety by unconsciously distorting reality. (p. 292)

deindividuation the loss of self-awareness and self-restraint occurring in group situations that foster arousal and anonymity. (p. 385)

déjà vu that eerie sense that "I've experienced this before." Cues from the current situation may unconsciously trigger retrieval of an earlier experience. (p. 191)

delusions false beliefs, often of persecution or grandeur, that may accompany schizophrenia and other disorders. (p. 340)

dendrites neuron extensions that receive messages and conduct impulses toward the cell body. (p. 28)

dependent variable the outcome factor; the variable that may change in response to manipulations of the independent variable. (p. 17)

depressants drugs (such as alcohol, barbiturates, and opiates) that reduce neural activity and slow body functions. (p. 326)

depth perception the ability to see objects in three dimensions, although the images that strike the retina are two-dimensional; allows us to judge distance. (p. 144)

developmental psychology a branch of psychology that studies physical, cognitive, and social change throughout the life span. (p. 64)

difference threshold the minimum difference between two stimuli required for detection 50 percent of the time. We experience the difference threshold as a *just noticeable difference* (or *jnd*). (p. 127)

discrimination in classical conditioning, the learned ability to distinguish between a conditioned stimulus and other irrelevant stimuli. (p. 162)

discrimination unjustifiable negative behavior toward a group and its members. (p. 388)

displacement psychoanalytic defense mechanism that shifts sexual or aggressive impulses toward a more acceptable or less threatening object or person, as when redirecting anger toward a safer outlet. (p. 293)

dissociative disorders disorders in which conscious awareness becomes separated (dissociated) from previous memories, thoughts, and feelings. (p. 322)

dissociative identity disorder (DID) a rare dissociative disorder in which a person exhibits two or more distinct and alternating personalities. Also called *multiple personality disorder*. (p. 323)

DNA (deoxyribonucleic acid) a molecule containing the genetic information that makes up the chromosomes. (p. 64)

double-blind procedure a procedure in which participants and research staff are ignorant (blind) about who has received the treatment or a placebo. (p. 17)

dream a sequence of images, emotions, and thoughts passing through a sleeping person's mind. (p. 57)

drive aroused, motivated state often created by deprivation of a needed substance. (p. 236)

drive-reduction theory the idea that a physiological need creates an aroused tension state (a drive) that motivates an organism to satisfy the need. (p. 236)

DSM-IV-TR the American Psychiatric Association's *Diagnostic and Statistical Manual of Mental Disorders*, a widely used system for classifying psychological disorders. Presently available in an updated, text-revised fourth edition. (p. 316)

dual processing the principle that information is often simultaneously processed on separate conscious and unconscious tracks. (p. 8)

E

eclectic approach an approach to psychotherapy that, depending on the client's problems, uses techniques from various forms of therapy. (p. 350)

Ecstasy (MDMA) a synthetic stimulant and mild hallucinogen. Produces euphoria and social intimacy, but with short-term health risks and longer-term harm to serotonin-producing neurons and to mood and cognition. (p. 330)

EEG (electroencephalogram) recording apparatus, using electrodes placed on the scalp, that records waves of electrical activity that sweep across the brain's surface. (The tracing of those brain waves is an *electroencephalogram*.) (p. 35)

effortful processing   encoding that requires attention and conscious effort. (p. 183)

ego   the largely conscious, "executive" part of personality that, according to Freud, balances the demands of the id, superego, and reality. The ego operates on the *reality principle*, satisfying the id's desires in ways that will realistically bring pleasure rather than pain. (p. 291)

egocentrism   in Piaget's theory, the preoperational child's difficulty taking another's point of view. (p. 74)

electroconvulsive therapy (ECT)   a biomedical therapy for severely depressed patients in which a brief electric current is sent through the brain of an anesthetized patient. (p. 367)

embryo   the developing human organism from about 2 weeks after fertilization through the second month. (p. 66)

emerging adulthood   a period from about age 18 to the mid-twenties, when many in Western cultures are no longer adolescents but have not yet achieved full independence as adults. (p. 89)

emotion   a response of the whole organism, involving (1) physiological arousal, (2) expressive behaviors, and (3) conscious experience. (p. 248)

emotional intelligence   the ability to perceive, understand, manage, and use emotions. (p. 221)

emotion-focused coping   attempting to alleviate stress by avoiding or ignoring a stressor and attending to emotional needs related to our stress reaction. (p. 276)

encoding   the processing of information into the memory system—for example, by extracting meaning. (p. 182)

endocrine [EN-duh-krin] **system**   the body's "slow" chemical communication system; a set of glands that secrete hormones into the bloodstream. (p. 33)

endorphins [en-DOR-fins]   "morphine within"—natural, opiatelike neurotransmitters linked to pain control and to pleasure. (p. 30)

environment   every external influence, from prenatal nutrition to social support in later life. (p. 65)

equity   a condition in which people receive from a relationship in proportion to what they give to it. (p. 398)

estrogens   sex hormones, such as estradiol, secreted in greater amounts by females than by males. In nonhuman female mammals, estrogen levels peak during ovulation, promoting sexual receptivity. (p. 109)

evolutionary psychology   the study of how our behavior and mind have changed in adaptive ways over time using principles of natural selection. (p. 117)

experiment   a method in which researchers vary one or more factors (independent variables) to observe the effect on some behavior or mental process (the dependent variable). (p. 16)

experimental group   the group in an experiment that is exposed to the treatment, that is, to one version of the independent variable. (p. 17)

explicit memory   memories of facts and personal events that you can consciously retrieve. (p. 189)

exposure therapies   behavioral techniques, such as systematic desensitization, that treat anxieties by exposing people (in imagination or actual situations) to the things they fear and avoid. (p. 354)

external locus of control   the perception that chance or outside forces beyond our personal control determine our fate. (p. 278)

extinction   in classical conditioning, the weakening of a conditioned response when an unconditioned stimulus does not follow a conditioned stimulus. (In operant conditioning, the weakening of a response when it is no longer reinforced.) (p. 161)

extrasensory perception (ESP)   the controversial claim that perception can occur apart from sensory input, such as through *telepathy, clairvoyance,* and *precognition.* (p. 151)

extrinsic motivation   a desire to perform a behavior to gain a reward or avoid a punishment. (p. 169)

F

facial feedback effect   the tendency of facial muscle states to trigger corresponding feelings such as fear, anger, or happiness. (p. 258)

factor   a cluster of behavior tendencies that occur together. (p. 299)

family therapy   therapy that treats the family as a system. Views an individual's unwanted behaviors as influenced by or directed at other family members. (p. 358)

feature detectors   nerve cells in the brain that respond to specific features of a stimulus, such as edges, lines, and angles. (p. 132)

feel-good, do-good phenomenon   our tendency to be helpful when already in a good mood. (p. 260)

fetal alcohol syndrome (FAS)   physical and cognitive abnormalities in children caused by a pregnant woman's heavy drinking. In severe cases, symptoms include noticeable facial misproportions. (p. 67)

fetus   the developing human organism from 9 weeks after conception to birth. (p. 66)

fight-or-flight   an emergency response, including activity of the sympathetic nervous system, that mobilizes energy and activity for attacking or escaping a threat. (p. 271)

figure-ground   the organization of the visual field into objects (the *figures*) that stand out from their surroundings (the *ground*). (p. 143)

fixation   the inability to see a problem from a new perspective; an impediment to problem solving. (p. 208)

fixation   according to Freud, a lingering focus of pleasure-seeking energies at an earlier psychosexual stage, in which conflicts were unresolved. (p. 292)

flashbulb memory   a clear memory of an emotionally significant moment or event. (p. 188)

flow   a completely involved, focused state, with lowered awareness of self and time; results from full engagement of our skills. (p. 407)

fluid intelligence   our ability to reason speedily and abstractly; tends to decrease during late adulthood. (p. 93)

fMRI (functional magnetic resonance imaging)   a technique for revealing bloodflow and, therefore, brain activity by comparing successive MRI scans. fMRI scans show brain function. (p. 35)

foot-in-the-door phenomenon   the tendency for people who have first agreed to a small request to comply later with a larger request. (p. 378)

formal operational stage   in Piaget's theory, the stage of cognitive development (normally beginning about age 12) during which people begin to think logically about abstract concepts. (p. 76)

framing   the way an issue is posed; framing can significantly affect decisions and judgments. (p. 208)

fraternal twins   twins who develop from separate fertilized eggs. They are genetically no closer than brothers and sisters, but they share a fetal environment. (p. 66)

free association in psychoanalysis, a method of exploring the unconscious in which the person relaxes and says whatever comes to mind, no matter how trivial or embarrassing. (p. 290)

frequency the number of complete wavelengths that pass a point in a given time (for example, per second). (p. 134)

frontal lobes portion of the cerebral cortex lying just behind the forehead; involved in speaking and muscle movements and in making plans and judgments. (p. 39)

frustration-aggression principle the principle that frustration—the blocking of an attempt to achieve some goal—creates anger, which can generate aggression. (p. 392)

fundamental attribution error the tendency, when analyzing another's behavior, to overestimate the influence of personal traits and underestimate the effects of the situation. (p. 376)

G

gender in psychology, the biologically and socially influenced characteristics by which people define *male* and *female*. (p. 103)

gender identity one's sense of being male or female. (p. 107)

gender role a set of expected behaviors for males or for females. (p. 107)

gender schema theory the theory that children learn from their cultures a concept of what it means to be male and female, and that they adjust their behavior accordingly. (p. 107)

gender typing taking on a traditional masculine or feminine role. (p. 107)

general adaptation syndrome (GAS) Selye's concept of the body's adaptive response to stress in three stages—alarm, resistance, exhaustion. (p. 271)

general intelligence (g) a general intelligence factor that, according to Spearman and others, underlies specific mental abilities and is therefore measured by every task on an intelligence test. (p. 218)

generalization in classical conditioning, the tendency, after conditioning, to respond similarly to stimuli that resemble the conditioned stimulus. (p. 162)

generalized anxiety disorder an anxiety disorder in which a person is continually tense, fearful, and in a state of autonomic nervous system arousal. (p. 318)

genes the biochemical units of heredity that make up the chromosomes; a segment of DNA. (p. 64)

genome the complete instructions for making an organism, consisting of all the genetic material in that organism's chromosomes. (p. 64)

gestalt an organized whole. Gestalt psychologists emphasized our tendency to integrate pieces of information into meaningful wholes. (p. 143)

glucose the form of sugar that circulates in the blood and provides the major source of energy for body tissues. When its level is low, we feel hunger. (p. 239)

group polarization the enhancement of a group's prevailing inclinations through discussion within the group. (p. 385)

grouping the perceptual tendency to organize stimuli into meaningful groups. (p. 143)

groupthink the mode of thinking that occurs when the desire for harmony in a decision-making group overrides a realistic appraisal of alternatives. (p. 386)

H

hallucinations false sensory experiences, such as hearing something in the absence of an external auditory stimulus. (p. 42)

hallucinogens psychedelic ("mind-manifesting") drugs, such as LSD, that distort perceptions and evoke sensory images in the absence of sensory input. (p. 330)

heredity the genetic transfer of characteristics from parents to offspring. (p. 64)

heritability the portion of variation among individuals that we can attribute to genes. The heritability of a trait may vary, depending on the range of populations and environments studied. (p. 226)

heuristic a simple thinking strategy that often allows us to make judgments and solve problems efficiently; usually speedier but also more error-prone than *algorithms*. (p. 206)

hierarchy of needs Maslow's pyramid of human needs; at the base are physiological needs that must be satisfied before higher-level safety needs, and then psychological needs, become active. (pp. 237, 297)

hindsight bias the tendency to believe, after learning an outcome, that one would have foreseen it. (Also known as the I-knew-it-all-along phenomenon.) (p. 10)

hormones chemical messengers that are manufactured by the endocrine glands, travel through the bloodstream, and affect other tissues. (p. 33)

hue the dimension of color that is determined by the wavelength of light; what we know as the color names *blue, green,* and so forth. (p. 129)

human factors psychology a subfield of I/O psychology that explores how people and machines interact and how machines and physical environments can be made safe and easy to use. (p. 408)

humanistic psychology emphasized the growth potential of healthy people and the individual's potential for personal growth. (p. 3)

hypnosis a social interaction in which one person (the hypnotist) suggests to another (the subject) that certain perceptions, feelings, thoughts, or behaviors will occur. (p. 139)

hypothalamus [hi-po-THAL-uh-muss] a neural structure lying below (*hypo*) the thalamus; directs several maintenance activities (eating, drinking, body temperature), helps govern the endocrine system via the pituitary gland, and is linked to emotion. (p. 38)

hypothesis a testable prediction, often implied by a theory. (p. 12)

I

id a reservoir of unconscious psychic energy that, according to Freud, strives to satisfy basic sexual and aggressive drives. The id operates on the *pleasure principle*, demanding immediate gratification. (p. 290)

identical twins twins who develop from a single fertilized egg that splits in two, creating two genetically identical siblings. (p. 66)

identification the process by which, according to Freud, children incorporate their parents' values into their developing superegos. (p. 292)

identity our sense of self; according to Erikson, the adolescent's task is to solidify a sense of self by testing and integrating various roles. (p. 86)

illusory correlation the perception of a relationship where none exists. (p. 16)

imagery mental pictures; a powerful aid to effortful processing, especially when combined with encoding meaning. (p. 185)

implicit memory   retaining learned skills or conditioning, often without conscious awareness of this learning. (p. 189)

inattentional blindness   failure to see visible objects when our attention is directed elsewhere. (p. 49)

incentive   a positive or negative environmental stimulus that motivates behavior. (p. 236)

independent variable   the experimental factor that is manipulated; the variable whose effect is being studied. (p. 17)

individualism   giving priority to our own goals over group goals and defining our identity in terms of personal traits rather than group membership. (p. 308)

industrial-organizational (I/O) psychology   the application of psychological concepts and methods to human behavior in workplaces. (p. 408)

ingroup   "Us"—people with whom we share a common identity. (p. 389)

ingroup bias   the tendency to favor our own group. (p. 389)

insight   a sudden realization of the solution to a problem; it contrasts with strategy-based solutions. (p. 206)

insomnia   recurring problems in falling or staying asleep. (p. 55)

intelligence   mental quality consisting of the ability to learn from experience, solve problems, and use knowledge to adapt to new situations. (p. 218)

intelligence quotient (IQ)   defined originally as the ratio of mental age (*ma*) to chronological age (*ca*) multiplied by 100 (thus, IQ = *ma/ca* × 100). On contemporary intelligence tests, the average performance for a given age is assigned a score of 100. (p. 223)

intelligence test   a method for assessing an individual's mental aptitudes and comparing them with those of others, using numerical scores. (p. 222)

intensity   the amount of energy in a light or sound wave, which we perceive as brightness or loudness, as determined by the wave's amplitude. (p. 129)

interaction   in psychology, occurs when the effect of one factor (such as environment) depends on another factor (such as heredity). (p. 66)

interference   the blocking of recall as old or new learning disrupts the recall of other memories. (p. 194)

internal locus of control   the perception that we control our own fate. (p. 278)

interneurons   neurons that communicate internally and intervene between the sensory inputs and motor outputs. (p. 31)

interpretation   in psychoanalysis, the analyst's noting supposed dream meanings, resistances, and other significant behaviors and events in order to promote insight. (p. 351)

intimacy   in Erikson's theory, the ability to form close, loving relationships; a primary developmental task in early adulthood. (p. 88)

intrinsic motivation   a desire to perform a behavior for its own sake. (p. 169)

J

James-Lange theory   the theory that our experience of emotion is our awareness of our physiological responses to emotion-arousing stimuli. (p. 249)

just-world phenomenon   the tendency of people to believe the world is just and that people therefore get what they deserve and deserve what they get. (p. 388)

K

kinesthesis [kin-ehs-THEE-sehs]   the system for sensing the position and movement of individual body parts. (p. 141)

L

language   our spoken, written, or signed words and the ways we combine them to communicate meaning. (p. 211)

latent content   according to Freud, the underlying meaning of a dream. (p. 57)

latent learning   learning that is not apparent until there is an incentive to demonstrate it. (p. 169)

learned helplessness   the hopelessness and passive resignation an animal or human learns when unable to avoid repeated aversive events. (p. 277)

learning   a relatively permanent change in behavior due to experience. (p. 157)

limbic system   neural system (including the *hippocampus, amygdala,* and *hypothalamus*) located below the cerebral hemispheres; associated with emotions and drives. (p. 37)

lobotomy   a psychosurgical procedure once used to calm uncontrollably emotional or violent patients. The procedure cut the nerves connecting the frontal lobes to the emotion-controlling centers of the inner brain. (p. 368)

long-term memory   the relatively permanent and limitless storehouse of the memory system. Includes knowledge, skills, and experiences. (p. 182)

long-term potentiation (LTP)   an increase in a synapse's firing potential. Believed to be a neural basis for learning and memory. (p. 187)

LSD   a powerful hallucinogenic drug; also known as *acid* (*lysergic acid diethylamide*). (p. 331)

lymphocytes   the two types of white blood cells that are part of the body's immune system: B *lymphocytes* release antibodies that fight bacterial infections; T *lymphocytes* attack cancer cells, viruses, and foreign substances. (p. 272)

M

major depressive disorder   a mood disorder in which a person experiences, in the absence of drugs or a medical condition, two or more weeks of significantly depressed moods, feelings of worthlessness, and diminished interest or pleasure in most activities. (p. 335)

mania   a mood disorder marked by a hyperactive, wildly optimistic state. (p. 335)

manifest content   according to Freud, the remembered story line of a dream. (p. 57)

maturation   biological growth processes leading to orderly changes in behavior, independent of experience. (p. 70)

medical model   the concept that diseases, in this case psychological disorders, have physical causes that can be *diagnosed, treated,* and, in most cases, *cured,* often through *treatment* in a *hospital.* (p. 315)

medulla [muh-DUL-uh]   the base of the brainstem; controls heartbeat and breathing. (p. 34)

memory   the persistence of learning over time through the storage and retrieval of information. (p. 181)

memory trace enduring physical changes in the brain as a memory forms. (p. 194)

menarche [meh-NAR-key] the first menstrual period. (p. 84)

menopause the end of menstruation. In everyday use, it can also mean the biological transition a woman experiences from before to after the end of menstruation. (p. 91)

mental age a measure of intelligence test performance devised by Binet; the chronological age that most typically corresponds to a given level of performance. Thus, a child who does as well as the average 8-year-old is said to have a mental age of 8. (p. 222)

mere exposure effect the phenomenon that repeated exposure to novel stimuli increases liking of them. (p. 394)

methamphetamine a powerfully addictive drug that stimulates the central nervous system, with speeded-up body functions and associated energy and mood changes; over time, appears to reduce baseline dopamine levels. (p. 329)

mirror neurons neurons that fire when we perform certain actions or observe others doing so. (p. 173)

mirror-image perceptions mutual views of each other often held by people in conflict. (p. 400)

misinformation effect a memory that has been corrupted by misleading information. (p. 196)

modeling the process of observing and imitating a specific behavior. (p. 173)

monocular cues depth cues, such as interposition and linear perspective, available to either eye alone. (p. 145)

mood-congruent memory the tendency to recall experiences that are consistent with your current good or bad mood. (p. 191)

mood disorders psychological disorders characterized by emotional extremes. See *major depressive disorder, mania,* and *bipolar disorder.* (p. 334)

motivation a need or desire that energizes and directs behavior. (p. 235)

motor cortex area at the rear of the frontal lobe; controls voluntary movements. (p. 40)

motor neurons neurons that carry outgoing information from the central nervous system to the muscles and glands. (p. 31)

MRI (magnetic resonance imaging) a technique that uses magnetic fields and radio waves to produce computer-generated images of soft tissue. MRI scans show brain anatomy. (p. 35)

N

narcolepsy sleep disorder in which a person has uncontrollable sleep attacks, sometimes lapsing directly into REM sleep. (p. 55)

natural selection the adaptive process; among the range of inherited trait variations, those that lead to increased reproduction and survival will most likely be passed on to succeeding generations. (p. 117)

naturalistic observation observing and recording behavior in naturally occurring situations without trying to manipulate and control the situation. (p. 14)

nature-nurture issue the longstanding controversy over the relative contributions that genes and experience make to the development of psychological traits and behaviors. Today's psychological science sees traits and behaviors arising from the interaction of nature and nurture. (p. 6)

near-death experience an altered state of consciousness reported after a close brush with death (such as through cardiac arrest); often similar to drug-induced hallucinations. (p. 331)

negative reinforcement increases behaviors by stopping or reducing negative stimuli, such as shock. A negative reinforcer is anything that, when *removed* after a response, strengthens the response. (Note: negative reinforcement is *not* punishment.) (p. 166)

nerves bundled axons that form neural "cables" connecting the central nervous system with muscles, glands, and sense organs. (p. 31)

nervous system the body's speedy, electrochemical communication network, consisting of all the nerve cells of the peripheral and central nervous systems. (p. 31)

neuron a nerve cell; the basic building block of the nervous system. (p. 28)

neurotransmitters neuron-produced chemicals that cross synapses to carry messages to other neurons or cells. (p. 29)

nicotine a stimulating and highly addictive psychoactive drug in tobacco. (p. 328)

normal curve the symmetrical bell-shaped curve that describes the distribution of many physical and psychological attributes. Most scores fall near the average, and fewer and fewer scores lie near the extremes. (p. 224)

O

object permanence the awareness that things continue to exist even when not perceived. (p. 74)

observational learning learning by observing others. (p. 173)

obsessive-compulsive disorder (OCD) an anxiety disorder characterized by unwanted repetitive thoughts (obsessions) and/or actions (compulsions). (p. 319)

occipital [ahk-SIP-uh-tuhl] **lobes** portion of the cerebral cortex lying at the back of the head; includes areas that receive information from the visual fields. (p. 40)

Oedipus [ED-uh-puss] **complex** according to Freud, a boy's sexual desires toward his mother and feelings of jealousy and hatred for the rival father. (p. 292)

one-word stage the stage in speech development, from about age 1 to 2, during which a child speaks mostly in single words. (p. 212)

operant behavior behavior that operates on the environment, producing consequences. (p. 165)

operant chamber a box (also known as a *Skinner box*) with an attached recording device to track the rate at which an animal presses the box's bar to obtain a reinforcer. Used in operant conditioning research. (p. 165)

operant conditioning a type of learning in which behavior is strengthened if followed by a reinforcer or diminished if followed by a punisher. (p. 165)

operational definition a statement of the procedures (operations) used to define research variables. For example, *human intelligence* may be operationally defined as what an intelligence test measures. (p. 12)

opiates opium and its derivatives, such as morphine and heroin; they depress neural activity, temporarily lessening pain and anxiety. (pp. 29, 328)

optic nerve the nerve that carries neural impulses from the eye to the brain. (p. 130)

optimism the anticipation of positive outcomes. Optimists are people who expect the best and expect their efforts to lead to good things. (p. 278)

organizational psychology a subfield of I/O psychology that examines organizational influences on worker satisfaction and productivity and facilitates organizational change. (p. 408)

outgroup "Them"—those perceived as different or apart from our group. (p. 389)

overconfidence the tendency to be more confident than correct—to overestimate the accuracy of your beliefs and judgments. (p. 208)

P

panic disorder an anxiety disorder marked by unpredictable minutes-long episodes of intense dread in which a person experiences terror and accompanying chest pain, choking, or other frightening sensations. (p. 319)

parallel processing the processing of many aspects of a problem or scene at the same time; the brain's natural mode of information processing for many functions, including vision. (p. 132)

parasympathetic nervous system the division of the autonomic nervous system that calms the body, conserving its energy. (p. 32)

parietal [puh-RYE-uh-tuhl] **lobes** portion of the cerebral cortex lying at the top of the head and toward the rear; receives sensory input for touch and body position. (p. 39)

partial (intermittent) reinforcement reinforcing a response only part of the time; results in slower acquisition but much greater resistance to extinction than does continuous reinforcement. (p. 167)

passionate love an aroused state of intense positive absorption in another, usually present at the beginning of a love relationship. (p. 397)

perception the process by which our brain organizes and interprets sensory information, transforming it into meaningful objects and events. (p. 125)

perceptual adaptation in vision, the ability to adjust to an artificially displaced or even inverted visual field. (p. 149)

perceptual constancy perceiving objects as unchanging (having consistent color, brightness, shape, and size) even as illumination and retinal images change. (p. 145)

perceptual set a mental predisposition to perceive one thing and not another. (p. 149)

peripheral nervous system (PNS) the sensory and motor neurons connecting the central nervous system (CNS) to the rest of the body. (p. 31)

personal control our sense of controlling our environment rather than feeling helpless. (p. 277)

personality an individual's characteristic pattern of thinking, feeling, and acting. (p. 289)

personality disorders psychological disorders characterized by inflexible and enduring behavior patterns that impair social functioning. (p. 324)

personnel psychology a subfield of I/O psychology that focuses on employee selection, placement, training, and appraisal. (p. 408)

pessimism the anticipation of negative outcomes. Pessimists are people who expect the worst and doubt that their goals will be achieved. (p. 278)

PET (positron emission tomography) scan a view of brain activity showing where a radioactive form of glucose goes while the brain performs a given task. (p. 35)

phobia an anxiety disorder marked by a persistent, irrational fear and avoidance of a specific object or situation. (p. 319)

physical dependence a physiological need for a drug, marked by unpleasant withdrawal symptoms when the drug is discontinued. (p. 326)

physiological needs basic bodily requirements. (p. 236)

pitch a tone's experienced highness or lowness; depends on frequency. (p. 135)

pituitary gland the endocrine system's most influential gland. Under the influence of the hypothalamus, the pituitary regulates growth and controls other endocrine glands. (p. 34)

placebo [pluh-SEE-bo; Latin for "I shall please"] an inert substance or condition that is assumed to be an active agent. (p. 17)

placebo effect results caused by expectations alone. (p. 17)

plasticity the brain's ability to change, especially during childhood, by reorganizing after damage or by building new pathways based on experience. (p. 44)

polygraph a machine, commonly used in attempts to detect lies, that measures several of the physiological responses accompanying emotion (such as changes in perspiration, heart rate, and breathing). (p. 253)

positive psychology the scientific study of human functioning, with the goals of discovering and promoting strengths and virtues that help individuals and communities to thrive. (p. 8)

positive reinforcement increases behaviors by presenting positive stimuli, such as food. A positive reinforcer is anything that, when *presented* after a response, strengthens the response. (p. 166)

post-traumatic stress disorder (PTSD) an anxiety disorder characterized by haunting memories, nightmares, social withdrawal, jumpy anxiety, and/or insomnia that lingers for four weeks or more after a traumatic experience. (p. 320)

prejudice an unjustifiable (and usually negative) attitude toward a group and its members. Prejudice generally involves stereotyped beliefs, negative feelings, and a predisposition to discriminatory action. (p. 388)

preoperational stage in Piaget's theory, the stage (from about 2 to 6 or 7 years of age) during which a child learns to use language but does not yet comprehend the mental operations of concrete logic. (p. 74)

primary reinforcer an event that is innately reinforcing, often by satisfying a biological need. (p. 167)

priming activating, often unconsciously, associations in our mind, thus setting us up to perceive or remember objects or events in certain ways. (p. 126)

problem-focused coping attempting to alleviate stress directly—by changing the stressor or the way we interact with that stressor. (p. 276)

projection psychoanalytic defense mechanism by which we disguise our own threatening impulses by attributing them to others. (p. 293)

projective test a personality test, such as the Rorschach test, that provides an unclear image designed to trigger projection of the test-taker's unconscious thoughts or feelings. (p. 294)

prosocial behavior positive, constructive, helpful behavior. The opposite of antisocial behavior. (p. 174)

psychoactive drug a chemical substance that alters perceptions and mood. (p. 325)

psychoanalysis Freud's theory of personality and therapeutic technique that attributes thoughts and actions to unconscious motives and conflicts. Freud believed the patient's free associations, resistances, dreams, and transferences—and the therapist's interpretations of them—released previously repressed feelings, allowing the patient to gain self-insight. (pp. 290, 350)

psychodynamic theory a Freud-influenced perspective that sees behavior, thinking, and emotions as reflecting unconscious motives. (p. 293)

psychodynamic therapy a Freud-influenced therapeutic perspective that sees behavior, thinking, and emotions in terms of unconscious motives. (p. 352)

psychological dependence a psychological need to use a drug, such as to relieve negative emotions. (p. 326)

psychological disorder deviant (atypical), distressful, and dysfunctional thoughts, feelings, or behaviors. (p. 314)

psychology the scientific study of behavior and mental processes. (p. 3)

psychoneuroimmunology (PNI) the study of how psychological, neural, and endocrine processes combine to affect our immune system and health. (p. 272)

psychosexual stages the childhood stages of development (oral, anal, phallic, latency, genital) during which, according to Freud, the id's pleasure-seeking energies focus on distinct erogenous zones. (p. 291)

psychosurgery surgery that removes or destroys brain tissue in an effort to change behavior. (p. 368)

psychotherapy treatment involving psychological techniques; consists of interactions between a trained therapist and someone seeking to overcome psychological difficulties or achieve personal growth. (p. 350)

puberty the period of sexual maturation, during which a person becomes capable of reproducing. (p. 84)

punishment an event that *decreases* the behavior it follows. (p. 168)

R

random assignment assigning participants to experimental and control groups by chance, thus minimizing any differences between them. (p. 16)

random sample a sample that fairly represents a population because each member has an equal chance of inclusion. (p. 13)

rationalization psychoanalytic defense mechanism that offers self-justifying explanations in place of the real, but more threatening, unconscious reasons for our actions. (p. 293)

reaction formation psychoanalytic defense mechanism by which the ego unconsciously switches unacceptable impulses into their opposites. Thus, we may express feelings that are the opposite of our anxiety-arousing unconscious feelings. (p. 293)

recall memory demonstrated by retrieving information learned earlier, as on a fill-in-the-blank test. (p. 190)

reciprocal determinism the interacting influences of behavior, internal personal factors, and environment. (p. 305)

recognition memory demonstrated by identifying items previously learned, as on a multiple-choice test. (p. 190)

reflex an unlearned, automatic response to a sensory stimulus. (p. 68)

refractory period a resting period after orgasm, during which a man cannot achieve another orgasm. (p. 109)

regression psychoanalytic defense mechanism in which an individual faced with anxiety retreats to an earlier stage of development. (p. 292)

rehearsal the conscious repetition of information, either to maintain it in consciousness or to encode it for storage. (p. 183)

reinforcement in operant conditioning, any event that *strengthens* the behavior it follows. (p. 165)

reinforcement schedule a pattern that defines how often a desired response will be reinforced. (p. 167)

relative deprivation the perception that we are worse off relative to those with whom we compare ourselves. (p. 263)

relearning memory demonstrated by time saved when learning material a second time. (p. 190)

reliability the extent to which a test yields consistent results, as assessed by the consistency of scores on two halves of the test, on alternate forms of the test, or on retesting. (p. 224)

REM (rapid eye movement) sleep recurring sleep stage during which vivid dreams commonly occur. Also known as *paradoxical sleep,* because the muscles are relaxed (except for minor twitches), but other body systems are active. (p. 51)

REM rebound the tendency for REM sleep to increase following REM sleep deprivation (created by repeated awakenings during REM sleep). (p. 58)

repetitive transcranial magnetic stimulation (rTMS) the application of repeated pulses of magnetic energy to the brain; used to stimulate or suppress brain activity. (p. 368)

replication repeating the essence of a research study, usually with different participants in different situations, to see whether the basic finding extends to other participants and circumstances. (p. 12)

repression in psychoanalytic theory, the basic defense mechanism that banishes anxiety-arousing thoughts, feelings, and memories from consciousness. (pp. 195, 292)

resistance in psychoanalysis, the blocking from consciousness of anxiety-laden material. (p. 351)

respondent behavior behavior that occurs as an automatic response to some stimulus. (p. 165)

reticular formation a nerve network in the brainstem that plays an important role in controlling arousal. (p. 36)

retina the light-sensitive inner surface of the eye; contains the receptor rods and cones plus layers of neurons that begin the processing of visual information. (p. 130)

retinal disparity a binocular cue for perceiving depth: By comparing images from the two eyeballs, the brain computes distance—the greater the disparity (difference) between the two images, the closer the object. (p. 145)

retrieval the process of getting information out of memory storage. (p. 182)

retrieval cue any stimulus (event, feeling, place, and so on) linked to a specific memory. (p. 190)

rods retinal receptors that detect black, white, and gray; necessary for peripheral and twilight vision, when cones don't respond. (p. 130)

role a set of expectations about a social position, defining how those in the position ought to behave. (pp. 106, 378)

Rorschach inkblot test the most widely used projective test, a set of 10 inkblots, designed by Hermann Rorschach; seeks to identify people's inner feelings by analyzing their interpretations of the blots. (p. 294)

S

savant syndrome a condition in which a person otherwise limited in mental ability has an exceptional specific skill, such as in computation or drawing. (p. 219)

scapegoat theory the theory that prejudice offers an outlet for anger by providing someone to blame. (p. 390)

schema a concept or framework that organizes and interprets information. (p. 73)

schizophrenia a group of severe disorders characterized by disorganized and delusional thinking, disturbed perceptions, and inappropriate emotions and actions. (p. 340)

selective attention focusing conscious awareness on a particular stimulus. (p. 48)

self your image and understanding of who you are; in modern psychology, the idea that this is the center of personality, organizing your thoughts, feelings, and actions. (p. 305)

self-actualization according to Maslow, the psychological need that arises after basic physical and psychological needs are met and self-esteem is achieved; the motivation to fulfill our potential. (p. 297)

self-concept all our thoughts and feelings about ourselves, in answer to the question, "Who am I?" (p. 298)

self-disclosure revealing intimate aspects of yourself to others. (p. 398)

self-esteem your feelings of high or low self-worth. (p. 306)

self-serving bias our readiness to perceive ourselves favorably. (p. 307)

self-transcendence according to Maslow, the striving for identity, meaning, and purpose beyond the self. (p. 297)

sensation the process by which our sensory receptors and nervous system take in stimulus energies from our environment. (p. 125)

sensorimotor stage in Piaget's theory, the stage (from birth to about 2 years of age) during which infants know the world mostly in terms of their sensory impressions and motor activities. (p. 74)

sensory adaptation reduced sensitivity in response to constant stimulation. (p. 128)

sensory cortex area at the front of the parietal lobes that registers and processes body touch and movement sensations. (p. 41)

sensory interaction the principle that one sense may influence another, as when the smell of food influences its taste. (p. 140)

sensory memory the immediate, very brief recording of sensory information in the memory system. (p. 182)

sensory neurons neurons that carry incoming information from the sensory receptors to the central nervous system. (p. 31)

serial position effect the tendency to recall best the last and first items in a list. (p. 184)

set point the point at which an individual's "weight thermostat" is supposedly set. When the body falls below this weight, an increase in hunger and a lowered metabolic rate may act to restore the lost weight. (p. 239)

sexual disorder a problem that consistently impairs sexual arousal or functioning. (p. 110)

sexual orientation an enduring sexual attraction toward members of either our own sex (homosexual orientation) or the other sex (heterosexual orientation). (p. 113)

sexual response cycle the four stages of sexual responding described by Masters and Johnson—excitement, plateau, orgasm, and resolution. (p. 109)

shaping an operant conditioning procedure in which reinforcers guide action closer and closer toward a desired behavior. (p. 165)

short-term memory activated memory that holds a few items briefly, such as the seven digits of a phone number while dialing, before the information is stored or forgotten. (p. 182)

sleep periodic, natural, reversible loss of consciousness—as distinct from unconsciousness resulting from a coma, general anesthesia, or hibernation. (Adapted from Dement, 1999.) (p. 51)

sleep apnea a sleep disorder in which a sleeping person repeatedly stops breathing until blood oxygen is so low it awakens the person just long enough to draw a breath. (p. 56)

social-cognitive perspective views behavior as influenced by the interaction between persons (and their thinking) and their social context. (p. 303)

social clock the culturally preferred timing of social events such as marriage, parenthood, and retirement. (p. 95)

social facilitation stronger responses on simple or well-learned tasks in the presence of others. (p. 384)

social leadership group-oriented leadership that builds teamwork, resolves conflict, and offers support. (p. 414)

social learning theory the theory that we learn social behavior by observing and imitating and by being rewarded or punished. (p. 107)

social loafing the tendency for people in a group to exert less effort when pooling their efforts toward attaining a common goal than when individually accountable. (p. 384)

social psychology the scientific study of how we think about, influence, and relate to one another. (p. 375)

social script culturally modeled guide for how to act in various situations. (p. 393)

somatic nervous system the division of the peripheral nervous system that controls the body's skeletal muscles. Also called the *skeletal nervous system*. (p. 31)

source amnesia linking the wrong source with an event you have experienced, heard about, read about, or imagined. (p. 197)

spacing effect the tendency for distributed study or practice to yield better long-term retention than is achieved through massed study or practice. (p. 184)

split brain condition in which the brain's two hemispheres are isolated by cutting the fibers (mainly those of the corpus callosum) connecting them. (p. 45)

spontaneous recovery the reappearance, after a pause, of an extinguished conditioned response. (p. 161)

spotlight effect overestimating others' noticing and evaluating our appearance, performance, and blunders (as if we presume a spotlight shines on us). (p. 306)

SQ3R a study method incorporating five steps: Survey, Question, Read, Rehearse, Review. (p. 22)

standardization defining meaningful scores by comparison with the performance of a pretested standardization group. (p. 224)

Stanford-Binet the widely used American revision (by Terman at Stanford University) of Binet's original intelligence test. (p. 222)

stereotype a generalized (sometimes accurate but often overgeneralized) belief about a group of people. (p. 388)

stereotype threat a self-confirming concern that we will be evaluated based on a negative stereotype. (p. 230)

stimulants drugs (such as caffeine, nicotine, and the more powerful amphetamines, cocaine, and Ecstasy) that excite neural activity and speed up body functions. (p. 328)

stimulus any event or situation that evokes a response. (p. 158)

storage the retention of encoded information over time. (p. 182)

stranger anxiety the fear of strangers that infants commonly display, beginning by about 8 months of age. (p. 76)

stress the process by which we perceive and respond to certain events, called *stressors*, that we appraise as threatening or challenging. (p. 270)

subjective well-being self-perceived happiness or satisfaction with life. Used along with measures of objective well-being (for example, physical and economic indicators) to evaluate our quality of life. (p. 260)

subliminal below our absolute threshold for conscious awareness. (p. 126)

substance-related disorders a maladaptive pattern of substance use leading to clinically significant impairment or distress. (p. 325)

superego the part of personality that, according to Freud, represents internalized ideals and provides standards for judgment (the conscience). (p. 291)

superordinate goals shared goals that override differences among people and require their cooperation. (p. 401)

survey a technique for ascertaining the self-reported attitudes or behaviors of people, usually by questioning a representative, random sample of them. (p. 13)

sympathetic nervous system the division of the autonomic nervous system that arouses the body, mobilizing its energy in stressful situations. (p. 32)

synapse [SIN-aps] the junction between the axon tip of the sending neuron and the dendrite or cell body of the receiving neuron. (p. 28)

systematic desensitization a type of exposure therapy that associates a pleasant relaxed state with gradually increasing, anxiety-triggering stimuli. Commonly used to treat phobias. (p. 354)

T

task leadership goal-oriented leadership that sets standards, organizes work, and focuses attention on goals. (p. 413)

telegraphic speech early speech stage in which a child speaks like a telegram—"go car"—using mostly nouns and verbs. (p. 212)

temperament a person's characteristic emotional reactivity and intensity. (p. 68)

temporal lobes portion of the cerebral cortex lying roughly above the ears; includes areas that receive information from the ears. (p. 40)

tend and befriend under stress, people (especially women) often provide support to others (*tend*) and bond with and seek support from others (*befriend*). (p. 272)

teratogens agents, such as chemicals and viruses, that can reach the embryo or fetus during prenatal development and cause harm. (p. 67)

testosterone the most important male sex hormone. Stimulates the growth of the male sex organs in the fetus and the development of the male sex characteristics during puberty. Females have testosterone, but less of it. (p. 106)

thalamus [THAL-uh-muss] area at the top of the brainstem; directs sensory messages to the cortex and transmits replies to the cerebellum and medulla. (p. 35)

THC the major active ingredient in marijuana; triggers a variety of effects, including mild hallucinations. (p. 331)

theory an explanation using an integrated set of principles that organizes observations and predicts behaviors or events. (p. 11)

theory of mind people's ideas about their own and others' mental states—about their feelings, perceptions, and thoughts, and the behaviors these might predict. (p. 75)

threshold the level of stimulation required to trigger a neural impulse. (p. 28)

token economy an operant conditioning procedure in which people earn a token for exhibiting a desired behavior and can later exchange the tokens for privileges or treats. (p. 356)

tolerance the diminishing effect with regular use of the same dose of a drug, requiring the user to take larger and larger doses before experiencing the drug's effect. (p. 325)

trait a characteristic pattern of behavior or a tendency to feel and act in a certain way, as assessed by self-reports on a personality test. (p. 299)

transduction changing one form of energy into another. In sensation, the transforming of stimulus energies, such as sights, sounds, and smells, into neural impulses our brains can interpret. (p. 126)

transference in psychoanalysis, the patient's transfer to the analyst of emotions linked with other relationships (such as love or hatred for a parent). (p. 351)

two-factor theory Schachter-Singer's theory that to experience emotion we must (1) be physically aroused and (2) cognitively label the arousal. (p. 249)

two-word stage beginning about age 2, the stage in speech development during which a child speaks mostly two-word statements. (p. 212)

Type A Friedman and Rosenman's term for competitive, hard-driving, impatient, verbally aggressive, and anger-prone people. (p. 275)

Type B Friedman and Rosenman's term for easygoing, relaxed people. (p. 275)

U

unconditional positive regard according to Rogers, an attitude of total acceptance toward another person. (p. 298)

unconditioned response (UR) in classical conditioning, the unlearned, naturally occurring response to the unconditioned stimulus (US), such as salivation when food is in the mouth. (p. 159)

unconditioned stimulus (US) in classical conditioning, a stimulus that unconditionally—naturally and automatically—triggers a response (UR). (p. 159)

unconscious according to Freud, a reservoir of mostly unacceptable thoughts, wishes, feelings, and memories. According to contemporary psychologists, information processing of which we are unaware. (p. 290)

V

validity the extent to which a test measures or predicts what it is supposed to. (p. 224)

vestibular sense the sense of body movement and position, including the sense of balance. (p. 142)

virtual reality exposure therapy An anxiety treatment that progressively exposes people to electronic simulations of their greatest fears, such as airplane flying, spiders, or public speaking. (p. 355)

visual cliff a laboratory device for testing depth perception in infants and young animals. (p. 144)

W

wavelength the distance from the peak of one light or sound wave to the peak of the next. (p. 129)

Weber's law the principle that, to be perceived as different, two stimuli must differ by a constant minimum proportion (rather than a constant amount). (p. 127)

Wechsler Adult Intelligence Scale (WAIS) the WAIS is the most widely used intelligence test; contains verbal and performance (nonverbal) subtests. (p. 223)

Wernicke's area a brain area, usually in the left temporal lobe, involved in language comprehension and expression; controls language reception. (p. 43)

withdrawal the discomfort and distress that follow discontinuing the use of an addictive drug. (p. 325)

working memory a newer understanding of short-term memory that involves conscious, active processing of incoming information, and of information retrieved from long-term memory. (p. 182)

X

X chromosome the sex chromosome found in both men and women. Females have two X chromosomes; males have one X chromosome and one Y chromosome. (p. 106)

Y

Y chromosome the sex chromosome found only in males. When paired with an X chromosome from the mother, it produces a male child. (p. 106)

Z

zygote the fertilized egg; it enters a 2-week period of rapid cell division and develops into an embryo. (p. 66)

Glosario

A

absolute threshold/umbral absoluto Estímulo mínimo necesario para detectar un estímulo particular el cincuenta por ciento del tiempo. (pág. 126)

achievement motivation/motivación de logro Deseo de lograr algo importante, con respecto a cosas, personas o ideas; deseo de lograr un alto estándar. (pág. 408)

achievement test/prueba de rendimiento Prueba diseñada para evaluar lo que una persona ha aprendido. (pág. 222)

acquisition/adquisición Según el condicionamiento clásico, etapa inicial en la que relacionamos un estímulo neutral con uno incondicionado, de tal modo que el estímulo neutral comienza a desencadenar la respuesta condicionada. (Según el condicionamiento operante, intensificación de una respuesta reforzada). (pág. 160)

action potential/potencial de acción Impulso nervioso. (pág. 28)

active listening/escucha activa Escucha empática en la que el oyente hace eco, reitera y clarifica. Una característica de la terapia de Rogers centrada en el cliente. (pág. 353)

adaptation-level phenomenon/fenómeno del nivel de adaptación Nuestra tendencia de formar juicios (de sonidos, de luces, de ingreso) relacionado a un nivel neutro definido por nuestra experiencia de antes. (pág. 262)

addiction/adicción Ansia y uso compulsivo de droga. (pág. 325)

adolescence/adolescencia Período de transición de la niñez a la madurez, extendiéndose de la pubertad a la independencia. (pág. 84)

adrenal glands/glándulas suprarrenales Par de glándulas endocrinas ubicadas sobre los riñones que segregan hormonas (epinefrina y norepinefrina) y contribuyen a la estimulación del cuerpo cuando hay estrés. (pág. 34)

aerobic exercise/ejercicios aeróbicos Actividad sostenida que aumenta la salud cardíaca y pulmonar; posiblemente reduce también la depresión y la ansiedad. (pág. 280)

aggression/agresión Comportamiento físico o verbal que tiene la intención de causar daño o destruir. (págs. 104, 391)

AIDS (acquired immune deficiency syndrome)/SIDA (síndrome de inmunodeficiencia adquirida) Infección peligrosa transmitida sexualmente y causada por *el virus de inmunodeficiencia humana* (VIH). El SIDA debilita el sistema de inmunidad y hace que el individuo se torne vulnerable a infecciones. (pág. 111)

alcohol dependence/dependencia alcohólica (conocida comúnmente como alcoholismo) Consumo de bebidas alcohólicas caracterizado por tolerancia, síntomas de abstinencia cuando se interrumpe el consumo y deseo de continuar bebiendo. (pág. 326)

algorithm/algoritmo Regla o procedimiento metódico y lógico que garantiza la resolución de un problema en particular. Contrasta con el empleo de la *heurística*, un método generalmente más rápido pero también más propenso a registrar errores. (pág. 206)

all-or-none response/respuesta de todo o nada Reacción que produce una neurona al activarse (con una respuesta de máxima intensidad) o al no activarse. (pág. 28)

alpha waves/ritmo alfa Ritmo con ondas cerebrales relativamente lentas que corresponden a un estado relajado y de vigilia. (pág. 51)

altruism/altruismo Consideración desinteresada por el bienestar de los demás. (pág. 398)

amphetamines/anfetaminas Drogas que estimulan la actividad neural, causando aceleración de las funciones corporales y de los niveles de energía asociadas con éstas así como cambios de humor. (pág. 328)

amygdala/amígdala Dos conjuntos de fibras nerviosas del tamaño de una haba que se hallan en el sistema límbico e intervienen en las emociones. (pág. 37)

anorexia nervosa/anorexia nerviosa Trastorno alimenticio en el cual una persona (generalmente una muchacha adolescente) se somete a una dieta de hambre a pesar de padecer de delgadez extrema (de un 15 por ciento o menos que el peso normal). (pág. 241)

antianxiety drugs/medicación antiansiedad Medicamentos recetados para aliviar los síntomas de la ansiedad y la agitación. (pág. 364)

antidepressant drugs/medicamentos antidepresivos Medicamentos recetados para tratar la depresión y ciertos trastornos de ansiedad. Los distintos tipos de medicamentos antidepresivos alteran la disponibilidad de diversos neurotransmisores. (pág. 365)

antipsychotic drugs/medicamentos antipsicóticos Medicación recetada para tratar la esquizofrenia y otros tipos de trastornos graves del pensamiento. (pág. 364)

antisocial personality disorder/trastorno antisocial de la personalidad Trastorno de la personalidad que se manifiesta cuando la persona (generalmente un hombre) no exhibe sentimiento de culpa por actuar con maldad, incluso hacia los amigos y miembros de la familia. Puede ser agresivo y cruel o un estafador listo. (pág. 324)

anxiety disorders/trastornos de ansiedad Trastornos psicológicos que se caracterizan por la preocupación y tensión crónicas o comportamientos desadaptados que reducen la ansiedad. (pág. 318)

aptitude test/prueba de aptitud Prueba diseñada para predecir la actuación de una persona en el futuro; la *aptitud* es la capacidad de aprender. (pág. 222)

association areas/áreas de asociación Áreas de la corteza cerebral principalmente relacionadas con las funciones mentales superiores como el aprendizaje, la memoria, el pensamiento y el habla. (pág. 42)

associative learning/aprendizaje asociativo El aprender que ciertos eventos ocurren juntos. Los eventos pueden ser dos estímulos (como en el condicionamiento clásico) o una respuesta y sus consecuencias (como en el condicionamiento operante). (pág. 158)

attachment/apego Vínculo emocional con otra persona; mostrado en niños pequeños quienes buscan cercanía física con la persona que los cuida y muestran angustia cuando se les separa de quien los cuida. (pág. 77)

attitude/actitud Sentimientos, a menudo basados en nuestras creencias que nos predisponen para responder de una manera particular a los objetos, las personas y eventos. (pág. 377)

audition/audición Sentido o acto de oír. (pág. 134)

autism/autismo Trastorno que se manifiesta en la niñez y que está marcado por una comunicación deficiente, falta de interacción social, y una incapacidad para entender el estado de ánimo de los otros. (pág. 75)

automatic processing/procesamiento automático Codificación inconsciente de información corriente, por ejemplo, de espacio, de tiempo, de frecuencia y de significados de palabras bien asimilados. (pág. 138)

autonomic nervous system/sistema nervioso autónomo División del sistema nervioso periférico que controla las glándulas y los músculos de los órganos (tales como el corazón). Su división simpática produce estimulación, y su división parasimpática produce relajación. (pág. 31)

availability heuristic/heurística de disponibilidad Acto de estimar la probabilidad de un evento, basándose en la facilidad con la que es rememorado. Si los casos vienen prontamente a la mente (quizás debido a su intensidad), presumimos que tales eventos son comunes. (pág. 207)

aversive conditioning/condicionamiento aversivo Paradigma de condicionamiento en el cual los efectos aversivos (naúsea) son asociados con estímulos externos no deseados (beber alcohol). (pág. 355)

axons/axones Prolongaciones de las neuronas que transmiten impulsos a otras neuronas o células. (pág. 28)

B

babbling stage/fase balbuciente Fase del desarrollo del lenguaje que se da aproximadamente a los cuatro meses de edad, y en la cual el infante espontáneamente emite sonidos que al principio no están relacionados con el idioma de la casa. (pág. 212)

barbiturates/barbitúricos Drogas que deprimen la actividad del sistema nervioso central, reduciendo la ansiedad; pero que afectan la memoria y el discernimiento. (pág. 328)

basal metabolic rate/tasa de metabolismo basal Cantidad de energía requerida por el organismo en reposo absoluto. (pág. 239)

basic trust/confianza básica Según Erik Erikson, la percepción de que el mundo es predecible y fidedigno; esta percepción se forma durante la infancia a través de experiencias apropiadas con cuidadores sensibles. (pág. 79)

behavior therapy/terapia del comportamiento Terapia que aplica los principios de aprendizaje para lograr la eliminación de comportamientos no deseados. (pág. 354)

behaviorism/conductismo Posición de que la psicología (1) debe ser una ciencia objetiva que (2) estudia el comportamiento sin referencia a los procesos mentales. La mayoría de los psicólogos en investigación hoy están de acuerdo con (1) pero no con (2). (págs. 3, 162)

belief perseverance/perseverancia en las creencias Empeño en mantener creencias e ignorar las evidencias que las desacreditan. (pág. 209)

binocular cues/claves binoculares Señales de profundidad, por ejemplo, la disparidad retiniana, que requieren el uso de los dos ojos. (pág. 144)

biofeedback/biorretroalimentación Sistema de registración, amplificación y reintroducción de información acerca de un estado fisiológico sutil, como la presión sanguínea o la tensión muscular. (pág. 281)

biological psychology/psicología biológica Especialidad de la psicología que estudia la relación entre la biología y el comportamiento. (pág. 27)

biomedical therapy/terapia biomédica Medicamentos recetados o procedimientos médicos. (pág. 350)

biopsychosocial approach/enfoque biopsicosocial Enfoque integrado que resulta de la incorporación de diversas ideas complementarias donde se combinan perspectivas biológicas, psicológicas y socioculturales. (pág. 6)

bipolar disorder/trastorno bipolar Trastorno que afecta el estado de ánimo; la persona alterna entre la desesperanza y el letargo de la depresión y el estado eufórico de la manía. (Anteriormente llamado trastorno maníaco-depresivo.) (pág. 355)

blind spot/punto ciego Punto en el cual el nervio óptico sale del ojo; esta parte de la retina es "ciega" porque carece de células receptoras. (pág. 130)

brainstem/tronco encefálico Parte más antigua y meollo del cerebro, empezando donde la médula espinal se inflama al entrar en el cráneo; el tronco encefálico es responsable por las funciones automáticas de supervivencia. (pág. 34)

Broca's area/área de Broca Parte del lóbulo frontal del cerebro, generalmente en el hemisferio izquierdo, que dirige los movimientos musculares relacionados con el habla y controla la expresión del lenguaje. (pág. 43)

bulimia nervosa/bulimia nerviosa Trastorno de alimentación que se caracteriza por episodios de ingestión excesiva de alimentos (generalmente de alto contenido calórico) seguidos de purgas (vómito o uso de laxantes), ayuno o ejercicios físicos excesivos. (pág. 241)

bystander effect/efecto espectador Tendencia que tienen las personas a no brindar ayuda si hay otras personas presentes. (pág. 399)

C

Cannon-Bard theory/teoría de Cannon–Bard Teoría de que un estímulo que despierta emociones simultáneamente puede provocar (1) respuestas fisiológicas y (2) la experiencia subjetiva de la emoción. (pág. 249)

case study/caso Técnica de observación en la cual se estudia a una persona a profundidad con la esperanza de revelar principios universales. (pág. 12)

catharsis/catarsis Liberación emocional. La hipótesis de la catarsis sostiene que al "liberar" la energía agresiva (mediante la acción o la fantasía) se alivian los impulsos agresivos. (pág. 259)

central nervous system (CNS)/sistema nervioso central El cerebro y la médula espinal. (pág. 31)

cerebellum/cerebelo Es el "cerebro pequeño" y está unido a la parte posterior del tronco cerebral. Sus funciones incluyen el procesamiento de la información sensorial y la coordinación de los movimientos y el equilibrio. (pág. 36)

cerebral cortex/corteza cerebral Capa delgada de neuronas conectadas entre sí, que forman los hemisferios cerebrales; es el principal centro de control y procesamiento de información del organismo. (pág. 39)

chromosomes/cromosomas Estructuras semejantes a hilos conformados de moléculas de ADN que contienen los genes. (pág. 64)

circadian rhythm/ritmo circadiano Reloj biológico; ritmos regulares del cuerpo (por ejemplo, temperatura y estado de vigilia) que ocurren en ciclos de 24 horas. (pág. 50)

classical conditioning/condicionamiento clásico Tipo de aprendizaje en el cual aprendemos a relacionar dos o más estímulos y a anticipar sucesos. (pág. 159)

client-centered therapy/terapia centrada en el cliente Tipo de terapia humanista creada por Carl Rogers, en la cual el terapeuta emplea técnicas tales como escuchar activamente dentro de un entorno genuino, con aceptación y empatía, para facilitar el crecimiento personal del cliente. (También se denomina *terapia centrada en la persona*). (pág. 352)

cochlea/cóclea Estructura tubular en forma de espiral, ósea y rellena de fluido que se halla en el oído interno; las ondas sonoras que pasan por el fluido coclear se convierten en impulsos nerviosos. (pág. 134)

cognition/cognición Todas las actividades mentales asociadas con el pensar, saber, recordar y comunicar. (págs. 73, 206)

cognitive dissonance theory/disonancia cognitiva Teoría según la cual llevamos a cabo una acción con el propósito de reducir la incomodidad (disonancia) que sentimos cuando tenemos dos pensamientos (cogniciones) contradictorios. Por ejemplo, cuando tenemos consciencia de que nuestra actitud y nuestras acciones entran en conflicto, cambiamos nuestra actitud para sentirnos más cómodos. (pág. 378)

cognitive map/mapa cognitivo Imagen mental del trazado de nuestro entorno. (pág. 169)

cognitive neuroscience/neurociencia cognitiva División de la psicología dedicada al estudio de las conexiones entre la actividad cerebral y los procesos del pensamiento, el saber, la memoria y la comunicación. (pág. 48)

cognitive therapy/terapia cognitiva Terapia que ayuda a los pacientes a pensar y actuar de un modo más realista y adaptativo. Está basada en el supuesto de que los pensamientos intervienen entre los eventos y nuestras reacciones emocionales. (pág. 357)

cognitive-behavior therapy/terapia cognitivo-conductual Terapia muy difundida e integrada que combina la terapia cognitiva (que cambia los pensamientos contraproducentes) con la terapia conductual (que cambia la conducta). (pág. 358)

collectivism/colectivismo Modo de dar prioridad a las metas del grupo (a menudo de la familia extendida o el grupo de trabajo) y de definir la identidad personal según dicta el grupo. (pág. 308)

color constancy/constancia de color El percibir que las superficies familiares parecen mantener la apariencia cromática incluso bajo condiciones luminosas muy diferentes. (pág. 145)

companionate love/amor compañero Apego afectuoso profundo que sentimos por aquéllos con quienes nuestras vidas se entrelazan. (pág. 398)

concrete operational stage/etapa del pensamiento lógico-concreto En la teoría de Piaget, la fase del desarrollo cognitivo (desde aproximadamente los 6 ó 7 años hasta los 11 años de edad) durante la cual los niños desarrollan las operaciones mentales que les permiten pensar lógicamente sobre eventos concretos. (pág. 76)

conditioned reinforcer/reforzador condicionado (También denominado *reforzador secundario*) Episodio que ha adquirido calidad de reforzador al ser asociado con un reforzador primario. (pág. 167)

conditioned response (CR)/respuesta condicionada En el condicionamiento clásico, la respuesta aprendida a un estímulo previamente neutral (pero ahora condicionado). (pág. 160)

conditioned stimulus (CS)/estímulo condicionado En el condicionamiento clásico, un estímulo originalmente irrelevante que, después de ser asociado con un estímulo incondicionado (EI) produce una respuesta condicionada. (pág. 160)

cones/conos Células receptoras que se concentran cerca del centro de la retina; con la luz del día o en lugares bien iluminados, los conos detectan detalles finos y producen las sensaciones del color. (pág. 130)

confirmation bias/sesgo confirmatorio Tendencia a buscar información que confirme nuestras ideas preconcebidas. (pág. 207)

conflict/conflicto Incompatibilidad percibida de acciones, metas o ideas. (pág. 400)

conformity/conformidad Tendencia a ajustar el comportamiento o la forma de pensar hasta hacerlos coincidir con las normas que tiene un grupo. (pág. 380)

consciousness/conciencia Percepción de nosotros mismos y de nuestro ambiente. (pág. 48)

conservation/conservación Principio de que las propiedades de masa, volumen y número no varían a pesar de los cambios en las formas de los objetos. (Piaget era de la opinión que éste formaba parte de la etapa operacional concreta). (pág. 74)

continuous reinforcement/refuerzo continuo El reforzar la respuesta deseada cada vez que ocurre. (pág. 167)

control group/grupo control En un experimento, el grupo de participantes que contrastan con las condiciones experimentales y que sirve de comparación para evaluar el efecto del tratamiento. (pág. 17)

coronary heart disease/enfermedad coronaria Obstrucción de los vasos que nutren el músculo cardíaco; causa principal de muerte en muchos países desarrollados, por ejemplo, en los países de América del Norte. (pág. 274)

corpus callosum/cuerpo calloso Banda grande de fibras neurales que conecta los dos hemisferios del cerebro y lleva mensajes entre ellos. (pág. 45)

correlation/correlación Medida del grado en que dos factores varían juntos y por ende, si es que uno de ellos es capaz de predecir el otro. El *coeficiente de correlación* es la expresión matemática de relación yendo de -1 a 1. (pág. 14)

counterconditioning/contracondicionamiento Técnica de terapia conductual que se basa en el empleo del condicionamiento clásico para provocar respuestas alternativas a estímulos que producen comportamientos no deseados; incluye *las terapias de exposición y el condicionamiento aversivo*. (pág. 354)

creativity/creatividad Capacidad para generar ideas novedosas y valiosas. (pág. 220)

critical period/período crítico Etapa después del nacimiento, en la cual son necesarios ciertos estímulos o experiencias para que se produzca el desarrollo apropiado del organismo. (pág. 71)

critical thinking/pensamiento crítico Forma de pensar en la que no se aceptan razones y conclusiones ciegamente; por el contrario, se examinan las suposiciones, se distinguen los valores escondidos, se evalúa la evidencia y se calculan las conclusiones. (pág. 5)

crystallized intelligence/inteligencia cristalizada Todo el conocimiento y capacidad verbal que hemos acumulado; tiende a aumentar con la edad. (pág. 93)

culture/cultura Ideas, actitudes, tradiciones y comportamientos duraderos que comparte un grupo de personas y que se trasmiten de una generación a otra. (págs. 6, 80)

D

defense mechanisms/mecanismos de defensa En la teoría psicoanalítica, los métodos de protección del ego para reducir la ansiedad distorsionando la realidad inconcientemente. (pág. 292)

deindividuation/desindividualización Pérdida de identidad personal y del sentido de responsabilidad en situaciones de grupo que fomentan la excitación y el anonimato. (pág. 385)

déjà vu/déjà vu Sensación de haber vivido antes una experiencia específica. Señales de la presente situación pueden de manera subconsciente activar la recuperación de una experiencia previa. (pág. 191)

delusions/delirios Creencias falsas, generalmente de persecución o grandeza, que son síntomas de esquizofrenia y otros trastornos psicológicos. (pág. 340)

dendrites/dendritas Prolongaciones de las neuronas que reciben mensajes y envían impulsos hacia el cuerpo neuronal. (pág. 28)

dependent variable/variable dependiente Factor resultante; el factor que puede cambiar en respuesta a cambios en la variable independiente. (pág. 17)

depressants/depresivos Drogas (como el alcohol, barbitúricos y opiatos) que hacen más lenta o reducen la actividad neuronal y física. (pág. 326)

depth perception/percepción de profundidad Habilidad de ver objetos en tres dimensiones aunque las imágenes percibidas por la retina son bidimensionales. Esto nos permite juzgar la distancia. (pág. 144)

developmental psychology/psicología del desarrollo Rama de la psicología que estudia el cambio físico, cognitivo y social a lo largo de la vida. (pág. 64)

difference threshold/umbral diferencial Diferencia mínima que un individuo es capaz de detectar entre dos estímulos la mitad de las veces. El umbral diferencial se experimenta como una *diferencia apenas perceptible* (o *jnd*, según sus siglas en inglés). (pág. 127)

discrimination/discriminación Según el condicionamiento clásico, capacidad aprendida de distinguir entre un estímulo condicionado y otros estímulos irrelevantes. (pág. 162)

discrimination/discriminación En las relaciones sociales, conducta negativa injustificada dirigida a un grupo y sus miembros. (pág. 388)

displacement/desplazamiento Mecanismo de defensa psicoanalítico mediante el cual se cambian los impulsos sexuales o agresivos hacia un objeto o persona más aceptable o menos amenazante, como el redirigir la ira hacia un escape más seguro. (pág. 293)

dissociative disorders/trastornos disociativos Trastornos en los que el conocimiento conciente se separa (se disocia) de los recuerdos, pensamientos y sentimientos anteriores. (pág. 322)

dissociative identity disorder (DID)/trastorno de identidad disociativo Trastorno disociativo poco común, en el cual una persona experimenta dos o más personalidades claramente definidas que se alternan entre sí. También se denomina *trastorno de personalidad múltiple*. (pág. 323)

DNA (deoxyribonucleic acid)/ADN (ácido desoxirribonucleico) Molécula que contiene la información genética de la que se constituyen los cromosomas. (pág. 64)

double-blind procedure/procedimiento doble ciego Procedimiento en el cual tanto los participantes como el personal de investigación ignoran (van a ciegas) quién ha recibido el tratamiento y quién el placebo. (pág. 17)

dream/sueño Sucesión de imágenes, emociones y pensamientos que fluyen en la mente de una persona dormida. (pág. 57)

drive/impulso Estado interno de estimulación y motivación causado a menudo por la privación de una sustancia necesaria. (pág. 236)

drive-reduction theory/teoría de la reducción del impulso Idea que una necesidad fisiológica crea un estado de excitación (un impulso) que motiva al organismo a satisfacer esta necesidad. (pág. 236)

DSM-IV-TR/DSM-IV *Manual estadístico y diagnóstico de trastornos mentales, Cuarta edición*, sistema ampliamente utilizado para clasificar los trastornos psicológicos. Hoy en día se distribuye en una "revisión del texto" actualizada (DSM-IV-TR). (pág. 316)

dual processing/procesamiento dual Principio que sostiene que la información a menudo se procesa simultáneamente en vías separadas conscientes e inconscientes. (pág. 8)

Ɛ

eclectic approach/aproximación ecléctica Enfoque de la psicoterapia que, dependiendo de los problemas del cliente, utiliza técnicas de distintas formas de terapia. (pág. 350)

Ecstasy (MDMA)/éxtasis (MDMA) Estimulante sintético y alucinógeno leve. Produce euforia e intimidad social, pero tiene riesgos de salud a corto plazo. Además, a largo plazo daña las neuronas que producen la serotonina, y afecta el ánimo y el proceso de cognición. (pág. 330)

EEG (electroencephalogram)/(EEG) electroencefalograma Aparato que emplea electrodos colocados sobre el cuero cabelludo y produce un registro de las ondas de actividad eléctrica que circulan por la superficie del cerebro. (El trazado de dichas ondas cerebrales es un *electroencefalograma*). (pág. 35)

effortful processing/procesamiento con esfuerzo Codificación que requiere atención y esfuerzo concientes. (pág. 183)

ego/ego Parte conciente y ejecutiva de la personalidad que, de acuerdo a Freud, media entre las demandas del id, el superego, y la realidad. El ego opera bajo el *principio de realidad,* satisfaciendo los deseos del id en formas que de manera realista le brindarán placer y no dolor. (pág. 291)

egocentrism/egocentrismo En la teoría de Piaget, la dificultad de los niños en la etapa preoperacional de aceptar el punto de vista ajeno. (pág. 74)

electroconvulsive therapy (ECT)/terapia electroconvulsiva (TEC) Terapia biomédica para pacientes severamente deprimidos en la que una corriente eléctrica de corta duración se envía a través del cerebro de un paciente anestesiado. (pág. 367)

embryo/embrión Etapa de desarrollo en el organismo humano a partir de las dos semanas de fertilización hasta el segundo mes. (pág. 66)

emerging adulthood/adultez emergente Etapa que se extiende desde los dieciocho hasta alrededor de los veinticinco años, durante la cual muchos individuos de los países occidentales ya no son adolescentes pero aún no han alcanzado la independencia plena de un adulto. (pág. 89)

emotion/emoción Reacción que involucra a todo el organismo, e incluye (1) excitación fisiológica, (2) comportamientos expresivos y (3) experiencia conciente. (pág. 248)

emotional intelligence/inteligencia emocional Habilidad de percibir, entender, administrar y utilizar las emociones. (pág. 221)

emotion-focused coping/superación con enfoque en las emociones Medidas para sobrellevar el estrés enfocadas en aliviar o ignorar una situación estresante y atender las necesidades emocionales relacionadas con nuestra reacción al estrés. (pág. 276)

encoding/codificación El procesar información al sistema de memoria—por ejemplo, extrayendo el significado. (pág. 182)

endocrine system/sistema endocrino Sistema "lento" de comunicación química del cuerpo; un conjunto de glándulas que secretan hormonas al torrente sanguíneo. (pág. 33)

endorphins/endorfinas "Morfina adentro"—neurotransmisores naturales similares a los opiatos que están asociados con el control del dolor y con el placer. (pág. 30)

environment/ambiente Toda influencia externa, desde la alimentación prenatal hasta el apoyo social que se recibe en la vejez. (pág. 65)

equity/equidad Condición en la cual las personas reciben de manera proporcional lo que aportan a una relación. (pág. 398)

estrogens/estrógenos Hormonas sexuales (por ejemplo, el estradiol) secretadas en mayor cantidad en la mujer que en el hombre. En las hembras de los animales mamíferos, los niveles de estrógeno alcanzan su nivel máximo durante la ovulación, facilitando la receptividad sexual. (pág. 109)

evolutionary psychology/psicología evolutiva Estudio de la evolución del comportamiento y la mente, que emplea los principios de la selección natural para una adaptación efectiva. (pág. 117)

experiment/experimento Método de investigación en el cual el investigador manipula uno o más factores (variables independientes) para observar su efecto en un comportamiento o proceso mental (variable dependiente). (pág. 16)

experimental group/grupo experimental Sujetos de un experimento que están expuestos al tratamiento, o sea, a una versión de la variable independiente. (pág. 17)

explicit memory/memoria explícita Memoria de hechos y experiencias personales que somos capaces de recuperar conscientemente. (pág. 17)

exposure therapies/terapias de exposición Técnicas conductuales, como la desensibilización sistemática, para tratar la ansiedad exponiendo a la persona (en situaciones imaginarias o reales) a las cosas que teme o evita. (pág. 354)

external locus of control/locus de control externo Impresión de que nuestro destino está determinado por el azar o por fuerzas que están más allá de nuestro control. (pág. 278)

extinction/extinción Según el condicionamiento clásico, disminución de una respuesta condicionada cuando un estímulo incondicionado no sigue a un estímulo condicionado. (En el condicionamiento operante, disminución de una respuesta cuando deja de ser reforzada). (pág. 161)

extrasensory perception (ESP)/percepción extrasensorial Idea polémica que propone que la percepción ocurre por una vía distinta de la estimulación de los sentidos, por ejemplo, por *telepatía, clarividencia y precognición*. (pág. 151)

extrinsic motivation/motivación extrínseca Deseo de realizar un comportamiento para obtener una recompensa o evitar un castigo. (pág. 169)

F

facial feedback effect/efecto de reacción facial Tendencia de los músculos faciales a provocar sentimientos correspondientes como el miedo, el enojo o la felicidad. (pág. 258)

factor/factor Conjunto de tendencias del comportamiento que ocurren al mismo tiempo. (pág. 299)

family therapy/terapia de familia Tipo de terapia que trata a la familia como sistema y considera que los comportamientos no deseados del individuo son influenciados por otros miembros de la familia o dirigidos a ellos. (pág. 358)

feature detectors/detectores específicos Células nerviosas del cerebro que responden a características específicas de un estímulo, por ejemplo, a bordes, líneas y ángulos. (pág. 132)

feel-good, do-good phenomenon/fenómeno de sentirse bien y hacer el bien Tendencia a ayudar a los demás cuando estamos de buen humor. (pág. 260)

fetal alcohol syndrome (FAS)/síndrome de alcoholismo fetal Anomalías físicas y cognitivas en los niños causadas por la ingestión de alcohol de las madres durante el embarazo. En casos agudos, los síntomas incluyen desproporciones faciales observables. (pág. 67)

fetus/feto Organismo humano en vías de desarrollo a partir de las 9 semanas de concepción hasta el nacimiento. (pág. 66)

fight-or-flight/respuesta de lucha o huida Reacción de emergencia que incluye actividad del sistema nervioso simpático y genera energía y actividad dirigidas a atacar o escapar de una amenaza. (pág. 271)

figure-ground/figura-fondo Organización del campo visual en objetos (*figuras*) que se distinguen de sus ambientes (*fondos*). (pág. 143)

fixation/fijación Incapacidad de ver un problema desde una perspectiva nueva; un impedimento para resolver problemas. (pág. 208)

fixation/fijación De acuerdo a Freud, un permanente foco de energía en busca de placer en una etapa psicosexual temprana cuando los conflictos todavía no estaban resueltos. (pág. 292)

flashbulb memory/memoria de flash Memoria clara de un momento o evento emocionalmente significativo. (pág. 188)

flow/fluidez Estado de total participación y concentración, con disminución de la conciencia de uno mismo y del tiempo, que ocurre cuando empleamos nuestras destrezas al máximo. (pág. 407)

fluid intelligence/inteligencia fluida Capacidad que tenemos de razonar de manera rápida y abstracta; tiende a disminuir en la vejez. (pág. 93)

fMRI (functional magnetic resonance imaging)/imágenes de resonancia magnética funcional Técnica para observar la circulación de la sangre, y por lo tanto, la actividad cerebral, que consiste en comparar sucesivas imágenes de resonancia magnética. Las imágenes de resonancia magnética funcional muestran el funcionamiento del cerebro. (pág. 35)

foot-in-the-door phenomenon/fenómeno de pie en la puerta Tendencia de la gente que ha accedido a algo pequeño en primer lugar, a después satisfacer una demanda más grande. (pág. 378)

formal operational stage/período operacional formal En la teoría de Piaget, el período en el desarrollo cognitivo (normalmente empieza a los 12 años) durante el que la persona empieza a pensar lógicamente sobre conceptos abstractos. (pág. 76)

framing/encuadre Forma en que se presenta un asunto; el encuadre puede influenciar considerablemente las decisiones y las opiniones. (pág. 208)

fraternal twins/mellizos Se desarrollan de dos óvulos fecundados distintos. Genéticamente no están más cercanos que los hermanos y hermanas; pero comparten un medio ambiente fetal. (pág. 66)

free association/asociación libre En psicoanálisis, un método de explorar el inconciente en el que la persona se relaja y dice lo primero que le viene a la mente, no importa cuán trivial o incómodo. (pág. 290)

frequency/frecuencia Número de ondas completas que pasan un punto en un tiempo dado (por ejemplo, por segundo). (pág. 134)

frontal lobes/lóbulos frontales Porción de la corteza cerebral que se halla inmediatamente detrás de la frente; se relaciona con el habla y los movimientos musculares y con la planificación y la formación de opiniones. (pág. 39)

frustration-aggression principle/principio de frustración-agresión Principio de que la frustración—el bloqueo de un intento para lograr alguna meta—crea ira, la cual puede generar agresión. (pág. 392)

fundamental attribution error/error fundamental de la atribución Tendencia de los observadores, cuando analizan el comportamiento ajeno, a sobrestimar el impacto de las características personales y subestimar el impacto de la situación. (pág. 376)

G

gender/género En psicología, las características biológicas y sociales por las cuales la sociedad define *hombre* y *mujer*. (pág. 103)

gender identity/identidad de género Sensación personal de ser hombre o mujer. (pág. 107)

gender role/rol de género Expectativas de cómo las mujeres y los hombres deben comportarse. (pág. 107)

gender schema theory/teoría de esquemas sexuales Teoría según la cual los niños aprenden los conceptos de masculinidad y feminidad de la cultura en la que viven y adaptan su comportamiento a esos conceptos. (pág. 107)

gender typing/tipificación sexual o de género Adopción de un papel masculino o femenino tradicional. (pág. 107)

general adaptation syndrome (GAS)/síndrome de adaptación general Término usado por Selye para la respuesta común del cuerpo al estrés que se da en tres etapas: alarma, resistencia, y agotamiento. (pág. 271)

general intelligence (g)/factor g de inteligencia general Factor de inteligencia general que de acuerdo a Spearman y otros subyace habilidades mentales específicas y es por lo tanto cuantificado por cada tarea de las pruebas de inteligencia. (pág. 218)

generalization/generalización Según el condicionamiento clásico, tendencia posterior al condicionamiento, de responder de manera similar a los estímulos que se parecen al estímulo condicionado. (pág. 162)

generalized anxiety disorder/trastorno de ansiedad generalizado Trastorno de ansiedad en el cual el individuo está constantemente tenso, asustado y con el sistema nervioso autónomo activado. (pág. 318)

genes/genes Unidades bioquímicas de la herencia que forman los cromosomas. Segmentos de ADN. (pág. 64)

genome/genoma Instrucciones completas para crear un organismo; consiste de todo el material genético en los cromosomas de ese organismo. (pág. 64)

gestalt/Gestalt Un todo organizado. Los psicólogos de la Gestalt ponen énfasis en nuestra tendencia a integrar segmentos de información en todos significativos. (pág. 143)

glucose/glucosa Forma de azúcar que circula en la sangre y provee de la mayor fuente de energía a los tejidos del cuerpo. Cuando su nivel es bajo, sentimos hambre. (pág. 239)

group polarization/efecto de polarización de grupo Solidificación y fortalecimiento de las posiciones imperantes en un grupo a través de discusiones del grupo. (pág. 385)

grouping/grouping/agrupamiento Tendencia de percepción que clasifica los estímulos en grupos que tienen sentido. (pág. 143)

groupthink/pensamiento del grupo Modo de pensar que ocurre cuando el deseo de armonía en un grupo de toma de decisiones anula la evaluación objetiva de las alternativas. (pág. 386)

H

hallucinations/alucinaciones Experiencias sensoriales falsas, por ejemplo, cuando una persona escucha algo sin recibir ningún estímulo auditivo externo. (pág. 42)

hallucinogens/alucinógenos Drogas psicodélicas ("que se manifiestan en la mente"), como el LSD, que distorsionan las percepciones y evocan imágenes sensoriales sin ninguna inducción sensorial. (pág. 330)

heredity/herencia Transferencia genética de características, de los padres a los hijos. (pág. 64)

heritability/heredabilidad Proporción de la variación entre individuos que es posible atribuir a los genes. La heredabilidad de un rasgo puede variar, según el número de poblaciones y ambientes que se estudien. (pág. 226)

heuristic/heurística Simple estrategia de pensamiento que nos permite formar juicios y resolver problemas de manera eficiente. Normalmente es más rápida que el utilizar *algoritmos*; pero también puede conducir a más errores. (pág. 206)

hierarchy of needs/jerarquía de necesidades Pirámide de Maslow de las necesidades humanas. En la base de la pirámide están las necesidades fisiológicas, que deben satisfacerse antes que las necesidades de seguridad personal; las necesidades psicológicas se activan por último, después de satisfacer las anteriores. (págs. 237, 297)

hindsight bias/distorsión retrospectiva Tendencia a creer después de saber un resultado, que uno lo habría previsto. (También conocido como el fenómeno de "ya yo lo sabía".) (pág. 10)

hormones/hormonas Mensajeros químicos producidos por las glándulas endocrinas, que circulan por la sangre y tienen efecto en los tejidos del cuerpo. (pág. 33)

hue/tono Dimensión del color determinada por la longitud de onda de luz; lo que conocemos como los nombre de los colores: azul, *verde*, etc. (pág. 129)

human factors psychology/psicología de factores humanos División de la psicología industrial y organizacional que explora la interacción entre las personas y las máquinas y las maneras de hacer que las máquinas y los entornos físicos sean más seguros y fáciles de utilizar. (pág. 408)

humanistic psychology/psicología humanista Perspectiva que enfatiza el potencial de crecimiento de las personas sanas y la capacidad de crecimiento personal del individuo. (pág. 3)

hypnosis/hipnosis Interacción social en la cual una persona (el hipnotizador) sugiere a otra (el sujeto) ciertas percepciones, sentimientos, pensamientos o comportamientos. (pág. 139)

hypothalamus/hipotálamo Estructura anterior localizada bajo (hipo) el tálamo; regula actividades como el comer, beber, y la temperatura del cuerpo; ayuda a dirigir el sistema endocrino a través de la glándula pituitaria; y está conectado a la emoción. (pág. 38)

hypothesis/hipótesis Predicción comprobable, a menudo implicada por una teoría. (pág. 12)

I

id/id Un depósito de energía psíquica inconciente que, según Freud, se esfuerza por satisfacer los impulsos sexuales y agresivos esenciales. El id opera bajo el *principio de placer*, exigiendo satisfacción inmediata. (pág. 290)

identical twins/gemelos Se desarrollan de un sólo huevo fertilizado que se parte en dos, creando dos organismos genéticamente idénticos. (pág. 66)

identification/identificación Proceso en el que, según Freud, los niños incorporan los valores de sus padres en sus súper-egos en vías de desarrollo. (pág. 292)

identity/identidad Sentido de uno mismo; de acuerdo con Erikson, la tarea del adolescente es de solidificar el sentido de sí mismo probando e integrando una variedad de roles. (pág. 86)

illusory correlation/correlación ilusoria Percepción de una relación dónde no hay ninguna. (pág. 16)

imagery/imágenes mentales Imágenes de la mente; ayuda poderosa en el procesamiento esforzado, especialmente cuando se combina con la codificación de significados. (pág. 185)

implicit memory/memoria implícita Retención de destrezas o condicionamientos aprendidos, que ocurre generalmente sin tener consciencia del aprendizaje. (pág. 189)

inattentional blindness/ceguera por falta de atención El no ver los objetos visibles cuando nuestra atención se dirige a otra parte. (pág. 49)

incentive/incentivo Estímulo positivo o negativo medioambiental que motiva el comportamiento. (pág. 236)

independent variable/variable independiente Factor experimental que se manipula; la variable cuyo efecto es el objeto de estudio. (pág. 17)

individualism/individualismo Manera de poner las metas personales antes que las metas del grupo y definir la identidad de acuerdo con las cualidades personales y no con la pertenencia al grupo. (pág. 308)

industrial-organizational (I/O) psychology/psicología industrial y organizacional Aplicación de conceptos y métodos psicológicos al comportamiento humano en ambientes laborales. (pág. 408)

ingroup/endogrupo "Nosotros"—personas con las que uno comparte una identidad común. (pág. 389)

ingroup bias/estereotipo de grupo propio Tendencia a favorecer al grupo al que se pertenece. (pág. 389)

insight/agudeza Entendimiento repentino de cómo se resuelve un problema; contrasta con las soluciones basadas en estrategias. (pág. 206)

insomnia/insomnio Problemas recurrentes para dormir o quedarse dormido. (pág. 55)

intelligence/inteligencia Calidad mental que consiste en la habilidad de aprender de la experiencia, resolver problemas y utilizar el conocimiento para adaptarse a nuevas situaciones. (pág. 218)

intelligence quotient (IQ)/coeficiente intelectual (CI) Número definido originalmente como la edad mental (*em*) dividida entre la edad cronológica (*ec*) y el resultado multiplicado por 100 (por lo tanto, CI = *em/ec* × 100). En las pruebas actuales de inteligencia, el rendimiento promedio para una edad dada recibe un puntaje de 100. (pág. 223)

intelligence test/prueba de inteligencia Método para evaluar las aptitudes mentales de un individuo y compararlas con las de otros utilizando puntajes numéricos. (pág. 222)

intensity/intensidad Cantidad de energía en una onda de luz o en una onda sonora que percibimos como brillo o fuerza ,determinada por la amplitud de la onda. (pág. 129)

interaction//interacción En psicología, ocurre la interacción cuando el efecto de un factor (por ejemplo, el ambiente) depende de otro factor (por ejemplo, la herencia). (pág. 66)

interference/teoría de interferencia Bloqueo de un recuerdo cuando un aprendizaje anterior o uno nuevo perturba la memoria de otros recuerdos. (pág. 194)

internal locus of control/locus de control interno Impresión de que controlamos nuestro propio destino. (pág. 278)

interneurons/interneuronas Neuronas que envían comunicaciones internas e intervienen en la estimulación sensorial y las respuestas motoras (pág. 31)

interpretation/interpretación En psicoanálisis, las observaciones del analista con relación al significado de los sueños, las resistencias, y otros comportamientos y eventos significativos, a fin de promover la sagacidad. (pág. 351)

intimacy/intimidad Según la teoría de Erikson, capacidad de formar relaciones cercanas y afectivas; tarea primordial del desarrollo al comienzo de la vida adulta. (pág. 88)

intrinsic motivation/motivación intrínseca Deseo de comportarse de una manera por el comportamiento en sí. (pág. 169)

J

James-Lange theory/teoría de James-Lange Teoría que nuestra experiencia emocional es nuestra conciencia de nuestras respuestas fisiológicas a los estímulos que despiertan nuestras emociones. (pág. 249)

just-world phenomenon/hipótesis del "mundo justo" Tendencia a creer que el mundo es justo y que las personas consiguen lo que se merecen y se merecen lo que consiguen. (pág. 388)

K

kinesthesis/cinética Sistema que siente la posición y el movimiento de las partes individuales de cuerpo. (pág. 141)

L

language/enguaje Palabras habladas, escritas o en señas y las maneras que se combinan para comunicar significado. (pág. 211)

latent content/contenido latente Según Freud, significado subyacente de un sueño. (pág. 57)

latent learning/aprendizaje latente Aprendizaje que no se demuestra hasta que aparece un incentivo para demostrarlo. (pág. 169)

learned helplessness/indefensión aprendida Desesperación y resignación pasiva que un animal o un ser humano desarrollan cuando son incapaces de evitar repetidos eventos de aversión. (pág. 277)

learning/aprendizaje Cambio relativamente permanente de comportamiento que resulta de la experiencia. (pág. 157)

limbic system/sistema límbico Sistema de neuronas (incluye el *hipocampo*, la *amígdala* y el *hipotálamo*), ubicado debajo de los hemisferios cerebrales; se lo asocia con las emociones y los impulsos. (pág. 37)

lobotomy/lobotomía Procedimiento psico-quirúrgico hoy en día inusual que se utilizó para calmar pacientes emocionalmente incontrolables o violentos. Este procedimiento separaba la conexión entre la corteza pre-frontal y el resto del cerebro. (pág. 368)

long-term memory/memoria a largo plazo Tipo de memoria relativamente permanente que mantiene grandes cantidades de información por un período largo de tiempo. Incluye el conocimiento, habilidades, y experiencias. (pág. 182)

long-term potentiation (LTP)/potenciación a largo plazo Aumento en la eficacia de una sinapsis para transmitir impulsos. Se considera la base nerviosa del aprendizaje y la memoria. (pág. 187)

LSD/ácido lisérgico Poderosa droga alucinógena; también se conoce como ácido (*ácido lisérgico y dietilamina*). (pág. 331)

lymphocytes/linfocitos Los dos tipos de glóbulos blancos que forman parte del sistema de inmunidad del organismo: Los *linfocitos B* liberan anticuerpos que combaten las infecciones bacterianas; los *linfocitos T* atacan las células cancerosas, los virus y las substancias extrañas al cuerpo. (pág. 272)

M

major depressive disorder/trastorno depresivo mayor Trastorno del estado de ánimo en el cual una persona—sin una condición médica y sin el uso de drogas—se siente deprimida, inútil y muestra poco interés o placer en la mayoría de las actividades por un período de por lo menos dos semanas. (pág. 335)

mania/manía Trastorno del estado de ánimo marcado por una condición hiperactiva y desenfrenadamente optimista. (pág. 335)

manifest content/contenido manifiesto Según Freud, argumento del sueño que se recuerda al estar despierto. (pág. 57)

maturation/maduración Procesos de crecimiento biológico que permiten cambios ordenados en el comportamiento y son independientes de la experiencia. (pág. 70)

medical model/modelo médico Concepto que afirma que las enfermedades, en este caso los trastornos psicológicos, tienen causas físicas que se pueden *diagnosticar, tratar* y, en la mayoría de los casos, *curar,* generalmente por medio de *tratamientos* que se llevan a cabo en un *hospital.* (pág. 315)

medulla/médula Base del bulbo raquídeo; controla el latido del corazón y la respiración. (pág. 34)

memory/memoria El aprender de manera persistente a través del tiempo usando almacenaje y recuperación de la información. (pág. 181)

memory trace/rastro de memoria Cambios físicos duraderos que ocurren en el cerebro al formarse un recuerdo. (pág. 194)

menarche/menarquía Primer período menstrual. (pág. 84)

menopause/menopausia Cesación de la menstruación. En el uso diario, el término se refiere a la transición biológica que experimenta una mujer desde antes hasta después de acabar de menstruar. (pág. 91)

mental age/edad mental Medida de desempeño en pruebas de inteligencia diseñada por Bidet. La edad cronológica normalmente corresponde a un nivel dado de desempeño. Por ende, una criatura que se desempeña como una persona normal de ocho años, tiene una edad mental de ocho años. (pág. 222)

mere exposure effect/efecto de la mera exposición (EME) Fenómeno que sostiene que la exposición repetida a estímulos novedosos aumenta su atracción. (pág. 394)

methamphetamine/metanfetamina Droga poderosamente adictiva que estimula el sistema nervioso central con funciones corporales aceleradas y cambios de energía y estado de ánimo. Aparentemente, con el tiempo reduce los niveles mínimos de dopamina. (pág. 329)

mirror neurons/neuronas espejo Neuronas que se activan cuando se llevan a cabo ciertas acciones o se observa a otras personas realizar una actividad. (pág. 173)

mirror-image perceptions/percepciones idénticas Opiniones mutuas que generalmente sostienen las personas que discrepan o experimentan conflictos entre sí. (pág. 400)

misinformation effect/efecto de información errónea Recuerdo que se deforma al recibir información engañosa. (pág. 196)

modeling/modelar Proceso de observar e imitar un comportamiento en particular. (pág. 173)

monocular cues/indicaciones monoculares Señales de profundidad como la interposición y la perspectiva lineal, que pueden ser extraídas de las imágenes de cada uno de los ojos. (pág. 145)

mood-congruent memory/memoria congruente con el estado de ánimo Tendencia a recordar experiencias que concuerdan con el buen o mal estado de ánimo que estamos experimentando. (pág. 191)

mood disorders/trastornos del estado de ánimo Categoría de trastornos psicológicos caracterizados por extremos de emociones. Ver *trastorno depresivo mayor, manía y trastorno bipolar.* (pág. 334)

motivation/motivación Necesidad o deseo que da energía y dirige el comportamiento. (pág. 235)

motor cortex/corteza motora Parte del cerebro en la parte posterior del lóbulo frontal, que controla los movimientos voluntarios. (pág. 40)

motor neurons/neuronas motrices Neuronas que llevan la información del sistema nervioso central hacia los músculos y glándulas. (pág. 31)

MRI (magnetic resonance imaging)/mágenes de resonancia magnética Técnica que emplea campos magnéticos y ondas de radio para producir imágenes de tejidos blandos generadas por una computadora. Las imágenes de resonancia magnética nos permiten ver la anatomía cerebral. (pág. 35)

N

narcolepsy/narcolepsia Trastorno caracterizado por ataques incontrolables de sueño, en el que a veces el individuo entra directamente en el sueño REM. (pág. 55)

natural selection/selección natural Proceso de adaptación; entre la variedad de rasgos heredados, aquellos que contribuyen al aumento de la reproducción y la supervivencia tienen mayor probabilidad de pasar a las generaciones futuras. (pág. 117)

naturalistic observation/observación naturalista El observar y registrar la conducta en situaciones reales sin tratar de manipular y controlar la situación. (pág. 14)

nature-nurture issue/debate naturaleza-crianza Antigua controversia acerca del aporte relativo que ejercen los genes y la experiencia en el desarrollo de los rasgos y comportamientos psicológicos. La ciencia psicológica actual opina que los rasgos y comportamientos tienen origen en la interrelación entre la naturaleza y la crianza. (pág. 6)

near-death experience/experiencia al borde de la muerte Estado de alteración experimentado por personas que llegan al borde de la muerte, o que parecen morir pero luego retornan a la vida (por ejemplo, cuando uno sufre un paro cardíaco). Son similares a las alucinaciones inducidas por las drogas. (pág. 331)

negative reinforcement/reforzamiento negativo Aumento en la expresión de comportamientos mediante la interrupción o reducción de estímulos negativos tales como golpes de corriente. Un reforzamiento negativo es cualquier cosa que, *eliminada* después de una respuesta, refuerza la respuesta. (Nota: reforzamiento negativo *no significa* castigo). (pág. 166)

nerves/nervios Haces de axones neuronales que forman "cables" de nervios y conectan el sistema nervioso central con los músculos, las glándulas y los órganos sensoriales. (pág. 31)

nervous system/sistema nervioso Veloz red electroquímica de comunicación del cuerpo que consiste de todas las células nerviosas del sistema periférico y del sistema nervioso central. (pág. 31)

neuron/neurona Célula nerviosa; el componente básico del sistema nervioso. (pág. 28)

neurotransmitters/neurotransmisores Químicos producidos por las neuronas que atraviesan las sinapsis y transmiten mensajes a otras neuronas o a las células del cuerpo. (pág. 29)

nicotine/nicotina Droga estimulante, altamente adictiva y psicoactiva que se halla en el tabaco. (pág. 328)

normal curve/curva normal Curva simétrica y en forma de campana que describe la distribución de muchos atributos físicos y psicológicos. La mayoría de los puntajes están cerca del promedio, disminuyendo en número conforme se acercan a los extremos. (pág. 224)

O

object permanence/permanencia de objeto Conocimiento que las cosas existen aunque no las veamos. (pág. 74)

observational learning/aprendizaje observacional El aprender observando a otros. (pág. 173)

obsessive-compulsive disorder (OCD)/trastorno obsesivo-compulsivo Trastorno de ansiedad caracterizado por pensamientos repetitivos no deseados (obsesiones) y/o acciones (compulsiones). (pág. 319)

occipital lobes/lóbulos occipitales Porción de la corteza cerebral ubicada en la parte posterior de la cabeza; incluye las áreas que reciben información de los campos visuales. (pág. 40)

Oedipus complex/complejo de Edipo Según Freud, los deseos sexuales de un muchacho hacia su madre y sentimientos de celos y odio para el padre rival. (pág. 292)

one-word stage/etapa holofrástica Etapa en el desarrollo del habla, entre el año y los dos años, en la que el niño se expresa principalmente en palabras aisladas. (pág. 212)

operant behavior/comportamiento operante Comportamiento que opera en el ambiente, produciendo consecuencias. (pág. 165)

operant chamber/cámara operante Caja con un aparato de grabación que registra la frecuencia con la que un animal dentro de la misma presiona una barra para obtener un refuerzo. Se emplea en experimentos de condicionamiento operante. (También se conoce como *caja de Skinner*). (pág. 165)

operant conditioning/condicionamiento operante Aprendizaje donde el comportamiento se consolida si está seguido por un refuerzo o se atenúa si está seguido por un castigo. (pág. 165)

operational definition/definición operacional Manifestación de los procedimientos (operaciones) utilizadas para definir las variables de investigación. Por ejemplo, la *inteligencia humana* puede ser operacionalmente definida como lo que mide una prueba de inteligencia. (pág. 12)

opiates/opiáceos El opio y sus derivados, como la morfina y la heroína, que deprimen la actividad neuronal y alivian temporalmente el dolor y la ansiedad. (págs. 29, 328)

optic nerve/nervio óptico Nervio que transporta los impulsos neuronales del ojo al cerebro. (pág. 130)

optimism/optimismo Anticipación de resultados positivos. Son optimistas las personas que esperan lo mejor y creen que sus esfuerzos conducen a obtener buenos resultados. (pág. 278)

organizational psychology/psicología organizacional Subdivisión de la psicología industrial y organizacional que examina las influencias organizacionales en la satisfacción y productividad de los trabajadores, y facilita cambios organizacionales. (pág. 408)

outgroup/grupo ajeno "Ellos", o sea, las personas a las que percibimos como distintas o separadas de nuestro grupo. (pág. 389)

overconfidence/exceso de confianza Tendencia a ser más confiado que acertado, o sea, a sobreestimar las creencias y las opiniones propias. (pág. 208)

P

panic disorder/trastorno de pánico Trastorno de ansiedad marcado por el inicio repentino y recurrente de episodios de aprehensión intensa o terror que pueden durar varios minutos. Incluyen dolor de pecho, sofocamiento, y otras sensaciones atemorizantes. (pág. 319)

parallel processing/procesamiento paralelo Procesamiento de varias partes de un problema o escena a la vez; modo natural del cerebro de procesar la información de varias funciones, incluida la visión. (pág. 132)

parasympathetic nervous system/sistema nervioso autonómico parasimpático División del sistema nervioso autonómico que calma el cuerpo conservando su energía. (pág. 32)

parietal lobes/lóbulos parietales Área de la corteza cerebral en la parte superior y hacia la parte posterior de la cabeza que recibe suministro sensorial para el tacto y la posición del cuerpo. (pág. 39)

partial (intermittent) reinforcement/refuerzo parcial (intermitente) Refuerzo a una respuesta sólo parte del tiempo; tiene como resultado la adquisición más lenta de una respuesta pero mucho más resistente a la extinción que el refuerzo continuo. (pág. 167)

passionate love/amor apasionado Estado excitado de intensa y positiva absorción en otro ser, normalmente presente al comienzo de una relación amorosa. (pág. 397)

perception/percepción Proceso mediante el cual el cerebro organiza e interpreta la información sensorial transformándola en objetos y sucesos que tienen sentido. (pág. 125)

perceptual adaptation/adaptación visual Habilidad de acomodarnos a un campo visual artificialmente desplazado o hasta invertido. (pág. 149)

perceptual constancy/constancia perceptiva Tendencia a percibir objetos como si fueran constantes e inalterables (como si mantuvieran el color, el brillo, la forma y el tamaño), a pesar de los cambios que se produzcan en la iluminación y las imágenes de la retina. (pág. 145)

perceptual set/predisposición perceptiva Predisposición mental para percibir una cosa y no otra. (pág. 149)

peripheral nervous system (PNS)/sistema nervioso periférico Neuronas sensoriales y motrices conectando el sistema nervioso central al resto del cuerpo. (pág. 31)

personal control/control personal Nuestro sentido de controlar nuestro ambiente en lugar de sentirnos impotentes. (pág. 277)

personality/personalidad Forma característica de pensar, sentir y actuar de un individuo. (pág. 289)

personality disorders/trastornos de la personalidad Trastornos psicológicos caracterizados por modelos de comportamiento inflexibles y duraderos que impiden el funcionamiento social. (pág. 324)

personnel psychology/psicología de personal Subdivisión de la psicología industrial y organizacional, que se encarga de la selección, ubicación, capacitación y evaluación de los empleados. (pág. 408)

pessimism/pesimismo Anticipación de resultados negativos. Son pesimistas las personas que dudan que sus metas se cumplirán. (pág. 278)

PET (positron emission tomography) scan/tomografía por emisión de positrones Muestra visual de la actividad cerebral que detecta por dónde va un tipo de glucosa radiactiva en el momento en que el cerebro realiza una función en particular. (pág. 35)

Phobia/fobia Trastorno de ansiedad marcado por un temor persistente e irracional y la evasión de un objeto o situación específicos. (pág. 319)

physical dependence/dependencia física Necesidad fisiológica de una droga, demostrada por un desagradable síndrome de abstinencia cuando se corta el suministro. (pág. 326)

physiological needs/necesidades fisiológicas Requerimientos básicos del cuerpo. (pág. 236)

pitch/tono Propiedad de los sonidos que los caracteriza como agudos o graves, en función de su frecuencia (pág. 135)

pituitary gland/glándula pituitaria Glándula más influyente del sistema endocrino. Bajo la influencia del hipotálamo, la pituitaria regula el crecimiento y controla otras glándulas endocrinas. (pág. 45)

placebo/placebo [En latín significa "yo complaceré"] Substancia o condición inactiva que se toma por agente activo. (pág. 17)

placebo effect/efecto placebo Resultados producidos únicamente por las expectativas. (pág. 17)

plasticity/plasticidad Capacidad del cerebro de modificarse, especialmente en los niños, reordenándose después de un daño cerebral o formando nuevas vías basadas en la experiencia. (pág. 44)

polygraph/detector de mentiras Máquina que se emplea comúnmente como medio para detectar mentiras y mide varias de las respuestas fisiológicas que acompañan las emociones (tales como los cambios en la transpiración, el ritmo cardíaco y la respiración). (pág. 253)

positive psychology/psicología positiva Estudio científico del funcionamiento humano, que tiene las metas de descubrir y promover la fortaleza y las virtudes que ayudan a los individuos y las comunidades a prosperar. (pág. 8)

positive reinforcement/reforzamiento positivo Aumento en la expresión de comportamientos mediante la presentación de estímulos positivos, por ejemplo, un alimento. Un reforzamiento positivo es cualquier cosa que, *presentada* después de una respuesta, refuerza la respuesta. (pág. 166)

post-traumatic stress disorder (PTSD)/trastorno de estrés post-traumático (TEPT) Trastorno de ansiedad caracterizado por recuerdos obsesionantes, pesadillas, aislamiento social, ansiedad asustadiza, y/o insomnio que dura por cuatro semanas o más después de una experiencia traumática. (pág. 320)

prejudice/prejuicio Actitud injustificable (y normalmente negativa) hacia un grupo y sus miembros. El prejuicio generalmente implica creencias estereotipadas, sentimientos negativos y una predisposición a acción discriminatoria. (pág. 388)

preoperational stage/etapa preoperacional En la teoría de Piaget, la etapa (desde los 2 hasta los 6 ó 7 años) durante la que el niño aprende a utilizar el lenguaje; pero todavía no comprende las operaciones mentales de lógica concreta. (pág. 74)

primary reinforcer/reforzador primario Suceso que es inherentemente reforzador y a menudo satisface una necesidad biológica. (pág. 167)

priming/preparación Activación de asociaciones en nuestra mente, que es a menudo inconsciente y nos dispone a percibir o recordar objetos o sucesos de una manera determinada. (pág. 126)

problem-focused coping/superación con enfoque en los problemas Intento de sobrellevar el estrés de manera directa cambiando ya sea la situación estresante o la forma en que nos relacionamos con dicha situación. (pág. 276)

projection/proyección Mecanismo de defensa psicológico que nos permite esconder nuestros impulsos intimidantes atribuyéndoselos a los demás. (pág. 293)

projective test/prueba de proyección Tipo de prueba de la personalidad, como la prueba de Rorschach, en la cual se proporciona a un individuo una imagen ambigua diseñada para provocar una proyección de pensamientos o sentimientos inconscientes. (pág. 294)

prosocial behavior/comportamiento prosocial Comportamiento positivo, constructivo, útil. Lo contrario del comportamiento antisocial. (pág. 174)

psychoactive drug/droga psicoactiva Sustancia química que altera las percepciones y el humor. (pág. 352)

psychoanalysis/psicoanálisis Teoría de la personalidad de Freud y la técnica terapéutica que atribuye los pensamientos y acciones a los motivos y conflictos inconcientes. Freud creía que las asociaciones libres del paciente, las resistencias, los sueños y la transferencia—y las interpretaciones del terapeuta sobre ellos—liberaban los sentimientos previamente reprimidos, permitiendo al paciente ganar introspección. (págs. 290, 350)

psychodynamic theory/teoría psicodinámica Perspectiva de influencia freudiana que considera que la conducta, el pensamiento y las emociones están basados en motivos inconscientes. (pág. 293)

psychodynamic therapy/terapia psicodinámica Perspectiva de influencia freudiana que considera que la conducta, el pensamiento y las emociones están basados en motivos inconscientes. (pág. 352)

psychological dependence/dependencia psicológica Necesidad psicológica de utilizar una droga, como para aliviar las emociones negativas. (pág. 326)

psychological disorder/trastorno psicológico Pensamientos, sentimientos o comportamientos desviados (anormales), angustiantes y disfuncionales. (pág. 314)

psychology/psicología Estudio científico del comportamiento y de los procesos mentales. (pág. 3)

psychoneuroimmunology (PNI)/psiconeuroinmunología Estudio de cómo se combinan en nuestro organismo los procesos psicológicos y las funciones del sistema nervioso y endocrino para influenciar el sistema de inmunidad y la salud en general. (pág. 272)

psychosexual stages/etapas psicosexuales Etapas del desarrollo infantil según Freud (oral, anal, fálica, latente, genital), durante las cuales la energía del id en busca de placer se enfoca en zonas erógenas específicas (pág. 291)

psychosurgery/psicocirugía Cirugía que remueve o destruye tejido cerebral para cambiar el comportamiento. (pág. 368)

psychotherapy/psicoterapia Tratamiento que consiste en la interacción entre un terapeuta calificado y una persona que desea superar dificultades psicológicas o lograr un crecimiento personal, mediante técnicas psicológicas. (pág. 350)

puberty/pubertad Período de maduración sexual durante el cual una persona adquiere la capacidad de reproducirse. (pág. 84)

punishment/castigo Evento que disminuye el comportamiento que le precede. (pág. 168)

R

random assignment/asignación aleatoria Asignación de participantes a grupos de control y experimentales, que se realiza al azar para minimizar las diferencias que hubiere entre los asignados. (pág. 16)

random sample/muestra aleatoria Muestra en la que cada elemento de la población tiene igual oportunidad de ser seleccionado. (pág. 13)

rationalization/racionalización   Mecanismo de defensa psicológico que nos proporciona justificaciones para reemplazar las verdaderas razones inconscientes de nuestras acciones, por ser éstas más intimidantes. (pág. 239)

reaction formation/formación de reacción   Mecanismo de defensa psicoanalítico en el que el ego inconcientemente cambia los impulsos inaceptables por sus opuestos. Así, nosotros podemos expresar sentimientos que son el opuesto de los sentimientos inconcientes que producen ansiedad. (pág. 293)

recall/recordación   Memoria que se demuestra recuperando información aprendida anteriormente, tal como en las pruebas que consisten en completar espacios en blanco. (pág. 190)

reciprocal determinism/determinismo recíproco   Influencias de la interacción entre la conducta, los factores internos de la personalidad y el ambiente. (pág. 305)

recognition/reconocimiento   Memoria que se demuestra identificando cosas que se aprendieron anteriormente, tal como en las pruebas de escogencia múltiple. (pág. 190)

reflex/reflejo   Respuesta no aprendida y automática a un estímulo sensorial. (pág. 68)

refractory period/período refractario   Fase de descanso después del orgasmo, en la que un hombre no es capaz de tener otro orgasmo. (pág. 109)

regression/regresión   Mecanismo de defensa psicológico en el cual un individuo que experimenta ansiedad regresa a una etapa anterior de su desarrollo. (pág. 292)

rehearsal/ensayo   Repetición conciente de información ya sea para mantenerla concientemente o para codificarla para almacenamiento. (pág. 183)

reinforcement/reforzamiento   Según el condicionamiento operante, todo suceso que *fortalece* el comportamiento al que sigue. (pág. 165)

reinforcement schedule/plan de refuerzo   Patrón que define la frecuencia con que se reforzará una respuesta deseada. (pág. 167)

relative deprivation/privación relativa   Impresión de que estamos en peor situación que aquellos con quienes nos comparamos. (pág. 263)

relearning/reaprendizaje   Memoria que se demuestra por el tiempo que se ahorra cuando se aprende un material por segunda vez. (pág. 190)

reliability/confiabilidad   Grado en el que una prueba produce resultados consistentes, comprobados por la consistencia en puntajes en dos mitades de la prueba, en formas alternas de la prueba, o al retomar la prueba. (pág. 224)

REM (rapid eye movement) sleep/sueño REM   Etapa recurrente del sueño en la cual generalmente ocurren sueños vívidos. También se conoce como *sueño paradójico* porque los músculos están relajados (excepto por unos temblores mínimos) pero los demás sistemas del cuerpo están activos. (pág. 51)

REM rebound/rebote de REM   Aumento marcado del sueño REM como consecuencia de la privación del sueño REM (producida por despertares repetidos durante el sueño REM). (pág. 58)

repetitive transcranial magnetic stimulation (rTMS)/estimulación magnética transcraneal repetitiva (EMTr)   Aplicación repetitiva de pulsos de energía magnética al cerebro; utilizada para estimular o suprimir la actividad cerebral. (pág. 368)

replication/replicación   El repetir la esencia de un estudio de investigación, usualmente con diferentes participantes y en diferentes situaciones para ver si las conclusiones básicas se extienden a otros participantes y circunstancias. (pág. 12)

repression/represión   En la teoría psicoanalítica, el mecanismo básico de defensa por medio del cual el sujeto elimina de su conciente aquellos pensamientos, emociones o recuerdos que le producen ansiedad. (págs. 195, 292)

resistance/resistencia   En psicoanálisis, el bloquear del conciente aquello que está cargado de ansiedad. (pág. 351)

respondent behavior/comportamiento de respuesta   Comportamiento que ocurre como respuesta automática a un estímulo. (pág. 165)

reticular formation/formación reticular   Red de nervios en el bulbo raquídeo que juega un papel importante en el control de la excitación. (pág. 36)

retina/retina   Superficie sensitiva a la luz en la parte interior del ojo que contiene los receptores de luz llamados bastoncillos y conos además de capas de neuronas que inician el procesamiento de la información visual. (pág. 130)

retinal disparity/disparidad retinal (también llamado diferencial)   Clave binocular que consiste en la diferencia en ángulo según una imagen entra por cada ojo (o sea, según se proyecta en la retina de cada ojo). Esa pequeña diferencia en ángulo es utilizada por el cerebro para calcular profundidad, a mayor diferencia de ángulo, menor la proximidad del objeto. (pág. 145)

retrieval/recuperación   Acto de sacar la información que está almacenada en la memoria. (pág. 182)

retrieval cue/clave de recuperación   Todo estímulo (suceso, sentimiento, lugar, etc.) relacionado con un recuerdo específico. (pág. 190)

rods/bastoncillos   Receptores de la retina que detectan el negro, blanco y gris; necesarios para la visión periférica y en la penumbra cuando los conos no responden. (pág. 130)

role/rol   Conjunto de expectativas acerca de una posición social, que definen la forma en que deben comportarse las personas que ocupan esa posición. (págs. 106, 378)

Rorschach inkblot test/test de Rorschach   Prueba proyectiva de amplio uso, un conjunto de 10 manchas de tinta, diseñado por Hermann Rorschach; busca identificar los sentimientos internos de las personas analizando sus interpretaciones de las manchas. (pág. 294)

S

savant syndrome/síndrome de savant   Condición según la cual una persona de habilidad mental limitada, tiene una destreza excepcional en un campo como la computación o el dibujo. (pág. 219)

scapegoat theory/teoría del chivo expiatorio   Teoría que el prejuicio ofrece un escape para la cólera porque nos brinda a alguien que resulta útil como depositario de la agresión. (pág. 390)

schema/esquema   Concepto o principio que organiza e interpreta la información. (pág. 73)

schizophrenia/esquizofrenia   Grupo de trastornos severos caracterizados por un pensamiento desorganizado y delirante, percepciones ofuscadas, así como emociones y acciones impropias. (pág. 340)

selective attention/atención selectiva   Capacidad de enfocar la consciencia en un estímulo en particular. (pág. 48)

self/yo Imagen que tenemos de nosotros mismos y entendimiento de quiénes somos. Según la psicología moderna, centro de la personalidad, de la organización de los pensamientos, sentimientos y acciones. (pág. 305)

self-actualization/autorrealización Según Maslow, necesidad psicológica que surge después de satisfacer las necesidades físicas y psicológicas y de lograr la autoestima; motivación para realizar nuestro potencial. (pág. 297)

self-concept/concepto de uno mismo Todo lo que pensamos y sentimos acerca de nosotros mismos cuando respondemos a la pregunta: "¿Quién soy?". (pág. 298)

self-disclosure/revelación de uno mismo Revelación a los demás de cosas que uno considera íntimas. (pág. 398)

self-esteem/autoestima Sentimientos de alto o bajo valor con los que nos valoramos a nosotros mismos. (pág. 306)

self-serving bias/parcialidad interesada Disposición para percibirnos a nosotros mismos favorablemente. (pág. 307)

self-transcendence/autotrascendencia Según Maslow, esfuerzo por alcanzar una identidad, un sentido y un propósito que vaya más allá de uno mismo. (pág. 297)

sensation/sensación Proceso mediante el cual los receptores sensoriales y el sistema nervioso reciben las energías de los estímulos de nuestro ambiente. (pág. 125)

sensorimotor stage/etapa sensorio-motriz En la teoría de Piaget, la etapa (0–2 años) durante la que los infantes conocen el mundo principalmente en términos de sus impresiones sensoriales y actividades motoras. (pág. 74)

sensory adaptation/adaptación sensorial Disminución en la sensibilidad como respuesta a la estimulación constante. (pág. 128)

sensory cortex/corteza sensorial Área de la parte frontal de los lóbulos parietales que registra y procesa las sensaciones de tacto y movimiento del cuerpo. (pág. 41)

sensory interaction/interacción sensorial Principio que un sentido puede influir a otro, como cuando el olor de la comida influye en su sabor. (pág. 140)

sensory memory/memoria sensorial Registro breve e inmediato de la información sensorial en el sistema de la memoria. (pág. 182)

sensory neurons/neuronas sensoriales Neuronas que reciben la información relacionada con las sensaciones, de los receptores la transportan al sistema nervioso central. (pág. 31)

serial position effect/efecto de posición serial Tendencia a recordar los elementos del comienzo y el final de una lista con mayor facilidad. (pág. 184)

set point/punto fijo Punto de equilibrio en el "termostato del peso" de un individuo. Cuando el cuerpo llega a un peso debajo de este punto, se produce un aumento en el hambre y una disminución en el índice metabólico, los cuales pueden actuar para restablecer el peso perdido. (pág. 239)

sexual disorder/trastorno sexual Problema que impide de manera consistente la excitación o funcionamiento sexual. (pág. 110)

sexual orientation/orientación sexual Atracción sexual duradera hacia miembros de nuestro mismo sexo (orientación homosexual) o del sexo opuesto (orientación heterosexual). (pág. 113)

sexual response cycle/ciclo de respuesta sexual Las cuatro etapas de respuesta sexual descritas por Masters y Johnson—excitación, meseta, orgasmo y resolución. (pág. 109)

shaping/modelamiento Procedimiento del condicionamiento operante en el cual los reforzadores conducen una acción con aproximaciones sucesivas hasta lograr un comportamiento deseado. (pág. 165)

short-term memory/memoria a corto plazo Memoria activada que retiene algunos elementos por un corto tiempo, tales como los siete dígitos de un número telefónico mientras se marca, antes que la información se almacene o se olvide. (pág. 182)

sleep/sueño Pérdida reversible del conocimiento que es periódica y natural. Esto es distinto de la inconsciencia que puede resultar del estado de coma, anestesia general, o hibernación. (Adaptado de Dement, 1999.) (pág. 51)

sleep apnea/apnea del sueño Trastorno del sueño en el que se interrumpe repetidamente la respiración hasta tal punto que el oxígeno en sangre llega a ser tan poco que la persona tiene que despertarse para respirar. (pág. 56)

social-cognitive perspective/perspectiva socio-cognoscitiva Ve la conducta como influida por la interacción entre los individuos (y sus pensamientos) y su contexto social. (pág. 303)

social clock/reloj social Manera que la sociedad tiene de marcar el tiempo adecuado de los eventos sociales, tales como matrimonio, paternidad y jubilación. (pág. 95)

social facilitation/facilitación social Respuestas más fuertes a las tareas simples o bien aprendidas en la presencia de otros. (pág. 384)

social leadership/liderazgo social Liderazgo orientado hacia el grupo que construye trabajo en grupo, media en el conflicto y ofrece apoyo. (pág. 414)

social learning theory/teoría de aprendizaje social Teoría que aprendemos la conducta social observando e imitando y al ser recompensados o castigados. (pág. 107)

social loafing/haraganería social Tendencia de las personas en un grupo de realizar menos esfuerzo cuando juntan sus esfuerzos para lograr una meta común que cuando son responsables individualmente. (pág. 384)

social psychology/psicología social Estudio científico del funcionamiento de la mente individual en un entorno social: pensamiento, influencia y relación entre las personas. (pág. 375)

social script/guión social Guías modeladas culturalmente acerca de cómo actuar en diversas situaciones. (pág. 393)

somatic nervous system/sistema nervioso somático División del sistema nervioso periférico que controla los músculos del esqueleto. También llamado *sistema nervioso del esqueleto*. (pág. 31)

source amnesia/amnesia de la fuente Situación en la que relacionamos una fuente equivocada con un suceso que hemos vivido, leído o imaginado, o del cual nos hemos enterado. (pág. 197)

spacing effect/efecto del aprendizaje espaciado Tendencia a que el estudio o práctica distribuidos logren mejor retención a largo plazo que la que se logra a través de estudio o prácticas masivas. (pág. 184)

split brain/cerebro dividido Condición en la que los dos hemisferios cerebrales se privan de la comunicación mediante el corte de las fibras que los conectan (principalmente las del cuerpo calloso). (pág. 45)

spontaneous recovery/recuperación espontánea Reaparición, después de una pausa, de una respuesta condicionada extinguida. (pág. 226)

spotlight effect/efecto reflector Sobreestimación de lo que los demás advierten y evalúan de nuestra apariencia, desempeño y desatinos (como si estuviéramos apuntados por un reflector). (pág. 306)

SQ3R/inspeccionar, preguntar, leer, recitar, repasar Método de estudio en el que se siguen los pasos de inspeccionar, preguntar, leer, recitar y repasar. (pág. 22)

Standardization/estandarización El definir puntajes significativos mediante la comparación del desempeño de un grupo examinado con anterioridad. (pág. 224)

Stanford-Binet/Stanford-Binet Revisión (por Terman en la Universidad de Stanford) de la prueba original de inteligencia de Binet. Esta prueba revisada es usada extensamente. (pág. 222)

Stereotype/estereotipo Creencia (a veces acertada; pero frecuentemente demasiado generalizada) sobre las características de un grupo. (pág. 388)

stereotype threat/amenaza de estereotipos Preocupación autoconfirmada de que seremos evaluados en base a un estereotipo negativo. (pág. 230)

stimulants/estimulantes Drogas (como cafeína, nicotina y las anfetaminas más poderosas, cocaína y éxtasis) que excitan la actividad neuronal y aceleran las funciones corporales. (pág. 328)

stimulus/estímulo Todo suceso o situación que provoca una respuesta. (pág. 158)

storage/almacenamiento Retención a través del tiempo de información codificada. (pág. 182)

stranger anxiety/miedo a los extraños Miedo a los extraños que los infantes normalmente expresan a partir de los ocho meses. (pág. 76)

stress/estrés Proceso a través del cual percibimos y respondemos a ciertos eventos llamados *estresores*, los cuales evaluamos como amenazantes o desafiantes. (pág. 270)

subjective well-being/bienestar subjetivo Felicidad o satisfacción con la vida de uno mismo. Se emplea junto con medidas de bienestar objetivo (por ejemplo, con indicadores físicos y económicos) para evaluar nuestra calidad de vida. (pág. 260)

subliminal/subliminal Aquello que ocurre por debajo de nuestro umbral absoluto de consciencia. (pág. 126)

substance-related disorders/trastornos causados por el abuso de sustancias adictivas Patrón desequilibrado de consumo de una sustancia que resulta en aflicciones o daños clínicos significativos. (pág. 325)

superego/superyó Según Freud, componente de la personalidad que representa ideales internalizados y proporciona parámetros de juicio (el consciente). (pág. 291)

superordinate goals/metas comunes Metas compartidas que hacen caso omiso de las diferencias entre las personas y que requieren su cooperación. (pág. 401)

survey/encuesta Técnica para verificar las actitudes o conductas reportadas por las personas; usualmente se pregunta a una muestra aleatoria y representativa. (pág. 13)

sympathetic nervous system/sistema nervioso simpático División del sistema nervioso autonómico que en situaciones estresantes despierta al cuerpo y moviliza su energía. (pág. 32)

synapse/sinapsis Intersección entre el extremo del axón de una neurona que envía un mensaje y la dendrita o cuerpo celular de la neurona receptora. (pág. 28)

systematic desensitization/desensibilización sistemática Tipo de terapia de exposición en la cual se asocia un estado tranquilo y agradable con estímulos que provocan ansiedad y que se aplican de manera gradual y en aumento. Se emplea comúnmente para tratar fobias. (pág. 354)

T

task leadership/liderazgo específico Liderazgo orientado a metas específicas que establece las normas, organiza el trabajo y centra la atención en metas. (pág. 413)

telegraphic speech/habla telegráfica Etapa del habla de un niño, que tiene forma de telegrama y está formada mayormente por sustantivos y verbos; por ejemplo, "voy carro". (pág. 212)

temperament/temperamento Característica de reactividad emocional e intensidad de una persona. (pág. 68)

temporal lobes/lóbulos temporales Porción de la corteza cerebral ubicada más o menos encima de las orejas; incluye las áreas que reciben información de los oídos. (pág. 40)

tend and befriend/cuidar y amigarse En situaciones de estrés, las personas (especialmente las mujeres) generalmente proporcionan apoyo y cuidan a los demás, a la vez que forman vínculos y buscan apoyo de los demás. (pág. 272)

teratogens/teratógenos Agentes químicos o virales que pueden afectar al embrión o al feto durante el desarrollo prenatal y causarle daño. (pág. 67)

testosterone/testosterona Principal hormona sexual masculina. Estimula el crecimiento de los órganos sexuales masculinos en el feto y el desarrollo de las características sexuales masculinas secundarias durante la pubertad. Las mujeres tienen menores cantidades de testosterona. (pág. 106)

thalamus/tálamo Área ubicada encima del tronco cerebral; dirige mensajes sensoriales a la corteza cerebral y transmite respuestas al cerebelo y la médula oblonga. (pág. 35)

THC/THC Principal sustancia activa encontrada en la marihuana, produce distintos efectos incluyendo alucinaciones leves. (pág. 331)

Theory/teoría Explicación que emplea un conjunto de principios integrados, organiza observaciones y predice comportamientos o sucesos. (pág. 11)

theory of mind/teoría de la mente Ideas que tienen las personas acerca de sus propios procesos mentales y los de los demás; es decir, de sus sentimientos, percepciones y pensamientos y los comportamientos que éstos podrían predecir. (pág. 75)

threshold/umbral Nivel de estímulo requerido para activar un impulso neuronal. (pág. 28)

token economy/economía de fichas Procedimiento conductual en el cual los individuos ganan una ficha cuando exhiben un comportamiento deseado y luego pueden intercambiar las fichas ganadas por privilegios o para darse algún gusto. (pág. 356)

tolerance/tolerancia Efecto decreciente de la misma dosis de una droga después de un tiempo de uso, requiriendo que el usuario aumente la dosis para poder experimentar el efecto de la droga. (pág. 325)

trait/rasgo Patrón de comportamiento característico o disposición a sentirse y actuar de cierta forma, según se evalúa en los autoinformes de una prueba de la personalidad. (pág. 299)

transduction/transducción Transformación de un tipo de energía en otro. En las sensaciones, transformación de la energía de los estímulos, como las imágenes, los sonidos y los olores, en impulsos nerviosos que el cerebro es capaz de interpretar. (pág. 126)

transference/transferencia En el psicoanálisis, la transferencia de emociones ligadas a otras relaciones, del paciente al analista (como el amor u odio hacia uno de los padres). (pág. 351)

two-factor theory/teoría de los dos factores   Teoría de Schachter y Singer que propone que para experimentar emociones debemos (1) recibir estimulación física y (2) identificar el estímulo a nivel cognitivo. (pág. 249)

two-word stage/etapa de dos palabras   A partir de los dos años, etapa del desarrollo del lenguaje durante la cual el niño emite mayormente frases de dos palabras. (pág. 212)

Type A/Tipo A   Término de Friedman y Rosenman para las personas competitivas, compulsivas, impacientes, verbalmente agresivas y con tendencia a enojarse. (pág. 275)

Type B/Tipo B   Término de Friedman y Rosenman para las personas tolerantes y relajadas. (pág. 275)

U

unconditional positive regard/consideración positiva incondicional   Según Rogers, una actitud de aceptación total hacia otra persona. (pág. 298)

unconditioned response (UR)/respuesta incondicionada (RI)   En el condicionamiento clásico, la respuesta no aprendida e innata que es producida por el estímulo incondicionado (EI) como la salivación cuando la comida está en la boca. (pág. 159)

unconditioned stimulus (US)/estímulo incondicionado (EI)   En el condicionamiento clásico, estímulo que provoca incondicionalmente una respuesta (RI) de manera natural y automática. (pág. 159)

unconscious/inconciente   Según Freud, un depósito de pensamientos, deseos, sentimiento y memorias en su mayoría inaceptables. Según los psicólogos contemporáneos, el procesamiento de información del cual no estamos alertas. (pág. 290)

V

validity/validez   Grado en que una prueba mide o predice lo que se supone debe medir o predecir. (pág. 224)

vestibular sense/sentido vestibular   Sentido de movimiento del cuerpo y posición, incluyendo el sentido de equilibrio. (pág. 142)

virtual reality exposure therapy/terapia de exposición a una realidad virtual   Tratamiento de ansiedad que progresivamente expone a las personas a simulaciones electrónicas de sus más grandes miedos, como volar en avión, arañas o hablar en público. (pág. 335)

visual cliff/precipicio visual   Dispositivo del laboratorio para examinar la percepción de profundidad en los infantes y animales jóvenes. (pág. 144)

W

wavelength/longitud de onda   Distancia entre la cresta de una onda de luz o de sonido y la cresta de la siguiente onda. (pág. 129)

Weber's law/ley de Weber   Principio que sostiene que para que dos estímulos se perciban como distintos, éstos deben diferir por una proporción mínima y constante (en vez de una cantidad constante). (pág. 127)

Wechsler Adult Intelligence Scale (WAIS)/escala de la Inteligencia de Wechsler para adultos   Prueba de inteligencia más ampliamente utilizada; contiene pruebas verbales y de desempeño (no verbales). (pág. 223)

Wernicke's area/área de Wernicke   Parte del cerebro generalmente ubicada en el lóbulo temporal izquierdo, que participa en la comprensión y la expresión del lenguaje, y controla la recepción del mismo. (pág. 43)

withdrawal/síndrome de abstinencia   Conjunto de síntomas que afectan a un individuo cuando se ve privado bruscamente de alguna droga adictiva. (pág. 325)

working memory/memoria operativa   Entendimiento más reciente de la memoria inmediata que supone un procesamiento consciente y activo de la infomación recibida y de información obtenida de la memoria remota. (pág. 182)

X

X chromosome/cromosoma X   Cromosoma sexual que se encuentra en el hombre y la mujer. Las mujeres tienen dos cromosomas X; los hombres tienen un cromosoma X y un cromosoma Y. (pág. 106)

Y

Y chromosome/cromosoma Y   Cromosoma del sexo encontrado sólo en los hombres. Cuando se aparea con un cromosoma X de la madre, produce un niño. (pág. 106)

Z

Zygote/cigoto   Huevo fertilizado, que atraviesa por un período de dos semanas de división celular rápida y se convierte en un embrión. (pág. 66)

References

Aas, H., & Klepp, K-I. (1992). Adolescents' alcohol use related to perceived norms. *Scandinavian Journal of Psychology, 33*, 315–325. (p. 334)

Abbey, A. (1991). Acquaintance rape and alcohol consumption on college campuses: How are they linked? *Journal of American College Health, 39*, 165–169. (p. 326)

Abrams, D. B. (1991). AIDS: What young people believe and what they do. Paper presented at the British Association for the Advancement of Science conference. (p. 279)

Abrams, D. B., & Wilson, G. T. (1983). Alcohol, sexual arousal, and self-control. *Journal of Personality and Social Psychology, 45*, 188–198. (p. 327)

Abrams, M. (2002, June). Sight unseen—Restoring a blind man's vision is now a real possibility through stem-cell surgery. But even perfect eyes cannot see unless the brain has been taught to use them. *Discover, 23*, 54–60. (p. 148)

Abramson, L. Y., Metalsky, G. I., & Alloy, L. B. (1989). Hopelessness depression: A theory-based subtype. *Psychological Review, 96*, 358–372. (p. 339)

Ackerman, D. (2004). *An alchemy of mind: The marvel and mystery of the brain.* New York: Scribner. (p. 28)

Adelmann, P. K., Antonucci, T. C., Crohan, S. F., & Coleman, L. M. (1989). Empty nest, cohort, and employment in the well-being of midlife women. *Sex Roles, 20*, 173–189. (p. 94)

Affleck, G., Tennen, H., Urrows, S., & Higgins, P. (1994). Person and contextual features of daily stress reactivity: Individual differences in relations of undesirable daily events with mood disturbance and chronic pain intensity. *Journal of Personality and Social Psychology, 66*, 329–340. (p. 261)

Aiello, J. R., Thompson, D. D., & Brodzinsky, D. M. (1983). How funny is crowding anyway? Effects of room size, group size, and the introduction of humor. *Basic and Applied Social Psychology, 4*, 193–207. (p. 384)

Ainsworth, M. D. S. (1973). The development of infant-mother attachment. In B. Caldwell & H. Ricciuti (Eds.), *Review of child development research (Vol. 3).* Chicago: University of Chicago Press. (p. 78)

Ainsworth, M. D. S. (1979). Infant-mother attachment. *American Psychologist, 34*, 932–937. (p. 78)

Ainsworth, M. D. S. (1989). Attachments beyond infancy. *American Psychologist, 44*, 709–716. (p. 78)

Albee, G. W. (1986). Toward a just society: Lessons from observations on the primary prevention of psychopathology. *American Psychologist, 41*, 891–898. (p. 371)

Albert, B., Brown, S., & Flanigan, C. M. (Eds.) (2003). *14 and younger: The sexual behavior of young adolescents.* Washington, DC: National Campaign to Prevent Teen Pregnancy. (p. 111)

Alcock, J. E. (1981). *Parapsychology: Science or magic?* Oxford: Pergamon. (p. 191)

Aldrich, M. S. (1989). Automobile accidents in patients with sleep disorders. *Sleep, 12*, 487–494. (p. 56)

Aldridge-Morris, R. (1989). *Multiple personality: An exercise in deception.* Hillsdale, NJ: Erlbaum. (p. 323)

Aleman, A., Kahn, R. S., & Selten, J-P. (2003). Sex differences in the risk of schizophrenia: Evidence from meta-analysis. *Archives of General Psychiatry, 60*, 565–571. (p. 342)

Allen, J. R., & Setlow, V. P. (1991). Heterosexual transmission of HIV: A view of the future. *Journal of the American Medical Association, 266*, 1695–1696. (p. 111)

Allen, L. S., & Gorski, R. A. (1992). Sexual orientation and the size of the anterior commisure in the human brain. *Proceedings of the National Academy of Sciences, 89*, 7199–7202. (p. 116)

Allen, N. B., & Badcock, P. B. T. (2003). The social risk hypothesis of depressed mood: Evolutionary, psychosocial, and neurobiological perspectives. *Psychological Bulletin, 129*, 887–913. (p. 335)

Allport, G. W. (1954). *The nature of prejudice.* New York: Addison-Wesley. (p. 12, 389)

Altman, L. K. (2004, November 24). Female cases of HIV found rising worldwide. *New York Times* (www.nytimes.com). (p. 274)

Alwin, D. F. (1990). Historical changes in parental orientations to children. In N. Mandell (Ed.), *Sociological studies of child development (Vol. 3).* Greenwich, CT: JAI Press. (p. 81)

AMA. (2004, November 11). Women lead in number of medical school applications. *Voice* (ama-assn.org). (p. 121)

Amabile, T. M. (1983). *The social psychology of creativity.* New York: Springer-Verlag. (p. 306)

Amabile, T. M., & Hennessey, B. A. (1992). The motivation for creativity in children. In A. K. Boggiano & T. S. Pittman (Eds.), *Achievement and motivation: A social-developmental perspective.* New York: Cambridge University Press. (p. 221)

Ambady, N., & Rosenthal, R. (1992). Thin slices of expressive behavior as predictors of interpersonal consequences: A meta-analysis. *Psychological Bulletin, 111*, 256–274. (p. 304)

Ambady, N., & Rosenthal, R. (1993). Half a minute: Predicting teacher evaluations from thin slices of nonverbal behavior and physical attractiveness. *Journal of Personality and Social Psychology, 64*, 431–441. (p. 304)

Amen, D. G., Stubblefield, M., Carmichael, B., & Thisted, R. (1996). Brain SPECT findings and aggressiveness. *Annals of Clinical Psychiatry, 8*, 129–137. (p. 391)

American Enterprise. (1992, January/February). Women, men, marriages & ministers. p. 106. (p. 309)

American Psychological Association. (1992). Ethical principles of psychologists and code of conduct. *American Psychologist, 47*, 1597–1611. (p. 20)

American Psychological Association. (2002). *Ethical principles of psychologists and code of conduct.* Washington, DC: American Psychological Association. (p. 20)

Andersen, S. M. (1998). *Service Learning: A National Strategy for Youth Development.* A position paper issued by the Task Force on Education Policy. Washington, DC: Institute for Communitarian Policy Studies, George Washington University. (p. 86)

Anderson, B. L. (2002). Biobehavioral outcomes following psychological interventions for cancer patients. *Journal of Consulting and Clinical Psychology, 70*, 590–610. (p. 274)

Anderson, C. A. (2004a). An update on the effects of playing violent video games. *Journal of Adolescence, 27*, 113–122. (p. 393)

Anderson, C. A., & Dill, K. E. (2000). Video games and aggressive thoughts, feelings, and behavior in the laboratory and in life. *Journal of Personality and Social Psychology, 78*, 772–790. (p. 393)

Anderson, C. A., Berkowitz, L., Donnerstein, E., Huesmann, L. R., Johnson, J. D., Linz, D., Malamuth, N. M., & Wartella, E. (2003). The influence of media violence on youth. *Psychological Science in the Public Interest, 4(3),* 81–110. (p. 175)

Anderson, C. A., Carnagey, N. L., Flanagan, M., Benjamin, A. J., Jr., Eubanks, J., & Valentine, J. C. (2004). Violent video games: Specific effects of violent content on aggressive thoughts and behavior. *Advances in Experimental Social Psychology, 36,* 199–249. (p. 393)

Anderson, C. A., Lindsay, J. J., & Bushman, B. J. (1999). Research in the psychological laboratory: Truth or triviality? *Current Directions in Psychological Science, 8,* 3–9. (p. 19)

Anderson, I. M. (2000). Selective serotonin reuptake inhibitors versus tricyclic antidepressants: A meta-analysis of efficacy and tolerability. *Journal of Affective Disorders, 58,* 19–36. (p. 366)

Anderson, R. C., Pichert, J. W., Goetz, E. T., Schallert, D. L., Stevens, K. V., & Trollip, S. R. (1976). Instantiation of general terms. *Journal of Verbal Learning and Verbal Behavior, 15,* 667–679. (p. 190)

Anderson, S. R. (2004). *Doctor Dolittle's delusion: Animals and the uniqueness of human language.* New Haven: Yale University Press. (p. 217)

Andreasen, N. C. (1997). Linking mind and brain in the study of mental illnesses: A project for a scientific psychopathology. *Science, 275,* 1586–1593. (p. 343)

Andreasen, N. C. (2001). *Brave new brain: Conquering mental illness in the era of the genome.* New York: Oxford University Press. (p. 343)

Angelsen, N. K., Vik, T., Jacobsen, G., & Bakketeig, L. S. (2001). Breast feeding and cognitive development at age 1 and 5 years. *Archives of Disease in Childhood, 85,* 183–188. (p. 16)

Antony, M. M., Brown, T. A., & Barlow, D. H. (1992). Current perspectives on panic and panic disorder. *Current Directions in Psychological Science, 1,* 79–82. (p. 321)

Antrobus, J. (1991). Dreaming: Cognitive processes during cortical activation and high afferent thresholds. *Psychological Review, 98,* 96–121. (p. 58)

Archer, J. (2004). Sex differences in aggression in real-world settings: A meta-analytic review. *Review of General Psychology, 8,* 291–322. (p. 104)

Arent, S. M., Landers, D. M., & Etnier, J. L. (2000). The effects of exercise on mood in older adults: A meta-analytic review. *Journal of Aging and Physical Activity, 8,* 407–430. (p. 281)

Aries, E. (1987). Gender and communication. In P. Shaver & C. Henrick (Eds.), *Review of Personality and Social Psychology, 7,* 149–176. (p. 105)

Arkowitz, H., & Lilienfeld, S. O. (2006, April/May). Psychotherapy on trial. *Scientific American: Mind,* pp. 42–49. (p. 362)

Armel, K. C., & Ramachandran, V. S. (2003). Projecting sensations to external objects: Evidence from skin conductance response. *Proceedings of the Royal Society of London. Series B. Biological Sciences, 270,* 1499–1506. (p. 137)

Armony, J. L., Quirk, G. J., & LeDoux, J. E. (1998). Differential effects of amygdala lesions on early and late plastic components of auditory cortex spike trains during fear conditioning. *Journal of Neuroscience, 18,* 2592–2601. (p. 322)

Arnett, J. J. (2000). Emerging adulthood: A theory of development from the late teens through the twenties. *American Psychologist, 55,* 469–480. (p. 89)

Aron, A., Melinat, E., Aron, E. N., Vallone, R. D., & Bator, R. J. (1997). The experimental generation of interpersonal closeness: A procedure and some preliminary findings. *Personality and Social Psychology Bulletin, 23,* 363–377. (p. 398)

Aronson, E. (2001, April 13). Newsworthy violence. E-mail to SPSP discussion list, drawing from *Nobody Left to Hate.* New York: Freeman, 2000. (p. 88)

Arseneault, L., Cannon, M., Poulton, R., Murray, R., Caspi, A., & Moffitt, T. E. (2002). Cannabis use in adolescence and risk for adult psychosis: Longitudinal prospective study. *British Medical Journal, 325,* 1212–1213. (p. 332)

Artiga, A. I., Viana, J. B., Maldonado, C. R., Chandler-Laney, P. C., Oswald, K. D., & Boggiano, M. M. (2007). Body composition and endocrine status of long-term stress-induced binge-eating rats. *Physiology and Behavior, 91,* 424–431. (p. 240)

Asch, S. E. (1955). Opinions and social pressure. *Scientific American,* pp. 193, 31–35. (p. 380)

Aserinsky, E. (1988, January 17). Personal communication. (p. 51)

ASHA. (2003). STD statistics. American Social Health Association (www.ashastd.org/stdfaqs/statistics.html). (p. 110)

Assanand, S., Pinel, J. P. J., & Lehman, D. R. (1998). Personal theories of hunger and eating. *Journal of Applied Social Psychology, 28,* 998–1015. (p. 239)

Atkinson, R. C., & Shiffrin, R. M. (1968). Human memory: A control system and its control processes. In K. Spence (Ed.), *The psychology of learning and motivation (Vol. 2).* New York: Academic Press. (p. 182)

Atwell, R. H. (1986, July 28). *Drugs on campus: A perspective.* Higher Education & National Affairs, p. 5. (p. 327)

Averill, J. R. (1983). Studies on anger and aggression: Implications for theories of emotion. *American Psychologist, 38,* 1145–1160. (p. 259)

Averill, J. R. (1993). William James's other theory of emotion. In M. E. Donnelly (Ed.), *Reinterpreting the legacy of William James.* Washington, DC: American Psychological Association. (p. 249)

Avery, R. D., & others. (1994, December 13). Mainstream science on intelligence. *Wall Street Journal,* p. A–18. (p. 227)

Ax, A. F. (1953). The physiological differentiation of fear and anger in humans. *Psychosomatic Medicine, 15,* 433–442. (p. 253)

Azar, B. (1998, June). Why can't this man feel whether or not he's standing up? *APA Monitor* (www.apa.org/monitor/jun98/touch.html). (p. 142)

Backman, L., & MacDonald, S. W. S. (2006). Death and cognition: Synthesis and outlook. *European Psychologist, 11,* 224–235. (p. 94)

Baddeley, A. D. (1982). *Your memory: A user's guide.* New York: Macmillan. (pp. 184)

Bagemihl, B. (1999). *Biological exuberance: Animal homosexuality and natural diversity.* New York: St. Martins. (p. 115)

Bahrick, H. P. (1984). Semantic memory content in permastore: 50 years of memory for Spanish learned in school. *Journal of Experimental Psychology: General, 111,* 1–29. (p. 193)

Bahrick, H. P., Bahrick, P. O., & Wittlinger, R. P. (1975). Fifty years of memory for names and faces: A cross-sectional approach. *Journal of Experimental Psychology: General, 104,* 54–75. (p. 190)

Bailenson, J. N., Iyengar, S., Yee, N., & Collins, N. (2008). Facial similarity as a voting heuristic. *Public Opinion Quarterly,* in press. (p. 395)

Bailey, J. M., Gaulin, S., Agyei, Y., & Gladue, B. A. (1994). Effects of gender and sexual orientation on evolutionary relevant aspects of human mating psychology. *Journal of Personality and Social Psychology,* 66, 1081–1093. (p. 118)

Bailey, J. M., Kirk, K. M., Zhu, G., Dunne, M. P., & Martin, N. G. (2000). Do individual differences in sociosexuality represent genetic or environmentally contingent strategies? Evidence from the Australian twin registry. *Journal of Personality and Social Psychology,* 78, 537–545. (p. 118)

Bailey, R. E., & Gillaspy, Jr., J. A. (2005). Operant psychology goes to the fair: Marian and Keller Breland in the popular press, 1947–1966. *The Behavior Analyst,* 28, 143–159. (p. 157)

Baillargeon, R. (1995). A model of physical reasoning in infancy. In C. Rovee-Collier & L. P. Lipsitt (Eds.), *Advances in infancy research* (Vol. 9). Stamford, CT: Ablex. (p. 74)

Baillargeon, R. (1998). Infants' understanding of the physical world. In M. Sabourin, F. I. M. Craik, & M. Roberts (Eds.), *Advances in psychological science, Vol. 2: Biological and cognitive aspects.* Hove, England: Psychology Press. (p. 74)

Baillargeon, R. (2004). Infants' physical world. *Current Directions in Psychological Science,* 13, 89–94. (p. 74)

Baker, T. B., Piper, M. E., McCarthy, D. E., Majeskie, M. R., & Fiore, M. C. (2004). Addiction motivation reformulated: An affective processing model of negative reinforcement. *Psychological Review,* 111, 33–51. (p. 167)

Bakermans-Kranenburg, M. J., van IJzendoorn, M. H., & Juffer, F. (2003). Less is more: Meta-analyses of sensitivity and attachment interventions in early childhood. *Psychological Bulletin,* 129, 195–215. (p. 78)

Bancroft, J., Loftus, J., & Long, J. S. (2003). Distress about sex: A national survey of women in heterosexual relationships. *Archives of Sexual Behavior,* 32, 193–208. (p. 110)

Bandura, A. (1982). The psychology of chance encounters and life paths. *American Psychologist,* 37, 747–755. (p. 95)

Bandura, A. (2005) The evolution of social cognitive theory. In K. G. Smith & M. A. Hitt (Eds.), *Great minds in management: The process of theory development.* Oxford: Oxford University Press. (p. 95, 173)

Bandura, A. (2008). An agentic perspective on positive psychology. In S. J. Lopez (Ed.), *The science of human flourishing.* Westport, CT: Praeger. (p. 63)

Bandura, A., Ross, D., & Ross, S. A. (1961). Transmission of aggression through imitation of aggressive models. *Journal of Abnormal and Social Psychology,* 63, 575–582. (p. 173)

Barinaga, M. B. (1997). How exercise works its magic. *Science,* 276, 1325. (p. 280)

Barlow, D. H. (1988). *Anxiety and its disorders: The nature and treatment of anxiety and panic.* New York: Guilford. (p. 322)

Barnes, M. L., & Sternberg, R. J. (1989). Social intelligence and decoding of nonverbal cues. *Intelligence,* 13, 263–287. (p. 257)

Barnett, P. A., & Gotlib, I. H. (1988). Psychosocial functioning and depression: Distinguishing among antecedents, concomitants, and consequences. *Psychological Bulletin,* 104, 97–126. (p. 339)

Barnier, A. J., & McConkey, K. M. (2004). Defining and identifying the highly hypnotizable person. In M. Heap, R. J. Brown, & D. A. Oakley (Eds.), *High hypnotisability: Theoretical, experimental and clinical issues.* London: Brunner-Routledge. (p. 139)

Baron, R. S., Cutrona, C. E., Hicklin, D., Russell, D. W., & Lubaroff, D. M. (1990). Social support and immune function among spouses of cancer patients. *Journal of Personality and Social Psychology,* 59, 344–352. (p. 280)

Barrett, L. F. (2006). Are emotions natural kinds? *Perspectives on Psychological Science,* 1, 28–58. (p. 252)

Bashore, T. R., Ridderinkhof, K. R., & van der Molen, M. W. (1997). The decline of cognitive processing speed in old age. *Current Directions in Psychological Science,* 6, 163–169. (p. 93)

Baskind, D. E. (1997, December 14). Personal communication, from Delta College. (p. 356)

Bass, L. E., & Kane-Williams, E. (1993). Stereotype or reality: Another look at alcohol and drug use among African American children. *U.S. Department of Health and Human Services, Public Health Reports,* 108 (Supplement 1), 78–84. (p. 333)

Bassett, D. R., Schneider, P. L., & Huntington, G. E. (2004). Physical activity in an Old Order Amish community. *Medicine and Science in Sports and Exercise,* 36, 79–85. (p. 245)

Baum, A., & Posluszny, D. M. (1999). Health psychology: Mapping biobehavioral contributions to health and illness. *Annual Review of Psychology,* 50, 137–163. (p. 274)

Baumeister, R. F. (1989). The optimal margin of illusion. *Journal of Social and Clinical Psychology,* 8, 176–189. (p. 208)

Baumeister, R. F. (2000). Gender differences in erotic plasticity: The female sex drive as socially flexible and responsive. *Psychological Bulletin,* 126, 347–374. (p. 114)

Baumeister, R. F., & Bratslavsky, E. (1999). Passion, intimacy, and time: Passionate love as a function of change in intimacy. *Personality and Social Psychology Review,* 3, 49–67. (p. 398)

Baumeister, R. F., & Exline, J. J. (2000). Self-control, morality, and human strength. *Journal of Social and Clinical Psychology,* 19, 29–42. (p. 278)

Baumeister, R. F., & Leary, M. R. (1995). The need to belong: Desire for interpersonal attachments as a fundamental human motivation. *Psychological Bulletin,* 117, 497–529. (pp. 247)

Baumeister, R. F., & Tice, D. M. (1986). How adolescence became the struggle for self: A historical transformation of psychological development. In J. Suls & A. G. Greenwald (Eds.), *Psychological perspectives on the self* (Vol. 3). Hillsdale, NJ: Erlbaum. (p. 88)

Baumeister, R. F., & Vohs, K. D. (2002). The pursuit of meaningfulness in life. In C. R. Snyder & S. Lopez (eds.), *Handbook of positive psychology.* New York: Oxford. (p. 280)

Baumeister, R. F., Campbell, J., Krueger, J. I., & Vohs, K. D. (2003). Does high self-esteem cause better performance, interpersonal success, happiness, or healthier lifestyles? *Psychological Science in the Public Interest,* 4(1), 1–44. (p. 306)

Baumeister, R. F., Campbell, J. D., Krueger, J. I., & Vohs, K. D. (2005, January). Exploding the self-esteem myth. *Scientific American,* pp. 84–91. (p. 306)

Baumeister, R. F., Catanese, K. R., & Vohs, K. D. (2001). Is there a gender difference in strength of sex drive? Theoretical views, conceptual distinctions, and a review of relevant evidence. *Personality and Social Psychology Review,* 5, 242–273. (p. 118)

Baumeister, R. F., Dale, K., & Sommer, K. L. (1998). Freudian defense mechanisms and empirical findings in modern personality and social psychology: Reaction formation, projection, displacement, undoing, isolation, sublimation, and denial. *Journal of Personality,* 66, 1081–1125. (p. 296)

Baumeister, R. F., Twenge, J. M., & Nuss, C. K. (2002). Effects of social exclusion on cognitive processes: Anticipated aloneness reduces intelligent thought. *Journal of Personality and Social Psychology,* 83, 817–827. (p. 248)

Baumgardner, A. H., Kaufman, C. M., & Levy, P. E. (1989). Regulating affect interpersonally: When low esteem leads to greater enhancement. *Journal of Personality and Social Psychology,* 56, 907–921. (p. 306)

Baumrind, D. (1982). Adolescent sexuality: Comment on Williams' and Silka's comments on Baumrind. *American Psychologist, 37*, 1402–1403. (p. 113)

Baumrind, D. (1996). The discipline controversy revisited. *Family Relations, 45*, 405–414. (p. 80)

Baumrind, D., Larzelere, R. E., & Cowan, P. A. (2002). Ordinary physical punishment: Is it harmful? Comment on Gershoff (2002). *Psychological Bulletin, 128*, 602–611. (p. 168)

Bavelier, D., Newport, E. L., & Supalla, T. (2003). Children need natural languages, signed or spoken. *Cerebrum, 5(1)*, 19–32. (p. 213)

Beaman, A. L., & Klentz, B. (1983). The supposed physical attractiveness bias against supporters of the women's movement: A meta-analysis. *Personality and Social Psychology Bulletin, 9*, 544–550. (p. 396)

Beardsley, L. M. (1994). Medical diagnosis and treatment across cultures. In W. J. Lonner & R. Malpass (Eds.), *Psychology and culture.* Boston: Allyn & Bacon. (p. 315)

Beardsley, T. (1996, July). Waking up. *Scientific American,* pp. 14, 18. (p. 54)

Beauchamp, G. K. (1987). The human preference for excess salt. *American Scientist, 75*, 27–33. (p. 240)

Beck, A. T., Rush, A. J., Shaw, B. F., & Emery, G. (1979). *Cognitive therapy of depression.* New York: Guilford Press. (p. 358)

Becklen, R., & Cervone, D. (1983). Selective looking and the noticing of unexpected events. *Memory and Cognition, 11*, 601–608. (p. 49)

Beckman, M. (2004). Crime, culpability, and the adolescent brain. *Science, 305*, 596–599. (p. 84)

Beeman, M. J., & Chiarello, C. (1998). Complementary right- and left-hemisphere language comprehension. *Current Directions in Psychological Science, 7*, 2–8. (p. 47)

Beitman, B. D., Goldfried, M. R., & Norcross, J. C. (1989). The movement toward integrating the psychotherapies: An overview. *American Journal of Psychiatry, 146*, 138–147. (p. 350)

Bell, A. P., Weinberg, M. S., & Hammersmith, S. K. (1981). *Sexual preference: Its development in men and women.* Bloomington: Indiana University Press. (p. 115)

Belsher, G., & Costello, C. G. (1988). Relapse after recovery from unipolar depression: A critical review. *Psychological Bulletin, 104*, 84–96. (p. 337)

Bem, D. J., & Honorton, C. (1994). Does psi exist? Replicable evidence for an anomalous process of information transfer. *Psychological Bulletin, 115*, 4–18. (p. 153)

Bem, D. J., Palmer, J., & Broughton, R. S. (2001). Updating the Ganzfeld database: A victim of its own success? *Journal of Parapsychology, 65*, 207–218. (p. 153)

Bem, S. L. (1987). Masculinity and femininity exist only in the mind of the perceiver. In J. M. Reinisch, L. A. Rosenblum, & S. A. Sanders (Eds.), *Masculinity/femininity: Basic perspectives.* New York: Oxford University Press. (p. 108)

Bem, S. L. (1993). *The lenses of gender.* New Haven: Yale University Press. (p. 108)

Benbow, C. P., Lubinski, D., Shea, D. L., & Eftekhari-Sanjani, H. (2000). Sex differences in mathematical reasoning ability at age 13: Their status 20 years later. *Psychological Science, 11*, 474–2000. (p. 229)

Bennett, W. I. (1995). Beyond overeating. *New England Journal of Medicine, 332*, 673–674. (p. 246)

Ben-Shakhar, G., & Elaad, E. (2003). The validity of psychophysiological detection of information with the guilt knowledge test: A meta-analytic review. *Journal of Applied Psychology, 88*, 131–151. (p. 254)

Benson, H. (1996). *Timeless healing: The power and biology of belief.* New York: Scribner. (p. 282)

Benson, K., & Feinberg, I. (1977). The beneficial effect of sleep in an extended Jenkins and Dallenbach paradigm. *Psychophysiology, 14*, 375–384. (p. 194)

Benson, P. L., Sharma, A. R., & Roehlkepartain, E. C. (1994). *Growing up adopted: A portrait of adolescents and their families.* Minneapolis: Search Institute. (p. 82)

Berger, B. G., & Motl, R. W. (2000). Exercise and mood: A selective review and synthesis of research employing the profile of mood states. *Journal of Applied Sports Psychology, 12*, 69–92. (p. 281)

Bergin, A. E. (1980). Psychotherapy and religious values. *Journal of Consulting and Clinical Psychology, 48*, 95–105. (p. 364)

Bergsholm, P., Larsen, J. L., Rosendahl, K., & Holsten, F. (1989). Electroconvulsive therapy and cerebral computed tomography. *Acta Psychiatrica Scandinavia, 80*, 566–572. (p. 368)

Berk, L. S., Felten, D. L., Tan, S. A., Bittman, B. B., & Westengard, J. (2001). Modulation of neuroimmune parameters during the eustress of humor-associated mirthful laughter. *Alternative Therapies, 7*, 62–76. (p. 279)

Berkel, J., & de Waard, F. (1983). Mortality pattern and life expectancy of Seventh Day Adventists in the Netherlands. *International Journal of Epidemiology, 12*, 455–459. (p. 283)

Berkowitz, L. (1983). Aversively stimulated aggression: Some parallels and differences in research with animals and humans. *American Psychologist, 38*, 1135–1144. (p. 392)

Berkowitz, L. (1989). Frustration-aggression hypothesis: Examination and reformulation. *Psychological Bulletin, 106*, 59–73. (p. 392)

Berndt, T. J. (1992). Friendship and friends' influence in adolescence. *Current Directions in Psychological Science, 1*, 156–159. (p. 105)

Berscheid, E. (1981). An overview of the psychological effects of physical attractiveness and some comments upon the psychological effects of knowledge of the effects of physical attractiveness. In G. W. Lucker, K. Ribbens, & J. A. McNamara (Eds.), *Psychological aspects of facial form (Craniofacial growth series)* Ann Arbor, MI (p. 396)

Berscheid, E., Gangestad, S. W., & Kulakowski, D. (1984). Emotion in close relationships: Implications for relationship counseling. In S. D. Brown & R. W. Lent (Eds.), *Handbook of counseling psychology.* New York: Wiley. (p. 398)

Bértolo, H., Paiva, T., Pessoa, L., Mestre, T., Marques, R., & Santos, R. (2003). Visual dream content, graphical representation and EEG alpha activity in congenitally blind subjects. *Cognitive Brain Research, 15*, 277–284. (p. 57)

Bettencourt, B. A., & Kernahan, C. (1997). A meta-analysis of aggression in the presence of violent cues: Effects of gender differences and aversive provocation. *Aggressive Behavior, 23*, p. 447–457. (p. 104)

Beyerstein, B., & Beyerstein, D. (Eds.) (1992). *The write stuff: Evaluations of graphology.* Buffalo, NY: Prometheus Books. (p. 302)

Bhatt, R. S., Wasserman, E. A., Reynolds, W. F., Jr., & Knauss, K. S. (1988). Conceptual behavior in pigeons: Categorization of both familiar and novel examples from four classes of natural and artificial stimuli. *Journal of Experimental Psychology: Animal Behavior Processes, 14*, 219–234. (p. 166)

Bianchi, S. M., Milkie, M. A., Sayer, L. C., & Robinson, J. P. (2000). Is anyone doing the housework? Trends in the gender division of household labor. *Social Forces, 79,* 191–228. (p. 121)

Bianchi, S. M., Robinson, J. P., & Milkie, M. A. (2006). *Changing rhythms of American family life.* New York: Russell Sage. (p. 121)

Bickman, L. (1999). Practice makes perfect and other myths about mental health services. *American Psychologist, 54,* 965–978. (p. 362)

Biello, S. M., & Dafters, R. I. (2001). MDMA and fenfluramine alter the response of the circadian clock to a serotonin agonist in vitro. *Brain Research, 920,* 202–209. (p. 330)

Binet, A. (1909). *Les idées mordermes sur les enfants.* Paris: Flammarion (quoted by A. Clarke & A. Clarke, Born to be bright. *The Psychologist, 19,* 409). (p. 222)

Birnbaum, S. G., Yuan, P. X., Wang, M., Vijayraghavan, S., Bloom, A. K., Davis, D. J., Gobeski, K. T., Sweatt, J. D., Manhi, H. K., & Arnsten, A. F. T. (2004). Protein kinase C overactivity impairs prefrontal cortical regulation of working memory. *Science, 306,* 882–884. (p. 187)

Biswas-Diener, R., & Diener, E. (2001). Making the best of a bad situation: Satisfaction in the slums of Calcutta. *Social Indicators Research, 55,* 329–352. (p. 262)

Bjork, R. A. (1999). Assessing our own competence: Heuristics and illusions. In D. Gopher & A. Koriat (Eds.), *Attention and performance XVII. Cognitive regulation of performance: Interaction of theory and application.* Cambridge, MA: MIT Press. (p. 184)

Bjork, R. A. (2000, July/August). Toward one world of psychological science. *APS Observer,* p. 3. (p. 4)

Bjorklund, D. F., & Green, B. L. (1992). The adaptive nature of cognitive immaturity. *American Psychologist, 47,* 46–54. (p. 76)

Blakemore, S-J., Wolpert, D. M., & Frith, C. D. (1998). Central cancellation of self-produced tickle sensation. *Nature Neuroscience, 1,* 635–640. (p. 137)

Blakeslee, S. (2005, February 8). Focus narrows in search for autism's cause. *New York Times* (www.nytimes.com). (p. 76)

Blanchard, R. (1997). Birth order and sibling sex ratio in homosexual versus heterosexual males and females. *Annual Review of Sex Research, 8,* 27–67. (p. 116)

Blanchard, R. (2001). Fraternal birth order and the maternal immunie hypothesis of male homosexuality. *Hormones and Behavior, 40,* 105–114. (p. 116)

Blascovich, J., Seery, M. D., Mugridge, C. A., Norris, R. K., & Weisbuch, M. (2004). Predicting athletic performance from cardiovascular indexes of challenge and threat. *Journal of Experimental Social Psychology, 40,* 683–688. (p. 270)

Blass, T. (1999). The Milgram paradigm after 35 years: Some things we now know about obedience to authority. *Journal of Applied Social Psychology, 29,* 955–978. (p. 382)

Bleustein, J. (2002, June 15). Quoted in "Harley retooled," by S. S. Smith, *American Way Magazine.* (p. 414)

Bloom, B. C. (Ed.). (1985). *Developing talent in young people.* New York: Ballantine. (p. 410)

Bloom, P. (2000). *How children learn the meanings of words.* Cambridge, MA: MIT Press. (p. 212)

Bodkin, J. A., & Amsterdam, J. D. (2002). Transdermal selegiline in major depression: A double-blind, placebo-controlled, parallel-group study in outpatients. *American Journal of Psychiatry, 159,* 1869–1875. (p. 366)

Boehm, K. E., Schondel, C. K., Marlowe, A. L., & Manke-Mitchell, L. (1999). Teens' concerns: A national evaluation. *Adolescence, 34,* 523–528. (p. 88)

Boesch-Achermann, H., & Boesch, C. (1993). Tool use in wild chimpanzees: New light from dark forests. *Current Directions in Psychological Science, 2,* 18–21. (p. 216)

Bogaert, A. F. (2003). Number of older brothers and sexual orientation: New texts and the attraction/behavior distinction in two national probability samples. *Journal of Personality and Social Psychology, 84,* 644–652. (p. 116)

Bogaert, A. F. (2006). Biological versus nonbiological older brothers and men's sexual orientation. *Proceedings of the National Academy of Sciences, 103,* 10771–10774. (pp. 114, 116)

Boggiano, A. K., Harackiewicz, J. M., Bessette, M. M., & Main, D. S. (1985). Increasing children's interest through performance-contingent reward. *Social Cognition, 3,* 400–411. (p. 170)

Boggiano, M. M., Chandler, P. C., Viana, J. B., Oswald, K. D., Maldonado, C. R., & Wauford, P. K. (2005). Combined dieting and stress evoke exaggerated responses to opioids in binge-eating rats. *Behavioral Neuroscience, 119,* 1207–1214. (p. 240)

Bolger, N., DeLongis, A., Kessler, R. C., & Schilling, E. A. (1989). Effects of daily stress on negative mood. *Journal of Personality and Social Psychology, 57,* 808–818. (p. 261)

Bonanno, G. A. (2001). Grief and emotion: Experience, expression, and dissociation. In M. Stroebe, W. Stroebe, R. O. Hansson, & H. Schut (Eds.), *New handbook of bereavement: Consciousness, coping, and care.* Cambridge: Cambridge University Press. (p. 96)

Bonanno, G. A. (2004). Loss, trauma, and human resilience: Have we underestimated the human capacity to thrive after extremely aversive events? *American Psychologist, 59,* 20–28. (pp. 96, 320)

Bonanno, G. A. (2005). Adult resilience to potential trauma. *Current Directions in Psychological Science, 14,* 135–137. (p. 320)

Bonanno, G. A., & Kaltman, S. (1999). Toward an integrative perspective on bereavement. *Psychological Bulletin, 125,* 760–777. (p. 96)

Bonanno, G. A., Galea, S., Bucciarelli, A., & Vlahov, D. (2006). Psychological resilience after disaster. *Psychological Science, 17,* 181–86. (p. 320)

Bond, M. H. (1988). Finding universal dimensions of individual variation in multi-cultural studies of values: The Rokeach and Chinese values surveys. *Journal of Personality and Social Psychology, 55,* 1009–1015. (p. 309)

Bond, R., & Smith, P. B. (1996). Culture and conformity: A meta-analysis of studies using Asch's (1952b, 1956) line judgment task. *Psychological Bulletin, 119,* 111–137. (p. 381)

Bono, J. E., & Judge, T. A. (2004). Personality and transformational and transactional leadership: A meta-analysis. *Journal of Applied Psychology, 89,* 901–910. (p. 413)

Booth, F. W., & Neufer, P. D. (2005). Exercise controls gene expression. *American Scientist, 93,* 28–35. (p. 242)

Boring, E. G. (1930). A new ambiguous figure. *American Journal of Psychology, 42,* 444–445. (p. 149)

Bornstein, M. H., Cote, L. R., Maital, S., Painter, K., Park, S-Y., Pascual, L., Pecheux, M-G., Ruel, J., Venute, P., & Vyt, A. (2004). Cross-linguistic analysis of vocabulary in young children: Spanish, Dutch, French, Hebrew, Italian, Korean, and American English. *Child Development, 75,* 1115–1139. (p. 213)

Bornstein, M. H., Tal, J., Rahn, C., Galperin, C. Z., Pecheux, M-G., Lamour, M., Toda, S., Azuma, H., Ogino, M., & Tamis-LeMonda, C. S.

(1992a). Functional analysis of the contents of maternal speech to infants of 5 and 13 months in four cultures: Argentina, France, Japan, and the United States. *Developmental Psychology, 28,* 593–603. (p. 83)

Bornstein, M. H., Tamis-LeMonda, C. S., Tal, J., Ludemann, P., Toda, S., Rahn, C. W., Pecheux, M-G., Azuma, H., Vardi, D. (1992b). Maternal responsiveness to infants in three societies: The United States, France, and Japan. *Child Development, 63,* 808–821. (p. 83)

Bornstein, R. F. (1989). Exposure and affect: Overview and meta-analysis of research, 1968–1987. *Psychological Bulletin, 106,* 265–289. (p. 394)

Bornstein, R. F. (1999). Source amnesia, misattribution, and the power of unconscious perceptions and memories. *Psychoanalytic Psychology, 16,* 155–178. (p. 394)

Bornstein, R. F., Galley, D. J., Leone, D. R., & Kale, A. R. (1991). The temporal stability of ratings of parents: Test-retest reliability and influence of parental contact. *Journal of Social Behavior and Personality, 6,* 641–649. (p. 192)

Boroditsky, R., Fisher, W., & Sand, M. (1995, July). Teenagers and contraception. Section of the Canadian contraception study. *Journal of the Society of Obstetricians and Gynaecologists of Canada, Special Supplement,* p. 22–25. (p. 108)

Boscarino, J. A. (1997). Diseases among men 20 years after exposure to severe stress: Implications for clinical research and medical care. *Psychosomatic Medicine, 59,* 605–614. (p. 270)

Bothwell, R. K., Brigham, J. C., & Malpass, R. S. (1989). Cross-racial identification. *Personality and Social Psychology Bulletin, 15,* 19–25. (p. 390)

Bouchard, T. J., Jr. (1995). Longitudinal studies of personality and intelligence: A behavior genetic and evolutionary psychology perspective. In D. H. Saklofske & M. Zeidner (Eds.), *International handbook of personality and intelligence.* New York: Plenum. (p. 226)

Bouchard, T. J., Jr. (1996). Behavior genetic studies of intelligence, yesterday and today: The long journey from plausibility to proof. *Journal of Biosocial Science, 28,* 527–555. (p. 226)

Bouchard, T. J., Jr. (2004). Genetic influence on human psychological traits. *Current Directions in Psychological Science, 13,* 148–151. (p. 69)

Bowden, E. M., & Beeman, M. J. (1998). Getting the right idea: Semantic activation in the right hemisphere may help solve insight problems. *Psychological Science, 9,* 435–440. (p. 47)

Bower, G. H., & Morrow, D. G. (1990). Mental models in narrative comprehension. *Science, 247,* 44–48. (p. 185)

Bower, J. E., Kemeny, M. E., Taylor, S. E., & Fahey, J. L. (1998). Cognitive processing, discovery of meaning, CD4 decline, and AIDS-related mortality among bereaved HIV-seropositive men. *Journal of Consulting and Clinical Psychology, 66,* 979–986. (pp. 274, 280)

Bower, J. M., & Parsons, L. M. (2003, August). Rethinking the "lesser brain." *Scientific American,* pp. 50–57. (p. 36)

Bowers, T. G., & Clum, G. A. (1988). Relative contribution of specific and nonspecific treatment effects: Meta-analysis of placebo-controlled behavior therapy research. *Psychological Bulletin, 103,* 315–323. (p. 362)

Bowles, S., & Kasindorf, M. (2001, March 6). Friends tell of picked-on but 'normal' kid. *USA Today,* p. 4A. (p. 248)

Bowman, H. (2003, Fall). Interactions between chimpanzees and their human caregivers in captive settings: The effects of gestural communication on reciprocity. *Friends of Washoe, 25(1),* 7–16. (p. 216)

Boyatzis, C. J., Matillo, G. M., & Nesbitt, K. M. (1995). Effects of the 'Mighty Morphin Power Rangers' on children's aggression with peers. *Child Study Journal, 25,* 45–55. (p. 176)

Braden, J. P. (1994). *Deafness, deprivation, and IQ.* New York: Plenum. (p. 228)

Bradley, D. R., Dumais, S. T., & Petry, H. M. (1976). Reply to Cavonius. *Nature, 261,* 78. (p. 143)

Brainerd, C. J. (1996). Piaget: A centennial celebration. *Psychological Science, 7,* 191–195. (p. 72)

Brandon, S., Boakes, J., Glaser, & Green, R. (1998). Recovered memories of childhood sexual abuse: Implications for clinical practice. *British Journal of Psychiatry, 172,* 294–307. (p. 199)

Brannon, L. A., & Brock, T. C. (1994). Perilous underestimation of sex partners' sexual histories in calculating personal AIDS risk. Paper presented to the American Psychological Society convention. (p. 110)

Bransford, J. D., & Johnson, M. K. (1972). Contextual prerequisites for understanding: Some investigations of comprehension and recall. *Journal of Verbal Learning and Verbal Behavior, 11,* 717–726. (p. 185)

Braun, S. (1996). New experiments underscore warnings on maternal drinking. *Science, 273,* 738–739. (p. 67)

Braun, S. (2001, Spring). Seeking insight by prescription. *Cerebrum,* pp. 10-21. (p. 330)

Bray, G. A. (1969). Effect of caloric restriction on energy expenditure in obese patients. *Lancet, 2,* 397–398. (p. 244)

Breedlove, S. M. (1997). Sex on the brain. *Nature, 389,* 801. (p. 115)

Brehm, S., & Brehm, J. W. (1981). *Psychological reactance: A theory of freedom and control.* New York: Academic Press. (p. 387)

Brewer, W. F. (1977). Memory for the pragmatic implications of sentences. *Memory & Cognition, 5,* 673–678. (p. 185)

Brewin, C. R., Andrews, B., Rose, S., & Kirk, M. (1999). Acute stress disorder and posttraumatic stress disorder in victims of violent crime. *American Journal of Psychiatry, 156,* 360–366. (p. 320)

Brickman, P., Coates, D., & Janoff-Bulman, R. J. (1978). Lottery winners and accident victims: Is happiness relative? *Journal of Personality and Social Psychology, 36,* 917–927. (p. 262)

Brief, A. P., & Weiss, H. M. (2002). Organizational behavior: Affect in the workplace. *Annual Review of Psychology, 53,* 279–307. (p. 410)

Brislin, R. (1993). *Understanding culture's influence on behavior.* Fort Worth, TX: Harcourt Brace. (p. 316)

Brislin, R. W. (1988). Increasing awareness of class, ethnicity, culture, and race by expanding on students' own experiences. In I. Cohen (Ed.), *The G. Stanley Hall Lecture Series.* Washington, DC: American Psychological Association. (p. 80)

British Psychological Society. (1993). Ethical principles for conducting research with human participants. *The Psychologist: Bulletin of the British Psychological Society, 6,* 33–36. (pp. 20, 302)

Brody, J. E. (1999, November 30). Yesterday's precocious puberty is norm today. *New York Times* (www.nytimes.com). (p. 84)

Brody, J. E. (2003, September). Addiction: A brain ailment, not a moral lapse. *New York Times* (www.nytimes.com). (p. 331)

Brody, J. E. (2003, December 23). Stampede of diabetes as U.S. races to obesity. *New York Times* (www.nytimes.com). (p. 245)

Brodzinsky, D. M., & Schechter, M. D. (Eds.) (1990). *The psychology of adoption.* New York: Oxford University Press. (p. 82)

Bronner, E. (1998, February 25). U.S. high school seniors among worst in math and science. *New York Times* (www.nytimes.com). (p. 229)

Brown, A. S. (2003). A review of the déjà vu experience. *Psychological Bulletin, 129,* 394–413. (p. 191)

Brown, A. S. (2004). *The déjà vu experience*. East Sussex, England: Psychology Press. (p. 191)

Brown, A. S., Begg, M. D., Gravenstein, S., Schaefer, C. A., Wyatt, R. J., Bresnahan, M., Babulas, V. P., & Susser, E. S. (2004). Serologic evidence of prenatal influenza in the etiology of schizophrenia. *Archives of General Psychiatry, 61*, 774–780. (p. 343)

Brown, A. S., Schaefer, C. A., Wyatt, R. J., Goetz, R., Begg, M. D., Gorman, J. M., & Susser, E. S. (2000). Maternal exposure to respiratory infections and adult schizophrenia spectrum disorders: A prospective birth cohort study. *Schizophrenia Bulletin, 26*, 287–295. (p. 343)

Brown, E. L., & Deffenbacher, K. (1979). *Perception and the senses*. New York: Oxford University Press. (p. 136)

Brown, G. K., Ten Have, T., Henriques, G. R., Xie, S. X., Hollander, J. E., & Beck, A. T. (2005). Cognitive therapy for the prevention of suicide attempts. *JAMA: Journal of the American Medical Association, 294*, 563–570. (p. 362)

Brown, J. D., Steele, J. R., & Walsh-Childers, K. (2002). *Sexual teens, sexual media: Investigating media's influence on adolescent sexuality*. Mahwah, NJ: Erlbaum. (p. 111)

Brown, S. W., Garry, M., Loftus, E., Silver, B., DuBois, K., & DuBreuil, S. (1996). People's beliefs about memory: Why don't we have better memories? Paper presented at the American Psychological Society convention. (p. 195)

Brownell, K. D., & Wadden, T. A. (1992). Etiology and treatment of obesity: Understanding a serious, prevalent, and refractory disorder. *Journal of Consulting and Clinical Psychology, 60*, 505–517. (p. 244)

Browning, C. (1992). *Ordinary men: Reserve police battalion 101 and the final solution in Poland*. New York: HarperCollins. (p. 383)

Brownmiller, S. (1975). *Against our will: Men, women, and rape*. New York: Simon and Schuster. (p. 113)

Bruck, M., & Ceci, S. (2004). Forensic developmental psychology: Unveiling four common misconceptions. *Current Directions in Psychological Science, 15*, 229–232. (p. 198)

Bruck, M., & Ceci, S. J. (1999). The suggestibility of children's memory. *Annual Review of Psychology, 50*, 419–439. (p. 198)

Bruer, J. T. (1999). *The myth of the first three years: A new understanding of early brain development and lifelong learning*. New York: Free Press. (p. 227)

Bryant, R. A. (2001). Posttraumatic stress disorder and traumatic brain injury: Can they co-exist? *Clinical Psychology Review, 21*, 931–948. (p. 199)

Buckingham, M. (2001, August). Quoted by P. LaBarre, "Marcus Buckingham thinks your boss has an attitude problem." *The Magazine* (fastcompany.com/online/49/buckingham.html). (pp. 411)

Buckingham, M., & Clifton, D. O. (2001). *Now, discover your strengths*. New York: Free Press. (pp. 409)

Buckley, C. (2007, January 3). Man is rescued by stranger on subway tracks. *New York Times* (www.nytimes.com). (p. 398)

Buckley, K. E., & Leary, M. R. (2001). Perceived acceptance as a predictor of social, emotional, and academic outcomes. Paper presented at the Society of Personality and Social Psychology annual convention. (p. 247)

Buehler, R., Griffin, D., & Ross, M. (1994). Exploring the "planning fallacy": Why people underestimate their task completion times. *Journal of Personality and Social Psychology, 67*, 366–381. (p. 208)

Buka, S. L., Goldstein, J. M., Seidman, L. J., Zornberg, G., Donatelli, J-A. A., Denny, L. R., & Tsuang, M. T. (1999). Prenatal complications, genetic vulnerability, and schizophrenia: The New England longitudinal studies of schizophrenia. *Psychiatric Annals, 29*, 151–156. (p. 343)

Bullough, V. (1990). The Kinsey scale in historical perspective. In D. P. McWhirter, S. A. Sanders, & J. M. Reinisch (Eds.), *Homosexuality/heterosexuality: Concepts of sexual orientation*. New York: Oxford University Press. (p. 114)

Buquet, R. (1988). Le reve et les deficients visuels (Dreams and the visually-impaired). *Psychanalyse-a-l'Universite, 13*, 319–327. (p. 57)

Bureau of Labor Statistics. (2004, September 14). *American time-user survey summary*. Washington, DC: United States Department of Labor (www.bls.gov). (p. 107)

Bureau of the Census. (2004). *Statistical abstract of the United States 2004*. Washington, DC: U.S. Government Printing Office. (p. 366)

Burger, J. M. (1987). Increased performance with increased personal control: A self-presentation interpretation. *Journal of Experimental Social Psychology, 23*, 350–360. (p. 414)

Burgess, M., Enzle, M. E., & Schmaltz, R. (2004). Defeating the potentially deleterious effects of externally imposed deadlines: Practitioners' rules-of-thumb. *Personality and Social Psychology Bulletin, 30*, 868–877. (p. 412)

Buri, J. R., Louiselle, P. A., Misukanis, T. M., & Mueller, R. A. (1988). Effects of parental authoritarianism and authoritativeness on self-esteem. *Personality and Social Psychology Bulletin, 14*, 271–282. (p. 80)

Burish, T. G., & Carey, M. P. (1986). Conditioned aversive responses in cancer chemotherapy patients: Theoretical and developmental analysis. *Journal of Counseling and Clinical Psychology, 54*, 593–600. (p. 163)

Burkholder, R. (2005a, January 11). Chinese far wealthier than a decade ago—but are they happier? *Gallup Poll News Service* (www.gallup.com). (p. 264)

Burkholder, R. (2005b, January 18). China's citizens optimistic, yet not entirely satisfied. *Gallup Poll News Service* (www.gallup.com). (p. 264)

Burns, B. C. (2004). The effects of speed on skilled chess performance. *Psychological Science, 15*, 442–447. (p. 211)

Bush, G. W. (2001, May 1). Speech to the National Defense University, Washington, DC. (p. 9)

Bushman, B. J. (1993). Human aggression while under the influence of alcohol and other drugs: An integrative research review. *Current Directions in Psychological Science, 2*, 148–152. (p. 392)

Bushman, B. J. (2002). Does venting anger feed or extinguish the flame? Catharsis, rumination, distraction, anger, and aggressive responding. *Personality and Social Psychology Bulletin, 28*, 724–731. (p. 260)

Buss, A. H. (1989). Personality as traits. *American Psychologist, 44*, 1378–1388. (p. 304)

Buss, D. M. (1994). The strategies of human mating: People worldwide are attracted to the same qualities in the opposite sex. *American Scientist*, p 238–249. (pp. 117, 118)

Buss, D. M. (1995). Evolutionary psychology: A new paradigm for psychological science. *Psychological Inquiry, 6*, 1–30. (p. 118)

Buss, D. M. (1996). Sexual conflict: Evolutionary insights into feminism and the "battle of the sexes." In D. M. Buss & N. M. Malamuth (Eds.), *Sex, power, conflict: Evolutionary and feminist perspectives*. New York: Oxford University Press. (p. 119)

Buss, D. M. (2000). *The dangerous passion: Why jealousy is as necessary as love and sex*. New York: Free Press. (p. 119)

Butler, R. A. (1954, February). Curiosity in monkeys. *Scientific American*, pp. 70–75. (p. 236)

Bynum, R. (2004, November 1). Associated Press article. (p. 137)

Byrne, D. (1982). Predicting human sexual behavior. In A. G. Kraut (Ed.), *The G. Stanley Hall Lecture Series* (Vol. 2). Washington, DC: American Psychological Association. (p. 110, 161)

Byrne, J. (2003, September 21). From correspondence reported by Michael Shermer, E-Skeptic for September 21, 2003, from The Skeptics Society. (p. 152)

Byrne, R. W. (1991, May/June). Brute intellect. *The Sciences*, pp. 42–47. (p. 216)

Cacioppo, J. T., Berntson, G. G., Klein, D. J., & Poehlmann, K. M. (1997). The psychophysiology of emotion across the lifespan. *Annual Review of Gerontology and Geriatrics, 17*, 27. (p. 252)

Cahill, L. (1994). (Beta)-adrenergic activation and memory for emotional events. *Nature, 371*, 702–704. (p. 187)

Cale, E. M., Lilienfeld, S. O. (2002). Sex differences in psychopathy and antisocial personality disorder: A review and integration. *Clinical Psychology Review, 22*, 1179–1207. (p. 324)

Call, K. T., Riedel, A. A., Hein, K., McLoyd, V., Petersen, A., & Kipke, M. (2002). Adolescent health and well-being in the twenty-first century: A global perspective. *Journal of Research on Adolescence, 12*, 69–98. (p. 111)

Callaghan, T., Rochat, P., Lillard, A., Claux, M. L., Odden, H., Itakura, S., Tapanya, S., & Singh, S. (2005). Synchrony in the onset of mental-state reasoning. *Psychological Science, 16*, 378–384. (p. 75)

Callicott, J. H., & 11 others. (2005). Variation in DISC1 affects hippocampal structure and function and increased risk for schizophrenia. *Proceedings of the National Academy of Sciences, 102*, 8627–8632. (p. 344)

Calvo-Merino, B., Glaser, D. E., Grèzes, J., Passingham, R. E., & Haggard, P. (2004). Action observation and acquired motor skills: An fMRI study with expert dancers. *Cerebral Cortex, 15*, 1243–1249. (p. 214)

Campbell, D. T. (1975). On the conflicts between biological and social evolution and between psychology and moral tradition. *American Psychologist, 30*, 1103–1126. (p. 263)

Campbell, D. T., & Specht, J. C. (1985). Altruism: Biology, culture, and religion. *Journal of Social and Clinical Psychology, 3*(1), 33–42. (p. 299)

Campbell, S. (1986). *The Loch Ness Monster: The evidence.* Willingborough, Northamptonshire, U.K.: Acquarian Press. (p. 150)

Camper, J. (1990, February 7). Drop pompom squad, U. of I. rape study says. *Chicago Tribune*, p. 1. (p. 326)

Camperio-Ciani, A., Corna, F., & Capiluppi, C. (2004). Evidence for maternally inherited factors favouring male homosexuality and promoting female fecundity. *Proceedings of the Royal Society of London B, 271*, 2217–2221. (p. 116)

Canli, T., Desmond, J. E., Zhao, Z., & Gabrieli, J. D. E. (2002). Sex differences in the neural basis of emotional memories. *Proceedings of the National Academy of Sciences, 99*, 10789–10794. (p. 257)

Cannon, W. B. (1929). *Bodily changes in pain, hunger, fear, and rage.* New York: Branford. (p. 271)

Cannon, W. B., & Washburn, A. (1912). An explanation of hunger. *American Journal of Physiology, 29*, 441–454. (p. 238)

Cantor, N., & Kihlstrom, J. F. (1987). *Personality and social intelligence.* Englewood Cliffs, NJ: Prentice Hall. (p. 221)

Caplan, N., Choy, M. H., & Whitmore, J. K. (1992, February). Indochinese refugee families and academic achievement. *Scientific American*, pp. 36–42. (pp. 82, 229)

Carducci, B. J., Cosby, P. C., & Ward, D. D. (1978). Sexual arousal and interpersonal evaluations. *Journal of Experimental Social Psychology, 14*, 449–457. (p. 397)

Carey, G. (1990). Genes, fears, phobias, and phobic disorders. *Journal of Counseling and Development, 68*, 628–632. (p. 322)

Carlson, M. (1995, August 29). Quoted by S. Blakeslee, In brain's early growth, timetable may be crucial. *New York Times*, pp. C1, C3. (p. 79)

Carlson, M., Charlin, V., & Miller, N. (1988). Positive mood and helping behavior: A test of six hypotheses. *Journal of Personality and Social Psychology, 55*, 211–229. (p. 400)

Carlson, S. (1985). A double-blind test of astrology. *Nature, 318*, 419–425. (p. 302)

Carrière, G. (2003). Parent and child factors associated with youth obesity. *Statistics Canada, Catalogue 82–003*, Supplement to Health Reports, 2003. (p. 244)

Carroll, J. (2006, August 7). American workers would be happier in same job with higher pay: Seventy-three percent of workers say they would be happier if they made more money. *Gallup Poll* (poll.gallup.com). (p. 262)

Carroll, J. (2007, August 16). Most Americans approve of interracial marriages. Gallup News Service (www.gallup.com). (p. 388)

Carroll, J. (2008, January 2). Time pressures, stress common for Americans. Gallup Poll (www.gallup.com). (p. 269)

Carter, R. (1998). *Mapping the mind.* Berkeley, CA: University of California Press. (p. 30)

Cartwright, R. D. (1978). *A primer on sleep and dreaming.* Reading, MA: Addison-Wesley. (p. 53)

CASA. (2003). *The formative years: Pathways to substance abuse among girls and young women ages 8–22.* New York, NY: National Center on Addiction and Substance Use, Columbia University. (pp. 327, 333)

Cash, T., & Janda, L. H. (1984, December). The eye of the beholder. *Psychology Today*, pp. 46–52. (p. 395)

Caspi, A., Harrington, H., Milne, B., Amell, J. W., Theodore, R. F., & Moffitt, T. E. (2003). Children's behavioral styles at age 3 are linked to their adult personality traits at age 26. *Journal of Personality, 71*, 496–513. (pp. 98, 338)

Cassidy, J., & Shaver, P. R. (1999). *Handbook of attachment.* New York: Guilford. (p. 78)

Castillo, R. J. (1997). *Culture and mental illness: A client-centered approach.* Pacific Grove, CA: Brooks/Cole. (pp. 313, 315)

Castonguay, L. G., & Goldfried, M. R. (1994). Psychotherapy integration: An idea whose time has come. *Applied & Preventive Psychology, 3*, 159–172. (p. 350)

Catanese, K. R., & Tice, D. M. (2005). The effect of rejection on antisocial behaviors: Social exclusion produces aggressive behaviors. In K. D. Williams, J. P. Forgas, & W. Von Hippel (Eds.), *The social outcast: Ostracism, social exclusion, rejection, and bullying.* New York: Psychology Press. (p. 392)

Cattell, R. B. (1963). Theory of fluid and crystallized intelligence: A critical experiment. *Journal of Educational Psychology, 54*, 1–22. (p. 93)

Cavalli-Sforza, L., Menozzi, P., & Piazza, A. (1994). *The history and geography of human genes.* Princeton, NJ: Princeton University Press. (p. 228)

Cavigelli, S. A., & McClintock, M. K. (2003). Fear of novelty in infant rats predicts adult corticosterone dynamics and an early death. *Proceedings of the National Academy of Sciences, 100*, 16131–16136. (p. 272)

Cawley, B. D., Keeping, L. M., & Levy, P. E. (1998). Participation in the performance appraisal process and employee reactions: A meta-analytic review of field investigations. *Journal of Applied Psychology, 83*, 615–633. (p. 414)

CDC. (2004). Teenagers in the United States: Sexual activity, contraceptive use, and childbearing, 2002. A fact sheet for series 23, number 24. DHHS Publication (PHS) 2005–1976. (pp. 108, 109)

Ceci, S. J. (1993). Cognitive and social factors in children's testimony. Master Lecture, American Psychological Association convention. (p. 198)

Ceci, S. J., & Bruck, M. (1993). Child witnesses: Translating research into policy. *Social Policy Report (Society for Research in Child Development), 7(3)*, 1–30. (p. 198)

Ceci, S. J., & Bruck, M. (1995). *Jeopardy in the courtroom: A scientific analysis of children's testimony.* Washington, DC: American Psychological Association. (p. 198)

Ceci, S. J., Huffman, M. L. C., Smith, E., & Loftus, E. F. (1994). Repeatedly thinking about a non-event: Source misattributions among preschoolers. *Consciousness and Cognition, 3*, 388–407. (p. 198)

Centers for Disease Control (2003). Who should get a flu shot (influenza vaccine). National Center for Infectious Diseases (www.cdc.gov/ncidod/diseases/flu/who.htm). (p. 343)

Centers for Disease Control (2007, accessed May 31). Basic statistics. www.cdc.gov/hib/topics/surveillance/basic.htm#hivaidsage (p. 111)

Centers for Disease Control (2008). [report showing that 1 in 4 14- to 19-year old women and half of those sexually active have STDs] Centers for Disease Control (2007, accessed May 31). Basic statistics. www.cdc.gov/hiv/topics/surveillance/basic.htm#hivaidsage. (p. 110)

Centers for Disease Control Vietnam Experience Study. (1988). Health status of Vietnam veterans. *Journal of the American Medical Association, 259*, 2701–2709. (p. 320)

Cerella, J. (1985). Information processing rates in the elderly. *Psychological Bulletin, 98*, 67–83. (p. 93)

CFI. (2003, July). International developments. Report. Amherst, NY: Center for Inquiry International. (p. 153)

Chamove, A. S. (1980). Nongenetic induction of acquired levels of aggression. *Journal of Abnormal Psychology, 89*, 469–488. (p. 175)

Chang, E. C. (2001). Cultural influences on optimism and pessimism: Differences in Western and Eastern construals of the self. In E. C. Chang (Ed.), *Optimism and pessimism.* Washington, DC: APA Books. (p. 279)

Chang, P. P., Ford, D. E., Meoni, L. A., Wang, N-Y., & Klag, M. J. (2002). Anger in young men and subsequent premature cardiovascular disease: The precursors study. *Archives of Internal Medicine, 162*, 901–906. (p. 275)

Chaplin, W. F., Phillips, J. B., Brown, J. D., Clanton, N. R., & Stein, J. L. (2000). Handshaking, gender, personality, and first impressions. *Journal of Personality and Social Psychology, 79*, 110–117. (p. 257)

Charles, S. T., Reynolds, C. A., & Gatz, M. (2001). Age-related differences and change in positive and negative affect over 23 years. *Journal of Personality and Social Psychology, 80*, 136–151. (p. 97)

Charpak, G., & Broch, H. (2004). *Debunked! ESP, telekinesis, and other pseudoscience.* Baltimore, MD: Johns Hopkins University Press. (p. 152)

Chartrand, T. L., & Bargh, J. A. (1999). The chameleon effect: The perception-behavior link and social interaction. *Journal of Personality and Social Psychology, 76*, 893–910. (p. 380)

Chaudhari, N., Landin, A. M., & Roper, S. D. (2000). A metabotropic glutamate receptor variant functions as a taste receptor. *Nature Neuroscience, 3*, 113–119. (p. 140)

Cheek, J. M., & Melchior, L. A. (1990). Shyness, self-esteem, and self-consciousness. In H. Leitenberg (Ed.), *Handbook of social and evaluation anxiety.* New York: Plenum. (p. 309)

Chess, S., & Thomas, A. (1987). *Know your child: An authoritative guide for today's parents.* New York: Basic Books. (p. 68)

Child Trends. (2001, August). Facts at a glance. (www.childtrends.org). (p. 111)

Chisholm, K. (1998). A three year follow-up of attachment and indiscriminate friendliness in children adopted from Romanian orphanages. *Child Development, 69*, 1092–1106. (p. 79)

Choi, I., & Choi, Y. (2002). Culture and self-concept flexibility. *Personality and Social Psychology Bulletin, 28*, 1508–1517. (p. 309)

Chomsky, N. (1972). *Language and mind.* New York: Harcourt Brace (p. 211)

Chorpita, B. F., & Barlow, D. H. (1998). The development of anxiety: The role of control in the early environment. *Psychological Bulletin, 124*, 3–21. (p. 321)

Christensen, A., & Jacobson, N. S. (1994). Who (or what) can do psychotherapy: The status and challenge of nonprofessional therapies. *Psychological Science, 5*, 8–14. (p. 363)

Christophersen, E. R., & Edwards, K. J. (1992). Treatment of elimination disorders: State of the art 1991. *Applied & Preventive Psychology, 1*, 15–22. (p. 355)

Chua, H. F., Boland, J. E., & Nisbett, R. E. (2005). Cultural variation in eye movements during scene perception. *Proceedings of the National Academy of Sciences, 102*, 12629–12633. (p. 376)

Chugani, H. T., & Phelps, M. E. (1986). Maturational changes in cerebral function in infants determined by 18FDG Positron Emission Tomography. *Science, 231*, 840–843. (p. 70)

CIA (2008). *The world factbook.* Washington, DC: Central Intelligence Agency (cia.gov/library/publications/the-world-factbook/geos/xx.html#People). (p. 92)

Cialdini, R. B. (1993). *Influence: Science and practice (3rd ed.).* New York: HarperCollins. (p. 378)

Cialdini, R. B., & Richardson, K. D. (1980). Two indirect tactics of image management: Basking and blasting. *Journal of Personality and Social Psychology, 39*, 406–415. (p. 390)

Clack, B., Dixon, J., & Tredoux, C. (2005). Eating together apart: Patterns of segregation in a multi-ethnic cafeteria. *Journal of Community and Applied Social Psychology, 15*, 1–16. (p. 401)

Clark, A., Seidler, A., & Miller, M. (2001). Inverse association between sense of humor and coronary heart disease. *International Journal of Cardiology, 80*, 87–88. (p. 279)

Coffey, C. E. (Ed.) (1993). *Clinical science of electroconvulsive therapy.* Washington, DC: American Psychiatric Press. (p. 368)

Cohen, D. (1995, June 17). Now we are one, or two, or three. *New Scientist,* pp. 14–15. (p. 323)

Cohen, H., Kaplan, Z., Kotler, M., Kouperman, I., Moisa, R., & Grisaru, N. (2005). Repetitive transcranial magnetic stimulation of the right dorsolateral prefrontal cortex in posttraumatic stress disorder: A double-blind, placebo-controlled study. *American Journal of Psychiatry, 16*, 515–524. (p. 369)

Cohen, K. M. (2002). Relationships among childhood sex-atypical behavior, spatial ability, handedness, and sexual orientation in men. *Archives of Sexual Behavior, 31*, 129–143. (p. 116)

Cohen, S. (1988). Psychosocial models of the role of social support in the etiology of physical disease. *Health Psychology, 7*, 269–297. (p. 280)

Cohen, S. (2004). Social relationships and health. *American Psychologist, 59*, 676–684. (p. 280)

Cohen, S., & Pressman, S. D. (2006b). Positive affect and health. *Current Directions in Psychological Science, 15*, 122–125. (p. 273)

Cohen, S., Alper, C. M., Doyle, W. J., Treanor, J. J., & Turner, R. B. (2006a). Positive emotional style predicts resistance to illness after experimental exposure to rhinovirus or influenza A virus. *Psychosomatic Medicine, 68*, 809–815. (p. 273)

Cohen, S., Doyle, W. J., & Skoner, D. P. (1999). Psychological stress, cytokine production, and severity of upper respiratory illness. *Psychosomatic Medicine, 61*, 175–180. (p. 273)

Cohen, S., Doyle, W. J., Skoner, D. P., Rabin, B. S., & Gwaltney, J. M., Jr. (1997). Social ties and susceptibility to the common cold. *Journal of the American Medical Association, 277*, 1940–1944. (p. 280)

Cohen, S., Doyle, W. J., Turner, R., Alper, C. M., & Skoner, D. P. (2003). Sociability and susceptibility to the common cold. *Psychological Science, 14*, 389–395. (p. 273)

Cohen, S., Kaplan, J. R., Cunnick, J. E., Manuck, S. B., & Rabin, B. S. (1992). Chronic social stress, affiliation, and cellular immune response in nonhuman primates. *Psychological Science, 3*, 301–304. (p. 273)

Colapinto, J. (2000). *As nature made him: The boy who was raised as a girl.* New York: HarperCollins. (p. 106)

Colarelli, S. M., Spranger, J. L., & Hechanova, M. R. (2006). Women, power, and sex composition in small groups: An evolutionary perspective. *Journal of Organizational Behavior, 27*, 163–184. (p. 104)

Colcombe, S. & Kramer, A. F. (2003). Fitness effects on the cognitive function of older adults: A meta-analytic study. *Psychological Science, 14*, 125–130. (p. 94)

Colcombe, S. J., Kramer, A. F., Erickson, K. I., Scalf, P., McAuley, E., Cohen, N. J., Webb, A., Jerome, G. J., Marquex, D. X., & Elavsky, S. (2004). Cardiovascular fitness, cortical plasticity, and aging. *Proceedings of the National Academy of Sciences, 101*, 3316–3321. (p. 94)

Coleman, P. D., & Flood, D. G. (1986). Dendritic proliferation in the aging brain as a compensatory repair mechanism. In D. F. Swaab, E. Fliers, M. Mirmiram, W. A. Van Gool, & F. Van Haaren (Eds.), *Progress in brain research (Vol. 20)*. New York: Elsevier. (p. 94)

Collins, D. W., & Kimura, D. (1997). A large sex difference on a two-dimensional mental rotation task. *Behavioral Neuroscience, 111*, 845–849. (p. 229)

Collins, R. L., Elliott, M. N., Berry, S. H., Danouse, D. E., Kunkel, D., Hunter, S. B., & Miu, A. (2004). Watching sex on television predicts adolescent initiation of sexual behavior. *Pediatrics, 114*, 280–289. (p. 15)

Collinson, S. L., MacKay, C. E., James, A. C., Quested, D. J., Phillips, T., Roberts, N., & Crow, T. J. (2003). Brain volume, asymmetry and intellectual impairment in relation to sex in early-onset schizophrenia. *British Journal of Psychiatry, 183*, 114–120. (p. 343)

Comer, R. J. (2004). *Abnormal psychology*. New York: Worth Publishers. (p. 314)

Consensus Conference. (1985). Electroconvulsive therapy. *Journal of the American Medical Association, 254*, 2103–2108. (p. 368)

Consumer Reports. (1995, November). Does therapy help? pp. 734–739. (p. 360)

Conway, M. A., Wang, Q., Hanyu, K., & Haque, S. (2005). A cross-cultural investigation of autobiographical memory. On the universality and cultural variation of the reminiscence bump. *Journal of Cross-Cultural Psychology, 36*, 739–749. (p. 92)

Cooke, L. J., Wardle, J., & Gibson, E. L. (2003). Relationship between parental report of food neophobia and everyday food consumption in 2–6-year-old children. *Appetite, 41*, 205–206. (p. 140)

Coopersmith, S. (1967). *The antecedents of self-esteem*. San Francisco: Freeman. (p. 80)

Coren, S. (1996). *Sleep thieves: An eye-opening exploration into the science and mysteries of sleep.* New York: Free Press. (pp. 53, 54, 55)

Corey, D. P., & 15 others. (2004). TRPA1 is a candidate for the mechanosensitive transduction channel of vertebrate hair cells. *Nature* (advance online publication, October 13, at www.nature.com). (p. 134)

Corina, D. P. (1998). The processing of sign language: Evidence from aphasia. In B. Stemmer & H. A. Whittaker (Eds.), *Handbook of neurolinguistics*. San Diego: Academic Press. (p. 47)

Corina, D. P., Vaid, J., & Bellugi, U. (1992). The linguistic basis of left hemisphere specialization. *Science, 255*, 1258–1260. (p. 47)

Corkin, S., quoted by R. Adelson (2005, September). Lessons from H. M. *Monitor on Psychology*, p. 59. (p. 181)

Correll, J., Park, B., Judd, C. M., & Wittenbrink, B. (2002). The police officer's dilemma: Using ethnicity to disambiguate potentially threatening individuals. *Journal of Personality and Social Psychology, 83*, 1314–1329. (p. 389)

Costa, P. T., Jr., Zonderman, A. B., McCrae, R. R., Cornoni-Huntley, J., Locke, B. Z., & Barbano, H. E. (1987). Longitudinal analyses of psychological well-being in a national sample: Stability of mean levels. *Journal of Gerontology, 42*, 50–55. (p. 97)

Costello, E. J., Compton, S. N., Keeler, G., & Angold, A. (2003). Relationships between poverty and psychopathology: A natural experiment. *Journal of the American Medical Association, 290*, 2023–2029. (p. 15)

Couli, J. T., Vidal, F., Nazarian, B., & Macar, F. (2004). Functional anatomy of the attentional modulation of time estimation. *Science, 303*, 1506–1508. (p. 408)

Courneya, K. S., & Carron, A. V. (1992). The home advantage in sports competitions: A literature review. *Journal of Sport and Exercise Psychology, 14*, 13–27. (p. 384)

Courtney, J. G., Longnecker, M. P., Theorell, T., & de Verdier, M. G. (1993). Stressful life events and the risk of colorectal cancer. *Epidemiology, 4*, 407–414. (p. 274)

Cowart, B. J. (1981). Development of taste perception in humans: Sensitivity and preference throughout the life span. *Psychological Bulletin, 90*, 43–73. (p. 140)

Crabbe, J. C. (2002). Genetic contributions to addiction. *Annual Review of Psychology, 53*, 435–462. (p. 333)

Crabtree, S. (2005, January 13). Engagement keeps the doctor away. *Gallup Management Journal* (gmj.gallup.com). (p. 411)

Crandall, C. S. (1994). Prejudice against fat people: Ideology and self-interest. *Journal of Personality and Social Psychology, 66*, 882–894. (p. 242)

Crandall, C. S. (1995). Do parents discriminate against their heavyweight daughters? *Personality and Social Psychology Bulletin, 21*, 724–735. (p. 242)

Crocker, J., & Major, B. (1989). Social stigma and self-esteem: The self-protective properties of stigma, *Psychological Review, 89,* 608–630. (p. 307)

Crocker, J., & Park, L. E. (2004). The costly pursuit of self-esteem. *Psychological Bulletin, 130,* 392–414. (p. 306)

Crocker, J., Thompson, L. L., McGraw, K. M., & Ingerman, C. (1987). Downward comparison, prejudice, and evaluation of others: Effects of self-esteem and threat. *Journal of Personality and Social Psychology, 52,* 907–916. (p. 390)

Croft, R. J., Klugman, A., Baldeweg, T., & Gruzelier, J. H. (2001). Electrophysiological evidence of serotonergic impairment in long-term MDMA ("Ecstasy") users. *American Journal of Psychiatry, 158,* 1687–1692. (p. 330)

Crook, T. H., & West, R. L. (1990). Name recall performance across the adult life-span. *British Journal of Psychology, 81,* 335–340. (p. 93)

Cross, S., & Markus, H. (1991). Possible selves across the life span. *Human Development, 34,* 230–255. (p. 305)

Cross-National Collaborative Group. (1992). The changing rate of major depression. *Journal of the American Medical Association, 268,* 3098–3105. (p. 338)

Crowell, J. A., & Waters, E. (1994). Bowlby's theory grown up: The role of attachment in adult love relationships. *Psychological Inquiry, 5,* 1–22. (p. 78)

Csikszentmihalyi, M. (1990). *Flow: The psychology of optimal experience.* New York: Harper & Row. (p. 407)

Csikszentmihalyi, M. (1999). If we are so rich, why aren't we happy? *American Psychologist, 54,* 821–827. (pp. 262, 407)

Csikszentmihalyi, M., & Hunter, J. (2003). Happiness in everyday life: The uses of experience sampling. *Journal of Happiness Studies, 4,* 185–199. (p. 88)

Cunningham, M. R., & others. (2005). "Their ideas of beauty are, on the whole, the same as ours": Consistency and variability in the cross-cultural perception of female physical attractiveness. *Journal of Personality and Social Psychology, 68,* 261–279. (p. 396)

Cunningham, W. A., Johnson, M. K., Raye, C. L., Gatenby, J. C., Gore, J. C., & Banaji, M. R. (2004). Separable neural components in the processing of Black and White faces. *Psychological Science, 15,* 806–813. (p. 389)

Curtis, G. C., Magee, W. J., Eaton, W. W., Wittchen, H-U., & Kessler, R. C. (1998). Specific fears and phobias: Epidemiology and classification. *British Journal of Psychiatry, 173,* 212–217. (p. 319)

Curtis, R. C., & Miller, K. (1986). Believing another likes or dislikes you: Behaviors making the beliefs come true. *Journal of Personality and Social Psychology, 51,* 284–290. (p. 396)

Cynkar, A. (2007, June). The changing gender composition of psychology. *Monitor on Psychology,* 46–47. (p. 107)

Dabbs, J. M., Jr. (2000). *Heroes, rogues, and lovers: Testosterone and behavior.* New York: McGraw-Hill. (p. 110)

Dabbs, J. M., Jr., Riad, J. K., & Chance, S. E. (2001a). Testosterone and ruthless homicide. *Personality and Individual Differences, 31,* 599–603. (p. 391)

Dabbs, J. M., Jr., Ruback, R. B., & Besch, N. F. (1987). Male saliva testosterone following conversations with male and female partners. Paper presented at the American Psychological Association convention. (p. 110)

Damasio, A. (2003). *Looking for Spinoza: Joy, sorrow, and the feeling brain.* New York: Harcourt. (p. 249)

Damasio, H., Grabowski, T., Frank, R., Galaburda, A. M., & Damasio, A. R. (1994). The return of Phineas Gage: Clues about the brain from the skull of a famous patient. *Science, 264,* 1102–1105. (p. 43)

Damon, W. (1995). *Greater expectations: Overcoming the culture of indulgence in America's homes and schools.* New York: Free Press. (p. 306)

Danner, D. D., Snowdon, D. A., & Friesen, W. V. (2001). Positive emotions in early life and longevity: Findings from the Nun Study. *Journal of Personality and Social Psychology, 80,* 804–813. (p. 279)

Danso, H., & Esses, V. (2001). Black experimenters and the intellectual test performance of white participants: The tables are turned. *Journal of Experimental Social Psychology, 37,* 158–165. (p. 230)

Darley, J. M., & Latané, B. (1968a). Bystander intervention in emergencies: Diffusion of responsibility. *Journal of Personality and Social Psychology, 8,* 377–383. (pp. 399, 400)

Darley, J. M., & Latané, B. (1968b, December). When will people help in a crisis? *Psychology Today,* pp. 54–57, 70–71. (p. 399)

Darrach, B., & Norris, J. (1984, August). An American tragedy. *Life,* pp. 58–74. (p. 324)

Darwin, C. (1859). *On the origin of species by means of natural selection.* London: John Murray. (p. 119)

Daum, I., & Schugens, M. M. (1996). On the cerebellum and classical conditioning. *Psychological Science, 5,* 58–61. (p. 189)

Davey, G. C. L. (1995). Preparedness and phobias: Specific evolved associations or a generalized expectancy bias? *Behavioral and Brain Sciences, 18,* 289–297. (p. 322)

Davidson, R. J. (2000). Affective style, psychopathology, and resilience: Brain mechanisms and plasticity. *American Psychologist, 55,* 1196–1209. (p. 253)

Davidson, R. J. (2003). Affective neuroscience and psychophysiology: Toward a synthesis. *Psychophysiology, 40,* 655–665. (p. 253)

Davidson, R. J., Kabat-Zinn, J., Schumacher, J., Rosenkranz, M., Muller, D., Santorelli, S. F., Urbanowski, F., Harrington, A., Bonus, K., & Sheridan, J. F. (2003). Alterations in brain and immune function produced by mindfulness meditation. *Psychosomatic Medicine, 65,* 564–570. (p. 283)

Davidson, R. J., Pizzagalli, D., Nitschke, J. B., & Putnam, K. (2002). Depression: Perspectives from affective neuroscience. *Annual Review of Psychology, 53,* 545–574. (p. 338)

Davidson, R. J., Putnam, K. M., & Larson, C. L. (2000). Dysfunction in the neural circuitry of emotion regulation—a possible prelude to violence. *Science, 289,* 591–594. (p. 391)

Davies, D. R., Matthews, G., & Wong, C. S. K. (1991). Aging and work. *International Review of Industrial and Organizational Psychology, 6,* 149–211. (p. 95)

Davies, P. (1992). *The mind of God: The scientific basis for a rational world.* New York: Simon & Schuster. (p. 120)

Davies, P. (1999). *The fifth miracle: The search for the origin and meaning of life.* New York: Simon & Schuster. (p. 120)

Davies, P. (2004, April 14). Into the 21st century. *Metaviews* (www.metanexus.net). (p. 120)

Davis, J. O., & Phelps, J. A. (1995a). Twins with schizophrenia: Genes or germs? *Schizophrenia Bulletin, 21,* 13–18. (p. 344)

Davis, J. O., Phelps, J. A., & Bracha, H. S. (1995b). Prenatal development of monozygotic twins and concordance for schizophrenia. *Schizophrenia Bulletin, 21,* 357–366. (p. 344)

Davis, S., Rees, M., Ribot, J., Moufarege, A., Rodenberg, C., & Purdie, D. (2003). Efficacy and safety of testosterone patches for the treatment of low sexual desire in surgically menopausal women. Presented to the American Society for Reproductive Medicine, San Antonio, October 11–15. (p. 110)

Dawes, R. M. (1994). *House of cards: Psychology and psychotherapy built on myth.* New York: Free Press. (p. 306)

de Boysson-Bardies, B., Halle, P., Sagart, L., & Durand, C. (1989). A cross linguistic investigation of vowel formats in babbling. *Journal of Child Language, 16*, 1–17. (p. 212)

de Courten-Myers, G. M. (2005, February 4). Personal correspondence (estimating total brain neurons, extrapolating from her carefully estimated 20 to 23 billion cortical neurons). (p. 32)

de Hoogh, A. H. B., den Hartog, D. N., Koopman, P. L., Thierry, H., van den Berg, P. T., van der Weide, J. G., & Wilderom, C. P. M. (2004). Charismatic leadership, environmental dynamism, and performance. *European Journal of Work and Organisational Psychology, 13*, 447–471. (p. 412)

De Koninck, J. (2000). Waking experiences and dreaming. In M. Kryger, T. Roth, & W. Dement (Eds.), *Principles and practice of sleep medicine, 3rd ed.* Philadelphia: Saunders. (p. 57)

de Waal, F. B. M. (1999, December). The end of nature versus nurture. *Scientific American*, pp. 94–99. (p. 121)

Deacon, B. J., & Abramowitz, J. S. (2004). Cognitive and behavioral treatments for anxiety disorders: A review of meta-analytic findings. *Journal of Clinical Psychology, 60*, 429–441. (p. 355)

Dean, G. A., Kelly, I. W., Saklofske, D. H., & Furnham, A. (1992). Graphology and human judgment. In B. Beyerstein & D. Beyerstein (Eds.), *The write stuff: Evaluations of graphology.* Buffalo, NY: Prometheus Books. (p. 302)

Deary, I. J., & Matthews, G. (1993). Personality traits are alive and well. *The Psychologist: Bulletin of the British Psychological Society, 6*, 299–311. (p. 304)

Deary, I. J., Thorpe, G., Wilson, V., Starr, J. M., & Whalley, L. J. (2003). Population sex differences in IQ at age 11: The Scottish mental survey 1932. *Intelligence, 31*, 533–541. (p. 229)

Deci, E. L., Koestner, R., & Ryan, R. M. (1999, November). A meta-analytic review of experiments examining the effects of extrinsic rewards on intrinsic motivation. *Psychological Bulletin, 125*(6), 627–668. (p. 169)

DeLoache, J. S., & Brown, A. L. (1987, October-December). Differences in the memory-based searching of delayed and normally developing young children. *Intelligence, 11*(4), 277–289. (p. 74)

DeLoache, J. S., Uttal, D. H., & Rosengren, K. S. (2004). Scale errors offer evidence for a perception-action dissociation early in life. *Science, 304*, 1027–1029. (p. 73)

Dement, W. C. (1978). *Some must watch while some must sleep.* New York: Norton. (pp. 51, 52, 56)

Dement, W. C. (1997, September). What all undergraduates should know about how their sleeping lives affect their waking lives. Stanford University: www.leland.stanford.edu/~dement/sleepless.html. (p. 54)

Dement, W. C. (1999). *The promise of sleep.* New York: Delacorte Press. (pp. 51, 54, 56)

Dement, W. C., & Wolpert, E. A. (1958). The relation of eye movements, body mobility, and external stimuli to dream content. *Journal of Experimental Psychology, 55*, 543–553. (p. 57)

Demir, E., & Dickson, B. J. (2005). Fruitless splicing specifies male courtship behavior in Drosophila. *Cell, 121*, 785–794. (p. 116)

Dempster, F. N. (1988). The spacing effect: A case study in the failure to apply the results of psychological research. *American Psychologist, 43*, 627–634. (p. 184)

DeNeve, K. M., & Cooper, H. (1998). The happy personality: A meta-analysis of 137 personality traits and subjective well-being. *Psychological Bulletin, 124*, 197–229. (p. 264)

Denton, K., & Krebs, D. (1990). From the scene to the crime: The effect of alcohol and social context on moral judgment. *Journal of Personality and Social Psychology, 59*, 242–248. (p. 326)

DePaulo, B. M. (1994). Spotting lies: Can humans learn to do better? *Current Directions in Psychological Science 3*, 83–86. (p. 257)

Dermer, M., & Pyszczynski, T. A. (1978). Effects of erotica upon men's loving and liking responses for women they love. *Journal of Personality and Social Psychology, 36*, 1302–1309. (p. 397)

Dermer, M., Cohen, S. J., Jacobsen, E., & Anderson, E. A. (1979). Evaluative judgments of aspects of life as a function of vicarious exposure to hedonic extremes. *Journal of Personality and Social Psychology, 37*, 247–260. (p. 264)

DeRubeis, R. J., & 10 others, (2005). Cognitive therapy vs. medications in the treatment of moderate to severe depression. *Archives of General Psychiatry, 62*, 409–416. (p. 362)

DeSteno, D., Dasgupta, N., Bartlett, M. Y., & Cajdric, A. (2004). Prejudice from thin air: The effect of emotion on automatic intergroup attitudes. *Psychological Science, 15*, 319–324. (p. 260)

DeSteno, D., Petty, R. E., Wegener, D. T., & Rucker, D. D. (2000). Beyond valence in the perception of likelihood: The role of emotion specificity. *Journal of Personality and Social Psychology, 78*, 397–416. (p. 191)

Deutsch, J. A. (1972, July). Brain reward: ESP and ecstasy. *Psychology Today*, 46–48. (p. 38)

Devilly, G. J., Gist, R., & Cotton, P. (2006). Ready! Fire! Aim! The status of psychological debriefing and therapeutic interventions: In the work place and after disasters. *Review of General Psychology, 10*, 318–345. (p. 321)

Devine, P. G. (1995). Prejudice and outgroup perception. In A. Tesser (Ed.), *Advanced social psychology.* New York: McGraw-Hill. (p. 395)

DeWall, C. N., Baumeister, R. F., Stillman, T. F., & Gaillot, M. T. (2007). Violence restrained: Effects of self-regulation and its depletion on aggression. *Journal of Experimental Social Psychology, 43*, 62–76. (p. 278)

Diamond, J. (1989, May). The great leap forward. *Discover*, pp. 50–60. (p. 211)

Diamond, J. (2001, February). A tale of two reputations: Why we revere Darwin and give Freud a hard time. *Natural History*, pp. 20–24. (p. 119)

Diamond, L. M. (2000). Sexual identity, attractions, and behavior among young sexual-minority women over a 2-year period. *Developmental Psychology, 36*, 241–250. (p. 114)

Diamond, L. M. (2003). Was it a phase? Young women's relinquishment of lesbian/bisexual identities over a 5-year period. *Journal of Personality and Social Psychology, 84*, 352–364. (p. 114)

Dickens, W. T., & Flynn, J. R. (2006). Black Americans reduce the racial IQ gap: Evidence from standardization samples. *Psychological Science, 17*, 913–920. (p. 227)

Dickler, J. (2007, January 18). Best employers, great returns. CNNMoney.com. (p. 410)

Dickson, B. J. (2005, June 3). Quoted in E. Rosenthal, For fruit flies, gene shift tilts sex orientation. *New York Times* (www.nytimes.com). (p. 116)

Diener, E., & Biswas-Diener, R. (2002). Will money increase subjective well-being? A literature review and guide to needed research. *Social Indicators Research, 57*, 119–169. (p. 263)

Diener, E., Diener, M., & Diener, C. (1995). Factors predicting the subjective well-being of nations. *Journal of Personality and Social Psychology, 69*, 851–864. (p. 396)

Diener, E., Emmons, R. A., & Sandvik, E. (1986). The dual nature of happiness: Independence of positive and negative moods. Unpublished manuscript, University of Illinois. (p. 97)

Diener, E., Oishi, S., & Lucas, R. E. (2003). Personality, culture, and subjective well-being: Emotional and cognitive evaluations of life. *Annual Review of Psychology, 54*, 403–425. (pp. 264, 265)

DiLalla, D. L., Carey, G., Gottesman, I. I., & Bouchard, T. J., Jr. (1996). Heritability of MMPI personality indicators of psychopathology in twins reared apart. *Journal of Abnormal Psychology, 105*, 491–499. (p. 338)

Dimberg, U., Thunberg, M., & Elmehed, K. (2000). Unconscious facial reactions to emotional facial expressions. *Psychological Science, 11*, 86–89. (pp. 173, 256, 259)

Dimberg, U., Thunberg, M., & Grunedal, S. (2002). Facial reactions to emotional stimuli: Automatically controlled emotional responses. *Cognition and Emotion, 16*, 449–472. (p. 173)

Dindia, K., & Allen, M. (1992). Sex differences in self-disclosure: A meta-analysis. *Psychological Bulletin, 112*, 106–124. (p. 105)

Dion, K. K., & Dion, K. L. (1993). Individualistic and collectivistic perspectives on gender and the cultural context of love and intimacy. *Journal of Social Issues, 49*, 53–69. (p. 309)

Dion, K. K., & Dion, K. L. (2001). Gender and cultural adaptation in immigrant families. *Journal of Social Issues, 57*, 511–521. (p. 107)

Dohrenwend, B., Pearlin, L., Clayton, P., Hamburg, B., Dohrenwend, B. P., Riley, M., & Rose, R. (1982). Report on stress and life events. In G. R. Elliott & C. Eisdorfer (Eds.), *Stress and human health: Analysis and implications of research* (A study by the Institute of Medicine/National Academy of Sciences). New York: Springer. (p. 271)

Dohrenwend, B. P., Turner, J. B., Turse, N. A., Adams, B. G., Koenen, K. C., & Marshall, R. (2006). The psychological risks of Vietnam for U.S. veterans: A revisit with new data and methods. *Science, 313*, 979–982. (p. 320)

Dolcos, F., LaBar, K. S., & Cabeza, R. (2004). Interaction between the amygdala and the medial temporal lobe memory system predicts better memory for emotional events. *Neuron, 42*, 855–863. (p. 187)

Dolezal, H. (1982). *Living in a world transformed*. New York: Academic Press. (p. 149)

Domhoff, G. W. (1996). *Finding meaning in dreams: A quantitative approach*. New York: Plenum. (p. 57)

Domhoff, G. W. (1999). New directions in the study of dream content using the Hall and Van de Castle coding system. *Dreaming, 9*, 115–137. (p. 57)

Domhoff, G. W. (2000). Moving Dream Theory Beyond Freud and Jung. Paper presented to the symposium "Beyond Freud and Jung?" Graduate Theological Union, Berkeley, CA, 9/23/2000. (p. 58)

Domhoff, G. W. (2003). *The scientific study of dreams: Neural networks, cognitive development, and content analysis*. Washington, DC: APA Books. (p. 58)

Domjan, M. (1992). Adult learning and mate choice: Possibilities and experimental evidence. *American Zoologist, 32*, 48–61. (p. 161)

Domjan, M. (1994). Formulation of a behavior system for sexual conditioning. *Psychonomic Bulletin & Review, 1*, 421–428. (p. 161)

Domjan, M. (2005). Pavlovian conditioning: A functional perspective. *Annual Review of Psychology, 56*. (p. 161)

Domjan, M., Blesbois, E., & Williams, J. (1998). The adaptive significance of sexual conditioning: Pavlovian control of sperm release. *Psychological Science, 9*, 411–415. (p. 161)

Donnellan, M. B., Trzesniewski, K. H., Robins, R. W., Moffitt, T. E., & Caspi, A. (2005). Low self-esteem is related to aggression, antisocial behavior, and delinquency. *Psychological Science, 16*, 328–335. (pp. 305, 306)

Donnerstein, E. (1998). Why do we have those new ratings on television. Invited address to the National Institute on the Teaching of Psychology. (pp. 175, 176)

Donnerstein, E., Linz, D., & Penrod, S. (1987). *The question of pornography*. New York: Free Press. (p. 176)

Doty, R. L., Shaman, P., Applebaum, S. L., Giberson, R., Siksorski, L., & Rosenberg, L. (1984). Smell identification ability: Changes with age. *Science, 226*, 1441–1443. (p. 92)

Dovidio, J. F., & Gaertner, S. L. (1999). Reducing prejudice: Combating intergroup biases. *Current Directions in Psychological Science, 8*, 101–105. (p. 401)

Doyle, R. (2005, March). Gay and lesbian census. *Scientific American*, p. 28. (p. 118)

Draguns, J. G. (1990a). Normal and abnormal behavior in cross-cultural perspective: Specifying the nature of their relationship. *Nebraska Symposium on Motivation 1989, 37*, 235–277. (p. 313)

Draguns, J. G. (1990b). Applications of cross-cultural psychology in the field of mental health. In R. W. Brislin (Ed.), *Applied cross-cultural psychology*. Newbury Park, CA: Sage. (pp. 313, 316)

Draguns, J. G. (1997). Abnormal behavior patterns across cultures: Implications for counseling and psychotherapy. *International Journal of Intercultural Relations, 21*, 213–248. (p. 313)

Druckman, D., & Bjork, R. A. (Eds.) (1994). *Learning, remembering, believing: Enhancing human performance*. Washington, DC: National Academy Press. (p. 139)

Duckworth, A. L., & Seligman, M. E. P. (2005). Discipline outdoes talent: Self-discipline predicts academic performance in adolescents. *Psychological Science, 12*, 939–944. (p. 409)

Duclos, S. E., Laird, J. D., Sexter, M., Stern, L., & Van Lighten, O. (1989). Emotion-specific effects of facial expressions and postures on emotional experience. *Journal of Personality and Social Psychology, 57*, 100–108. (p. 259)

Duenwald, M. (2004, October 26). The dorms may be great, but how's the counseling? *New York Times* (www.nytimes.com). (p. 366)

Duffy, M. (2003, June 9). Weapons of mass disappearance. *Time*, pp. 28–33. (p. 379)

Duggan, J. P., & Booth, D. A. (1986). Obesity, overeating, and rapid gastric emptying in rats with ventromedial hypothalamic lesions. *Science, 231*, 609–611. (p. 239)

Dugger, C. W. (2005, January 18). U.N. proposes doubling of aid to cut poverty. *New York Times* (www.nytimes.com). (p. 210)

Duncan, B. L. (1976). Differential social perception and attribution of intergroup violence: Testing the lower limits of stereotyping of blacks. *Journal of Personality and Social Psychology, 34*, 590–598. (p. 388)

Dunn, A. L., Trivedi, M. H., Kampert, J. B., Clark, C. G., & Chambliss, H. O. (2005). Exercise treatment for depression: Efficacy and dose response. *American Journal of Preventive Medicine, 28*, 1–8. (p. 281)

Dunson, D. B., Colombo, B., & Baird, D. D. (2002). Changes with age in the level and duration of fertility in the menstrual cycle. *Human Reproduction, 17,* 1399–1403. (p. 91)

Dush, C. M. K., Cohan, C. L., & Amato, P. R. (2003). The relationship between cohabitation and marital quality and stability: Change across cohorts? *Journal of Marriage and Family, 65,* 539–549. (p. 94)

Dutton, D. G., & Aron, A. P. (1974). Some evidence for heightened sexual attraction under conditions of high anxiety. *Journal of Personality and Social Psychology, 30,* 510–517. (p. 397)

Dutton, D. G., & Aron, A. (1989). Romantic attraction and generalized liking for others who are sources of conflict-based arousal. *Canadian Journal of Behavioural Sciences, 21,* 246–257. (p. 397)

Eagly, A. H., & Johnson, B. T. (1990). Gender and leadership style: A meta-analysis. *Psychological Bulletin, 108,* 233–256. (p. 104)

Eagly, A. H., & Wood, W. (1999). The origins of sex differences in human behavior: Evolved dispositions versus social roles. *American Psychologist, 54,* 408–423. (p. 120)

Eagly, A. H., Ashmore, R. D., Makhijani, M. G., & Kennedy, L. C. (1991). What is beautiful is good, but . . . : A meta-analytic review of research on the physical attractiveness stereotype. *Psychological Bulletin, 110,* 109–128. (p. 395)

Ebbesen, E. B., Duncan, B., & Konecni, V. J. (1975). Effects of content of verbal aggression on future verbal aggression: A field experiment. *Journal of Experimental Social Psychology, 11,* 192–204. (p. 260)

Ebbinghaus, H. (1885). Über das Gedachtnis. Leipzig: Duncker & Humblot. Cited in R. Klatzky (1980), *Human memory: Structures and processes.* San Francisco: Freeman. (p. 193)

Eberhardt, J. L. (2005). Imaging race. *American Psychologist, 60,* 181–190. (p. 389)

Eckensberger, L. H. (1994). Moral development and its measurement across cultures. In W. J. Lonner & R. Malpass (Eds.), *Psychology and culture.* Boston: Allyn and Bacon. (p. 86)

Eckersley, R. (2000). The mixed blessings of material progress: Diminishing returns in the pursuit of happiness. *Journal of Happiness Studies, 1,* 267–292. (p. 263)

Eckert, E. D., Heston, L. L., & Bouchard, T. J., Jr. (1981). MZ twins reared apart: Preliminary findings of psychiatric disturbances and traits. In L. Gedda, P. Paris, & W. D. Nance (Eds.), *Twin research: Vol. 3. Pt. B. Intelligence, personality, and development.* New York: Alan Liss. (p. 322)

Economist. (2001, December 20). An anthropology of happiness. *The Economist* (www.economist.com/world/asia). (p. 247)

Edelman, S., & Kidman, A. D. (1997). Mind and cancer: Is there a relationship? A review of the evidence. *Australian Psychologist, 32,* 1–7. (p. 274)

Edwards, C. P. (1981). The comparative study of the development of moral judgment and reasoning. In R. H. Munroe, R. L. Munroe, & B. B. Whiting (Eds.), *Handbook of cross-cultural human development.* New York: Garland Press. (p. 86)

Edwards, C. P. (1982). Moral development in comparative cultural perspective. In D. A. Wagner & H. W. Stevenson (Eds.), *Cultural perspectives on child development.* San Francisco: Freeman. (p. 86)

Egan, M. F., & 16 others. (2004). Variation in GRM3 affects cognition, prefrontal glutamate, and risk for schizophrenia. *Proceedings of the National Academy of Sciences, 101,* 12604–12609. (p. 345)

Ehrlichman, H., & Halpern, J. N. (1988). Affect and memory: Effects of pleasant and unpleasant odors on retrieval of happy and unhappy memories. *Journal of Personality and Social Psychology, 55,* 769–779. (p. 141)

Eisenberg, N., & Lennon, R. (1983). Sex differences in empathy and related capacities. *Psychological Bulletin, 94,* 100–131. (p. 257)

Eisenberger, R., & Rhoades, L. (2001). Incremental effects of reward on creativity. *Journal of Personality and Social Psychology, 81,* 728–741. (p. 170)

Ekman, P. (1994). Strong evidence for universals in facial expressions: A reply to Russell's mistaken critique. *Psychological Bulletin, 115,* 268–287. (p. 258)

Ekman, P., Friesen, W. V. (1975). *Unmasking the face.* Englewood Cliffs, NJ: Prentice Hall. (p. 258)

Ekman, P., Friesen, W. V., O'Sullivan, M., Chan, A., Diacoyanni-Tarlatzis, I., Heider, K., Krause, R., LeCompte, W. A., Pitcairn, T., Ricci-Bitti, P. E., Scherer, K., Tomita, M., & Tzavaras, A. (1987). Universals and cultural differences in the judgments of facial expressions of emotion. *Journal of Personality and Social Psychology, 53,* 712–717. (p. 258)

El-Alayli, A., Lystad, A. L., Webb, S. R., Hollingsworth, S. L., & Ciolli, J. L. (2006). Reigning cats and dogs: A pet-enhancement bias and its link to pet attachment, pet-self similarity, self-enhancement, and well-being. *Basic and Applied Social Psychology, 28,* 131–143. (p. 307)

Elbert, T., Pantev, C., Wienbruch, C., Rockstroh, B., & Taub, E. (1995). Increased cortical representation of the fingers of the left hand in string players. *Science, 270,* 305–307. (p. 71)

Elfenbein, H. A., & Ambady, N. (1999). Does it take one to know one? A meta-analysis of the universality and cultural specificity of emotion recognition. Unpublished manuscript, Harvard University. (p. 258)

Elfenbein, H. A., & Ambady, N. (2002). On the universality and cultural specificity of emotion recognition: A meta-analysis. *Psychological Bulletin, 128,* 203–235. (p. 258)

Elfenbein, H. A., & Ambady, N. (2003a). When familiarity breeds accuracy: Cultural exposure and facial emotion recognition. *Journal of Personality and Social Psychology, 85,* 276–290. (p. 258)

Elfenbein, H. A., & Ambady, N. (2003b). Universals and cultural differences in recognizing emotions. *Current Directions in Psychological Science, 12,* 159–164. (p. 258)

Elkin, I., Shea, T., Watkins, J. T., Imber, S. D., Sotsky, S. M., Collins, J. F., Glass, D. R., Pilkonis, P. A., Leber, W. R., Docherty, J. P., Fiester, S. J., & Parloff, M. B. (1989). National Institute of Mental Health treatment of depression collaborative research program. *Archives of General Psychiatry, 46,* 971–983. (p. 362)

Elkind, D. (1970). The origins of religion in the child. *Review of Religious Research, 12,* 35–42. (p. 85)

Elkind, D. (1978). *The child's reality: Three developmental themes.* Hillsdale, NJ: Erlbaum. (p. 85)

Ellis, A. (1980). Psychotherapy and atheistic values: A response to A. E. Bergin's "Psychotherapy and religious values." *Journal of Consulting and Clinical Psychology, 48,* 635–639. (p. 364)

Ellis, A., & Becker, I. M. (1982). *A guide to personal happiness.* North Hollywood, CA: Wilshire Book Co. (p. 164)

Ellis, B. J. (2004). Timing of pubertal maturation in girls: An integrated life history approach. *Psychological Bulletin, 130,* 920–958. (p. 88)

Ellis, B. J., Bates, J. E., Dodge, K. A., Fergusson, D. M., John, H. L., Pettit, G. S., & Woodward, L. (2003). Does father absence place daughters at special risk for early sexual activity and teenage pregnancy? *Child Development, 74,* 801–821. (p. 112)

Ellis, L., & Ames, M. A. (1987). Neurohormonal functioning and sexual orientation: A theory of homosexuality-heterosexuality. *Psychological Bulletin, 101,* 233–258. (p. 116)

Emerging Trends. (1997, September). *Teens turn more to parents than friends on whether to attend church.* Princeton, NJ: Princeton Religion Research Center, p. 5. (p. 88)

Emery, G. (2004). Psychic predictions 2004. Committee for the Scientific Investigation of Claims of the Paranormal (www.csicop.org). (p. 152)

Emmons, S., Geisler, C., Kaplan, K. J., & Harrow, M. (1997). *Living with schizophrenia.* Muncie, IN: Taylor and Francis (Accelerated Development). (p. 313,, 341)

Endler, N. S. (1982). *Holiday of darkness: A psychologist's personal journey out of his depression.* New York: Wiley. (p. 339)

Engemann, K. M., & Owyang, M. T. (2005, April). So much for that merit raise: The link between wages and appearance. *Regional Economist* (www.stlouisfed.org). (p. 395)

Engen, T. (1987). Remembering odors and their names. *American Scientist, 75,* 497–503. (p. 141)

Epley, N., Keysar, B., Van Boven, L., & Gilovich, T. (2004). Perspective taking as egocentric anchoring and adjustment. *Journal of Personality and Social Psychology, 87,* 327–339. (p. 74)

EPOCH. (2000). Legal reforms: Corporal punishment of children in the family (www.stophitting.com/laws/legalReform.php). (p. 168)

Epstein, J., Stern, E., & Silbersweig, D. (1998). Mesolimbic activity associated with psychosis in schizophrenia: Symptom-specific PET studies. In J. F. McGinty (Ed.), *Advancing from the ventral striatum to the extended amygdala: Implications for neuropsychiatry and drug use: In honor of Lennart Heimer.* Annals of New York Academy of Sciences, 877, 562–574. (p. 343)

Epstein, S. (1983a). Aggregation and beyond: Some basic issues on the prediction of behavior. *Journal of Personality, 51,* 360–392. (p. 304)

Epstein, S. (1983b). The stability of behavior across time and situations. In R. Zucker, J. Aronoff, & A. I. Rabin (Eds.), *Personality and the prediction of behavior.* San Diego: Academic Press. (p. 304)

Erdberg, P. (1990). Rorschach assessment. In G. Goldstein & M. Hersen (Eds.), *Handbook of psychological assessment, 2nd ed.* New York: Pergamon. (p. 295)

Erdelyi, M. H. (1985). *Psychoanalysis: Freud's cognitive psychology.* New York: Freeman. (p. 296)

Erdelyi, M. H. (1988). Repression, reconstruction, and defense: History and integration of the psychoanalytic and experimental frameworks. In J. Singer (Ed.), *Repression: Defense mechanism and cognitive style.* Chicago: University of Chicago Press. (p. 296)

Erickson, M. F., & Aird, E. G. (2005). *The motherhood study: Fresh insights on mothers' attitudes and concerns.* New York: The Motherhood Project, Institute for American Values. (p. 94)

Ericsson, K. A. (2001). Attaining excellence through deliberate practice: Insights from the study of expert performance. In C. Desforges & R. Fox (Eds.), *Teaching and learning: The essential readings.* Malden, MA: Blackwell Publishers. (p. 409)

Ericsson, K. A. (2002). Attaining excellence through deliberate practice: Insights from the study of expert performance. In C. Desforges & R. Fox (Eds.), *Teaching and learning: The essential readings.* Malden, MA: Blackwell Publishers. (p. 220)

Ericsson, K. A., & Lehmann, A. C. (1996). Expert and exceptional performance: Evidence of maximal adaptations to task constraints. *Annual Review of Psychology, 47,* 273–305. (p. 220)

Ericsson, K. A., Krampe, R. T., & Heizman, S. (1993). Can we create gifted people? In G. R. Bock & K. Ackrill (Eds.), *Ciba Foundation Symposium 178: The origins and development of high ability.* New York: Wiley. Cited by M. J. A. Howe, J. W. Davison, & J. A. Siobada (1998). Innate talents: Reality or myth? *Behavioral and Brain Sciences, 21,* 399–442. (p. 409)

Erikson, E. H. (1963). *Childhood and society.* New York: Norton. (p. 86)

Ernsberger, P., & Koletsky, R. J. (1999). Biomedical rationale for a wellness approach to obesity: An alternative to a focus on weight loss. *Journal of Social Issues, 55,* 221–260. (p. 245)

Escobar-Chaves, S. L., Tortolero, S., Markham, C., Low, B., Eitel, P., & Thitckstun, P. (2005). Impact of the media on adolescents attitudes and behaviors. *Pediatrics, 116,* 303–326. (p. 112)

Esser, J. K., & Lindoerfer, J. S. (1989). Groupthink and the space shuttle *Challenger* accident: Toward a quantitative case analysis. *Journal of Behavioral Decision Making, 2,* 167–177. (p. 386)

Esterling, B. A., L'Abate, L., Murray, E. J., & Pennebaker, J., W. (1999). Empirical foundations for writing in prevention and psychotherapy: Mental and physical health outcomes. *Clinical Psychology Review, 19,* 79–96. (p. 280)

Esterson, A. (2001). The mythologizing of psychoanalytic history: Deception and self-deception in Freud's accounts of the seduction theory episode. *History of Psychiatry, 12,* 329–352. (p. 296)

Eszterhas, J. (2002, August 9). Hollywood's responsibility for smoking deaths. *New York Times* (www.nytimes.com). (p. 328)

Evans, C. R., & Dion, K. L. (1991). Group cohesion and performance: A meta-analysis. *Small Group Research, 22,* 175–186. (p. 414)

Ewing, R., Schmid, T., Killingsworth, R., Zlot, A., & Raudenbush, S. (2003). Relationship between urban sprawl and physical activity, obesity, and morbidity. *American Journal of Health Promotion, 18,* 47–57. (p. 245)

Exner, J. E. (2003). *The Rorschach: A comprehensive system, 4th edition.* Hoboken, NJ: Wiley. (p. 295)

Eysenck, H. J. (1952). The effects of psychotherapy: An evaluation. *Journal of Consulting Psychology, 16,* 319–324. (p. 361)

Eysenck, H. J. (1990, April 30). An improvement on personality inventory. *Current Contents: Social and Behavioral Sciences, 22*(18), 20. (p. 300)

Eysenck, H. J. (1992). Four ways five factors are not basic. *Personality and Individual Differences, 13,* 667–673. (p. 300)

Eysenck, H. J., Wakefield, J. A., Jr., & Friedman, A. F. (1983). Diagnosis and clinical assessment: The DSM-III. *Annual Review of Psychology, 34,* 167–193. (p. 317)

Eysenck, M. W., MacLeod, C., & Mathews, A. (1987). Cognitive functioning and anxiety. *Psychological Research, 49,* 189–195. (p. 305)

Eysenck, S. B. G., & Eysenck, H. J. (1963). The validity of questionnaire and rating assessments of extraversion and neuroticism, and their factorial stability. *British Journal of Psychology, 54,* 51–62. (p. 300)

Faber, N. (1987, July). Personal glimpse. *Reader's Digest,* p. 34. (p. 220)

Fagan, J. F., III. (1992). Intelligence: A theoretical viewpoint. *Current Directions in Psychological Science, 1,* 82–86. (p. 228)

Fairburn, C. G., Cowen, P. J., & Harrison, P. J. (1999). Twin studies and the etiology of eating disorders. *International Journal of Eating Disorders, 26,* 349–358. (p. 241)

Farah, M. J., Rabinowitz, C., Quinn, G. E., & Liu, G. T. (2000). Early commitment of neural substrates for face recognition. *Cognitive Neuropsychology, 17,* 117–124. (p. 44)

Farina, A. (1982). The stigma of mental disorders. In A. G. Miller (Ed.), *In the eye of the beholder*. New York: Praeger. (pp. 315, 317)

Farley, M., Baral, I., Kiremire, M., & Sezgin, U. (1998). Prostitution in five countries: Violence and post-traumatic stress disorder. *Feminism and Psychology, 8,* 405–426. (p. 320)

Farrington, D. P. (1991). Antisocial personality from childhood to adulthood. *The Psychologist: Bulletin of the British Psychological Society, 4,* 389–394. (p. 324)

FBI. (2004). *Crime in the United States 2003, Five-Year Arrest Trends by Sex, 1999–2003.* Table 35. (p. 104)

Feder, H. H. (1984). Hormones and sexual behavior. *Annual Review of Psychology, 35,* 165–200. (p. 109)

Feeney, J. A., & Noller, P. (1990). Attachment style as a predictor of adult romantic relationships. *Journal of Personality and Social Psychology, 58,* 281–291. (p. 79)

Feingold, A. (1990). Gender differences in effects of physical attractiveness on romantic attraction: A comparison across five research paradigms. *Journal of Personality and Social Psychology, 59,* 981–993. (p. 395)

Feingold, A. (1992). Good-looking people are not what we think. *Psychological Bulletin, 111,* 304–341. (p. 395)

Feingold, A., & Mazzella, R. (1998). Gender differences in body image are increasing. *Psychological Science, 9,* 190–195. (p. 241)

Fenton, W. S., & McGlashan, T. H. (1991). Natural history of schizophrenia subtypes: II. Positive and negative symptoms and long-term course. *Archives of General Psychiatry, 48,* 978–986. (p. 342)

Fenton, W. S., & McGlashan, T. H. (1994). Antecedents, symptom progression, and long-term outcome of the deficit syndrome in schizophrenia. *American Journal of Psychiatry, 151,* 351–356. (p. 342)

Fergusson, D. M., & Woodward, L. G. (2002). Mental health, educational, and social role outcomes of adolescents with depression. *Archives of General Psychiatry, 59,* 225–231. (p. 337)

Fernandez, E., & Turk, D. C. (1989). The utility of cognitive coping strategies for altering pain perception: A meta-analysis. *Pain, 38,* 123–135. (p. 138)

Fernandez-Dols, J-M., & Ruiz-Belda, M-A. (1995). Are smiles a sign of happiness? Gold medal winners at the Olympic Games. *Journal of Personality and Social Psychology, 69,* 1113–1119. (p. 258)

Ferris, C. F. (1996, March). The rage of innocents. *The Sciences,* pp. 22–26. (p. 79)

Feynman, R. (1997). Quoted by E. Hutchings (Ed.), *"Surely you're joking, Mr. Feynman."* New York: Norton. (p. 9)

Fiedler, F. E. (1981). Leadership effectiveness. *American Behavioral Scientist, 24,* 619–632. (p. 413)

Fiedler, F. E. (1987, September). When to lead, when to stand back. *Psychology Today,* pp. 26–27. (p. 413)

Fiedler, K., Nickel, S., Muehlfriedel, T., & Unkelbach, C. (2001). Is mood congruency an effect of genuine memory or response bias? *Journal of Experimental Social Psychology, 37,* 201–214. (p. 191)

Field, A. P. (2006). Is conditioning a useful framework for understanding the development and treatment of phobias? *Clinical Psychology Review, 26,* 857–875. (p. 321)

Field, T. (2001). Massage therapy facilitates weight gain in preterm infants. *Current Directions in Psychological Science, 10,* 51–54. (p. 71)

Field, T., Hernandez-Reif, M., Diego, M., Feijo, L., Vera, Y., & Gil, K. (2004). Massage therapy by parents improves early growth and development. *Infant Behaviour and Development, 27,* 435–442. (p. 71)

Fincham, F. D., & Bradbury, T. N. (1993). Marital satisfaction, depression, and attributions: A longitudinal analysis. *Journal of Personality and Social Psychology, 64,* 442–452. (p. 376)

Fink, M. (1998). ECT and managed care. *Journal Watch Psychiatry, 4,* 73, 76. (p. 368)

Finzi, E., & Wasserman, E. (2006). Treatment of depression with botulinum toxin A: A case series. *Dermatological Surgery, 32,* 645–650. (p. 259)

Fischhoff, B. (1982). Debiasing. In D. Kahneman, P. Slovic, & A. Tversky (Eds.), *Judgment under uncertainty: Heuristics and biases.* New York: Cambridge University Press. (p. 208)

Fischhoff, B., Slovic, P., & Lichtenstein, S. (1977). Knowing with certainty: The appropriateness of extreme confidence. *Journal of Experimental Psychology: Human Perception and Performance, 3,* 552–564. (p. 208)

Fisher, H. E. (1993, March/April). After all, maybe it's biology. *Psychology Today,* pp. 40–45. (p. 94)

Fisher, H. T. (1984). Little Albert and Little Peter. *Bulletin of the British Psychological Society, 37,* 269. (p. 355)

Fleming, I., Baum, A., & Weiss, L. (1987). Social density and perceived control as mediator of crowding stress in high-density residential neighborhoods. *Journal of Personality and Social Psychology, 52,* 899–906. (p. 277)

Fleming, J. H. (2001, Winter/Spring). Introduction to the special issue on linkage analysis. *The Gallup Research Journal,* pp. i–vi. (p. 412)

Fleming, J. H., & Scott, B. A. (1991). The costs of confession: The Persian Gulf War POW tapes in historical and theoretical perspective. *Contemporary Social Psychology, 15,* 127–138. (p. 258)

Fletcher, G. J. O., Fitness, J., & Blampied, N. M. (1990). The link between attributions and happiness in close relationships: The roles of depression and explanatory style. *Journal of Social and Clinical Psychology, 9,* 243–255. (p. 376)

Flora, S. R. (2004). *The power of reinforcement.* Albany, NJ: SUNY Press. (p. 170)

Flynn, J. R. (2003). Movies about intelligence: The limitations of g. *Current Directions in Psychological Science, 12,* 95–99. (p. 226)

Foa, E. B., & Kozak, M. J. (1986). Emotional processing of fear: Exposure to corrective information. *Psychological Bulletin, 99,* 20–35. (p. 356)

Ford, E. S. (2002). Does exercise reduce inflammation? Physical activity and B-reactive protein among U.S. adults. *Epidemiology, 13,* 561–569. (p. 280)

Foree, D. D., & LoLordo, V. M. (1973). Attention in the pigeon: Differential effects of food-getting versus shock-avoidance procedures. *Journal of Comparative and Physiological Psychology, 85,* 551–558. (p. 170)

Forgas, J. P., Bower, G. H., & Krantz, S. E. (1984). The influence of mood on perceptions of social interactions. *Journal of Experimental Social Psychology, 20,* 497–513. (p. 191)

Foss, D. J., & Hakes, D. T. (1978). *Psycholinguistics: An introduction to the psychology of language.* Englewood Cliffs, NJ: Prentice Hall. (p. 296)

Foster, R. G. (2004). Are we trying to banish biological time? *Cerebrum, 6(2),* 7–26. (p. 50)

Foulkes, D. (1999). *Children's dreaming and the development of consciousness.* Cambridge, MA: Harvard University Press. (p. 58)

Fouts, R. S. (1992). Transmission of a human gestural language in a chimpanzee mother-infant relationship. *Friends of Washoe, 12/13,* pp. 2–8. (p. 217)

Fouts, R. S. (1997). *Next of kin: What chimpanzees have taught me about who we are.* New York: Morrow. (p. 217)

Fouts, R. S., & Bodamer, M. (1987). Preliminary report to the National Geographic Society on "Chimpanzee intrapersonal signing." *Friends of Washoe, 7(1),* 4–12. (p. 217)

Fowler, M. J., Sullivan, M. J., & Ekstrand, B. R. (1973). Sleep and memory. *Science, 179,* 302–304. (p. 194)

Fowles, D. C. (1992). Schizophrenia: Diathesis-stress revisited. *Annual Review of Psychology, 43,* 303–336. (p. 342)

Fox, B. H. (1998). Psychosocial factors in cancer incidence and prognosis. In P. M. Cinciripini & others (Eds.), *Psychological and behavioral factors in cancer risk.* New York: Oxford University Press. (p. 274)

Fox, E., Lester, V., Russo, R., Bowles, R. J., Pichler, A., & Dutton, K. (2000). Facial expression of emotion: Are angry faces detected more efficiently? *Cognition and Emotion, 14,* 61–92. (p. 257)

Fox, J. L. (1984). The brain's dynamic way of keeping in touch. *Science, 225,* 820–821. (p. 44)

Fracassini, C. (2000, August 27). Holidaymakers led by the nose in sales quest. *Scotland on Sunday.* (p. 141)

Fraley, R. C. (2002). Attachment stability from infancy to adulthood: Meta-analysis and dynamic modeling of developmental mechanisms. *Personality and Social Psychology Review, 6,* 123–151. (p. 79)

Frank, J. D. (1982). Therapeutic components shared by all psychotherapies. In J. H. Harvey & M. M. Parks (Eds.), *The Master Lecture Series: Vol. 1. Psychotherapy research and behavior change.* Washington, DC: American Psychological Association. (p. 363)

Frankenburg, W., Dodds, J., Archer, P., Shapiro, H., & Bresnick, B. (1992). The Denver II: A major revision and restandardization of the Denver Developmental Screening Test. *Pediatrics, 89,* 91–97. (p. 72)

Frankl, V. E. (1962). *Man's search for meaning: An introduction to logotherapy.* Boston: Beacon Press. (p. 280)

Frasure-Smith, N., & Lespérance, F. (2005). Depression and coronary heart disease: Complex synergism of mind, body, and environment. *Current Directions in Psychological Science, 14,* 39–43. (p. 275)

Frattaroli, J. (2006). Experimental disclosure and its moderators: A meta-analysis. *Psychological Bulletin, 132,* 823–865. (p. 280)

Fredrickson, B. L. (2002). Positive emotions. In C. R. Snyder & S. J. Lopez (Eds.), *Handbook of positive psychology.* New York: Oxford. (p. 261)

Fredrickson, B. L. (2003). The value of positive emotions. *American Scientist, 91,* 330–335. (p. 261)

Freedman, D. J., Riesenhuber, M., Poggio, T., & Miller, E. K. (2001). Categorical representation of visual stimuli in the primate prefrontal cortex. *Science, 291,* 312–316. (p. 215)

Freedman, J. L. (1988). Television violence and aggression: What the evidence shows. In S. Oskamp (Ed.), *Television as a social issue.* Newbury Park, CA: Sage. (p. 176)

Freedman, J. L., & Perlick, D. (1979). Crowding, contagion, and laughter. *Journal of Experimental Social Psychology, 15,* 295–303. (p. 384)

Freeman, W. J. (1991, February). The physiology of perception. *Scientific American,* pp. 78–85. (p. 134)

Freud, S. (1935; reprinted 1960). *A general introduction to psychoanalysis.* New York: Washington Square Press. (p. 94)

Freyd, J. J., Putnam, F. W., Lyon, T. D., Becker-Blease, K. A., Cheit, R. E., Siegel, N. B., & Pezdek, K. (2005). The science of child sexual abuse. *Science, 308,* 501. (p. 79)

Friedman, M., & Ulmer, D. (1984). *Treating Type A behavior—and your heart.* New York: Knopf. (pp. 274, 282)

Friedrich, O. (1987, December 7). New age harmonies. *Time,* pp. 62–72. (p. 314)

Friend, T. (2004). *Animal talk: Breaking the codes of animal language.* New York: Free Press. (p. 217)

Frith, U., & Frith, C. (2001). The biological basis of social interaction. *Current Directions in Psychological Science, 10,* 151–155. (p. 76)

Fromkin, V., & Rodman, R. (1983). *An introduction to language (3rd ed.).* New York: Holt, Rinehart & Winston. (p. 212)

Fry, A. F., & Hale, S. (1996). Processing speed, working memory, and fluid intelligence: Evidence for a developmental cascade. *Psychological Science, 7,* 237–241. (p. 93)

Fuhriman, A., & Burlingame, G. M. (1994). Group psychotherapy: Research and practice. In A. Fuhriman & G. M. Burlingame (Eds.), *Handbook of group psychotherapy.* New York: Wiley. (p. 359)

Fujita, F., & Diener, E. (2005). Life satisfaction set point: Stability and change. *Journal of Personality and Social Psychology, 88,* 158–164. (p. 265)

Fuller, M. J., & Downs, A. C. (1990). *Spermarche is a salient biological marker in men's development.* Poster presented at the American Psychological Society convention. (p. 84)

Funder, D. C., & Block, J. (1989). The role of ego-control, ego-resiliency, and IQ in delay of gratification in adolescence. *Journal of Personality and Social Psychology, 57,* 1041–1050. (p. 86)

Furlow, F. B., & Thornhill, R. (1996, January/February). The orgasm wars. *Psychology Today,* p. 42–46. (p. 109)

Furnham, A. (1982). Explanations for unemployment in Britain. *European Journal of Social Psychology, 12,* 335–352. (p. 377)

Furnham, A., & Baguma, P. (1994). Cross-cultural differences in the evaluation of male and female body shapes. *International Journal of Eating Disorders, 15,* 81–89. (p. 242)

Furr, R. M., & Funder, D. C. (1998). A multimodal analysis of personal negativity. *Journal of Personality and Social Psychology, 74,* 1580–1591. (p. 340)

Gaertner, L., & Iuzzini, J. (2005). Rejection and entitativity: A synergistic model of mass violence. In K. D. Williams, J. P. Forgas, & W. von Hippel (Eds.). *The social outcast: Ostracism, social exclusion, rejection, and bullying.* New York: Psychology Press. (p. 392)

Gaillot, M. T., & Baumeister, R. F. (2007). Self-regulation and sexual restraint: Dispositionally and temporarily poor self-regulatory abilities contribute to failures at restraining sexual behavior. *Personality and Social Psychology Bulletin, 33,* 173–186. (p. 278)

Galambos, N. L. (1992). Parent-adolescent relations. *Current Directions in Psychological Science, 1,* 146–149. (p. 88)

Galanter, E. (1962). Contemporary psychophysics. In R. Brown, E. Galanter, E. H. Hess, & G. Mandler (Eds.), *New directions in psychology.* New York: Holt Rinehart, & Winston. (p. 126)

Gallup. (2002, June 11). Poll insights: The gender gap—post Sept. 11th fear. The Gallup Organization (www.gallup.com/poll/pollInsights). (p. 318)

Gallup Brain. (2008, accessed February 20). Woman for president: Question qn2f, March, 2007 wave. Brain.Gallup.com., (p. 388)

Gallup Organization. (2003, July 8). American public opinion about Iraq. *Gallup Poll News Service* (www.gallup.com) (p. 379)

Gallup Organization. (2004, August 16). 65% of Americans receive NO praise or recognition in the workplace. E-mail from Tom Rath: bucketbook@gallup.com. (p. 412)

Gallup, G. H. (1972). *The Gallup poll: Public opinion 1935–1971 (Vol. 3).* New York: Random House. (p. 401)

Gallup, G., Jr. (2002, April 30). Education and youth. *Gallup Tuesday Briefing* (www.gallup.com/poll/tb/educaYouth/20020430.asp). (p. 175)

Gangestad, S. W., & Simpson, J. A. (2000). The evolution of human mating: Trade-offs and strategic pluralism. *Behavioral and Brain Sciences, 23,* 573–587. (p. 119)

Garcia, J., & Gustavson, A. R. (1997, January). Carl R. Gustavson (1946–1996): Pioneering wildlife psychologist. *APS Observer,* pp. 34–35. (p. 163)

Garcia, J., & Koelling, R. A. (1966). Relation of cue to consequence in avoidance learning. *Psychonomic Science, 4,* 123–124. (p. 162)

Gardner, H. (1983). *Frames of mind: The theory of multiple intelligences.* New York: Basic Books. (p. 218)

Gardner, H. (1998, March 19). An intelligent way to progress. *The Independent (London),* p. E4. (pp. 82, 219)

Gardner, H. (1999). *Multiple views of multiple intelligence.* New York: Basic Books. (pp. 218, 222)

Gardner, R. A., & Gardner, B. I. (1969). Teaching sign language to a chimpanzee. *Science, 165,* 664–672. (p. 216)

Gardner, R. M., & Tockerman, Y. R. (1994). A computer-TV video methodology for investigating the influence of somatotype on perceived personality traits. *Journal of Social Behavior and Personality, 9,* 555–563. (p. 242)

Garfield, C. (1986). *Peak performers: The new heroes of American business.* New York: Morrow. (p. 214)

Garner, D. M., & Wooley, S. C. (1991). Confronting the failure of behavioral and dietary treatments for obesity. *Clinical Psychology Review, 11,* 729–780. (p. 245)

Garry, M., Manning, C. G., Loftus, E. F., & Sherman, S. J. (1996). Imagination inflation: Imagining a childhood event inflates confidence that it occurred. *Psychonomic Bulletin & Review, 3,* 208–214. (p. 197)

Gates, W. (1998, July 20). Charity begins when I'm ready (interview). *Fortune* (www.pathfinder.com/fortune/1998/980720/bil7.html). (p. 219)

Gawin, F. H. (1991). Cocaine addiction: Psychology and neurophysiology. *Science, 251,* 1580–1586. (p. 329)

Gazzaniga, M. S. (1967, August). The split brain in man. *Scientific American,* pp. 24–29. (p. 45)

Gazzaniga, M. S. (1983). Right hemisphere language following brain bisection: A 20-year perspective. *American Psychologist, 38,* 525–537. (p. 46)

Gazzaniga, M. S. (1988). Organization of the human brain. *Science, 245,* 947–952. (p. 46)

Geary, D. C. (1995). Sexual selection and sex differences in spatial cognition. *Learning and Individual Differences, 7,* 289–301. (p. 229)

Geary, D. C. (1996). Sexual selection and sex differences in mathematical abilities. *Behavioral and Brain Sciences, 19,* 229–247. (p. 229)

Geary, D. C. (1998). *Male, female: The evolution of human sex differences.* Washington, DC: American Psychological Association. (p. 119)

Geary, D. C., Salthouse, T. A., Chen, G-P., & Fan, L. (1996). Are East Asian versus American differences in arithmetical ability a recent phenomenon? *Developmental Psychology, 32,* 254–262. (p. 228)

Geen, R. G., & Quanty, M. B. (1977). The catharsis of aggression: An evaluation of a hypothesis. In L. Berkowitz (Ed.), *Advances in experimental social psychology (Vol. 10).* New York: Academic Press. (p. 260)

Geen, R. G., & Thomas, S. L. (1986). The immediate effects of media violence on behavior. *Journal of Social Issues, 42(3),* 7–28. (p. 176)

Gehring, W. J., Wimke, J., & Nisenson, L. G. (2000). Action monitoring dysfunction in obsessive-compulsive disorder. *Psychological Science, 11(1),* 1–6. (p. 322)

Genevro, J. L. (2003). *Report on bereavement and grief research.* Washington, DC: Center for the Advancement of Health. (p. 96)

Gentile, D. A., Lynch, P. J., Linder, J. R., & Walsh, D. A. (2004). The effects of violent video game habits on adolescent hostility, aggressive behaviors, and school performance. *Journal of Adolescence, 27,* 5–22. (pp. 175, 393)

George, L. K., Ellison, C. G., & Larson, D. B. (2002). Explaining the relationships between religious involvement and health. *Psychological Inquiry, 13,* 190–200. (p. 284)

George, L. K., Larson, D. B., Koenig, H. G., & McCullough, M. E. (2000). Spirituality and health: What we know, what we need to know. *Journal of Social and Clinical Psychology, 19,* 102–116. (p. 284)

George, M. S. (2003, September). Stimulating the brain. *Scientific American,* pp. 67–73. (p. 370)

Gerbner, G. (1990). Stories that hurt: Tobacco, alcohol, and other drugs in the mass media. In H. Resnik (Ed.), *Youth and drugs: Society's mixed messages.* Rockville, MD: Office for Substance Abuse Prevention, U.S. Department of Health and Human Services. (p. 334)

Gerhart, K. A., Koziol-McLain, J., Lowenstein, S. R., & Whiteneck, G. G. (1994). Quality of life following spinal cord injury: Knowledge and attitudes of emergency care providers. *Annals of Emergency Medicine, 23,* 807–812. (p. 262)

Gerrard, M., & Luus, C. A. E. (1995). Judgments of vulnerability to pregnancy: The role of risk factors and individual differences. *Personality and Social Psychology Bulletin, 21,* 160–171. (p. 111)

Gershoff, E. T. (2002). Parental corporal punishment and associated child behaviors and experiences: A meta-analytic and theoretical review. *Psychological Bulletin, 128,* 539–579. (p. 168)

Gershon, J., Anderson, P., Graap, K., Zimand, E., Hodges, L., & Rothbaum, B. O. (2002). Virtual reality exposure therapy in the treatment of anxiety disorders. *Scientific Review of Mental Health Practice, 1,* 76–81. (p. 356)

Gibbons, F. X. (1986). Social comparison and depression: Company's effect on misery. *Journal of Personality and Social Psychology, 51,* 140–148. (p. 264)

Gibson, E. J., & Walk, R. D. (1960, April). The "visual cliff." *Scientific American,* pp. 64–71. (p. 144)

Gigerenzer, G. (2004). Fast and frugal heuristics: The tools of bounded rationality. In D. Koehler & N. Harvey (Eds.), *Handbook of judgment and decision making.* Oxford, UK: Blackwell. (pp. 209, 210)

Gilbert, D. T. (2006). *Stumbling on happiness.* New York: Knopf. (pp. 95, 211, 308)

Gilbert, D. T., Pinel, E. C., Wilson, T. D., Blumberg, S. J., & Wheatley, T. P. (1998). Immune neglect: A source of durability bias in affective forecasting. *Journal of Personality and Social Psychology, 75,* 617–638. (p. 261)

Gilligan, C. (1982). *In a different voice: Psychological theory and women's development.* Cambridge, MA: Harvard University Press. (p. 105)

Gilligan, C., Lyons, N. P., & Hanmer, T. J. (Eds.). (1990). *Making connections: The relational worlds of adolescent girls at Emma Willard School.* Cambridge, MA: Harvard University Press. (p. 105)

Gilovich, T. (1991). *How we know what isn't so: The fallibility of human reason in everyday life.* New York: Free Press. (p. 16)

Gilovich, T. D. (1996). The spotlight effect: Exaggerated impressions of the self as a social stimulus. Unpublished manuscript, Cornell University. (p. 306)

Gilovich, T., & Medvec, V. H. (1995). The experience of regret: What, when, and why. *Psychological Review, 102,* 379–395. (p. 97)

Gilovich, T., & Savitsky, K. (1999). The spotlight effect and the illusion of transparency: Egocentric assessments of how we are seen by others. *Current Directions in Psychological Science, 8,* 165–168. (p. 306)

Gingerich, O. (1999, February 6). Is there a role for natural theology today? *The Real Issue* (www.origins.org/real/n9501/natural.html). (p. 120)

Gladue, B. A. (1990). Hormones and neuroendocrine factors in atypical human sexual behavior. In J. R. Feierman (Ed.), *Pedophilia: Biosocial dimensions.* New York: Springer-Verlag. (p. 116)

Gladue, B. A. (1994). The biopsychology of sexual orientation. *Current Directions in Psychological Science, 3,* 150–154. (p. 116)

Glass, R. I. (2004). Perceived threats and real killers. *Science, 304,* 927. (p. 210)

Glass, R. M. (2001). Electroconvulsive therapy: Time to bring it out of the shadows. *Journal of the American Medical Association, 285,* 1346–1348. (p. 368)

Glater, J. D. (2001, March 26). Women are close to being majority of law students. *New York Times* (www.nytimes.com). (p. 107)

Gleaves, D. H. (1996). The sociocognitive model of dissociative identity disorder: A reexamination of the evidence. *Psychological Bulletin, 120,* 42–59. (p. 323)

Glenn, N. D. (1975). Psychological well-being in the postparental stage: Some evidence from national surveys. *Journal of Marriage and the Family, 37,* 105–110. (p. 95)

Godden, D. R., & Baddeley, A. D. (1975). Context-dependent memory in two natural environments: On land and underwater. *British Journal of Psychology, 66,* 325–331. (pp. 190, 191)

Goel, V., & Dolan, R. J. (2001). The functional anatomy of humor: Segregating cognitive and affective components. *Nature Neuroscience, 4,* 237–238. (p. 44)

Goff, D. C., & Simms, C. A. (1993). Has multiple personality disorder remained consistent over time? *Journal of Nervous and Mental Disease, 181,* 595–600. (p. 323)

Gold, M., & Yanof, D. S. (1985). Mothers, daughters, and girlfriends. *Journal of Personality and Social Psychology, 49,* 654–659. (p. 88)

Goldapple, K., Segal, Z., Garson, C., Lau, M., Bieling, P., Kennedy, S., & Mayberg, H. (2004). Modulation of cortical-limbic pathways in major depression. *Archives of General Psychiatry, 61,* 34–41. (p. 367)

Goldberg, J. (2007, accessed May 31). Quivering bundles that let us hear, by J. Goldberg. Howard Hughes Medical Institute (www.hhmi.org/senses/c120.html). (p. 134)

Goldfried, M. R., & Padawer, W. (1982). Current status and future directions in psychotherapy. In M. R. Goldfried (Ed.), *Converging themes in psychotherapy: Trends in psychodynamic, humanistic, and behavioral practice.* New York: Springer. (p. 363)

Goldfried, M. R., Raue, P. J., & Castonguay, L. G. (1998). The therapeutic focus in significant sessions of master therapists: A comparison of cognitive-behavioral and psychodynamic-interpersonal interventions. *Journal of Consulting and Clinical Psychology, 66,* 803–810. (p. 363)

Golding, J. M. (1999). Sexual-assault history and the long-term physical health problems: Evidence from clinical and population epidemiology. *Current Directions in Psychological Science, 8,* 191–194. (p. 320)

Goldstein, I. (2000, August). Male sexual circuitry. *Scientific American,* pp. 70–75. (p. 33)

Goldstein, I., Lue, T. F., Padma-Nathan, H., Rosen, R. C., Steers, W. D., & Wicker, P. A. (1998). Oral sildenafil in the treatment of erectile dysfunction. *New England Journal of Medicine, 338,* 1397–1404. (pp. 17, 392)

Goleman, D. (1980, February). 1,528 little geniuses and how they grew. *Psychology Today,* pp. 28–53. (p. 409)

Goleman, D. (1995). *Emotional intelligence.* New York: Bantam. (p. 253)

Gonsalves, B., Reber, P. J., Gitelman, D. R., Parrish, T. B., Mesulam, M-M., & Paller, K. A. (2004). Neural evidence that vivid imagining can lead to false remembering. *Psychological Science, 15,* 655–659. (p. 197)

Goodale, M. A., & Milner, D. A. (2004). *Sight unseen: An exploration of conscious and unconscious vision.* Oxford: Oxford University Press. (p. 8)

Goodale, M. A., & Milner, D. A. (2006). One brain—two visual systems. *The Psychologist, 19,* 660–663. (p. 8)

Goodall, J. (1986). *The chimpanzees of Gombe: Patterns of behavior.* Cambridge, MA: Harvard University Press. (p. 390)

Goode, E. (1999, April 13). If things taste bad, 'phantoms' may be at work. *New York Times* (www.nytimes.com). (p. 138)

Goode, E. (2003, January 28). Even in the age of Prozac, some still prefer the couch. *New York Times* (www.nytimes.com). (p. 352)

Goodhart, D. E. (1986). The effects of positive and negative thinking on performance in an achievement situation. *Journal of Personality and Social Psychology, 51,* 117–124. (p. 279)

Goodman, G. S., Ghetti, S., Quas, J. A., Edelstein, R. S., Alexander, K. W., Redlich, A. D., Cordon, I. M., & Jones, D. P. H. (2003). A prospective study of memory for child sexual abuse: New findings relevant to the repressed-memory controversy. *Psychological Science, 14,* 113–118. (p. 199)

Goodman, G. S., Rudy, L., Bottoms, B. L., & Aman, B. (1990). Children's concerns and memory: Issues of ecological validity in the study of children's eyewitness testimony. In R. Fivush & J. A. Hudson (Eds.), *Knowing and remembering in young children.* New York: Cambridge University Press. (p. 198)

Goodwin, F. K., & Morrison, A. R. (1999). Scientists in bunkers: How appeasement of animal rights activism has failed. *Cerebrum, 1*(2), 50–62. (p. 20)

Goranson, R. E. (1978). The hindsight effect in problem solving. Unpublished manuscript, cited by G. Wood (1984), Research methodology: A decision-making perspective. In A. M. Rogers & C. J. Scheirer (Eds.), *The G. Stanley Hall Lecture Series* (Vol. 4). Washington, DC: American Psychological Association. (p. 10)

Gore-Felton, C., Koopman, C., Thoresen, C., Arnow, B., Bridges, E., & Spiegel, D. (2000). Psychologists' beliefs and clinical characteristics: Judging the veracity of childhood sexual abuse memories. *Professional Psychology: Research and Practice, 31,* 372–377. (p. 199)

Gortmaker, S. L., Must, A., Perrin, J. M., Sobol, A. M., & Dietz, W. H. (1993). Social and economic consequences of overweight in adolescence and young adulthood. *New England Journal of Medicine, 329,* 1008–1012. (p. 242)

Gosling, S. D., Ko, S. J., Mannarelli, T., & Morris, M. E. (2002). A room with a cue: Personality judgments based on offices and bedrooms. *Journal of Personality and Social Psychology, 82,* 379–398. (p. 304)

Gotlib, I. H., & Hammen, C. L. (1992). Psychological aspects of depression: Toward a cognitive-interpersonal integration. New York: Wiley. (p. 340)

Gottesman, I. I. (1991). *Schizophrenia genesis: The origins of madness.* New York: Freeman. (p. 344)

Gottesman, I. I. (2001). Psychopathology through a life span—genetic prism. *American Psychologist, 56,* 867–881. (p. 344)

Gottfredson, L. S. (2002a). Where and why g matters: Not a mystery. *Human Performance, 15,* 25–46. (p. 220)

Gottfredson, L. S. (2002b). g: Highly general and highly practical. In R. J. Sternberg & E. L. Grigorenko (Eds.), *The general factor of intelligence: How general is it?* Mahwah, NJ: Erlbaum. (p. 220)

Gottfredson, L. S. (2003a). Dissecting practical intelligence theory: Its claims and evidence. *Intelligence, 31,* 343–397. (p. 220)

Gottfredson, L. S. (2003b). On Sternberg's "Reply to Gottfredson." *Intelligence, 31,* 415–424. (p. 220)

Gould, S. J. (1997, June 12). Darwinian fundamentalism. *The New York Review of Books, XLIV(10),* 34–37. (p. 119)

Grady, C. L., & McIntosh, A. R., Horwitz, B., Maisog, J. M., Ungeleider, L. G., Mentis, M. J., Pietrini, P., Schapiro, M. B., & Haxby, J. V. (1995). Age-related reductions in human recognition memory due to impaired encoding. *Science, 269,* 218–221. (p. 193)

Graham, J. W., Marks, G., & Hansen, W. B. (1991). Social influence processes affecting adolescent substance use. *Journal of Applied Psychology, 76,* 291–298. (p. 334)

Gray-Little, B., & Burks, N. (1983). Power and satisfaction in marriage: A review and critique. *Psychological Bulletin, 93,* 513–538. (p. 398)

Gray-Little, B., & Hafdahl, A. R. (2000). Factors influencing racial comparisons of self-esteem: A quantitative review. *Psychological Bulletin, 126,* 26–54. (p. 307)

Green, J. T., & Woodruff-Pak, D. S. (2000). Eyeblink classical conditioning: Hippocampal formation is for neutral stimulus associations as cerebellum is for association-response. *Psychological Bulletin, 126,* 138–158. (p. 189)

Greenfeld, L. A. (1998). *Alcohol and crime: An analysis of national data on the prevalence of alcohol involvement in crime.* Washington, DC: Document NCJ–168632, Bureau of Justice Statistics (www.ojp.usdoj.gov/bjs). (p. 392)

Greenwald, A. G. (1992). Subliminal semantic activation and subliminal snake oil. Paper presented to the American Psychological Association Convention, Washington, DC. (p. 127)

Greenwald, A. G., McGhee, D. E., & Schwartz, J. L. K. (1998). Measuring individual differences in implicit cognition: The implicit association test. *Journal of Personality and Social Psychology, 74,* 1464–1480. (p. 389)

Greenwald, A. G., Oakes, M. A., & Hoffman, H. (2003). Targets of discrimination: Effects of race on responses to weapons holders. *Journal of Experimental Social Psychology, 39,* 399. (p. 389)

Greenwald, A. G., Spangenberg, E. R., Pratkanis, A. R., & Eskenazi, J. (1991). Double-blind tests of subliminal self-help audiotapes. *Psychological Science, 2,* 119–122. (p. 127)

Greenwood, M. R. C. (1989). Sexual dimorphism and obesity. In A. J. Stunkard & A. Baum (Eds.). *Perspectives in behavioral medicine: Eating, sleeping, and sex.* Hillsdale, NJ: Erlbaum. (p. 242)

Greers, A. E. (2004). Speech, language, and reading skills after early cochlear implantation. *Archives of Otolaryngology—Head & Neck Surgery, 130,* 634–638. (p. 213)

Gregory, R. L. (1978). *Eye and brain: The psychology of seeing (3rd ed.).* New York: McGraw-Hill. (p. 148)

Gregory, R. L., & Gombrich, E. H. (Eds.). (1973). *Illusion in nature and art.* New York: Charles Scribner's Sons. (p. 151)

Greif, E. B., & Ulman, K. J. (1982). The psychological impact of menarche on early adolescent females: A review of the literature. *Child Development, 53,* 1413–1430. (p. 84)

Greist, J. H., Jefferson, J. W., & Marks, I. M. (1986). *Anxiety and its treatment: Help is available.* Washington, DC: American Psychiatric Press. (p. 319)

Grèzes, J., & Decety, J. (2001). Function anatomy of execution, mental simulation, observation, and verb generation of actions: A meta-analysis. *Human Brain Mapping, 12,* 1–19. (p. 214)

Grilo, C. M., & Pogue-Geile, M. F. (1991). The nature of environmental influences on weight and obesity: A behavior genetic analysis. *Psychological Bulletin, 110,* 520–537. (p. 244)

Grobstein, C. (1979, June). External human fertilization. *Scientific American,* pp. 57-67. (p. 66)

Gross, A. E., & Crofton, C. (1977). What is good is beautiful. *Sociometry, 40,* 85–90. (p. 396)

Grossberg, S. (1995). The attentive brain. *American Scientist, 83,* 438–449. (p. 150)

Grossman, M., & Wood, W. (1993). Sex differences in intensity of emotional experience: A social role interpretation. *Journal of Personality and Social Psychology, 65,* 1010–1022. (p. 257)

Gruder, C. L. (1977). Choice of comparison persons in evaluating oneself. In J. M. Suls & R. L. Miller (Eds.), *Social comparison processes.* New York: Hemisphere. (p. 264)

Grunebaum, M. F., Ellis, S. P., Li, S., Oquendo, M. A., Mann, J. J. (2004). Antidepressants and suicide risk in the United States, 1985–1999. *Journal of Clinical Psychiatry, 65,* 1456–1462. (p. 367)

Guerin, B. (1986). Mere presence effects in humans: A review. *Journal of Personality and Social Psychology, 22,* 38–77. (p. 384)

Guerin, B. (2003). Language use as social strategy: A review and an analytic framework for the social sciences. *Review of General Psychology, 7,* 251–298. (p. 211)

Gustafson, D., Lissner, L., Bengtsson, C., Björkelund, C., & Skoog, I. (2004). A 24-year follow-up of body mass index and cerebral atrophy. *Neurology, 63,* 1876–1881. (p. 242)

Gustafson, D., Rothenberg, E., Blennow, K., Steen, B., & Skoog, I. (2003). An 18-year follow-up of overweight and risk of Alzheimer disease. *Archives of Internal Medicine, 163,* 1524–1528. (p. 242)

Gustavson, C. R., Garcia, J., Hankins, W. G., & Rusiniak, K. W. (1974). Coyote predation control by aversive conditioning. *Science, 184,* 581–583. (p. 163)

Gustavson, C. R., Kelly, D. J., & Sweeney, M. (1976). Prey-lithium aversions I: Coyotes and wolves. *Behavioral Biology, 17,* 61–72. (p. 163)

Guttmacher Institute. (1994). *Sex and America's teenagers.* New York: Alan Guttmacher Institute. (p. 89, 110)

Guttmacher Institute. (2000). *Fulfilling the promise: Public policy and U.S. family planning clinics.* New York: Alan Guttmacher Institute. (p. 89)

H., Sally. (1979, August). Videotape recording number T–3, Fortunoff Video Archive of Holocaust Testimonies. New Haven, CT: Yale University Library. (p. 296)

Haber, R. N. (1970, May). How we remember what we see. *Scientific American,* pp. 104–112. (p. 81)

Haidt, J. (2006). *The happiness hypothesis: Finding modern truth in ancient wisdom.* New York: Basic Books. (p. 85)

Hakuta, K., Bialystok, E., & Wiley, E. (2003). Critical evidence: A test of the critical-period hypothesis for second-language acquisition. *Psychological Science, 14,* 31–38. (p. 213)

Halberstadt, J. B., Niedenthal, P. M., & Kushner, J. (1995). Resolution of lexical ambiguity by emotional state. *Psychological Science, 6,* 278–281. (p. 150)

Haldeman, D. C. (1994). The practice and ethics of sexual orientation conversion therapy. *Journal of Consulting and Clinical Psychology, 62,* 221–227. (p. 114)

Haldeman, D. C. (2002). Gay rights, patient rights: The implications of sexual orientation conversion therapy. *Professional Psychology: Research and Practice, 33,* 260–264. (p. 114)

Hall, C. S., & Lindzey, G. (1978). *Theories of personality (2nd ed.).* New York: Wiley. (p. 295)

Hall, C. S., Dornhoff, W., Blick, K. A., & Weesner, K. E. (1982). The dreams of college men and women in 1950 and 1980: A comparison of dream contents and sex differences. *Sleep, 5,* 188–194. (p. 57)

Hall, G. (1997). Context aversion, Pavlovian conditioning, and the psychological side effects of chemotherapy. *European Psychologist, 2,* 118–124. (p. 163)

Hall, J. A. (1984). *Nonverbal sex differences: Communication accuracy and expressive style.* Baltimore: Johns Hopkins University Press. (p. 257)

Hall, J. A. (1987). On explaining gender differences: The case of nonverbal communication. In P. Shaver & C. Hendrick (Eds.), *Review of Personality and Social Psychology, 7,* 177–200. (p. 105, 257)

Hall, S. S. (2004, May). The good egg. *Discover,* pp. 30–39. (p. 66)

Halpern, C. T., Joyner, K., Udry, J. R., & Suchindran, C. (2000). Smart teens don't have sex (or kiss much either). *Journal of Adolescent Health, 26,* 213–225. (p. 112)

Halpern, D. F. (1991). Cognitive sex differences: Why diversity is a critical research issue. Paper presented to the American Psychological Association convention. (p. 229)

Halpern, D. F. (2000). *Sex-related ability differences: Changing perspectives, changing minds.* Mahwah, NJ: Erlbaum. (p. 229)

Hamann, S., Monarch, E. S., & Goldstein, F. C. (2002). Impaired fear conditioning in Alzheimer's disease. *Neuropsychologica, 40,* 1187–1195. (p. 187)

Hammersmith, S. K. (1982, August). Sexual preference: An empirical study from the Alfred C. Kinsey Institute for Sex Research. Paper presented at the meeting of the American Psychological Association, Washington, DC. (p. 115)

Hampson, R. (2000, April 10). In the end, people just need more room. *USA Today,* p. 19A. (p. 245)

Hankin, B. L., & Abramson, L. Y. (2001). Development of gender differences in depression: An elaborated cognitive vulnerability-transactional stress theory. *Psychological Bulletin, 127,* 773–796. (p. 339)

Hansen, C. H., & Hansen, R. D. (1988). Finding the face-in-the-crowd: An anger superiority effect. *Journal of Personality and Social Psychology, 54,* 917–924. (p. 257)

Hare, R. D. (1975). Psychophysiological studies of psychopathy. In D. C. Fowles (Ed.), *Clinical applications of psychophysiology.* New York: Columbia University Press. (p. 324)

Harkins, S. G., & Szymanski, K. (1989). Social loafing and group evaluation. *Journal of Personality and Social Psychology, 56,* 934–941. (p. 384)

Harlow, H. F., Harlow, M. K., & Suomi, S. J. (1971). From thought to therapy: Lessons from a primate laboratory. *American Scientist, 59,* 538–549. (p. 77)

Harmon-Jones, E., Abramson, L. Y., Sigelman, J., Bohlig, A., Hogan, M. E., & Harmon-Jones, C. (2002). Proneness to hypomania/mania symptoms or depression symptoms and asymmetrical frontal cortical responses to an anger-evoking event. *Journal of Personality and Social Psychology, 82,* 610–618. (p. 253)

Harris, B. (1979). Whatever happened to Little Albert? *American Psychologist, 34,* 151–160. (p. 164)

Harris, J. R. (1998). *The nurture assumption.* New York: Free Press. (pp. 78, 82)

Harris, R. J. (1994). The impact of sexually explicit media. In J. Brant & D. Zillmann (Eds.), *Media effects: Advances in theory and research.* Hillsdale, NJ: Erlbaum. (p. 394)

Harrison, Y., & Horne, J. A. (2000). The impact of sleep deprivation on decision making: A review. *Journal of Experimental Psychology: Applied, 6,* 236–249. (p. 54)

Harter, J. K. (2000, Winter/Spring). The linkage of employee perceptions to outcomes in a retail environment—cause and effect? *Gallup Research Journal,* pp. 25–38. (p. 411)

Harter, J. K., Schmidt, F. L., & Hayes, T. L. (2002). Business-unit-level relationship between employee satisfaction, employee engagement, and business outcomes: A meta-analysis. *Journal of Applied Psychology, 87,* 268–279. (p. 410)

Hartmann, E. (1981, April). The strangest sleep disorder. *Psychology Today,* pp. 14, 16, 18. (p. 56)

Hatfield, E. (1988). Passionate and companionate love. In R. J. Sternberg & M. L. Barnes (Eds.), *The psychology of love.* New Haven: Yale University Press. (pp. 397, 398)

Hatfield, E., & Sprecher, S. (1986). *Mirror, mirror . . . The importance of looks in everyday life.* Albany: State University of New York Press. (p. 395)

Haxby, J. V. (2001, July 7). Quoted by B. Bower, Faces of perception. *Science News,* pp. 10–12. See also J. V. Haxby, M. I. Gobbini, M. L. Furey, A. Ishai, J. L. Schouten & P. Pietrini, Distributed and overlapping representations of faces and objects in ventral temporal cortex. *Science, 293,* 2425–2430. (p. 132)

Hebl, M. R., & Mannix, L. M. (2003). The weight of obesity in evaluating others: A mere proximity effect. *Personality and Social Psychology Bulletin, 29,* 28–38. (p. 243)

Hedges, L. V., & Nowell, A. (1995). Sex differences in mental test scores, variability, and numbers of high-scoring individuals. *Science, 269,* 41–45. (p. 229)

Heider, F. (1958). *The psychology of interpersonal relations.* New York: Wiley. (p. 376)

Heiman, J. R. (1975, April). The physiology of erotica: Women's sexual arousal. *Psychology Today,* 90–94. (p. 112)

Heine, S. J., & Hamamura, T. (2007). In search of East Asian self-enhancement. *Personality and Social Psychology Review, 11,* 4–27. (p. 307)

Helmreich, W. B. (1992). *Against all odds: Holocaust survivors and the successful lives they made in America.* New York: Simon & Schuster. (p. 296)

Helmreich, W. B. (1994). Personal correspondence. Department of Sociology, City University of New York. (p. 296)

Helms, J. E., Jernigan, M., & Mascher, J. (2005). The meaning of race in psychology and how to change it: A methodological perspective. *American Psychologist, 60,* 27–36. (p. 228)

Helmuth, L. (2001). Boosting brain activity from the outside in. *Science, 292,* 1284–1286. (p. 369)

Henderlong, J., & Lepper, M. R. (2002). The effects of praise on children's intrinsic motivation: A review and synthesis. *Psychological Bulletin, 128,* 774–795. (p. 170)

Henkel, L. A., Franklin, N., & Johnson, M. K. (2000, March). Cross-modal source monitoring confusions between perceived and imagined events. *Journal of Experimental Psychology: Learning, Memory, & Cognition, 26,* 321–335. (p. 197)

Herman, C. P., & Polivy, J. (1980). Restrained eating. In A. J. Stunkard (Ed.), *Obesity.* Philadelphia: Saunders. (p. 246)

Herrnstein, R. J., & Loveland, D. H. (1964). Complex visual concept in the pigeon. *Science, 146,* 549–551. (p. 166)

Herrnstein, R. J., & Murray, C. A. (1994). *The bell curve: Intelligence and class structure in American life.* NY: Free Press. (p. 227)

Hertenstein, M. J. (2002). Touch: Its communicative functions in infancy. *Human Development, 45, 70–94.* (p. 78)

Herz, R. S. (2001). Ah sweet skunk! Why we like or dislike what we smell. *Cerebrum, 3(4),* 31–47. (p. 141)

Hess, E. H. (1956, July). Space perception in the chick. *Scientific American,* pp. 71–80. (p. 149)

Hettema, J. M., Neale, M. C., & Kendler, K. S. (2001). A review and meta-analysis of the genetic epidemiology of anxiety disorders. *American Journal of Psychiatry, 158,* 1568–1578. (p. 322)

Hickok, G., Bellugi, U., & Klima, E. S. (2001, June). Sign language in the brain. *Scientific American,* pp. 58–65. (p. 47)

Hill, C. E., & Nakayama, E. Y. (2000). Client-centered therapy: Where has it been and where is it going? A comment on Hathaway. *Journal of Clinical Psychology, 56,* 961–875. (p. 354)

Hines, M. (2004). *Brain gender.* New York: Oxford University Press. (p. 106)

Hingson, R. W., Heeren, T., & Winter M. R. (2006). Age at drinking onset and alcohol dependence. *Archives of Pediatrics & Adolescent Medicine, 160,* 739–746. (p. 327)

Hingson, R. W., Heeren, T., Zakocs, R. C., Kopstein, A., & Wechsler, H. (2002). Magnitude of alcohol-related mortality and morbidity among U.S. college students ages 18–24. *Journal of Studies on Alcohol, 63,* 136–144. (p. 328)

Hinz, L. D., & Williamson, D. A. (1987). Bulimia and depression: A review of the affective variant hypothesis. *Psychological Bulletin, 102,* 150–158. (p. 241)

Hirsch, J. (2003). Obesity: Matter over mind? *Cerebrum, 5(1),* 7–18. (p. 244)

Hobson, J. A. (2003). *Dreaming: An introduction to the science of sleep.* New York: Oxford. (p. 58)

Hobson, J. A. (2004). *13 dreams Freud never had: The new mind science.* New York: Pi Press. (p. 58)

Hoebel, B. G., & Teitelbaum, P. (1966). Effects of forcefeeding and starvation on food intake and body weight in a rat with ventromedial hypothalamic lesions. *Journal of Comparative and Physiological Psychology, 61,* 189–193. (p. 239)

Hoffman, C., & Hurst, N. (1990). Gender stereotypes: Perception or rationalization? *Journal of Personality and Social Psychology, 58,* 197–208. (p. 389)

Hoffman, D. D. (1998). *Visual intelligence: How we create what we see.* New York: Norton. (p. 133)

Hoffman, H. G. (2004, August). Virtual-reality therapy. *Scientific American,* pp. 58–65. (pp. 138, 356)

Hogan, R. (1998). Reinventing personality. *Journal of Social and Clinical Psychology, 17,* 1–10. (p. 304)

Hoge, C. W., Castro, C. A., Messer, S. C., McGurk, D., Cotting, D. I., & Koffman, R. L. (2004). Combat duty in Iraq and Afghanistan, mental health problems, and barriers to care. *New England Journal of Medicine, 35,* 13–22. (p. 320)

Hogg, M. A. (1996). Intragroup processes, group structure and social identity. In W. P. Robinson (Ed.), *Social groups and identities: Developing the legacy of Henri Tajfel.* Oxford: Butterworth Heinemann. (p. 389)

Hohmann, G. W. (1966). Some effects of spinal cord lesions on experienced emotional feelings. *Psychophysiology, 3,* 143–156. (p. 249)

Hokanson, J. E., & Edelman, R. (1966). Effects of three social responses on vascular processes. *Journal of Personality and Social Psychology, 3,* 442–447. (p. 260)

Holden, C. (1993). Wake-up call for sleep research. *Science, 259,* 305. (p. 54)

Holliday, R. E., & Albon, A. J. (2004). Minimizing misinformation effects in young children with cognitive interview mnemonics. *Applied Cognitive Psychology, 18,* 263–281. (p. 198)

Hollis, K. L. (1997). Contemporary research on Pavlovian conditioning: A "new" functional analysis. *American Psychologist, 52,* 956–965. (p. 161)

Hollon, S. D., & 10 others. (2005). Prevention of relapse following cognitive therapy vs. medications in moderate to severe depression. *Archives of General Psychiatry, 62,* 417–422. (p. 362)

Hollon, S. D., Thase, M. E., & Markowitz, J. C. (2002). Treatment and prevention of depression. *Psychological Science in the Public Interest, 3,* 39–77. (p. 367)

Holstege, G., Georgiadis, J. R., Paans, A. M. J., Meiners, L. C., van der Graaf, F. H. C. E., & Reinders, A. A. T. S. (2003a). Brain activation during male ejaculation. *Journal of Neuroscience, 23,* 9185–9193. (p. 109)

Holstege, G., Reinders, A. A. T., Paans, A. M. J., Meiners, L. C., Pruim, J., & Georgiadis, J. R. (2003b). *Brain activation during female sexual orgasm. Program No. 727.7.* Washington, DC: Society for Neuroscience. (p. 109)

Home Office. (2003). *Prevalence of drug use: Key findings from the 2002/2003 British Crime Survey.* London: Research, Development and Statistics Directorate, Home Office. (p. 329)

Hooper, J., & Teresi, D. (1986). *The three-pound universe.* New York: Macmillan. (p. 38)

Horn, J. L. (1982). The aging of human abilities. In J. Wolman (Ed.), *Handbook of developmental psychology.* Englewood Cliffs, NJ: Prentice Hall. (p. 93)

Horner, V., Whiten, A., Flynn, E., & de Waal, F. B. M. (2006). Faithful replication of foraging techniques along cultural transmission chains by chimpanzees and children. *Proceedings of the National Academy of Sciences, 103,* 13878–13883. (p. 216)

Horrey, W. J., & Wickens, C. D. (2006). Examining the impact of cell phone conversations on driving using meta-analytic techniques. *Human Factors and Ergonomics Society, 48,* 196–205. (p. 49)

Horwood, L. J., & Fergusson, D. M. (1998). Breastfeeding and later cognitive and academic outcomes. *Pediatrics, 101(1).* (p. 15)

House, J. S., Landis, K. R., & Umberson, D. (1988). Social relationships and health. *Science, 241,* 540–545. (p. 280)

House, R. J., & Singh, J. V. (1987). Organizational behavior: Some new directions for I/O psychology. *Annual Review of Psychology, 38,* 669–718. (p. 412)

Houts, A. C., Berman, J. S., & Abramson, H. (1994). Effectiveness of psychological and pharmacological treatments for nocturnal enuresis. *Journal of Consulting and Clinical Psychology, 62,* 737–745. (p. 355)

Howe, M. L. (1997). Children's memory for traumatic experiences. *Learning and Individual Differences, 9,* 153–174. (p. 198)

Hu, F. B., Li, T. Y., Colditz, G. A., Willett, W. C., & Manson, J. E. (2003). Television watching and other sedentary behaviors in relation to risk of obesity and type 2 diabetes mellitus in women. *Journal of the American Medical Association, 289,* 1785–1791. (p. 245)

Hubel, D. H., & Wiesel, T. N. (1979, September). Brain mechanisms of vision. *Scientific American,* pp. 150–162. (p. 132)

Hublin, C., Kaprio, J., Partinen, M., Heikkila, K., & Koskenvuo, M. (1997). Prevalence and genetics of sleepwalking—A population-based twin study. *Neurology, 48,* 177–181. (p. 56)

Hublin, C., Kaprio, J., Partinen, M., & Koskenvuo, M. (1998). Sleeptalking in twins: Epidemiology and psychiatric comorbidity. *Behavior Genetics, 28,* 289–298. (p. 56)

Hucker, S. J., & Bain, J. (1990). Androgenic hormones and sexual assault. In W. Marshall, R. Law, & H. Barbaree (Eds.), *The handbook on sexual assault.* New York: Plenum. (p. 110)

Hughes, H. C. (1999). *Sensory exotica: A world beyond human experience.* Cambridge, MA: MIT Press. (p. 126)

Hugick, L. (1989, July). Women play the leading role in keeping modern families close. *Gallup Report, No. 286,* p. 27–34. (p. 105)

Hull, J. M. (1990). *Touching the rock: An experience of blindness.* New York: Vintage Books. (pp. 190, 396)

Hummer, R. A., Rogers, R. G., Nam, C. B., & Ellison, C. G. (1999). Religious involvement and U.S. adult mortality. *Demography, 36,* 273–285. (p. 283)

Hunsley, J., & Di Giulio, G. (2002). Dodo bird, phoenix, or urban legend? The question of psychotherapy equivalence. *Scientific Review of Mental Health Practice, 1,* 11–22. (p. 362)

Hunt, C., Slade, T., & Andrews, G. (2004). Generalized anxiety disorder and major depressive disorder comorbidity in the *National Survey of Mental Health and Well-Being. Depression and Anxiety, 20,* 23–31. (p. 318)

Hunt, J. M. (1982). Toward equalizing the developmental opportunities of infants and preschool children. *Journal of Social Issues, 38*(4), 163–191. (p. 227)

Hunt, M. (1974). *Sexual behavior in the 1970s.* Chicago: Playboy Press. (p. 112)

Hunt, M. (1990). *The compassionate beast: What science is discovering about the humane side of humankind.* New York: William Morrow. (p. 4)

Hunt, M. (1993). *The story of psychology.* New York: Doubleday. (pp. 1, 2)

Huston, A. C., Donnerstein, E., Fairchild, H., Feshbach, N. D., Katz, P. A., & Murray, J. P. (1992). *Big world, small screen: The role of television in American society.* Lincoln, NE: University of Nebraska Press. (p. 175)

Hyde, J. S. (1983, November). Bem's gender schema theory. Paper presented at GLCA Women's Studies Conference, Rochester, IN. (p. 196)

Hyde, J. S., Fennema, E., & Lamon, S. J. (1990). Gender differences in mathematics performance: A meta-analysis. *Psychological Bulletin, 107,* 139–155. (p. 229)

Hyman, R. (1981). Cold reading: How to convince strangers that you know all about them. In K. Frazier (Ed.), *Paranormal borderlands of science.* Buffalo, NY: Prometheus. (p. 302)

Ickes, W., Snyder, M., & Garcia, S. (1997). Personality influences on the choice of situations. In R. Hogan, J. Johnson, & S. Briggs (Eds.), *Handbook of Personality Psychology.* San Diego, CA: Academic Press. (p. 305)

Idson, L. C., & Mischel, W. (2001). The personality of familiar and significant people: The lay perceiver as a social-cognitive theorist. *Journal of Personality and Social Psychology, 80,* 585–596. (p. 376)

Ikonomidou, C., Bittigau, P., Ishimaru, M. J., Wozniak, D. F., Koch, C., Genz, K., Price, M. T., Stefovska, V., Hoerster, F., Tenkova, T., Dikranian, K., & Olney, J. W. (2000). Ethanol-induced apoptotic neurodegeneration and fetal alcohol syndrome. *Science, 287,* 1056–1060. (p. 67)

Immen, W. (1995, July 16). Canadians ignore "safe sex" warning. *Toronto Globe and Mail* (in *Grand Rapids Press,* p. A22). (p. 111)

Ingham, A. G., Levinger, G., Graves, J., & Peckham, V. (1974). The Ringelmann effect: Studies of group size and group performance. *Journal of Experimental Social Psychology, 10,* 371–384. (p. 384)

Inglehart, R. (1990). *Culture shift in advanced industrial society.* Princeton, NJ: Princeton University Press. (pp. 97, 247, 277, 408)

Insana, R. (2005, February 21). Coach says honey gets better results than vinegar (interview with Larry Brown). *USA Today,* p. 4B. (p. 412)

Inzlicht, M., & Ben-Zeev, T. (2000). A threatening intellectual environment: Why females are susceptible to experiencing problem-solving deficits in the presence of males. *Psychological Science, 11,* 365–371. (p. 230)

IPU. (2005). Women in national parliaments: Situation as of 28 February 2005. *Inter-Parliamentary Union* (www.ipu.org). (p. 104)

Ironson, G., Solomon, G. F., Balbin, E. G., O'Cleirigh, C., George, A., Kumar, M., Larson, D., & Woods, T. E. (2002). The Ironson-Woods spiritual/religiousness index is associated with long survival, health behaviors, less distress, and low cortisol in people with HIV/AIDS. *Annals of Behavioral Medicine, 24,* 34–48. (p. 283)

Irwin, M., Mascovich, A., Gillin, J. C., Willoughby, R., Pike, J., & Smith, T. L. (1994). Partial sleep deprivation reduces natural killer cell activity in humans. *Psychosomatic Medicine, 56,* 493–498. (p. 54)

ISR. (2003, Spring). Drug use: Religion plays role for White as well as Black teens (data from 70,000 seniors surveyed 1997–2001, ISR Monitoring the Future Study). Ann Arbor, MI: Institute for Social Research Newsletter, University of Michigan. (p. 333)

Ito, T. A., Miller, N., & Pollock, V. E. (1996). Alcohol and aggression: A meta-analysis on the moderating effects of inhibitory cues, triggering events, and self-focused attention. *Psychological Bulletin, 120,* 60–82. (p. 392)

Iversen, L. L. (2000). *The science of marijuana.* New York: Oxford. (p. 332)

Iyengar, S. S., & Lepper, M. R. (2000). When choice is demotivating: Can one desire too much of a good thing? *Journal of Personality and Social Psychology, 79,* 995–1006. (p. 278)

Izard, C. E. (1977). *Human emotions.* New York: Plenum Press. (pp. 258, 259)

Izard, C. E. (1994). Innate and universal facial expressions: Evidence from developmental and cross-cultural research. *Psychological Bulletin, 114,* 288–299. (p. 258)

Jablensky, A. (1999). Schizophrenia: Epidemiology. *Current Opinion in Psychiatry, 12,* 19–28. (p. 343)

Jackson, J. M., & Williams, K. D. (1988). Social loafing: A review and theoretical analysis. Unpublished manuscript, Fordham University. (p. 384)

Jacobs, B. L. (1987). How hallucinogenic drugs work. *American Scientist, 75,* 386–392. (p. 331)

Jacobs, B. L. (1994). Serotonin, motor activity, and depression-related disorders. *American Scientist, 82,* 456–463. (p. 339)

Jacoby, L. L., Bishara, A. J., Hessels, S., & Toth, J. P. (2005). Aging, subjective experience, and cognitive control: Dramatic false remembering by older adults. *Journal of Experimental Psychology: General, 154,* 131–148. (p. 196)

Jacques, C., & Rossion, B. (2006). The speed of individual face categorization. *Psychological Science, 17,* 485–492. (p. 125)

Jaffe, E. (2004, October). Peace in the Middle East may be impossible: Lee D. Ross on naive realism and conflict resolution. *APS Observer,* pp. 9–11. (p. 151)

Jakicic, J. M., Winters, C., Lang, W., & Wing R. R. (1999). Effects of intermittent exercise and use of home exercise equipment on adherence, weight loss, and fitness in overweight women. *Journal of the American Medical Association, 282,* 1554–1560. (p. 246)

James, W. (1890). *The principles of psychology (Vol. 2).* New York: Holt. (pp. 136, 200, 258, 249)

Jameson, D. (1985). Opponent-colors theory in light of physiological findings. In D. Ottoson & S. Zeki (Eds.), *Central and peripheral mechanisms of color vision.* New York: Macmillan. (p. 145)

Jamison, K. R. (1993). *Touched with fire: Manic-depressive illness and the artistic temperament.* New York: Free Press. (p. 337)

Jamison, K. R. (1995a). *An unquiet mind.* New York: Knopf. (p. 349, 368)

Jamison, K. R. (1995b, February). Manic-depressive illness and creativity. *Scientific American,* pp. 62–67. (p. 337)

Janicak, P. G. (2005). Treating psychiatric disorders using transcranial magnetic stimulation. *Psychiatric Annals, 35,* 102–108. (p. 369)

Janis, I. L. (1982). *Groupthink: Psychological studies of policy decisions and fiascoes.* Boston: Houghton Mifflin. (p. 386)

Janis, I. L. (1986). Problems of international crisis management in the nuclear age. *Journal of Social Issues, 42(2),* 201–220. (p. 206)

Javitt, D. C., & Coyle, J. T. (2004, January). Decoding schizophrenia. *Scientific American,* pp. 48–55. (p. 342)

Jeffery, R. W., Drewnowski, A., Epstein, L. H., Stunkard, A. J., Wilson, G. T., Wing, R. R., & Hill, D. R. (2000). Long-term maintenance of weight loss: Current status. *Health Psychology, 19,* No. 1 (Supplement), 5–16. (p. 245)

Jenkins, J. G., & Dallenbach, K. M. (1924). Obliviscence during sleep and waking. *American Journal of Psychology, 35,* 605–612. (pp. 194)

Jenkins, J. M., & Astington, J. W. (1996). Cognitive factors and family structure associated with theory of mind development in young children. *Developmental Psychology, 32,* 70–78. (p. 75)

Jensen, J. P., & Bergin, A. E. (1988). Mental health values of professional therapists: A national interdisciplinary survey. *Professional Psychology: Research and Practice, 19,* 290–297. (p. 364)

John, O. P., & Srivastava, S. (1999). The Big Five trait taxonomy: History, measurement, and theoretical perspectives. In L. A. Pervin & O. P. John (Eds.), *Handbook of personality: Theory and research.* New York: Guilford. (p. 301)

Johnson, D. L., Wiebe, J. S., Gold, S. M., Andreasen, N. C., Hichwa, R. D., Watkins, G. L., & Ponto, L. L. B. (1999). Cerebral blood flow and personality: A Positron Emission Tomography study. *American Journal of Psychiatry, 156,* 252–257. (p. 300)

Johnson, D. W., & Johnson, R. T. (1989). *Cooperation and competition: Theory and research.* Edina, MN: Interaction Book. (p. 401)

Johnson, D. W., & Johnson, R. T. (1994). Constructive conflict in the schools. *Journal of Social Issues, 50(1),* 117–137. (p. 401)

Johnson, E., with Novak, W. (1993). *My life.* New York: Random House. (p. 279)

Johnson, J. A. (2007, June 26). Not so situational. Commentary on the SPSP listservm (spsp-discuss@stolaf.edu). (p. 387)

Johnson, J. G., Cohen, P., Kotler, L., Kasen, S., & Brook, J. S. (2002). Psychiatric disorders associated with risk for the development of eating disorders during adolescence and early adulthood. *Journal of Consulting and Clinical Psychology, 70,* 1119–1128. (p. 241)

Johnson, J. S., & Newport, E. L. (1991). Critical period effects on universal properties of language: The status of subjacency in the acquisition of a second language. *Cognition, 39,* 215–258. (pp. 213, 214)

Johnson, L. C. (2001, July 10). The declining terrorist threat. *New York Times* (www.nytimes.com). (p. 209)

Johnson, M. H., & Morton, J. (1991). *Biology and cognitive development: The case of face recognition.* Oxford: Blackwell Publishing. (p. 68)

Johnston, L. D., O'Malley, P. M., Bachman, J. G., & Schulenberg, J. E. (2005). *Monitoring the future: National results on adolescent drug use: Overview of key findings, 2004.* Bethesda, MD: National Institute on Drug Abuse. (pp. 329, 333)

Jones, J. M. (2003, February 12). Fear of terrorism increases amidst latest warning. *Gallup News Service* (www.gallup.com/releases/pr030212.asp). (p. 318)

Jones, J. M., & Moore, D. W. (2003, June 17). Generational differences in support for a woman president. The Gallup Organization (www.gallup.com). (p. 388)

Jones, J. T., Pelham, B. W., Carvallo, M., & Mirenberg, M. C. (2004). How do I love thee? Let me count the Js: Implicit egotism and interpersonal attraction. *Journal of Personality and Social Psychology, 87,* 665–683. (p. 394)

Jones, M. C. (1924). A laboratory study of fear: The case of Peter. *Journal of Genetic Psychology, 31,* 308–315. (p. 355)

Jones, M. V., Paull, G. C., & Erskine, J. (2002). The impact of a team's aggressive reputation on the decisions of association football referees. *Journal of Sports Sciences, 20,* 991–1000. (p. 150)

Jones, S. S., Collins, K., & Hong, H-W. (1991). An audience effect on smile production in 10–month-old infants. *Psychological Science, 2,* 45–49. (p. 258)

Jordan, C. H., Spencer, S. J., Zanna, M. P., Hoshino-Browne, E., & Correll, J. (2003). Secure and defensive high self-esteem. *Journal of Personality and Social Psychology, 85,* 969–978. (p. 306)

Judge, T. A., Thoresen, C. J., Bono, J. E., & Patton, G. K. (2001). The job satisfaction/job performance relationship: A qualitative and quantitative review. *Psychological Bulletin, 127,* 376–407. (p. 410)

Kagan, J. (1976). Emergent themes in human development. *American Scientist, 64,* 186–196. (p. 79)

Kagan, J. (1984). *The nature of the child.* New York: Basic Books. (p. 77)

Kagan, J. (1995). On attachment. *Harvard Review of Psychiatry, 3,* 104–106. (p. 78)

Kagan, J. (1998). *Three seductive ideas.* Cambridge, MA: Harvard University Press. (p. 98)

Kagan, J., & Snidman, N. (2004). *The long shadow of temperament.* Cambridge, MA: Belknap Press. (p. 68)

Kagan, J., Lapidus, D. R., & Moore, M. (December, 1978). Infant antecedents of cognitive functioning: A longitudinal study. *Child Development*, 49(4), 1005–1023. (p. 98)

Kahneman, D. (1999). Assessments of objective happiness: A bottom-up approach. In D. Kahneman, E. Diener, & N. Schwartz (Eds.), *Understanding well-being: Scientific perspectives on enjoyment and suffering*. New York: Russell Sage Foundation. (p. 138)

Kahneman, D. (2005, January 13). What were they thinking? Q&A with Daniel Kahneman. *Gallup Management Journal* (www.gmj.gallup.com). (p. 207)

Kahneman, D. (2005, February 10). Are you happy now? *Gallup Management Journal* interview (www.gmj.gallup.com). (p. 262)

Kahneman, D., Fredrickson, B. L., Schreiber, C. A., & Redelmeier, D. A. (1993). When more pain is preferred to less: Adding a better end. *Psychological Science*, 4, 401–405. (p. 138)

Kahneman, D., Krueger, A. B., Schkade, D. A., Schwarz, N., & Stone, A. A. (2004). A survey method for characterizing daily life experience: The day reconstruction method. *Science*, 306, 1776–1780. (p. 261)

Kail, R. (1991). Developmental change in speed of processing during childhood and adolescence. *Psychological Bulletin*, 109, 490–501. (p. 93)

Kaiser Family Foundation. (2003, October 28). New study finds children age zero to six spend as much time with TV, computers and video games as playing outside. www.kff.org/entmedia/entmedia102803nr.cfm. (p. 15)

Kalin, N. H. (1993, May). The neurobiology of fear. *Scientific American*, pp. 94–101. (p. 253)

Kamarck, T., & Jennings, J. R. (1991). Biobehavioral factors in sudden cardiac death. *Psychological Bulletin*, 109, 42–75. (p. 275)

Kamena, M. (1998). Repressed/false childhood sexual abuse memories: A survey of therapists. Paper presented to the Sexual Abuse memories Symposium at the American Psychological Association convention. (p. 198)

Kaminski, J., Cali, J., & Fischer, J. (2004). Word learning in a domestic dog: Evidence for "fast mapping." *Science*, 304, 1682–1683. (p. 216)

Kandel, E. R., & Schwartz, J. H. (1982). Molecular biology of learning: Modulation of transmitter release. *Science*, 218, 433–443. (p. 187)

Kann, L., Warren, W., Collins, J. L., Ross, J., Collins, B., & Kolbe, L. J. (1993). Results from the national school-based 1991 Youth Risk Behavior Survey and progress toward achieving related health objectives for the nation. U.S. Department of Health and Human Services, *Public Health Reports*, 108 (Supplement 1), 47–55. (p. 333)

Kaplan, A. (2004). Exploring the gene-environment nexus in anorexia, bulimia. *Psychiatric Times*, 21 (www.psychiatrictimes.com/p040801b.html). (p. 241)

Kaplan, H. I., & Saddock, B. J. (Eds.). (1989). *Comprehensive textbook of psychiatry*, V. Baltimore, MD: Williams and Wilkins. (p. 365)

Kaplan, R. M., & Kronick, R. G. (2006). Marital status and longevity in the United States population. *Journal of Epidemiology and Community Health*, 60, 760–765. (p. 280)

Kaprio, J., Koskenvuo, M., & Rita, H. (1987). Mortality after bereavement: A prospective study of 95,647 widowed persons. *American Journal of Public Health*, 77, 283–287. (p. 271)

Karacan, I., Goodenough, D. R., Shapiro, A., & Starker, S. (1966). Erection cycle during sleep in relation to dream anxiety. *Archives of General Psychiatry*, 15, 183–189. (p. 52)

Karau, S. J., & Williams, K. D. (1993). Social loafing: A meta-analytic review and theoretical integration. *Journal of Personality and Social Psychology*, 65, 681–706. (p. 384)

Kark, J. D., Shemi, G., Friedlander, Y., Martin, O., Manor, O., & Blondheim, S. H. (1996). Does religious observance promote health? Mortality in secular vs. religious kibbutzim in Israel. *American Journal of Public Health*, 86, 341–346. (p. 283)

Kaufman, J. C., & Baer, J. (2002). I bask in dreams of suicide: Mental illness, poetry, and women. *Review of General Psychology*, 6, 271–286. (p. 337)

Kaufman, J., & Zigler, E. (1987). Do abused children become abusive parents? *American Journal of Orthopsychiatry*, 57, 186–192. (p. 79)

Kaufman, L., & Kaufman, J. H. (2000). Explaining the moon illusion. *Proceedings of the National Academy of Sciences*, 97, 500–505. (p. 147)

Kazdin, A. E., & Benjet, C. (2003). Spanking children: Evidence and issues. *Current Directions in Psychological Science*, 12, 99–103. (p. 168)

Keesey, R. E., & Corbett, S. W. (1983). Metabolic defense of the body weight set-point. In A. J. Stunkard & E. Stellar (Eds.), *Eating and its disorders*. New York: Raven Press. (p. 239)

Keller, M. B., McCullough, J. P., Klein, D. N., Arnow, B., Dunner, D. L., Gelenberg, A. J., Markowitz, J. C., Nemeroff, C. B., Russell, J. M., Thase, M. E., Trivedi, M. H., & Zajecka J. (2000), A comparison of nefazodone, the cognitive behavioral-analysis system of psychotherapy, and their combination for the treatment of chronic depression. *New England Journal of Medicine*, 342, 1462–1470. (p. 367)

Kellerman, J., Lewis, J., & Laird, J. D. (1989). Looking and loving: The effects of mutual gaze on feelings of romantic love. *Journal of Research in Personality*, 23, 145–161. (p. 257)

Kellermann, A. L. (1997). Comment: Gunsmoke—changing public attitudes toward smoking and firearms. *American Journal of Public Health*, 87, 910–913. (p. 391)

Kellermann, A. L., Rivara, F. P., Rushforth, N. B., Banton, H. G., Feay, D. T., Francisco, J. T., Locci, A. B., Prodzinski, J., Hackman, B. B., & Somes, G. (1993). Gun ownership as a risk factor for homicide in the home. *New England Journal of Medicine*, 329, 1084–1091. (p. 391)

Kellermann, A. L., Somes, G. Rivara, F. P., Lee, R. K., & Banton, J. G. (1998). Injuries and deaths due to firearms in the home. *Journal of Trauma*, 45, 263-267. (p. 391)

Kelley, J., & De Graaf, N. D. (1997). National context, parental socialization, and religious belief: Results from 15 nations. *American Sociological Review*, 62, 639–659. (p. 82)

Kelling, S. T., & Halpern, B. P. (1983). Taste flashes: Reaction times, intensity, and quality. *Science*, 219, 412–414. (p. 140)

Kellner, C. H., & 15 others. (2005). Relief of expressed suicidal intent by ECT: A consortium for research in ECT study. *American Journal of Psychiatry*, 162, 977–982. (p. 368)

Kelly, A. E. (2000). Helping construct desirable identities: A self-presentational view of psychotherapy. *Psychological Bulletin*, 126, 475–494. (p. 358)

Kelly, I. W. (1997). Modern astrology: A critique. *Psychological Reports*, 81, 1035–1066. (p. 302)

Kelly, I. W. (1998). Why astrology doesn't work. *Psychological Reports*, 82, 527–546. (p. 302)

Kelly, T. A. (1990). The role of values in psychotherapy: A critical review of process and outcome effects. *Clinical Psychology Review*, 10, 171–186. (p. 364)

Kempermann, G., Kuhn, H. G., & Gage, F. H. (May, 1998). Experience-induced neurogenesis in the senescent dentate gyrus. *Journal of Neuroscience*, 18(9), 3206–3212. (p. 94)

Kendall-Tackett, K. A., Williams, L. M., & Finkelhor, D. (1993). Impact of sexual abuse on children: A review and synthesis of recent empirical studies. *Psychological Bulletin, 113,* 164–180. (pp. 79, 199)

Kendler, K. S. (1997). Social support: A genetic-epidemiologic analysis. *American Journal of Psychiatry, 154,* 1398–1404. (p. 305)

Kendler, K. S. (1998, January). Major depression and the environment: A psychiatric genetic perspective. *Pharmacopsychiatry, 31*(1), 5–9. (p. 337)

Kendler, K. S., Jacobson, K. C., Myers, J., & Prescott, C. A. (2002a). Sex differences in genetic and environmental risk factors for irrational fears and phobias. *Psychological Medicine, 32,* 209–217. (p. 322)

Kendler, K. S., Karkowski, L. M., & Prescott, C. A. (1999). Fears and phobias: Reliability and heritability. *Psychological Medicine, 29,* 539–553. (p. 322)

Kendler, K. S., Myers, J., & Prescott, C. A. (2002b). The etiology of phobias: An evaluation of the stress-diathesis model. *Archives of General Psychiatry, 59,* 242–248. (p. 322)

Kendler, K. S., Neale, M. C., Kessler, R. C., Heath, A. C., & Eaves, L. J. (1992). Generalized anxiety disorder in women: A population-based twin study. *Archives of General Psychiatry, 49,* 267–272. (p. 322)

Kendler, K. S., Neale, M. C., Thornton, L. M., Aggen, S. H., Gilman, S. E., & Kessler, R. C. (2002). Cannabis use in the last year in a U.S. national sample of twin and sibling pairs. *Psychological Medicine, 32,* 551–554. (p. 333)

Kendler, K. S., Thornton, L. M., & Gardner, C. O. (2001). Genetic risk, number of previous depressive episodes, and stressful life events in predicting onset of major depression. *American Journal of Psychiatry, 158,* 582–586. (p. 337)

Kennedy, S., & Over, R. (1990). Psychophysiological assessment of male sexual arousal following spinal cord injury. *Archives of Sexual Behavior, 19,* 15–27. (p. 33)

Kenrick, D. T., & Funder, D. C. (1988). Profiting from controversy: Lessons from the person-situation debate. *American Psychologist, 43,* 23–34. (p. 304)

Kenrick, D. T., & Gutierres, S. E. (1980). Contrast effects and judgments of physical attractiveness: When beauty becomes a social problem. *Journal of Personality and Social Psychology, 38,* 131–140. (p. 112)

Kenrick, D. T., Gutierres, S. E., & Goldberg, L. L. (1989). Influence of popular erotica on judgments of strangers and mates. *Journal of Experimental Social Psychology, 25,* 159–167. (p. 112)

Kenrick, D. T., Nieuweboer, S., & Bunnk, A. P. (in press). Universal mechanisms and cultural diversity: Replacing the blank slate with a coloring book. In M. Schaller, S. Heine, A. Norenzayan, T. Yamagishi, & T. Kameda (Eds.), *Evolution, culture, and the human mind.* Mahwah, NJ: Erlbaum. (p. 117)

Keough, K. A., Zimbardo, P. G., & Boyd, J. N. (1999). Who's smoking, drinking, and using drugs? Time perspective as a predictor of substance use. *Basic and Applied Social Psychology, 2,* 149–164. (p. 291)

Kernis, M. H. (2003). Toward a conceptualization of optimal self-esteem. *Psychological Inquiry, 14,* 1–26. (p. 306)

Kerr, N. L., & Bruun, S. E. (1983). Dispensability of member effort and group motivation losses: Free-rider effects. *Journal of Personality and Social Psychology, 44,* 78–94. (p. 384)

Kessler, M., & Albee, G. (1975). Primary prevention. *Annual Review of Psychology, 26,* 557–591. (p. 371)

Kessler, R. C. (2000). Posttraumatic stress disorder: The burden to the individual and to society. *Journal of Clinical Psychiatry, 61*(suppl. 5), 4–12. (p. 320)

Kessler, R. C. (2001). Epidemiology of women and depression. *Journal of Affective Disorders, 74,* 5–13. (p. 339)

Kessler, R. C., Foster, C., Joseph, J., Ostrow, D., Wortman, C., Phair, J., & Chmiel, J. (1991). Stressful life events and symptom onset in HIV infection. *American Journal of Psychiatry, 148,* 733–738. (p. 274)

Keynes, M. (1980, December 20/27). Handel's illnesses. *The Lancet,* pp. 1354–1355. (p. 337)

Keys, A., Brozek, J., Henschel, A., Mickelsen, O., & Taylor, H. L. (1950). *The biology of human starvation.* Minneapolis: University of Minnesota Press. (p. 238)

Khan, A., Warner, H. A., & Brown, W. A. (2000). Symptom reduction and suicide risk inpatients treated with placebo in antidepressant clinical trials. *Archives of General Psychiatry, 57,* 311–317. (p. 367)

Kho, K. H., van Vreeswijk, M. F., Simpson, S., & Zwinderman, A. H. (2003). A meta-analysis of electroconvulsive therapy efficacy in depression. *Journal of ECT, 19,* 139–147. (p. 368)

Kiecolt-Glaser, J. K., & Glaser, R. (1995). Psychoneuroimmunology and health consequences: Data and shared mechanisms. *Psychosomatic Medicine, 57,* 269–274. (p. 274)

Kiecolt-Glaser, J. K., Page, G. G., Marucha, P. T., MacCallum, R. C., & Glaser, R. (1998). Psychological influences on surgical recovery: Perspectives from psychoneuroimmunology. *American Psychologist, 53,* 1209–1218. (p. 273)

Kihlstrom, J. F. (1990). The psychological unconscious. In L. A. Pervin (Ed.), *Handbook of personality: Theory and research.* New York: Guilford Press. (p. 296)

Kihlstrom, J. F. (2005). Dissociative disorders. *Annual Review of Clinical Psychology, 1,* 227–253. (p. 323)

Kim, B. S. K., Ng, G. F., & Ahn, A. J. (2005). Effects of client expectation for counseling success, client-counselor worldview match, and client adherence to Asian and European American cultural values on counseling process with Asian Americans. *Journal of Counseling Psychology, 52,* 67–76. (p. 364)

Kimata, H. (2001). Effect of humor on allergen-induced wheal reactions. *Journal of the American Medical Association, 285,* 737. (p. 279)

King, R. N., & Koehler, D. J. (2000). Illusory correlations in graphological interference. *Journal of Experimental Psychology: Applied, 6,* 336–348. (p. 302)

Kinnier, R. T., & Metha, A. T. (1989). Regrets and priorities at three stages of life. *Counseling and Values, 33,* 182–193. (p. 97)

Kinsey, A. C., Pomeroy, W., & Martin, C. (1948). *Sexual behavior in the human male.* Philadelphia: Saunders. (p. 109)

Kinsey, A. C., Pomeroy, W., Martin, C., & Gebhard, P. (1953). *Sexual behavior in the human female.* Philadelphia: Saunders. (p. 109)

Kirby, D. (2002). Effective approaches to reducing adolescent unprotected sex, pregnancy, and childbearing. *Journal of Sex Research, 39,* 51–57. (p. 112)

Kirsch, I., & Sapirstein, G. (1998). Listening to Prozac but hearing placebo: A meta-analysis of antidepressant medication. *Prevention and Treatment, 1,* posted June 26 at ⟨journals.apa.org/prevention/volume1⟩. (pp. 17, 367)

Kirsch, I., Moore, T. J., Scoboria, A., & Nicholls, S. S. (2002, July 15). New study finds little difference between effects of antidepressants and placebo. *Prevention and Treatment* ⟨journals.apa.org/prevention⟩. (p. 367)

Klayman, J., & Ha, Y-W. (1987). Confirmation, disconfirmation, and information in hypothesis testing. *Psychological Review, 94,* 211–228. (p. 207)

Klein, S. B., & Kihlstrom, J. F. (1998). On bridging the gap between social-personality psychology and neuropsychology. *Personality and Social Psychology Review, 2*, 228–242. (p. 76)

Kleinfeld, J. (1998). *The myth that schools shortchange girls: Social science in the service of deception.* Washington, DC: Women's Freedom Network. Available from ERIC, Document ED423210, and via www.uaf.edu/northern/schools/myth.html. (p. 229)

Kleinke, C. L. (1986). Gaze and eye contact: A research review. *Psychological Bulletin, 1000*, 78–100. (p. 257)

Kleinmuntz, B., & Szucko, J. J. (1984). A field study of the fallibility of polygraph lie detection. *Nature, 308*, 449–450. (p. 254)

Kleitman, N. (1960, November). Patterns of dreaming. *Scientific American,* pp. 82–88. (p. 51)

Klemm, W. R. (1990). Historical and introductory perspectives on brainstem-mediated behaviors. In W. R. Klemm & R. P. Vertes (Eds.), *Brainstem mechanisms of behavior.* New York: Wiley. (p. 35)

Kline, D., & Schieber, F. (1985). Vision and aging. In J. E. Birren & K. W. Schaie (Eds.), *Handbook of the psychology of aging.* New York: Van Nostrand Reinhold. (p. 91)

Kline, G. H., Stanley, S. M., Markman, J. H., Olmos-Gallo, P. A., St. Peters, M., Whitton, S. W., & Prado, L. M. (2004). Timing is everything: Pre-engagement cohabitation and increased risk for poor marital outcomes. *Journal of Family Psychology, 18*, 311–318. (p. 94)

Kline, N. S. (1974). *From sad to glad.* New York: Ballantine Books. (p. 340)

Klineberg, O. (1984). Public opinion and nuclear war. *American Psychologist, 39*, 1245–1253. (p. 401)

Kluft, R. P. (1991). Multiple personality disorder. In A. Tasman & S. M. Goldfinger (Eds.), *Review of Psychiatry,* (Vol. 10). Washington, DC: American Psychiatric Press. (p. 323)

Klüver, H., & Bucy, P. C. (1939). Preliminary analysis of functions of the temporal lobes in monkeys. *Archives of Neurology and Psychiatry, 42*, 979–1000. (p. 37)

Knapp, S., & VandeCreek, L. (2000, August). Recovered memories of childhood abuse: Is there an underlying professional consensus? *Professional Psychology: Research and Practice, 31*, 365–371. (p. 199)

Knickmeyer, E. (2001, August 7). In Africa, big is definitely better. *Associated Press (Seattle Times,* p. A7). (p. 241)

Knight, W. (2004, August 2). Animated face helps deaf with phone chat. NewScientist.com. (p. 140)

Koenig, H. G., & Larson, D. B. (1998). Use of hospital services, religious attendance, and religious affiliation. *Southern Medical Journal, 91*, 925–932. (p. 283)

Koenig, L. B., McGue, M., Krueger, R. F., & Bouchard, T. J., Jr. (2005). Genetic and environmental influences on religiousness: Findings for retrospective and current religiousness ratings. *Journal of Personality, 73*, 471–488. (p. 82)

Koestner, R., Lekes, N., Powers, T. A., & Chicoine, E. (2002). Attaining personal goals: Self-concordance plus implementation intentions equals success. *Journal of Personality and Social Psychology, 83*, 231–244. (p. 412)

Kohlberg, L. (1981). *The philosophy of moral development: Essays on moral development (Vol. I).* San Francisco: Harper & Row. (p. 85)

Kohlberg, L. (1984). *The psychology of moral development: Essays on moral development (Vol. II).* San Francisco: Harper & Row. (p. 85)

Kohler, I. (1962, May). Experiments with goggles. *Scientific American,* pp. 62–72. (p. 149)

Köhler, W. (1925; reprinted 1957). *The mentality of apes.* London: Pelican. (p. 215)

Kohn, P. M., & Macdonald, J. E. (1992). The survey of recent life experiences: A decontaminated hassles scale for adults. *Journal of Behavioral Medicine, 15*, 221–236. (p. 271)

Kolata, G. (1987). Metabolic catch-22 of exercise regimens. *Science, 236*, 146–147. (p. 246)

Kolata, G. (2004, September 30). Health and money issues arise over who pays for weight loss. *New York Times* (www.nytimes.com). (p. 245)

Kolb, B. (1989). Brain development, plasticity, and behavior. *American Psychologist, 44*, 1203–1212. (p. 44)

Kolb, B., & Whishaw, I. Q. (1998). Brain plasticity and behavior. *Annual Review of Psychology, 49*, 43–64. (p. 71)

Kolker, K. (2002, December 8). *Video violence disturbs some; others scoff at influence.* Grand Rapids Press, pp. A1, A12. (p. 393)

Kolodziej, M. E., & Johnson, B. T. (1996). Interpersonal contact and acceptance of persons with psychiatric disorders: A research synthesis. *Journal of Consulting and Clinical Psychology, 64*, 1387–1396. (p. 317)

Koltko-Rivera, M. E. (2006). Rediscovering the later version of Maslow's hierarchy of needs: Self-transcendence and opportunities for theory, research, and unification. *Review of General Psychology, 10*, 302–317. (p. 237)

Koole, S., & Spijker, M. (2000). Overcoming the planning fallacy through willpower: Effects of implementation intentions on actual and predicted task-completion times. *European Journal of Social Psychology, 30*, 873–888. (p. 412)

Kopta, S. M., Lueger, R. J., Saunders, S. M., & Howard, K. I. (1999). Individual psychotherapy outcome and process research: Challenges leading to greater turmoil or a positive transition? *Annual Review of Psychology, 30*, 441–469. (p. 361)

Kosslyn, S. M., & Koenig, O. (1992). *Wet mind: The new cognitive neuroscience.* New York: Free Press. (p. 32)

Kotchick, B. A., Shaffer, A., & Forehand, R. (2001). Adolescent sexual risk behavior: A multi-system perspective. *Clinical Psychology Review, 21*, 493–519. (p. 111)

Kotkin, M., Daviet, C., & Gurin, J. (1996). The Consumer Reports mental health survey. *American Psychologist, 51*, 1080–1082. (p. 360)

Kotva, H. J., & Schneider, H. G. (1990). Those "talks"—general and sexual communication between mothers and daughters. *Journal of Social Behavior and Personality, 5*, 603–613. (p. 111)

Kraft, R. (1996, December 2, and 1994, July 20). Personal correspondence (from Otterbein College) regarding Holocaust memories. (p. 295)

Kraft, R. N. (2002). *Memory perceived: Recalling the Holocaust.* Westport, CT: Praeger. (p. 200)

Kraus, N., Malmfors, T., & Slovic, P. (1992). Intuitive toxicology: Expert and lay judgments of chemical risks. *Risk Analysis, 12*, 215–232. (p. 209)

Kraut, R. E., & Johnston, R. E. (1979). Social and emotional messages of smiling: An ethological approach. *Journal of Personality and Social Psychology, 37*, 1539–1553. (p. 258)

KRC Research & Consulting. (2001, August 7). Memory isn't quite what it used to be (survey for General Nutrition Centers). *USA Today,* p. D1. (p. 93)

Krijn, M., Emmelkamp, P. M. G., Olafsson, R. P., & Biemond, R. (2004). Virtual reality exposure therapy of anxiety disorders: A review. *Clinical Psychology Review, 24,* 259–281. (p. 356)

Kring, A. M., & Gordon, A. H. (1998). Sex differences in emotion: Expression, experience, and physiology. *Journal of Personality and Social Psychology, 74,* 686–703. (p. 257)

Kroll, R., Danis, S., Moreau, M., Waldbaum, A., Shifren, J., & Wekselman, K. (2004). Testosterone transdermal patch (TPP) significantly improved sexual function in naturally menopausal women in a large Phase III study. Presented to the American Society of Reproductive Medicine annual meeting, Philadelphia, October. (p. 110)

Kruger J., Epley, N., Parker, J., & Ng, Z-W. (2005). Egocentrism over e-mail: Can we communicate as well as we think? *Journal of Personality and Social Psychology, 89,* 925-936. (p. 74)

Krützen, M., Mann, J., Heithaus, M. R., Connor, R. C., Bejder, L., & Sherwin, W. B. (2005). Cultural transmission of tool use in bottlenose dolphins. *Proceedings of the National Academy of Sciences, 102,* 8939–8943. (p. 216)

Kubey, R., & Csikszentmihalyi, M. (2002, February). Television addiction is no mere metaphor. *Scientific American,* pp. 74–80. (p. 175)

Kübler, A., Winter, S., Ludolph, A. C., Hautzinger, M., & Birbaumer, N. (2005). Severity of depressive symptoms and quality of life in patients with amyotrophic lateral sclerosis. *Neurorehabilitation and Neural Repair, 19*(3), 182–193. (p. 262)

Kuhl, P. K., & Meltzoff, A. N. (1982). The bimodal perception of speech in infancy. *Science, 218,* 1138–1141. (p. 212)

Kuncel, N. R., Nezlett, S. A., & Ones, D. S. (2004). Academic performance, career potential, creativity, and job performance: Can one construct predict them all? *Journal of Personality and Social Psychology, 86,* 148–161. (p. 220)

Kunkel, D. (2001, February 4). *Sex on TV.* Menlo Park, CA: Henry J. Kaiser Family Foundation (www.kff.org). (p. 111)

Kutas, M. (1990). Event-related brain potential (ERP) studies of cognition during sleep: Is it more than a dream? In R. R. Bootzin, J. F. Kihlstrom, & D. Schacter (Eds.), *Sleep and cognition.* Washington, DC: American Psychological Association. (p. 52)

Lacayo, R. (1995, June 12). Violent reaction. *Time.* pp. 25–39. (p. 13)

Lachman, M. E., & Weaver, S. L. (1998). The sense of control as a moderator of social class differences in health and well-being. *Journal of Personality and Social Psychology, 74,* 763–773. (p. 278)

Laird, J. D. (1974). Self-attribution of emotion: The effects of expressive behavior on the quality of emotional experience. *Journal of Personality and Social Psychology, 29,* 475–486. (p. 258)

Laird, J. D. (1984). The real role of facial response in the experience of emotion: A reply to Tourangeau and Ellsworth, and others. *Journal of Personality and Social Psychology, 47,* 909–917. (p. 258)

Laird, J. D., Cuniff, M., Sheehan, K., Shulman, D., & Strum, G. (1989). Emotion specific effects of facial expressions on memory for life events. *Journal of Social Behavior and Personality, 4,* 87–98. (p. 258)

Lambird, K. H., & Mann, T. (2006). When do ego threats lead to self-regulation failure? Negative consequences of defensive high self-esteem. *Personality and Social Psychology Bulletin, 32,* 1177–1187. (p. 306)

Lampinen, J. M. (2002). What exactly is déjà vu? *Scientific American* (scieam.com/askexpert/biology/biology63). (p. 191)

Landauer, T. (2001, September). Quoted by R. Herbert, You must remember this. *APS Observer,* p. 11. (p. 200)

Landauer, T. K., & Whiting, J. W. M. (1979). Correlates and consequences of stress in infancy. In R. Munroe, B. Munroe, & B. Whiting (Eds.), *Handbook of Cross-Cultural Human Development.* New York: Garland. (p. 270)

Landry, M. J. (2002). MDMA: A review of epidemiologic data. *Journal of Psychoactive Drugs, 34,* 163–169. (p. 330)

Lang, E. V., Benotsch, E. G., Fick, L. J., Lutgendorf, S., Berbaum, M. L., Logan, H., & Spiegel, D. (2000). Adjunctive non-pharmacological analgesia for invasive medical procedures: A randomised trial. *Lancet, 355,* 1486–1490. (p. 139)

Langer, E. J. (1983). *The psychology of control.* Beverly Hills, CA: Sage. (p. 277)

Langer, E. J., & Abelson, R. P. (1974). A patient by any other name . . . : Clinician group differences in labeling bias. *Journal of Consulting and Clinical Psychology, 42,* 4–9. (p. 317)

Langer, E. J., & Imber, L. (1980). The role of mindlessness in the perception of deviance. *Journal of Personality and Social Psychology, 39,* 360–367. (p. 317)

Langlois, J. H., Kalakanis, L., Rubenstein, A. J., Larson, A., Hallam, M., & Smoot, M. (2000). Maxims or myths of beauty? A meta-analytic and theoretical review. *Psychological Bulletin, 126,* 390–423. (pp. 395, 396)

Langlois, J. H., Roggman, L. A., Casey, R. J., Ritter, J. M., Rieser-Danner, L. A., & Jenkins, V. Y. (1987). Infant preferences for attractive faces: Rudiments of a stereotype? *Developmental Psychology, 23,* 363–369. (p. 395)

Larkin, K., Resko, J. A., Stormshak, F., Stellflug, J. N., & Roselli, C. E. (2002). Neuroanatomical correlates of sex and sexual partner preference in sheep. Society for Neuroscience convention. (p. 115)

Larson, R. W., & Verma, S. (1999). How children and adolescents spend time across the world: Work, play, and developmental opportunities. *Psychological Bulletin, 125,* 701–736. (p. 228)

Larzelere, R. E. (1996). A review of the outcomes of parental use of nonabusive or customary physical punishment. *Pediatrics, 78,* 824–828. (p. 168)

Larzelere, R. E. (2000). Child outcomes of non-abusive and customary physical punishment by parents: An updated literature review. *Clinical Child and Family Psychology Review, 3,* 199–221. (p. 168)

Larzelere, R. E., Kuhn, B. R., & Johnson, B. (2004). The intervention selection bias: An underrecognized confound in intervention research. *Psychological Bulletin, 130,* 289–303. (p. 168)

Latané, B. (1981). The psychology of social impact. *American Psychologist, 36,* 343–356. (p. 384)

Latané, B., & Dabbs, J. M., Jr. (1975). Sex, group size and helping in three cities. *Sociometry, 38,* 180–194. (p. 399)

Lau, C., & Kramer, L. (2005). *Die relativitätstheorie des glücks: Über das leben von lottomillinären (The relativity of luck: About the life of lottery millionaires).* Herbolzheim: Centaurus. (p. 262)

Laumann, E. O., Gagnon, J. H., Michael, R. T., & Michaels, S. (1994). *The social organization of sexuality: Sexual practices in the United States.* Chicago: University of Chicago Press. (p. 118)

Lazarus, R. S. (1990). Theory-based stress measurement. *Psychological Inquiry, 1,* 3–13. (p. 271)

Lazarus, R. S. (1991). Progress on a cognitive-motivational-relational theory of emotion. *American Psychologist, 46,* 352–367. (p. 256)

Lazarus. R. S. (1998). Fifty years of the research and theory of R. S. Lazarus: An analysis of historical and perennial issues. Mahwah, NJ: Erlbaum. (pp. 256, 270)

Lea, S. E. G. (2000). Towards an ethical use of animals. *The Psychologist,* 13, 556–557. (p. 20)

Leach, P. (1993). Should parents hit their children? *The Psychologist: Bulletin of the British Psychological Society,* 6, 216–220. (p. 168)

Leach, P. (1994). *Children first.* New York: Knopf. (p. 168)

Leary, M. R. (1999). The social and psychological importance of self-esteem. In R. M. Kowalski & M. R. Leary (Eds.), *The social psychology of emotional and behavioral problems.* Washington, DC: APA Books. (p. 306)

Leary, M. R., Haupt, A. L., Strausser, K. S., & Chokel, J. T. (1998). Calibrating the sociometer: The relationship between interpersonal appraisals and state self-esteem. *Journal of Personality and Social Psychology,* 74, 1290–1299. (p. 247)

Leary, W. E. (1998, September 28). Older people enjoy sex, survey says. *New York Times* (www.nytimes.com). (p. 92)

LeDoux, J. (1996). *The emotional brain: The mysterious underpinnings of emotional life.* New York: Simon & Schuster. (p. 189)

LeDoux, J. E., & Armony, J. (1999). Can neurobiology tell us anything about human feelings? In D. Kahneman, E. Diener, & N. Schwartz (Eds.), *Well-being: The foundations of hedonic psychology.* New York: Sage. (p. 256)

Lee, L., Frederick, S., & Ariely, D. (2006). Try it, you'll like it: The influence of expectation, consumption, and revelation on preferences for beer. *Psychological Science,* 17, 1054–1058. (p. 150)

Lefcourt, H. M. (1982). *Locus of control: Current trends in theory and research.* Hillsdale, NJ: Erlbaum. (p. 278)

Legrand, L. N., Iacono, W. G., & McGue, M. (2005). Predicting addiction. *American Scientist,* 93, 140–147. (p. 333)

Lehman, A. F., Steinwachs, D. M., Dixon, L. B., Goldman, H. H., Osher, F., Postrado, L., Scott, J. E., Thompson, J. W., Fahey, M., Fischer, P., Kasper, J. A., Lyles, A., Skinner, E. A., Buchanan, R., Carpenter, W. T., Jr., Levine, J., McGlynn, E. A., Rosenheck, R., & Zito, J. (1998). Translating research into practice: The schizophrenia patient outcomes research team (PORT) treatment recommendations. *Schizophrenia Bulletin,* 24, 1–10. (p. 365)

Lehman, D. R., Wortman, C. B., & Williams, A. F. (1987). Long-term effects of losing a spouse or child in a motor vehicle crash. *Journal of Personality and Social Psychology,* 52, 218–231. (p. 96)

Leigh, B. C. (1989). In search of the seven dwarves: Issues of measurement and meaning in alcohol expectancy research. *Psychological Bulletin,* 105, 361–373. (p. 327)

Leitenberg, H., & Henning, K. (1995). Sexual fantasy. *Psychological Bulletin,* 117, 469–496. (p. 110, 113)

Lemonick, M. D. (2002, June 3). Lean and hungrier. *Time,* p. 54. (p. 239)

Lennox, B. R., Bert, S., Park, G., Jones, P. B., & Morris, P. G. (1999). Spatial and temporal mapping of neural activity associated with auditory hallucinations. *Lancet,* 353, 644. (p. 42)

Lenzenweger, M. F., Dworkin, R. H., & Wethington, E. (1989). Models of positive and negative symptoms in schizophrenia: An empirical evaluation of latent structures. *Journal of Abnormal Psychology,* 98, 62–70. (p. 365)

Leserman, J., Jackson, E. D., Petitto, J. M., Golden, R. N., Silva, S. G., Perkins, D. O., Cai, J., Folds, J. D., & Evans, D. L. (1999). Progression to AIDS: The effects of stress, depressive symptoms, and social support. *Psychosomatic Medicine,* 61, 397–406. (p. 274)

Leucht, S., Barnes, T. R. E., Kissling, W., Engel, R. R., Correll, C., & Kane, J. M. (2003). Relapse prevention in schizophrenia with new-generation antipsychotics: A systematic review and exploratory meta-analysis of randomized, controlled trials. *American Journal of Psychiatry,* 160, 1209–1222. (p. 366)

LeVay, S. (1991). A difference in hypothalamic structure between heterosexual and homosexual men. *Science,* 253, 1034–1037. (p. 115)

LeVay, S. (1994, March). Quoted in D. Nimmons, Sex and the brain. *Discover,* p. 64–71. (p. 115)

Levenson, R. W. (1992). Autonomic nervous system differences among emotions. *Psychological Science,* 3, 23–27. (p. 253)

Levin, I. P., & Gaeth, G. J. (1988). How consumers are affected by the framing of attribute information before and after consuming the product. *Journal of Consumer Research,* 15, 374–378. (p. 209)

Levine, R. V., & Norenzayan, A. (1999). The pace of life in 31 countries. *Journal of Cross-Cultural Psychology,* 30, 178–205. (p. 14)

Levine, R., Sato, S., Hashimoto, T., & Verma, J. (1995). Love and marriage in eleven cultures. *Journal of Cross-Cultural Psychology,* 26, 554–571. (p. 398)

Lewinsohn, P. M., & Rosenbaum, M. (1987). Recall of parental behavior by acute depressives, remitted depressives, and nondepressives. *Journal of Personality and Social Psychology,* 52, 611–619. (p. 192)

Lewinsohn, P. M., Hoberman, H., Teri, L., & Hautziner, M. (1985). An integrative theory of depression. In S. Reiss & R. Bootzin (Eds.), *Theoretical issues in behavior therapy.* Orlando, FL: Academic Press. (p. 337)

Lewinsohn, P. M., Rohde, P., & Seeley, J. R. (1998). Major depressive disorder in older adolescents: Prevalence, risk factors, and clinical implications. *Clinical Psychology Review,* 18, 765–794. (p. 337)

Lewis, D. O., Yeager, C. A., Swica, Y., Pincus, J. H., & Lewis, M. (1997). Objective documentation of child abuse and dissociation in 12 murderers with dissociative identity disorder. *American Journal of Psychiatry,* 154, 1703–1710. (p. 323)

Lewis, M. (1992). Commentary. *Human Development,* 35, 44–51. (p. 192)

Lewontin, R. (1976). Race and intelligence. In N. J. Block & G. Dworkin (Eds.), *The IQ controversy: Critical readings.* New York: Pantheon. (p. 228)

Lewontin, R. (1982). *Human diversity.* New York: Scientific American Library. (p. 228)

Li, J., Laursen, T. M., Precht, D. H., Olsen, J., & Mortensen, P. B. (2005). Hospitalization for mental illness among parents after the death of a child. *New England Journal of Medicine,* 352, 1190–1196. (p. 96)

Lichtman, S. W., Pisarska, K., Berman, E. R., Pestone, M., Dowling, H., Offenbacher, E., Weisel, H., Heshka, S., Matthews, D. E., & Heymsfield, S. B. (1992). Discrepancy between self-reported and actual caloric intake and exercise in obese subjects. *New England Journal of Medicine,* 327, 1893–1898. (p. 244)

Lieberman, J. A., & 11 others. (2005). Effectiveness of antipsychotic drugs in patients with chronic schizophrenia. *New England Journal of Medicine,* 353, 1209–1223. (p. 365)

Lilienfeld, S. O., Lynn, S. J., Kirsch, I., Chaves, J. F., Sarbin, T. R., Ganaway, G. K., & Powell, R. A. (1999). Dissociative identity disorder and the sociocognitive model: Recalling the lessons of the past. *Psychological Bulletin,* 125, 507–523. (p. 323)

Linville, P. W., Fischer, G. W., & Fischhoff, B. (1992). AIDS risk perceptions and decision biases. In J. B. Pryor & G. D. Reeder (Eds.), *The social psychology of HIV infection.* Hillsdale, NJ: Erlbaum. (p. 208)

Lippa, R. A. (2005). *Gender, nature, and nurture (2nd ed.).* Mahwah, NJ: Erlbaum. (p. 105)

Lippa, R. A. (2006). The gender reality hypothesis. *American Psychologist, 61*, 639–640. (p. 105)

Livingstone, M., & Hubel, D. (1988). Segregation of form, color, movement, and depth: Anatomy, physiology, and perception. *Science, 240*, 740–749. (p. 132)

Locke, E. A., & Latham, G. P. (2002). Building a practically useful theory of goal setting and task motivation. *American Psychologist, 57*, 705–717. (p. 412)

Loehlin, J. C., & Nichols, R. C. (1976). *Heredity, environment, and personality.* Austin: University of Texas Press. (p. 69)

Loehlin, J. C., McCrae, R. R., & Costa, P. T., Jr. (1998). Heritabilities of common and measure-specific components of the Big Five personality factors. *Journal of Research in Personality, 32*, 431–453. (p. 301)

Loewenstein, G., & Furstenberg, F. (1991). Is teenage sexual behavior rational? *Journal of Applied Social Psychology, 21*, 957–986. (p. 167)

Loftus, E. F. (1979). The malleability of human memory. *American Scientist, 67*, 313–320. (p. 196)

Loftus, E. F. (1995, March/April). Remembering dangerously. *Skeptical Inquirer,* pp. 20–29. (p. 295)

Loftus, E. F. (2001, November). Imagining the past. *The Psychologist, 14*, 584–587. (p. 197)

Loftus, E. F., & Palmer, J. C. (October, 1974). Reconstruction of automobile destruction: An example of the interaction between language and memory. *Journal of Verbal Learning & Verbal Behavior, 13*(5), 585–589. (p. 196)

Loftus, E. F., Milo, E. M., & Paddock, J. R. (1995). The accidental executioner: Why psychotherapy must be informed by science. *The Counseling Psychologist, 23*, 300–309. (p. 198)

Loftus, G. R. (1992). When a lie becomes memory's truth: Memory distortion after exposure to misinformation. *Current Directions in Psychological Science, 1*, 121–123. (p. 296, 196)

Logan, T. K., Walker, R., Cole, J., & Leukefeld, C. (2002). Victimization and substance abuse among women: Contributing factors, interventions, and implications. *Review of General Psychology, 6*, 325–397. (p. 333)

Logue, A. W. (1998a). Laboratory research on self-control: Applications to administration. *Review of General Psychology, 2*, 221–238. (p. 167)

Logue, A. W. (1998b). Self-control. In W. T. O'Donohue, (Ed.), *Learning and behavior therapy.* Boston, MA: Allyn & Bacon. (p. 167)

London, P. (1970). The rescuers: Motivational hypotheses about Christians who saved Jews from the Nazis. In J. Macaulay & L. Berkowitz (Eds.), *Altruism and helping behavior.* New York: Academic Press. (p. 174)

Looy, H. (2001). Sex differences: Evolved, constructed, and designed. *Journal of Psychology and Theology, 29*, 301–313. (p. 119)

Lopes, P. N., Brackett, M. A., Nezlek, J. B., Schutz, A., Sellin, II, & Salovey, P. (2004). Emotional intelligence and social interaction. *Personality and Social Psychology Bulletin, 30*, 1018–1034. (p. 221)

Lord, C. G., Lepper, M. R., & Preston, E. (1984). Considering the opposite: A corrective strategy for social judgment. *Journal of Personality and Social Psychology, 47*, 1231–1247. (p. 209)

Lord, C. G., Ross, L., & Lepper, M. (1979). Biased assimilation and attitude polarization: The effects of prior theories on subsequently considered evidence. *Journal of Personality and Social Psychology, 37*, 2098–2109. (p. 209)

Louie, K., & Wilson, M. A. (2001). Temporally structured replay of awake hippocampal ensemble activity during rapid eye movement sleep. *Neuron, 29*, 145–156. (p. 58)

Lourenco, O., & Machado, A. (1996). In defense of Piaget's theory: A reply to 10 common criticisms. *Psychological Review, 103*, 143–164. (p. 76)

Lovaas, O. I. (1987). Behavioral treatment and normal educational and intellectual functioning in young autistic children. *Journal of Consulting and Clinical Psychology, 55*, 3–9. (p. 357)

Lubinski, D., & Benbow, C. P. (1992). Gender differences in abilities and preferences among the gifted: Implications for the math-science pipeline. *Current Directions in Psychological Science, 1*, 61–66. (p. 229)

Luborsky, L., Rosenthal, R., Diguer, L., Andrusyna, T. P., Berman, J. S., Levitt, J. T., Seligman, D. A., & Krause, E. D. (2002). The dodo bird verdict is alive and well—mostly. *Clinical Psychology: Science and Practice, 9*, 2–34. (p. 362)

Lucas, A., Morley, R., Cole, T. J., Lister, G., & Leeson-Payne, C. (1992). Breast milk and subsequent intelligence quotient in children born preterm. *Lancet, 339*, 261–264. (p. 16)

Lucas, R. E. (2005). Long-term disability has lasting effects on subjective well-being: Evidence from two nationally representative longitudinal studies. Unpublished manuscript, Michigan State University. (p. 262)

Lucas, R. E., Clark, A. E., Georgellis, Y., & Diener, E. (2003). Re-examining adaptation and the setpoint model of happiness: Reactions to changes in marital status. *Journal of Personality and Social Psychology, 84*, 527–539. (Figure courtesy of R. E. Lucas.) (p. 96)

Lucas, R. E., Clark, A. E., Georgellis, Y., & Diener, E. (2004). Unemployment alters the set point for life satisfaction. *Psychological Science, 15*, 8–13. (p. 264)

Ludwig, A. M. (1995). *The price of greatness: Resolving the creativity and madness controversy.* New York: Guilford Press. (p. 337)

Luria, A. M. (1968). In L. Solotaroff (Trans.), *The mind of a mnemonist.* New York: Basic Books. (p. 181)

Lustig, C., & Buckner, R. L. (2004). Preserved neural correlates of priming in old age and dementia. *Neuron, 42*, 865–875. (p. 189)

Lutgendorf, S. K., Russell, D., Ullrich, P., Harris, T. B., & Wallace, R. (2004). Religious participation, Interleukin-6, and mortality in older adults. *Health Psychology, 23*, 465–475. (p. 283)

Luthar, S. S., & Latendresse, S. J. (2005). Children of the affluent: Challenges to well-being. *Current Directions in Psychological Science, 14*, 49–53. (p. 262)

Lyall, S. (2005, November 29). What's the buzz? Rowdy teenagers don't want to hear it. *New York Times* (www.nytimes.com). (p. 92)

Lykken, D. T. (1991). Science, lies, and controversy: An epitaph for the polygraph. Invited address upon receipt of the Senior Career Award for Distinguished Contribution to Psychology in the Public Interest, American Psychological Association convention. (p. 254)

Lykken, D. T. (1995). *The antisocial personalities.* Hillsdale, NJ: Erlbaum. (p. 391)

Lykken, D. T. (1999). *Happiness.* New York: Golden Books. (p. 225)

Lykken, D. T., & Tellegen, A. (1993). Is human mating adventitious or the result of lawful choice? A twin study of mate selection. *Journal of Personality and Social Psychology, 65*, 56–68. (p. 95)

Lykken, D. T., & Tellegen, A. (1996). Happiness is a stochastic phenomenon. *Psychological Science, 7*, 186–189. (p. 265)

Lynch, G. (2002). Memory enhancement: The search for mechanism-based drugs. *Nature Neuroscience, 5* (suppl.), 1035–1038. (p. 187)

Lynch, G., & Staubli, U. (1991). Possible contributions of long-term potentiation to the encoding and organization of memory. *Brain Research Reviews, 16,* 204–206. (p. 187)

Lynn, M. (1988). The effects of alcohol consumption on restaurant tipping. *Personality and Social Psychology Bulletin, 14,* 87–91. (p. 326)

Lynn, R. (1991, Fall/Winter). The evolution of racial differences in intelligence. *The Mankind Quarterly, 32,* 99–145. (p. 227)

Lynn, R. (2001). *Eugenics: A reassessment.* Westport, CT: Praeger/Greenwood. (p. 227)

Lyons, L. (2002, June 25). Are spiritual teens healthier? *Gallup Tuesday Briefing,* Gallup Organization (www.gallup.com/poll/tb/religValue/20020625b.asp). (p. 283)

Lyons, L. (2005, January 4). Teens stay true to parents' political perspectives. *Gallup Poll News Service* (www.gallup.com). (p. 88)

Lytton, H., & Romney, D. M. (1991). Parents' differential socialization of boys and girls: A meta-analysis. *Psychological Bulletin, 109,* 267–296. (p. 107)

Lyubomirsky, S. (2001). Why are some people happier than others? The role of cognitive and motivational processes in well-being. *American Psychologist, 56,* 239–249. (p. 263)

Lyubomirsky, S., King, L., & Diener, E. (2005). The benefits of frequent positive affect: Does happiness lead to success? *Psychological Bulletin, 131,* 803–855. (p. 261)

Maas, J. B. (1999). *Power sleep. The revolutionary program that prepares your mind for peak performance.* New York: HarperCollins. (p. 54)

Maccoby, E. E. (1990). Gender and relationships: A developmental account. *American Psychologist, 45,* 513–520. (p. 105)

Maccoby, E. E. (1995). Divorce and custody: The rights, needs, and obligations of mothers, fathers, and children. *Nebraska Symposium on Motivation, 42,* 135–172. (p. 107)

Maccoby, E. E. (1998). *The paradox of gender.* Cambridge, MA: Harvard University Press. (p. 105)

MacDonald, T. K., Zanna, M. P., & Fong, G. T. (1995). Decision making in altered states: Effects of alcohol on attitudes toward drinking and driving. *Journal of Personality and Social Psychology, 68,* 973–985. (p. 326)

MacFarlane, A. (1978, February). What a baby knows. *Human Nature,* pp. 74–81. (p. 68)

MacKinnon, D. W., & Hall, W. B. (1972). Intelligence and creativity. In *Proceedings, XVIIth International Congress of Applied Psychology* (Vol. 2). Brussels: Editest. (p. 220)

MacLeod, C., & Campbell, L. (1992). Memory accessibility and probability judgments: An experimental evaluation of the availability heuristic. *Journal of Personality and Social Psychology, 63,* 890–902. (p. 207)

Maes, H. H. M., Neale, M. C., & Eaves, L. J. (1997). Genetic and environmental factors in relative body weight and human adiposity. *Behavior Genetics, 27,* 325–351. (p. 244)

Maestripieri, D. (2003). Similarities in affiliation and aggression between cross-fostered rhesus macaque females and their biological mothers. *Developmental Psychobiology, 43,* 321–327. (p. 69)

Magnusson, D. (1990). Personality research—challenges for the future. *European Journal of Personality, 4,* 1–17. (p. 324)

Major, B., Carrington, P. I., & Carnevale, P. J. D. (1984). Physical attractiveness and self-esteem: Attribution for praise from an other-sex evaluator. *Personality and Social Psychology Bulletin, 10,* 43–50. (p. 396)

Major, B., Schmidlin, A. M., & Williams, L. (1990). Gender patterns in social touch: The impact of setting and age. *Journal of Personality and Social Psychology, 58,* 634–643. (p. 105)

Malamuth, N. M., & Check, J. V. P. (1981). The effects of media exposure on acceptance of violence against women: A field experiment. *Journal of Research in Personality, 15,* 436–446. (p. 112)

Malan, D. H. (1978). The case of the secretary with the violent father. In H. Davanloo (Ed.), *Basic principles and techniques in short-term dynamic psychotherapy.* New York: Spectrum. (p. 352)

Malinosky-Rummell, R., & Hansen, D. J. (1993). Long-term consequences of childhood physical abuse. *Psychological Bulletin, 114,* 68–79. (p. 79)

Malloy, E. A. (1994, June 7). Report of the Commission on Substance Abuse at Colleges and Universities, reported by *Associated Press.* (p. 327)

Malmquist, C. P. (1986). Children who witness parental murder: Posttraumatic aspects. *Journal of the American Academy of Child Psychiatry, 25,* 320–325. (p. 296)

Malnic, B., Hirono, J., Sato, T., & Buck, L. B. (1999). Combinatorial receptor codes for odors. *Cell, 96,* 713–723. (p. 141)

Mandel, D. (1983, March 13). One man's holocaust: Part II. The story of David Mandel's journey through hell as told to David Kagan. *Wonderland Magazine (Grand Rapids Press),* pp. 2–7. (p. 238)

Manson, J. E. (2002). Walking compared with vigorous exercise for the prevention of cardiovascular events in women. *New England Journal of Medicine, 347,* 716–725. (p. 280)

Maquet, P. (2001). The role of sleep in learning and memory. *Science, 294,* 1048–1052. (p. 58)

Marangell, L. B., Rush, A. J., George, M. S., Sackeim, H. A., Johnson, C. R., Husain, M. M., Nahas, Z., & Lisanby, S. H. (2002). Vagus nerve stimulation (VNS) for major depressive episodes: One year outcomes. *Biological Psychiatry, 51,* 280–287. (p. 369)

Marcus, B., Machilek, F., & Schütz, A. (2006). Personality in cyberspace: Personal web sites as media for personality expressions and impressions. *Journal of Personality and Social Psychology, 90,* 1014–1031. (p. 304)

Margolis, M. L. (2000). Brahms' lullaby revisited: Did the composer have obstructive sleep apnea? *Chest, 118,* 210–213. (p. 56)

Markus, H., & Kitayama, S. (1991). Culture and the self: Implications for cognition, emotion, and motivation. *Psychological Review, 98,* 224–253. (p. 309)

Markus, H., & Nurius, P. (1986). Possible selves. *American Psychologist, 41,* 954–969. (p. 305)

Marlatt, G. A. (1991). Substance abuse: Etiology, prevention, and treatment issues. Master lecture, American Psychological Association convention. (p. 327)

Marschark, M., Richman, C. L., Yuille, J. C., & Hunt, R. R. (1987). The role of imagery in memory: On shared and distinctive information. *Psychological Bulletin, 102,* 28–41. (p. 185)

Marshall, M. J. (2002). *Why spanking doesn't work.* Springville, UT: Bonneville Books. (p. 168)

Marteau, T. M. (1989). Framing of information: Its influences upon decisions of doctors and patients. *British Journal of Social Psychology, 28,* 89–94. (p. 208)

Martin, C. L., & Ruble, D. (2004). Children's search for gender cues. *Current Directions in Psychological Science, 13,* 67–70. (p. 108)

Martin, C. L., Ruble, D. N., & Szkrybalo, J. (2002). Cognitive theories of early gender development. *Psychological Bulletin, 128,* 903–933. (p. 108)

Martin, J. L. R., Barbanojh, M. J., Schlaepfer, T. E., Thompson, E., Perez, V., & Kulisevsky, J. (2005). Repetitive transcranial magnetic stimulation for the treatment of depression: Systematic review and meta-analysis. *British Journal of Psychiatry, 182,* 480–491. (p. 369)

Martin, R. J., White, B. D., & Hulsey, M. G. (1991). The regulation of body weight. *American Scientist, 79,* 528–541. (p. 239)

Martino, S. C., Collins, R. L., Kanouse, D. E., Elliott, M., & Berry, S. H. (2005). Social cognitive processes mediating the relationship between exposure to television's sexual content and adolescents' sexual behavior. *Journal of Personality and Social Psychology, 89,* 914–924. (p. 112)

Martins, Y., Preti, G., Crabtree, C. R., & Wysocki, C. J. (2005). Preference for human body odors is influenced by gender and sexual orientation. *Psychological Science, 16,* 694–701. (p. 116)

Maslow, A. H. (1970). *Motivation and personality (2nd ed.).* New York: Harper & Row. (pp. 237, 297)

Maslow, A. H. (1971). *The farther reaches of human nature.* New York: Viking Press. (p. 237)

Mason, C., & Kandel, E. R. (1991). Central visual pathways. In E. R. Kandel, J. H. Schwartz, & T. M. Jessell (Eds.), *Principles of neural science (3rd ed.).* New York: Elsevier. (p. 31)

Mason, H. (2003, March 25). Wake up, sleepy teen. *Gallup Poll Tuesday Briefing* (www.gallup.com). (p. 54)

Mason, H. (2003, September 2). Americans, Britons at odds on animal testing. *Gallup Poll News Service* (www.gallup.com). (p. 20)

Mason, H. (2005, January 25). Who dreams, perchance to sleep? *Gallup Poll News Service* (www.gallup.com). (p. 54)

Mason, R. A., & Just, M. A. (2004). How the brain processes causal inferences in text. *Psychological Science, 15,* 1–7. (p. 47)

Masse, L. C., & Tremblay, R. E. (1997). Behavior of boys in kindergarten and the onset of substance use during adolescence. *Archives of General Psychiatry, 54,* 62–68. (p. 333)

Massimini, M., Ferrarelli, F., Huber, R., Esser, S. K., Singh, H., & Tononi, G. (2005). Breakdown of cortical effective connectivity during sleep. *Science, 309,* 2228–2232. (p. 51)

Masters, W. H., & Johnson, V. E. (1966). *Human sexual response.* Boston: Little, Brown. (p. 109)

Mastroianni, G. R. (2002). Milgram and the Holocaust: A reexamination. *Journal of Theoretical and Philosophical Psychology, 22,* 158–173. (p. 382)

Masuda, T., & Kitayama, S. (2004). Perceiver-induced constraint and attitude attribution in Japan and the US: A case for the cultural dependence of the correspondence bias. *Journal of Experimental Social Psychology, 40,* 409–416. (p. 376)

Mataix-Cols, D., Rosario-Campos, M. C., & Leckman, J. F. (2005). A multidimensional model of obsessive-compulsive disorder. *American Journal of Psychiatry, 162,* 228–238. (p. 322)

Mataix-Cols, D., Wooderson, S., Lawrence, N., Brammer, M. J., Speckens, A., & Phillips, M. L. (2004). Distinct neural correlates of washing, checking, and hoarding symptom dimensions in obsessive-compulsive disorder. *Archives of General Psychiatry, 61,* 564–576. (p. 322)

Mather, M., & Carstensen, L. L. (2003). Aging and attentional biases for emotional faces. *Psychological Science, 14,* 409–415. (p. 97)

Mather, M., Canli, T., English, T., Whitfield, S., Wais, P., Ochsner, K., Gabrieli, J. D. E., & Carstensen, L. L. (2004). Amygdala responses to emotionally valenced stimuli in older and younger adults. *Psychological Science, 15,* 259–263. (p. 97)

Matsumoto, D., & Ekman, P. (1989). American-Japanese cultural differences in intensity ratings of facial expressions of emotion. *Motivation and Emotion, 13,* 143–157. (p. 258)

Maurer, D., & Maurer, C. (1988). *The world of the newborn.* New York: Basic Books. (p. 68)

May, C., & Hasher, L. (1998). Synchrony effects in inhibitory control over thought and action. *Journal of Experimental Psychology: Human Perception and Performance, 24,* 363–380. (p. 50)

May, P. A., & Gossage, J. P. (2001). Estimating the prevalence of fetal alcohol syndrome: A summary. *Alcohol Research and Health, 25,* 159–167. (p. 67)

Mayberg, H. S., Lozano, A. M., Voon, V., McNeely, H. E., Seminowicz, D., Hamani, C., Schwalb, J. M., & Kennedy, S. H. (2005). Deep brain stimulation for treatment-resistant depression. *Neuron, 45,* 651–660. (p. 369)

Mayberry, R. I., Lock, E., & Kazmi, H. (2002). Linguistic ability and early language exposure. *Nature, 417,* 38. (p. 214)

Mayer, J. D. Salovey, P., & Caruso, D. (2002). *The Mayer-Salovey-Caruso emotional intelligence test (MSCEIT).* Toronto: Multi-Health Systems, Inc. (p. 221)

Mazure, C., Keita, G., & Blehar, M. (2002). *Summit on women and depression: Proceedings and recommendations.* Washington, DC: American Psychological Association (www.apa.org/pi/wpo/women&depression.pdf). (p. 339)

Mazzoni, G., & Memon, A. (2003). Imagination can create false autobiographical memories. *Psychological Science, 14,* 186–188. (p. 197)

McAneny, L. (1996, September). Large majority think government conceals information about UFOs. *Gallup Poll Monthly,* pp. 23–26. (p. 191)

McBurney, D. H. (1996). *How to think like a psychologist: Critical thinking in psychology.* Upper Saddle River, NJ: Prentice Hall. (p. 42)

McBurney, D. H., & Gent, J. F. (1979). On the nature of taste qualities. *Psychological Bulletin, 86,* 151–167. (p. 140)

McCann, I. L., & Holmes, D. S. (1984). Influence of aerobic exercise on depression. *Journal of Personality and Social Psychology, 46,* 1142–1147. (p. 281)

McCaul, K. D., & Malott, J. M. (1984). Distraction and coping with pain. *Psychological Bulletin, 95,* 516–533. (p. 138)

McCauley, C. R. (2002). Psychological issues in understanding terrorism and the response to terrorism. In C. E. Stout (Ed.), *The psychology of terrorism, Vol. 3.* Westport, CT: Praeger/Greenwood. (p. 386)

McCauley, C. R., & Segal, M. E. (1987). Social psychology of terrorist groups. In C. Hendrick (Ed.), *Group processes and intergroup relations.* Beverly Hills, CA: Sage. (p. 386)

McClearn, G. E., Johansson, B., Berg, S., Pedersen, N. L., Ahern, F., Petrill, S. A., & Plomin, R. (1997). Substantial genetic influence on cognitive abilities in twins 80 or more years old. *Science, 276,* 1560–1563. (p. 226)

McClure, E. B. (2000). A meta-analytic review of sex differences in facial expression processing and their development in infants, children, and adolescents. *Psychological Bulletin, 126,* 424–453. (p. 229)

McConnell, R. A. (1991). National Academy of Sciences opinion on parapsychology. *Journal of the American Society for Psychical Research, 85,* 333–365. (p. 152)

McCool, G. (1999, October 26). Mirror-gazing Venezuelans top of vanity stakes. *Toronto Star* (via web.lexis-nexis.com). (p. 395)

McCormick, C. M., & Witelson, S. F. (1991). A cognitive profile of homosexual men compared to heterosexual men and women. *Psychoneuroendocrinology*, 16, 459–473. (p. 116)

McCrae, R. R. (2001). Trait psychology and culture. *Journal of Personality*, 69, 819–846. (p. 301)

McCrae, R. R., & Costa, P. T., Jr. (1994). The stability of personality: Observations and evaluations. *Current Directions in Psychological Science*, 3, 173–175. (p. 98)

McCrae, R. R., & Costa, P. T., Jr. (1999). A five-factor theory of personality. In L. A. Pervin & O. P. John (Eds.), *Handbook of personality: Theory and research*. New York: Guilford. (p. 301)

McCrae, R. R., Costa, P. T., Jr., de Lirna, M. P., Simoes, A., Ostendorf, F., Angleitner, A., Marusic, I., Bratko, D., Caprara, G. V., Barbaranelli, C., Chae, J-H., & Piedmont, R. L. (1999). Age differences in personality across the adult life span: Parallels in five cultures. *Developmental Psychology*, 35, 466–477. (p. 301)

McCrae, R. R., Costa, P. T., Jr., Ostendorf, F., Angleitner, A., Hrebickova, M., Avia, M. D., Sanz, J., Sanchez-Bernardos, M. L., Kusdil, M. E., Woodfield, R., Saunders, P. R., & Smith, P. B. (2000). Nature over nurture: Temperament, personality, and life span development. *Journal of Personality and Social Psychology*, 78, 173–186. (p. 68)

McCrae, R. R., Terracciano, A., & 78 others. (2005). Universal features of personality traits from the observer's perspective: Data from 50 cultures. *Journal of Personality and Social Psychology*, 88, 547–561. (p. 301)

McCullough, M. E., & Laurenceau, J-P. (2005). Religiousness and the trajectory of self-rated health across adulthood. *Personality and Social Psychology Bulletin*, 31, 560–573. (p. 283)

McCullough, M. E., Hoyt, W. T., Larson, D. B., Koenig, H. G., & Thoresen, C. (2000). Religious involvement and mortality: A meta-analytic review. *Health Psychology*, 19, 211–222. (p. 283)

McGaugh, J. I. (2003). *Memory and emotion: The making of lasting memories.* New York: Columbia University Press. (p. 187)

McGaugh, J. L. (1994). Quoted by B. Bower, Stress hormones hike emotional memories. *Science News*, 146, 262. (p. 187)

McGhee, P. E. (June, 1976). Children's appreciation of humor: A test of the cognitive congruency principle. *Child Development*, 47(2), 420–426. (p. 76)

McGrath, J. J., & Welham, J. L. (1999). Season of birth and schizophrenia: A systematic review and meta-analysis of data from the Southern hemisphere. *Schizophrenia Research*, 35, 237–242. (p. 343)

McGrath, J., Welham, J., & Pemberton, M. (1995). Month of birth, hemisphere of birth and schizophrenia. *British Journal of Psychiatry*, 167, 783–785. (p. 343)

McGue, M., & Bouchard, T. J., Jr. (1998). Genetic and environmental influences on human behavioral differences. *Annual Review of Neuroscience*, 21, 1–24. (p. 69)

McGue, M., Bouchard, T. J., Jr., Iacono, W. G., & Lykken, D. T. (1993). Behavioral genetics of cognitive ability: A life-span perspective. In R. Plomin & G. E. McClearn (Eds.), *Nature, nurture and psychology*. Washington, DC: American Psychological Association. (pp. 225, 226)

McGuire, W. J. (1986). The myth of massive media impact: Savings and salvagings. In G. Comstock (Ed.), *Public communication and behavior.* Orlando, FL: Academic Press. (p. 176)

McGurk, H., & MacDonald, J. (1976). Hearing lips and seeing voices. *Nature*, 264, 746–748. (p. 140)

McHugh, P. R. (1995a). Witches, multiple personalities, and other psychiatric artifacts. *Nature Medicine*, 1(2), 110–114. (p. 323)

McKenna, K. Y. A., & Bargh, J. A. (1998). Coming out in the age of the Internet: Identity "demarginalization" through virtual group participation. *Journal of Personality and Social Psychology*, 75, 681–694. (p. 386)

McLaughlin, C. S., Chen, C., Greenberger, E., & Biermeier, C. (1997). Family, peer, and individual correlates of sexual experience among Caucasian and Asian American late adolescents. *Journal of Personality and Social Psychology: Journal of Research on Adolescence*, 7, 33–53. (p. 108)

McMurray, C. (2004, January 13). U.S., Canada, Britain: Who's getting in shape? *Gallup Poll Tuesday Briefing* (www.gallup.com). (p. 281)

McNally, R. J. (2003). *Remembering trauma.* Cambridge, MA: Harvard University Press. (p. 199)

McNally, R. J., Bryant, R. A., & Ehlers, A. (2003). Does early psychological intervention promote recovery from posttraumatic stress? *Psychological Science in the Public Interest*, 4, 45–79. (pp. 320, 321)

McNeil, B. J., Pauker, S. G., & Tversky, A. (1988). On the framing of medical decisions. In D. E. Bell, H. Raiffa, & A. Tversky (Eds.), *Decision making: Descriptive, normative, and prescriptive interactions.* New York: Cambridge, 1988. (p. 208)

Meador, B. D., & Rogers, C. R. (1984). Person-centered therapy. In R. J. Corsini (Ed.), *Current psychotherapies (3rd ed.).* Itasca, IL: Peacock. (p. 354)

Medical Institute for Sexual Health. (1994, April). Condoms ineffective against human papilloma virus. *Sexual Health Update*, 2. (p. 111)

Mednick, S. A., Huttunen, M. O., & Machon, R. A. (1994). Prenatal influenza infections and adult schizophrenia. *Schizophrenia Bulletin*, 20, 263–267. (p. 343)

Mehl, M. R., & Pennebaker, J. W. (2003). The sounds of social life: A psychometric analysis of students' daily social environments and natural conversations. *Journal of Personality and Social Psychology*, 84, 857–870. (p. 14)

Mehl, M. R., Gosling, S. D., & Pennebaker, J. W. (2006). Personality in its natural habitat: Manifestations and implicit folk theories of personality in daily life. *Journal of Personality and Social Psychology*, 90, 862–877. (p. 304)

Meichenbaum, D. (1977). *Cognitive-behavior modification: An integrative approach.* New York: Plenum Press. (p. 359)

Meichenbaum, D. (1985). *Stress inoculation training.* New York: Pergamon. (p. 359)

Meltzoff, A. N. (1988). Infant imitation after a 1-week delay: Long-term memory for novel acts and multiple stimuli. *Developmental Psychology*, 24, 470–476. (p. 173)

Meltzoff, A. N., & Moore, M. K. (1989). Imitation in newborn infants: Exploring the range of gestures imitated and the underlying mechanisms. *Developmental Psychology*, 25, 954–962. (p. 173)

Meltzoff, A. N., & Moore, M. K. (1997). Explaining facial imitation: A theoretical model. *Early Development and Parenting*, 6, 179–192. (p. 173)

Melzack, R. (1992, April). Phantom limbs. *Scientific American*, pp. 120–126. (p. 137)

Melzack, R. (1993). Distinguished contribution series. *Canadian Journal of Experimental Psychology*, 47, 615–629. (p. 137)

Melzack, R. (1998, February). Quoted in Phantom limbs. *Discover*, p. 20. (p. 137)

Mendle, J., Turkheimer, E., & Emery, R. E. (2007). Detrimental psychological outcomes associated with early pubertal timing in adolescent girls. *Developmental Review, 27,* 151–171. (p. 84)

Merari, A. (2002). Explaining suicidal terrorism: Theories versus empirical evidence. Invited address to the American Psychological Association. (p. 386)

Merskey, H. (1992). The manufacture of personalities: The production of multiple personality disorder. *British Journal of Psychiatry, 160,* 327–340. (p. 323)

Merton, R. K., & Kitt, A. S. (1950). Contributions to the theory of reference group behavior. In R. K. Merton & P. F. Lazarsfeld (Eds.), *Continuities in social research: Studies in the scope and method of the American soldier.* Glencoe, IL: Free Press. (p. 264)

Mestel, R. (1997, April 26). Get real, Siggi. *New Scientist* (www.newscientist.com/ns/970426/siggi.html). (p. 58)

Meston, C. M., & Frohlich, P. F. (2000). The neurobiology of sexual function. *Archives of General Psychiatry, 57,* 1012–1030. (p. 110)

Meston, C. M., Trapnell, P. D., & Gorzalka, B. B. (1996). Ethnic and gender differences in sexuality: Variations in sexual behavior between Asian and non-Asian university students. *Archives of Sexual Behavior, 25,* 33–72. (p. 108)

Meyer-Bahlburg, H. F. L. (1995). Psychoneuroendocrinology and sexual pleasure: The aspect of sexual orientation. In P. R. Abramson & S. D. Pinkerton (Eds.), *Sexual nature/sexual culture.* Chicago: University of Chicago Press. (p. 116)

Mezulis, A. M., Abramson, L. Y., Hyde, J. S., & Hankin, B. L. (2004). Is there a universal positivity bias in attributions? A meta-analytic review of individual, developmental, and cultural differences in the self-serving attributional bias. *Psychological Bulletin, 130,* 711–747. (p. 307)

Middlebrooks, J. C., & Green, D. M. (1991). Sound localization by human listeners. *Annual Review of Psychology, 42,* 135–159. (p. 136)

Mikulincer, M., & Shaver, P. R. (2001). Attachment theory and intergroup bias: Evidence that priming the secure base schema attenuates negative reactions to our-groups. *Journal of Personality and Social Psychology, 81,* 97–115. (p. 390)

Mikulincer, M., & Shaver, P. R. (2005). Attachment theory and emotions in close relationships: Exploring the attachment-related dynamics of emotional reactions to relational events. *Personal Relationships, 12,* 149–168. (p. 79)

Milan, R. J., Jr., & Kilmann, P. R. (1987). Interpersonal factors in premarital contraception. *Journal of Sex Research, 23,* 289–321. (p. 111)

Miles, D. R., & Carey, G. (1997). Genetic and environmental architecture of human aggression. *Journal of Personality and Social Psychology, 72,* 207–217. (p. 391)

Milgram, S. (1963). Behavioral study of obedience. *Journal of Abnormal & Social Psychology, 67(4),* 371–378. (p. 381)

Milgram, S. (1974). *Obedience to authority.* New York: Harper & Row. (pp. 381, 383, 386)

Miller, E. J., Smith, J. E., & Trembath, D. L. (2000). The "skinny" on body size requests in personal ads. *Sex Roles, 43,* 129–141. (p. 243)

Miller, G. (2004). Axel, Buck share award for deciphering how the nose knows. *Science, 306,* 207. (p. 141)

Miller, G. A. (1956). The magical number seven, plus or minus two: Some limits on our capacity for processing information. *Psychological Review, 63,* 81–97. (p. 186)

Miller, G. A. (1962). *Psychology: The science of mental life.* New York: Harper & Row. (p. 296)

Miller, J. G., & Bersoff, D. M. (1995). Development in the context of everyday family relationships: Culture, interpersonal morality and adaptation. In M. Killen and D. Hart (Eds.), *Morality in everyday life: A developmental perspective.* New York: Cambridge University Press. (p. 86)

Miller, K. I., & Monge, P. R. (1986). Participation, satisfaction, and productivity: A meta-analytic review. *Academy of Management Journal, 29,* 727–753. (p. 277)

Miller, L. (2005, January 4). U.S. airlines have 34 deaths in 3 years. *Associated Press.* (p. 210)

Miller, L. K. (1999). The Savant Syndrome: Intellectual impairment and exceptional skill. *Psychological Bulletin, 125,* 31–46. (p. 219)

Miller, N. E., & Brucker, B. S. (1979). A learned visceral response apparently independent of skeletal ones in patients paralyzed by spinal lesions. In N. Birbaumer & H. D. Kimmel (Eds.), *Biofeedback and self-regulation.* Hillsdale, NJ: Erlbaum. (p. 281)

Miller, P. C., Lefcourt, H. M., Holmes, J. G., Ware, E. E., & Saleh, W. E. (1986). Marital locus of control and marital problem solving. *Journal of Personality and Social Psychology, 51,* 161–169. (p. 278)

Mills, M., & Melhuish, E. (1974). Recognition of mother's voice in early infancy. *Nature, 252,* 123–124. (p. 68)

Milton, J., & Wiseman, R. (2002). A response to Storm and Ertel (2002). *Journal of Parapsychology, 66,* 183–185. (p. 153)

Mineka, S. (1985). The frightful complexity of the origins of fears. In F. R. Brush & J. B. Overmier (Eds.), *Affect, conditioning and cognition: Essays on the determinants of behavior.* Hillsdale, NJ: Erlbaum. (p. 321)

Mineka, S., & Zinbarg, R. (1996). Conditioning and ethological models of anxiety disorders: Stress-in-dynamic-context anxiety models. In D. Hope (Ed.), *Perspectives on anxiety, panic, and fear.* Nebraska symposium on motivation. Lincoln, NE: University of Nebraska Press. (pp. 320, 322)

Mineka, S., & Zinbarg, R. (2006). A contemporary learning theory perspective on the etiology of anxiety disorders: It's not what you thought it was. *American Psychologist, 61,* 10–26. (p. 321)

Miner-Rubino, K., Winter, D. G., & Stewart, A. J. (2004). Gender, social class, and the subjective experience of aging: Self-perceived personality change from early adulthood to late midlife. *Personality and Social Psychology Bulletin, 30,* 1599–1610. (p. 97)

Mischel, W. (1968). *Personality and assessment.* New York: Wiley. (p. 303)

Mischel, W. (1984). Convergences and challenges in the search for consistency. *American Psychologist, 39,* 351–364. (p. 303)

Mischel, W. (2004). Toward an integrative science of the person. *Annual Review of Psychology, 55,* 1–22. (p. 303)

Mischel, W., Shoda, Y., & Peake, P. K. (1988). The nature of adolescent competencies predicted by preschool delay of gratification. *Journal of Personality and Social Psychology, 54,* 687–696. (p. 86)

Mischel, W., Shoda, Y., & Rodriguez, M. L. (1989). Delay of gratification in children. *Science, 244,* 933–938. (p. 86, 167)

Mita, T. H., Dermer, M., & Knight, J. (1977). Reversed facial images and the mere-exposure hypothesis. *Journal of Personality and Social Psychology, 35,* 597–601. (p. 394)

Moffitt, T. E., Caspi, A., Harrington, H., & Milne, B. J. (2002). Males on the life-course-persistent and adolescence-limited antisocial pathways: Follow-up at age 26 years. *Development and Psychopathology, 14,* 179–207. (p. 98)

Moghaddam, F. M. (2005). The staircase to terrorism: A psychological exploration. *American Psychologist, 60,* 161–169. (p. 386)

Mohn, J. K., Tingle, L. R., & Finger, R. (2003). An analysis of the causes of the decline in non-marital birth and pregnancy rates for teens from 1991 to 1995. *Adolescent and Family Health, 3,* 39–47. (p. 109)

Mondloch, C. J., Lewis, T. L., Budreau, D. R., Maurer, D., Dannemiller, J. L., Stephens, B. R., & Kleiner-Gathercoal, K. A. (1999). Face perception during early infancy. *Psychological Science, 10,* 419–422. (p. 68)

Money, J. (1987). Sin, sickness, or status? Homosexual gender identity and psychoneuroendocrinology. *American Psychologist, 42,* 384–399. (p. 116)

Money, J., Berlin, F. S., Falck, A., & Stein, M. (1983). *Antiandrogenic and counseling treatment of sex offenders.* Baltimore: Department of Psychiatry and Behavioral Sciences, The Johns Hopkins University School of Medicine. (p. 110)

Moody, R. (1976). *Life after life.* Harrisburg, PA: Stackpole Books. (p. 331)

Mook, D. G. (1983). In defense of external invalidity. *American Psychologist, 38,* 379–387. (p. 19)

Moorcroft, W. H. (2003). *Understanding sleep and dreaming.* New York: Kluwer/Plenum. (pp. 51, 55)

Moore, D. W. (2003, November 23). Many Americans deluding themselves about weight. *Gallup Poll* (poll.gallup.com). (p. 245)

Moore, D. W. (2004, December 17). Sweet dreams go with a good night's sleep. *Gallup News Service* (www.gallup.com). (p. 53)

Moreland, R. L., & Beach, S. R. (1992). Exposure effects in the classroom: The development of affinity among students. *Journal of Experimental Social Psychology, 28,* 255–276. (p. 394)

Moreland, R. L., & Zajonc, R. B. (1982). Exposure effects in person perception; Familiarity, similarity, and attraction. *Journal of Experimental Social Psychology, 18,* 395–415. (p. 394)

Morell, V. (1995). Attacking the causes of "silent" infertility. *Science, 269,* 775–776. (p. 110)

Morell, V. (1995). Zeroing in on how hormones affect the immune system. *Science, 269,* 773–775. (p. 273)

Morelli, G. A., Rogoff, B., Oppenheim, D., & Goldsmith, D. (1992). Cultural variation in infants' sleeping arrangements: Questions of independence. *Developmental Psychology, 26,* 604–613. (p. 81)

Morey, R. A., Inan, S., Mitchell, T. V., Perkins, D. O., Lieberman, J. A., & Belger, A. (2005). Imaging frontostriatal function in ultra-high-risk, early, and chronic schizophrenia during executive processing. *Archives of General Psychiatry, 62,* 254–262. (p. 342)

Morgan, A. B., & Lilienfeld, S. O. (2000). A meta-analytic review of the relation between antisocial behavior and neuropsychological measures of executive function. *Clinical Psychology Review, 20,* 113–136. (p. 325)

Morrison, A. R. (2003). The brain on night shift. *Cerebrum, 5*(3), 23–36. (p. 52)

Mortensen, E. L., Michaelsen, K. F., Sanders, S. A., & Reinisch, J. M. (2002). The association between duration of breastfeeding and adult intelligence. *Journal of the American Medical Association, 287,* 2365–2371. (p. 16)

Mortensen, P. B. (1999). Effects of family history and place and season of birth on the risk of schizophrenia. *New England Journal of Medicine, 340,* 603–608. (p. 343)

Moruzzi, G., & Magoun, H. W. (1949). Brain stem reticular formation and activation of the EEG. *Electroencephalography and Clinical Neurophysiology, 1,* 455–473. (p. 36)

Moscovici, S. (1985). Social influence and conformity. In G. Lindzey & E. Aronson (Eds.), *The handbook of social psychology* (3rd ed). Hillsdale, NJ: Erlbaum. (p. 387)

Mosher, D. L., & Anderson, R. D. (1986). Macho personality, sexual aggression, and reactions to guided imagery of realistic rape. *Journal of Research in Personality, 20,* 77–94. (p. 326)

Mosher, W. D., Chandra, A., & Jones, J. (2005, September 15). Sexual behavior and selected health measures: Men and women 15–44 years of age, United States, 2002. *Advance Data from Vital and Health Statistics,* No. 362. (p. 114)

Moss, H. A., & Susman, E. J. (1980). Longitudinal study of personality development. In O. G. Brim, Jr., & J. Kagan (Eds.), *Constancy and change in human development.* Cambridge, MA: Harvard University Press. (p. 98)

Moyer, K. E. (1983). The physiology of motivation: Aggression as a model. In C. J. Scheier & A. M. Rogers (Eds.), *G. Stanley Hall Lecture Series* (Vol. 3). Washington, DC: American Psychological Association. (p. 391)

Mroczek, D. K. (2001). Age and emotion in adulthood. *Current Directions in Psychological Science, 10,* 87–90. (p. 97)

Mroczek, D. K., & Spiro, A., III. (2005). Change in life satisfaction during adulthood: Findings from the Veterans Affairs normative aging study. *Journal of Personality and Social Psychology, 88,* 189–202. (p. 265)

Muller, J. E., & Verrier, R. L. (1996). Triggering of sudden death—Lessons from an earthquake. *New England Journal of Medicine, 334,* 461. (p. 270)

Mullin, C. R., & Linz, D. (1995). Desensitization and resensitization to violence against women: Effects of exposure to sexually violent films on judgments of domestic violence victims. *Journal of Personality and Social Psychology, 69,* 449–459. (p. 176)

Mulrow, C. D. (1999, March). Treatment of depression—newer pharmacotherapies, summary. *Evidence Report/Technology Assessment, 7.* Agency for Health Care Policy and Research, Rockville, MD. (www.ahrq.gov/clinic/deprsumm.htm). (p. 366)

Murray, C. A., & Herrnstein, R. J. (1994, October 31). Race, genes and I.Q.—An apologia. *New Republic,* pp. 27–37. (p. 227)

Murray, H. (1938). *Explorations in personality.* New York: Oxford University Press. (p. 408)

Murray, H. A., & Wheeler, D. R. (1937). A note on the possible clairvoyance of dreams. *Journal of Psychology, 3,* 309–313. (pp. 19, 152)

Murray, R., Jones, P., O'Callaghan, E., Takei, N., & Sham, P. (1992). Genes, viruses, and neurodevelopmental schizophrenia. *Journal of Psychiatric Research, 26,* 225–235. (p. 343)

Murray, S. L., Bellavia, G. M., Rose, P., & Griffin, D. W. (2003). Once hurt, twice hurtful: How perceived regard regulates daily marital interactions. *Journal of Personality and Social Psychology, 84,* 126–147. (p. 150)

Murray, S. L., Rose, P., Bellavia, G. M., Holmes, J. G., & Kusche, A. G. (2002). When rejection stings: How self-esteem constrains relationship-enhancement processes. *Journal of Personality and Social Psychology, 83,* 556–573. (p. 306)

Musick, M. A., Herzog, A. R., & House, J. S. (1999). Volunteering and mortality among older adults: Findings from a national sample. *Journals of Gerontology, 54B,* 173–180. (p. 283)

Mustanski, B. S., & Bailey, J. M. (2003). A therapist's guide to the genetics of human sexual orientation, *Sexual and Relationship Therapy, 18,* 1468–1479. (p. 116)

Myers, D. G. (1993). *The pursuit of happiness.* New York: Avon Books. (pp. 261, 262, 264)

Myers, D. G. (2000). *The American paradox: Spiritual hunger in an age of plenty.* New Haven: Yale University Press. (pp. 264, 392)

Myers, D. G. (2005). *Social psychology (8th ed).* New York: McGraw-Hill. (p. 307)

Myers, D. G., & Bishop, G. D. (1970). Discussion effects on racial attitudes. *Science, 169,* 78–779. (p. 385)

Myers, D. G., & Diener, E. (1995). Who is happy? *Psychological Science, 6,* 10–19. (p. 264)

Myers, D. G., & Diener, E. (1996, May). The pursuit of happiness. *Scientific American.* (p. 264)

Myers, D. G., & Scanzoni, L. D. (2005). *What God has joined together?* San Francisco: HarperSanFrancisco. (p. 94, 114)

Nacos, B. L., Bloch-Elkon, Y., & Shapiro, R. Y. (2007). Post-9/11 terrorism threats, news coverage, and public perceptions in the United States. *International Journal of Conflict and Violence, 1*(2), 105–126. (p. 205)

Nagourney, A. (2002, September 25). For remarks on Iraq, Gore gets praise and scorn. *New York Times* (www.nytimes.com). (p. 377)

Napolitan, D. A., & Goethals, G. R. (1979). The attribution of friendliness. *Journal of Experimental Social Psychology, 15,* 105–113. (p. 376)

National Academy of Sciences. (2001). *Exploring the biological contributions to human health: Does sex matter?* Washington, DC: Institute of Medicine, National Academy Press. (p. 106)

National Center for Health Statistics. (1990). *Health, United States, 1989.* Washington, DC: U.S. Department of Health and Human Services. (p. 92)

National Center for Health Statistics. (2004, December 15). Marital status and health: United States, 1999–2002 (by Charlotte A. Schoenborn). *Advance Data from Vital and Human Statistics, number 351.* Centers for Disease Control and Prevention. (p. 280)

National Institute of Mental Health. (1982). *Television and behavior: Ten years of scientific progress and implications for the eighties.* Washington, DC: U. S. Government Printing Office. (p. 176)

National Institute of Mental Health (2008). The numbers count: Mental disorders in America (nimh.nih.gov). (pp. 313, 314)

National Research Council. (1987). *Risking the future: Adolescent sexuality, pregnancy, and childbearing.* Washington, DC: National Academy Press. (p. 111)

National Safety Council. (2006). Transportation mode comparisons, from *Injury Facts* (via correspondence with Kevin T. Fearn, Research & Statistical Services Department). (p. 205)

Neese, R. M. (1991, November/December). What good is feeling bad? The evolutionary benefits of psychic pain. *The Sciences,* pp. 30–37. (pp. 137, 163)

Neisser, U. (1979). The control of information pickup in selective looking. In A. D. Pick (Ed.), *Perception and its development: A tribute to Eleanor J. Gibson.* Hillsdale, NJ: Erlbaum. (p. 49)

Neisser, U., Boodoo, G., Bouchard, T. J., Jr., Boykin, A. W., Brody, N., Ceci, S. J., Halpern, D. F., Loehlin, J. C., Perloff, R., Sternberg, R. J., & Urbina, S. (1996). Intelligence: Knowns and unknowns. *American Psychologist, 51,* 77–101. (p. 230)

Nelson, G., Hoon, M. A., Chandrashekar, J., Zhang, Y., Ryba, N. J., Nicholas, J. P., & Zuker, C. S. (2001). Mammalian sweet taste receptors. *Cell, 106,* 381–390. (p. 140)

Nelson, M. D., Saykin, A. J., Flashman, L. A., & Riordan, H. J. (1998). Hippocampal volume reduction in schizophrenia as assessed by magnetic resonance imaging. *Archives of General Psychiatry, 55,* 433–440. (p. 343)

Nelson, N. (1988). *A meta-analysis of the life-event/health paradigm: The influence of social support.* Philadelphia: Temple University Ph.D. dissertation. (p. 280)

Nesca, M., & Koulack, D. (1994). Recognition memory, sleep and circadian rhythms. *Canadian Journal of Experimental Psychology, 48,* 359–379. (p. 194)

Neumann, R., & Strack, F. (2000). "Mood contagion": The automatic transfer of mood between persons. *Journal of Personality and Social Psychology, 79,* 211–223. (p. 259)

Nevin, J. A. (1988). Behavioral momentum and the partial reinforcement effect. *Psychological Bulletin, 103,* 44–56. (p. 167)

Newberg, A., & D'Aquili, E. (2001). *Why God won't go away: Brain science and the biology of belief.* New York: Simon and Schuster. (p. 282)

Newcomb, M. D., & Harlow, L. L. (1986). Life events and substance use among adolescents: Mediating effects of perceived loss of control and meaninglessness in life. *Journal of Personality and Social Psychology, 51,* 564–577. (p. 333)

Newman, A. J., Bavelier, D., Corina, D., Jezzard, P., & Neville, H. J. (2002). A critical period for right hemisphere recruitment in American Sign Language processing. *Nature Neuroscience, 5,* 76–80. (p. 214)

Newport, E. L. (1990). Maturational constraints on language learning. *Cognitive Science, 14,* 11–28. (p. 214)

Newport, F. (2002, July 29). Bush job approval update. *Gallup News Service* (www.gallup.com/poll/releases/pr020729.asp). (p. 401)

Newport, F. (2007, May 11). The age factor: Older Americans most negative about Iraq war (www.galluppoll.com). (p. 104)

Newport, F., Moore, D. W., Jones, J. M., & Saad, L. (2003, March 21). Special release: American opinion on the war. *Gallup Poll Tuesday Briefing* (www.gallup.com). (p. 379)

Neylan, T. C., Metzler, T. J., Best, S. R., Weiss, D. S., Fagan, J. A., Liberman, A., Rogers, C., Vedantam, K., Brunet, A., Lipsey, T. L., & Marmar, C. R. (2002). Critical incident exposure and sleep quality in police officers. *Psychosomatic Medicine, 64,* 345–352. (p. 55)

Nezlek, J. B. (2001). Daily psychological adjustment and the planfulness of day-to-day behavior. *Journal of Social and Clinical Psychology, 20,* 452–475. (p. 278)

Ng, W. W. H., Sorensen, K. L., & Eby, L. T. (2006). Locus of control at work: A meta-analysis. *Journal of Organizational Behavior, 27,* 1057–1087. (p. 278)

NIDA. (2002). Methamphetamine abuse and addiction. *Research Report Series.* National Institute on Drug Abuse, NIH Publication Number 02–4210. (p. 328)

NIDA. (2005, May). Methamphetamine. *NIDA Info Facts.* National Institute on Drug Abuse. (p. 328)

Nier, J. A. (2004). Why does the "above average effect" exist? Demonstrating idiosyncratic trait definition. *Teaching of Psychology, 31,* 53–54. (p. 307)

NIH. (2001, July 20). Workshop summary: Scientific evidence on condom effectiveness for sexually transmitted disease (STD) prevention. Bethesda, MD: National Institute of Allergy and Infectious Diseases, National Institutes of Health. (p. 111)

Nisbett, R. (2003). *The geography of thought: How Asians and Westerners think differently . . . and why.* New York: Free Press. (p. 376)

Noel, J. G., Forsyth, D. R., & Kelley, K. N. (1987). Improving the performance of failing students by overcoming their self-serving attributional biases. *Basic and Applied Social Psychology, 8,* 151–162. (p. 278)

Nolen-Hoeksema, S. (2001). Gender differences in depression. *Current Directions in Psychological Science, 10,* 173–176. (p. 339)

Nolen-Hoeksema, S. (2003). *Women who think too much: How to break free of overthinking and reclaim your life.* New York: Holt. (p. 339)

Nolen-Hoeksema, S., & Davis, C. G. (2002). Positive responses to loss: Perceiving benefits and growth. In C.R. Snyder & S. Lopez (Eds.), *Handbook of positive psychology.* New York: Oxford. (p. 280)

Nolen-Hoeksema, S., & Larson, J. (1999). *Coping with loss.* Mahwah, NJ: Erlbaum. (p. 96)

Norem, J. K. (2001). *The positive power of negative thinking: Using defensive pessimism to harness anxiety and perform at your peak.* New York: Basic Books. (p. 279)

Novin, A. F. (2006, December 21). Hard work paying off. NCAAsports.com. (p. 269)

Nowak, R. (1994). Nicotine scrutinized as FDA seeks to regulate cigarettes. *Science, 263,* 1555–1556. (p. 328)

NSF. (2001, October 24). Public bounces back after Sept. 11 attacks, national study shows. *NSF News,* National Science Foundation (www.nsf.gov/od/lpa/news/press/ol/pr0185.htm). (p. 270)

Nuttin, J. M., Jr. (1987). Affective consequences of mere ownership: The name letter effect in twelve European languages. *European Journal of Social Psychology, 17,* 381–402. (p. 394)

O'Connor, P., & Brown, G. W. (1984). Supportive relationships: Fact or fancy? *Journal of Social and Personal Relationships, 1,* 159–175. (p. 363)

O'Donnell, L., Stueve, A., O'Donnell, C., Duran, R., San Doval, A., Wilson, R. F., Haber, D., Perry, E., & Pleck, J. H. (2002). Long-term reduction in sexual initiation and sexual activity among urban middle schoolers in the reach for health service learning program. *Journal of Adolescent Health, 31,* 93–100. (p. 112)

Oaten, M., & Cheng, K. (2006a). Longitudinal gains in self-regulation from regular physical exercise. *British Journal of Health Psychology, 11,* 717–733. (p. 278)

Oaten, M., & Cheng, K. (2006b). Improved self-control: The benefits of a regular program of academic study. *Basic and Applied Social Psychology, 28,* 1–16. (p. 278)

Oettingen, G., & Seligman, M. E. P. (1990). Pessimism and behavioural signs of depression in East versus West Berlin. *European Journal of Social Psychology, 20,* 207–220. (p. 277)

Offer, D., Ostrov, E., Howard, K. I., & Atkinson, R. (1988). *The teenage world: Adolescents' self-image in ten countries.* New York: Plenum. (p. 88)

Ogden, C. L., Fryar, C. D., Carroll, M. D., & Flegal, K. M. (2004, October 27). Mean body weight, heights, and body mass index, Unites States 1960–2002. *Advance Data from Vital and Health Statistics,* No. 347. (p. 245)

Öhman, A. (1986). Face the beast and fear the face: Animal and social fears as prototypes for evolutionary analyses of emotion. *Psychophysiology, 23,* 123–145. (p. 322)

Öhman, A., Lundqvist, D., & Esteves, F. (2001). The face in the crowd revisited: A threat advantage with schematic stimuli. *Journal of Personality and Social Psychology, 80,* 381–396. (p. 257)

Oishi, S., Diener, E. F., Lucas, R. E., & Suh, E. M. (1999). Cross-cultural variations in predictors of life satisfaction: Perspectives from needs and values. *Personality and Social Psychology Bulletin, 25,* 980–990. (p. 237)

Olds, J. (1975). Mapping the mind onto the brain. In F. G. Worden, J. P. Swazey, & G. Adelman (Eds.), *The neurosciences: Paths of discovery.* Cambridge, MA: MIT Press. (p. 38)

Olds, J., & Milner, P. (1954). Positive reinforcement produced by electrical stimulation of the septal area and other regions of rat brain. *Journal of Comparative and Physiological Psychology, 47,* 419–427. (p. 38)

Olfson, M., Gameroff, M. J., Marcus, S. C., & Jensen, P. S. (2003). National trends in the treatment of attention deficit hyperactivity disorder. *American Journal of Psychiatry, 160,* 1071–1077. (p. 367)

Oliner, S. P., & Oliner, P. M. (1988). *The altruistic personality: Rescuers of Jews in Nazi Europe.* New York: Free Press. (p. 174)

Olshansky, S. J., Passaro, D. J., Hershow, R. C., Layden, J., Carnes, B. A., Brody, J., Hayflick, L., Butler, R. N., Allison, D. B., & Ludwig, D. S. (2005). A potential decline in life expectancy in the United States in the 21st century. *New England Journal of Medicine, 352,* 1138–1145. (p. 242)

Olsson, A., & Phelps, E. A. (2004). Learned fear of "unseen" faces after Pavlovian, observational, and instructed fear. *Psychological Science, 15,* 822–828. (p. 321)

Osborne, L. (1999, October 27). A linguistic big bang. *New York Times Magazine* (www.nytimes.com). (p. 213)

Ost, L. G., & Hugdahl, K. (1981). Acquisition of phobias and anxiety response patterns in clinical patients. *Behaviour Research and Therapy, 16,* 439–447. (p. 321)

Ostfeld, A. M., Kasl, S. V., D'Atri, D. A., & Fitzgerald, E. F. (1987). *Stress, crowding, and blood pressure in prison.* Hillsdale, NJ: Erlbaum. (p. 277)

Owen, A. M., Coleman, M. R., Boly, M., Davis, M. H., Laureys, S., & Pickard, J. D. (2006). Detecting awareness in the vegetative state. *Science, 313,* 1402. (p. 34)

Owen, R. (1814). First essay in *New view of society or the formation of character.* Quoted in *The story of New Lamark.* New Lamark Mills, Lamark, Scotland: New Lamark Conservation Trust, 1993. (p. 413)

Oxfam (2005, March 26). Three months on: New figures show tsunami may have killed up to four times as many women as men. *Oxfam Press Release* (www.oxfam.org.uk). (p. 107)

Ozer, E. J., & Weiss, D. S. (2004). Who develops posttraumatic stress disorder. *Current Directions in Psychological Science, 13,* 169–172. (p. 320)

Ozer, E. J., Best, S. R., Lipsey, T. L., & Weiss, D. S. (2003). Predictors of posttraumatic stress disorder and symptoms in adults: A meta-analysis. *Psychological Bulletin, 129,* 52–73. (p. 320)

Pacifici, R., Zuccaro, P., Farre, M., Pichini, S., Di Carlo, S., Roset, P. N., Ortuno, J., Pujadus, M., Bacosi, A., Menoyo, E., Segura, J., & de la Torre, R. (2001). Effects of repeated doses of MDMA ("Ecstasy") on cell-mediated immune response in humans. *Life Sciences, 69,* 2931–2941. (p. 330)

Padgett, V. R. (1989). Predicting organizational violence: An application of 11 powerful principles of obedience. Paper presented to the American Psychological Association convention. (p. 382)

Paivio, A. (1986). *Mental representations: A dual coding approach.* New York: Oxford University Press. (p. 185)

Palace, E. M. (1995). Modification of dysfunctional patterns of sexual response through autonomic arousal and false physiological feedback. *Journal of Consulting and Clinical Psychology, 63,* 604–615. (p. 255)

Pallier, C., Colomé, A., & Sebastián-Gallés, N. (2001). The influence of native-language phonology on lexical access: Exemplar-based versus abstract lexical entries. *Psychological Science, 12*, 445–448. (p. 212)

Pandey, J., Sinha, Y., Prakash, A., & Tripathi, R. C. (1982). Right-left political ideologies and attribution of the causes of poverty. *European Journal of Social Psychology, 12*, 327–331. (p. 377)

Panksepp, J. (1982). Toward a general psychobiological theory of emotions. *Behavioral and Brain Sciences, 5*, 407–467. (p. 253)

Pantelis, C., Velakoulis, D., McGorry, P. D., Wood, S. J., Suckling, J., Phillips, L. J., Yung, A. R., Bullmore, E. T., Brewer, W., Soulsby, B., Desmond, P., & McGuire, P. K. (2002). Neuroanatomical abnormalities before and after onset of psychosis: A cross-sectional and longitudinal MRI comparison. *The Lancet*, published online at image.thelancet.com/extras/01art9092web.pdf. (p. 343)

Park, D. C., Lautenschlager, G., Hedden, T., Davidson, N. S., Smith, A. D., & Smith, P. K. (2002). Models of visuospatial and verbal memory across the adult life span. *Psychology and Aging, 17*, 299–320. (p. 93)

Park, R. L. (1999). Liars never break a sweat. *New York Times*, July 12, 1999 (www.nytimes.com). (p. 254)

Parker, C. P., Baltes, B. B., Young, S. A., Huff, J. W., Altmann, R. A., LaCost, H. A., & Roberts, J. E. (2003). Relationships between psychological climate perceptions and work outcomes: A meta-analytic review. *Journal of Organizational Behavior, 24*, 389–416. (p. 410)

Parker, E. S., Cahill, L., & McGaugh, J. L. (2006). A case of unusual autobiographical remembering. *Neurocase, 12*, 35–49. (p. 192)

Patterson, D. R. (2004). Treating pain with hypnosis. *Current Directions in Psychological Science, 13*, 252–255. (p. 139)

Patterson, D. R., & Jensen, M. (2003). Hypnosis for clinical pain control. *Psychological Bulletin, 129*, 495–521. (p. 139)

Patterson, F. (1978, October). Conversations with a gorilla. *National Geographic*, pp. 438–465. (p. 217)

Patterson, G. R., Chamberlain, P., & Reid, J. B. (1982). A comparative evaluation of parent training procedures. *Behavior Therapy, 13*, 638–650. (pp. 168, 392)

Patterson, G. R., Reid, J. B., & Dishion, T. J. (1992). *Antisocial boys*. Eugene, OR: Castalia. (p. 392)

Patterson, M., Warr, P., & West, M. (2004). Organizational climate and company productivity: The role of employee affect and employee level. *Journal of Occupational and Organizational Psychology, 77*, 193–216. (p. 410)

Patton, G. C., Coffey, C., Carlin, J. B., Degenhardt, L., Lynskey, M., & Hall, W. (2002). Cannabis use and mental health of young people: Cohort study. *British Medical Journal, 325*, 1195–1198. (p. 332)

Paulos, J. A. (1995). *A mathematician reads the newspaper*. New York: Basic Books. (p. 367)

Paus, T., Zijdenbos, A., Worsley, K., Collins, D. L., Blumenthal, J., Giedd, J. N., Rapoport, J. L., & Evans, A. C. (1999) Structural maturation of neural pathways in children and adolescents: In vivo study. *Science, 283*, 1908–1911. (p. 70)

Pavlov, I. (1927). *Conditioned reflexes: An investigation of the physiological activity of the cerebral cortex*. Oxford: Oxford University Press. (p. 159)

Pekkanen, J. (1982, June). Why do we sleep? *Science, 82*, 86. (p. 55)

Pelham, B. W. (1993). On the highly positive thoughts of the highly depressed. In R. F. Baumeister (Ed.), *Self-esteem: The puzzle of low self-regard*. New York: Plenum. (p. 306)

Pendick, D. (1994, January/February). The mind of violence. *Brain Work: The Neuroscience Newsletter*, pp. 1–3, 5. (p. 391)

Pennebaker, J. (1990). *Opening up: The healing power of confiding in others*. New York: William Morrow. (pp. 280, 296)

Pennebaker, J. W. (2002, January 28). Personal communication. (p. 401)

Pennebaker, J. W., & O'Heeron, R. C. (1984). Confiding in others and illness rate among spouses of suicide and accidental death victims. *Journal of Abnormal Psychology, 93*, 473–476. (p. 280)

Pennebaker, J. W., & Stone, L. D. (2003). Words of wisdom: Language use over the life span. *Journal of Personality and Social Psychology, 85*, 291–301. (p. 97)

Pennebaker, J. W., Barger, S. D., & Tiebout, J. (1989). Disclosure of traumas and health among Holocaust survivors. *Psychosomatic Medicine, 51*, 577–589. (p. 280)

Peplau, L. A., & Garnets, L. D. (2000). A new paradigm for understanding women's sexuality and sexual orientation. *Journal of Social Issues, 56*, 329–350. (p. 114)

Perkins, A., & Fitzgerald, J. A. (1997). Sexual orientation in domestic rams: Some biological and social correlates. In L. Ellis and L. Ebertz (Eds.), *Sexual orientation: Toward biological understanding*. Westport, CT: Praeger Publishers. (p. 115)

Perls, T., & Silver, M. H., with Lauerman, J. F. (1999). *Living to 100: Lessons in living to your maximum potential*. Thorndike, ME: Thorndike Press. (p. 276)

Person, C., Tracy, M., & Galea, S. (2006). Risk factors for depression after a disaster. *Journal of Nervous and Mental Disease, 194*, 659–666. (p. 320)

Pert, C. B., & Snyder, S. H. (1973). Opiate receptor: Demonstration in nervous tissue. *Science, 179*, 1011–1014. (p. 30)

Peschel, E. R., & Peschel, R. E. (1987). Medical insights into the castrati in opera. *American Scientist, 75*, 578–583. (p. 110)

Peters, T. J., & Waterman, R. H., Jr. (1982). *In search of excellence: Lessons from America's best-run companies*. New York: Harper & Row. (p. 171)

Peterson, C., & Barrett, L. C. (1987). Explanatory style and academic performance among university freshmen. *Journal of Personality and Social Psychology, 53*, 603–607. (p. 278)

Peterson, C., Peterson, J., & Skevington, S. (1986). Heated argument and adolescent development. *Journal of Social and Personal Relationships, 3*, 229–240. (p. 85)

Peterson, L. R., & Peterson, M. J. (1959). Short-term retention of individual verbal items. *Journal of Experimental Psychology, 58*, 193–198. (p. 186)

Petitto, L. A., & Marentette, P. F. (1991). Babbling in the manual mode: Evidence for the ontogeny of language. *Science, 251*, 1493–1496. (p. 212)

Pettegrew, J. W., Keshavan, M. S., & Minshew, N. J. (1993). 31P nuclear magnetic resonance spectroscopy: Neurodevelopment and schizophrenia. *Schizophrenia Bulletin, 19*, 35–53. (p. 342)

Petticrew, C., Bell, R., & Hunter, D. (2002). Influence of psychological coping on survival and recurrence in people with cancer: Systematic review. *British Medical Journal, 325*, 1066. (p. 274)

Petticrew, M., Fraser, J. M., & Regan, M. F. (1999). Adverse life events and risk of breast cancer: A meta-analysis. *British Journal of Health Psychology, 4*, 1–17. (p. 274)

Pettigrew, T. F. (1969). Racially separate or together? *Journal of Social Issues, 25*, 43–69. (p. 401)

Pettigrew, T. F. (2004). Justice deferred a half century after Brown v. Board of Education. *American Psychologist, 59,* 521–529. (p. 401)

Pew. (2003). *Views of a changing world 2003. The Pew Global Attitudes Project.* Washington, DC: Pew Research Center for the People and the Press (people-press.org/reports/pdf/185.pdf). (p. 107)

Pew. (2006). Remembering 9/11. Pew Research Center (pewresearch.org). (p. 188)

Pew. (2007, January 24). Global warming: A divide on causes and solutions. Pew Research Center for the People and the Press. (p. 205)

Phelps, J. A., Davis J. O., & Schartz, K. M. (1997). Nature, nurture, and twin research strategies. *Current Directions in Psychological Science, 6,* 117–120. (p. 344)

Philip Morris Companies, Inc. (1999, Oct. 13). Referenced in Myron Levin, "Philip Morris' new campaign echoes medical experts," *Los Angeles Times.* (p. 328)

Piaget, J. (1932). *The moral judgment of the child.* New York: Harcourt, Brace & World. (p. 85)

Pickar, D., Labarca, R., Linnoila, M., Roy, A., Hommer, D., Everett, D., & Payl, S. M. (1984). Neuroleptic-induced decrease in plasma homovanillic acid and antipsychotic activity in schizophrenic patients. *Science, 225,* 954–957. (p. 365)

Pido-Lopez, J., Imami, N., & Aspinall, R. (2001). Both age and gender affect thymic output: More recent thymic migrants in females than males as they age. *Clinical and Experimental Immunology, 125,* 409–413. (p. 273)

Piliavin, J. A. (2003). Doing well by doing good: Benefits for the benefactor. In C. L. M. Keyes & J. Haidt (Eds.), *Flourishing: Positive psychology and the life well-lived.* Washington, DC: American Psychological Association. (p. 86)

Pillemer, D. G. (1998). *Momentous events, vivid memories.* Cambridge: Harvard University Press, 1998. (p. 93)

Pillsworth, M. G., Haselton, M. G., & Buss, D. M. (2004). Ovulatory shifts in female desire. *Journal of Sex Research, 41,* 55–65. (p. 110)

Pincus, H. A. (1997) Commentary: Spirituality, religion, and health: Expanding, and using the knowledge base. *Mind/Body Medicine, 2,* 49. (p. 284)

Pingitore, R., Dugoni, B. L., Tindale, R. S., & Spring, B. (1994). Bias against overweight job applicants in a simulated employment interview. *Journal of Applied Psychology, 79,* 909–917. (p. 243)

Pinker, S. (1995). The language instinct. *The General Psychologist, 31,* 63–65. (p. 217)

Pinker, S. (1998). Words and rules. *Lingua, 106,* 219–242. (p. 211)

Pinkerton, S. D., & Abramson, P. R. (1997). Condoms and the prevention of AIDS. *American Scientist, 85,* 364–373. (p. 111)

Pipe, M-E. (1996). Children's eyewitness memory. *New Zealand Journal of Psychology, 25,* 36–43. (p. 198)

Pipe, M-E., Lamb, M. E., Orbach, Y., & Esplin, P. W. (2004). Recent research on children's testimony about experienced and witnessed events. *Developmental Review, 24,* 440–468. (p. 198)

Pipher, M. (2002). *The middle of everywhere: The world's refugees come to our town.* New York: Harcourt Brace. (p. 247)

Plomin, R. (2001). Genetics and behaviour. *The Psychologist, 14,* 134–139. (p. 225)

Plomin, R., & Crabbe, J. (2000). DNA. *Psychological Bulletin, 126,* 806–828. (p. 65)

Plomin, R., & Daniels, D. (1987). Why are children in the same family so different from one another? *Behavioral and Brain Sciences, 10,* 1–60. (p. 82)

Plomin, R., & DeFries, J. C. (1998, May). The genetics of cognitive abilities and disabilities. *Scientific American,* pp. 62–69. (p. 226)

Plomin, R., & McGuffin, P. (2003). Psychopathology in the postgenomic era. *Annual Review of Psychology, 54,* 205–228. (p. 338)

Plomin, R., Corley, R., Caspi, A., Fulker, D. W., & DeFries, J. (1998). Adoption results for self-reported personality: Evidence for nonadditive genetic effects? *Journal of Personality and Social Psychology, 75,* 211–219. (p. 69)

Plomin, R., DeFries, J. C., McClearn, G. E., & Rutter, M. (1997). *Behavioral genetics.* New York: Freeman. (pp. 226, 244, 344)

Plotkin, H. (1994). *Darwin machines and the nature of knowledge.* Cambridge, MA: Harvard University Press. (p. 338)

Plous, S., & Herzog, H. A. (2000). Poll shows researchers favor lab animal protection. *Science, 290,* 711. (p. 20)

Polivy, J., & Herman, C. P. (1985). Dieting and binging: A causal analysis. *American Psychologist, 40,* 193–201. (p. 246)

Polivy, J., & Herman, C. P. (1987). Diagnosis and treatment of normal eating. *Journal of Personality and Social Psychology, 55,* 635–644. (p. 246)

Polivy, J., & Herman, C. P. (2002). Causes of eating disorders. *Annual Review of Psychology, 53,* 187–213. (p. 241)

Pollak, S., Cicchetti, D., & Klorman, R. (1998). Stress, memory, and emotion: Developmental considerations from the study of child maltreatment. *Developmental Psychopathology, 10,* 811–828. (p. 162)

Polusny, M. A., & Follette, V. M. (1995). Long-term correlates of child sexual abuse: Theory and review of the empirical literature. *Applied & Preventive Psychology, 4,* 143–166. (p. 79)

Poole, D. A., & Lindsay, D. S. (1995). Interviewing preschoolers: Effects of nonsuggestive techniques, parental coaching and leading questions on reports of nonexperienced events. *Journal of Experimental Child Psychology, 60,* 129–154. (p. 198)

Poon, L. W. (1987). *Myths and truisms: Beyond extant analyses of speed of behavior and age.* Address to the Eastern Psychological Association convention. (p. 93)

Pope, H. G., & Yurgelun-Todd, D. (1996). The residual cognitive effects of heavy marijuana use in college students. *Journal of the American Medical Association, 275,* 521–527. (p. 332)

Popenoe, D. (1993). *The evolution of marriage and the problem of stepfamilies: A biosocial perspective.* Paper presented at the National Symposium on Stepfamilies, Pennsylvania State University. (p. 309)

Popenoe, D., & Whitehead, B. D. (2002). *Should We Live Together?* (2nd ed). New Brunswick, NJ: The National Marriage Project, Rutgers University. (p. 94)

Porter, S., Birt, A. R., Yuille, J. C., & Lehman, D. R. (2000, Nov.). Negotiating false memories: Interviewer and rememberer characteristics relate to memory distortion. *Psychological Science, 11,* 507–510. (p. 197)

Posavac, H. D., Posavac, S. S., & Posavac, E. J. (1998). Exposure to media images of female attractiveness and concern with body weight among young women. *Sex Roles, 38,* 187–201. (p. 241)

Posner, M. I., & Carr, T. H. (1992). Lexical access and the brain: Anatomical constraints on cognitive models of word recognition. *American Journal of Psychology, 105,* 1–26. (p. 44)

Powell, K. E., Thompson, P. D., Caspersen, C. J., & Kendrick, J. S. (1987). Physical activity and the incidence of coronary heart disease. *Annual Review of Public Health, 8*, 253–287. (p. 280)

Powell, L. H., Schahabi, L., & Thoresen, C. E. (2003). Religion and spirituality: Linkages to physical health. *American Psychologist, 58*, 36–52. (p. 284)

Powell, R. A., & Boer, D. P. (1994). Did Freud mislead patients to confabulate memories of abuse? *Psychological Reports, 74*, 1283–1298. (p. 296)

Presley, C. A., Meilman, P. W., & Lyerla, R. (1997). *Alcohol and drugs on American college campuses: Issues of violence and harrassment.* Carbondale, IL: Core Institute, Southern Illinois University. (p. 326)

Prince Charles (2000). BBC Reith Lecture. (p. 9)

Prioleau, L., Murdock, M., & Brody, N. (1983). An analysis of psychotherapy versus placebo studies. *The Behavioral and Brain Sciences, 6*, 275–310. (p. 363)

Pronin, E., Lin, D. Y., & Ross, L. (2002). The bias blind spot: Perceptions of bias in self versus others. *Personality and Social Psychology Bulletin, 28*, 369–381. (p. 307)

Pryor, J. H., Hurtado, S., Saenz, V. B., Korn, J. S., Santos, J. L., & Korn, W. S. (2006). *The American freshman: National norms for Fall 2006.* Los Angeles, UCLA Higher Education Research Institute. (pp. 105, 339)

Pryor, J. H., Hurtado, S., Saenz, V. B., Lindholm, J. A., Korn, W. S., & Mahoney, K. M. (2005). *The American freshman: National norms for fall 2005.* Los Angeles: Higher Education Research Institute, UCLA. (p. 118)

Psychologist. (2003, April). Who's the greatest? *The Psychologist, 16*, 17. (p. 76)

Puetz, T. W., O'Connor, P. J., & Dishman, R. K. (2006). Effects of chronic exercise on feelings of energy and fatigue: A quantitative synthesis. *Psychological Bulletin, 132*, 866-876. (p. 281)

Putnam, F. W. (1991). Recent research on multiple personality disorder. *Psychiatric Clinics of North America, 14*, 489–502. (p. 323)

Putnam, F. W. (1995). Rebuttal of Paul McHugh. *Journal of the American Academy of Child and Adolescent Psychiatry, 34*, 963. (p. 323)

Pyszczynski, T. A., Solomon, S., & Greenberg, J. (2002). *In the wake of 9/11: The psychology of terror.* Washington, DC: American Psychological Association. (p. 390)

Qirko, H. N. (2004). "Fictive kin" and suicide terrorism. *Science, 304*, 49–50. (p. 386)

Quinn, P. C., Bhatt, R. S., Brush, D., Grimes, A., & Sharpnack, H. (2002). Development of form similarity as a Gestalt grouping principle in infancy. *Psychological Science, 13*, 320–328. (p. 143)

Quinn, P. J., Williams, G. M., Najman, J. M., Andersen, M. J., & Bor, W. (2001). The effect of breastfeeding on child development at 5 years: A cohort study. *Journal of Pediatrics & Child Health, 3*, 465–469. (p. 16)

Rahman, Q., & Wilson, G. D. (2003). Born gay? The psychobiology of human sexual orientation. *Personality and Individual Differences, 34*, 1337–1382. (pp. 115, 117)

Rahman, Q., Wilson, G. D., & Abrahams, S. (2003). Biosocial factors, sexual orientation and neurocognitive functioning. *Psychoneuroendocrinology, 29*, 867–881. (p. 116)

Raine, A. (1999). Murderous minds: Can we see the mark of Cain? *Cerebrum: The Dana Forum on Brain Science, 1*(1), 15–29. (pp. 324, 391)

Raine, A., Lencz, T., Bihrle, S., LaCasse, L., & Colletti, P. (2000). Reduced prefrontal gray matter volume and reduced autonomic activity in antisocial personality disorder. *Archives of General Psychiatry, 57*, 119–127. (p. 325)

Ralston, A. (2004). Enough rope. Interview for ABC TV, Australia, by Andrew Denton (www.abc.net.au/enoughrope/stories/s1227885.htm). (p. 235)

Ramachandran, V. S., & Blakeslee, S. (1998). *Phantoms in the brain: Probing the mysteries of the human mind.* New York: Morrow. (pp. 32, 45)

Ramirez, J. M., Bonniot-Cabanac, M-C., & Cabanac, M. (2005). Can aggression provide pleasure? *European Psychologist, 10*, 136–145. (p. 260)

Randi, J. (1999, February 4). 2000 Club mailing list e-mail letter. (p. 153)

Rapoport, J. L. (1989, March). The biology of obsessions and compulsions. *Scientific American*, pp. 83–89. (p. 322)

Räsänen, S., Pakaslahti, A., Syvalahti, E., Jones, P. B., & Isohanni, M. (2000). Sex differences in schizophrenia: A review. *Nordic Journal of Psychiatry, 54*, 37–45. (p. 342)

Ray, J. (2005, April 12). U.S. teens walk away from anger: Boys and girls manage anger differently. The Gallup Organization (www.gallup.com). (p. 260)

Raynor, H. A., & Epstein, L. H. (2001). Dietary variety, energy regulation, and obesity. *Psychological Bulletin, 127*, 325–341. (p. 239)

Reason, J. (1987). The Chernobyl errors. *Bulletin of the British Psychological Society, 40*, 201–206. (p. 386)

Reason, J., & Mycielska, K. (1982). *Absent-minded? The psychology of mental lapses and everyday errors.* Englewood Cliffs, NJ: Prentice Hall. (p. 150)

Reed, P. (2000). Serial position effects in recognition memory for odors. *Journal of Experimental Psychology: Learning, Memory, and Cognition, 26*, 411–422. (p. 184)

Reeve, C. L., & Hakel, M. D. (2002). Asking the right questions about g. *Human Performance, 15*, 47–74. (p. 220)

Regier, D. A., Kaelber, C. T., Rae, D. S., Farmer, M. E., Knauper, B., Kessler, R. C., & Norquist, G. S. (1998). Limitations of diagnostic criteria and assessment instruments for mental disorders: Implications for research and policy. *Archives of General Psychiatry, 55*, 109–115. (p. 317)

Reichman, J. (1998). *I'm not in the mood: What every woman should know about improving her libido.* New York: Morrow. (p. 110)

Reiner, W. G., & Gearhart, J. P. (2004). Discordant sexual identity in some genetic males with cloacal exstrophy assigned to female sex at birth. *New England Journal of Medicine, 350*, 333–341. (p. 106)

Reisenzein, R. (1983). The Schachter theory of emotion: Two decades later. *Psychological Bulletin, 94*, 239–264. (p. 255)

Reiser, M. (1982). *Police psychology.* Los Angeles: LEHI. (p. 152)

Remley, A. (1988, October). From obedience to independence. *Psychology Today*, pp. 56–59. (p. 81)

Reneman, L., Lavalaye, J., Schmand, B., De Wolff, F. A., Van Den Brink, W., Den Heeten, G., & Booij, J. (2001). Cortical serotonin transporter density and verbal memory in individuals who stopped using 3, 4-methylenedioxy-methampetamine. *Archives of General Psychiatry, 58*, 901–908. (p. 330)

Renner, M. J. (1992). Curiosity and exploration. In L. R. Squire (Ed.), *Encyclopedia of Learning and Memory.* New York: Macmillan. (p. 236)

Renner, M. J., & Renner, C. H. (1993). Expert and novice intuitive judgments about animal behavior. *Bulletin of the Psychonomic Society, 31*, 551–552. (p. 71)

Renner, M. J., & Rosenzweig, M. R. (1987). *Enriched and impoverished environments: Effects on brain and behavior.* New York: Springer-Verlag. (p. 70)

Rentfrow, P. J., & Gosling, S. D. (2003). The Do Re Mi's of everyday life: The structure and personality correlates of music preferences. *Journal of Personality and Social Psychology, 84,* 1236–1256. (p. 304)

Repetti, R. L., Taylor, S. E., & Seeman, T. E. (2002). Risky families: Family social environments and the mental and physical health of offspring. *Psychological Bulletin, 128,* 330–366. (p. 270)

Resnick, M. D., Bearman, P. S., Blum, R. W., Bauman, K. E., Harris, K. M., Jones, J., Tabor, J., Beuhring, T., Sieving, R., Shew, M., Bearinger, L. H., & Udry, J. R. (1997). Protecting adolescents from harm: Findings from the National Longitudinal Study on Adolescent Health. *Journal of the American Medical Association, 278,* 823–832. (pp. 15, 88)

Resnick, R. A., O'Regan, J. K., & Clark, J. J. (1997). To see or not to see: The need for attention to perceive changes in scenes. *Psychological Science, 8,* 368–373. (p. 49)

Resnick, S. M. (1992). Positron emission tomography in psychiatric illness. *Current Directions in Psychological Science, 1,* 92–98. (p. 342)

Reuters. (2000, July 5). Many teens regret decision to have sex (National Campaign to Prevent Teen Pregnancy survey). www.washingtonpost.com. (p. 111)

Rhee, S. H., & Waldman, I. D. (2002). Genetic and environmental influences on antisocial behavior: A meta-analysis of twin and adoption studies. *Psychological Bulletin, 128,* 490–529. (p. 324)

Rhodes, S. R. (1983). Age-related differences in work attitudes and behavior: A review and conceptual analysis. *Psychological Bulletin, 93,* 328–367. (p. 92)

Rholes, W. S., & Simpson, J. A. (Eds.) (2004). *Adult attachment: Theory, research, and clinical implications.* New York: Guilford. (p. 79)

Rice, B. (1985, September). Performance review: The job nobody likes. *Psychology Today,* pp. 30–36. (p. 377)

Rieff, P. (1979). *Freud: The mind of a moralist* (3rd ed.). Chicago: University of Chicago Press. (p. 295)

Rieger, G., Chivers, M. L., & Bailey, J. M. (2005). Sexual arousal patterns of bisexual men. *Psychological Science, 16,* 579–584. (p. 114)

Riis, J., Loewenstein, G., Baron, J., Jepson, C., Fagerlin, A., & Ubel, P. A. (2005). Ignorance of hedonic adaptation to hemodialysis: A study using ecological momentary assessment. *Journal of Experimental Psychology: General, 134,* 3–9. (p. 262)

Ring, K. (1980). *Life at death: A scientific investigation of the near-death experience.* New York: Coward, McCann & Geoghegan. (p. 331)

Riskind, J. H., Beck, A. T., Berchick, R. J., Brown, G., & Steer, R. A. (1987). Reliability of DSM-III diagnoses for major depression and generalized anxiety disorder using the structured clinical interview for DSM-III. *Archives of General Psychiatry, 44,* (p. 316)

Rizzolatti, G., Fadiga, L., Fogassi, L., & Gallese, V. (2002). From mirror neurons to imitation: Facts and speculations. In A. N. Meltzoff & W. Prinz (Eds.), *The imitative mind: Development, evolution, and brain bases.* Cambridge: Cambridge University Press, 2002. (p. 173)

Roberts, B. W., & DelVecchio, W. F. (2000). The rank-order consistency of personality traits from childhood to old age: A quantitative review of longitudinal studies. *Psychological Bulletin, 126,* 3–25. (p. 303)

Roberts, B. W., Caspi, A., & Moffitt, T. E. (2001). The kids are alright: Growth and stability in personality development from adolescence to adulthood. *Journal of Personality and Social Psychology, 81,* 670–683. (p. 98)

Roberts, B. W., Caspi, A., & Moffitt, T. E. (2003). Work experiences and personality development in young adulthood. *Journal of Personality and Social Psychology, 84,* 582–593. (p. 98)

Roberts, B. W., Walton, K. E., & Viechtbauer, W. (2006). Patterns of mean-level change in personality traits across the life course: A meta-analysis of longitudinal studies. *Psychological Bulletin, 132,* 1–25. (p. 98)

Robins, R. W., & Trzesniewski, K. H. (2005). Self-esteem development across the lifespan. *Current Directions in Psychological Science, 14(3),* 158–162. (p. 97)

Robins, R. W., Trzesniewski, K. H., Tracy, J. L., Gosling, S. D., & Potter, J. (2002). Global self-esteem across the lifespan. *Psychology and Aging, 17,* 423–434. (p. 87)

Roberts, L. (1988). Beyond Noah's ark: What do we need to know? *Science, 242,* 1247. (p. 277)

Roberts, T-A. (1991). Determinants of gender differences in responsiveness to others' evaluations. *Dissertation Abstracts International, 51(8–B).* (p. 105)

Robinson, F. P. (1970). *Effective study.* New York: Harper & Row. (p. 22)

Robinson, T. N. (1999). Reducing children's television viewing to prevent obesity. *Journal of the American Medical Association, 282,* 1561–1567. (p. 245)

Robinson, V. M. (1983). Humor and health. In P. E. McGhee & J. H. Goldstein (Eds.), *Handbook of humor research: Vol. II. Applied studies.* New York: Springer-Verlag. (p. 279)

Rochat, F. (1993). How did they resist authority? Protecting refugees in Le Chambon during World War II. Paper presented at the American Psychological Association convention. (p. 383)

Rock, I., & Palmer, S. (1990, December). The legacy of Gestalt psychology. *Scientific American,* pp. 84–90. (p. 143)

Rodin, J. (1986). Aging and health: Effects of the sense of control. *Science, 233,* 1271–1276. (pp. 277)

Roediger, H. L., III, Wheeler, M. A., & Rajaram, S. (1993). Remembering, knowing, and reconstructing the past. In D. L. Medin (Ed.), *The psychology of learning and motivation: Advances in research and theory* (Vol. 30). Orlando, FL: Academic Press. (p. 196)

Roehling, M. V. (1999). Weight-based discrimination in employment: Psychological and legal aspects. *Personnel Psychology, 52,* 969–1016. (p. 243)

Roehling, P. V., Roehling, M. V., & Moen, P. (2001). The relationship between work-life policies and practices and employee loyalty: A life course perspective. *Journal of Family and Economic Issues, 22,* 141–170. (p. 414)

Roenneberg, T., Kuehnle, T., Pramstaller, P. P., Ricken, J., Havel, M., Guth, A., & Merrow, M. (2004). A marker for the end of adolescence. *Current Biology, 14,* R1038–9. (p. 50)

Roese, N. J., & Summerville, A. (2005). What we regret most . . . and why. *Personality and Social Psychology Bulletin, 31,* 1273–1285. (p. 97)

Roesser, R. (1998). What you should know about hearing conservation. *Better Hearing Institute* (www.betterhearing.org). (p. 135)

Rogers, C. R. (1958). Reinhold Niebuhr's The self and the dramas of history: A criticism. *Pastoral Psychology, 9,* 15–17. (p. 307)

Rogers, C. R. (1961). *On becoming a person: A therapist's view of psychotherapy.* Boston: Houghton Mifflin. (p. 352)

Rogers, C. R. (1980). *A way of being.* Boston: Houghton Mifflin. (pp. 298, 352, 354)

Rohan, M. J., & Zanna, M. P. (1996). Value transmission in families. In C. Seligman, J. M. Olson, & M. P. Zanna (Eds.), *The psychology of values: The Ontario Symposium* (Vol. 8). Mahwah, NJ: Erlbaum. (p. 82)

Rohner, R. P. (1986). *The warmth dimension: Foundations of parental acceptance-rejection theory.* Newbury Park, CA: Sage. (p. 83)

Rohner, R. P., & Veneziano, R. A. (2001). The importance of father love: History and contemporary evidence. *Review of General Psychology, 5,* 382–405. (p. 78)

Roiser, J. P., Cook, L. J., Cooper, J. D., Rubinsztein, D. C., & Sahakian, B. J. (2005). Association of a functional polymorphism in the serotonin transporter gene with abnormal emotional processing in ecstasy users. *American Journal of Psychiatry, 162,* 609–612. (p. 330)

Rose, J. S., Chassin, L., Presson, C. C., & Sherman, S. J. (1999). Peer influences on adolescent cigarette smoking: A prospective sibling analysis. *Merrill-Palmer Quarterly, 45,* 62–84. (p. 82)

Rose, R. J., Kaprio, J., Winter, T., Dick, D. M., Viken, R. J., Pulkkinen, L., & Koskenvuo, M. (2002). Femininity and fertility in sisters with twin brothers: Prenatal androgenization? Cross-sex socialization? *Psychological Science, 13,* 263–266. (p. 116)

Rose, S. (1999). Precis of Lifelines: Biology, freedom, determinism. *Behavioral and Brain Sciences, 22,* 871–921. (p. 119)

Rose, S., Bisson, J., & Wessely, S. (2003). A systematic review of single-session psychological interventions ("debriefing") following trauma. *Psychotherapy and Psychosomatics, 72,* 176–184. (pp. 82, 321)

Roselli, C. E., Larkin, K., Schrunk, J. M., & Stormshak, F. (2004). Sexual partner preference, hypothalamic morphology and aromatase in rams. *Physiology and Behavior, 83,* 233–245. (p. 115)

Roselli, C. E., Resko, J. A., & Stormshak, F. (2002). Hormonal influences on sexual partner preference in rams. *Archives of Sexual Behavior, 31,* 43–49. (p. 115)

Rosenhan, D. L. (1973). On being sane in insane places. *Science, 179,* 250–258. (p. 317)

Rosenthal, R., Hall, J. A., Archer, D., DiMatteo, M. R., & Rogers, P. L. (1979). The PONS test: Measuring sensitivity to nonverbal cues. In S. Weitz (Ed.), *Nonverbal communication (2nd ed.).* New York: Oxford University Press. (pp. 229, 257)

Rosenzweig, M. R. (1984). Experience, memory, and the brain. *American Psychologist, 39,* 365–376. (p. 70)

Rossi, P. J. (1968). Adaptation and negative after effect to lateral optical displacement in newly hatched chicks. *Science, 160,* 430–432. (p. 149)

Rostosky, S. S., Wilcox, B. L., Wright, M. L. C., & Randall, B. A. (2004). The impact of religiosity on adolescent sexual behavior: A review of the evidence. *Journal of Adolescent Research, 19,* 677–697. (p. 112)

Rothbart, M. K., Ahadi, S. A., & Evans, D. E. (2000). Temperament and personality: Origins and outcomes. *Journal of Personality and Social Psychology, 78,* 122–135. (p. 68)

Rothbart, M., Fulero, S., Jensen, C., Howard, J., & Birrell, P. (1978). From individual to group impressions: Availability heuristics in stereotype formation. *Journal of Experimental Social Psychology, 14,* 237–255. (p. 390)

Rothbaum, B. O., Hodges, L., Anderson, P. L., Price, L., & Smith, S. (2002). Twelve-month followup of virtual reality and standard exposure therapies for the fear of flying. *Journal of Consulting and Clinical Psychology, 70,* 428–432. (p. 356)

Rothman, A. J., & Salovey, P. (1997). Shaping perceptions to motivate healthy behavior: The role of message framing. *Psychological Bulletin, 121,* 3–19. (p. 208)

Rovee-Collier, C. (1989). The joy of kicking: Memories, motives, and mobiles. In P. R. Solomon, G. R. Goethals, C. M. Kelley, & B. R. Stephens (Eds.), *Memory: Interdisciplinary approaches.* New York: Springer-Verlag. (p. 72)

Rovee-Collier, C. (1999). The development of infant memory. *Current Directions in Psychological Science, 8,* 80–85. (p. 72)

Rowe, D. C. (1990). As the twig is bent? The myth of child-rearing influences on personality development. *Journal of Counseling and Development, 68,* 606–611. (p. 69)

Rowe, D. C. (2005). Under the skin: On the impartial treatment of genetic and environmental hypotheses of racial differences. *American Psychologist, 60,* 60–70. (p. 228)

Rowe, D. C., Almeida, D. M., & Jacobson, K. C. (1999). School context and genetic influences on aggression in adolescence. *Psychological Science, 10,* 277–280. (p. 391)

Rowe, D. C., Jacobson, K. C., & Van den Oord, E. J. C. G. (1999). Genetic and environmental influences on vocabulary IQ: Parental education level as moderator. *Child Development, 70(5),* 1151–1162. (p. 226)

Rozin, P., Dow, S., Mosovitch, M., & Rajaram, S. (1998). What causes humans to begin and end a meal? A role for memory for what has been eaten, as evidenced by a study of multiple meal eating in amnesic patients. *Psychological Science, 9,* 392–396. (p. 240)

Ruback, R. B., Carr, T. S., & Hopper, C. H. (1986). Perceived control in prison: Its relation to reported crowding, stress, and symptoms. *Journal of Applied Social Psychology, 16,* 375–386. (p. 277)

Rubenstein, J. S., Meyer, D. E., & Evans, J. E. (2001). Executive control of cognitive processes in task switching. *Journal of Experimental Psychology: Human Perception and Performance, 27,* 763–797. (p. 49)

Rubin, D. C., Rahhal, T. A., & Poon, L. W. (1998). Things learned in early adulthood are remembered best. *Memory and Cognition, 26,* 3–19. (p. 92)

Rubin, L. B. (1985). *Just friends: The role of friendship in our lives.* New York: Harper & Row. (p. 105)

Rubin, Z. (1970). Measurement of romantic love. *Journal of Personality and Social Psychology, 16,* 265–273. (p. 257)

Ruchlis, H. (1990). *Clear thinking: A practical introduction.* Buffalo, NY: Prometheus Books. (p. 206)

Ruffin, C. L. (1993). Stress and health—little hassles vs. major life events. *Australian Psychologist, 28,* 201–208. (p. 271)

Rule, B. G., & Ferguson, T. J. (1986). The effects of media violence on attitudes, emotions, and cognitions. *Journal of Social Issues, 42(3),* 29–50. (p. 176)

Rumbaugh, D. M. (1977). *Language learning by a chimpanzee: The Lana project.* New York: Academic Press. (p. 217)

Rumbaugh, D. M., & Savage-Rumbaugh, S. (1994, January/February). Language and apes. *Psychology Teacher Network,* pp. 2–5, 9. (p. 217)

Rumbaugh, D. M., & Washburn, D. A. (2003). *Intelligence of apes and other rational beings.* New Haven, CT: Yale University Press. (p. 218)

Rush, A. J., & 15 others. (2005). Vagus nerve stimulation for treatment-resistant depression: A randomized, controlled acute phase trial. *Biological Psychiatry, 58,* 347–354. (p. 369)

Rushton, J. P. (1998). The "Jensen effect" and the "Spearman-Jensen hypothesis" of black-white IQ differences. *Intelligence, 26,* 217–225. (p. 227)

Rushton, J. P. (2003). Race, brain size, and IQ: The case for consilience. *Behavioral and Brain Sciences, 26,* 648–649. (p. 227)

Russell, B. (1930/1985). *The conquest of happiness.* London: Unwin Paperbacks. (p. 264)

Rutter, M., and the English and Romanian Adoptees (ERA) study team. (1998). Developmental catch-up, and deficit, following adoption after severe global early privation. *Journal of Child Psychology and Psychiatry, 39,* 465–476. (p. 79)

Ryan, R. M., & Deci, E. L. (2004). Avoiding death or engaging life as accounts of meaning and culture: Comment on Pyszczynski et al. (2004). *Psychological Bulletin, 130,* 473–477. (p. 306)

Ryckman, R. M., Robbins, M. A., Kaczor, L. M., & Gold J. A. (1989). Male and female raters' stereotyping of male and female physiques. *Personality and Social Psychology Bulletin, 15,* 244–251. (p. 242)

Saad, L. (2001, December 17). Americans' mood: Has Sept. 11 made a difference? *Gallup Poll News Service* (www.gallup.com/poll/releases/pr011217.asp). (p. 270)

Saad, L. (2002, November 21). Most smokers wish they could quit. *Gallup News Service* (www.gallup.com). (p. 328)

Saad, L. (2006, September 6). "Grin and bear it" is motto for most air travelers. *Gallup News Service* (www.gallup.com). (p. 205)

Sabbagh, M. A., Xu, F., Carlson, S. M., Moses, L. J., & Lee, K. (2006). The development of executive functioning and theory of mind. *Psychological Science, 17,* 74–81. (p. 75)

Sabini, J. (1986). Stanley Milgram (1933–1984). *American Psychologist, 41,* 1378–1379. (p. 382)

Sachdev, P., & Sachdev, J. (1997). Sixty years of psychosurgery: Its present status and its future. *Australian and New Zealand Journal of Psychiatry, 31,* 457–464. (p. 370)

Sacks, O. (1985). *The man who mistook his wife for a hat.* New York: Summit Books. (pp. 142, 188)

Salovey, P. (1990, January/February). Interview. *American Scientist,* pp. 25–29. (p. 261)

Salovey, P., & Grewal, D. (2005). The science of emotional intelligence. *Current Directions in Psychological Science, 14,* 281–285. (p. 221)

Salthouse, T. A. (2004). What and when of cognitive aging. *Current Directions in Psychological Science, 13,* 140–144. (p. 93)

Sampson, E. E. (2000). Reinterpreting individualism and collectivism: Their religious roots and monologic versus dialogic person–other relationship. *American Psychologist, 55,* 1425–1432. (p. 309)

Sanders, G., & Wright, M. (1997). Sexual orientation differences in cerebral asymmetry and in the performance of sexually dimorphic cognitive and motor tasks. *Archives of Sexual Behavior, 26,* 463–479. (p. 116)

Sandfort, T. G. M., de Graaf, R., Bijl, R., & Schnabel, P. (2001). Same-sex sexual behavior and psychiatric disorders. *Archives of General Psychiatry, 58,* 85–91. (p. 114)

Sandler, W., Meir, I., Padden, C., & Aronoff, M. (2005). The emergence of grammar: Systematic structure in a new language. *Proceedings of the National Academy of Sciences, 102,* 2261–2265. (p. 213)

Sanford, A. J., Fray, N., Stewart, A., & Moxey, L. (2002). Perspective in statements of quantity, with implications for consumer psychology. *Psychological Science, 13,* 130–134. (p. 209)

Sanz, C., Blicher, A., Dalke, K., Gratton-Fabri, L., McClure-Richards, T., & Fouts, R. (1998, Winter–Spring). Enrichment object use: Five chimpanzees' use of temporary and semi-permanent enrichment objects. *Friends of Washoe, 19*(1,2), 9–14. (p. 216)

Sanz, C., Morgan, D., & Gulick, S. (2004). New insights into chimpanzees, tools, and termites from the Congo Basin. *American Naturalist, 164,* 567–581. (p. 216)

Sapadin, L. A. (1988). Friendship and gender: Perspectives of professional men and women. *Journal of Social and Personal Relationships, 5,* 387–403. (p. 105)

Sapolsky, B. S., & Tabarlet, J. O. (1991). Sex in primetime television: 1979 versus 1989. *Journal of Broadcasting and Electronic Media, 35,* 505–516. (pp. 379, 393)

Sapolsky, R. (2005). The influence of social hierarchy on primate health. *Science, 308,* 648–652. (p. 277)

Savage-Rumbaugh, E. S., Murphy, J., Sevcik, R. A., Brakke, K. E., Williams, S. L., & Rumbaugh, D. M., with commentary by Bates, E. (1993). Language comprehension in ape and child. *Monographs of the Society for Research in Child Development, 58* (233), 1–254. (p. 217)

Savic, I., Berglund, H., & Lindstrom, P. (2005). Brain response to putative pheromones in homosexual men. *Proceedings of the National Academy of Sciences, 102,* 7356–7361. (p. 115)

Savitsky, K., & Gilovich, T. (2003). The illusion of transparency and the alleviation of speech anxiety. *Journal of Experimental Social Psychology, 39,* 618–625. (p. 306)

Savitsky, K., Epley, N., & Gilovich, T. (2001). Do others judge us as harshly as we think? Overestimating the impact of our failures, shortcomings, and mishaps. *Journal of Personality and Social Psychology, 81,* 44–56. (p. 306)

Savoy, C., & Beitel, P. (1996). Mental imagery for basketball. *International Journal of Sport Psychology, 27,* 454–462. (p. 214)

Scarr, S. (1984, May). What's a parent to do? A conversation with E. Hall. *Psychology Today,* pp. 58–63. (p. 227)

Scarr, S. (1989). Protecting general intelligence: Constructs and consequences for interventions. In R. J. Linn (Ed.), *Intelligence: Measurement, theory, and public policy.* Champaign: University of Illinois Press. (p. 220)

Scarr, S. (1993, May/June). Quoted by *Psychology Today,* Nature's thumbprint: So long, superparents, p. 16. (p. 82)

Schab, F. R. (1991). Odor memory: Taking stock. *Psychological Bulletin, 109,* 242–251. (p. 141)

Schachter, S., & Singer, J. E. (1962). Cognitive, social and physiological determinants of emotional state. *Psychological Review, 69,* 379–399. (pp. 249, 253)

Schacter, D. L. (1992). Understanding implicit memory: A cognitive neuroscience approach. *American Psychologist, 47,* 559–569. (p. 188)

Schacter, D. L. (1996). *Searching for memory: The brain, the mind, and the past.* New York: Basic Books. (pp. 92, 188, 198, 295)

Schacter, D. L. (1999). The seven sins of memory: Insights from psychology and cognitive neuroscience. *American Psychologist, 54,* 182–201. (p. 192)

Schall, T., & Smith, G. (2000, Fall). Career trajectories in baseball. *Chance,* pp. 35–38. (p. 91)

Scheier, M. F., & Carver, C. S. (1992). Effects of optimism on psychological and physical well-being: Theoretical overview and empirical update. *Cognitive Therapy and Research, 16,* 201–228. (p. 278)

Schein, E. H. (1956). The Chinese indoctrination program for prisoners of war: A study of attempted brainwashing. *Psychiatry, 19,* 149–172. (p. 378)

Scherer, K. R., Banse, R., & Wallbott, H. G. (2001). Emotion inferences from vocal expression correlate across languages and cultures. *Journal of Cross-Cultural Psychology, 32,* 76–92. (p. 257)

Schiffenbauer, A., & Schiavo, R. S. (1976). Physical distance and attraction: An intensification effect. *Journal of Experimental Social Psychology, 12,* 274–282. (p. 384)

Schimel, J., Arndt, J., Pyszczynski, T., & Greenberg, J. (2001). Being accepted for who we are: Evidence that social validation of the intrinsic self reduces general defensiveness. *Journal of Personality and Social Psychology, 80,* 35–52. (p. 299)

Schkade, D., Sunstein, C. R., & Hastie, R. (2006). What happened on deliberation day? University of Chicago Law and Economics, Olin Working Paper No. 298. (p. 386)

Schmitt, D. P. (2005). Sociosexuality from Argentina to Zimbabwe: A 48-nation study of sex, culture, and strategies of human mating. *Behavioral and Brain Sciences, 28,* 247–311. (p. 118)

Schmitt, D. P., & Pilcher, J. J. (2004). Evaluating evidence of psychological adaptation: How do we know one when we see one? *Psychological Science, 15,* 643–649. (p. 67)

Schnaper, N. (1980). Comments germane to the paper entitled "The reality of death experiences" by Ernst Rodin. *Journal of Nervous and Mental Disease, 168,* 268–270. (p. 331)

Schneider, S. L. (2001). In search of realistic optimism: Meaning, knowledge, and warm fuzziness. *American Psychologist, 56,* 250–263. (p. 279)

Schneiderman, N. (1999). Behavioral medicine and the management of HIV/AIDS. *International Journal of Behavioral Medicine, 6,* 3–12. (p. 274)

Schoeneman, T. J. (1994). Individualism. In V. S. Ramachandran (Ed.), *Encyclopedia of human behavior.* San Diego: Academic Press. (p. 309)

Schofield, J. W. (1986). Black-White contact in desegregated schools. In M. Hewstone & R. Brown (Eds.), *Contact and conflict in intergroup encounters.* Oxford: Basil Blackwell. (p. 401)

Schonfield, D., & Robertson, B. A. (1966). Memory storage and aging. *Canadian Journal of Psychology, 20,* 228–236. (p. 93)

Schooler, J. W., Gerhard, D., & Loftus, E. F. (1986). Qualities of the unreal. *Journal of Experimental Psychology: Learning, Memory, and Cognition, 12,* 171–181. (p. 196)

Schuman, H., & Scott, J. (June, 1989). Generations and collective memories. *American Sociological Review, 54(3),* 359–381. (p. 93)

Schwartz, B. (1984). *Psychology of learning and behavior (2nd ed.).* New York: Norton. (pp. 163, 321)

Schwartz, B. (2000). Self-determination: The tyranny of freedom. *American Psychologist, 55,* 79–88. (p. 277)

Schwartz, B. (2004). *The paradox of choice: Why more is less.* New York: Ecco/HarperCollins. (p. 277)

Schwartz, J. M., Stoessel, P. W., Baxter, L. R., Jr., Martin, K. M., & Phelps, M. E. (1996). Systematic changes in cerebral glucose metabolic rate after successful behavior modification treatment of obsessive-compulsive disorder. *Archives of General Psychiatry, 53,* 109–113. (pp. 359, 370)

Schwartz, J., & Estrin, J. (2004, November 7). Living for today, locked in a paralyzed body. *New York Times* (www.nytimes.com). (p. 262)

Schwarz, N., Strack, F., Kommer, D., & Wagner, D. (1987). Soccer, rooms, and the quality of your life: Mood effects on judgments of satisfaction with life in general and with specific domains. *European Journal of Social Psychology, 17,* 69–79. (p. 191)

Sclafani, A. (1995). How food preferences are learned: Laboratory animal models. *Proceedings of the Nutrition Society, 54,* 419–427. (p. 240)

Scott, D. J., & others. (2004, November 9). U-M team reports evidence that smoking affects human brain's natural "feel good" chemical system (press release by Kara Gavin). University of Michigan Medical School (www.med.umich.edu). (p. 328)

Scott, W. A., Scott, R., & McCabe, M. (1991). Family relationships and children's personality: A cross-cultural, cross-source comparison. *British Journal of Social Psychology, 30,* 1–20. (p. 83)

Sdorow, L. M. (2005). The people behind psychology. In B. Perlman, L. McCann, & W. Buskist (Eds.), *Voices of experience: Memorable talks from the National Institute on the Teaching of Psychology.* Washington, DC: American Psychological Society. (p. 294)

Sechrest, L., Stickle, T. R., & Stewart, M. (1998). The role of assessment in clinical psychology. In A. Bellack, M. Hersen (Series eds.) & C. R. Reynolds (Vol. ed.), *Comprehensive clinical psychology: Vol 4: Assessment.* New York: Pergamon. (p. 294)

Seeman, P., Guan, H-C., & Van Tol, H. H. M. (1993). Dopamine D4 receptors elevated in schizophrenia. *Nature, 365,* 441–445. (p. 342)

Segall, M. H., Dasen, P. R., Berry, J. W., & Poortinga, Y. H. (1990). *Human behavior in global perspective: An introduction to cross-cultural psychology.* New York: Pergamon. (pp. 76, 107, 118)

Segerstrom, S. C., Taylor, S. E., Kemeny, M. E., & Fahey, J. L. (1998). Optimism is associated with mood, coping, and immune change in response to stress. *Journal of Personality and Social Psychology, 74,* 1646–1655. (p. 279)

Seidlitz, L., & Diener, E. (1998). Sex differences in the recall of affective experiences. *Journal of Personality and Social Psychology, 74,* 262–271. (p. 339)

Self, C. E. (1994). *Moral culture and victimization in residence halls.* Dissertation: Thesis (M.A.). Bowling Green University. (p. 334)

Seligman, M. E. P. (1975). *Helplessness: On depression, development and death.* San Francisco: Freeman. (p. 277)

Seligman, M. E. P. (1991). *Learned optimism.* New York: Knopf. (pp. 277, 339)

Seligman, M. E. P. (1994). *What you can change and what you can't.* New York: Knopf. (pp. 280, 296, 306)

Seligman, M. E. P. (1995). The effectiveness of psychotherapy: The Consumer Reports study. *American Psychologist, 50,* 965–974. (pp. 360, 362)

Seligman, M. E. P. (2002). *Authentic happiness: Using the new positive psychology to realize your potential for lasting fulfillment.* New York: Free Press. (pp. 8, 306, 359)

Seligman, M. E. P., & Yellen, A. (1987). What is a dream? *Behavior Research and Therapy, 25,* 1–24. (p. 51)

Seligman, M. E. P., Steen, T. A., Park, N., & Peterson, C. (2005). Positive psychology progress: Empirical validation of interventions. *American Psychologist, 60,* 410–421. (p. 8)

Selye, H. (1936). A syndrome produced by diverse nocuous agents. *Nature, 138,* 32. (p. 271)

Selye, H. (1976). *The stress of life.* New York: McGraw-Hill. (p. 271)

Senghas, A., & Coppola, M. (2001). Children creating language: How Nicaraguan Sign Language acquired a spatial grammar. *Psychological Science, 12,* 323–328. (p. 213)

Sengupta, S. (2001, October 10). Sept. 11 attack narrows the racial divide. *New York Times* (www.nytimes.com). (p. 401)

Serdula, M. K., Mokdad, A., Williamson, D. F., Galuska, D. A., Mendlein, J. M., & Heath, G. W. (1999). Prevalence of attempting weight loss and strategies for controlling weight. *Journal of the American Medical Association, 282,* 1353–1358. (p. 245)

Service, R. F. (1994). Will a new type of drug make memory-making easier? *Science, 266,* 218–219. (p. 187)

Shadish, W. R., & Baldwin, S. A. (2005). Effects of behavioral marital therapy: A meta-analysis of randomized controlled trials. *Journal of Consulting and Clinical Psychology, 73,* 6–14. (p. 362)

Shadish, W. R., Matt, G. E., Navarro, A. M., & Phillips, G. (2000). The effects of psychological therapies under clinically representative conditions: A meta-analysis. *Psychological Bulletin, 126,* 512–529. (p. 361)

Shafir, E., & LeBoeuf, R. A. (2002). Rationality. *Annual Review of Psychology, 53,* 491–517. (p. 210)

Shamir, B., House, R. J., & Arthur, M. B. (1993). The motivational effects of charismatic leadership: A self-concept based theory. *Organizational Science, 4*(4), 577–594. (p. 412)

Shanahan, L., McHale, S. M., Osgood, D. W., & Crouter, A. C. (2007). Conflict frequency with mothers and fathers from middle childhood to late adolescence: Within- and between-families comparisons. *Developmental Psychology, 43,* 539–550. (p. 88)

Sharma, A. R., McGue, M. K., & Benson, P. L. (1998). The psychological adjustment of United States adopted adolescents and their non-adopted siblings. *Child Development, 69,* 791–802. (p. 82)

Shaw, H. L. (1989–90). Comprehension of the spoken word and ASL translation by chimpanzees (Pan troglodytes). *Friends of Washoe, 9*(1/2), 8–19. (p. 217)

Sheehan, S. (1982). *Is there no place on earth for me?* Boston: Houghton Mifflin. (p. 341)

Shelton, J. N., & Richeson, J. A. (2005). Intergroup contact and pluralistic ignorance. *Journal of Personality and Social Psychology, 88,* 91–107. (p. 401)

Shenton, M. E. (1992). Abnormalities of the left temporal lobe and thought disorder in schizophrenia: A quantitative magnetic resonance imaging study. *New England Journal of Medicine, 327,* 604–612. (p. 343)

Shepard, R. N. (1990). *Mind sights.* New York: Freeman. (p. 21)

Shepherd, C. (1999, June). News of the weird. *Funny Times,* p. 21. (p. 245)

Sherif, M. (1966). *In common predicament: Social psychology of intergroup conflict and cooperation.* Boston: Houghton Mifflin. (p. 401)

Sherman, P. W., & Flaxman, S. M. (2001). Protecting ourselves from food. *American Scientist, 89,* 142–151. (p. 242)

Shettleworth, S. J. (1973). Food reinforcement and the organization of behavior in golden hamsters. In R. A. Hinde & J. Stevenson-Hinde (Eds.), *Constraints on learning.* London: Academic Press. (p. 170)

Shettleworth, S. J. (1993). Where is the comparison in comparative cognition? Alternative research programs. *Psychological Science, 4,* 179–184. (p. 186)

Showers, C. (1992). The motivational and emotional consequences of considering positive or negative possibilities for an upcoming event. *Journal of Personality and Social Psychology, 63,* 474–484. (p. 279)

Sieff, E. M., Dawes, R. M., & Loewenstein, G. (1999). Anticipated versus actual reaction to HIV test results. *The American Journal of Psychology, 112,* 297–313. (p. 262)

Siegel, J. M. (2003, November). Why we sleep. *Scientific American,* pp. 92–97. (p. 55)

Siegel, R. K. (1977, October). Hallucinations. *Scientific American,* pp. 132–140. (p. 331)

Siegel, R. K. (1980). The psychology of life after death. *American Psychologist, 35,* 911–931. (p. 331)

Siegel, R. K. (1982, October). Quoted by J. Hooper, Mind tripping. *Omni,* pp. 72–82, 159–160. (p. 331)

Siegel, R. K. (1984, March 15). Personal communication. (p. 331)

Siegel, R. K. (1990). Intoxication. New York: Pocket Books. (pp. 329, 332)

Siegler, R. S., & Ellis, S. (1996). Piaget XE "Piaget, J." on childhood. *Psychological Science, 7,* 211–215. (p. 73)

Silbersweig, D. A., Stern, E., Frith, C., Cahill, C., Holmes, A., Grootoonk, S., Seaward, J., McKenna, P., Chua, S. E., Schnorr, L., Jones, T., & Frackowiak, R. S. J. (1995). A functional neuroanatomy of hallucinations in schizophrenia. *Nature, 378,* 176–179. (p. 342)

Silva, A. J., Stevens, C. F., Tonegawa, S., & Wang, Y. (1992). Deficient hippocampal long-term potentiation in alpha-calcium-calmodulin kinase II mutant mice. *Science, 257,* 201–206. (p. 187)

Silva, C. E., & Kirsch, I. (1992). Interpretive sets, expectancy, fantasy proneness, and dissociation as predictors of hypnotic response. *Journal of Personality and Social Psychology, 63,* 847–856. (p. 139)

Silver, M., & Geller, D. (1978). On the irrelevance of evil: The organization and individual action. *Journal of Social Issues, 34,* 125–136. (p. 387)

Silverman, I., & Eals, M. (1992). Sex differences in spatial abilities: Evolutionary theory and data. In J. H. Barkow, L. Cosmides, & J. Tooby (Eds.), *The adapted mind: Evolutionary psychology and the generation of culture.* New York: Oxford University Press. (p. 229)

Silverman, I., & Phillips, K. (1998). The evolutionary psychology of spatial sex differences. In C. Crawford & D. L. Krebs (Eds.), *Handbook of Evolutionary Psychology: Ideas, Issues, and Applications.* Mahwah, NJ: Erlbaum. (p. 229)

Silverman, K., Evans, S. M., Strain, E. C., & Griffiths, R. R. (1992). Withdrawal syndrome after the double-blind cessation of caffeine consumption. *New England Journal of Medicine, 327,* 1109–1114. (p. 328)

Simon, H. (2001, February). Quoted by A. M. Hayashi, "When to trust your gut." *Harvard Business Review,* pp. 59–65. (p. 211)

Simons, D. J. (1996). In sight, out of mind: When object representations fail. *Psychological Science, 7,* 301–305. (p. 49)

Simons, D. J., & Ambinder, M. S. (2005). Change blindness: Theory and consequences. *Current Directions in Psychological Science, 14,* 44–48. (p. 49)

Simons, D. J., & Chabris, C. F. (1999). Gorillas in our midst: Sustained inattentional blindness for dynamic events. *Perception, 28,* 1059–1074. (p. 49)

Simonton, D. K. (1988). Age and outstanding achievement: What do we know after a century of research? *Psychological Bulletin, 104,* 251–267. (p. 93)

Simonton, D. K. (1990). Creativity in the later years: Optimistic prospects for achievement. *The Gerontologist, 30,* 626–631. (p. 93)

Simonton, D. K. (1992). The social context of career success and course for 2,026 scientists and inventors. *Personality and Social Psychology Bulletin, 18,* 452–463. (p. 221)

Simonton, D. K. (2000). Creativity: Cognitive, personal, developmental, and social aspects. *American Psychologist, 55,* 151–158. (pp. 176, 220)

Sinclair, R. C., Hoffman, C., Mark, M. M., Martin, L. L., & Pickering, T. L. (1994). Construct accessibility and the misattribution of arousal: Schachter and Singer revisited. *Psychological Science, 5,* 15–18. (p. 255)

Singelis, T. M., & Sharkey, W. F. (1995). Culture, self-construal, and embarrassability. *Cross-Cultural Psychology, 26,* 622–644. (p. 309)

Singelis, T. M., Bond, M. H., Sharkey, W. F., & Lai, C. S. Y. (1999). Unpackaging culture's influence on self-esteem and embarrassability: The role of self-construals. *Journal of Cross-Cultural Psychology, 30,* 315–341. (p. 309)

Singer, T., Seymour, B., O'Doherty, J., Kaube, H., Dolan, R. J., & Frith, C. (2004). Empathy for pain involves the affective but not sensory components of pain. *Science, 303,* 1157–1162. (p. 173)

Singh, D. (1995). Female health, attractiveness, and desirability for relationships: Role of breast asymmetry and waist-to-hip ratio. *Ethology and Sociobiology, 16,* 465–481. (p. 119)

Singh, S. (1997). *Fermat's enigma: The epic quest to solve the world's greatest mathematical problem.* New York: Bantam Books. (p. 220)

Singh, S., & Riber, K. A. (1997, November). Fermat's last stand. *Scientific American,* pp. 68–73. (p. 221)

Sipski, M. L., & Alexander, C. J. (1999). Sexual response in women with spinal cord injuries: Implications for our understanding of the able bodied. *Journal of Sex and Marital Therapy, 25,* 11–22. (p. 33)

Sjöstrum, L. (1980). Fat cells and body weight. In A. J. Stunkard (Ed.), *Obesity.* Philadelphia: Saunders. (p. 243)

Skinner, B. F. (1953). *Science and human behavior.* New York: Macmillan. (p. 167)

Skinner, B. F. (1956). A case history in scientific method. *American Psychologist, 11,* 221–233. (p. 168)

Skinner, B. F. (1983, September). Origins of a behaviorist. *Psychology Today,* pp. 22–33. (p. 170)

Skinner, B. F. (1986). What is wrong with daily life in the western world? *American Psychologist, 41,* 568–574. (p. 171)

Skinner, B. F. (1988). The school of the future. Address to the American Psychological Association convention. (p. 171)

Skinner, B. F. (1989). Teaching machines. *Science, 243,* 1535. (p. 171)

Skitka, L. J., Bauman, C. W., & Mullen, E. (2004). Political tolerance and coming to psychological closure following the September 11, 2001, terrorist attacks: An integrative approach. *Personality and Social Psychology Bulletin, 30,* 743–756. (p. 260)

Sklar, L. S., & Anisman, H. (1981). Stress and cancer. *Psychological Bulletin, 89,* 369–406. (p. 274)

Skov, R. B., & Sherman, S. J. (1986). Information-gathering processes: Diagnosticity, hypothesis-confirmatory strategies, and perceived hypothesis confirmation. *Journal of Experimental Social Psychology, 22,* 93–121. (p. 207)

Slater, L. (2000, November 19). How do you cure a sex addict? *New York Times Magazine* (www.nytimes.com). (p. 366)

Slavin, R. E., Hurley, E. A., & Chamberlain, A. (2003). Cooperative learning and achievement: Theory and research. In W. M. Reynolds & G. E. Miller (Eds.), *Handbook of psychology: Educational psychology,* Vol. 7. New York: Wiley. (p. 401)

Sloan, R. P. (2005). Field analysis of the literature on religion, spirituality, and health. Columbia University (available at www.metanexus.net/tarp). (p. 283)

Sloan, R. P., & Bagiella, E. (2002). Claims about religious involvement and health outcomes. *Annals of Behavioral Medicine, 24,* 14–21. (p. 283)

Sloan, R. P., Bagiella, E., & Powell, T. (1999). Religion, spirituality, and medicine. *Lancet, 353,* 664–667. (p. 283)

Sloan, R. P., Bagiella, E., VandeCreek, L., & Poulos, P. (2000). Should physicians prescribe religious activities? *New England Journal of Medicine, 342,* 1913–1917. (p. 283)

Slovic, P., Finucane, M., Peters, E., & MacGregor, D. G. (2002). The affect heuristic. In T. Gilovich, D. Griffin, & D. Kahneman (Eds.), *Intuitive judgment: Heuristics and biases.* New York: Cambridge University Press. (p. 328)

Slutske, W. S. (2005). Alcohol use disorders among U.S. college students and their non-college-attending peers. *Archives of General Psychiatry, 62,* 321–327. (p. 327)

Small, M. F. (1997). Making connections. *American Scientist, 85,* 502–504. (p. 81)

Small, M. F. (2002, July). What you can learn from drunk monkeys. *Discover,* pp. 40–45. (p. 333)

Smedley, A., & Smedley, B. D. (2005). Race as biology is fiction, racism as a social problem is real: Anthropological and historical perspectives on the social construction of race. *American Psychologist, 60,* 16–26. (p. 228)

Smelser, N. J., & Mitchell, F. (Eds.) (2002). *Terrorism: Perspectives from the behavioral and social sciences.* Washington, DC: National Research Council, National Academies Press. (p. 390)

Smith, A. (1983). Personal correspondence. (p. 342)

Smith, D. V., & Margolskee, R. F. (2001, March). Making sense of taste. *Scientific American,* pp. 32–39. (p. 140)

Smith, E., & Delargy, M. (2005). Locked-in syndrome. *British Medical Journal, 330,* 406–409. (p. 262)

Smith, J. E., Waldorf, V. A., & Trembath, D. L. (1990). "Single white male looking for thin, very attractive . . ." *Sex Roles, 23,* 675–685. (p. 243)

Smith, M. B. (1978). Psychology and values. *Journal of Social Issues, 34,* 181–199. (p. 299)

Smith, M. L., & Glass, G. V. (1977). Meta-analysis of psychotherapy outcome studies. *American Psychologist, 32,* 752–760. (p. 362)

Smith, M. L., Glass, G. V., & Miller, R. L. (1980). *The benefits of psychotherapy.* Baltimore: Johns Hopkins Press. (pp. 361, 362)

Smith, P. B., & Tayeb, M. (1989). Organizational structure and processes. In M. Bond (Ed.), *The cross-cultural challenge to social psychology.* Newbury Park, CA: Sage. (p. 414)

Smith, P. F. (1995). Cannabis and the brain. *New Zealand Journal of Psychology, 24,* 5–12. (p. 332)

Smith, T. W. (1998, December). American sexual behavior: Trends, sociodemographic differences, and risk behavior. National Opinion Research Center GSS Topical Report No. 25. (pp. 108, 112, 114)

Smith, T. W. (2005). Troubles in America: A study of negative life events across time and sub-groups. GSS Topical Report No 40., National Opinion Research Center, University of Chicago. (p. 360)

Smith, T. W., & Ruiz, J. M. (2002). Psychosocial influences on the development and course of coronary heart disease: Current status and implications for research and practice. *Journal of Consulting and Clinical Psychology, 70,* 548–568. (p. 275)

Smoreda, Z., & Licoppe, C. (2000). Gender-specific use of the domestic telephone. *Social Psychology Quarterly, 63,* 238–252. (p. 105)

Snarey, J. R. (1985). Cross-cultural universality of social-moral development: A critical review of Kohlbergian research. *Psychological Bulletin, 97,* 202–233. (p. 86)

Snarey, J. R. (1987, June). A question of morality. *Psychology Today,* pp. 6–7. (p. 86)

Snodgrass, S. E., Higgins, J. G., & Todisco, L. (1986). The effects of walking behavior on mood. Paper presented at the American Psychological Association convention. (p. 259)

Snyder, F., & Scott, J. (1972). The psychophysiology of sleep. In N. S. Greenfield & R. A. Sterbach (Eds.), *Handbook of psychophysiology.* New York: Holt, Rinehart & Winston, (p. 53)

Snyder, M. (1984). When belief creates reality. In L. Berkowitz (Ed.), *Advances in experimental social psychology (Vol. 18).* New York: Academic Press. (pp. 28, 317)

Snyder, S. H. (1986). *Drugs and the brain.* New York: Scientific American Library. (p. 368)

Solomon, D. A., Keitner, G. I., Miller, I. W., Shea, M. T., & Keller, M. B. (1995). Course of illness and maintenance treatments for patients with bipolar disorder. *Journal of Clinical Psychiatry, 56,* 5–13. (p. 368)

Solomon, J. (1996, May 20). Breaking the silence. *Newsweek,* pp. 20–22. (p. 317)

Solomon, M. (1987, December). Standard issue. *Psychology Today,* pp. 30–31. (p. 395)

Söndergard, L., Kvist, K., Andersen, P. K., & Kessing, L. V. (2006a). Do antidepressants precipitate youth suicide? A nationwide pharmacoepidemiological study. *European Journal of Adolescent Psychiatry, 15,* 232–240. (p. 367)

Söndergard, L., Kvist, K., Andersen, P. K., & Kessing, L. V. (2006b). Do antidepressants prevent suicide? *International Clinical Psychopharmacology, 21,* 211–218. (p. 367)

Sonenstein, F. L. (1992). Condom use. *Science, 257,* 861. (p. 111)

Soussignan, R. (2001). Duchenne smile, emotional experience, and autonomic reactivity: A test of the facial feedback hypothesis. *Emotion, 2,* 52–74. (p. 259)

Spector, P. E. (1986). Perceived control by employees: A meta-analysis of studies concerning autonomy and participation at work. *Human Relations, 39,* 1005–1016. (p. 414)

Spencer, K. M., Nestor, P. G., Perlmutter, R., Niznikiewicz, M. A., Klump, M. C., Frumin, M., Shenton, M. E., & McCarley, R. W. (2004). Neural synchrony indexes disordered perception and cognition in schizophrenia. *Proceedings of the National Academy of Sciences, 101,* 17288–17293. (p. 342)

Spencer, S. J., Steele, C. M., & Quinn, D. M. (1999). Stereotype threat and women's math performance. *Journal of Experimental Social Psychology, 3,* 4–28. (p. 230)

Sperling, G. (1960). The information available in brief visual presentations. *Psychological Monographs, 74* (Whole No. 498). (p. 186)

Sperry, R. W. (1964). Problems outstanding in the evolution of brain function. James Arthur Lecture, American Museum of Natural History, New York. Cited by R. Ornstein (1977), *The psychology of consciousness (2nd ed.).* New York: Harcourt Brace Jovanovich. (p. 46)

Speulda, N., & McIntosh, M. (2004, May 13). Global gender gaps. Pew Global Attitudes Project. Pew Research Center (pewglobal.org). (p. 109)

Spiegel, K., Leproult, R., & Van Cauter, E. (1999). Impact of sleep debt on metabolic and endrocrine function. *Lancet, 354,* 1435–1439. (p. 54)

Spielberger, C., & London, P. (1982). Rage boomerangs. *American Health, 1,* 52–56. (p. 275)

Sprecher, S. (1989). The importance to males and females of physical attractiveness, earning potential, and expressiveness in initial attraction. *Sex Roles, 21,* 591–607. (p. 395)

Sprecher, S., & Sedikides, C. (1993). Gender differences in perceptions of emotionality: The case of close heterosexual relationships. *Sex Roles, 28,* 511–530. (p. 257)

Spring, B., Pingitore, R., Bourgeois, M., Kessler, K. H., & Bruckner, E. (1992). The effects and non-effects of skipping breakfast: Results of three studies. Paper presented at the American Psychological Association convention. (p. 246)

Srivastava, S., John, O. P., Gosling, S. D., & Potter, J. (2003). Development of personality in early and middle adulthood: Set like plaster or persistent change? *Journal of Personality & Social Psychology, 84,* 1041–1053. (pp. 98, 301)

St. Clair, D., Xu, M., Wang, P., Yu, Y., Fang, Y., Zhang, F., Zheng, X., Gu, N., Feng, G., Sham, P., & He, L. (2005). Rates of adult schizophrenia following prenatal exposure to the Chinese famine of 1959–1961. *Journal of the American Medical Association, 294,* 557–562. (p. 343)

Stafford, R. S., MacDonald, E. A., & Finkelstein, S. N. (2001). National patterns of medication treatment for depression, 1987 to 2001. *Primary Care Companion Journal of Clinical Psychiatry, 3,* 232–235. (p. 367)

Stanford University Center for Narcolepsy. (2002). Narcolepsy is a serious medical disorder and a key to understanding other sleep disorders (www.med.stanford.edu/school/Psychiatry/narcolepsy). (p. 56)

Stanovich, K. (1996). *How to think straight about psychology.* New York: HarperCollins. (p. 290)

Statistics Canada. (2003). *Victims and persons accused of homicide, by age and sex.* Table 253–0003. www.statcan.ca (p. 104)

Staub, E. (1989). *The roots of evil: The psychological and cultural sources of genocide.* New York: Cambridge University Press. (p. 378)

Steele, C. (1990, May). A conversation with Claude Steele. *APS Observer,* pp. 11–17. (p. 227)

Steele, C. M., Spencer, S. J., & Aronson, J. (2002). Contending with group image: The psychology of stereotype and social identity threat. *Advances in Experimental Social Psychology, 34,* 379–440. (p. 230)

Steinberg, L. (1987, September). Bound to bicker. *Psychology Today,* pp. 36–39. (p. 88)

Steinberg, L., & Morris, A. S. (2001). Adolescent development. *Annual Review of Psychology, 52,* 83–110. (pp. 84, 88)

Steinberg, L., & Scott, E. S. (2003). Less guilty by reason of adolescence: Developmental immaturity, diminished responsibility, and the juvenile death penalty. *American Psychologist, 58,* 1009–1018. (p. 84)

Steinberg, N. (1993, February). Astonishing love stories (from an earlier United Press International report). *Games,* p. 47. (p. 395)

Stern, M., & Karraker, K. H. (1989). Sex stereotyping of infants: A review of gender labeling studies. *Sex Roles, 20,* 501–522. (p. 151)

Stern, S. L., Dhanda, R., & Hazuda, H. P. (2001). Hopelessness predicts mortality in older Mexican and European Americans. *Psychosomatic Medicine, 63,* 344–351. (p. 279)

Sternberg, R. J. (1988). Applying cognitive theory to the testing and teaching of intelligence. *Applied Cognitive Psychology, 2,* 231–255. (p. 220)

Sternberg, R. J., & Grajek, S. (1984). The nature of love. *Journal of Personality and Social Psychology, 47,* 312–329. (p. 398)

Sternberg, R. J., & Kaufman, J. C. (1998). Human abilities. *Annual Review of Psychology, 49,* 479–502. (p. 218)

Sternberg, R. J., & Lubart, T. I. (1991). An investment theory of creativity and its development. *Human Development,* 1–31. (p. 220)

Sternberg, R. J., & Lubart, T. I. (1992). Buy low and sell high: An investment approach to creativity. *Psychological Science, 1,* 1–5. (p. 220)

Sternberg, R. J., Grigorenko, E. L., & Kidd, K. K. (2005). Intelligence, race, and genetics. *American Psychologist, 60,* 46–59. (p. 228)

Stetter, F., & Kupper, S. (2002). Autogenic training: A meta-analysis of clinical outcome studies. *Applied Psychophysiology and Biofeedback, 27,* 45–98. (p. 281)

Stevenson, H. W. (1992, December). Learning from Asian schools. *Scientific American,* pp. 70–76. (p. 228)

Stewart, B. (2002, April 6). Recall of the wild. *New York Times* (www.nytimes.com). (p. 20)

Stice, E., & Shaw, H. E. (1994). Adverse effects of the media portrayed thin-ideal on women and linkages to bulimic symptomatology. *Journal of Social and Clinical Psychology, 13,* 288–308. (p. 241)

Stice, E., Spangler, D., & Agras, W. S. (2001). Exposure to media-portrayed thin-ideal images adversely affects vulnerable girls: A longitudinal experiment. *Journal of Social and Clinical Psychology, 20,* 270–288. (p. 241)

Stickgold, R. (2000, March 7). Quoted by S. Blakeslee, For better learning, researchers endorse "sleep on it" adage. *New York Times,* p. F2. (p. 58)

Stickgold, R., Hobson, J. A., Fosse, R., & Fosse, M. (2001). Sleep, learning, and dreams: Off-line memory processing. *Science, 294,* 1052–1057. (p. 58)

Stickgold, R., Malia, A., Maquire, D., Roddenberry, D., & O'Connor, M. (2000, October 13). Replaying the game: Hypnagogic images in normals and amnesics. *Science, 290,* 350–353. (p. 58)

Stith, S. M., Rosen, K. H., Middleton, K. A., Busch, A. L., Lunderberg, K., & Carlton, R. P. (2000). The intergenerational transmission of spouse abuse: A meta-analysis. *Journal of Marriage and the Family, 62,* 640–654. (p. 174)

Stockton, M. C., & Murnen, S. K. (1992). Gender and sexual arousal in response to sexual stimuli: A meta-analytic review. Presented at the American Psychological Society convention. (p. 112)

Stone, A. A., & Neale, J. M. (1984). Effects of severe daily events on mood. *Journal of Personality and Social Psychology, 46,* 137–144. (p. 261)

Stoppard, J. M., & Gruchy, C. D. G. (1993). Gender, context, and expression of positive emotion. *Personality and Social Psychology Bulletin, 19,* 143–150. (p. 257)

Storm, L. (2000). Research note: Replicable evidence of psi: A revision of Milton's (1999) meta-analysis of the ganzfeld data bases. *Journal of Parapsychology, 64,* 411–416. (p. 153)

Storm, L. (2003). Remote viewing by committee: RV using a multiple agent/multiple percipient design. *Journal of Parapsychology, 67,* 325–342. (p. 153)

Storms, M. D. (1983). *Development of sexual orientation.* Washington, DC: Office of Social and Ethical Responsibility, American Psychological Association. (p. 115)

Storms, M. D., & Thomas, G. C. (1977). Reactions to physical closeness. *Journal of Personality and Social Psychology, 35,* 412–418. (p. 384)

Strack, F., Martin, L., & Stepper, S. (1988). Inhibiting and facilitating conditions of the human smile: A nonobtrusive test of the facial feedback hypothesis. *Journal of Personality and Social Psychology, 54,* 768–777. (p. 259)

Strange, B. A., & Dolan, R. J. (2004). b-Adrenergic modulation of emotional memory-evoked human amygdala and hippocampal responses. *Proceedings of the National Academy of Sciences, 101,* 11454–11458. (p. 187)

Stratton, G. M. (1896). Some preliminary experiments on vision without inversion of the retinal image. *Psychological Review, 3,* 611–617. (p. 149)

Straub, R. O., Seidenberg, M. S., Bever, T. G., & Terrace, H. S. (1979). Serial learning in the pigeon. *Journal of the Experimental Analysis of Behavior, 32,* 137–148. (p. 217)

Straus, M. A., & Gelles, R. J. (1980). *Behind closed doors: Violence in the American family.* New York: Anchor/Doubleday. (p. 168)

Straus, M. A., Sugarman, D. B., & Giles-Sims, J. (1997). Spanking by parents and subsequent antisocial behavior of children. *Archives of Pediatric Adolescent Medicine, 151,* 761–767. (p. 168)

Strawbridge, W. J., Shema, S. J., Cohen, R. D., & Kaplan, G. A. (2001). Religious attendance increases survival by improving and maintaining good health behaviors, mental health, and social relationships. *Annals of Behavioral Medicine, 23,* 68–74. (p. 283)

Strayer, D. L., & Johnston, W. A. (2001). Driven to distraction: Dual-task studies of simulated driving and conversing on a cellular telephone. *Psychological Science, 12,* 462–466. (p. 49)

Strayer, D. L., Drews, F. A., & Johnston, W. A. (2003). Cell phone-induced failures of visual attention during simulated driving. *Journal of Experimental Psychology: Applied, 9,* 23–32. (p. 49)

Striegel-Moore, R. H., Silberstein, L. R., & Rodin, J. (1993). The social self in bulimia nervosa: Public self-consciousness, social anxiety, and perceived fraudulence. *Journal of Abnormal Psychology, 102,* 297–303. (p. 241)

Stroebe, M., Stroebe, W., & Schut, H. (2001). Gender differences in adjustment to bereavement: An empirical and theoretical review. *Review of General Psychology, 5,* 62–83. (p. 96)

Stroebe, M., Stroebe, W., Schut, H., Zech, E., & van den Bout, J. (2002). Does disclosure of emotions facilitate recovery from bereavement? Evidence from two prospective studies. *Journal of Consulting and Clinical Psychology, 70,* 169–178. (p. 96)

Stroebe, W., Schut, H., & Stroebe, M. S. (2005). Grief work, disclosure and counseling: Do they help the bereaved? *Clinical Psychology Review, 25,* 395–414. (p. 96)

Strupp, H. H. (1986). Psychotherapy: Research, practice, and public policy (How to avoid dead ends). *American Psychologist, 41,* 120–130. (p. 363)

Stumpf, H., & Jackson, D. N. (1994). Gender-related differences in cognitive abilities: Evidence from a medical school admissions testing program. *Personality and Individual Differences, 17,* 335–344. (p. 229)

Stunkard, A. J., Harris, J. R., Pedersen, N. L., & McClearn, G. E. (1990). A separated twin study of the body mass index. *New England Journal of Medicine, 322,* 1483–1487. (p. 244)

Suddath, R. L., Christison, G. W., Torrey, E. F., Casanova, M. F., & Weinberger, D. R. (1990). Anatomical abnormalities in the brains of monozygotic twins discordant for schizophrenia. *New England Journal of Medicine, 322,* 789–794. (p. 344)

Sue, S. (2006). Research to address racial and ethnic disparities in mental health: Some lessons learned. In S. Il. Donaldson, D. E. Berger, & K.

Pezdek (Eds.), *Applied psychology: New frontiers and rewarding careers.* Mahwah, NJ: Erlbaum. (p. 364)

Suedfeld, P. (1998). Homo invictus: The indomitable species. *Canadian Psychology, 38,* 164–173. (p. 320)

Suedfeld, P. (2000). Reverberations of the Holocaust fifty years later: Psychology's contributions to understanding persecution and genocide. *Canadian Psychology, 41,* 1–9. (p. 320)

Suedfeld, P., & Mocellin, J. S. P. (1987). The "sensed presence" in unusual environments. *Environment and Behavior, 19,* 33–52. (p. 331)

Suhail, K., & Chaudry, H. R. (2004). Predictors of subjective well-being in an Eastern Muslim culture. *Journal of Social and Clinical Psychology, 23,* 359. (p. 262)

Suinn, R. M. (1997). Mental practice in sports psychology: Where have we been, Where do we go? *Clinical Psychology: Science and Practice, 4,* 189–207. (p. 214)

Sullivan, P. F., Neale, M. C., & Kendler, K. S. (2000). Genetic epidemiology of major depression: Review and meta-analysis. *American Journal of Psychiatry, 157,* 1552–1562. (p. 338)

Suls, J. M., & Tesch, F. (1978). Students' preferences for information about their test performance: A social comparison study. *Journal of Experimental Social Psychology, 8,* 189–197. (p. 264)

Summers, M. (1996, December 9). Mister clean. *People Weekly,* pp. 139–142. (p. 313)

Sundstrom, E., De Meuse, K. P., & Futrell, D. (1990). Work teams: Applications and effectiveness. *American Psychologist, 45,* 120–133. (p. 414)

Suomi, S. J. (1986). Anxiety-like disorders in young nonhuman primates. In R. Gettleman (Ed.), *Anxiety disorders of childhood.* New York: Guilford Press. (p. 322)

Suomi, S. J. (1987). Genetic and maternal contributions to individual differences in rhesus monkey biobehavioral development. In N. A. Krasnegor & others (Eds.), *Perinatal development: A psychobiological perspective.* Orlando, FL: Academic Press. (p. 293)

Surgeon General. (1986). *The Surgeon General's workshop on pornography and public health, June 22–24.* Report prepared by E. P. Mulvey & J. L. Haugaard and released by Office of the Surgeon General on August 4, 1986. (p. 394)

Susser, E. S., Herman, D. B., & Aaron, B. (2002, August). Combating the terror of terrorism. *Scientific American,* pp. 70–77. (p. 320)

Susser, E., Neugenbauer, R., Hoek, H. W., Brown, A. S., Lin, S., Labovitz, D., & Gorman, J. M. (1996). Schizophrenia after prenatal famine. *Archives of General Psychiatry, 53*(1), 25–31. (p. 343)

Sutherland, A. (2006). *Bitten and scratched: Life and lessons at the premier school for exotic animal trainers.* New York: Viking. (p. 157)

Sutherland, A. (2006, June 25). What Shamu taught me about a happy marriage. *New York Times* (www.nytimes.com). (p. 157)

Swann, Jr., W. B., Chang-Schneider, C., & McClarty, K. L. (2007). Do people's self-views matter: Self-concept and self-esteem in everyday life. *American Psychologist, 62,* 84–94. (p. 306)

Sweat, J. A., & Durm, M. W. (1993). Psychics: Do police departments really use them? *Skeptical Inquirer, 17,* 148–158. (p. 152)

Swerdlow, N. R., & Koob, G. F. (1987). Dopamine, schizophrenia, mania, and depression: Toward a unified hypothesis of cortico-stiato-pallido-thalamic function (with commentary). *Behavioral and Brain Sciences, 10,* 197–246. (p. 342)

Symond, M. B., Harris, A. W. F., Gordon, E., & Williams, L. M. (2005). "Gamma synchrony" in first-episode schizophrenia: A disorder of temporal connectivity? *American Journal of Psychiatry, 162,* 459–465. (p. 342)

TADS (Treatment for Adolescents with Depression Study Team). (2004). Fluoxetine, cognitive-behavioral therapy, and their combination for adolescents with depression: Treatment for adolescents with depression study (TADS) randomized controlled trial. *Journal of the American Medical Association, 292,* 807–820. (p. 367)

Taha, F. A. (1972). A comparative study of how sighted and blind perceive the manifest content of dreams. *National Review of Social Sciences, 9*(3), 28. (p. 57)

Taheri, S. (2004). The genetics of sleep disorders. *Minerva Medica, 95,* 203–212. (p. 54)

Tajfel, H. (Ed.). (1982). *Social identity and intergroup relations.* New York: Cambridge University Press. (p. 389)

Talarico, J. M., & Rubin, D. C. XE "Rubin, D. C." (2003). Confidence, not consistency, characterizes flashbulb memories. *Psychological Science, 14,* 455–461. (p. 188)

Tang, S-H., & Hall, V. C. (1995). The overjustification effect: A meta-analysis. *Applied Cognitive Psychology, 9,* 365–404. (p. 169)

Tangney, J. P., Baumeister, R. F., & Boone, A. L. (2004). High self-control predicts good adjustment, less pathology, better grades, and interpersonal success. *Journal of Personality, 72,* 271–324. (p. 278)

Tannen, D. (1990). *You just don't understand: Women and men in conversation.* New York: Morrow. (pp. 28, 105)

Tannenbaum, P. (2002, February). Quoted by R. Kubey & M. Csikszentmihalyi, Television addiction is no mere metaphor. *Scientific American,* pp. 74–80. (p. 128)

Tarmann, A. (2002, May/June). Out of the closet and onto the Census long form. *Population Today, 30,* p. 1, 6. (p. 114)

Taubes, G. (1994). Will new dopamine receptors offer a key to schizophrenia? *Science, 265,* 1034–1035. (p. 365)

Taubes, G. (2001). The soft science of dietary fat. *Science, 291,* 2536–2545. (p. 246)

Taubes, G. (2002, July 7). What if it's all been a big fat lie? *New York Times* (www.nytimes.com). (p. 246)

Taylor, S. E. (1983). Adjustment to threatening events: A theory of cognitive adaptation. *American Psychologist, 38,* 1161–1173. (p. 280)

Taylor, S. E. (1989). *Positive illusions.* New York: Basic Books. (pp. 208, 279)

Taylor, S. E. (2006). Tend and befriend: Biobehavioral bases of affiliation under stress. *Current Directions in Psychological Science, 15,* 273–277. (p. 272)

Taylor, S. E., Cousino, L. K., Lewis, B. P., Gruenewald, T. L., Gurung, R. A. R., & Updegraff, J. A. (2000). Biobehavioral responses to stress in females: Tend-and-befriend, not fight-or-flight. *Psychological Review, 107,* 411–430. (p. 272)

Taylor, S. E., Pham, L. B., Rivkin, I. D., & Armor, D. A. (1998). Harnessing the imagination: Mental simulation, self-regulation, and coping. *American Psychologist, 53,* 429–439. (p. 215)

Taylor, S. P., & Chermack, S. T. (1993). Alcohol, drugs and human physical aggression. *Journal of Studies on Alcohol, Supplement No. 11,* 78–88. (p. 392)

Taylor, S., Kuch, K., Koch, W. J., Crockett, D. J., & Passey, G. (1998). The structure of posttraumatic stress symptoms. *Journal of Abnormal Psychology, 107,* 154–160. (p. 320)

Tedeschi, R. G., & Calhoun, L. G. (2004). Posttraumatic growth: Conceptual foundations and empirical evidence. *Psychological Inquiry, 15,* 1–18. (p. 320)

Teerlink, R., & Ozley, L. (2000). *More than a motorcycle: The leadership journey at Harley-Davidson.* Cambridge, MA: Harvard Business School Press. (p. 414)

Teghtsoonian, R. (1971). On the exponents in Stevens' law and the constant in Ekinan's law. *Psychological Review, 78,* 71–80. (p. 127)

Teran-Santos, J., Jimenez-Gomez, A., & Cordero-Guevara, J. (1999). The association between sleep apnea and the risk of traffic accidents. *New England Journal of Medicine, 340,* 847–851. (p. 56)

Terracciano, A., Costa, Jr., P. T., & McCrae, R. R. (2006). Personality plasticity after age 30. *Personality and Social Psychology Bulletin, 32,* 999–1009. (p. 98)

Terrace, H. S. (1979, November). How Nim Chimpsky changed my mind. *Psychology Today,* pp. 65–76. (p. 217)

Tesser, A., Forehand, R., Brody, G., & Long, N. (1989). Conflict: The role of calm and angry parent-child discussion in adolescent development. *Journal of Social and Clinical Psychology, 8,* 317–330. (p. 88)

Thatcher, R. W., Walker, R. A., & Giudice, S. (1987). Human cerebral hemispheres develop at different rates and ages. *Science, 236,* 1110–1113. (pp. 70, 89)

Thiele, T. E., Marsh, D. J., Ste. Marie, L., Bernstein, I. L., & Palmiter, R. D. (1998). Ethanol consumption and resistance are inversely related to neuropeptide Y levels. *Nature, 396,* 366–369. (p. 333)

Thomas, A., & Chess, S. (1986). The New York Longitudinal Study: From infancy to early adult life. In R. Plomin & J. Dunn (Eds.), *The study of temperament: Changes, continuities, and challenges.* Hillsdale, NJ: Erlbaum. (p. 98)

Thomas, L. (1992). *The fragile species.* New York: Scribner's. (pp. 213, 361)

Thompson, G. (1998, December 14). As obesity in children increases, so do cases of adult-onset diabetes. *New York Times* (www.nytimes.com). (p. 245)

Thompson, J. K., Jarvie, G. J., Lahey, B. B., & Cureton, K. J. (1982). Exercise and obesity: Etiology, physiology, and intervention. *Psychological Bulletin, 91,* 55–79. (p. 246)

Thompson, P. M., Giedd, J. N., Woods, R. P., MacDonald, D., Evans, A. C., & Toga, A. W. (2000). Growth patterns in the developing brain detected by using continuum mechanical tensor maps. *Nature, 404,* 190–193. (p. 70)

Thompson, R., Emmorey, K., & Gollan, T. H. (2005). "Tip of the fingers" experiences by deaf signers. *Psychological Science, 16,* 856–860. (p. 194)

Thorndike, A. L., & Hagen, E. P. (1977). *Measurement and evaluation in psychology and education.* New York: Macmillan. (p. 223)

Thorne, J., with Larry Rothstein. (1993). *You are not alone: Words of experience and hope for the journey through depression.* New York: HarperPerennial. (p. 313)

Thornton, B., & Moore, S. (1993). Physical attractiveness contrast effect: Implications for self-esteem and evaluations of the social self. *Personality and Social Psychology Bulletin, 19,* 474–480. (p. 396)

Thorpe, W. H. (1974). *Animal nature and human nature.* London: Metheun. (p. 218)

Tiedens, L. Z. (2001). Anger and advancement versus sadness and subjugation: The effect of negative emotion expressions on social status conferral. *Journal of Personality and Social Psychology, 80,* 86–94. (p. 261)

Time. (1997, December 22). Greeting card association data, p. 19. (p. 105)

Time/CNN Survey. (1994, December 19). Vox pop: Happy holidays, *Time.* (p. 335)

Tirrell, M. E. (1990). Personal communication. (p. 161)

Tondo, L., Jamison, K. R., & Baldessarini, R. J. (1997). Effect of lithium maintenance on suicidal behavior in major mood disorders. In D. M. Stoff & J. J. Mann (Eds.), *The neurobiology of suicide: From the bench to the clinic.* New York: New York Academy of Sciences. (p. 368)

Toni, N., Buchs, P.-A., Nikonenko, I., Bron, C. R., & Muller, D. (1999). LTP promotes formation of multiple spine synapses between a single axon terminal and a dendrite. *Nature, 402,* 421–42. (p. 187)

Torrey, E. F. (1986). *Witchdoctors and psychiatrists.* New York: Harper & Row. (p. 363)

Torrey, E. F., & Miller, J. (2002). *The invisible plague: The rise of mental illness from 1750 to the present.* New Brunswick, NJ: London: Rutgers University Press. (p. 343)

Torrey, E. F., Miller, J., Rawlings, R., & Yolken, R. H. (1997). Seasonality of births in schizophrenia and bipolar disorder: A review of the literature. *Schizophrenia Research, 28,* 1–38. (p. 343)

Totterdell, P., Kellett, S., Briner, R. B., & Teuchmann, K. (1998). Evidence of mood linkage in work groups. *Journal of Personality and Social Psychology, 74,* 1504–1515. (p. 380)

Tovee, M. J., Mason, S. M., Emery, J. L., McCluskey, S. E., & Cohen-Tovee, E. M. (1997). Supermodels: Stick insects or hourglasses? *The Lancet, 350,* 1474–1475. (p. 241)

Treffert, D. A., & Wallace, G. L. (2002). Island of genius—The artistic brilliance and dazzling memory that sometimes accompany autism and other disorders hint at how all brains work. *Scientific American, 286,* 76–86. (p. 219)

Treisman, A. (1987). Properties, parts, and objects. In K. R. Boff, L. Kaufman, & J. P. Thomas (Eds.), *Handbook of perception and human performance.* New York: Wiley. (p. 143)

Triandis, H. C. (1994). *Culture and social behavior.* New York: McGraw-Hill. (pp. 309, 392)

Triandis, H. C., Bontempo, R., Villareal, M. J., Asai, M., & Lucca, N. (1988). Individualism and collectivism: Cross-cultural perspectives on self-ingroup relationships. *Journal of Personality and Social Psychology, 54,* 323–338. (p. 309)

Trickett, P. K., & McBride-Chang, C. (1995). The developmental impact of different forms of child abuse and neglect. *Developmental Review, 15,* 311–337. (p. 79)

Trimble, J. E. (1994). Cultural variations in the use of alcohol and drugs. In W. J. Lonner & R. Malpass (Eds.), *Psychology and culture.* Boston: Allyn & Bacon. (p. 333)

Triplett, N. (1898). The dynamogenic factors in pacemaking and competition. *American Journal of Psychology, 9,* 507–533. (p. 384)

Trolier, T. K., & Hamilton, D. L. (1986). Variables influencing judgments of correlational relations. *Journal of Personality and Social Psychology, 50,* 879–888. (p. 16)

Tsang, Y. C. (1938). Hunger motivation in gastrectomized rats. *Journal of Comparative Psychology, 26,* 1–17. (p. 238)

Tsuang, M. T., & Faraone, S. V. (1990). *The genetics of mood disorders.* Baltimore, MD: Johns Hopkins University Press. (p. 338)

Tuber, D. S., Miller, D. D., Caris, K. A., Halter, R., Linden, F., & Hennessy, M. B. (1999). Dogs in animal shelters: Problems, suggestions, and needed expertise. *Psychological Science, 10,* 379–386. (p. 20)

Tucker, K. A. (2002). I believe you can fly. *Gallup Management Journal* (www.gallupjournal.com/CA/st/20020520.asp). (p. 411)

Turner, J. C. (1987). Rediscovering the social group: A self-categorization theory. New York: Basil Blackwell. (p. 389)

Turner, N., Barling, J., & Zacharatos, A. (2002). Positive psychology at work. In C. R. Snyder & S. J. Lopez (Eds.), *The handbook of positive psychology.* New York: Oxford University Press. (p. 413)

Tversky, A. (1985, June). Quoted in K. McKean, Decisions, decisions. *Discover,* pp. 22–31. (p. 207)

Tversky, A., & Kahneman, D. (1974). Judgment under uncertainty: Heuristics and biases. *Science, 185,* 1124–1131. (p. 207)

Twenge, J. M. (1997). Changes in masculine and feminine traits over time: A meta-analysis. *Sex Roles 36(5–6),* 305–325. (p. 103)

Twenge, J. M. (2000). The age of anxiety? Birth cohort change in anxiety and neuroticism, 1952–1993. *Journal of Personality and Social Psychology, 79,* 1007–1021. (p. 322)

Twenge, J. M., & Campbell, W. K. (2001). Age and birth cohort differences in self-esteem: A cross-temporal meta-analysis. *Personality and Social Psychology Review, 5,* 321–344. (p. 87)

Twenge, J. M., & Crocker, J. (2002). Race and self-esteem: Meta-analyses comparing Whites, Blacks, Hispanics, Asians, and American Indians and comment on Gray-Little and Hafdahl (2000). *Psychological Bulletin, 128,* 371–408. (p. 307)

Twenge, J. M., & Nolen-Hoeksema, S. (2002). Age, gender, race, socioeconomic status, and birth cohort differences on the children's depression inventory: A meta-analysis. *Journal of Abnormal Psychology, 111,* 578–588. (p. 87)

Twenge, J. M., Baumeister, R. F., Tice, D. M., & Stucke, T. S. (2001). If you can't join them, beat them: Effects of social exclusion on aggressive behavior. *Journal of Personality and Social Psychology, 81,* 1058–1069. (pp. 248, 392)

Twenge, J. M., Catanese, K. R., & Baumeister, R. F. (2002). Social exclusion causes self-defeating behavior. *Journal of Personality and Social Psychology, 83,* 606–615. (pp. 248, 392)

Twenge, J. M., Catanese, K. R., & Baumeister, R. F. (2003). Social exclusion and the deconstructed state: Time perception, meaninglessness, lethargy, lack of emotion, and self-awareness. *Journal of Personality and Social Psychology, 85,* 409–423. (p. 392)

Tyler, K. A. (2002). Social and emotional outcomes of childhood sexual abuse: A review of recent research. *Aggression and Violent Behavior, 7,* 567–589. (p. 79)

U.S. Senate Select Committee on Intelligence. (2004, July 9). *Report of the U.S. Intelligence Community's prewar intelligence assessments on Iraq.* www.gpoaccess.gov/serialset/creports/iraq.html (pp. 207, 386)

Uchino, B. N., Cacioppo, J. T., & Kiecolt-Glaser, J. K. (1996). The relationship between social support and physiological processes: A review with emphasis on underlying mechanisms and implications for health. *Psychological Bulletin, 119,* 488–531. (p. 280)

Uchino, B. N., Uno, D., & Holt-Lunstad, J. (1999). Social support, physiological processes, and health. *Current Directions in Psychological Science, 8,* 145–148. (p. 280)

Udry, J. R. (2000). Biological limits of gender construction. *American Sociological Review, 65,* 443–457. (p. 106)

UK ECT Review Group. (2003). Efficacy and safety of electroconvulsive therapy in depressive disorders: A systematic review and meta-analysis. *Lancet, 361,* 799–808. (p. 368)

Ulrich, R. E. (1991). Animal rights, animal wrongs and the question of balance. *Psychological Science, 2,* 197–201. (p. 20)

UNAIDS. (2008). *Report on the global AIDS epidemic.* United Nations (www.unaids.org). (p. 111)

Urbany, J. E., Bearden, W. O., & Weilbaker, D. C. (1988). The effect of plausible and exaggerated reference prices on consumer perceptions and price search. *Journal of Consumer Research, 15,* 95–110. (p. 209)

Urry, H. L., Nitschke, J. B., Dolski, I., Jackson, D. C., Dalton, K. M., Mueller, C. J., Rosenkranz, M. A., Ryff, C. D., Singer, B. H., & Davidson, R. J. (2004). Making a life worth living: Neural correlates of well-being. *Psychological Science, 15,* 367–372. (p. 253)

USAID. (2004, January). *The ABCs of HIV prevention.* www.usaid.gov. (p. 274)

Vaidya, J. G., Gray, E. K., Haig, J., & Watson, D. (2002). On the temporal stability of personality: Evidence for differential stability and the role of life experiences. *Journal of Personality and Social Psychology, 83,* 1469–1484. (p. 301)

Vaillant, G. E. (2002). *Aging well: Surprising guideposts to a happier life from the landmark Harvard study of adult development.* Boston: Little, Brown. (p. 280)

Valenstein, E. S. (1986). *Great and desperate cures: The rise and decline of psychosurgery.* New York: Basic Books. (p. 369)

Vallone, R. P., Griffin, D. W., Lin, S., & Ross, L. (1990). Overconfident prediction of future actions and outcomes by self and others. *Journal of Personality and Social Psychology, 58,* 582–592. (p. 10)

van den Boom, D. (1990). Preventive intervention and the quality of mother-infant interaction and infant exploration in irritable infants. In W. Koops, H. J. G. Soppe, J. L. van der Linden, P. C. M. Molenaar, & J. J. F. Schroots (Eds.), *Developmental psychology research in The Netherlands.* The Netherlands. (p. 78)

van den Bos, K., & Spruijt, N. (2002). Appropriateness of decisions as a moderator of the psychology of voice. *European Journal of Social Psychology, 32,* 57–72. (p. 414)

Van Dyke, C., & Byck, R. (1982, March). Cocaine. *Scientific American,* pp. 128–141. (p. 329)

van Engen, M. L., & Willemsen, T. M. (2004). Sex and leadership styles: A meta-analysis of research published in the 1990s. *Psychological Reports, 94,* 3–18. (p. 104)

van IJzendoorn M. H., & Kroonenberg, P. M. (1988). Cross-cultural patterns of attachment: A meta-analysis of the strange situation. *Child Development, 59,* 147–156. (p. 78)

Van Ijzendoorn, M. H., & Juffer, F. (2005). Adoption is a successful natural intervention enhancing adopted children's IQ and school performance. *Current Directions in Psychological Science, 14,* 326–330. (p. 226)

Van Ijzendoorn, M. H., & Juffer, F. (2006). The Emanual Miller Memorial Lecture 2006: Adoption as intervention. Meta-analytic evidence for massive catch-up and plasticity in physical, socio-emotional, and cognitive development. *Journal of Child Psychology and Psychiatry, 47,* 1228–1245. (p. 226)

Van Leeuwen, M. S. (1978). A cross-cultural examination of psychological differentiation in males and females. *International Journal of Psychology, 13,* 87–122. (p. 107)

Van Rooy, D. L., & Viswesvaran, C. (2004). Emotional intelligence: A meta-analytic investigation of predictive validity and nomological net. *Journal of Vocational Behavior, 65,* 71–95. (p. 221)

van Schaik, C. P., Ancrenaz, M., Borgen, G., Galdikas, B., Knott, C. D., Singleton, I., Suzuki, A., Utami, S. S., & Merrill, M. (2003). Orangutan cultures and the evolution of material culture. *Science, 299,* 102–105. (p. 216)

Van Yperen, N. W., & Buunk, B. P. (1990). A longitudinal study of equity and satisfaction in intimate relationships. *European Journal of Social Psychology, 20,* 287–309. (p. 398)

Vance, E. B., & Wagner, N. N. (1976). Written descriptions of orgasm: A study of sex differences. *Archives of Sexual Behavior, 5,* 87–98. (p. 109)

Vandenberg, S. G., & Kuse, A. R. (1978). Mental rotations: A group test of three-dimensional spatial visualization. *Perceptual and Motor Skills, 47,* 599–604. (p. 230)

Vanman, E. J., Saltz, J. L., Nathan, L. R., & Warren, J. A. (2004). Racial discrimination by low-prejudiced Whites. *Psychological Science, 15,* 711–714. (p. 389)

Vaughn, K. B., & Lanzetta, J. T. (1981). The effect of modification of expressive displays on vicarious emotional arousal. *Journal of Experimental Social Psychology, 17,* 16–30. (p. 259)

Vazire, S., & Gosling, S. D. (2004). e-Perceptions: Personality impressions based on personal websites. *Journal of Personality and Social Psychology, 87,* 123–132. (p. 304)

Vecera, S. P., Vogel, E. K., & Woodman, G. F. (2002). Lower region: A new cue for figure-ground assignment. *Journal of Experimental Psychology: General, 13,* 194–205. (p. 146)

Vekassy, L. (1977). Dreams of the blind. *Magyar Pszichologiai Szemle, 34,* 478–491. (p. 57)

Verhaeghen, P., & Salthouse, T. A. (1997). Meta-analyses of age-cognition relations in adulthood: Estimates of linear and nonlinear age effects and structural models. *Psychological Bulletin, 122,* 231–249. (p. 93)

Viding, E., Blair, R., James, R., Moffitt, T. E., & Plomin, R. (2005). Evidence for substantial genetic risk for psychopathy in 7-year-olds. *Journal of Child Psychology & Psychiatry, 46,* 592–597. (p. 324)

Vigliocco, G., & Hartsuiker, R. J. (2002). The interplay of meaning, sound, and syntax in sentence production. *Psychological Bulletin, 128,* 442–472. (p. 212)

Vitello, P. (2006, June 12). A ring tone meant to fall on deaf ears. *New York Times* (www.nytimes.com). (p. 92)

von Senden, M. (1932). *The perception of space and shape in the congenitally blind before and after operation.* Glencoe, IL: Free Press. (p. 148)

Wade, K. A., Garry, M., Read, J. D., & Lindsay, D. S. (2002). A picture is worth a thousand lies: Using false photographs to create false childhood memories. *Psychonomic Bulletin & Review, 9,* 597–603. (p. 197)

Wade, N. G., Worthington, Jr., E. L., & Vogel, D. L. (2007). Effectiveness of religiously tailored interventions in Christian therapy. *Psychotherapy Research, 17,* 91–105. (p. 364)

Wagner, U., Gais, S., Haider, H., Verleger, R., & Born, J. (2004). Sleep inspires insight. *Nature, 427,* 352–355. (p. 55)

Wagstaff, G. (1982). Attitudes to rape: The "just world" strikes again? *Bulletin of the British Psychological Society, 13,* 275–283. (p. 377)

Wahlberg, D. (2001, October 11). We're more depressed, patriotic, poll finds. *Grand Rapids Press,* p. A15. (p. 270)

Wakefield, J. C., & Spitzer, R. L. (2002). Lowered estimates—but of what? *Archives of General Psychiatry, 59,* 129–130. (p. 321)

Walker, M. P., & Stickgold, R. (2006). Sleep, memory, and plasticity. *Annual Review of Psychology, 57,* 139–166. (p. 55)

Walker, W. R., Skowronski, J. J., Gibbons, J. A., Vogl, R. J., & Thompson, C. P. (2003). On the emotions that accompany autobiographical memories: Dysphoria disrupts the fading affect bias. *Cognition and Emotion, 17,* 703–723. (p. 97)

Wall, B. (2002, August 24–25). Profit matures along with baby boomers. *International Herald Tribune,* p. 13. (p. 396)

Wallace, D. S., Paulson, R. M., Lord, C. G., & Bond, C. F., Jr. (2005). Which behaviors do attitudes predict? Meta-analyzing the effects of social pressure and perceived difficulty. *Review of General Psychology, 9(3),* 214–227. (p. 377)

Wallach, M. A., & Wallach, L. (1983). *Psychology's sanction for selfishness: The error of egoism in theory and therapy.* New York; Freeman. (p. 299)

Wallach, M. A., & Wallach, L. (1985, February). How psychology sanctions the cult of the self. *Washington Monthly,* pp. 46–56. (p. 299)

Wallis, C. (1983, June 6). Stress: Can we cope? *Time,* pp. 48–54. (p. 271)

Walster (Hatfield), E., Aronson, V., Abrahams, D., & Rottman, L. (1966). Importance of physical attractiveness in dating behavior. *Journal of Personality and Social Psychology, 4,* 508–516. (p. 395)

Wampold, B. E. (2001). *The great psychotherapy debate: Models, methods, and findings.* Mahwah, NJ; Erlbaum. (p. 363)

Ward, A., & Mann, T. (2000). Don't mind if I do: Disinhibited eating under cognitive load. *Journal of Personality and Social Psychology, 78,* 753–763. (p. 246)

Ward, C. (1994). Culture and altered states of consciousness. In W. J. Lonner & R. Malpass (Eds.), *Psychology and culture.* Boston: Allyn & Bacon. (p. 325)

Ward, K. D., Klesges, R. C., & Halpern, M. T. (1997). Predictors of smoking cessation and state-of-the-art smoking interventions. *Journal of Social Issues, 53,* 129–145. (p. 329)

Wardle, J., Cooke, L. J., Gibson, L., Sapochnik, M., Sheiham, & A., Lawson, M. (2003). Increasing children's acceptance of vegetables; a randomized trial of parent-led exposure. *Appetite, 40,* 155–162. (p. 140)

Warner, J., McKeown, E., Johnson, K., Ramsay, A., Cort, C., & King, M. (2004). Rates and predictors of mental illness in gay men, lesbians and bisexual men and women. *British Journal of Psychiatry, 185,* 479–485. (p. 114)

Warren, R. M. (1984). Perceptual restoration of obliterated sounds. *Psychological Bulletin, 96,* 371–383. (p. 150)

Wason, P. C. (1960). On the failure to eliminate hypotheses in a conceptual task. *Quarterly Journal of Experimental Psychology, 12,* 129–140. (p. 207)

Wason, P. C. (1981). The importance of cognitive illusions. *The Behavioral and Brain Sciences, 4,* 356. (p. 207)

Wasserman, E. A. (1993). Comparative cognition: Toward a general understanding of cognition in behavior. *Psychological Science, 4,* 156–161. (p. 166)

Wasserman, E. A. (1995). The conceptual abilities of pigeons. *American Scientist, 83,* 246–255. (p. 215)

Watson, D. (2000). *Mood and temperament*. New York: Guilford Press. (p. 261)

Watson, D., Suls, J., & Haig, J. (2002). Global self-esteem in relation to structural models of personality and affectivity. *Journal of Personality and Social Psychology, 83*, 185–197. (p. 306)

Watson, J. B. (1913). Psychology as the behaviorist views it. *Psychological Review, 20*, 158–177. (pp. 162, 164)

Watson, J. B. (1924). The unverbalized in human behavior. *Psychological Review, 31*, 339–347. (p. 164)

Watson, J. B., & Rayner, R. (1920). Conditioned emotional reactions. *Journal of Experimental Psychology, 3*, 1–14. (p. 164)

Watson, R. I., Jr. (1973). Investigation into deindividuation using a cross-cultural survey technique. *Journal of Personality and Social Psychology, 25*, 342–345. (p. 385)

Watson, S. J., Benson, J. A., Jr., & Joy, J. E. (2000). NEWS AND VIEWS—Marijuana and medicine: Assessing the science base; A summary of the 1999 Institute of Medicine report. *Archives of General Psychiatry, 57*, 547–553. (p. 332)

Wayment, H. A., & Peplau, L. A. (1995). Social support and well-being among lesbian and heterosexual women: A structural modeling approach. *Personality and Social Psychology Bulletin, 21*, 1189–1199. (p. 94)

Weaver, J. B., Masland, J. L., & Zillmann, D. (1984). Effect of erotica on young men's aesthetic perception of their female sexual partners. *Perceptual and Motor Skills, 58*, 929–930. (p. 112)

Webb, W. B. (1992). *Sleep: The gentle tyrant*. Bolton, MA; Anker Publishing. (pp. 53, 55)

Webb, W. B., & Campbell, S. S. (1983). Relationships in sleep characteristics of identical and fraternal twins. *Archives of General Psychiatry, 40*, 1093–1095. (p. 53)

Wechsler, H., Davenport, A., Dowdall, G., Moeykens, B., & Castillo, S. (1994). Health and behavioral consequences of binge drinking in college. *Journal of the American Medical Association, 272*, 1672–1677. (p. 327)

Wechsler, H., Lee, J. E., Kuo, M., Seibring, M., Nelson, T. F., & Lee, H. (2002). Trends in college binge drinking during a period of increased prevention efforts. *Journal of American College Health, 50*, 203–217. (p. 327)

Weed, W. S. (2001, May). Can we go to Mars without going crazy? *Discover*, pp. 31–43. (p. 408)

Weingarten, G. (2002, March 10). Below the beltway. *Washington Post*, p. W03. (p. 407)

Weinstein, N. D. (1980). Unrealistic optimism about future life events. *Journal of Personality and Social Psychology, 39*, 806–820. (p. 279)

Weinstein, N. D. (1982). Unrealistic optimism about susceptibility to health problems. *Journal of Behavioral Medicine, 5*, 441–460. (p. 279)

Weinstein, N. D. (1996, October 4). 1996 optimistic bias bibliography. Distributed via internet (weinstein_c@aesop.rutgers.edu). (p. 279)

Weissman, M. M. (1999). Interpersonal psychotherapy and the health care scene. In D. S. Janowsky (Ed.), *Psychotherapy indications and outcomes*. Washington, DC: American Psychiatric Press. (p. 352)

Weissman, M. M., Bland, R. C., Canino, G. J., Faravelli, C., Greenwald, S., Hwu, H-G., Joyce, P. R., Karam, E. G., Lee, C-K., Lellouch, J., Lepine, J-P., Newman, S. C., Rubio-Stepic, M., Wells, J. E., Wickramaratne, P. J., Wittchen, H-U., & Yeh, E-K. (1996). Cross-national epidemiology of major depression and bipolar disorder. *Journal of the American Medical Association, 276*, 293–299. (p. 338)

Welch, W. W. (2005, February 28). Trauma of Iraq war haunting thousands returning home. *USA Today* (www.usatoday.com). (p. 320)

Wellings, K., Collumbien, M., Slaymaker, E., Singh, S., Hodges, Z., Patel, D., & Bajos, N. (2006). Sexual behaviour in context: A global perspective. *Lancet, 368*, 1706–1728. (p. 108)

Wellman, H. M., & Gelman, S. A. (1992). Cognitive development: Foundational theories of core domains. *Annual Review of Psychology, 43*, 337–375. (p. 74)

Wells, G. L. (1981). Lay analyses of causal forces on behavior. In J. Harvey (Ed.), *Cognition, social behavior and the environment*. Hillsdale, NJ: Erlbaum. (p. 158)

Wender, P. H., Kety, S. S., Rosenthal, D., Schulsinger, F., Ortmann, J., & Lunde, I. (1986). Psychiatric disorders in the biological and adoptive families of adopted individuals with affective disorders. *Archives of General Psychiatry, 43*, 923–929. (p. 338)

Wener, R., Frazier, W., & Farbstein, J. (1987, June). Building better jails. *Psychology Today*, pp. 40–49. (p. 277)

Westen, D. (1996). Is Freud really dead? Teaching psychodynamic theory to introductory psychology. Presentation to the Annual Institute on the Teaching of Psychology, St. Petersburg Beach, Florida. (p. 294)

Westen, D. (1998). The scientific legacy of Sigmund Freud: Toward a psychodynamically informed psychological science. *Psychological Bulletin, 124*, 333–371. (p. 295)

Weuve, J., Kang, J. H., Manson, J. E., Breteler, M. M. B., Ware, J. H., & Grodstein, F. (2004). Physical activity, including walking, and cognitive function in older women. *Journal of the American Medical Association, 292*, 1454–1460. (p. 94)

Whalen, P. J., Kagan, J., Cook, R. G., Davis, F. C., Kim, H., Polis, S., McLaren, D. G., Somerville, L. H., McLean, A. A., Maxwell, J. S., & Johnstone, T. (2004). Human amygdala responsibility to masked fearful eye whites. *Science, 302*, 2061. (p. 256)

White, G. L., & Kight, T. D. (1984). Misattribution of arousal and attraction: Effects of salience of explanations for arousal. *Journal of Experimental Social Psychology, 20*, 55–64. (p. 397)

White, H. R., Brick, J., & Hansell, S. (1993). A longitudinal investigation of alcohol use and aggression in adolescence. *Journal of Studies on Alcohol, Supplement No. 11*, 62–77. (p. 392)

White, L., & Edwards, J. (1990). Emptying the nest and parental well-being: An analysis of national panel data. *American Sociological Review, 55*, 235–242. (p. 95)

White, P. H., Kjelgaard, M. M., & Harkins, S. G. (1995). Testing the contribution of self-evaluation to goal-setting effects. *Journal of Personality and Social Psychology, 69*, 69–79. (p. 412)

Whitehead, B. D., & Popenoe, D. (2001). *The state of our unions 2001: The social health of marriage in America*. Rutgers University; The National Marriage Project. (p. 94)

Whiten, A., & Boesch, C. (2001, January). Cultures of chimpanzees. *Scientific American*, pp. 60–67. (p. 216)

Whiting, B. B., & Edwards, C. P. (1988). *Children of different worlds: The formation of social behavior*. Cambridge, MA; Harvard University Press. (p. 81)

Whitley, B. E., Jr. (1999). Right-wing authoritarianism, social dominance orientation, and prejudice. *Journal of Personality and Social Psychology, 77*, 126–134. (p. 389)

WHO. (2008). *Schizophrenia*. Geneva: World Health Organization (www.who.int). (pp. 313, 342)

WHO. (2004). *Women, girls, HIV, and AIDS.* World Health Organization, Western Pacific Regional Office. (p. 111)

Whooley, M. A., & Browner, W. S. (1998). Association between depressive symptoms and mortality in older women. *Archives of Internal Medicine, 158,* 2129–2135. (p. 275)

Wichman, H. (1992). *Human factors in the design of spacecraft.* Stony Brook, NY: State University of New York, (p. 408)

Wickelgren, I. (2005). Autistic brains out of sync? *Science, 308,* 1856–1858. (p. 76)

Wickelgren, W. A. (1977). *Learning and memory.* Englewood Cliffs, NJ: Prentice Hall. (p. 185)

Widom, C. S. (1989a). Does violence beget violence? A critical examination of the literature. *Psychological Bulletin, 106,* 3–28. (p. 79)

Widom, C. S. (1989b). The cycle of violence. *Science, 244,* 160–166. (p. 79)

Wiens, A. N., & Menustik, C. E. (1983). Treatment outcome and patient characteristics in an aversion therapy program for alcoholism. *American Psychologist, 38,* 1089–1096. (p. 356)

Wierson, M., & Forehand, R. (1994). Parent behavioral training for child noncompliance: Rationale, concepts, and effectiveness. *Current Directions in Psychological Science, 3,* 146–149. (p. 171)

Wierzbicki, M. (1993). Psychological adjustment of adoptees: A meta-analysis. *Journal of Clinical Child Psychology, 22,* 447–454. (p. 82)

Wiesel, T. N. (1982). Postnatal development of the visual cortex and the influence of environment. *Nature, 299,* 583–591. (p. 148)

Wigdor, A. K., & Garner, W. R. (1982). *Ability testing: Uses, consequences, and controversies.* Washington, DC; National Academy Press. (p. 230)

Wilcox, A. J., Baird, D. D., Dunson, D. B., McConnaughey, D. R., Kesner, J. S., & Weinberg, C. R. (2004). On the frequency of intercourse around ovulation: Evidence for biological influences. *Human Reproduction, 19,* 1539–1543. (p. 110)

Wilder, D. A. (1981). Perceiving persons as a group: Categorization and intergroup relations. In D. L. Hamilton (Ed.), *Cognitive processes in stereotyping and intergroup behavior.* Hillsdale, NJ; Erlbaum. (p. 389)

Williams, J. E., & Best, D. L. (1990). *Measuring sex stereotypes: A multination study.* Newbury Park, CA; Sage. (p. 104)

Williams, J. E., Paton, C. C., Siegler, I. C., Eigenbrodt, M. L., Nieto, F. J., & Tyroler, H. A. (2000). Anger proneness predicts coronary heart disease risk: Prospective analysis from the artherosclerosis risk in communities (ARIC) study. *Circulation, 101,* 17, 2034–2040. (p. 275)

Williams, K. D. (2002). *Ostracism: The power of silence.* New York; Guilford. (p. 247)

Williams, K. D. (2007). Ostracism. *Annual Review of Psychology, 58,* 425–452. (p. 247)

Williams, K. D., & Zadro, L. (2001). Ostracism: On being ignored, excluded and rejected. In M. Leary (Ed.), *Rejection.* New York; Oxford University Press. (p. 247)

Williams, R. (1993). *Anger kills.* New York: Times Books. (p. 275)

Williams, S. L. (1987). Self-efficacy and mastery-oriented treatment for severe phobias. Paper presented to the American Psychological Association convention. (p. 356)

Willmuth, M. E. (1987). Sexuality after spinal cord injury: A critical review. *Clinical Psychology Review, 7,* 389–412. (p. 112)

Wilson, A. E., & Ross, M. (2001). From chump to champ: People's appraisals of their earlier and present selves. *Journal of Personality and Social Psychology, 80,* 572–584. (p. 307)

Wilson, C. M., & Oswald, A. J. (2002). How does marriage affect physical and psychological health? A survey of the longitudinal evidence. Working paper, University of York and Warwick University. (p. 280)

Wilson, R. S. (1979). Analysis of longitudinal twin data: Basic model and applications to physical growth measures. *Acta Geneticae medicae et Gemellologiae, 28,* 93–105. (p. 71)

Windholz, G. (1989, April–June). The discovery of the principles of reinforcement, extinction, generalization, and differentiation of conditional reflexes in Pavlov's laboratories. *Pavlovian Journal of Biological Science, 26,* 64–74. (p. 162)

Windholz, G. (1997). Ivan P. Pavlov: An overview of his life and psychological work. *American Psychologist, 52,* 941–946. (p. 160)

Wiseman, R. (2002). *Laugh Lab—final results.* University of Hertfordshire (www.laughlab.co.uk). (p. 206)

Witvliet, C. V. O., & Vrana, S. R. (1995). Psychophysiological responses as indices of affective dimensions. *Psychophysiology, 32,* 436–443. (p. 253)

Witvliet, C. V. O., Ludwig, T., & Vander Laan, K. (2001). Granting forgiveness or harboring grudges: Implications for emotions, physiology, and health. *Psychological Science, 12,* 117–123. (p. 261)

Wixted, J. T., & Ebbesen, E. B. (1991). On the form of forgetting. *Psychological Science, 2,* 409–415. (p. 193)

Wolfson, A. R., & Carskadon, M. A. (1998). Sleep schedules and daytime functioning in adolescents. *Child Development, 69,* 875–887. (p. 58)

Woll, S. (1986). So many to choose from: Decision strategies in video-dating. *Journal of Social and Personal Relationships, 3,* 43–52. (p. 395)

Wolpe, J. (1958). *Psychotherapy by reciprocal inhibition.* Stanford, CA: Stanford University Press. (p. 355)

Wolpe, J., & Plaud, J. J. (1997). Pavlov's contributions to behavior therapy: The obvious and the not so obvious. *American Psychologist, 52,* 966–972. (p. 355)

Wong, D. F., Wagner, H. N., Tune, L. E., Dannals, R. F., & others. (1986). Positron emission tomography reveals elevated D2 dopamine receptors in drug-naive schizophrenics. *Science, 234,* 1588–1593. (p. 342)

Wong, M. M., & Csikszentmihalyi, M. (1991). Affiliation motivation and daily experience: Some issues on gender differences. *Journal of Personality and Social Psychology, 60,* 154–164. (p. 105)

Wood, J. (2003, May 19). Quoted by R. Mestel, Rorschach tested: Blot out the famous method? Some experts say it has no place in psychiatry. *Los Angeles Times* (www.latimes.com). (p. 295)

Wood, J. M., Bootzin, R. R., Kihlstrom, J. F., & Schacter, D. L. (1992). Implicit and explicit memory for verbal information presented during sleep. *Psychological Science, 3,* 236–239. (p. 195)

Wood, J. M., Nezworski, M. T., Garb, H. N., & Lilienfeld, S. O. (2006). The controversy over the Exner Comprehensive System and the Society for Personality Assessment's white paper on the Rorschach. *Independent Practitioner,* in press. (p. 295)

Wood, W. (1987). Meta-analytic review of sex differences in group performance. *Psychological Bulletin, 102,* 53–71. (p. 105)

Wood, W., & Eagly, A. (2002). A cross-cultural analysis of the behavior of women and men: Implications for the origins of sex differences. *Psychological Bulletin, 128,* 699–727. (pp. 103, 104, 105, 120)

Wood, W., Lundgren, S., Ouellette, J. A., Busceme, S., & Blackstone, T. (1994). Minority influence: A meta-analytic review of social influence processes. *Psychological Bulletin, 115,* 323–345. (p. 387)

Woods, N. F., Dery, G. K., & Most, A. (1983). Recollections of menarche, current menstrual attitudes, and premenstrual symptoms. In S. Golub (Ed.), *Menarche: The transition from girl to woman.* Lexington, MA; Lexington Books. (p. 84)

Woodward, B. (2002). *Bush at war.* New York: Simon & Schuster. (p. 9)

World Health Organization. (1979). *Schizophrenia: An international follow-up study.* Chicester, England; Wiley. (p. 342)

World Health Organization (2000). *Global strategy for infant and young child feeding.* Geneva: WHO. (p. 17)

World Health Organization. (2001, December 1). Mental and neurological disorders. Fact Sheet Number 265. (p. 335)

Worthington, E. L., Jr. (1989). Religious faith across the life span: Implications for counseling and research. *The Counseling Psychologist, 17,* 555–612. (p. 85)

Worthington, E. L., Jr., Kurusu, T. A., McCullogh, M. E., & Sandage, S. J. (1996). Empirical research on religion and psychotherapeutic processes and outcomes: A 10-year review and research prospectus. *Psychological Bulletin, 119,* 448–487. (p. 364)

Wortman, C. B., & Silver, R. C. (1989). The myths of coping with loss. *Journal of Consulting and Clinical Psychology, 57,* 349–357. (p. 96)

Wren, C. S. (1999, April 8). Drug survey of children finds middle school a pivotal time. *New York Times* (www.nytimes.com). (p. 334)

Wright, I. C., Rabe-Hesketh, S., Woodruff, P. W. R., David, A. S., Murray, R. M., & Bullmore, E. T. (2000). Meta-analysis of regional brain volumes in schizophrenia. *American Journal of Psychiatry, 157,* 16–25. (p. 343)

Wright, P. H. (1989). Gender differences in adults' same- and cross-gender friendships. In R. G. Adams & R. Blieszner (Eds.), *Older adult friendships: Structure and process.* Newbury Park, CA; Sage. (p. 105)

Wright, P., Takei, N., Rifkin, L., & Murray, R. M. (1995). Maternal influenza, obstetric complications, and schizophrenia. *American Journal of Psychiatry, 152,* 1714–1720. (p. 343)

Wrzesniewski, A., & Dutton, J. E. (2001). Crafting a job: Revisioning employees as active crafters of their work. *Academy of Management Review, 26,* 179–201. (p. 407)

Wrzesniewski, A., McCauley, C. R., Rozin, P., & Schwartz, B. (1997). Jobs, careers, and callings: People's relations to their work. *Journal of Research in Personality, 31,* 21–33. (p. 407)

Wuethrich, B. (2001, March). Features—GETTING STUPID—Surprising new neurological behavioral research reveals that teenagers who drink too much may permanently damage their brains and seriously compromise their ability to learn. *Discover, 56,* 56–64. (p. 327)

Wulsin, L. R., Vaillant, G. E., & Wells, V. E. (1999). A systematic review of the mortality of depression. *Psychosomatic Medicine, 61,* 6–17. (p. 275)

Wyatt, J. K., & Bootzin, R. R. (1994). Cognitive processing and sleep: Implications for enhancing job performance. *Human Performance, 7,* 119–139. (p. 194)

Wynne, C. D. L. (2004). *Do animals think?* Princeton, NJ: Princeton University Press. (p. 217)

Xu, Y., & Corkin, S. (2001). H.M. revisits the Tower of Hanoi puzzle. *Neuropsychology, 15,* 69–79. (p. 188)

Yamagata, S. & 11 others (2006). Is the genetic structure of human personality universal? A cross-cultural twin study from North America, Europe, and Asia. *Journal of Personality and Social Psychology, 90,* 987–998. (p. 301)

Yarnell, P. R., & Lynch, S. (1970, April 25). Retrograde memory immediately after concussion. *Lancet,* pp. 863–865. (p. 187)

Yates, W. R. (2000). Testosterone in psychiatry. *Archives of General Psychiatry, 57,* 155–156. (p. 110)

Ybarra, O. (1999). Misanthropic person memory when the need to self-enhance is absent. *Personality and Social Psychology Bulletin, 25,* 261–269. (p. 306)

Yirmiya, N., Erel, O., Shaken, M., & Solomonica-Levi, D. (1998). Meta-analyses comparing theory of mind abilities of individuals with autism, individuals with mental retardation, and normally developing individuals. *Psychological Bulletin, 124,* 283–307. (p. 76)

Zajonc, R. B. (1965). Social facilitation. *Science, 149,* 269–274. (p. 384)

Zajonc, R. B. (1980). Feeling and thinking: Preferences need no inferences. *American Psychologist, 35,* 151–175. (p. 255)

Zajonc, R. B. (1984a). On the primacy of affect. *American Psychologist, 39,* 117–123. (p. 255)

Zajonc, R. B. (1984b, July 22). Quoted by D. Goleman, Rethinking IQ tests and their value. *New York Times,* p. D22. (p. 222)

Zajonc, R. B. (1998). Emotions. In D. Gilbert, S. T. Fiske, & G. Lindzey (Eds.), *Handbook of social psychology,* (4th ed.). New York: McGraw-Hill. (p. 395)

Zajonc, R. B. (2001). Mere exposure: A gateway to the subliminal. *Current Directions in Psychological Science, 10,* 224–228. (p. 394)

Zammit, S., Allebeck, P., Andreasson, S., Lundberg, I., & Lewis, G. (2002). Self reported cannabis use as a risk factor for schizophrenia in Swedish conscripts of 1969: Historical cohort study. *British Medical Journal, 325,* 1199. (p. 332)

Zauberman, G., & Lynch, J. G., Jr. (2005). Resource slack and propensity to discount delayed investments of time versus money. *Journal of Experimental Psychology: General, 134,* 23–37. (p. 208)

Zeidner, M. (1990). Perceptions of ethnic group modal intelligence: Reflections of cultural stereotypes or intelligence test scores? *Journal of Cross-Cultural Psychology, 21,* 214–231. (p. 227)

Zhang, H., & Xu, Y. (2006). Teaching of psychology to university students in China. *International Journal of Psychology, 41,* 17–23. (p. 4)

Zilbergeld, B. (1983). *The shrinking of America: Myths of psychological change.* Boston: Little, Brown. (p. 361)

Zillmann, D. (1986). Effects of prolonged consumption of pornography. Background paper for *The Surgeon General's workshop on pornography and public health,* June 22–24. Report prepared by E. P. Mulvey & J. L. Haugaard and released by Office of the Surgeon General on August 4, 1986. (p. 255)

Zillmann, D. (1989). Effects of prolonged consumption of pornography. In D. Zillmann & J. Bryant (Eds.), *Pornography: Research advances and policy considerations.* Hillsdale, NJ; Erlbaum. (pp. 112, 393)

Zillmann, D., & Bryant, J. (1984). Effects of massive exposure to pornography. In N. Malamuth & E. Donnerstein (Eds.), *Pornography and sexual aggression.* Orlando, FL: Academic Press. (p. 394)

Zimbardo, P. (2007, September). Person × situation × system dynamics. *The Observer* (Association for Psychological Science), p. 43. (p. 378)

Zimbardo, P. G. (1970). The human choice: Individuation, reason, and order versus deindividuation, impulse, and chaos. In W. J. Arnold & D. Levine (Eds.), *Nebraska Symposium on Motivation, 1969.* Lincoln, NE; University of Nebraska Press. (p. 385)

Zimbardo, P. G. (1972, April). Pathology of imprisonment. *Transaction/Society*, pp. 4–8. (p. 378)

Zimbardo, P. G. (2001, September 16). Fighting terrorism by understanding man's capacity for evil. Op Ed Essay distributed by spsp-discuss@stolaf.edu. (p. 390)

Zimbardo, P. G. (2004, May 25). Journalist interview re: Abu Ghraib prison abuses; Eleven answers to eleven questions. Unpublished manuscript, Stanford University. (p. 378)

Zornberg, G. L., Buka, S. L., & Tsuang, M. T. (2000). At issue: The problem of obstetrical complications and schizophrenia. *Schizophrenia Bulletin, 26*, 249–256. (p. 343)

Zubieta, J-K., Heitzeg, M. M., Smith, Y. R., Bueller, J. A., Xu, K., Xu, Y., Koeppe, R. A., Stohler, C. S., & Goldman, D. (2003). COMT val158met genotype affects μ-opioid neurotransmitter responses to a pain stressor. *Science, 299*, 1240–1243. (p. 138)

Zucker, G. S., & Weiner, B. (1993). Conservatism and perceptions of poverty: An attributional analysis. *Journal of Applied Social Psychology, 23*, 925–943. (p. 377)

Zuckerman, M. (1979). *Sensation seeking: Beyond the optimal level of arousal*. Hillsdale, NJ; Erlbaum. (p. 236)

Zvolensky, M. J., Feldner, M. T., Leen-Feldner, E. W., & McLeish, A. C. (2005). Smoking and panic attacks, panic disorder, and agoraphobia: A review of the empirical literature. *Clinical Psychology Review, 25*, 761–789. (p. 319)

Name Index

Subject Index

COMPLETE INDEX OF EVERYDAY LIFE APPLICATIONS